LET'S GO

www.letsgo.com

EUROPE TOP 10 CITIES

research managers
Linda Buehler
Billy Marks
Dorothy McLeod

managing editors
Sarah Berlow
Chris Kingston

editors
Spencer Burke
Michael Goncalves
Mary Potter

staff writers

Audrey Anderson
Matthew Beck
Sarah Berlow
Linda Buehler
Holly Cao
Madeline Ford
Beatrice Franklin
Amy Friedman
Nora Garry
Michael Goncalves

Anna Hopper
Sanders Isaac-Berstein
Devi K. Lockwood
Lange Luntao
Mikia Manley
Katrina Malakhoff
Taylor Nickel
Bronwen O'Herin
Emily Pereira
Alexandra Perloff-Giles

Eleanor Regan
Delphine Rodrik
Emelyn Rude
Katherine Savarese
Jane Seo
Mark Warren
Natania Wolansky
Roland Yang
Qichen Zhang

researcher-writers

Beatrice Franklin
Michal Labik
Patrick Lauppe
Graham Lazar
Taylor Nickel

Michelle Oing
Sofia Tancredi
Katharine Vidt
Mark Warren
Roland Yang

CONTENTS

EUROPE TOP 10 CITIES

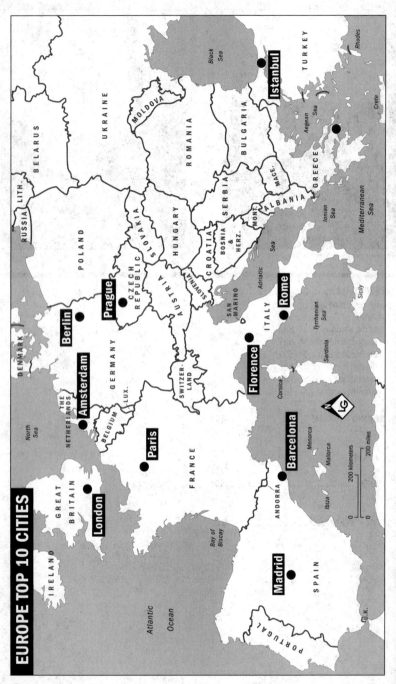

RESEARCHER-WRITERS

BEATRICE FRANKLIN. Beatrice Franklin is to *Let's Go* as JK Rowling is to Britain. As a wee freshman she worked on *Let's Go Thailand 2009; as* a jolly junior, she took on *Let's Go Amsterdam and Brussels 2011;* for her final LG adventure, this decorated veteran headed to London. Between hipster hunting in the East End and avoiding cheeky pick-up lines in the West End, Beatrice truly embraced her inner Brit. She even learned to walk on the proper side of the road.

MICHAL LABIK. While in college, Michal Labik had an illustrious (get it?) career drawing comics for his school newspaper, and we think this probably helped develop the keen wit that pervades all of his writing for *Let's Go.* His fluency in Czech certainly added an insiders' element to the Prague guide: we can't even pronounce most of the addresses he gave us, but we do know they're correct.

PATRICK LAUPPE. Patrick Lauppe was born to be a researcher for *Let's Go Berlin,* assuming he was born with all the colorful pants that he owns today. We didn't hesitate to give him the job, especially once we heard that his spirit animal is an ostrich. Unfortunately, only after he was hired did we realize the risk of injury that his blogs and listings pose to readers (split sides, broken funny bones, etc.).

GRAHAM LAZAR. Along with his bougie alter ego Winston Shrewsbury, Graham Lazar attacked the streets of Madrid with an aplomb hitherto unheard of—at least, that's how Winston would say it. Overcoming such obstacles as solo-tackling the communal Spanish dinner, foodie Graham held every restaurant to the highest of gourmet standards and kept his copy sharp for the duration of his route.

TAYLOR NICKEL. This *Let's Go* veteran returned to France to conquer Paris's streets and woo its women with his savvy wit. When he wasn't sipping on a *demi-pêche* or resting up in his apartment in the 14ème, Taylor was finding the perfect local hangouts and the best bargains. Though it's slightly more stressful than the French countryside, Paris will always be Taylor's home away from home.

MICHELLE OING. A true academic at heart, Michelle flexed her superior art-historian muscles, beautifully depicting 14th-century wooden crosses, martyrdoms, and the ever-popular Roman ruins. Despite her hatred of Ms. Hepburn, she starred in her own Roman holiday, partying in Termini, fawning over the ubiquitous stray cats, and endlessly searching for the perfect Roman bath(room).

SOFIA TANCREDI. After leaving her broken computer in the hands of a stranger named Carlo, Sofia showed Florence how budget travel should be done. When she wasn't on her eternal quest for Wi-Fi, she pulled out all the stops, donning the most conservative of conservative outfits to infiltrate churches, monasteries, and Tuscan towers. Through epic travels and innumerable pints of gelato, Sofia discovered she can take herself anywhere.

KATHARINE VIDT. From providing X-rated research notes to cycling around on her bicycle, Kat embraced the true spirit of Amsterdam. She proved she could pry information from anyone, whether a stony-faced hostel owner or just a plain stoner. Though Kat could probably write books solely on Electric Ladyland, Albert Heijns, and *stroopwafel* ice cream, she conquered the whole city, and did it with swag.

MARK WARREN. A *Let's Go* veteran, Mark Warren found most of his stationary stay in Barcelona to be a cakewalk, especially since he speaks every language remotely related to the city. Easily handling even the parts of his visit that were decidedly not a cakewalk—discovering local dives and dueling armed muggers—Mark is a posterboy for LG stardom.

ROLAND YANG. This staff writer-turned-researcher (who also goes by RoRo) taught the Istanbulites a thing or two about their own city. Dodging bears and haggling in markets, Roland left no road unexplored in the city. Whether concocting Turkish fast food or charming his way into clubs, Roland crushed his route with class.

EUROPE TOP 10 CITIES

We live in an era of lists—top 100 songs of the '90s, top 20 TV shows canceled before their time (*Firefly*, we miss you!), top five foods that will give you a coronary of joy—why not apply the philosophy to travel? You're going to Europe, but you don't have the time or money to tour every podunk town in France, even though they all seem to have at least three art museums. With so much to see and do, there's no shame in settling for the greatest hits.

Make no mistake—these cities are heavy hitters. Amsterdam will satisfy your cravings for culture and a few other things. Hit the beach all day and the bars all night in Barcelona. Berlin is Europe's champion of cool, but it won't try too hard to show it or anything. You can't walk down the street in Florence without running into an artistic masterpiece. Four names, three empires, and two continents make Istanbul one of a kind. Despite all the tradition, tea, and tweed, London moves like no other city. You can spend the whole day in Madrid's country-sized museums, but don't be late for dinner (at midnight). Nearly everyone in the world idealizes Paris, but it's more than a city of ideals. Prague is magic—ex-communist, post-Kafka, pre-*Harry Potter* magic. Not even Carthage could conquer Rome, but you're welcome to try.

Every which way, we've got you covered. Grab your *Best of Queen* or *Worst of Jefferson Airplane* CD, your seven favorite T-shirts, and your three best friends. You're going to see the top 10 cities Europe has to offer.

when to go

Summer is the busiest time to travel in Europe. The season's many festivals can jack up prices, but it might be worth it to catch Bastille Day in Paris or London's Proms. Late spring and early autumn bring fewer tourists and cheaper airfare—meaning they're good times to go, if you can get the days off. Winter travel is great for those looking to hit the ski ranges around the mountains, but not the best time to take a walking tour through Prague. Plus, you'll find that some hotels, restaurants, and sights have limited hours or are on vacation—from you.

best of europe's top 10 cities

You're visiting the *crème de la crème* of European cities. Now you can top that by doing the best of the best in each metropolis, from partying at the coolest club to snacking on the tastiest treat. After completing all of this epic one-upping, we doubt you'll have ever felt more superior over superlatives.

AMSTERDAM: The works at the Van Gogh Museum (p. 43) will have you mourning the artist's early death. You might understand it once you see titles like *Skull of a Skeleton with Burning Cigarette,* though.

BARCELONA: Ogle the Sagrada Família (p. 118); bask at a *platja* (p. 127); and brood at Barcelona Pipa Club (p. 145), where smoking accoutrements decorated by Dalí make it all so much cooler.

BERLIN: Forget Checkpoint Charlie and go to the Berliner Mauer Dokumentationszentrum (p. 213) for a sense of pre-Wall times. Come nightfall hit up Club Tresor (p. 238) to witness Berlin's famous techno scene.

FLORENCE: You will meet your dream man in this city. His name will be David (p. 288). Also, make the requisite trip to the Uffizi (p. 281). (You will not meet David here.)

ISTANBUL: The Blue Mosque (p. 351) will most likely make your jaw drop. If it doesn't, get that mandible looked at.

LONDON: This city is all about converting you—from modern-art hater to gaga for Andy Warhol at the Tate Modern (p. 428), from snore-through-Shakespeare to I-heart-Hamlet at the Globe Theatre (p. 429).

MADRID: If you do not see *Guernica, The Garden of Earthly Delights,* or *Las Meninas,* you have done something very wrong (p. 505). Almost as wrong as not munching on *chocolates con churros* at dawn after a whole night of partying.

PARIS: It's so cliché, but stick with the tried-and-true here. The Eiffel Tower (p. 595) will have you wanting to sweep someone off her feet (just don't drop her off the edge), the Latin Quarter (p. 573) is just grand, and the croissants are orgasmic.

PRAGUE: Yes, the Charles Bridge (p. 682) and Prague Castle (p. 691) are overrun with tourists—it's because they're awesome. Save some money for the sights by buying beer (it's cheaper than water!).

ROME: Rome is for cosplay tourists and carb-lovers: gladiators at the Colosseum (p. 764) will happily playfight for your euro, and the dishes at Cacio e Pepe (p. 790) will make all other pastas you have ever tasted seem inadequate.

what to do

HERE COMES THE SUN

Sometimes, the best sights are all around you. Put the book down for a few minutes—we forgive you!—and explore the outdoors.

- **ISTANBUL:** For the best views the city has to offer, cross the **Galata Bridge** (p. 352) over the Golden Horn, or climb **Çamlıca Hill** (p. 360) on the Asian side. For the best view of city life, look no further than the **bazaars** (p. 384).

- **AMSTERDAM:** Rent a bike (p. 84) near Centraal Station and ride down **Haarlemmerstraat,** which is full of cheap eats, stores, and coffeeshops. Then head south through the quaint streets of **Jordaan.** Take a breather at a canal-side cafe. Smell that? No, not pot. Freedom. Or maybe pot.

- **ROME:** All roads lead to Rome, so don't worry about getting lost on the **Appian Way** (p. 781). If you're sick of crumbling monuments, the **Villa Borghese** (p. 778) has enough green for days.

- **BARCELONA:** The entire strip between Torre San Sebastiá and Parc de Diagonal-Mar is lined with public beaches. Our favorites are **Platja de la Barceloneta** (p. 128) and **Platja Mar Bella** (p. 128), the city's only official ❧**nude beach.**

THE GREAT INDOORS

Let's be real: you didn't come to Europe for the trees—except the ones in the background of the *Mona Lisa.* Each of these cities' museums could keep you distracted for a lifetime or four.

- **PARIS:** **Musée Rodin** (p. 596), **Musée d'Orsay** (p. 597), and, of course, the **Louvre** (p. 587)—we promise it was famous before *The Da Vinci Code.*

- **LONDON:** In the **British Museum** (p. 434), the **National Gallery** (p. 424), the **Tate Modern** (p. 428), and the **Victoria and Albert Museum** (p. 430), priceless works somehow translate to free admission. Yay, socialism!

- **MADRID:** If the Avenida del Arte were a bowling lane, you could knock out three world-class museums with one ball: the **Prado** (p. 505), the **Reina Sofía** (p. 505), and the **CaixaForum** (p. 506).

- **PRAGUE:** Choose between the history of central European art at **Veletržní Palác** (p. 695), the old *nouveau* at the **Alfons Mucha Museum** (p. 678), or the contemporary scene at **DOX** (p. 695)—or be indecisive and do all three!

OM NOM NOM

No, u cant haz cheezburger, because European food is as diverse as it is delicious.

- **FLORENCE:** *Bistecca alla fiorentina* and gelato are fantastic everywhere in the city, but only **Cibréo Teatro del Sale** (p. 303) combines gourmet dinner with a brilliant show.

- **MADRID:** If you pinch your pennies eating at tapas joints in **Las Huertas** (p. 490), you can save up to try the suckling pig Hemingway ate at **El Sobrino de Botín** (p. 511).

- **ROME:** Pizza (**Antica Pizzeria de Roma;** p. 794), pasta (**Cacio e Pepe;** p. 790), and pastries (**Pasticceria Strabbioni Roma;** p. 794). Need we say more?

- **PARIS:** Feeling crepe-d out? **Thabthim Siam's** tasty Thai (p. 613), **Le Jip's** creative Cuban-African-Brazilian fusion (p. 607), and **L'As du Falafel's** legendary falafel (p. 608) draw all the locals.

student superlatives

- **MOST BLING:** The Pope's crib (a.k.a. Vatican City, p. 772), where you'll find the sickest frescoes and some Swiss guards in tricked out uniforms.

- **MOST EMBARRASSING MUSEUM TO VISIT WITH YOUR FAMILY (ESPE-CIALLY CREEPY UNCLE NICK):** The Amsterdam Sex Museum (p. 36).

- **BEST PLACE TO FIND A HIPSTER HUSBAND:** Hackescher Markt (p. 210)—or really anywhere in Berlin.

- **BEST PLACE TO TAKE A SIESTA:** Parque del Buen Retiro (p. 506)—or really anywhere in Madrid.

- **BEST PLACE TO GET SO FRESH AND SO CLEAN:** Getting pummelled by a nearly naked hairy Turkish man in one of Istanbul's hamams is actually a lot more relaxing than you'd think (p. 382).

- **MOST LIKELY TO SUCK UP ALL YOUR TIME:** La Cité Libreria Café in Florence has everything you'd ever need: food, cheap beer, live music, and comfortable seating (p. 315).

- **BEST PLACE TO GET ARSE-ACHE:** Shakespeare's Globe Theatre in London (p. 429).

- **BEST PLACE TO BUY A PARROT AND A SUNFLOWER ON THE SAME BLOCK:** Barcelona's Las Ramblas (p. 98).

- **BEST PLACE TO ASK SOMEONE TO SLEEP WITH YOU WITHOUT GETTING SLAPPED:** Paris's Moulin Rouge (p. 634). Thanks, Christina Aguilera!

- **BEST PLACE TO KISS:** Below the ear. Just kidding—under the metronome in Prague's Letná Park (p. 695).

LAST FRIDAY NIGHT

Oh, hey. Have we met? You look awfully familiar...

- **AMSTERDAM:** Were you at **Paradiso** (p. 65) the other day? You know, the club in a converted church? Or were you chilling with the locals at **Studio 80** (p. 67)?

- **BERLIN:** Well, if you're a techno-lover, you must have been at **Sanitorium 23** (p. 236). Was that you grooving inside and then playing ping pong outside **Rosi's** (p. 235) in Friederichshain?

- **ISTANBUL:** With swanky friends at **Anjelique** (p. 376)? On the beer terrace at **Peyote** (p. 375)? Puffing the night away at **Asmalı Sohbet Çay Evi** (p. 374)?

- **PRAGUE:** Well, we give up. Let's go to **Cross Club** (p. 726). Repeat after us: *"Pĕt piv, prosím!"* (Five beers, please!)

BEYOND TOURISM

Take, take, take. Have you had enough? No? Well, you'll get a lot out of giving back, and there are plenty of opportunities to do so. For even more on studying, volunteering, and working abroad, flip to **Beyond Tourism** (p. 843).

- **BOĞAZIÇI UNIVERSITY:** Head to Istanbul to study at the oldest American university outside of the United States (p. 846).

- **ROME UNIVERSITY OF FINE ARTS:** If the Sistine Chapel's ceiling leaves you inspired, come to RU to embrace your inner Michelangelo (p. 848).

- **PINK POINT:** Help GLBT travelers have a fulfilling Amsterdam experience at this information kiosk (p. 850).
- **EUROINTERNS:** Work in Madrid with major companies like Amnesty International and American Express (p. 854).

suggested itineraries

THE GRAND TOUR *(1 month)*

Brace yourself. Seeing all 10 of these cities in one month is going to be a serious trip. Fortunately, you have us to suggest an order and timeframe for each city. Refer to the itineraries above for the key things you have to see in each city and for many of the transportation links between them.

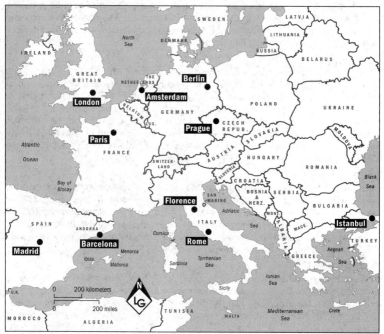

london *(3 days)*

Load up on history, culture, and tea. Go shop at Harrod's or catch a play in the West End. If you time your trip right, you can even see the Olympic Games return to the city. When you've seen enough royalty and mastered your Cockney slang, catch a bus (UK£37) to Amsterdam. Be aware that the bus takes about 12hr., so you're losing half of one of your precious Eurotripping days. The train is a faster option, though you'll have to transfer at Brussels and shell out over UK£100.

amsterdam *(3 days)*

Depending on what you want out of the city, Amsterdam can be very similar or completely different from London. It has imperial history, renowned artistic pedigree, and a great music scene, just like London. Of course, it also has coffeeshops and legalized prostitution. For the proper Amsterdam experience. you need to explore both sides. Done? Hop on the 3hr. train to Paris.

paris *(4 days)*

The quintessential European city! A word of warning, though: it's rougher and less idealized than you might think. Don't feel like you have to stay within shouting distance of the Seine at all times—you'll be surprised by what you find in places like Pigalle and Montparnasse. To continue the tour, head to Barcelona. You could catch a train from the Gare d'Austerlitz, but it costs over €100. Ryanair runs flights from Beauvais airport (85km north of Paris), and if you book in advance you can get a ticket for not much more than you pay for a coffee along the Champs-Élysées.

barcelona *(3 days)*

You'll be hard-pressed to leave this city of beaches and modernisme. Gaze up at the never-ending construction of La Sagrada Família and stroll through the medieval streets of Barri Gótic in search of a damsel in distress and a dragon to slay (or just an exquisite Catalan meal). When it's time to discover other Spanish frontiers, taking a long, cheap bus ride with a service like Alsa, or a shorter but more expensive train ride on the national Spanish train sytem.

madrid *(3 days)*

This restless, youthful city will have you living the infectious *madrileño* way in no time. Eat dinner at 10pm, go out until sunrise, and explore under the warm, inviting sun. Fill up on *bocaditos* and join the 20-somethings haunting the cool cafes, pubs, and bars of Las Huertas. Bring your newfound night-owl skills to Rome via a budget airline flight. Ryanair has flights at €45, which we think is quite a steal.

rome *(4 days)*

You may think that you've seen a lot of old things so far, but get ready for Rome to put them all to shame. Be amazed at how intact some of the ruins are (the Colosseum is certainly in much better shape than the Circus Maximus). Engage in Rome's modern culture at the bars of Centro Storico or the clubs of Testaccio. Don't forget to eat as the Romans do. Set aside €45 and a couple of hours for the train to Florence.

florence *(2 days)*

Throw yourself into the Renaissance, which seems to live on in every Florentine building. The most compact of these 10 cities, Florence doesn't require quite as much time, but that doesn't mean it's any less rewarding. You'll take to the air again for the next leg of your trip, catching a flight to Prague. Air One (Alitalia's budget subsidiary) offers flights from Pisa Airport (a 1hr. bus ride from Florence) to Prague for €70.

prague *(3 days)*
The gritty post-communism side seeps through the tourist-happy tinsel of Prague's recent renovations. In New Town you can find the window where the Hussites began a Czech tradition of defenestration. The neighborhood of Holešovice is becoming one of the most happening places in Prague, and its nightclubs should not be missed. Good to go? Hop on a €30 bus at the Florenc ÚAN bus terminal.

berlin *(3 days)*
Falafel and schnitzel, East and West, Potter and Voldemort... ok, maybe not that last one. Look out for horn-rimmed glasses and cardigans among Friedrichshain's nightclubs, which are housed in former DDR buildings. Tiergarten in the middle of Berlin will make you forget you're in a metropolis. Thank the Turkish immigrants in Kreuzberg for your cheap shawarma and ludicrously inexpensive flights to Istanbul, your last, but in no way least exciting, stop.

istanbul *(3 days)*
Europe-d out? Asia is a cheap ferry ride away. Experience the city that has been fought over for millennia, and see the effect that all these influences have had on its culture. Spend the final night of your trip watching the sun set over the domes of Istanbul's mosques, and remember the extraordinary things you've seen along the way. Then go party it up one last time in some swanky nightclubs. You've earned some serious revelry by now.

CITY HOPPING
If tackling 10 cities at once seems a little daunting, don't worry—you've got a whole lifetime of travel ahead to hit them all. For now, focus on a selection of the cities that can easily be visited together.

london, paris, and amsterdam
These cities in the north of Europe are not the ones you come to for the weather. The list of reasons not to go ends there, and lucky for you they can easily be visited together. If you start in London, you can hop on the Eurostar train to Paris. Tickets

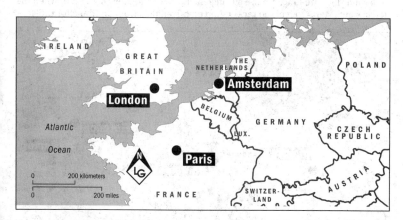

are much cheaper if bought well in advance and can be as low as £38, or as high as £100. When you manage to tear yourself away from the beauty of Paris, catch a

Thalys train to Amsterdam. If booked more than a month in advance, you can get a ticket for €35, but again prices rise a lot closer to the date of travel.

prague, berlin, and istanbul

Despite the long distances between them, these cities are surprisingly easy to travel between. Berlin is separated from Prague by a 4½hr., €30 bus ride—that's the perfect interval of time to play Go Fish with your new bus friends before you get sick of each other. If you're going in the other direction, try the 1425Kč train to Berlin. Traveling from Berlin to Istanbul doesn't really sound like city-hopping, but thanks to the large number of Turkish immigrants in Germany, there are regular cheap flights connecting the cities. Pegasus Airlines has flights for as low as €50.

madrid, barcelona, florence, and rome

If your travel checklist includes art, sun, and Catholicism, Spain and Italy are ideal destinations. From Madrid, Barcelona is a hop, skip, and 3hr. train away. Although the trains run frequently, they can be expensive (€120 expensive). Buses take about 6hr. but only cost €30. A third option is plane travel, which takes 1½hr. and, if you're lucky, costs as low as €60. From Barcelona to Florence, flying may be the best option; train rides are long, require a transfer, and can sometimes cost €200. When the Renaissance starts to feel too recent, hop on a Trenitalia train to Rome for €15-45.

WEEKEND GETAWAYS

You're a very busy and important person with only two days to spare for gallivanting around your European city of choice. Fear not—we'll make sure you hit all the highlights. Or string a few of these together to make your own adventure!

amsterdam

In your two days in the city of van Gogh, canals, and legal prostitution, you're going to be busy. Start with sunflowers and ear wounds at the **Van Gogh Museum** (p. 43), then jazz it up mightily with a trip to **Electric Ladyland** (p. 42). Jump on a **bike** while you're here—it's the most Dutch thing you can do. **Westerkerk** church (p. 38) is one of Amsterdam's finest, while the architecture of the **Golden Bend** (p. 41) is a lesson in both design and history. You aren't here for the food, but load up on the city's cheap and delicious sandwiches.

Don't tire yourself out too much during the days, since evenings in Amsterdam are one of the city's biggest attractions. One night, try the **Red Light District** (p. 60) on for size (as long as you can handle all the British bachelor parties doing the same). The other night, allow the gravitational pulls of **Leidseplein** (p. 65) or **Rembrandtplein** (p. 67) to draw you in; good luck choosing among their dozens of bars and clubs.

barcelona

You may be melting in the sun along with all that twisted modernisme architecture, but these two days in Barcelona will be some of the most surreal of your life. Start with **Parc Güell** (p. 123), wander through Gaudí's trippy sculptures, fountains, and mosaics, and hike up to the park's summit to get a vista of the entire city. Then head off to the neighborhood of Gràcia to house hunt famed modernista casas, and stop by **Un Lugar de Gràcia** for one of the best lunch specials in Barcelona. Hop on the metro to peruse **Museu Picasso's** (p. 116) extensive collection, then bar hop along El Born.

Begin your second day with some Roman ruins **Museu d'Història de la Ciutat** (p. 112) and a vista from the top of Columbus Tower. Then hit the beaches of Barcelona, where you can play pick-up volleyball with the locals or sunbathe (in the nude, if you like). At night, the clubs along Barceloneta come alive, so don't let a long train ride the next morning stop you from joining in the debauchery.

berlin

The hippest city in Europe has way too many things for you to see in just two days, but don't let that keep you from trying. Tornado through Mitte's Museum Island (don't skip the **Neue Nationalgalerie** or the **Pergamon Museum** p. 207), before heading over to Hackescher Markt and bobbing through waves of flannel and horn-rimmed glasses that roll into cool cafes, bookstores, and art galleries. At night, join **Kaffee Burger's** (p. 231) crowd of 20-somethings in band T-shirts for heavy techno, poetry readings, and dancing in drunken sloppiness.

Delve into Kreuzberg's graffiti-lined streets and Soviet sights with a deliciously cheap döner kebab from one of the street vendors in hand, then Friedrichshain's **East Side Gallery** (p. 213), the world's largest open-air gallery that contains the longest remaining portion of the Wall. After a quick nap, start with house music at the indoor-outdoor **Rosi's** (p. 235), pay a visit to the Transformers action figures at **Astro-Bar** (p. 236), and brace yourself for the trip out to **K-17** (p. 236), a massive *Diskothek* that the tourists haven't discovered yet.

florence

Get your Renaissance on during your two days in one of the artistic capitals of Europe. You don't have much time, so make a reservation in advance for the **Uffizi** (p. 281) to avoid wasting your trip standing in line. Then explore the free art and people-watching potential in the central **Piazza della Signoria**. In case you don't have time to visit the real *David* in the **Accademia** (p. 288), get a good luck at his replica here. Visit the city's crowning glory: the **Duomo** (p. 279). Admire its remarkable facade, then climb its dome for a stunning panorama of the whole city. Reward yourself for conquering all those steps with Florence's greatest form of sustenance: gelato.

Don't let the Arno River be a barrier to your exploration. Cross the famous **Ponte Vecchio** (try not to waste too much money in all its gold shops) to the Oltrarno and pay a visit to the **Palazzo Pitti** complex (p. 293). The Boboli Gardens are a remarkably green oasis in the city. Florence's nightlife is less structured than in other cities, so go with the flow by settling in a *piazza* with the locals. **Piazza Sant'Ambrogio** in Santa Croce is a particularly good bet.

istanbul

Istanbul is the city to visit when other European destinations are starting to blend together. No more cathedrals for you. Try Istanbul's two greatest mosques: the **Haggia Sophia** and the **Blue Mosque** (p. 351). The maze of Sultanahmet, the oldest neighborhood of one of the oldest cities in Europe, will captivate you. Visit the **Grand Bazaar** (p. 385) for a shopping experience like no other. Now take the cheapest intercontinental cruise in the world to visit the Asian half of the city. It's not the most exciting part of town, but crossing the Bosphorus alone is a remarkable experience.

In the evening, the clubs of **Beşiktaş** (p. 376) are entertaining both as social microcosms and as nightspots. Spend at least half a day in **Beyoğlu** (p. 340), the heart of modern Istanbul. Catch a contemporary vision of the city at the **Istanbul Museum of Modern Art** (p. 356) and take your time exploring Istanbul's liveliest street, **İstiklal Caddesi**. For a really Turkish experience, try visiting a **hamam** (p. 382). On your last evening, smoke some *nargile* in **Sultanahmet** (p. 372), or just hit up **Beyoğlu's bars** (p. 374) for nightlife as good as in any European city.

london

During your time in London, try to talk to as many people as possible. Firstly, British people are interesting. Secondly, after all those strange continental languages, it will be an amazing relief speaking to people whom you can (just about) understand. When you aren't stuck in conversation, make sure to run between as many of London's free museums as possible. The **National Gallery** (p. 424), the **Victoria and Albert Museum** (p. 430), and the **British Museum** (p. 434) are just three of our favorites.

You're obviously going to want to see the iconic sights (Buckingham Palace, Big Ben, the Tower, Platform Nine and Three Quarters), but we encourage you not to waste your money on hefty admission fees. Instead, save up for a night out in the West End. Catching a blues show at **Ain't Nothin' But** then dancing at **The Borderline** (p. 451) sounds like a great plan to us. When hunger strikes, sample some of London's hugely varied ethnic food offerings (that whole empire thing was the best thing that ever happened to British cuisine).

madrid

Meander with the crowds of tourists hankering to see Picasso's *Guernica* at the **Reina Sofía** (p. 505) and join the crowd of wild *el botellón* by night. No experience in Madrid is complete without walking the tree-lined **Avenida del Arte** (p. 505) and popping through the various world-class museums (so much Velázquez). For a respite, saunter over to **Parque del Buen Retiro** (p. 506), where you can check out a couple of palaces, row in the artificial pond, or just siesta in the shade. Come nightfall, head over to **Kapital** (p. 531) and choose from seven floors of trashy fun that play everything from house to Spanish pop to hip hop. Stay out until sunrise and dig into *churros con chocolate*.

After an early-morning nap (you probably won't have enough time for a real sleep), start off your day with an **Egyptian temple** (p. 508) and then check out Franco's former place of residence in **El Pardo** (p. 508). Gallivant through Malasaña, a playground of the best nightlife, live music, and dining in the city—it's the place to experience the '70s counter-culture movement, La Movida, particularly at **La Vía Láctea** (p. 538). Plus, you won't have to pay cover if you arrive before 1am.

paris

Welcome to the busiest two days of your life. Stroll the elegant Champs-Élysées, Paris's most famous boulevard, and be awed by the **Arc de Triomphe** (p. 598) towering above you. Once you're warmed up on Parisian sightseeing, continue on to the **Louvre** (p. 587). Don't try to see everything here; you might as well give up on the rest of your trip and set up a tent next to the *Venus de Milo* if you insist on covering the whole collection. Try not to panic that your time in Paris is already a quarter over, and head to **Notre Dame** (p. 584) for one of Europe's greatest cathedrals. If you must, pose for a photo as a hunchback. Complete your collection of great Paris monuments at the **Eiffel Tower** (p. 595), which is beautiful to look at and even better to look from.

Make sure to leave the postcard-ready monuments behind at some stage and get to know a more authentic side of the city. Tour the intellectual **Latin Quarter** to unleash your inner Hemingway and Sartre. Grab some brie and a baguette for a traditional Parisian picnic in the **Jardin du Luxembourg** (p. 592). If you can face more museums, the **Musée d'Orsay** (p. 597) is full of works by artists considered not good enough for the Louvre, including untalented hacks like Monet, Manet, and van Gogh. If you have any energy left (and if you're ever going to dig deep for stamina, now's the time to do it), indulge in **Paris's nightlife** (p. 622). Head to the Marais or enjoy the student-friendly scene in the Latin Quarter.

prague

The Disneyland of Europe, Prague is a lot of fairytale and, unlike Space Mountain, very little disappointment. Hit the major sights of Old Town, like the **Astronomical Clock** (p. 683), the Art Deco **Municipal House** (p. 683), and the **Charles Bridge** (p. 682). Next, saunter over to the nearby **Jewish Quarter** (p. 685) to see the various synagogues, but don't hold your breath for a Golem. End the night at **Rudolfinum** (p. 728), the home of the Czech Philharmonic Orchestra.

The next day, conquer **Prague Castle** (p. 691) and **Saint Vitus Cathedral** (p. 691)—which took six centuries to build and only two hours for you to see. Make your way over to **Café Louvre** (p. 702), where Kafka and his friends used to sit around being intellectual. Finally, choose your own adventure among the enormous rooms of **Cross Club** (p. 726), considered one of Europe's best nightclubs.

rome

Rome is famous for its ancient monuments, and you won't want to miss the **Colosseum** and **Roman Forum** (p. 765). When you move onto the Centro Storico area, navigate by monument rather than by map and you'll be less likely to get lost and you'll definitely see more sights. The **Pantheon** and **Piazza Navona** (p. 768) are unmissable. In case you need reminding, remember to try some of the incredible local pasta or pizzas. Spend one evening visiting the **Trevi Fountain** (it's less busy and more impressive after dark) and hanging out with the young crowd on the **Spanish Steps** (p. 771).

Rome wasn't built in a day and you didn't manage to see it all in one, so on the second morning head over to Vatican City. Explore the majestic **Vatican Museums** and **Sistine Chapel,** and maybe try to stop by **Saint Peter's Basilica** during mass (p. 773). This is a great neighborhood for food, so load up on calories at a **trattoria** (p. 790). On your last evening, throw yourself into the throbbing nightlife scene. Bars litter the Centro Storico, or head south to **Testaccio** for its clubs (p. 807).

how to use this book

CHAPTERS

In the next few pages, the travel coverage chapters—the meat of any *Let's Go* book—begin with **Amsterdam,** which is thriving in refined, artistic culture in addition to being a pothead's paradise. Next we'll give you a taste for Catalonia culture in **Barcelona,** and then head to Germany to explore the fast-paced city of **Berlin.** In our first Italian adventure, come face to face with *David* in **Florence.** We'll throw in some European/Asian fusion in **Istanbul** before heading to the place where a hip underground scene meets posh royalty: **London.** We'll next head the intellectual and cultural centers of two neighboring countries: **Madrid,** full of Old World palaces and cathedrals, and **Paris,** whose museums have more artwork than you could see in a month. The journey continues in **Prague,** full of towers, castles, and medieval-meets-modern charm. Our Top 10 tour concludes by returning to Italy to play gladiator-for-a-day in **Rome.**

But that's not all, folks. We also have a few extra chapters for you to peruse:

CHAPTER	DESCRIPTION
Discover Europe Top 10 Cities	Discover tells you what to do, when to do it, and where to go for it. The absolute coolest things about any destination get highlighted in this chapter at the front of all *Let's Go* books.
Essentials	Essentials contains the practical info you need before, during, and after your trip—visas, regional transportation, health and safety, phrasebooks, and more.
Beyond Tourism	As students ourselves, we at *Let's Go* encourage studying abroad, or going beyond tourism more generally, every chance we get. This chapter lists ideas for how to study, volunteer, or work abroad with other young travelers in Europe to get more out of your trip.

LISTINGS

Listings—a.k.a. reviews of individual establishments—constitute a majority of *Let's Go* coverage. Our Researcher-Writers list establishments in order from **best to worst value**—not necessarily quality. (Obviously a five-star hotel is nicer than a hostel, but it would probably be ranked lower because it's not as good a value.) Listings pack in a lot of information, but it's easy to digest if you know how they're constructed:

ESTABLISHMENT NAME type of establishment $$$$

Address ☎phone number; website

Editorial review goes here.

✣ Directions to the establishment. ℹ Other practical information about the establishment, like age restrictions at a club or whether breakfast is included at a hostel. $ Prices for goods or services. ⏰ Hours or schedules.

ICONS

First things first: places and things that we absolutely love, sappily cherish, generally obsess over, and wholeheartedly endorse are denoted by the all-empowering 👍 **Let's Go thumbs-up.** In addition, the icons scattered at the end of a listing (as you saw in the sample above) can serve as visual cues to help you navigate each listing:

👍	*Let's Go* recommends	☎	Phone numbers	✣	Directions
ℹ	Other hard info	$	Prices	⏰	Hours

PRICE DIVERSITY

A final set of icons corresponds to what we call our "price diversity" scale, which approximates how much money you can expect to spend at a given establishment. For **accommodations,** we base our range on the cheapest price for which a single traveler can stay for one night. For **food,** we estimate the average amount one traveler will spend in one sitting. The table below tells you what you'll *typically* find in Europe at the corresponding price range, but keep in mind that no system can allow for the quirks of individual establishments.

ACCOMMODATIONS	WHAT YOU'RE LIKELY TO FIND
$	Campgrounds and dorm rooms, both in hostels and actual universities. Expect bunk beds and a communal bath. You may have to provide or rent towels and linens.
$$	Upper-end hostels or lower-end hotels. You may have a private bathroom, or there may be a sink in your room and a communal shower in the hall.
$$$	A small room with a private bath. Should have decent amenities, such as phone and TV. Breakfast may be included.
$$$$	Large hotels or chains. If it's $$$$ and it doesn't have the perks you want (and more), you've paid too much.
FOOD	WHAT YOU'RE LIKELY TO FIND
$	Probably street food, kebabs, crepes, or gelato, but also university cafeterias and bakeries (yum). Usually takeout, but you may have the option of sitting down.
$$	Sandwiches, pizza, appetizers at a bar, or low-priced entrees and tapas. Most ethnic eateries and trattorias are $$. Either takeout or a sit-down meal, but only slightly more fashionable decor.
$$$	A somewhat fancy restaurant. Entrees tend to be heartier or more elaborate, but you're really paying for decor and ambience. Since you'll have the luxury of a waiter, the tip will set you back a little extra.
$$$$	Your meal might cost more than your room, but there's a reason—it's something fabulous, famous, or both. Slacks and dress shirts may be expected. Offers fancier food and a decent wine list. Don't order a PB and J!

AMSTERDAM

Tell someone you're going to Amsterdam, and you'll be met with a chuckle and a knowing smile. Yes, everyone will think you're going for the hookers and weed, but there's much more to Amsterdam. The Netherlands's permissive attitudes are the product of a long history of liberalism and tolerance that dates back far before the advent of drug tourism and prostitutes' unions. A refuge for Protestants and Jews in the 16th and 17th centuries, Amsterdam earned tremendous wealth as the center of a trading empire that stretched from the New York (sorry: New Amsterdam) to Indonesia. The city's wealth served as an incubator for the artistic achievements of the Dutch Golden Age and the economic and political birth of modern Europe. Today, Amsterdam is a diverse and progressive city as famous for its art museums and quaint canal-side cafes as for its coffeeshops and prostitution.

As you stroll the streets, savor the culture and vitality of this pretty city. You can walk or bike it in a day, moving from the peaceful canals of the Jordaan to the gaudy peepshows of the Red Light District. Old trading money lives on in graceful mansions, while, a few blocks away, repurposed squats house clubs and cinemas. Whether you're obsessed with van Gogh, want to dance all night at GLBT clubs, or always wanted to learn all about the history of flourescent art, you're guaranteed to have a good time in Amsterdam.

greatest hits

- **DRINK THROUGH THE PLEIN.** Head to **Weber** in Leidseplein for a drink or two, then explore the area's many fun student bars (p. 65).

- **LET'S (VAN) GOGH.** The **Van Gogh Museum** will make you empathize with one of the Netherlands's greatest artists. It's not hard; he left enough self-portraits behind (p. 43).

- **ITS ELECTRIC! Electric Ladyland,** the world's "First Museum of Fluorescent Art," will take you on an unforgettably weird trip into the world of glowing rocks and "participatory art" (p. 42).

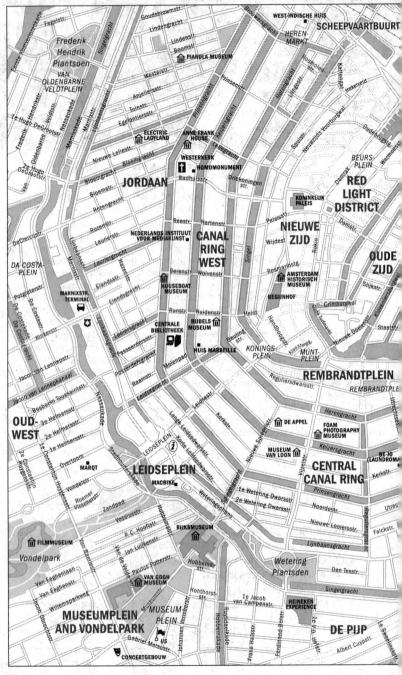

amsterdam

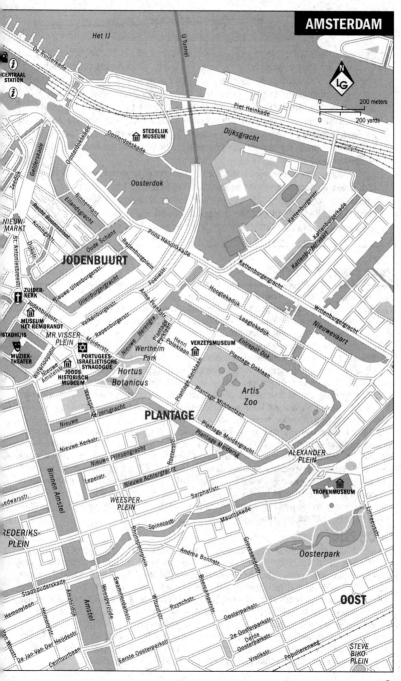

AMSTERDAM

0   200 meters
0   200 yards

Het IJ

De Ruijterkade

CENTRAAL
STATION

U Tunnel

Piet Heinkade

STEDELIJK
MUSEUM

Oosterdokskade

Dijksgracht

Oosterdok

Kattenburgerstr.

Kattenburgerkade

Kattenburgervaart

Zeedijk

Geldersekade

Oosterdokskade

NIEUW-
MARKT

Binnenkant

Eilandsgracht

Oude Schans

Prins Hendrikkade

Rapenburgerplein

St. Antoniesbreestr.

Dijkstr.

Recht Boomssloot

Kattenburgergracht

Wittenburgergracht

JODENBUURT

Nieuwe Uilenburgerstr.

Uilenburgergracht

Foeliestr.

Hoogtekadijk

Laagtekadijk

Nieuwevaart

ZUIDER-
KERK

Jodenbreestr.

Valkenburgerstr.

Anne Frankstr.

MUSEUM
HET REMBRANDT

Rapenburgerstr.

Plantage Kerklaan

Nieuwe Herengracht

Entrepot Dok

STADHUIS

MR VISSER
PLEIN

Muiderstr.

Henri
Polaklaan

VERZETSMUSEUM

Plantage Doklaan

MUZIEK-
THEATER

Waterlooplein

Nieuwe Amstel

PORTUGEES-
ISRAELIETISCHE
SYNAGOGUE

Wertheim
Park

JOODS
HISTORISCH
MUSEUM

Hortus
Botanicus

Plantage Kerklaan

Plantage Middenlaan

Artis
Zoo

Nieuwe

Waterlooplein

Zwanenburgwal

PLANTAGE

Plantage Muidergracht

Plantage Muiderstr.

Nieuwe Kerkstr.

Plantage Muidergracht

Nieuwe Prinsengracht

Roetersstr.

ALEXANDER
PLEIN

Lepelstr.

Nieuwe Achtergracht

WEESPER-
PLEIN

Sarphatistr.

TROPENMUSEUM

EDWARSSTR.

Binnen Amstel

Spinozastr.

Mauritskade

REDERIKS-
PLEIN

Rhijnspoorplein

Andrea Bonnstr.

's Gravesandestr.

Oosterpark

Stadhouderskade

Amstel

Weesperzijde

Swammerdamstr.

Wibautstr.

Ruyschstr.

Bleekerstr.

OOST

Hemonylaan

Hemonystr.

Van Woustr.

2e Jan Der Heijdestr.

Ceintuurbaan

Oosterparkstr.

2e Oosterparkstr.

Derde
Oosterparkstr.

Eerste Oosterparkstr.

Vrolikstr.

Populierenweg

Linnaeusstr.

STEVE
BIKO
PLEIN

It's hard to think of a city as friendly to students as Amsterdam. Student scenes and discounts are easy to find, while the wealth of things to do means young people never need constrain themselves to any one place or activity. The Dutch make their cultural institutions extremely accessible to those under 26, offering them a 50% discount on the **Museumjaarkaart,** which gives unlimited access to most of the country's museums. Many places actively court student customers. If you're hungry, try 'Skek, where you'll receive a 33% discount by showing a student ID. This might be the first place in the world where people try to borrow IDs from people who are actually under 21.

Of course, one of the most (in)famous attractions in Amsterdam is its nightlife. Fortunately, it doesn't disappoint and helps drive Amsterdam's reputation as a great student city. Parties rage nightly in Leidseplein and Rembrandtplein, while the central areas like the Red Light District offer a seedier, but uniquely "Amsterdam," experience. Load up on student life in Amsterdam, as it simply doesn't get any better than this.

orientation

The first step to getting a handle on Amsterdam's geography is to understand its canals. The Singel wraps around the heart of the Centrum, which is made up from east to west of the Oude Zijd, Red Light District, and Nieuwe Zijd. Barely 1km in diameter, the Centrum's skinny streets overflow with bars, brothels, clubs, and tourists—many of whom won't leave this area during their whole stay in Amsterdam.

The next set of canals, running in concentric circles, are Herengracht, Keizergracht, and Prinsengracht (hint: "gracht" means "canal", so if you're looking for a "gracht" street and you don't see water, you're lost). These enclose a somewhat classier area filled with locals, tasty restaurants, and plenty of museums (some very worthwhile, others completely ridiculous). Rembrandtplein and Leidseplein, the twin hearts of Amsterdam's and party scene, are also nestled here.

To the east of the canal ring are Jodenbuurt and Plantage, the city's old Jewish quarter. Moving southwest you get to De Pijp, an artsy neighborhood filled with immigrants and hipsters, then Museumplein and Vondelpark, home to the city's largest park and most important museums. Working back north to the west of the center you'll find Oud-West and Westerpark, two largely residential neighborhoods that are experiencing a boom in popularity and culture. In between Westerpark and the canal ring is the reliably chic Jordaan. Finally, to the north, in between Jordaan and Centraal Station, lies Scheepvaartbuurt, the city's old shipping quarter.

OUDE ZIJD

Many will delight in telling you that the Oude Zijd ("Old Side") is in fact newer than the Nieuwe Zijd ("New Side"). That doesn't really say much about the character of the neighborhood, which is sandwiched between the wild Red Light District and the more relaxed, local-dominated Jodenbuurt and feels like a balance between the two. A mini-kinda-Chinatown stretches along the northern part of **Zeedijk,** which spills into **Nieuwmarkt,** a lovely square dominated by a medieval ex-fortress. The bars and cafes lining Nieuwmarkt's perimeter are popular places for tourists and locals to rub elbows over a beer. Farther south is **Kloveniersburgwal,** a canal lined with genteel 17th-century buildings (many now occupied by the University of Amsterdam). Fancier hotels and cafes start to replace the tourist-traps and faux-British pubs where the canal hits the Amstel.

amsterdam

RED LIGHT DISTRICT

Once defined by the sailors who frequented Amsterdam's port, the Red Light District dates back to the 13th century, when business-savvy ladies began to capitalize on the crowds of sex-starved seamen. Today, the only sailors you'll find are the fake ones in the gay porn and costume shops, but the sex industry still flourishes here. The neighborhood is remarkably well regulated and policed, but this is definitely no Disneyland (though the number of families sightseeing here might surprise you). The **Oudezijds Achterburgwal,** with its live sex shows and porn palaces, is the Red Light's major artery. The streets perpendicular to this main thoroughfare are lined with girl-filled windows, stretching to **Oudezijds Voorburgwal** and **Warmoesstraat.** Some sex stores and theaters have set up camp on these western streets, but for the most part they provide bars for male tourists to get liquored up before venturing through one of the neon-lit doors. Those not looking for prostitution can still carouse in the Red Light District's endless sea of bars and coffeeshops. You'll also find an immense army of the infamous Dutch public urinals, as well as the type of traveler who feels comfortable using them. To see the hedonism at its peak, come on a Friday or Saturday night; for a less overwhelming visit, try strolling through on a weekday afternoon.

NIEUWE ZIJD

Older than the Oude Zijd (but home to a church that's younger than the Oude Kerk, thus explaining the neighborhoods' confusing name swap), the Nieuwe Zijd offers a mix of history, culture, and a whole lot of tourists. **Damrak,** its eastern edge, stretches from **Centraal Station** to **Dam Square** and then turns into **Rokin.** These are some of the busiest streets in the city, full of souvenir shops and shawarma stands; they're best tackled on foot, as this is the one part of Amsterdam where bikes don't rule the road. As you head west to **Spuistraat,** the streets become less crowded and more hip. **Kalverstraat,** one of the city's prime shopping streets for centuries, is now home to department stores and international chains. The Nieuwe Zijd is tourist central, full of huge hostels and coffeeshops, and you're much more likely to run into drug-ready backpackers and elderly tourists taking pictures than any locals.

SCHEEPVAARTBUURT

Scheepvaartbuurt, which would create quite a round on *Wheel of Fortune,* is Amsterdam's old shipping quarter. It was traditionally a working-class neighborhood with a lot of immigrants and had a reputation as one of the rougher parts of the city. Nowadays, despite looking difficult to pronounce (it's actually not that bad... it's like "shape-fart-burt"), Scheepvaartbuurt is a pleasant area full of young people and largely devoid of tourists. Remnants of the neighborhood's salty seadog past—like bronze propellers, anchors, and steering wheels—dot the sidewalks, and you can almost detect a faint whiff of the sea breeze that once blew ships to this shore. There aren't any real sights, but it's worth a visit for the local shops that line **Haarlemmerplein,** which becomes **Haarlemmerdijk** as you move east toward residential Westerpark.

CANAL RING WEST

The Canal Ring West lies around—spoiler alert—a ring of three canals: the **Herengracht, Keizersgracht,** and **Prinsengracht** (helpful hint: they go in alphabetical order from the center of the city toward the west). It extends from Brouwersgracht in the north down to the Leidseplein. Chock-full of grand canal houses and quaint houseboats, the neighborhood provides a nice escape from the more crowded Nieuwe Zijd next door. Three major sights draw visitors: the **Anne Frank House, Westerkerk,** and the **Homomonument.** The **Nine Streets,** small lanes running from the Prinsengracht to the Singel, south of Raadhuisstraat, are packed with more unique stores and vibrant cafes than we can fit in this guidebook.

orientation

CENTRAL CANAL RING

The Central Canal Ring tends to get overshadowed by its neighbors: Museumplein outshines its sights, Rembrandtplein and Leidseplein outdo its nightlife, and De Pijp offers a more exciting culinary scene. However, this neighborhood—the area from **Leidsestraat** to the **Amstel**, bordered on the north by the **Singel** and on the south by **Weteringschans**—enjoys the best parts of its surrounds without suffering their crowds, high prices, and soul- and cash-sucking tourist traps. **Utrechtsestraat** in particular offers lively cafes, restaurants, and stores, all frequented by a mix of locals and tourists, while the **Golden Bend** boasts some of Amsterdam's most impressive architecture. Along the Southern border, **Weteringplantsoen** and **Frederiksplein** provide some small but pretty green spaces to stop and rest your feet.

LEIDSEPLEIN

The Leidseplein, an almost exclusively commercial rectangle south of the Central Canal Ring, has a polarizing effect on those who pass through it, inspiring either devotion or disapproval. It's a busy, toristy part of town that lies in the area between the Nassaukade, Spiegelgracht, Prinsengracht, and Leidsegracht. During the day, the square is packed with street performers and promoters for pub crawls and other assorted evening entertainments. At night, the revelry continues in a bath of neon light and cheap beer. The few streets running through the Leidseplein's interior are packed with ethnic restaurants, theaters, bars, and clubs. Among the sushi and salsa, there are also a number of very Dutch establishments to be found. Numerous transport connections, including the elusive night bus, make this neighborhood a convenient as well as fun part of town. There are no sights to speak of, though look out for the enigmatic inscription *"Homo sapiens non urinat in ventum"* ("A wise man does not piss into the wind") on the pillars above **Max Euweplein Square.** While many Dutch will frown in pity if you spend much of your trip here, the best part about Leidseplein is that some of those frown-bearers will secretly be living it up here all weekend, too.

REMBRANDTPLEIN

For our purposes, the Rembrandtplein neighborhood comprises the square itself, plus the area stretching from Herengracht to the Amstel, and the part of Reguliersdwarstraat between Vijzelstraat and the Bloemenmarkt. Once upon a time (a.k.a. the late 17th century), the area now known as Rembrandtplein was home to Amsterdam's butter market *(Botermarkt)*. The construction of a few hotels in the 20th century brought tourists, and with the tourists came booze (and euro-trance). With a few noteworthy exceptions, food and accommodations in Rembrandtplein often cost more than they're worth. The real reason to come here is the nightlife. Rembrandtplein's bars and clubs are as popular and numerous as in the Leidseplein, but tend to be larger and more exclusive, with more locals and GLBT establishments. Europe's largest LCD TV screen, located above Amsterdam's largest club, **Escape,** lights up the square at night. From the middle of the square, a statue of **Rembrandt van Rijn** looks benevolently down at the madness. When you get tired of bar-hopping, take a rest in nearby **Thorbeckeplein,** a grassy stretch of trees, named for Johan Rudolph Thorbecke (1798-1872), known colloquially as the first prime minister of the Netherlands. "Thorbeckeplein" is also the name of a song written by the popular Dutch singer Robert Long about a bittersweet gay love affair.

JORDAAN

Once a staunchly working-class neighborhood, the Jordaan has been transformed into one of Amsterdam's prettiest and most fashionable areas. It provides a nice escape from the overwhelming hordes of tourists in the Red Light District to its east and has more energy than the more residential Westerpark to the (what do you think?) west. Streets are narrow, canals are leafy, and gabled houses are clumped together in colorful rows. You won't find any of Amsterdam's most famous sights here (well, except for **Electric Ladyland**), but the Jordaan's restaurants and cafes are not to be missed. Establishments in the northern part of the neighborhood are more often filled with locals, while tourists tend to wander over from Westermarkt into the area near **Rozengracht.**

WESTERPARK AND OUD-WEST

Westerpark is a residential neighborhood northeast of the main city center; its eponymous park is a serene stretch of green that makes for a pleasant break from the urban jungle. It has a loyal and vocal community—just don't expect to hear any English—and is becoming increasingly popular among young people and art-ists, bringing ever-exciting cultural projects and nightlife to its streets. South of Westerpark lies the Oud-West, still dominated by locals but with a few large streets (**Kinkerstraat** and **Overtoom** in particular) full of small ethnic cafes and cheap chain stores that keep the area busy. The northern part of Oud-West is a little grungy, but the area farther south—north of Vondelpark, close to the Leidseplein—is probably the most tourist-friendly part of the neighborhood.

MUSEUMPLEIN AND VONDELPARK

Museumplein and Vondelpark lie just south of the main canal ring, close to the city center yet somewhat removed from its hectic nature. Vondelpark is a gorgeous green space with some fine hostels not far from the excitement of Leidseplein and the ethnic eateries of the Oud-West. Museumplein, meanwhile, feels distinctly different from the rest of the city, attracting older and more af-fluent tourists than the backpacker-swarmed areas to the north. **P. C. Hooftstraat** is lined with designer stores like Prada and Tiffany. But just because you're young and on a budget doesn't mean you should shy away. Museumplein is a large, grassy field lined with some of the best museums in the world—no visit to Amsterdam is complete without a trip to the **Van Gogh Museum** and **Rijksmuseum.** Most of the tourist-friendly action is sandwiched between Stadhouderskade to the north and Van Baerlestraat (which contains the Museumplein tram stop) to the south. Come here to get some space, culture, and class—three things that feel far away when you're downing Heinekens with the masses in a hostel bar on Warmoesstraat.

DE PIJP

De Pijp ("duh pipe") may lack history and sights, but it more than makes up for that with modern culture. A mix of immigrants, students, and artists creates a haven of excellent ethnic restaurants, fun cafes, and relatively inexpensive housing. **Albert Cuypstraat** hosts the city's largest open-air market, along with a cluster of cafes, clothing stores, and cheap eats. Intersecting Albert Cuypstraat to the west is **Ferdinard Bolstraat,** which is home to a high concentration of restau-rants and leads to the avoidable **Heineken Experience.** Still a little bit rough around the edges, De Pijp has all the charm of the Jordaan in a much younger and more urban environment.

JODENBUURT AND PLANTAGE

A high concentration of sights and museums is the real draw here, but don't overlook the few excellent restaurants and small bars. The open space in these neighborhoods is a great antidote to the over-crowded city center. Jodenbuurt, centered around **Waterlooplein,** was historically the home of Amsterdam's Jewish population. Plantage, home to wide streets and numerous parks, stretches around Jodenbuurt to the east. Most commercial establishments can be found on the streets near the **Artis Zoo** or near the **Rembrandt House.**

accommodations

When lodging in Amsterdam, chances are you'll either be staying in a big backpacker hostel or a small hotel in a converted canal house. For the most part, anything you find in the city center is a decent option, but there's a huge range of value—some rooms are simply small white boxes with a bed, while others are lovingly decorated with attention to cozy details or an interesting theme. To get the most for your euro, consider staying in one of the neighborhoods outside of the main canal ring. If you didn't come to Amsterdam to find a 24hr. party, avoid hostels in the Red Light District. If you came to get down all day and all of the night, centrally located hostels, often with late-night bars attached, will provide plenty of opportunities to meet fellow travelers with similar missions.

Room rates fluctuate according to season and day of the week. The closer you get to the cold of winter, the cheaper your room will be—except for the days surrounding Christmas and New Year's, when prices skyrocket. While we don't advise showing up without having booked a room, especially during the summer, owners with too many unoccupied beds have been known to radically slash prices at less busy times.

OUDE ZIJD

The Oude Zijd isn't home to as many accommodations as the nearby Red Light District or Nieuwe Zijd, but it's home to two of the city's best.

▨ SHELTER CITY   HOSTEL $
Barndesteeg 21   ☎020 625 32 30; www.shelter.nl

Shelter City is a large Christian hostel (with no religious requirements for guests) in the heart of the Oude Zijd. All rooms are single-sex, most with shared baths, a few with ensuites. The beds are a bit reminiscent of those in army barracks, but the well-decorated common spaces, including a cafe, breakfast room, and courtyard garden, encourage guests to make new friends. Shelter City is popular with a wide array of young backpackers, from the quiet museum lover to the rabid party-goer.

⚲ Ⓜ Nieuwmarkt. Just off the southwestern edge of the square. *i* Breakfast included. Free Wi-Fi. No drugs or alcohol allowed. Ⓢ Beds €15-34. Discounts available for longer stays. ⚿ Security 24hr.

▨ STAYOKAY AMSTERDAM STADSDOELEN (HI)   HOSTEL $
Kloveniersburgwal 97   ☎020 624 68 32; www.stayokay.com/stadsdoelen

Enjoy professional, upbeat staff and some cushy amenities rarely found in hostels: washing and drying machines, a TV room complete with foosball table, and a substantial breakfast including fruit and cornflakes (different varieties of cornflakes!). Rooms are plain and clean in this huge hostel—with over 150 beds, look here when your whole Varsity Marching Band needs a place to stay in Amsterdam. Located in an old canal building in a tranquil part of the Oude Zijd, this hostel is nearer to Jodenbuurt but still just a short walk from Dam Sq., the Red Light District, and Rembrandtplein.

⚲ Tram #4, 9, 16, 24, or 25 to Muntplein. Walk down Nieuwe Doelenstraat; Kloveniersburgwal is on the right over the bridge. *i* Breakfast included. Free Wi-Fi. Ⓢ Co-ed or single-sex 8- to 20-bed dorms €15-30, depending on season and day; private rooms €39-70. HI discount.

RED LIGHT DISTRICT

Sure, this neighborhood is obsessed with sex, but the high concentration of hotels and hostels on Warmoesstraat means that there is an industry for the less red-blooded traveler as well. These are great places to stash your pack and go unabashedly wild with fellow backpackers. While the prices vary seasonally, rates in the Red Light District also tend to fall drastically in the middle of the week.

THE GREENHOUSE EFFECT HOTEL — HOTEL $$$

Warmoesstraat 55 — ☎020 624 49 74; www.greenhouse-effect.nl

The Greenhouse Effect has some of the nicest rooms in Amsterdam, definitely miles above average for the Red Light District. Each room is decorated according to its own whimsical theme: there's "1001 Nights," with gauzy wall hangings and an exotic chandelier; the "Sailor's Cabin," done up ship-shape with deep blue walls and brass accents; and the "Outer Space" room, with a translucent neon green light-up sink, to name a few. Guests recieve discounts at the bar below and the coffeeshop next door.

From Centraal Station, walk south on Damrak, turn right onto Brugsteeg, and left onto Warmoesstraat. ***i*** *Breakfast included. Most rooms have ensuite bath. Free Wi-Fi in the bar.* [S] *Singles €65-75; doubles €95-110; triples €130.*

DURTY NELLY'S HOSTEL — HOSTEL $

Warmoesstraat 115-117 — ☎020 638 01 25; www.durtynellys.nl

A popular hostel over a convivial pub, Durty Nelly's boasts co-ed dorms that are (ironically) very clean. The rooms aren't terribly spacious, but they feel more cozy than cramped. Guests receive a discount at the pub below.

From Centraal Station, walk south on Damrak, turn right onto Brugsteeg, and right onto Warmoesstraat. ***i*** *Breakfast included. Free Wi-Fi. Large lockers available.* [S] *4- to 10-bed dorms €25-50.*

HOTEL WINSTON — HOSTEL $$

Warmoesstraat 129 — ☎020 623 13 80; www.winston.nl

Hotel Winston feels more modern and continental than the other boozing-and-snoozing complexes on the street, thanks in part to the attached sleek bar and trendy club. Always busy, Winston fills up fast with backpackers and young people. It's not the cheapest place on the block and doesn't have the most interesting rooms, but it is perfect for larger groups and those who prefer the club scene to the pubs connected to most of Winston's competitors.

From Centraal Station, walk south on Damrak, turn right onto Brugsteeg, and right onto Warmoesstraat. ***i*** *Breakfast included. Free Wi-Fi.* [S] *Dorms €32-40; singles €73-95; doubles €88-114.*

MEETING POINT YOUTH HOSTEL — HOSTEL $

Warmoesstraat 14 — ☎020 627 74 99; www.hostel-meetingpoint.nl

Meeting Point's location near Centraal Station and its low prices make it popular with young backpackers. Be warned: anarchy frequently reigns in the 24hr. bar downstairs. Female travelers take note that there are no single-sex dorms, and the hostel tends to attract a rowdier crowd that isn't suited for the faint of heart. Those looking for peace and quiet would do best to look elsewhere.

From Centraal Station, turn left onto Prins Hendrikkade, right onto Nieuwebrugsteeg, and right onto Warmoesstraat. ***i*** *Breakfast €2.50. Lockers available, lock rentals €2 per stay. Free Wi-Fi.* [S] *18-bed dorms €18-25; 8-bed €25-30.*

HOTEL INTERNATIONAAL — HOTEL $$$

Warmoesstraat 1-3 — ☎020 624 55 20; www.hotelinternationaal.com

Although it's similar to other small bar-hotel setups along the street, Hotel Internationaal stands out thanks to its extra-amicable staff and pastel-green walls. The rooms are otherwise nondescript—though those on the top floor have cool Tudor-style beams—but are perfectly functional and comfortable. All rooms include a sink, while some have ensuite baths. Despite being a hotel rather than a hostel, the atmosphere is only a couple of decibels quieter than the party-hard complexes down the street.

From Centraal Station, turn left onto Prins Hendrikkade, right onto Nieuwebrugsteeg, and right onto Warmoesstraat. ***i*** *Free Wi-Fi. Computers available.* [S] *Doubles €65-85, with bath €85-110; quads €120-140.*

HOTEL VIJAYA   HOTEL $$

Oudezijds Voorburgwal 44   ☎020 626 94 06; www.hotelvijaya.com

This hotel at the edge of the Red Light District, not far from the Oude Kerk, offers some of the cheapest private rooms in the area. Singles are somewhat small but still a bargain, especially midweek when prices fall. Breakfast is served in a spacious dining room.

✈ *From Centraal Station, turn left onto Prins Hendrikkade and then bear right onto Nieuwebrug-steeg. Continue straight and Nieuwebrugsteeg will become Oudezijds Voorburgwal.* ℹ *Breakfast included. All rooms have ensuite bath. Free Wi-Fi.* ⑤ *Singles €35-80; doubles €50-105.*

OLD NICKEL HOTEL   HOTEL $$$

Nieuwebrugsteeg 11   ☎020 624 19 12; www.oldquarter.com/oldnickel

At the northern tip of the Red Light District, Old Nickel remains close to the activity but maintains some peace and quiet for guests. The plaid coverlets on the beds and nature wallpaper can almost fool you into thinking you're in a British country inn—the pub downstairs certainly adds to that impression. Slanted ceilings add a nice sense of coziness to the rooms on the top floor.

✈ *From Centraal Station, turn left onto the far side of Prins Hendrikkade, then turn right onto Nieuwebrugsteeg.* ℹ *Breakfast included. All rooms have shared bath. Free Wi-Fi.* ⑤ *Singles €50-75; doubles €60-85.*

NIEUWE ZIJD

The Nieuwe Zijd is packed with accommodations, making it easy to stumble straight from Centraal Station into your room. Hotels here tend to be pricey, but top-notch hostels abound.

▨ FLYING PIG DOWNTOWN   HOSTEL $

Nieuwendijk 100   ☎020 420 68 22; www.flyingpig.nl

A lively bar, a comfy smoking lounge, and spacious dorms make this party hostel a perennial favorite among backpackers. The youthful staff and frequent events—like live DJs, drink specials, and televised sports games—help to drive a social atmosphere. Guests are referred to as "piggies," but don't worry, it's meant to be endearing. Queen-sized bunk beds (perfect for couples, "special" friends, or maybe even "just friends") are available in some dorms and must be booked for two people.

✈ *From Centraal Station, walk toward Damrak. Pass the Victoria Hotel and take the 1st alley on the right, which leads to Nieuwendijk.* ℹ *Breakfast included. Towels included. Kitchen available. Free Wi-Fi. Computers available.* ⑤ *4- to 18-bed dorms €20-30. Significant discounts online and in the low season.*

▨ AIVENGO YOUTH HOSTEL   HOSTEL $

Spuistraat 6   ☎020 421 36 70; www.aivengoyouthhostel.com

Aivengo isn't just one of the closest hostels to Centraal Station—it's also one of the nicest. Deep colors and gauzy purple curtains give some dorms a decadent, *Arabian Nights* vibe, while others have clean, crisp interiors that are more reminiscent of Ikea. A mix of bunks and normal beds fills the large and sociable dorms. Somewhat humorously (misogynistically, some might say), the all-female dorms are the only ones equipped with kitchens—other dorms include only a fridge and microwave. Two private doubles are also available, one with a roof terrace and a hot tub.

✈ *From Centraal Station, walk down Martelarsgraacht and keep straight onto Hekelveld, which becomes Spuistraat.* ℹ *Free Wi-Fi. Computers available.* ⑤ *Summer dorms €20-35; winter from €12. Private rooms €70-110.*

▨ BOB'S YOUTH HOSTEL   HOSTEL $

Nieuwezijds Voorburgwal 92   ☎020 624 63 58; www.bobsyouthhostel.nl

A slightly hippie-er counterpart to the Flying Pig, Bob's Youth Hostel attracts flocks of young travelers who enjoy lounging in the graffiti-filled bar and strumming their guitars outside on the steps. The dorms are decorated with cheeky, colorful murals by visiting artists. An apartment with a kitchen and bath is available for two or three people. Though it used to operate on a first-come-first-served, ultra-free-spirit-style system, the new management now accepts advance reservations.

‡ *From Centraal Station, go down Martelaarsgracht and bear left as it becomes Nieuwezijds Voorburgwal.* **i** *Breakfast included. Wi-Fi €3 per hr., €4 per day. Computers available.* Ⓢ *4- to 16-bed dorms €25-35; apartment €90-120.* Ⓩ *Bar open until 3am.*

HOSTEL AROZA   HOSTEL $

Nieuwendijk 23   ☎020 620 91 23; www.aroza.nl

Trippy murals in the halls give this place definite charm, although the "Don't Worry, Be Sexy" signs might be a little too charming for some tastes. The downstairs bar is a popular hangout and features a guestbook and colored pencils for guests to record their visit for future generations, or just so they can amuse themselves after an evening of coffeeshop-hopping.

‡ *From Centraal Station, turn right, left at Martelaarsgracht, and right onto Nieuwendijk.* **i** *Breakfast included. Lockers included. Single-sex and co-ed dorms available. Free Wi-Fi. Computer with internet in the bar.* Ⓢ *Dorms €25-30.*

HOTEL BROUWER   HOTEL $$$

Singel 83   ☎020 624 63 58; www.hotelbrouwer.nl

If you want to know what it's like to live in an old Dutch canal house, Hotel Brouwer is your best bet (and value). Each room is named for a Dutch artist, but the "Bosch" room, a small double, is the real delight, with antique furniture in the living room and a traditional box bed set into the wall. The other rooms, which all overlook the pretty Singel Canal, are less distinctive but still spacious and well decorated. All of them make for a nice change of pace from the seedier hostels and hotels of the Nieuwe Zijd.

‡ *From Centraal Station, cross the water, turn right onto Prins Hendrikkade, and left onto Singel.* **i** *Breakfast included. Free Wi-Fi.* Ⓢ *Singles €60; doubles €95.*

HOTEL GROENENDAEL   HOTEL $$

Nieuwendijk 15   ☎020 624 48 22; www.hotelgroenendael.com

This conveniently located hotel offers some of the cheapest singles in the city. The simple rooms include large windows and a few small terraces.

‡ *From Centraal Station, turn right, go left at Martelaarsgracht, and turn right onto Nieuwendijk.* **i** *Breakfast included. Reservations by phone only. Free Wi-Fi.* Ⓢ *Singles €35; doubles €60; triples €90.*

SCHEEPVAARTBUURT

Scheepvaartbuurt lacks the stellar hostels of nearby Nieuwe Zijd, but it does have one of the best hotels in the city.

🏅 FREDERIC RENT-A-BIKE   HOTEL $$

Brouwersgracht 78   ☎020 624 55 09; www.frederic.nl

Three homey and uniquely decorated rooms, each named after a different artist, sit at the back of Frederic's bike-rental shop. The Mondrian room steals the show with a double **waterbed** and a **hot tub** in the brightly tiled bathroom. Frederic also rents out a number of houseboats and apartments throughout the area. The supremely helpful owners know the city inside-out and will enthusiastically dispense some of the best Amsterdam advice you can find. They also have some great stories to tell; make sure to ask about their experiences with other luminaries of the travel-writing world.

‡ *From Centraal Station, turn right, cross the Singel, and walk 2 blocks down Brouwersgracht.* **i** *Breakfast included with hotel rooms. Small rooms have shared bath.* Ⓢ *Smaller rooms as singles €40-50; as doubles €60-70. Mondrian room €90-100. Houseboats €100-225, with 15% reservation fee.*

accommodations

HOTEL MY HOME HOTEL $$$

Haarlemmerstraat 82 ☎020 624 23 20; www.amsterdambudgethotel.com

This place has been around for a while, as you can tell by their prime piece of internet real estate. The rooms are small and simple, but the yellow walls and patterned bedspreads brighten things up a bit. The relaxed common space includes a pool table. Most rooms are private, but some dorms are available.

➜ From Centraal Station, turn right, cross the Singel, and walk down Haarlemmerstraat. ℹ Breakfast included (and includes more than toast!). Free Wi-Fi. $ 5-bed dorms €28-33; Doubles €55-70; triples €84-99; quints €140-165.

RAMENAS HOTEL HOTEL $$$

Haarlemmerdijk 61 ☎020 624 60 30; www.hotelramenas.nl

Near Haarlemmerplein, Ramenas sits above a cafe of the same name. The rooms are nothing special, but the low ceilings and wooden window frames embrace the cozier side of Amsterdam. Ramenas Hotel isn't a terrible option if more interesting hotels are booked.

➜ Tram #3 to Haarlemmerplein. Cross Harlemmerplein to reach Haarlemmerdijk, then continue walking east. Reception is in the cafe downstairs. ℹ Breakfast included. Some rooms with bath. Free Wi-Fi. $ Singles €50-75; doubles €60-100. Additional 5% tourist tax.

CANAL RING WEST

Raadhuisstraat is a row of hotel after hotel, making it a great place to try and find a private room if everywhere else is full. Many hotels are more charming than the busy traffic below might suggest (although almost all have mountainous Amsterdam staircases, so if your grandma is coming along, you might want to spare her). For a quieter and more picturesque location, try one of the accommodations on the **Nine Streets.**

👍 **HOTEL CLEMENS** HOTEL $$

Raadhuisstraat 39 ☎020 624 60 89; www.clemenshotel.com

Every room in this small hotel is decorated with French-patterned wallpaper and tiered curtains, many revealing great views; some have cushioned window seats, and all have both a fridge and a safe. Enjoy breakfast on the balcony with a view of Westerkerk. Best of all, Hotel Clemens is a great value.

➜ Tram #13, 14, or 17 to Westermarkt. Walk across the bridge and it's on the right. ℹ Breakfast included. Free Wi-Fi. $ Singles €40-60; doubles €60-120; triples €120-150.

👍 **NADIA HOTEL** HOTEL $$$

Raadhuisstraat 51 ☎020 620 15 50; www.nadia.nl

Nadia Hotel boasts luxurious rooms with thick red bedspreads, large windows, and built-in wooden shelves. The gorgeous breakfast room is full of hanging plants and a baller view of Westermarkt. The double overlooking the canal will make you feel like you're on a boat. Some deluxe rooms have balconies and views of the canal or Westerkerk. All rooms have desks, coffee and tea makers, safes, and ensuite bathrooms.

➜ Tram #13, 14, or 17 to Westermarkt. Walk across the bridge and it will be on your right. ℹ Breakfast included. Free Wi-Fi. Computer available. $ Singles €50-90; doubles €65-100.

HOTEL WESTERTOREN HOTEL $$

Raadhuisstraat 35B ☎020 624 46 39; www.hotelwestertoren.nl

The most exciting room here is the seven-person ensemble, which has two lofted double beds, a single bed underneath, and another double against the opposite wall. Have fun building a fort with your friends—it definitely beats the average hostel. Each room is decorated with traces of the old luxe charm that once characterized this canal house (think red curtains, floral bedspreads, and romantic paintings).

➜ Tram #13, 14, or 17 to Westermarkt. Walk across the bridge and it's on the right. ℹ Breakfast included, and can be delivered to your room. Free Wi-Fi. All rooms have fridges. Some rooms have balconies. $ Singles €40-60; 7-person room €35 per person (must be booked as a group).

HOTEL PAX

HOTEL $$

Raadhuisstraat 37B   ☎020 624 97 35; www.hotelpax.nl

The common spaces in Hotel Pax are brightly painted and decorated with mirrors and prints, giving it a much nicer feel than most budget hotels in the neighborhood. The no-frills rooms are outfitted with plain metal-frame beds but are spacious and airy.

✈ *Tram #13, 14, or 17 to Westermarkt. Cross the bridge and it's on the right.* ℹ️ *Computer available for a fee. All rooms have cable TV.* Ⓢ *Singles from €35; doubles €60-90; quads €120-150.*

HOTEL BELGA

HOTEL $$

Hartenstraat 8   ☎020 624 90 80; www.hotelbelga.nl

Tucked among hip cafes and quirky shops on one of the Nine Streets, this cannabis-friendly hotel remains popular with young travelers. The rooms are large, if a bit plain, but abstract floral paintings brighten up the white walls. Some rooms have slightly slanted floors, which can seem either charming or disorienting depending on your degree of dyspraxia.

✈ *Tram #13, 14, or 17 to Westermarkt. Cross Keizersgracht, make a right, and then a left onto Hartenstraat.* ℹ️ *Breakfast included. Free Wi-Fi.* Ⓢ *Singles with shared bath €45-55; doubles €60-100.*

HOTEL HEGRA

HOTEL $$$

Herengracht 269   ☎020 623 78 77; www.hotelhegra.nl

Hegra's pretty canal-side location is a bit inconvenient, though it does remove you from the sound of traffic. You'll pay a bit more here than at comparable hotels in the neighborhood. Rooms are clean and simple, with plush red carpeting underfoot and pretty floral tiles.

✈ *Tram #1, 2, 5, 13, 14, or 17 to Dam. Continue along Raadhuisstraat and make a left onto Herengracht.* ℹ️ *Breakfast included. Free Wi-Fi.* Ⓢ *Doubles €49-119.*

CENTRAL CANAL RING

Stay in the Central Canal Ring if you're looking for private rooms in a relatively quiet atmosphere. You'll still be close to the action of Museumplein, Leidseplein, and Rembrantplein, but you won't have to pay the hefty surcharge that can accompany the short stumbling-distance.

HEMP HOTEL

HOTEL $$$

Fredericksplein 15   ☎020 625 44 25; www.hemp-hotel.com

Each of Hemp Hotel's rooms has a different geographic theme—the Caribbean, Tibet, and India are all represented—brought to life by hemp fabrics, handmade wood carvings, and vibrant pictures. The Hemple Temple bar downstairs serves a dozen varieties of hemp beer, along with drinks derived from less infamous crops. If you don't mind stained carpets and unpainted wood, it's a great place to hang out and meet chilled-out travelers. Book far in advance—there are a surprising number of travelers who are very excited about showering with hempseed soap and eating hemp rolls for breakfast.

✈ *Tram #4, 7, 10, or 25 to Fredericksplein. Walk diagonally across the square.* ℹ️ *Breakfast included. Free Wi-Fi.* Ⓢ *Singles €60; doubles €70, with bath €75.*

THE GOLDEN BEAR

HOTEL $$$

Kerkstraat 37   ☎020 624 47 85; www.goldenbear.nl

Since 1948, this has been Amsterdam's premier gay hotel (about 75% of the guests are male, though women and straight guests are certainly welcome). Besides the fun atmosphere, the hotel is notable for its welcoming staff and well-decorated rooms—if you're lucky, you might get the one with fur on the wall.

✈ *Tram #1, 2, or 5 to Keizersgracht. Continue down Leidsestraat and turn right.* ℹ️ *Breakfast included. Free Wi-Fi.* Ⓢ *Singles with shared bath €65-70; doubles €73-90, with bath €90-130.*

accommodations

HOTEL KAP HOTEL $$

Den Texstraat 5B ☎020 624 59 08; www.kaphotel.nl

Hotel Kap is an especially attractive option in the summer, when you can eat breakfast or relax in the leafy garden out back. The rooms have high ceilings and large windows, though the furnishings are rather plain. It's one of the best deals you'll find in this neighborhood and a good place to look if other hotels are booked, even if the single "student rooms" are a bit cramped.

 # Tram #4, 7, 10, 16, 24, or 25 to Weteringcircuit. Walk down Weteringschans, turn right onto 2e Weteringplantsoen, and left onto Den Texstraat. i Breakfast included. All rooms have private showers; singles and some doubles have shared toilet. Wi-Fi €5 per stay. [$] Singles €40-65; doubles €60-95.

HOTEL ASTERISK HOTEL $$$

Den Texstraat 16 ☎020 624 17 68; www.asteriskhotel.nl

Hotel Asterisk offers well-priced rooms in a great location, a pocket of calm between touristy neighborhoods. Rooms with good furniture, pretty paintings, and nice curtains are kept very clean. The simpler twins and singles might feel a little small, but the deluxe rooms with bath are quite spacious.

 # Tram #4, 7, 10, 16, 24, or 25 to Weteringcircuit. Walk down Weteringschans, turn right onto 2e Weteringplantsoen, and left onto Den Texstraat. i Breakfast included. Free Wi-Fi. [$] Singles €59-68; doubles €60-79, deluxe €89-129.

LEIDSEPLEIN

The best hotels in the Leidseplein are found down **Marnixstraat** and around the bend of the **Leidsekade.**

BACKSTAGE HOTEL HOTEL $$

Leisegracht 114 ☎020 624 40 44; www.backstagehotel.com

Popular with musicians in town for shows at nearby clubs, the decor at Backstage adheres to a concert-venue theme: backboards are made to look like trunks, lamps resemble spotlights, lights have drum lampshades, and some rooms have dressing tables that even Lady Gaga would envy. Some suites are quads and quints big enough to house the whole band. Autographed concert posters line the walls and stairways, and reception is accompanied by a bar, pool table, and piano. Open-mic nights are held every Tuesday, and the staff is happy to talk up Amsterdam as well as the hotel's concert schedule. Guitars are available for jamming, and Guitar Hero for pretend jamming.

 # Tram #1, 2, or 5 to Leidseplein. Head away from the sqaure toward Leidsegracht. i Most rooms with private bath. Free Wi-Fi. Computer available. [$] Singles €35-85; doubles €50-150; quads €150-210; quints €150-250.

FREELAND HOTEL $$$

Marnixstraat 386 ☎020 622 75 11; www.hotelfreeland.com

The small, 17-room Freeland feels miles apart from the crowds and grit of the Leidseplein, though the neighborhood's bustling center is just a block away. Rooms are airy and floral, and each one is stocked with amenities like DVD players and coffee makers. Ask if the special double with sunroom is available. Book early, as this place's charm isn't a well-kept secret.

 # Tram #1, 2, 5, 7, or 10 to Leidseplein; or #7 or 10 to Raamplein. i Breakfast included. Free Wi-Fi. [$] Singles €55-82; doubles €75-125.

INTERNATIONAL BUDGET HOSTEL HOSTEL $

Leidsegracht 76 ☎020 624 27 84; www.internationalbudgethostel.com

This place is popular with students and backpackers, yet still significantly toned down from the Red Light District's party hostels. Maybe things are quieter because everybody is too busy partying outside the hostel in the bars just across the canal. Each dorm has four single beds and lockers. Two private doubles (with shared bath) are also available. The lounge has couches, a TV, and vending machines. Breakfast (€3-8) is served until noon in the canteen.

‡ Tram #7 or 10 to Raamplein. Continue walking down Marnixstraat and turn left at the canal. You can also take tram #1, 2, or 5 to Prinsengracht. Turn right and walk along Prinsengracht and then turn left after you cross the bridge. i Free Wi-Fi. [S] Dorms €20-32.

KING HOTEL HOTEL $$$

Leidsekade 85-86 ☎020 624 96 03; www.hotel-king.nl

Warmly decorated, impeccably clean rooms with glossy wood and orange curtains fill this hotel, which is located in an old canal house along the bend of the Leidsekade. Some rooms have spectacular views of the water (though you'll pay extra to enjoy them).

‡ Tram #1, 2, 5, 7, or 10 to Leidseplein. Walk down Marnixstraat and turn left at the canal; the hotel is around the bend. i Breakfast included. Free Wi-Fi. [S] Singles €50-75; doubles €75-125.

HOTEL QUENTIN HOTEL $$

Leidsekade 89 ☎020 622 75 11; www.quentinhotels.com

Located in a beautiful renovated mansion overlooking the Leidsekade, this hotel sets itself apart with the funky, abstract furniture and posters of musicians (not to mention flatscreen TVs) that fill its comfortable rooms. The hotel bar serves coffee, alcohol, and soft drinks.

‡ Tram #1, 2, 5, 7, or 10 to Leidseplein. Walk down Marnixstraat and turn left at the canal. The hotel is around the bend. i Free Wi-Fi. [S] Singles €35-55, with bath €40-60; doubles €50-85.

REMBRANDTPLEIN

Rembrandtplein's reputation as a popular nightspot can be both a blessing and a curse. On the one hand, living here means it's easy to stumble home after a long night; on the other, prices and noise levels can be high (especially on weekends).

HOTEL THE VETERAN HOTEL $$

Herengracht 561 ☎020 620 26 73; www.veteran.nl

Hotel the Veteran is a bare-bones establishment, but all the essentials are here. The rooms are clean and cozy with floral bedspreads and wood paneling, which seems to be the go-to tactic for creating welcoming sleeping environments in this city. The hotel sits at the corner of a beautiful stretch of the Herengracht Canal and Thorbeckeplein's strip of bars. Be advised: to enter some rooms you must climb an external staircase next to a bunch of bars, which may be uncomfortable for some travelers returning to their rooms at night. That said, this is one of the cheapest places to stay around Rembrandtplein.

‡ Tram #9 or 14 to Rembrandtplein. At the corner of Thorbeckeplein and Herengracht. i Breakfast included. Singles all have shared bath; both shared and ensuite doubles available; triples all ensuite. Wi-Fi available. [S] Singles €35-65; doubles from €50; triples and family rooms from €65.

CITY HOTEL HOTEL $$$$

Utrechtstraat 2 ☎020 627 23 23; www.city-hotel.nl

City Hotel boasts large, clean rooms, brightly decorated with colorful bedspreads and oversized pictures of flowers. Some rooms have balconies, and those on the top floor have great views of Rembrandtplein and the rest of the city. Many of the rooms are made for five to eight people (some with bunk beds), but none feel cramped. City is popular with groups of young backpackers, since you can find much better values if you're only looking for a double or triple (there are no singles). Breakfast is available—for an extra charge—in a chic dining area with red leather seats.

‡ Tram #9 or 14 to Rembrandtplein. City Hotel is off the southeast corner of the main square. i Breakfast €7.50. All rooms have safe. Free Wi-Fi and free public computer in dining room. [S] Doubles from €100; triples from €135; 6-person rooms €270.

HOTEL MONOPOLE
HOTEL $$$

Amstel 60 ☎020 624 62 71

A few blocks removed from the madness of Rembrandtplein, this hotel has simple but pretty pastel rooms, many with canal views (ask ahead). Rooms have the added luxury of breakfast delivered to your door. There's also a cushy common space on the first floor.

⚓ *Tram #9 or 14 to Rembrandtplein. Cut through 1 of the alleyways on the northern side of the square to get to the canal side. i Breakfast included. Free Wi-Fi.* ⓢ *Singles €65-105; doubles €75-125.*

JORDAAN

If you want to live like a local but not commute like one, camp out here.

▧ SHELTER JORDAAN
HOSTEL $

Bloemstraat 179 ☎020 624 47 17; www.shelter.nl

Smaller and in a quieter location than its sister hostel in the Oude Zijd, the Shelter Jordaan has the same excellent prices, clean facilities, and comfortable atmosphere. They cater to Christian travelers (though all are welcome), so the rooms are single-sex, and drugs and alcohol are forbidden. With speakers blaring an uninterrupted stream of Christian rock, this hostel isn't for everybody, but it's in a good location and feels safe. The rooms are large and bright, with colorful beds and lockers. The large cafe and garden provide cozy places to hang out and enjoy the free breakfast, which often features pancakes and french toast.

⚓ *Tram #10 to Bloemstraat or tram #13, 14, or 17 to Westermarkt. Follow Lijnbaansgracht for 50m, then turn right onto Bloemstraat. i Breakfast included. All rooms with shared bath. Lockers available, though you'll have to bring your own lock or purchase one for €4. Free Wi-Fi.* ⓢ *4- to 8-bed dorms €17-30.*

HOTEL VAN ONNA
HOTEL $$

Bloemgracht 104 ☎020 626 58 01; www.vanonna.nl

The rooms on the top floor of this hotel are truly remarkable, with slanted ceilings, exposed wood beams, and views over the rooftops of the whole Jordaan. You'll need to hike up the stairs to reach them, but at least the staircase is lined with lovely black-and-white photos of the city. The rooms are impeccably clean, though the ones downstairs are dull compared to those upstairs.

⚓ *Tram #10 to Bloemgracht or tram #13, 14, or 17 to Westermarkt. Cross Prinsengracht and turn right; Bloemgracht is 2 blocks away. i Breakfast included. Free Wi-Fi.* ⓢ *Singles €50; doubles €90; triples €135. Credit cards add 5%.*

HOTEL ACACIA
HOTEL $$$

Lindengracht 251 ☎020 622 14 60; www.hotelacacia.nl

Tucked in a tranquil corner of the picturesque northern Jordaan, Acacia is nonetheless the epitome of bland and boring. Small studio apartments, which come with a kitchenette and living area, feel a little less institutional.

⚓ *Tram #3 or 10 to Marnixplein. Cross the small canal and make a left onto Lijnbaansgracht; Acacia will be on the right. i Breakfast included. All rooms with full bath. Free Wi-Fi.* ⓢ *Doubles €60-90; studios €70-110.*

WESTERPARK AND OUD-WEST

Westerpark is almost exclusively residential with relatively few accommodations. The section of the Oud-West closest to the Leidseplein has a smattering of small hotels, but make sure to bring a good pair of walking shoes or learn how to use the tram if you plan on staying out here. Accommodations cost about the same as their competitors closer to the canal ring, but they are far less crowded and noisy.

HOTEL JUPITER HOTEL $$

2e Helmersstraat 14 ☎020 618 71 32; www.jupiterhotel.nl

This hotel sits on one of the small streets parallel to Overtoom, so it's close to transportation and grocery shopping but removed from the bustle and noise of the main thoroughfare. Rooms are sleek and bare, but they're only a 5min. walk from the Leidseplein. Breakfast is included, but the staff can be grouchy.

⇟ Tram #3 or 12 to Overtoom or #1 tp 1e Con. Huygensstraat. Walk 2 blocks away from Vondelpark on 1e Con. Huygensstraat and turn right. $ High-season singles €54, with bath €64; doubles €74/99. Low-season singles €39/49; doubles €59/79. Triples and quads also available.

HOTEL ABBA HOTEL $$

Overtoom 116-122 ☎020 618 30 58; www.hotel-abba.nl

The rooms here are simple: white walls and gray concrete. This "smoker-friendly" hotel has a very practical location right above an Albert Heijn supermarket. Cable TV (in every room) and breakfast are included. Free safety deposit boxes are available at reception, where the friendly staff will help you arrange trips and tours.

⇟ Tram #1 to 1e Con. Huygensstraat. Above the Albert Heijn. $ High-season singles €50, with bath €60; doubles €70/85. Low-season singles €35/40; doubles €60/70.

MUSEUMPLEIN AND VONDELPARK

You can get your hostel fix without facing the noise and crowds of the Centrum at one of Vondelpark's two excellent backpacker lodgings. Hotels in the neighborhood are removed from the city's best restaurants and bars, but they ooze residential luxury.

✔ STAYOKAY AMSTERDAM VONDELPARK HOSTEL $

Zandpad 5 ☎020 589 89 96; www.stayokay.nl/vondelpark

This is a huge hostel—the size makes it feel slightly institutional, but it's clean and well managed. Each room has its own bathroom (the larger rooms have two). Downstairs, an affordable bar with foosball tables, vending machines, and pool tables is a popular hangout. The staff is happy to answer questions about the city, and with so many guests, it won't be hard to find some buddies to venture to nearby Leidseplein with you.

⇟ Tram #1, 2, 5, 7, or 10 to Leidseplein. Walk across the canal toward the Marriott, take a left, then make a right onto Zandpad after 1 block. ℹ Breakfast included. Single-sex dorms available. Free Wi-Fi. $ 2- to 20-bed dorms €20-34; singles €50-80.

✔ FLYING PIG UPTOWN HOSTEL $

Vossiusstraat 46-47 ☎020 400 41 87; www.flyingpig.nl

We find it a little confusing that Flying Pig Uptown is actually south of Flying Pig Downtown (in Nieuwe Zijd), but then again, we can't quite wrap our heads around the fact that the Nile runs south to north... no matter. This is the original Flying Pig, and with a tranquil location across from Vondelpark, this winged swine is a little less rowdy than its younger sibling. Nevertheless, it's still phenomenally popular. The quality of the dorms vary—some are just plain walls and metal-frame bunks—but they're all comfortable and clean, and they each have their own bathrooms. The downstairs boasts a bar with a TV lounge on one side and a smoking room on the other. With proximity to the Leidseplein, guests frequently start off here before going pubbing and clubbing.

⇟ Tram #2, 3, 5, or 12 to Van Baerlestraat. Walk down Van Baerlestraat toward Vondelpark and turn right onto Vossiusstraat. ℹ Breakfast included. Linens and towel included. Free lockers. Free Wi-Fi. Kitchen available. $ Dorms €12-40. ⏰ Bar open until 3am.

HOTEL BEMA
HOTEL $$

Concertgebouwplein 19B ☎020 679 13 96; www.bemahotel.com

Just across from the stunning Concertgebouw and the major museums on the Museumplein, Hotel Bema boasts elegant rooms with high ceilings, crystal chandeliers, and old-fashioned floral wallpaper. Chambers on the ground floor have antique-style furniture to boot. They'll even deliver breakfast to your room. It's amazing that you can get such luxury at these prices, but no one seems to be arguing with it.

 # Tram #3, 5, 12, 16, or 24 to Museumplein. Walk down the left side of the Concertgebouw and cross the street. i Breakfast included. Free Wi-Fi. [$] Singles €40-45; doubles €65-75, with bath €85-90.

HOTEL MUSEUMZICHT
HOTEL $$$

Jan Luijkenstraat 22 ☎020 671 29 54; www.hotelmuseumzicht.com

Staying here is a bit like staying in your cool grandmother's house—if your grandmother has a perfect view of the Rijksmuseum and serves a traditional Dutch breakfast every day. Old wooden furniture, oriental carpets, and decorative curtains adorn each room. Museumzicht caters to the individual or celibate traveler—there are no double beds, though twins can be pushed together.

 # Tram #2 or 5 to Hobbemastraat. Walk away from the Rijksmuseum and turn left onto Jan Luykenstraat. i Breakfast included. Free Wi-Fi. [$] Singles €55; doubles €75-85, with bath €85-125.

DE PIJP

Though far from the city center, De Pijp has character and easy transportation options, making it a good place to get a feel for local life in a hip up-and-coming neighborhood.

BICYCLE HOTEL
HOTEL $$

Van Ostadestraat 123 ☎020 679 34 52; www.bicyclehotel.com

A certain current of yuppie environmentalism runs through De Pijp, so it's appropriate that this eco-conscious hotel is located here. We couldn't be happier: not only does the hotel have solar panels and a "green roof" (plants grow on it and it saves energy—the owners explain it better than we can), but the theme of clean freshness permeates the entire building. The rooms have lavender sheets and pastel prints on the walls, while large windows overlook leafy gardens and let in sun and fresh air. There are even some balconies to sit on. Plus, the per-day bike rental costs the same as a 24hr. transport ticket, so there's no excuse for you not to go green as well.

 # Tram #3, 12, or 25 to Ceinturbaan/Ferdinand Bolstraat. Continue 1 block down Ferdinand Bolstraat and turn left onto Van Ostadestraat. i Breakfast included. Free Wi-Fi. [$] Singles €35-70; doubles €40-85, with bath €60-120. Bike rental €7.50 per day.

HOTEL VIVALDI
HOTEL $$$

Stadhouderskade 76 ☎020 577 63 00

Location is everything at this hotel, which sits at the northern end of the main part of De Pijp, across from the Central Canal Ring. The rooms are minimally furnished (don't worry, there's still a bed), but a few will surprise you with stained-glass windows and great canal views.

 # Tram #16 or 24 to Stadhouderskade. Walk toward the water, veer left, and Hotel Vivaldi is on the left. i Breakfast included. Free Wi-Fi. [$] Singles €45-120; doubles €60-150.

JODENBUURT AND PLANTAGE

Staying in these neighborhoods, slightly removed from the city center (though in pocket-sized Amsterdam you're never really far from anything), will give you a more local experience. However, you can expect to pay a little (or a lot) extra for the tranquility.

BRIDGE HOTEL

HOTEL $$$$

Amstel 107-111 ☎020 623 70 68; www.thebridgehotel.nl

The nicest hotel in this pricey neighborhood, Bridge's massive, comfortable rooms will easily accommodate you and all the shoes you didn't need to pack. The staff is eager to help you settle into what feels more like a modern Amsterdam apartment than a hotel room (actual apartments with kitchens are also available). The location may feel remote, but you're really just across the bridge from Rembrandtplein.

 # Tram #9 or 14 to Waterlooplein or Mr. Visserplein. Walk down Waterlooplein toward the bridge and turn left onto Amstel. ***i*** *Breakfast included. Free Wi-Fi.* [$] *Singles €85-115; doubles €98-140.*

HERMITAGE HOTEL

HOTEL $$$

Nieuwe Keizersgracht 16 ☎020 623 82 59; www.hotelhermitageamsterdam.nl

A new addition to the area, Hermitage has a younger feel than most of the neighboring hotels. Somehow managing to combine two of Amsterdam's predominant hotel aesthetics—modern minimalist and old-fashioned floral—Hermitage covers its walls in stylized silver-and-black flowered wallpaper for a cozy, but urban, feel.

 # Tram #9 or 14 to Waterlooplein or Mr. Visserplein. Walk down Waterlooplein toward the bridge, turn left onto Amstel, and then left onto Nieuwe Keizersgracht. ***i*** *Breakfast €9. Free Wi-Fi.* [$] *Singles €44-90; doubles €55-120.*

sights

Between the pretty old churches, quaint canals, and nightly showcases of revelry and debauchery, Amsterdam is a sight in and of itself. You can see and learn a lot about the city, even with zero euro. For a little more, you can see Museumplein's excellent art museums (showcasing everything from Northern Renaissance masterpieces to newer avant-garde works), modern photography exhibitions held in hip ex-squat studios and 14th-century churches, and a slew of museums and monuments devoted to remembering WWII. If you're dead set on shunning anything remotely highbrow, there are still plenty of things to see (the Sex Museum and the Hash, Marijuana, and Hemp Museum). Drug-loving tourists shouldn't miss **Electric Ladyland,** the First Museum of Fluorescent Art—more a trip than a sight, but still highly recommended.

If you're planning on visiting a number of museums, save some euro by investing in the Museumjaarkaart (www.museumjaarkaart.nl). For €40 (or €20 if you're under 26) you get free entrance to most museums in Amsterdam and the Netherlands for a whole year. With the Museumjaarkaart, there's nothing to stop you from popping into one of the many small and weird museums and then popping right back out if it's not up to snuff. You cannot get the card at the tourist office (it's a great deal rarely advertised to tourists), but it's sold at some of the bigger participating museums.

OUDE ZIJD

While the best museums in Amsterdam are found elsewhere, the Oude Zijd is home to some worthwhile architecture and history. Make some erudite observations on these landmarks on your way to the Red Light District.

✓ NIEUWMARKT

SQUARE

Dominated by the largest still-standing medieval building in Amsterdam, Nieuwmarkt is a calm square lined with cafes and bars, making it one of the best places in the city for some relaxed people-watching. Originally a fortress gate, **De Waag,** the 15th-century castle-like structure in Nieuwmarkt's center, has housed a number of establishments over the years, including a weighing house, a gallery for surgical dissections (Rembrandt's *The Anatomy Lesson of Dr. Tulp* depicts one such event), the **Jewish Historical Museum,** and, today, a swanky restaurant. Nieuwmarkt is beloved by tourists and locals alike: heavy rioting erupted in 1975 in response to a proposal to build a highway through the square. Daily markets here sell everything from souvenirs to organic food, especially on weekends.

[M]Nieuwmarkt, or from Centraal Station walk 10min. down Zeedijk.

AMSTERDAMS CENTRUM VOOR FOTOGRAFIE — GALLERY

Bethanienstraat 39 ☎020 622 48 99; www.acf-web.nl

Tucked in a small street between Nieuwmarkt and the Red Light District, this gallery showcases the work of young Dutch photographers, many just out of art school. Exhibits vary greatly in topic and quality, but since it's free, it's worth poking your head in if you're in the neighborhood. The center also holds lectures, workshops, and master classes—all in Dutch.

[M]Nieuwmarkt. Walk south on Kloveniersburgwal and make a right. $ Free. Open Th-Sa 1-5pm.

OOST-INDISCH HUIS — DUTCH HISTORY

Kloveniersburgwal 48

For almost two centuries, the *Vereenigde Oostindische Compagnie*, or Dutch East India Company—the world's first multinational corporation—wielded quasi-governmental powers and a whole lot of cash. Beginning in 1606, they set up shop in this building along Kloveniersburgwal. Its Dutch Renaissance design is a trademark of Hendrik de Keyser, the architect to whom the building has been (convincingly) attributed. Today, the University of Amsterdam occupies this national monument, and the students loitering and smoking outside take away much of the building's gravitas.

[M]Nieuwmarkt. Kloveniersburgwal is on the southwestern edge of the sqaure.

RED LIGHT DISTRICT

Many tourists treat the Red Light District as a sight in and of itself, wandering through the crowded streets while pretending not to look at window prostitutes. But there are plenty of other worthwhile opportunities for travelers to learn about parts of Dutch history and culture that don't involve sex, drugs, and drunk frat boys.

OUDE KERK — CHURCH

Oudekerksplein 23 ☎020 625 82 84; www.oudekerk.nl

Since its construction in 1306, Oude Kerk, the oldest church in Amsterdam, has endured everything from the Protestant Reformation to the growth of the Red Light District, which today encroaches naughtily on its very square. (Case in point: the bronze relief of a hand caressing a breast set into the cobblestones outside.) Oude Kerk didn't escape all this history unscathed; during the Reformation of 1578, the church lost much of its artwork and religious figures. However, it remains a strikingly beautiful structure, with massive vaulted ceilings and gorgeous stained glass that betray the building's Catholic roots. You can occasionally hear concerts played on the grandiose **Vater-Muller organ,** which dates back to 1724, but Oude Kerk is now used mainly for art and photography exhibitions, including the display of the prestigious **World Press Photo** prizewinners. Whether you come for the art, music, or the sanctuary, tread lightly—you're walking on 35 generations of Amsterdam's dead.

From Centraal Station, walk down Damrak, turn left onto Oudebrugsteeg, and right onto Warmoesstraat; the next left leads to the church. i Check the website for a calendar of performances. $ €7.50; students, seniors, and under 13 €5.50; with Museumjaarkaart free. Open M-Sa 10am-5:30pm, Su 1-5:30pm.

subprime tulip crisis

What can tulips tell us about the current global financial situation? A lot, actually. In 1593, tulips were brought from Turkey to the Netherlands, where they soon contracted the "mosaic" virus, which caused flames of color to develop on the petals. The colorful flowers became increasingly desirable, and, in just one month, tulips increased 20 times in value. At the height of tulip mania, you could trade a single tulip for an entire estate. Pubs turned into tulip exchanges at night, and people from all social strata staked their homes and livelihoods on the precious bulbs in a frenzy of what the Dutch call *windhandel,* or "trading in the wind"—speculating without any actual goods to back it up.

When the market inevitably crashed overnight in 1637, prices took a nosedive. A tulip was suddenly worth no more than an onion. The whole credit system fell apart and the Netherlands experienced a major depression whose reverberations were felt across Europe.

Today, Amsterdam hosts tours about tulip mania. Bankers and investors could definitely learn a thing or two from these pretty, but financially deadly, flowers.

[✓] ONS' LIEVE HEER OP SOLDER — MUSEUM

Oudezijds Voorburgwal 40 ☎020 624 66 04; www.opsolder.nl

The Ons' Lieve Heer op Solder ("Our Lord in the Attic") museum commemorates a beautiful Catholic church... in an attic. Built by a merchant in the 17th century, when Catholicism was officially banned in the Netherlands, the church was once regularly packed with secret worshippers. The museum includes three houses whose connected offices house the church, featuring art and furniture from the period. In contrast to the Catholic lavishness of Oude Kerk around the corner, Ons' Lieve Heer op Solder highlights the more muted Catholicism of the post-Reformation era. The church contains an impressive organ and a beautiful altarpiece by the famous painter **Jacob de Wit,** but the real appeal is the understanding you'll gain of broader trends in Dutch history and culture.

⇞ From Centraal Station, turn left onto Prins Hendrikkade and then right onto Nieuwebrugsteeg. Continue straight as Nieuwebrugsteeg becomes Oudezijds Voorburgwal. $ €7, students €5, under 18 €1, under 5 and with Museumjaarkaart free. ⏰ Open M-Sa 10am-5pm, Su 1-5pm.

BROUWERIJ DE PRAEL — BREWERY

Oudezijds Voorburgwal 30 ☎020 408 44 70; www.deprael.nl

If you love beer but find yourself asking "what's a hops?" come get a quick and easy crash course with a tour of this favorite local brewery. All the beer is organic, unfiltered, and unpasteurized, and all are named after classic *levensliederen*, sappy Dutch love songs (aww). A brewery that does more than make beer, de Prael was founded by two former psychiatrists and now employs over 60 people with a history of mental illness. The attached store sells de Prael's beers and other merchandise.

⇞ From Centraal Station, turn left onto Prins Hendrikkade and then right onto Nieuwebrugsteeg. Continue straight as it becomes Oudezijds Voorburgwal. $ Tour with 1 beer €7.50, with tasting menu €16.50. ⏰ Brewery open M-F 9am-5pm. Tasting room open Tu-Su 11am-11pm.

CANNABIS COLLEGE
Oudezijds Achterburgwal 124   ☎020 423 44 20; www.cannabiscollege.com

MUSEUM

Get your druggie "diploma" (a bachelor's in blunts? a master's in marijuana? a doctorate in doobies?) by taking a short quiz on all things cannabis. If you want cold, hard, sticky-icky facts, this is a repository of any information you could ever want to know about hemp and marijuana, especially regarding growing the plants themselves. Friendly volunteers, who are knowledge-able enough to provide training workshops to coffeeshop owners, are happy to answer questions about the history, science, and use of the drug. If you're dying to see some of the plants in person, check out the garden downstairs—otherwise, save the couple of euro and check out the pictures on their website. If you're looking for more kitsch, try the **Hash Marijuana Hemp Museum** just a few doors down (Oudezijds Achterburgwal 148; www.hashmuseum.com Ⓢ €9).

⚑ *From Dam Sq., walk east on Dam and make a left onto Oudezijds Achterburgwal.* Ⓢ *Free. Garden €2.50.* ✪ *Open daily 11am-7pm.*

NIEUWE ZIJD
The Nieuwe Zijd (despite its name) is one of the oldest parts of the city. Go back in time at the Amsterdam Historical Museum, then get a rude awakening into the present at some of the area's gimmicky attractions, such as Madame Tussaud's and the Sex Museum.

NIEUWE KERK
Dam Sq.   ☎020 638 69 09; www.nieuwekerk.nl

CHURCH, MUSEUM

Built in 1408 when the Oude Kerk became too small for the city's growing population, the Nieuwe Kerk is a commanding Gothic building that holds its own amid the architectural extravaganza of Dam Sq. Inside, the church is all vaulted ceilings and massive windows. Don't miss the intricate organ case designed by Jacob van Campen, architect of the Koninklijk Palace. Today, the Nieuwe Kerk is the site of royal inaugurations (the most recent one being Queen Beatrix's in 1980) and some royal weddings (like Prince Willem-Alexander's in 2002). Most of the year, however, the space serves as a museum. Each winter, the church holds exhibits on foreign cultures, spe-cifically focusing on world religions (recent topics have included Islam and Ancient Egypt). The space is also used for temporary exhibits by prominent Dutch museums like the Stedelijk and Rijksmuseum. Organ concerts are held here every Sunday, while shorter and more informal organ recitals are performed on Thursday afternoons.

⚑ *Any tram to Dam Sq. Nieuwe Kerk is on the northeastern edge of the square.* Ⓢ *€5, students €4, with Museumjaarkaart free. Organ concerts €8.50; recitals €5.* ✪ *Open daily 10am-5pm. Recitals Th 12:30pm. Concerts Su 8pm.*

AMSTERDAM SEX MUSEUM
Damrak 18   ☎020 622 83 76; www.sexmuseumamsterdam.nl

MUSEUM

Unless you were previously unaware that people have been having sex since mankind's origin, there's not much new information about sex or sexu-ality in this museum. (The brief "Sex Through the Ages" presentation is hilariously simplistic, though the elegant British-accented narration is priceless.) But let's face it: who needs information when you've got smut? Tons of pornographic photographs, paintings, and life-sized dolls fill the museum, along with models of various sexual icons: Marilyn Monroe with her skirt fluttering over the subway vent, a 1980s pimp, and even a 🔦**flasher** who thrills the audience every few seconds. The museum attracts crowds of tourists who react quite differently: some leave slightly offended by the hardcore porn-and-fetish room, some find the farting dolls funny, and others inexplicably insist on having their picture taken with one of the giant model penises. If you really want to see a parade of pictures of people having sex, you could just visit a sex shop in the Red Light District, but at least the Sex Museum charges a low rate for its high kitsch factor. Be warned: after you see (and hear) the mannequins of a Dutch girl giving a handjob in a public urinal, you may never look at one of those Dutch "curlies" the same way again.

From Centraal Station, walk straight down Damrak. ***i*** *16+.* *$ €4.* *Open daily 9:30am-11:30pm.*

AMSTERDAM HISTORICAL MUSEUM MUSEUM

Nieuwezijds Voorburgwal 359 ☎020 523 18 22; www.amsterdammuseum.nl

People, schmeople. This museum is about Amsterdam as a city. Through paintings, artifacts, and multimedia presentations, the museum's "Grand Tour" will show you how Amsterdam changed from 1350 to the present (spoiler: it changed a lot). Don't miss the room dedicated to Golden Age art and its stomach-churning paintings of anatomy lessons, which were apparently all the rage in the 17th century. Also fascinating is the corner that shows various city planning designs from the past century, driving home the fact that Amsterdam is an entirely man-made city. Only true history buffs will really be intrigued enough to read the placards about mercantile ships, but accessible and interesting temporary exhibits make up for some of the slower material. If you want to get to know the city a little better, this is a great place to start.

Tram #1, 2, or 5 to Spui/Nieuwezijds Voorburgwal. Head up Nieuwezijds Voorburgwal and the museum is on the right. *$ €10, seniors €7.50, students and ages 6-18 €5, under 6 and with Museumjaarkaart free. Audio tour €4.50.* *Open M-F 10am-5pm, Sa-Su 11am-5pm.*

BEGIJNHOF COURTYARD, CHURCH

Begijnhof www.begijnhofamsterdam.nl

The Beguines were small groups of Catholic laywomen who took vows of chastity and chose to serve the Church, though they didn't retreat from the world and formally join a convent. After seeing this beautiful 14th-century courtyard, surrounded by the Beguines' homes, you'll agree that they made a good call: this is a pretty sweet crib. Tour groups, bicycles, and photographs aren't allowed, so take in the place's original tranquility. During the Alteration, the original chapel was turned into a Protestant place of worship. The women responded by using a secret Catholic church, the **Begijnhofkapel,** built within two of the houses. Today, the cute but unremarkable chapel is an English Presbyterian church (the Belgians would be livid) and is open to respectful visitors.

Tram #1, 2, or 5 to Spui/Nieuwezijds Voorburgwal. Walk down Gedempte Begijnsloot and the gardens are on the left. *$ Free.* *Open daily 9am-5pm.*

DAM SQUARE SQUARE

Once upon a time, Amsterdam was just two small settlements on either side of the Amstel River. One day the villagers decided to connect their encampments with a dam. Since then, Dam Sq. has been the heart of the city, home to markets, the town hall, a church, and a weigh house (until Napoleon's brother had it torn down because it blocked his view). The obelisk on one end is the **Nationaal Monument,** erected in 1956 to honor the Dutch victims of WWII. The wall surrounding the monument contains soil from cemeteries and execution sites in each of the Netherlands's 12 provinces, as well as the Dutch East Indies. Across from the monument, next to the Nieuwe Kerk, you'll find the **Koninklijk Palace** (www.paleisamsterdam.nl), where you can see what it's like to be Dutch royalty. Louis Napoleon took it over in 1808, deciding that the building (constructed in the 17th century as Amsterdam's town hall) would make an excellent fixer-upper. Since then, it has been a royal palace, although Queen Beatrix only uses it for official functions. Too bad—she's wasting a unique view of the crowds, street performers, and occasional concerts in the square below.

Tram #1, 2, 4, 5, 9, 13, 14, 16, 17, 24, or 25 to Dam (remember when we said this was the center of the city?). $ Palace €7.50; ages 5-16, over 65, and students €6.50; with Museumjaarkaart free. ⏰ Palace usually open noon-5pm; check website for details.

CANAL RING WEST

The Canal Ring West is home to a few must-see sights (the Anne Frank House and nearby Westerkerk should be near the top of your list) along with some wackier ones like the Nationaal Brilmuseum and the National Spectacles Museum (Gasthuismolensteeg; www.brilmuseumamsterdam.nl).

ANNE FRANK HOUSE — MUSEUM

Prinsengracht 267 — ☎020 556 71 00; www.annefrank.nl

This is one of the most frequently visited sights in the city, and for good reason. It is the house where Anne Frank and her family lived in hiding from 1942 to 1944, when they were finally arrested by the Nazis. The well-organized museum route takes you through the family's hiding place, starting behind the moveable bookcase that masked their secret annex. Displays include pages of Anne's famous diary and a model of the rooms in 1942—Anne's father Otto requested that the museum not re-furnish the actual annex rooms after the Nazis seized all the original furnishings. Videos featuring interviews with those who knew the family make the story even more tangible. The end of the route includes information and interactive displays on contemporary issues in human rights and discrimination, reflecting the museum's mission as a center for activism and education as well as remembrance. This is one of the few museums in Amsterdam that opens early and stays open late, and we recommend you take advantage of it: the cramped attic gets packed with visitors in the middle of the day, and you'll want to be able to move around and take your time in such a thought-provoking place.

Tram #13, 14, or 17 to Westermarkt. Walk away from Keizersgracht down Westermarkt, then take a right onto Prinsengradcht. $ €8.50, ages 10-17 €4, under 10 and with Museumjaarkaart free. ⏰ Open daily July-Aug 9am-10pm; Sept 1-14 9am-9pm; Sept 15-March 14 9am-7pm; March 15-June 9am-9pm.

WESTERKERK — CHURCH

Prinsengracht 281 — ☎020 624 77 66; www.westerkerk.nl

Westerkerk's 85m tower, the Westerkerkstoren, stands far above central Amsterdam's other buildings. A trip up it in a 30min. guided tour is a must. The patient staff will pause to accommodate your huffing and puffing until you finish the climb and step out to behold the best view in Amsterdam. The tower also houses 47 bells, one of which weighs in at an astonishing 7509kg. The church was completed in 1631, a gift to the city from Maximilian of Austria (whose crown can be seen on the tower) in thanks for the city's support of the Austro-Burgundian princes. The church's brick-and-stone exterior is a fine example of Dutch late-Renaissance architecture. Inside, its plain white walls and clear glass windows are typical of the clean Calvinist aesthetic. The only real decorations are the shutters on the organ, which are beautifully painted by Gerard de Lairesse. The tower's carillon plays between noon and 1pm on Tuesdays, free organ concerts are held every Friday at 1pm, and the church hosts many other concerts throughout the year. Queen Beatrix and Prince Claus were married here in 1966, and Rembrandt is buried somewhere within the church—although no one seems to know exactly where. (Yeah, we don't know how they forgot where they put one of the most famous painters of all time either.)

Tram #13, 14, or 17 to Westermarkt. Walk away from Keizersgracht and turn right onto Prinsengradcht. $ Free. Tower tour €7. ⏰ Open Apr-June M-F 10am-6pm, Sa 10am-8pm; July-Sept M-Sa 10am-8pm; Oct M-F 11am-4pm, Sa 10am-6pm. Tower tours every 30min.

HOMOMONUMENT MONUMENT

Westermarkt www.homomonument.nl

The Homomonument is the culmination of a movement to erect a memorial honoring homosexual victims of Nazi persecution, but it's also meant to stand for all people, past and present, who've been oppressed for their sexuality. Designed by Karin Daan and officially opened in 1987, the monument consists of three pink granite triangles (in remembrance of the symbol the Nazis forced homosexuals to wear), connected by thin lines of pink granite to form a larger triangle. The Homomonument was designed to merge seamlessly with the daily life of the city, so it can be hard to discern under picnicking tourists and whizzing bikes. One triangle is set down into the water of the Keizergracht and points toward the National War Monument in Dam Sq., representing the present. The raised triangle stands for the future and points toward the headquarters of the COC, a Dutch gay rights group founded in 1946 and the oldest continuously operating gay and lesbian organization in the world. The third triangle points toward the Anne Frank House, symbolizing the past; it is engraved with the words "*Naar Vriendschap Zulk een Mateloos Verlangen*" ("such an endless desire for friendship"), a line from the poem "To a Young Fisherman" by the gay Dutch Jewish poet Jacob Israel de Haan (1881-1924).

Tram #13, 14, or 17 to Westermarkt. The Homomonument is between Westerkerk and the Keizersgracht. $ Free.

MULTATULI MUSEUM MUSEUM

Korsjespoortsteeg 20 ☎020 638 19 38; www.multatuli-museum.nl

This museum is dedicated to the Netherlands's most famous writer, Eduard Douwes Dekker, who was born here in 1820. Dekker was better known by his pen name, Multatuli—Latin for "I have endured much." He was a rather unsuccessful lad, and after failing at school and a trade clerkship, he was carted off to Indonesia by his sea captain father. Here, he finally exhibited some talent in the civil service, rising through the ranks and marrying a baroness along the way. Disgusted by the abuses of imperialism, he eventually quit his job, returned to a penniless life in Europe, and wrote the autobiographical novel *Max Havelaar* to expose the evils of colonialism and the Dutch East India Company. Ironically, *Max Havelaar* became a massive hit, not due to its message of reform (which was largely ignored by the contemporary public) but because of Multatuli's entertaining, well-written prose. In time, the work came to be cited as one of the most important books to influence reform movements. Today, *Max Havelaar* remains the most popular Dutch novel, and has been translated into more than 40 languages. Multatuli is considered a crucial intellectual forefather to the atmosphere of tolerance for which the Netherlands is so famous today.

The dedicated proprietor of the museum, who cares passionately about Multatuli's legacy, will gladly tell you everything about the author's life in the form of personal and funny stories. The free museum is worth a stop for literary fiends, those who want a quick brush-up on Dutch history, or those curious to learn more about the brain inside the enormous head replicated in the big statue over the Singel.

Tram #1, 2, 5, 13, or 17 to Nieuwezijds Kolk. Walk to the Herengracht and make a right. $ Free (but don't forget to tip the guide!). ⏰ Open Tu 10am-5pm, Sa-Su 10am-5pm.

NEDERLANDS INSTITUUT VOOR MEDIAKUNST MUSEUM

Keizersgracht 264 ☎020 623 71 01; www.nimk.nl

The Netherlands Media Art Institute puts on four 10-week exhibitions each year to showcase the works of Dutch and international artists who use film, video, the internet, and other media technology. If you're planning a visit, be prepared to invest some time, as pieces can sometimes run for 20min. or more, but most are interesting enough that you'll want to see the whole thing. The institute also runs a number of smaller exhibitions that involve more experimental performances and symposia. The museum is in the same building as the **Mediatheque,** which houses a huge collection of books and media pieces.

🚋 Tram #13, 14, or 17 to Westermarkt. Follow Keizergracht and the museum will be on your right. [$] €4.50, students and seniors €2.50. Mediatheque free. ⏰ Open Tu-F 11am-6pm, Sa and every 1st Su 1-6pm. Mediatheque open M-F 1-5pm.

BIJBELS MUSEUM MUSEUM

Herengracht 366-368 ☎020 624 24 36; www.bijbelsmuseum.nl

This bizarre museum provides glimpses into two radically different worlds: ancient biblical culture and 17th-century Dutch life. The centerpiece is the Tabernacle model, the life work of minister Leendert Schouten (1828-1905), who based the original museum around public Tabernacle viewings. The top floor has Egyptian artifacts—sculptures, sarcophagi, even a mummy—that are meant to illustrate the Israelite presence in Egypt. Some exhibits also deal with the history of Islam and Judaism. The ground floor shows artifacts of 17th-century domestic life. Adjacent are two reading rooms and the somewhat perplexing **Aroma Room,** which has samples of biblical scents like cedar and myrrh free for the sniffing.

🚋 Tram #1, 2, or 5 to Koningsplein. Walk down Koningsplein toward the bridge, then make a right onto Herengracht. [$] €8, students €4.75, ages 13-17 €4, with Museumjaarkart free. ⏰ Open M-Sa 10am-5pm, Su 11am-5pm.

poezenboot

At first, Henriette van Weelde was your typical cat lady. In 1966, she took in a family of stray cats she found across from her home. Then she took in another. And another. After a while, she realized she had a bit of a space issue–namely, too many cats, too little space. So, Henriette did the reasonable thing: she bought her feline friends a sailing barge. The cats never stopped coming, so she upgraded the boat a few times over the years. By 1987, the boat was named an official cat sanctuary. Today, it meets all the requirements for an animal shelter. The Poezenboot (Cat Boat) has room for 30 kitties, and they adopt out an average of 15 per month. If you find yourself looking for a different kind of pussy in Amsterdam, stop by to offer one a good home. (Singel 38G ☎020 625 87 94; www.poezenboot.nl ⏰ Open M-Tu 1-3pm, Th-Sa 1-3pm.)

CENTRAL CANAL RING

The grand buildings in the center of the canal ring, architectural landmarks themselves, house a few historical museums as well as art galleries that lean toward the avant-garde. For kitsch aficionados, come here for some of the quirkier museums in the city, like the **Cat's Cabinet** (see below) or the **Museum of Bags and Purses** (Herengracht 573 ☎020 524 64 52; http://www.tassenmuseum.nl).

[icon] FOAM — MUSEUM

Keizersgracht 609 ☎020 551 65 00; www.foam.org

Foam—the **Fo**tografiemuseum **Am**sterdam—showcases new photography, from gritty photojournalism to glossy fashion photos. Work by renowned and up-and-coming photographers is displayed in an expansive wood-and-metal space. Grab a coffee and try to blend in with the artsy students hanging out here.

🚋 Tram #4, 16, 24, or 25 to Keizersgracht. Foam is about 50m east of the stop. $ €8, students and seniors €5.50, under 12 and with Museumjaarkaart free. ⏰ Open M-W 10am-6pm, Th-F 10am-9pm, Sa-Su 10am-6pm. Cafe open daily 11am-5pm.

GOLDEN BEND — ARCHITECTURE

Herengracht, between Leidsestraat and Vijzelstraat

If Amsterdam's tiny, teetering canal houses are beginning to make you feel claustrophobic, head to this scenic stretch of the canal ring, removed from the noisy center but still only 15min. south of Dam Sq. In the 17th century, expanding the canals meant the city needed wads of cash, so they allowed the rich to build houses twice as wide as before in order to encourage investment. Termed the "Golden Bend" for the wealth that subsequently flocked here, this stretch of former residences features Neoclassical facades and glimpses of sparkling chandeliers through latticed windows. Today, most of these former mansions are inhabited by banks, life insurance agencies, and a few very lucky (and very wealthy) residents. To get a peek inside one of the swanky buildings, you may have to stifle your suppressed fear of crazy cat ladies and visit **Cat's Cabinet** (Herengracht 497 ☎020 626 53 78; www.kattenkabinet.nl). This bizarre museum was created a Golden Bend house after the owner's beloved cat—fittingly named JP Morgan—passed away. For some reason, the apparently distraught owner felt the world needed a museum devoted to all things feline. For a less idiosyncratic peek inside, **Open Garden Days** each June allow visitors to tour many of the houses' gardens (for more info, check out www.opentuinendagen.nl).

🚋 Tram #1, 2, or 5 to Koningsplein. $ Cat's Cabinet €6, ages 4-12 €3. ⏰ Cat's Cabinet open M-F 10am-4pm, Sa-Su noon-5pm.

MUSEUM WILLET-HOLTHUYSEN — MUSEUM

Herengracht 605 ☎020 523 18 22; www.willetholthuysen.nl

Not technically on the "Golden Bend" but just as elegant and opulent, this building has been preserved by the Amsterdam Historical Museum. The museum's goal is to demonstrate what wealthy Dutch life was like in the 19th century as seen through the eyes of **Abraham Willet** and **Louisa Willet-Holthuysen,** the house's last inhabitants. Visitors gawk and admire three floors of wealth on display, including the Willets' art collection and a stately garden. Those less interested in history might tire of all the tidbits from the meticulously chronicled lives of Louisa and Abe, but if you've got a few minutes and a Musuemjaarkaart, the inside offers a new perspective on the famous canal houses. The museum will leave you wondering if all the tall skinny abodes you trek past are this ridiculously grand.

🚋 Tram #9 or 14 to Rembrandtplein. Walk down Utrechtsestraat and turn left. $ €8, ages 6-18 €4, under 6 and with Museumjaarkaart free. ⏰ Open M-F 10am-5pm, Sa-Su 11am-5pm.

JORDAAN

The Jordaan is home to some of Amsterdam's quirkiest sights. Those uninterested in the psychedelic trip that is **Electric Ladyland** can visit the **Pianola Museum,** dedicated to self-playing pianos. Even if you just pass through, look for the **Hofjes,** and some of the most beautiful canal views in the city.

👍 ELECTRIC LADYLAND — MUSEUM

Tweede Leliedwarsstraat 5 ☎020 420 37 76; www.electric-lady-land.com

Electric Ladyland, the "First Museum of Fluorescent Art," is a sight unlike any other. The passionate and eccentric owner, Nick Padalino, will happily spend hours explaining the history, science, and culture of fluorescence to each and every visitor who walks through the door. The museum consists of a one-room basement full of Padalino's own art and other artifacts, including rocks and minerals from New Jersey to the Himalayas that glow all kinds of colors under the lights. The most intriguing part though, is the fluorescent cave-like sculpture that Padalino terms "participatory art." Don a pair of foam slippers and poke around the glowing grottoes and stalactites; flick the lights on and off to see different fluorescent and phosphorescent stones; and look for the tiny, hidden Hindu sculptures. Upstairs, you can buy your own fluorescent art and blacklight kits. When a tour is in progress, you may have to ring the doorbell for a few minutes, but trust us: it's worth any wait.

🚋 Tram #13, 14, or 17 to Westermarkt. Cross Prinsengracht and walk 1 block down Rozengracht, then make a right and walk a few blocks. The museum is just before you reach Egelantiersgracht. $ €5. ⏰ Open Tu-Sa 1-6pm.

STEDELIJK MUSEUM BUREAU AMSTERDAM (SMBA) — MUSEUM

Rozenstraat 59 ☎020 422 04 71; www.smba.nl

There's no telling what you'll find at the Stedelijk Museum's project space, but it seems to usually be some kind of art. Local artists have the chance to showcase artwork in rotating exhibits; during *Let's Go*'s last visit it was "The Marx Lounge"—a red room with a table full of books on critical theory. Special lectures and movie screenings are also sponsored occasionally. Check the website for current events or simply take your chances and drop by—after all, it's free.

🚋 Tram #13, 14, or 17 to Westermarkt. Cross Prinsengracht, turn left, and walk 1 block. $ Free. ⏰ Open Tu-Su 11am-5pm.

HOFJES — GARDENS, DUTCH HISTORY

The northern third of the Jordaan

Tucked behind the neighborhood's closed doors are some of the oldest and prettiest gardens in the city. *Hofjes* are courtyard gardens, surrounded by almshouses originally built to provide housing for impoverished old women. These old gardens are scattered throughout the Jordaan, and many are now open to the public. In the northern part of the Jordaan, at Palmgracht 28-38, you can find the **Raepenhofje,** and a few blocks down is the **Karthuizerhof** (Karthuizersstraat 21-131). This larger *hofje* has two flowering gardens dotted with benches and a pair of old-fashioned water pumps. Finally, head to Egelantiersgracht 107-145 for the **Sint-Andrieshof.** These gardens are surrounded by residences, so be quiet and respectful.

🚋 From Raepenhofje, take tram #3 to Nieuwe Willemstraat, cross Lijnbaansgracht, make a left, and turn right onto Palmgracht. $ Free. ⏰ Open M-Sa 9am-6pm.

WESTERPARK AND OUD-WEST

Visitors to this area can relax in the park that gives the neighborhood its name, while art-lovers could check out two of the city's more idiosyncratic destinations, to the north and east of the park.

MUSEUM HET SCHIP — MUSEUM

Spaarndammerplantsoen 140 ☎020 418 28 85; www.hetschip.nl

This museum commemorates "The Ship," a housing project designed by Amsterdam School architect Michel de Klerk in 1919. Inspired by Socialist ambitions, de Klerk added unusual shapes and fanciful brickwork to his building, believing that Amsterdam's working class was overdue for "something beautiful." The first floor houses an old post office designed by de Klerk, as well as a re-creation of what one of the original apartments looked like. Be sure to take the free tour, as knowledgeable staff can point out quirky details in the architecture that are otherwise easily missed. Across the street, a lunchroom serves food amid an exhibit of Amsterdam School photography and sculptures.

🚏 Tram #3 to Haarlemmerplein. Walk across the canal toward Westerpark, up Spaarndammerstraat, then take a left onto Zaanstraat; the building will be a few blocks down the street. $ €7.50, students €5, with Museumjaarkaart free. 🕐 Open Tu-Su 11am-5pm. Tours every hr. 11am-4pm, though they can usually be joined late.

WESTERGASFABRIEK — CULTURAL PARK

Pazzanistraat 41 ☎020 586 07 10; www.westergasfabriek.nl

Westergasfabriek, a so-called "cultural park" right next to Westerpark, serves as a center for local artists and trendy restaurants. Originally a 19th-century gasworks, its imposing brick buildings are now open to all manner of cultural projects, and currently house art studios and galleries, restaurants, theaters, and nightclubs. Check the website for upcoming showings and special events like film festivals, art showings, and market days.

🚏 Just east of Westerpark. Tram #10 to Van Hallstraat. Cross the bridge and turn right to get to the main cluster of buildings.

MUSEUMPLEIN AND VONDELPARK

The Museumplein is filled with museums—surprise! Plus, the beautiful **Concertgebouw,** at the southern end of Museumplein, is worth checking out even when the music isn't playing (see **Arts and Culture**).

👍 VAN GOGH MUSEUM — MUSEUM

Paulus Potterstraat 7 ☎020 570 52 00; www.vangoghmuseum.nl

Van Gogh only painted for about a decade, yet he left a remarkable legacy of paintings and drawings. There's a lot more here than the pictures on the walls: one exhibit has a graphic novel depicting van Gogh's tumultuous personal life, while another details how the paintings have changed over the years with recreations of the masterpieces as the painter himself would've seen them. The museum dedicates considerable space to the artists who influenced van Gogh; including Toulouse-Lautrec, Gauguin, Renoir, Manet, Seurat, and Pissarro. On the flip side there are some paintings influenced by van Gogh, from artists like Derain and Picasso. Of course, the highlight of the museum is its impressive collection of van Gogh's own work—the largest in the world—ranging from the dark, gloomy works like the *Potato Eaters* and *Skull of a Skeleton with Burning Cigarette* to the delicate *Branches of an Almond Tree in Blossom.* The exhibits are arranged chronologically, and wall plaques do an excellent job tracking the artist's biography alongside the paintings, concluding with the artist's descent into depression and suicide. We think this may be the best museum in Amsterdam—unfortunately, so do a lot of other people. The lines can get pretty painful; to avoid them, reserve tickets on the museum's website or arrive when the crowds thin at around 10:30am or 4pm. But don't let the fear of crowds deter you—this is hands down one of the city's must-sees, and it's absolutely worth the wait.

🚏 Tram #2, 3, 5, or 12 to Van Baerlestraat. Walk 1 block up Paulus Potterstraat. $ €14, under 18 and with Museumjaarkaart free. Audio tour €5. 🕐 Open M-Th 10am-6pm, F 10am-10pm, Sa-Su 10am-6pm. Last entry 30min. before close.

👍 RIJKSMUSEUM — MUSEUM

Jan Luijkenstraat 1 ☎020 674 70 00; www.rijksmuseum.nl

When you first see the commanding facade of the Rijksmuseum, it looks like the type of place you could get lost in for hours (if not days). Luckily—if a bit disappointingly—the museum is undergoing extensive renovations (scheduled to be completed in 2013), so only highlights of the collection are currently on display. It's still well worth a visit, though. Current displays feature art and artifacts from the Middle Ages through the 19th century, a comprehensive exhibit on Dutch history, and a collection of Asian art. There is also an enormous selection of furniture, Delftware, silver, and decorative objects (including two enormous dollhouses that probably cost more than some apartments). The exhibits on the ground floor trace the Netherlands's history as it grew from a small republic to a world power, commanding more than a fair share of the seas and international trade. The heart of the museum, however, is the second-floor gallery of art from the Dutch Golden Age. Numerous still lifes—cheese figures prominently, typical Dutch—landscapes, and portraits set the tone for 17th-century Dutch art, reflecting the same trends as the history lesson on the first floor. They pull out the big guns in a room full of beautiful works by **Rembrandt** and his pupils, evocative landscapes by Jacob van Ruisdael, and four luminous paintings by **Vermeer,** including *The Milkmaid.* The big finish is the room devoted to the **Night Watch,** probably Rembrandt's most famous painting. Only in Amsterdam would the old master be exhibited alongside a modern sculpture that looks like metal magic mushrooms hanging upside-down. Two audio tours are available to guide you through the museum. One is more traditional and led by the museum director, while the other is narrated by the Dutch artist, actor, and director Jeroen Krabbé, who gives a more personal view of the artists and paintings.

 # Tram #2 or 5 to Hobbemastraat. Alternatively, tram #7 or 10 to Spiegelgracht. The museum is directly across the canal. **i** *Lines are shorter after 4pm.* [$] *€12.50, under 18 and with Museumjaarkaart free. Audio tour €5.* ⏰ *Open daily 9am-6pm.*

✓ VONDELPARK — PARK

Rolling streams, leafy trees, and inviting grass make the 120-acre Vondelpark central Amsterdam's largest and most popular open space. Established in the 1880s to provide a place for the city's residents to walk and ride, the park is now a hangout for skaters, senior citizens, stoners, soccer players, and sidewalk acrobats. Head here on the first sunny day of spring to see the whole city out in full force. The park is named after Joost van den Vondel, a 17th-century poet and playwright often referred to as the "Dutch Shakespeare." Vondelpark is also home to excellent cafes and an open-air theater (www.openluchttheater.nl), which offers free music and performances in the summer. If you're looking for a different sort of outdoor entertainment, you should know that in 2008 the Dutch police decided that it's legal to ✓**have sex** in Vondelpark—so long as it's not near a playground and condoms are thrown away. Even without a bit of afternoon delight, this is still a delightful place to picnic and take a break from the bustling city.

 # Tram #2, 3, 5, or 12 to Van Baerlestraat. Walk down Van Baerlestraat to the bridge over the park and take the stairs down.

DE PIJP

De Pijp's sights are of a decidedly different variety than those in nearby Museumplein. Rather than staring at paintings you'll never own, haggle for wares at **Albert Cuypmarkt** (see **Shopping**). Or, instead of contemplating what life would be like in the Dutch Golden Age, find out what it's like being a bottle of beer at the **Heineken Experience.**

SARPHATIPARK — PARK

In the 1860s, Amsterdam's chief architect was convinced that the center of the city would move south, and that this spot in De Pijp (then just marshlands and a windmill or two) would be the ideal place for Centraal Station. We all know how that one turned out (though we wonder what would have happened to the Red Light District if visitors couldn't stumble straight into it from the station). Not one to be deterred, the architect decided to build a park instead. Sarphatipark is fairly small, but its crisscrossing paths and central monument give it a genteel, 19th-century feel. It's rarely as crowded as Vondelpark, so you can have more grassy sunbathing space to yourself. The monument commemorates the park's namesake, the Jewish philanthropist and doctor Samuel Sarphati.

🚊 Tram #3 or 25 to 2e Van der Helstraat.

HEINEKEN EXPERIENCE — MUSEUM

Stadhouderskade 78 ☎020 523 92 22; www.heinekenexperience.com

They can't call it a museum, because it isn't informative enough, and they can't call it a brewery, because beer hasn't been made here since 1988. So, welcome to the Heineken "Experience." Four floors of holograms, multimedia exhibits, and virtual-reality machines tell you everything you'll ever want to know about the green-bottled stuff. Highlights include a ride that replicates the experience of actually becoming a Heineken beer. (There's something very Zen-alcoholic about the whole "in order to enjoy the beer you must BE the beer" idea.) In the end, this is a big tourist trap where you pay €15 to watch an hour of Heineken commercials. On the other hand, there's something quintessentially Dutch about the whole "experience"—these are, after all, the people who invented capitalism.

🚊 Tram #16 or 24 to Stadhouderskade, or tram #4, 7, 10, or 25 to Weterincircuit. From Weterincircuit, cross the canal and you'll see the building. $ €15. ⏰ Open daily 11am-7pm. Last entry 5:30pm.

JODENBUURT AND PLANTAGE

Some lesser-known but still worthwhile museums fill Jodenbuurt, historically the city's Jewish Quarter and now home to several sights focusing on Jewish culture and identity. Spacious Plantage, meanwhile, is home to the Botanical Gardens and Artis Zoo. The phenomenal Brouwerij 't IJ is in the north, by the water.

swimming with the fishes

Move over, Atlantis. Rather than searching for the fabled underwater paradise, Dutch architects and city engineers have taken matters into their own hands. In 2018, construction will begin on an underwater city buried under canals. The underwater buildings would mostly be used for parking, shopping, and entertainment. The architects, Zwarts and Jansma, claim the project will be completely eco-friendly, and that the air filtration techniques will improve Amsterdam's above-ground air. Objectors to the project oppose the idea of living like moles under the earth—but we're pretty excited by the idea of living like mermen and mermaids, to be honest.

🏆 VERZETSMUSEUM (DUTCH RESISTANCE MUSEUM) — MUSEUM

Plantage Kerklaan 61 ☎020 620 25 35; www.verzetsmuseum.org

This museum chronicles the five years the Netherlands spent under Nazi occupation during WWII. The permanent exhibit centers on the question that people faced in this period, "What do we do?" In the early days of the occupation, many struggled to decided whether to adapt to their relatively unchanged life under Nazi rule or to resist. As time went on, the persecution of Jews, gypsies, and homosexuals intensified, and as repression grew, so did the resistance. The museum masterfully presents individuals' stories with interactive exhibits and an extensive collection of artifacts and video footage. The museum pays tribute to the ordinary Dutch citizens who risked (and often lost) their lives to publish illegal newspapers, hide Jews, or pass information to Allied troops. A smaller portion of the exhibit details the effects of the war on Dutch colonies in East Asia. Verzetsmuseum is well worth your time and money, even if you're not a history buff.

Tram #9 or 14 to Plantage Kerklaan. Across from Artis Zoo. $ €7.50, ages 7-15 €4, under 7 and with Museumjaarkaart free. ⏰ Open M 11am-5pm, Tu-F 10am-5pm, Sa-Su 11am-5pm.

TROPENMUSEUM MUSEUM

Linnaeusstraat 2 ☎020 568 82 00; www.tropenmuseum.nl

In a palatial building that is part of the Koninklijk Instituut voor de Tropen (Dutch Royal Institute of the Tropics), this immense museum provides an anthropological look at the world's tropical regions from the distant past to today. A running theme throughout the exhibits is the complicated relationship between Europe and the tropics during the rise and fall of Western imperialism. An astounding collection of cultural artifacts like Thai bridal jewelry and African presidential folk cloths give a sense of life in these regions. An extensive portion of the first floor is devoted to the Dutch colonial experience in Indonesia (from the perspective of both the colonizers and colonized). There are also some cool interactive exhibits like drum kits to make early African music. That one's probably for the kids, but if you find yourself rocking out, we won't tell.

Tram #9, 10, or 14 to Alexanderplein. Cross the canal and walk left along Mauritskade. $ €9, students €5, under 18 and with Museumjaarkaart free. ⏰ Open daily 10am-5pm.

JOODS HISTORISCH MUSEUM (JEWISH HISTORICAL MUSEUM) MUSEUM

Nieuwe Amstelstraat 1 ☎020 531 03 10; www.jhm.nl

Four 17th- and 18th-century Ashkenazi synagogues were incorporated to form this museum dedicated to the history and culture of Dutch Jews. One part of the museum highlights the religious life of the community using artifacts (including a number of beautifully decorated Torahs), explanations of Jewish traditions, and videos that recount personal anecdotes. Another exhibit explores the history of the community between 1600 and 1900, from the first settlements in this unusually tolerant city to later struggles to gain full civil and political liberties. The period surrounding WWII is also covered. The museum holds two temporary exhibition spaces that host art shows. The JHM Children's Museum introduces kids to Jewish life and culture through the reconstruction of a typical Jewish family, with friendly Max the Matzo as their guide.

Trams #9 or 14 or [M]Waterlooplein. Walk down Waterlooplein and turn right onto Wesperstraat. Nieuwe Amstelstraat is on the right. $ €9, students and seniors €6, ages 13-17 €4.50, under 13 and with Museumjaarkaart free. Special exhibits may cost extra. ⏰ Open daily 11am-5pm.

BROUWERIJ 'T IJ BREWERY

Funenkade 7 ☎020 622 83 25; www.brouwerijhetij.nl

What could be more Dutch than drinking beer at the base of a windmill? Even better, the beer brewed and served here is much, much tastier than the more internationally famous Dutch brands. Once a bathhouse, this building was taken over as a squat in the 1980s. Today, its brewers craft 10 organic, unfiltered, and non-pasteurized beers. You can try a glass or three of their wares at the massive outdoor terrace of the on-site pub, or at cafes and bars throughout the city. The brewers are proud of their beers, which range from a golden triple beer to a pilsner; proud of their brewery, which you can scope out on a free tour; and even prouder of their huge collection of beer bottles, purportedly one of Europe's largest.

Tram #10 to Hoogte Kadijk or #14 to Pontanusstraat. Head toward the windmill. $ Beer €2. ⏰ Pub open daily 3-8pm. Free brewery tours F and Su 4pm.

REMBRANDT HOUSE MUSEUM
Jodenbreestraat 4

MUSEUM

☎020 520 04 00; www.rembrandthuis.nl

Flush with success at the height of his popularity, Rembrandt van Rijn bought this massively expensive house in 1639. Twenty years later, after a decline in sales and failure to pay his mortgage, he was forced to sell it along with many of his possessions. His misfortune turned out to be a great boon for historians—the inventory of Rembrandt's worldly goods gave curators the ability to reconstruct his house almost exactly as it was when he lived there. Now visitors can see where Rembrandt slept, entertained guests, made paintings, sold paintings, and got attacked by his mistress after a fight over alimony (that would be the kitchen). The most interesting rooms are on the top floor: Rembrandt's massive studio (with many of his original tools) and the room where he stored his *objets d'art*—armor, armadillos, and everything in between. Paintings by his talented contemporaries and students adorn the walls, and the museum holds a collection of hundreds of Rembrandt's etchings. Guides reenact his etching and printing techniques on the third floor every 45min.

✢ Tram #9 or 14 or Ⓜ Waterlooplein. Walk down Waterlooplein, around the stadium, then turn right and continue until you reach Jodenbreestraat. The museum is on the right. Ⓢ €9, with ISIC card €6, ages 6-17 €2.50, under 6 and with Museumjaarkaart free. ⌚ Open daily 10am-5pm.

HORTUS BOTANICUS
Plantage Middenlaan 2A

GARDENS

☎020 638 16 70; www.dehortus.nl

One of the oldest botanical gardens in the world, Hortus Botanicus began in 1638 as a place for growing medicinal herbs (no, not that kind). Now it's grown to include over 4000 species of plant life. Thanks to the Dutch East India company, the gardens gathered exotic species from all around the world, and some of those original plants (such as the Eastern Cape giant cycad) are still around today. The "crown jewels" section is the place to go to catch a glimpse of extremely rare species such as the *Victoria amazonica*, a water lily that only opens at dusk. Nicely landscaped ponds and paths make this a pleasant place to wander for an afternoon, and the butterfly house might be the closest you'll get to some steamy summer weather in Amsterdam.

✢ Tram #9 or 14 to Mr. Visserplein. Walk down Plantage Middenlaan. The gardens are on the right. Ⓢ €7.50, seniors and ages 5-14 €3.50. Tours €1. ⌚ Open July-Aug M-F 9am-7pm, Sa-Su 10am-7pm; Sept-June M-F 9am-5pm, Sa-Su 10am-5pm. Tours Su 2pm.

food

For some reason, when we think "Northern Europe," we don't think "awesome food." It's telling that in the vast world of Amsterdam restaurants, not too many of them actually serve Dutch cuisine. (Here's a quick run-down of what that looks like: pancakes, cheese, herring, and various meat-and-potato combinations.) Luckily, Amsterdam's large immigrant populations have brought Indonesian, Surinamese, Ethiopian, Algerian, Thai, and Chinese food to the banks of the canals. Finally, Amsterdam has this thing with sandwiches—they're everywhere, and they tend to be really, really good.

De Pijp, Jordaan, and the Nine Streets in Canal Ring West boast the highest concentration of quality eats, and De Pijp is the cheapest of the three. If you really want to conserve your cash, the supermarket chain Albert Heijn is a gift from the budget gods (find the nearest location at www.ah.nl). Keep in mind that most supermarkets close around 8pm. If you need groceries late at night (we can only guess why), try De Avondmarkt near Westerpark.

food

OUDE ZIJD

Zeedijk is overrun with restaurants, but if you shop around to avoid touristy rip-offs, you can land a great meal.

👍 **'SKEK** — CAFE, GLOBAL $$

Zeedijk 4-8 — ☎020 427 05 51; www.skek.nl

A "cultural eetcafe" where students (with ID) get a 33% discount, ' Skek prepares healthy, hearty cuisine, with rotating options like a Japanese hamburger with wasabi mayonnaise, grilled vegetable lasagna, and braised eggplant. The interior is on a mission to be hip, with whimsical fantasy board games painted on the tables, student art on the walls, and occasional live music. Come for the free Wi-Fi and student discount, stay for the not-bad food—just don't accidentally order the hamburger made out of carrots.

 # From Centraal Station, follow Prins Hendrikkade to Zeedjik. $ Lunch dishes around €5-7. Dinner entrees around €13. ⏰ Open M-Th noon-1am, F-Sa noon-3am, Su noon-1am.

👍 **LATEI** — CAFE $

Zeedijk 143 — ☎020 625 74 85; www.latei.net

Colorful and eccentric, Latei is filled with mismatched furniture and interesting knick-knacks—which just so happen to all be for sale. But save your money for the simple, filling, and tasty food: sandwiches are made with artisan bread and the cafe's own olive oil and topped with fresh cheese or veggies. (Note: Dutch "sandwiches" usually only include one slice of bread.) Indian cuisine makes a guest appearance at dinner Thursday to Saturday nights.

 # [M]Nieuwmarkt. Zeedijk is along the northwestern corner of the square. $ Sandwiches €3-5. Desserts €3-4. ⏰ Open M-W 8am-6pm, Th-F 8am-10pm, Sa 9am-10pm, Su 11am-6pm.

BIRD — THAI $$

Zeedijk 72-74 — ☎020 620 14 42; www.thai-bird.nl

Zeedijk may be considered Amsterdam's Chinatown, but the best Asian restaurant in town might be this Thai eatery. Across the street from the main restaurant is a simpler snack bar version, which sells many of the same dishes for a few euro less. The menu is full of all your favorite Thai classics, including some special dishes from the northeast. *Let's Go* really likes their green curry.

 # [M]Nieuwmarkt. $ Entrees €8-14. Snack bar cash only. ⏰ Open daily 5-11pm. Snack bar open daily 2-10pm.

IN DE WAAG — ITALIAN, DUTCH $$$

Nieuwmarkt 4 — ☎020 452 77 72; www.indewaag.nl

Located inside De Waag, Nieuwmarkt's distinctive 15th-century castle, this restaurant presents quite the dining experience—with prices to match. During the summer, sit on the large terrace and admire the architecture and bustle of the square. When it's cold out, the modernized medieval interior, lit by hundreds of candles, is just as enticing. The food is Mediterranean with a Dutch twist—lots of lamb, beef, and fish, with some vegetarian pastas and polentas.

 # [M]Nieuwmarkt. $ Lunch entrees €7.50-14; dinner entrees €18-22. ⏰ Open daily 10am-1am.

RED LIGHT DISTRICT

Gluttony is one of the few sins you can't indulge in the Red Light District. There are plenty of snack shops selling plastic-looking pizzas and imitation falafel, but there are also some good, reasonably priced cafes. If you're looking for a quality meal, head next door to the Oude Zijd.

DE BAKKERSWINKEL — CAFE $

Warmoesstraat 69 — ☎020 489 80 00; www.debakkerswinkel.nl

This place is as cute and homey as the surrounding streets are neon and sordid. In the large pastel dining room, you can enjoy quiche, breakfast, or homemade sourdough bread and cheese. High tea is also available, with different combinations of scones, sweets, and sandwiches. Dessert here is a special treat, befitting the general decadence of the neighborhood.

From Centraal Station, walk down Damrak, turn left onto Oudebrugsteeg, and then right onto Warmoesstraat. [$] Sandwiches €4. Slice of quiche €5. Breakfast menus €6-12. High teas €14-40. ⏰ Open Tu-F 8am-6pm, Sa 8am-5pm, Su 10am-5pm.

SI CHAUN KITCHEN — CHINESE $

Warmoesstraat 17 — ☎020 420 78 33

Chinese is probably the best deal for a substantial meal in the Red Light District, and Si Chaun is marginally cozier, cheaper, and tastier than many of its competitors. This place offers standard favorites like fried rice and noodle dishes alongside house specialties and plenty of vegetarian options.

From Centraal Station, walk down Damrak, turn left onto Oudebrugsteeg, and left onto Warmoesstraat. [$] Most entrees €7-12. ⏰ Open daily 3-11:30pm.

NIEUWE ZIJD

Eating in the Nieuwe Zijd is less than ideal: the area is packed with overpriced, low-quality tourist traps. Try the southern half of **Spuistraat** or head to one of the shopping-center cafeterias nearby for a quick lunch. Otherwise, save your money and head to the Canal Ring West instead.

CAFE SCHUIM — CAFE $

Spuistraat 189 — ☎020 638 93 57

This artsy cafe offers a nice break from the neighborhood's usual big chains, with old movie posters adorning the walls and massive, padded leather chairs. Try the smoked chicken and avocado club for lunch, or the creative pasta or steak at dinner. Cafe Schuim is popular at night, too, when young professionals and hipsters crowd the bar and picnic tables outside. Live music and DJs perform a few times per month.

Tram #1, 2, 5, or 14 to Dam/Paleisstraat. Walk down Paleisstraat toward Singel and make a left onto Spuistraat. [$] Sandwiches €4-7. Pasta €9.50-13. Beer from €2.20. ⏰ Open M-Th noon-1am, F-Sa noon-3am, Su 1pm-1am.

LA PLACE — CAFETERIA $

Kalverstraat 203 — ☎020 622 01 71; www.laplace.nl

In most parts of Amsterdam, cute cafes tend to be the best informal dining choice. In the Nieuwe Zijd, many of those cafes will charge €10 for a sandwich, so embrace the rampant commercialism and head to this immense multi-level cafeteria inside the giant **Vroom and Dreesmann** department store. You'll be rewarded with a vast, affordable buffet of pizza, pasta, salad, sandwiches, meats, and pastries. Grab a tray and help yourself, then head to one of several seating areas, including an outdoor terrace. Of the many cafeterias and food courts nearby, this is the biggest and the grandest.

Tram #4, 9, 14, 16, 24, or 25 to Muntplein. Note the giant V and D store, and enter through the Kalverstraat door. The entrance to the cafeteria is on the left. [$] Sandwiches €3-5. Pizzas €7. Entrees typically €3-8. ⏰ Open M 11am-8pm, Tu-W 10am-8pm, Th 10am-9pm, F-Sa 10am-8pm, Su noon-8pm.

RISTORANTE CAPRESE — ITALIAN $$

Spuistraat 259-261 — ☎020 620 00 59

The service here is leisurely at best, but that just makes it feel more authentically Italian. With the massive wall mural of the Bay of Naples, you might even be convinced that you're a few countries to the south. Ristorante Caprese serves traditional Italian food done well, from the excellent tomato sauce to the organically raised meat.

Tram #1, 2, or 5 to Spui/Nieuwezijds Voorburgwal. Cross over to Spuistraat and turn right. [$] Pasta €9-14. Meat entrees €18-22. House wine from €4. ⏰ Open daily noon-11pm.

SIE JOE
INDONESIAN $

Gravenstraat 24 ☎020 624 18 30; www.siejoe.com

This unassuming Indonesian spot in the shadow of the Nieuwe Kerk is one of the best cheap options for a sit-down meal in the area. The limited menu contains a half-dozen rice dishes, some soups, and meat satays. For vegetarians, the *gado gado* (mixed vegetables and tofu in peanut sauce) is a good option.

🧭 From Dam Sq., walk up Nieuwezijds Voorburgwal and turn left onto Gravenstraat. Sie Joe is directly behind the church. $ Entrees €6.75-9.25. ⏰ Open M-W noon-7pm, Th noon-8pm, F-Sa noon-7pm.

SCHEEPVAARTBUURT

Haarlemmerstraat and **Haarlemmerdijk** are lined with restaurants, from cheap sandwich joints to upscale bistros. You'll have no problem finding somewhere to eat, but don't disregard the quality options off the main streets.

👍 HARLEM: DRINKS AND SOUL FOOD
AMERICAN $$

Haarlemmerstraat 77 ☎020 330 14 98

No, they didn't leave out a vowel: this place is the Dutch outpost of good ol' American soul food (or, at least, as close to it as you'll get in the Netherlands). At Harlem, you can indulge your culinary homesickness without the shame of being seen in a Burger King. Fill up on a variety of club sandwiches, soups, and salads at lunch or sup on dishes like fried chicken at dinner. As the night wears on, patrons stick around to imbibe and listen to the grooving soul and funk on the stereo, making Harlem one of Scheepvaartbuurt's livelier places come nightfall.

🧭 From Centraal Station, turn right, cross the Singel, and walk down Haarlemmerstraat a few blocks. Harlem is on the corner with Herenmarkt. $ Sandwiches €5-8. Entrees €12-18. ⏰ Open M-Th 10am-1am, F-Sa 10am-3am, Su 10am-1am. Kitchen closes at 10pm.

OPEN CAFE-RESTAURANT
MEDITERRANEAN $$

Westerdoksplein 20 ☎020 620 10 10; www.open.nl

This restaurant inhabits one of the coolest locations in Amsterdam—a renovated segment of a train bridge perched high above the water, between Westerdok and the IJ. You can sit in the glossy interior (lined with windows and green leather booths), on a walkway terrace, or on the sidewalk right by the water. The Mediterranean-style food is elegant, and includes dishes like lamb ravioli, stewed oxtail, and sea-bass salad. Most dishes come in both half and full portions.

🧭 From Haarlemmerstraat, walk from Korte Prinsengracht through the tunnel under the train tracks and then cross the bridge. Open is on the right. $ Sandwiches and salads €7-14. Half-entrees €7-14; full €14-22. ⏰ Open daily 10am-10:30pm.

LE SUD
VEGETARIAN, MEDITERRANEAN $

Haarlemmerdijk 118 ☎064 019 04 49; www.lesud.nl

This counter near Haarlemmerplein sells a variety of salads and vegetarian sandwiches filled with things like hummus, grilled eggplant, and falafel. There's also a tremendous array of deli items, including olives, cheeses, dolmades (stuffed grape leaves), tapenades, and more hummus. Food is primarily for takeout.

🧭 Tram #3 to Haarlemmerplein. Cross Haarlemmerplein to reach Haarlemmerdijk, then continue walking east. $ Sandwiches €3. Salads €1.25-2.50 per 100g. ⏰ Open M-Sa 10am-6pm.

CANAL RING WEST

This is one of the best places for high-quality eats in Amsterdam. The Nine Streets area is packed with hip and delicious cafes.

'T KUYLTJE
SANDWICHES $

Gasthuismolensteeg 9 ☎020 620 10 45; www.kuyltje.nl

This no-frills takeout spot makes tremendous, filling Belgian *broodjes* (sandwich rolls). The proprietor used to be a butcher, a fact which is immediately evident from the fresh and flavorful meats (roast beef, pastrami, speck, etc.) hanging from the ceiling.

🚋 *Tram #1, 2, 5, 13, 14, or 17 to Dam/Radhuisstraat. Continue down Radhuisstraat and make a left at the Singel.* ⑤ *Sandwiches €3-4.* ⌚ *Open M-F 7am-4pm.*

---

dutch nom nom

Ordering a meal at a Dutch restaurant is no easy affair. The names of many Dutch dishes contain more letters than the dishes do calories. Educate yourself on the meanings of these common Dutch delicacies in order to ensure you get a sweet deal.

- **JAN-IN-DE-ZAL.** This "john in the bag" is no evil twin to SNL's "dick in a box." Also known as "plum duff," this dessert consists of a ball of dough stuffed with candied lemon peels and slices of roasted almonds, all cooked in a pot of boiling water. Before you ask, changing the name to "ball in a pot" probably wouldn't help with the sexual connotations.

- **BOERENJONGENS.** Is this just us, or does this all sound like sex stuff? Boerenjongens are just brandied raisins, and frequently appear at the bottom of a cup of eggnog.

- **KAPUCIJNERS.** This bean is not for cappuccino-lovers. Rather than deriving its name from any coffee drink, the pea-like Kapucijners gets its name from its color, which is reminiscent of the habits of Capuchin monks.

- **KIP MET SLAGROOMSAUS.** This isn't some Martian version of *When Harry Met Sally*. This dish, which translates to "chicken with whipped cream sauce," involves a light, airy cream usually made with onions or mushrooms.

TASCA BELLOTA
SPANISH $$

Herenstraat 22 ☎020 420 29 46; www.tascabellota.com

Spanish restaurants are hugely popular in Amsterdam, but few match the quality and value of this tapas-and-wine bar. The menu features delicious dishes like spicy lamb meatballs, peppers stuffed with lentils and Manchego cheese, and dates with bacon. The interior is intimate, and its murals have a bullfighter fetish that would put Hemingway to shame. Strongly recommended by locals, Tasca Bellota also hosts live music some nights.

🚋 *Tram #1, 2, 5, 13, or 17 to Nieuwezijds Kolk. Cross Spuistraat and the Singel and continue on Herenstraat.* ⑤ *Small dishes €5-10.* ⌚ *Open Tu-Su 6-10pm.*

DE KAASKAMER
CHEESE $$

Runstraat 7 ☎020 623 34 83; www.kaaskamer.nl

Wallace and Gromit's dream come true, this store is packed floor-to-ceiling with hundreds of types of cheese. Hard cheese, soft cheese, French cheese, Dutch cheese, red cheese, blue cheese—if you can make it out of milk, they have it. Because man cannot live on cheese alone (though one ill-fated *Let's Go* researcher tried it a few years back), the shop also sells wine, bread, olives, and other cheese-complementing snacks. This is Holland: you want to go to a cheese shop. Go to this one.

🚋 *Tram #13, 14, or 17 to Westermarkt. Walk down Prinsengracht and Runstraat will be on the left.* ⑤ *Most cheeses €2-5 per 100g, €7-9 per 500g. Cash only.* ⌚ *Open M noon-6pm, Tu-F 9am-6pm, Sa 9am-5pm, Su noon-5pm.*

food

THE PANCAKE BAKERY — DUTCH $$

Prinsengracht 191 — ☎020 625 13 33; www.pancake.nl

Many swear that this canal-side restaurant serves the best pancakes in Amsterdam. The menu has a dizzying list of sweet and savory options, from the standard ham and cheese to international concoctions like the Indonesian (with chicken, peanut sauce, and sprouts). Enjoy these flaky, gooey wonders in the wooden interior or at a table by the water. The bakery also serves beer and cherry jenever—because the only thing better than fat and happy is fat, happy, and drunk.

➡ Tram #13, 14, or 17 to Westermarkt. Make a right up Prinsengracht. $ Pancakes €7-14. ⏰ Open daily noon-9:30pm.

VENNINGTON — CAFE $

Prinsenstraat 2 — ☎020 625 93 98

Vennington is an inexpensive, diner-esque restaurant that serves breakfast and lunch. There's nothing particularly gourmet going on here; it's just a place to get full and have a nice greasy meal for as few euro as possible. They have an extensive selection of sandwiches breakfast items, coffee, and shakes.

➡ From the Westerkerk, walk up Prinsengracht and make a right. $ Sandwiches €2.50-7. Coffee from €1.50. Shakes €3-4. ⏰ Open daily 8am-5:30pm.

CENTRAL CANAL RING

You'll eat well in the Central Canal Ring, where restaurants are affordable, tourist crowds are low, and you're never too far from Amsterdam's major sights. Try window-food-shopping down **Utrechtsestraat,** which is full of tasty ethnic eateries, Dutch cheese shops, and bakery fronts piled high with pastries—it's a little like food porn's answer to the Red Light District.

👍 ZUIVERE KOFFIE — CAFE $

Utrechtsestraat 39 — ☎020 624 99 99

There's an expression in Dutch, "*dat is geen zuivere koffie*," which translates to, "that's no pure coffee," but really means something like, "that's totally suspicious." This cozy store is the opposite, offering good coffee and delicious homemade croissants, desserts, and sandwiches. The apple pie is a thing of beauty. Feel comfortably European while enjoying it all in the gorgeous garden seating area.

➡ Tram #4, 16, 24, or 25 to Keizersgracht. Walk east on Keizersgracht and make a left onto Utrechtsestraat. $ Sandwiches €5. Apple pie €3.50. Drinks €2-4. ⏰ Open M-F 8am-5pm, Sa 9am-5pm.

👍 GOLDEN TEMPLE — VEGETARIAN $$

Utrechtsestraat 126 — ☎020 626 85 60; www.restaurantgoldentemple.com

Golden Temple offers a new-age soundtrack, yoga classes, and a tiny roof terrace with sofas and Indian artwork. But none of that will matter once you taste the food. The dinner menu features vegetarian cuisine, from salads to Italian pizzas to Mediterranean *mezze.* The food is a bit on the pricey side, but Golden Temple takes its ingredients seriously, and the meals are delicious and filling.

➡ Tram #4, 7, 10, or 25 to Fredericksplein. Walk diagonally through the square and up Utrechtsestraat. i Free Wi-Fi. $ Entrees €8-17. ⏰ Open daily 5-9:30pm.

B AND B LUNCHROOM — CAFE, SANDWICHES $

Leidsestraat 44 — ☎020 638 15 42

It's hard to walk by this storefront window heaped high with pastries and muffins and not drool with desire. Unlike so many bakeries in town, most people can actually afford to step inside this one and indulge. You can probably even afford a real meal too. Filling sandwiches feature healthy and tasty combinations like roast beef and "citron mayonnaise," or gorgonzola and asparagus. Soups and salads complete the extensive menu printed on blackboards across the store. In the afternoon, you may have to take your food to go, as the store gets busy with locals on lunch break.

🚊 *Tram #1, 2, or 5 to Keizersgracht. The cafe is on the southwestern corner.* Ⓢ *Sandwiches €3.50-6. Salads €6.50-7.50.* 🕐 *Open daily 10am-6pm.*

LEIDSEPLEIN

Korte and Lange Leidsedwarsstraat are stuffed with restaurants of every kind. Most post menus and prices (and sometimes enthusiastic, soliciting hostesses) outside, making it a little easier to shop around and avoid rip-offs. For the best values, look for restaurants that have special set menus or daily deals, or just grab a sandwich and snack from a grocery store. At night, places like **Maoz** and **Wok to Walk** (both on Leidsestraat, toward Prinsengracht) stay open late and are surprisingly tasty and affordable.

BOJO
INDONESIAN $$

Lange Leidsedwarsstraat 49 ☎020 643 44 43

Come here for great deals on delectable Indonesian cuisine. Bojo offers several special combo deals, including your choice of meat, noodle or rice dish, and a satay skewer (€10). The portions are ample, and the staff knows it—there's a note on the menu encouraging visitors to ask for a doggy bag. The bamboo walls and low-hanging lanterns will make you think you're oceans away from chilly Amsterdam.

🚊 *Tram #1, 2, 5, 7, or 10 to Leidseplein. Walk down Leidseplein, turn left onto Leidsekruisstraat, and then left onto Lange Leidsekruisstraat.* Ⓢ *Entrees €8-14.* 🕐 *Open M-F 4-9pm, Sa-Su noon-9pm.*

DE ZOTTE
BELGIAN $$

Raamstraat 29 ☎020 626 86 94; www.dezotte.nl

De Zotte is unusual among the infinite alcohol-focused establishments around the Leidseplein thanks to its attention to quality, not just quantity. It offers a wide selection of beers and a menu full of hearty Belgian food to go with them. Choose from steak, sausages, and pâté or cheese served with wonderful country bread. Less artery-clogging options like quiche are also available.

🚊 *Tram #7 or 10 to Raamplein. Raamstraat is 1 block away from the Leidsegracht. Or tram #1, 2, or 5 to Leidseplein. Walk down Marnixstraat and Raamstraat is on the right after the canal.* Ⓢ *Appetizers (some are filling enough to be a meal) from €3. Entrees €10-17.* 🕐 *Open M-Th 4pm-1am, Sa-Su 4pm-3am. Kitchen open daily 6-9:30pm.*

THE PANTRY
DUTCH $$

Leidsekruisstraat 21 ☎020 620 09 22; www.thepantry.nl

Designed to feel like an old Dutch living room, with traditional paintings and cozy wooden tables, The Pantry fills up with locals, as well as tourists brave enough to try some authentic Dutch dishes, like salted herring and *boerenkoolstamppot* (mashed potatoes mixed with kale, served with a smoked sausage or meatball).

🚊 *Tram #1, 2, 5, 7, or 10 to Leidseplein. Make a right onto Korte Leidsedwarsstraat and Leidsekruisstraat is on the left.* Ⓢ *Entrees €12-17.* 🕐 *Open daily noon-9pm.*

J. J. OOIJEVAAR
DELI $

Lange Leidsedwarsstraat 47 ☎020 623 55 03

This is the place for the cheapest sandwiches on the Leidseplein—perhaps in all of Amsterdam. Rolls start at €1.30, and all kinds of fillings (cheeses, meats, vegetables, etc.) are available to stuff inside them. They also sell dirt-cheap grocery and convenience items.

🚊 *Tram #1, 2, 5, 7, or 10 to Leidseplein. Walk down Leidseplein, take a left onto Leidsekruisstraat, and another left onto Lange Leidsekruisstraat.* Ⓢ *Sandwiches €1.30-3.50. 6-pack of beer €6.* 🕐 *Open M-F 8:30am-6pm.*

food

REMBRANDTPLEIN

Rembrandtplein, like the Leidseplein, is packed with enormous international restaurants and oversized cafes, but here there are fewer small, affordable eateries scattered into the mix. Below are the noteworthy exceptions.

🍴 VAN DOBBEN
SANDWICHES $

Korte Reguliersdwarsstraat 5-9   ☎020 624 42 00; www.eetsalonvandobben.nl

An old-school deli and cafeteria that is everything most restaurants in Rembrandtplein are not: cheap, fast, and simple. The black and white ceramic tiling and chrome accents are a good match for the food's simplicity. Choose from a long list of sandwiches or a more limited selection of soups, salads, and omelettes. We're not sure how this place stays in business, seeing as everywhere else nearby seems to charge five times as much, but keep it in mind when looking for a satisfying meal for under €10 in this neighborhood.

🚋 *Tram #9 or 14 to Rembrandtplein. The easiest way to find the small street is to get onto Reguliersdwarsstraat heading away from Rembrandtplein, and then look for where the street veers off on the right.* **i** *Free Wi-Fi.* Ⓢ *Sandwiches €2.50-5.* ⏰ *Open M-W 10am-9pm, Th 10am-1am, F-Sa 10am-2am, Su 11:30am-8pm.*

🍴 RISTORANTE PIZZERIA FIRENZE
ITALIAN $

Halvemaansteeg 9-11   ☎020 627 33 60; www.pizzeria-firenze.nl

The plentitude of pizzas and murals of Italian scenery on the walls will make you feel like you're actually in *Italia*. By no means is it the world's best pizza, but when you can get a huge pie for only €5-7, no one's complaining. With dozens of choices for both pizza and pasta, as well as some meat and fish dishes, Pizzeria Firenze is definitely one of the best values for a restaurant meal around Rembrandtplein.

🚋 *Tram #9 or 14 to Rembrandtplein. Halvemaansteeg is the street to the left of the line of buildings with the giant TV screen.* Ⓢ *Pizza and pasta €5-11. House wine €2.50 per glass.* ⏰ *Open daily 1-11pm.*

ROSE'S CANTINA
MEXICAN $$

Reguliersdwarsstraat 40   ☎020 625 97 97; www.rosescantina.com

A bright interior with salsa music and an outdoor patio make this a livelier option among the similarly overpriced restaurants around Rembrandtplein. They have a good selection of appetizers and standard Mexican entrees. The large bar serves up a long list of summery cocktails.

🚋 *Tram #9 or 14 to Rembrandtplein or tram #1, 2, or 5 to Koningsplein.* Ⓢ *Appetizers €5.50-7.50. Entrees €14-21. Mixed drinks €7-9.50.* ⏰ *Open M-Th 5-10:30pm, F-Sa 5pm-2am, Su 5-10:30pm. Kitchen closes F-Sa at 11pm.*

JORDAAN

The Jordaan has very few truly budget food options, but few overpriced ones either. Establishments here are frequented more by loyal regulars than by tourists.

🍴 RAINARAI
ALGERIAN $$

Prinsengracht 252   ☎020 624 97 91; www.rainarai.nl

The Algerian dishes at this small food counter change daily, and the staff will explain the day's offerings to you. A standard plate (get the medium) comes with generous servings of rice or couscous, a meat dish, and a vegetable dish, including items like spicy lamb meatballs, grilled asparagus, stuffed artichokes, and curry. Take-out is available, and serious fans can take home the store's cookbook or some Algerian spices from the mini grocery.

🚋 *Tram #13, 14, or 17 to Westermarkt. Cross Prinsengracht and turn left.* Ⓢ *Medium entree plate €13.50.* ⏰ *Open Tu-Su noon-10pm.*

DE VLIEGENDE SCHOTEL

VEGETARIAN $$

Nieuwe Leliestraat 162-168 ☎020 625 20 41; www.vliegendeschotel.com

With hearty dishes and generous portions, De Vliegende Schotel, "The Flying Saucer," is the perfect place to grab dinner after exploring **Electric Ladyland.** The organic and vegan-friendly menu changes seasonally, but often includes dishes like Ayurvedic curry, seitan goulash, or lasagna. You may have to wait for your food—after all, it's prepared from scratch in the open kitchen by the eccentric old proprietor.

Tram #10 to Bloemgracht. Cross Lijnbaansgracht, turn left, and then right onto Nieuwe Leliestraat. $ Entrees €11-13. Open daily 4-11:30pm. Kitchen closes at 10:45pm.

WINKEL

CAFE $$

Noordermarkt 43 ☎020 623 02 23; www.winkel43.nl

It's all about the famous apple pie here, renowned across the city and served with a heap of fluffy whipped cream. Don't be surprised if every person inside has a plate of it. Enjoy your pie and the view from the outdoor patio, or step into the quaint interior and chat with locals. Not up for dessert? Winkel serves up sandwiches, soups, and stews, and occasionally hosts live music and dancing. Besides the pie, the food isn't too memorable, but it has a nice location and isn't too expensive.

Tram #3 or 10 to Marnixplein. Cross Lijnbaangracht, walk up Westerstraat, and make a left onto Noordermarkt Sq. $ Entrees €6-15. Open M 7am-1am, Tu-Th 8am-1am, F 8am-3am, Sa 7am-3am, Su 10am-1am.

TOSCANINI

ITALIAN $$$$

Lindengracht 75 ☎020 623 28 13; www.diningcity.nl/toscanini

Quite a few locals swear backward and forward that this is the best Italian food in Amsterdam. The menu is strongly authentic: instead of pizza, you'll find homemade pastas like ravioli with lemon and saffron, or *secondi* like pan-fried pork with *vin santo*.The bright, sky-lit interior lacks the gimmickry of faux-Italian trattorias the world over. Since it's been around for over 20 years, Toscanini is no longer a secret, so reservations are almost always required.

Tram #3 to Nieuwe Willemstraat. Cross Lijnbaansgracht to Willemstraat, turn right onto Palmdwarsstraat, and then left onto Lindengracht. $ Appetizers €11-15. Primi €8-15. Secondi €18-23. Open M-Sa 6-10:30pm.

WESTERPARK AND OUD-WEST

Some of the best-quality food can be found in these residental neighborhoods, where you're likely to be the only foreigner at the table.

TOMATILLO

MEXICAN $

Overtoom 261 ☎020 683 30 86; www.tomatillo.nl

Fresh ingredients, generous portions, and prices perfect for the budget-conscious set Tomatillo apart from the rest of the ethnic fast-food eateries along Overtoom. Familiar Tex-Mex is prepared in an open-air kitchen, visible from the clean, crisp dining area. The food steers clear of the greasy, over-cheesiness of many gringo attempts at Mexican cuisine. The tacos are an especially good deal, consisting of two small tortillas and a heap of fillings that add up to a satisfying lunch. You may feel strange listening to "Georgia on Your Mind" while you eat, but the English menu makes this a good option in a neighborhood that's not always foreigner-friendly.

Tram #1 to J. P. Heijestraat. Tomatillo is between Jan Pieter Heijestraat and G. Brandstraat, a block north of Vondelpark. $ Tacos €2.75-3.50. Burritos and tostadas €7.50-9.50. Desserts €2-4. Open Tu-Su noon-9pm.

BELLA STORIA

ITALIAN $$

Bentinckstraat 28 ☎020 488 05 99; www.bellastoria.info

For people who miss their Italian granny's home cooking (or missed out on having an Italian granny entirely), this is the place to be. It's truly a family affair, run by a mother and her sons who chatter in Italian as they roll out dough. Since the restaurant sits in the middle of an extremely residential area, expect to have the place to yourself during a weekday lunch and to be surrounded by locals at dinner. The daily specials aren't always listed on the menu, so check the blackboard or ask the waitress when you come in. We promise you won't be disappointed.

Tram #10 to Van Limburg Stirumplein. Facing Limburg Stirumstraat, Bentinckstraat is on your right. [$] Pasta €10-17. Open daily 10am-10pm

DE AVONDMARKT GROCERY STORE $

De Wittenkade 94-96 ☎020 686 49 19; www.deavondmarkt.nl

One of the most frustrating things about the Netherlands can be the lack of 24hr. stores, but "The Evening Market" helps fill the bellies of night owls (at least until midnight). De Avondmarkt sells standard but high-quality groceries, wine, beer, cheeses, and prepared foods like lasagna. De Avondmarkt will also appeal to travelers looking for organic, cage-free, and vegan foods at affordable prices.

Tram #10 to De Wittenkade. On the mainland side of De Wittenkade, at the corner of Van Limburg Stirumstraat. Open M-F 4pm-midnight, Sa 3pm-midnight, Su 2pm-midnight.

PEPERWORTEL DELI $$

Overtoom 140 ☎020 685 10 53; www.peperwortel.nl

The type of bountiful gourmet market you'd expect to find in Italy or France, Peperwortel offers prepared foods such as quiche, pasta, hummus, soup, and more exotic dishes like Indonesian beef. Order an entree as a meal, and it comes with a starch and vegetable. A wide variety of vegetarian options and a good wine selection round out the menu. Limited seating is available outside, but the grass of Vondelpark a few blocks away makes for an even better table.

Tram #1 to 1e Con. Huygensstraat. Peperwortel is on the corner of Overtoom and 2e Con. Huygensstraat. [$] Entrees €9-14. Desserts €3. Wines from €7. Open M-F 4-9pm, Sa-Su 3-9pm.

CAFE NASSAU CAFE, ITALIAN $$

De Wittenkade 105A ☎020 684 35 62; www.cafenassau.com

Get your cute European cafe fix at this local favorite. Ingredients are fresh, and the helpful staff will guide you though the all-Dutch menu. Quaint outdoor patio furniture and picnic tables allow you to dine canal-side, and if you're lucky you can even land the table for two with the covered porch swing, perfect for taking that hostel romance to a classier level. Try the *broodje* (with spicy Italian sausage, grilled eggplant, parmesan, and arugula), sip on a Dutch coffee, or order a drink from the cafe's full bar.

Tram #10 to De Wittenkade. At the corner of De Wittenkade and 2e Nassaustraat. [$] Sandwiches from €5. Entrees €10-20. Open M-Th 11:30am-midnight, F-Sa 11:30am-1am, Su 11:30am-midnight.

breakfast sprinkles

Though the limited toast and jam in your hostel may suggest otherwise, the Dutch are pretty big on breakfast. They also have a fondness for desserts (name a culture that doesn't). In the 1930s, supposedly in response to a very persistent five-year-old boy who kept writing letters asking for a chocolate breakfast item, a Dutch company invented a great way to combine the two: *hagelslag*.

This confection is essentially chocolate sprinkles, but it provides a socially acceptable way to eat a ton of chocolate first thing in the morning: just sprinkle a thick layer of *hagelslag* on a piece of buttered toast. In addition to the original chocolate flavor, vanilla and fruit combinations exist. Still, legally, *hagelslag* must be over 35% cacao to be called *chocolat hagelslag*. Otherwise, the appropriate term is "cacao fantasy *hagelslag*"—which sounds like something unicorns eat.

MUSEUMPLEIN AND VONDELPARK

Museumplein seems to be the one area of Amsterdam that consistently attracts real grown-ups, so food here tends to be a bit pricey. A long day of museum-hopping can be strenuous though, and the **Albert Heijn** supermarket right behind the van Gogh museum is the place to refuel on the cheap.

🍴 CAFE VERTIGO — CAFE, MEDITERRANEAN $$

Vondelpark 3 — ☎020 612 30 21; www.vertigo.nl

Cafe Vertigo is housed in a remarkable, ornate building with a seemingly endless patio that makes it look like it should be more expensive than it is. On a summer day, there's no better place to enjoy a sandwich and a drink—except, perhaps, for the grass of Vondelpark itself. Sandwiches (like goat cheese with red onion compote) and soups (try the chickpea with lamb) make a great lunch. There's a full bar as well, so you can enjoy the atmosphere with just a drink too.

🚊 Tram #1, 3, or 12 to 1e Con. Huygensstraat/Overtoom. Walk down 1e Con. Huygensstraat, make a right onto Vondelstraat, enter the park about 1 block down, and the cafe is on the left. [$] Soups and sandwiches €3.50-6.75. Entrees €12-20. ⏰ Open daily 10am-1am.

🍴 PASTA TRICOLORE — ITALIAN $

P.C. Hooftstraat 52 — ☎020 664 83 14; www.pastatricolore.nl

If you want something a bit snazzier than Albert Heijn, Pasta Tricolore's front counter brims with a mouth-watering selection of salads, antipasti, lasagna, and desserts. You can also head to the back of the shop to order from a long list of Italian sandwiches (with filling combinations of salami, cheeses, and grilled vegetables). Limited seating is available, but it's nicest to take your meal to go and enjoy it in Vondelpark or Museumplein.

🚊 Tram #2 or 5 to Hobbemastraat. Walk down Hobbemastraat away from the Rijksmuseum and make a left onto P.C. Hooftstraat. [$] Sandwiches and salads from €4. ⏰ Open M-Sa 9am-7pm, Su noon-7pm.

DE PIJP

If you could somehow eat every meal in De Pijp, you would be a happy camper. In a radius of just a few blocks, you'll find a tremendous variety of cuisine dished up at significantly lower prices than in most other parts of the city. **Albert Cuypstraat** and **Ferdinand Bolstraat** are good places to start, but there are plenty of great options on side streets as well. Many of the bars in De Pijp also whip up surprisingly good food.

🍴 CAFE DE PIJP — MEDITERRANEAN $

Ferdinand Bolstraat 17-19 — ☎020 670 41 61; www.goodfoodgroup.nl

A catch-all local hostpot, Cafe De Pijp is usually swarmed with 20-somethings lingering over drinks, dinner, or more drinks. The menu has tapas-style offerings, like *merguez* (sausage) with Turkish bread and aioli, but also more substantial dishes, dishes like eggplant parmesan. On weekend nights, DJs spin dance tunes to help you work off your meal.

🚊 Tram #16 or 24 to Stadhouderskade. Walk 2 blocks down Ferdinand Bolstraat. Cafe De Pijp is on the left. [$] Entrees €5.50-8. ⏰ Open M-Th 3:30pm-1am, F 3:30pm-3am, Sa noon-2am, Su noon-1am.

🍴 HET IJSPALEIS — ICE CREAM $

1e Sweelinckstraat 20 — ☎061 204 16 17

This is a gleaming white "Ice Palace" that looks awfully tempting on a hot day, especially after trawling through the crowds of Albert Cuypmarkt. They serve up about a dozen fresh, homemade flavors in cups or cones, along with coffee and tea if you get too chilly. Keeping to the neighborhood's hipster ambience, they offer exotic flavors like rooibos, but don't miss the stroopwafel ice cream.

🚊 Tram #16 or 24 to Albert Cuypmarkt. Walk through the market and turn right. [$] Scoops from €1.10. ⏰ Open daily 11am-8pm.

👍 BAZAR — MIDDLE EASTERN $$

Albert Cuypstraat 182 ☎020 675 05 44; www.bazaramsterdam.com

When the crush of Albert Cuypmarkt starts to feel a little overwhelming, pop into this church-cum-restaurant for inexpensive and tasty Middle Eastern. You can be basic with falafel or less basic with creative dinner specials like saffron veggie kebab. The vaulted ceilings are now decorated with Arabic Coca-Cola signs and old Dutch advertisements. Seating is available on the ground floor and in the old balconies above.

➜ Tram #16 or 24 to Albert Cuypstraat. Walk through the market about 3 blocks. $ Sandwiches and lunch entrees €4-10. Dinner entrees €12-16. ⏰ Open M-Th 11am-midnight, F 11am-1am, Sa 9am-1am, Su 9am-midnight.

WARUNG SPANG MAKANDRA — INDONESIAN $

Gerard Doustraat 39 ☎020 670 50 81; www.spangmakandra.nl

Imperialism had more than a few downsides, but it was good at fostering new culinary combinations, like the Indonesian-Surinamese cuisine at this neighborhood favorite. Enjoy noodle and rice dishes, satays, and *rotis*—pancakes with meat and vegetable fillings—for incredibly low prices.

➜ Tram #16 or 24 to Albert Cuypstraat. Walk 1 block north on Ferdinand Bolstraat and take the 1st left. The restaurant is on the left. $ Entrees €5.50-9. ⏰ Open M-Sa 11am-10pm, Su 1-10pm.

DE SOEPWINKEL — SOUP $

1e Sweelinckstraat 19F ☎020 673 22 83; www.soepwinkel.nl

Modern minimalism meets home cooking at this soup shop. Enjoy one of De Soepwinkel's six marvelous rotating soups (at least one is always vegetarian) inside the airy store or on the outside patio. They prepare quiches, tarts, and sandwiches as well.

➜ Tram #3, 4, or 25 to Ceinturbaan/Van Woutstraat. Walk toward the park, turn right onto Sarphatipark, continue for 1½ blocks, and turn left onto 1e Sweelinckstraat. Alternatively, take tram #16 or 24 to Albert Cuypstraat. Walk a few blocks through the market and turn right onto 1e Sweelinckstraat. $ Soups from €4. Menu with soup, a slice of quiche, and a drink €8.50. ⏰ Open M-F 11am-8pm, Sa 11am-6pm.

BURGERMEESTER — BURGERS $

Albert Cuypstraat 48 ☎020 670 93 39; www.burgermeester.eu

Thankfully, the burgers here are better than the store's punny name (*burgemeester* is "mayor" in Dutch). This is something of a designer-burger bar—you can get a patty made from fancy beef, lamb, salmon, falafel, or Manchego cheese and hazelnuts, then top it with Chinese kale, truffle oil, or buffalo mozzarella. Burgers can be ordered normal-sized or miniature. They sell salads, too, but who goes to a burger joint for a salad?

➜ Tram #16 or 24 to Albert Cuypstraat. Walk down the street away from the market. $ Burgers €6.50-8.50. Toppings €0.50-1. ⏰ Open daily noon-11pm.

WILD MOA PIES — PIES $

Van Ostadestraat 147 ☎064 291 40 50; www.pies.nu

We didn't know that New Zealand had much national cuisine, but apparently it does, and it's pie-centric. This Kiwi-owned store sells six types of meat pie (one made from real New Zealand beef) and three vegetarian types (we like the Three P's—pumpkin, sweet potato, and paprika). One large table is available if you want to eat your pies in the store, but you can also take them across the street to Sarphatipart.

➜ Tram #3 or 25 to 2e Van der Helstraat. Walk 1 block south, away from the park. Von Ostadestraat is on the right. $ Pies €3. ⏰ Open Tu-Sa 9am-5:30pm.

JODENBUURT AND PLANTAGE

◪ EETKUNST ASMARA
ERITREAN $$

Jonas Daniel Meijerplein 8   ☎020 627 10 02

Jodenbuurt started out as a neighborhood of immigrants, and this East African restaurant is a testament to the area's continuing diversity. The menu consists of varieties of delicately spiced meat and vegetables, all served with delicious *injera*, a traditional spongy, slightly tangy bread. Each dish is accompanied by an assortment of lentils and other veggies, so one entree could feed two people. This is one of the best values around and a nice break from Amsterdam's unending parade of sandwiches.

🚊 *Tram #9 or 14 or ⓂWaterlooplein. Walk down Waterlooplein and turn right onto Wesperstraat. Jonas Daniel Mieijerplein is on the right, 1 street after the Jewish Historical Museum.* ⓈEntrees €9.50-11.50. Beer €1.50. ☼ Open daily 6-11pm.*

PLANCIUS
CAFE, SANDWICHES, FRENCH $$

Plantage Kerklaan 61A   ☎020 330 94 69; www.restaurantplancius.nl

Right across from the zoo, Plancius is a stylish one-stop shop for everything from breakfast to after-dinner drinks. The menu rotates seasonally, but lunch always offers creative spins on the traditional sandwich, while dinner tends more toward formal French fare like lamb shank and shrimp croquettes.

🚊 *Tram #9 or 14 to Plantage Kerklaan.* Ⓢ *Sandwiches €2.50-8.50. Appetizers €8. Entrees €15-19.* ☼ *Open daily 11am-11pm. Lunch menu served until 6pm.*

SOEP EN ZO
SOUP $

Jodenbreestraat 94A   ☎020 422 22 43; www.soupenzo.nl

This small outpost of an Amsterdam chain serves fresh soups and a few salads. Soups come with bread and toppings like coriander and cheese. Take advantage of their outside patio when the weather's nice.

🚊 *Tram #9 or 14 or ⓂWaterlooplein.* Ⓢ *Soups €3-7.* ☼ *Open M-F 11am-8pm, Sa-Su noon-7pm.*

nightlife

Experiencing Amsterdam's nightlife is an essential part of visiting the city. Sure, you can go to the Rijksmuseum and see a dozen Rembrandts, but there's nothing like stumbling out of a bar at 5am and seeing the great man staring down at you from his pedestal in the middle of Rembrandtplein. That square and its debaucherous cousin, Leidseplein, have all the glitzy clubs, rowdy tourist bars, and live DJs you could ever hope for. For a mellower night out, *bruin cafes* are cafe-pub combinations populated by old Dutch men or hipster students, depending on which neighborhood you're in. The closer you get to the Red Light District, the fewer locals you find, the more British bros on bachelor party trips you're forced to interact with. GLBT venues are a very visible and prominent part of Amsterdam's nightlife, and it's worth bearing in mind that in this city famous for tolerance, virtually every bar and club is ◪**GLBT-friendly.**

NL20 is a free publication that lists the week's happenings—it's only in Dutch, but it's pretty easy to decipher the names of clubs and DJs. You can find it outside most stores, supermarkets, and tobacco shops. The English-language *Time Out Amsterdam* provides monthly calendars of nightlife, live music, and other events. It can be purchased at newsstands and bookstores.

OUDE ZIJD

Though the Oude Zijd is a little tamer at night than certain nearby neighborhoods, its close proximity to the Red Light District ensures consistent energy and some revelling tourists, especially along **Zeedijk.** If you're looking for a place to grab a drink here, both Zeedijk and **Nieuwmarkt** are lined with pubs and cafe-bars. Follow the rainbow flags to find a smattering of **GLBT** bars in the northern part of Zeedijk, near Centraal Station.

👍 CAFE DE ENGELBEWAARDER — BAR

Kloveniersburgwal 59 ☎020 625 37 72; www.cafe-de-engelbewaarder.nl

The "Guardian Angel" Cafe takes its (exclusively) Belgian beer selection pretty seriously—and so should you. Located on the first floor of a canal house with a handsome, candle-lit seating area by the water, it's the perfect place to converse with artsy young locals. Despite the hipness, welcoming bartenders will gladly help you find the perfect drink. The walls inside are postered with advertisements for local goings-on that will bring you up to speed on all that's, well, going on.

➡ [M]Nieuwmarkt. ℹ Live jazz Su 4:30pm. Occasional art showings; check website for details. $ Beer from €3. ⏰ Open M-Th 11am-1am, F-Sa 11am-3am, Su 11am-1am.

👍 HET ELFDE GEBOD — BAR

Zeedijk 5 ☎020 622 35 77; www.hetelfdegebod.com

For a country that produces so much beer, the Dutch can be surprisingly unpatriotic in their selections. Het Elfde Gebod is another all-Belgian-beer affair, this time with seven on tap and over 50 in bottles (many of which come served in their own special glasses). Don't worry if you're overwhelmed by the choices; the knowledgeable bartenders are happy to provide recommendations. The bar gets crowded on weekend nights with jolly, well-dressed locals.

➡ At the beginning of Zeedijk, near Centraal Station. $ Beer from €3. Wine and spirits from €4. ⏰ Open M 5pm-1am, W-Su 3pm-1am.

CAFE DE JAREN — BAR

Nieuwe Doelenstraat 20-22 ☎020 625 57 71; www.cafedejaren.nl

Popular with locals and tourists alike, Cafe de Jaren has an expansive interior and a two-tiered terrace overlooking the Amstel. It seems to be trying hard to be the coolest place in town, so it looks a lot more expensive than it is.

➡ Tram #4, 9, 16, 24, or 25 to Muntplein. Cross the Amstel and walk ½ a block. $ Beer from €2.50. Wine from €3. Also serves lunch and dinner €15-20. ⏰ Open M-Th 9:30am-1am, F-Sa 9:30am-2am, Su 9:30am-1am.

CAFE "OOST-WEST" — BAR

Zeedijk 85 ☎020 422 70 80

The Cafe "Oost-West" prides itself on being an old-fashioned pub where the jokes flow as freely as the booze. The music is unabashedly cheesy and often hilarious (we particularly enjoyed the Dutch techno cover of "Sweet Caroline"), which is just how the slightly rowdy crowd of older locals—often dressed in similarly ridiculous fashion—likes it.

➡ [M]Nieuwmarkt. $ Beer from €2.50. ⏰ Open M-Th 11am-1am, F-Sa 11am-3am, Su 11am-1am.

RED LIGHT DISTRICT

Ah, the Red Light District at night. Most of the neon glow bathes **Oudezijds Achterburgwal** and the nearby alleyways. Farther over on **Warmoesstraat,** you can still get a tinge of the lascivious luminescence but will find fewer sex-related establishments. Especially on weekends, the whole area is filled with slow-moving crowds of predominantly male tourists. Despite getting very busy, the hotel bars on Warmoesstraat and Oudezijds Voorburgwal can be fun places to mingle with fellow backpackers. Despite police frequently strolling through, the area can turn into a meeting place for dealers and junkies late on weekends.

WYNAND FOCKINK

BAR

Pijlsteeg 31 ☎020 639 26 95; www.wynand-fockink.nl

Many people avoid small alleyways in the Red Light District for fear of up-close-and-personal contact with a red-lit window, but this one holds a unique draw—an over-300-year-old distillery and tasting room that makes the best *jenever* in the city. Perfect for day-drinking, Wynand Fockink has no music, no flatscreen TV, and not even any chairs: just rows of bottles on creaking shelves behind the small bar. Dozens of liquors are available, with flavorings like cinnamon, rose petals, bergamot, and strawberry. Most are complex blends with names like "Forget Me Not" and "The Bride's Tears," which often come with humorous histories. With as much focus on educating as getting crunk, this bar promises to answer all your burning questions about how the drinks are made—just ask the bartender or take a tour of the distillery.

From Dam Sq., walk down Dam to Oudezijds Voorburgwal, make the 1st left, and turn left onto Pijlsteeg. $ Spirits from €2.50. Open daily 3-9pm. Tours in English Sa 12:30pm.

DURTY NELLY'S PUB

IRISH PUB

Warmoesstraat 115-117 ☎020 638 01 25; www.durtynellys.nl

Right underneath Durty Nelly's Hostel, this pub attracts backpackers from upstairs, students from around the world, and drunkards from the official Red Light District pub crawl. There's plenty to keep you entertained, from watching international sports on the TVs to playing pool, foosball, and darts yourself. The atmosphere is fun-loving and rowdy, making it a great place for a pint or six. Durty Nelly's also serves standard pub food, including full Irish breakfast (which, big surprise, includes Guinness).

From Centraal Station, go south on Damrak, turn right onto Brugsteeg, and turn onto Warmoesstraat. i Strict no-smoking policy (tobacco or otherwise). $ Beer from €2. Open M-Th 8am-1am, F-Sa 8am-3am, Su 8am-1am.

CAFE AEN'T WATER

BAR

Oudezijds Voorburgwal 2A ☎020 652 06 18

Smack in the middle of the two busiest Red Light District drags, you'll be surprised by how relaxed you feel and how much Dutch you hear in Cafe Aen't Water. The drunkest and loudest of the Euro-tripping backpackers have been weeded out, making for a casual, quiet atmosphere. The large outdoor patio, which hugs a bend in the canal, is a perfect spot for sipping and people-watching.

From Centraal Station, turn left onto Prins Hendrikkade, and right onto Nieuwebrugsteeg. Continue straight as it becomes Oudezijds Voorburgwal. $ Beer from €2. Open M-Th noon-1am, F-Sa noon-3am, Su noon-1am.

CLUB WINSTON

CLUB

Warmoesstraat 129 ☎020 625 39 12; www.winston.nl

One of the largest and hippest of the many hostel bars and clubs on the block, Winston fills up with tireless dancers. There's also a lounge area across the dance floor, but people tend to stay on their feet. DJs spin everything from rock and metal to indie pop and hip hop—whatever people will get down to. Live acts sometimes play earlier in the evening; check their website for the schedule.

From Centraal Station, go south on Damrak, turn right onto Brugsteeg, and left onto Warmoesstraat. $ Cover for live shows varies by event, usually around €5. Beer from €2.50. Hours vary by event, but usually open 9pm-4am.

GETTO GLBT-FRIENDLY, BAR

Warmoesstraat 51 ☎020 421 51 51; www.getto.nl

A fun, everyone's-welcome cocktail bar crossed with a diner, Getto offers a phenomenal drink menu featuring homemade infused vodka (flavors range from vanilla to cucumber). The sedate atmosphere of this GLBT-friendly bar doesn't quite live up to its claims to "put the Cock in Cocktail."

⇅ From Centraal Station, go south on Damrak, turn right onto Brugsteeg, and left onto Warmoesstraat. ℹ DJ party Su from 5pm, includes special cocktail deals. $ Cocktails from €6; happy hour €4.50. ⏰ Open Tu-Th 4pm-1am, F-Sa 4pm-2am, Su 4pm-midnight. Happy hour Tu-Sa 5-7pm.

NIEUWE ZIJD

The Nieuwe Zijd has some decent nightlife, but it's not very concentrated. **Spuistraat** is the place to go for artsier cafes and bars, while **Dam Square** and **Rokin** are lined with larger, rowdier pubs. The small streets in the southern part of the neighborhood are home to good beer bars and a couple of energetic clubs. However, with fewer people around, it can feel a little less safe at night than the jam-packed Leidesplein and Red Light District.

👍 PRIK BAR, CLUB, GLBT

Spuistraat 109 ☎020 320 00 02; www.prikamsterdam.nl

Voted both best bar and best gay bar in Amsterdam on multiple occasions, Prik attracts a mostly male crowd. Its atmosphere is about as light and fun as its name ("bubble" in Dutch—get your minds out of the gutter, English speakers). Come for cocktail specials all day Thursday and on Sunday evenings, or to hear DJs spin pop, house, and disco classics on the weekends.

⇅ Tram #1, 2, 5, or 14 to Dam/Paleisstraat. Walk down Paleisstraat and turn right onto Spuistraat. $ Beer from €2. Cocktails from €6. ⏰ Open M-Th 4pm-1am, F-Sa 4pm-3am, Su 4pm-1am. Kitchen open until 11pm.

👍 BELGIQUE BAR

Gravenstraat 2 ☎020 625 19 74; www.cafe-belgique.nl

If you can muscle your way through to the bar—it tends to be packed in here, even on weekdays—you'll be rewarded by a choice of eight draft beers and dozens more Belgian and Dutch brews in bottles. "But I'm in the Netherlands," you say, "should I really be at a bar called 'Belgium'?" Be quiet and enjoy your beer.

⇅ From Dam Sq., walk down Zoutsteeg. The bar is behind the Nieuwe Kerk, in between Nieuwendijk and Nieuwezijds Voorburgwal. $ Beer from €2.50. ⏰ Open daily 2pm-1am.

👍 DANSEN BIJ JANSEN CLUB

Handboogstraat 11-13 ☎020 620 17 79; www.dansenbijjansen.nl

A student-only club, Dansen bij Jansen attracts students from the nearby University of Amsterdam as well as backpackers from local hostels. The music on the crowded dance floor is a slightly cheesy mix of Top 40, R and B, and disco. Upstairs, another bar offers a range of electronic music.

⇅ Tram #1, 2, or 5 to Koningsplein. Cross the canal, walk up Heiligeweg, and turn left onto Handboogstraat. ℹ Must have a student ID or be accompanied by someone who does. $ Cover M-W €2; Th-Sa €5. Beer from €2. ⏰ Open M-Th 11pm-4am, F-Sa 11pm-5am.

👍 BITTERZOET BAR, CLUB

Spuistraat 2 ☎020 421 23 18; www.bitterzoet.nl

Not as reliably popular as the larger clubs to the south, Bitterzoet is one of the best parties you can find this close to Centraal Station. The crowd is mostly young people jamming to a steady mix of dance, bouncy house, smooth reggae, classic hip hop, and occasional live acts. There's a simple dance room with a cool balcony and smoking room upstairs, creating a generally unpretentious atmosphere.

⇅ From Centraal Station, walk down Martelaarsgracht, which becomes Hekelweg and then Spuistraat. $ Cover €5-8. Beer from €2. ⏰ Open M-Th 8pm-3am, F-Sa 8pm-4am, Su 8pm-3am.

GOLLEM BAR

Raamsteeg 4 ☎020 676 71 17; www.cafegollem.nl

This is not a bar for the indecisive. Beer aficionados from all across the city (and the world) flock to Gollem's slightly Gothic interior for the specialty brews. Way back in the '70s, this was one of the first cafes in Amsterdam to serve now-trendy Belgian beers. Nowadays, the bar offers over 200 varieties, with eight on tap. You can find Trappist ales, fruit lambics, doubles, triples—pretty much anything they make in Belgium with yeast and hops. They even have the famed **Westvleteren,** made by reclusive monks in incredibly small batches and only sold at the monastery itself.

 # Tram #1, 2, or 5 to Spui/Nieuwezijds Voorburgwal. Walk up Spui and turn left onto Raamsteeg. $ Beer from €2.50. ⏰ Open M-F 4pm-1am, Sa-Su 2pm-2am.

THE TARA IRISH PUB

Rokin 85-89 ☎020 421 26 54; www.thetara.com

This Irish pub is large enough to be called a complex. The Tara keeps multiple bars running, so the Guinness flows all night long. Different parts of the building have different themes—go from a hunting lodge to a downtown lounge without even stepping outside. It still attracts enough people for the tourists to be spilling out into the streets. Come here if you're determined to avoid any semblance of local culture.

 # Tram #4, 9, 14, 16, 24, or 25 to the Spui/Rokin stop. Walk a few blocks up Rokin. The Tara is on the right. $ Beer from €2.70. ⏰ Open M-Th 10am-1am, F-Sa 10am-3am, Su 11am-1am.

jenever fever

Amsterdam may be famous for a certain kind of herbal intoxication, but don't let the siren call of coffeeshops prevent you from trying another one of Holland's delights: jenever. A juniper-based alcohol and ancestor of gin, jenever was first sold as a medicine, and then took off as a different kind of remedy once people figured out it tasted good and got you drunk.

Nowadays, some locals swear by a quick two shots of chilled jenever to get you ready for a night on the town. A more common method of imbibing it is a *kopstoot* ("headbutt"), which is a shot of jenever followed by a pint of beer. Most Dutch bars will have one or two generic jenever brands, but for a real authentic selection, head to the centuries-old distillery Wynand Fockink (Pijlsteeg 31-43 ☎020 639 26 95; www.wynand-fockink.nl) in the Red Light District.

CLUB NL CLUB

Nieuwezijds Voorburgwal 169 ☎020 622 75 10; www.clubnl.nl

Club NL is a swanky lounge club with a surprisingly low cover. Patrons are slinkily dressed, and we advise you to spruce up a bit before trying to get in, especially later on weekend nights. Music goes from ambient house to more energetic dance tunes; check their website for guest DJ appearances. The carefully crafted cocktail menu is just as image-conscious as the club itself, with delicious results.

 # Tram #1, 2, 5 or 14 to Dam/Paleisstraat. Walk east down Rozengracht and then right onto Nieuwezijds Voorburgwal. Club NL is south of the stop on Nieuwezijds Voorburgwal. $ Cover F-Sa €5. Beer from €2.50. Cocktails from €8. ⏰ Open M-Th 10pm-3am, F-Sa 10pm-4am, Su 10pm-3am.

SCHEEPVAARTBUURT

Nightlife in Scheepvaartbuurt isn't exactly happening. After dark, those who do stick around tend to congregate in the coffeeshops on **Haarlemmerstraat.** However, there are a few pleasant places to stop for a quiet drink.

◙ DULAC
BAR

Haarlemmerstraat 118   ☎020 624 42 65; www.restaurantdulac.nl

This bar is popular with local and international students (maybe the 50% student discount on food helps with that). The exterior kind of blends into the background of Haarlemmerstraat, but follow the young Dutch kids to find it. You'll know you're in the right place if you find crazy sculptures and many miscellaneous objects inside. There's a nice garden terrace in the back.

� ✸ *From Centraal Station, turn right, cross the Singel, and walk down Haarlemmerstraat.* Ⓢ *Beer from €2.50. Entrees €10-18.* Ⓐ *Open M-Th 3pm-1am, F 3pm-3am, Sa 12pm-3am, Su 12pm-1am.*

CANAL RING WEST

The Canal Ring West doesn't go wild after sunset, but the pubs along the water are great places to grab a cheap beer and befriend some locals.

◙ DE PRINS
BAR

Prinsengracht 124   ☎020 624 93 82; www.deprins.nl

De Prins attracts artsy types, young locals, and savvy tourists with its classic *bruin cafe* atmosphere. An extensive lunch and dinner menu complements the broad drink selection, which includes five beers on tap. Enjoy your brew at the canal-side seating or inside the wooden interior, which inexplicably features portraits of Al Pacino along with the usual pictures of Queen Beatrix.

✸ *Tram #13, 14, or 17 to Westermarkt. 2 blocks up Prinsengracht, on the far side.* Ⓢ *Beer €2-3.50. Liquor €3.50-5.* Ⓐ *Open daily 10am-1am. Kitchen closes at 10pm.*

THIRSTY DOGG
BAR

Oude Leliestraat 9   ☎064 512 22 72

A small bar in the Nine Streets that puts the extra "g" in "dogg," Thirsty Dogg is popular with young locals and the type of tourist who didn't come to Amsterdam to see art museums. The bar has an excellent selection of liquor, including six types of absinthe. During the week, the bartender dictates the music selection, which tends toward heavy hip hop; on some weekend nights a live DJ brings in trip hop and dubstep. Some travelers consider Thirsty Dogg a marijuana-friendly environment.

✸ *Tram #13, 14, or 17 to Westermarkt. Walk down Raadhuisstraat, make a left onto Herengracht, and then a right onto Oude Leliestraat.* Ⓢ *Beer €2.50. Wine €3. Absinthe €4.* Ⓐ *Open M-Th 4pm-1am, F-Sa 4pm-3am, Su 4pm-1am.*

CAFE BRANDON
BAR

Keizersgracht 157   ☎065 434 71 36

The owners of this tiny bar took an 18-year hiatus when they won the lottery... twice in one year. Maybe they blew all the money, because Cafe Brandon has now reopened, much to the joy of the locals who pack it to the brim on weekends. A pool table fills the back room, and the walls are covered in Dutch memorabilia. Comfy outdoor seating includes benches with large cushions, but when this place fills up, most people just stand around looking hip.

✸ *Tram #13, 14, or 17 to Westermarkt. 1 block up Keizersgracht, on the corner with Leliegracht.* Ⓢ *Beer €2.50.* Ⓐ *Open M-Th 11am-1am, F-Sa 11am-3am, Su 11am-1am.*

CENTRAL CANAL RING

With the meccas of Leidseplein and Rembrandtplein at its corners, the Central Canal Ring doesn't have much in the way of its own nightlife. Given their proximity to the larger squares, **Spiegelgracht** and **Utrechtsestraat** house most of the neighborhood bars, including some decent places to have a quiet drink.

CAFE BRECHT — CAFE, BAR

Weteringschans 157 ☎020 627 22 11; www.cafebrecht.nl

Cafe Brecht delivers everything you'd expect from a place named after a Marxist poet, playwright, and theorist (Bertolt Brecht). The cafe prides itself on its beer, which comes from an old Czech brewery, and most of the ingredients on the daytime soup-and-sandwich menu are organic and local. Brecht hosts free poetry readings and live music on the first Monday of each month. Though we aren't sure what exactly it has to do with a bar or German art, you can get a haircut here on Wednesdays.

➡ Tram #7 or 10 to Spiegelgracht. Walk down Weteringschans and it's on the right. $ Beer from €2. ⏰ Open M-Th noon-1am, F-Sa noon-3am, Su noon-1am. Poetry nights start at 10:30pm.

MANKIND — GLBT-FRIENDLY, BAR

Weteringstraat 60 ☎020 638 47 55; www.mankind.nl

In a quiet spot just a few blocks from Leidseplein and the Rijksmuseum, Mankind is an ideal bar to grab an afternoon or evening beer. Two outdoor patios, one facing Weteringstraat and the other adjacent to the canal, allow you to people-watch by land or by sea. Mankind draws local regulars but also caters to tourists with an extremely friendly staff happy to give recommendations. Mankind serves the usual menu of Dutch bar snacks (*bitterballen*, *tostis*, etc.), as well as a more substantial meal-of-the-day. Though it's advertised as GLBT-friendly, the bar's crowd is not exclusively gay.

➡ Tram #7 or 10 to Spiegelgracht. Walk down Weteringschans and turn left. $ Beer from €2. ⏰ Open M-Sa noon-11pm. Kitchen closes at 8pm.

LEIDSEPLEIN

"Leidseplein" roughly translates to "more diverse nightlife per sq. ft. than anywhere else in the city" (don't listen to anyone who feeds you a story about how it means something to do with a road to the city of Leiden). Some native Amsterdammers scoff at this area, considering it a sea of drunken British and American tourists. But the bars that cater to these liquored-up crowds are primarily confined to the Korte and Lange Leidsedwarsstraats. The rest of the area hosts some very hip and friendly bars as well as a few terrific nightclubs. You can also find several bastions of incredible live music scattered throughout the neighborhood, and, unless you're going to a big-name event at **Paradiso** or **Melkweg,** prices are extremely reasonable. Many establishments are just as full of locals as they are of tourists. If you want to be one of the revelers that gives the Leidseplein its bad name, check out the Leidseplein Pub Crawl (promoters lurk in the main square all day long).

👍 **WEBER** — BAR

Marnixstraat 397 ☎020 622 99 10

Tremendously popular with young locals and a few stylish tourists, Weber is the place to be. Come early or late (after people have departed for the clubs) if you want to get a seat on a weekend night. Frilly red lampshades and vintage pornographic art give the place a cheeky bordello feel, complemented by jazzy French pop. But don't be fooled: this bar steers clear of the tawdriness that plagues so much of Amsterdam's nightlife.

➡ Tram #1, 2, 5, 6, 7, or 10 to Leidseplein. Walk south of the main square and make a right onto Marnixstraat. $ Beer from €2.50. Spirits from €4. ⏰ Open M-Th 8pm-3am, F-Sa 8pm-4am, Su 8pm-3am.

👍 **PARADISO** — CLUB, CONCERT VENUE

Weteringschans 6-8 ☎020 626 45 21; www.paradiso.nl

You can have a very good Friday in this former church. Paradiso began in 1968 as the "Cosmic Relaxation Center Paradiso," and its laid-back vibe (at least, as laid-back as you get in one of the city's most popular clubs) keeps this place true to its roots. The club generally attracts less well-known artists than nearby Melkweg, though it has played host to big names like Wu-Tang Clan and Lady Gaga. Check out the live music every day and club nights five nights per week—including *Noodlanding!* ("emergency landing!"), a party with "alternative dance hits" on Thursdays.

🚋 Tram #1, 2, 5, 6, 7, or 10 to Leidseplein. Take a left onto Weteringschans. $ Concert tickets €5-20, plus €3 monthly membership fee. Cover for club nights €5-20. ⏰ Hours vary by event; check website for details.

🎉 SUGAR FACTORY — CLUB

Lijnbaansgracht 238 ☎020 626 50 06; www.sugarfactory.nl

Billing itself as a *nachttheater*, Sugar Factory is, at its core, just a very sweet place to dance. Music is the main focus here: it tends to outshine that of larger clubs nearby, and includes house, electro, and "club jazz." Live music and DJs are accompanied by mind-bending video displays and dancers. The sizeable dance floor fills with a mix of young Dutch hipsters, older locals, and clusters of tourists. Check the website for upcoming events, though it's safe to assume that there's something going on Friday and Saturday from midnight to 5am.

🚋 Tram #1, 2, 5, 6, 7, or 10 to Leidseplein. Turn down the small street to the left of the Stadsschouwburg theater. $ Cover varies depending on event; usually €8-12. Beer from €3. Cocktails €6.50. ⏰ Hours vary depending on event; check website for details.

🎉 MELKWEG — CLUB, CONCERT VENUE

Lijnbaansgracht 234A ☎020 531 81 81; www.melkweg.nl

The name translates to "milky way"—a pun on the fact that this cultural center is housed in an old milk factory. One of Amsterdam's legendary nightspots and concert venues, Melkweg hosts rock, punk, pop, indie, reggae, electronic... basically any type of music that exists in the big Milky Way has probably been played in this little one. Popular events sell out quickly, so keep an eye on the website if you're planning a visit. Club nights follow the concerts on Friday and Saturday. The building is also home to theater performances, photography exhibits, and a restaurant.

🚋 Tram #1, 2, 5, 6, 7, or 10 to Leidseplein. Turn down the small street to the left of the Stadsschouwburg theater. $ Tickets €10-30, plus €3.50 monthly membership fee. ⏰ Hours vary depending on event, but concerts usually start at 8 or 9pm. Clubbing gets going around 11pm or midnight.

DE PIEPER — BRUIN CAFE

Prinsengracht 424 ☎020 626 47 75

One of Amsterdam's oldest cafes, De Pieper lives in a building that's been around since the 17th century. The low ceilings and dark paneling reflect the building's age, but De Pieper also makes quirky nods to modernity, with strings of fairy lights and posters from performances at nearby venues. This is a place to escape from the bustle of the Leidseplein in a dark, subdued *bruin cafe* (though who comes to Leidseplein for that?).

🚋 Tram #1, 2, or 5 to Prinsengracht or #7 or 10 to Raamplein. At the corner of Prinsengracht and Leidsegracht. $ Beer from €2.50. ⏰ Open M-Th 11am-1am, F-Sa 11am-3am.

BOURBON STREET — BLUES CLUB

Leidsekruisstraat 6-8 ☎020 623 34 40

One of the better touristy joints in the square, Bourbon Street is a bustling home to nightly live blues, soul, and funk shows. The walls are packed with memorabilia and photos from past events. They host jam nights on Monday, Tuesday, and Sunday, where all are welcome to bring their own instruments and play along—these tend to be high-quality, since if you're willing to haul your gear to the Leidseplein, you're probably pretty good.)

🚋 Tram #1, 2, 5, 6, 7, or 10 to Leidseplein. Make a right onto Korte Leidsedwarsstraat and Leidsekruisstraat is on the left. $ Cover varies, up to €5. Beer from €3. ⏰ Open M-Th 10pm-4am, F-Sa 10pm-5am, Su 10pm-4am. Music starts M-Th 10:30pm, F-Sa 11pm, Su 10:30pm.

PUNTO LATINO CLUB, SALSA

Lange Leidsedwarsstraat 35 ☎020 420 22 35

Punto Latino is a small salsa club that's popular on the weekends for fiery Latin music and dancing. It attracts a crowd of young tourists and older locals, many of Spanish or Latin origin.

🚋 Tram #1, 2, 5, 6, 7, or 10 to Leidseplein. $ Beer €2.50. ⏰ Open daily 11pm-4am.

REMBRANDTPLEIN

Rembrandtplein *is* its nightlife. Yeah, there's a pretty sweet statue of Rembrandt in the middle of this square, but if you were interested in the man himself, then you would be at one of Amsterdam's many fine museums, none of which can be found here. This is home to the art of looking good and getting down, not the art of the Dutch Renaissance. The square itself is lined with massive bars and clubs, while the streets that fan out from it are home to smaller establishments. **Reguliersdwarstraat,** known as "the gayest street in Amsterdam," is lined with a diverse array of gay bars and clubs, though many can be found on neighboring streets as well. Whatever you're looking for in nightlife can be found here: Irish pub, sleek bar, chic club, grungy dive, gay cafe, tourist dance party. Just walk around until you hear some music that you like. Rembrandtplein is conveniently serviced by night buses #355, 357, 359, 361, and 363; taxis also loiter around the main square at all hours.

👍 **STUDIO 80** CLUB

Rembrandtplein 17 www.studio-80.nl

Many swear that Studio 80 *is* Amsterdam nightlife. A grungier alternative to the more polished clubs around Rembrandtplein, Studio 80 is extremely popular with students and young Dutch hipsters, and with good reason—the emphasis here is squarely on good music and good dancing. This is also where young Amsterdammers flock to have a wild night out on the town, and where in-the-know tourists come to get a taste of the action.

🚋 Tram #9 or 14 to Rembrandtplein. The entrance is next to Escape (see below), under the large balcony. $ Cover depends on the night, usually €6-10. Beer €2.50. ⏰ Open W-Th 11pm-3:30am, F-Sa 11pm-5am.

👍 **VIVE LA VIE** BAR, GLBT

Amstelstraat 7 ☎020 624 01 14; www.vivelavie.net

This long-established lesbian bar draws a diverse crowd of mostly young women and a few of their male friends. The atmosphere is refreshingly unpretentious, focusing on dancing and having a good time. The excellent drink selection includes the Clit on Fire shot (€4). Music ranges from indie rock and bluesy country in the early evening, toward more dance and hip hop as the night progresses.

🚋 Tram #9 or 14 to Rembrandtplein. $ Beer from €2.20. Spirits from €3. ⏰ Open M-Th 4pm-3am, F-Sa 4pm-4am, Su 4pm-3am.

ESCAPE CLUB

Rembrandtplein 11 ☎020 622 11 11; www.escape.nl

This is Amsterdam's biggest club, with a capacity for thousands. Although it may no longer be the hottest spot in town, it still draws reliably large crowds and excellent DJs. Escape is an institution—its hulking form dominates Rembrandtplein—and it has the cover and drink prices to match. The main dance floor features a massive stage (VIP area behind the DJ) and platforms scattered throughout for those brave enough to take the dancing spotlight. Upstairs, there's a lounge, another dance space, and a balcony from which to observe the bacchanalia below. The music varies depending on the DJ but generally tends toward house, electro, and trance. The crowd is a mix of droves of tourists and young-to-middle-aged Dutch. Lines can get long on weekends after 1am: some suggest that upping your style will increase your chances of getting in.

⚑ Tram #9 or 14 to Rembrandtplein. Almost impossible to miss, under the huge TV screen. Ⓢ Cover €5-16. Beer from €2.60 (in a tiny glass). Spirits €3.80-5.80. ⏰ Open Th 11pm-4am, F-Sa 11pm-5am, Su 11pm-4:30am.

DE DUIVEL
BAR

Reguliersdwarsstraat 87   ☎020 626 61 84; www.deduivel.nl

Amsterdam's premier hip-hop joint has attracted the likes of Public Enemy, Cypress Hill, and Ghost Face, but even without famous guests, De Duivel remains a nighttime favorite, with expert DJs drawing a diverse group of music-lovers. The intimidating stained-glass devil that gives the bar its name overlooks the small dance floor, but most patrons seem to be more interested in chilling and nodding their heads to the music than in showcasing their dance moves.

⚑ Tram #9 or 14 to Rembrandtplein. Ⓢ Beer €2.50. ⏰ Open M-Th 10pm-3am, F-Sa 10pm-4am, Su 10pm-3am.

MONTMARTRE
BAR, GLBT

Halvemaansteeg 17   ☎020 625 55 65; www.cafemontmartre.nl

A sinfully luxurious Garden of Eden-inspired interior provides the backdrop for this popular spot, regularly voted the best gay bar in Amsterdam. The crowd is dominated by gay men, but all are welcome. As the night wears on, the dancing heats up to Euro and American pop and bouncy disco. Special theme nights spice up each day of the week.

⚑ Tram #9 or 14 to Rembrandtplein. Off of the northwest corner of the square. Ⓢ Beer from €2.50. Liquor from €3.50. ⏰ Open M-Th 5pm-1am, F-Sa 5pm-3am, Su 5pm-1am.

LELLEBEL
BAR, GLBT

Utrechtstraat 4   ☎020 427 51 39; www.lellebel.nl

Outrageous drag queens preside over this bar just off the square, where the decor is as campy as the costumes. Lellebel plays host to a variety of theme nights—karaoke, "Transgender Cafe," Miss Lellebel contests, and a Eurovision party, to name a few—and attracts a mostly older, gay male crowd.

⚑ Tram #9 or 14 to Rembrandtplein. Just off the southeast corner of the square. 𝑖 Karaoke Tu. "Transgender Cafe" W. Red Hot Salsa Night Th. Ⓢ Beer €2.50. ⏰ Open M-Th 8pm-3am, F-Sa 8pm-4am, Su 8pm-3am.

JORDAAN

Nightlife in the Jordaan is much more relaxed than in Leidseplein or Nieuwe Zijd, but that doesn't mean it's not popular or busy. Establishments tend more toward cafe-bars or local pubs than clubs, though some excellent music can be found in the neighborhood's southern stretches. If you're looking to seriously mingle with the locals, try one of the lively-on-weekends places along **Lijnbaansgracht** and **Noordermarkt**.

▨ FESTINA LENTE
BAR

Looiersgracht 40B   ☎020 638 14 12; www.cafefestinalente.nl

Looking something like a bar stuck in the middle of an elegant vintage living room, this spot is enduringly popular with fun and cultured young Amsterdammers who want to "make haste, slowly." Bookshelves line the walls, and games of chess and checkers are readily available—if you can find a spot to play. Poetry contests and live concerts are held often (check the website for details). The menu features *lentini*, small Mediterranean dishes, and an astonishing selection of bruschettas (on homemade bread!). No wonder it's always so crowded.

⚑ Tram #7, 10, or 17 to Elandsgracht. Go straight on Elandsgracht and turn right onto Hazenstraat; the bar is 2 blocks down on the corner. Ⓢ Beer from €2. Wine from €3.30 per glass. ⏰ Open M noon-1am, Tu-Th 10:30am-1am, F-Sa 10:30am-3am, Su noon-1am. Kitchen closes at 10:30pm.

👍 SAAREIN — BRUIN CAFE, GLBT

Elandsstraat 119 — ☎020 623 49 01; www.saarein.info

A classic *bruin cafe* in the Jordaan tradition but with a GLBT focus, Saarein mainly attracts a local group of older lesbians, but no matter what your gender or orientation, you're sure to have fun. Saarein hosts a variety of events, including a pool competition every Tuesday and a bi-weekly "underground disco party."

➜ Tram #7, 10, or 17 to Elandsgracht. Make a left onto Lijnbaansgracht and walk 2 blocks. ℹ Free Wi-Fi, and a computer available. $ Beer from €2. ⏰ Open Tu-Th 4pm-1am, F 4pm-2am, Sa noon-2am, Su noon-1am.

'T SMALLE — CAFE, BRUIN CAFE

Egelantiersgracht 12 — ☎020 623 96 17

't Smalle was founded in 1780 as a spot to taste the products of a nearby *jenever* distillery. It's one of the most revered and popular *bruin cafes* in the city, but be warned: "revered and popular" can manifest itself in the form of stuffy middle-aged people chilling. Enjoy your drink or snacks like "Doritos with sauce" on the airy upper level of the old-fashioned interior, or, if you can get a spot, outside at one of the many tables lining Egelantiersgracht, one of the prettiest canals in Amsterdam.

➜ Tram #13, 14, or 17 to Westermarkt. Cross Prinsengracht, turn right, and walk a few blocks. $ Beer from €2. Wine and spirits €4-5. ⏰ Open M-Th 10am-1am, F-Sa 10am-2am, Su 10am-1am.

CAFE CHRIS — BAR

Bloemstraat 42 — ☎020 624 59 42; www.cafechris.nl

Workers building the tower of the nearby Westerkerk used to stop here to pick up (and then probably spend) their paychecks—the bar first opened its doors in 1624, making it the oldest in the Jordaan. Come today to mingle with the local after-work crowd and let the gloomy dark wood interior transport you back in time to an era before electricity and indoor plumbing—okay, maybe not that far back.

➜ Tram #13, 14, or 17 to Westermarkt. Cross Prinsengracht, make a right, and walk 1 block. $ Beer €3-5. ⏰ Open M-Th 3pm-1am, F-Sa 3pm-2am, Su 3-9pm.

WESTERPARK AND OUD-WEST

Large swathes of this area are dead at night, but you can brush shoulders with the locals for cheap if you know the right spots. Look for posters advertising weekend parties, as many of the establishments here keep irregular hours.

👍 OT301 — CLUB

Overtoom 301 — www.ot301.nl

Home to everything even remotely entertaining—a temporary handicrafts store, a cinema, live music, yoga and acrobatic classes, a vegan restaurant, and excellent DJ parties on most weekend nights—OT301 provides an escape from the typical tourist to-do list. The building was occupied by squatting artists in the late '90s, and OT301 eventually became a destination for Amsterdam's hippest residents. A diverse and laid-back crowd congregates for OT301's parties, which feature music ranging from electro house to soul and funk.

➜ Tram #1 to J. Pieter Heijestraat. ℹ Check the website for upcoming events, or just wander in and peruse the decorated handbills. $ Cover €3-5 most nights. ⏰ Hours vary depending on programming; check website for details.

PACIFIC PARC — BAR, CONCERT VENUE

Polonceaukade 23 — ☎020 488 77 78; www.pacificparc.nl

"Industrial honky-tonk" is the best phrase we can think of to describe this large bar on the end of the Westergasfabriek. Iron staircases and a massive stove in one corner recall the building's factory roots, while the cowhide coverings on the window shades will make you feel as if you're home, home on the range. The who-knows-what-the-hell-it's-made-of chandelier has to be seen to be believed. Spread out on plenty of tables and cushioned benches as you enjoy a drink amid a local, late-20s crowd. There's also space for dancing to the blues and old-school country rock. They have live music some nights, beginning at 11pm. Pacific Parc doubles as a restaurant during the day.

 # Tram #10 to Van Limburg Stirumstraat or Van Hallstraat. Either way, walk to the Haarlemmerweg and cross over; it's at the corner of the Westergasfabriek that is farthest from Westerpark. $ Beer from €2.50. Wine and spirits from €3. ⏰ Open M-Th 11am-1am, F-Sa 11am-3am, Su 11am-11pm.

bike 'n' beer

Want to drink beer, get to where you want to go, and be ecologically friendly, all at the same time? The Dutch seem to share the same extremely specific desires. The **Beer-Bike Bar** is a creation that allows 10-19 people to sit around a bar as they are pedaled through the streets. The multi-tasking and extremely in-shape bartender serves the drinks as he pedals the contraption.

Recently, there has been some backlash against the drink-while-you-go philosophy because of several accidents involving distracted beer-bikers. Thankfully, these concerns have influenced a new law requiring no more than 30 liters of beer on any bike bar, no matter how many people are riding. That means passengers may only drink half a keg en route to another bar—a tragedy, really.

MUSEUMPLEIN AND VONDELPARK

The museums don't often stay open past 6pm, so there's not much reason to come to Museumplein in the evening. Vondelpark has a handful of spots for grabbing a drink and enjoying the scenery, but if you're looking for a lively night out, you'd best head elsewhere.

BLAUWE THEEHUIS BAR

Vondelpark 5 ☎020 662 02 54; www.blauwetheehuis.nl

This bar looks a bit like a UFO that's just crash-landed on Earth. Alien or not, 't Blawe Theehuis is probably the only bar in the city center where you can drink while surrounded by trees and greenery. Enjoy the view from the large circular patio outside or the terrace above.

 # Tram #2 to Jacob Obrechtstraat. Enter Vondelpark, walk straight, cross the footbridge, and you should see the building ahead. $ Beer from €2.30. Spirits from €2.40. Wine from €3. ⏰ Open M-Th 9am-10:30pm, F-Sa 9am-midnight, Su 9am-10pm.

DE PIJP

De Pijp does laid-back hipster bars with good beer, good food, and good company—and it does them very well.

CHOCOLATE BAR BAR

1e Van Der Helststraat 62A ☎020 675 76 72; www.chocolate-bar.nl

While most bars in the neighborhood have a cafe vibe, Chocolate Bar is more like a cocktail lounge. The long, glossy bar and seating area peppered with small, chic tables make the place classy. An outdoor patio with couches and picnic tables provides a prime place to survey the De Pijp scene. On weekends, DJs spin laid-back dance tunes inside.

🚊 *Tram #16 or 24 to Albert Cuypstraat. Walk 1 block down Albert Cuypstraat and turn right.* Ⓢ *Beer from €2. Cocktails €7.* 🕐 *Open M-Th 10am-1am, F-Sa 10am-3am, Su 11am-1am.*

TROUW AMSTERDAM   CLUB
Wibautstraat 127   ☎020 463 77 88; www.trouwamsterdam.nl

Housed in the former office building of the newspaper *Trouw*, this complex includes a restaurant, exhibition space, and club. It's gritty, industrial, and extremely popular with local students. The music ranges from dubstep to house and more; check the website for specific events. If you just can't stop partying, you'll be pleased to know they occasionally host after-parties beginning at 6am.

🚊 *Tram #3 or Ⓜ Wibautstraat. Walk a few blocks south on Wibautstraat and watch out for a giant white office building that says "Trouw" on the upper corner.* Ⓢ *Cover €10-17.* 🕐 *Open F-Sa 10:30pm-5am (sometimes Th and Su as well). Check website for specifics.*

KINGFISHER   BAR
Ferdinand Bolstraat 24   ☎020 671 23 95

One of the bars responsible for the initial cool-ification of De Pijp, Kingfisher hasn't let the popularity go to its head. They've got a good selection of international beers and a spacious wood interior. It gets crowded on weekend nights, but on a sunny afternoon you should still be able to grab one of the coveted outside tables.

🚊 *Tram #16 or 24 to Stadhouderskade. Walk 1 block down Ferdinand Bolstraat.* Ⓢ *Beer from €2.* 🕐 *Open M-Th 11am-1am, F-Sa 11am-3am, Su noon-1am.*

JODENBUURT AND PLANTAGE
This is not the neighborhood for rowdy nightlife. If you're looking for a big night out, you'd do better to head to nearby Rembrandtplein or Nieuwmarkt.

🏛 DE SLUYSWACHT   BAR
Jodenbreestraat 1   ☎020 625 76 11; www.sluyswacht.nl

This tiny, tilting 17th-century building houses the kind of bar you'd expect to find on a lone seacoast, not a bustling street. The outdoor patio sits right above the canal, with giant umbrellas ready in case it starts to rain. When it gets really inclement, the plain wooden interior is invitingly snug. This bar is perfect for day-drinking and people-watching, with a good selection of draft and bottled beers.

🚊 *Tram #9 or 14 or Ⓜ Waterlooplein. Walk north from the stop and turn left onto Jodenbreestraat.* Ⓢ *Beer €2-4.* 🕐 *Open M-Th 11:30am-1am, F-Sa 11:30am-3am, Su 11:30am-7pm.*

arts and culture

Amsterdam offers a whole host of cultural attractions, many of which are very affordable. The music, film, and arts festivals that take place throughout the summer, along with countless top-notch underground music venues, make the city an absolute paradise for art-lovers. In a city where the most cutting-edge photography exhibits are held in a 17th-century canal house, the performing arts in Amsterdam predictably run the gamut from traditional to bizarre. Many establishments provide significant student discounts or rush tickets so that, even on a budget, you can take a trip to the theater or see the famed Concertgebouw, which some say has the best acoustics in the world.

CLASSICAL MUSIC AND OPERA

Classical music is a strong presence in Amsterdam, thanks to the various high-caliber orchestras and innovative chamber ensembles that call this city home. Churches (especially the **Oude Kerk**) regularly hold organ and choral concerts and are particularly nice in the summer, when a lot of the concert halls close. Use this guide to begin your exploration of Amsterdam's arts scene, but, as with nightlife, keep an eye out for posters advertising upcoming events.

◪ CONCERTGEBOUW   MUSEUMPLEIN AND VONDELPARK
Concertgebouwplein 2-6   ☎020 573 05 73; www.concertgebouw.nl

Home to the highly renowned **Royal Concertgebouw Orchestra,** this performance space boasts some of the best acoustics in the world. They manage to fit in 900 concerts each year—primarily classical but also some jazz and world music. You can catch rehearsal concerts for free on Wednesdays at 12:30pm during the summer.

☷ *Tram #3, 5, 12, 16, or 24 to Museumplein.* ⓘ *Guided tours available.* ⓢ *Varies by concert, but generally €15-100.* ⏰ *Ticket office open M-F 1-7pm, Sa-Su 10am-7pm.*

MUZIEKTHEATER   JODENBUURT AND PLANTAGE
Waterlooplein 22   ☎625 54 55; www.het-muziektheater.nl

This large complex in Jodenbuurt is the best place in Amsterdam to see opera and classical ballet—it's the home turf of both the **Netherlands Opera** and the **Dutch National Ballet.** Muziektheater also hosts performances by visiting companies and some more modern works. Rush tickets are available for students 1½hr. before curtain for the ballet (€10) and opera (€15).

☷ *ⓂWaterlooplein.* ⓢ *Most tickets €15-100.* ⏰ *Box office open early Sept-July M-Sa 10am-6-pm, Su 11:30am-2:30pm, and before curtain on performance days. Check for information about free summer concerts.*

MUZIEKGEBOUW AAN'T IJ   JODENBUURT AND PLANTAGE
Piet Heinkade 1   ☎020 788 20 00; www.muziekgebouw.nl

This is the prime spot in the city for cutting-edge classical music. In addition to their main concert hall, performances are also held in a smaller hall that houses a newly renovated, 31-tone Fokker organ. They clearly have the interests of young people at heart, as they set aside a certain number of "Early Bird" tickets (€10) for those under 30. If you miss out on those, you can still try to get under-30 rush tickets (also €10) 30min. before performances.

☷ *Tram #25 or 26 to Muziekgebouw Bimhuis. Make a hairpin turn around the small inlet of water to get to the theater.* ⓢ *Most tickets €18.* ⏰ *Box office open from mid-Aug to June M-Sa noon-6pm.*

LIVE MUSIC

It's not hard to find great live music in Amsterdam. Many local artists tend toward electronic, techno, and house music, but you'll find home-grown bands and international indie, punk, pop, and hip-hop acts as well. Small jazz and blues joints can be found throughout the city. Leidseplein and the Oud-West boast particularly high concentrations of quality venues, ranging from large all-purpose clubs and concert halls to cozy bars and repurposed squats. In the summer, festivals explode in Amsterdam and the surrounding cities, often centered around electronic or reggae (Amsterdam has this thing with reggae, we can't imagine why). Check the websites of major venues, look for posters around the city, and consult the newspapers *NL20* or *Time Out Amsterdam* for the most up-to-date listings.

◪ DE NIEUWE ANITA   WESTERPARK AND OUD-WEST
Frederick Hendrikstraat 111   ☎064 150 35 12; www.denieuweanita.nl

De Nieuwe Anita's popularity exploded recently when people realized that the cushy room at the front wasn't just some tasteful person's private living room. It's actually a great bar filled with creative and intellectual types with a super-cool music room attached. American and Dutch underground and indie bands draw gangs of young local hipsters, while more diverse crowds show up for cheap movie screenings and readings.

🚊 Tram #3 to Hugo de Grootplein. Or take tram #10, 13, 14, or 17 to Rozengracht. Head north on Marnixstraat, make the 1st left before the Bloemgracht stop, cross the canal, and make another left at the traffic circle. $ Usually €5-10. ⏰ Hours vary; check website for details.

👍 MELKWEG — LEIDSEPLEIN

Lijnbaansgracht 234A — ☎020 531 81 81; www.melkweg.nl

Melkweg is a legendary venue for all kinds of live music as well as clubbing. See the full listing in **Nightlife.**

🚊 Tram #1, 2, 5, 6, 7, or 10 to Leidseplein. Turn down the small street to the left of the Stadsschouwburg theater. $ Tickets generally €10-30; €3.50 monthly membership required. ⏰ Hours vary, but concerts usually start around 8 or 9pm.

👍 PARADISO — LEIDSEPLEIN

Weteringschans 6-8 — ☎020 626 45 21; www.paradiso.nl

Paradiso hosts shows by everyone from big-name pop acts to experimental DJs. See the full listing in **Nightlife.**

🚊 Tram #1, 2, 5, 6, 7, or 10 to Leidseplein. Take a left onto Weteringschans. $ Tickets usually €5-20; €3 monthly membership required. ⏰ Hours vary; check website for details.

👍 ALTO — LEIDSEPLEIN

Korte Leidsedwarsstraat 115 — ☎020 626 32 49; www.jazz-cafe-alto.nl

Amsterdam's most respected jazz joint, Alto is small, dark, and intimate. Look for the giant saxophone outside. With a loyal following and nightly performances by renowned artists, this place fills up quickly, so show up early to get a good seat.

🚊 Tram #1, 2, 5, 6, 7, or 10 to Leidseplein. Korte Leidsedwarsstraat is in the corner of the square. ⏰ Open M-Th 9pm-3am, F-Sa 9pm-4am, Su 9pm-3am. Music starts daily at 10pm.

COTTON CLUB — NIEUWE ZIJD

Nieuwmarkt 5 — ☎020 626 61 92; www.cottonclubmusic.nl

Cotton Club is an old and storied jazz club on the edge of Nieuwmarkt. Come every Saturday between 5 and 8pm to hear free concerts by the house band (often joined by special guests). There are occasionally other shows, but for most of the week this is just a relaxed place to enjoy a drink.

🚊 Ⓜ Nieuwmarkt. $ Beer from €2.50. Weekly concerts are free. ⏰ Open M-Th noon-1am, F-Sa noon-2am, Su noon-1am.

MALOE MELO — LEIDSEPLEIN

Lijnbaansgracht 163 — ☎020 420 45 92; www.maloemelo.nl

This small bar with a simple stage seems more like New Orleans than Amsterdam. Maloe Melo is run by a father and son team—the dad sometimes joins performers on the accordion. There's live music every night and frequent jam sessions throughout the week. This is a good place to hear some decent blues along with a smattering of jazz and country.

🚊 Tram #7, 10, or 17 to Elandsgracht. Walk up the Jordaan side of Lijnbaansgracht a few blocks. $ Weekend cover to music room €5-7.50. Beer from €2. ⏰ Open M-Th 9pm-3am, F-Sa 9pm-4am, Su 9pm-3am. Music room opens 10:30pm.

THEATER AND COMEDY

Traditional theater and musicals don't have the same presence in Amsterdam as they do in many other cities. The comedy scene is perhaps more varied and vibrant. For entertainment you can picnic to, don't miss the **Open Air Theater** in Vondelpark in July.

BOOM CHICAGO — LEIDSEPLEIN

Leidseplein 12 ☎020 423 01 01; www.boomchicago.nl

Boom Chicago is the place for extremely popular improv comedy with plenty of audience participation. English-only shows manage to poke fun at Dutch as well, which you'll probably appreciate after spending a while in Amsterdam. Wednesday is student night: up to four students can get in using one regular ticket.

➡ Tram #1, 2, 5, 7, or 10 to Leidseplein. At the far corner of the square. $ Tickets €20-25. ⏰ Most shows begin 8 or 9pm; check website for details.

COMEDY THEATER — RED LIGHT DISTRICT

Nes 110 ☎020 422 27 77; www.comedytheater.nl

The three comedy troupes based here offer standup in both Dutch and English. Comedy Theater sometimes host international guests as well. Open-mic nights take place a few times per month, so start practicing now. Jokes at the expense of Germans will probably go down well.

➡ Tram #4, 9, 14, 16, 24, or 25 to Spui/Rokin. Cross the canal and make a left onto Nes. $ Most tickets up to €20. ⏰ Shows start beween 7:30 and 9pm. Box office open W-Th 5:30-8:30pm, F-Sa 5:30-11:30pm.

STADSSCHOUWBURG — LEIDSEPLEIN

Leidseplein 26 ☎020 624 23 11; www.ssba.nl

A prime spot for catching theater in Amsterdam and the base for the **Holland Festival** in June, Stadsschouwburg also hosts opera and dance performances. The attached cafe that spills out onto the Leidseplein is almost as popular as the theater itself.

➡ Tram #1, 2, 5, 7, or 10 to Leidseplein. $ Tickets €10-20. ⏰ Box office open M-Sa noon-6pm.

> **surprise cinema**
>
> Pop-ups come in bad (porn ads when your dad looks over your shoulder) and good (birthday cards with $50 stuffed inside) flavors. Cinema41, a pop-up movie theater, definitely falls in the latter category. The smallest cinema in the world, Cinema41 is open to anyone at anytime—just email cinema41@golfstromen.nl to make a reservation. You'll receive an email with the exact location of the theater. The movies vary, but expect to see some classics. At a mere €3, including soda and popcorn, it's a great way to spend a rainy Amsterdam afternoon.

FILM

It's easy to catch a wide variety of old, new, and totally out-there films in Amsterdam. Most English-language movies are screened with Dutch subtitles. Look out for film festivals in the summer, like EYE institute's **North by Northwest.**

EYE INSTITUTE — MUSEUMPLEIN AND VONDELPARK

Vondelpark 3 ☎020 589 14 00; www.eyefilm.nl

This elegant theater at the edge of Vondelpark mostly shows new indie flicks from around the world. They also play classics, organize retrospectives on important actors and directors, and host occasional exhibits. The institute also has an extensive library, located across the street.

➡ Tram #1, 3, or 12 to 1e Con. Huygensstraat/Overtoom. Walk down 1e Con. Huygensstraat, turn right onto Vondelstraat, and enter the park about a block down. The Institute is on the left. $ Screenings €8, students and with Museumjaarkaart €6.70. ⏰ Open M-F 9am-10pm, Sa-Su from 1hr. before the 1st show to 10:15pm. Library open M-Tu 1-5pm, Th-F 1-5pm.

PATHE TUSCHINSKI
REMBRANDTPLEIN
Reguliersbreestraat 26-28   ☎020 626 26 33; www.tuschinski.nl

One of Europe's first experiments with Art Deco design, this 1921 theater maintains its original luxury, but now boasts better technology. Watch new Hollywood releases from the comfort of some of the biggest, cushiest seats you'll ever sit in. Catch artsier fare at the **Tuschinski Arthouse** next door.

✚ *Tram #9 or 14 to Rembrandtplein. Walk down Reguliersbreestraat, and you'll see the cinema on the right.* Ⓢ *Tickets €7.80-10.* ⏰ *Open daily from 11:30am.*

SAUNAS AND SPAS

Saunas and spas fall into two categories: those intended for indulgent pampering, and gay saunas where people go to indulge in the other pleasures of the flesh. It should be fairly obvious which are which, but, if you want to be sure, a quick Google search never hurt anyone.

SAUNA DECO
CANAL RING WEST

Herengracht 115   ☎020 623 82 15; www.saunadeco.nl

Inside a stunning Art Deco interior (with ornaments from the original Le Bon Marché store on rue de Sèvres in Paris), bathers enjoy a sauna, steam room, plunge bath, and spa offering services from massages to facials. The patio garden and lounge beds make it the perfect place to relax even on dry land. All bathing is unisex.

✚ *Tram #1, 2, 5, 14, or 17 to Nieuwezijds Kolk. Walk east, cross the Singel, and turn left onto Herengracht.* Ⓢ *Sauna €21. Towel rental €2. 25min. massage €30, 55min. €55. Cash only.* ⏰ *Open M noon-11pm, Tu 3-11pm, W-Sa noon-11pm, Su 1-7pm.*

THERMOS
LEIDSEPLEIN

Raamstraat 33   ☎020 623 91 58; www.thermos.nl

Thermos is one of the oldest and largest gay saunas in Europe. Its day and night branches were recently fused together into one complex, making it possible to stay from lunchtime till breakfast the next day (although you'd likely get pretty pruney). It has a Finnish sauna, Turkish steam bath, whirlpool, swimming pool, video room, private rooms, beauty salon, bar, and restaurant. Depending on the season, there may be a lot of tourists, but Thermos generally attracts a slightly older clientele.

✚ *Tram #7 or 10 to Raamplein.* ⓘ *16+. Men only.* Ⓢ *€19.50, under 25 and over 65 €10.* ⏰ *Open daily noon-8am.*

COFFEESHOPS

Once upon a time, Amsterdam allowed tourists from far and wide to flock to its canals for cheap, legal drugs at its famous "coffeeshops." But those days have come and gone, and, as of late 2011, Dutch officials were planning to limit the use of legal marijuana to Dutch citizens. New regulations aside, coffeeshops and the relative permissability of soft drugs in the Netherlands provide a fascinating window into Dutch culture and society. The listings that follow represent but a small introduction to the vast world of Amsterdam coffeeshops. If you happen to be Dutch, or if the government suddenly backtracks, you'll be able to get into them. The exact impact of the new regulations is hard to predict at the time of publishing, so we encourage you to do some research if you're interested in learning more about coffeeshops. Finally, though we may list a number of coffeeshops, *Let's Go* does not recommend drug use in any form.

PARADOX
JORDAAN

1e Bloemdwarsstraat 2   ☎020 623 56 39; www.paradoxcoffeeshop.com

Come to this local gem for the product, and stay for the chill atmosphere. The walls and furniture are covered in oddball art (one table is adorned with a painting of a bare-breasted, two-headed mermaid), while bongs, vaporizers, and bowls

arts and culture

are on hand. Select from over a dozen types of weed and an usually broad selection of joints. A helpful menu describes the effects of each variety, making it easy to get exactly what you want. If you're still confused, the staff is happy to help.

 # Tram #13, 14, or 17 to Westermarkt. Cross Prinsengracht and continue on Rozengracht, then make a left onto 1e Bloemdwarsstraat. $ Joints €3-5; weed €5.50-11 per g; hash €7-15 per g; space cakes €6. ⏰ Open daily 10am-8pm.

move over, mushrooms

Holland may have a reputation as the land where "anything goes," but every country has its limits. In December 2008, in an effort to save face internationally, the government outlawed magic mushrooms. Dutch smartshops have lived up to their name, out-smarting the ban by turning instead to truffles. Also known as Philosopher's Stones, truffles can be eaten raw like mushrooms, and, because they contain the same hallucinogenic compounds (psilocin and psilocybin), they have a similar psychoactive effect. Some truffles might make you laugh, while others will give you a more mystical or contemplative high, and some will have you seeing brightly colored kaleidoscopic patterns everywhere you look. *Let's Go* never recommends drug use, but if you are considering trying truffles, talk to the people at the smartshop about the safest way to experience them.

✓ AMNESIA — CANAL RING WEST

Herengracht 133 — ☎020 427 78 74

Amnesia is a well-regarded coffeeshop with a gorgeous canal view and high-quality products, highlighted by nine Cannabis Cup winners. There's also a large coffee bar for those who prefer the stimulating effects of caffeine to those of the other drugs on offer.

 # Tram #1, 2, 5, 13, 14, or 17 to Dam/Radhuisstraat. Continue along Radhuisstraat and turn right onto Herengracht. $ Joints €4-6; weed €8.50-13 per g; specialty brands €13-17 per g. ⏰ Open daily 10am-1am.

✓ AZARIUS — CENTRAL CANAL RING

Kerkstraat 119 — ☎020 489 79 14; www.azarius.net

The best thing about this smartshop (a shop that sells psychoactive drugs rather than marijuana) is its knowledgeable staff, who are eager to answer any questions about their products. They sell magic truffles, salvia, herbal XTC, and other herbs and extracts as well as cannabis seeds and various smoking paraphernalia. If you can't find what you're looking for, Azarius also runs the world's largest online smartshop.

 # Tram #1, 2, or 5 to Prinsengracht. Walk 1 block up Leidsestraat and make a right onto Kerkstraat. $ Truffles €10-14. ⏰ Open in summer daily noon-9pm; fall-spring M-Tu noon-9pm, Th-Sa noon-9pm.

DE TWEEDE KAMER — NIEUWE ZIJD

Heisteeg 6 — ☎020 422 22 36

It looks like a regular Dutch *bruin cafe*, but don't be fooled—De Tweede Kamer has one of the most extensive menus of any coffeeshop in Amsterdam, categorized by type, smell, flavor, and quality of the high. Plus, there's something fun about smoking in a store named after one of the Dutch chambers of Parliament.

 # Tram #1, 2, or 5 to Spui/Nieuwezijds Voorburgwal. Walk down to Spui, up Spuistraat, and turn left onto Heisteeg. $ Joints €3-9; weed €4-13 per g; hash €8-40 per g; space cakes and muffins €6. ⏰ Open daily 10am-1am.

TWEEDY

MUSEUMPLEIN AND VONDELPARK

2e Constantijn Huygensstraat 76 ☎020 618 03 44

Tweedy is located just a short walk from a classy museum (the Van Gogh Museum), a beautiful park (Vondelpark), and a repurposed squat (OT301). Hit all of them plus this coffeeshop in one day, and you'll have seen just about everything that matters in Amsterdam. Tweedy's selection is small but cheap and includes quality favorites like White Widow. A steady stream of reggae will join you in the relaxing basement-like smoking area.

🚊 Tram #1 to 1e Con. Huygensstraat or tram #3 or 12 to Overtoom. Walk down Overtoom and make a left onto 2e Con. Huygensstraat. $ Joints €3.50; weed €5-11 per g; hash €6-10 per g. ⏰ Open daily 11am-11pm.

THE BUSH DOCTOR

REMBRANDTPLEIN

Thorbeckeplein 28 ☎020 330 74 75

This small store boasts two floors and outdoor seating that spills out onto Thorbeckeplein. The drug menu caters to the serious and experienced smoker, making it one of the best places to try specialty strains of weed and hash. Not only does the Bush Doctor have a variety of their own potent mixes, various fruity options, and organic wares, but they also carry half a dozen kinds of the infamous ice-o-lator hash. The best part of this shop is its location, just a short distance away from Studio 80 and the other clubs of Rembrandtplein, and not too far from the bars in Leidseplein.

🚊 Tram #9 or 14 to Rembrandtplein. Thorbeckeplein is across the square from the giant TV screen. $ Joints €4-6; weed €7.50-12.50 per g; hash €10-12 per g, ice-o-lator €22-55 per g; space cakes €7. ⏰ Open daily 9am-1am.

shopping

With shopping, as with pretty much everything else, Amsterdam accommodates both snooty European intellectuals and renegade rasta men. The Nine Streets just south of Westerkerk are packed with vintage stores and interesting boutiques. Haarlemmerstraat, in Scheepvaartbuurt, is an up-and-coming design district. For more established brands, look to Kalverstraat, with its string of international chains and large department stores. For something really pricey, P. C. Hooftstraat, near Museumplein, is home to all the big-name designers. On the other end of the spectrum, markets like Albert Cuypmarkt and Waterlooplein offer dirt-cheap and, at times, flat-out bizarre clothing and other miscellaneous wares.

CLOTHING AND JEWELRY

SPRMRKT — JORDAAN

Rozengracht 191-193 — ☎020 330 56 01; www.sprmrkt.nl

Too cool for school (or for vowels, at least), this large store in the Jordaan sells excruciatingly hip streetwear for men and women. The store-within-the-store, SPR+, sells even nicer designer pieces.

🚋 Tram #10, 13, 14, or 17 to Rozengracht/Marnixstraat. Walk a few blocks down Rozengracht; the store is on the right. ⏰ Open Tu-W 10am-6pm, Th 10am-8pm, F-Sa 10am-6pm, Su noon-6pm.

STUDIO 88 — DE PIJP

Gerard Douplein 88 — ☎020 770 65 84; www.fashionstudio88.nl

Sometimes it feels like affordable Albert Cuypmarkt isn't a deal, because you won't even wear the clothes. The items at Studio 88 might not have the same rock-bottom prices, but the overstock and sample attire let you get high-end pieces for a fraction of the original cost. The store mostly carries women's clothes, with a few racks of men's things in the back and a small selection of kid's attire.

🚋 Tram #16 or 24 to Albert Cuypstraat. Walk 1 block up (toward the canal) and turn right onto Gerard Doustraat. The store is up 2 blocks on the right. $ Shirts around €20. Dresses around €40. ⏰ Open M 1-6pm, Tu-F 11am-6pm, Sa 10am-6pm.

VEZJUN — JORDAAN

Rozengracht 110 — www.vezjun.nl

Vezjun is a small store that specializes in clothing from young, independent Dutch designers. The clothes are occasionally a little out there, but they are well constructed, fresh, and modern. You can be sure no one else will be wearing the same thing at the next party—but you'll be paying for that peace of mind.

🚋 Tram #10, 13, 14, or 17 to Rozengracht/Marnixstraat. Walk a few blocks east on Rozengracht; the store is on the left. $ Dresses €70-90. ⏰ Open Tu-F noon-7pm, Sa 11am-6pm.

BOOKS

THE BOOK EXCHANGE — OUDE ZIJD

Kloveniersburgwal 58 — ☎020 626 62 66; www.bookexchange.nl

The Book Exchange stocks a tremendous inventory of secondhand books, ranging from New Age philosophy to poetry. They have a particularly large selection of paperback fiction. The knowledgeable expat owner is more than happy to chat at length with customers. As the name suggests, the shop also buys and trades books.

🚋 From Nieuwmarkt, cross to the far side of Kloveniersburgwal and make a left. ⏰ Open M-Sa 10am-6pm, Su 11:30am-4pm.

AMERICAN BOOK CENTER NIEUWE ZIJD

Spui 2 ☎020 625 55 37; www.abc.nl

A centrally located English-language bookstore with a wide range of new and classic titles, American Book Center also has an excellent selection of maps of Amsterdam, from the simple to the more-detailed-than-you-could-ever-have-need-for.

🚋 Tram #1, 2, or 5 to Spui/Nieuwezijds Voorburgwal. It's on the northern edge of the square. ℹ 10% discount for students and teachers with ID. ⏰ Open M 11am-8pm, Tu-W 10am-8pm, Th 10am-9pm, F-Sa 10am-8pm, Su 11am-6:30pm.

THE ENGLISH BOOKSHOP JORDAAN

Lauriergracht 71 ☎020 626 42 30; www.englishbookshop.nl

This small, cozy shop in the Jordaan draws a vibrant community of regulars who enjoy coffee, tea, and fresh pastries while browsing the wide selection of English-language books. The store hosts events like writing workshops, a monthly book club, and the quirky 👍**literary Trivial Pursuit.**

🚋 Tram #10, 13, 14, or 17 to Rozengracht/Marnixstraat. Cross Lijnbaansgracht, make a right, and then a left onto Lauriergracht. ⏰ Open Tu-Sa 11am-6pm.

ANTIQUES AND VINTAGE CLOTHING

The **Nine Streets** area in Canal Ring West is the place to find quirky stores selling antiques and vintage swag. For slightly cheaper options, check out the smaller stores on **Haarlemmerstraat.**

👍 **LAURA DOLS** CANAL RING WEST

Wolvenstraat 7 ☎020 624 90 66; www.lauradols.nl

Laura Dols specializes in vintage gowns, including taffeta prom dresses, fluffy shepherdess numbers, and things you could actually get away with wearing outside of the house. It also sells shoes, bags, and old-school lingerie (including some awesome metallic bras).

🚋 Tram #1, 2, or 5 to Spui/Nieuwezijds Voorburgwal. Walk west to the far side of Herengracht, make a right, and then turn left onto Wolvenstraat. $ Most dresses €30-60. ⏰ Open M-W 11am-6pm, Th 11am-9pm, F-Sa 11am-6pm, Su 1-6pm.

👍 **PETTICOAT** JORDAAN

Lindengracht 99 ☎020 623 30 65

Come to Petticoat for a good selection of secondhand men's and women's clothing, some from fairly upscale brands. It's unusual to find such an affordable option in the Jordaan, or anywhere in the city for that matter.

🚋 Tram #3 to Nieuwe Willemstraat. Cross Lijnbaansgracht, make a right, and then turn left onto Lindengracht. $ Tops from €10. Bottoms from €15. ⏰ Open M 11am-6pm, W-F 11am-6pm, Sa 11am-5pm.

LADY DAY CANAL RING WEST

Hartenstraat 9 ☎020 623 58 20; www.theninestreets.com/ladyday

An established go-to spot for '50s, '60s, and '70s vintage style, Lady Day offers a massive collection of men's and women's clothes: tweed jackets, cocktail dresses, bathing suits, sweaters, tops, scarves, and much more. Most of the clothes are still quite fashionable, and the things that aren't are still really cheap.

🚋 Tram #13, 14, or 17 to Westermarkt. Walk down Radhuisstraat to the far side of Keizersgracht, make a right, and then turn left onto Hartenstraat. $ Dresses around €25. Sweaters €20. Scarves €1. ⏰ Open M-W 11am-6pm, Th 11am-9pm, F-Sa 11am-6pm, Su 1-6pm.

MARKETS

◪ ALBERT CUYPMARKT
DE PIJP

Albert Cuypstraat

Stretching almost half a mile along the length of Albert Cuypstraat, this is the most famous market in the city. Need a motorcycle helmet, sundress, and cinnamon all in one afternoon? Albert Cuypmarkt is the place to go. The clothes can be hit-or-miss, but for produce or knick-knacks, it's a great option. Rows of stores behind the market stalls sell similar items at slightly higher prices (though the clothes are a bit more wearable). Be sure to come early if you want to see the full display—some vendors start packing up as early as 4pm.

♯ *Tram #16 or 24 to Albert Cuypstraat.* ☼ *Open M-Sa 9am-6pm.*

◪ NOORDERMARKT
JORDAAN

Noordermarkt   www.boerenmarktamsterdam.nl

This organic market pops up every Saturday in a picturesque northern corner of the Jordaan to sell produce, cheese, baked goods, herbs, homeopathic remedies, and some hippie-esque clothes. Noordermarkt is a great place to shop or browse when you can't afford the Jordaan's classy indoor boutiques.

♯ *Tram #3 to Nieuwe Willemstraat. Cross Lijnbaansgracht, walk up Willemstraat, make a right onto Brouwersgracht, and then another right onto Prinsengracht. The market is about a block down.* ☼ *Open Sa 9am-4pm.*

DAPPERMARKT
OUTSKIRTS

Dapperstraat   www.dappermarkt.nl

Dappermarkt exudes the vibrant local flavor of Amsterdam East, blending the city's old charm with the cultures of its North African and Middle Eastern immigrant communities. Come here to find vegetables, spices, cloth, furniture, clothes, and more at cheaper prices than the touristy markets in the city center. It's near Oosterpark, just south of Plantage.

♯ *Tram #3 or 7 to Dapperstraat. Walk south on Wijttenbachstraat and make the 1st right onto Dapperstraat.* ☼ *Open M-Sa 9am-5pm.*

SMOKING ACCESSORIES AND MUSIC

Smartshops and larger coffeeshops often have wide selections of drug toys, from pipes to bongs to one-hitters in all colors, shapes, and sizes. Amsterdam also has some excellent music stores and quirky secondhand music can be found at some of the markets.

◪ CONCERTO
CENTRAL CANAL RING

Utrechtsestraat 52-60   ☎020 623 52 28; www.platomania.eu

Multiple storefronts make up this huge complex with the biggest music selection in Amsterdam. Concerto sells records, DVDs, and secondhand CDs in almost every genre imaginable. It's also a great place to check out flyers and posters for upcoming concerts and festivals. You can even purchase some show tickets here.

♯ *Tram #4, 7, 10, or 25 to Frederiksplein. Walk diagonally across the square and up Utrechtsestraat.* ☼ *Open M-W 10am-6pm, Th 10am-9pm, F-Sa 10am-6pm, Su noon-6pm.*

SOUTH MIAMI PLAZA
DE PIJP

Albert Cuypstraat 116   ☎020 662 28 17; www.southmiamiplaza.nl

Come here for a fine selection of pop, blues, reggae, R and B, world music, and a special section of Dutch classics (trust us, browsing the covers alone is a worthwhile endeavor). They also have plenty of DVDs. Bargain bins hold an eclectic mix of CDs that start at just €1.

♯ *Tram #16 or 24 to Albert Cuypstraat. Walk through the market and the store is on the right.* ☼ *Open M-Sa 10am-6pm.*

got wood?

Wooden shoes may sound bizarre, but this is Amsterdam, so obviously that isn't stopping them. The traditional shoes can be traced back to the Germanic tribes who were the original occupants of the Netherlands. Over a century ago, they were used to protect the feet of factory workers, miners, and farmers. Known as *klompen*, these clogs can withstand almost anything that would threaten a worker's feet with harm, including sharp objects and acid.

You're not likely to find a native strolling the city in this old-fashioned style, but they are still a common (and cliché) souvenir among tourists. And some people do indeed wear them while working in the garden or on the farm. Have a green thumb yourself? Take a pair home, and garden like the Dutch.

THE OLD MAN   NIEUWE ZIJD
Damstraat 16   ☎020 627 00 43; www.theoldman.com

This large store near Dam Sq. sells smoking accessories, boardsport equipment, and knives—we just hope no one uses all three at once. Paraphernalia ranges from tiny pipes to bongs to grinders. The Old Man's products aren't necessarily better than what you'd find at a smartshop, but there's a wider variety and quirkier options. Case in point: the bong in the shape of a clog—clearly the Dutch souvenir your grandmother is hoping for.

✈ *1 of the many trams to Dam. Walk to the end of the square and make a left.* ◘ *Open M-W 10am-6pm, Th-F 10am-9pm, Sa-Su 10am-6pm.*

VELVET MUSIC   JORDAAN
Rozengracht 40   ☎020 422 87 77; www.velvetmusic.nl

Velvet carries the latest releases and older music in virtually every genre, with an especially good selection of the diverse kinds of sounds that get lumped together as "indie". Smaller than Concerto, but less overwhelming to navigate, the shop also buys used music and has a large selection of vinyl.

✈ *Tram #13, 14, or 17 to Westermarkt. Cross Prinsengracht and walk down Rozengracht.* ◘ *Open M noon-6pm, Tu-Sa 10am-6pm.*

essentials

PRACTICALITIES

- **TOURIST OFFICES: VVV** provides information on sights, museums, performances, and accommodations. They also sell the **I Amsterdam** card, which gives you unlimited transport and free admission to many museums for a set number of days. For other transportation information, you're better off going to the **GVB office** next door. The lines at the office by Centraal Station can be unbearably long, so unless you need information right after you step off the train, try the one in Leidseplein instead. (Stationsplein 10 ☎020 201 88 00; www.iamsterdam.com ✈ Across from the eastern part of Centraal Station, near tram stops #1-4. ◘ Open July-Aug daily 9am-7pm; Sept-June M-Sa 9am-6pm, Su 9am-5pm.) Other locations at **Schiphol Airport** (Aankomstpassage 40, in Arrival Hall 2 ◘ Open daily 7am-10pm.) and **Leidseplein 26.** (◘ Open M-F 10am-7:30pm, Sa 10am-6pm, Su noon-6pm.)

- **GLBT RESOURCES: GAYtic** is a tourist office that specializes in GLBT info, and is authorized by the VVV. (Spuistraat 4 ☎020 330 14 61; www.gaytic.nl 🚋 Tram #1, 2, 5, 13, or 17 to Nieuwezijds Kolk. Walk 1 block west to Spuistraat; the office is inside the Gays and Gadgets store. ⏰ Open M-Sa 11am-8pm, Su noon-8pm.) **Pink Point** provides information on GLBT issues, events, and attractions in the city, and sells all kinds of GLBT souvenirs. (Westermarkt, by the Homomonument ☎020 428 10 70; www.pinkpoint.org 🚋 Tram #13, 14, or 17 to Westermarkt. ⏰ Open daily 10am-6pm; reduced hours in winter.) **Gay and Lesbian Switchboard** provides anonymous assistance for any GLBT-related questions or concerns. (☎020 623 65 65; www.switchboard.nl ⏰ Operates M-F 2-6pm.)
- **LAUNDROMATS: Rozengracht Wasserette** sells detergent and provides self-service and next-day laundry. (Rozengracht 59 ☎020 063 59 75 🚋 Tram #13, 14, or 17 to Westermarkt. Cross Prinsengracht and walk a few blocks down Rozengracht. $ Wash €8, dry €7. ⏰ Open daily 9am-9pm.) **Powders Laundrette.** (Kerkstraat 56 ☎062 630 60 57; www.powders.nl 🚋 Tram #1, 2, 5, 7, or 10 to Leidseplein. Walk up Leidsestraat and make a right. ℹ Detergent for sale. Wi-Fi. $ Wash €4.50 per hr.; dry €0.50 per 11min. 5kg wash, dry, and fold €10. ⏰ Self-service open daily 7am-10pm. Full-service open M-W 8am-5pm, F 8am-5pm, Sa-Su 9am-3pm.)
- **INTERNET: Openbare Bibliotheek Amsterdam** provides free Wi-Fi and free use of computers that can be reserved through the information desk. (Oosterdokskade 143 ☎020 523 09 00; www.oba.nl 🚋 From Centraal Station, walk east, sticking close to the station building. You'll cross a canal, and the street will become Oosterdokskade. ⏰ Open daily 10am-10pm.) **The Mad Processor** is popular with gamers. (Kinkerstraat 11-13 ☎020 612 18 18; www.madprocessor.nl 🚋 Tram #7, 10, or 17 to Elandsgracht. Cross Nassaukade onto Kinkerstraat. ℹ Computers with Skype. Fax machines and scanners available. $ Internet €1 per 30min. Printing €0.20 per page. ⏰ Open daily noon-2am.)
- **POST OFFICES:** The main branch can deal with all of your postal needs, plus it has banking services and sells phone cards. (Singel 250 ☎020 556 33 11; www.tntpost.nl 🚋 Tram #1, 2, 5, 13, 14, or 17 to Dam. Walk on Raadhuisstraat away from the square and make a left onto Singel. The post office is in the basement. ⏰ Open M-F 7:30am-6:30pm, Sa 7:30am-5pm.) You can also buy stamps and send packages from any store that has the orange and white TNT sign (including many grocery stores and tobacco shops).
- **POSTAL CODES:** Range from 1000 AA to 1099 ZZ. Check http://maps.google.nl or www.tntpost.com to find out the code for a specific address.

EMERGENCY

- **EMERGENCY NUMBER:** ☎112.
- **POLICE: Politie Amsterdam-Amstelland** is the Amsterdam police department. Dialing ☎0900 8844 will connect you to the nearest station or rape crisis center. The following stations are located in and around the city center. **Lijnbaansgracht.** (Lijnbaansgracht 219 🚋 Tram #7 or 10 to Raamplein. Walk 1 block south and make a left onto Leidsegracht. ⏰ Open 24hr.) **Nieuwezijds Voorburgwal.** (Nieuwezijds Voorburgwal 104-108 🚋 Tram #1, 2, 5, 13, or 17 to Nieuwezijds Kolk. Walk 1 block down Nieuwezijds Voorburgwal, away from Centraal Station. ⏰ Open 24hr.) **Prinsengracht.** (Prinsengracht 1109 🚋 Tram #4, 7, 10, or 25 to Frederickplein. Walk north diagonally through the square, up Utrechtsestraat, and make a

right onto Prinsengracht. ⏰ Open 24hr.) From outside the Netherlands, you can call the Amsterdam police at ☎+31 20 559 91 11.

- **CRISIS HOTLINES: Telephone Helpline** provides general counseling services. (☎020 675 75 75 ⏰ Operates 24hr.) **Amsterdam Tourist Assistance Service** provides help for victimized tourists, generally those who have been robbed. They offer assistance with transferring money, replacing documents, and finding temporary accommodations. (Nieuwezijds Voorburgwal 104-08 ☎020 625 32 46; www.stichtingatas.nl 🚋 Tram #1, 2, 5, 13, or 17 to Nieuwezijds Kolk. Walk 1 block down Nieuwezijds Voorburgwal. It's inside the police station. ⏰ Open daily 10am-10pm.) **Sexual Abuse Hotline** provides information and assistance to victims of domestic violence, abuse, and rape. (☎020 611 60 22 ⏰ Operates 24hr.)
- **LATE-NIGHT PHARMACIES: Afdeling Inlichtingen Apotheken Hotline** provides information about which pharmacies are open late on a given day. (☎020 694 87 09 ⏰ Operates 24hr.) You can also check posted signs on the doors of closed pharmacies to find the nearest one open in the area. There are no specifically designated 24hr. pharmacies, but there are always a few open at any given time.
- **HOSPITALS/MEDICAL SERVICES: Academisch Meidisch Centrum** is one of two large university hospitals in Amsterdam. Located southeast of the city, past the Amsterdam Arena stadium. (Meibergdreef 9 ☎020 566 91 11; www.amc.uva.nl 🚋 Bus #45, 47, 355 or Metro trains #50 or 54 to Holendrecht. The hospital is directly across. ⏰ Open 24hr.) **Tourist Medical Service** provides doctor's visits for guests at registered hotels and runs a 24hr. line to connect tourists to non-emergency medical care. (☎020 592 33 55; www.tmsdoctor.nl ⏰ Operates 24hr.)

GETTING THERE

by plane

Schiphol Airport (AMS) is the main international airport for both Amsterdam and the Netherlands. (☎020 900 01 41 from the Netherlands, +31 207 940 800 from elsewhere; www.schiphol.nl) It's located 18km outside the city center. The easiest way to reach Centraal Station from the airport is by **train.** ($ €4.20. ⏰ 15-20min.; 4-10 per hr. 6am-1am, 1 per hr. 1am-6am.) The train station is located just below the airport; you can buy tickets at machines with cards or coins, or from the ticket counter with cash. Buses also leave from the airport, which can be useful for travelers who are staying outside the city center. Bus #370 passes by Leidseplein, and other buses travel to Amsterdam and neighboring towns.

by train

Within the Netherlands, the easiest way to reach Amsterdam is by train, which will almost certainly run to **Centraal Station.** (Stationsplein 1 ☎020 900 92 92; www.ns.nl) Trains arrive from The Hague ($ €10.20. ⏰ 1 hr., 3-6 per hr. 4:45am-12:45am.), Rotterdam ($ €13.40. ⏰ 1hr.; 3-8 per hr. 5:30am-12:45am, 1 per hr. 12:45am-5:30am.), and Utrecht. ($ €6.70. ⏰ 30min.; 4 per hr. 6am-midnight, 1 per hr. midnight-6am.) International trains from Belgium and Paris are operated by **Thalys** (www.thalys.com), which runs trains from Brussels ($ €29-69. ⏰ 2hr., 1 per hr. 7:50am-8:50pm.) and Paris. ($ €35-120. ⏰ 3hr.)

You'll need to shop around for the best deals on trains to Amsterdam from other major European cities. Check Rail Europe (www.raileurope.com) to compare prices for most companies. Like Dutch trains, all international trains run to the glorious potpourri of travelers known as Centraal Station. Train tickets range from €100-300 depending on the destination, and rise rapidly as the date of departure approaches.

by bus

While buses aren't a great way to get around the Netherlands, they can be cheaper for international travel. **Eurolines** (☎020 560 87 88; www.eurolines.com) is the best choice, and runs buses from Brussels ($ €25, under 25 €19. ⏰ 3-4½hr., 7-12 per day.) and Bruges ($ €25, under 25 €19. ⏰ 5hr., 1 per day.) to the **Amsterdam Amstel station,** which is connected to the rest of the city by Metro and tram #12.

If you want to travel to Amsterdam by bus from major cities such as London ($ €42.), Munich ($ €42.), and Paris ($ €84.), you will almost definitely have to go through Brussels, Bruges, and the above-mentioned stops on the way. Eurolines often has deals for those who book in advance.

GETTING AROUND

Tram, bus, and Metro lines extend out from Centraal Station, while more trams and buses cross those routes perpendicularly, or circumnavigate the canal rings. Trams are generally the fastest and easiest mode of transport in Amsterdam, serving almost all major points within the city center. The Red Light District and Oude Zijd only have stops on their northern or southern ends. Buses are good if you are heading outside of the center or to more residential parts of the city, though trams extend to some of these as well. The Metro is rarely useful for tourists, as it only goes down the eastern side of the city and has few stops within the center.

Tickets and information can be found at **GVB.** (☎020 460 60 60; www.gvb.nl ➡ On Stationsplein across from the eastern end of Centraal Station next to the VVV tourist office. ⏰ Open M-F 7am-9pm, Sa-Su 10am-6pm.) The lines here can be long, but it's the easiest place to buy transport tickets. The **OV-chipkaart** (www.ov-chipkaart.nl) has replaced the strippenkaart as the only type of ticket used on Amsterdam public transport. Disposable tickets can be purchased when boarding trams and buses. ($ 1hr. ticket €2.60, 1- to 7-day tickets €7-30.) A personalized OV-chipkaart, featuring the owner's picture and allowing perks like automatically adding value when the balance is low, is a good option if you're staying in Amsterdam for a long time. You're more likely, however, to get an anonymous card, which can be purchased for €7.50 (plus an extra €5 as a starting balance), and can be reloaded at machines located throughout the city (most visibly in major supermarkets like Albert Heijn).

You must both tap in and tap out with your chipkaart to avoid being charged for more than you actually travel. With the chipkaart, a ride on the bus, tram, or Metro costs €0.79 plus €0.10 per km. Most rides within the city center will cost around €1-2. Most transport runs 5am-midnight; after that, there are 12 night bus lines that run once per hour, twice per hour on weekend nights. An ordinary chipkaart does not work on night buses; you must buy special tickets (€4; 12 for €30) or one of the one- to seven-day passes.

bike rentals

FREDERIC RENT-A-BIKE SCHEEPVAARTBUURT

Brouwersgracht 78 ☎020 624 55 09; www.frederic.nl

In addition to rooms and general wisdom re: all things Amsterdam (see **Accommodations**), come here for bike repairs and rentals.

➡ From Centraal Station, cross the canal, make a right on Prins Hendrikkade, cross the Singel, make a left on Singel, and then a right onto Brouwersgracht. ℹ Prices include lock and insurance. No deposit required, just a copy of a credit card or passport. $ Bike rentals €10 per day; €16 per 2 days; €40 per week; €100 per month. ⏰ Open daily 9am-5:30pm.

BIKE CITY JORDAAN

Bloemgracht 68-70 ☎020 626 37 21; www.bikecity.nl

Rentals cost a bit more here than at other shops, but they are well worth it, because the bikes come free from the plastered advertisements attached to most rented bikes in the city. You may even be able to blend in as a local with one of Bike City's plain black rides.

*🚋 Tram #13, 14, or 17 to Westermarkt. Cross Prinsengracht, make a right, and then a left onto Bloemgracht. **i** ID and deposit of a credit card or €50 required. $ Bike rentals from €10 per 4hr.; €13.50 per 24hr.; up to €43.50 per 5 days. Insurance €2.50 per day. ⏰ Open daily 9am-6pm.*

DAMSTRAAT RENT-A-BIKE — RED LIGHT DISTRICT

Damstraat 22 — ☎020 625 50 29; www.bikes.nl

Damstraat rents multiple kinds of bikes, including tandems, and also sells new and secondhand bikes.

*🚋 1 of the many trams to Dam. Walk to the end of the square and make a left onto Damstraat. **i** Copy of credit card or ID and €25 deposit required. $ From €6.50 per 3hr.; €9.50 per 24hr.; €31 per 6 days. Sells bikes from €160. ⏰ Open daily 9am-6pm.*

MONEY

tipping

In the Netherlands, service charges are included in the bill at restaurants. This means that waiters do not depend on tips for their livelihood, and you need not fear a proletariat revolution if you choose not to tip. Still, leaving 5-10% for exceptional service is common practice. Tip any higher than that, and you're just showing off. Tipping in bars is rare. For cab drivers, tip around 10%.

taxes

Advertised prices in the Netherlands include **value added tax** (VAT, or BTW in Dutch). This tax on goods is generally levied at 19%, although some goods are subject to a lower rate of 6%.

SAFETY AND HEALTH

drugs and alcohol

It hardly needs to be stated that attitudes toward conscience-altering substances are quite different in Amsterdam from in other areas of the world, though the city is taking active measures to change this image. The Dutch take a fairly liberal attitude toward alcohol, with the drinking age set at 16 (for alcohol content under 15%—for hard liquor it's 18). Public drunkenness, however, is frowned upon and is a sure way to mark yourself as a tourist.

When it comes to drugs other than alcohol, things get a little more interesting. Whatever anyone standing outside of a club at 4am might tell you, hard drugs are completely illegal, and possession or consumption of substances like heroin and cocaine will be harshly punished. Soft drugs, such as marijuana, are tolerated, but consumption is confined to certain legalized zones, namely coffeeshops (for marijuana) and smartshops (for herbal drugs). However, the age of the coffeeshop is, in some ways, coming to a close. Under new laws passed by the Dutch government, only Dutch residents over the age of 18 will be allowed to enter coffeeshops. As of 2012, customers will have to sign up for a one-year membership, or "dope pass," in order to use the shops, which have been blamed in recent years for encouraging drug trafficking and criminal activity.

prostitution

The "world's oldest profession" has flourished in the Netherlands, particularly in Amsterdam's famous Red Light District. Legal prostitution comes in two main forms. Window prostitution, which involves scantily clad women tempting passersby from small chambers fronted by a plate-glass window, is by far the most visible. Another option is the legalized brothels. The term usually refers to an establishment centered around a bar. Women, or men, will make your acquaintance—and are then available for hour-long sessions.

The best place to go for information about prostitution in Amsterdam is the **Prostitution Information Centre.** (Enge Kerksteeg 3, in the Red Light District behind the Oude Kerk ☎020 420 7328; www.pic-amsterdam.com ☒ Open Sa 4-7pm. Available at other times for group bookings, call ahead.) Founded in 1994 by Mariska Majoor (once a prostitute herself), the center fills a niche, connecting the Red Light District with its eager visitors.

glbt travelers

In terms of sexual diversity, in Amsterdam, anything goes—and goes often. Darkrooms and dungeons rub elbows with saunas and sex clubs, though much more subdued options are the standard, Despite this openness, certain travelers—including drag queens and kings, other cross-dressers, and transgendered visitors more generally—should take extra caution walking the streets at night, especially around and in the Red Light District. All GLBT visitors to Amsterdam should also be aware that, though the city is a haven of homosexual tolerance, the recent infusion of fundamentalist religiosity into the Dutch political dialogue has created an environment detrimental to complete acceptance of GLBT behaviors and visibility.

minority travelers

Despite Amsterdam being known for its openness, there's a lot of hullabaloo about ethnic minorities coming into the Netherlands. Immigrants aren't always welcomed with open arms. Although foreign tourists of all stripes are sometimes treated with suspicion (understandably so, given the regular nuisance they become in the Red Light District), it's mostly non-white visitors who occasionally encounter hostility. Muslims, or those who appear Muslim, seem to run into the most problems. The city is still generally tolerant, but sadly racism is not unheard of.

amsterdam 101

HISTORY

built on beer (1200-1648)

Amsterdam first took root sometime in the 13th century as a humble fishing village at the mouth of the River Amstel. Inhabitants soon tired of getting their feet wet and decided to build a dam to protect themselves from the river's flooding. Thus was born Amsterdam, "the dam on the Amstel." Amsterdammers eventually realized that switching to the trade business could net them a better income and reduce that awful fish smell. The city got rich quick on the booming beer trade, and became an important site of pilgrimage for Roman Catholics after the so-called **Miracle of Amsterdam**. From what we gather, this involved a dying man puking and something not catching on fire, but you might need to ask a local for the lowdown on why this was so important. The Spanish Empire took over the region in 1506, but the Dutch quickly came to resent the high taxes and religious intolerance imposed by their faraway Catholic overlords. Their ensuing struggle for independence, known as the **80 Years' War,** ended in 1648 when they established the Dutch Republic as a refuge for Europe's religiously persecuted.

death by gold (1648-1700)

The 17th century is now known as the **Dutch Golden Age.** This era was marked by loads of trade, some scientific innovation, military expansion, and a Baroque trend in art that infiltrated everything from still lifes to genre paintings. The city's merchants built Amsterdam into the undisputed commercial hub of Northern Europe. The **Dutch East India Company** (*Vereenigde Oost-Indische Compagnie*), the world's first publicly traded multinational corporation, sent ships around

the world and established outposts from Japan to South Africa. The city's afflu-ence encouraged a renaissance in art and architecture that gave birth to painters like **Rembrandt** and **Vermeer.** While Amsterdam's merchant fleet brought wealth to the city, it also introduced the Bubonic Plague. The epidemic killed 10% of the population from 1663-1666. Amsterdam's mayors, exhibiting all the useful-ness we've come to associate with local government, advised inhabitants not to consume salad, spinach, or prunes and recommended tobacco smoke as a protection against the plague.

growing pains (1701-1945)

Amsterdam's fabulous wealth encouraged competition, and the Dutch fought a series of wars with rival colonial powers in the 18th century. It turned out the Dutch were much better businessmen than soldiers. They lost many of their overseas colonies to the British and French, and Amsterdam entered a period of economic stagnation and political upheaval. Having been handed Belgium and Luxembourg after the defeat of Napoleon in 1815, the Netherlands man-aged to lose them both by 1830, leaving the Netherlands as the small country we know today.

Amsterdam began to get its mojo back during the Industrial Revolution, but new development led to its own growing pains. New jobs in the city attracted large numbers of peasants from the countryside who soon made up a militant socialist base. Violence between protesters and police became something of a weekly affair.

The Netherlands remained neutral in WWI, though it still suffered from dra-matic food shortages. The Dutch didn't get off so easily when WWII hit Europe. The Nazis occupied Amsterdam and shattered Amsterdam's tradition of religious tolerance, sending more than 100,000 Amsterdam Jews to concentration camps. Though many Jews, including **Anne Frank,** went into hiding, the majority did not survive the war, and Amsterdam's formerly robust Jewish community was decimated.

sex, drugs, and rock and roll (1946-2000)

After a long period of limping recovery after the war, Amsterdam was reborn in the cultural revolution of the 1960s and '70s. The city became known as the *magisch centrum* (magical center) of Europe. Soft drugs were legalized, anarchists and squatters laid claim to the streets, and yuppies took over old working-class neighborhoods. This last development marked an important transition in Amsterdam's economy from industry to service and sparked the growth of wealth and finance in the city.

Amsterdam's demographics have shifted dramatically in recent decades. Nearly a third of the city's residents are immigrants, hailing mainly from Turkey, North Africa, and former Dutch colonies in the Caribbean. Strict social tolerance laws with harsh penalties were imposed to mollify the cultural tension that accompanied early immigration.

a turn toward the past (2000-present)

Recent years have seen some scaling back of Amsterdam's famed permissiveness. A third of the Red Light District's brothels were shut down in 2006 amid accusations of promoting criminality. In 2008, the central government ordered the city to shut down coffeehouses located within 500m of a school. The cultivation and sale of magic mushrooms was banned in the same year. In the past year, the government focused on banning tourists from its famous coffeeshops. For more information on this era-ending legislation, see **Drugs and Alcohol** above.

CUSTOMS AND ETIQUETTE

We know you're expecting some culture shock in the Red Light District, but there's plenty to be aware of in your more "professional" encounters with Hollanders. When you are introduced to someone, a firm handshake is customary. Close friends greet each other with three kisses, *comme le style français*. When sharing a meal, men commonly wait for women to be seated.

FOOD AND DRINK

The typical Dutch *ontbijt* (breakfast) consists of bread topped with cold cuts and slices of local cheese, and a dab of *appelstroop* (syrup made from apple juice). If you're looking to satisfy your morning sweet tooth, top your toast with *hagelslag* (chocolate, aniseed, or fruit-flavored sprinkles).

Lunch includes rolls, sandwiches, or soup, eaten at one of the city's thousands of cafes. *Erwtensoep* (pea soup) is a cold-weather favorite and is often made with chunks of smoked sausage. You might also find *uitsmijter,* or Dutch fried eggs sunny-side-up (for some reason the name translates to "out-thrower" or "bouncer," as in the doorman at a club). A *broodje haring* (herring sandwich) garnished with onions and pickles is particularly tasty—you'll find one at fish stalls throughout the city. *Diner* is served in Dutch homes around 5 or 6pm. A meat entree is traditionally accompanied by two vegetable side dishes, though you might encounter a *stamppot*, which combines meat, vegetables, and gravy in a mash.

For dessert, you will find fruit, yogurt, or a cold custard followed by *kaffie* (coffee). The distinction between cafe and bar doesn't exist in the Netherlands. You can order a Heineken on its own turf, or sample some of the other famous Dutch pale lagers. *Eet smakelijk* (enjoy your meal)!

HOLIDAYS AND FESTIVALS

HOLIDAY OR FESTIVAL	DESCRIPTION	DATE
Amsterdam International Fashion Week (AIFW)	A week of invitation-only catwalks and hoity-toity gatherings alongside public exhibitions and disco parties where you can show off your finest attire (and take the time to admire everyone else).	Late January
The Queen's Birthday	A day of national pride. Orange clothing and street parties everywhere. Though Queen Beatrix was actually born in January, she decided to keep the holiday on the springtime birthdate of the previous queen (her mother).	April 30 (April 29 if the 30th is a Sunday)
World Press Photo Exhibit	*Oude Kerk* hosts this celebration of the world's best photojournalism, often juxtaposing disturbing images of warfare with the serene beauty of the natural world.	Late April to mid-June
WWII Remembrance Day	A solemn day to remember the Netherlands' WWII victims. Two minutes of silence are observed at 8pm.	May 4
Liberation Day	A day of public festivities to celebrate the country's liberation from Nazi occupation.	May 5
National Windmill Day	Windmills throw open their doors, and many have special (often educational) events.	2nd Tuesday in May
Amsterdam Gay Pride	Three days of tolerance and partying, with a parade and street festivals for all sexual orientations.	Early August
Aalsmeer Flower Parade	Flower floats, flower art, and flower power in the world's tulip capital.	Early September
High Times Cannabis Cup	One long tokefest. At the end of the festival, awards are given to the best hash and marijuana.	November
Sinterklaas Eve	Dutch Santa Claus delivers candy and gifts to nice Dutch children. According to local lore, naughty kids are kidnapped (hope you're on the nice list).	December 5

amsterdam 101

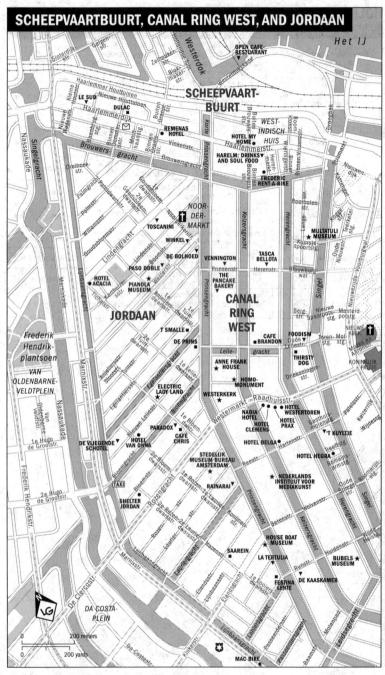

SCHEEPVAARTBUURT, CANAL RING WEST, AND JORDAAN

Het IJ

OPEN CAFÉ-RESTAURANT

SCHEEPVAART-BUURT

LE SUD
DULAC

WEST-INDISCH HUIS

REMENAS HOTEL
HOTEL MY HOME
HARELM: DRINKS AND SOUL FOOD

FREDERIC RENT-A-BIKE

NOOR-DER-MARKT

MULTATULI MUSEUM

TOSCANINI
WINKEL
DE BOLHOED
PASO DOBLE
HOTEL ACACIA
PIANOLA MUSEUM

VENNINGTON

TASCA BELLOTA

THE PANCAKE BAKERY

JORDAAN

CANAL RING WEST

Frederik Hendrik-plantsoen

VAN OLDENBARNE-VELDTPLEIN

T SMALLE
DE PRINS

CAFÉ BRANDON

FOODISM

THIRSTY DOG

ELECTRIC LADY LAND

ANNE FRANK HOUSE

HOMO-MONUMENT

WESTERKERK

NADIA HOTEL
HOTEL CLEMENS
HOTEL PRAX

HOTEL WESTERTOREN

'T KUYLTJE

PARADOX
CAFÉ CHRIS
HOTEL VAN ONNA
DE VLIEGENDE SCHOTEL

HOTEL BELGA

HOTEL HEGRA

STEDELIJK MUSEUM BUREAU AMSTERDAM

NEDERLANDS INSTITUUT VOOR MEDIAKUNST

TAXI
SHELTER JORDAN

RAINARAI

HOUSE BOAT MUSEUM

SAAREIN

LA TERTULIA

BIJBELS MUSEUM

DE KAASKAMER

FESTINA LENTE

DA COSTA-PLEIN

0   200 meters

0   200 yards

MAC BIKE

90 www.letsgo.com

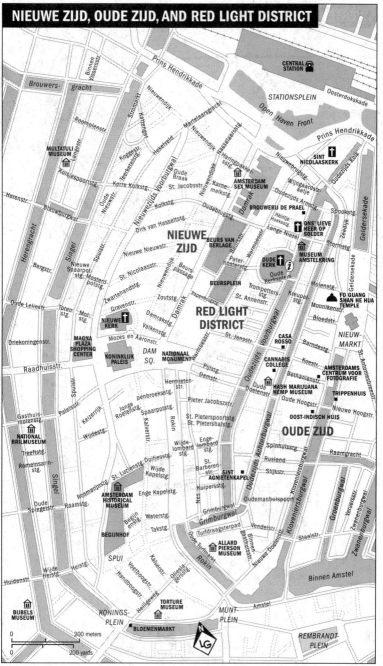

nieuwe zijd, oude zijd, and red light district map

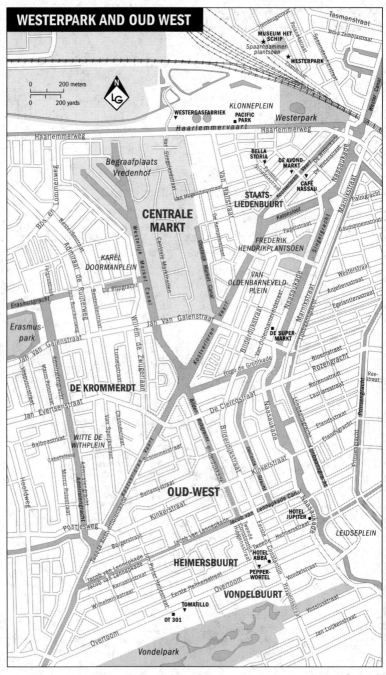

WESTERPARK AND OUD WEST

MUSEUM HET SCHIP
Spaarndammer-plantsoen
WESTERPARK

Hembrugstraat
Tasmanstraat
Nova-Zemblastraat

0   200 meters
0   200 yards

N
LG

Wester Canal

KLONNEPLEIN

WESTERGASFABRIEK   PACIFIC PARK
Haarlemmervaart   Westerpark
Haarlemmerweg   Haarlemmerweg

Haarlemmerweg

Begraafplaats Vredenhof

BELLA STORIA
DE AVOND-MARKT
CAFÉ NASSAU

STAATS-LIEDENBUURT

Katensloot
Fagelstraat

CENTRALE MARKT

FREDERIK HENDRIKPLANTSOEN

Westelijk Market Canal

Centrale Markthallen

Oosterse Basket Canal

Westerstraat
Anjeliersstraat
Egelantiersstraat

KAREL DOORMANPLEIN

De Rijpgracht

VAN OLDENBARNEVELD PLEIN

Bos en Lommerweg
Erasmusgracht

Erasmus-park

Admiraal de Ruijterweg

DE SUPER-MARKT

Bloemstraat
Rozengracht
Rozenstraat
Laurierstraat

Jan van Galenstraat

Hugo de Grootkade

Ree-straat

Koetvierloren Vaart

DE KROMMERDT

De Clercqstraat

Elandsstraat
Elandsgracht

Jan Everstenstraat

WITTE DE WITHPLEIN

Bilderdijkstraat
Kinkerstraat

Prinsengracht

Hoofdweg

Postjesweg

OUD-WEST

Kinkerstraat

HOTEL JUPITER

LEIDSEPLEIN

Jacob van Lennepkade Canal

HEIMERSBUURT

HOTEL ABBA

PEPPER-WORTEL

Overtoom

VONDELBUURT

Jacob van Lennepkade
Kanaalstraat
Wilhelminastraat

Eerste Heimerstraat

TOMATILLO

OT 301

Overtoom

Vondelpark

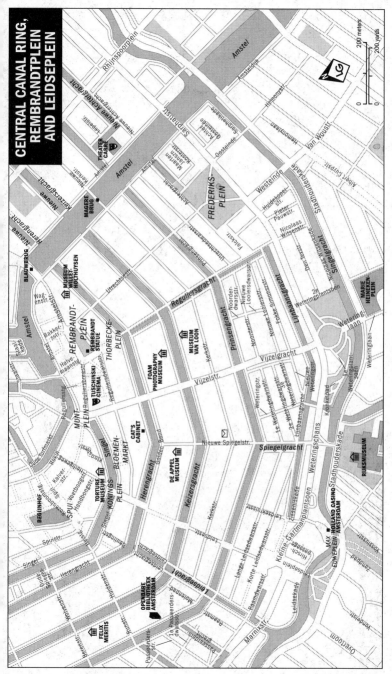

CENTRAL CANAL RING, REMBRANDTPLEIN AND LEIDSEPLEIN

central canal ring, rembrandtplein and leideseplein map

MUSEUMPLEIN AND VONDELPARK

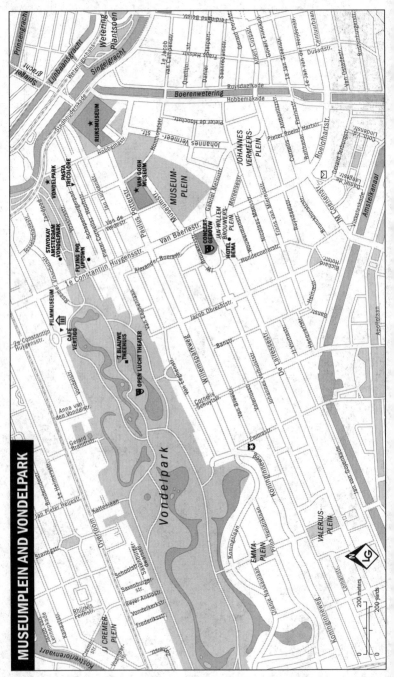

Prinsengracht

Spiegel gracht

Lijnbaansgracht

Weteringschans

Singelgracht

Wetering Plantsoen

Feldingand Bolstr.

1e Jacob van Campenstr.

Daniel Stalpertstr.

Frans Halsstr.

Gerard Doustr.

Saenredamstr.

Albert Cuypstr.

Gevert Flinckstr.

Ruysdaelkade

Hobbemakade

Boerenwetering

Pieter de Hoochstr.

Ruysdaelstr.

1e Jan van der Heijdenstr.

2e Jan Steenstr.

Hanthostr.

Jacob Obrechtstr.

Van Ostadestr.

Rustenburgerstr.

★ RIJKSMUSEUM

Stadhouderskade

Hobbemastr.

Johannes Vermeerstr.

JOHANNES VERMEERS-PLEIN

Cornelis Troostpl.

Pieter Aertszstr.

Baltasar Floriszstr.

Gerard Terborgstr.

Cornelis Anthoniszstr.

Ruysdaelstr.

Roelofhartstr.

Daniel de Lairessestr.

Van den Coornhertstr.

Lindenstr.

★ VONDELPARK PACVA TROLLORE

Zandpad

Vossiusstr.

Jan Luijkenstr.

Schapenburgerpad

Paulus Potterstr.

★ VAN GOGH MUSEUM

Museumstr.

MUSEUM-PLEIN

Gabriel Metsustr.

JAN WILLEM PLEIN

Moreelsestr.

Anstelkanaal

IM Coenenstr.

STAYOKAY AMSTERDAM ● VONDELPARK

FLYING PIG UPTOWN ●

Tesselschadestr.

Van de Veldestr.

Pieter Cornelisz Hooftstr.

Honthorststr.

CONCERT GEBOUW

BROUWERS ● PLEIN

HOTEL ● BEMA

Nicolaas Maesstr.

Frans van Mierisstr.

Wouwermanstr.

Roelofhartstr.

Heinzestr.

Dansstr.

Richard Holstr.

1e Constantijn Huygensstr.

Vondelstr.

Alexander Boersstr.

Jacob Obrechtstr.

FILMMUSEUM 🏛

CAFÉ VERTIGO ●

2e Constantijn Huygensstr.

Van Eeghenstr.

Willemsparkweg

Bartstr.

Banstr.

'T BLAUWE THEEHUIS ■

★ OPEN LUCHT THEATER

Cornelis Schuytstr.

Johannes Verhulststr.

De Lairessestr.

Apollolaan

Anna van den Vondelstr.

Gerard Brandtstr.

Vondelpark

Van Baerlestr.

Van Breestr.

Valeriusstr.

Johannes Verhulststr.

Emmastr.

Koninginneweg

Van Eeghenlaan

Roemer Visscherstr.

Jan Pieter Heijestr.

Tweede Helmersstr.

Overtoom

Kattenlaan

Starstr.

Anna van den Vondelstr.

Koningslaan

Prins Hendriklaan

EMMA-PLEIN

VALERIUS-PLEIN

Jan van Goyenkade

Lomanstr.

Koninginneweg

Kostverlorenvaart

JJ CREMER PLEIN

Rhijnvis Feithstr.

Kinkerstr.

Schoolstr.

Saxenburger gwarsstr.

Saxenburger str.

Reyer Anslostr.

Vondelkerkstr.

Frederiksstr.

Orange Nassaulaan

Overtoom

★ 200 meters

200 yards

0

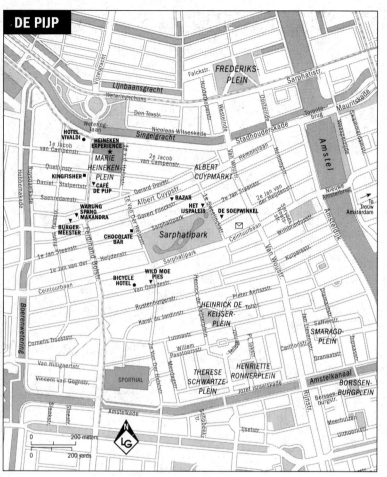

de pijp map

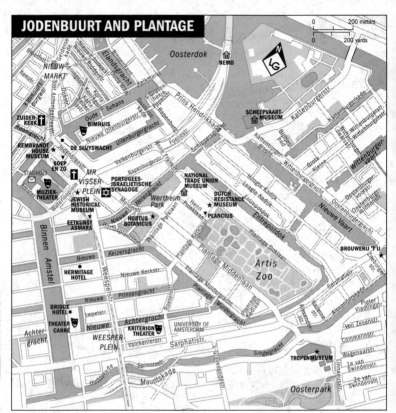

JODENBUURT AND PLANTAGE

Oosterdok

NEMO

NIEUW-
MARKT

Elandsgracht

Bloetstraat

Koestr.

Geldersekade

Nieuwe-Jonkerstr.

Nieuwe-Brugsteeg

purgwal

Sint Antoniesbreestr.

Kattenburgerstr.

Kattenburgerstr.

Kattenburgerstr.kade

Korte

Kolksteeg

Korte

Oude Schans

SCHEEPVAART-
MUSEUM

Kattenburger
gracht

Buiten-
Kadijk

Pad

Wittenburgerstr.

Wittenburgerstr.kade

Wittenburgerstr.

Prins Hendrikkade

Kalkmarkt

Grote
Bickersstr.

Peper

Rapenburg

Oosterburgergracht

Groote
Kadijk

Kleine

Wittenburgergracht

Nieuwe Vaart

Nieuwe-Uilenburgergracht

Anna Paulowna

Foeliestr.

Schippersgracht

ZUIDER-
KERK

Jodenbreestr.

BIMHUIS

Oude

REMBRANDT
HOUSE
MUSEUM

DE SLUYSWACHT

SOEP
EN ZO

Uilenburgergracht

Valkenburgerstr.

Hoogte Kadijk

Laagte Kadijk

Entrepotdok

Oostenburger-
gracht

Oostenburger-
poort

Oostenburger-
middenstr.

STADHUIS

MR
VISSER-
PLEIN

PORTUGEES-
ISRAELIETISCHE
SYNAGOGE

Rapenburgerstr.

NATIONAL
TRADE UNION
MUSEUM

DUTCH
RESISTANCE
MUSEUM

Nieuwe Vaart

MUZIEK-
THEATER

JEWISH
HISTORICAL
MUSEUM

Midden Herengracht

*Wertheim
Park*

PLANCIUS

Entrepotdok

Plantage Doklaan

BROUWERIJ 'T IJ

Zeeburgerstr.

EETKUNST
ASMARA

HORTUS
BOTANICUS

Nieuwe Herengracht

Henri
Polaklaan

Plantage Kerklaan

Binnen
Amstel

Nieuwe Keizersgracht

*Artis
Zoo*

Sarphatistr.

Alexanderkade

Hermitage
HOTEL

Nieuwe Kerkstr.

Plantage Middenlaan

Plantage Muidergracht

Plantage Kadijk

Weesperstr.

Nieuwe Prinsengracht

Plantage Parklaan

Alexanderstr.

Pieter
Vlamingstr.

BRIDGE
HOTEL

Lepelstr.

Achtergracht

UNIVERSITY OF
AMSTERDAM

Kastanjestr.

Von Zesenstr.

Commelinstr.

THEATER
CARRÉ

Nieuwe
Prinsengracht

KRITERION
THEATER

's Gravesandestr.

Wagenaarstr.

Achter-
gracht

WEESPER-
PLEIN

Vatckenierstr.

Sarphatistr.

Singelgracht

1e van
Swindenstr.

TROPENMUSEUM

2e van
Swindenstr.

Hugokade

Spinozastr.

Mauritskade

Oosterpark

Linneausstr.

200 meters

200 yards

BARCELONA

Benvolgut a Barcelona! Welcome to a city more exquisite, more idiosyncratic, more bold, and more fun than you ever thought a city could be. There's a whole lot more to Barcelona than Gaudí's architecture and the incredible clubs, and *Let's Go* will show you the way—at the end of the day, you've always got Gaudí and the clubs to fall back on.

You'll find that the locals consider themselves Catalan first and Spanish a distant second. Barcelona is quite proud of its Catalan culture and language, which is the default and which you'll probably hear much more frequently than *castellano*. Everybody in Catalonia speaks Spanish—they just generally prefer not to—and even if your Spanish-language skills don't extend beyond *hola* and *cerveza*, you'll get by just fine.

Whether you're strolling through the broad tree-and-*modernista*-building-lined avenues of l'Eixample by day, bar-hopping beneath the walls of Gothic churches of the Ciutat Vella at night, or napping off that hangover in one of Gràcia's shady plazas, if you take a second to look around you'll be mesmerized by the city's ubiquitous charm. Oh, and did we mention there's also a beach? Save it for last, because once you head to the beach, you'll never see anything else.

greatest hits

- **EMERGENCY STAY. Hostal Maldà** only books 60% of its space via reservations, so check here if you need an awesome, last-minute room (p. 102).

- **THE GAUDIEST.** Parc Güell (p. 123) is to Barcelona as buffalo sauce is to chicken wings.

- **ALL OF THE FRUITS. La Boqueria** in Las Ramblas has 'em (p. 130).

- **MIRA, MIRA.** Sip a cocktail with the jaw-dropping backdrop of Barcelona at **Mirablau** (p. 161).

orientation

Though a large and complex city, Barcelona's *barris* (neighborhoods) are fairly well-defined. The **Ciutat Vella** (old city) is the city's heart, comprised of **El Raval** (west of Las Ramblas), **Barri Gòtic** (between **Las Ramblas** and Via Laietana), **El Born** (between Via Laietana and Parc de la Ciutadella), and **La Barceloneta** (the peninsula south of El Born). Farther down the coast (to the left as you look at a map with the sea at the bottom) from the *Ciutat Vella* is the park-mountain **Montjuïc,** and the small neighborhood of **Poble Sec** between Montjuïc and Avda. Paral·lel. Farther inland from the *Ciutat Vella* is the large, central, rigidly gridded zone of **l'Eixample,** and still farther away from the sea is **Gràcia.** The **Plaça de Catalunya** is one of the city's most central points, located where Las Ramblas meets the Passeig de Gràcia; it is essentially the meeting point of El Raval, Barri Gòtic, and l'Eixample.

BARRI GÒTIC AND LAS RAMBLAS

You will get lost in Barri Gòtic. Knowing this, the best way to properly orient yourself in the confusing neighborhood, where streets still follow their medieval routes, is to take a day to learn your way around. **Las Ramblas** provides the western boundary of the neighborhood, stretching from the waterfront to **Plaça de Catalunya. Via Laietana** marks the eastern border, running nearly parallel to Las Ramblas. The primary east-west artery running between Las Ramblas and V. Laietana is known as **Carrer de Ferran** between Las Ramblas and the central **Plaça de Sant Jaume,** and as **Carrer de Jaume I** between Pl. Sant Jaume and V. Laietana. Of the many plazas hiding in the Barri Gòtic, **Plaça Reial** (take the tiny C. de Colom off Las Ramblas) and Plaça de Sant Jaume are the grandest. The neighborhood is better known, though, for its more cramped spaces, like the narrow alleys covered with arches or miniature *placetas* in the shadows of parish churches. The **L3** and **L4** Metro lines serve this neighborhood, with ⓂDrassanes, ⓂLiceu, and ⓂCatalunya along Las Ramblas (L3), and ⓂJaume I at the intersection of C. Jaume I and V. Laietana.

EL BORN

El Born, which makes up the eastern third of the **Ciutat Vella,** is celebrated for being slightly less touristy than the Barri Gòtic and slightly less prostitute-y than El Raval. The neighborhood is renowned for its confusing medieval streets, whose ancient bends hide fashionable boutiques and restaurants both traditional and modern. The **Passeig del Born,** the lively hub of this quirky *barri*, makes for a good bar- and restaurant-lined starting point.

barcelona

EL RAVAL

There's no point beating around the bush: El Raval is one of Barcelona's more dangerous neighborhoods. By no means should you avoid it, just be careful and aware—even during the day—and be prepared to deal with persistent drug dealers and aggressive prostitutes. In particular, avoid **Carrer de Sant Ramon.** Clearly, El Raval does not lack character, and it is actually one of the city's most interesting neighborhoods. Everything tends to be significantly less expensive than on the other side of Las Ramblas, and a large student population supports a bevy of quirky restaurants and bars. Areas around the **Rambla del Raval** and the **Carrer de Joaquim Costa** hide small unique bars and late-night cafes frequented by Barcelona's alternative crowd. For daytime shopping, check out **Riera Baixa,** a street lined entirely with secondhand shops that also hosts a flea market on Saturdays, or the ritzier neighborhood around **Carrer del Doctor Dou, Carrer del Pintor Fortuny,** and **Carrer Elisabets** for higher-end (though still reasonably priced) shops.

L'EIXAMPLE

In this posh neighborhood (pronounced leh-SHAM-plah), big blocks, wide avenues, and dazzling architecture mean lots of walking and lots of exciting storefronts. *Modernista* buildings line **Passeig de Gràcia** (first word pronounced pah-SAYCH), which runs from north to south through the neighborhood's center (Ⓜ Diagonal, Ⓜ Passeig de Gràcia, Ⓜ Catalunya), with **L'Eixample Dreta** encompasses the area to the east around the **Sagrada Família,** and **Eixample Esquerra** comprises the area closer to the **University,** uphill from **Plaça de la Universitat.** Though the former contains some surprisingly cheap accommodations for those willing to make the hike, the Eixample Esquerra is somewhat more pedestrian-friendly and more interesting to walk around. While this neighborhood is notoriously expensive, there are some cheaper and more interesting options as you get closer to Pl. Universitat. The stretch of **Carrer del Consell de Cent** west of Pg. de Gràcia boasts vibrant nightlife, where many "hetero-friendly" bars, clubs, and hotels give it the nickname **Gaixample.**

BARCELONETA

Barceloneta, the triangular peninsula that juts out into the Mediterranean, is a former mariners' and fishermen's neighborhood, built on a sandbank at the beginning of the 18th century to replace the homes destroyed by the construction of the *ciutadella.* The grid plan, a consequence of Enlightenment city planning, gives the neighborhood's narrow streets a distinct character, seasoned by the salty sea breezes that whip through the urban canyons. Tourists and locals are drawn to unconventional Barceloneta by the restaurants and views along the **Passeig Joan de Borbó,** by the renowned beaches on the other side along the **Passeig Marítim de la Barceloneta,** and by the *discotecas* at the **Port Olímpic.**

GRÀCIA

Gràcia is hard to navigate by Metro. While this may at first seem like a negative, the poor municipal planning is actually a bonus. Filled with artsy locals, quirky shops, and a few lost travelers, Gràcia is a quieter, more out-of-the-way neighborhood, best approached by foot. Ⓜ **Diagonal** will drop you off at the northern end of the Pg. de Gràcia; follow it across Avda. Diagonal as it becomes **Carrer Gran de Gràcia,** one of the neighborhood's main thoroughfares. Ⓜ **Fontana** lies further up on C. Gran de Gràcia. If you're heading uphill on C. Gran de Gràcia, any right turn will take you into the charmingly confusing grid of Gràcia's small streets, of which **Carrer de Verdi,** running parallel to C. Gran de Gràcia several blocks away, is probably the most scenic. For bustling *plaças* both day and night, your best bets are **Plaça de la Vila de Gràcia** (more commonly known as Pl. Rius i Taulet), **Plaça del Sol,** and **Plaça de la Revolució de Setembre de 1868,** off of C. de Ros de Olano.

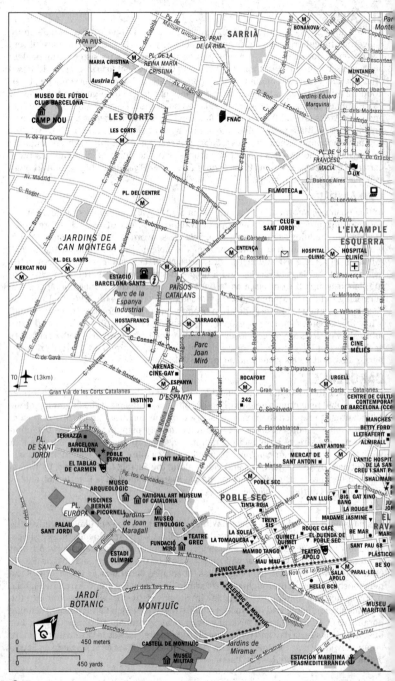

barcelona

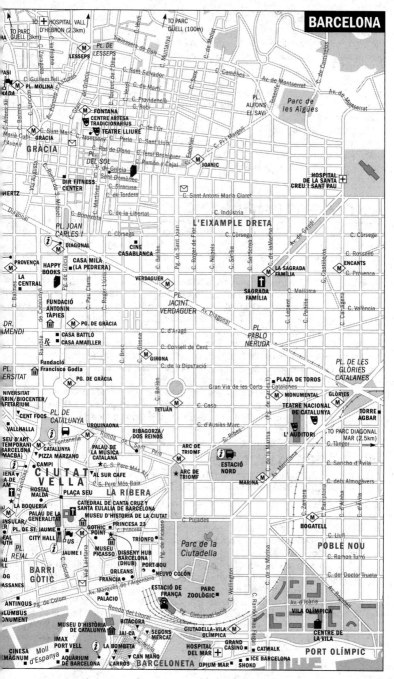

BARCELONA

barcelona overview map

MONTJUÏC AND POBLE SEC

Montjuïc, the mountain just down the coast from the old center of Barcelona, is one of the city's chief cultural centers. Its slopes are home to **public parks,** some of the city's best museums, theaters that host everything from classical music to pop, and a 👍**kick-ass castle** on its peak. Montjuïc (old Catalan for "mountain of the Jews," possibly for the Jewish cemetery once located there) also has some of the most incredible views of the city. Many approach the mountain from the **Plaça de Espanya,** passing between the two towers to ascend toward the museums and other sights; others take the funicular from [M]Paral·lel.

The small neighborhood of **Poble Sec** (Catalan for "dry village") lies at the foot of Montjuïc, between the mountain and **Avinguda del Paral·lel.** Tree-lined, sloping streets characterize the largely residential neighborhood, with the **Plaça del Sortidor** as its heart and the pedestrian-friendly, restaurant-lined **Carrer de Blai** as its commercial artery.

accommodations

You can find accommodation in any of the neighborhoods that *Let's Go* lists, and they will all have their pros and cons. The main reasons to stay in the Barri Gòtic are its convenience (few sights are out of walking distance), its beauty, and the sheer preponderance of accommodations. However, if being surrounded by hordes of tourists is likely to annoy you, you may want to check out a less central neighborhood. **El Born's** options are reasonably priced and varied, but be sure to scout out your hotel's location ahead of time, as this neighborhood's narrow streets can disorient even the most experienced traveler. Though **El Raval** is grittier than the other areas of the Ciutat Vella, its *hostales* and *pensiónes* generally cost as much as or more than their counterparts in Barri Gòtic and El Born. The pure abundance of accommodation options in **L'Eixample** means it's likely you'll end up staying there: however, it is pricey and less pedestrian-friendly than some. If it's the beach you crave, you might think **Barceloneta** is your best bet: however it's generally cheaper and better to stay in El Born or **Barri Gòtic** if you want to be near the clubs and beaches of Barceloneta. **Gràcia** is a good choice if you anticipate getting sick of the tourists around Las Ramblas and want more of a neighborhood feel. **Poble Sec,** in the shadow of Montjuïc, doesn't offer much in the way of tourist attractions, but it does have a couple of backpackers' hostels close to the Metro that make good bases for exploring the rest of the city.

BARRI GÒTIC AND LAS RAMBLAS

If you can see through the tourist crowds to the neighborhood's true charm—or if you just want to blend in with the hordes—the Barri Gòtic is for you.

👍 HOSTAL MALDÀ — HOSTEL $

C. Pi, 5 — ☎933 17 30 02; www.hostalmalda.jimdo.com

Hostal Maldà provides a dirt-cheap home away from home, complete with kitschy clocks, ceramics, confusing knick-knacks, and your grandmother's cat. A comfy lounge with books and a TV feels more like a living room than a dorm common space. Unlike many *hostales*, the prices don't change with the season, nor will Maldà be booked months in advance during the summer—knowing their audience and popularity, the owners only accept reservations for up to 60% capacity, so try stopping by if you're stranded or weren't quick enough to snag a room beforehand.

➤ [M]Liceu. Begin walking away from Las Ramblas in front of the house with the 📷**dragon** *and take an immediate left onto C. Casañas. Stay on this road as it passes in front of the church and through the Pl. Pi. Enter the Galerias Maldà (interior shopping mall) and follow the signs to the hostel.* ℹ *Linens included. Luggage storage available. All rooms have shared bath; some have ensuite showers.* [$] *Singles €15, with shower €20; doubles €30; triples €45; quads €60. Cash only.* ⏰ *Reception 24hr.*

👍 HOSTEL SUN & MOON — HOSTEL $$

C. Ferran, 17 — ☎932 70 20 60; www.sunandmoonhostel.com

Though the prices may seem far too high given the crowded dorms and with rental linens, blankets, and towels, Hostel Sun & Moon is actually a pretty good deal for the neighborhood. More importantly, it has a popcorn machine (€1). Located on one of the the Barri Gòtic's main drags, the recently renovated hostel has an incredibly lively atmosphere, thanks to its endless stream of young travelers. A deal with a nearby restaurant allows it to offer €4 meals as well. Watch out for the 10-bed dorm, though, where 10 guests share a single bathroom.

➔ [M]Liceu. Walk toward the sea on Las Ramblas and take a left onto C. Ferran. ℹ Breakfast included. Linens €2. Towels €2. Blankets €3. Luggage storage €2. Free Wi-Fi. Full kitchen for guest use. [$] Dorms €14-28; doubles (across the street) €75; triples €85; quads €95. ⏰ Reception 24hr.

KABUL YOUTH HOSTEL — HOSTEL $$

Pl. Reial, 17 — ☎933 18 51 90; www.kabul.es

One of the biggest and most popular hostels in Barcelona, the Kabul Youth Hostel has hosted nearly one million backpackers since it opened in 1985. The hostel offers bare-bones dorms—many with balconies over Pl. Reial—and a rooftop terrace. Lower-capacity rooms are often cramped and more expensive, but if you can get one with a balcony (just ask), it's worth the added expense. The common space boasts backpacker photo galleries, a pool table, foosball, music, and a never-ending swarm of chatty younger travelers who are genuinely excited to meet each other. Complimentary breakfast and dinner make these rooms a steal.

➔ [M]Liceu. Walk toward the sea on Las Ramblas and turn left onto C. Ferran. Take the 1st right and enter the Pl. Reial. Kabul Youth Hostel will be on the far left, with well-marked glass doors. ℹ Breakfast and dinner included. Linens €2. Lockers €15 deposit. Luggage storage and laundry facilities available. 20min. free internet per day. Guestlist access to local nightclubs. [$] Dorms €15-29. ⏰ Reception 24hr.

ALBERG PALAU — HOSTEL $$

C. Palau, 6 — ☎934 12 50 80; www.bcnalberg.com

Alberg Palau's clean dorms with pleasant views onto the street and courtyard below fit four to eight people. Rooms have cheerily colored ceilings and wooden floors, and some include balconies—perfect for scoping out fellow travelers, restaurants, or the nearby souvenir shop. The common space provides a bright, if boring seating area in which to veg out in front of the TV, grab snacks from the vending machine, or meet fellow hostelmates over a board game.

➔ [M]Liceu. Walk down C. de Ferran and take a right onto C. Palau when you reach Pl. Sant Jaume. ℹ Breakfast and lockers included. Linens €2. Free Wi-Fi. Kitchen open 7-10pm. [$] 4- to 8-bed dorms €13-25; doubles €28-55. ⏰ Reception 24hr.

HOSTAL-RESIDÈNCIA REMBRANDT — HOSTEL $$

C. Portaferissa, 23 — ☎933 18 10 11; www.hostalrembrandt.com

Hostal-Residència has a variety of large rooms with great additions. Many include large windows or balconies looking out over the corner of the street or into the courtyard, and one triple even has a loft. For once, it's worth paying for an ensuite bathroom—even the ones that aren't equipped with jacuzzis are still big enough to spend an entire week relaxing in. The rooms are a real steal in the low season, and the location and charm are still worth it in the high season.

➔ [M]Liceu. Walk down Las Ramblas toward Pl. Catalunya and take a right onto C. Portaferissa; the hostal is by Galerias Maldà. ℹ Linens and towels included. Free Wi-Fi. Internet use on hostal computers €2 per 30min., €3 per hr. [$] Singles €20-30, with bath €25-35; doubles €35-40; triples €60-75; quads €100. ⏰ Reception 9am-11pm.

HOSTAL-RESIDENCIA LAUSANNE HOSTEL $$

Avda. Portal de l'Àngel, 24 ☎933 02 11 39; www.hostallausanne.es

A beautiful stairway (marble stairs, blue and gold tiles, stained glass at each landing) leads to equally impressive rooms. Each has an excellent view, but try to get one that faces the patio—the view is better and it will be quieter at night, so long as your hostelmates aren't total hooligans. Enjoy the view from your room; chat up some fellow travelers in the bohemian common space with free internet, microwave, and TV; or chill out on the back patio overlooking the neighboring rooftops.

✦ Ⓜ*Catalunya. From the Metro, walk toward El Corte Inglés. Upon reaching the far corner of the square, turn right onto Avda. Portal de l'Àngel.* *i* *Towels, linens, and toiletries included. Fridge and luggage storage available.* Ⓢ *Singles €24-35, with bath €35-50; doubles €42-53/48-70; triples €60-75/69-95. Call for up-to-date rates.* ⌚ *Reception 24hr.*

QUARTIER GOTHIC HOSTEL $$

C. Avinyó, 42 ☎933 18 79 45; www.hotelquartiergothic.com

Flags from around the world and the hostel's own regalia decks the halls of Quartier Gothic. Rooms overlooking the courtyard have the best vistas and the least noise from the night-long cacophony of the Barri Gòtic. Though the private baths are more spacious than those in comparable hostels in the area, the shared bath is practically a room of its own (one at a time, please). This hostel shows up many in its price range in terms of amenities (some TVs and DVD players, a fairly impressive breakfast) while still being in a central location.

✦ Ⓜ*Drassanes. Head toward Pl. Catalunya on Las Ramblas. Turn right onto C. Escudellers, then right onto C. Avinyó.* *i* *Breakfast €3. Linens included. Rooms have safes. Lockers available for day after checkout €2. Free Wi-Fi.* Ⓢ *Singles €16-29; doubles €28-45, with bath €42-62; triples €42-75. Discounts available online.* ⌚ *Reception 24hr.*

HOSTAL FERNANDO HOSTEL, PENSIÓN $$

C. de Ferran, 31 ☎933 01 79 93; www.hfernando.com

The *Alberg de Joventut* (Youth Hostel) portion of Hostal Fernando is composed of big, clean, and bright dormitories with bunk beds. It offers the amenities you'd expect from a nicer hostel: comfortable common spaces, complimentary breakfast, and daily activities such as walking tours and discounts at clubs. The private rooms (the *pensión* part) are similarly modern but unremarkable.

✦ Ⓜ*Liceu. From Las Ramblas, take a left onto C. Ferran. Hostal Fernando is on the left.* *i* *Breakfast and linens included. Towels €1.50. Lockers €1.50 per day; safes in private rooms. Free Wi-Fi in common area; internet €1 per 30min. Credit card required for 1st night reservation. Walking tour daily 10:45am.* Ⓢ *Dorms €18-25; singles €45-55; doubles €60-75; triples €75-95; 4- to 6-person family rooms €90-160.* ⌚ *Reception 24hr.*

ARCO YOUTH HOSTEL (ALBERGUE ARCO) HOSTEL $

L'Arc Santa Eulàlia, 1 ☎934 12 54 68

Offering rooms with lockers for six, eight, and 18 (!) people, the Arco Youth Hostel provides a bunk to crash in and breakfast to wake you up. Sunny Japanese-themed murals of cherry blossoms greet tired guests, and a full communal kitchen provides a stage for your own Iron Chef battles. The smaller common space has couches, books, and a TV—just hope that no one is using their "gym," a.k.a. the exercise bike squeezed along the wall. The prices are rock-bottom for this neighborhood, but be sure to abide by their extensive check-in and cancellation policies to avoid fees.

✦ Ⓜ*Liceu. Walk down C. Boqueria; L'Arc Santa Eulàlia is the 3rd right.* *i* *Breakfast included. Linens €1.70. Lockers €10 deposit. Free Wi-Fi and internet use. Kitchen available. Call ahead if arrival time is different than originally noted. Fee for canceled reservations with less than 48hr. in advance or no show; cancellations must be via email (not phone or fax).* Ⓢ *Dorms €20-23.* ⌚ *Reception 24hr.*

EL BORN

Many accommodations in this area are found just off **Via Laietana** or concentrated on **Avinguda del Marquès de l'Argentera,** near Estació de França. Scout out your hotel's location ahead of time, as this neighborhood's narrow streets can disorient even the most experienced traveler.

GOTHIC POINT YOUTH HOSTEL
HOSTEL $

C. Vigatans, 5 ☎932 68 78 08; www.gothicpoint.com

This youth hostel's social life is as vibrant as its lime green walls, with a ping-pong table on the huge terrace for those nights when you just need to duke it out. The place is trying way too hard to be that one super-cool social hostel with the quirky-but-not-quite-kitschy decor and the lived-in college-hangout feel. Sometimes it succeeds, but generally it just comes off looking toolish. The chutes-and-ladders-esque bedrooms provide standard youth hostel fare with one significant improvement: beds come with curtains for a little bit of privacy on those steamy hostel nights. (BYO Barry White CDs.)

✣ ⓂJaume I. Walk down C. Argenteria and take a left onto C. Vigatans. *i* Kitchen available. Inquire about working to pay for your stay. Linens €2. Towels €2. Ⓢ Dorms €15-25. ⌚ Reception 24hr.

HOTEL TRIUNFO
HOTEL $$$

Pg. Picasso, 22 ☎933 10 40 85; www.atriumhotels.com

The musty darkness of an apartment building's stairwell is shattered by the gleaming lights and colors of this sleek hotel. Chic but small rooms are a steal and boast curtains that actually match the covers, luxurious bathrooms with slick black tubs, and flatscreen TVs. Be sure to request a room with a window, as some have only a narrow slit facing the tiny, dark courtyard. A small common room with black leather couches, a bright white sculpture, and posters of art exhibitions from around the world provide the perfect place to prep before heading across the street to catch a classical performance in the Parc de la Ciutadella.

✣ ⓂArc de Triomf. Walk down Pg. Lluís Companys through the arch and toward the Parc. Follow the curve to the right once it meets the park to get on Pg. Picasso. Hotel Triunfo is on the right underneath the arcade. *i* All rooms have private baths. Ⓢ Singles €40-45; doubles €60-70; triples €90-100. Ask about discounts M-F. ⌚ Reception 24hr.

HOSTAL ORLEANS
HOSTEL $$$

Avda. Marquès l'Argentera, 13 ☎933 19 73 82; www.hostalorleans.com

This large *hostal* (a good bet if other places are full) is a simple and comfortable option, though the hallway floors get a little Escher-esque in places—watch for unexpected steps and inexplicable inclines. The decor is humble but clean, and it just feels a little bit nicer than its competitors.

✣ ⓂBarceloneta. Walk on Plà Palau away from the water and take a right onto Avda. Marquès de l'Argentera. The hostal is on the left at the corner of C. Comerç. Ⓢ Singles €45, with private bath €55; doubles €60-70; triples €70-80. ⌚ Reception 24hr.

HOSTAL RIBAGORZA
HOSTEL $$$

C. Trafalgar, 39, 1st fl. ☎933 19 19 68; www.hostalribagorza.com

Simple rooms decorated with bland art and some ceramic knick-knacks make for an unexciting but perfectly pleasant stay. Let this place spoil you with clean rooms, balconies, and surprisingly large shared bathrooms.

✣ ⓂArc de Triomf. Stand on the far side of the Arc farthest from the Parc with your back to the arch. C. Trafalgar is the 1st street on the left. Ⓢ Doubles €45, with bath €50-62; triples €60-€75. ⌚ Reception 24hr.

accommodations

EL RAVAL

👍 HOTEL PENINSULAR — HOTEL $$$$

C. Sant Pau, 34 ☎933 02 31 38; www.hotelpeninsular.net

Austere rooms—the hotel was formerly a monastery—are situated off a sky-lit four-story-high atrium, with seating below, plants above, and mint green paint everywhere. There's still a secret passageway connecting the former monastery to the church across the street, though its use has been quite infrequent since the building's conversion to a hotel for the 1876 Exposició Universal. Though at the higher end of the *Let's Go* pricing scale, this is your chance to get a taste of old-world grandeur for a reasonable rate.

🧭 ⓂLiceu. Walk away from Pl. Catalunya on Las Ramblas. C. Sant Pau is on the right. ℹ Free Wi-Fi. Ensuite bathrooms. $ Singles €50-60; doubles €65-80; triples €85; quads €100. Cash only. ⏰ Reception 24hr.

BE SOUND HOSTEL — HOSTEL $$

C. Nou de la Rambla, 91 ☎931 85 08 00; www.behostels.com/sound

This laid-back hostel deep in El Raval offers a range of amenities, fairly large dorm rooms, and a huge common room in the basement with foosball, leather sofas, and a flatscreen TV. When you're done watching TV, head out on one of the two free daily walking tours of the city, or just go up to the rooftop terrace (open daily 8am-11pm).

🧭 ⓂParal·lel. Follow Avda. Paral·lel briefly toward the water and turn left on C. Nou de la Rambla. ℹ Linens and towels €2.50 each, €3.50 for both. Lockers included. Free Wi-Fi and internet. Kitchen available. $ 6- or 8-person dorms in winter €16; in summer €29. Rates average €2 higher on weekends. ⏰ Reception 24hr.

BE MAR HOSTEL — HOSTEL $$

C. Sant Pau, 80 ☎933 24 85 30; www.barcelonamar.com

The clean and cheerily painted Be Mar appears to be the livelier, more energetic cousin of Be Sound a couple of blocks away (it must be something in the complimentary breakfast). The dorms are large—some have 16 beds—but not cramped, and the common areas are similarly spacious.

🧭 ⓂParal·lel. From Avda. Paral·lel, take C. Sant Pau (not Ronda Sant Pau). ℹ Breakfast and lockers included. Linens and towels €2.50 each, €3.50 for both. Free internet and Wi-Fi. Free walking tours daily. Kitchen for guests' use. $ 6-, 8-, 10-, 14-, or 16-bed dorms in winter €14; in summer €29. Rates average €2 higher on weekends. ⏰ Reception 24hr.

IDEAL YOUTH HOSTEL — HOSTEL $$

C. Unió, 12 ☎933 42 61 77; www.idealhostel.com

An industrial-chic common space with foosball and amoeba-like couches hosts a revolving door of vibrant young backpackers. The bathroom facilities in this standard youth hostel smell soapy so you know they must be clean. The young staff will point you in the right direction and may even end up joining you to show you the ropes.

🧭 ⓂLiceu. Walk toward the water on Las Ramblas and take a right onto C. Unió. ℹ Breakfast included. Safes available. Free WiFi 30min. $ Dorms €19-27; private rooms €27-32. €9.50 deposit. Cash only. ⏰ Reception 24hr.

DOWNTOWN PARAISO HOSTEL — HOSTEL $$$$

C. Junta de Comerç, 13 ☎933 02 61 34

Beautiful, hip artwork by an Argentine artist covers the already colorful walls of this lively *hostal*. There's more turquoise and orange beneath the high ceilings than you're likely to see this side of Santa Fe, and the common room and sunny terrace are perfect for hiding from the madness of El Raval. Downtown Paraiso is not inexpensive, but it more than lives up to its rates.

🧭 ⓂLiceu. Follow C. Hospital and take a left on C. Junta de Comerç. ℹ Linens included. Towels €2. Kitchen for guests' use. Free Wi-Fi and internet. $ Singles €50-60, with bath €55-80; doubles €70-90. ⏰ Reception 24hr.

L'EIXAMPLE

In an awful twist, you'll likely end up staying in Barcelona's priciest and least pedestrian-friendly neighborhood, because of its abundance of accommodations. Learn to love *modernisme*.

⚑ SANT JORDI: HOSTEL ARAGÓ   HOSTEL $$

C. Aragó, 268   ☎932 15 67 43; www.santjordihostels.com/hostel-arago

Kick back in the gloriously bright and homey kitchen and common room, or gather round on one of the couches and listen to hostelmates play covers of Bob Dylan and Andrew Bird on the communal guitar. Any hostel with quotes from Guy Debord, Wittgenstein, and Nietzsche on its board has to be a little different, and Hostel Aragó is—in only the best way. Modern wooden and steel bunks offer little more than a place to rest your head, but nightly outings and a solid community ensure you'll be spending little time in them.

✦ ⓂPasseig de Gràcia. Walk up Pg. de Gràcia away from Pl. Catalunya and take a left onto C. Aragó. *i* Linens, lockers, and luggage storage included. Towels €2. Laundry available. Free Wi-Fi and internet. ⑤ Dorms €18-35. ☒ Reception 24hr.

⚑ SANT JORDI: SAGRADA FAMÍLIA   HOSTEL $$

C. Freser, 5   ☎934 46 05 17; www.santjordihostels.com/apt-sagrada-familia/

For those sick of dining on takeout, coffee, and beer, Sant Jordi's apartment-style lodging offers the chain's characteristic laid-back style, communal guitars, employees dedicated to organizing nightly parties, and social hostelmates guaranteed to be as cool as you. Each apartment includes a private bath, stylish and comfy living room, free washing machine, and stocked kitchen, with the added benefit of hostel-style sociability. With rooms for one, two, or four people, you can pick your privacy without *pensión*-style isolation. If you long for that traditional hostel feel, they also have air-conditioned six-, eight-, 10-, and 12-person dorms in the next building, whose common areas include Seussian wall niches and a small halfpipe on the terrace.

✦ ⓂSant Pau/Dos de Maig. Walk downhill on C. Dos de Maig toward C. Còrsega. Take a left onto C. Rosselló and stay left as the road splits to C. Freser. *i* Lockers and linens included. Free Wi-Fi. ⑤ 4-bed dorms €16-28; singles €20-38; doubles €36-64. Hostel dorms €16-35. ☒ Reception 24hr. Quiet hours after 10pm.

⚑ HOSTAL OLIVA   HOSTEL $$$

Pg. de Gràcia, 32   ☎934 88 01 62; www.hostaloliva.com

If you think the interior view of Oliva's sunlit atrium from the period wooden elevator is impressive, ask for a room facing the street. Large windows facing the grandiose Pg. de Gràcia offer peep shows of the architectural orgasm of the Manzana de Discòrdia. Though lacking the fantastic views, interior rooms make up for their shortcomings with more space. Huge rooms with marble floors and the view of Gaudí's Casa Batlló make this *hostal* well worth the few extra euro.

✦ ⓂPasseig de Gràcia. Walk up Pg. de Gràcia away from Pl. Catalunya; Hostal Oliva is on the right at the corner of C. Diputació and Pg. de Gràcia. *i* Free Wi-Fi. ⑤ Singles €39; doubles €68-87; triples €120. Cash only.

ROOMS4RENT   HOSTEL $

Gran Via de les Corts Catalanes, 602 ☎933 17 01 49; 686 34 28 68; www.rooms4rentbcn.com

This hostel isn't easy to spot—no sign marks its door, and you'll have to look for its sticker on the buzzer. Inside, you'll find a near-blinding assortment of primary colors that match an equally vibrant and young clientele. Plenty of cozy common space fills out this charming old place, complete with turn-of-the-century doorways with stained glass and original fixtures.

✦ ⓂUniversitat. Facing the university, walk to your right along Gran Via de les Corts Catalanes. Look for the name on the buzzer. *i* Breakfast and linens included. Kitchen available for guests' use. Free Wi-Fi. ⑤ Dorms €17-25; doubles €50. Private rooms available to rent for €300 per month. ☒ Reception 24hr.

accommodations

HOSTAL CENTRAL
HOSTEL $$$

Ronda Universitat, 11 ☎933 02 24 20; www.hostalcentral.net

Hostal Central has large, slightly quirky rooms between Pl. Universitat and Pl. Catalunya. Some rooms use their sunny enclosed porches for lazy mornings, while in the more crowded rooms these areas become fanciful sleeping spots, complete with lace curtains for a dose of privacy.

✦ ⓂUniversitat. Facing the university, walk to the right, parallel to Gran Via de les Corts Catalanes, to exit the plaza. Ronda Universitat runs diagonally to the right. *i* Breakfast included. Free Wi-Fi. ⓢ Singles €25-38, with bath €40-55; doubles €35-45/50-62. Extra bed €15. ⧖ Reception 24hr.

EQUITY POINT CENTRIC
HOSTEL $$

Pg. de Gràcia, 33 ☎932 15 65 38; www.equity-point.com

Equity Point's location can't be beat, especially for the price. Though the sheer number of rooms and the gargantuan reception area in this *modernista* building might intimidate you, the hostel website would prefer to think of it "like a cuckoo that's muscled into the very plushest of nests." Great views from the dorms and a ton of amenities, including a terrace and bar, provide the perfect escape if for some reason you don't feel like spending the day on Pg. de Gràcia.

✦ ⓂPasseig de Gràcia. Walk along Pg. de Gràcia away from Pl. Catalunya and El Corte Inglés. Equity Point is on the corner of C. Consell de Cent and Pg. de Gràcia. *i* Linens €2. Lockers available. Free Wi-Fi; computers with internet free for 20min. ⓢ Dorms €19-32. ⧖ Reception 24hr.

GRAFFITI HOSTAL
HOSTEL $

C. Aragó, 527 ☎932 88 24 99

True to its name, this hostel is covered in graffiti, which ranges from impressive works of art spanning entire walls to mundane scratchings by drunk hostelmates. An ironically unmarked door (on C. Aragó, next to Bar Giralda) hides some of the cheapest rooms in Barcelona, complete with lockers (BYO padlock), two outdoor terraces, and a common room with computers and a TV. It's got a much less clean-cut feel than the other hostels you're likely to find in Barcelona, but what else would you expect with a name like Graffiti Hostal?

✦ ⓂClot. Facing the rocket-shaped Agbar Tower, head to the right along C. Aragó. Or, ⓂEncants. Walk along C. Dos de Maig toward Agbar Tower and take a left onto C. Aragó. *i* Linens €2. Free Wi-Fi. ⓢ Dorms €15-20. ⧖ Common areas closed midnight-8am.

BARCELONA URBANY HOSTEL
HOSTEL $$

Avda. Meridiana, 97 ☎935 03 60 04; www.barcelonaurbany.com

Young people swarm this hostel, guaranteeing an exciting Barcelona experience. The free gym and pool access and nightly clubbing outings simply heighten this potential. Rooms are supermodern, but you'll probably spend most of your time on the terrace bar sipping cheap beer and sangria.

✦ ⓂClot. Walk along Avda. Meridiana toward the rocket-shaped Agbar Tower. Urbany is on the right, on the corner of Avda. Meridiana and C. Corunya. *i* Breakfast included. Luggage storage and laundry available. ⓢ Women-only dorms €23-34; co-ed €20-31. Singles and doubles €68-94. ⧖ Reception 24hr.

HOSTEL SOMNIO
HOSTEL $$

C. Diputació, 251 ☎932 72 53 08; www.somniohostels.com

This ultra-sleek *hostal* offers the best of both worlds—beautifully decorated private rooms and cost-efficient dorms. Wooden floors and modern decor will leave you expecting higher rates, but, thankfully, both the dorms and the private rooms are remarkably cheap for the neighborhood.

✦ ⓂPasseig de Gràcia. Walk down Pg. de Gràcia toward Pl. Catalunya and turn right on C. Diputació. *i* Breakfast €2. Linens and locker included. Free Wi-Fi. ⓢ Dorms €26; singles €44; doubles €78, with bath €87. ⧖ Reception 24hr.

BARCELONETA

⬛ PENSIÓN PALACIO
PENSIÓN $

Pg. Isabel II, 10 ☎933 19 36 09; www.pensionpalacio.com

This refreshingly colorful and inexpensive *pensión* with a deceiving laundry list of rules and fees (they're actually laid-back, we promise) is just a 5min. walk from the hip neighborhood of El Born and the sandy beaches of Barceloneta. Balconies overlook the pleasant and breezy Pg. Isabel II.

✦ ⓂBarceloneta. With your back to the beach, walk to the left on Pg. Isabel II. Pensión Palacio is under the arcade on the left. *i* Safes included. Laundry wash €5, dry €2. Kitchen €1 per day. Free Wi-Fi. Internet computers available. ⓢ Rooms €13-25 per person. ⓒ Reception 24hr. Computer room open 8am-11pm.

SEA POINT
HOSTEL $

Pl. Mar, 1-3 ☎932 31 20 45; www.equity-point.com

Sea Point is just seconds from San Sebastian beach, making it the only youth hostel bordering the water this side of Barceloneta. Tumble out of one of the solid metal bunk beds (no annoying midnight squeaks here) and onto the sand. Though clean, bright, and lively, these accommodations aren't as spiffy as other Barcelona hostels in the chain.

✦ ⓂBarceloneta. Follow Pg. Joan de Borbó until Pl. Mar (near the beach) and enter the hostel through the cafe on the right side of the building. *i* Breakfast included. Lockers €3. Linens €2. Luggage storage. Free 20min. internet access. Kitchen available. ⓢ Dorms €15-25.

GRÀCIA

⬛ ALBERGUE-RESIDENCIA LA CIUTAT
HOSTEL $

C. Alegre de Dalt, 66 ☎932 13 03 00; www.laciutat.com

This large (room for 180), busy, and cheerfully decorated hostel is a little off the typical tourist's path—but we don't see this as a negative in the least. The simple, brightly painted dorms are some of the cheapest beds in the area, and it's close enough to the lively heart of Gràcia for you to enjoy the neighborhood, while still far enough away that its revelers won't keep you up at night (unless they're in your dorm room). Complimentary breakfast should give you the energy to make it to the Metro in order to explore the rest of the city.

✦ ⓂJoanic. Walk along C. Escorial for 5-10min., passing through the plaza. Take a right onto C. Marti before the Clinic and take the 1st left onto C. Alegre de Dalt. *i* Towels and linens €1.80. Lockers €1.50 per day, €5 deposit. Free Wi-Fi and internet. Kitchens and shared bathrooms on each floor. ⓢ 4- to 10-bed dorms €17-20; singles €35-50; doubles €52-60. 1st night deposit required for online booking. ⓒ Reception 24hr.

HOSTAL SAN MEDÍN
HOSTEL $$

C. Gran de Gràcia, 125 ☎932 17 30 68; www.sanmedin.com

Big beds and rooms make San Medín feel more like a bed and breakfast than a budget *hostal*. Pictures of Barcelona's famous architecture cover the newly papered walls, and bright chandeliers add some sparkle to your sleeping space. Snag a room with a balcony; otherwise you'll be looking onto a drab (though quiet) scene: the classic light well.

✦ ⓂFontana. Take a left onto C. Gran de Gràcia. San Medín is 1 block down on the right, just after Rambla de Prat. *i* Free Wi-Fi. ⓢ Singles €32, with bath €45; doubles €50/65; triples €70/80.

PENSIÓN NORMA
PENSIÓN $$

C. Gran de Gràcia, 87 ☎932 37 44 78

Meticulously maintained rooms in an unbeatable location provide a relaxing place to return to after a night of marching the *modernista*-studded Pg. de Gràcia nearby. A few pieces of "art" give the somewhat bland rooms a splash of color and ease you out of the overwhelming artistry of the city beyond the *pensión*'s walls. If traveling with lots of luggage, be warned: it's a three-story walk-up.

✈ ⓂFontana. Take a left onto C. Gran de Gràcia. Pensión Norma is a few blocks down on the right. *i* Linens included. Ⓢ Singles €30; doubles €45, with bathroom €50; triples €66. ⓉReception 24hr.

MONTJUÏC AND POBLE SEC

HELLO BCN HOSTEL
HOSTEL $$

C. Lafont, 8-10 ☎934 42 83 92; www.hellobcnhostel.com

This hostel has a huge common area for those who want to relax, and a gym—unusual for hostels—for those who want to bring the energy up a level. Hello BCN's brightly painted common spaces and four-, six-, and eight-bed dorms have served the Barna backpacker community well, and they keep travelers coming back.

✈ ⓂParal·lel. Follow C. Nou de la Rambla up into Poble Sec past Apolo Theater and turn left on C. Vilà i Vilà and right onto C. Lafont. *i* Breakfast, linens, and lockers included. Towels €3. Key deposit €10. Free Wi-Fi and internet. Kitchen and gym available. Ⓢ Dorms €13-30; doubles €75-90. ⓉReception 24hr.

MAMBO TANGO YOUTH HOSTEL
HOSTEL $$

C. Poeta Cabanyes, 23 bis ☎934 42 51 64; www.hostelmambotango.com

Colorful rooms and even more vibrant bedding make for the most vivid hostel in town. A common area with the plushest sofas you've ever seen make it tough to leave, but the fun-loving staff will make sure you do.

✈ ⓂParal·lel. Follow Avda. Paral·lel away from the water past the small plaza on the left and turn left up C. Poeta Cabanyes. *i* Linens and lockers included. Towels for rent. Free Wi-Fi and internet. Kitchen for guests' use. Ⓢ Dorms €15-30. ⓉReception 24hr.

OUTSKIRTS

Though a trek from the city center, the following youth hostels and campgrounds offer astounding views and amenities at prices that would get you a basic bed with a view of the wall in the more touristy areas of Barcelona. You're not stuck out in the boonies, either—with bus and train stations nearby, the city is just a short and cheap ride away. In fact, almost all of Barcelona's campgrounds come equipped with a baffling assortment of amenities—even the most rugged campsites have bathing and laundry facilities as well as a supermarket and restaurant. If you're traveling with a group that appreciates rustic charm, but not outdoorsy amenities, go for a four- to six-person bungalow, which usually comes with a kitchen and a bathroom. Some have minimum stay requirements, so be prepared to kick back for a few days.

🏯 MARE DE DÉU DE MONTSERRAT YOUTH HOSTEL (HI)
HOSTEL $

Pg. Mare de Déu del Coll, 41-51 ☎934 83 83 63; www.xanascat.cat

Once a bourgeois country home, this renovated *modernista* palace near Parc Güell is now owned and operated by the government. Basic rooms offer huge lockers for all of your hiking gear, but the real draw is the breathtaking stained glass and neo-Moorish detail in the foyer and common rooms; it's worth the visit even if you're staying elsewhere.

✈ Buses #28, 92, and N5 stop across the street. Behind Parc Güell. *i* Breakfast, linens, and luggage storage included. Lockers and safes available. Laundry €4.50. Free internet. Ⓢ Dorms €17-22; singles, doubles, and triples with ensuite bathrooms €20-25 per person. ⓉReception 24hr.

CAMPING CARAVANNING TRES ESTRELLAS
CAMPGROUND $

Autovía Castelldefells, km. 186.2, Gavà ☎936 33 06 37; www.camping3estrellas.com

If you got any closer to the beach, you'd be washed out to sea at high tide. Camping facilities dot the beautiful beach of Gavà Mar, 15km from the city center

barcelona

(40min. by bus). The extensive facilities include not one but two swimming pools (in case you're afraid of sharks or jellyfish), volleyball nets, and a grill area, along with the usual suspects—a supermarket, bar, and restaurant.

From Pl. Catalunya, take bus #L94 or L95 (every 20min. 7am-10pm) to Gavà Platges/Tres Estrellas. Take the pedestrian walkway across the highway, and, as you face the highway, head to the right along the highway about 300m. i Wi-Fi €1 per 15min. $ Camping €6.10-8.30 per person; €7.80-9.40 per tent. 2-person cabin €26-38; 4-person cabin €38-60. ⏰ Open from mid-Mar to mid-Oct.

CAMPING BARCELONA CAMPGROUND $

Carretera N-II, km. 650, Mataró ☎937 90 47 20; www.campingbarcelona.com

Just across the highway from Mataró beach (frequent free buses connect the campground to the shore) and about 45min. from Barcelona by train, Camping Barcelona is comfy enough that you might want to just skip that whole "Barcelona" thing altogether. A beachside restaurant doubles as a club at night, and shady grassy plots look onto the nearby shore. The campground covers all of the bases with a swimming pool, internet cafe, laundromat, restaurant, supermarket, and farm with goats and rabbits for those looking for a little animal companionship (by the way, pets are allowed, so you can also bring your own). The management tries to avoid neighborly conflict by splitting up the campers into areas: Spaniards in one area, teens in another, etc.

Rodalies: Mataró. Free shuttle from Mataró train station to campground every hr. 9:10am-11:10pm. Bus #N82 stops outside the campground every hr. 11pm-6am. The bus from the campground to Pl. Catalunya takes 45min., departs the campground daily at 9:15am, returns from Pl. Catalunya at 7:45pm July-Aug €3; Mar-Jun and Sep-Nov free. i 6A power supply access. Bike rental available. Free Wi-Fi. Free shuttle to Mataró Beach every 15-30min. $ €5.50-9.50 per person. 2-person bungalow and car €59-169; 4-person bungalow and car €79-169; 6-person bungalow and car €99-169. Electricity €4.25-5.50. Down payment of 35% and €150 deposit for bungalows. Reduced rates for longer stays. ⏰ Open Mar-Nov.

sights

Sights in Barcelona run the gamut from Cathedrals to *casas* to museums and more. Here's a brief overview of what each neighborhood has to offer. **El Gòtic** is Barcelona's most tourist-ridden neighborhood: despite the crowds of foreigners, however, the Gothic Quarter is filled with alley after alley of medieval charm. Beginning along the sea and cutting straight through to Pl. de Catalunya, **Las Ramblas** is Barcelona's world-famous tree-lined pedestrian throughfare that attracts thousands of visitors daily. **El Born** is a sight in itself, with ancient streets surrounded by sloping buildings or crumbling arches suddenly opening onto secluded *placetes*. **El Raval** has its own beauties, from the medieval Hospital de la Santa Creu i Sant Pau to the present day artwork housed in the modern buildings of MACBA and CCCB. **L'Eixample's** sights are mostly composed of marvelous examples of *modernista* architecture; in particular, the Sagrada Família is a must-see. **Barceloneta** is filled with Catalan pride, from the red-and-yellow flags hanging on apartment balconies to the museum devoted to Catalonia and its history. **Gràcia** contains the epic mountain-*modernista*-retreat Parc Güell, as well as a few independent examples of this historic Barcelonan style. Finally, **Montjuïc**—you know, that big hill with the castle on it that you can see from just about anywhere in Barcelona—is home to some phenomenal museums, a model Spanish village, and, of course, that **castle.**

BARRI GÒTIC AND LAS RAMBLAS

barri gòtic

El Gòtic is Barcelona's most tourist-ridden neighborhood. Despite the crowds of foreigners, the Gothic Quarter is filled with alley after alley of medieval charm. The neighborhood is so convoluted that some areas still manage to remain largely unsullied by tourists; good luck finding them!

👍 MUSEU D'HISTÒRIA DE LA CIUTAT — HISTORY, ROMAN RUINS

Pl. Rei — ☎932 56 21 00; www.museuhistoria.bcn.es

If you thought the winding streets of the Barri Gòtic were old school, check out the Museu d'Història de la Ciutat's Roman ruins, hidden 20m underneath Pl. del Rei. Beneath the medieval plaza lies the excavation site of the archaeological remains of ancient Barcino, the Roman city from which Barcelona evolved; get into the elevator/time-machine that's so cheesy it's awesome (who needs a DeLorean?) and go back in time as you descend in altitude. Once under the plaza, a massive ruin lies before you, with elevated walks allowing you to pass through the entire site. One thing has remained the same since Roman times—the people of Barcelona love their booze, and huge ceramic wine flasks can be seen dotting the intricate floor mosaics in the strikingly well-preserved ruins dating from the first to sixth centuries CE. The second part of the museum features the comparatively new **Palacio Reial Major,** a 14th-century palace for Catalan-Aragonese monarchs, built in part using materials from the fourth-century CE Roman walls. Inside the palace, the expansive and impressively empty Gothic **Saló de Tinell** (Throne Room) is the seat of legend: here Columbus was received by Fernando and Isabel after his journey to the New World. The **Capilla de Santa Àgata** avoids the fame of kitschy tales and goes right for the goods, hosting rotating exhibits about modern Barcelona.

⇄ [M]Jaume I. ℹ Free multilingual audio guides. $ Museum and exhibition €7, students and ages 16-25 €5, under 16 free. ⏰ Open Apr-Oct Tu-Sa 10am-7pm, Su 10am-8pm; Nov-Mar Tu-Sa 10am-5pm, Su 10am-8pm.

👍 AJUNTAMENT DE BARCELONA (CITY HALL) — GOVERNMENT

Pl. Sant Jaume, enter on C. Font de Sant Miquel — ☎934 02 70 00; www.bcn.es

The stolid 18th-century Neoclassical facade facing the Pl. Sant Jaume hides a more interesting 15th-century Gothic one, located at the old entrance to the left of the building (where the tourist office is on C. Ciutat). You can only get into the City Hall building on Sundays 10am-1:30pm, or if you get voted in (municipal elections are usually held in May), but once you're inside, it's marvelous. The lower level of this bureaucratic palace is home to many pieces of sculpture from modern Catalan masters, while the upper level showcases elaborate architecture, vivid stained glass, and lavish rooms like the *Saló de Cent,* from which the *Consell de Cent* (Council of One Hundred) ruled the city from 1372 to 1714.

⇄ [M]Jaume I. Follow C. Jaume I to Pl. Sant Jaume; City Hall is on your left. ℹ Tourist info available at entrance. To enter, take alley to the left of City Hall and take a right onto C. Font de Sant Miquel. $ Free. ⏰ Open Su 10am-1:30pm. Tours every 30min. in Spanish or Catalan.

CATEDRAL DE BARCELONA — CATHEDRAL

Pl. Seu — ☎933 42 82 60; www.catedralbcn.org

Behold: la Catedral de la Santa Creu i Santa Eulàlia (the Cathedral of the Holy Cross and Saint Eulalia, or La Seu, for short) and its ever-present construction accoutrements. This is Barcelona's only cathedral and it is a marvel of beauty and perseverance. The impressive scaffolding rig and skeletal spire drawing attention away from the Gothic facade are actually signs of what you'll see advertised with the "Sponsor a Stone" campaign in the interior—costly renovations that began in 2005 and are racing at a snail's pace to beat the construction on the Sagrada

Família. The cathedral is no stranger to drawn-out construction projects, though. Work on the cathedral began in 1298, but the main building wasn't finished until 1460, the front facade until 1889, and the central spire until 1913.

Once you've been funneled through the scaffolding and into the main interior, almost all signs of construction disappear. Soaring vaulted ceilings mark the nave, and decadent chapels—28 in all—line the central space. The most important of these chapels is the *cathedra* (bishop's throne). Found on the altar, the *cathedra* designates this building as a cathedral. Don't miss the crypt of St. Eulàlia, located at the bottom of the stairs in front of the altar.

To the right of the altar is the entrance to the cloister, a chapel-laden courtyard enclosing palm trees and 13 white ducks meant to remind visitors of St. Eulàlia's age at the time of her martyrdom. Here you will find the cathedral's museum, which hides various religious paintings and altarpieces in various stages of restoration; a very gold monstrance (used during communion); and, in the Sala Capitular, Bartolomé Bermejo's *Pietà*. If you only have a couple of euro to spend, take the lift to the terrace instead—you'll get up close and personal with one of the church's spires and find yourself with a churchbell's-eye view of the city.

� ⓜ*Jaume I. From the Metro, go left onto Via Laietana and then left onto Avda. Catedral.* ⓢ *Cathedral free. Museum €2. Elevator to terrace €2.50.* ⓩ *Free admission to Cathedral M-F 8am-12:45pm and 5:15-7:30pm, Sa 8am-12:45pm and 5:15-8pm, Su 8am-1:45pm and 5:15-8pm. Inquire about guided visit to museum, choir, rooftop terraces, and towers, as hours vary.*

PALAU DE LA GENERALITAT   GOVERNMENT
Pl. Sant Jaume   ☎902 40 00 12; www.gencat.cat/generalitat/eng/guia/palau

Facing the Pl. de Sant Jaume and the Ajuntament, the Palau de la Generalitat provides a second reason explaining this plaza's incredible popularity with protestors and petitioners. The 17th-century exterior conceals a Gothic structure that was obtained by the Catalan government in 1400. Although the majority of visitors will be stuck admiring its wonderfully authoritative feel from the exterior, with a bit of magic in the way of good timing and advance planning, it's possible to see the interior. There, visitors will find a Gothic gallery, an orange tree courtyard, St. George's Chapel, a bridge to the house of the President of the Generalitat, many historic sculptures and paintings, and the **Palau's carillon,** a 4898kg instrument consisting of 49 bells that is played on holidays and during special events.

✝ ⓜ*Jaume I. Take C. Jaume I after exiting the station. Once in Pl. Sant Jaume, Palau is on your right.* ⓢ *Free.* ⓩ *Open to the public on Apr 23, Sept 11, and Sept 24, and on 2nd and 4th Su of each month from 10am-2pm. Make reservations online at least 2 weeks in advance.*

GRAN TEATRE DEL LICEU   THEATER
Las Ramblas, 51-59   ☎934 85 99 00; www.liceubarcelona.com

Though La Rambla itself is one of Europe's grandest stages, the highbrow Liceu specializes in opera and classical music. The Baroque interior of the auditorium will leave you gawking at the fact that it dates to 1999, when it was reconstructed following a 1995 fire—you can't say they don't make 'em like they used to. A 20min. tour provides a glimpse of the ornate *Sala de Espejos* (Room of Mirrors), where Apollo and the Muses look down upon opera-goers during intermission, and the five-story auditorium, where, if you're lucky, you may catch a director yelling furiously during a rehearsal. For a more in-depth tour that won't leave you spending half of your time looking at stackable chairs in the foyer or being told about the donors list (though it does include the venerable Plácido Domingo), come for the 1hr. tour at 10am, arrange a behind-the-scenes tour with the box office, or attend a performance in person.

✝ ⓜ*Liceu.* ⓘ *Discounted tickets available.* ⓢ *20min. tour €4, 1hr. tour €8.* ⓩ *Box office open M-F 2-8:30pm. 20min. tours start every 30min. daily 11:30am-1pm; 1hr. tour daily at 10am.*

sights

las ramblas

Beginning along the sea and cutting straight through to Pl. Catalunya, Las Ramblas is Barcelona's world-famous tree-lined pedestrian throughfare that attracts thousands of visitors daily. Marked by shady trees, cafes, tourist traps, human statues, beautiful buildings, animal vendors, and ever-present pickpockets, the five distinct promenades combine seamlessly to create the most lively and exciting pedestrian area in Barcelona—perhaps in all of Europe. The *ramblas,* in order from Pl. Catalunya to the Columbus Monument are: **La Rambla de les Canaletes, La Rambla dels Estudis, La Rambla de Sant Josep, La Rambla dels Caputxins,** and **La Rambla de Santa Mònica.**

COLUMBUS MONUMENT — TOWER

Portal Pau — ☎933 02 52 24

The *Mirador de Colom,* at the coastal end of Las Ramblas, offers a phenomenal view of the city and a heart attack for those afraid of heights, small spaces, or tourists. The 60m statue was constructed 1882-88 for Barcelona's World's Fair in order to commemorate Christopher Columbus meeting in Barcelona with King Ferdinand and Queen Isabella upon his return from the New World. Though some say the 7.2m statue at the top of the tower points west to the Americas, it actually points east, supposedly to his hometown of Genoa. Reliefs around the base of the column depict the journey, as do bronze lions that are guaranteed to be mounted by tourists on any given hour.

 # [M]Drassanes. Entrance located in base facing water. [$] €4, seniors and children €3. ⏰ Open daily May-Oct 9am-7:30pm, Nov-Apr 9am-6:30pm.

LA RAMBLA DE LES CANALETES — PROMENADE

The head of Las Ramblas when walking from Pl. Catalunya to the water, this *rambla* is named after the fountain that marks its start: Font de les Canaletes. Surprisingly unceremonious, the fountain is not a spewing spectacle of lights and water jets but instead a fancy drinking fountain with four spouts, rumored to make those who drink its water fall in love with the city. These days the fountain has (amusingly) run dry, so you'll have to fill your Nalgene elsewhere, sans love potion.

 # [M]Catalunya.

LA RAMBLA DELS ESTUDIS — PROMENADE

Named for the university that was once located here, the path is now closer to a lesson in animal taxonomy than more philosophical topics. Known colloquially as "Las Ramblas dels Ocells" (literally, "of the birds"), the shops along this stretch of pavement sell everything from rabbits to guinea pigs, iguanas to turtles, ducks to parrots, and much more. Here's your chance to pick up a pigeon, and, with some good training, you may soon be able to sidestep Spain's postal service. This area has understandably become a target of Barcelona's active and outraged animal rights proponents, but there seems to be no indication that La Rambla dels Estudis will be any less furry, fluffy, feathery, or adorable anytime soon.

 # [M]Catalunya. Walk toward the water.

LA RAMBLA DE SANT JOSEP — PROMENADE

If you're looking for a bouquet for that special someone, or you've just decided that your hostel bed could really benefit from a few rose petals, La Rambla de Sant Josep is your place. Flower shops line this stretch of the pedestrian avenue, giving it the nickname "La Rambla de les Flors." Boqueria market (see **Food**) is also found along this stretch, along with the once grand but now practically gutted **Betlem Church.** The end of this promenade is marked by Joan Miró's mosaic in the pavement at Pl. Boqueria.

 # [M]Liceu. Walk toward Pl. Catalunya.

LA RAMBLA DELS CAPUTXINS — PROMENADE

La Rambla dels Caputxins boasts access to [M]Liceu and a straight shot to the Pl. Sant Jaume via C. Ferran, which runs directly through the center of the Gothic Quarter. Cafes and restaurants line this portion of Las Ramblas, and eager business owners will try desperately to pull you into their lair—if "tapas" and specials listed in English and 10 other languages don't do it first. Littered with eye candy such as the **Casa Bruno Cuadros** (corner of C. Boqueria and Las Ramblas, the one with the 👍**dragon** in front), Teatre Liceu, and a mosaic by Joan Miró, this portion of Las Ramblas is often the busiest.

➜ *[M]Liceu. Walk toward the sea.*

LA RAMBLA DE SANTA MÒNICA — PROMENADE

Ending at the feet of Christopher Columbus himself, La Rambla de Santa Mònica leads the promenade to the waterfront. This portion of the path is the widest and, unlike its saintly name would suggest, the most packed with vices and temptation. Filled with artists peddling their takes on Miró, your face, or dolphins in the shape of letters during the day, at night the area becomes thick with aggressive prostitutes. In the same debaucherous spirit, Santa Mònica is also the go-to *Rambla* for peep shows.

➜ *[M]Drassanes.*

EL BORN

This part of the *ciutat vella* is a sight in itself, with ancient streets surrounded by sloping buildings or crumbling arches suddenly opening onto secluded *placetes*. In addition to the joys of just walking through the neighborhood, there are certain sights you just can't miss.

👍 PALAU DE LA MÚSICA CATALANA — MUSIC HALL

C. Palau de la Música, 4-6 — ☎902 44 28 82; www.palaumusica.org

Home to both Barcelona's Orfeó Choir and the Catalan musical spirit, the Palau is Barcelona's most spectacular music venue. But forget about saving up for a live concert—the building itself is the sight to behold. Lluís Domènech i Montaner, contemporary of Gaudí and architect of the **Hospital de Sant Pau, Casa Fuster,** and the 👍**Castell dels Tres Dragons,** crafted this awe-inspiring *modernista* masterpiece from the humble materials of brick, ceramic, stone, iron, and glass. True to the *modernista* movement's principles, the building (1905-08) is covered inside and out with organic motifs. It's hard to get a good view of the outside because of the narrow width of the streets flanking the structure, but the stunning interior more than makes up for this shortcoming. The breathtaking inverted dome of the stained-glass ceiling and the tall stained-glass windows make the luminous interior shimmer. Columns pose as abstracted trees, while intricate ceramic flowers decorate the ceiling. Behind the stage, angelic muses emerge from the walls, part flat ceramic tiles, part stone sculpture. Above and around the stage, angels interact with trees, the riding Valkyries, and musicians such as Wagner and Beethoven. Back in commission after a 30-year hiatus, the Palau's 3772-pipe organ stands front and center in the upper portion of the hall. The Palau offers reduced-admission concerts regularly, but if you're dying to hear the legendary acoustics, just ask your tour guide—chances are they'll play a pre-programmed song on the organ for your group.

➜ *[M]Jaume I. On Via Laietana, walk toward the Cathedral for about 5min. and then take a right onto C. Sant Pere Mas Alt. Palau de la Música Catalana will be on the left.* ***i*** *Schedule of events and ticketing info on website.* [$] *Guided tours €12, students €10.* ⏰ *Guided tours 50min. daily 10am-3:30pm, with English every hr. and Catalan and Spanish every 30min. Aug and Easter week tours 10am-6pm. Box office open 9am-9pm.*

MUSEU PICASSO — MUSEUM

C. Montcada, 15-23 ☎932 56 30 00; www.museupicasso.bcn.es

Tucked away among the bodegas and medieval charms of the old city is the Museu Picasso—five beautiful connected mansions dedicated to showcasing Picasso's entire career, not just the funky faces with eyes in all the wrong places. Works from his early years are organized chronologically, providing insight into his development. Paintings from his time in Paris and afterward show the French influence, while several works from his Blue and Rose periods help to—literally—paint a picture of his past. The museum also contains a work whose title (unclear whether it was Picasso's or added later) represents the greatest disjunction between image and description yet encountered by *Let's Go:* a small but graphic depiction of two women *in flagrante*—and in ecstasy—is dubbed *Two Women and A Cat.* The highlight of the collection is easily the room of the artist's 58 renditions of Velázquez's *Las Meninas,* where the iconic work is spiked and contorted into a nightmarish landscape of typically Picasso forms. Temporary exhibits highlight the work of Picasso's contemporaries, providing some context for the permanent collection. Expect a long wait along the crowded C. Montcada any day of the week but especially on Sundays when the museum is free. To beat the throngs, try hitting up the museum early or waiting until the later hours.

➔ From [M]Jaume I, walk down C. Princesa and turn right onto C. Montcada. $ Admission €10, 16-24 and retired €6, under 16 and teachers free. 1st Su of each month free, other Su free after 3pm. ⏰ Open Tu-Su 10am-8pm. Last entry 30min. before close.

PARC DE LA CIUTADELLA — PARK, MUSEUM

Between Pg. Picasso, C. Pujades, and C. Wellington

Once the site of a Spanish fortress built by King Philip V in the 18th century, the park was transformed into its current state after the citadel was leveled in preparation for the Universal Exhibition of 1888. This sprawling complex designed by Josep Fontserè includes plenty of green space as well as various *modernista* buildings. Points of architectural interest are located in two areas: the old fort holds the governor's palace (now a medical school), the arsenal (today home of the **Parlament de Catalunya**), and chapel, while the 1888 Exhibition area showcases century-old gems. Many of these are still in use today: the steel and glass **Hivernacle,** a greenhouse-turned-civic-space near the Pujades entrance, maintains its original function as well as its newer one as a concert venue. The **Natural History Museum** (Museu de Ciències Naturals ☎933 19 69 12) continues to educate crowds and complete conservation work. The **Museu Martorell** functions as a geology museum, and the **Castell dels Tres Dragons,** designed by Lluís Domènech i Montaner (of Palau de la Música Catalana and Hospital de Santa Creu fame) houses the **Zoological Museum** and the entrance to the **Barcelona Zoo** (☎902 45 75 45; www.zoobarcelona.cat). The extravagant **Cascada Monumental** fountain, designed in part by Antoni Gaudí, still provides a spectacle. Though a newer addition, the mastodon near the entrance of the zoo makes for an excellent photo op.

For those just looking to use the park as, well, a park, bike trails run around the exterior walls, and dirt pedestrian paths break up the lush grass and tree-shaded pockets. Expect to see nearly every corner covered in picnickers during the summer months, and be sure to stop by and join the locals for a bath in the fountain. Most awesome is that the typical pigeons are joined by quite atypical green parrots.

➔ [M]Arc de Triomf. Walk through the arch and down the boulevard to enter the park. ℹ Free Wi-Fi available at the Geological Museum, Parliament building, and Zoological Museum. $ Park free. Museums €4.10-7, Su 3-8pm free. Zoo €17. ⏰ Park open daily 10am-dusk. Natural History Museum open Tu-F 10am-7pm, Sa-Su 10am-8pm. Zoo open daily May 16-Sept 15 10am-7pm; Sept 16-Oct 29 10am-6pm; Oct 30-Mar 26 10am-5pm; Mar 27-May 15 10am-6pm.

DISSENY HUB BARCELONA (DHUB)
C. Montcada, 12

☎932 56 23 00; www.dhub-bcn.cat

Split over two buildings nearly a town apart, Disseny Hub Barcelona showcases Barcelona's cutting edge contemporary art with a commercial twist through historical displays, video supplements, and a creative laboratory that fosters the budding designer in even the least creative visitor. The **Montcada branch,** located across from the Museu Picasso, houses temporary exhibitions of design and fashion. Just across town, its sister museum in the Palau de Pedralbes hosts the **Museu de les Arts Decoratives** and the **Museu Tèxtil i d'Indumentària** (Avda. Diagonal, 686 ☎932 56 34 65), both of which highlight the evolution of art objects and fashion from the Romanesque to the Industrial Revolution with enough quirky artifacts and period dress to make it worth the trek. Currently, DHUB's ground-floor exhibition space on C. Montcada is free while the Pedralbes branch costs €5 (free 1st Su of month, other Su 3-6pm), but look for both to be housed under the same roof in the upcoming year as the primary home of the Disseny Hub Barcelona is finished in Pl. Glòries Catalanes. There's currently a model of DHUB's future home on display, and, when it opens, it will be one handsome museum.

⚑ *Montcada: From* Ⓜ*Jaume I, walk down C. Princesa and turn right onto C. Montcada. Pedralbes:* Ⓜ*Palau Reial.* *i* *New combined museum to open in 2012 in Pl. Glòries.* Ⓢ *Free.* ⓩ *Montcada open Tu-F 11am-7pm, Su 11am-8pm. Pedralbes open Tu-Su 10am-6pm.*

ARC DE TRIOMF
Between Pg. Lluís Companys and Pg. Sant Joan

For a proper greeting from the city of Barcelona, be sure to arrive by bus and get dropped off at the **Arc de Triomf Station.** If you're coming by other means, cheat and come here anyway. At first glance you'll know that this is most definitely not Paris's Arc de Triomphe; the differences between the two encapsulate why Paris is Paris and Barcelona is awesome. Situated at the beginning of a wide boulevard leading to the **Parc de la Ciutadella,** the arch not only frames the palm tree- and *modernista*-building-lined road and its incredible terminus but also literally embraces visitors with a sculptural frieze by Josep Reynés inscribed with the phrase *"Barcelona rep les nacions,"* or "Barcelona welcomes the nations." This declaration was made with the arch's construction for the 1888 Universal Exhibition, when it served as the main entrance to the fairgrounds in the Parc.

Today the arch serves as little more than a historical artifact, but it's worth a look if you're in the area. The triumphant brick arch was designed by Josep Jilaseca i Cassanovas in the Moorish revival style. Its exterior is decked out with sculptures of 12 women representing fame and a relief by Josep Lllimona that depicts the award ceremony.

⚑ Ⓜ*Arc de Triomf.* Ⓢ *Free.*

EL RAVAL

🏛 PALAU GÜELL
C. Nou de la Rambla, 3-5

☎934 72 57 75; www.palauguell.cat

Commissioned by Eusebi Güell, the wealthy industrialist of Parc Güell fame, Güell Palace was designed by Antoni Gaudí and completed in 1888. The Palau Güell holds the distinction of being the only building that Gaudí himself completed, and it hasn't been significantly altered since, though it reopened in May 2011 after being closed for restoration. Palau Güell represents an early phase in Gaudí's career in which he began to develop his own architectural style. Its roots in the Islamic-Hispanic architectural tradition are visible in many of the windows, which look like Moorish horseshoe arched windows that have been elongated and smoothed out with a typical Gaudí twist. Be sure to look up in the Saló Central to see another example of this: tiny holes in the conical ceiling

sights

allow in rays of light, reminiscent of an Arabesque bath. The rooftop is perhaps the most impressive aspect of the palace, with its colorful, typically Gaudían ceramic-tiled chimneys.

🚶 Ⓜ️Liceu. Walk toward the water on Las Ramblas and take a right onto C. Nou de la Rambla. *i* Rooftop closed when raining. Ⓢ €10, students €8. Free 1st Su of month. Audio tour free. 🕐 Open Tu-Su Apr-Sep 10am-8pm; Oct-Mar 10am-5:30pm. Last entry 1hr. before close.

🏛️ MUSEU D'ART CONTEMPORANI DE BARCELONA (MACBA)　　　　MUSEUM
Pl. Àngels, 1　　　　　　　　　　　　　　　　　☎934 12 08 10; www.macba.cat

If the teeny art galleries and student-studded restaurants around El Raval have struck your fancy, consider checking out the culture hub that helped spawn them. Bursting out of the narrow streets and into its own spacious plaza, American architect Richard Meier's bright white geometric building has made an indelible mark on the land, both literally and figuratively, by turning the area into a regional cultural and artistic center. The stark, simple interior displays an impressive collection of contemporary art, with particular emphasis on Spanish and Catalan artists, including a world-renowned collection of the interwar avant-garde and a selection of works by Miró and Tàpies. With its prime location near the Universitat and its undeniable appeal to local youth, MACBA prides itself on hip happenings, so check the website to see if there are any evening events coming up. As if these weren't enough, the museum completely transforms during Barcelona's Sónar music festival every year, converting into the Sónar Complex stage and denying admittance to those without a festival ticket.

🚶 Ⓜ️Universitat. Walk down C. Pelai, take the 1st right and then turn left onto C. Tallers. Take a right onto C. Valldonzella and a left onto C. Montalegre. *i* Admission includes English-language tour. Ⓢ Entrance to all exhibits €7.50, students €6. Temporary exhibits €6, students €4.50. 1-year pass €12. 🕐 Open June 24-Sept 24 M 11am-8pm, W-F 11am-8pm, Sa 10am-8pm, Su 10am-3pm; Sept 25-June 23 M 11am-7:30pm, W-F 11am-7:30pm, Sa 10am-8pm, Su 10am-3pm.

L'EIXAMPLE

🏛️ CASA BATLLÓ　　　　　　　　　　　　　　　　　　ARCHITECTURE
Pg. de Gràcia, 43　　　　　　　　　　　　　　☎932 16 03 06; www.casabatllo.es

From the spinal-column stairwell that holds together the scaly building's interior to the undulating dragon's back curve of the ceramic rooftop to the skull-like balconies on the facade, the Casa Batlló will have you wondering what kinds of drugs Gaudí was on and where one might go about acquiring them. This remarkable building has hardly a right angle inside or out; every surface—stone, wood, glass, anything—is soft and molten. This architectural wonderland was once an apartment complex for the fantastically rich and is now the busiest of the three *modernista* marvels in the **Manzana de la Discòrdia** on Pg. de Gràcia. A free audio tour lets you navigate the dream-like space at your own pace, so be sure to spend some time with the curved wood and two-toned stained glass of each of the doors (from both sides—the glass changes color), the soft scaled pattern of the softly bowed walls, and the swirly light fixture that pulls at the entire ceiling, rippling into its center. Gaudí's design ranges from the incredibly rational to the seemingly insane, including a blue lightwell that passes from deep navy at the top to sky blue below in order to distribute light more evenly.

🚶 Ⓜ️Passeig de Gràcia. Walk away from Pl. Catalunya on Pg. de Gràcia; Casa Batlló is on the left. *i* Tickets available at box office or through TelEntrada. Admission includes audio tour. Ⓢ €18.15, students and BCN cardholders €14.55. 🕐 Open daily 9am-8pm.

🏛️ SAGRADA FAMÍLIA　　　　　　　　　　　　　　　ARCHITECTURE
C. Mallorca, 401　　　　　　　　　　　　　　☎932 08 04 14; www.sagradafamilia.cat

If you know Barcelona, you know the Sagrada Família—its eight completed towers and fanciful forms befitting its Gaudí nametag have been plastered on tourist magazines, featured in movies, and included in every panorama of the city ever photographed in the modern era. And 130 years of construction have made the cranes surrounding the Sagrada Família complex as iconic as the church itself.

Although still very much a work in progress, Sagrada Família's construction began way back in 1882. The super-pious, super-conservative Spiritual Association for Devotion to St. Joseph (or the Josephines) commissioned the building as a reaction to the liberal ideas spreading through Europe in the decades prior. It was intended as an Expiatory Temple for Barcelona in commemoration of the sacred family—Mary, Jesus, and Joseph. The Josephines originally picked Diocesan architect Francisco de Paula del Villar, but the relationship quickly soured, and one year later, after the Gothic foundations had already been laid, the church replaced Villar with Gaudí.

At the time of his employment, Gaudí was just 30 years old, and he would continue to work on the building until his death over 40 years later. Modest private donations funded the construction of the church in the beginning, but after the completion of the **crypt** in 1889, the church received an incredibly generous private donation that allowed Gaudí to step up his game. This extra cash gave birth to the design that would make the building both the most ambitious and the most difficult to complete in Barcelona. After building the **Nativity Facade,** a drop in private donations slowed construction, and in 1909 temporary schools were built next to the church for workers' children. Gaudí set up shop on-site a few years later, working next to his incomplete masterpiece until his brutal death by tram just outside of the church's walls in 1926. He was buried inside the **Carmen Chapel** of the crypt.

Gaudí's bizarre demise marked the start of a tragic period for the temple. The Civil War brought construction entirely to a halt, and in 1936 arsonists raided Gaudí's tomb, smashed the plaster models of the site, and burned every document in the workshop, effectively destroying all records of the architect's design. Since then, plans for the construction have been based on the few remaining reconstructed plaster models, and, more recently, on computer analyses of Gaudí's complex mathematics. Currently, the building remains under the auspices of the Josephines, and architect **Jordi Bonet,** whose father worked directly with Gaudí, is in charge of the overall direction.

The Cubist **Passion Facade** faces Pl. Sagrada Família, and was completed by Josep Marià Subirachs in 1998. Its angular and abstracted forms are a far cry from Gaudí's 1911 plans for the facade and provide a stark contrast to his more traditional Nativity Facade. The first mass was held inside the then-gutted church in 2000 for celebration of the millennium, and the interior was completed in 2010; on November 7, 2010, Pope Benedict XVI consecrated the Sagrada Família as a basilica.

If all goes well, the projected completion date is 2030, but we wouldn't bet on it. The final structure will look radically different from what you see today: there will be two more facades of four towers, with five even taller towers in the middle around one massive tower that will be almost twice as tall as those already standing. Until that glorious and perhaps apocryphal day arrives, drawings and projections of the completed building can be seen in the adjacent museum, and an exhibit dedicated to the mathematical models lets you imagine the completed building.

✦ Ⓜ Sagrada Família. *i* Towers closed during rain. Ⓢ €13, students €11, under 10 free. Elevator €2.50. Audio tour €4. Combined ticket with Casa-Museu Gaudí (in Parc Güell) €15, students €14. ☏ Open daily Apr-Sept 9am-8pm; Oct-Mar 9am-6pm. Last elevator to the tower 15min. before close. Guided tours in English May-Oct at 11am, 1, 3, and 4pm; Nov-Apr at 11am and 1pm.

sights

La Sagrada Família is a popular tourist stop for most travelers in Barcelona. But more interesting than the Church itself is Gaudí's taste in models. In hopes of finding inspiration for the donkey carrying Mary and Jesus in the main portal, the architect viewed the finest asses in Barcelona, but was displeased with all of them. Eventually he settled on modeling an old donkey that belonged to a woman who sold sand. Humble donkey carrying a humble cargo—appropriate.

For the scene of the soldier and the innocents on the Nativity facade of the church, Gaudí used the corpses of dead 2-to-3-day-old babies, and for his soldier he used a man with 11 toes. Try to identify the six-toed guy among an array of other crazy Gaudí sculptures.

CASA MILÀ (LA PEDRERA)
ARCHITECTURE

Pg. de Gràcia, 92; C. Provença, 261-265   ☎934 84 59 00; www.lapedreraeducacio.org

No, this building's facade didn't melt in the Barcelona sun, though it has garnered some equally unflattering theories. Its nickname "La Pedrera" literally means "the quarry," and stems from popular jokes, criticism, and caricatures about the house upon its construction a century ago. Wealthy businessman Pere Milà hired Gaudí after being impressed by his nearby Casa Battló, but his wife began to loathe this building as construction progressed and eventually refused to let the costly venture proceed. Not one to let a difficult couple have the last word, Gaudí sued the rich pair over fees and gave his winnings from the suit to the poor. Not ones to let Gaudí have the last say, the couple then looked elsewhere to complete their home's interior, making La Pedrera the only house designed by Gaudí that isn't graced by his furniture.

La Pedrera still functions as a home for the rich, famous, and patient—the waitlist for an apartment is over two decades long—as well as the offices of the Caixa Catalunya bank. Many portions of the building are open to the public, including an apartment decorated with period furniture (true to the house, not designed by Gaudí) and the main floor. The attic, a space known as **Espai Gaudí**, boasts a mini-museum to the man himself, including helpful exhibits explaining the science behind his beloved caternary arches and what exactly it means for the architect to be "inspired by natural structures." Up top, a terrace holds the perfect photo op, whether it be with the desert-like sculptural outcroppings or of the view overlooking Barcelona to the Sagrada Família. During the summer, the terrace lights up with jazz performances on Friday and Saturday nights in a series known as *Nits d'Estiu a La Pedrera*.

✦ ⓂDiagonal. Walk down Pg. de Gràcia away from Avda. Diagonal; La Pedrera is on the right.
𝒊 Purchase tickets to Nits d'Estiu a La Pedrera online via Telentrada at www.telentrada.com.
Ⓢ €14, students and seniors €10. Audio tour €4. Nits d'Estiu a La Pedrera €25; includes access to Espai Gaudí. ⌚ Open daily Mar-Oct 9am-8pm; Nov-Feb 9am-6:30pm. Last entry 30min. before close. Concerts mid-June to late Aug, some F and Sa 8:30pm.

CASA AMATLLER
ARCHITECTURE

Pg. de Gràcia, 41   ☎934 96 12 45; www.amatller.org

The more rational—but no less whimsical—counterpart to Gaudí's neighboring acid-trip Casa Batlló, Casa Amatller was the first in the trio of buildings now known as the **Manzana de la Discòrdia**. In 1898, chocolate mogul Antoni Amatller commissioned **Josep Puig i Cadafalch** to build his palatial home along Pg. de Gràcia, and out popped a mix of Catalan, Neo-Gothic, Islamic, and Dutch architecture

barcelona

in a strict geometric plane. A carving of Sant Jordi battling that pesky dragon appears over the front door, accompanied by four figures engaged in painting, sculpting, and architecture. The building's entrance is free to see—note the ornate lamps and amazing stained-glass ceiling in the stairwell, created by the same artist that did the ceiling of the Palau de la Música Catalana. The rest of the building is even more spectacular and is well worth the €10 tour; unfortunately it is closed for restorations and isn't scheduled to reopen until 2013 (womp womp).

⚑ Ⓜ*Passeig de Gràcia. Walk away from Pl. Catalunya on Pg. de Gràcia; Casa Amatller is a couple of blocks up on the left.* ⓘ *Reservation by phone or email required for tour.* **Closed for restoration; expected to reopen in 2013.** Ⓢ *Tours €10.* Ⓩ *Guided tours M-F at 10am, 11am, noon, 1, 3, 4, 5, and 6pm.*

HOSPITAL DE LA SANTA CREU I SANT PAU   ARCHITECTURE
C. Sant Antoni Maria Claret, 167   ☎902 07 66 21; www.santpau.es

Considered the most important piece of *modernista* public architecture, this hospital is anything but *nouveau*. Dating back to 1401, the Hospital de la Santa Creu i Sant Pau is the newer embodiment of the medical practice formerly housed in the Antic Hospital de la Santa Creu in El Raval. Wealthy benefactor Pau Gil bequested funds for the building with strict instructions, including the name appendage. Construction then began in 1902 under the direction of Lluís Domènech i Montaner, who in almost Gaudían fashion, died before its completion. His son saw the work to fruition, giving the hospital 48 large pavilions connected by underground tunnels and bedazzled with luxurious modern sculptures and paintings. Although the hospital still functions as a world-class medical facility, you won't need to break a leg to appreciate its beauty. Guided tours (€10) are offered daily as a part of Barcelona's Ruta de Modernisme, or you can just waltz in and have a look around. Much of the complex is currently closed for renovation, but it's still worth a visit.

⚑ Ⓜ*Guinardó/Hospital de Sant Pau. Walk down C. Sant Quintí and turn right onto C. Sant Antoni Maria Claret.* Ⓢ *Free. Tours €10.* Ⓩ *Guided tours in English daily at 10, 11am, noon, and 1pm. Information desk open daily 9:30am-1:30pm.*

sights

torre agbar

There's no need to fear. That larger-than-life Technicolor bullet doesn't mean you've accidentally wandered into a groovy *Honey, I Shrunk the Tourists: Gaza Edition.* Go ahead and take off those vaguely hipster 3D movie glasses—but keep the golden buttery popcorn. Your stomach might hunger for a snack as your eyes drink in the architectural oddity that is the Torre Agbar.

Marking the entrance of Barcelona's blossoming technological district since 2005, the Torre Agbar wasted no time rushing into the international spotlight with some pretty shiny lights of its own. Though the architects have pointed to the nearby Montserrat mountain and an erupting geyser as inspiration, some Barcelonans point to the toilet with the nickname "El Supositori." The Torre Agbar's nocturnal illumination silences—or at least blinds—the local critics that harp in Catalan about the building's phallic and fecal resemblance.

The Torre Agbar is more than just a trophy wife—it has as much substance and style as Barcelona itself. True, the psychedelic interior may hold corporate offices. Nevertheless, the glittering multidimensional shell rises 38 stories as a beacon for the Catalan culture in central Barcelona (no glasses required).

FUNDACIÓ ANTONI TÀPIES — ARCHITECTURE, MUSEUM

C. Aragó, 255 — ☎934 87 03 15; www.fundaciotapies.org

Housed in a building by *modernista* architect Lluís Domènech i Montaner, the Fundació Antoni Tàpies is unmissable thanks to its mess of wire and steel atop the low brick roofline. Made by the museum's namesake, Antoni Tàpies, it's actually a sculpture entitled *Núvol i Cadira* (Cloud and Chair; 1990) that supposedly shows a chair jutting out of a large cloud. Once inside, the lowest and highest levels are dedicated to temporary exhibitions on modern and contemporary artists and themes—recent shows have included work by Eva Hesse and Steve McQueen—while the middle floors hold Tàpies' own work. Start upstairs and work your way down, watching the descent from Surrealistic-Symbolist beauty into a misshapen chaos of not so well-seeming forms.

➜ [M]Passeig de Gràcia. Walk uphill on Pg. de Gràcia and take a left onto C. Aragó. $ €7, students €5.60. Free May 18 and Sept 24. ⏰ Open Tu-Su 10am-7pm.

BARCELONETA

MUSEU D'HISTÒRIA DE CATALUNYA — MUSEUM

Pl. Pau Vila, 3 — ☎932 25 47 00; www.mhcat.net

If you've had "Catalonia is not Spain" pounded into your head without a proper explanation of what that could possibly mean, stop by the impressive, if slightly proselytizing, Museu d'Història de Catalunya. Located on the threshhold between the Old City and touristy Barceloneta, this informative museum doubles as regional propaganda, attempting to inform anyone and everyone about Catalonia's history, politics, and culture in a way that is both patriotic and informative. Hands-on and 3D displays, complete with English captions and vivid dioramas, recount the city's history and shed light on the layers of ruins that you've seen throughout the city. But this museum is more than a mere supplement to *Let's Go: Barcelona;* it's an introduction for the uninitiated and for Catalans alike to the unique identity of the region. The museum recounts Catalonia's history from prehistoric flint tools to the birth of Catalan (the first written use of the term is traced to the 12th century) to Franco's crackdown on the region, followed by Catalonia's subsequent resurgence after the Generalíssimo's demise. Don't be surprised if you walk out of this museum wrapped in the *senyera* (Catalonia's flag).

➜ [M]Barceloneta. Museum is located along the water on Pg. Joan de Borbó. $ €4, students and under 18 €3, college students free with ID. 1st Su of month free. ⏰ Open Tu 10am-7pm, W 10am-8pm, Th-Sa 10am-7pm, Su 10am-2:30pm. Last entry 30min. before close.

GRÀCIA

Some of the most defining features of Gràcia's cityscape are the cafe-lined **plaças** that seem to appear out of nowhere around every corner. The **Plaça de la Vila de Gràcia** (also known as Pl. Rius i Taulet) is one of the largest and most beautiful, with a massive 19th-century clocktower ([M]Fontana; take a left down C. Gran de Gràcia and then a left onto C. Sant Domènec). With your back to the powder-blue municipal building, head up the street running along the right side of the plaza, and in a few blocks you'll get to the **Plaça del Sol,** the neighborhood's most lively square, especially at night. Two blocks east of that (follow C. Ramon i Cajal) is the **Plaça de la Revolució de Setembre de 1868,** a long, open square with the word "Revolució" engraved in the pavement. Head up C. Verdi from Pl. Revolució de Setembre 1868 and take a left at the third intersection, which will bring you to the shady **Plaça del Diamant,** while a right will bring you to the true gem that is the **Plaça de la Virreina.**

Main entrance on C. Olot

Now a mecca for countless tourists and outdoor- or architecture-loving locals, Parc Güell was originally intended for the eyes of a select few. Catalan industrialist, patron of the arts, and all-around man of disgusting wealth Eusebi Güell called upon his go-to architect Antoni Gaudí in 1900 to collaborate on a project completely unlike previous commissions. The patron envisioned a luxurious community of 60 lavish homes enclosed by an English-inspired Eden overlooking Barcelona—rich, elite, and pleasantly removed from the city and its riffraff. Unfortunately for Güell and his endeavor, other members of Barcelona's upper class weren't convinced; they weren't about to abandon the amenities of the city for a cut-off hunk of grass dotted by Gaudí's seemingly deranged buildings, which at the time lacked even basic luxuries. Construction came to a halt in 1914, with only two homes completed: Güell's and Gaudí's. In 1918, the Barcelona City Council bought the property and made it into a park. It was opened to the public in 1923 and has since been declared a UNESCO World Heritage Site. Buses bring flocks of visitors directly to the **Palmetto Gate,** a structure flanked by a giftshop and guardhouse-turned-museum (the one that looks like a gingerbread house on LSD). Musicians in the acoustically remarkable alcove across from the guardhouse provide ethereal soundtracks for most visits. Those with sturdy shoes and no fear of heights often choose to take the Metro and climb the escalators to the nature-clad side entrance (from Avda. República Argentina, take C. Agramunt, which becomes Baixada Glòria).

The park's main attractions are the brightly colored mosaics and fountains, such as the colorful drac (dragon) fountain just across from Palmetto Gate. The pillar forest of the **Hall of One Hundred Columns (Teatre Griego)**—dotted with sculptural pendants by Josep Maria Jujol, musicians, and vendors peddling fake handbags—has come close to its intended purpose as the garden-city's marketplace. The intricate vaults of the hall support the **Plaça de la Nauturalesa,** which is enclosed by the winding serpentine bench decked out in colorful ceramics, including 21 distinct shades of white that were castoffs from the **Casa Milà.** If you catch yourself wondering how a ceramic bench can be so comfortable, thank the woman rumored to have sat bare-bottomed in clay for Jujol to provide the form.

Paths to the park's summit provide amazing views, and one in particular showcases what the park has to offer aside from the spectacular entrance: walk to the right when facing the dragon fountain from its base. Follow the wide path and veer right toward the shaded benches, continuing uphill to come across the **Casa-Museu Gaudí** (C. d 'Olot, 7 ☎934 57 22 84; www.casa-museugaudi.org) where the architect lived for about two decades. As you continue, another original building of the complex, Juli Batllevell's **Casa Trias** lies inconspicuously ahead, still privately owned by the Domènech family. Continuing on the long, winding route, **El Turó de les Tres Creus** greets visitors at the top of the path. This, the park's highest point with appropriately incredible views, was originally intended to be the residents' church and now serves instead to mark the end of the ascent—or the beginning of the descent, if you arrive from the Baixada de la Glòria.

Although the main areas of the park are regularly full during the dog days of summer, it's possible to ditch the toddlers and fannypacks by showing up at or before the park's opening—chances are they won't turn you away, and, even if you have to wait, at least there's an incredible view to enjoy while you do so.

✝ Ⓜ︎Lesseps. Walk uphill on Travessera Dalt and take a left to ride escalators. Or Ⓜ︎Vallcarca. Walk down Avda. República Argentina and take a right onto C. Agramunt, which becomes the partially

sights

be-escalatored Baixada Glòria. Bus #24 from Pl. Catalunya stops just downhill from the park. ⑤ Free. Guardhouse €2, students €1.50. Free Su after 3pm and 1st Su of month. Casa-Museu Gaudí €5.50, students €4.50. ✪ Park open daily May-Aug 10am-9pm; Sept 10am-8pm; Oct 10am-7pm, Nov-Feb 10am-6pm; Mar 10am-7pm; Apr 10am-8pm. Guardhouse open daily Apr-Oct 10am-8pm; Nov-Mar 10am-4pm. Casa-Museu Gaudí open daily Apr-Sept 10am-8pm; Oct-Mar 10am-6pm.

CASA VICENS   ARCHITECTURE
C. Carolines, 24
Built in the 1880s for wealthy industrialist Manuel Vicens, this house is Antoni Gaudí's first major work. Though lacking the fluid forms that would character- ize his later projects, Casa Vicens hardly lacks his typical exuberance: colored tiles, made in Vicens' factory, cover the eclectic neo-Moorish facade. While you can't visit the interior, this private residence is up for sale—the asking price at time of writing is rumored to be around €27 million. So you can always pretend to be a Russian oil magnate and try to get the real estate company to give you a tour.
⚑ ⓂLesseps. Follow C. Gran de Gràcia downhill from Pl. Lesseps, then right on C. Carolines.

CASA FUSTER   ARCHITECTURE
Pg. de Gràcia, 132
The last building Lluís Domènech i Montaner built in Barcelona, the Casa Fuster (1908-11) was a gift from the incredibly wealthy Mariano Fuster to his wife. (Guys, step it up.) The *modernista* aspects of the building are a bit understated from the outside, but the interior, now a luxury hotel, is all *modernisme*. Check out the lobby if you get a chance; if not, it's still a great sight from the street.
⚑ ⓂDiagonal. Follow Pg. de Gràcia across Avda. Diagonal.

CASA COMALAT   ARCHITECTURE
Avda. Diagonal, 442; rear facade C. Còrsega, 316
No, it's not so hot out that the building started to melt; it's just *modernisme*. The Casa Comalat (1909-11), built by architect Salvador Valeri i Pupurull, clearly owes much of its form (curving facades, parabolic arches, ceramic mosaics) to the work of contemporary Gaudí. Nevertheless, it is a fantastic example of the *modernista* style; the rear facade in particular, with its irregular wooden galleries, showcases Valeri's inventiveness.
⚑ ⓂDiagonal. Take a right on Avda. Diagonal. To see the rear facade, cross Avda. Diagonal and take a right on C. Còrsega.

MONTJUÏC AND POBLE SEC

▨ FUNDACIÓ MIRÓ   MUSEUM
Parc de Montjuïc   ☎934 43 94 70; www.fundaciomiro-bcn.org
From the outside in, the Fundació serves as both a shrine to and a celebration of the life and work of Joan Miró, one of both Catalonia and Spain's most beloved contemporary artists. The bright white angles and curves of the Lego-esque Rationalist building were designed by Josep Lluís Sert, a close friend of Joan Miró. Since it first opened, the museum has expanded beyond Miró's original collection to include pieces inspired by the artist. A collection of over 14,000 works now fills the open galleries, which have views of the grassy exterior and adjacent **Sculpture Park.** The collection includes whimsical sculptures, epic paint- ings, and gargantuan *sobreteixims* (paintings on tapestry) by Miró as well as works by Calder, Duchamp, Oldenburg, and Léger. Have fun gazing at Calder's politically charged **mercury fountain,** which was exhibited alongside Picasso's *Guernica* at the 1937 World's Fair in Paris. Like much of Barcelona, the founda- tion refuses to be stuck in its past—although an impressive relic of a previous era, Fundació Miró continues to support contemporary art. Temporary exhibi- tions have recently featured names such as Olafur Eliasson, Pipllotti Rist, and

Kiki Smith, while the more experimental **Espai 13** houses exhibits by emerging artists selected by freelance curators. Overwhelmed? You should be. This is one of the few times we recommend paying for the audio tour (€4).

[M]Paral·lel. From the Metro, take the funicular to the museum. $ €9, students €6, under 14 free. Temporary exhibits €4, students €3. Espai 13 €2.50. Sculpture garden free. Open Jul-Sep Tu-W 10am-8pm, Th 10am-9:30pm, F-Sa 10am-8pm, Su 10am-2:30pm; Oct-Jun Tu-W 10am-7pm, Th 10am-9:30pm, F-Sa 10am-7pm, Su 10am-2:30pm. Last entry 15min. before close.

MUSEU NACIONAL D'ART DE CATALUNYA (MNAC) MUSEUM

Palau Nacional, Parc de Montjuïc ☎936 22 03 76; www.mnac.cat

This majestic building perched atop Montjuïc isn't quite as royal as it first appears. Designed by Enric Catà and Pedro Cendoya for the 1929 International Exhibition, the Palau Nacional has housed the Museu Nacional d'art de Catalunya (MNAC) since 1934. The sculpture-framed view over Barcelona from outside the museum can't be beat, and more treasures await on the inside. Upon entrance you'll be dumped into the gargantuan colonnaded **Oval Hall,** which, though empty, gets your jaw appropriately loose to prepare for its drop in the galleries. The wing to the right houses a collection of Catalan Gothic art, complete with paintings on wood panels and sculptures that Pier 1 would die to replicate. To the left in the main hall is the museum's impressive collection of Catalan Romanesque art and frescoes, removed from their original settings in the 1920s and installed in the museum—a move that was probably for the best considering the number of churches devastated in the Civil War just a decade later. More modern attractions grace the upstairs, with modern art to the left, numismatics (coins, for you non-collectors) to the near right, and drawings, prints, and posters to the far right. For those intoxicated by the quirky architecture of the city, Catalan *modernisme* and *noucentisme* works dot the galleries, from Gaudí-designed furniture to Picasso's

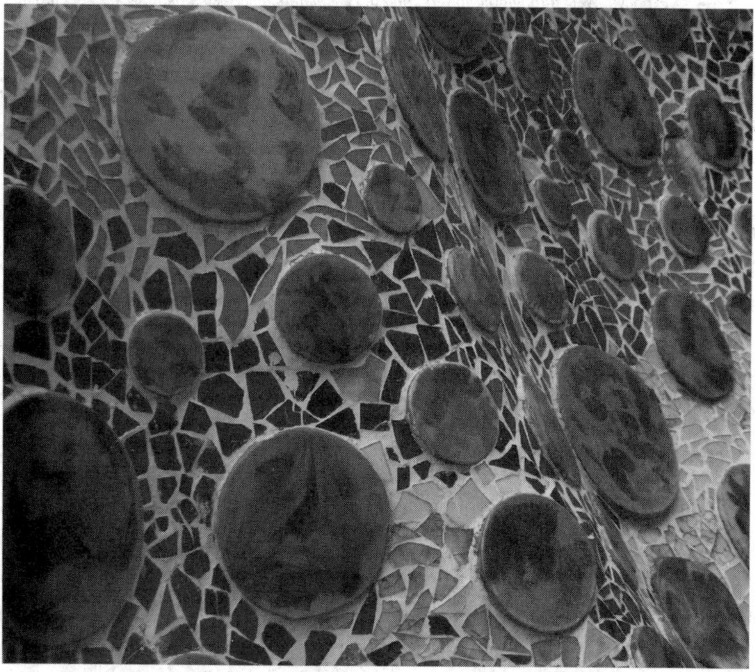

Cubist *Woman in Fur Hat and Collar.* The collection, which spans the 19th and early 20th century, includes an impressive selection from the underappreciated Joaquim Mir, and a couple of large, fascinating works by the more renowned José Gutiérrez Solana. If art isn't your thing, check out the currency collection—though beauty may be in the eye of the beholder, this 140,000-piece brief in the history of Catalan coins will have hardly any detractors.

✚ Ⓜ*Espanya. Walk through the towers and ride the escalators to the top; the museum is the palace-like structure.* Ⓢ *Permanent exhibits €8.50, students €6, under 16 free. Annual subscription (permanent and temporary exhibits) €14. Combined ticket with Poble Espanyol €15. Audio tour €3.10. 1st Su of each month free.* ⌚ *Open Tu-Sa 10am-7pm, Su 10am-2:30pm. Last entry 30min. before close.*

POBLE ESPANYOL   ARCHITECTURE
Avda. Francesc Ferrer i Guàrdia, 13   ☎935 08 63 00; www.poble-espanyol.com

One of the few original relics from the 1929 International Exhibition that still dots the mountain, the Poble Espanyol originally aimed to present a unified Spanish village. Inspired by *modernista* celebrity Josep Puig i Cadafalch, the four architects and artists in charge of its design visited over 1600 villages and towns throughout the country to find models to copy in constructing the village's 117 full-scale buildings, streets, and squares. Though intended simply as a temporary arts pavilion, the outdoor architectural museum was so popular that it was kept open as a shrine (or challenge) to the ideal of a united Spain that never was. It's perfect for those traveling only to Barcelona but want to get some idea of what the rest of the country looks like—the "Barri Andaluz" feels like a Sevillian street with whitewashed walls and arches. Nowadays, artists' workshops peddle goods along the winding roads, spectacles take place during the day and parties rage at night.

✚ Ⓜ*Espanya. Walk through the towers, ride the escalators, and take a right.* Ⓢ *€9.50, students €6.60, at night €5.50. Combined visit with National Art Museum of Catalonia €15. Audio tour €3.* ⌚ *Open M 9am-8pm, Tu-Th 9am-2am, F 9am-4am, Sa 9am-5am, Su 9am-midnight. Last entry 1hr. before close. Workshops and shops open daily in summer 10am-8pm; in fall 10am-7pm; in winter 10am-6pm; in spring 10am-7pm.*

BARCELONA PAVILION   ARCHITECTURE
Avda. Francesc Ferrer i Guàrdia, 7   ☎934 23 40 16; www.miesbcn.com

Though the original Barcelona Pavilion was dismantled when the International Exhibition ended in 1930, this faithful 1986 reconstruction recreates the original feel perfectly. **Ludwig Mies van der Rohe's** iconic, start 1929 structure of glass, steel, and marble reminds us that "less is more." The open interior is populated solely by the famous Barcelona chair and a reflecting pool with a bronze reproduction of Georg Kolbe's *Alba.* This pavilion—simple, tranquil, sleek—changed modern architecture, modern design, and the way we look at both, whether we realize it or not.

✚ Ⓜ*Espanya. Walk through the towers and take the escalators up Montjuïc. Barcelona Pavilion is on the 1st landing to the right—follow the signs.* Ⓢ *€4.60, students €2.50, under 18 free.* ⌚ *Open M 4-8pm, Tu-Su 10am-8pm.*

CASTLE OF MONTJUÏC   CASTLE
Carretera Montjuïc, 66   ☎932 56 44 45; www.bcn.cat/castelldemontjuic

Built in 1640 during the revolt against Philip IV, this former fort and castle has been involved in its fair share of both Catalan and Spanish struggles. The fortress first saw action in 1641 against Castilian forces and continued its function as a military post until 1960 when it was ceded to the city and refurbished as a military museum by Franco. Despite being handed to the city, the fort was controlled by the army until 2007, when its direction was finally handed to the Barcelona City Council. Since then, Barcelona has really enjoyed having a castle—maybe a little too much. A current exhibition named "Barcelona té castell!" (Barcelona has a castle!) explores and celebrates the possibilities for the space, while the castle itself remains, well, a castle. Incredible views of the harbor and city as well as a moat-turned-beautifully-manicured-garden await those that make the hike (or shell out for the gondola to the top). Bring your own cannonballs and help guard the city!

✣ ⓜEspanya. Montjuïc telefèric on Avda. Miramar. ⓢ Free. ◷ Open daily Apr 1-Sept 30 9am-9pm; Oct 1-Mar 31 9am-7pm.

the great outdoors

BEACHES

For basic information on all of the city beaches, contact the **city beach office**. (☎932 21 03 48; http://ves.bcn.cat/platja ◷ Lifeguards on duty at all beaches June-Sept daily 10am-7pm; Mar-June Sa-Su 10am-7pm.) Tents, motorcycles, loud music, littering, and dogs—though we've seen plenty of the latter two—are all prohibited. Showers, bathrooms, police, first aid, and basic info are available at each beach (June-Sept 10am-7pm). Lockers are available at the police station during certain hours. For the gym rats and juice heads, almost all beaches have some sort of outdoor workout facility.

lookin' for gaudies

Don't let the nude or topless beaches fool you—the government of Barcelona is cracking down on people baring flesh. Once you leave the confines of a swimming pool or beach you better cover up that bikini, or you could be fined as much as €500. The city became uncomfortable with the number of people walking around the city in skimpy bikinis and has put up signs and passed laws to require people to cover up.

PLATJA DE SANT SEBASTIÀ   BARCELONETA
Pl. Mar to end of Barceloneta peninsula

The slightly more remote nature of this beach makes it a better bet in your quest to find a square foot of sand during the packed summer weekends. All the way at the end of the peninsula of Barceloneta, this is where most local Barcelonans who choose to stay in the city come for their tanning. Bathe in sea and sun under the shimmering auspices of the new W Hotel, nicknamed *la vela* ("the sail") for obvious reasons.

✣ ⓜBarceloneta. Take bus #17, 39, or 64 all the way down Pg. Joan de Borbó to Pg. Escullera. ⓢ Free. ◷ Open 24hr. Wheelchair-accessible bathing services available daily from July to early Sept 11am-2pm; June and late Sept Sa-Su and holidays 11am-2pm.

PLATJA DE SANT MIQUEL   BARCELONETA
Pl. Mar to C. Almirall Aixada

Walk through Barceloneta parallel to Pg. Joan de Borbó, and you'll eventually hit this beach, at the urban area's southernmost tip. This is where city meets sea, with some beautiful beach in between. The beach is the site of the now iconic *Homenatge a la Barceloneta* monument by German artist Rebecca Horn (the one that looks like a skyscraper after a mild earthquake) and is one of the most crowded spots in Barcelona in the summer.

✣ ⓜBarceloneta. Take bus #17, 39, or 64 down Pg. Joan de Borbó to Pl. Mar. ⓢ Free. ◷ Open 24hr.

PLATJA DE LA BARCELONETA

BARCELONETA

Pg. Marítim de la Barceloneta, from C. Almirall Aixada to Parc de la Barceloneta

The most popular (read: crowded) beach in Barcelona, Platja de la Barceloneta attracts a vibrant mix of visitors, tourists, and brave locals regardless of the weather. In short, good luck finding a place to sunbathe—even when there's no sun to be seen. If you're looking for a little exercise, pick-up volleyball games abound on the public courts.

✷ Ⓜ*Barceloneta. Buses #35, 45, 57, 59, or 157 to Pg. Marítim.* Ⓢ *Free.* ◷ *Open 24hr.*

PLATJA DEL SOMORROSTRO

BARCELONETA

Pg. Marítim de la Barceloneta, Parc de la Barceloneta to Port Olímpic

Once the site of a 15,000-person shantytown, Somorrostro is now one of the busiest beaches at all hours. Come during the day to take advantage of the *biblioplatja* (beach library) and athletic facilities, or stumble out of the clubs at 3am for a late-night swim; you'll be in good company.

✷ Ⓜ*Barceloneta or Ciutadella/Vila Olímpica. Buses #36, 45, 57, 59, or 157 to Pg. Marítim/C. Trelawny.* 𝒊 *Book rental. Volleyball courts, gym, and sports areas available.* Ⓢ *Free.* ◷ *Open 24hr.*

PLATJA MAR BELLA

POBLENOU

From Mar Bella Pier to Bac de Roda Pier

Past the Bogatell naval base, rocky outcroppings provide cover for Barcelona's only designated nude beach. Beyond this short stretch of plentiful skin is a gay beach, marked by a rainbow flag flying at the beachside restaurant. Mostly frequented by younger and local people, the two sections provide a perfect place to shed some inhibitions (among other things).

✷ Ⓜ*Poblenou. Bus #41.* 𝒊 *Ping-pong tables, skating area, biblioplatja (beach library), and basketball courts available.* Ⓢ *Free.* ◷ *Open 24hr.*

beach sightseeing

Barcelona's beaches are some of the best in the world. In fact, *National Geographic* put it in the top 10, and the Discovery channel crowned it champ in 2005. If you're like us, you like doing and seeing, but mostly in a way you can reassure yourself (or your parents) that you are actually getting some culture, and not just partying the days away. Here are some more artistic/literary sights to see while in the process of your lazy, sun-bleached day-drinking at the beach:

- **HOMENATGE A LA BARCELONETA:** See that rusty, three-story-tall iron structure that brings up images of a post-apocalyptic Planet of the Apes world? It's actually a tribute to the city by the eclectic German artist Rebecca Horn. Fear not, the apes haven't taken over. Yet.

- **PEIX D'OR:** Named "goldfish," this not-so-guppy of a sculpture rests in between Barcelona's two tallest towers in Port Olympic. American architect Frank Gehry thought this one up... well... because he liked fish. No sarcasm, his art is heavily influenced by the shapes of fish. Whatever floated his boat, we guess.

- **DON QUIXOTE DE LA MIERDA:** In book two of the fully titled *The Ingenius Gentleman Don Quixote of the Mancha*, the white pristine sand of Barceloneta is described when Quixote comes ashore. You'll have to refer back to Miguel de Cervantes' description in the novel because today, the World Health Organization has some interesting questions as to the health quality of the sand.

PLATJA NOVA MAR BELLA

Bac de Roda Pier to Selva de Mar Pier

One of urban Barcelona's most distant beaches and consequently the least crowded, Platja Nova Mar Bella is the stomping ground of local teenagers and students. Still easily accessible by Metro, this beach boasts a more relaxing alternative to the tourist-shoving death-match of Platja de la Barceloneta, especially on weekends.

🚇 Ⓜ Selva de Mar. Bus #41. Ⓢ Free. 🕒 *Open daily from July to early Sept 11am-6pm. Wheelchair-accessible bathing services available from June to late Sept Sa-Su and holidays.*

PARKS

PARC DE COLLSEROLA

Crta. de l'Església, 92 ☎ 932 80 35 52; www.parccollserola.net

On Barcelona's outskirts lies the world's largest metropolitan park—though that distinction gives its urban counterparts short shrift, as the Parc de Collserola is really more of a suburban forest than anything else. The park stretches along the **Collserola mountain range** from the **Besòs River** to the **Llobregat River,** between Barcelona and **Sant Cugat del Vallès** farther inland. Although the park is easily accessible by public transportation, few non-Barcelonans visit, so don't expect information in English.

The park's 80 sq. km. include diverse flora and fauna, like wild boars and badgers and such naughtily named birds as woodpeckers, whitethroats, and the small but perky blue tits. For a greatest-hits showcase of the park's variety, the 13km trail from **Parc del Laberint d'Horta** (Ⓜ Mundet) to **Sant Cugat** is highly recommended. Collserola is a good place to work off those tapas with a ton of hiking trails and the **Carertera de les Aigües** (Water Highway), a cycling track that follows the ridge of the mountain range and has stunning views of the city to the south and the valley to the north.

For those who do not find never-ending delight in the birds and the bees, the park is littered with places to eat, benches to relax on, and historic architecture and ruins to mentally digest. History buffs will want to check out the 12th-century *ermitas* (dwellings) of **Sant Adjutori** and **Sant Medir,** while those interested in the modern should be sure to stop at the **Collserola Tower,** a telecommunications tower designed by architect Norman Foster for the '92 Olympics. Although the games have long past, the 10th-floor observation deck and unbeatable location on Vilana Hill make it an ideal place to look out over Barcelona, Montserrat, and, if the day is clear, the Pyrenees.

🚇 *FGC: Baixador de Vallvidrera for Information Center (S1, S2), FGC: Peu de Funicular (S1, S2), FGC: Les Planes (S1, S2), FGC: La Floresta (S1, S2, S5, S55), or* Ⓜ *Mundet (L3).* 𝒊 *Tourist information center, museum, and restaurant near FGC: Baixador de Vallvidrera entrance. Other museums and restaurants scattered throughout; see website for full list.* Ⓢ *Free.* 🕒 *Tours daily 10am-2pm. Info center open daily 9:30am-3pm.*

PARC DE LA GUINEUETA

Pl. Llucmajor www.bcn.cat/parcsijardins

Though a bit out of the way, this narrow but beautiful park draws visitors from all over the city; it's surprisingly busy considering its distance from the center. Occupying a natural gully, the lower part of the park offers isolation, while a large plaza at the park's summit serves as a popular place for meetings, demonstrations, and *sardanes* (traditional dances).

🚇 Ⓜ *Llucmajor. Follow Pg. Verdum toward Pl. Llucmajor.* Ⓢ *Free.* 🕒 *Open daily 10am-dusk.*

the great outdoors

food

Given the cosmopolitan character of Barcelona, you can find just about any food you crave. The cheapest options are chain supermarkets (Dia, Caprabo, and Spar, to name a few), and local groceries that tend to run a few eurocents cheaper still; in terms of prepared food, **kebab** restaurants are some of the cheapest and most plentiful. Local **Catalan cuisine** is varied and includes food from land and sea: some of the most traditional dishes are *botifarra amb mongetes* (Catalan pork sausage with beans), *esqueixada* (cod with tomato and onion), *llonganissa* (a kind of salami), and *coques* (somewhere between a pizza and an open-faced sandwich; singular *coca*). The simplest and most prevalent dish is **pa amb tomàquet** (bread smeared with tomato, garlic, olive oil, salt, and pepper). Note also that the Catalan for "salad" is *amanida*; this bears no relation to the word in English or Spanish, which confuses some travelers poring over a menu in search of *ensalada*.

BARRI GÒTIC AND LAS RAMBLAS

Avoid the tourist traps along Las Ramblas and let *Let's Go* show you the ones worth going to, both on and off the beaten path.

LA BOQUERIA (MERCAT DE SANT JOSEP)   MARKET $
Las Ramblas, 89

If you're looking for the freshest tomatoes, leeks the size of a well-fed child's arm, fruit prickly enough that it could second as a shuriken, a whole sheep's head (eyes included), or maybe just some nuts, the Boqueria has you covered in the most beautiful way—just look for the stained-glass archway facing Las Ramblas. Though each neighborhood in Barcelona has its own *mercat*, the Mercat de Sant Josep is not only the biggest and most impressive in the city, it's the largest open air market in all of Spain, a remarkable distinction given the country's abundance of open-air markets. As a consequence, though, be ready to fight your way through wildebeest-like hordes to get to those cherished lychees (or whatever exotic fruit you might fancy) for your beach picnic. If filling your stomach from the glowing rows of perfectly arranged, perfectly ripe produce doesn't satisfy your famished gut, restaurants surrounding the market offer meals made from produce straight from the nearby vendors.

✦ ⓜ*Liceu. Walk on Las Ramblas toward Pl. Catalunya and take a left onto Pl. Sant Josep.* ☒ *Open M-Sa 8am-8pm, though certain vendors stay open after 9pm.*

ATTIC   MEDITERRANEAN $$$
Las Ramblas, 120   ☎933 02 48 66; www.angrup.com

After a long day along Las Ramblas, Attic provides a soothing and incredibly orange world away from the performers, pickpockets, and never-ending construction. It serves fresh, delectable food at downright reasonable prices for the quality and the presence of cloth napkins. Attic has no dress code, but you should probably change out of that pit-stained T-shirt and the Tevas. Sit on the rooftop terrace overlooking Las Ramblas at dinner for a truly memorable experience.

✦ ⓜ*Liceu. On Las Ramblas toward Pl. Catalunya.* ⓢ *Appetizers €4.50-12; meat entrees €8-14, fish €10-13.* ☒ *Open daily 1-4:30pm and 7pm-12:30am.*

ESCRIBÀ   BAKERY $
Las Ramblas, 83   ☎933 01 60 27; www.escriba.es

Grab a coffee and ogle the stained-glass peacock or one of the impressive works of art waiting to be devoured in the front display case. With tarts, croissants, cakes, and lifelike rings made of caramel, Escribà is waiting to tempt you from every corner of its beautiful *modernista*-style store. If you're not in the mood for sweets, try a savory dish, such as the croissant with blue cheese, caramelized apple, and walnuts (€4.50) or the "bikini" bread mold with ham and brie (€3.50).

✴ Ⓜ*Liceu. Walk toward Pl. Catalunya. Escribà is on the left.* Ⓢ *Sandwiches €3.50. Salads €3. Menú €5.90. Sweets €3-5.* *i* *Open daily 8:30am-9pm. Kitchen open M-Th noon-5pm and 8-11pm, F-Sa noon-5pm and 8pm-midnight, Su noon-5pm.*

i prefer my vegetables cowardly

If there's a food that captures Barcelona's essence, it may be *patatas bravas*. Literally translated as "fierce potatoes," this dish of fried quartered spuds is popular all over the country—in tapas bars and foofy restaurants alike. While the recipes vary based on which of Spain's 17 autonomous communities you're in, the Catalonian is the most feisty. Barcelonans cook their *patatas* in a sauce of olive oil, red pepper, paprika, and vinegar, which, needless to say, packs a punch. Generally speaking, the greasier the potatoes, the better. It's hard to find a watering hole within the city limits that doesn't serve a mean batch. Disclaimer: extended ingestion of said potatoes may very well cause a coronary by the age of 30, but they're so delicious it may be worth the risk.

ARC CAFÉ   FUSION $$
C. Carabassa, 19   ☎933 02 52 04; www.arccafe.com

Down the narrow C. d'en Carabassa, Arc Café is easy to miss. For this reason, it's a great stop when you're sick of the fanny packs and sneakers that crowd Las Ramblas—it's virtually guaranteed to be tourist-free. The restaurant boasts a vegetarian-friendly menu that rotates every three months as well as popular Thai nights on Thursdays and Fridays (regular menu still available). Luckily, their curries are always available—choose between chicken and tofu with jasmine rice (€11-12)—just be sure to order a mojito with Malibu to cool off (€6) if you're brave enough to go for spice. There's also a cheaper midday *menú* daily (€9.60).

✴ Ⓜ*Drassanes. Walk toward the sea on Las Ramblas and take a left onto C. Josep Anselm Clavé. Walk 5min. as the road becomes C. Ample. Take a left onto Carabassa. Arc Café is on the right.* *i* *Reservations recommended on weekends. Free Wi-Fi.* Ⓢ *Appetizers €4.50-6.90; entrees €8.50-12. Wine €2. Beer €2-3.* ⏱ *Open M-Th 10am-1am, F 10am-3am, Sa 11am-3am, Su 11am-1am.*

L'ANTIC BOCOI DEL GÒTIC   CATALAN $$$
Baixada Viladecols, 3   ☎933 10 50 67; www.bocoi.net

Enter the lair of L'Antic Bocoi del Gòtic, where walls of rustic stone and exposed ancient brick surround diners in cave-like intimacy. The restaurant specializes in Catalan cuisine with fresh, seasonal ingredients and prides itself on bringing new ideas to traditional food. The staff recommends the selection of cheeses and their own take on the *coques de recapte*, a regional dish made of a thin dough with delicious fresh produce and thickly layered meats (€8.50-9). This fancy joint fills up quickly after opening, so make reservations.

✴ Ⓜ*Jaume I. Follow C. Jaume I toward Pl. Sant Jaume, then left onto C. Dagueria, which becomes C. dels Lledó, which becomes Baixada Viladecols.* *i* *Reservations recommended.* Ⓢ *Appetizers €7-10; entrees €10-21.* ⏱ *Open M-Sa 8:30pm-midnight.*

food

CAFÈ DE L'ACADÈMIA

C. Lledó, 1

CATALAN $$$

☎933 19 82 53

This Barri Gòtic staple on Pl. Sant Just has been a local favorite since it opened some 30 years ago, and has remained a locals' secret—until now. The high-quality food at surprisingly reasonable prices draws everyone from business-men and government bureaucrats from the *ajuntament* up the street to more casual groups of friends out for a bite. Sit in the dark, cellar-like interior, or in the summer months enjoy the *plaça* outside in one of the least touristy corners of the Barri Gòtic. This place has such disdain for tourists that they close on the weekends and for most of August.

✦ ⓂJaume I. Follow C. Jaume I toward Pl. Sant Jaume, then left onto C. Dagueria, which becomes C. Lledó. *i* Reservations recommended. Ⓢ Entrees €14-30. Menú €15, at the bar €10. ☼ Open M-F 1:30-4pm and 8:30-11:30pm. Closed 3 weeks in Aug.

CAFÉ VIENA

Las Ramblas, 115

SANDWICHES $

☎933 17 14 92; www.viena.es

This incongruously named cafe—it has nothing to do with the Austrian capital—has earned much renown for a fulsome 2006 *New York Times* article whose author raved for several paragraphs about Viena's *flauta ibèric* (Iberian ham sandwich; €6.60), calling it "the best sandwich I've ever had." The sandwich's secret, which the article's author almost figured out but couldn't quite pin down, is that the *flauta* comes on *pa amb tomàquet*, the staple of the Catalan kitchen that involves smearing tomato on bread before seasoning with salt, pepper, olive oil, and garlic. And it is a damn good sandwich, the sort that melts in your mouth with each bite, though *Let's Go* isn't sure that ham is supposed to do that.

✦ ⓂCatalunya. Follow Las Ramblas toward the sea. Ⓢ Sandwiches €2.40-9.30 (most under €4). Coffee €1.30-2.40. ☼ Open M-Th 8am-11:30pm, F-Sa 8am-12:30am, Su 8am-11:30pm.

XALOC

C. Palla, 13-17

TAPAS $$

☎933 01 19 90; www.xalocrestaurant.com

When you walk into Xaloc, you see a clean, modern interior, with one catch: the walls are covered in legs of Iberian ham. And, thank the gods, what you see is what you get. Try one of the sampler plates of Catalan sausages (€7) or anything that includes the word *"jamón"* (ham). This is what Spain is famous for—you can't leave here without trying *pernil ibèric*. Seriously, they will stop you at the airport.

✦ ⓂLiceu. Walk down C. Boqueria and take a left onto C. Cardenal Casañas. Stay on this road in front of the church and through the Pl. Pi. Stay right as it leaves the square and becomes C. Palla. Xaloc is located where C. Palla merges with C. Banys Nous. Ⓢ Tapas €2-13. Sandwiches €3.80-5.50. ☼ Open M-F 10:30am-midnight, Sa-Su 11am-midnight.

JUICY JONES

C. Cardenal Casañas, 7

VEGETARIAN, INDIAN $$

☎933 02 43 30

Juice bar and vegan haven, Juicy Jones serves a variety of veggie-stuffed sand-wiches, vegan pizzas and lasagnas, daily specials, and a *menú* (appetizer, entree, dessert, and wine; €8.50). If you have a strong stomach, chill out in the back seating area, where it looks like a kaleidoscope full of acid exploded in a 1950s diner. Keep an eye out for "Turtle Jones" chillin' on a wall. Otherwise, sit among dreadlocked locals at the fruit-filled bar in the front and sip on one of the freshly made delicious juice combinations or milkshakes; the adventurous can create their own (€3-5).

✦ ⓂLiceu. From the Metro, walk down C. Boqueria. Take a left onto C. Cardenal Casañas. Ⓢ Tapas €3.50. Sandwiches €4.50. Salads €5. Thali €6. Plate of the day €6.25. Juice €2.50-5. Cash only. ☼ Open daily 10am-midnight.

PASTA BAR — PASTA $$

C. Escudellers, 47

Assemble your own steaming bowl of fresh pasta, made to order right in front of you. Pick a pasta and a sauce, add ingredients (cheese is free), and take your pasta to go or eat it under one of the chic hanging lamps made from wine bottles. Most *Let's Go* readers will understand the value of refueling with lots of inexpensive carbohydrates after an exhausting day of sightseeing; Pasta Bar is a delicious and convenient stop to do just that.

➜ Ⓜ Liceu. Walk on Las Ramblas toward the water. Take a left onto C. Escudellers. $ Pasta €3.90-7.90 depending on sauce; extra ingredients €0.30-2 each. Pasta of the week €5.90. Desserts €3.90. Menú €9.90. ⏰ Open daily noon-1am.

TUCCO PASTAS FRESCAS — PASTA $

C. Aglà, 6 — ☎933 01 51 91; www.tuccopastasfrescas.com

True to its name, Tucco "fresh pasta" offers just that—a selection of fresh pastas topped with your choice of sauce and cheese (€3.95). The limited seating in the teeny store serves as a revolving door for hip, young locals and internationals wandering far off the beaten path. If pasta isn't your thing, a selection of wallet-friendly sandwiches, pizzas, salads, and snacks loaded with veggies attempts to fill the nutritional void that a meal of carbs creates. Don't expect to sit if you come at mealtime; instead, take your plasticware and hit the road.

➜ Ⓜ Liceu. Walk on Las Ramblas toward the water. Take a left onto C. Escudellers. Left onto C. Aglà. $ Pasta €3.95. Pizza from €9. ⏰ Open M-F 1-11:30pm, Sa 1-6pm.

LA CLANDESTINA — TEA $

Baixada Viladecols, 2bis — ☎933 19 05 33

A hidden—dare we say, clandestine?—tea house with the most relaxed atmosphere in all the Barri Gòtic. An artsy feel is nearly as pervasive as the thick air, fragrant from the freshly brewed tea and occasionally from smoking hookahs. The cavernous *teteria* makes for a great place to take a short (or long) reprieve from the frenetic pace of the Gothic Quarter.

➜ Ⓜ Jaume I. Follow C. Jaume I toward Pl. Sant Jaume, then left onto C. Dagueria, which becomes C. Lledó, which becomes Baixada Viladecols. ℹ Free Wi-Fi. $ Sandwiches €4.20-4.40. Teas €2.50-6; pots €10-15. Juices €2.70-3.60. Cash only. ⏰ Open M-Th 10am-10pm, F-Sa 10am-midnight, Su 11am-10pm.

EL BORN

This chic neighborhood is full of restaurants of nearly every genre imaginable, from traditional Catalan food to Basque *pintxos* to meat fondue and crunchy vegetarian co-ops.

👍 **EL XAMPANYET** — TAPAS $$

C. Montcada, 22 — ☎933 19 70 03

This is as authentic as it gets, with sheepskin wine bags, an overwhelming selection of *cava*, and crunchy old locals spilling out the door and onto the street at all hours. Inside, it's a museum of casks, blackened bottles, and kitschy bottle openers displayed against handpainted ceramic tiles. We recommend you try the cask-fresh *cerveza* (€3.50) or the house wine *xampanyet* (€2), and pad your stomach with some of the delicious tapas.

➜ Ⓜ Jaume I. Walk down C. Princesa and take a right onto C. Montcada, toward the Museu Picasso. Xampanyet is on the right before the Placeta Montcada. $ Tapas €1.10-13. Beer €3.50. Wine and cava from €2. ⏰ Open Tu-Sa noon-4pm and 7-11pm, Su noon-4pm.

👍 **PETRA** — RESTAURANT $$

C. Sombrerers, 13 — ☎933 19 99 99

With dark wood, stained glass, Art Nouveau prints, menus pasted onto wine bottles, and chandeliers made of silverware, Petra's eccentric decor will have you expecting an expensive meal. Luckily, the lively bohemian feel is matched by bohemian prices. Pasta dishes like the rich gnocchi with mushrooms and hazelnut oil (€5.20) and entrees such as the duck with lentils (€7.90) are easy on the wallet, as is the midday *menú* of a main course (varies daily), salad, and wine for €6.60—a true steal.

➥ [M]Jaume I. Walk down C. Princesa and take a right onto C. Pou de la Cadena. Take an immediate left onto C. Barra de Ferro and a right onto C. Banys Vells. Petra is located where C. Banys Vells ends at C. Sombrerers. $ Menú €6.50. Appetizers €4.90-7.10; entrees €7.90. ⏰ Open Tu-Sa 1:30-4pm and 9-11:30pm, Su 1:30-4pm.

👍 LA BÁSCULA — VEGETARIAN $$

C. Flassaders, 30 — ☎933 19 98 66

This working cooperative serves vegetarian sandwiches, *empanadas*, salads, and more—the menu changes daily. Doors laid flat serve as communal tables, and a mixture of art, environmentally friendly sodas, and protest flyers set this restaurant apart. Though discretely robed in the same antique exterior as more expensive places, Báscula provides a more reasonably priced alternative to the upscale eateries. Hours and seating availability may change as the restaurant fights for its right to serve in-house, but takeout is available no matter the outcome.

➥ [M]Jaume I. Walk down C. Princesa and take a right onto C. Flassaders. $ Entrees and salads €7-9. Sandwiches and soups €4-5. Piadinas €6. Cash only. ⏰ Open W-Sa 1pm-midnight, Su 1-8pm.

👍 LA PARADETA — SEAFOOD $$$

C. Comercial, 7 — ☎932 68 19 39; www.laparadeta.com

For the highest quality seafood, this hybrid fish market/restaurant is where Barcelona goes. The line often stretches down C. Comercial, but it's worth the wait to walk into the simple interior and pick out fresh fish to be cooked to your liking. When they call your number, head up and grab your meal, then sit back down and enjoy.

➥ [M]Jaume I. Follow C. Princesa all the way to C. Comerç, then right, then left at C. Fusina (just before the market), then right on C. Comercial. $ Market prices. ⏰ Open Tu-Th 1-4pm and 8-11:30pm, F-Sa 1-4pm and 8pm-midnight, Su 1-4pm.

HOFMANN PASTISSERIA — BAKERY $$

C. Flassaders, 44 — ☎932 68 82 21; www.hofmann-bcn.com

Pastry school meets storefront in this Seussian mindbender. Drift through the door, take a deep breath, and let that wonderful smell of freshly baked sweets fill your lungs. Watch artisans work on delectable goods ion the surreal spiral staircase above, while glass cases and wooden cabinets wait below filled with adorable gelatos (€3.50), precious marmalade jars (€8), and a selection of not-so-sickeningly-cute-but-utterly-delectable tarts and cakes wait below. If you're lucky, Chef Eric will have whipped up some fantastical 3D chocolate scene.

➥ [M]Jaume I. Walk down C. Princesa and take a right onto C. Flassaders. You'll see Hofmann right before crossing Pg. Born. $ Croissants €1-1.50. Gelato €3.50. Marmalades €8. Chocolates €1-5. Coffee €1.20-1.50. ⏰ Open M-Th 9am-2pm and 3:30-8pm, F 9am-2pm and 3:30-8:30pm, Sa 9am-8:30pm, Su 9am-2:30pm.

LA LLAVOR DELS ORIGENS — CATALAN $$

C. Vidriería, 6 — ☎934 53 11 20; www.lallavordelsorigens.com

La Llavor dels Origens serves traditional Catalan fare with a picture menu that lets you see your meal in painstaking detail before you eat it, with even more excruciatingly specific written descriptions of each dish—these guys take food seriously. Seasonal menus change every two months, while the regular menu changes every six, ensuring that there will always be something new to try (and maybe cook yourself—all recipes are available on the website). Drawings from customers young and not-so-young deck the walls, undermining the sleek decor.

➥ [M]Jaume I. Walk down C. Princesa and take a right onto C. Montcada. Upon crossing Pg. Born, C. Vidriería is the street directly in front of you. ℹ Organic meat available on request. $ Entrees €6-11. Beer €3. Wine €3.50. 15% discount for takeout. 10% surcharge for sitting outside. ⏰ Open daily 12:30pm-1am.

AL SUR

CAFE $

C. Sant Pere Més Alt, 4   ☎933 10 12 86; www.alsurcafe.com

Directly across from the Palau de la Música Catalana, Al Sur whips up cheap and tasty *bocadillos* and *empanadas* that please empty pockets. Free Wi-Fi, an iBar with Apple TV, and a small but comfy loft-lounge encourage you to kick back and relax, while hot, filling sandwiches are perfect for on-the-go diners. The baristas can put together a mean coffee, too—look for lunch combos that include a sandwich or *empanadas*, a drink, and a coffee for just a handful of euro.

✚ ⓂUrquinaona. Walk down C. Jonqueres and take a right onto C. Sant Pere Més Alt. Al Sur is directly across from the Palau. *i* Free Wi-Fi. Ⓢ Combo food and drink specials €4.10-6.50. ⓏOpen M-Th 8:30am-1:30am, F 8:30am-3am, Sa 10am-3am, Su 10am-1:30am.

EL RAVAL

Kebab is a major food group in El Raval, and it's always a good, cheap option. For those looking for more of a traditional Barcelonan meal, though, El Raval has much to offer.

🏛 CAN LLUÍS

CATALAN $$$

C. Cera, 49   ☎934 41 11 87

Can Lluís? Yes he can! (Just kidding: *Can* is Catalan for *Chez*). This crowded restaurant has been an El Raval staple since its founding in the 1920s, when this neighborhood was Barcelona's Chinatown. It's stayed in the family for three generations and today it looks today like many of the customers have been around since the early days, too—try to get there when it opens, as the usual suspects have dibs on most of the tables. Don't be intimidated by the fact that everyone already knows each other, or by the fact that you'll almost certainly be spoken to in Catalan. Just remember: "Què vols?" ("What do you want?") is your cue to order.

✚ ⓂSant Antoni. Follow Ronda Sant Antoni toward Mercat de Sant Antoni, bear left on Ronda Sant Pau, and then head left on C. Cera. Ⓢ Appetizers €4.90-15; entrees €9.90-24. Lunch menú €9.30. ⓏOpen M-Sa 1:30-4pm and 8:30-11:15pm. Closed 3 weeks in Aug.

🏛 SOHO

PITA, HOOKAH $

C. Ramelleres, 26

A welcome recent addition to the neighborhood, Soho serves cheap and simple with meat and vegetarian options (€2) without rushing you out of the place. It feels very impromptu, with everything written by hand and a lot of exposed plywood, but, at prices this low, it's definitely here to stay. Low-slung seats around low wooden tables in a simple dining room make for a no-frills dining experience, while smaller, intimate rooms are perfect for test-driving a hookah (€10) from the impressive wall of smoking paraphernalia.

✚ ⓂUniversitat. Walk down C. Tallers and take a right onto C. Ramelleres. Ⓢ Pita and drink €3.50. Cash only. ⓏOpen M-Sa 1pm-midnight.

🏛 JUICY JONES

VEGETARIAN $$

C. Hospital, 74   ☎934 43 90 82; www.juicyjones.com

The big brother of the Juicy Jones in the Barri Gòtic, this version of the vegetarian eatery fits into its surroundings more appropriately—daily specials of Indian dahl and curries that seemed a bit out of place in la Gòtic fit right into El Raval's culinary landscape. If you've ever wondered what M.C. Escher's art would have looked like if he used more color and took more shrooms, the interior will satisfy your curiosity.

✚ ⓂLiceu. Walk down C. Hospital. Juicy Jones is on the right at the corner of C. Hospital and C. En Roig, before Rambla del Raval. Ⓢ Daily thali plate €6. Tapas €2-3.50. Sandwiches €3.90-4.50. Menú €8.50. ⓏOpen daily 1-11:30pm.

food

NARIN MIDDLE EASTERN $

C. Tallers, 80 ☎933 01 90 04

Sitting discreetly among the shops and cafes of C. Tallers, Narin is hiding the best baklava (€1) in Barcelona as well as equally scrumptious falafel, shawarma, and kebabs. If you can't stand the heat, get out of the kitchen—the inside resembles a sauna with wooden walls and sweaty customers. Luckily, beers come cold and cheap (€1.80) for those looking to brave the bar, and a tiled dining room provides a reprieve from the buzz of the electric shawarma shaver.

⇆ [M]Universitat. Walk down C. Tallers. [$] Pitas €2.90-4. Durums €3.50-4.50. Entrees €6.50-7.40. ⏰ Open M-Th 11am-2am, F-Sa 11am-3am, Su 11am-2am.

HELLO SUSHI JAPANESE $$

C. Junta de Comerç, 14 ☎934 12 08 30; www.hello-sushi.com

The large, semi-industrial interior, decorated with both modern and traditional Japanese art, offers a cheap daily *menú* (€8.50) and sushi platters at reasonable prices, luring a young clientele into its dark, pillow-padded lair. Dine at the bar, grab a table, or sit on the floor in the foyer and admire the paintings while the smell of tempura and teriyaki tempt you to stay for another round.

*⇆ [M]Liceu. Walk down C. Hospital and take a left onto C. Junta de Comerç. **i** Sometimes hosts live music; check website for schedule. [$] Entrees €8-14. Sushi rolls €4-8; combos €12-32. ⏰ Open Tu-Sa 12:30-4:30pm and 8:30pm-12:30am, Su 8:30pm-12:30am.*

SHALIMAR PAKISTANI, INDIAN $$

C. Carme, 71 ☎933 29 34 96

Shalimar serves authentic Pakistani and Indian dishes tandoori-style. Generous portions and delicious meat-based curries (€7-9) punctuate a menu that would make any vegetarian happy. Hand-painted tiles and warm lighting perk up the simple interior, and lace curtains block out the busy streets of Raval.

⇆ [M]Liceu. Walk down C. Hospital and take a right onto C. En Roig, then a left onto C. Carme. Shalimar is on the left before the fork. [$] Appetizers €2-8; entrees €6.80-9.20. Beer €2. ⏰ Open M-Tu 8pm-midnight, W-Su 1-4pm and 8pm-midnight.

MADAME JASMINE CAFE $$

Rambla del Raval, 22

Allow yourself to be seduced by either the hip 19th-century French-brothel-chic interior or the scrumptious *bocadillos* (€5.50). Orange and red lighting sets the mood, incense fills the nostrils, and a selection of sultry Latin, electro, and lounge music may just convince you to partake in the less legal red-light activities lining the streets of Raval.

⇆ [M]Liceu. Walk down C. Hospital and take a left onto Rambla del Raval. Madame Jasmine is on the right nearly ¾ of the way down. [$] Salads €7. Cocktails €5. Beer €2-3. ⏰ Open M-F 5:30pm-2:30am, Sa-Su 1:30pm-2:30am. Kitchen open daily until 12:30am.

MENDIZABAL FAST FOOD $

C. Junta de Comerç, 2

A crowd of young, artsy students out front and vibrant multicolored tiles in the back make this otherwise inconspicuous foodstand hard to miss. Take your cheap eats to go, or grab a seat on the terrace in the neighboring *plaça* for an extra 10% (look for the coordinating chairs). Some vegetarian-friendly options are available—we recommend the tomato, brie, and avocado sandwich (€3.60).

⇆ [M]Liceu. Walk down C. Hospital. Mendizabal is on the left at the corner of C. Hospital and C. Junta de Comerç. [$] Bocadillos €3-4. Beer €2.50. Cocktails €4.50. Cash only. ⏰ Open daily 8:30am-1am.

ORGANIC
MEDITERRANEAN $$

C. Junta de Comerç, 11   ☎933 01 09 02; www.antoniaorganickitchen.com

For once, you won't have to worry about space for seating—Organic has enough room to fit an entire youth hostel and its luggage. A vegan buffet (€7) surprises and delights with croquettes, pasta, and salad fixings, while all-vegetarian Mediterranean dishes will please even the most outspoken carnivores. Be sure to say thanks to Mother Earth as you leave—she'll be on your left looking down on you approvingly, surrounded by peas, earth, and fire.

✚ ⓂLiceu. Walk down C. l'Hospital and take a left onto C. Junta de Comerç. Ⓢ Vegan salad buffet €7. Pizza €9. Menú €9.50-12. ☒ Open daily 12:30pm-midnight.

L'EIXAMPLE

🔖 LA RITA
CATALAN $$

C. Aragó, 279   ☎934 87 23 76; www.laritarestaurant.com

La Rita serves traditional Catalan dishes with a twist, like potatoes and black sausage in mushroom sauce, and duck with apples, raspberry *coulis*, and mango chutney. Though the price is dirt-cheap given the quality and quantity of food, the interior is anything but—expect an upscale but relaxed ambience (think piano music) that will make you wish you had changed out of that sweaty T-shirt.

✚ ⓂPasseig de Gràcia. Walk up Pg. de Gràcia away from Pl. Catalunya and turn right onto C. Aragó. Ⓢ Appetizers €5-7.50; entrees €7-12. ☒ Open daily 1-3:45pm and 8:30-11:30pm.

🔖 LISBOA
PORTUGUESE $$

C. Comte Borrell, 145   ☎934 51 00 27; www.lisboaenbarcelona.com

Incredibly rich and delicious Portuguese fare will make anyone who's been to Portugal nostalgic—and will make anyone who hasn't book a ticket for the next flight to Lisbon. The only traditional Portuguese restaurant in Barcelona, Lisboa serves the expected *bacalhau* (cod) dishes as well as *alheira* (chicken sausage; €11), which is nearly impossible to find outside of Portugal. Wash it all down with a shot of Lisbon's classic liqueur, sour cherry *ginja* (€2).

✚ ⓂUrgell. With your back to the rocket-shaped Agbar Tower, walk along Gran Via de les Corts Catalanes and take a right onto C. Comte Borrell. Ⓢ Entrees €9-16. Lunch menú Tu-F €9.90. ☒ Open Tu-Sa 1-4pm and 8-11pm, Su 1-4pm.

🔖 OMEÍA
MIDDLE EASTERN $$

C. Aragó, 211   ☎934 52 31 79; www.omeia.es

When you're tired of cheap shawarma stands, stop into Omeía for some authentic Middle Eastern fare. Start off with their roasted red pepper soup (€6.50), then fill up with one of the traditional Jordanian dishes (€11-13). Pick something you haven't got a chance of pronouncing correctly and hope for the best!

✚ ⓂUniversitat. Walk up C. Aribau to the left of the University building and turn right onto C. Aragó. Ⓢ Appetizers €6.30-7; entrees €7.50-13. Lunch menú €7.50. ☒ Open daily 10am-4pm and 8pm-1am.

CAMPECHANO
GRILL $$

C. València, 286   ☎932 15 62 33; www.campechanobarcelona.com

If you've ever wondered what it's like to picnic at a Barcelonan *merendero* (outdoor bar and lunch area), Campechano may not quite satisfy your curiosity—but it will try. The restaurant offers *carnes a la brasa* (grilled meat) beside a courtyard campfire. Peek through the painted trees to peep mountainside campers and prepare to chow down on delicious, relatively cheap eats.

✚ ⓂDiagonal. Head downhill on Pg. de Gràcia and turn left onto C. València. Ⓢ Salads €4-6. Entrees €8.50-18. Lunch menú €10. ☒ Open M 1-4pm, Tu-F 1-4pm and 8:30-midnight, Sa 1:30-4pm and 8:30-midnight.

food

EL JAPONÉS
JAPANESE $$

Passatge Concepció, 2 ☎934 87 25 92; www.grupotragaluz.com

This sushi may cost more than your hostel bunk, but if you appreciate quality, it's worth the splurge. Bulk up on noodles or rice and order a mixed sushi platter (€20) for a slightly more economical—though by no means cheap—alternative. Trendy hardly begins to describe the clients and the interior; definitely leave the backpack in your hostel.

✚ ⓜDiagonal. Walk down Pg. de Gràcia and turn right onto Passatge Concepció, which is the 1st narrower road on the right. ⓢ Appetizers €6-10; entrees €8-16. Sushi €5-10. ⓩ Open M-W 1:30-4pm and 8:30pm-midnight, Th 1:30-4pm and 8pm-midnight, F-Sa 1:30-4pm and 8pm-12:30am, Su 1:30-4pm and 8:30pm-midnight.

CAFÉ CHAPULTEPEC
MEXICAN $$

C. Comte Borrell, 152 ☎934 51 92 85; www.cafechapultepec.com

Cheap burritos (€4.30-5.40) and other Mexican dishes, along with free internet, make this cafe a pleasant retreat from generally overpriced l'Eixample. Grab some *chilaquiles de pollo* (€6), or try one of the flavored hotcakes with ham or bacon (€4.80).

✚ ⓜUrgell. With your back to the rocket-shaped Agbar Tower, walk along Gran Via de les Corts Catalanes and turn right onto C. Comte Borrell. ⓢ Appetizers €3.60-5.90; entrees €4.30-8.50. ⓩ Open Tu-F 10am-4pm and 7-11pm, Sa 12:30-4:30pm and 7-11pm, Su 12:30-4:30pm.

MUSSOL
CATALAN $$

C. Casp, 19 ☎933 01 78 10

Mussol serves delicious and inexpensive traditional fare in a massive den filled with businessmen, families, and 10 ft. wine casks. With tchotchkes lining the wall and *faux-bois* decor, it doesn't quite achieve a down-home feel, but the prices are remarkably low.

✚ ⓜCatalunya. Head up Pg. de Gràcia and turn right onto C. Casp. ⓢ Appetizers €4.60-10; entrees €5.80-17 (most under €12). Daily specials €4-10. ⓩ Open M-F 7:45-noon and 1pm-1am, Sa 1pm-1am, Su 1pm-midnight.

FRIDA'S
MEXICAN $$

C. Bruc, 115 ☎934 57 54 09

Renowned as the most authentic Mexican restaurant in l'Eixample, Frida's serves anti-Tex-Mex quesadillas, *tostadas*, and a range of traditional dishes including *cochinita pibil* (€12) and *michoacan carnitas* (€12). Kick back with a margarita (€5.70) at the bar under a portrait of Frida Kahlo, or take your food to-go for a picnic along nearby Pg. de Gràcia.

✚ ⓜGirona. Walk down C. Girona past C. Aragó and take a left onto C. Mallorca. Frida's is on the corner of Mallorca and Bruc. ⓘ 5 tacos €9 on Th and F. ⓢ Tostadas and quesadillas €3. Entrees €7.80-12. Lunch menú €11. ⓩ Open Tu-Sa 1-4pm and 8:30pm-midnight.

GINZA
JAPANESE $$

C. Provença, 205 ☎934 51 71 93

Ginza is a tastier and cheaper alternative to the multitude of all-you-can-eat Japanese restaurants in the area. Fresh, delicious dishes are served amid paper lamps and woodblock prints. Look up at the photograph of sumo wrestlers under blossoming cherry trees as you sip miso soup (€3), fill up on *teppanyaki* (€6-12), and wash it all down with a cup of sake.

✚ ⓜDiagonal. Walk away from Pg. de Gràcia on C. Rosselló. Take a left onto C. Balmes and a right onto C. Provença. ⓢ Appetizers €3-9.60; entrees €6-12. Sushi €6.50. ⓩ Open daily 1-4pm and 8pm-midnight.

MAURI
BAKERY, DELI, TEA $$

Rambla Catalunya, 102 and 103   ☎932 15 10 20; www.pasteleriasmauri.com

This tripartite pastry-deli-dessert shop has something to satisfy any craving, whether sweet or savory. Dine on little sandwiches, croquettes, croissants, and more cakes than you've seen in one place at Rambla Catalunya, 102, or order something from the deli next door and dine in the wood and plaster salon. Across the street, you'll find Mauri's *bombonería* and tearoom, which sells gift baskets perfect for wooing cute hostelmates.

✚ ⓂDiagonal. Walk away from Pg. de Gràcia and take a right onto Rambla Catalunya. The pastry shop is on the right; the tea shop on the left. Ⓢ Pastries and snacks €1.50-2.50. Tapas €3.20-8. Sandwiches €2-3. Lunch menú €13. ☒ Open M-Sa 9am-9pm, Su 9am-3pm.

LAIE BOOKSTORE CAFÉ
CAFE, CATALAN $$

C. Pau Claris, 85   ☎933 02 73 10; www.laie.es/restaurante/pau-claris/8

Perfect for the bibliophilic foodie—or just anyone looking for a cafe to chill with her copy of *Let's Go*. Head to the sunny yellow back room with palm trees and burlap shades, or chill out on the couches hovering around the bookstore's entrance. A vegetarian-friendly snack bar with gourmet mini-sandwiches and pastries provides snacks during the odd hours, while a full-on restaurant serves inexpensive dishes come mealtime.

✚ ⓂCatalunya. Follow Pg. de Gràcia away from Pl. Catalunya and turn right onto C. Casp and then left onto C. Pau Claris. *i* Internet €1 per 15min. Ⓢ Coffee and snacks €1.40-4.50. Food €7-10. Lunch menú M-F €14, Sa-Su €17. Beer €2.60. Wine €1.60-3. ☒ Open M-F 9am-10pm, Sa 10am-10pm.

EL ÚLTIMO AGAVE
MEXICAN $$

C. Aragó, 193   ☎934 54 93 43; www.elultimoagave.com

Wrapped in brick and tastefully crumbling red plaster—less tastefully covered in customers' graffiti—this very Mexican joint (note the shrine to the Virgin of Guadalupe), whips up tacos, enchiladas, and the Último Agave (€14), which it claims is better than any other fajita. (We claim it's more expensive but worth the extra euro.) Let the pole of *coronita* caps guide your path through their selection of Mexican beers, or simply opt for a margarita.

✚ ⓂUniversitat. Head up C. Aribau to the left of the University building. Turn left onto C. Aragó. Ⓢ Appetizers €7-11; entrees €9-17. Desserts €4.50-5. ☒ Open daily 1pm-3am.

LA FLAUTA
TAPAS, SANDWICHES $$

C. Aribau, 23   ☎933 23 70 38

La Flauta takes its name from the crispy Catalan sandwich made with *pa amb tomàquet* (tomato squeezed onto the bread) that puts all other *bocadillos* to shame. This is not the stale bread with two slices of cheese that you drunkenly paid €4 for at 3am; these sandwiches are stuffed with mouthwatering veggies, meat, and cheese. If you'd prefer your food on a toothpick or tiny piece of bread instead of between two big slices, the restaurant's tapas are just as famous as its *flautas* and attract a crowd that spills out onto the street in the evening.

✚ ⓂUniversitat. Walk down C. Aribau, the road to the left of the University. La Flauta is 1 block down on the left. Ⓢ Entrees €4.50-8. Sandwiches €3.70-9.50. Weekday lunch menú €11. ☒ Open M-Sa 7am-1:30am.

LA MUSCLERIA
SEAFOOD $$

C. Mallorca, 290   ☎934 58 98 44; www.muscleria.com

Would you eat them in a can? Would you, could you, in a van? Would you eat them in a boat? Could you eat them in a moat? Although you probably won't be able to answer these questions, La Muscleria will let you try—they offer more mussel options than you knew existed, though you'll have to order takeout (at a 20% discount) to try the aforementioned eating locales. Other seafoods (cala-

food

mari and oysters, to name a few) and *cocas* (think love child of an open-faced sandwich and pizza) round out the menu.

✈ ⓂGirona. Walk along C. Girona past C. Aragó and take a left onto C. Mallorca. La Muscleria is on the corner on the left. ⓢ Mussels €10. ⌚ Open M-Sa 1-4pm and 8:30-11:30pm, Su 1-4pm.

LA PULPERÍA
SEAFOOD $$

C. Consell de Cent, 329 ☎924 87 53 98; www.restaurantelapulperia.com

In a masochistic turn of events, this restaurant lets you eat fantastic *pulpo* (octopus; €8.50-33), under the watchful eye of an eight-legged friend (admittedly, he's painted and presumably holds no grudge). Just to be sure there are no hard feelings, a selection of non-octopus Galician tapas are available around the dark wooden bar, and there's always room to escape his gaze on the terrace.

✈ ⓂPasseig de Gràcia. Walk up Pg. de Gràcia and take a left onto C. Consell de Cent. ⓢ Tapas €4-9.50. Entrees €11-19. ⌚ Open M-Th noon-midnight, F-Sa noon-2am.

BARCELONETA

Barceloneta is nearly surrounded by the Mediterranean, so it's no surprise that its cuisine involves an abundance of seafood, ranging from the homeliest tapas bars to the swankiest restaurants, with everything in between.

🏴 BOMBETA
TAPAS $$

C. Maquinista, 3 ☎933 19 94 45

Take heed of the warning scrawled above the bar, *"No hablamos inglés, pero hacemos unas bombas cojonudas"*—or, for those who don't speak Spanish, "We don't speak English, but we make *bombas* that are out of this world." The retro facade is plastered with menu listings, and a no-frills dining room inside offers typical Spanish fare like *tostadas*, tortillas, and tapas, but really—just get the *bombas* (fried potato balls with spicy ground beef inside; €3.50 for two).

✈ ⓂWalk down Pg. Juan de Borbó (toward the beach) and take a left onto C. Maquinista. ⓢ Appetizers €3-9.50; entrees €5-18. ⌚ Open M-Tu 10am-midnight, Th-Su 10am-midnight.

🏴 SOMORROSTRO
SEAFOOD $$$

C. Sant Carles, 11 ☎932 25 00 10; www.restaurantesomorrostro.com

This extraordinary restaurant assembles a new menu every day based on selections from the catch of the day that the young chefs have selected—though "artists" might be a more appropriate term—Jordi Limón and Andrés Gaspar. Somorrostro is not cheap—its rotating menu of seafood dishes, paella, curries, and other dishes runs about €13-20 per entree, but the nighttime *menú* (€15-17) of the chefs' gastronomical experiments is the real treat. The kitchen is in full view right behind the bar, so you can watch the masters at work and ask them questions like, "How the hell did you manage to make a solid bar of gazpacho?"

✈ ⓂBarceloneta. Walk on Plà Palau over Ronda Litoral, following the harbor. After crossing Litoral, take the 5th left onto C. Sant Carles. ⓢ Appetizers €6-14; entrees €13-20. Weekday lunch buffet €13 per kg. Dinner menú €15-17. Wine €3-5. ⌚ Open M 8-11:30pm, W-Sa 8-11:30pm, Su 2-4pm and 8-11:30pm.

L'ARRÒS
PAELLA $$$

Pg. Joan de Borbó, 12 ☎932 21 26 46; www.larros.es

At first glance, L'Arròs ("Rice") appears to be a typical tourist trap along Barceloneta's main drag, but don't let the uninspired decor and multilingual menu of this *arrocería* fool you. What the restaurant lacks in atmosphere it makes up for with its paella, which Barcelona natives claim is some of the best in town.

✈ ⓂBarceloneta. Walk on Plà Palau over Ronda Litoral and follow Pg. Joan de Borbó. ⓢ Appetizers €8-17; entrees €14-20. ⌚ Open daily noon-11:30pm.

BAR JAI-CA

TAPAS, SEAFOOD $$

C. Ginebra, 13 ☎932 68 32 65

This unassuming tapas bar serves fresh seafood and local flavor to swarms of locals. Ceramic jars and houses line the shelves, while signed photographs of F.C. Barcelona legends look down from overhead. Grab a single *bomba* (fried potato ball with spicy ground beef; €1.40) or wash down a plateful of crunchy sea critters (€3-6) with some cheap beer (€1.80).

✢ ⓂBarceloneta. Walk on Plà Palau over Ronda Litoral to follow the harbor. After crossing Litoral, take the 2nd left onto C. Ginebra. *i* Credit card min. €10. Ⓢ Tapas €1.30-8. ☼ Open Tu-Sa 9am-11:30pm, Su 9am-10:30pm.

BAR BITÁCORA

TAPAS $

C. Balboa, 1 ☎933 19 11 10

During the summer months, the giant neon eyeball of this establishment looks onto a small terrace full of young people who flock from the beach like pigeons to a tasty chunk of bread. The 10% surcharge to sit in the courtyard terrace is worth every cent. A simple interior offers plenty of seating for those looking to get out of the sun, with a cheap but filling daily *menú* (entree with salad and *patatas bravas*, bread, a drink, and dessert; €5).

✢ ⓂBarceloneta. Walk down Pg. Joan de Borbó (towards the beach) and take the 1st left after Ronda del Litoral onto C. Balboa. Ⓢ Tapas €2.50-8. Sangria €3. Menú del día €5-7. ☼ Open M-W 9am-midnight, Th-F 9am-2am, Sa 10am-2am, Su noon-midnight.

SEGONS MERCAT

SEAFOOD $$$

C. Balboa, 16 ☎933 10 78 80; www.segonsmercat.com

On the aging streets of Barceloneta, this sleek and clean restaurant stands apart. The menu and prices vary each day, as the name (*segons mercat* is Catalan for market price) suggests. Dine in the shiny interior with businessmen on their lunch breaks and other diners who appreciate the best seafood, even if they have to shell out (get it?) a little extra.

✢ ⓂBarceloneta. Walk on Plà Palau over Ronda Litoral to follow the harbor. Take the 1st left after crossing Litoral, onto C. Balboa. Ⓢ Tapas €4-7.50. Entrees €7.90-17. Wines €2.50-4. ☼ Open M-F 7:30am-1:30am, Sa-Su 1pm-midnight.

GRÀCIA

Gràcia's pedestrian *plaças* and cute streets are home to some of Barcelona's most vibrant cafes. Almost every establishment will have tapas, even if they aren't the house specialty, but don't miss out on the more traditional meals that Gràcia has to offer.

◾ UN LUGAR DE GRACIA

CATALAN $$

C. Providència, 88 ☎932 19 32 89

Un Lugar de Gracia has the best-priced and most ample lunch special in the neighborhood by far: any two dishes from the midday *menú*—no distinction between first and second courses, so the very hungry may essentially order two main courses at no extra cost—bread, water or wine, and dessert cost €9.50. For that amount of food at that price, you'd expect mediocre fare in a depressing bar, but this is a brightly colored, and lively meeting place, with locals returning often for the great food and company.

✢ ⓂJoanic. From the Metro, follow C. Escorial uphill and take a left onto C. Providència. Ⓢ Entrees €6-11. ☼ Open M 8:15am-4:30pm, W-Th 8:15am-4:30pm and 7:30pm-midnight, F 8:15am-4:30pm and 7:30pm-2am, Sa 11am-4:30pm and 7:30pm-2am, Su 11am-4:30pm. Also open for F.C. Barcelona matches.

food

👍 **SAMSARA** TAPAS $$

C. Terol, 6 ☎932 85 36 88

Samsara has a long regular menu with some of the best tapas in the neighborhood as well as about a half dozen "novetats": daily tapas specials listed on the chalkboard. The restaurant's feel would be date-like, were it not for the often communal tables: low wooden tables surrounded by even lower cushioned ottomans accommodate as many as can squeeze in, so be prepared to make new friends.

➡ ⓂFontana. Head downhill on C. Gran de Gràcia, then turn left on C. Ros de Olano, which becomes C. Terol. [$] Tapas €4.40-7.50. Beer €2-3.20. Wine €3-4. ⏰ Open M-W 8:30pm-1am, Th 8:30pm-2am, F-Sa 8:30pm-3am, Su 7:30pm-1am.

LA NENA CAFE $

C. Ramón y Cajal, 36 ☎932 85 14 76

La Nena has an extensive menu of gourmet chocolates, ice creams, crepes, sandwiches, and quiches at ridiculously low prices. Don't try ordering a cold beer to beat the heat, though—the huge banner overhead alerts visitors that this may be the only spot in Barcelona that doesn't serve alcohol. This is a *xocolateria*, and as such, it specializes in that thick and excellent Spanish hot chocolate (€2.50-3.50). For a more savory treat, try one of the *tostadas*, like the goat cheese with tomato and mushroom, which will have you wishing you, too, had an extra stomach for more room.

➡ ⓂFontana. Follow C. Astúries away from C. Gran de Gràcia and take a right onto C. Torrent de l'Olla. Walk a few blocks and take a left onto C. Ramón y Cajal. [$] Sandwiches €3-6. Quiches €5.50. Pastries €1.80-2.50. Cash only. ⏰ Open M-W 9am-2pm and 4-10pm, Th-Su 9am-10:30pm.

GAVINA PIZZA $$

C. Ros de Olano, 17 ☎934 15 74 50

Gavina is Gràcia's most heavenly pizzeria: winged cherubs above the door welcome you, and a further host of angels and saints watches benevolently as you eat, while a giant plastic hand of God scoops through the wall, about to pick you up. The big draw, though, is not the impressive kitsch but the gigantic, delicious pizzas (€6.50-14). Try the namesake Gavina (potatoes, ham, onion, and mushrooms; €12) or the pizza of the day—but be sure to bring friends or an otherworldly appetite.

➡ ⓂFontana. From the Metro, walk downhill on C. Gran de Gràcia and take a left onto C. Ros de Olano. [$] Pizza €6.50-14. Midday menú €10. ⏰ Open M-Th 1pm-1am, F-Sa 1pm-2am, Su 1pm-1am.

IKASTOLA BAR, CAFE $

C. Perla, 22

If you don't like the specials, just write your own on the chalkboard menu—but don't expect the cook to take heed. Every night young locals gather at Ikastola (Basque for "nursery school") to chat, pound out tunes on the upright piano, and scribble everything from love notes to apartment listings on the walls of this cafe. Lively and quick with cheap and famous *bocatas* (sandwiches; €4.50) on view behind the bar, Ikastola is the perfect place to start the night before embarking on more mature shenanigans.

➡ ⓂFontana. Follow C. Astúries away from C. Gran de Gràcia, then take a right onto C. Torrent de l'Olla and left onto C. Perla. [$] Salads €7. Beer €1.70-2.30. Wine €2. Cash only. ⏰ Open M-Th 7pm-midnight, F-Sa 7pm-1am, Su 7pm-midnight.

CHIDO ONE MEXICAN $$

C. Torrijos, 30 ☎932 85 03 35; www.chidoone.es

If the colorful Oaxacan wooden animals lining the walls don't tip you off that this place means business, the *mole* (spicy chocolate-based sauce) will. The tacos, served in tiny flour tortillas, are the best on this side of the Atlantic, and the *mole*-drowned enchiladas "Santa Rosa" (€12) are absolutely divine. Grab a Mexican beer (€2-4) to wash it all down.

✈ Ⓜ*Fontana. Follow C. Astúries away from C. Gran de Gràcia to Pl. Virreina. In the middle of the right side of the plaza, take a right down C. Torrijos.* Ⓢ *Appetizers €8.50-9.50; entrees €10-13. Cash only.* 🕗 *Open M-Th 1-5pm and 7pm-1am, F-Su 1pm-2am.*

L'ILLA DE GRÀCIA
VEGETARIAN $$

C. Sant Domènec, 19   ☎932 38 02 29; www.illadegracia.cat

A haven for vegetarians, this modern eatery just off the Pl. Vila de Gràcia serves meatless meals worlds away from the *queso bocadillos* you've been trying to enjoy while your friends savored their delicious *jamón*. The restaurant offers vegetarian versions of Catalan classics, including spinach *canelons* and seitan dishes served in personal crocks (€5-8).

✈ Ⓜ*Fontana. From the Metro, head downhill 5 blocks on C. Gran de Gràcia and turn left onto C. Sant Domènec.* Ⓢ *Salads €5-6. Entrees €3.70-8.* 🕗 *Open Tu-F 1-4pm and 9pm-midnight, Sa-Su 2-4pm and 9pm-midnight.*

pa amb tomáquet

Forget about Butterfingers, butterflies, and butterfaces. Stop believing in I Can't Believe It's Not Butter. If you go searching for the classic bread and butter combination in Barcelona, you'll be disappointed.

Here, *pa amb tomáquet* rules the day—or at least the dinner table. The traditional accompaniment in Barcelonan and Catalan cuisine, toasted bread is converted into the storied *pa amb tomáquet* through a vigorous tomato rubdown, followed by a thorough olive oil and garlic seasoning. *Pa amb tomáquet* is widely heralded as a symbol of the Catalan culture—and it can be tough to escape. Ignore the vague resemblance to strawberry jam and dig right in—just don't go asking for butter. And please, don't call it bruschetta.

food

CAFÈ DEL TEATRE
BAR $

C. Torrijos, 41   ☎934 16 06 51

This corner cafe's name is a bit misleading: don't come here expecting stuffy old-world pomp, because you're going to find a cool little bar with lots of shiny black surfaces and its name boldly stated in lime-green translucent plastic. The only hint of anything classic is found in the colorfully updated interpretations of vintage wallpaper. Drop by for the cheap *menú* (€6.40-6.90) and the even cheaper beer (€1-3).

✈ Ⓜ*Fontana. Follow C. Astúries away from C. Gran de Gràcia to Pl. Virreina. In the middle of the right side of the plaza, take a right down C. Torrijos.* Ⓢ *Entrees and sandwiches €4.90-6.50. Menú €6.40-6.90. Beer €1-3. Cash only.* 🕗 *Open daily 11am-3am.*

MIRIOT
MEDITERRANEAN $$

C. Francisco Giner, 54   ☎933 68 26 05; www.miriot.com

Miriot serves delicious Catalan and Mediterranean food, often with a bit of a twist (for example, the duck *canelons*; €8). The place itself approaches the level of swanky but it stays quite within the budget traveler's reach thanks to the incongruously low prices. The decor is simple—plain brick walls punctuated by the obligatory photographs of Gaudí buildings—but the effort not spent on elaborate design has been put into the food.

✈ Ⓜ*Diagonal. Follow Pg. de Gràcia uphill across Avda. Diagonal. Take a right onto C. Bonavista and then a left onto C. Francisco Giner.* Ⓢ *Salads €6-10. Entrees €9.20-17. Menú M-F €10, Sa €13. Credit card min. €15.* 🕗 *Open M-Sa 1-4pm and 9pm-midnight.*

BARCELONA REYKJAVÍK
BAKERY $

C. Astúries, 20   ☎933 02 09 21; www.barcelonareykjavik.com

This bakery is perfect for the discerning backpacker who's tired of white bread and those sugary, mass-produced *magdalenas*. Barcelona Reykjavík bakes mind-blowing breads—if you've been in Spain long enough, you'll find the sourdough a godsend—as well as delicious muffins, brioche, and other baked goods. Ingredients and potential allergens for each are listed, making the lives of those with dietary restrictions a little easier, if only for a second before they venture back out into the world of meat, cheese, sugar, and gluten. Be prepared to eat on your feet or save it for later—this little storefront has no seating.

✦ ⓂFontana. Follow C. Astúries away from C. Gran de Gràcia. Ⓢ Items sold by weight. Breads normally €3-5. Baked goods €1-2. ☼ Open M-Sa 10:30am-9:30pm, Su 10:30am-8pm.

MONTJUÏC AND POBLE SEC

The neighborhood of **Poble Sec** hides a number of inexpensive restaurants and bars—perfect for those who don't feel like breaking the bank to eat at a museum cafe up on Montjuïc, or for those looking to explore a lovely neighborhood a bit off the beaten track.

🔲 QUIMET I QUIMET
TAPAS, BAR $$

C. Poeta Cabanyes, 25   ☎934 42 31 42

This pocket-sized tapas bar has walls lined with alcohol going all the way up to its very high ceiling, a crowd spilling out onto the street at tapas time, and the best tapas in Poble Sec—possibly in the entire city. Push your way through to the bar, order whatever looks good, and get the dark house beer if you're getting sick of Estrella Damm.

✦ ⓂParal·lel. Follow Avda. Paral·lel away from the water past the small plaça on the left, then head left up C. Poeta Cabanyes. Ⓢ Tapas €1.90-5.50. Beer €2-4. Cash only. ☼ Open M-F noon-4pm and 7-10:30pm, Sa noon-4pm.

TRENTA SIS
BAR $$

C. Margarit, 36   ☎935 05 87 97

The meals at Trenta Sis are fancy but not at all expensive. As advertised outside, Trenta Sis is *"rico y baratito"*—delicious and very cheap. The handwritten specials on the chalkboard outside change frequently, but they generally don't break the €7 barrier, and the midday lunch *menú* (Tu-F) is just €6.

✦ ⓂPoble Sec. Follow Avda. Paral·lel toward the water and turn right on C. Margarit. Ⓢ Entrees €3.80-6.90. Cash only. ☼ Open Tu-Th 1pm-2am, F-Sa 1pm-3am, Su 1pm-2am.

EL DUENDE DE POBLE SEC
SPANISH $$

C. Poeta Cabanyes, 11   ☎936 00 59 00

The glass floor with a minuscule fairy world underneath (*duende* is Spanish for a kind of fairy) is a huge hit with the kids, and the inexpensive but delicious Spanish cuisine keeps the grown-ups coming back. Fake ivy and new brick trying to look old envelop diners in the humble restaurant whose real attraction is the food. And the fairies.

✦ ⓂParal·lel. Follow Avda. Paral·lel away from the water past the small plaça on the left, then left up C. Poeta Cabanyes. Ⓢ Salads €5.90-7.80. Tapas €2.80-6.90. Entrees €7.50-19. Menú €9.90. Cash only. ☼ Open Tu-Sa 1-4pm and 8pm-midnight, Su 1-4pm.

nightlife

Nightlife in Barcelona is ubiquitous and hardcore, though there are plenty of bars and pubs for those less likely to make it to dawn. The **Barri Gòtic's** dark corners and confusing lattice of streets hide many quirky and colorful bars that you're not likely to come across unless you know they're there—even then, your chances of finding them aren't great. **El Born's** nightlife involves hopping from bar to bar, past medieval churches and Baroque palaces, in what is sure to be one of the most beautiful nights out you've ever experienced. Given the outrageously lewd (and often illicit) nature of **El Raval** during daylight hours, it's no surprise that this *barri* gets wild at night. **L'Eixample** is known colloquially as "Gaixample," and this is why: a majority of the nightlife spots in this neighborhood are geared toward the GLBT community. **Barceloneta's** clubs are on the beach, and that's about all you need to know. **Gràcia's** strong neighborhood vibe and effectively pedestrian-only streets make it a natural hotbed of nightlife and bar culture. The nightlife of **Poble Sec** is of high quality but limited quantity, and it's often hard to find unless you know to go down empty streets and into barely marked doorways. Some of the nightclubs are a little more obvious, and the few to be found here are among the city's most popular. **Tibidabo** isn't really a neighborhood but a mountain that is home to some of Barcelona's finest clubs. You'll probably have to take a cab, but it will probably be worth it.

BARRI GÒTIC AND LAS RAMBLAS

⚐ BARCELONA PIPA CLUB
BAR, CLUB

Pl. Reial, 3   ☎933 02 47 32; www.bpipaclub.com

With pipes from four continents, smoking accoutrement decorated by Dalí, and an "ethnological museum dedicated to the smoking accessory," the only pipe-related article missing from this club—albeit somewhat appropriately—is René Magritte's *Ceci n'est pas une pipe*. Despite its cryptic lack of signage and the furtive ambience of a secret society, the combination bar, pool room, and music lounge boasts a surprisingly high number of travelers. The dark wood, low lights, and provincial furnishings make for a perfect place to transport yourself away from the more collegiate nightlife of the Pl. Reial, even if your previous smoking experience amounts to time spent with a candy cigarette.

⚑ Ⓜ*Liceu. Walk on Las Ramblas toward the water and turn left onto C. Colom to enter Pl. Reial. Pipa Club is an unmarked door to the right of Glaciar Bar. To enter, ring the bottom bell.* **i** *Rotating selection of tobacco available for sale. Special smoking events. Tango and salsa lessons M and Th 8:30-10:30pm.* Ⓢ *Beer €4-5. Wine €4-5. Cocktails €7.50-9. Cash only.* Ⓧ *Open daily 6pm-6am.*

⚐ HARLEM JAZZ CLUB
JAZZ CLUB, BAR

C. Comtessa de Sobradiel, 8   ☎933 10 07 55; www.harlemjazzclub.es

With live performances nightly and often a drink included in the cover (check the schedule), this is a budget-conscious music lover's paradise. A performance schedule online and at the door lets you choose whether you'll drop in to hear lovesick English crooning or a little saucier Latin flavor. Acts range from Bossa Nova to gypsy punk, and the crowd is just as eclectic.

⚑ Ⓜ*Liceu. Walk toward the water on Las Ramblas and take a left onto C. Ferran, a right onto C. Avinyó, and a left onto C. Comtessa de Sobradiel.* **i** *Live music usually begins at 10 or 11pm. Calendar of events available online or at the door.* Ⓢ *Cover €5-6; sometimes includes 1 drink. Beer €3.80. Cocktails €7.80. Cash only.* Ⓧ *Open M-Th 8pm-4am, F-Sa 9pm-5am, Su 9pm-4am.*

free things, sketchiness included

Be careful walking through Las Ramblas. A lot of sketchy things go down on Barcelona's perpetually busy pedestrian walkway—especially after dark. Club promoters typically hang out in the area and pass out free drink coupons or entrance passes to tourists, which may strike you as gimmicky. To an extent, it is, but it also means that very few tourists pay to get into clubs or bars. Use your judgment, of course, but don't be afraid to accept a coupon or two if you want to save those euro.

SINCOPA — BAR

C. Avinyò, 35

At night this music-themed bar—rumored to have once been owned by none other than Manu Chao—plays host to as many nationalities as it has currencies and secondhand instruments on its walls. Of Barri Gòtic's bars, Sincopa has some of the most colorful decor and clientele. One night the crowd might be baked and chilling to *Dark Side of the Moon*, and the next they'll all be salsa dancing.

‡ [M]Liceu. Walk on Las Ramblas toward the water and take a left onto C. Ferran and a right onto C. Avinyò. [$] Beer €2-3. Cocktails €7. Juices €2.50. Cash only. ⏰ Open M-Th 6pm-2:30am, F-Sa 6pm-3am.

MANCHESTER — BAR

C. Milans, 5 ☎663 07 17 48; www.manchesterbar.com

The names of the drinks posted on the front door—Joy Division, The Cure, Arcade Fire, The Smiths, and many, many more—let you know what you're in for once you enter. After passing the spinning turntable when you walk in, you'll find a dark, red-lit world of intimate seating, band references, and people chatting and drinking the night away. The happy hour with €1.50 Estrella Damms will have you crooning "This Charming Man" before the evening's up.

‡ [M]Liceu. Walk toward the water on Las Ramblas and head left on C. Ferran, right on C. Avinyó, and left onto C. Milans, before C. Ample. Manchester is at the bend in the street. [$] Beers €2-4; happy hour €1.50. Shots from €2.50. Cocktails €6. Cash only. ⏰ Open M-Th 7pm-2:30am, F-Sa 7pm-3am, Su 7pm-2:30am. Happy hour daily 7-10pm.

LAS CUEVAS DEL SORTE — BAR

C. Gignàs, 2 ☎687 76 50 83

The eponymous caves (accentuated by miniature stalactites on the ceiling) are filled with alcohol and revelers. Exquisite mosaics crop up in the most unexpected places, including the bathrooms. Downstairs, small tables and another bar surround a be-disco-balled dancefloor.

‡ [M]Liceu. Walk toward the water on Las Ramblas and head left on C. Ferran, right onto C. Avinyó, and left on C. Gignàs. [$] Cocktails €6-7; before 10pm €4.50. ⏰ Open M 7pm-2am, W-Th 7pm-2am, F-Sa 7pm-3am, Su 7pm-2am.

EL 13 — BAR

C. Lleona, 13

If you can fight your way through the crowd of international 20-somethings into this pocket-sized hangout, El 13 offers the self-proclaimed and *Let's Go*-confirmed best mojitos in Barcelona (€6). Exposed brick walls show off local artwork and an assorted selection of vinyl and dismembered mannequin body parts, including a set of legs that stick out over the restroom door and a torso that serves as the primary light source. Hits from the '80s abound, and a projector plays a selection of music videos and YouTube clips over the heads of the clientele. Watch out for the vintage porn over the bar and door.

✈ [M]Liceu. Walk toward the sea on Las Ramblas and head left onto C. Ferran, right onto C. Avinyó, and left on C. Lleona. $ Beer €2-3. Cocktails €6-7. Shots €2.50. ⏰ Open M-Th 7pm-3am, F-Sa 7pm-5:30am, Su 7pm-3am.

SHANGÓ BAR

C. en Groch, 9 ☎662 10 51 65

Tucked down a poorly lit alley, Shangó's bright black-and-yellow door provides a warm, sunny beacon that beckons revelers throughout the night. Free salsa lessons and a neverending supply of spicy Latin tunes complement cheap mojitos (€4.50) and beer. Meanwhile, the comfortably full upper level of chairs and couches provides a relaxing place to grab a drink, meet some strangers, and soak in the sensation of being inside a big, sugary lemon.

✈ [M]Jaume I. Walk down Via Laietana toward the water. Take a right onto C. En Gignàs and right onto C. En Groch. i Free salsa lessons Tu-W 11pm-midnight. $ Beer €1.50-3. Mojitos €4.50. Cocktails €6; M and Su €4. ⏰ Open daily 9pm-3am.

OVISO CAFE, BAR

C. Arai, 5 ☎637 58 92 69; www.barnawood.com

Ancient Roman villa meets bohemian dive bar at Oviso. Frescoes adorn the walls, depicting peacocks, mythology, and a curious scene in which a man appears to be putting the moves on a lion. Benches and larger tables invite clients to continue the period theme and lounge at their discretion like a drunken Bacchus. Oviso serves a delicious variety of food and juices during the day, while at night the bar fills up quickly with locals from the Pl. Trippy (actual name Pl. George Orwell, a theme elaborated on by the live video feed of the bar visible on the website).

✈ [M]Liceu. Walk toward the water on Las Ramblas and head left onto C. Ferran, right onto C. Avinyó, and right onto C. Arai. Oviso is on the right as you enter the plaça. $ Beer €3. Cocktails €7. Cash only. ⏰ Open M-Th 10am-2:30am, F-Sa 10am-3am, Su 10am-2:30am.

TRESFLORES BAR

C. Correu Vell, 10 ☎666 76 76 76

Some of the cheapest cocktails in the neighborhood draw huge crowds of young partiers to this lively bar on the nightlife (or *Botellón*) hub of the Pl. Traginers. Once inside, ancient brick arches embrace the revelry below, but you'll be too distracted by the crowd and the shockingly low drink prices to notice.

✈ [M]Jaume I. Take C. Jaume I and go left on C. Dagueria, which becomes C. Lledó, which becomes Baixada Viladecols. Take a right at the bottom of the plaça. $ Cocktails €3.50. Beer €2. Cash only. ⏰ Open Tu-Th 8pm-2:30am, F-Sa 8pm-3am.

SMOLL BAR BAR

C. Comtessa de Sobradiel, 9 ☎933 10 31 73

The chic, updated '60s decor and friendly, burly bartenders combine to please an ever-present hip, gay-friendly, and young crowd. When there's room at the bar, squeeze in tight and try one of over 25 cocktails or a signature shot. The Rasmokov (vodka shot with a lime wedge topped in sugar and espresso; €2.50) will leave you caffeinated, sugar-buzzed, and full of fuzzy, extroverted feelings.

✈ [M]Liceu. Walk toward the water on Las Ramblas. Take a left onto C. Ferran, a right onto C. Avinyó, and a left onto C. Comtessa de Sobradiel. $ Beer €3.50. Cocktails €5.60. Cash only. ⏰ Open M-Th 9:30pm-2:30am, F-Sa 9:30pm-3am.

LA RIA BAR

C. Milans, 4 ☎933 10 00 92

A bright white interior, upright seating, and an entirely local clientele make for cheap booze, cheap food, and a refreshing—albeit grittier—alternative to the dressed up places in Pl. Reial. Order from the street and hang outside if the noisy sounds of Catalan from within intimidate you.

➡ Ⓜ Jaume I. Walk on Via Laietana toward the water and take a right onto C. en Gignàs. La Ria will be on the corner of C. En Gignàs and C. Milans. $ Beer €1-2.50. Wine €1.50-1.80. Tapas €4-12. Menú €6.50. Cash only. ⏰ Open M-Th 10am-1am, F 10am-3am, Sa 6pm-3am.

JAMBOREE JAZZ CLUB

Pl. Reial, 17 ☎933 19 17 89; www.masimas.com/jamboree

A hall-of-fame assortment of jazz musicians on the walls of the lower level will leave you with no guesses as to where this club's allegiances lie, even when its grotto-like halls are filled with Americans singing Aaliyah. The club offers nightly jazz and blues performances and welcomes a younger set after the shows end at midnight. After this witching hour, be prepared for everything from hip hop to Shania Twain.

➡ Ⓜ Liceu. Walk on Las Ramblas toward the water. Left on C. Colom to enter Pl. Reial. ℹ Calendar of events and concerts on the website. Flyers provide discounts. $ Dance club cover €10. Event tickets €4-12. Tarantos (upstairs, mostly flamenco) cover €6. Beer €5. Cocktails €9-10. ⏰ Dance club open M-Th 12:30pm-5am, F-Sa 12:30pm-6am, Su 12:30pm-5am. Music club open daily 9pm-1am, shows at 9 and 11pm. Tarantos open daily 8-11pm.

HEAVEN BAR

C. Escudellers, 20

€1 shots. Any questions?

➡ Ⓜ Liceu. Walk toward the water on Las Ramblas and take a left on C. Escudellers. $ Shots €1. Cocktails €4. Cash only. ⏰ Open M-Tu 8pm-2:30am, Th 8pm-2:30am, F-Sa 8pm-3am, Su 8pm-2:30am.

EL BORN

👍 EL CASO BORN BAR

C. Sant Antoni dels Sombrerers, 7 ☎932 69 11 39

This is a quieter alternative for those too cool to bother with the packed houses and inflated prices of nearby Pg. Born. Cheap drinks tempt travelers, while relaxed seating, a chill crowd, and a drinks menu with cocktails named for the Bourne movies (the name is a pun on *El Caso Bourne*, the Spanish title of *The Bourne Identity*) provide ample reasons to start the night here.

➡ Ⓜ Jaume I. Walk down C. Princesa and take a right onto C. Montcada. Upon entering Pg. Born, take a right onto C. Sombrerers and then take the 1st right onto C. Sant Antoni dels Sombrerers. $ Cava €1.80. Beer €2. Cocktails €5-7. ⏰ Open Tu-Th 6pm-2:30am, F-Sa 6pm-3am.

👍 ESPAI BARROC BAR

C. Montcada, 20 ☎933 10 06 73; www.palaudalmases.com

Nobody wants to pay €12 for a cocktail, but consider it a €6 drink with a €6 entrance fee. The space is what you're really paying for anyway. Espai Barroc is in the courtyard and ground floor of the Palau Dalmases, a 17th-century palace whose simple facade hides one of the most beautiful patios in existence, with a jaw-dropping carved staircase and an overall elegance that makes this an obligatory stop. Get the cheapest drink you can find (if €6 of the drink price is for the setting, the beer is just €1!), relax, and drink like royalty.

➡ Ⓜ Jaume I. Walk down C. Princesa and take a right onto C. Montcada. ℹ Flamenco M and W 9:30pm (€20; includes 1 drink). Live opera Th 11pm. Piano and jazz Su 9pm. $ Beer €7. Cocktails €12. ⏰ Open Tu-Th 8pm-2am, F-Sa 8pm-3am, Su 6-10pm.

LA LUNA
C. Abaixadors, 10   BAR
☎932 95 55 13; www.lalunabcn.com

Another of Barcelona's most beautiful bars, La Luna sits under timeless vaulted brick arches, with dim lighting and mirrors behind the bar making it seem even larger. Comfortable lounge seating in front makes the front a good place to camp out and take in the bar's beauty. The tropical mojito (with coconut rum; €7) and the mojito de fresa (€7.30), which replaces the lime with strawberries, are both quite popular.

✢ Ⓜ Jaume I. Take C. Argenteria to Santa Maria del Mar, then take a sharp right onto C. Abaixadors. Ⓢ Beer €2-3. Mixed drinks €6-8. ☒ Open M-W 6pm-1:30am, Th-F 6pm-2:30am, Sa 1pm-2:30am, Su 1pm-1:30am.

LA FIANNA
C. Banys Vells, 15   BAR
☎933 15 18 10; www.lafianna.com

A glass partition divides the restaurant and bar, but be prepared to push your way through on weekend nights no matter where you choose to wine or dine. Unlike at other places in the area, finding a seat at the bar is a distinct possibility; getting a spot on one of the comfy couches, where patrons kick off their shoes and settle in, is another story altogether. Patience pays off with large mojitos (€7) made with special bitters.

✢ Ⓜ Jaume I. Walk down C. Princesa and take a right onto C. Montcada. Upon entering Pg. Born, take a right onto C. Sombrerers and then another right onto C. Banys Vells. *i* All cocktails €4.50 M-Th 6-9pm. Discounted tapas M-Th 7pm-12:30am, F-Sa 7-11:30pm, and Su 7pm-12:30am. Ⓢ Tapas €2-4.80. Beer €2.50-3.40. Shots €4. Cocktails €6-7. ☒ Open M-W 6pm-1:30am, Th-Sa 6pm-2:30am, Su 6pm-1:30am.

EL COPETÍN
Pg. Born, 19   LATIN BAR
☎607 20 21 76

This dance floor just won't quit: Latin beats blare all night long, attracting a laid-back, fun-loving crowd that knows how to move. A narrow, tightly packed bar up front provides little reprieve for those who need a drink, as the waitstaff will probably be too busy dancing anyway to tend to your every beck and call.

✢ Ⓜ Jaume I. Walk down C. Princesa and take a right onto C. Montcada. Follow to Pg. Born. Ⓢ Mixed drinks €7. Cash only. ☒ Open M-Th 6pm-2:30am, F-Sa 6pm-3am, Su 6pm-2:30am.

BERIMBAU
Pg. Born, 17   BRAZILIAN BAR
☎646 00 55 40

This *copas* bar, reportedly the oldest Brazilian bar in Spain (founded 1978), offers a range of drinks you won't easily find this side of the Atlantic. Try the *guaraná* with whiskey (€8), an orange and banana juice with vodka (€9), or the tried and true (and damn good) caipirinha (€7). Samba and Brazilian electronic music fill the room with a *brasileiro* feel, and the wicker furniture and stifling heat complete the scene.

✢ Ⓜ Jaume I. Walk down C. Princesa and take a right onto C. Montcada. Follow to Pg. Born, then take a left. Ⓢ Cocktails €7-10. Beer €2.50-3. ☒ Open daily 6pm-2:30am.

CACTUS BAR
Pg. Born, 30   BAR
☎933 10 63 54; www.cactusbar.cat

Cactus Bar is renowned along Pg. Born for its phenomenally delicious, large, and potent mojitos (€8). If you can get a bartender's attention over the clamor, you generally don't need to specify which drink you want: just use your fingers to indicate how many mojitos it'll be. The constant stream—or devastating flood, perhaps more accurately—of customers means the bartenders work as a team, creating a mojito assembly line that churns out over a dozen of the minty beverages at a time.

✢ Ⓜ Jaume I. Walk down C. Princesa and take a right onto C. Montcada. Follow until you hit Pg. Born, then take a left. *i* DJs M and W. Ⓢ Beer €3. Cocktails €8. Breakfast €1.50. Sandwiches €2.50-3.70. Tapas €1.80-6.50. ☒ Open daily 4pm-2:30am.

nightlife

EL RAVAL

The nightlife in El Raval is mostly centered on the bars on and around **Rambla del Raval** and **Carrer de Joaquin Costa.**

👍 MARSELLA BAR — BAR

C. Sant Pau, 65 — ☎934 42 72 63

Walls lined with antique mirrors, cabinets, old advertisements, and ancient liquor bottles that have probably been there since the age of *modernisme* will have you just waiting to witness your first saloon brawl. Luckily, the crowd is genial and friendly, even after a few absinthes (€5)—not that there's room to fight in this crowded place anyway. Paint falling from the ceiling and fuzzy chandeliers will have you feeling every month of the bar's 190 years of business.

➜ Ⓜ Liceu. Follow C. Sant Pau from Las Ramblas. $ Beer €3. Mixed drinks €5-6.50. Cash only. ⏰ Open M-Th 11pm-2am, F-Sa 11pm-3am.

👍 MOOG — CLUB

C. Arc del Teatre, 3 — ☎933 19 17 89; www.masimas.com/moog

One of Europe's premier clubs for electronic music, Moog—named for the synth that is the backbone of electronic music—caters both to electrotrash aficionados and lost souls just trying to find a place to dance. Come on Wednesdays and weekends for the biggest crowds, or drop in earlier in the week for house DJ sets. If you're looking for older hits or just want to get away from the throbbing mass on the dance floor, check out the upstairs, which plays a mix of older electro, disco, and techno.

➜ Ⓜ Drassanes. Walk away from the water on Las Ramblas and left onto C. Arc del Teatre. i Discount flyers often available on Las Ramblas. $ Cover €10. ⏰ Open M-Th midnight-5am, F-Sa midnight-6am, Su midnight-5am.

👍 PLÁSTICO BAR — BAR

C. Sant Ramón, 23 — ☎938 94 13 33; www.myspace.com/plasticobar

This tiny but hip bar, hidden on one of El Raval's seediest back streets, will accommodate as many people as are cool enough to enter. Dark paisley walls with a green-lit bar usher you in, but squeeze through to the back portion where the real life awaits. The upper level is for lounging, while the scratchy sound system of the lower portion pumps a mix of modern indie and '60s rock to a dance-ready crowd.

➜ Ⓜ Liceu. Walk on Las Ramblas toward the sea. Take a right onto C. Nou de la Rambla and right onto C. Sant Ramón. $ Shots €3. Beer €3-3.50. Mixed drinks €6. Cash only. ⏰ Open Tu-Th 7pm-2:30am, F-Sa 7pm-3am.

BAR BIG BANG — BAR, LIVE MUSIC

C. Botella, 7 — www.bigbangbcn.net

The back room attracts a collegiate crowd who watch free nightly jazz, standup, and vaudeville-esque theater. Out front, customers are serenaded by big band favorites—both local and national—from the stereo and black-and-white projector screen. Outsider art and vintage photographs line the walls, adding a little something extra to the sensory overload.

➜ Ⓜ Sant Antoni. Walk down C. Sant Antoni Abad and take a right onto C. Botella. i Schedule of performances and special events on website. Variety show on Tu. DJ F-Sa midnight. $ Shots €3. Beer €3-4. Cocktails €6.50. All cheaper before 11pm. Cash only. ⏰ Open Tu-Su 9:30pm-2:30am.

BETTY FORD'S BAR

C. Joaquin Costa, 56 ☎933 04 13 68

This ain't your dad's Betty Ford's. During the earlier hours of the evening, this bar and restaurant stuffs the crowds of local students coming in with relatively cheap and famously delicious burgers (€6.50). Happy hour (6-9pm) provides cheap drinks, and later in the night the place gets packed with a young, noisy crowd.

🧭 ⓂUniversitat. Walk down Ronda de Sant Antoni and take a slight left onto C. Joaquin Costa. $ Beer €3. Mixed drinks €5-6; happy hour €4. Burgers €6.50. Shakes €3.50. Cash only. 🕒 Open M 6pm-1:30am, Tu-Th 11am-1:30am, F-Sa 11am-2:30am. Happy hour M-Sa 6-9pm.

LLETRAFERIT BAR, BOOKSTORE

C. Joaquin Costa, 43 ☎933 01 19 61

A haven of calm in the frenetic, off-beat nightlife of C. Joaquin Costa, Lletraferit (Catalan for "bookworm") offers a little bit of literature to accompany your alcohol binge. Chill up front with a cocktail (€6-7.50) in comfy leather armchairs or head around to the back, where a cozy library and bookstore awaits. Settle in with a good book and watch the schwasted passersby while smugly sipping a drink.

🧭 ⓂUniversitat. Walk down Ronda Sant Antoni and take a slight left onto C. Joaquin Costa. $ Cocktails €6-7.50. Cash only. 🕒 Open M-Th 4pm-1:30am, F-Sa 4pm-3am, Su 4pm-1:30am.

VALHALLA CLUB DE ROCK BAR, LIVE MUSIC

C. Tallers, 68

Be prepared to see burly men air-guitaring Slayer in the area where you'd usually find a dance floor. A concert hall some nights, this dark and industrial nightclub is a haven for those looking for something a little more metal after all the flashing lights and throbbing techno. Free entry on non-show nights means you can use the cash you save to try the entire selection of *chupitos del rock*, specialty shots named after bands from Elvis to Whitesnake (€1).

🧭 ⓂUniversitat. Walk down C. Tallers. ℹ Search for Valhalla Club de Rock on Facebook to find a calendar of concerts and special events. $ Shots €1-2. Beer €1.50-2.50, after 10pm €2.50-5. Mixed drinks €6-7. Cash only. 🕒 Open daily 6:30pm-2:30am.

SANT PAU 68 BAR

C. Sant Pau, 68 ☎934 41 31 15

Sant Pau 68 is an absurdist bar with an identity crisis. The wall of ears—be careful what you say, the walls here literally have ears—and gas-tank-inspired lights and a metal chandelier with circuit board cutouts cast geek-chic patterns of light across the stairwell. If you're looking to get away from the crowd, grab a Bloody Mary (€6) and head upstairs to scrawl your regards on the graffiti wall.

🧭 ⓂLiceu. Follow C. Sant Pau away from Las Ramblas. $ Beer €2.20. Mixed drinks €6-7. 🕒 Open M-Th 8pm-2:30am, F-Sa 8pm-3:30am, Su 8pm-2:30am.

LA ROUGE BAR

Rambla Raval, 10 ☎933 29 54 45

Push your way through the packed bar area to lounge in the dark seating in back, or look down on the masses from the loft. Cocktails start at €5, while the house shot *chupito la rouge* will cost you €3.50. Electronic dance music plays over the stereo to please the younger crowd.

🧭 ⓂLiceu. Walk on C. Hospital and take a left onto Rambla Raval. La Rouge will be on the right. $ Beer €2.50. Cava €4. Cocktails €5-6. Tapas €1.50-6.50. Cash only. 🕒 Open M-Th 8pm-2am, F-Sa 8pm-3am.

L'EIXAMPLE

☒ LES GENTS QUE J'AIME
BAR

C. València, 286bis   ☎932 15 68 79

Come down the stairs into this sultry red-velvet underworld, redolent of gin and *modernisme*, where you'll be transported back some hundred years into a *fin-de-siècle* fiesta. Black-and-white photographs, cool jazz, and vintage chandeliers set the mood for you to partake of sinful pleasures. Not sure where to head for the rest of the night? Cozy up next to the palm-reader or have your tarot cards read to avoid making the decision yourself.

✦ ⓜDiagonal. Head downhill on Pg. de Gràcia and turn left onto C. València. Les Gents Que J'aime is downstairs, just past Campechano. *i* Palm reading and tarot M-Sa. ⓢ Wine €3. Beer €3.50. Cocktails €7. Palm reading €30. Tarot €25. ⏰ Open M-Th 7pm-2:30am, F-Sa 7pm-3am, Su 7pm-2:30am.

☒ LA FIRA
CLUB

C. Provença, 171   ☎933 23 72 71

Decorated entirely with pieces from the old Apolo Amusement Park in Barcelona, this club is that creepy carnival from *Scooby Doo*, but with a bar instead of a g-g-g-ghooooost. Spend a little extra time in the Mystery Machine before entering, and this club will be one of Barcelona's most memorable. Chill with a drink and the carousel horses, or dance until you just can't handle this place anymore.

✦ ⓜHospital Clínic. Walk away from the engineering school along C. Rossello and take a right onto C. Villarroel. Take the 1st left onto C. Provença; La Fira is a few blocks down. *i* Often hosts shows or parties, sometimes with entrance fee or 1-drink min. ⓢ Cover sometimes €10; includes 1 drink. Beer €5. Cocktails €8. Cash only. ⏰ Open W-Sa 11:30pm-3am.

LA CHAPELLE
BAR, GLBT

C. Muntaner, 67   ☎934 53 30 76

A wall of devotional figurines, crosses, and paintings with mostly nude men in front allows La Chapelle to show a gayer side of the sacrament. Solemn red lighting mixed with modern bubble lights cut through the veil of testosterone—apparently debaucherous religious imagery is bait for bears, or maybe it's the video of naked male models on the flatscreen. Get a little closer to God while getting a lot closer to some grizzly guys.

✦ ⓜUniversitat. Face the University building and walk left on Gran Via de les Corts Catalanes. Turn right onto C. Muntaner; La Chapelle is 2 blocks up. ⓢ Beer €2.50. Mixed drinks €5. ⏰ Open daily 4pm-2:30am.

LE CYRANO
BAR

C. Aribau, 154   ☎932 31 79 09

Don't you just hate it when you watch the bartender pour your drink, and you're all like, okay, enough, that's good, really, ENOUGH? And then you're forced to sip the drink you just paid way too much for and could have done a better job making yourself? Well, this is the bar for you—for no more than €5 (usually €4) you get an empty glass and get to make your own cocktail, ranging from a 95%-Coke Cuba Libre to the *Let's Go* pregame special: vodka with a splash of juice. Free popcorn keeps you busy while you wait some 40min. for the ever-packed bar to clear so you can get your next round.

✦ ⓜDiagonal. Facing downhill on Pg. de Gràcia, head right on C. Rosselló 3 blocks, then right up C. Aribau. ⓢ All drinks €4-5. ⏰ Open Th-Sa 11pm-3am.

DOW JONES
BAR

C. Bruc, 97   ☎934 76 38 31; www.bardowjones.es

During the day, this bar has enough TV screens to keep every *fútbol* fan happy, no matter her allegiance. At night, the bar lights up with raucous foreigners (mainly American, British, and Irish) trying desperately to order their favorite drink before the price spikes—like the stock market, drink prices here vary based on their popularity throughout the day. Wait for the prices to crash if you're craving a winner, or keep buying low and be glad the staff speaks English for when you start slurring your Spanish (or your English).

✦ ⓂGirona. Follow C. Consell de Cent 1 block toward Pg. de Gràcia and turn right up C. Bruc. Ⓢ Beer €2-5.50. Cocktails €4-7. Food €2.80-7.50. Prices vary by demand. ⓩ Open M-F 7am-2:30am, Sa-Su noon-3am.

ÁTAME
BAR, GLBT

C. Consell de Cent, 257 ☎934 34 92 73; www.facebook.com/bar.atame

Dietrich Gay Teatro Café's life partner, Atame's simple, dark interior, accented by sparkly rainbow flags, pulses with '80s hits and a mostly male crowd that loves to sing along (and encourages you to sing with them). The dance floor in back is crowded when drag shows aren't in session, while the front of the bar provides a pack of men lying in wait for unsuspecting newcomers.

✦ ⓂUniversitat. Face the University building and walk left on Gran Via de les Corts Catalanes. Turn right onto C. Aribau, walk 2 blocks, and turn left onto C. Consell de Cent; Atame is 1 block down. *i* Drag shows and other events Tu-F and Su. Call for more info. Ⓢ Mixed drinks €5, happy hour €4. ⓩ Open M-Th 6:30pm-2:30am, F-Sa 7pm-3am, Su 6:30pm-2:30am. Happy hour daily until 11pm.

AIRE (SALA DIANA)
CLUB, GLBT

C. València, 236 ☎934 54 63 94; www.arenadisco.com/aire.htm

If you're looking for a gay party spot that isn't overwhelmingly male (read: the rest of L'Eixample), check out Aire for all of the female company the neighborhood seemed to be lacking. This huge club is packed almost as soon as its doors open and continues to party with a mix of pop hits, R and B, and electronica well into the night. You generally don't even need to pay the cover to meet someone, as the party spills out onto C. València. Don't worry about feeling left out—no matter your gender or orientation, the club is, as the owner says, "for her and her male friends."

✦ ⓂPasseig de Gràcia. Head uphill toward Avda. Diagonal and turn left onto C. València; Aire is 2½ blocks down on the left. Ⓢ Cover €5-10; includes 1 drink. ⓩ Open Th-Sa 11pm-3am.

LUZ DE GAS
CLUB, CONCERT HALL

C. Muntaner, 246 ☎932 09 77 11; www.luzdegas.com

One of the most renowned clubs in the city, and for good reason. Red velvet walls, gilded mirrors, and sparkling chandeliers will have you wondering how you possibly got past the bouncer, while the massive purple-lit dance floor surrounded by bars will remind you what you're here for. Big name jazz, blues, and soul performers occasionally take the stage during the evening hours, while after 1am it turns into your typical *discoteca* (only better dressed). Ritzy young things dance to deafening pop from Outkast to Nancy Sinatra in the lower area, while the upstairs lounge provides a much-needed break for both your feet and ears.

✦ ⓂDiagonal. Take a left on Avda. Diagonal and a right on C. Muntaner after a few blocks. *i* For show listings and times, check the Guía del Ocio or the club's website. Ⓢ Cover €18; includes 1 drink. Beer €7. Cocktails €10. ⓩ Open daily 11:30pm-5:30am.

PLATA BAR
BAR

C. Consell de Cent, 233 ☎934 52 46 36

Flatscreens over two floors play a simulcast of jacked models, and the chic interior is spiced up with rainbow flags and colored lights. Order a mojito (€9.50) from one of the ripped bartenders, and settle into this upmarket gay bar before heading over to shake a tailfeather elsewhere.

✦ ⓂUniversitat. Face the University building and walk to the left up C. Aribau for 2 blocks. Turn left onto C. Consell de Cent; Plata Bar is 2 blocks down. Ⓢ Beer €3.50. Cocktails €9.50. ⓩ Open daily 7pm-3am.

nightlife

ANTILLA
LATIN CLUB

C. Aragó, 141 ☎934 51 45 64; www.antillasalsa.com

Be careful when entering—this Latin bar and dance club is so full of energy that dancers often dance right out the door. Little Cuban *maracas*, bongos, and cowbells are littered along the sandy bar, and painted palm trees dot the walls. For those intimidated by the frantic shimmying, salsa lessons are offered before the club opens to the public (Tu-Sa 5-11pm) so you can shake it like a pro—or at least make it look like you know a bachata from a rumba.

☞ ⓜUrgell. Walk along Gran Via de les Corts Catalanes and take a right up C. Comte d'Urgell. Walk 3 blocks and take a left onto C. Aragó. *i* W-Th 1-drink min. ⓢ Cover F-Sa €10; includes 1 drink. Beer €6. Cocktails €8. ⓐ Open W 11pm-4am, Th 11pm-5am, F-Sa 11pm-6am, Su 7pm-1am.

ESPIT CHUPITOS (ARIBAU)
BAR

C. Aribau, 77 www.espitchupitos.com

If you want shots, they've got 'em—580 different delectable little devils will let you party as if you'd gone to Cancún instead of Barcelona. Be prepared for a little more than just drinking, though, as most involve fire. Spectacle shots such as the Harry Potter literally light up the night, while others have the bartenders getting down and dirty. For a good laugh, order the Monica Lewinsky for somebody else, and thank us later.

☞ ⓜUniversitat. Walk up C. Aribau to the left of the university building; Espit Chupitos is 4 blocks uphill. ⓢ Shots €2-4. Cocktails €8.50. ⓐ Open M-Th 8pm-2:30am, F-Sa 8pm-3am, Su 8pm-2:30am.

ZELTAS
BAR, GLBT

C. Casanova, 75 ☎934 50 84 69

Like a story lifted from a sultry romance novel about an all-male harem with impeccable taste, Zeltas pleases the eyes in more ways than one. An all-black interior accented with blue lighting sets the tone, while chic white couches and a bar seemingly built for those looking to dance shirtless sets the mood. Musky cologne floats through the air, and beefy male dancers in tight black spankies make the air somehow thicker.

☞ ⓜUniversitat. Face the University building and walk left on Gran Via de les Corts Catalanes. Turn right onto C. Casanova; Zeltas is 2 blocks up. *i* Male dancers nightly. ⓢ Beer €5. Cocktails €7.50. ⓐ Open daily 11pm-6am.

MOJITO CLUB
LATIN CLUB

C. Rosselló, 217 ☎654 20 10 06; www.mojitobcn.com

A salsa-inspired club for the younger set, Mojito can't be as easily defined as its Latin-beat-blasting counterparts. Low leather couches and semi-private alcoves dot the foyer, while the dance floor pulses to everything from hip hop to rumba, depending on the night. Stop by during the day to take a salsa lesson from the **Buenavista Dance Studio** (☎932 37 65 28) or just come to the Brazil party on Wednesday nights, when free samba lessons start at 11:30pm.

☞ ⓜDiagonal. Facing down Pg. de Gràcia toward Pl. Catalunya, C. Rosselló is to the right. Mojito is near the intersection of C. Balmes, on the far side. *i* Th and Sa 1-drink min. Salsa night on Th, salsa on F-Sa until 1:30am. Check the website for special events. ⓢ Cover F-Sa €12; includes 1 drink. Beer €7. Cocktails €9. ⓐ Open daily 11pm-5am.

DBOY/LA MADAME/DMIX CLUB, GLBT

Ronda Sant Pere, 19-21 ☎934 53 05 82; www.matineegroup.com

Three clubs in one, this spot hosts a downright confusing variety of nightlife options depending on the night. **DBoy** is men-only, with a young and lively gay crowd dancing in a laser-lit mosh pit. **La Madame** is geared toward women, but that doesn't deter the DBoy regulars from getting their groove on. **DMix** supplies just like what it promises—a crowd of both genders, with some straighter action going on as well. Check the website to see what you can expect on a given night.

⇄ [M]Urquinaona. Head along Ronda Sant Pere away from Pl. Catalunya and toward Arc de Triomf. Follow it a few short steps and look for the LED sign. $ Cover €10-15. ⏰ DBoy open in summer F-Sa midnight-6am. La Madame open in summer Su midnight-5am. Demix open Sept-July F-Su midnight-6am.

DIETRICH GAY CAFÉ BAR

C. Consell de Cent, 225 ☎934 51 77 07; www.facebook.com/dietrichcafe

Rainbow flags, a cheery staff, and an unquestionably classy—but overly graphic—portrait of a fishnet-clad Marlene Dietrich greet you as you walk in the door. Despite the lighthearted atmosphere at the bar in front, a serious dance floor waits in back, complete with a Bacardi-cooler-turned-sculpture presiding. Some nights are hit-or-miss—the house is packed during their special events but can be an echoing shell on nights off. If the bar seems too empty for your tastes, hop next door to the club's other portion, Átame, for a guaranteed full house.

⇄ [M]Universitat. Face the University building and walk left on Gran Via de les Corts Catalanes. Turn right onto C. Aribau, walk 2 blocks, and turn left onto C. Consell de Cent. ℹ Drag shows, acrobatics, and dancers on some nights. Check for event schedule. $ Beer €3.50. Mixed drinks €4.50 before 1:30pm, after €5.50-7.50. ⏰ Open from Oct to mid-July F-Sa 10:30pm-3am; from mid-July to Sept daily 10:30pm-3am.

BAR CENTRIK BAR

C. Aribau, 30 ☎630 23 15 03; www.centrik.es

A sleek bar in the heart of Gaixample, Centrik has an appropriately almost-all-male clientele. Prepare to be enveloped in an overwhelming sea of purple, accented with shiny retro bubbles and rays of purple light. Let the photograph of a "Gay St." over the bar distract you while the rest of the bar checks you out before heading to the dance floor in back to party.

⇄ [M]Universitat. Face the University building and head left on Gran Via de les Corts Catalanes. Turn right onto C. Aribau; Bar Centrik is 1 block down. $ Beer €3-4. Cocktails €6-8. Cash only. ⏰ Open Th 11pm-2:30am, F-Sa 11pm-3am.

TOPXI CLUB

C. València, 358 ☎932 07 01 20

One of the few places you'll find Elton John playing on the stereo as a drag queen performs a strip tease, this subterranean bar-club has something for everyone: foosball tables, dart boards, and—the best part—instead of an expensive cover there's a one-drink minimum. Sometimes the programming switches up and a non-drag male takes the silver-curtained stage. Checkered tile floors, red walls, and a sweet bar staff will have you feeling like you're in a friendly hangout back home instead of some underground bar with transvestite strippers in a foreign city.

⇄ [M]Verdaguer. Walk toward Avda. Diagonal on Pg. Sant Joan and take a right onto C. València. Topxi is 1 block down on the left. ℹ Dancers F-Sa at 3:30am. 1-drink min. $ Beer €3-5. Cocktails €6-8. Cash only. ⏰ Open daily noon-5am.

SNOOKER BAR
BAR, POOL HALL

C. Roger de Llúria, 42 ☎933 17 97 60; www.snookerbarcelona.com

With award-winning interior decor in the bar and an equally impressive pool hall in back, Snooker is like what your smoky bowling-alley-slash-pool-hall back home would look like after an episode of "Pimp My Smoky Bowling-Alley-Slash-Pool-Hall." Sit back in one of the custom-designed red velvet chairs with one of Snooker's many scotches and wait for some sucker to challenge you foolishly to a round of what the English call "the beautiful game."

✦ Ⓜ*Passeig de Gràcia. Facing Pl. Catalunya, head left on Gran Via de les Corts Catalanes for 2 blocks and turn left onto C. Roger de Llúria. ⓘ Singles night W 8pm. Salsa dancing Th 6:30, 7:30pm; Su 6, 7pm. Ⓢ Mixed drinks €8. Beer €3-4. ☼ Open M-Th 7pm-2:30am, F-Sa 7pm-3am, Su 7pm-2:30am.*

BARCELONETA

🏴 ABSENTA
BAR

C. Sant Carles, 36 ☎932 21 36 38; www.kukcomidas.com/absenta.html

Not for the easily spooked, Absenta is like an episode of *The Twilight Zone* if you were trapped inside the TV looking out and were also experiencing a touch of that wormwood hallucination. Staticky TV sets with flickering faces dot the walls, and vintage proscriptions against the consumption of the vivid green liquor scold you from above the bar while you sinfully sip the eponymous absinthe (€4-7). A young crowd brings this *modernisme*-inspired beauty up-to-date in an appropriately artsy manner.

✦ Ⓜ*Barceloneta. Walk down Pg. Joan de Borbó toward the beach and take a left onto C. Sant Carles. Ⓢ Beer €2.30. Mixed drinks €7. Absinthe €4-7. ☼ Open M 11am-2am, Tu 6pm-2am, W-Th 11am-2am, F-Sa 11am-3am, Sa-Su 11am-2am.*

¿KÉ?
BAR

C. Baluard, 54 ☎932 24 15 88

Plop down on a cushioned keg chair or the comfiest barstool you'll ever experience. This small bar attracts internationals and provides a calm alternative to the crowded beaches and throbbing bass of the *platja*. Shelves doubling as upside-down tables, fruit decals along the bar, and a playful group of faces peering down from overhead will have you wondering "¿Ké? " as well.

✦ Ⓜ*Barceloneta. Walk down Pg. Joan de Borbó toward the sea and take a left onto C. Sant Carles. Take a left onto C. del Baluard once you enter the plaça. Ⓢ Beer €2.50. Cocktails €6. ☼ Open M-Th 11am-2:30am, F 11am-3am, Sa noon-3am, Su noon-2:30am.*

CATWALK
DISCOTECA

C. Ramón Trias Fargas, 2-4 ☎932 24 07 40; www.clubcatwalk.net

One of Barcelona's most famous clubs, Catwalk has two packed floors of *discoteca*. Downstairs, bikini-clad dancers gyrate to house and techno in neon-lit cages while a well-dressed crowd floods the dance floor. Upstairs, club-goers attempt to dance to American hip hop and pop in very close quarters. Dress well if you want to get in—really well if you want to try to get in without paying the cover—and don't bother trying to get the attention of a bartender at the first bar upon entering; there are about six others, and they're all less busy.

✦ Ⓜ*Ciutadella/Vila Olímpica. ⓘ No T-shirts, ripped jeans, or sneakers permitted. Events listing on website. Ⓢ Cover €15-20; includes 1 drink. Beer €7. Mixed drinks €12. ☼ Open Th midnight-5am, F-Sa midnight-6am, Su midnight-5am.*

OPIUM MAR
CLUB, RESTAURANT

Pg. Marítim de la Barceloneta, 34 ☎902 26 74 86; www.opiummar.com

Slick restaurant by day and even slicker club by night, this lavish indoor and outdoor party spot is a favorite in the Barça nightlife scene. Renowned guest DJs spin every Wednesday, but the resident DJs every other night of the week keep the dance floor sweaty and packed, while six bars make sure the party maintains a base level of schwasty.

❦ Ⓜ*Ciutadella/Vila Olímpica.* *i* *Events listing on website.* Ⓢ *Cover €20; includes 1 drink.* Ⓣ *Restaurant open daily 1pm-1am. Club open M-Th midnight-5am, F-Sa 1-6am, Su midnight-5am.*

SHÔKO
CLUB, RESTAURANT

Pg. Marítim de la Barceloneta, 36 ☎932 25 92 00; www.shoko.biz

The younger, cheaper, raunchier sister of the Port Olímpic club scene. Entrance won't cost you a dime (though you'll still need to dress to impress), and, when it comes to dancing, the utilitarian black floors and wooden platform are only gritty when compared to ritzier clubs nearby. For prime booty-shaking time, drop in after 2am, or come by for Sexy Sundays.

❦ Ⓜ*Ciutadella/Vila Olímpica.* *i* *No sneakers, beach clothes, or lame shirts.* Ⓢ *Beer €6. Mixed drinks €10.* Ⓣ *Restaurant open daily 7pm-midnight. Club open daily midnight-3:30am.*

an atypical olympic event

When the Olympics comes to town, there's a lot of prep work that needs to be done: stadiums must be built, airports refurbished, new flavors of Gatorade invented, etc. But Barcelona took preparations for the 1992 Summer Olympics one step further. In the interest of fighting the city's image as a no-holds-barred, scandalously sinful, 24hr. party mecca, the Catalonian government declared a war on prostitution. Barcelona had to clean up its image, and the first step was taking care of the world's oldest profession.

Don't worry, no one sent out Spanish stormtroopers to prowl the streets of Barcelona looking for high heels and fishnets—the "war" ended up being peaceful, friendly, and quite polite. In typical European fashion, the government sent the ladies on vacation. Two weeks before the games began, the Olympic Committee drove around Barceloneta (at the time, the skeeziest of neighborhoods) in a coach bus, picked up all of the courtesans, and dropped them off at hotels on the outskirts of town for a month-long complimentary holiday. Problem solved!

Not. Today, prostitution remains a sensitive subject for locals. Last year, pictures that were printed by a major newspaper of British holiday-makers in uncompromising positions with Barcelonan ladies of the night caused quite an uproar. Barcelona attracts fun-seekers, but it's not classless, city leaders argue. Maybe there is such a thing as too much fun?

ICEBARCELONA
BAR

C. Ramón Trias Fargas, 2 ☎932 24 16 25; www.icebcn.com

You don't have to be in Barcelona long before you tire of the sticky humidity and the even sweatier *discotecas.* Fortunately, there's an alternative: adjacent to the beach and to the other Port Olímpic clubs is Icebarcelona, a bar made entirely of ice, whose temperature hovers between -2° and -10°C. Your €15 cover includes winter wear, so you can sip your ice-cold drink while sitting on a chair made of ice, sitting at a bar made of ice, gazing at sculptures made of ice, in a room made entirely of ice. And if you think this place is just too cool for you, chill outside on the beach terrace, which requires neither cover nor overcoat.

❦ Ⓜ*Ciutadella/Vila Olímpica.* *i* *Reservations recommended for weekends after midnight.* Ⓢ *€15 cover; includes coat, gloves, and 1 drink. No cover for beach terrace. Beer €4. Mixed drinks €8.* Ⓣ *Open daily June-Sept noon-3am; Oct-May noon-2:30am.*

nightlife

GRÀCIA

EL RAÏM
BAR

C. Progrès, 48
www.raimbcn.com

It may be a little far from Gràcia's roaring plazas, but this confused time capsule is well worth the short trek. A mix between a Catalan bodega and '50s Cuban bar, this traditional winery has been in business since 1886, when it served as the diner for the factory across the street. Since then, the owner has transformed the place into a shrine to Cuban music and memorabilia that consistently attracts down-to-earth locals with its rum drinks, like the incredible mojitos (€6).

Ⓜ️Fontana. Walk downhill on C. Gran de Gràcia and make a left onto C. Ros de Olano. Walk for about 4 blocks and take a right onto C. Torrent de l'Olla. Take the 4th left onto Siracusa; El Raïm is on the corner at the intersection with C. Progrès. Ⓢ *Beer €2.30-3. Wine €2. Shots €2-3.50. Mixed drinks €5.50.* ⏰ *Open daily 8pm-2:30am.*

VINILO
BAR

C. Matilde, 2
☎669 17 79 45

Those expecting a fetish club—whether for LPs or something a little kinkier—may be disappointed. Though this is certainly no shrine to a musical era past (or present), the warm lighting and comfy pillows make it the perfect place to kick back and watch the movie of the day in the orange neon light. Feel free to geek out over their giant phonograph or the Velvet Underground song playing over the speakers—chances are the hip clientele will understand.

Ⓜ️Fontana. Head downhill on C. Gran de Gràcia, turn left on Travessera Gràcia, and take the 2nd right onto C. Matilde. Ⓢ *Beer €3-3.50. Mixed drinks €5.* ⏰ *Open in summer M-Th 8pm-2am, F-Sa 8pm-3am; in winter M-Th 8pm-2am, F-Sa 8pm-3am, Su 8pm-2am.*

EL CHATELET
BAR

C. Torrijos, 54
☎932 84 95 90

A cozy corner bar lit by candles, tiny hanging paper lamps, and dim but sparkly chandeliers, El Chatelet serves drinks so big and so strong they'll have you climbing the walls—look up and to your right as you come in to see previous revelers' footsteps. Sit at the bar under the auspices of the funky painted lizard on the wall behind you, or move to the back, where big windows provide excellent views of the partiers along C. Torrijos and C. Perla.

Ⓜ️Fontana. Head downhill on C. Gran de Gràcia and turn left onto C. Montseny. Follow it as it turns into C. Perla and turn right onto C. Torrijos. Ⓢ *Beer €2-3. Mixed drinks €6.* ⏰ *Open M-Th 6pm-2:30am, F-Sa 6pm-3am, Su 6pm-2:30am.*

ASTROLABI
BAR, LIVE MUSIC

C. Martínez de la Rosa, 14

You might need to break out your astrolabe to find this place, but once there, it's worth the voyage. Maps, clocks, and miniature ships help to explain away your drunk dizziness as "seasickness." Drop in early in the night for some entertainment, with a small and dedicated following crammed into the watering hole to watch underground and up-and-probably-never-quite-coming acoustic acts croon over lost loves and anachronisms. If you need an ear to listen, shrunken heads dangle over the bar for your disposal.

Ⓜ️Diagonal. Take a left onto Pg. de Gràcia, cross Avda. Diagonal, and turn right onto C. Bonavista before Pg. de Gràcia becomes C. Gran de Gràcia. Take a left onto C. Martínez de la Rosa. 𝒊 *Live music daily 10pm.* Ⓢ *Beer €2.50-3. Wine from €1. Mixed drinks €6. Cash only.* ⏰ *Open M-Th 8pm-2:30am, F-Sa 8pm-3am, Su 8pm-2:30am.*

LA CERVERSERA ARTESANA
BAR, BREWERY

C. Sant Agustí, 14
☎932 37 95 94; www.lacervesera.net

No matter what vows you've taken with PBR, when you visit the only pub in Barcelona that makes its own beer, you better order the house brew. With a huge variety—dark, amber, honey, spiced, chocolate, peppermint, fruit-flavored, and more—there's literally something for any beer-lover. If beer isn't your thing, come for the *fútbol* that perpetually plays on the flatscreen TVs.

 # Ⓜ Diagonal. Head uphill on Pg. de Gràcia and take a right onto C. Corsega at the roundabout where Pg. de Gràcia meets Avda. Diagonal. C. Sant Agustí is the 3rd left. $ House brews €4.80-5. Other beers €3-4.50. ⏰ Open M-Th 6pm-2am, F-Sa 6pm-3am, Su 6pm-2am.

VELCRO BAR BAR

C. Vallfogona, 10 ☎610 75 47 42

Though Velcro Bar is a bit of a walk from Gràcia's popular plazas, its screenings of nightly movies attract a young and hip clientele that ends up paying little attention to the screen. Politically charged poster-style art covers the wall opposite the bar, where the real discussions take place. Though somewhat hokey, the bar's name represents the tight (and sometimes noisy) connections made by its patrons.

 # Ⓜ Fontana. Follow C. Astúries and turn right onto C. Torrent de l'Olla. Walk 3 blocks and turn left onto C. Vallfogona. $ Beer €2. Mixed drinks €6. ⏰ Open daily 7pm-2:30am.

OTTO ZUTZ CLUB

C. Lincoln, 15 ☎932 38 07 22; www.ottozutz.com

Like a layer cake with an impeccably designed party inside (or maybe a recreation of Dante's *Inferno*, depending on the night), three floors of dancing and drinks await. At least four different DJs pound out a huge variety of music for a chic and shiny crowd. Watch out—during the summer this heaven gets hellishly hot.

 # Ⓜ Fontana. Walk along Rambla de Prat and take a left as it dead-ends into Via Augusta. Take the 1st right onto C. Laforja and the 1st right again onto C. Lincoln. $ Cover €10-15; includes 1 drink. Beer €6. Mixed drinks €6-12. ⏰ Open M midnight-6am, W-Sa midnight-6am.

THE SUTTON CLUB CLUB

C. Tuset, 13 ☎934 14 42 17; www.thesuttonclub.com

To get into the swankiest club this side of Diagonal, be sure to put on your finest duds (that's what nice clothes are called, right?), slick back your hair, and affect the snootiest air you can muster. Once you're in the door, though, all bets are off; four bars provide mass quantities of alcohol to a dance floor that gets sloppier as the night goes on.

 # Ⓜ Diagonal. Turn left on Avda. Diagonal, walk about 4 blocks, and turn right on C. Tuset. $ Cover €12-18; includes 1 drink. Beer €5. Mixed drinks €8-12. ⏰ Open W midnight-5am, Th midnight-5:30am, F-Sa midnight-6am, Su 10:30pm-4am.

KGB CLUB

C. Alegre de Dalt, 55 ☎932 10 59 06

In Soviet Russia, the club hits you! But seriously, folks—the only indications of the Eastern Bloc are the KGB posters hanging from the walls and the sheer austerity of the decorations—expect lots of black, lots of metal, and little sparkle. Scrappy youth join the bartenders and live DJ and VJ in a sweaty countdown to get down. Entrance is free with a flyer; otherwise you'll ironically pay €12-15 to join this Party.

 # Ⓜ Joanic. Walk along C. Pi i Maragall and take the 1st left. $ Cover with 1 drink €12, with 2 drinks until 3am €15; free with flyer. Beer €4. Mixed drinks €9. Cash only. ⏰ Open F-Sa midnight-6am and for musical performances.

CAFÉ DEL SOL CAFE, BAR

Pl. Sol, 16 ☎932 37 14 48

One of the many tapas bars lining the Pl. Sol, the Cafe del Sol offers cheap and delicious eats in an ambience well-suited to the square's unbeatable outdoor cafe nightlife. Botero-esque figures line the wall along the bar, while a back room provides a cozy shelter for those looking for respite from the square.

 # Ⓜ Fontana. Walk downhill on C. Gran de Gràcia, make a left onto C. Ros de Olano, and turn right onto C. Virtut. $ Beer €2.20-2.80. Mixed drinks €6-7. Tapas €3.50-7.50. Entrees €3.50-5.80. ⏰ Open daily 12:30pm-3am.

MONTJUÏC AND POBLE SEC

▨ ROUGE CAFÉ
BAR

C. Poeta Cabanyes, 21 ☎934 42 49 85

When you walk into a sultry red-lit lounge—think oversized photo darkroom—decked in leather chairs and a cavalcade of vintage decor (including a shoddy copy of Jan van Eyck's *The Arnolfini Wedding*), you know you're doing something right. Luckily, a crowd of hip, friendly locals is there to join you. The prettiest drinks in the city are some of the most delicious, so try the melon Absolut Porno (€6) or the syrupy vodka-based Barcelona Rouge (€6.50).

✦ Ⓜ*Paral·lel. With Montjuïc to your left, walk along Avda. Paral·lel. Take a left onto C. Poeta Cabanyes. Rouge Café is on the left before Mambo Tango Youth Hostel.* Ⓢ *Beer €2-3.50. Wine €2.50-4. Cocktails €6-8.* ☑ *Open daily in summer 7pm-3am; in winter 8pm-3am.*

▨ MAU MAU
BAR

C. Fontrodona, 35 ☎934 41 80 15; www.maumaunderground.com

The epicenter of Barcelona's underground, Mau Mau is best known for its online guide to art, film, and other hip happenings around the city, but the real-life bar is worth the trip up C. Fontrodona. Mau Mau takes its gin and tonics (from €8) very seriously—with 20 gins and nine brands of tonic water, the list takes some time just to read, let alone drink. The bartenders can also throw together a mean dark and stormy (€8) as well as its proletarian counterpart, the Moscow Mule (dark and stormy with vodka instead of rum; €8). Expect to see artsy 20-somethings reclining on this cool warehouse-turned-lounge's comfy white couches before and after concerts at the nearby Sala Apolo, or maybe for a Herzog screening (movies Th-Sa at 10pm).

✦ Ⓜ*Paral·lel. Facing Montjuïc, walk right along Avda. Paral·lel and take a left onto C. Fontrodona. Follow the street as it zigzags; Mau Mau is just a few blocks down.* Ⓢ *1-year membership (includes discounts at Mau Mau and at various clubs, bars, and cultural destinations around the city) €12. No cover for visitors. Beer €2.50-3. Mixed drinks from €6.* ☑ *Open Th-Sa 10pm-2:30am and other days of the week for special events.*

SALA APOLO
CLUB

C. Nou de la Rambla, 113 ☎934 41 40 01; www.sala-apolo.com

Looking to party, but lamenting the fact that it's Monday? Sulk no more—for a number of years, Sala Apolo has been drawing locals to start the week off right with Nasty Mondays, featuring a mix of rock, pop, indie, garage, and '80s. In fact, the night is so popular that it has spawned Crappy Tuesdays (indie and electropop), which take over after the American one-woman show *Anti-Karaoke*. Stop by later in the week when just about anybody and everybody is around, and check the website to see which of the latest big-ish-name indie groups may be rolling through.

✦ Ⓜ*Paral·lel. Walk along Paral·lel with Montjuïc to your right. Take a right onto C. Nou de la Rambla. Not to be confused with Teatre Apolo, which is on Avda. Paral·lel.* ⓘ *Anti-Karaoke €8. Nasty M €11. Crappy Tu €10-12.* Ⓢ *Other tickets €15-23. Cover usually includes 1 drink. Beer €5. Mixed drinks from €8.* ☑ *Open daily midnight-6am and for concerts and events earlier in the evening; check website for schedule.*

LA TERRRAZZA
CLUB

Avda. Marquès de Comillas, 13 ☎687 96 98 25; www.laterrrazza.com

One of the most popular clubs in Barcelona, La Terrrazza lights up the Poble Espanyol after the artisans and sunburned tourists call it a day. The open-air dance floor gets packed early with everyone from the does-Spain-enforce-the-drinking-age young to the does-this-club-even-have-bouncers old, and everything in between, but nobody really cares because the Ibiza-style nightclub is so remarkable.

🚇 Ⓜ*Espanya. Head through the Venetian towers and ride the escalators. Follow the signs to Poble Espanyol.* *i* *Free bus from Pl. Catalunya (Hard Rock Café) to club every 20min. 12:20am-3:20am; free bus from Terrrazza to Pl. Catalunya non-stop 5:30am-6:45am.* Ⓢ *Cover €18, with flyer €15; includes 1 drink. Beer €6. Mixed drinks €8-10.* 🕐 *Open Th 11pm-5am, F-Sa midnight-6am.*

242 ###### CLUB

C. Entença, 37 ☎932 28 90 73; www.myspace.com/club242

You know that feeling of utter disappointment when that prudish club shuts down at the way-too-soon hour of 6am? If you're one of the select few who can party harder than Barna's *discotecas*, the best remedy is an "after"—a club that opens once the rest close down. One of the longest running afters in Barcelona, 242 opens at 6am, which means you never have to come down off your partying buzz. Once the other clubs close, a crowd trickles in to enjoy drinks and some serious underground electronica that would impress at any hour.

🚇 Ⓜ*Espanya. Walk away from Montjuïc on Gran Via de les Corts Catalanes and take a right onto C. Entença. 242 is just before the intersection with C. Sepúlveda.* Ⓢ *Cover €15; includes 1 drink. Beer €5. Mixed drinks €10.* 🕐 *Open F-Su 6am-whenever the party stops.*

TIBIDABO

Tibidabo—the mountain that rises behind Barcelona—is easily reached by a combination of FGC and tram during the day, but a seriously long uphill hike once trams stop running at 10pm. A cab from Pl. Lesseps to Pl. Doctor Andreu is about €8; from Pl. Catalunya, it's about €13. Once you figure out a safe way to get home, head here for a night of incredible views that seem to twinkle more with every drink.

▨ MIRABLAU ###### BAR, CLUB

Pl. Doctor Andreu, S/N ☎934 18 56 67; www.mirablaubcn.com

With easily the best view in Tibidabo—and arguably the best in Barcelona—Mirablau is a favorite with posh internationals and the younger crowd, so dress well. It also happens to be near the mountain's peak, so we only recommend walking up here if you prefer to sip your cocktails while drenched in sweat. The glimmering lights of the metropolis and the bar's quivering candles create a dreamlike aura that earns Mirablau a *Let's Go* thumbpick. If the club is more your style, head downstairs where pretty young things spill out onto the terrace to catch their breath from the crowded dance floor.

🚇 *L7 to FGC: Avda. de Tibidabo. Take the Tramvia Blau up Avda. Tibidabo to Pl. Doctor Andreu.* *i* *Th-Sa credit card min. €4.70. Drinks discounted M-Sa before 11pm, Su before 6pm.* Ⓢ *Beer and wine €1.80-6. Cocktails €7-9.50.* 🕐 *Open M-Th 11am-4:30am, F-Sa 11am-5:30am.*

MERBEYÉ ###### BAR

Pl. Doctor Andreu, 2 ☎934 17 92 79; www.merbeye.net

Merbeyé provides a dim, romantic atmosphere on an outdoor terrace along the cliff. With the lights in the lounge so low that seeing your companion may be a problem, Merbeyé is the perfect place to bring an unattractive date. Smooth jazz serenades throughout, and with just one Merbeyé cocktail (cava, cherry brandy, and Cointreau; €9-10), you'll be buzzed real quick.

🚇 *L7 to FGC: Avda. de Tibidabo. Take the Tramvía Blau up Avda. Tibidabo to Pl. Doctor Andreu.* Ⓢ *Beer €2.50-4. Cocktails €9-10. Food €2-7.60.* 🕐 *Open Th 5pm-2am, F-Sa 11am-3am, Su 11am-2am.*

arts and culture

There's no doubt that Barcelona is one of the global capitals of culture. Hopefully you were looking forward to this, but even if you just came for the beaches and clubs, you'll discover that the artistic side of Barcelona life is pretty inescapable. Just look at the banners hanging from lampposts throughout the city—the variety of concerts and theater productions can be overwhelming. Every week, it seems, there's another festival, from the small (indie comics) to the massive (Sónar music festival). Whatever genre of music you're into, the big names generally pass through Barcelona at some point, so check those concert schedules like a fiend. Theater options are more limited for those who speak only English, though no less fascinating or entertaining. Various public festivals dot the annual calendar; they close down stores and restaurants during the day but turn into phenomenal fiestas at night. And of course, there's always FC Barcelona, the *fútbol* club that is Barcelona's pride and joy; on game days, FCB fever grips the city—or, at least, its bars.

MUSIC AND DANCE

For comprehensive guides to large events and information on cultural activities, contact the **Guía del Ocio** (www.guiadelociobcn.com) or the **Institut de Cultura de Barcelona (ICUB).** (Palau de la Virreina, Las Ramblas, 99 ☎933 16 10 00; www.bcn.cat/cultura ☼ Open daily 10am-8pm.) If you're able to glean basic information from Catalan websites, check out **www.butxaca.com,** a comprehensive bimonthly calendar with film, music, theater, and art listings, or **www.maumaunderground.com,** which lists local music news, reviews, and events. The website **www.infoconcerts.cat/ca** (available in English) provides even more concert listings. For tickets, check out **ServiCaixa** (☎902 33 22 11; www.servicaixa.com ☼ Open M-F 8am-2:30pm.), located at any branch of the Caixa Catalonia bank; **TelEntrada** (☎902 10 12 12; www.telentrada.com); or **Ticketmaster** (www.ticketmaster.es).

Although a music destination year-round, Barcelona especially perks up during the summer with an influx of touring bands and music festivals. The biggest and baddest of these is the three-day electronic music festival **Sónar** (www.sonar.es), which takes place in mid-June. Sónar attracts internationally renowned DJs, electronica fans, and partiers from around the world. From mid-June to the end of July, the **Grec** summer festival (http://grec.bcn.cat) hosts international music, theater, and dance at multiple venues throughout the city, while the indie-centric **Primavera Sound** (www.primaverasound.com) at the end of May is also a regional must-see. *Mondo Sonoro* (www.mondosonoro.com) has more information, and lists musical happenings across the Spanish-speaking world.

classical and opera

PALAU DE LA MÚSICA CATALANA   EL BORN
C. Sant Francesc de Paula, 2   ☎902 44 28 82; www.palaumusica.org

Although the Bach- and Verdi-studded stage still hosts primarily classical concerts, this *modernista* structure welcomes a surprising variety of musical acts almost every night. Over 300 performances of choral and orchestral pieces, pop, acoustic, jazz, and flamenco grace the palau's stage every year, including those from its very own Orfeo Català (Catalan choir), for which the building was constructed. If you're just looking for an excuse to see the breathtaking *Secret Garden*-esque interior without a tour (or you just really like giant air-driven instruments), drop by for one of the cheap and frequent organ performances.

♯ ⓜUrquinaona. Follow Via Laietana toward the water and take the 1st left onto C. Sant Francesc de Paula. *i* Visit www.guiadelociobcn.com for listings. Ⓢ Tickets €8-175. ☼ Box office open M-Sa 10am-9pm, Su 2hr. before curtain. No concerts in Aug.

L'AUDITORI

C. Lepant, 150 ☎932 47 93 00; www.auditori.com

Built in 1999 by world-renowned architect Rafael Moneo, this auditorium is now home to the Symphonic Orchestra of Barcelona (OBC). Glass, steel, and concrete reverberate with various highbrow genres of music, including classical, chamber, and jazz. In addition to the regular program, a number of festivals are held here throughout the year, including the World Music Festival, International Percussion Festival of Catalonia, Festival of Old Music of Barcelona, and even the electronic Sónar.

✦ Ⓜ*Marina. Walk down Avda. Meridiana toward Pl. Glòries and turn left onto C. Lepant.* ⓘ *Tickets available by phone, at the box office, or through ServiCaixa or TelEntrada.* Ⓢ *Tickets €4-40.* Ⓩ *Box office open M-Sa noon-9pm, Su 1hr. before curtain.*

GRAN TEATRE DEL LICEU

Las Ramblas, 51-59 ☎934 85 99 13; www.liceubarcelona.com

A Barcelona institution since its founding in 1847, the Gran Teatre del Liceu has been actively reclaiming its role as the premier venue for upscale performances after a fire closed it down in 1994. Classical, opera, and ballet grace the stage of its impressively restored auditorium, while a smaller reception room hosts smaller events and discussions about the pieces. Drop in for a tour and you may catch a sneak-peak of the rehearsal for the night's performance.

✦ Ⓜ*Liceu. Walk 1 block toward the water; Teatre is on the right.* ⓘ *Tickets available at box office, online, or through ServiCaixa.* Ⓩ *Box office open M-F 1:30-8pm.*

pop and rock

RAZZMATAZZ

C. Pamplona, 88 and Almogàvers, 122 ☎932 72 09 10; www.salarazzmatazz.com

This massive labyrinth of a converted warehouse hosts popular acts from reggae to electropop to indie to metal. The massive nightclub complex spans multiple stories in two buildings, connected by industrial stairwells and a rooftop walkway—definitely not intended for the navigationally challenged. The big room packs the popular draw (with bands like Motörhead, Alice in Chains, and Gossip), while the smaller rooms hide up-and-comers like The Pretty Reckless (we see you, *Gossip Girl*), up-and-cames like MGMT, never-made-its like Casiotone for the Painfully Alone, and has-beens-making-comebacks like Face to Face and Skunk Anansie. If there isn't a concert, you can still find a young crowd pulsing to the beat of one of the nightly DJs.

✦ Ⓜ*Bogatell. Walk down C. Pere IV away from the plaza and take the 1st slight left onto C. Pamplona. Razzmatazz is on the right.* ⓘ *Tickets available online through website, TelEntrada, or Ticketmaster.* Ⓢ *Tickets €12-22.*

SALA APOLO

C. Nou de la Rambla, 113 ☎934 41 40 01; www.sala-apolo.com

Sala Apolo hosts major indie acts (think Crystal Castles and The Pains of Being Pure at Heart) as well as hip hop and electronica artists. A regular rumba club on Wednesday nights features a different band every week, and popular Nasty Mondays (cover €11) and Nasty Tuesdays (€10-12) shake up weeknights.

✦ Ⓜ*Paral·lel. With Montjuïc to your right, walk along Avda. Paral·lel and take a hard right onto C. Nou de la Rambla. Not to be confused with Teatre Apolo, which is on Avda. Paral·lel.* ⓘ *Purchase tickets online.* Ⓢ *Rumba tickets €6-10. Other concert tickets €15-23. Beer €5. Mixed drinks from €8.*

folk and jazz

JAMBOREE

Pl. Reial, 17 ☎933 19 17 89; www.masimas.com

The black-and-white portraits of jazz musicians lining the walls hint at Jamboree's reputation. The club has hosted jazz acts for more than 50 years and

arts and culture

manages to mix this rich history with a surprising dose of relevant contemporary artists—expect to hear a Billie Holiday tribute one night and the Markus Strickland Quartet the next. If you're looking for something a little less predictable, their WTF Jam Sessions are popular with local musicians and cost only €4.

♯ ⓂLiceu. Walk down Las Ramblas toward the water and turn left onto C. Colom to enter Pl. Reial. *i* Tickets available through TelEntrada. WTF Jam Sessions M 9pm-1:30am. Jazz performances Tu-Su 9, 11pm; check website for exact times. ⓈJazz tickets €10-25. Su jam session €4. Flamenco €6. Beer €5. Cocktails €9-10. ⓒ Tarantos (upstairs) holds flamenco shows daily 8:30, 9:30, and 10:30pm.

CENTRE ARTESÁ TRADICIONÀRIUS (CAT)   GRÀCIA
Travessia Sant Antoni, 6-8   ☎932 18 44 85; www.tradicionarius.com

This mini-convention center serves as a one-stop shop for traditional Catalan music in a relaxed setting. Whether you're looking to drop in for a Barcelonan singing to a ukulele, or just to track down the next outdoor rumba session or Catalan folk festival, CAT can provide. Each winter the center helps to organize the Festival Tradicionàrius, which highlights a smorgasbord of Catalan music, dance, and art from January to March.

♯ ⓂFontana. Head down C. Gran de Gràcia and turn left onto C. Montseny. Take a left onto Travessia Sant Antoni. *i* Events often located elsewhere in the city; check website for details. Ⓢ Events €6-20. ⓒ Box office open M-F 11am-2pm and 5-9pm.

CINEMA

CINEMA VERDI   GRÀCIA
C. Verdi, 32   ☎932 38 79 90; www.cines-verdi.com/barcelona

This is Barcelona's first theater to run movies in their original language. The cinema, along with its annex a few streets over on C. Torrijos, makes for a cinephile's mecca in Gràcia, with 10 screens featuring independent and foreign films.

♯ ⓂFontana. Walk down C. Astúries and turn right onto C. Verdi. *i* Schedule available on website. Ⓢ Tickets €5.50-8.

FESTIVALS

Barcelona loves to party. Although *Let's Go* fully supports the city's party agenda, we still need to include some nitty-gritty things like accommodations and, you know, food, so we can't possibly list all of the annual festivals. Stop by the tourist office for a full list of what's going on during your visit. As a teaser, here are a few of the biggest, most student-relevant shindigs:

FESTA DE SANT JORDI   LAS RAMBLAS
Las Ramblas

A more intelligent, civil alternative to Valentine's Day, this festival celebrates both St. George (the dragon-slayer and patron saint of Barcelona) and commemorates the deaths of Shakespeare and Cervantes. On this day, Barcelona gathers along Las Ramblas in search of flowers and books to give to lovers.
ⓒ Apr 23.

FESTA DE SANT JOAN   BARCELONETA, POBLENOU
The beachfront

These days light a special fire in every pyromaniac's heart as fireworks, bonfires, and torches light the city and waterfront in celebration of the coming of summer.
ⓒ Night of June 23; June 24.

BARCELONA PRIDE   CITYWIDE, L'EIXAMPLE
Parade ends in Avda. Maria Cristina, behind Pl. Espanya

This week is the biggest GLBT celebration in the Mediterranean, and Catalonia is no exception. Multiple venues throughout the region take active part in the

festival, which culminates with a parade through "Gaixample" and a festival.
🗓 *Last week of June.*

FESTA MAJOR
GRÀCIA

Pl. Rius i Taulet (Pl. Vila de Gràcia)

Festa Major is a community festival in Gràcia in which the artsy intellectuals put on fun happenings in preparation for the Assumption of the Virgin. Expect parades, concerts, floats, arts and crafts, dancing, and—of course—parties.
🗓 *End of Aug.*

LA DIADA
EL BORN

C. Fossar de les Moreres

Catalonia's national holiday celebrates the end of the Siege of Barcelona in 1714 as well as the reclaiming of regional identity after the death of Franco. Parties are thrown, flags are waved, and Estrella Damm is imbibed.
🗓 *Sept 11.*

FESTA MERCÈ
CITYWIDE, EL BORN

Pl. Sant Jaume

This massive outpouring of joy for one of Barcelona's patron saints (Our Lady of Mercy) is the city's main annual celebration. More than 600 free performances take place in multiple venues. There is also a **castellers competition** in the Pl. Sant Jaume; competitors attempt to build *castells* (literally "castles"; here, human towers) several humans high, which small children clad in helmets and courage then attempt to climb.
🗓 *Weeks before and after Sept 24.*

FÚTBOL

Although Barcelona technically has two *fútbol* teams, **Fútbol Club Barcelona (FCB)** and the **Real Club Deportiu Espanyol de Barcelona (RCD),** you can easily go weeks in the city without hearing mention of the latter. It's impossible to miss the former, though, and for good reason. Besides being a really incredible athletic team, FCB lives up to its motto as "more than a club."

During the years of Francisco Franco, FCB was forced to change its name and crest in order to avoid nationalistic references to Catalonia and thereafter became a rallying point for oppressed Catalan separatists. The original name and crest were reinstated after Franco's fall in 1974, and the team retained its symbolic importance; it's still seen as a sign of democracy, Catalan identity, and regional pride.

This passion is not merely patriotic or altruistic, though—FCB has been one of the best teams in the world in recent years. In 2009, they were the first team to win six out of six major competitions in a single year; in 2010, they won Spain's Super Cup trophy; in 2010 and in 2011, FCB took Spain's La Liga trophy; and in 2011, they beat Manchester United to win the UEFA Champion's League, cementing their status as the best club in the world. Their world-class training facilities (a legacy of the 1992 Olympics) supply many World Cup competitors each year, leaving some Barcelonans annoyed that Catalonia is not permitted to compete as its own nation, much like England, Wales, and Scotland do in the United Kingdom. In fact, Spain's 2010 World Cup victory disappointed some hardheaded FCB fans.

Because FCB fervor is so pervasive, you don't need to head to their stadium, the Camp Nou, to join in the festivites—almost every bar off the tourist track boasts a screen dedicated to their games. Kick back with a brew and be sure not to root for the competition.

shopping

Whether you're gawking at the high fashion on the Pg. de Gràcia or enjoying less mainstream shopping in the backstreets of El Raval, you'll find whatever it is that you're looking for and probably a good deal more. El Born is where you're most likely to stumble across cute boutique and vintage shops (pause for squeals), particularly on and around **Carrer Flassaders;** rapidly gentrifying Gràcia is another good place to look for the same. El Raval is the best for vintage and secondhand shopping, particularly on and around **Carrer Riera Baixa** (where there is also a weekly flea market on Saturdays) and **Carrer Tallers;** slightly more upscale shopping can be done around **Carrer Pintor Fortuny** and **Carrer Doctor Dou.** More tourist-oriented and overpriced shopping fills the Barri Gòtic, though it's hardly a complete wasteland, and you can find your Gucci (along with more affordable Zara and Desigual) on the **Passeig de Gràcia** in **L'Eixample.**

BOOKS

🏷 LA CENTRAL DEL RAVAL
EL RAVAL

C. Elisabets, 6 ☎902 88 49 90; www.lacentral.com

A massive bookstore and cafe set in the 17th-century Casa de la Misericòrdia, selling a wide selection of titles in different languages. This expansive bookstore is as close to Carlos Ruiz Zafón's Cemetery of Forgotten Books as you'll get.

✦ ⓂCatalunya. Follow Las Ramblas away from Pl. Catalunya and turn right onto C. Elisabets. ⏰ Open M-F 9:30am-9pm, Sa 10am-9pm.

HIBERNIAN BOOKS
GRÀCIA

C. Montseny, 17 ☎932 17 47 96; www.hibernian-books.com

This secondhand, English-language bookstore is a godsend for bibliophiles. With an alarmingly broad selection, Hibernian is the perfect place to stock up on cheap paperbacks for a long flight home.

✦ ⓂFontana. Head downhill on C. Gran de Gràcia and turn left onto C. Montseny. ⏰ Open Jan-July M 4-8:30pm, Tu-Sa 10:30am-8:30pm; Aug Tu-Sa 11am-2pm and 5-9pm; Sept-Dec M 4-8:30pm, Tu-Sa 10:30am-8:30pm.

COME IN LLIBRERIA ANGLESA
L'EIXAMPLE

C. Balmes, 129 ☎934 53 12 04; www.libreriainglesa.com

Out of English books? Don't worry, it happens to all of us. Don't cave and get an e-reader—head to the English-language bookstore. And while you're there, request that they order large shipments of *Let's Go*.

✦ ⓂDiagonal. From Pg. de Gràcia facing downhill, turn right onto C. Rosselló. Come In is 2 blocks down. ⏰ Open M-Sa 10am-2pm and 4:30-8pm.

CLOTHING

boutiques

CLINK
GRÀCIA

C. Verdi, 14 ☎933 02 88 68

C. Verdi is home to many a cute boutique, but Clink stands out with its collection of brightly colored dresses (€20-30) with distinct prints and fabrics. Clink also has an excellent selection of women's hats and a variety of accessories.

✦ ⓂFontana. Follow C. Astúries away from C. Gran de Gràcia, then right down C. Verdi. ⏰ Open M-Sa 10am-10pm.

INSTINTO
GRÀCIA

C. Astúries, 15 ☎932 17 92 99

This women's clothing store has clothes in exuberant colors, made of exceptionally soft fabrics. It's a great place to pick up a present to take home to your mom—and who knows? You might luck out and find something that you like, too.

✚ Ⓜ*Fontana. Follow C. Astúries away from C. Gran de Gràcia.* ⌚ *Open M-F 10:30am-2:30pm and 5-9pm, Sa 11am-2:30pm and 5-9pm.*

EL PIANO TINA GARCIA
GRÀCIA

C. Verdi, 20 ☎934 15 51 76

This boutique has a selection of distinctive garments for women. The menswear version, **El Piano Man,** is across the street at C. Verdi, 15.

✚ Ⓜ*Fontana. Follow C. Astúries away from C. Gran de Gràcia, then right down C. Verdi.* ⌚ *Open M-Sa 10am-9:30pm.*

SOMBRERIA MIL
BARRI GÒTIC

C. Fontanella, 20 ☎933 01 84 91

Sombreria Mil is great excuse to say the word "milliner." It's also a great place to try on hats and take funny pictures. Maybe you'll even buy a handsome fedora—we've leave that up to you.

✚ Ⓜ*Catalunya or* Ⓜ*Urquinaona. On C. Fontanella between Pl. Catalunya and Pl. Urquinaona.* ⌚ *Open M-Sa 9:30am-8:45pm.*

secondhand

🏷 GALLERY
GRÀCIA

C. Torrent de l'Olla, 117 ☎935 51 01 91

Gallery sells vintage clothing of all shapes, sizes, and colors. It's the sort of place you want to save for the end of the day, because you won't be able to leave.

✚ Ⓜ*Fontana. Head downhill on C. Gran de Gràcia, then left on C. Montseny, then right on C. Torrent de l'Olla.* ⌚ *Open M 5-9pm, Tu-Sa 11am-2pm and 5-9pm.*

LOISAIDA
EL BORN

C. Flassaders, 42 ☎932 95 54 92; www.loisaidabcn.com

Hip Loisaida has secondhand and vintage clothing inspired by New York's Lower East Side, along with new international brands and clothes of its own label.

✚ Ⓜ*Jaume I. Follow Pg. Born to the end farthest from the church, and take a left near the end onto C. Flassaders.* ⌚ *Open M-Sa 11am-9pm.*

MARKETS

🏷 MERCAT RAVAL
EL RAVAL

Rambla del Raval www.mercatraval.com

A clothing, art, and design market with booths of funky dresses, designer T-shirts, and trendy accessories. Almost as odd and alternative as its locale.

✚ Ⓜ*Liceu. Follow C. Hospital and take a left onto Rambla del Raval.* ⌚ *Open Sa-Su 11am-9pm.*

LA BOQUERIA (MERCAT DE SANT JOSEP)
LAS RAMBLAS

Las Ramblas, 89

Barcelona's main food market is an absolute treat to browse. See **Food** for more information.

✚ Ⓜ*Liceu. Walk toward Pl. Catalunya on Las Ramblas and take a left onto Pl. Sant Josep.* ⌚ *Open M-Sa 8am-8pm, though certain vendors stay open after 9pm.*

RIERA BAIXA
EL RAVAL

C. Riera Baixa www.facebook.com/pages/Riera-Baixa

A street lined entirely with secondhand shops, Riera Baixa is a mecca for any bargain or vintage shopper. The main attraction happens on Saturdays when clothes, records, trinkets, cameras, and an unfathomable amount of other stuff combine with El Raval's large student population to give birth to the most exciting flea market in the city.

✚ Ⓜ*Liceu. Walk down C. Hospital and take a slight right onto C. Riera Baixa.* ⌚ *Flea market open Sa 11am-9pm.*

shopping

essentials

PRACTICALITIES

- **TOURIST OFFICES: Plaça de Catalunya** is the main office, offering free maps and brochures, last-minute booking service for accommodations, currency exchange, and box office, Caixa de Catalunya. (Pl. de Catalunya, 17-S ☎932 85 38 34; www.barcelonaturisme.com ✚ ⓂCatalunya, underground, across from El Corte Inglès. Look for the pillars with the letter "i" on top. ☼ Open daily 8:30am-8:30pm.) **Plaça de Sant Jaume.** (C. Ciutat, 2 ☎932 70 24 29 ✚ ⓂJaume I. Follow C. Jaume I to Pl. de Sant Jaume. Located in the Ajuntament building on the left. ☼ Open M-F 8:30am-8:30pm, Sa 9am-7pm, Su and holidays 9am-2pm.) **Oficina de Turisme de Barcelona.** (Palau Robert, Pg. de Gràcia, 107 ☎932 38 80 91, toll-free in Catalonia ☎012; www.gencat.es/probert ✚ ⓂDiagonal. ☼ Open M-Sa 10am-7pm, Su 10am-2:30pm.) **Institut de Cultura de Barcelona (ICUB).** (Palau de la Virreina, La Rambla, 99 ☎933 16 10 00; www.bcn.cat/cultura ✚ ⓂLiceu. ☼ Open daily 10am-8pm.) **Estació Barcelona-Sants.** (Pl. Països Catalans ☎902 24 02 02 ✚ ⓂSants-Estació. ☼ Open June 24-Sept 24 daily 8am-8pm; Sept 25-June 23 M-F 8am-8pm, Sa-Su 8am-2pm.)

- **TOURS:** Self-guided tours of Gothic, Romanesque, *modernista*, and contemporary Barcelona are available; pick up pamphlets in tourism offices. A wide variety of guided tours also exist, check the brochures at the tourism office. The **Plaça de Catalunya tourist office** hosts its own walking tours of the Barri Gótic and has info about bike tours. (☎932 85 38 32 ✚ ⓂCatalunya, underground across from El Corte Inglès. Look for the pillars with the letter "i" on top. Ⓢ €12, ages 4-12 €5. ☼ English tours daily 10am, Spanish and Catalan Sa noon.) **Picasso tours** of Barcelona are given in English, Spanish, and Catalan and include entry to **Museu Picasso.** (☎932 85 38 32 ✚ ⓂCatalunya Ⓢ €19, ages 4-12 €7. ☼ In English Tu, Th, Sa 4pm; Spanish or Catalan available Sa 4pm with booking in advance.)

- **LUGGAGE STORAGE: Estació Barcelona-Sants.** (ⓂSants-Estació. Ⓢ Lockers €3-4.50 per day. ☼ Open daily 5:30am-11pm.) **Estació Nord.** (ⓂArc de Triomf. *i* Max 90 days. Ⓢ Lockers €3.50-5 per day.) **El Prat Airport.** (Ⓢ €3.80-4.90 per day.)

- **GLBT RESOURCES: GLBT tourist guide,** available at the Pl. Catalunya tourist office, includes a section on GLBT bars, clubs, publications, and more. **GayBarcelona** (www.gaybarcelona.net) and **Infogai** (www.colectiugai.org) have up-to-date info. **Antinous** specializes in gay and lesbian books and films. (C. Josep Anselm Clavé, 6. ☎933 01 90 70; www.antinouslibros.com ✚ ⓂDrassanes. ☼ Open M-F 10:30am-2pm and 5-8:30pm, Sa noon-2pm and 5-8:30pm.)

- **INTERNET ACCESS:** The **Barcelona City Government** (www.bcn.es) offers free Wi-Fi at over 500 locations, including museums, parks, and beaches. **Easy Internet Café** has decent rates and around 300 terminals. (Las Ramblas, 31 ☎933 01 75 07 ✚ ⓂLiceu. Ⓢ €2.10 per hr., min. €2. Day pass €7; week €15; month €30. ☼ Open daily 8am-2:30am.)

- **POST OFFICE:** Pl. Antonio López. ☎934 86 83 02; www.correos.es. ✚ⓂJaume I or Barceloneta. Ⓢ Open M-F 8:30am-9:30pm, Sa 8:30am-2pm.

- **POSTAL CODE:** 08001.

EMERGENCY

- **EMERGENCY NUMBERS:** ☎112. **Ambulance:** ☎061.

- **POLICE: Local police:** ☎092. **Mossos d'Esquadra (regional police):** ☎088. **National police:** ☎091. **Tourist police:** Las Ramblas, 43 ☎932 56 24 30 ⚔ Ⓜ Liceu. ⏰ Open 24hr.

- **LATE-NIGHT PHARMACY:** Rotates. Check any pharmacy window for the nearest on duty, contact the police, or call **Información de Farmacias de Guardia** (☎010 or ☎934 81 00 60; www.farmaciesdeguardia.com).

- **HOSPITALS/MEDICAL SERVICES: Hospital Clínic i Provincal.** (C. Villarroel, 170 ☎932 27 54 00 ⚔ Ⓜ Hospital Clínic. Main entrance at C. Roselló and C. Casanova.) **Hospital de la Santa Creu i Sant Pau.** (☎932 91 90 00; emergency ☎91 91 91 ⚔ Ⓜ Vall d'Hebron.) **Hospital del Mar.** (Pg. Marítim, 25-29. ☎932 48 30 00 ⚔ Ⓜ Ciutadella-Vila Olímpica.)

LOCAL LAWS AND POLICE

Travelers are not likely to break major laws unintentionally while visiting Spain. You can contact your embassy if arrested, although they often can't do much beyond helping you find legal counsel. You should feel comfortable approaching the police, although few officers speak English. There are three types of police in Spain. The **Policía Nacional** wear blue or black uniforms and white shirts; they deal with crime investigation (including theft), guard government buildings, and protect dignitaries. The **Policía Local** wear blue uniforms, deal more with local issues, and report to the mayor or town hall in each municipality. The **Guardia Civil** wear olive-green uniforms and are responsible for issues more relevant to travelers: customs, crowd control, and national security.

drugs and alcohol

Recreational drugs are illegal in Spain, and police take these laws seriously. The legal **drinking age** is 18. Spain has the highest road mortality rate and one of the highest rates of drunk driving deaths in Europe. Recently, Spanish officials have started setting up checkpoints on roads to test drivers' blood alcohol levels. Do not drive while intoxicated, and be cautious on the road.

GETTING THERE

by plane

There are two possible airports you may use to reach Barcelona. The first, **Aeroport del Prat de Llobregat** (BCN, Terminal 1. ☎934 78 47 04; Terminal 2B ☎934 78 05 65), is located slightly closer to the city, though both necessitate bus rides. To get to Pl. Catalunya from the airport, take the **Aerobus** in front of terminals 1 or 2. (☎924 15 60 20; www.aerobusbcn.com Ⓢ €5.30, round-trip ticket valid for 9 days €9.15. ⏰ 35-40min.; every 5-20min. to Pl. Catalunya 6am-1am, to airport 5:30am-12:10am.) To get to the airport, the **A1** bus goes to Terminal 1 and **A2** bus goes to Terminal 2. For early morning flights, the Nitbus **N17** runs from Pl. Catalunya to all terminals. (Ⓢ €1.45. ⏰ From Pl. Catalunya every 20min. 11pm-5am, from airport every 20min. 9:50pm-4:40am.) The **RENFE Rodalies** train is cheaper and usually a bit faster than the Aerobus. (☎902 24 34 02; www.renfe.es Ⓢ €1.45, free with T10 transfer from Metro. ⏰ 20-25min. to Estació Sants, 25-30min. to Pg. de Gràcia; every 30min. from airport 5:40am-11:38pm, from Estació Sants to airport 5:10am-11:09pm.) To reach the train from Terminal 2, take the pedestrian overpass in front of the airport (with your back to the entrance, it's to the left). For those arriving at Terminal 1, there's a shuttle bus outside the terminal that goes to the train station.

The **Aeroport de Girona-Costa Brava** (GRO; ☎902 40 47 04; www.barcelona-girona-

essentials

airport.com) is technically located in Girona, a city outside of Barcelona. However, many budget airlines fly into this airport, so it may be your best bet for getting to Barcelona on the cheap. The **Barcelona Bus** goes from the airport in Girona to Estació d'Autobusos Barcelona Nord. (☎902 36 15 50; www.barcelonabus.com ℹ Buses from the airport to Barcelona Nord are timed to match flight arrivals. Buses from Barcelona Nord arrive at Girona Airport approximately 3hr. before flight departures. $ €12, round-trip €21. 🕐 1½hr.)

by train

Depending on the destination, trains can be economical. **Estació Barcelona-Sants** (Pl. Països Catalans ➡ ⓂSants Estació) serves most domestic and international traffic, while **Estació de França** (Avda. Marqués de l'Argentera ➡ ⓂBarceloneta) serves regional destinations and a few international locations. Note that trains often stop before the main stations; check the schedule. **RENFE** (reservations and info ☎902 24 02 02; international ☎902 24 34 02; www.renfe.es) runs to Bilbao (€65); Madrid (€118); Sevilla (€143); Valencia (€40-45); and many other destinations in Spain. Trains also travel to Milan, ITA (€135) via Girona, Figueres, Perpignan, and Turin; Montpellier, FRA (€60); Paris, FRA (€146); and Zurich, CHE (€136) via Geneva and Bern. There's a 20% discount on round-trip tickets, and domestic trains usually have discounts for reservations made more than two weeks in advance. Call or check website for schedules.

by bus

Buses are often considerably cheaper than the train. The city's main bus terminal is **Estació d'Autobuses Barcelona Nord.** (☎902 26 06 06; www.barcelonanord.com ➡ ⓂArc de Triomf or #54 bus.) Buses also depart **Estació Barcelona-Sants** and the airport. **Sarfa** (ticket office at Ronda Sant Pere, 21 ☎902 30 20 25; www.sarfa.es) is the primary line for regional buses in Catalonia, but **Eurolines** (☎932 65 07 88; www.eurolines.es) also goes to Paris, FRA (€80) via Lyon and offers a 10% discount to travelers under 26 or over 60. ALSA (☎902 42 22 42; www.alsa.es) is Spain's main bus line. Buses go to Bilbao (€43); Madrid (€29-34); Sevilla (€79-90); Valencia (€26-31); and many other Spanish cities.

by ferry

Ferries to the Balearic Islands (Ibiza, Mallorca, and Minorca) leave daily from the port of Barcelona at **Terminal Drassanes** (☎933 24 89 80) and **Terminal Ferry de Barcelona** (☎932 95 91 82 ➡ ⓂDrassanes) The most popular ferries are run by **Trasmediterránea** (☎902 45 46 45; www.trasmediterrana.es) in Terminal Drassanes. They go to Ibiza ($ €90. 🕐 9½hr.) and Mallorca. ($ €83. 🕐 8hr.)

GETTING AROUND

by metro

The most convenient mode of transportation in Barcelona is the **Metro.** The Metro is made up of three main companies: **Transports Metropolitans de Barcelona** (TMB ☎933 18 70 74; www.tmb.cat), whose logo is an M in a red diamond; **Ferrocarrils de la Generalitat de Catalunya** (FGC ☎932 05 15 15; www.fgc.cat), whose logo is an orange square; and **Tramvia de Barcelona** (Tram ☎900 70 11 81; www.trambcn.com), whose logo is a green square with a white T. The TMB lines are the most used. Thankfully, all three companies are united, along with the bus system and Rodalies train system, under the **Autoritat del Transport Metropolità** (www.atm.cat), which means that you only need one card for all forms of transport, and that you get free transfers. Most Metro lines are identified with an L (L1, L2, etc.), though some FGC lines begin with S, and all Tram lines begin with T. ($ 1 day €6.20, 10 rides €8.25, 50 rides €33.50, 1 month €51. 🕐 Trains run M-Th 5am-midnight, F 5am-2am, Sa 24hr., Su 5am-midnight.)

by bus

For journeys to more remote places, the bus may be an important complement to the Metro. The **NitBus** is the most important: it runs all night long after the Metro closes. Look for bus lines that begin with an N. Barcelona's tourist office also offers a **tourist bus** (http://bcnshop.barcelonaturisme.com [$] 1 day €23, 2 days €30.) that hits major sights and allows riders to hop on and off. Depending on how much you plan to use the route (and how much you fear being spotted on a red double decker labeled "Tourist Bus"), a pass may be a worthwhile investment.

by bike, motorcycle, or scooter

Motocicletas (scooters, and less frequently motorcycles—*motos* for short) are a common sight in Barcelona, and **bicycles** are also becoming more popular. Many institutions rent *motos*, but you need a valid driver's license recognized in Spain (depends on the company, but this sometimes means an international driver's license as well as a license from your home country) in order to rent one. Many places also offer bike rental. If you will be staying in the city for an extended period, it is possible to buy a bike secondhand (try **www.loquo.com**) or register for **Bicing** (☎902 31 55 31; www.bicing.cat), the municipal red and white bikes located throughout the city.

by taxi

When other cheaper and more exciting options fail, call **Radio Taxi** (☎932 25 00 00).

PHRASEBOOK

ENGLISH	CATALAN	PRONUNCIATION
Please.	Sisplau.	sees-PLOW
Sorry/Excuse me.	Perdó.	pahr-DOH
Good morning/good day.	Bon dia.	bohn DEE-ah
Good afternoon.	Bona tarda.	BOH-nah TAHR-dah
How are you?	Què tal?	keh tahl?
Where are the toilets?	On són els lavabos?	ohn sohn als la-BAH-boos?
How do I get to the Carrer dels Banys Vells?	Cóm s'arriba al Carrer dels Banys Vells?	kom sah-REE-bah ahl kah-RREH dahls bahny(uh)s beh-ys?
What time is it?	Quina hora és?	KEE-nah OH-rah ehs?
It is five thirty.	Són dos quarts de sis.	sohn dohs kwarts dah sees (literally, "it is two quarters of six")
Don't shoot, I'm an American!	No dispari sóc un nord-americá/una nord-americana!	noh dees-PAH-ree, sohk oon nohrd-ah-mah-ree-KAH / OO-na nohrd-ah-mah-ree-KAH-nah
It is too expensive.	És massa car.	ehs MAH-sah kahr
I was born in New York.	Vaig néixer a Nova York.	bahch NEH-shah ah NOH-vah york
They told me it never rained in Barcelona. Where can I buy an umbrella?	M'habian dit que mai plou a Barcelona. On puc comprar un paraiguas?	mah-BEE-ahn deet kah my ploh ah bahr-sah-LOH-nah. ohn pook koom-PRAH oon pah-RYE-gwahs?
The brothel is right next to the church.	El bordell és al costat de la església.	ahl boor-DEY ehs ahl koo-STAHT dah lah ehs-GLEH-zee-ah
My hovercraft is full of eels.	El meu aerodeslizador està ple d'anguiles.	ahl MEH-oo eh-roh-dehs-lee-zah-DOH eh-STAH pleh dahn-GWEE-lahs
It/that hashish/your child is not mine.	Això/aquell haixix/el teu nen, no és meu.	ah-SHOH / ah-KAY ah-SHEESH / ahl TEH-oo nehn, noh ehs MEH-oo

essentials

barcelona 101

HISTORY

sailors, a golden fleece, and... hercules? (stone age-third century BCE)

As far as archaeologists can tell, humans have lived near the modern site of Barcelona since the end of the Stone Age—and really, you'd have to be of the *homo ineptus* species to pass up a spot on a coast this beautiful. Small settlements on the coastal areas (and the hills now known as Montjuïc) have been around since Neolithic times, but things didn't really heat up until around the 13th century BCE. Like most great cities of the world, Barcelona has a particularly colorful foundation myth, and the origins of the city are said to have roots in Greek and Roman mythology. Legend has it that, in the course of his fabled 12 labors, **Hercules** linked up with Jason, the Argonauts, and their nine boats as they prepared for an epic Mediterranean voyage to find the mythical golden fleece. Off the coast of Catalonia, one of the boats lost its way in a storm and shipwrecked. Hercules, demigod that he was, braved the storm to find the beached crew who—lo and behold—were perfectly safe and having a grand ol' time on the beautiful *playa*. In honor of their good luck, the crewmen founded *Barca Nona* at the site, a city named for that ninth boat.

the new jersey turnpike, but less smelly (third century BCE-717 CE)

Let's Go favors most things epic, but scholars agree that there's little evidence to support the Hercules story. In the third century BCE, locals called the Laietani founded a small settlement named Barkeno, which was soon conquered by rampaging **Carthaginians** on their way to sack Rome. It took a century or two, but the Empire eventually struck back, and by 19 BCE, **Caesar Augustus** had gained control of the entire Iberian Peninsula. With the Romans in power, Barkeno was renamed Colonia Faventia Julia Augusta Pia Barcino, proving once and for all that "brevity is the soul of wit."

Throughout the Roman occupation, Barcelona flourished, mainly because of its central location on the **Via Augusta** (Ancient Rome's answer to our interstate highway). Nevertheless, the city played second fiddle to other, more important settlements like Zaragoza and Tarragona. Basically, in the interstate highway of our metaphor, Barcelona was a rest stop: a McDonald's, a restroom, and a place to get gas. Needless to say, the Romans paid the city little attention—they were too busy conquering the known world.

Barcelona's residents have the **Visigoths** to thank for shortening the name of the city to **Barcinona** following their takeover in 414 CE. The Visigoths, initially a huge pain for the Western Roman Empire, became Rome's best frenemies when a whole new crop of rampaging Germanic tribes showed up. For the next four centuries the Visigoths hung on tightly to their city by the sea.

please, sir, i'd like some moor (717-1162)

After almost 1000 years of European bickering interspersed with the occasional period of peace, a new player emerged on the scene: **the Moors.** The Muslim forces, originally from North Africa, jumped the Strait of Gibraltar in 711 and steadily took control of the peninsula until around 717. The Moors initiated a golden age in Spanish history: they constructed the **Alhambra** near Granada, introduced sophisticated Islamic art and science, and heralded a time of **convivencia,** or relative religious tolerance.

Expectedly, though, European leaders began to freak out as the Moors amassed more and more (har, har) land. Barcelona emerged as the frontline in what would become known as **the Reconquista.** The Moors only held Barcelona for about a century, until **Louis the Pious** recaptured the city in 801. From then on, Barcelona became a center for the Christian forces to wage war against Islamic Spain, increasing the city's prominence. Ruled by the **Counts of Barcelona,** who were originally installed as royal administrators and eventually became royalty themselves, the port city became rich and famous.

royally confusing (1162-1462)

In a normal history book, the next 300 years would read like a soap opera: this prince marries this princess and their kingdoms unite; this kingdom goes to war with that kingdom; revenge, adultery, assassination, dragons, treason...you get the gist. Thankfully, this is not a normal history book. For the quiz bowl nerds out there, we will say this: in 1162, **Ramon Berenguer IV,** Count of Barcelona, married **Petronila of Aragon.** Their son, **Alfonso II,** became King of Aragon, which now included Catalonia. (We dare you to remember all three of those names and their full titles.) If you can't keep track of those crazy royals, at least remember that as the Moors continued to push southward (off of the Peninsula), Catalonia became integrated royally and economically into the larger **Crown of Aragon.**

sibling rivalries (1462-1936)

By the beginning of the Renaissance, power in fragmented Christian Spain was split between two major centers: Barcelona and Madrid. In 1462, two Spanish royals who you're probably familiar with got hitched and Barcelona stumbled into a four-century slump from which it's still recovering. When **Ferdinand II** and **Isabella I** married, Spain took a major step toward becoming fully unified, and the country's political center shifted to Madrid. Then, to add insult to injury, the new royal couple set their sights westward, fronting some money for this crazy bro **Columbus.** When Europe turned toward the newly-discovered Americas, Barcelona's power as a Mediterranean trading port began to wane.

Barcelona was not to be ignored, though, and it tried its best to make trouble. In the **War of the Spanish Succession,** Catalan nobility sided against the Bourbon **King Felipe V,** who had the support of the Castilian elite. Boy, did they choose wrong.

Two hundred years later, Catalan independence was just as fierce (and just as feisty). In 1936, as Nazi Berlin was preparing to host the Summer Olympics, left-wing Barcelona offered to host their own **People's Olympiad.** Conceived as a protest against Nazism and fascism, artists and athletes began pouring in from around the world—George Orwell and Ernest Hemingway among them. When the conservative Nationalist army under **Francisco Franco** began a **civil war** in 1936, the games were cancelled and the city turned into a staunch Republican bastion. Barcelona fought off the Franquistas until January 26, 1939, and the war soon ended.

[title redacted for treasonous material] (1936-75)

Oh, the Franco years. Such a wonderful time for freedom of speech, women's rights, religious liberty, and democracy. Without risking too much political controversy, we can safely say that most of the country is happy to be done with this period in Spanish history. Barcelona, in particular, suffered under Franco's regime. The Catalan language was prohibited and political autonomy was abolished, which dealt a severe blow to the area's culture.

free at last? (1975-now)

Franco died in 1975. Since then, Barcelona has been at the forefront in calling for reform and has led attempts at political recovery. A degree of Catalan autonomy has been restored, and the left-leaning government has since become a full member of the **European Union.** Happy ending? We're not that naïve—Barcelona has its problems, just like everywhere else. But we can say with confidence that now is a pretty good time to be a Barcelonan, and an even better time to visit.

CUSTOMS AND ETIQUETTE

the personal bubble

For cold and independent Americans (or non-Americans who share a general anxiety over personal space), Barcelona may seem quite chummy. Expect a kiss on both cheeks as a greeting, and try not to throw a fit if you see friends of both genders arm-in-arm or hand-in-hand on the street. This all comes with a caveat, however, and that caveat is **pickpocketers.** Be wary of people who are *too* close in crowded areas like the subway.

how to avoid misrepresenting an entire culture

A few things to clarify: Yes, Catalan is a completely separate language compared to the Spanish (Castellano) that you may remember from high school. Both Catalan and Spanish work for daily life. No, Catalan is not a dialect, and, if you read the **History** section of this chapter, you'll know that Catalan culture is a fiercely defended part of what it means to be a Barcelonan. While it probably won't end friendships, insensitivity to Catalan identity and the question "why can't you all just speak Spanish?" should generally be avoided.

this is how barcelona protests

In the fall of 2010, the Pope came to town to consecrate La Sagrada Família, the behemoth Catholic church in central Barcelona designed by Antoni Gaudí. Expectedly, it was a big deal that the basilica, which had its groundbreaking in 1882, was finally being consecrated. Pope Benedict arrived with all the fanfare that the Gucci-heeled Holy Father is known for (Mercedes Benz Popemobile and all) to find an unexpected welcoming party—a group of queer-rights activists. As the Pope drove by La Sagrada Família, around 200 gay and lesbian couples staged a kiss-in in an attempt to call awareness to the Catholic Church's socially conservative politics. In the process, they scandalized religious leaders and caused the Pope to condemn Spain's progressive marriage legislation (same-sex marriage has been legal since 2005). Takeaway? 1) Barcelonans don't shy away from controversy. 2) Be prepared to pucker up if you want to participate.

FOOD AND DRINK

tapas, but only as a last resort

Catalan cuisine differs subtly from other regional Spanish cuisines. Observe: **tapas** (small dishes). While tapas are native to southern and central Spain, you'll find that a variety of restaurants in Barcelona also serve them. You're welcome to try them, but Barcelona's better known for its simple staples: **pa amb tomàquet** (bread with tomato and garlic) and **paella,** a rice dish cooked with Mediterranean seafood. Overall, it's typical for restaurants to serve a fixed-price **menú del día** (menu of the day) with an appetizer, main dish, drink, and dessert rather than small dishes.

timing is everything

As with the rest of Spain, meals in Barcelona are long, leisurely, and eminently social. You won't be surprised by the time for *l'esmorzar* (breakfast, roughly 7-11am) or *dinar* (lunch, roughly 11am-3pm), but be careful about managing the *migdiada* (midday) restaurant closings (4-8pm). Apart from international chains and tapas bars, it'll be a challenge to find a good meal during this witching hour—so save your appetite for a late-night *sopa* (dinner).

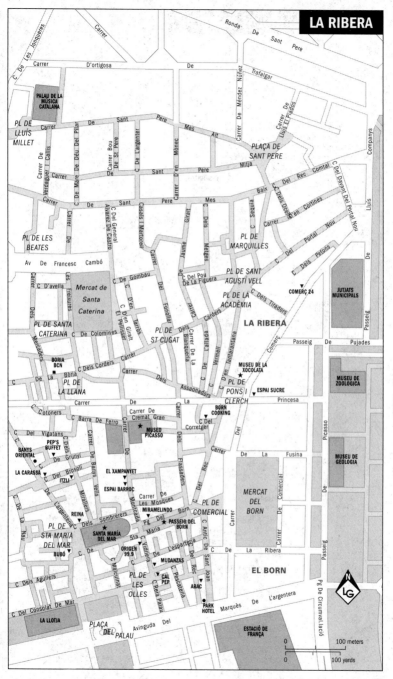

LA RIBERA

Ronda De Sant Pere

Carrer D'ortigosa

De

Carrer De Méndez Núñez

Trafalgar

Carrer De Lluís El Piadós

PALAU DE LA MÚSICA CATALANA

PL DE LLUÍS MILLET

Carrer De Verdaguer Callís

Carrer De

C De Mare De Déu Del Pilar

C De General Alvarez De Castro

Carrer Bou De St Pere

C De L'argenter

Carrer D'en Mònec

Sant Pere Mes Alt

PLAÇA DE SANT PERE

Companys

Sant Pere Mitja

C Del Rec Comtal

Baix

Carrer D'en Cortines

Lluís

PL DE LES BEATES

C D'avella

Les Freixures

Casals I Martorell

Sant Pere Mes Baix

Sèquia

C Del Portal Nou

De

C Dels Patons

Passeig

Av De Francesc Cambó

Mercat de Santa Caterina

C De Gombau

C Del Pou De La Figuera

PL DE MARQUILLES

PL DE SANT AGUSTÍ VELL

C D'en Tantarantana

C Dels Tiradors

COMERÇ 24

JUTJATS MUNICIPALS

PL DE SANTA CATERINA

C De Colomines

C D'en Giralt El Pellisser

C D'en Tartos

Del Fonollar

PL DE ST CUGAT

Carrers

PL DE LA ACADÈMIA

LA RIBERA

BORIA BCN

C Dels Corders

Carrer

Dels

Carrer De La Blanqueria

Vermell

MUSEU DE LA XOCOLATA

Passeig

De Pujades

MUSEU DE ZOOLÒGICA

PL DE LA LLANA

C De La

Assaonadors

D'en Tantarantana

PL DE PONS I CLERCH

ESPAI SUCRE

Comerç

Passeig

Cotoners

C Barra De Ferro

Carrer De Cremat Gran

La

Princesa

Picasso

C Del Vigatans

MUSEO PICASSO

C Del Corretger

BORN COOKING

De

La Fusina

MUSEU DE GEOLOGIA

BANYS ORIENTAL

PEP'S BUFFET

C Dels

De Grunyi

EL XAMPANYET

ESPAI BARROC

Carrer De Les Mosques

Carrer De Banys Vells

Flassaders

Carrer De

Born

Carrer De

MERCAT DEL BORN

Comercial

LA CARASSA

ITZLI

C Del Brosoli

Mirallers

MIRAMELINDO

Pg. De

PL DE COMERCIAL

C Antic De Sant Joan

REINA

Dels

Sombrerers

PASSEIG DEL BORN

Carrer

De

PL DE STA MARIA DEL MAR

SANTA MARÍA DEL MAR

Sta Maria

Vidriera

De L'esparteria

Del Rec

La Ribera

EL BORN

Passeig

Pg De Circunval.lació

BUBÓ

C De La Nau

ORIGEN 99.9

MUDANZAS

C Dels Aguilers

PL DE LES OLLES

CAL PEP

ABAC

De La Pescateria

C De Sant Joan

De

L'argentera

C Del Consolat De Mar

C De Malcuinat

C Dera Palau

PARK HOTEL

Marquès De

LA LLOTJA

PLAÇA DEL PALAU

Avinguda Del

ESTACIÓ DE FRANÇA

N LG

0 — 100 meters

0 — 100 yards

la ribera map

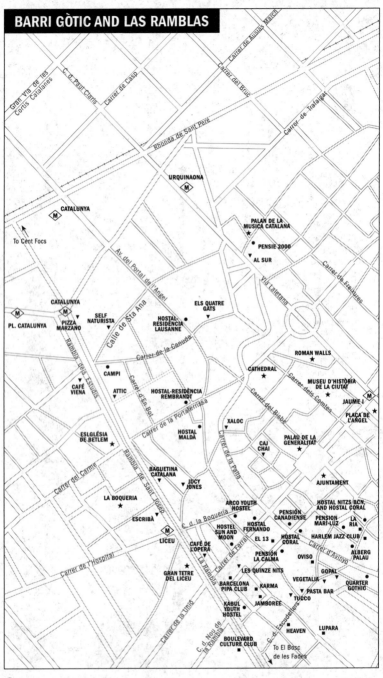

BARRI GÒTIC AND LAS RAMBLAS

Gran Via de les Corts Catalanes

C. d' Paul Claris

Carrer de Casp

Carrer del Bruc

Carrer de Ausiàs March

Carrer de Trafalgar

Rhonda de Sant Peré

Carrer de Fradikers

URQUINAONA Ⓜ

CATALUNYA Ⓜ

To Cent Focs

PALAN DE LA MUSICA CATALANA ■

PENSIE 2000 ●

AL SUR ●

Via Laietana

Av. del Portal de l'Angel

ELS QUATRE GATS ■

CATALUNYA Ⓜ

PL. CATALUNYA Ⓜ

PIZZA MARZANO ▼

SELF NATURISTA ▼

Calle de Sta Ana

HOSTAL-RESIDÈNCIA LAUSANNE ●

ROMAN WALLS ★

Carrer de la Canuda

CATHEDRAL ★

Carrer dels Comtes

MUSEU D'HISTÒRIA DE LA CIUTAT ■

Carrer del Bisbe

JAUME I Ⓜ

CAMPI ●

CAFÉ VIENA ▼

ATTIC ▼

Carrer d'En Bot

HOSTAL-RESIDÈNCIA REMBRANDT ■

Carrer de la Portaferrissa

XALOC ▼

PLAÇA DE L'ANGEL ★

ESLGLÉSIA DE BETLEM ★

Rambla dels Estudis

HOSTAL MALDA ■

CAJ CHAI ▼

Carrer de la Palla

PALAU DE LA GENERALITAT ★

Carrer del Carme

BAGUETINA CATALANA ▼

Rambla de Sant Josep

JUCY JONES ▼

AJUNTAMENT ★

LA BOQUERIA ★

ARCO YOUTH HOSTEL ■

PENSIÓN CANADIENSE ■

HOSTAL NITZS BCN, AND HOSTAL CORAL ■

ESCRIBÀ ▼

C. d. la Boqueria

HOSTEL SUN AND MOON ■

HOSTAL FERNANDO ■

PENSION MARI-LUZ ■

LA RIA ▼

LICEU Ⓜ

CAFÉ DE L'OPERA ▼

EL 13 ▼

HOSTAL CORAL ■

HARLEM JAZZ CLUB ●

Carrer de l'Hospital

PENSIÓN LA CALMA ■

OVISO ●

Carrer d'Avinyo

ALBERG PALAU ■

GRAN TETRE DEL LICEU ★

LES QUINZE NITS ▼

VEGETALIA ▼

GOPAL ▼

QUARTER GOTHIC ▼

Carrer de Ferran

BARCELONA PIPA CLUB ■

KARMA ●

PASTA BAR ▼

La Rambla

KABUL YOUTH HOSTEL ■

JAMBOREE ●

TUCCO ▼

Carrer de la Unió

C. d. Nou de la Rambla

BOULEVARD CULTURE CLUB ■

HEAVEN ●

LUPARA ●

C. d. Escudellers

To El Bosc de les Fades

barcelona

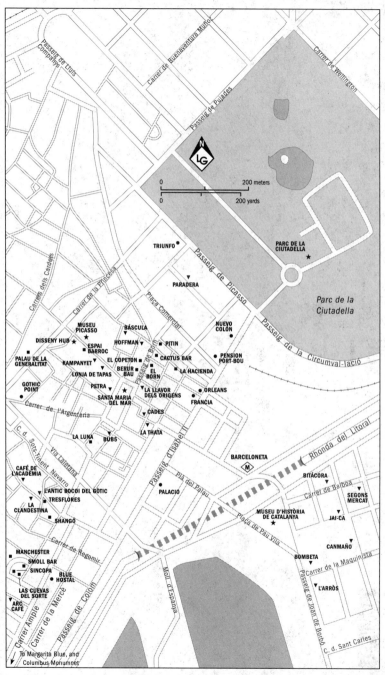

barri gòtic and las ramblas map

TRIUNFO ●

PARADERA ▼

PARC DE LA
CIUTADELLA ★

Parc de la
Ciutadella

MUSEU
PICASSO ★

DISSENY HUB ★

BÁSCULA ▼

HOFFMAN ▼   PITIN ▼

ESPAI
BARROC ▼

NUEVO
COLÓN ●

PALAU DE LA
GENERALITAT ■

KAMPANYET ▼   EL COPETÓN ▼   CACTUS BAR ■

PENSION
PORT-BOU ●

BERUR
BAU ■   EL
BORN ■

LONJA DE TAPAS ▼

LA HACIENDA ▼

GOTHIC
POINT ●

PETRA ▼

SANTA MARIA
DEL MAR ★

LA LLAVOR
DELS ORIGENS ▼

ORLEANS ●

FRANCIA ●

CADES ▼

Carrer de l'Argenteria

LA LUNA ▼   BUBS ■

LA THATA ▼

BARCELONETA
Ⓜ

Rhonda del Litoral

CAFÉ DE
L'ACADEMIA ▼

L'ANTIC BOCOÍ DEL GÒTIC ■

TRESFLORES ▼

BITÁCORA ▼

Carrer de Balboa

SEGONS
MERCAT ▼

LA
CLANDESTINA ▼

SHANGO ■

PALACIO ●

MUSEU D'HISTÒRIA
DE CATALUNYA ★

JAI-CA ▼

MANCHESTER ■

SMOLL BAR ■

SINCOPA ■

BLUE
HOSTAL ●

CANMAÑO ▼

BOMBETA ●

LAS CUEVAS
DEL SORTE ▼

ARC
CAFÉ ▼

L'ARRÒS ▼

C. d. Sant Carles

To Margarita Blue, and
Columbus Monumnet

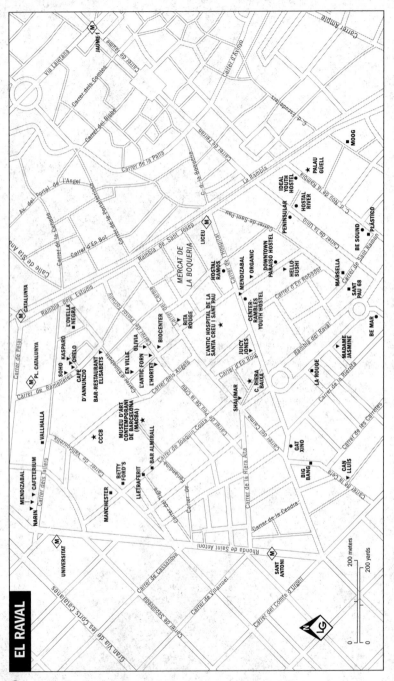

EL RAVAL

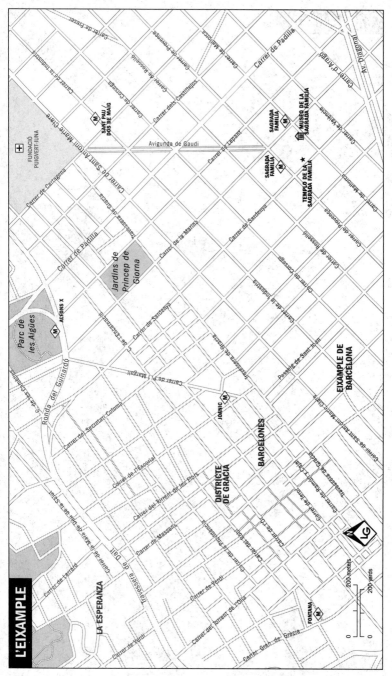

L'EIXAMPLE

Parc de les Aigües

Jardins de Princep de Giorna

DISTRICTE DE GRACIA

LA ESPERANZA

BARCELONÈS

EIXAMPLE DE BARCELONA

SAGRADA FAMÍLIA

SAGRADA FAMÍLIA

MUSEO DE LA SAGRADA FAMÍLIA

TEMPLO DE LA SAGRADA FAMÍLIA ★

FUNDACIÓ PUIGVERT-IUNA

Carrer de Padilla

Carrer de Mallorca

Carrer de Provença

Carrer de Rosselló

Carrer de Còrsega

Carrer dels Castillejos

Avinguda de Gaudí

Carrer de Lepant

Carrer de la Marina

Carrer de Sardenya

Carrer de Pàdua

Carrer de la Indústria

Passatge de Sant Joan

Carrer del Secretari Coloma

Ronda del Guinardó

Carrer de Cartagena

Carrer de Sant Antoni Maria Claret

Carrer de la Indústria

Carrer de Sardenya

Carrer de Còrsega

Carrer de Provença

Carrer de Mallorca

Carrer de Padilla

Carrer d'Aragó

Av. Diagonal

Carrer de València

Carrer de Rosselló

Carrer de l'Escorial

Carrer del Torrent de les Flors

Carrer de les Massens

Carrer de Besalú

Carrer de Verdi

Carrer del Torrent de n'Olla

Carrer Gran de Gràcia

Passatge de D.D.

Passatge de Sant Joan

Carrer de Bailèn

Carrer de Girona

Carrer de P.I. Margall

Carrer de Terrassa

Carrer de Mare de Déu del Coll

SANT PAU / DOS DE MAIG (M)

ALFONS X (M)

JOANIC (M)

FONTANA (M)

LG (M)

L'EIXAMPLE map

200 meters

200 yards

0

0

www.letsgo.com

Ø 179

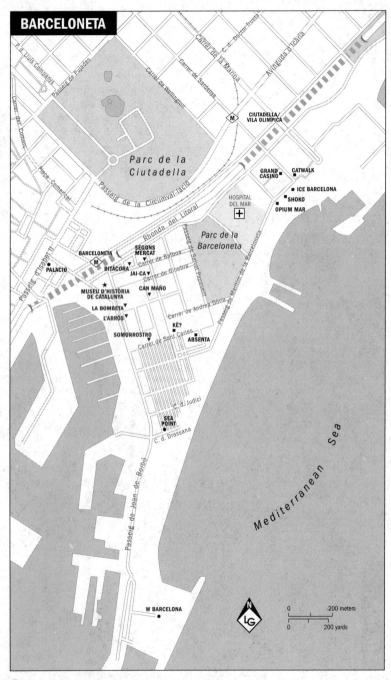

BARCELONETA

Carrer de la Marina

Carrer de la C. t. Doctor Trueta

Carrer de Sardenya

Avinguda d' Icaria

P. d. Lluis Companys

Passeig de Pujades

Carrer de Wellington

Carrer del Comerç

Ⓜ CIUTADELLA/
VILA OLIMPICA

Parc de la Ciutadella

Passeig de la Circumval·lació

GRAND CASINO ■   ■ CATWALK

■ ICE BARCELONA

HOSPITAL
DEL MAR
✚   ■ SHOKO
OPIUM MAR ■

Rhonda del Litoral

Parc de la Barceloneta

Plaça Comercial

BARCELONETA   SEGONS
MERCAT ▾

Carrer de Balboa

Passeig d' Isabel II

PALACIO   Ⓜ BITÁCORA

JAI-CA ▾

Carrer de Ginebra

Passeig de Sant Paname

★ MUSEU D'HISTÒRIA
DE CATALUNYA

CAN MAÑO

LA BOMBETA ▾

L'ARRÒS ▾

Carrer de Andrea Dòria

Passeig de Martim de la Barceloneta

SOMORROSTRO

KÈ? ■

Carrer de Sant Carles   ABSENTA

C. e. d' Judici

SEA
POINT ■

C. d. Drassana

Mediterranean Sea

Passeig de Joan de Borbó

N
LG

0   200 meters

0   200 yards

W BARCELONA ●

barcelona

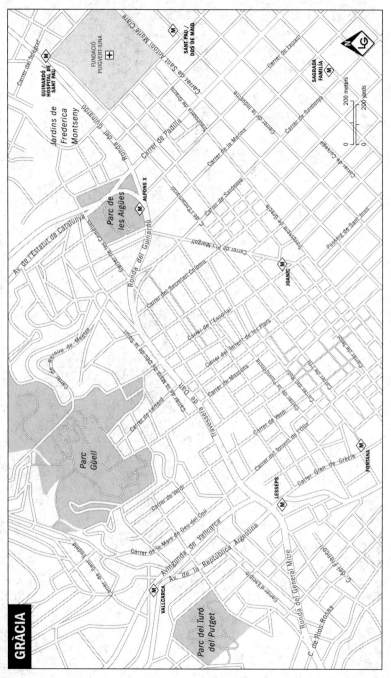

GRÀCIA

gràcia map

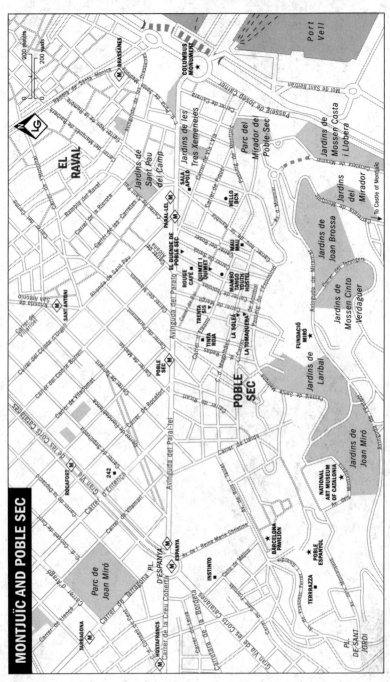

MONTJUÏC AND POBLE SEC

BERLIN

So you've decided to visit Berlin. Congratulations. Your pretentious friends went to Paris. Your haughty friends went to London. And your lost friends went to Belarus. But you decided on Berlin. You've probably heard that Berlin is the coolest city in the world, or that it has one of the best clubs in Europe, or that it sleeps when the sun comes up. Well, don't believe the hype. It's not the coolest city in the world; it's several of the coolest cities in the world. It doesn't have one of the best clubs in Europe; it has 10. And Berlin *never* sleeps.

Berlin's rise began with some normal history, taken to epic heights. King Friedrich II and his identically named progeny ruled from canal-lined boulevards, built palaces like middle-fingers to all the haters, and developed Prussia into an Enlightened European powerhouse, with Berlin at the helm. But after centuries of captaining Europe, Berlin went crazy in the 20th. As the seat of Hitler's terror, and with WWII drama in its streets, Berlin rebooted in the '50s, only to become a physical manifestation of Cold War divisions. The Wall rose in '61, slicing the city and breeding the enmity of a radical student and punk population. Ten years after the Wall crumbled in '89, the German government decided to relocate from Bonn to Berlin. And from there, Berlin became today's European champion of cool.

Sorry about your friends.

greatest hits

- **THREE RINGS. Circus Hostel** in Mitte is exactly what it sounds like (p. 193).
- **OLD SCHOOL.** See ancient ruins in their full glory (and size) at the **Pergamon Museum** (p. 207).
- **MUNCH'N'WATCH. Das Film Café** offers both good food and indie film screenings, at the same time! (p. 223)
- **BI-WINING. The Weinerei: Forum** lets you sample as much wine as you want for a flat fee! (p. 233)

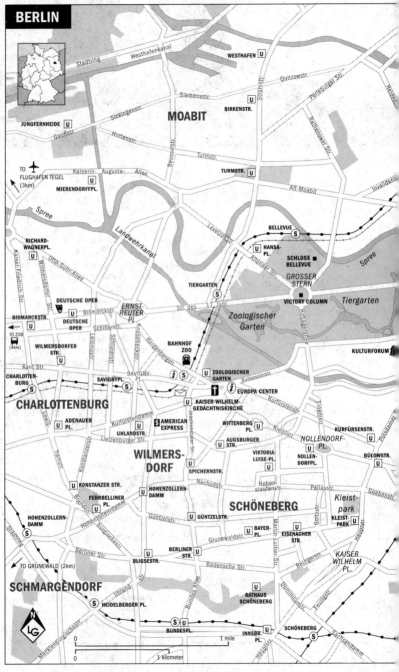

BERLIN

WESTHAFEN Ⓤ

Stadtring   Westhafenkanal

Siemensstr.

JUNGFERNHEIDE Ⓤ   **MOABIT**   BIRKENSTR.

Quitzowstr.

Sickingenstr.

Gaußstr.   Huttenstr.

Turmstr.

TO ✈ FLUGHAFEN TEGEL (3km)

Kaiserin- Augusta- Allee

TURMSTR. Ⓤ

MIERENDORFFPL.

Alt-Moabit

Invaliden

Spree

Landwehrkanal

Levetzowstr.

BELLEVUE Ⓢ

RICHARD-WAGNERPL. Ⓤ

HANSA-PL. Ⓤ

SCHLOSS BELLEVUE ■

Spree

Kaiser-Friedrich-Str.

Otto-Suhr-Allee

Wilmersdorfer Str.

TIERGARTEN

GROSSER STERN

DEUTSCHE OPER ♱

Bismarckstr.

ERNST-REUTER-PL.

Str. des 17. Juni   VICTORY COLUMN ◆   Tiergarten

BISMARCKSTR. Ⓤ

DEUTSCHE OPER Ⓤ

Schillerstr.

Zoologischer Garten

TO ZOB (4km)

WILMERSDORFER STR. Ⓤ

Leibnizstr.   Schlüterstr.   Krumme str.   Hardenbergstr.

BAHNHOF ZOO

KULTURFORUM ♱

Kant Str.

CHARLOTTEN-BURG Ⓢ

SAVIGNYPL. Ⓢ

SAVIGNY PL.

ⓘ Ⓢ

Ⓤ ZOOLOGISCHER GARTEN

Budapesterstr.

Hofjägerallee

CHARLOTTENBURG

✉

ⓘ EUROPA CENTER

KAISER-WILHELM-GEDÄCHTNISKIRCHE

Kurfürstenstr.

Friedrich

KÜRFÜRSTENSTR. Ⓤ

ADENAUER PL. Ⓤ

Kurfürstendamm

Ⓢ AMERICAN EXPRESS

WITTENBERG PL. Ⓤ

Kleiststr.

NOLLENDORF-PL. Ⓤ

Potsdamer str.

UHLANDSTR. Ⓤ

Lietzenburger Str.

Joachimstaler Str.

AUGSBURGER STR.

NOLLEN-DORFPL. Ⓤ

BÜLOWSTR. Ⓤ

WILMERS-DORF

VIKTORIA-LUISE-PL. Ⓤ

SPICHERNSTR. Ⓤ

Hohen-staufenstr.

Pallasstr.

Goebenstr.

KONSTANZER STR. Ⓤ

HOHENZOLLERN-DAMM

Nachodstr.

SCHÖNEBERG

Kleist-park

KLEIST-PARK Ⓤ

FEHRBELLINER PL. Ⓤ

Güntzelstr.

GÜNTZELSTR. Ⓤ

Grunewaldstr.

Hohenzollerndamm

Brandenburgischestr.

Konstanzerstr.

BAYER. PL. Ⓤ

EISENACHER STR. Ⓤ

Gothstr.

Belziger str.

KAISER WILHELM PL.

HOHENZOLLERN-DAMM Ⓢ

Berliner Str.

BERLINER STR. Ⓤ

Bädensche Str.

TO GRÜNEWALD (2km)

BLISSESTR. Ⓤ

Uhland str.

SCHMARGENDORF

HEIDELBERGER PL. Ⓢ

Bundes Allee

RATHAUS SCHÖNEBERG Ⓤ

Dominicus-str.

Teutstr.

Sachsendamm

Stadtring

N

LG

0   1 mile

0   1 kilometer

BUNDESPL. Ⓢ Ⓤ

INNSBR. PL. Ⓤ

SCHÖNEBERG Ⓢ

Mecklenburgischestr.

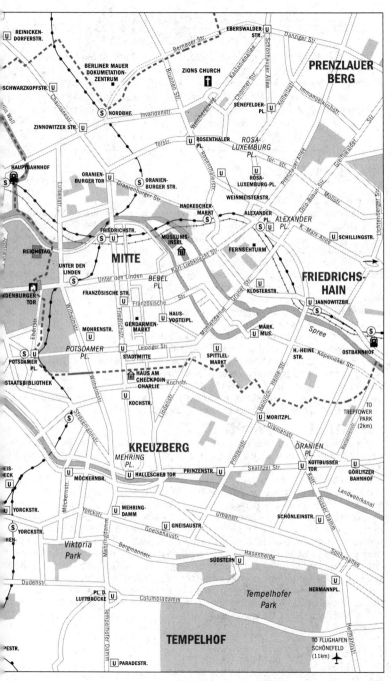

REINICKEN-
DORFERSTR. U

BERLINER MAUER
DOKUMETATION-
ZENTRUM

ZIONS CHURCH

EBERSWALDER U
STR.

Danziger Str.

PRENZLAUER
BERG

SCHWARZKOPFSTR. U

Bernauer Str.

Kastanienallee

Choriner Str.

Schönhauser Allee

Kollwitzstr.

Immanuelkirchstr.

S NORDBHF.

SENEFELDER-
PL.

Invalidenstr.

ZINNOWITZER STR. U

Torstr.

ROSENTHALER
PL.

ROSA-
LUXEMBURG
PL.

Tor- str.

HAUPTBAHNHOF

ORANIEN-
BURGER TOR U

ORANIEN-
BURGER STR.

Oranienburger Str.

ROSA-
LUXEMBURG-PL.

Prenzlauer Allee

Greifswalder Str.

WEINMEISTERSTR.

Otto-Brau.-Str.

Mollstr.

REICHSTAG

FRIEDRICHSTR.
S U

HACKESCHER-
MARKT
S

MUSEUMS-
INSEL

ALEXANDER
PL. S U

ALEXANDER
PL.

K.-Marx-Allee

SCHILLINGSTR. U

Lichtenberger Str.

MITTE

FERNSEHTURM

FRIEDRICHS-
HAIN

UNTER DEN
LINDEN S

Unter den Linden

BEBEL
PL.

Str.

Karl-Liebknecht-Str.

FRANZÖSISCHE STR. U

Str.

KLOSTERSTR. U

JANNOWITZBR. U

FRANZÖSISCHE.

HAUS-
VOGTEIPL. U

Grüner Str.

Mühlendamm

Spree

OSTBAHNHOF S

MOHRENSTR. U

GENDARMEN-
MARKT

Leipziger Str.

MÄRK.
MUS.

H.-HEINE
STR. U

Köpenicker Str.

POTSDAMER
PL.

STADTMITTE U

SPITTEL-
MARKT U

Reichenb. Heine-Str.

POTSDAMER
PL. S U

STAATSBIBLIOTHEK

Ebertstr.

Wilhelmstr.

HAUS AM
CHECKPOIN
CHARLIE

Kochstr.

TO
TREPTOWER
PARK
(2km)

KOCHSTR. U

Lindenstr.

MORITZPL. U

Oranienstr.

ORANIEN
PL.

Stresemannstr.

S

KREUZBERG

MEHRING
PL.

PRINZENSTR. U

Prinzenstr.

Skalitzer Str.

KOTTBUSSER
TOR U

GÖRLITZER
BAHNHOF

EIS-
ECK U

MÖCKERNBR. U

HALLESCHES TOR U

Kottb.

Büsser Damm

Landwehrkanal

YORCKSTR. U

MEHRING-
DAMM U

Urbanstr.

SCHÖNLEINSTR. U

YORCKSTR. S

Yorckstr.

GNEISAUSTR. U

Gneisenaustr.

HEN-

Viktoria
Park

Bergmannstr.

Hasenheide

Sonnenallee

SÜDSTERN U

HERMANNPL. U

Dudenstr.

PL. D.
LUFTBRÜCKE U

Columbiadamm

Tempelhofer
Park

Hermannstr.

PESTR.

TEMPELHOF

TO FLUGHAFEN
SCHÖNEFELD
(11km) ✈

PARADESTR. U

If we had to recommend one neighborhood to the student travelers of Berlin, it would probably be Kreuzberg. With the cheapest food (can we get a hell yeah for döner kebabs?) and the coolest, grungiest clubs, it seems to be designed specifically for the young budget traveler. Check out **Mustafa's** for arguably the best ethnic food in Berlin, followed up by visits to both **Club Tresor** and **Club der Visionaere,** which will hopefully introduce you to some of the rock-star locals.

orientation

CHARLOTTENBURG

Should you forget that Berlin is an old European capital, venture into Charlottenburg. Originally a separate town founded around the grounds of Friedrich I's palace, it became an affluent cultural center during the Weimar years and the Berlin Wall era thanks to Anglo-American support. The neighborhood retains its original old-world opulence, from the upscale Beaux-Arts apartments to the shamelessly extravagant **Kurfürstendamm,** Berlin's main shopping strip. **Ku'damm,** as the locals call it, runs from east to west through southern Charlottenburg. It's home to Europe's largest department store, **KaDeWe,** which comprises five massive floors that keep patrons expertly dressed and lavishly fed with gourmet delicacies. Close to central Charlottenburg is the elephantine **Bahnhof Zoo,** a favorite among families, cute animal enthusiasts, and taxidermists (R.I.P., Knut). Along with the zoo, the Ku'damm, and its never-ending flow of teenagers darting in and out of H and M, is one of the youngest and liveliest areas in Charlottenburg. Other popular sights include the Spree River in the northwest and the absurdly splendiferous **Schloß Charlottenburg** to the north. Otherwise, the neighborhood's high rents keep out most young people and students, so the Charlottenburg crowd tends to be old and quiet, and prefers the sidewalk seating of an expensive Ku'Damm restaurant to crazy ragers in one of the area's few clubs.

SCHÖNEBERG AND WILMERSDORF

South of Ku'damm, Schöneberg and Wilmersdorf are primarily quiet residential neighborhoods, remarkable for their world class cafe culture, bistro tables, relaxed diners, and coffee shops spilling onto virtually every cobblestone street. There's a reason that no Starbucks has popped up in Schöneberg: the coffee here is delicious, cheap, and sometimes made with so much love that a heart appears in the foam. Also, nowhere else in Berlin, and perhaps in all of Germany, is the GLBT community quite as spectacularly ready to party as in the area immediately surrounding **Nollendorfplatz.** Here, the gay nightlife scene varies from chill to crazy, and the various bars scattered across the northern part of Schöneberg are often packed beyond capacity. To the west lies one of Berlin's most convenient outdoor getaways: **Grunewald** rustles with city dwellers trading their daily commute for peaceful strolls with the family dog among the pines. But if you don't have the time for the 20min. bus or tram ride—or a palm reader once predicted that you would be mauled by dogs in a German forest— then Schöneberg and Wilmersdorf offer a gracious handful of shady parks scattered among their apartment facades where you can sit back in the grass and kick back the cups of joe.

MITTE

True to its name ("center" in English), Mitte is without a doubt Berlin's political, historical, cultural, and tourist-ical center. Boasting the **Brandenburg Gate,** the **Reichstag,** the **Jewish Memorial,** the **Rotes Rathaus,** the **Victory Column,** and the **Berliner Dom,** Mitte is crawling with tourists wearing the names of other cities on their T-shirts, passing through to get a glimpse of some of the world's worthiest sights. The area also has Berlin's best cultural institutions; **Museum Island** piles some of the world's most awe-inspiring museums practically on top of each other, with the too-well-preserved-to-be-true **Pergamon Museum** atop the heap. Some of the world's most famous performance halls, including the **Berlin Philharmonic** and the **Deutscher Staatsoper,** grace this cultural capital with their cultural capital. Then, of course, there's the forest-like **Tiergarten** at the center of Mitte, which shelters sunbathers, barbecuers, pensive wanderers, and probably several breeds of magical creatures. The main street cutting through the Tiergarten, **Straße des 17 Juni,** serves as a popular gathering place where carnivals, markets, protests, and public viewings of the World Cup take precedent over constant traffic.

What's perhaps most fun about Mitte is tracing the history of Berlin down its streets and through its buildings. One of the most common phrases in relation to every Mitte sight is "heavily damaged in WWII," and constructions and reconstructions are often difficult to distinguish. The **Berlin Wall** once ran directly through Mitte, and, though the signs of the divide fade with every passing year, there are still many remnants of a more fragmented Berlin, like the DDR-built **Fernsehturm,** which, for better or worse, is Mitte's most incessantly visible landmark. One of the longest still-standing stretches of wall deteriorates in the south, an unsightly sign of unsettling recent times.

But Mitte ain't just about the capital-S Sights: it also burns brightly from night until morning with some of Berlin's most prized techno clubs, many of which are named after baked goods for whatever reason (e.g. **Cookies**). Plus, with shopping centers both ritzy (**Friedrichstraße**) and intimidatingly hip (**Hackescher Markt**), Mitte can serve as a pricey place to replace your threads with something more flannel or form-fitting; that way, entry into the sometimes exclusive nightlife options is only a flashy strut away.

mitte in the middle

Mitte didn't become the center of Berlin by accident. A historically important borough before the 20th century and once a center of Kaiser Wilhelm's Reich empire, Mitte continued its rise to the top after WWII, when it hosted East Germany's architecturally atrocious (and now thankfully destroyed) Palace of the Republic.

As a symbol of reunification after the fall of the Berlin Wall, the West Berlin city government moved from Schöneberg Town Hall into the former home of the communist city government. The red bricks and tower of **Rotes Rathaus** (Red Town Hall) in Mitte, now make for a convenient landmark, in case you get lost in the middle of Berlin's urban jungle.

PRENZLAUER BERG

Like the history of all things trendy, the history of Prenzlauer Berg in the 20th century is reversal after reversal after reversal. When the Wall fell, Prenzlauer Berg was in ruins. Though it had suffered little damage from Allied bombs compared to its neighbors during WWII, its early DDR days were as filled with neglect as Hansel and

Gretel: buildings fell into piles of graffitied bread crumbs, and it wasn't until the '70s that people started sweeping up the mess. But as any home-owner with a neighbor who doesn't mow their lawn knows, neglect means lower rents, and lower rents draw students and the younger in years. By the current millennium, Prenzlauer Berg had become the hippest of the hippest, populated by dreadlock-laden grungesters shopping at secondhand clothing stores, tight-jeaned post-teens drinking cheap black coffee from sidewalk cafe tables, and enough flannel to make a lumberjack chuckle. But hip, by definition, never lasts, and as the noughts progressed, Prenzlauer Berg steadily began to gentrify: students became parents, hippies gave way to yuppies, and parks became playgrounds. Today, Prenzlauer Berg is overrun with toddlers and has one of the highest birth rates in the country. Jungle gyms, strollers, and daycares share the streets with the vestiges of a younger, edgier age, like the tiny, pricey fashion and secondhand stores that line **Kastanienallee** and the countless cafes spilling onto every sidewalk around **Helmholtzplatz**. Though it's changed, Prenzlauer Berg hasn't completely lost its cool: with the best bar scene of any of the neighborhoods, including a wine place where you choose how much to pay, a ping-pong bar, and more vintage sofas than *Mad Men*, P'Berg can still be pretty unbelievable. One recommendation for maximizing your time here: rent a bike. With only about four Metro stations, this Berg is most accessible on two wheels.

FRIEDRICHSHAIN

Friedrichshain's low rents and DDR edge draw a crowd of punks and metal-heads ever eastward. From the longest still-standing remnant of the Berlin Wall, which runs along the Spree, to the stark, towering architecture of the neighborhood's central axis, **Frankfurter Allee,** the ghost of the former Soviet Union still haunts the 'Hain. Fortunately, this ghost only seems to scare the population out into the night, when any crumbling factory, any cobwebbed train station, and any complex of graffiti and grime is fair game for F'Hain's sublimely edgy nightlife. Some locals complain that gentrification has found its way even here, as traditional residential buildings pop up, clubs become tame and touristy, and chic 20-somethings set up shop on the cafe-ridden **Simon-Dach-Strasse** and **Boxhagenerplatz.** Nonetheless, Friedrichshain is still wonderfully inexpensive and unique. Travelers should keep a lookout at night, though, because Friedrichshain's often desolate infrastructure can hide shady characters.

KREUZBERG

If Mitte is Manhattan, Kreuzberg is Brooklyn. Graffiti adorns everything, and the younger population skulks around while chowing down on street food fit for a last supper. The parties start later, go later, and sometimes never stop. Kreuzberg was spawned during the 1860s, when industrialization crammed the previously unpopulated area to Berlin's southeast with dense, low-income housing and brick factories, many of which still stand today. During its 20th-century teens, Kreuzberg ruled as the center of punkdom and counterculture in Berlin. Its old warehouses and factories housed *Hausbesetzer* (squatters) in the 1970s, until a conservative city government forcibly evicted them in the early '80s. Riots ensued, and, during Reagan's 1985 visit to the city, authorities so feared protests in Kreuzberg that they locked down the entire district. While time has tamed Kreuzberg, the neighborhood's alternative soul sticks around like an especially persistent squatter. Underground clubs in abandoned basements, burned-out apartment buildings, and oppressive warehouse complexes shake off their dust when the sun disappears and rage until well after it reappears; the clubs that party the hardest, the latest, and the best in Berlin all find shelter in Kreuzberg. Kreuzberg is also home to most of Berlin's enormous Turkish population (hence the nickname "Little Istanbul"). Döner kebabs, the salty scraps cut from those gigantic meaty beehives in every other storefront, go for €2-3 all across this district, and the **Turkish Market** along the southern bank of the **Landwehrkanal** is one of the most exciting, raucous, cheap, and authentic markets in Western Europe. If you want to learn about Berlin, head to Mitte. If you want to not remember what you learned, come to Kreuzberg.

accommodations

Berlin's accommodations run the gamut from trashy to classy, so it's all up to you (and your wallet) to decide where you fall. And in this big, booming metropolis, most neighborhoods will guarantee you something to do or see—or at least a convenient U-Bahn stop. Travelers with just a few nights in Berlin should consider shelling out for a room in Mitte to be nearby the city's major sights and nightlife. Central Charlottenburg is dotted with cheap pensions and hostels, and the neighborhood's relative affluence practically ensures that you won't stumble into a shady part of town. Schöneberg and Wilmersdorf can be pricey for a solo backpacker, so come with your wolf pack (not the one-man kind) to get the most for your money. Prenzlauer Berg's few hostels are among the best in town: for only a couple bucks more than their counterparts down south in Mitte, you can claim a bed in one of several hostels with a hip staff, spacious rooms, and great proximity to the neighborhood's world-class bars and cafes as well as public transportation that can take you quickly south. A variety of cheap options for backpackers in Friederichshain provide more than a place to crash after dancing yourself clean—even though that's probably all you'll be doing at the neighborhood's techno clubs. If you're looking to meet fellow travelers, the hostels in Kreuzberg have a great sense of community, and they're just a quick leap to Mitte's sights and an even quicker leap to Berlin's best clubs come nightfall.

CHARLOTTENBURG

✎ BEROLINA BACKPACKER — HOSTEL $$

Stuttgarter Pl. 17 — ☎030 327 09 072; www.berolinabackpacker.de

This quiet hostel rejects the generic with pastel walls and bunk-free dorms. The high ceilings and big windows are a necessary foil to the narrow rooms, some of which even have balconies and intricate molding. Surrounding cafes and close proximity to the U-Bahn and S-Bahn make up for its distance from the rush of the city. Relax and enjoy a breakfast buffet (€7), or the "backpackers' breakfast" (a roll with sausage, cheese, and coffee; €3) in the popular, pale blue dining area, or cook your own food in one of the hostel's many kitchens (communal €1 per day, private €9.50).

🚆 S3, S5, S9, or S75: Charlottenburg or U7: Wilmersdorfer Str. ℹ Free Wi-Fi. Internet access on the hostel computer first 30min. free, €0.50 per 15min. thereafter. $ Dorms €17; singles €30-36; doubles €37-47; triples €40-55; quads €46-60. ⏰ Reception 8am-1:30am.

HOTEL PENSION CITYBLICK — PENSION $$$

Kantstr. 71 — ☎030 323 03 282; www.hotel-cityblick.de

Rich ochre decor, surprisingly large rooms, and exposed timbers make this cheap, conveniently located pension a pleasant surprise. The dark wood paneling that lines the classy breakfast room will make you feel like you're kickin' it in a posh Ku'damm hotel rather than an upper Charlottenburg faux-tel. Just be aware that prices may vary steeply from one week (or even day) to the next. To avoid surprises, email ahead to verify rates at hotel-cityblick@gmx.de.

🚆 S3, S5, S7 or S75: Charlottenburg, or U7: Wilmersdorfer Str. $ Singles from €35; doubles from €58; triples from €75; quads from €100. ⏰ Reception 8am-10pm.

accommodations

A & O HOSTEL — HOSTEL $

Joachimstaler Str. 1-3 ☎030 809 47 5300; www.aohostels.com

On a busy, commercial street, A & O may not have an ideal location unless you plan on visiting the Erotik Museum 40m away. Its cheap and spacious rooms, dominated by boxy furniture and low ceilings, are reliable despite their surroundings. After all, A & O owns several hostels in Germany, so any possible personality is wiped clean by standardization. The lobby and bar are packed nightly, as is the roof patio despite its resemblance to a dilapidated minigolf course.

➤ 30m from Bahnhof Zoo. ℹ Breakfast buffet €6. Linens €6. Wi-Fi €5 per day. [$] 8-10 bed dorms from €10; smaller dorms from €15. Singles from €78; doubles from €50. Prices may change significantly in busy months. ⏰ Reception 24hr.

FRAUENHOTEL ARTEMISIA — HOTEL $$$$

Brandenburgische Str. 18 ☎030 873 89 05; www.frauenhotel-berlin.de

This quiet hotel for women was the first of its kind in Germany. Located four flights up in a modern apartment building, its enormous carpeted rooms peek through wide windows onto a silent courtyard. But the city is never far: the rooftop terrace attached to the breakfast room allows a priceless view of the trees and towers of lower Charlottenburg. Named after Italian painter Artemisia Gentileschi, the hotel hosts rotating art exhibitions.

➤ U7: Konstanzer Str. ℹ Breakfast buffet €8. Free Wi-Fi. [$] Singles €98-108, with bath €128-158; doubles €78-108. Extra bed €20. ⏰ Reception daily 7am-8pm.

JUGENDHOTEL BERLIN — HOSTEL $$$$

Kaiserdamm 3 ☎030 322 10 11; www.sportjugendhotel-berlin.de

Though mostly booked by traveling school groups, Jugendhotel Berlin is an uninteresting option that benefits from its proximity to public transportation. Clean, small rooms with lots of light suffer from an unfortunate lack of decoration and character, exemplified by the bare, boxy furniture that looks like it came from an IKEA shopping spree gone wrong. All rooms have full baths and more than half have balconies.

➤ U2: Sophie-Charlotte-Pl. ℹ Breakfast and linens included. Substantial discounts for groups of 10 or more, email for details. [$] Singles €36-49 per person; doubles €32-35 per person; triples €23-30 per person. ⏰ Reception 24hr.

CITY PENSION BERLIN — PENSION $$$$

Stuttgarter Pl. 9 ☎030 277 410; www.city-pension.de

The value of proximity to public transportation can never be underestimated, and this hotel is directly across the street from the Charlottenburg U-Bahn/train hub. Oh, and there are rooms too! Travelers at City Pension get ensuite baths, televisions, and small carpeted rooms sans bunk beds. The pension itself is tiny and quiet, and walking through its yellow-lit halls is like eating toffee with your eyes. Also only a block away from the strip mall-lined Wilmersdorfer Pl., City Pension is a convenient and intimate non-hostel option for groups that can keep you all under budget.

➤ S3, S5, S7, or S75: Charlottenburg, or U7: Wilmersdorfer Str. ℹ Breakfast included. Free Wi-Fi. [$] Singles €54; doubles €76; triples €89; quads €104. ⏰ Reception 24hr.

SCHÖNEBERG AND WILMERSDORF

👍 JUGENDHOTEL BERLINCITY — HOSTEL $$$$

Crellestr. 22 ☎030 787 02 130; www.jugendhotel-berlin.de

Jugendhotel Berlincity, which does not offer dorms, is quite a splurge for solo travelers. Fortunately, it's an unforgettable one. Sky-high brick ceilings, wall-consuming windows, stained wood floors, colorful furniture, and quirky paintings make it a real charmer. Check out the painting in the huge breakfast room to see what we mean: it's *The Last Supper*, staged with Disney and Looney Tunes characters, featuring Mickey as Jesus. The hostel strictly prohibits smoking and alcohol, and it's popular with younger groups, but the mere 5min. walk to the U-Bahn provides a quick escape. Plus, the employees tend to be absurdly charismatic, so seek them out if you want some over-20 conversation.

*U7: Kleistpark. **i** Linens and large breakfast buffet included. Wi-Fi €1 per 30min., €5 per 24hr. (can be used over several days). $ Singles €38, with bath €52; doubles from €60/79; triples €87/102; quads €112/126; quints €124/150; 6-person rooms €146/168. ⏰ Reception 24hr., although sparse in the late morning and early afternoon.*

JETPAK HOSTEL $

Pücklerstr. 54 ☎030 832 501; www.jetpak.de

You might need a jetpack to reach it, but JetPAK is definitely the most unique hostel you'll find in Schöneberg or Wilmersdorf. Hidden in the Grunewald (Berlin's own extensive forest) and secluded from the city by a 15-minute bus ride and seven-minute hike, JetPAK resembles the summer camp where you lost your virginity more than it does the hostel in which you contracted bedbugs. JetPAK comes complete with long tables and bench seating, a collection of bikes, a woodpile, and a small field where you can emulate your favorite *Fußball* players. Originally an old German army camp, the hostel has been warmed up with colorful walls, comfortable beds, and ubiquitous sofas. And with showers heated by the hostel's own solar panels, JetPAK is also one of Berlin's most environmentally conscious places to kick back and reap the benefits of nature.

*U3: Fehrbelliner Pl. or U9: Güntzselstr. Then, bus #115 (dir. Neuruppiner Str.): Pücklerstr. Follow the signs to Grunewald, and turn left on Pücklerstr. Turn left again at the JetPAK sign, just before the road turns to dirt. **i** Breakfast, linens, and internet included. $ 8-bed dorms €14; doubles €23.*

JETPAK CITY HOSTEL HOSTEL $$

Pariserstr. 58 ☎030 784 43 60; www.jetpak.de

There's nothing like large rooms with pine bunks, big windows, and brightly colored walls to lessen the institutional hostel feel. Owned by the same people who started JetPAK in the Grunewald, this hostel is much more practical and central, if not as one-of-a-kind. The bathrooms are newly tiled, and the common room has couches and a foosball table (they call it "Kicker" in Deutschland). There's even a small cafe on the first floor that serves as the reception area during the day. The rates make this place popular with backpackers, so be sure to book ahead online.

*U3 or U9: Spichernstr. **i** Most breakfast items (including croissants) €1. Linens included. $ 8-bed dorms from €17; 6-bed from €19; 4-bed from €20. ⏰ Reception 8am-midnight.*

JUGENDGÄSTEHAUS CENTRAL HOSTEL $$

Nikolsburger Str. 2-4 ☎030 873 01 88 89; www.jugendgaestehaus-central.de

With around 450 beds, Jugendgästehaus is one of Berlin's largest hostels. Due to a heavy student demographic—think the younger, field-trip-taking kind—this hostel is very helpful for the newly arrived, complete with a courteous English-speaking staff, a huge street and train map of Berlin on one of its entrance walls, and its own ATM. Breakfast is included, and seven separate dining rooms cater to the hostel's tremendous population. The rooms are tiny, forgettable, and around 50 years old, but, at these prices, we'll forgive them.

*U3: Hohenzollernpl. or U9: Güntzelstr. **i** Linens €2.50 for stays of under 3 nights, included for stays of 3 nights or more. $ Mar-Oct dorms with breakfast €24, with ½-board €28, with full board €31; singles €30/34/37. Nov-Feb dorms with breakfast €20, with ½-board €24, with full board €26; singles €26/30/32. ⏰ Reception 24hr.*

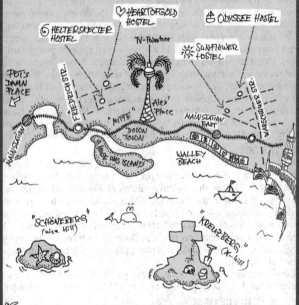

SUNSHINEHOUSE BERLIN

HOSTEL $$

Wexstr. 8 ☎030 826 20 79; www.sunshinehouse-berlin.de

Three three-story buildings and a reception house dot the grassy grounds of Sunshinehouse Berlin, which means that there is, appropriately, plenty of sunshine to be had. Unfortunately, the hostel lies right next to the freeway, so a morning jaunt will leave your ears ringing. But Sunshinehouse provides a solution: common kitchens on every floor of every building allow you to stay inside all day, making yourself breakfast after breakfast. And though you're about as far south as you can get in Schöneberg, a nearby U-Bahn stop keeps you connected to the city above.

🚇 U4: Innsbrucker Pl. ℹ Bathrooms with showers shared between 2 rooms. $ 2- to 3-bed dorms €20; singles €30. ⏰ Reception 9am-9pm.

ART-HOTEL CONNECTION

HOTEL $$$$

Fuggerstr. 33 ☎030 210 21 8800; www.arthotel-connection.de

With deep purple walls, crystal chandeliers, chairs so silver you can nearly see your reflection, and dark wood floors, this hotel is (almost) nothing but class. A gay hotel that describes itself as "hetero-friendly," Art-Hotel boasts some of the most sophisticated style in Schöneberg, especially after recently outfitting all rooms with flatscreens and DVD players. Lest we get too serious, this hotel also offers "playrooms," with slings and other sex toys. Plus, with breakfast offered until 4pm, you can stay in and enjoy the furnishings without missing a meal.

🚇 U1, U2, or U15: Wittenbergpl. ℹ Free Wi-Fi. $ Singles €49-70, with bath €59-80; doubles with shower €79-120, with full bath €89-130; suites €99-130. ⏰ Reception 8am-10pm.

MITTE

👍 CIRCUS HOSTEL

HOSTEL $$

Weinbergsweg 1A ☎030 200 03 939; www.circus-berlin.de

You'll know this hostel by the lobby's red-and-white-striped circus tent of a ceiling. Especially clean and colorful rooms are far more fun than their namesake, featuring tremendous wood floors, couches, tables, and a line of wide windows looking down on a broad and bustling intersection. Rooms come with a ton of "extras": podcast audio tours, jogging route maps, quality food recommendations, and outstandingly helpful staff really do make a difference. Plus, a huge basement bar with lounge space may spare you the cost of a U-Bahn ride to find nightlife. The breakfast buffet (€5) is probably the freshest and biggest you'll find in Mitte's hostels.

🚇 U8: Rosenthaler Pl. It's visible right as you exit the Metro. ℹ Lockers €10 deposit. Linens included. Towels €1. $ 8- to 10-bed dorms €19; 4-bed €23. Singles €86; doubles €56. €2 service charge when paying with credit card. Bikes €12 per day. Segways €35 per day. ⏰ Reception 24hr.

👍 HELTER SKELTER

HOSTEL $

Kalkscheunenstr. 4-5 ☎030 280 44 997; www.helterskelterhostel.de

The receptionist's warning: "The bar's open all day, but if you're too drunk at breakfast, we cut you off." Though the furniture is worn and the sheets are old, this hostel is so drunkenly social that you probably won't mind (or notice). Every night, a huge common room fills to the brim with booze-thirsty backpackers, joining the partying skeletons painted on the wall. Rooms are spacious and colorful, and a lack of individual door keys makes the hostel feel more communal (but less secure) than most. If hostel-wide drinking games and late nights are your thing, then take a chance on this place, and years from now (though perhaps not the morning after) you'll remember it as a Berlin highlight.

🚇 U6: Oranienburger Tor. From the Metro, head south on Friedrichstr. and take a left on Johannisstr. The hostel is on the 3rd floor through a courtyard. Follow the signs. ℹ Breakfast €3; free for stays longer than 3 days. Linens, towel, coffee, and tea included. Free Wi-Fi. Smoking allowed in common area. Kitchen available. 1st 10min. of computer use free, €1 per 30min. thereafter. $ Megadorm €10-14; singles €34; doubles €22-27. ⏰ Reception 24hr.

WOMBAT'S CITY HOSTEL HOSTEL $$$

Alte Schönhauser Str. 2 ☎030 847 10 820; www.wombats-hostels.com

Mod, spotless, comfortable, and with a rooftop bar and terrace—if Wombat's is wrong, we don't want to be right. Though the prices are only a bit higher than average, every detail screams nice hotel, from cushy furniture to sparkling ensuite bathrooms. Relax on the beanbags in the lobby and enjoy the feeling of cleanliness. And if the higher price is still nagging you, keep in mind that your first beer at the rooftop bar is free once you book a bed.

🚇 U2: Rosa-Luxemburg-Pl. From the Metro, head through the alleyway across from a small grassy area. ℹ Breakfast €3.70. Linens, lockers, and luggage storage included. Free Wi-Fi. Towels €2, free in doubles and apartments. Laundry €4.50. Internet stations €.50 per 20min. Guest kitchen. Non-smoking. $ 4- to 6-bed dorms €22-24; doubles €58-70; apartments €40-50 per person. ⏰ Reception 24hr.

HEART OF GOLD HOSTEL HOSTEL $

Johannisstr. 11 ☎030 290 03 300; www.heartofgold-hostel.de

This isn't a hostel to which you'll simply say, "So long, and thanks for all the fish," but a place that will last especially long in your memory bank, even relative to the rest of Mitte's distinctive offerings. Deeply space-ious rooms, each with a window that actually takes the place of an entire wall, provide all the joys of the final frontier, while an open courtyard and some rooms with balconies provide a perfect vantage point for stargazing. If your nerd powers haven't kicked in by now, this hostel is based entirely on Douglas Adams's *The Hitchhiker's Guide to the Galaxy*, which we hope is your second favorite travel guide. The breakfast and common room may contain more than 42 references to this beloved sci-fi series.

🚇 S1, S2, or S25: Oranienburger Str. From the Metro, head south on Tucholskystr., then right on Johannisstr. ℹ Breakfast €3.50, free for stays over 3 days. Lockers and towels included. Linens deposit €5. Laundry €4. Key deposit €5. Free Wi-Fi. Padlock deposit €10. $ Megadorms from €10; 7- to 8-bed €12; 4-bed €16. Singles €32; doubles €56. ⏰ Reception 24hr.

BAXPAX DOWNTOWN HOTEL/HOSTEL HOSTEL, HOTEL $

Ziegelstr. 28 ☎030 278 74 880; www.baxpax.de

Baxpax Downtown has a bag full of fun hostel tricks. Two above-ground pools are revealed in the summer (one on the lower patio, the other on the roof, where there's a sweet minibar and a spectacular view of the skyline). Downstairs there's a bar with lots of cheap food (€2-9) and there's a club in the basement. Like everything else in the building, the rooms are brightly colored, and spotless wood floors provide a reassuringly classy click to your step. Plus, in a location that manages to be both quiet *and* just a few minutes' walk from iconic Mitte attractions (like Museum Island!), baxpax Downtown promises both a great night and an easy sleep.

🚇 U6: Oranienburger Tor. From the Metro, head south on Friedrichstr., then turn left on Ziegelstr. ℹ Breakfast €5.50. Linens €2.50. Towels €1, free in doubles and singles. Laundry self-service €5, full-service €8. Key deposit €5. Non-smoking. $ 20-bed dorms €8-31; 8-bed-dorms with showers €12-33; 5-bed dorms with ensuite bathrooms and showers €15-36. Singles €29-92; doubles €54-132. ⏰ Reception 24hr.

CITYSTAY HOSTEL $$

Rosenstr. 16 ☎030 236 24 031; www.citystay.de

A central location, a beautiful, well-kept courtyard, and an expansive cafe lounge separate this hostel from the pack. Rooms are small, smell like several generations of backpackers, and lack any furniture or decoration other than a couple of plastic chairs, but they benefit from huge windows and cushy beds. You know what really seals the deal? A 2min. walk to Museum Island, Unter den Linden, and Alexanderpl.

🚇 U5, U8, S5, S7, S9, or S75: Alexanderpl. From the Metro, head south on Karl-Liebknecht-Str., then turn right halfway down the block onto Rosenstr. ℹ Lockers €10 deposit. Linens €2.50, with ISIC free. Laundry €5. Towels €5 deposit. 5 computers in lobby €3 per hr. $ 8-bed dorms €17; 4-bed €21. Doubles €50, with private shower €65. ⏰ Reception 24hr.

ST. CHRISTOPHER'S
HOSTEL $

Rosa Luxembourg Str. 41   ☎030 814 53 960; www.st-christophers.co.uk

It's rare you find a hostel bar with €1 Jager shots, but St. Christopher's delivers this and the inevitable crazy Jager nights. A roomy bar complemented by indoor and outdoor seating and a broad loft space with a pool table and loads of lounging space ensure that your stay won't lack social time. Rooms, though, are small and boring, with cheesy plastic furniture and fuzzy blue carpeting that scream "hostel." Still, it's a bargain for backpackers, and apartments with kitchens are a cheap option for long-term stays.

⚓ *U2: Rosa-Luxemburg-Pl. Right next to the Metro.* *i* *Breakfast, luggage storage, lockers, and linens included. Towels €1. Internet €2 per hr. Non-smoking.* ⓢ *Dorms €9-20; doubles €35-50; quads €60-96. Prices can vary by day based on availability.* ☒ *Reception 24hr. Bar open daily until 3am. Happy Hour daily 5-10pm.*

THREE LITTLE PIGS HOSTEL
HOSTEL $

Stresemannstr. 66   ☎030 326 62 955; www.three-little-pigs.de

An enormous century-old former abbey serves as this hostel's lobby. Hidden far back in a silent courtyard, Three Little Pigs guarantees a quiet place to sleep, although consequently provides little in the way of nightlife. Tremendously spacious and bright rooms gain some color with floral designs, and large windows allow you to gaze quietly on the beautiful brick complex that surrounds you. Unfortunately, with a 3min. walk between the hostel and a non-central S-Bahn station, staying here will require a hefty commute to reach prime Mitte destinations (20min. or so).

⚓ *S1, S2, or S25: Anhalter Bahnhof. From the Metro, head south on Stresemannstr. and turn left into a long courtyard.* *i* *Breakfast €5. Linens €2.50. Towel €1. Lockers included. Free Wi-Fi. Laundry €5. 4 computers with Internet access €2 per hr. Bike rental €12 per day. Guest kitchen. Parking available.* ⓢ *6- to 8-bed dorms €11-17; singles €34-36; doubles €44-48.* ☒ *Reception 24hr.*

BAXPAX MITTE
HOSTEL $

Chausseestr. 102   ☎030 283 90 965; www.baxpax.de/mittes-backpacker

Recently refurbished and repainted rooms make baxpax Mitte one of the most interesting places to catch some zzzs. Hallways covered from floor to ceiling with mystical murals, including a glittery mountainscape, lead to some of the quirkiest themed dorms and private rooms you'll find. The "Beetle Room" features a tangled, metal sculpture in the center of its ceiling; the "Miró Room" hides a jittery mural based on the abstract work of its namesake; and the "Fruit of the Loom" room may make you crave fruit-snacks more than underwear with its fruity, neon stripes. A small common room with a tiny kitchen fails to match the social spaces of other Mitte hostels, and the area is too far north to guarantee nearby nightlife, but you may be too busy studying the wall behind your roommate's bed to notice.

⚓ *U6: Naturkundemuseum. From the Metro, head north on Chausseestr.* *i* *Guest kitchen available. Breakfast €5.50. Linens €2.50. Towels €1. Full-service laundry €7. 2 Internet kiosks €2 per hr. Key deposit €10. Happy hour at small in-house bar 7-8pm. Non-smoking.* ⓢ *10- to 12-bed dorms €6-31; 8-bed €7-33; 6-bed €9-34. Doubles €50-86, with private toilet €56-92.* ☒ *Reception 24hr.*

PRENZLAUER BERG

▧ PFEFFERBETT
HOSTEL $

Christinenstr. 18-19   ☎030 939 35 858; www.pfefferbett.de

This 19th-century brick building features high, arched ceilings, giant pillars, exposed beams, and a cathedral-sized common room. This may sound a little scary and impersonal, but, fortunately, green walls, two patios (one in a shaded garden), a fireplace, and an energetic staff with a taste for house music fill this huge space with a requisite amount of warmth. The rooms feature some of the highest brick ceilings you'll have seen in a hostel and accommodate massive metal bunks. Some fun features, including sports projected on the common room wall, a pool table, and a fully stocked bar, promise constant entertainment between your assaults on the town.

⇟ U2: Senefelderpl. From the Metro, exit through the southernmost exit. Look immediately to your right, and there will be a sign in a large doorway directing you to Pfefferbett. Go up the left flight of stairs, turn right at the top, and walk to the back of the shaded, cluttered courtyard. Turn left at the back. The hostel is just around the corner. ℹ Breakfast €4. Linens €2.50. Free Wi-Fi in common room. Women-only dorms available. $ 8-bed dorms from €12; 6-bed from €15, with shower from €19; 4-bed from €20. Singles with bath from €47; doubles with bath €64. ⏰ Reception 24hr.

👍 EAST SEVEN HOSTEL HOSTEL $$

Schwedter Str. 7 ☎030 936 22 240; www.eastseven.de

A strict no-bunk policy makes this retro hostel an especially comfortable place to lay your head. The indoor lounge area and the gorgeous, grill-bedecked back patio are popular hangouts for backpackers who appreciate cold beer specials (€1) and the finer things. Rooms are spacious, with hardwood floors, old windows, and subtle-hued stripes that would make Martha Stewart proud. The young, personable staff even make checking in and out a real treat; be sure to take advantage of their refreshingly opinionated expertise on the city.

⇟ U2: Senefelderpl. From the Metro, exit through the northernmost entrance, and you'll be near Schwedter Str. Cross Schönhauser Allee to the west side, then walk west on Schwedter Str. The hostel is on the right. ℹ Linens included. Free Wi-Fi. Internet terminals €0.50 per 20min. $ Mar-Oct 8-bed dorms €18; 4-bed with bath €22. Singles €38; doubles €52; triples €68. Nov-Feb 8-bed dorms €14; 4-bed with bath €19. Singles €31; doubles 44; triples €57. Bike rental €10 per day. ⏰ Reception 7am-midnight.

LETTE'M SLEEP HOSTEL HOSTEL $$

Lettestr. 7 ☎030 447 33 623; www.backpackers.de

As one of Berlin's very first hostels, Lette'm Sleep knows what it's doing. A huge amount of floor space ensures that you won't awkwardly brush up against your dorm-mates in the morning, and wide windows admit the sights and sounds of Helmholtzpl., which is home to a shady park and P'Berg's highest concentration of cool cafes. The fluorescent paint job, a communal kitchen with mattress-like couches, and a staff that actually enjoys conversing with guests make this far more than just a place to crash.

⇟ U2: Eberswalder Str. From the Metro, head east on Danziger Str., turn left on Lynchener Str., then turn right on Lettestr., which is immediately past the park. The hostel will be on your left. ℹ Linens included. Each room has a sink. Free Wi-Fi. $ Apr-Oct 3- to 7-bed dorms €17-21; doubles with kitchenette €49; triples with kitchenette €84. Nov-Mar 4- to 7-bed dorms €16-20; doubles with kitchenette €40; triples with kitchenette €75. ⏰ Reception 24hr.

ALCATRAZ HOSTEL $$

Schönhauser Allee 133a ☎030 484 96 815; www.alcatraz-backpacker.de

Don't worry: Alcatraz is no island prison. It has a great, accessible location, and your roommates will only have committed several murders *in your imagination.* Plus, a cozy "Chill-Out Room," outfitted with a foosball table, a TV, and several couches will make you feel far more comfortable than that time you spent the night in jail for "public drunkenness." Unfortunately, the rooms are so small and bare that you might begin to suspect that the name has more accuracy than you'd hoped. Instead of sitting in your room contemplating your remorse, check out the beautiful central courtyard and the bright, cartoonish murals lining the halls, or bake a cake in the common kitchen.

⇟ U2: Eberswalder Str. From the Metro, head north on Schönhauser Allee. The hostel will be on the left. ℹ Free Wi-Fi. Fully equipped kitchen. Breakfast €2. Linens €2. Bike rental €10 per day. $ Mar-Oct 8-bed dorms €16; 4-bed €18. Singles €40; doubles €50; triples €69. Nov-Feb 8-bed dorms €13; 4-bed €15. Singles €35; doubles €44; triples €57. Cash only. ⏰ Reception 24hr.

FRIEDRICHSHAIN

⚑ SUNFLOWER HOSTEL   HOSTEL $
Helsingforser Str. 17   ☎030 440 44 250; www.sunflower-hostel.de
In one hall, Darth Vader kicks an arcade game. In another, Sesame Street
characters and pixelated Space Invaders battle for your attention. The
lobby's young, personable staff and indie electro mix are all just one Hab-
ermas book away from a college cafe. The sum of all of these elements?
A real blossom of a hostel. Each room and hallway is ecstatically and
hilariously painted with the best breed of Berlin quirkiness. Yet with tremendous windows and a wealth of floor space that just invites cartwheels,
these rooms aren't only about the walls. Seven minutes from the Simon-
Dach restaurant strip, and about five from the club scene, this hostel is
only somewhat off the beaten path but far enough off its rocker to make a
lasting impression.
   ✈ *U1, S3, S5, S7, S9 or S75: Warschauer Str. From the Metro, walk north on Warschauer
   Str., turn left on Helsingforser Str., and the hostel will be on your right.* **i** *Breakfast €3.
   Linens and padlocks €3 deposit. Laundry €4.50. Free Wi-Fi.* ⑤ *7- to 8-bed dorms €10-15;
   5- to 6-bed €13-17. Singles €30-37; doubles €38-48; apartments €70-75. Bikes €12 per
   day.* ☒ *Reception 24hr.*

GLOBETROTTER HOSTEL ODYSSEE   HOSTEL $$
Grünberger Str. 23   ☎030 290 00 081; www.globetrotterhostel
Hi-scary-ous medieval statues and walls covered in jagged fragments of
old wooden crates greet you as you enter Globetrotter Hostel's spacious
lobby, where a chalkboard calendar lists the concerts and parties in Berlin
for every day of the week. Though some of these details, along with the
dark brown paint job, may seem disconcertingly metal at first, they are
only part of this bright and busy hostel. Muraled walls, an ivy facade, and
a shaded courtyard out back are highlights, along with a 22-bed dorm,
which, by virtue of well-placed barriers and clever bed positioning, actually feels far more private than most 8-bed dorms.
   ✈ *U5: Frankfurter Tor. From the Metro, walk south on Warschauer Str., then turn right on
   Grünberger Str. The hostel will be on your right, halfway down the block.* **i** *Breakfast €8.
   Linens €3 deposit. Free Wi-Fi. Internet terminals €0.50 per 20min.* ⑤ *22-bed dorms €13-
   19; 8-bed €14-20; 6-bed €16-22; 4- to 5-bed €18-24. Singles €36-49; doubles €47-59,
   with shower €54-69. Prices vary, so check the calendar on the website for precise rates.
   Credit card min. €25.* ☒ *Reception 24hr.*

U INN BERLIN HOSTEL   HOSTEL $$
Finowstr. 36   ☎030 330 24 410; www.uinnberlinhostel.com
The crowning detail of this tiny hostel is probably that every Friday at
7pm, the employees and guests come together to cook organic food in the
guest kitchen. If this is your idea of a memorable Friday evening, then this
is definitely the hostel for you. U Inn Berlin doesn't consider itself a party
hostel: there's a no-alcohol policy, and quiet hours start at 10pm. But with
only two floors, a beautiful little common room, and potted plants galore,
it's a wonderfully homey community to join for a couple days. Plus, the
small and somewhat dim rooms benefit from eclectic paint coats based on
different U- and S-Bahn lines.
   ✈ *U5: Frankfurter Allee. From the Metro, walk west on Frankfurter Allee, then turn left
   on Finowstr. The hostel is hidden to the left.* **i** *Breakfast €2. Linens €2. Hostel internet
   terminals €1 per 20min. Daily supplement to pay for "greening" the cleaning supplies and
   buying fair trade, organic coffee €0.50.* ⑤ *Apr-Oct 8-bed dorms €15; 5-bed €18; 4-bed
   €19. Singles €29; doubles €50; triples €69. Nov-Mar 8-bed dorms €13; 5-bed €16; 4-bed
   €17. Singles €25; doubles €46; triples €63.* ☒ *Reception 7am-1am.*

accommodations

ALL IN HOSTEL HOSTEL $

Grünberger Str. 54 ☎030 288 76 83; www.all-in-hostel.com

Right in the midst of the Simon-Dach restaurant strip, this hostel has the best location of any on the list, but not by quite enough of a margin to make up for otherwise underwhelming facilities. Dorms are some of the tiniest: bunks are actually pressed up against each other, and moving around with several other people in the room is a tight squeeze. Though the rooms may be small, the massive common room contains a fleet of spotless tables, a bar, a pool table, two TVs, and a smoking room.

🚇 U5: Frankfurter Tor. From the Metro, walk south on Warschauer Str., turn left on Grünberger Str., and look for a slightly inconspicuous, orange-lettered sign on your right. The hostel is set back from the street by a small courtyard. [i] Breakfast €5. Linens €3 for 1st night. Wi-Fi €1 per hr., €5 per 24hr. Hostel internet terminal €1 per 20min. [$] 10-bed dorms €10; 6-bed with bath €18. Singles with bath €39; doubles with bath €44. ⏰ Reception 24hr.

OSTEL HOSTEL $$

Wriezener Karree 5 ☎030 257 68 660; www.ostel.eu

No, it's not a typo. "Ost" means "east" in German, and this hostel delivers more east than Easter. Located in a DDR flat and filled with original DDR furniture and wallpaper (think glossy, boxy bookshelves and orange-striped walls that are so 1950s, they'll make you want to mow your lawn and have seven kids), Ostel is a respectable attempt at recreating daily life from before the wall's fall. Though a bit of a splurge, a stay in the "Pioneer Camp" dorm is like living in a condo with people you don't know: it consists of two huge six-bed rooms with large tables and ensuite bathrooms. Perhaps the only detail that will remind you you're still living in a post-wall Berlin is the beach volleyball court out front.

🚇 S3, S5, S7, S9, or S75: Ostbahnhof. From the Metro, walk north on Str. der Pariser Kommune, and turn right at the Ostel Restaurant. Follow the sidewalk to the next building, and turn left into the narrow street with the beach volleyball court. [i] Breakfast €6.50. Linens and towels included. [$] "Pioneer Camp" 12-bed dorms €15; singles €33; doubles €54. Bikes €9 per day. ⏰ Reception 24hr.

EASTERN COMFORT HOSTEL HOSTEL $$

Mühlenstr. 73-77 ☎030 667 63 806; www.eastern-comfort.com

Grab your swim trunks and your flippy-floppies, 'cause this hostel-boat is straight flowin' on the Spree. Guests rent rooms in cabins, with fold-down beds and portals for windows. Rooms are closet-sized, but you're on a boat, backpacker! The truly adventurous can rent a tent and sleep on the top deck for the cheapest view of the big blue watery road. Every Wednesday, travelers enjoy a Language Party, where guests get together to enjoy the hostel's international clientele.

🚇 U1, S3, S5, S7, S9, or S75: Warschauer Str. [i] Breakfast €4.50. Linens €5. Free Wi-Fi. Internet €1 per 30min. 2-night min. stay on weekends. [$] Tents €12; 4- or 5-bed dorms €16; singles with bath €50; doubles with bath €58; triples with bath €69; quads with bath €76. ⏰ Reception 8am-midnight.

KREUZBERG

COMEBACKPACKERS HOSTEL HOSTEL $$

Adalbertstr. 97 ☎030 600 57 527; www.comebackpackers.com

In a long, curved building on a busy square, this hostel looks futuristic but delivers a refreshing dose of the basics: light, space, and entertainment. Windows take up nearly three walls of the common room and an entire wall of each spacious bedroom, so there's plenty of sunlight to wake you up when you accidentally set your phone's alarm clock to PM. The roof terrace that lines the common room has only dead plants, rocks, and a bird cage with plastic birds, but it provides a great view of the bustle below, a perfect place to smoke or drink, and, in the summer, grill. Jittery wall murals and couches in the hall add some interest, as does a funny, young staff with an affinity for hardcore punk. Let's hope this is what hostels are like in the future.

U1 or U8: Kotbusser Tor. From the Metro, walk up Adalbertstr. and turn into the curved alleyway to your left. The hostel is on the left. [i] Continental breakfast €3. Coffee and linens included. Free Wi-Fi. Full-service laundry €5. Towel €2. Key deposit €10. $ Dorms €14-20. Cash only. ⏰ Reception 24hr.

METROPOL HOSTEL — HOSTEL $

Mehringdamm 32 ☎030 259 40 890; www.metropolhostel-berlin.com

So you're in a total food coma from eating *zwei Würste ohne Darm* at **Curry 36** and then wandering about 5 ft. and downing a dürüm (Turkish wrap filled with döner kebab) at **Mustafa's.** Where, oh, where can you sleep this off? Well, turn around, my friend, because Metropol Hostel is right behind you. Don't let the century-old doors fool you: this hostel opened in July 2010 and as mod as they come. The long common room overlooks the busy Mehringdamm, and a bar, some booths, and fleets of cushy seats add hominess. The rooms are almost too spacious, but wide wood floors make you appreciate the emptiness. Almost universally ensuite bathrooms, Wi-Fi everywhere, and spotless rooms make this huge hostel feel more like a hotel.

U6 or U7: Mehringdamm. From the Metro, cross to the west side of Mehringdamm and walk south past the building that looks like a cartoon version of a Medieval castle. The hostel is on the 4th floor of a well-labeled building. [i] Breakfast, lockers, luggage storage, safe, and towels included. Linens €2. Free Wi-Fi. Shower and toilet in every room. $ 6-to 10-bed dorms €9-21, with bath €12-29; singles €39-69; doubles €50-79. ⏰ Reception 24hr.

HOSTEL X BERGER — HOSTEL $

Schlesische Str. 22 ☎030 695 31 863; www.hostelxberger.com

For the quickest jump to the coolest clubs in Berlin, no one outdoes Hostel X Berger, which is right along the canal. The rooms are small, the bunks old, and the mattresses frayed, but thick curtains block out the sun from your inevitably blood-shot eyes. A foggy downstairs smoking room with a pool table feels like an underground club filled with punks, potheads, and people with pink hair. Some unique extra features let you play hard, like a late check-out time (2pm), free coffee for your after-party blues, and a communal kitchen where you can grab a snack before you hit the hay.

U1: Schlesisches Tor. From the Metro, head southeast on Schlesische Str. The hostel is on the right, just before the canal. [i] Linens €2. Laundry €4. Towel €1. Luggage storage included. 2 internet computers. Lock rental €1. Key deposit €10. Free Wi-Fi. $ 16-bed dorms €8-13, 4-bed €15-19. Singles €30-37; doubles €38-48. ⏰ Reception 24hr. Guest kitchen open 24hr.

BAXPAX KREUZBERG — HOSTEL $$

Skalitzer Str. 104 ☎030 695 18 322; www.baxpax.de

If we were measuring by common space, baxpax Kreuzberg would take the proverbial hostel cake. A huge lobby with a bar and couches; a venti-sized interior common room with all sorts of cushy lounge furniture, foosball, and a flatscreen; and a long, bright common kitchen connected to a frighteningly agreeable roof terrace guarantee some space to converse. Each room has a different country as a theme, and, like countries, not all rooms are created equal: while the Italian room is spacious, bright, and covered in football posters, most of the German room is taken up by a vintage Volkswagen Bug with a bed inside. The Wi-Fi can be unreliable, but otherwise this fun, colorful hostel is a real rose.

U1: Görlitzer Bahnhof. From the Metro, cross to the north side of Skalitzer Str. and walk about halfway down the block. Enter the labeled courtyard to the left; the hostel will be at the end of the courtyard, to the right, on the 3rd floor. [i] Breakfast €1-2.50. Linens and towel €2.50. Internet terminals €2 per hr. Laundry €7. Lockers, luggage storage, and safe included. Guests can smoke in the common room after 6pm. $ 32-bed dorms €8-28; 8-bed €12-33. Singles €25-54; doubles €40-98, with bath €48-120; quads €64-176. ⏰ Reception 24hr.

MEININGER

HOSTEL $

Hallesches Ufer 30 ☎030 983 21 075; www.meininger-hotels.com

Meininger can only approximate the sense of community at some of its Kreuzberg peers, but it does provide top-notch service and plenty of common space. Graffiti-lined walls lead to a quaint guest kitchen that never closes, all-you-can-eat breakfast graces a roomy roof terrace, and a relaxed bar serves drinks daily after 7pm. The rooms definitely beat the mean: each has a TV and the carpets are as spotless as a summer sky. With proximity to a vertical/horizontal U-Bahn crossroads, this hostel ensures that Mitte is just a quick hop away, assuming you can figure out which train to take.

🚇 U1 or U6: Hallesches Tor. From the Metro, head west on Gitschiner Str., cross Mehringdamm, and continue heading west on Hallesches Ufer. ℹ Linens and lockers included. Breakfast €4. Laundry €5. Towel €1, plus €5 deposit. Lock deposit €5. Late riser fee €5. [$] 8-bed dorms €12-18; 4-bed €14-21. Singles €42-55; doubles €54-66. ⏰ Reception 24hr. Roof terrace open daily until 10pm.

ALETTO'S

HOSTEL $$$$

Tempelhofer Ufer 8-9 ☎030 259 30 480; www.aletto.de

In spite of a logo that resembles a dildo with a boomerang through its head (ouch!...ouch!), Aletto keeps it clean for groups of travelers. Though rooms accommodate multiple guests, each is private and must be booked in its entirety. The Hostel Oscar (Hoscar?) nominees for Best Amenities at an Aletto in Kreuzberg are: large free breakfast, starring eggs; the mini-cinema, starring free DVD rentals; and the huge common spaces, starring free Wi-Fi, a full service bar, and a foosball table. Light pine bunks and proud pictures of that rascally dildo enchant every room.

🚇 U1 or U6: Hallesches Tor. From the Metro, cross to the south side of the canal, then head west, crossing over Mehringdamm to reach Tempelhofer Ufer. The hostel will be about half-way down the block. ℹ Linens, luggage storage, and towels included. Internet terminals €2 per hr. ATM available in lobby. [$] Singles €35-55; doubles €39-75; quads €64-124. ⏰Reception 24hr.

HOSTEL 36 ROOMS

HOSTEL $$

Spreewaldpl. 8 ☎030 530 86 398; www.36rooms.com

A preserved 1878 townhouse is the site of this gorgeous hostel, with wood floors, high ceilings, and beautiful molding. Large, bright rooms and an outdoor patio are robbed of some fun by the hostel's no-outside-alcohol policy, but guests can get a beer at the hostel bar or wait until Thursday, Friday, and Saturday, when an underground club rocks in the hostel's basement. Hot travelers (like you) can also dip in the wave pool across the street at the hostel's discounted price (€4 per hr., students €3 per hr.). The Old-World rooms are adorned with chandeliers and vintage furniture but unfortunately may carry a similarly Old-World smell.

🚇 U1: Görlitzer Bahnhof. From the Metro, head east on Skalitzer Str. Turn right on Spreewaldpl., just before the park. ℹ Locker rental €2. Linens €2.50. Towels €2. Key deposit €10. [$] 8-bed dorms €14-16; 4-bed €18-20. Singles €35-38; doubles €50-56. Bike rental €10 per day. ⏰ Reception 24hr. Patio and kitchen open daily until 10pm.

sights

Berlin is bursting at the seams with memorable sights, most of which won't even cost you a euro. All of the memorials, picturesque streets, and most of the churches are open for your unlimited and untaxed viewing pleasure. Check Mitte for by far the greatest concentration of sights, many of which are free. Head to Charlottenburg if it's a Baroque palace you're after, or retreat to Schöneberg's Grunewald for a pastoral escape. Prenzlauer Berg is better known for hip shops and cafes than sights, but the city's premier Wall museum, Berliner Mauer Dokumentationszentrum, is a must-see. Friederichshain offers more Cold War era sights, including the Stasi Museum and the East Side Gallery, which contains the longest remaining portion of the Berlin Wall. Kreuzberg is less known for its sights, but there are a handful of memorials, museums, and parks worth visiting if you're in the area. So grab a map and get going.

CHARLOTTENBURG

Most of Berlin's sights are located outside of the more residential Charlottenburg, closer to the center of the city. That said, Charlottenburg has certain sights that recommend themselves to the traveler with more than a day or two to spend in Berlin. Unique museums, grand palaces, and one of the world's most historic stadiums are spread out all over the neighborhood—and we mean *all* over.

SCHLOß CHARLOTTENBURG — PALACE

Spandauer Damm 10-22 ☎030 320 92 75

This expansive Baroque palace, commissioned by Friedrich I in the 1600s as a gift for his wife, Sophia-Charlotte, could have been one of the more indulgent summer homes featured on 17th-century *Cribs*. **Altes Schloß,** the Schloß's oldest section (marked by a blue dome in the middle of the courtyard), flaunts historic furnishings (much of them reconstructed after WWII), elaborate gilding, and neck-strainingly splendid ceiling murals. **Neuer Flügel** (New Wing) will make you feel poor and tiny with basketball-court-sized receiving rooms and the more somber royal chambers. **Neuer Pavillon** houses a museum dedicated to Prussian architect Karl Friedrich Schinkel. Other sections include the **Belvedere,** a small building containing the royal family's obscenely extensive porcelain collection, and the **Mausoleum,** where the remains of most of the family, well, remain. Behind the palace you'll find the exquisitely manicured Schloßgarten, full of small lakes, fountains, and those secretive, forested paths you've always wanted to walk along.

🚏 Bus #M45 from Bahnhof Zoo to Luisenpl./Schloß Charlottenburg or U2: Sophie-Charlotte Pl. $ Altes Schloß €12, students €8; Neuer Flügel €6/5; Belvedere €3/2.50; Mausoleum free. A Tageskarte (day ticket; €15, students €11) covers them all. Audio tours (available in English) included with admission. ⏰ Altes Schloß open Apr-Oct Tu-Su 10am-6pm; Nov-Mar Tu-F 10am-5pm, Sa-Su noon-4pm. Neuer Flügel open year-round M and W-Su 10am-6pm. Belvedere open Apr-Oct daily 10am-6pm, Nov-Mar daily noon-5pm. Mausoleum open Apr-Oct 10am-6pm.

KÄTHE-KOLLWITZ-MUSEUM — MUSEUM

Fasanenstr. 24 ☎030 882 52 10; www.kaethe-kollwitz.de

Through both World Wars, Käthe Kollwitz, a member of the Berlin *Sezession* (Secession) movement and one of Germany's most prominent 20th-century artists, protested war and the situation of the working class with haunting sketches, etchings, woodcuts, sculptures and charcoal drawings of death, poverty, and starvation. The series of works entitled "A Weaver's Revolt" on the second floor are the drawings that skyrocketed Kollwitz to fame. The death of the artist's own son, who was killed in Russia in WWII, provides a wrenching emotional authenticity to her depictions of death, pregnancy, and starvation as well as her bleak self-portraits. Her almost entirely black works contrast powerfully with the museum's bright, all-white interior.

🚏 U1: Uhlandstr. $ €6, students €3. ⏰ Open daily 11am-6pm.

sights

MUSEUM BERGGRUEN
MUSEUM

Schloßstr. 1 ☎030 326 95 80

Think Picasso is a jerk whose art doesn't deserve the hype? This sunny museum will obliterate your anti-Picasso sentiments. The first and second floors are Picasso-packed, with the occasional foray into Matisse and African masks. The third floor showcases intensely abstract paintings by Bauhaus teacher Paul Klee, as well as Alberto Giacometti's super-skinny sculptures of the human form. A wide spectrum of works from across Picasso's career allows you to track the development of the big-lipped, warped-faced figures that have always confounded you, displayed most beautifully in *Le matador et femme nue* (The matador and the nude woman).

🚌 Bus #M45 from Bahnhof Zoo to Luisenpl./Schloß Charlottenburg or U2: Sophie-Charlotte Pl. ℹ Ticket covers entry to Berggruen Museum, Bröhanmuseum, and Sammlung Scharf-Gerstenberg on the same day. $ €8, students €4, children free. Audio guide included. ⏰ Open Tu-Su 10am-6pm.

OLYMPIASTADION
STADIUM

Olympischer Pl. 3 (Visitors Center) ☎030 250 02 322; www.olypiastadion-berlin.de

This massive Nazi-built stadium comes in a close second to Tempelhof Airport in the list of monumental Third Reich buildings in Berlin. It was erected for the infamous 1936 Olympic Games, in which African-American track and field athlete Jesse Owens won four gold medals. Hitler refused to congratulate Owens, who has since been honored with a Berlin street, Jesse-Owens-Allee. Owens' name has also been engraved into the side of the stadium with the other 1936 gold medal winners. The six stone pillars flanking the stadium were originally intended to signify the unity of the six "tribes" of ethnicities that Hitler believed fed into true German heritage. Recent uses have included the 2006 World Cup final. The independently operated **Glockenturm** (bell tower) houses an exhibit on the history of German athletics and provides a great lookout point.

🚌 S5, S7, or U2: Olympia-Stadion. For Glockenturm, S5 or S7: Pichelsburg. $ €4, students €3. Guided tour €8, students €7, under 6 free. Audioguides €3.50. ⏰ Open daily Apr-May 9am-7pm, from June to mid-Sept 9am-8pm; from mid-Sept to Oct 9am-7pm; Nov-Mar 9am-4pm. Last entry 30min. before close. Glockenturm open daily 9am-6pm.

BRÖHANMUSEUM
MUSEUM

Schloßstr. 1A ☎030 326 90 600; www.broehan-museum.de

If you're wondering where all the stuff you couldn't sell at your great-aunt's estate sale went, here it is. Though a museum dedicated to bro version of Dragonball Z might have been more captivating, these Art Nouveau and Art Deco paintings, housewares, and furniture will still wow you. Along with figurines and lampshades that resemble the knicknacks you sneered at (and now regret not buying) at neighborhood garage sales, the ground floor also pairs several groupings of period furniture with paintings from the same era (1889-1939). However, don't expect the highest of the high: these paintings, like the household objects that surround them, are sometimes absurdly grounded in their time, including giggle-worthy idealizations of factory workers. The second floor is a small gallery dedicated to the modernist Berlin *Sezession* painters, and the top floor houses special exhibitions, like a recent all-silver exhibit.

🚌 Bus #M45 from Bahnhof Zoo to Luisenpl./Schloß Charlottenburg or U2: Sophie-Charlotte Pl. The museum is next to the Bergguen, across from the Schloß. $ €6, students €4. Ticket covers entry to Berggruen Museum, Bröhanmuseum, and Sammlung Scharf-Gerstenberg on the same day. ⏰ Open Tu-Su 10am-6pm.

ZOOLOGISCHER GARTEN
ZOO

8 Hardenberg Pl. ☎030 254 010; www.zoo-berlin.de; www.aquarium-berlin.de

Germany's oldest zoo houses around 14,000 animals of 1500 species, most in open-air habitats connected by winding pathways under dense cover of trees. Unfortunately, the zoo's biggest asset, über-cute polar cub 🏆**Knut,** recently died,

berlin

but there are still some fluffy options, like the white wolf, who somehow pulls off a dangerous combination of adorable and badass. Also, there is highly contested talk that Knut may be stuffed in the near future, so keep your eyes peeled. With a few uninteresting tanks (and one obese shark), the **Aquarium**, which lies inside the zoo, proves that fish may actually be boring after all.

🚇 U2 or U9: Zoological Garten, or S5, S7 or S75: Bahnhof Zoo. Main entrance is across from the Europa Center. $ Zoo €13, students €10, children €6.50. Aquarium €12, students €9, children €6. Combination to zoo and aquarium €20/15/10. ⏰ Open daily Jan 1-Mar 19 9am-5pm; Mar 20-Oct 3 9am-7pm; Oct 4-Dec 31 9am-5pm. Last entry 1hr. before close.

SCHÖNEBERG AND WILMERSDORF

Schöneberg sights are a mix of pastoral parks and whatever cultural tidbits ended up in this largely residential neighborhood. Travelers with limited time in Berlin should note that attractions here are few and far between, and aren't easily and efficiently visited. If you want to visit them all, or at least the majority, map them and attack them in groups.

👍 GRUNEWALD AND THE JAGDSCHLOß — PARK

Am Grunewaldsee 29 (Access from Pücklerstr.) ☎030 813 35 97; www.spsg.de

This 3 sq. km park, with winding paths through wild underbrush, gridded pines, and a peaceful lake, is popular dog-walking turf and a great change from the rest of bustling Berlin. About a 1km walk into the woods is the **Jagdschloß**, a restored royal hunting lodge that houses a gallery of portaits and paintings by German artists like Anton Graff and Lucas Cranach the Elder. The lodge is the picture of understated elegance, surrounded by even more blooming botany. The one-room hunting lodge is worth skipping, unless you find pottery shards particularly earth-shattering. Instead, walk around the grounds, or take a hike north in the forest to **Teufelsberg** ("Devil's Mountain"), the highest point in Berlin, made of rubble from WWII piled over a Nazi military school.

🚇 U3 or U7: Fehrbelliner Pl., or S45 or S46: Hohenzollerndamm, then bus #115 (dir. Neuruppiner Str. of Spanische Alle/Potsdamer): Pücklerstr. Turn left on Pücklerstr., follow the signs, and continue straight into the forest to reach the lodge. ℹ Check the Jagdschloß visitors center for a map. $ Hunting lodge €4, students €3. Tours in German (€1) offered on the weekends. ⏰ Open in winter Sa-Su 10am-4pm; in spring-fall Tu-Su 10am-6pm. Last entry 30min. before close.

BRÜCKE MUSEUM — MUSEUM

Bussardsteig 9 ☎030 831 20 29; www.brueckemusuem.de

Die Brücke (The Bridge) was a short-lived but influential part of German Expressionism, a period when figuration had begun to break down into thick lines and simple patterns, creating disorienting and intricate abstractions. What resulted were the energetic colors and the fierce brushstrokes jutting out from the canvases of this museum, which makes up for its lack of a permanent exhibition with engaging special exhibitions, like the gripping landscape works of Karl Schmidt-Rottluff that will grace the walls into 2012. The museum is tiny and requires a substantial trek to find, but it is a rare privilege to enjoy these paintings in an angular modern building nestled in the whispering woods of the Grunewald.

🚇 U3 or U7: Fehberlliner Pl., then bus #115 (dir. Neuruppiner Str. to Spanische Allee/Potsdammer): Finkenstraße, then walk back up Clayallee for about 50 ft. and turn left on the footpath leading into the woods; signs will lead you from there. $ €5, students €3. Cash only. ⏰ Open M 11am-5pm, W-Su 11am-5pm.

ALTER SANKT-MATTHÄUS-KIRCHHOF — CEMETERY

On Großgörschen Str., right next to the lower Yorckstr. S-Bahn Station entrance.

This expansive, sloping cemetery isolated from the city by tall trees and hushed gardens conceals the graves of some of Germany's most famous, including renowned linguists, folklorians, and general academic badasses the Brothers

Grimm and Romantic composer Max Bruch. A grand, mid-19th-century chapel juts out from the shrubbery, as do a number of gigantic and increasingly impressive structures that old Berlin families built for their deceased. On your way out, stop by the cafe and flower shop to freshen up from all that grave hunting.

🚇 U7, S2, S25: Yorckstr. ⏰ Hours vary by month, but approximately: winter M-F 8am-4pm, Sa-Su 9am-8pm; summer M-F 8am-8pm, Sa-Su 9am-8pm. Cafe open M-Sa 9am-6pm.

MITTE

If you're anything like us, 95% of your time in Mitte will be spent screaming obscenities at Segway tours. For the other 5%, here's a modest list of suggestions for the sights that make Mitte a way to Seg.

architecture and landmarks

FERNSHEHTURM TOWER

Panoramastr. 1A ☎030 242 33 33; www.tv-turm.de

At 368m, the Fernshehturm (literally "TV Tower") trumps all other sky-pokers in the EU. It's shaped like a lame 1950s space probe on purpose: the East Berliners wanted their neighbors to the west to remember Sputnik every time they looked out their windows in the morning. For better or worse, capitalism has since co-opted the DDR's biggest erection, giving you the chance to rocket up into the tower's crowning Christmas ornament for a steep fee. Fortunately, in spite of the hordes of tourists that will inevitably get in your way, the view is incredible, and especially worth checking out at the end of your stay once you have a working vocabulary of Mitte's sights. Otherwise, it's just a big, beautiful mess of towers and roofs.

🚇 U2, U5, or U8: Alexanderpl. $ €11, ages 3-16 €7, under 3 free. ⏰ Open daily Mar-Oct 9am-midnight; Nov-Feb 10am-midnight.

BERLINER DOM CHURCH

Am Lustgarten ☎030 202 69 119; www.berlinerdom.de

You may cringe upon paying to enter a church (damn it), but in this case it's completely worth it. Though *Dom* means "cathedral" in German, this 1905 church belongs to the Protestants, so it's technically not a cathedral. Nonetheless, when it comes to grandeur, it crushes most of the cathedrals you've seen. A museum upstairs shows various failed incarnations of the church, and if you climb some back stairs that seem to get sketchier and sketchier as you proceed, you can actually get to a spectacular roof terrace lookout. Don't forget the basement with the most splendiferous crypt you've ever seen, which houses the ghosts of lightweights like the Hohenzollern kings.

🚇 U2, U5, or U8: Alexanderpl. From the Metro, walk southwest on Karl-Liebknecht-Str. $ €5, students €3. ⏰ Open Apr-Sept M-Sa 9am-8pm, Su noon-8pm; Oct-Mar M-Sa 9am-7pm, Su noon-7pm.

ROTES RATHAUS CITY HALL

Rathausstr. 15 ☎030 90 260

Fortunately not quite as horrifying as a house for rats, this "Red Town Hall" used to be East Berlin's city hall. Today it houses the Berlin Senate. Berlin, after all, is its own state, so each district has individual state senators who meet at the Rathaus every week. Inside, there are rolls of red carpet and a few small, loosely related exhibits for intrepid tourists, like a series of aerial photographs of central Berlin from 1943 to 2004. Make sure to check the place out at night: its four brightly glowing clock faces make it look like a robot owl monster.

🚇 U2: Klosterstr., then head north. Or U2, U5, or U8: Alexanderpl. ⏰ Open daily 8am-6pm.

MARIENKIRCHE
CHURCH

Karl-Liebknecht-Str. 8 ☎030 242 44 67; www.marienkirche-berlin.de

The oldest still-standing medieval church in Berlin (built in 1270) has one of the most frightening murals you'll ever see: in it, a line of saints and kings perform the dance of death alongside a line of skeletons who look more like *X-Files* aliens than Christian iconography. There's a Dan Brown novel here just waiting to be written.

✚ U2, U5, or U8: Alexanderpl. *From the Metro, walk southwest along Karl-Liebknecht-Str.* Ⓢ *Free.* Ⓞ *Open daily in summer 10am-8pm; in winter 10am-6pm.*

SAINT HEDWIG'S CATHEDRAL
CATHEDRAL

Hinter der Katholischen Kirche 3 ☎030 203 48 10; www.hedwigs-kathedrale.de

Named after Harry Potter's owl (okay, maybe not), the biggest and oldest Catholic cathedral in the city is like no cathedral you've seen before: with a billowing dome and an angled overhang, it looks more like God's baseball cap. Due to money troubles, it took about 140 years to build (1747-1887), only to be destroyed about 60 years later by British bombs and eventually reconstructed in the 1960s. As a result, it's got '60s written all over the interior, with long strings of glowing glass balls and abstract stained glass. It's a beautiful cathedral to see, both inside and out, and due to some acoustic miracle, it might be the quietest place you'll find to read this book.

✚ U2: Hausvogteipl. *From the Metro, walk north along Oberwallstr. Look for the copper dome.* Ⓢ *Free.* Ⓞ *Open M-F 10am-5pm, Su 1-5pm.*

NEPTUNBRUNNEN
FOUNTAIN

Alexanderpl.

Located in the wide square just southwest of the Fernshehturm, this fountain, built in 1891, depicts the Roman god Neptune getting in a water fight with slimy creatures of the deep, including a crocodile and a snake—gross. He's also surrounded by four women, each of whom represents one of the main rivers of Prussia: the Elbe, the Rhine, the Vistula, and the Oder. Fun activity: move around until the Fernshehturm is sticking out of Neptune's head!

✚ S3, S5, S75, U2, U5, or U8: Alexanderpl. Ⓢ *Free—it's a fountain.* Ⓞ *Open 24hr.*

REICHSTAG
PARLIAMENT

Pl. der Republik 1 ☎030 227 32 152; www.bundestag.de

Visitors to the German parliament building can climb the roof's 1200-ton glass dome that looks down into the main chamber to symbolize the "openness" of German democracy. It also serves to focus sunlight into the government chambers via an aggressive spire of mirrored fragments that juts down toward the floor. A free, automated audio tour tracks your movements up and down the nearly 300m ramp—fortunately it's not yet advanced enough to follow your furtive eye movements. Stop off at the top for a swell view of the Berlin skyline and to marvel at the fact that this dome—and therefore the Reichstag—is roofless. Rain, snow, and sleet all fall into the building and land in a giant "cone" located on the dome's floor. Visitors can trek around the roof terrace while avoiding the solar panels that make the Reichstag the world's only zero-emission congress.

✚ Bus #100: Pl. der Republik. U55: Reichstag. *i To access the roof, you must reserve an appointment online at least 2 days before.* Ⓢ *Free.* Ⓞ *Open daily 8am-10pm.*

memorials

🖎 **MEMORIAL TO THE MURDERED JEWS OF EUROPE**
MEMORIAL

Cora-Berliner-Str. 1 ☎030 263 94 311; www.stiftung-denkmal.de

Stark concrete blocks arranged in a grid pattern across an entire city block commemorate the Jews killed by the Nazis. Though the commotion of the busy streets surrounding the memorial may seem to discourage reflection, as you

sights

walk deeper into the gradually growing blocks, the city recedes into silence. Lose yourself on the uneven paths of the memorial, then head below ground for a moving, informative exhibit on the history of Judaism during WWII. Especially devastating is the "family" room, which presents pre-war Jewish family portraits and then investigates the individual fates of the family members. The last room continuously plays one of thousands of compiled mini-biographies of the six million individuals killed in the Holocaust. To read the bios of every murdered Jew would take over six years.

⇄ *U2: Potsdamer Pl. From the Metro, walk north on Ebertstr.* $ *Free.* ⏰ *Open daily Apr-Sept 10am-8pm; Oct-Mar 10am-7pm.*

👍 HOMOSEXUAL MEMORIAL — MEMORIAL

On Ebertstr. — www.stiftung-denkmal.de/en/homosexualmemorial

While Berlin's acceptance of homosexuality is matched by few other places in the world, it wasn't so until 1969. Before that, homosexuality was illegal in both East and West Germany under a law passed by the Nazis. As a result, homosexuals were not included in many WWII memorials. This memorial, which opened in 2008, consists of a giant block of gray stone, like a misplaced part of the Memorial to the Murdered Jews of Europe across the street, but with one big difference: if you gaze fixedly into a small window, you can watch a video of two men kissing in slow motion projected on a permanent loop. While containing a definite middle-finger-to-Hitler message, the looped video is also intensely humanizing, and worth looking into, quite literally.

⇄ *U2: Potsdamer Pl. From the Metro, walk north on Ebertstr. The memorial will be on your left, in the garden.* ⏰ *Open 24hr.*

SOVIET MEMORIAL — MEMORIAL

Str. des 17 Juni

WWII tanks and anti-aircraft guns flank this memorial, which was built by the Soviets in 1945. A larger-than-life-sized copper soldier reaches out to the air before him on the peak of a gate held up by rectangular pillars and covered in Cyrillic. After taking several photos of a writing system you can't even sound out, make sure to check out the tiny outdoor exhibit behind the memorial to get some historical context that has been translated into English. Haunting photos of a desolate post-war Berlin (the Reichstag, the Soviet Memorial, and the Brandenburger Tor stand spookily on a barren field now covered by the trees of the Tierpark) and of Soviet battlefields covered with bodies make this memorial more than just an overbearing sign of Soviet militarism.

⇄ *Bus #100: Pl. der Republik. Head south through Tiergarten to Str. des 17 Juni and take a right.* $ *Free.* ⏰ *Open 24hr.*

NEUE WACHE — MEMORIAL

Unter den Linden 4 — ☎030 250 025

Neue Wache was built as a guard house for the nearby city palace (hence, "New Watch"). Since then, it's been used as a number of different memorials, and in 1969 the remains of an unknown soldier and an unknown concentration camp victim were laid to rest here. Since 1993, the Neue Wache has served as the central memorial of the Federal Republic of Germany for the Victims of War and Tyranny, and it now contains a sculpture by Käthe Kollwitz depicting a mother holding her dead son inside of a hauntingly empty room. An open skylight that exposes her to the elements symbolizes civilian suffering under Nazism.

⇄ *U2: Hausvogteipl. From the Metro, walk north along Oberwallstr.* $ *Free.* ⏰ *Open daily 10am-6pm. The interior of the monument is still visible when the gate is closed.*

museums

👍 PERGAMON MUSEUM
MUSEUM

Am Kupfergraben 5 ☎030 209 05 577; www.smb.museum

As long as it kept its two main exhibits, the Pergamon Altar and the Ishtar Gate, the rest of this museum could display cotton balls, and it'd still be worth it. Pergamon was the capital of a Hellenistic kingdom of the same name, and the museum reconstructs its temple to nearly its full size, so that you can walk up its steep steps. The battle relief on the wall displays jagged-toothed snakes ripping off heroes' arms while titans rip lions' mouths apart, so epic-leptics beware. The Mesopotamian Ishtar Gate, reconstructed tile-by-original-tile, rises 30m into the air, then stretches 100m down a hallway. You'll hardly believe it.

➡ S5, S7, S9, or S75: Hackescher Markt. From the Metro, head south on Burgstr., turn right on Bodestr., and then right again on Kupfergraben after crossing the bridge. $ €10, students €5. A Tageskarte (€16, students €8) grants entry to all museums on Museum Island on the day of purchase. ⏰ Open M-W 10am-6pm, Th 10am-10pm, F 10am-6pm.

👍 NEUE NATIONALGALERIE
MUSEUM

Potsdamer Str. 50 ☎030 266 424 510; www.smb.museum

With some of the most famous and inspired works of the early German Modernists, this museum is a rare look at the masterpieces of early 20th-century painting. Works by Franz Marc, Max Ernst, and Ernst Ludwig Kirchner are just a few of the highlights. Sadly, key works were labeled "degenerate" by the Nazis in the 1930s and have since disappeared from the collection. Missing works appear as black-and-white photocopies throughout the gallery. The permanent exhibition fills the basement, while the spacious "Temple of Light and Glass" that greets you on the ground floor holds spectacular contemporary exhibits.

➡ U2: Potsdamer Pl. From the Metro, head west on Potsdamer Str. and follow it as it curves south. $ €10, students €5; with Tageskarte €16/8. Admission includes audio tour. ⏰ Open M-W 10am-6pm, Th 10am-10pm, F-Su 10am-6pm.

👍 TOPOGRAPHY OF TERROR
MUSEUM

Niederkirchner Str. 8 ☎030 254 50 950; www.topographie.de

This exhibit opened in May 2010 and tracks the origins, development, and deployment of Nazi terror from 1930 to 1946. Spreading across the first floor of a glassy modern building, the exhibit consists of an extended series of maps, graphs, photographs, and an enormous amount of context—you could spend an entire afternoon reading through all the captions and explanations, which are fortunately provided in both German and English. Travelers with weak stomachs be warned: no detail or image is deemed off-limits. That said, the images are so consistently powerful—and the exhibition so unbelievably exhaustive—that it is a must for any nuanced understanding of the development of Nazi terror. Outside, a newer exhibition of the development of Nazi influence in Berlin runs along the block-long remaining segment of the Berlin Wall: it too, is tremendously affecting, especially when many of the sights you've just seen are shown in ruins or surrounded by Hitler-heiling mobs.

➡ U6: Kochstr. or U2: Potsdamer Pl. From the Metro, head east on Leipziegerstr. and take a right on Wilhelmstr. $ Free. ⏰ Open daily 10am-8pm.

NEUES MUSEUM
MUSEUM

Bodestr. 1 ☎030 266 424 242; www.neues-museum.de

One of the top museums in the city, this collection of Egyptian and Greek antiquities contains a variety of unbelievably well-preserved artifacts from the ancient world, from jewelry to sculpture to the most intricate coffins you've ever seen. Mummies run rampant, sarcophagi multiply, and somewhere in it all, that famous bust of Nefertiti—yeah, that one—sits glowing in her own gallery. The building was heavily damaged in WWII, and this new New Museum incorporates the old collection into a spectacularly modern complex. Wander into the central chamber on the second floor, and you might just feel like the slab of granite you're standing on is floating through some esoteric Egyptian incantation. To avoid the lines, reserve a ticket online.

U6: Friedrichstr. S5,S7,S75, or S9: Hackescher Markt. From the S-Bahn, head south on Burgstr., then turn right on Bodestr. The museum will be on your right, but the ticket office is on the left before the river. ***i*** *Tickets correspond to a time; once they've been purchased, visitors must return at the time printed on their ticket.* $ *€10, students €5; with Tageskarte €16/8.* ⏰ *Open M-W 10am-6pm, Th-Sa 10am-8pm, Su 10am-6pm.*

TACHELES GALLERY

Oranienburger Str. 53 ☎030 282 61 85; www.tacheles.de

An unforgettable experience day or night, this bombed-out department store has become a living, breathing street-art Metropolis. Bars, galleries, a movie theater, a faux beach exterior, and a sculpture garden and workshop are all covered in graffiti art, human piss, or both. *But it's worth it.* Though it no longer has quite the revolutionary artsiness it once had now that the original artists have uprooted for other digs, recent political developments toward tearing Tacheles down should force it toward the top of your Berlin bucket list. It may smell like an outhouse, but you'll probably never experience something like this anywhere else.

U6: Oranienburger Tor. From the Metro, head east on Oranienburgerstr. Tacheles will be on your right. $ *Free to enter; most galleries also free.* ⏰ *Open 8am-late.*

jelly doughnut conspiracy

In the days of the Berlin Wall, any US president worth his salt had to give some dramatic speech about it. One of the most famous was JFK's "*Ich bin ein Berliner*" ("I am a Berliner") speech, delivered in 1963 to express US support for West Berlin in the wake of the Wall's construction. West Berliners lived on an island in the sea of Soviet-dominated East Germany. To drive his point home, Kennedy claimed to be a symbolic citizen of Berlin, pronouncing *"Ich bin ein Berliner!"* in his Boston accent. Afterward, several journalists claimed that by including the word "*ein*" Kennedy had mistakenly said "I am a jelly-filled doughnut," since *Berliner* could also refer to this jam-filled confection. The amusing argument that followed between linguists over whether or not Kennedy had indeed claimed to be a delicious pastry ultimately concluded that regardless of the wording, JFK had gotten his point across. But with all the debate, maybe it would have been better to stick to English.

THE KENNEDYS MUSEUM

Pariser Pl. 4A ☎030 206 53 570; www.thekennedys.de

An exhibit of photographs and rare memorabilia follows this little-known family that had such strong ties to Berlin. You may end up learning more about the Kennedys than you ever wanted to know, and the exhibition can often seem far too starry-eyed for its handsome protagonist, but the photographs are engaging, especially the ones you don't already recognize. The other artifacts that grace the exhibit, like original letters and notes, are also rare enough to invite a look. One paper even shows the first time Kennedy scrawled out his (in)famous phrase, "Ich bin ein Berliner."

🚆 S1, S25, or U55: Brandenburger Tor. From the Metro, walk west toward Brandenburg Gate, then turn right in the square immediately before the Gate. $ €7, students €3.50. ⏰ Open daily 10am-6pm.

HAMBURGER BAHNHOF MUSEUM MUSEUM

Invalidenstr. 50-51 ☎030 397 83 439; www.hamburgerbahnhof.de

This massive museum, stretching the entire length of the old station house, pairs modern masterworks, like gigantic Andy Warhol prints (a very colorful Chairman Mao included) and several pioneering Minimalist works, with boldly (and often annoyingly) conceptual works. You may find yourself playing a Guitar Hero version of a one-note Lamont Young piece. You may find yourself lost and trembling in the back of a dark tunnel. Wherever you are, it will take a lot of walking to get back to the entrance, because this museum stretches for leagues in every direction. A unique home for a unique collection, it's full of old people with sweaters around their necks looking to get their culture back.

🚆 S5, S7, S9, or S75: Hauptbahnhof. From the Metro, exit through the northern exit, then walk northeast on Invalidenstr. On the left, the museum is set back in a small court hidden by vegetation. $ €12, students €6. ⏰ Open Tu-F 10am-6pm, Sa 11am-8pm, Su 11am-6pm.

museum nightlife

If you find yourself craving culture when the sun goes down, Berlin's got your back. Besides the bevy of clubs and concerts, over 100 museums across the city open from 6pm to 2am twice per year (usually in late January and August) for the **Long Night of the Museums.** Stay up all night with special programs, guided tours, readings, and performances, but don't expect a quiet evening: sleepless locals crowd the exhibits. Tickets include entry to all museums and a free shuttle service that connects them.

ALTE NATIONALGALERIE GALLERY

Bodestr. 1-3 ☎030 209 05 577; www.smb.museum

This wide collection of mostly German *fin de siècle* and early 20th-century art does special justice to masters like Adolph Menzel, whose Realist canvases are all over the first floor, including a grotesque painting of his own feet. The exhibition is also very Romanticism-heavy, so you may get a little tired of the same idealized golden cliffs and imaginary castles after you've seen them several times over. Music fans will note the famous portrait of Richard Wagner. One of the museum's main strengths is its small assortment of French Impressionism on the second floor, including absolute beauts by Monet, Manet, Munet (okay, maybe not Munet), and Renoir.

🚆 S3, S5, or S75: Hackescher Markt. From the Metro, head south on Burgstr. and turn right on Bodestr. The museum will be the 1st on your right. $ €10, students €5; with Tageskarte €16/8. ⏰ Open M-W 10am-6pm, Th 10am-10pm, F-Su 10am-6pm.

ALTES MUSEUM MUSEUM

Am Lustgarten www.smb.museum

This "old" museum, smiling widely with its pillar teeth next to the Berliner Dom, is filled with Roman and Etruscan antiquities, including a wide range of pottery, sculpture, jewelry, and other artifacts from the daily lives of the long dead. After seeing the Pergamon and the Neues Museum, you might feel a little relieved once a gilded bronze victory goddess waves goodbye at the end of this permanent exhibition. But don't let this museum be overshadowed by its flashier neighbors. Its rebuilt central hall, with imposing marble busts surrounding you at every angle, may induce euphoria.

 # U2, U5, or U8: Alexanderpl. From the Metro, head southwest on Karl-Liebknecht-Str., and turn right after the Berliner Dom. $ €10, students €5; with Tageskarte €16/8. ⏰ Open M-W 10am-6pm, Th 10am-10pm, F-Su 10am-6pm.

parks, squares, and streets

HACKESCHER MARKT — SQUARE

Hackescher Markt

Guitarists strum and didgeridooers drone for cash. Restaurants spill their outdoor seating far out onto the cobblestones, heavily flanneled 20-year-olds play badminton at 2am, and hip storefronts extend in every direction from this bee-hive-busy square along the S-Bahn tracks. If the square isn't enough for your massive appetite for culture, check out the quiet shops and cafes of the **Hackesche Höfe** (that is, courts) just up Rosenthaler Str., as well as the little courtyard next-door, where film houses, restaurants, bookstores, cafes, and art exhibitions join together in a heavily graffitied, Tacheles-like complex.

 # S5, S7, S9, or S75: Hackescher Markt.

FRIEDRICHSTRASSE — STREET

Friedrichstr.

About as unpretentious as its Hohenzollern namesake, Friedrichstraße is Mitte's Fifth Avenue, where marble collonades cover the sidewalks and high-end franchises fight for your attention and your wallet. A block-wide Mercedes Benz showroom and a five-floor behemoth of a music and bookstore are only two of the jewels in this tremendous corporate crown. Come for the glass facades, but don't stay very long—otherwise, you might have to buy something.

 # S1, S2, S3, S5, S75, or U6: Friedrichstr.

TIERGARTEN — PARK

Tiergarten — www.berlin.de/orte/sehenswuerdigkeiten/tiergarten

Stretching from the Brandenburg Gate in the east to the Bahnhof Zoo in the west, this enormous park at the heart of Berlin contains some of its most iconic monuments, including the Victory Column and the **Soviet Memorial.** Str. des 17 Juni bisects the park from east to west, and frequently hosts parades, celebrations, and markets. During the 2010 World Cup, the city blocked off the entire street in June and July and broadcast the World Cup on 10 enormous screens to thousands of fans. The park also contains some beautiful paths, ponds, and gardens that can offer solace from the heat and the hordes of hipsters.

 # Bus #100, #200, S1, or S2: Brandenburger Tor. From the Metro, head west on Unter den Linden.

GENDARMENMARKT — SQUARE

Gendarmenmarkt

This plaza contains Konzerthaus Berlin, where the Berlin Philharmonic Symphony performs, and the Französischer Dom, an 18th-century church built for French Huguenots (Protestants). In July, the Berlin Symphony Orchestra plays free night concerts outside, while in December, the Markt hosts one of Berlin's most popular Christmas markets, guaranteed to make you feel like a kid again. Regardless of the season, it's a broad, bustling, and beautiful square. For a kick, read some of the menus of the fancy cafes around the square that try to be "bourgeois hip" and offer such pairings as currywurst and champagne.

 # U2: Hausvogteipl. $ Französischer Dom Tower €2.50. ⏰ Tower open daily 10am-6pm.

BRANDENBURG GATE
MONUMENT

Pariser Pl. ☎030 226 33 017

You've already seen its image obnoxiously covering the windows of every U-Bahn train, but upon approaching the real Brandenburg Gate for the first time, trumpets may still blare in your head. During the day, tourists swarm this famous 18th-century gate; however, the wise traveler will return at night to see it ablaze in gold. Friedrich Wilhelm II built the gate as a symbol of military victory, but Germans these days prefer to shy away from that designation, due to their weak 20th-century batting average. A system of gates once surrounded it, but today only this most famous gate remains.

⇟ S1, S2, or S25: Brandenburger Tor.

HUMBOLDT UNIVERSITY
UNIVERSITY

Unter den Linden 6 www.hu-berlin.de

Home to some of the greatest thinkers of the modern age, including Freud and Einstein, this university is closed to the public and doesn't make much of a tourist sight, but it's neat to stop by and feel like you're somehow involved in something. During the day, vendors sell used books out front. Maybe you'll find Einstein's old unread copy of *The Mayor of Casterbridge.*

⇟ U2: Hausvogteipl, then walk north along Oberwalstr. and turn left on Unter den Linden. Or U6, S3, S5, or S7: Friedrichstr., then walk south on Friedrichstr.

VICTORY COLUMN
MONUMENT

Großer Stern 1 ☎030 391 29 61; www.monument-tales.de

This 27m monument celebrates Prussia's victory over France in 1880. The statue of Victoria at the top is made of melted-down French cannons, and during WWII, Hitler had the statue moved to its present location to increase its visibility. Inside, you can now find a worthless exhibit on world monuments, complete with a fleet of mundane miniatures, but the real value of the price of admission is the view from the top of the column. Though your calves will protest against the 250+ stairs that spiral up a narrow shaft, your eyes will thank you for the spectacular view of the entire Tiergarten and the skylines of practically every Berlin neighborhood.

*⇟ U9: Hansapl. From the Metro, walk southeast on Altonaer Str. **i** Present your ticket at the cafe to get a €0.50 drink discount. $ €2.20, students €1.50. ⏰ Open Apr-Oct M-F 9:30am-6:30pm, Sa-Su 9:30am-7pm; Nov-Mar M-F 10am-5pm, Sa-Su 10am-5:30pm.*

SCHLOßPLATZ
SQUARE

Schloßpl.

Schloßpl. is a sight where even the castles themselves feud. The Berliner Schloß (the Hohenzollern imperial palace) stood on this spot until the Communists tore it down in 1950 to build the Palast der Republick. After reunification, the Palast der Republick was torn down, this time to make way for a replica of the Berliner Schloß. Construction is set to start in 2013 and finish in 2019. Currently, the field sits open, divided by a network of boardwalks accessible to the public, while some sections are under archaeological excavation. Placards mounted around the boardwalk provide information in German and English about the building-to-be, while a free tour of the dig site (in German) is offered every Friday at 2pm.

*⇟ U2: Hausvogteipl. From the Metro, walk north along Oberwalstr. and take a right on Französische Str. Stay on Französische Str. and cross the canal bridge. **i** Meet in front of Schlosspl. 1 for the tour.*

DOROTHEEN MUNICIPAL CEMETERY
CEMETERY

Chausseestr. 126

Hegel, one of the most notorious haunts of college syllabi, has reached synthesis with the earth here, as has Bertolt Brecht, whose grave unfortunately does not force you to take a position. A map near the entrance points out graves of interest, so you won't have to keep searching past nightfall.

U6: Oranienburger Tor. From the U-Bahn, head north on Chausseestr. ⏰ Open daily 8am-dusk.

high sights

The only thing better than seeing Berlin? Seeing Berlin high. Conquer your fear of heights and scale these landmarks for the best views in town.

- **GET CLOSER TO YOUR MAKER:** Climb the spiral stairs of the **Franzosischer Dom,** Berlin's French Cathedral. You will see Mitte and the surrounding square, but views of heaven are not guaranteed.
- **POLITICIZE** at the **Reichstag.** To some, Norman Foster's modern glass dome may stick out like an anachronistic eyesore, but the top of the Reichstag still has dazzling views of the city and less-dazzling views of the parliamentary debates below.
- **CELEBRATE** the 1871 German victory over France atop the **Victory Column.** From 66m up, you can also celebrate the calories you've burned going up the stairs.
- **CLIMB** Berlin's tallest hills for the 30m **Muggelturm**. Originally planned as a TV tower, this ugly building ended up serving as a listening post for East Germany's Stasi. You don't have to be a spy (or a wizard) to trek up the steps and enjoy distant views of Berlin, framed by suburbs and greenery.
- **UNLEASH YOUR INNER OLYMPIAN** at **Glockenturm,** the Bell Tower at the Olympiastadion. Thanks to the 2006 World Cup, the tower sports a new glass lift and a historical exhibition. Want 24/7 eyes on Berlin? Check out the live webcam at www.olympiastadion-berlin.de.

PRENZLAUER BERG

Tourists who can't shake the itch to take snapshots tend to flock to the brick-tastic but yawn-sensational **Kulturbrauerei** on Schönhauser Allee, the actually interesting **Berliner Mauer Dokumentationszentrum** in the north, and the towering **Wasserturm.** Generally, other than our two thumbpicks, P'Berg's sights are only worth a brief pass by between buying shoes and drinking brews.

👍 MAUERPARK — PARK

Extends north of the intersection between Eberswalder Str. and Schwedter Str.

Like Berlin, Mauerpark on a hot afternoon is an amalgam of a thousand different things that shouldn't exist in the same world, let alone on the same flat surface, but somehow do so in the most colorful way possible. Hipsters, punks, goths, hippies, bros, drunkards, lovers, the shirtless, and everything in between flatten the dry grass with blankets, lawn chairs, card tables, portable barbecues, African drums, and enough bottles to fill the stadium next door. Footballs, tennis balls, basketballs, and clouds of smoke soar through the air. Every inanimate surface (and several animate ones) are coated with thick graffiti. A rock climbing wall crowns one end, while a gigantic, multicolored edifice of logs writhes with the adventurous children of the hip at the other. Taken in full, Mauerpark is contemporary Berlin's thesis statement spoken through a distorted megaphone.

U2: Eberswalder Str. From the Metro, walk west on Eberswalder Str. Mauerpark will extend far to the north after you pass the stadium. $ Free.

BERLINER MAUER DOKUMENTATIONSZENTRUM — MUSEUM, MEMORIAL

Bernauer Str. 111 — ☎030 464 10 30; www.berliner-mauer-gedenkstaette.de

A remembrance complex, museum, chapel, and entire city block of the preserved Berlin Wall come together as a memorial to "victims of the Communist tyranny." The church is made of an inner oval of poured cement walls, lit from above by a large skylight and surrounded by a see-through skeleton of two-by-fours. The museum has assembled a comprehensive collection of all things Wall, including original recordings, telegrams, blueprints, film footage, and photos. Climb up a staircase to see the wall from above.

U8: Bernauer Str. From the Metro, walk north on Brunnen Str., then turn left on Bernauer Str. The church and memorial are on the left before Ackerstr., and the Dokumentationszentrum and exhibition are on the right immediately after Ackestr. $ Free. ⏰ Open Tu-Su Apr-Oct 9:30am-7pm; Nov-Mar 9:30am-6pm.

KOLLWITZPLATZ — PARK, MONUMENT

Directly below Wörther Str.

This little triangle of greenery is one big playground, with toddlers climbing over tree stumps, jungle gyms, and even the lap of Käthe Kollwitz's statue. Nearby, a magical little playground with a small bridge, stream, and willow trees is another popular destination for young moms with energetic kids. Non-parents are drawn by the upscale market on Saturdays, where vendors sell everything from boar meat sausage to handmade ravioli.

U2: Senefelderpl. From the Metro, walk north on Kollwitzstr. until you reach Knaackstr. The park is on the left. $ Free.

FRIEDRICHSHAIN

VOLKSPARK FRIEDRICHSHAIN — PARK

Volkspark Friedrichshain may lose out to the Tiergarten in a battle of bulk, but as Berlin's oldest park, it makes the Tiergarten look like a youthful dabbler. It's huge too: with 52 hectares, it's too large to feel crowded, even with masses of dog-walkers and suntanners filling the paths and lawns. Since opening in 1840, monuments and memorials have cropped up here and there; today it seems part-park, part-museum. In 1913 the **Märchenbrunnen** or "Fairy Tale Fountain" was completed, depicting 10 characters from the tales of the Brothers Grimm around a tremendous cascade of water. **Mount Klemont,** which now occasionally serves as a platform for open-air concerts and movie screenings, gains its mass from the enormous pile of rubble swept beneath it in 1950 from two bomb-destroyed, WWII bunkers. With perhaps too much history for its own good, the park still draws thousands from their homes on nice days, so people-watching provides several afternoons' worth of entertainment.

S8 or S10: Landsberger Allee or U5: Strausbgr. Pl. From Strausbgr. Pl., walk north on Lichtenberger Str. Bounded by Am Friedrichshain to the north, Danziger Str. to the east, Landsberger Allee to the south, and Friedenstr. Str. to the south.

EAST SIDE GALLERY — GALLERY, MONUMENT

Along Mühlenstr. — www.eastsidegallery.com

The longest remaining portion of the Berlin Wall, this 1.3km stretch of cement slabs has been converted into the world's largest open-air art gallery. The Cold War graffiti no longer exists; instead, the current murals hail from an international group of artists who gathered in 1989 to celebrate the wall's fall. One of the most famous contributions is by artist Dmitri Wrubel, who depicted a wet, wrinkly kiss between Leonid Brezhnev and East German leader Erich Honecker. The stretch of street remains unsupervised and, on the Warschauer Str. side, open at all hours, but vandalism is surprisingly rare.

U1, U15, S3, S5, S6, S7, S9, or S75: Warschauer Str. or S5, S7, S9, or S75: Ostbahnhof. From the Metro, walk back toward the river. $ Free.

STASI MUSEUM — MUSEUM

Ruschestr. 103, Haus 1 — ☎030 553 68 54; www.stasimuseum.de

This Lichtenberg suburb harbors perhaps the most hated and feared building of the DDR regime: the headquarters of the East German secret police, the **Staatssicherheit** or **Stasi.** During the Cold War, the Stasi kept dossiers on some six million of East Germany's own citizens, an amazing feat and a testament to the huge number of civilian informers in a country of only 16 million people. Since a 1991 law made the records public, the "Horror Files" have rocked Germany, exposing millions of informants and wrecking careers, marriages, and friendships at every level of German society. Officially known today as the Forschungs-und Gedenkstätte Normannenstrasse, the building retains its oppressive Orwellian gloom and much of its worn 1970s aesthetic. The museum exhibition, housed until 2012 in a temporary space across a courtyard from the actual headquarters during renovations, presents a wide array of original Stasi artifacts, among which is the mind-blowing collection of concealed microphones and cameras. All we want to know is how nobody noticed the bulky microphone concealed in a tie.

🚇 U5: Magdalenenstr. $ €4, students €3. Exhibits in German; English info booklet €3. ⏰ Open M-F 11am-6pm, Sa-Su 2-6pm.

KREUZBERG

Most of Kreuzberg's sights are skippable, especially in comparison to their glamorous cousins up north, but if you're in the area during the day, there are several museums, parks, and buildings you should definitely stop by. In addition to the sights we've listed, Kreuzberg also has several beautiful 19th-century churches that are worth a look, including **Saint-Michael-Kirche** (Michaelkirchpl.), the **Heilig-Kreuz-Kirche** (Zossener Str. 65), and **Saint Thomas-Kirche** (Bethaniendamm 23-27).

👍 DEUTSCHES TECHNIKMUSEUM BERLIN — MUSEUM

Trebbiner Str. 9 — ☎030 902 54 0; www.sdtb.de

Don't tell the National Air and Space Museum about this place. With 30 full-sized airplanes, 20 boats—including a full-sized Viking relic—and a train from every decade since 1880, this museum could be a city in itself. Though the prime demographic that enjoys these behemoths of progress includes your five-year-old brother and your dad, there's something to appeal to anyone's sense of awe in this absurdly large collection. Five floors of large machinery include an original WWII German rocket (hopefully deactivated), a U-boat (the last haven for Kreuzberg squatters), and a turn-of-the-century model for a balloon that would carry an entire city (what we dub the "Balloon of Babel.") You won't have dropped your jaw this much since the Pergamon Museum.

🚇 U1 or U2: Gleisdreieck. From the Metro, head east on Luckenwalder Str. and turn right on Tempelhofer Ufer. Walk under the train tracks and turn right onto Trebbiner Str. The entrance is about ¾ of the way down Trebbiner Str. ℹ Many exhibits in English. $ €6, students €3. ⏰ Open Tu-F 9am-5:30pm, Sa-Su 10am-6pm.

👍 SOVIET WAR MEMORIAL — MEMORIAL

Treptower Park

This 20,000 sq. m memorial, built in 1949 to commemorate the Soviet soldiers lost in the Battle of Berlin, makes Mitte's **Soviet Memorial** seem teeny in comparison. Two jagged triangular slabs, each bearing the hammer and sickle, guard a tremendous rectangular square lined by exquisitely cut shrubs and surrounded by marble reliefs of Soviet soldiers helping the poor and the huddled. Quotations from Stalin in the original Russian and in German translation encircle you at every step. But the most impressive piece stands at the end of the square: a tremendous grassy mound bears a giant bronze statue of a Soviet soldier, crushing a broken swastika and lugging a sword. After a jaunt around the place, you'll either be horrified, ready to unite the working classes of the world, or a little bit of both.

🚇 U1 or U15: Schlesisches Tor. From the Metro, walk southeast on Schlesische Str. Cross both canals, and continue until you reach a fork in the road, between Puschkinallee and Am Treptower Park. Take Puschkinallee, and walk along the park until you reach a large semicircular courtyard with an entrance gate. Turn into this courtyard; the memorial is on the left. $ Free. ⏰ Open 24hr.

TEMPELHOFER PARK PARK

At Columbiadamm and Tempelhofdamm ☎030 700 90 688; www.tempelhoferfreiheit.de

Once an airport (and drop point for the Berlin Airlift), Tempelhof closed forever in 2008. In 2010, it was converted into a park and reopened to the public. Now, this flat, expansive plot of land covered in tall grass and wide runways provides plenty of legroom, and some of the most pastoral paths on which to enjoy a bike ride, a jog, or, appropriately, a kite-fly. Before or after spending a quiet, breezy afternoon on the taxiway, make sure to check out the **Berlin Airlift Memorial** just to the northwest: it looks like a rainbow under construction.

🚇 U6: Pl. der Luftbrücke. From the Metro, walk south on the left side of Tempelhofer Damm and pass by the old airport parking lot. There will be signs indicating the park's entrance. ℹ The dog that you brought on your backpacking trip must stay on a leash. $ Free. ⏰ Open daily dawn-dusk.

go on a spree

Forget the fact that it flows past 250 mi. of industrial lands, forests, and fields. The Spree is best known where it hits Berlin, before joining the Havel River in the suburbs. Unfortunately, due to the decrepit drains that support the city's sewage system, occasional torrential rain means that sewage often mixes with river water. Not to worry, though. Since 2008, the Spree 2011 project has worked to contain the overflow waste and clean up the water. For now, here are some ways to enjoy the river without sharing the water with your favorite coliform bacteria.

- **FANCY A FLOAT?** Book a river cruise and tour Berlin from the (dis)comfort of your boat. Avid rowers can rent their own rowboats at **Rent-a-Boat** (☎177 299 32 62; www.rent-a-boat-berlin.com) at the entrance to the Abtei Bridge in Treptower Park. Several companies also run tours.
- **HOW ABOUT A DIP?** The Spree might be too polluted for casual bathing, but you can still swim on the river if you head to the **Arena Pool.** This converted shipping container holds a clean swimming pool, floating next to a sandy area with a bar and lounge. In the winter, massage areas and two saunas will keep you sweating in the covered pool. If it's too crowded to do your laps, grab a cocktail and lap up views of the Berlin skyline instead.
- **HIT THE BAR.** The sandbar, that is. Complete with beach chairs, parasols, and exotic palm trees, 30 beaches dot the Spree, so you can work on your tan without leaving the city.

OBERBAUMBRÜCKE BRIDGE

At the south end of Warschauer Str.

Massive twin brick towers rise from this late 19th-century double-decker bridge that spans the Spree River. Once a border crossing into East Berlin, it now connects Kreuzberg to Friedrichshain. Residents of the rival neighborhoods duke it out on the bridge every July 27, when thousands of people chuck rotten vegetables at each other in order to establish which 'hood is edgier.

🚇 U1 or U15: Schlesisches Tor. From the Metro, follow Oberbaum Str. as it curves north.

JEWISH MUSEUM MUSEUM

Lindenstr. 9-14 ☎030 259 93 300; www.jmberlin.de

Modern, interactive exhibits treat subjects ranging from the Torah to the philosophies of Moses Mendelssohn to discrimination against Jews under Charles V. Architect Daniel Libeskind designed the museum's building to reflect the discomfort, pain, and the inherent voids in Jewish history, including tremendous, triangular shafts, inaccessible rooms, and uneven floors. One tall room is piled with metal faces (Menashe Kadishman's *Fallen Leaves*) that make a terrible racket as you walk across them. It's an amazing museum that actually succeeds at being "experiential": it's disorienting, frightening, and historical.

 # U1 or U6: Hallesches Tor. From the station, head east on Gitschinerstr. and take a left at Lindenstr. [$] €5, students €2.50, under 6 free. Audio tours €3. ⏰ Open M 10am-10pm, Tu-Su 10am-8pm. Last entry 1hr. before close.

SCHWULES MUSEUM (GAY MUSEUM) MUSEUM

Mehringdamm 61 ☎030 695 99 050; www.schwulesmuseum.de

This small museum is the world's only state-funded exhibit on homosexual persecution. Temporary exhibits take up over half of the museum, and the permanent exhibition is tiny but packs a big punch with its presentation of interesting, lesser-known history and materials you probably won't find anywhere else. Penises are common, but so are 19th-century canvases; issues of *Der Eigene*, the world's first gay newspaper; and the mug shots of gay men prosecuted by the Nazis. Plus, the temporary exhibitions are actually worth seeing: the most recent, on Wittgenstein, featured everything from the eminent philosopher's thoughts on his tweed blazer to what to do with friends that you haven't talked to for a while.

*# U6 or U7: Mehringdamm. From the Metro, head south on Merhringdamm. The museum will be through a courtyard on the left in the block after Gneisenaustr. **i** English exhibit guide available. [$] €5, students €3. ⏰ Open M 2-6pm, W-F 2-6pm, Sa 2-7pm, Su 2-6pm.*

food

German food may not sound appealing in theory, but in practice, we think you'll find the opposite to be true. It's not just about beer and sausage anymore: check ethnic eateries for great deals on pho, döner, burritos, and more. Wealthy Charlottenburg is not known for its budget-friendly fare, so head north to the neighborhood Moabit for cheap, authentic Turkish or Vietnamese food. Check out Schöneberg's relaxed cafe culture around the intersection of **Maaßenstrasse** and **Winterfeldstrasse.** In Mitte, it's best to avoid overpriced restaurants and cafes near major sights. Instead, look north of Alexanderpl. for the best value, where streets like **Alte Schönhauserstrasse** and **Rosa-Luxemburg-Strasse** are lined with delicious, modern restaurants that offer all types of cuisine for less than €10. Prenzlauer Berg is another cafe capital: check out **Kastanienallee** or the streets around **Helmholtzplatz** for the highest concentration of caffeine. Some of Friedrichshain's narrow cobblestone streets are lined with cheap cafes, ice cream joints, and reasonably priced restaurants, which makes it simple to find something that piques your appetite without stealing too much of your cash. The intersection of **Simon-Dach-Strasse** and **Grünbergerstrasse** is a good place to start. For the best international cuisine in a city known for cheap ethnic fare, head to Kreuzberg, where incredible restaurants line **Oranienstraße, Bergmannstraße,** and **Schlesische Straße.**

CHARLOTTENBURG

👍 SCHWARZES CAFE — BAR, CAFE $$$

Kantstr. 148 — ☎030 313 80 38

Pharmacies, grocery stores, and even whole neighborhoods might close down at night, but Schwarzes will still be open. As you sit on one of the two packed, candlelit floors, you might begin to forget how much of a tab you're building up sampling the extravagant menu. Kick back an absinthe and watch the artistically peeling paint on the exquisitely molded ceilings dance to the folk-rock mix. Then chase your massive drinkage with breakfast when the sun comes up or, if you prefer, at a more bohemian hour: all meals are served around the clock.

🚏 S3, S5, S7, S9, or S75: Savignypl. $ Weekly specials €7-13 served 11:30am-8pm. Breakfast €5-8.50. Drinks €3-7. Cash only. ⏰ Open M 24hr., Tu 11am-3am, W-Su 24hr.

FAM DANG — VIETNAMESE $$

Hutten Str. 5 — ☎030 755 67 526

Located in a predominantly Vietnamese area, Fam Dang's bright rooms, outdoor patio, and ridiculously inexpensive daily menu make it a must. Drop by in the busy noon hour to watch the waitresses careen around with tremendous white bowls as they rapidly rail in accented German at a middle-aged, professional crowd on its lunch break. The soup menu includes a wide variety of Vietnamese favorites, like glass noodle soup. Portions are gigantic, so make sure to come starving and dehydrated.

🚏 Bus M27: Turnstr./Beusselstr. $ Entrees €5. Cash only. ⏰ Open M-F 11am-9pm, Sa noon-9pm.

KASTANIE — BEER GARDEN $$

Schloßstr. 22 — ☎030 321 50 34; www.kastanie-berlin.de

Nestled between the high apartment facades that line Schloßstr., Kastanie offers a little piece of Bavaria on the cheap. A changing entree menu (€3.50-6.50) includes all the old German favorites, including delectable Nürnberger sausages and yummy *Käsespätzle* (späzle with cheese and onions). The weathered wooden tables spread across the shaded, gravel grounds exude authenticity, while the colorful wooden masks hanging above suggest a quaint quirkiness. Kastanie is the *echt deutsch* place to enjoy a beer and quiet conversation on a sunny early afternoon.

🚏 U2: Sophie-Charlotte Pl., then walk up Schloßstr. toward the Schloß. $ Breakfast €4-6. Beer €3. Cash only. ⏰ Open daily 10am-1am. Breakfast served 10am-2pm.

AREPERIA — COLOMBIAN $

Stuttgarter Pl. 18 — ☎030 310 10 626; www.la-areperia.de

With only three menu options, it may not have the widest selection, but Areperia delivers in quality and quantity what it lacks in variety. Choose between *arepas* (the root of the title; €3), empanadas (3 for €4), *patacónes* (delicious fried banana patties; 3 for €4), or a combination thereof, all with a variety of tasty and filling options, like avocado or cold cheese. Though it looks like some generic franchise runoff from Wilmersdorfer Str., Areperia is anything but. The neon orange and lime green walls, modern furniture, and photographs for sale on the walls put the cool back in postcolonial.

🚏 S3, S5, S7, S75: Charlottenburg; U7: Wilmersdorfer Str. $ Cash only. ⏰ Open M-Sa noon-9pm, Su 1-6pm.

ABBAS — MIDDLE EASTERN $

Huttenstr. 71 — ☎030 343 47 770

Abbas and the restaurants around it, like Fam Dang, belong to Middle Eastern and Asian immigrants attracted by the area's low rent. This sprawling sweet and nut shop sells a wide range of authentic Middle Eastern desserts on the cheap, from chocolate-covered lentils to pistachio-cashew pastries. Try the specialty baklava (2 pieces €1.30; sizeable box €3)—you'll be licking your fingers for hours.

🚏 Bus M27: Turmstr./Beusseistr. $ Cash only. ⏰ Open M-Th 10am-5pm, F-Sa noon-8pm. Cash only.

MENSA TU CAFETERIA $

Hardenbergerstr. 34 ☎030 939 39 7439

It's a cafeteria, but the Hardenbergerstr. Mensa offers the cheapest hot meal around, with three entree choices as well as vegetarian options. And our favorite part: your portion size is as much food as you can fit on a plate. Accordingly, it's overrun by university students, who chat in the sunny, modern complex and read on the ubiquitous benches. The food is nothing special, but, like any cafeteria, it's meant for folks on a budget, and it probably won't poison you (fingers crossed!). The slightly higher-priced cafeteria downstairs should be avoided.

🚏 U2: Ernst-Reuter-Pl. or bus #245: Steinpl. A 10min. walk from Bahnhof Zoo. $ Meals €4-5, students €2-3. Cash only. ⏰ Upstairs cafeteria open M-F 11:30am-3:30pm. Coffee bar M-F 11am-6pm. Cake shop M-F 7:30am-2:30pm. Downstairs open M-F 11am-2:30pm.

PARIS BAR BISTRO $$$$

Kantstr. 152 ☎030 313 80 52; www.parisbar.de

Formerly one of West Berlin's favorite hip gathering places, the Paris Bar is now a stuffy and formal restaurant (pronounced rest-owe-RAW) that's geared more toward art patrons than artists. The frenzy of Surrealist canvases and quirky posters that line the walls seem misplaced among a collared, older crowd downing entrees with obscene prices. The black and white linoleum floors and dark wood walls are certainly nice, but at what cost? A hefty one, that's what.

🚏 U1: Uhlandstr. $ Soups from €5.50. Appetizers €6.50-14.50; entrees €12-25. Drinks €4-12. ⏰ Open daily noon-2am. Kitchen closes at 1am.

LA PETIT FRANCE CROISSANTERIE CAFE $

Nürnberger Str. 24A ☎017 817 11 3826

Fresh, inexpensive lunches are sometimes difficult to come by in sprawling Charlottenburg. This pocket-sized French bistro has some stellar baguettes and classic Francophone music to transport you across the Rhine. Try the small baguettes with a variety of toppings, including tomato, mozzarella, and basil.

🚏 U3 to Ausgburger Str. $ Baguettes €2.50, large €3.30. Quiche and salad combo €4.50. Cash only. ⏰ Open M-Sa 8am-6:30pm.

SCHÖNEBERG AND WILMERSDORF

If you manage to burn through all the cafes on **Maaßenstrasse** and **Winterfeldstrasse,** more popular cafes and inexpensive restaurants crowd the **Akazienstrasse,** which runs from the U-Bahn station at Eisenacherstr. to Hauptstr. All in all, come for the foamy coffee, stay for the eclectic foreign cuisine.

👍 **CAFE BILDERBUCH** CAFE $$

Akazienstr. 28 ☎030 787 06 057; www.cafe-bilderbruch.de

Even if you couldn't eat here, Cafe Bilderbuch's antique cabinets, fringed lamps, deep-cushioned sofas, and adjoining library would still make this a place to visit. Fortunately, their unbeatable Sunday brunch menu, named after different fairy tales, has us shoving grandmothers out of the way to get in the door. Our favorite combo is *"Der Froschkönig "* (The Frog Prince), which includes salmon, trout, caviar, and a glass of prosecco. The menu, printed on their own press, doubles as a weekly newspaper.

🚏 U7: Eisenacher Str. ℹ Free Wi-Fi. $ Soup from €3.70. Salads from €6. Entrees €8. Coffee €1.50. Cash only. ⏰ Open M-Sa 9am-midnight, Su 10am-midnight. Kitchen closes daily 11pm.

👍 BAHARAT FALAFEL TURKISH $$

Winterfeldtstr. 37 ☎030 216 83 01

This isn't your average döner stand. First, it doesn't serve döner. Second, this vegetarian Turkish restaurant makes all of its falafel fried to order, in fluffy pita with lots of tomatoes, lettuce, and mango or chili sauce (€3-4). Wash down Baharat's plates (hummus, tabouleh, and salad) with fresh-squeezed *Gute-Laune Saft* (good-mood juice, €1-2), which tastes sublimely refreshing in a land where even water is a soft drink. Indoor seating with a map of Iraq on the bright walls or an outdoor bench under a striped awning are comfortable settings for your messy nom-nom-nomming.

🚇 U1, U3, U4, or U9: Nollendorfpl. $ Entrees €6-8. Cash only. ⏰ Open M-Sa 11am-2am, Su noon-2am.

👍 HIMALI TIBETAN, NEPALESE $$

Crellestr. 45 ☎030 787 16 175; www.himali-restaurant.de

A tandoori oven spits out piping hot Nepali and Tibetan classics. Entrees are never short on spices, either in quantity or variety, which are grown and ground by hand. Himali offers a tremendous range of vegetarian dishes, curried or grilled, with tofu, vegetables, naan and your choice of seasonings. The Nepali tea (€2.50) makes English Breakfast seem like child's play.

🚇 U7: Kleistpark, walk up (quite literally) Langenscheidtstr. and turn right on Crellestr. $ Entrees €6.50-10. ⏰ Open daily noon-midnight.

DOUBLE EYE CAFE $

Akazienstr. 22 ☎017 945 66 960; www.doubleeye.de

For coffee purists, this is an inexpensive way to enjoy the best kind of brew. This small and quick coffee bar has a line of locals snaking out the door all day, waiting to order the no-syrup-added daily brews covered in enough bright-white foam to build a Santa disguise. Baristas prepare each espresso with surgical precision and take pride on their top-quality "latte-art": designs traced into the inch-thick crowns of foam. And yes, they've got victory plaques behind the bar to back up that smack.

🚇 U7: Eisenacher Str. $ All drinks €1-3. Soup-bowl-sized coffee with milk only €2.20. Cash only. ⏰ Open M-F 8:45am-6:30pm, Sa 9am-6pm, Su 8:45am-6:30pm.

CAFÉ EINSTEIN VIENNESE CAFE $$$

Kurfurstenstr. 58 ☎030 261 50 96; www.cafeeinstein.com

You don't have to be a rocket scientist to enjoy Café Einstein, which is Berlin's premier Viennese coffeeshop and an obligatory stop for tourists, impeccably dressed locals playing hard-to-get in their books, and intelligent, good-looking *Let's Go* travelers alike (oh, we know: we shouldn't have). Large windows refract the light bouncing off of Einstein's private garden, where you can sip a splurge-worthy home-roasted coffee (cappuccino €4.30; *Milchkaffee* €3.80). You'll want time to slow down as you cherish a small cake or an 👍**Apfelstrudel**, which are the least expensive (but perhaps the tastiest) ways to enjoy the cafe's dark wood-paneled walls and detailed molding, and will set you back about €4.

🚇 U1, U3, U4, or U9: Nollendorfpl. $ Entrees €15-22. Breakfast from €5.80. Su brunch bar €13. ⏰ Open daily 6am-1am.

BERLIN BURRITO COMPANY BURRITOS $

Pallasstr. 21 ☎030 236 24 990; www.berlin-burrito-company.de

Alright, we see you. You're narrowing your eyes and muttering self-righteously to yourself, "Burritos have nothing to do with Berlin." It's okay, we forgive you. Other than the same first syllable, they don't. But for those college kids who have spent an entire year eating a burrito for every meal, locating the nearest cheap burrito place could be life-saving. Plus, this place is cheap and delicious, with a variety of interesting fillings (like lime chicken and spicy tomato habañero sauce) to complicate the usual way you stuff your face. And with see-through barber shop chairs and some dark electro tunes you've never heard before, this little burrito place has a definite Berlin flavor.

✈ *U1, U2, U3, U4: Nollendorfpl., then walk down Maasenstr. toward the church, and turn right on Pallasstr.* Ⓢ *Burritos €3.30, with meat €5. Cash only.* ⏰ *Open M-Sa noon-11pm, Su 1-10pm.*

BAR TOLUCCI
ITALIAN $$

Eisenacher Str. 86   ☎030 214 16 07; www.bar-tolucci.de

With stone-oven-cooked pizzas and outdoor seating on wood-slated bistro tables along the quiet street corner, this restaurant is casual eating and generous portions at their finest. The pizzas are cheap (€5.50-8.20) and eclectic (smoked salmon? Bitte!). Be sure to arrive after the oven starts firing at 5pm; non-pizza options can be a bit pricier. Double-fist your pizza slices in a warm, red interior or a small garden.

✈ *U7: Eisenacher Str.* Ⓢ *Pizzas €5.50-8.20. Entrees €7-12.* ⏰ *Open M-F 10am-midnight. Garden open noon-midnight. Pizza oven in use M-F 5pm-midnight.*

the glories of meat

We can thank Berlin for developing many of the meaty staples of German cuisine, although some may seem more palatable than others. If you are ready to delve into this gastronomical adventure, we must warn you about one of the meats you're likely to encounter: **Eisbein.** Literally "ice legbone," *Eisbein* is a boiled dish made from pickled ham hock (a.k.a. pig knuckles). It's best to order this dish on an empty stomach, since *Eisbein* comes in huge portions, covered in a thick layer of fat with the soft skin left on. You're not supposed to eat that part, though, so be sure to peel the skin off. In order to soften the meat, *Eisbein* must be cooked for many hours, giving it a distinctive and aromatic flavor that makes up for the appearance (or so we hope).

MITTE

◪ MONSIEUR VUONG
VIETNAMESE $$

Alte Schönhauserstr. 46   ☎030 992 96 924; www.monsieurvuong.de

The prices are a little high compared to most Vietnamese places, and the portions are not as fantastically large, but Monsieur Vuong rationalizes its stinginess with some of the tastiest and most beautifully presented Vietnamese food you'll find. With a menu that changes every two days, Monsieur Vuong has developed a wide popularity among regulars who just can't stop coming back for the next fix... er, dish. The delicious and cheap Vietnamese coffee (€2) made with condensed milk and a little bit of 'Nam will prevent you from having to say "Goodnight, Saigon."

✈ *U2: Rosa-Luxemburg-Pl. From the Metro, take the alleyway from the park across Rosa-Luxemburg-Str., then turn left on Alte Schönhauserstr.* Ⓢ *Entrees €6-9.80. Vietnamese "shakes" €3.40-5.80.* ⏰ *Open daily noon-midnight.*

BERLINER MARCUS BRÄU
GERMAN $$

1-3 Münzstr.   ☎030 247 69 85; www.brau-dein-bier.de

Though Marcus Bräu has only been brewing since 1982, the *Bier* tastes like what your German grandpa was drinking before German history went crazy. The home-brewed liqueurs (especially the coffee liqueur) taste as good as your mom smells, assuming she smells great. The decor's a little kitschy (as in, framed religious slogans kitschy) and entrees tend to hover around €10, but several delicious varieties of wienerschnitzel from only €9.20 are a rare and belly-filling bargain. Try the beer—it goes down smoother than air.

✈ U2, U5, U8, S5, S7, S9, or S75: Alexanderpl. From the Metro, head north on Karl-Liebknecht-Str., then turn left on Münzstr. Ⓢ Entrees €7.50-11. Drinks €1-7. Beer €2.40 per 0.3L, €6.70 per L. ⓘ Good daily noon-late.

GOOD MORNING VIETNAM   VIETNAMESE $$
Alte Schonhauserstr. 60   ☎030 308 82 973; www.good-morning-vietnam.de

The name is great. The explanation for the name is even better: "A yesterday's movie title, a salutation that reminds us of the past, a past full of starvation and war..." Brimming with such great food, this restaurant is hardly about starvation, although it may start a war among your friends when you must decide between this place and Monsieur Vuong down the street. Entrees are cheaper than their MV counterparts, and include crispy duck, mango chicken skewers, and tofu platters. While the food may not dance in your mouth quite as wonderfully as at Monsieur Vuong, the larger portions will definitely please your belly.

✈ U2: Rosa-Luxemburg-Pl. From the Metro, take the alleyway across Rosa-Luxemburg-Str. from the park. Ⓢ Entrees €7.50. ⓘ Open daily noon-midnight.

TIPICA   MEXICAN $$
Rosenstr. 19   ☎030 250 99 440; www.tipica.mx

Tipica (pronounced TEE-pee-ca) is built around a DIY taco menu. Large portions of meat, cilantro, onion, and lime come with four tortillas; you add the sides and salsas and roll your own creations. The meats get crazy (veal tacos!), but the portions stay large and the selection crowd-pleasing. Get any meat Alcurbie style—fried with peppers, onions, and bacon—for no extra charge.

✈ S5, S7, S9, or S75: Hackescher Markt. From the station, head east and turn right at An der Spandauer Brucke immediately after the Markt. Follow it 100m or so as it curves to the right. Ⓢ Tacos €6-7. Sides €2. Salsa €1. ⓘ Open M-Th 11am-11pm, F-Sa 11am-1am, Su 11am-11pm.

DOLORES BURRITOS   MEXICAN FUSION $
Rosa-Luxemburg-Str. 7   ☎030 280 99 597; www.dolores-online.de

Modeled after the Mexican fusion model of Baja Fresh or Chipotle, this "California Burrito" shop sells hulking tubes under €5. While we won't go so far as to call these suckers "Californian," we will say that they're appropriately tremendous, which always tickles our fancy. The place supplies a hefty and distinctive menu of chipotle chicken, spiced *carnitas*, and vegetables and lets you combine them in burrito (€4), bowl (€4), or quesadilla (€3.70). Also, the blown-up map of the Mission District in San Francisco that covers the walls may convince you that you've stepped through a portal to sunnier climes...or it may just baffle your sense of direction more completely.

✈ U2, U5, U8, S5, S7, S9, or S75: Alexanderpl. From the Metro, head north on Rosa-Luxemburg-Str. Ⓢ Burritos from €5; prices vary depending on your ingredients. Cash only. ⓘ Open M-Sa 11:30am-10pm, Su 1-10pm.

DADA FALAFEL   FALAFEL $
Linienstr. 132   ☎030 275 96 927; www.dadafalafel.de

Ever stood in line at a falafel place and thought, "This place could use more Duchamp!"? Well, even if you haven't, this is the place for you. The high walls and ceiling of this tiny takeout place are covered in thick multicolored paint swirls, as if to reflect the smear of sauces that will soon cover your face. The falafel (€3.50) is appropriately packed with flavor, the plates (€5) are beautifully and smearfully arranged, and everything just seems to taste better with the classic jazz playing from the speakers. After feasting your belly, feast your eyes on "Derdasdie," the Dada art exhibit next to the restaurant.

✈ U6: Oranienburger Tor. Ⓢ Cash only. ⓘ Open M-Sa 9am-6pm.

food

FASSBENDER AND RAUSCH CHOCOLATIERS
CHOCOLATE $$$

Charlottenstr. 60 ☎030 204 58 443; www.fassbender-rausch.de

To prepare for his fall into Wonka's chocolate river, Augustus Gloop must have jumped into F and R's chocolate volcano (real), took a ride on their chocolate Titanic (real, though it might be the Lusitania), and commented on the Baroque idealism of their chocolate Berliner Dom. Established in 1863, this is a giant bustling chocolate house where every inch is filled with confections so delicious, they make Wonka seem like an amateur. You'll wish that all your friends and family were just chocolate replicas here so you could feast on their delicious flesh. Truffles (€0.50-0.80) come in 100 flavors, and it's hard to go wrong with any of them.

🔴 U2 or U6: Stadtmitte. ⓢ Chocolate €0.50-300. ☑ Open M-Sa 10am-8pm, Su 11am-8pm.

ROSENTHALER GRILL
FAST FOOD $

Torstr. 125 ☎030 283 21 53

Outstanding deals and quality Berlin street food at a nice outdoor cafe. Big eaters or families of five, get pumped: an entire chicken costs €5. Gigantic döner kebabs (like a gyro, but made with cabbage; €3.40) and pizzas (€3-5) are also tasty and dirt cheap (without the dirt). Quick tip: the place never closes, and the large döner is the perfect hangover prevention if you eat it on the way home from a crazy night.

🔴 U8: Rosenthaler Pl. ⓢ Menu €1-6. Cash only. ☑ Open 24hr.

ARABESKE
LEBANESE $

Kastanienallee 59 ☎030 440 12 770; www.arabeske.berlin.de

A solid meal at a great price with no frills and one thrill (the salad dressing! No joke, it kills). Safe bets include shawarma (€5.50), which comes with hummus and salad, or its sandwich counterpart (€2.70), which is a packed, burrito-sized wrap that can be easily eaten while holding onto a subway railing for dear life. Vegetarians take comfort in falafel (€4) and the fact that they only indirectly contribute to the deaths of millions of innocent animals.

🔴 U8: Rosenthaler Pl. From the U-Bahn, head northeast up Weinbergsweg. ⓢ Entrees €4-6. ☑ Open daily 11am-late.

HUMBOLDT UNIVERSITY NEW LIBRARY CAFETERIA
CAFETERIA $

Geschwister-Scholl-Str. 1 ☎030 209 399 399; www.ub.hu-berlin.de

Amid the most tourist-bespeckled sidewalks in all of Mitte—where a cup of coffee costs €4—sits the quiet, seemingly off-limits library of Humboldt University. You'll find no one but students inside this absurdly narrow cafeteria in the library's entrance hall (conveniently located before the security checkpoint) that has the lowest prices anywhere in central Berlin. Bockwurst (€1.50), salads with chicken and egg (€2), pastries (€1-2), and coffee (€0.85-1.70) must be state-subsidized at these prices. They even have a tray of powders to construct your very own "curry bockwurst." Frequently packed tables may make you feel like the cafeteria outcast all over again, but there's always a small bar with quick turnover or the steps outside.

🔴 U6: Friedrichstr. From the station, take Friedrichstr. north and make a right just past the tracks. ⓢ Entrees €1-2. Cash only. ☑ Open M-F 9am-8pm, Sa-Su noon-5pm.

PRENZLAUER BERG

Prenzlauer Berg is smitten with its cafes: nearly every street hides a cafe (or six), so a cheap, tasty cup of joe or a small, inexpensive meal are never hard to come by. If your place is kitchen-equipped, stock up at **Fresh'N' Friends** grocery store. (Kastanienallee 26 ☎030 440 40 670; www.freshnfriends.com ☑ Open 24hr.)

W—DER IMBISS

VEGETARIAN $$

Kastanienallee 49   ☎030 443 52 206; www.w-derimbiss.de

Maybe it's Indian food, or maybe it's Mexican. We can't really tell, but one thing we do know: it's tasty. W specializes in fusing ethnic food types to make something novel, extremely popular, and damn good. Its specialty is the *naan* pizza (€2-8)—freshly baked in a tandoori oven and spread with anything from pesto to avocado to chipotle sauce and piled high with arugula and feta or mozzarella. They also sell cold wraps, quesadillas, and burritos to go.

🕈 *U8: Rosenthaler Pl. From the Metro, walk north on Weinbergsweg until it becomes Kastanienallee. The restaurant is on the left.* Ⓢ *Cold or grilled wraps €4-6. Burritos €6. Cash only.* ☼ *Open daily May-Aug noon-midnight; Sept-Apr 12:30-11:30pm.*

DAS FILM CAFÉ

BURGERS, THEATER $$

Schliemannstr. 15   ☎030 810 19 050; www.dasfilmcafe.de

Das Film Café serves homemade burgers to fans hungry for a good meal and even better movies. With screenings of indie and international films nearly every night in a small, high-resolution theater downstairs, this cafe proves that you can enjoy burgers while still "understanding" culture. Sometimes they even combine their specialties: "Eat the Movie" film breakfasts (cheese, ham, fruit, prosecco, and movie ticket; €9.90) precede the Sunday 2pm showing, while a monthly "film quiz" is, according to the waitress, a quiz that's about film. Films are never dubbed and are usually in English.

🕈 *U2: Eberswalder Str. From the Metro, head north on Pappelallee, turn right on Raumerstr., turn left before the park on Lychenerstr., then turn right immediately so you're walking along the park. Take a left on Schliemannstr. The cafe will be on the right.* Ⓢ *Burgers €7. Breakfast €4.90-8.50. Hummus plates €5.50. Cappuccino €2. Tickets €4.50, students €4. Film quiz €5. Cash only.* ☼ *Open M-F 3pm-late, Sa-Su 11am-late.*

SUICIDE SUE

CAFE $$

Dunckerstr. N2   ☎030 648 34 745; www.suicidesue.com

Based on an extended backstory of some *Kill-Bill*-like, samurai-sword-wielding woman who gave up slicing Yakuza brains to slice bread, Suicide Sue is a bright and beautiful place (re: intricate molding) to enjoy some inexpensive internet, coffee, and lunch. Sizable *Stullen* (sandwiches) comprise the main food options, but they're large enough, cheap enough, and varied enough that they transcend the thousands of other sandwiches that Prenzlauer Berg offers. When you're not surfing the web, check out the coffee table books on photography and film.

🕈 *U2: Eberswalder Str. From the Metro, walk east on Danziger Str., then take the 3rd left on Dunckerstr. Suicide Sue is immediately on the right.* Ⓢ *Stullen €3-5. Breakfasts €2.40-8.50. Cake €2-3 per slice. Cash only.* ☼ *Open M-F 8am-6pm, Sa 9am-6pm, Su 10am-6pm.*

THE BIRD

BURGERS $$$

Am Falkpl. 5   ☎030 510 53 283; www.thebirdinberlin.com

With a bar made of old wood and exposed brick, this seemingly quintessential European restaurant is anything but. Opened by two New York transplants, The Bird makes some of the only honest-to-goodness, criminally huge burgers in Berlin. Everything is made from scratch daily, including the sauce for the aptly named "napalm wings." Locals appreciate "Angry Hour," 6-8pm, when all beer is buy one, get one free. Get it? It's a reference to Angry Birds, right?

🕈 *U8: Bernauer Str. From the Metro, head east on Bernauer Str. and turn left into Mauerpark. Walk along the long grassy area in the park until you reach the gigantic jungle gym of colorful logs. Turn right onto the sidewalk, and walk in front of the stadium until you reach Am Falkpl. on the other side. Turn left onto Am Falkpl., and The Bird will be immediately on your right.* Ⓢ *Burgers €9.50-13. Wings €6. Cash only.* ☼ *Open M-Th 6-11pm, F 5pm-midnight, Sa noon-midnight, Su noon-11pm.*

food

ANNA BLUME
CAFE $$

Kollwitzstr. 83   ☎030 440 48 749; www.cafe-anna-blume.de

"Blume" means "flower" in German, and, though "Anna" doesn't mean "coffee," flowers and coffee are this corner cafe's specialties. Outdoor tables blossom out into the street to accommodate a hefty lunch crowd, and multiple coffee blends keep the clientele awake and ready for more. The jam-packed crepes (sometimes quite literally) are a crazy sweet snack; the Alphonso combines mango, orange sauce, peach yogurt, and mango ice cream in one sensational crepacorpia (€6.50). But the real forget-me-not is the flower shop next door, where you can buy some blooms for your loved ones at the height of your coffee buzz.

� *U2: Eberswalder Str. From the Metro, head east on Danziger Str., then turn right on Kollwitzstr. The cafe is on the right, at the southwest corner of Kollwitzstr. and Stredzkistr.* ⑤ *Breakfast €4-8. Crepes €4-8.50. Coffee €2-3.* ⏰ *Open daily 8am-2am.*

KREUZBURGER
BURGERS $

Pappelallee 19   ☎030 746 95 737; www.kreuzburger.de

Okay, so it's not Kreuzberg. Get over it: when you're drunk and stumbling at 2am, you won't give a damn what *Bezirk* you're in anyway. And though we don't want to support your drunk munchies too enthusiastically, there's no better place in P'Berg to prevent a hangover with some tasty fried foods. Bigger and greasier make the morning after easier!

� *U2: Eberswalder Str. From the Metro, head northeast on Pappelallee and take the 1st right onto Raumerstr. Kreuzburger is on the corner of Raumerstr. and Pappelallee.* ⑤ *Burgers €4-8. Fries €2. Cash only.* ⏰ *Open daily noon-3am.*

FRIEDRICHSHAIN

If you're staying somewhere with a kitchen, check out **Viv BioFrischeMarkt** (Boxhagener Str. 103 ☎030 521 30 688; www.viv-biofrischemarkt.de ⏰ Open M-Sa 9am-9pm.) to get your grocery fix.

▨ FRITTIERSALON
GERMAN $$

Boxhagener Str. 104   ☎030 259 33 906

Yes, we know: ever since you set foot in Berlin, you've been drowning in bratwurst, currywurst, and fried potatoes. Still, this all-organic "frying salon" is unique enough to merit a visit. In addition to a traditional prize-winning Berliner currywurst, this restaurant serves German classics with a twist: try the wheat-based vegetarian currywurst or bratwurst, or a hamburger or veggie burger with strawberries and avocado. All sauces and french fries are homemade, and all dishes are cooked to order.

� *U5: Frankfurter Tor. From the Metro, walk south on Warschauer Str. and turn left on Boxhagener Str.; the restaurant will be along the 2nd block on the left.* ⑤ *Bratwurst and currywurst €2.20. Burgers €3.90-7.80. Cash only.* ⏰ *Open M-Th 5pm-midnight, F-Su 1pm-midnight.*

▨ AUNT BENNY
CAFE $

Oderstr. 7   ☎030 664 05 300

Frequented by moms who take their children to the playground across the street, students who are wild about Wi-Fi, and anyone who's serious about the art of carrot cake, this cafe is always booming with indie rock and buzzing with caffeine. Regulars are almost aggressive with their enthusiasm for the cafe's *bricher-muesli*—a kind of Swiss cereal, containing nuts, fresh apples, and oats, soaked overnight, served with yogurt, and usually sold out by 4pm. The carrot cake will spoil you for any other attempts at buttercream frosting.

� *U5: Frankfurter Allee. From the Metro, walk west on Frankfurter Allee, then turn left on Jessnerstr. The restaurant is on the left, opposite the park.* ⑤ *Smoothies €4.20-4.80. Bagels €1.60. Cake €3.10 per slice. Coffee €1.60. Su brunch €8. Cash only.* ⏰ *Open Tu-F 9am-7pm, Sa-Su 10am-7pm.*

VÖNER VEGETARIAN $

Boxhagener Str. 56 ☎030 992 65 423; www.voener.de

The fries are cut from organic potatoes, the fridge is stocked with more organic smoothies than your spacy aunt's garage, and the employees wear jeans that somehow manage to be skinnier than their legs. Everything on the menu is vegetarian—in fact, most of it is vegan. Veggie döners (vöners), veggie burgers (vurgers?), and veggie currywurst (not even gonna try) all compare quite nicely to their more murderous cousins.

🚇 U5: Samariter Str. From the Metro, head south on Colbestr., then turn left on Boxhagener Str., and follow it down until you pass Wühlischstr. [$] Vöners €3.40. Veggie burgers €3. Organic soft drinks and smoothies €1.80. ⏰ Open M-F 11:30am-11pm, Sa-Su 1:30-11pm.

CARAMELLO EIS ICE CREAM $

Wühlischerstr. 31 ☎030 503 43 105; www.caramello-dopamino.de

Caramello Eis scoops some of the best ice cream in town all night long to a following of devoted students. All of Caramello's ice cream is handmade, organic, and vegan, except for the flavor with bacon bits (we kid). Don't leave Friedrichshain without trying the dark chocolate *Eis* with chili powder—the staff says it's the best chocolate ice cream in all of Berlin, and we're not about to argue, as our mouths are too full.

🚇 U5: Frankfurter Tor. [$] Cones €1. Coffee €1-2.60. Smoothies €2-3. Cash only. ⏰ Open M-Th 11am-10pm, F-Sa 11am-1am, Su 11am-10pm.

FLIEGENDER TISCH ITALIAN $$

Mainzer Str. 10 ☎030 297 76 489

Though it lacks any of the "flying tables" that its name entails, this cozy, candlelit eatery serves inexpensive Italian food to local devotees. The pizza is cooked fresh in a Dutch oven, like their very own Fliegender Tisch pizza (bacon, onions, pickled peppers, feta cheese, and yumminess; €6.80). The restaurant's fans swear by the risotto (€5.60-6.50), and you just might swear when discussing how great it tastes. A small restaurant with a few small tables, jazz music, and low, brightly lit ceilings, Fliegender Tisch feels a lot nicer than the low prices might suggest.

🚇 U5: Samariter Str. [$] Pizza €5. Pasta €4.30-6.60. Cash only. ⏰ Open daily 5-11pm.

HOPS AND BARLEY MICROBREWERY $

Wühlischstr. 22/23 ☎030 293 67 534; www.hopsandbarley-berlin.de

This microbrewery makes its own cider, pilsner, and lager on site for hordes of thirsty locals. The bar gets wonderfully packed for German football games, when the bar opens early (3pm) and stays open late enough for the hangovers to kick in. The guys here also make their own bread daily, so you can drink your grain and eat it too.

🚇 U5: Samariter Str. From the Metro, walk west on Frankfurter Allee, then turn left on Mainzer Str. Follow the same street as it turns into Gärtner Str., then turn left on Wühlischstr. [$] Beer €2.80 per 0.5L. Cash only. ⏰ Open daily 5pm-3am.

CAFE CORTADO CAFE $

Simon-Dach-Str. 9

Flowers and board games on breezy patio tables and a cozy, sofa-covered backroom draw a young crowd with a taste for international coffee blends. Cafe Cortado's mosaic bar serves Turkish and Portuguese coffee by day and beer and cocktails by night. A variety of chai teas, a berry torte, and a handful of deliciously gooey ciabattas prepared fresh daily are highlights best enjoyed simultaneously.

🚇 U5: Frankfurter Tor. From the Metro, walk south on Warschauer Str., turn left on Grünberger Str., and turn right on Simon-Dach-Str. The cafe is in the long line of restaurants on your left. [$] Beer €3. Mixed drinks from €6. Coffee €1.70. Bagels €3.50. Brownies €2. Cash only. ⏰ Open M-F 9am-9pm, Sa-Su 9am-midnight.

YOBARCA

FROZEN YOGURT $

Simon-Dach-Str. 40 ☎017 096 99 737; www.yobarca.com

This is the first frozen-yogurt place to have opened in Friedrichshain, and while the locals may still be figuring it out, we love it. Try toppings from berries to Haribo fruit snacks and Kinder chocolate. Started by an Italian ice-cream maker, this small and shockingly yellow fro-yo-to-go joint also serves a tasty take on frozen yogurt's hippest cousin: bubble tea. Eat, drink, and be yuppie.

🚇 *U5: Frankfurter Tor.* 💲 *Small yogurt with 1 topping €2.50. Extra toppings €0.50. Bubble tea €2.50. Cash only.* 🕐 *Open daily noon-8pm. Also, closed when it rains, which is sad, because isn't that when we need a sweet treat the most?*

KREUZBERG

🏔 MUSTAFA'S

MIDDLE EASTERN $

Mehringdamm 32 www.mustafas.de

Some say that this place serves the best döner kebabs in the city—that's debatable, but Mustafa's does undoubtedly have the best dürüm (Turkish wrap filled with döner kebab; €4). Brimming with a spectacular variety of grilled and raw vegetables, plus some tasty cheese and loads of spices, a Mustafa's dürüm is what no other fast food even tries to be: nuanced. Vegetarians who usually scrounge through various falafel options will rejoice at the delicious grilled vegetables in the veggie dürüm (€3.10).

🚇 *U6 or U7: Mehringdamm. From the Metro, cross to the west side of Mehringdamm, then walk south past the big building that looks like a cartoon Medieval castle. Mustafa's is in the little stand on the sidewalk immediately past the castle.* 💲 *Entrees €2.50-5. Cash only.* 🕐 *Open 24hr.*

🏔 SANTA MARIA

MEXICAN $$

Oranienstr. 170 ☎030 922 10 027; www.lasmarias.de

Started by an Australian and run by a hip, young staff from everywhere but Mexico, this Mexican restaurant defies logic with its amazingly authentic food. A few bites of anything from the long and diverse menu may convince you that you're south of the border, rather than south of the Wall. The *choriqueso* (€6.50) is a pot of melted cheese and sausage...just think about that for a second. The standard issue grub like fat Mexican sandwiches (€6), burritos (€5-7), delicious tacos (€5.50-6.50), and margaritas (€5) are also on hand, and they're all so flavorful that you'll want to savor them for hours. The exposed grill, electro beats, and candlelight make this an unbeatable evening hangout.

🚇 *U8: Moritzpl. From the Metro, head southeast on Oranienstr. The restaurant is on the left after Oranienpl.* ℹ️ *Taco Tu (€1 tacos).* 💲 *Entrees €5-8. Cash only.* 🕐 *Open daily noon-late. Happy hour (margaritas; €4) daily 8-10pm.*

🏔 CAFÉ MORGENLAND

CAFE $$

Skalitzer Str. 35 ☎030 611 32 91; www.cafemorgenland.eu

The Parisian breakfast—a fresh butter croissant, a large dish of perfect vanilla custard with fresh fruit, and the best milk coffee you've ever had—breaks the laws of economics at just €5. The all-you-can-eat brunch buffet (€9.50) on the weekends will literally make your jaw drop: eight types of meat, five types of bread, 15 spreads, five types of cereal (including German fruit loops), sausages, eggs, curries, potatoes, fish, vegetables, fruits—it's paradise. The few tables packed into this small, bright cafe and lining its sidewalk are predictably full, so unless you want to risk a long wait or an empty tummy, call ahead to make a reservation. Your salivary glands will thank you.

🚇 *U1: Görlitzer Bahnhof. From the Metro, walk west on Skalitzer Str. The cafe is in the little square next to the intersection between Skalizter Str. and Manteufel Str.* 💲 *Entrees €5-15. Cash only.* 🕐 *Open M-F 9am-1am, Sa-Su 10am-1am. Brunch Sa-Su 10am-4pm. Business lunch M-F noon-4pm.*

🍴 RESTAURANT RISSANI — MIDDLE EASTERN $

Spreewaldpl. 4 — ☎030 616 29 433

With a thousand döner places in Kreuzberg to choose from, all of them screaming how "authentic" they are, it's difficult to find the stand-out at which to throw your gold. Well, Rissani doesn't serve döners, only chicken shawarma sandwiches, but they're twice as delicious and half as expensive (€2) as their döner cousins. Dinner plates (€5-6) with shawarma, falafel, tabbouleh, hummus, and salad will make you forget your bad day.

🚇 U1: Görlitzer Bahnhof. From the station, head east down Skalitzer str. and take a right at Spreewaldpl. [$] Entrees €2-5. Cash only. ⏰ Open M-Th 11am-3am, F-Sa 11am-5am, Su 11am-3am.

🍴 HENNE ALT-BERLINER WIRTSHAUS GASTSTÄTTEN — GERMAN $$

Leuschnerdamm 25 — ☎030 614 77 30; www.henne-berlin.de

Henne provides the most German experience imaginable. Inside an antler-lined parlor crammed with plaid tablecloths, sturdy German damsels haul mugs of beer, and the menu bears only a single dinner (€7.90): a piece of bread, creamy potato salad, and enormous, perfectly crispy, internationally renowned chicken that will forever redefine fried food. The chicken skin whispers, "You don't need family, friends, or love in your life. You only need ME!" Frankly, it's got a pretty compelling case.

*🚇 U1 or U8: Kottbusser Tor. From the station, head northwest on Oranienstr. Take a right at Oranienpl. and follow the park about halfway to St. Michael's Church. The restaurant is at the corner of Leuschnerdamm and Waldemarstr. **i** Reservations required for outdoor seating; they're a good idea for indoor seating as well. [$] Sausage €2.40-3.50. Beer €2.60-3.60. Wine €4. Cash only. ⏰ Open Tu-Sa 7pm-late, Su 5pm-late. Kitchen open Tu-Sa 7-11pm, Su 5-10pm.*

CURRY 36 — CURRYWURST $

Mehringdamm 36 — ☎030 251 73 68; www.curry36.de

The best currywurst in Berlin means the best currywurst in the world. The standard recipe of sausage, ketchup, and curry spices becomes a holy trinity with some of the most tender, flavorful sausage in *Wurstland* and a uniquely zesty blend of spices—the ketchup's the only ingredient you'll have tasted before. Be brave: take it with fries and an enormous glob of mayo.

🚇 U6 or U7: Mehringdamm. From the Metro, head south on Mehringdamm. The fast-food stand is on the right just before Yorck/Gneisenaustr. [$] Organic currywurst €1.80. French fries €1.30. Cash only. ⏰ Open daily 9am-5am.

OREGANO — PIZZA, MIDDLE EASTERN $$

Oranienstr. 19 — ☎030 614 01 096

This Orianienstr. takeout place serves cheap, delicious pizza baked fresh in a stone oven with toppings prepared before your eyes in gigantic, flaming skillets. Oregano is also a kebab place on the side, so many of its pizza and menu options reflect their "Little Istanbul" surroundings with some distinctly Middle Eastern ingredients. The "Oriental" pizza bears spinach, lamb, and yogurt (€5.30), while the *rolle* (calzone; €3-5) and *pide* (calzone with egg; €3.60-5.80) each hold some infinitely edible combination of cheese, spinach, lamb, and mushrooms.

🚇 U1 or U8: Kottbusser Tor. From the Metro, head northeast on Adalbertstr. and turn right on Oranienstr. The restaurant is on the left, near the end of the block. [$] Pizzas €3-6. Cash only. ⏰ Open M-Th 11:30am-3am, F-Sa 11:30am-5am, Su 11:30am-3am.

SK KREUZBERG FOOD 24 GMBH — STREET FOOD $

Schlesischestr. 1-2 — ☎030 610 76 000

Home of the amazing €1 personal pizza and the €3 impersonal pizza (so disaffected), SK gets flooded by post-clubbers and pre-clubbers every evening. While the food may remind the careful taster of something pulled from a TV dinner, what matters most is the fact that it's hot, gooey, and filling. No need to look further; this is Kreuzberg's cheapest drunk food.

🚇 U1: Schlesisches Tor. From the Metro, cross the south lane of Skalitzer Str. along Schlesische Str. The restaurant is on the corner of Schlesiche Str. and Skalitzer Str. $ Pasta, sandwiches €3-5. Cash only. ⏰ Open 24hr.

courting the currywurst

More cult than sausage, currywurst, the fried goodness of pork and beef topped with curry and ketchup, has kept Berliners happy and their stomachs full for over 60 years. As if the city's more than 2000 currywurst stands weren't enough, Berlin also opened the **Currywurst Museum** dedicated to its beloved street food. The ticket includes—no surprise—currywurst in a cup.

Also, look out for the **Grillwalker,** a franchise of currywurst vendors who carry around their grills, freezers, gas tanks, and assorted currywurst condiments and paraphernalia, as they walk around selling the goodies. With so many options, let your gut be your guide, and don't forget to wash the curry concoction down with some champagne, the latest trend in this sausage-obsessed city.

nightlife

If you're reading this section and thinking "I'm not sure I *want* to go clubbing in Berlin," then stop it. Stop it right now. Take a hint from Lady Gaga, patron saint of Berlin, and just dance...you won't regret it. The true *Diskotheken* await in the barren cityscape of Friederichshain and notoriously nocturnal Kreuzberg. Mitte does not disappoint—its tremendous multi-room clubs filled with exquisitely dressed 20-somethings are generally worth the heftier covers. The major parties in Schöneberg are at the GLBT clubs in the northern part of the neighborhood. For tamer nightlife, try the jazz clubs in Charlottenburg or the bar scene in Prenzlauer Berg.

CHARLOTTENBURG

Charlottenburg's quiet cafes and music venues cater to the 30-something set. The neighborhood is great for a mellow evening or some live jazz, but the real parties are eastward. The **Ku'damm** is best avoided after sunset, unless you enjoy fraternizing with drunk businessmen.

A TRANE — BAR, CLUB

Bleibtreustr. 1 — ☎030 313 25 50; www.a-trane.de

A Trane is small in size and big in history. With walls covered in signed black and white photographs of past jazz legends who have performed on its stage (Herbie Hancock, Wynton Marsalis) and a rack of albums recorded live there, A Trane has a long reputation as one of Berlin's premier jazz clubs. But, with dying legends and fading interest, the Trane has derailed a bit by pursuing popularity over prowess (Red Hot Chili Peppers jazz covers? No thanks!). Skip the fads and sit in on a Saturday jam session; these tend to extend well into Sunday morning.

🚇 S3, S5, S7, S9, or S75: Savignypl. $ Cover €10-15, students €8-13. Sa no cover after 12:30am. Cash only. ⏰ Open M-Th 9pm-1am, F-Sa 9pm-late, Su 9pm-1am.

CASCADE — CLUB

Fasanenstr. 81 — ☎030 318 00 940; www.cascade-club.de

The walk down to the large basement club is bordered by steps flooded by flowing, pink water (hence Cascade). With a high cover, this club might be a bit of a splurge, but in return patrons get a dance floor of underlit blocks (a la *Saturday Night Fever*), a wall-to-wall bar, and a young crowd, which happen to be the three basic ingredients of a good dance party. There are ways to get around the high cover charge: stop by on a Friday and pick up a voucher for free entry, which is good the next evening or even the next weekend.

U1: Uhlandstr. $ Cover €10, F no cover until 1am. Beer €3.50. Shots €4. Cash only. ⏰ Open F-Sa 11am-late.

QUASIMODO CLUB

Kantstr. 12A ☎030 312 80 86; www.quasimodo.de

The upside here is that Quasimodo showcases live music in a variety of genres, including soul, R and B, folk, and jazz, nearly every night of the week. The music choices are wildly eclectic, but each act guarantees a long night of entertainment. The downside is that the older crowd sometimes gives the club a kind of office-party energy. A spacious basement room with a large bar and stage lets all those awkward coworkers dance right up close to the performers.

*U2, S5, S7, S9, or S75: Zoologischer Garten. **i** Check the website for music schedule. $ Cover for concerts €8-30, cheaper if reserved in advance. Drinks €2.50-4.50. Cash only. ⏰ Open daily 12:30pm-late.*

ANDA LUCIA BAR, RESTAURANT

Savignypl. 2 ☎030 540 271; www.andalucia-berlin.de

So you're wandering around the streets of Berlin after hours, thinking, "Hey, you know what I'm in the mood for? A little Latin flavor! I wonder where I could nosh on tapas and show off my salsa at 2am!" (Don't say we don't know our readers.) We've found the perfect place for you: Anda Lucia may not have a dance floor, but that doesn't keep guests and staff from dancing around tables to salsa tunes blasting late into the heat of the night. There's also outdoor patio seating for those on a dance siesta and in the mood for a late night tapas. If Anda Lucia's not hoppin' on a particular night, there are, eerily, three more tapas places in Savignypl. from which to choose.

S5, S7, or S75: Savignypl. $ Wines from €4 per glass. Tequila €3. Tapas €3.70-5. ⏰ Kitchen open 5pm-midnight. Tapas bar open 5pm-late.

SALZ CLUB

Salzufer 20 ☎017 028 33 504; www.salz-club.de

You'll have to go a little out of your way to find a more upbeat and youthful bunch in low-key Charlottenburg—and by "a little out of your way" we mean a 20min. walk from the nearest U-Bahn station. But if you're looking to stay in the neighborhood and see someone dancing under the age of 32, this is the place to go. Exposed brick walls keep the disco-ball-lit floor looking classy at this salt-warehouse-turned-techno-club. Out front find a beautiful patio lit with multi-colored lights and tiki torches.

*U2: Ernst-Reuter-Pl. Walk down Str. des 17 Juni to Satzufer. Turn left and walk along the river to Salz. **i** Check the website for music schedules. $ No cover. Cash only. ⏰ Open Th 8pm-late.*

SCHÖNEBERG AND WILMERSDORF

Schöneberg is still Berlin's unofficial gay district, therefore it's full of GLBT nightlife. A couple of distinctive cocktail bars may be worth visiting in the interest of broadening your buzz, but the neighborhood's real parties happen at the GLBT clubs and bars in northern Schöneberg.

HAFEN BAR, GLBT

Motzstr. 19 ☎030 211 41 18; www.hafen-berlin.de

Nearly 20 years old, this bar has become a landmark for Berlin's gay community. The sign outside may only specifically invite "drop dead gorgeous looking tourists," but you'll find plenty of locals all along the spectrum of attractiveness.

Dancing neon lights grace the walls of an expansive bar with a large supply of tables and a consistently high level of volume and energy from its clean, drum-machine-heavy tunage. The weekly pub quiz (M 8pm; 1st M of the month in English) is wildly popular, and every Wednesday features a new DJ. On April 30th, Hafen hosts their largest party of the year, in honor of the Queen of the Netherlands. They promise us that the "Queen" makes an appearance.

U1, U3, U4, or U9: Nollendorfpl. $ No cover. ⏰ Open daily 8am-4am. Cash only.

SLUMBERLAND — BAR

Goltstr. 24 ☎030 216 53 49

So normally we like a little more authenticity in our bars, but we're not going to pretend that we don't appreciate an island escape in the middle of land-locked Berlin, and the locals aren't either. So what if you didn't come to Germany for reggae, palm trees, and sand in your shoes? By the way, if you were confused with that last part, the floor is covered with sand. Try an obligatory beach favorite, like a piña colada or a Sex on the Beach (both €6.50), or go tropical in a new direction with a fruit-flavored African beer (DjuDju, €3.90).

U1 , U3, U4, or U9: Nollendorfpl. $ Most drinks €2-7. ⏰ Open M-Th 6pm-2am, F 6pm-4am, Sa 11am-4am, Su 6pm-2am.

PRINZKNECHT — BAR, GLBT

Fuggerstr. 33 ☎030 236 27 444; www.prinzknecht.de

A huge wooden bar dancing with disco ball reflections is the beating heart of this ecstatic gay bar. Even with levels upon levels of bar stools and couches extending far back into its neon-lit interior, the bar fills up way past capacity on event nights, and people begin to resemble waves on the street. A mostly male clientele spread between 20-somethings and 50-year-olds nods to the almost oppressively loud beats inside, while others cool off on the long benches that stretch across the pavement outside. Check the website for upcoming events, including an incredibly popular ABBA night.

U1 or U2: Wittenbergpl. $ 2-for-1 drinks W 7-9pm. Cash only. ⏰ Open M-F 2pm-3am, Sa and Su 3pm-3am.

BEGINE — BAR, GLBT

Potsdamer Str. 139 ☎030 215 14 14; www.begine.de

In a neighborhood dominated by male gay clubs, Begine is a welcome retreat for women. Named after a now-defunct Lesbian WC, Berlin's biggest lesbian community center has a popular, low-key cafe and bar with comfortable sofas and features readings and live music at night. Dim yellow lighting and an acre of empty floor space make for a quiet bar that offers a short and unremarkable list of beers, coffee, and cocktails. The bar is far removed from the nightlife center over by Nollendorfpl., but maybe that's precisely the point. An older crowd proudly patronizes this respectable neighborhood rarity.

U2: Bülowstr. ⏰ Open M-F 5pm-late, Sa 3pm-late, Su 7pm-late.

TRAIN — BAR

On the corner of Potsdamer Str. and Willmanndamm ☎030 017 734 441 23

You know those terrible restaurants that our parents took you to when you were a kid, ya know, the ones inside of old train cars? Well, this cocktail bar, located inside a good ol' locomotive, may bring back those mundane memories. Sure, it's gimmicky, but it's also decked out in aluminum foil ceilings and chandeliers, and totally packed with sexy 20-somethings! With a ton of train-themed drinks listed in the sleek black menu, like the fruity Train Fever (rum, lime juice, lemon juice, maracuja syrup, mango juice; €6), you might easily wake up the next morning feeling like you were run over by several trains. Choo choo!

U7: Kleistpark. $ All cocktails €6, €5 on M-Tu and Su nights. Cash only. ⏰ Open daily 1pm-late.

HEILE WELT BAR, GLBT

Motzstr. 5 ☎030 219 17 507

Even with the addition of two enormous, quiet sitting rooms, the 20-something clientele still pack the bar and take over the street. As a foil to the frenetic energy of **Hafen,** which lies a little further down Motzstr., Heile Welt keeps its cool with a fur-covered wall, chandeliers, gold tassels darkening the street window, and a row of comfy armchairs. But without much of the glamor or volume of its competitors, Heile Welt can seem dull at times, so arrive once your buzz has begun to mellow.

🚇 U1, U3, U4, or U9: Nollendorfpl. $ Beers €2.50 per liter. Cash only. ⏰ Open daily 6pm-4am, sometimes later.

MITTE

👍 COOKIES CLUB

Friedrichstr. 158 ☎030 274 92 940; www.cookies-berlin.de

Hot, sweaty, sexy, and packed, Cookies is housed in a former Stasi bunker that operates as a restaurant during the day. Locals claim that this party originally started in some guy's basement before moving to more permanent digs. Three bars lubricate your dancing joints with a long list of trendy, expensive cocktails, such as the Watermelonman (Smirnoff, watermelon liqueur, grenadine, lemon juice, orange juice; €7.50). Once you're all messy and unbalanced, choose between a huge dance floor with light, clean techno and a tiny room with heavy American hip hop. The party don't start 'til 1am, so save your tears if you show up alone at midnight. Also, invest in some plaid or a cardigan beforehand, because the bouncers tend to select the more hipsterly attired.

🚇 U6: Französische Str. From the Metro, head north on Friedrichstr. along the left side of the street. The club is unmarked, so look for a group of darkly dressed dudes around a door as you near Dorotheenstr. $ Cover €5-15. Cocktails €7.50-€10. Coat check €1. Unfortunately, no baked goods. ⏰ Open Tu 10:30pm-6am, Th 10:30pm-6am.

👍 LEVEE CLUB

Neue Promenade 10 www.levee-club.com

This dark and smoky techno club, hidden under the S-Bahn tracks in a nook just off of Hackescher Markt, is tremendously popular among 20-something locals. And there's no wonder why. There are two very different dance floors: the one on the ground floor is large and surrounded by a huge bar, while the one downstairs is cramped (or intimate, depending on your tastes) and better dressed. The ground floor's techno is heavy; upstairs it's heavier. The cover can be difficult to, well, cover at popular hours, but you'll want to stay here all night once it gets packed around 1 or 2am. Check the website for guest DJs, concerts, and special events.

🚇 S5, S7, S9, or S75: Hackescher Markt. From the Metro, walk west and enter the 1st street that runs under the S-Bahn tracks. $ Cover free-€20. Beer €4. Cash only. ⏰ Open F-Sa 11pm-late.

KAFFEE BURGER CLUB

Torstr. 58-60 ☎030 280 46 495; www.kaffeeburger.de

So it's a Wednesday night and you're buzzed from the hostel bar, but can't find anywhere to show off your moves: Kaffee Burger is the perfect place to stumble into. There's a small dance floor packed by 20-year-olds in band T-shirts and scarves right next to 40- and 50-year-olds showing off how crazy they can still be. With a quieter, smokier "Burger Bar" next door with plenty of cushy furniture to lounge on and a cocktail called the "Drunken Rihanna" (€7), Kaffee Burger will transform your weeknight from a bleak night into a freak night. Weekly programs include poetry readings, film screenings, and drunken sloppiness.

🚇 U6: Rosa-Luxemburg-Pl. From the Metro, walk 1 block to the east on Torstr. $ Cover M-Th €1, F-Sa €5, Su €1. Beer €2.50. Shots €3-4. Cocktails €6-7. Cash only. ⏰ Open M-F 8pm-late, Sa 9pm-late, Su 7pm-late.

WEEK END CLUB

Alexanderpl. 5 ☎030 246 31 676; www.week-end-berlin.de

Two words: rooftop bar. It may not be the rooftop of the Park Inn nearby, but this club with the neon "Sharp" sign in the smaller skyscraper just off Alexanderpl. lets you cool off from the bangin' dance floor while enjoying a spectacular view of Mitte's nightscape. Downstairs in the actual club, a tremendous bar borders a small dance floor with some of the coolest lighting you'll find outside of a Lady Gaga concert. One downside is the annoyingly large tourist population invited by this club's central location, none of whom are adequately acclimated to the heavy techno. Plus, with skyscraping cover and drink prices, you may not want to spend every weekend at Week End.

🚏 U6: Alexander Pl. From the Metro, head northeast to the "Sharp" building. $ Cover €10-20. Coat check €1.20. ⏰ Open F-Su 11pm-late.

CLÄRCHENS BALLHAUS CLUB

Auguststr. 24 ☎030 282 92 95; www.ballhaus.de

For travelers who enjoy the type of dancing that gets worse as the night wears on, this 1930s-style ballroom has cha cha, salsa, and other programs Sunday through Thursday. Friday and Saturday DJs play "hipper" music. Come early for a drink in the beautiful patio garden, or come late to watch the surprisingly talented steppers of all generations kick it old school in a tremendous hall surrounded by silver tassels.

🚏 U8: Oranienburger Str. From the Metro, head north on Tucholsky Str. and turn right on Auguststr. $ M-Th, Su programs €8, students €6, after midnight free; F-Sa €3. ⏰ Open daily 10am-late. Dance programs start 7-8:30pm, depending on the day of the week. Check the website for more details.

8MM BAR
BAR

Schönhauser Allee 177B   ☎030 405 00 624; www.8mmbar.com

8MM is a dim, smoky hipster bar where you can chat about how ironic you are or just play a round of pool. Art films projected on the wall, guest performers, and live DJs make this more than just a place to wear flannel and look disaffected, although there's still plenty of that to go around. Crowd levels vary, but when it's bustling, it's bustling.

✴ *U2: Senefelderpl. From the Metro, head south on Schönhauser Allee.* Ⓢ *Beer €2.50-6. Mixed drinks €4-7. Cash only.* 🕐 *Open M-Th 8pm-late, F-Su 9pm-late.*

DELICIOUS DOUGHNUTS
CLUB

Rosenthaler Str. 9   ☎030 280 99 274; www.delicious-doughnuts.de

No, it's not a doughnut shop. Yes, it's a hip backpacker hangout with a late-20s crowd of locals. There's not much room to dance here, but there are plenty of couches and space enough to relax, talk, drink, and smoke. Plus, there's a gigantic bar with pretty much any drink you can think of, all under a mess of tree branches and a stuffed owl. If your friends are boring, escape to the pinball machine in the corner. After all, a small steel ball is friend enough for anyone.

✴ *U8: Rosenthaler Pl. From the Metro, head south on Rosenthaler Str. It's the club on the corner of Rosenthaler Str. and Auguststr. labeled with a donut with three crosshatches.* Ⓢ *Cover €5-10. Cocktails €6-8.* 🕐 *Open daily 10pm-late.*

NEUE ODESSA BAR
BAR

Torstr. 89   ☎017 183 98 991

Black-and-white-striped wallpaper, dimly lit vintage parlors furnished with cushy, classy furniture, and a dazzling bar invite you to this glamorous and heavily populated hipster bar. The bar is small and there will constantly be several layers of the perfectly dressed keeping you from it, but plenty of table space spread across two large rooms and lining the sidewalk outside means that it won't be difficult to find a niche. A live DJ spinning electropoppy American indie rock completes the scene.

✴ *U6: Rosa-Luxemburg-Pl. From the Metro, walk 2 blocks east on Torstr. to the corner of Torstr. and Chorinerstr.* Ⓢ *No cover. Beer €3. Cocktails €6-8. Cash only.* 🕐 *Open daily 7pm-late.*

TAPE
CLUB

Heidestr. 14   ☎030 284 84 873; www.tapeberlin.de

The huge open spaces of this converted warehouse keep it cool when the party hits a hard boil. And it always does. The party starts (and goes) very late. Tape derives some of its hip powers from its remote location: be sure to check the website calendar before making the long trek, because after an hour-long quest, you don't want to find it closed for the night.

✴ *U8: Hauptbahnhof. From the Metro, walk north on Heidestr. for about 10min. Tape will be on your right, in an old warehouse building.* Ⓢ *Cover varies. Cash only.* 🕐 *Open F-Sa 11pm-late.*

PRENZLAUER BERG

With less techno, more lounging, and far earlier quiet hours (midnight-1am) than other parts of Berlin, Prenzlauer Berg's nightlife is calm but worth checking out. The bars are some of the most unforgettable in town, and, since they fill and empty a bit earlier, they're perfect before you head out to later, clubbier climes.

◩ THE WEINEREI: FORUM
BAR

Fehrbelliner Str. 57   ☎030 600 53 072; www.weinerei.com

This unmarked wine bar has been catapulted from local secret to local legend thanks to its comfortable elegance and unique payment system. Pay €2 for a glass, sample all the wines, and then sample again and again. Before leaving, just pay what you think you owe. Only in Berlin! Enjoy your vintage at an outdoor table or on an indoor sofa, but be warned: this place is so absurdly (and understandably) popular that you'll definitely have trouble finding a seat.

🚇 U2: Senefelderpl. From the Metro, exit by the northern stairs, then head west on Schwedter Str. Turn left on Kastanienalle, then veer right onto Veteranenstr. a block down the hill. The bar is on the corner of Veteranenstr. and Fehrbelliner Str. $ Depends on how drunk you get. Cash only. ⏰ Open M-Sa 10am-late, Su 11am-late, but the wine flows 8pm-midnight every night, so let that guide you.

👍 DR. PONG — BAR, PING-PONG

Eberswalder Str. 21 — www.drpong.net

Under falling fluorescent lights, in the middle of a concrete room with peeling paint, stands a single ping-pong table, the centerpiece of this minimal bar. Intense hipsters ring the table, gripping their paddles, motivated by nothing other than the thrill of victory over a ring of unsteady strangers. All are welcome, including beginners and the severely intoxicated.

🚇 U2: Eberswalder Str. From the Metro, head east on Eberswalder Str. The bar is on the left. $ Cover €3.50; includes 1 beer. Beer €2.70. Cocktails €4.50-5.50. Cash only. ⏰ Open M-Sa 8pm-late, Su 6pm-late.

👍 KLUB DER REPUBLIK (KDR) — CLUB

Pappelallee 81 — www.myspace.com/klubderrepublik

There are few museums that have as many authentic Soviet artifacts as KDR has hanging on its walls. Once the showroom of a DDR carpet and linoleum supplier, KDR kept the old Formica bar and leaded glass, and added lamps from the original Palast Republik, as it was being torn down. The furniture is from the DDR landmark Café Moscow. Eclectic DJs play everything from punk to trance to something known as "cosmic disco," which is probably as ahead-of-its-time as Sputnik. Huge crowds of P'Berg's hippest comrades arrive late and stay late, so end your night at KDR, and you won't be disappointed.

*🚇 U2: Eberswalder Str. Turn into what looks like a deserted parking lot and climb the metal stairs. **i** DJs W-Su. Check the website for a schedule of events. $ Long drinks €5-6. Beer €2.30-3. Spirits €3.50-5. Cash only. ⏰ Open from "dark to light." In more definite terms, that's around 9pm-late in the summer, 8pm-late in the winter.*

SCOTCH AND SOFA — BAR

Kollwitzstr. 18 — ☎030 440 42 371

Exactly what the name promises. This bar channels gold-foiled '70s glamour and serves classic drinks on vintage sofas. Far from stuffy, Scotch and Sofa relaxes to some mellow tunes—big band and reggae sound especially refreshing in a land of house—and grand French doors open up to a quiet street lined with patio seating.

*🚇 U2: Senefelderpl. From the Metro, exit by the northern stairs, then head southeast on Metzer Str. After passing the grocery store, turn left on Kollwitzstr. The bar is on the right, about half a block up Kollwitzstr. **i** Happy hour cocktail of the day €3.80. $ Scotch from €5. ⏰ Open daily 6pm-very late. Happy hour daily 6-7pm.*

WOHNZIMMER — BAR

Lettestr. 6 — ☎030 445 54 58; www.wohnzimmer-bar.de

Wohnzimmer means "living room," and it's not hard to see why this bar goes by that name, given its wide wood-planked floors, glassware cabinets, and vintage lounge chairs. Settle into a velvety Victorian sofa with a mixed drink among a crowd split between nostalgic 50-year-olds and 25-year-olds wishing they had something to feel nostalgic about.

🚇 U2: Eberswalder Str. From the Metro, head east on Danziger Str., turn left on Lychener Str., then turn right on Lettestr., just past the park. The bar is on the left, at the corner of Lettestr. and Schliemannstr. $ Cocktails €4-5. Beer €2.50-3. Cash only. ⏰ Open daily 9am-4am.

DUNCKER CLUB

Dunckerstr. 64 ☎030 445 95 09; www.dunckerclub.de

Suits of armor, chainmail, and retro bead curtains hang from the high ceilings of this horse-stable-turned-club. A gigantic metal bat keeps a watchful perch above the small corner stage—who knows, it may even come alive on "Dark Monday." Duncker heats up at around 1am, when it draws punkish crowds with an insider vibe and great sound. Ring the bell for entry.

🚇 U2: Eberswalder Str. From the Metro, head east on Danziger Str., then turn left on Dunckerstr. Walk north on Dunckerstr. until you reach the bridge over the train tracks. The club is on the left, in the darkened building, immediately past the bridge. ***i*** *Goth music on M. Eclectic DJs Tu-W. Live bands on Th. "Independent dance music" F-Sa. Throwback DJs on Su. "Dark Market" goth flea market on Su 1pm.* $ *Cover M-W €2.50, F €4, Sa €4.50, Su €2.50. No cover on Th. Beers €2.50. Long drinks €4.50. F-Sa all drinks max €2. Cash only.* ⏰ *Open M-W 9pm-late, Th 10pm-late, F-Sa 11pm-late, Su 10pm-late.*

WHITE TRASH FAST FOOD BAR, CLUB, TATTOOS

Schönehauser Allee 6-7 ☎030 503 48 668; www.whitetrashfastfood.com

White Trash Fast Food cakes the irony on so disgustingly thick that it may be hard to tell whether you're actually enjoying yourself. Four floors filled with intentionally kitschy paintings, obscene Americanisms, and dark, candlelit hallways mean that entering this restaurant/bar/club/tattoo parlor complex feels like descending into some haunted funhouse. Fortunately, it can be a lot of fun. International punk bands, rock bands, and DJs fill the place with distorted noise every night of the week, and the wide, greasy, hilarious menu is worth sampling. Is this how Americans seem to the world? Hell yeah.

🚇 U2: Senefelderpl. From the Metro, exit by the southern steps, then head south on Schönhauser Allee. The bar is on the left as you approach Torstr. $ *Cover €5. Beers €2.80-3.50. Specialty drinks from €8. Burgers €7.50-13. Cash only.* ⏰ *Open M-F noon-late, Sa-Su 6pm-late.*

MORGENROT BAR

Kastanienallee 85 ☎030 443 17 844; www.cafe-morgenrot.de

This little cafe is trying to save the world, and they're having a great time doing it. Owned by a five-person work collective, Morgenrot makes vegan, organic, fair-trade food by day (including a weekend brunch buffet where guests pay €5-9, according to what they can afford) and serves beer, frosty vodka shots, and live house music by night. Deep teal walls and climbing plants on the outside pull in black-clothed crowds to brood over how much capitalism has destroyed their souls.

🚇 U2: Eberswalder Str. From the Metro, head southwest on Kastanienallee. The bar is about half-way down the 2nd block on the left. $ *Shots €2. Beer €2.50-3. Spirits €3.60. Cash only.* ⏰ *Open Tu-Th noon-1am, F-Sa 11am-3am, Su 11am-1am.*

FRIEDRICHSHAIN

With its heavily graffitied walls and blinding floodlights, industrial Friedrichshain may not be the most inviting neighborhood to navigate in the dead of night, but it hides some of Berlin's biggest and most bangin' techno clubs. The old warehouses along **Revaler Strasse** hold the lion's share of sprawling dance floors, but you might want to branch out a little to avoid a double-digit cover. Fortunately for those with two left feet (or three for that matter) Friedrichshain isn't only about its *Diskotheken:* the area around **Simon-Dach-Strasse** provides plenty of popular bars to liven your night without stretching your legs.

👍 **ROSI'S** CLUB

Revaler Str. 29 www.rosis-berlin.de

Walking into this indoor-outdoor club complex is like a kid walking into a candy store with great house music playing over the speakers: there are a ton of things to do, and, like we said, there's great house music playing over the speakers!

Outdoor features include a fire pit, ping-pong, a small dance floor, and a tiny grill. Indoor features include Indiana Jones pinball, a high-ceilinged dance floor, and, still, great house music playing over the speakers. Rosi's is way at the opposite end of Revaler Str. from the main club complex, meaning that natural selection weeds out most of the tourist riff-raff on the dark walk over. Plus, parties start and end super late, so this is a perfect place to end your night.

U1, S3, S5, S7, S9, or S75: Warschauer Str. From the Metro, walk north on Warschauer Str., turn right on Revaler Str., and walk for about 10min; Rosi's will be on your right. $ Cover €3-7. Cash only. ⏰ Open Th-Sa 11pm-late.

ASTRO-BAR BAR

Simon-Dach-Str. 40 www.myspace.com/astrobar

If your religion requires that you only enter houses of debauchery with Transformers action figures nailed behind the bar, then enter Astro-Bar with ease. Light-years of lounge and table space line the walls, while the dim lighting from orb-shaped lamps may make you feel lost in space. With a new DJ every night, Astro-Bar provides a ton of tunage, from punk to powerpop to Britfunk to every head-scratching subgenre under the sun. Astro-Bar is an extremely popular bar with the 20-something set; the kids just keep coming back for the booze, the tunes, and the feeling that they're floating in space.

U5: Frankfurter Tor. From the Metro, head south on Warschauer Str., turn right on Grünberger Str., and then turn right on Simon-Dach-Str. $ Beer from €2.50. Mixed drinks from €5. Cash only. ⏰ Open daily 6pm-late.

K-17 CLUB

Pettenkoferstr. 17 www.k17.de

This towering club has a spacious dance floor and bar on each of its four floors. It's a long trip from any of the nightlife centers in Friedrichshain, but this ensures fewer tourists on the hunt for their first *Diskothek* experience. Metal and all things loud and crunchy blast from the speakers of each floor, attracting a mostly black-clad crowd that will inevitably think you're preppy. Concerts are usually once per week, so keep an eye on the website for dates and prices.

U5: Frankfurter Allee. Once you're on Pettenkoferstr., keep an eye out for signs; the club is off the road on your right. $ Cover €6. Beer €2.50. Vodka and coke €3.50. ⏰ Open F-Sa 10pm-late.

ABGEDREHT BAR

Karl-Marx-Allee 140 ☎030 293 81 911; www.abgedreht.net

Though it caters particularly to a metal crowd, with enough churning guitars on the speakers to make any grandma faint, this dim and dark wooden bar serves up enough good beer and loud company to attract a wider set of locals than just the ones wearing black. Sheet music papers the walls, and leather couches clump around antique sewing tables, all of which are puzzling in a bar whose name means "high" in colloquial German. Though its crowd generally falls in the 30+ range, and though you might get a couple of disapproving stares when you walk in wearing that lime-green button-up that your mom bought you, this is one of the more accessible points of entry into F'Hain's metal scene.

U5: Frankfurter Tor. From the Metro, walk west on Karl-Marx-Allee until you pass the building with the huge, copper tower. $ Beer €3-4 per 0.5L. Happy hour cocktails €4. Traditional German foods like bratwurst and wienerschnitzel around €9. Cash only. ⏰ Open daily 5pm-late. Happy hour 7-9pm.

SANITORIUM 23 BAR

Frankfurter Allee 23 ☎030 420 21 193; www.sanatorium23.de

If you're looking to experience the techno scene but don't know if you're ready for the Revalerstr. riot, get your feet wet at Sanitorium 23. This bar plays light, almost clinical techno to guests that lounge on sleek, backless couches shaped like cubes. It's almost like they're all sitting on a life-sized version of the menu, which is cleverly designed to look like the periodic table of elements.

✈ U5: Frankfurter Tor. Ⓢ Cocktails €5.50-8. Beer €2.50-3.50. Cash only. ◷ Open M-Th 3pm-2am, F-Sa 4pm-4am, Su 4pm-2am.

FRITZ CLUB   CLUB

Prinzessinnenstr. 1   ☎030 698 12 80; www.fritzclub.com

It's a testament to how touristy this place is that the American Top 40 dance floor is constantly and completely packed, while the techno floor remains sparsely attended. That said, the club's three tremendous dance floors—the other one plays American arena rock, which is not quite a dealbreaker in our book—provide plenty of space and opportunity for you to try your feet at some different dance cuisine, and the whole place is a constant bustle of activity and colored lights. A huge outdoor rock garden that's more desert than oasis provides some space to lounge and let your sweat evaporate, while bars strewn liberally about the complex prevent you from going dry. Though it's a bit far and we have our reservations, a relatively cheap cover and a constant stream of 20-year-olds ready to pump their fists make this one of the highlights off Mühlenstr.

✈ S3, S5, or S75: Ostbahnhof. From the Metro, walk south on Str. der Pariser Kommune, turn left on Mühlenstr., and take the first left toward the big complex of warehouses. The club will be on the right side of these warehouses. Ⓢ Beer €3-3.50. Cover €6. Cash only. ◷ Concerts start at 9pm. Club open F-Su 11pm-late and select weekdays. Check the website for a calendar of events.

RED ROOSTER   BAR

Grünbergerstr. 23   ☎030 290 03 310; www.redroosterbar.de

Since it's linked to the Odysee Hostel next door, the Red Rooster fills every night with an international crowd of backpackers, who spill out onto the outdoor patio and porch swing. Inside, from behind an old wood countertop and under exposed brick ceilings and pipelines, bartenders serve cider and Czech beers from the tap. For the particularly outgoing or desperate backpacker, "perform 4 stay" events invite you to sing for a free beer—or even a free bed! The drunken crowing that results is where we assume the name comes from.

✈ U5: Frankfurter Tor. Walk south on Warschauer Str. and turn right on Grünberger Str. Ⓢ Beer from €2.50-3. Cash only. ◷ Open M-Th 5pm-1am, F-Sa 5pm-3am, Su 5pm-1am.

CASSIOPEIA   CLUB, BEER GARDEN, RESTAURANT, LIVE MUSIC

Revaler Str. 99   ☎030 473 85 949; www.cassiopeia-berlin.de

A sprawling nightlife oasis in an abandoned train factory with space for about 3000 guests, this all-in-one entertainment complex may as well have its own government. Outdoor couches and a climbing wall let you take a break from the huge indoor dance floor, not that you'll want to—the tunes are unstoppable. Occasionally, the club hosts concerts, usually starting around 8pm; check out the list of bands you've never heard of on the website. Unfortunately, with a cover that can move into the high teens during prime time, the budget traveler may have to remain content with gazing at the Cassiopeia in the sky, rather than gaining entry to this piece of club heaven on earth.

✈ U1, S3, S5, S7, S9, or S75: Warschauer Str. Ⓢ Cover €5-16. Beer €2.50-3. Vodka €2.50. Cash only. ◷ Open W-Sa 11pm-late.

JÄGERKLAUSE   BAR, BEER GARDEN

Grünbergerstr. 1   ☎017 622 286 892; www.jaegerklause-berlin.de

Jägerklause is frequented by pin-up stylers, leather-clad bikers, and the old T-shirt and ripped-jeans crowd. Hence the mounted antlers and disco ball combo. This bar is known for its large beer garden lined with tall shrubs, where guests can lounge in canvas chairs under strands of outdoor lights while sniffing the bratwurst and steaks sizzling on the grill. The connected pub has a dance floor, and features

nightlife

live bands, like the chart-topping stylings of a band called Cannabis Corpse from Wednesday to Saturday. Check the website calendar for dates and deets.

U5: Frankfurter Tor. Beer garden open daily 3pm-late. Pub open daily 6pm-late.

KREUZBERG

Kreuzberg is world-renowned for its unbelievable techno scene. Converted warehouses, wild light displays, destructive speaker systems, and dance floors so packed they look like Dante's *Inferno* cluster around **Schlesisches Tor,** but some of the best are scattered more widely. Kreuzberg is one of Berlin's most notoriously nocturnal neighborhoods, so expect the parties to rage from about 2am to well past dawn.

CLUB TRESOR — CLUB

Köpenicker Str. 70 — ☎030 629 08 750; www.tresorberlin.com

Club Tresor, like many of Berlin's best, contains two dance floors in an old warehouse. Apart from that, there is no comparison to be made between this superb club and its peers. The basement dance floor manages to provide plenty of dancing and breathing room in one of the most oppressive environments of any Berlin club. Intense strobe lights cut up the time continuum, exposed pipeline caverns hide unseen techno monsters, and the beats are so heavy, they practically dislodge the drywall. Upstairs, a brighter, redder, and more comfortable floor plays tight house tracks, which serve as a perfect warm-up or cool-down. Make the trek, stay all night, and have your nightmares later.

U8: Heinrich Heinestr. $ Cover €8-15. Cash only. Usually open W 10pm-late, F-Sa 10pm-late. Check the website for a schedule.

CLUB DER VISIONAERE — CLUB, BAR

Am Flutgraben 1 — ☎030 695 18 942; www.clubdervisionaere.com

Though this riverfront cabana/bar/club/boat is packed, the experience is well worth the sweaty armpits. A DJ spins inside a mini indoor club, but the fun's definitely outside, where you can sip rum drinks, dip your feet in the river, and share large pizzas (€8) with friends, preferably all at once. This club is like a mix of the Bayou, New York, and Cancun, but it could never exist in any of them. So relaxing, so visionary, so Berlin.

U1: Schlesisches Tor. From the Metro head southeast on Schlesischestr. Cross the 1st canal, and, when you reach the 2nd, the club will be on the left next to the bridge. $ Cover €4-15. Beer €2.50-3.50. Long drinks €5.50. Cash only. Open M-F 2pm-late, Sa-Su noon-late.

HORST KRZBRG — CLUB

Tempelhofer Ufer 1 — www.horst-krzbrg.de

Though it's not a tremendous, multi-level, self-sufficient community like many of Kreuzberg's clubs, Horst Krzbrg offers an excess of two club fundamentals: delicious beats and room to dance. This club is the place to be when you're fed up with the incessant pulse of house that hounds you from every bar and club you pass. The drum kicks here are all over the place and not necessarily where you expect them to be, yielding music that's just as unsettling as it is danceable—that is, extremely. The spacious, black-and-white tiled dance floor allows a young, bohemian crowd to spread out and go crazy—think punks, scene kids, and misplaced dudes in baggy jeans and old Adidas flailing their limbs. Though it'll take some commuting, Horst Krzbrg is a worthy place to spend any (or all) of your weekend nights.

U1, U6: Hallesches Tor. From the Metro, cross to the south side of the river, then turn right on Tempelhofer Ufer. $ Cover €8-12. Shots €2.50-3. Beer €3. Long drinks €6-7. Cash only. Hours vary, but normally open Th-Sa midnight-late.

ARENA CLUB CLUB

Eichenstr. 4 ☎030 533 20 30; www.arena-club.de

Part of the awesome indoor/outdoor complex of Arena, which includes a pool floating on the Spree and a gigantic venue for concerts and events, Arena Club inhabits an old, two-story factory building, in which some of the old machinery is still intact. Plenty of lounge space, with cushy, square booths for snuggling, fills every corner of the labyrinthine floor plan, along with two bars and two dance floors that spin a wide range of techno. The factory aesthetic is good retro fun (check out the throwback glass tiles on the second floor), the tunes are some of Kreuzberg's finest, and the whole place promises a memorable night of raging and relaxing in alternation.

🚇 U1: Schlesisches Tor. From the Metro, head south on Schlesischestr. across both canal bridges. The Arena complex is the large industrial set of buildings on the left after the 2nd bridge. $ Cover €5-10. Cash only. ⏰ Party hours vary but usually open F-Sa midnight-late.

WATERGATE CLUB

Falckensteinstr. 49 ☎030 612 80 396; www.water-gate.de

Even if we don't recommend it, we understand: you'll probably end up going anyway. As Berlin's most exclusive club, this is a must for anyone who needs something to brag about on Facebook. From about 1am on (and we mean *on*), a long line (30min.-1hr.) will greet you at the door. If not perfectly gender-balanced or heavy on the women, groups should split up: the bouncer is ruthless. Inside, you'll find a gorgeous Spree-level view, a boat to cool off on, and a dance floor that's so packed, so loud, and so long, that you'll probably momentarily forget the world while you're there. The whole place is spectacular and enticing, but for authenticity's sake, we urge you to seek some other Kreuzberg clubs. Watergate is like Nixon's presidency: ruined by nosy Americans. So if you're looking for somewhere more local, look around.

🚇 U1: Schlesisches Tor. From the Metro, head toward the bridge. It's the unmarked door at the top of the stairs just before the river. There'll be a line. $ Cover €8-20. Mixed drinks €6.50. Cash only. ⏰ Open W midnight-late, F-Sa midnight-late.

RITTER BUTZKE CLUB

Ritterstr. 24 www.ritterbutzke.de

One of Berlin's only clubs to feature a *Gästeliste*, or guest list, in addition to regular admission for n00bs and natives without friends in high places, Ritter Butzke's three-dance-floor complex nestled in the alleyways of an old factory building is one of Kreuzberg's most well-known and best-kept secrets. Word about this place doesn't often reach tourists, so it's one of your best bets for kickin' it with local *Volk*. Floors vary from small and intimate to medium-sized and cramped to expansive and accommodating of even the most notorious toe steppers.

🚇 U1: Prinzenstr. From the Metro, head northeast on Prinzenstr. for 2 blocks, then turn left on Ritterstr. Halfway down the block, turn into the courtyard shaded by trees on the right. The entrance to the club is at the end of this courtyard. $ Cover around €10. Shots €2-2.50. Beer €2-3. Long drinks €5-6. Cash only. ⏰ Hours vary, but generally open F midnight-late, Sa 10pm-late. Check the website for a full calendar of events.

LUZIA BAR, CAFE

Oranienstr. 34 ☎030 817 99 958; www.luzia.tc

This huge bar is tremendously popular among a 20-something, hipster clientele, and understandably so. Gold-painted walls glow softly in a dim space flickering with candles. A huge, L-shaped design allows for long lines of vintage, threadbare lounge chairs, cafe tables, and a bar so long that it can easily fit even the crowd that swarms at peak hours. The tables out on the sidewalk are always packed, with skinny-jeaned barhoppers replacing skinny-jeaned cafe-dwellers at sundown. Sipping absinthe in a dilapidated armchair to '80s synth? Yeah, you're in Berlin.

U1 or U8: Kotbusser Tor. From the Metro, head northeast up Aldabertstr. and turn left on Oranienstr. The bar is on the right. The only sign is a large, black rectangle with a gold coat-of-arms in the middle. $ Beer €2.50-3.50. Long drinks €5-6. Absinthe €3-7. Cash only. ⏰ Open daily noon-late.

MAGNET CLUB CLUB, LIVE MUSIC

Falckensteinstr. 48 ☎030 440 08 140; www.magnet-club.de

This club's guests break down into two groups: cool locals who come for the DJs and frequent live bands, and angry tourists who got rejected from Watergate next door. Indie bands play on a short, shallow stage that makes it seem as though they're part of the crowd, and DJs spin a much lighter mix than their Kreuzberg counterparts—think indie electropop. A little too "indie" for its own good, Magnet Club repels the vicious dancers, but its softer steps and three-bar complex attract those looking for a quieter night than Kreuzberg normally allows.

U1: Schlesisches Tor. From the Metro, head toward the bridge. An "M" hangs above the door. $ Cover €3-7. Beer Shots €2-2.50. €2.50-3. Long drinks €6-6.50. ⏰ Usually open Tu-Su from 10pm. Check online for exact schedule.

SO36 BAR, CLUB, LIVE MUSIC

Oranienstr. 190 ☎030 614 01 306; www.so36.de

SO36 sees itself less as a club, and more as an organization with an attitude. The various parties, live shows, and cultural presentations that fill this huge hall attract a mixed gay/straight clientele whose common denominator is that they like to party hardy. Gayhane, a gay cabaret that performs the last Saturday of every month, has become a staple of the Berlin GLBT scene and can get pretty epic.

U1 or U8: Kottbusser Tor. From the Metro, walk north on Adalbertstr. and turn right on Oranienstr. The club is on the right. $ Cover varies. Shots €2.20. Beer €2.80-3.50. Wine €3. Long drinks €5.50, with Red Bull €6. Cash only. ⏰ Hours vary, but usually open F-Sa 10pm-late.

ROSES BAR, GLBT

Oranienstr. 187 ☎030 615 65 70

Fuzzy pink walls, a fuzzy pink ceiling, ubiquitous tiger print, and a curious collection of Christian iconograpy make this small gay bar a real treat. Gay men, some lesbian women, and a couple of straight groups (there to camp out in campy glory) join together for small talk over some clean electro. The bar's small size makes mingling easy, and the endless assortment of wall trinkets (glowing mounted antlers, twinkling hearts, a psychedelic Virgin Mary) keeps everyone giggling.

U1 or U8: Kottbusser Tor. From the Metro, head northwest on Oranienstr. past Mariannenstr. The bar is on the left. $ Beer €2.50. Cocktails €5, with Red Bull €6. Cash only. ⏰ Open daily 9pm-late.

MILCHBAR BAR

Manteuffelstr. 40/41 ☎030 611 70 67; www.milchbar-berlin.de

Despite an unfortunate lack of *Clockwork Orange* references to match its milky title, Milchbar draws a sampling of the punk spectrum to lounge, drink, and listen to hardcore music throughout the night. For some inexplicable reason the walls are painted blue and covered by murals of sea creatures. Foosball and pinball in a back room provide some entertainment in case you get lost at sea.

U1: Görlitzer Bahnhof. From the Metro, head west on Skalitzer Str., then turn right on Manteuffelstr. The bar is on the left. $ Beer €3. Spirits €2-5. ⏰ Open M-Sa 9am-late.

arts and culture

As the old saying goes, "where there be hipsters, there be Arts and Culture." Though the saying's origins are unclear, it certainly applies to Berlin. Whether it's opera, film, or Brecht in the original German that you're after, Berlin has got you covered. For a magical evening at the symphony, grab a standing-room-only ticket to see the Berliner Philharmoniker or grab a rush seat to see the Deutsche Oper perform Wagner's four-opera cycle, *The Ring of the Nibelung*. If rock, pop, indie, or hip hop are more your style, head to Kreuzberg to check out Festsaal Kreuzberg and Columbiahalle. Nearby English Theater Berlin will satisfy any Anglophone's theater cravings, while the Deutsches Theater in Mitte hosts performances of the German classics as well as the English canon in translation. The truly hip should head straight to Lichtblick Kino or Kino Babylon to find radical documentaries, avant-garde films, and a sea of flannel and retro frames.

doing it in public

Had too many beers and can't make it back to the hotel in time? No worries. Berlin has various public facilities that cater to your needs. Some are paid, some are free, but all will get the job done.

- **MEAN, GREEN PISSING MACHINES.** These *pissoirs* conceal their function behind their elegant octagonal walls, but the rust and smell probably give it away. Historically significant (who knew urinals could be landmarks?), they were established in the 19th century and are now privately run. Toilet-goers-to-be beware: of the 30 *pissoirs* left standing, some are only for men.

- **DO IT IN STYLE.** In front of the C&A Store in Mitte's Alexanderpl., a modern temple to bodily fluids flatters worshippers with stainless steel, glass, and artsy photographs of the city.

- **KEEP IT IN YOUR PANTS.** No matter how badly you have to go, always remember where you are. In the few months after its 2005 opening, drunken fans and opportunistic visitors availed themselves behind the privacy of the 2711 concrete slabs at Berlin's Holocaust Memorial. Not cool.

MUSIC AND OPERA

👍 BERLINER PHILHARMONIE — MITTE

Herbert-von-Karajan-Str. 1 ☎030 254 88 999; www.berlin-philharmonic.com

It may look strange from the outside, but acoustically, this yellow building is pitch-perfect. Every audience member seated around the massive pentagonal hall gets a full view and even fuller sound. But the hall can only be as good as the music that fills it: fortunately, the **Berliner Philharmoniker,** led by the eminent Sir Simon Rattle, is one of the world's finest orchestras. It's tough to get a seat, so check the website for availability. For sold-out concerts, some tickets and standing room may be available 90min. before the concert begins, but only at the box office. Stand in line, get some cheap tickets if you're lucky, and enjoy some of the sweetest sounds known to mankind.

🚇 S1, S2, S25, or U2: Potsdamer Pl. From the Metro, head west on Potsdamer Str. $ Tickets for standing room from €7, for seats from €15. ⏰ Open from July to early Sept. Box office open M-F 3-6pm, Sa-Su 11am-2pm.

DEUTSCHE STAATSOPER — MITTE

Unter den Linden 7 ☎030 203 54 555; www.staatsoper-berlin.de

The Deutsche Staatsoper is East Berlin's leading opera theater. Though it suffered during the years of separation, this opera house is rebuilding its reputation and its repertoire of classical Baroque opera and contemporary pieces. Unfortunately, it's exterior is under extensive renovation until 2013, but performances will continue as usual. Recent performances have included productions of Mozart and Strauss, so you know you're in good hands.

🚇 U6: Französische Str. Or bus #100, 157, or 348: Deutsche Staatsoper. $ Tickets €14-260. For certain seats, students can get a ½-price discount, but only within 4 weeks of the performance, and only at the box office. Unsold tickets €13, 30min. before the show. ⏰ Open from Aug to mid-July. Box office open daily noon-7pm and 1hr. before performances.

DEUTSCHE OPER BERLIN — CHARLOTTENBURG

Bismarckstr. 35 ☎030 343 84 343; www.deutscheoperberlin.de

The Deutsche Oper Berlin's original home, the Deutsches Opernhaus was built in 1911 but decimated by Allied bombs. Today performances take place in Berlin's newest opera house, which looks like a gigantic concrete box. If you have the chance, don't pass up a cheap ticket to see one of Berlin's most spectacular performances. The 2011-2012 season includes Wagner's four-opera cycle, *The Ring of the Nibelung*, and Puccini's *Tosca*, along with a variety of other canonical German and Italian productions.

🚇 U2: Deutsche Oper. $ Tickets €16-122. 25% student discount when you buy tickets at the box office. Unsold tickets €13, 30min. before the show. ⏰ Open Sept-June. Box office open M-Sa 11am until beginning of the performance, or 11am-7pm on days without performances; Su 10am-2pm. Evening tickets available 1hr. before performances.

FESTSAAL KREUZBERG — KREUZBERG

Skalitzerstr. 130 ☎030 611 01 313; www.festsaal-kreuzberg.de

Free jazz, indie rock, swing, electropop—you never know what to expect at this absurdly hip venue. A tremendous chasm of a main hall accommodates acts of all shapes and sizes, plus an overflowing crowd of fans packed together on the main floor and hanging from the mezzanine. A dusty courtyard out front features a bar, some busy chill-out space, and novelty acts like fire throwers. Poetry readings, film screenings, and art performances fill out the program with some appropriately eclectic material, making this one of Berlin's most exciting venues.

🚇 U1 or U8: Kottbusser Tor. From the U-Bahn, head east on Skalitzerstr. The venue is on the left. $ Tickets €5-20. Shots €2. Long drinks €6. ⏰ Hours vary. Usually open F-Sa 9pm-late. Check website for details.

COLUMBIAHALLE KREUZBERG

Columbiadamm 13-21 ☎030 698 09 80; www.columbiahalle.de

Any venue that features Snoop Dogg, The Specials, and Bon Iver in a matter of a couple months has a special place in our hearts. With a wildly eclectic collection of superstars and indie notables from all over the world, Columbiahalle's calendar is bound to make you gasp and say, "Oh I definitely wanna see that," at least twice. Once a gym for American service members in south Kreuzberg, Columbiahalle may look dated and innocuous, but its standing-room-only floor and mezzanine sure can rage.

🚇 U6: Pl. der Luftbrücke. From the Metro, head east on Columbiadamm. The venue is in the 1st block on the right. $ Tickets €20-60, depending on the act. ⏰ Hours and dates vary, but concerts tend to start at 8pm. Check the website for more details.

FILM

Finding English films in Berlin is almost as easy as finding the Fernsehturm. On any night, choose from over 150 different films, marked **O.F.** or **O.V.** for the original version (meaning not dubbed in German), **O.m.U** for original version with German subtitles, or **O.m.u.E.** for original film with English subtitles.

LICHTBLICK KINO PRENZLAUER BERG

Kastanienallee 77 ☎030 440 58 179; www.lichtblick-kino.org

This 32-seat theater specializes in avant-garde films and radical documentaries, with a range of movies that crosses decades, borders, and the lines of polite society. English films are intermixed with all sorts of other international fare, and all films are shown with the original sound and accompanied by German subtitles, so you won't need to perform any amazing feats of lip-reading in order to enjoy a movie whose dialogue is in a language you can actually understand. Directors stop by frequently. This is the quintessential art-house experience.

🚇 U8: Eberswalder Str. From the Metro, walk southwest on Kastanienallee, past Oderberger Str. The theater is near the end of the next block on the left. $ Tickets €5, students €4.50. ⏰ 2-5 films shown every night, usually 5-10pm. Check the website for a full calendar.

KINO BABYLON MITTE

Rosa-Luxemburg-Str. 30 ☎030 242 59 69; www.babylonberlin.de

Americans and Berliners alike flock to this spunky independent film house with a commitment to classic international cinema. Silent films, fiction readings, and constant themed retrospectives—like a recent exposition of Lithuanian films—guarantee that you'll have a chance to see something new and interesting alongside the classics. Occasional summer screenings happen outdoors on the beautiful Rosa-Luxemburg-Pl.—and epic screenings of *Rocky Horror Picture Show* go down regularly. Unfortunately, outside of the frequent American classics, English is a bit hard to come by, as most subtitles are in German.

🚇 U2: Rosa-Luxemburg-Pl. From the Metro, walk south on Rosa-Luxemburg-Str. $ Tickets €4-8. ⏰ The schedule changes daily; check website for details. Box office open M-F from 5pm until the 1st film of the evening.

ARSENAL MITTE

In the Filmhaus at Potsdamer Pl. ☎030 269 55 100; www.arsenal-berlin.de

Run by the founders of Berlinale and located just below the **Museum for Film and Television**, Arsenal showcases independent films and some classics. Discussions, talks, and frequent appearances by guest directors make the theater a popular meeting place for Berlin's filmmakers. With the majority of films in the original with English subtitles, the English "purist" can get her fix.

🚇 U2, S1, S2, or S25: Potsdamer Pl. From the Metro, head west on Potsdamer Str. and go into the building labeled "Deutsche Kinemathek." Take the elevator down to the 2nd basement level. $ Tickets €6.50, students €5. ⏰ 3-5 films shown each night. Films usually start 4-8pm. Check the website for a full calendar.

THEATER

ENGLISH THEATER BERLIN — KREUZBERG

Fidicinstr. 40 ☎030 693 56 92; www.etberlin.de

For over 20 years, Berlin's only completely English-language theater has been defying German-language totalitarianism with everything from festivals of 10min. contemporary shorts to full-length canonical productions. Leave your *umlauts* at home.

🚇 U6: Pl. der Luftbrücke. From the Metro, head north on Mehringdamm for 2 blocks and turn right on Fidicinstr. The theater is on the left within the 1st block. $ €14, students €8. ⏰ Box office opens 1hr. before show. Shows are at 8pm unless otherwise noted. Check the website for a calendar of performances.

DEUTSCHES THEATER — MITTE

Schumann Str. 13a ☎030 284 41 225; www.deutschestheater.de

Built in 1850, this world-famous theater that legendary director Max Reinhardt once controlled is still a cultural heavy hitter in Berlin. With even the English drama in translation (Shakespeare and Beckett are rockstars here), English speakers shouldn't expect to understand any of the words, but the productions are gorgeous enough that they're worth seeing in spite of the language barrier.

🚇 U6: Oranienburger Tor. From the U-Bahn, head south on Friederichstr., take a right on Reinhartstr. and another right on Albrechtstr. $ €5-30. ⏰ Box office open M-Sa 11am-6:30pm, Su 3-6:30pm. Shows at 8pm unless otherwise noted.

shopping

Though you'll probably have trouble finding room in your pack for new merch, Berlin's shopping scene is worth several broken zippers. Appropriate to its opulent West Berlin background, **Ku'Damm** in Charlottenburg is considered Berlin's quintessential shopping center, although the stores are generally high-class franchises, and the prices are more western than Plato in a cowboy hat. **Friedrichstraße** in Mitte is Ku'Damm's East Berlin twin, although with more glamorous marble colonnades, and the book/music chain behemoth **Dussmann. Kastanienallee** in Prenzlauer Berg or **Hackescher Markt** in Mitte are the places to prowl if you want to return home several degrees hipper than you left, with genitalia-crushing skinny jeans and ill-fitting v-necks in every stark storefront. Kastanienallee quakes with record stores as well—it's the place to go for either new CD releases or vintage LPs. In line with its "street"-ier reputation, **Kreuzberg** is strewn with some impressive skate shops, which are pricey, but offer the best selection of hoodies and threads to wear while robbing a gas station. Thrift stores are spread widely without a specific "thrift-strict," where you can hunt for secondhand clothes, books, and music, but the best options are located in **Schöneberg** and **Prenzlauer Berg.** Otherwise, any flea market will oblige, with the exception of the **Turkish Market,** which is more focused on food. If you want a more complete, although less discerning, guide to clothes shopping in Berlin, ask the clerk at any clothing store for a free Berlin shopping guide. Meanwhile, here are our favorites.

CLOTHING

department stores

KADEWE — CHARLOTTENBURG

Tauentzienstr. 21-24 ☎030 212 10

If a zombie infestation occurs, KaDeWe is the place to hole up with the rest of the uninfected. With seven floors of food, groceries, books, toys, make-up, and clothes, you'll have at least a year's worth of stuff to begin rebuilding human civilization before supplies start running out. But, zombie invasions aside, we question

berlin

KaDeWe's worth. Due to the unrelenting prices, it serves only as a jaw-dropping spectacle to anyone who has any budget conscience whatsoever. But with Chanel, Prada, and Cartier flashing from every window display, it may be worth checking out if you don't feel quite poor enough after a visit to **Schloß Charlottenburg.**

🚇 U1, U2, or U3: Wittenbergpl. ⏰ Open M-Th 10am-8pm, F 10am-9pm, Sa 9:30am-8pm.

OVERKILL KREUZBERG

Köpenicker Str. 195a ☎030 695 06 126; www.overkillshop.com

This two-story shoe store lives up to its name by offering an uncommonly excessive selection of two quintessentially Kreuzbergian accessories: bright shoes and even brighter spray paint. Until you have these in tow, you may as well be a pathetic tool on a bus tour in the eyes of most Kreuzbergers, so Overkill is a good place to start out on the right foot. On the sleek ground level, a floor-to-ceiling display of the hippest kicks by Nike, New Balance, Adidas, Fred Perry, and other big names squares off against another floor-to-ceiling display of the largest spray-paint rainbow you'll ever lay eyes on. The second floor is an abrupt contrast, with more shoes and some expensive skater clothes spread around a gorgeous old Berlin apartment, bearing vintage leather furniture, stained wood floors, and intricate wallpaper. It's a beautiful home to a dazzling collection of merchandise.

🚇 U1: Schlesiches Tor. From the Metro, begin walking west on Köpenicker Str. The store is on the left. [$] Shoes €90-180. Shirts €45. ⏰ Open M-Sa 11am-8pm.

secondhand

Unfortunately, there's no central grouping of secondhand stores in Berlin where you can go and spend an entire vintage afternoon: the best ones are spread all over the place, and the *best* one happens to be located in rich, old West Berlin (lots of rich old ladies donating their rich old clothes). You'll definitely find the largest number in Prenzlauer Berg, particularly around **Kastanienallee,** but otherwise, you should plan on hitting our recommendations one at a time as you navigate the different neighborhoods. Request a free Berlin shopping guide at any of these places: your wardrobe will thank you.

GARAGE SCHÖNEBERG

Ahornstr. 2 ☎030 211 27 60

American Apparel wishes it were this legit. With quirky posters (Beastie Boys tour '92!), silver tassels hanging from the ceiling, shopping carts full of socks, disaffected mannequins, and a sea of circular racks arranged neatly by color, Garage will raise your hipster cred simply by walking in. And with one of the best deals in town (€15 per kg of clothes from the largest portion of the store), it'll make you want to return again and again, extra-large shopping bags in tow.

🚇 U1, U2, U3, U4, or U9: Nollendorfpl. ℹ "Happy Hour" W 11am-1pm add an extra 30% off to those criminally low prices you're already enjoying. ⏰ Open M-F 11am-7pm, Sa 11am-6pm.

STIEFELKOMBINAT-BERLIN PRENZLAUER BERG

Eberswalder Str. 21/22 ☎030 510 51 234; www.stiefelkombinat.de

This packed, double-address thrift store (one for men, one for women) hawks merch from the '40s through the '90s, including the usual quirky options to complete your outfit, plus a hilarious collection of all sorts of eclectic antiques, many of them inexplicably pertaining to vintage American cartoons. This means you can finally get that Garfield shirt (the comic strip, not the movie), gigantic Smurf action figure (the TV show, not *Avatar*), or plastic Snoopy with an electric fan in his nose you were deprived of during childhood. The shoe selection, though mostly dress shoes priced in the upper double-digits, is unbeatably wide for anyone looking to put some class in his step.

🚇 U2: Eberswalder Str. From the Metro, head west on Eberswalder Str. The thrift store is about a quarter of the way down the block on the left. [$] Garfield shirts €10-25. Dress shoes €50-100. Blazers €40-80. ⏰ Open M-Th 10am-10pm, F-Sa 10am-midnight.

MACY'Z

Mommsenstr. 2   ☎030 881 13 63

Mommsenstr. is Berlin's secondhand designer-label mecca, and Macy'z may have the best collection around. Everything the store carries is less than two years old, and designed by the biggest names in the industry—think Gucci bags and Prada shoes for half the original price or less. (Just to clarify, half-price on a Burberry coat might still set you back €500.) But for the truly devoted, a (very relative) deal can be found.

🚉 *U1: Uhlandstr.* 🕐 *Open M-Sa noon-6:30pm, Su noon-4pm.*

flea markets

Basically, if there is a Berlin square and it's warm out, come early afternoon on a weekend or holiday and you can pretty much guarantee a flea market. Most are small, and many contain the same boring assortment of books, LPs, and kitchenware, so if you want to find a wide selection of good, cheap merchandise—plus extra features like free fruit and street musicians—stick with our recommendations.

🏴 TURKISH MARKET

Along the south bank of the Landwehrkanal

Entering this market is like entering a shouting match in several different languages you don't understand. Fruit sellers scream melon prices in Turkish-infused German, and clothes hawkers announce deals on shoes in German-infused Turkish. Some shop owners even sing, overflowing with enthusiasm at the prospect of an incessantly dense crowd. The Turkish Market is not just an amazing place to find great deals on fruit and clothing—it's one of the best experiences of the entire city. The fruit stands have fruits you've never seen (that may cost as little as €1), and many of them feature free samples, meaning an agile traveler can assemble a free fruit salad during a spin through the market. The clothing stands have deals like three pairs of socks for the price of one, and confectionary stands serve substantial hunks of Turkish delight for gutter prices (€1 per 100g).

🚉 *U1: Kottbusser Tor. From the Metro, head south toward the canal.* 🕐 *Open Tu noon-6pm, F noon-6pm.*

🏴 FLEA MARKET ON MAUERPARK

Bernauerstr. 63-64   ☎017 629 250 021; www.mauerparkmarkt.de

The Flea Market on Mauerpark is the biggest and best-known in all of Berlin. A labyrinth of booths and stalls hides everything from hand-ground spices to used clothing to enamel jewelry to old power tools. Hordes of bargain hunters, hipsters, and gawking tourists crowd the park, drinking fresh-squeezed orange juice and listening to street musicians. Like all secondhand stores in Prenzlauer Berg, Mauerpark's prices are hardly secondhand. You can still find good values, but don't expect to come away feeling like you just legally robbed several people.

🚉 *U2: Eberswalden Str. From the Metro, head west on Eberswalder Str. The flea market will be on your right, immediately after you pass Mauerpark.* 🕐 *Open Sunday 9am-5pm.*

ARKONAPLATZ

Arkonapl.   ☎030 786 97 64; www.troedelmarkt-arkonaplatz.de

Craftsmen sell jewelry. Farmers juice oranges. That guy down the street hawks his CDs from a towel. Arkonapl. brings out the weird, the old, the desperate, and the people who want to buy stuff from all of them. Despite the modest size of the square, the market itself is packed together and features an incredible range of wares: DDR relics, bolts of fabric, pictures of vendors' babies, antique space hats, etc. Stick around in the afternoons when the Irish guy comes by with a karaoke machine on his bike. He's been doing it for years.

🚉 *U8: Bernauerstr. From the Metro, walk south on Brunnenstr. and take the 1st left on Rheinsberger Str. Take the 3rd right on Wolliner Str. Arkonapl. is on the right.* 🕐 *Open Su 10am-6pm.*

AM KUPFERGRABEN

On Am Kupfergraben, across from the Bodemuseum

Stroll along Museum Island while you shop at secondhand tents, and cross your fingers that you'll come across Nefertiti's Bust among the wares. The market is tiny and consists of almost exclusively books and LPs, but if you're looking to pick up a cheap German book the selection is unrivalled and extremely cheap. A requisite collection of steins will remind you that Berlin happens to be located in Germany.

🚉 *S3, S5, S7, or S75: Hackesher Markt. From the Metro, walk south on Burgstr., turn right on Bodestr. After you pass across Museum Island and cross the Spree for the 2nd time, Am Kupfergraben is on the right.* 🕙 *Open Sa-Su 11am-5pm.*

books

Finding English books in Berlin is about as easy as finding someone who speaks English: they're everywhere, but they're not always very good. Secondhand is the way to go to offset the extra cost of English books.

🏴 ST. GEORGE'S BOOKSTORE

PRENZLAUER BERG

Wörtherstr. 27 ☎030 817 98 333; www.saintgeorgesbookshop.com

You'll be hard-pressed to find a better English-language bookstore on the continent. St. George's owner makes frequent trips to the UK and the US to buy the loads of titles that fill the towering shelves so that his customers can find anything they're looking for and then some. Over half of the books are used and extremely well-priced (paperbacks €4-8), with a number of books for just €1. This shop also carries new books and can order absolutely any title they don't already carry. If you're searching for a book to make you look mysterious in your hostel's lobby, there's absolutely no better place. Pay in euro, British pounds, or American dollars (oh my!).

🚉 *U2: Senefelderpl. From the Metro, head southeast on Metzerstr. and turn left on Prenzlauer Allee. Follow Prenzlauer Allee for 3 blocks, then turn left on Wörtherstr. The bookstore will be halfway down the block, on your right.* Ⓢ *Used hardcovers €10.* 🕙 *Open M-F 11am-8pm, Sa 11am-7pm.*

ANOTHER COUNTRY

KREUZBERG

Riemannstr. 7 ☎030 694 01 160; www.anothercountry.de

Browsing this cluttered secondhand English bookstore feels a little like walking around some guy's house, but a wide and unpredictable collection rewards searching, especially since all books are €2-5. Another Country doesn't just want to be that forgettable place where you can buy a cheap copy of *Twilight* (€5); it wants to be a local library and cultural center. Ten to fifteen percent of the books are labeled "lending only," meaning they're priced a little higher (around €10), and you get back the entire price minus €1.50 when you return them. Plus, live acoustic performances, readings, and trivia add a further incentive to return again and again. Check out the wide selection of "Evil Books," which includes a copy of L. Ron Hubbard's *Dianetics*, *The Quotable Richard Nixon*, and a book entitled *Bradymania*.

🚉 *U7: Gneisenaustr.* 🕙 *Open Tu-F 11am-8pm, Sa-Su noon-4pm.*

music

🏴 SPACE HALL

KREUZBERG

Zossenerstr. 33, 35 ☎030 694 76 64; www.spacehall.de

They don't make them like this anymore in the States—maybe they never did. With two addresses (one of just CDs, the other strictly vinyl), Space Hall makes it nearly impossible *not* to find what you're looking for, plus 1001 things you aren't looking for. The vinyl store never misses a beat, with the longest interior of any Berlin record store (painted to resemble a forest, of course), and easily one of the widest selections to boot. They also have an inspiring collection of rubber duckies.

🚉 *U7: Gneisenaustr. From the Metro, head south on Zossenerstr. The record store is on the left.* Ⓢ *CDs regular €10-20, discounted €3-10. LPs €10-30.* 🕙 *Open M-W 11am-8pm, Th-F 11am-10pm, Sa 11am-8pm.*

shopping

HARD WAX KREUZBERG

Paul-Lincke-Ufer 44a ☎030 611 30 111; www.hardwax.com

Walk down a silent alleyway, through an eerily quiet courtyard, up three flights of dim, graffitied stairs, and suddenly, you're in one of Berlin's best record stores for electronic music. Bare brick and concrete walls make it feel aggressively nonchalant, while an entire back room dedicated to private listening stations for patrons show that Hard Wax is dedicated to helping you get out of the House. Dubstep, IDM, ambient, and subgenres upon subgenres of all shapes and sizes confound you from the shelves, but fortunately, nearly every CD and LP bears a short description in English courtesy of Hard Wax's experts, so you never feel like you're randomly flipping through a lot of crap. Though the selection is small compared to some of Berlin's other electro record stores, the offerings seem hand-picked.

🚇 U1 or U8: Kottbusser Tor. From the U-Bahn, head south on Kottbusserstr. Take a left just before the canal, then enter the courtyard on the left just after crossing Mariannenstr. $ Records €5-30, but mostly €8-12. CDs €10-20. ⏰ Open M-Sa noon-8pm.

FIDELIO SCHÖNEBERG

Akazienstr. 30 ☎030 781 97 36

For those looking to develop their finer tastes, or seeking to butcher the names of the world's greatest composers (give Rozhdestvensky a try—we dare you), Fidelio is the place to go. An extensive selection of classical CDs lines the walls, along with a smaller, but still impressive collection of jazz. If you've only just recently been inspired to give Wagner a listen, the staff here are more than happy to point newcomers in the right direction. Here and there, some vintage vinyl makes an appearance, but the major commodities are the CDs. Prices vary widely, but most CDs fall between €12 and €20.

🚇 U7: Eisenacherstr. From the Metro, head east on Grunewaldstr. and turn right on Akazienstr. Follow Akazienstr. for 2 blocks. The store will be on your right near the end of the 3rd block. ⏰ Open M-F 11am-7pm, Sa 10am-3pm.

MELTING POINT PRENZLAUER BERG

Kastanienallee 55 ☎030 440 47 131; www.meltingpoint-berlin.de

Berlin DJs frequent this small, whitewashed storefront for one of the most tremendous selections of international techno vinyl in Berlin. The records you can flip your grimy little fingers through are only the tip of the iceberg: a packed library extends back behind the clerk. If your techno tastes are obscure enough, you may have a chance to plumb the depths.

🚇 U8: Rosenthaler Pl. From the Metro walk northeast up Weinbergsweg, which becomes Kastanienallee. The store is at the corner of Kastanienallee and Fehrbelliner Str. $ Records €5-30. Cash only. ⏰ Open M-Sa noon-8pm.

FRANZ AND JOSEF SCHEIBEN PRENZLAUER BERG

Kastanienallee 48 ☎030 417 14 682

If you're looking for '80s punk and rock, this secondhand vinyl store will have what you're looking for. If you're looking for anything else, you're pretty much out of luck (sorry, bro-fi fans). The owner will tell you to expect to pay somewhere between €1 and €1000 for the vinyl, but most records thankfully fall into the lower part of that range (€10-30). Some real antiques hide in the €1-5 bins out front: they feature a wide selection of embarrassing Christmas albums that you can bring home for your grandma.

🚇 U2: Senefelderpl. From the Metro, exit from the northern steps, and head northeast on Schwedter Str. Walk 4 blocks and turn left on Kastanienallee. The store will be on your right. $ Cash only. ⏰ Open M-Sa 1-8pm.

essentials

PRACTICALITIES

- **TOURIST OFFICES:** Now privately owned, tourist offices merely give you some commercial flyer or refer you to a website instead of guaranteeing human contact. Visit **www.berlin.de** for reliable info on all aspects of city life. **Tourist Info Centers.** (Berlin Tourismus Marketing GmbH, Am Karlsbad 11 ☎030 25 00 25; www.visitberlin.de ⚢ On the ground floor of the Hauptbahnhof, next to the northern entrance. *i* English spoken. *Siegessäule, Blu,* and *Gay-Yellowpages* have GLBT event and club listings. ⓢ Transit maps free; city maps €1-2. The monthly *Berlin Programm* lists museums, sights, restaurants, and hotels as well as opera, theater, and classical music performances, €1.75. *Tip,* provides full listings of film, theater, concerts, and clubs in German, €2.70. *Ex-Berliner* has English-language movie and theater reviews, €2. ⏰ Open daily 8am-10pm.)

- **STUDENT TRAVEL OFFICES: STA** books flights and hotels and sells ISICs. (Dorotheenstr. 30 ☎030 201 65 063 ⚢ S3, S5, S7, S9, S75, or U6: Friedrichstr. From the Metro, walk 1 block south on Friedrichstr., turn left on Dorotheenstr., and follow as it veers left. STA will be on the left. ⏰ Open M-F 10am-7pm, Sa 11am-3pm.) **Second location.** (Gleimstr. 28 ☎030 285 98 264 ⚢ S4, S8, S85, or U2: Schönhauser Allee. From the Metro, walk south on Schönhauser Allee and turn right on Gleimstr. ⏰ Open M-F 10am-7pm, Sa 11am-4pm.) **Third location.** (Hardenbergstr. 9 ☎030 310 00 40 ⚢ U2: Ernst-Reuter-Pl. From the Metro, walk southeast on Hardenbergstr. ⏰ Open M-F 10am-7pm, Sa 11am-3pm.) **Fourth location.** (Takustr. 47. ⚢ U3: Dahlem-Dorf. From the Metro, walk north on Brümmerstr., turn left on Königin-Luise Str., then turn right on Takustr. ☎030 831 10 25 ⏰ Open M-F 10am-7pm, Sa 10am-2pm.)

- **POST OFFICES: Bahnhof Zoo.** (Joachimstaler Str. 7 ☎030 887 08 611 ⚢ Down Joachimstaler Str. from Bahnhof Zoo on the corner of Joachimstaler Str. and Kantstr. ⏰ Open M-Sa 9am-8pm.) **Alexanderplatz.** (Rathausstr. 5, by the Dunkin Donuts. ⏰ Open M-F 9am-7pm, 9am-4pm.) **Tegel Airport.** (⏰ Open M-F 8am-6pm, Sa 8am-noon.) **Ostbahnhof.** (⏰ Open M-F 8am-8pm, Sa-Su 10am-6pm.) To find a post office near you, visit the search tool on their website, www.standorte.deutschepost. de/filialen_verkaufspunkte, which is confusing, and in German, but eventually could help.

- **POSTAL CODE:** 10706.

EMERGENCY

- **POLICE:** Pl. der Luftbrücke 6. ⚢ U6: Pl. der Luftbrücke.

- **EMERGENCY NUMBERS:** ☎110. **Ambulance and Fire:** ☎112. **Non-emergency advice hotline:** ☎030 466 44 664.

- **MEDICAL SERVICES:** The American and British embassies list English-speaking doctors. The **emergency doctor** (☎030 31 00 31 or ☎018 042 255 23 62) service helps travelers find English-speaking doctors. **Emergency dentist,** (☎030 890 04 333).

- **CRISIS LINES:** English spoken at most crisis lines. **American Hotline** (☎017 781 41 510) has crisis and referral services. **Poison Control** (☎030 192 40) **Berliner Behindertenverband** has resources for the disabled. (Jägerstr. 63d ☎030 204 38 47; www.bbv-ev.de ⏰ Open W noon-5pm and by appointment.) **Deutsche AIDS-Hilfe.** (Wilhelmstr. 138 ☎030 690 08 70; www.aidshilfe.de) **Drug Crisis Hotline.**

essentials

(☎030 192 37 ☼ 24hr.) **Frauenkrisentelefon** Women's crisis line. (☎030 615 4243; www.frauenkrisentelefon.de ☼ Open M 10am-noon, Tu-W 7-9pm, Th 10am-noon, F 7-9pm, Sa-Su 5-7pm.) **Lesbenberatung** offers counseling for lesbians. (Kulmer Str. 20a ☎030 215 20 00; www.lesbenberatung-berlin.de) **Schwulen-beratung** offers counseling for gay men. (Mommenstr. 45 ☎030 194 46; www.schwulenberatungberlin.de.)

GETTING THERE

by plane
Capital Airport Berlin Brandenburg International (BBI) will open in southeast Berlin in June of 2012. Until then, **Tegel Airport** will continue to serve travelers. (Take express bus #X9 or #109 from U7: Jakob-Kaiser Pl., bus #128 from U6: Kurt-Schumacher-Pl., or bus TXL from S42, S41: Beusselstr. Follow signs in the airport for ground transportation. ☎018 050 00 186; www.berlin-airport.de.)

by train
International trains (☎972 226 150) pass through Berlin's **Hauptbahnhof** and run to: Amsterdam, NTH (Ⓢ €130. ☼ 7hr., 16 per day); Brussels, BEL (Ⓢ €140. ☼ 7hr., 16 per day); Budapest, HUN (Ⓢ €140. ☼ 13hr., 4 per day); Copenhagen, DNK (Ⓢ €135. ☼ 7hr., 7 per day.); Paris, FRA (Ⓢ €200. ☼ 9hr., 9 per day.); Prague, CZR; (Ⓢ €80. ☼ 5hr., 12 per day); Vienna, AUT. (Ⓢ €155. ☼ 10hr., 12 per day.)

beware of bikes

Painted or paved in red, Berlin's bike lanes skip the roads and take up space on and right next to the sidewalks. Stay off the red and stick to the gray pedestrian paths when walking to avoid nasty looks, ringing bells, and loss of life and limb.

GETTING AROUND

by public transportation: the bvg
The two pillars of Berlin's Metro are the **U-Bahn** and **S-Bahn** trains, which cover the city in spidery and circular patterns, (somewhat) respectively. **Trams** and **buses** (both part of the U-Bahn system) scuttle around the remaining city corners. (BVG's 24hr. hotline ☎030 194 49; www.bvg.de.) Berlin is divided into three transit zones. **Zone A** consists of central Berlin, including Tempelhof Airport. The rest of Berlin lies in **Zone B; Zone C** covers the larger state of Brandenburg, including Potsdam. An **AB** ticket is the best deal, since you can later buy extension tickets for the outlying areas. A **one-way** ticket is good for 2hr. after validation. (Ⓢ Zones AB €2.30, BC €2.70, ABC €3, under 6 free.) Within the validation period, the ticket may be used on any S-Bahn, U-Bahn, bus, or tram.

Most train lines don't run Monday through Friday 1-4am. S-Bahn and U-Bahn lines do run Friday and Saturday nights, but less frequently. When trains stop running, 70 night buses take over, running every 20-30min. generally along major transit routes; pick up the free Nachtliniennetz **map** of bus routes at a **Fahrscheine und Mehr** office. The letter "N" precedes night bus numbers. Trams continue to run at night.

Buy tickets, including monthly passes, from machines or ticket windows in Metro stations or from bus drivers. **Be warned:** machines don't give more than €10 change, and many machines don't take bills, though some accept credit cards. **Validate** your ticket by inserting it into the stamp machines before boarding. Failure to validate becomes a big deal when plainclothes policemen bust you and charge you €40 for freeloading. If you bring a bike on the U-Bahn or S-Bahn, you must buy it a child's ticket. Bikes are prohibited on buses and trams.

Single-ride tickets are a waste of money. A **Day Ticket** (Ⓢ AB €6.30, BC €6.60, ABC €6.80) is good from the time it's stamped until 3am the next day. The BVG also sells **7-day tickets** (Ⓢ AB €27.20, BC €28, ABC €33.50) and **month-long passes** (Ⓢ AB €74, BC €75, ABC €91). The popular tourist cards are another option. The **WelcomeCard** (sold at tourist offices) buys unlimited travel (Ⓢ AB 48hr. €17, ABC €19; 72hr. €23/26) and includes discounts on 130 sights. The **CityTourCard** is good within zones AB (Ⓢ 48hr. €16, 72hr. €22) and offers discounts at over 50 attractions.

LOCAL LAWS AND POLICE

Certain regulations may seem harsh and unusual (practice some self-control, city-slickers, **jaywalking** is a €5 fine), but abide by all local laws while in Germany as your respective embassy won't necessarily get you off the hook. Be sure to carry a valid passport with you as police have the right to ask for identification.

drugs and alcohol

The drinking age in Germany is 16 for beer and wine and 18 for hard alcohol. The maximum blood alcohol content for drivers is 0.05%. It's 0.00% for drivers who have only recently gotten their licenses. Avoid public drunkenness: it can jeopardize your safety and earn the disdain of locals.

If you use insulin, syringes, or any prescription drugs, carry a copy of the prescriptions and a doctor's note. Needless to say, illegal drugs are best avoided. While possession of **marijuana** or **hashish** is illegal, possession of small quantities for personal consumption is decriminalized in Germany. Each region has interpreted "small quantities" differently; the limit in Berlin is 10g. Carrying drugs across an international border—considered to be drug trafficking—is a serious offense that could land you in prison.

PHRASEBOOK

Nothing can replace a full-fledged phrasebook or pocket English-German dictionary, but this phrasebook will provide you with a few essentials. German features both an informal and formal form of address; in the tables below, the polite form follows the familiar form in parentheses. In German, nouns can be one of three genders: masculine (taking the article **der**; pronounced DARE), feminine (**die**; pronounced DEE), and neuter (**das**; pronounced DAHSS). All plural nouns take the article *die*, regardless of their gender in the singular. (Revolution girl-style!)

greetings

ENGLISH	GERMAN	ENGLISH	GERMAN
Good morning.	Guten Morgen.	**My name is...**	Ich heiße...
Good afternoon.	Guten Tag.	**What is your name?**	Wie heißt du (heißen Sie)?
Good evening.	Guten Abend.	**Where are you from?**	Woher kommst du (kommen Sie)?
Good night.	Guten Nacht.	**How are you?**	Wie geht's (geht es Ihnen)?
Excuse me/Sorry.	Enthschuldigung/Sorry.	**I'm well.**	Es geht mir good.
Could you please help me?	Kannst du (Können Sie) mir helfen, bitte?	**Do you speak English?**	Sprichst du (Sprechen Sie) Englisch?
How old are you?	Wie alt bist du (sind Sie)?	**I don't speak German.**	Ich spreche kein Deutsch.

essentials

useful phrases

ENGLISH	GERMAN	PRONUNCIATION
Hello!/Hi!	Hallo!/Tag!	Hahllo!/Tahk!
Goodbye!/Bye!	Auf Wiedersehen!/Tschüss!	Owf VEE-der-zain!/Chuess!
Yes.	Ja.	Yah.
No.	Nein.	Nine.
Sorry!	Es tut mir leid!	Ess toot meer lite!
EMERGENCY		
Go away!	Geh weg!	Gay veck!
Help!	Hilfe!	HILL-fuh!
Call the police!	Ruf die Polizei!	Roof dee Pol-ee-TSEI!
Get a doctor!	Hol einen Arzt!	Hole EIN-en Ahrtst!

CARDINAL NUMBERS										
0	1	2	3	4	5	6	7	8	9	10
null	eins	zwei	drei	vier	fünf	sechs	sieben	acht	neun	zehn

CARDINAL NUMBERS										
11	12	20	30	40	50	60	70	80	90	100
elf	zwölf	zwanzig	dreißig	vierzig	fünfzig	sechzig	siebzig	achtzig	neunzig	hundert

FOOD AND RESTAURANT TERMS			
bread	Brot	water	Wasser
roll	Brötchen	tap water	Leitungswasser
jelly	Marmelade	juice	Saft
meat	Fleisch	beer	Bier
beef	Rindfleisch	wine	Wein
pork	Schweinfleisch	coffee	Kaffee
chicken	Huhn	tea	Tee
sausage	Wurst	soup	Suppe
cheese	Käse	potatoes	Kartoffeln
fruit	Obst	milk	Milch
vegetables	Gemüse	sauce	Soße
cabbage	Kohl	french fries	Pommes frites
I would like to order...	Ich hätte gern...	Another beer, please.	Noch ein Bier, bitte.
It tastes good.	Es schmeckt gut.	It tastes awful.	Es schmeckt widerlich.
I'm a vegetarian.	Ich bin Vegetarier (m)/ Vegetarierin (f).	I'm a vegan.	Ich bin Veganer (m)/ Veganerin (f).
Service included.	Bedienung inklusiv.	Daily special	Tageskarte
Check, please.	Rechnung, bitte.	Give me a Nutella sandwich.	Geben Sie mir ein Nutel-labrötchen.

RIDICULOUS(LY) USEFUL PHRASES			
Here's looking at you, kid.	Schau mich in die Augen, Kleines.	Many thanks for the pleasure ride in your patrol car.	Vielen Dank für den Ausritt in Ihrem Streifen-wagen.
May I buy you a drink, darling?	Darf ich dir ein Getränk kaufen, Liebling?	I'm hung over.	Ich habe einen Kater.
Cheers!	Prost!	There is a disturbance in the force.	Es gibt eine Störung in der Kraft.
You're delicious.	Du bist lecker.	Inconceivable!	Quatsch!
That's cool.	Das ist ja geil/crass.	Hasta la vista, baby.	Bis später, Baby.

berlin

berlin 101

HISTORY

back in the day (750-1700)

In 750 CE, a settlement named **Spandau** was founded in the region now known as Berlin. Control over this town flip-flopped between Slavic and German rule for the next 350 years until the Germans finally gained power in the 12th century.

In 1150, Albert the Bear inherited most of the region and, under his reign, the Slavic and German tribes began to intermarry, slowly diminishing the distinction between the two. In fact, it turns out they really enjoyed each other's company—as things proceeded relatively peacefully, the population grew steadily, reaching roughly 8000 in the 15th century.

The 16th century, on the other hand, was not Berlin's happiest. Thirty-eight Jews were burned in 1510 after allegedly stealing the bread of the Holy Communion. Further persecution took place as Berlin was officially declared Lutheran during the **Protestant Reformation** of 1540. The **Bubonic Plague**—always a hit—struck the city in 1576. Just when Berlin had replenished its population, the **Thirty Years' War**—another favorite—rolled in from 1618 to 1648. What began as a religious conflict grew into a war of no purpose resulting in mega-destruction and the death of half of Berlin's population. The French saw this as a rare real estate opportunity, and, by 1700, 20% of the population was French. *C'est la vie.*

one frederick after another (1700-1870)

In the aftermath of the Thirty Years' War, Elector Frederick III decided that he would like to be called **Frederick I, King of Prussia.** He built himself a castle, renamed the region the "Royal Capital and Residence of Berlin," and did little else for the city. Things changed during the rule of his son, **Frederick William I,** and Prussia began to emerge as an important military force. Enlightenment thinking reached Berlin during the rule of **Frederick the Great,** but his son, **Frederick William II** enforced censorship and repression after he came to power in 1786. Berlin did see some liberalization, with its first public elections, the founding of the **Berlin University,** and reforms that allowed Jews to hold any job. Also, the revolution fever spreading across Europe reached Berlin in the mid-1800s, where it was quelled by Frederick William IV. In 1861, **Kaiser Wilhelm I** took the reins and so began the events that any student of modern European history is painfully familiar with.

it gets worse: from the empire to the third reich (1871-1940)

Wilhelm I appointed **Otto von Bismarck** as Chancellor in 1871. Bismarck had been instrumental in winning the **Danish-Prussian** and **Austro-Prussian wars,** in 1864 and 1866 respectively, and completed German unification by defeating France in 1871. The rest of the 19th century was a time of development in Germany: important infrastructure such as the **U-Bahn** and **S-Bahn** were built, the economy grew, and, in 1884, the **Reichstag** was built. At the end of WWI, the Weimar Republic was declared and conflicts between the Social Democrats (SPD) and the communist party (KDP) began to brew.

In 1933 **Adolf Hitler** was appointed Chancellor of Germany and Berlin became the capital of the **Third Reich.** In the years leading up to WWII, Hitler made sure all Berlin citizens knew who was boss. He disbanded the Weimar Constitution, increased his power immensely, showed off the Nazi regime for the rest of the world during the **1936 Olympics** and ordered the murder of six million European Jews, homosexuals, gypsies, socialists, and others.

berlin 101

berlin's favorite drink

You've all heard of German beer, and Berlin is no slacker when it comes to the celebration of this beverage. Berlin has its own unique specialty beer known as Berliner Weisse (Berlin White), a fizzy, sour wheat beer with about 3% alcohol. The beverage dates back to 16th-century Berlin, when Cord Broihan developed the beverage and was subsequently copied by the doctor J.S. Elsholz, who prescribed it to his patients. His patients enjoyed drinking the beer so much that they decided to share it with the healthy. By the 19th century, it became the most popular drink in Berlin, with about 700 breweries producing it. Popular legend claims that Napoleon's troops dubbed it the "champagne of the North." Now the beer has become rarer, with only two Berlin breweries still producing it. Due to its sour nature, beer aficionados typically mix in flavored syrups like raspberry or woodruff (the sweet flavoring also used in brandy, jam, and herbal tea), creating a drink known as *Weiss mit Schuss* (White with a shot). For a true beer drinking experience, sample some Berliner Weisse at the **International Berlin Beer Festival,** the longest beer garden in the world, held annually in August.

war and no peace (1940-45)

WWII hit Berlin hard. 1940 saw the first Allied **air raid** on Berlin. By 1943, Berlin had become a major target for bombardment. Thousands of Jews around Germany continued to be sent to concentration camps, and Berlin was a major site of deportation. By 1943, only 1200 (out of a previous 160,000) Jews were left in Berlin. As the war came to a close, the Allied powers raced each other to reach Berlin, an obvious political target. The **Red Army** got there first, and, soon after they moved in, Hitler committed suicide.

the aftermath (1945-90)

Conflict didn't end with the declaration of peace. Berlin was divided into four sectors, one each for the US, the UK, France, and the Soviet Union. Tensions rose in 1948, and, angered by the fact that the Americans wouldn't pay reparations and that the Allies wanted to join their sectors, the Soviets blocked off ground access to West Berlin, known as the **Berlin Blockade.** Though the blockade was eventually lifted, the Soviets decided they didn't want to share the city anymore. In 1949, they announced that they would independently govern their sector, now known as **East Berlin.** For years, the Soviets struggled to keep people from fleeing to West Berlin. They eventually decided a physical separation was necessary, and, on August 13, 1961, the first brick of the **Berlin Wall** was laid, essentially putting East Berlin in a permanent time-out. In the 28 years that the Wall stood, there were only 5000 successful escapes to West Berlin, while 192 people were murdered and 200 seriously wounded as they tried to cross. Meanwhile, the popularity of **student movements** increased, with young radicals starting parties in the shadow of the Wall. Riots and revolts were common, especially in the **Kreuzberg.**

The Wall stood strong until November 9, 1989. After a misleading press statement that led guards to believe the Wall would be opened, hundreds rushed the Wall, dancing and celebrating. Almost immediately, citizens took to the structure with hammers and chisels, and it was rapidly destroyed. Germany was officially declared reunited on October 3, 1990, after the Soviet Union collapsed throughout Europe.

life after the wall (1990-present day)

After the fall of the Wall, **Chancellor Helmut Kohl** led a unified Germany and, in 1994, Russian and Allied troops finally withdrew from Berlin. The rest of the 20th century and the start of the 21st was a somewhat tumultuous time politically for the country, with various resignations and transfers of power. In 1999, the German parliament made the move from Bonn to Berlin, restoring the city to its pre-war status as the nation's capital. Although it has come far since then—2005 saw **Angela Merkel** become the first female Chancellor—Berlin still struggles with many of the same issues facing the rest of the world. The economic slump of 2008 forced Germany into recession (from which it is still, understandably, recovering), and, in May 2011, the German government announced plans to phase out nuclear power over the next 11 years. With Germany as a leading world power, Berlin continues to be an important player in global affairs.

CUSTOMS AND ETIQUETTE

In Berlin, as in the rest of Germany, frankness should not be mistaken for rudeness. Simply put, Berliners are nice—just don't expect too much emotion, or get all sappy with them, and you should be fine.

r-e-s-p-e-c-t

When meeting someone for the first time, it is customary to lock lips. Just kidding. A quick (but firm) handshake will do. Make sure you are on time for your meeting—Germans put an emphasis on punctuality. Titles are also important to Germans, so it's a good idea to use *Herr* (Mr.) and *Frau* (Mrs.) followed by a surname unless invited to use a first name. Don't be intimidated by Berliners' tendency toward intense eye-contact—it's just a sign that they're *really* listening (and you would be wise to return the stare).

honor the haus

It is customary to bring a small gift when visiting a German's house—just like pretty much everywhere else in the world, flowers are a common one. Keep in mind that red ones (especially roses) imply romantic intentions. If you bring wine, opt for an imported one—bringing German wine screams "whatever you have to offer isn't good enough!"

If you're staying for a meal, don't be the first to seat yourself unless invited to do so. Your host will likely initiate a toast. Some common ones include "*Zum Wohl!*" (cheers) when drinking wine and "*Prosit!*" (toast) when drinking beer.

around town

When entering a small store, it's polite to say *Guten Tag* to the clerk, even if he is busy with another customer. And though English is spoken in most places, using German phrases such as *bitte* (please) and *danke* (thank you) for please and thank you are considered courteous.

At restaurants, it's preferred to hand your check and money directly to your waiter rather than leaving it on the table. When venturing to the bathroom, know that H stands for *Herren* (gentlemen) and D for *Damen* (ladies).

FOOD AND DRINK

What do Germans eat? In a word, meat. And more meat. And some more meat. **Currywurst,** slices of sausage served in a curry sauce, is an extremely common option throughout the city, sold on street corners and in restaurants alike. **Bratwurst,** another common street food, resembles an American hotdog. Traditionally it is made from pork, but today, it's frequently made from a combination of meats. **Kassler** is a cured and smoked slice of pork. Simple but yummy.

But fret not if meat isn't your thing. **Vegetarian** options are becoming increasingly popular in Berlin restaurants, if not among street vendors. If you look beyond meat and sit-down meals, you'll find a rich **coffeehouse culture** in Berlin. Berliners (and Germans in general) prefer their coffee thin, dark, and bitter. If you're unable to wrap your American head around the idea of a black coffee, you can order a **Milchkaffe** (that's right—coffee with milk); just don't complain when the locals scoff. Berliners also take pride in their pastries, particularly the **jelly-filled doughnut** (one of JFK's favorites). Outside of Berlin, it's called a *Berliner*, but in the city, they're usually referred to as **Pfannkuchen.**

And of course there's **beer.** Germans take their beer seriously. In fact, all beer is brewed in accordance with *Reinheitsgebot* or "beer purity law," which regulates the ingredients. If you're looking for something uniquely Berlin, order a **Berliner Weisse.** This pale, sour wheat beer is often served with a shot of flavored syrup to cut the tartness and presented in a bowl-shaped glass. And if your beer comes with a straw, ditch it. It's your waiter's way of saying, "I can tell you're a tourist."

HOLIDAYS AND FESTIVALS

HOLIDAY OR FESTIVAL	DESCRIPTION	DATE
Berlinale Film Festival	Berlin's version of the Oscars—but with trophies shaped like bears instead of little men.	February
Labor Day / May Day	An internationally recognized holiday honoring workers.	May 1st
Berlin Carnival of Cultures	An annual celebration of the melting pot that is Berlin. (Also, an excuse to dress up and get drunk.)	June
Berlin Beer Festival	Pretty self-explanatory, this festival is a good warm-up for Oktoberfest.	August
Jewish Cultural Days	An annual event honoring Berlin's Jewish population and educating the community about Jewish heritage.	September
Unity Day	This national holiday marks the official anniversary of German reunification in 1990.	October 3rd
Berlin Festival of Lights	A citywide celebration that involves laser displays and fireworks around major monuments, squares, towers, streets...and, of course, lots of beer.	October
Oktoberfest	Head to Munich for this world-famous beer fest. Book your tickets and hostel far in advance.	October

ART AND ARCHITECTURE

museums, manifold and multifarious

Europe and art go together like Alfalfa and Darla, and Berlin is no exception. The city boasts over 170 museums visited by millions of people each year. A good place to start is **Museumsinsel**—a mini island nested in the middle of the city that is home to some of its most famous museums. The **Bode Museum** holds a collection of sculptures, coins, medals, and Byzantine art. The **Alte Nationalgalerie** contains works from the eras of Classicism, Romanticism, and Impressionism as well as some early modern work. The collection at the **Altes Museum** is focused on classical antiquities, while the **Neues Museum** contains ancient Egyptian and prehistoric works. Last but not least, there's the **Pergamon Museum**, the most visited museum in Europe. The antiquities collection boasts actual sections of the **Pergamon Altar**, the **Gate of Miletus**, and the **Ishtar Gate.** Don your best sandals and loincloth a la King Nebuchadnezzar II (who commissioned the Ishtar Gate in Babylon in 575 BCE) for the full effect.

history: it's all around you

As you walk around the city it's hard to ignore its striking monuments. The nave of the Berlin Cathedral, better known as the **Berliner Dom,** is spectacular in its own right, but be sure to head downstairs if you enjoy the company of dead guys—it's home to the sarcophagi of roughly 90 Prussian royals. Other monuments of note include the **Victory Column,** representing the unification that followed the Prussian wars, the **Brandenburg Gate,** representing the unification of East and West Germany, and the **Reichstag,** which, after being razed by Nazi supporters, bombed by the Allies, and stormed by Russian troops, was renovated in 1999 as a symbol of—you guessed it—German unification. The **Olympiastadion** is a particularly eerie sight.

important graffiti (not an oxymoron)

Perhaps the most famous and extravagant graffiti in Berlin today is on the crumbling fragments of the Wall, which acts as a canvas for social, political, and artistic thoughts. There are paintings from before and after the fall that include sayings ("Crack is Wack" and "We Are The Wall"), cartoons (everything from raindrops to penises), and truly beautiful artwork by artists from around the world. The Wall embodies the youthful spirit that is quickly enveloping Berlin while simultaneously paying homage to the city's rich history. The **East Side Gallery** in Friederichshain preserves a portion of the Wall with graffiti by international artists made at the time of its fall in 1989.

dada art: the very first memes?

Berlin Dada artists served as inspiration for future snarky Photoshoppers with their cut-and-paste method of political satire. During the Weimar era, prominent German artists marked their moment in art history with photo collage, putting today's memes to shame. Here are a few names you should know:

- **GEORGE GROSZ.** Famous for his colorful yet macabre portraits, Grosz became a household name with his transvestite depiction of a famous German journalist Sylvia von Harden, portraying her with a man's face with protruding teeth and a monocle. In later years, Grosz's portrait patronage fell dramatically. We can't imagine why.

- **RAOUL HAUSMANN.** A known sexist, Hausmann was also considered a huge Casanova and created many male-centric pieces during his career. In one of his most famous sculptures, *Mechanical Head: The Spirit of Our Age,* he tacked rulers, tape measures, and other devices onto a wooden head. Some people like to read it as a critique of technology's domination in "our age," but ignoring the phallic symbols won't make them go away.

- **HANNAH HÖCH.** Notorious for her large-scale *Cut with the Kitchen Knife through the Last Weimar Beer-Belly Cultural Epoch in Germany,* Hannah Höch is considered the most famous female artist in Berlin Dada.

- **OTTO DIX.** Returning to Berlin after a stint at the front during WWI, Dix began making grotesque pieces of soldiers with their faces ripped off. Known for his anti-war critiques and pictures of human organs and dangling body parts, Dix gave new meaning to the acronym "TMI."

berlin 101

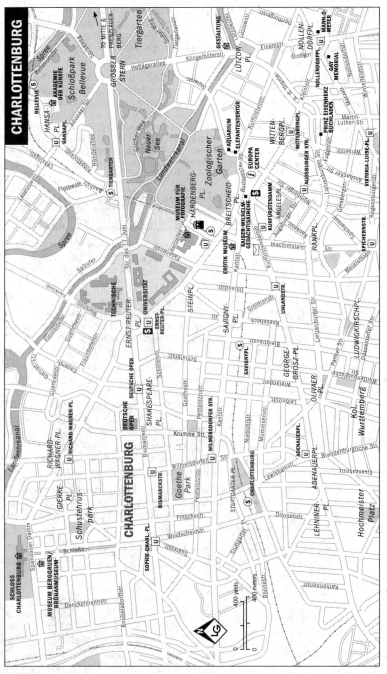

CHARLOTTENBURG

berlin

Tiergarten

TO MITTE & PRENZLAUER BERG

GROSSER STERN

Hofjägerallee

Schloßpark Bellevue

Spree

Bellevuestr.

AKADEMIE DER KÜNSTE

BELLEVUE Ⓢ

HANSA- Ⓤ PL. HANSAPL.

GESTALTUNG

NOLLENDORFPL. Ⓤ MANN-O-MEYER

Einemstr.

Klingelhöferstr.

LÜTZOW- PL.

GAY MEMORIAL

NOLLENDORFPL. ■

Großgörschenstr.

Martin-Luther-Str.

PRINZ EISENHERZ BUCHLADEN

WITTEN- BERGPL. Ⓤ

WITTENBERGPL. Ⓢ

AUGSBURGER STR. Ⓤ

VIKTORIA-LUISE-PL. Ⓤ

Neuer See

Landwehrkanal

AQUARIUM

ELEFANTENTOR

Zoologischer Garten

EUROPA CENTER ⓘ

KAISER-WILHELM- GEDÄCHTNISKIRCHE

Budapester Str.

S

KURFÜRSTENDAMM

Joachimstaler Str.

RANKPL.

SPICHERNSTR. Ⓤ

MUSEUM FÜR FOTOGRAFIE

HARDENBERG- PL.

BREITSCHEID- PL.

ANGELESPA

KURFÜRSTENDAMM Ⓤ

Kantstr.

ZOO Ⓢ

EROTIK MUSEUM

Hardenbergstr.

Fasanenstr.

Uhlandstr. Ⓤ

STEINPL.

SAVIGNY- PL.

Grolmanstr.

Knesebeckstr.

Schlüterstr.

Bleibtreustr.

Pestalozzistr.

TECHNISCHE UNIVERSITÄT

Str. des 17. Juni

ERNST-REUTER- PL.

ERNST- REUTER-PL. Ⓤ Ⓢ

SAVIGNYPL. Ⓢ

GEORGE- GROSZ-PL.

OLIVAER PL.

Leibnizstr.

Wielandstr.

Lietzenburger Str.

Pariser Str.

DEUTSCHE OPER Ⓤ

SHAKESPEARE- PL.

Schillerstr.

Goethestr.

Niebuhrstr.

Mommsenstr.

Wittenbergplatz Str.

DEUTSCHE OPER

Bismarckstr.

WILMERSDORFER STR. Ⓤ

Krumme Str.

Kantstr.

ADENAUERPL. Ⓤ

Brandenburgische Str.

Eisenzahnstr.

BISMARCKSTR. Ⓤ

RICHARD- WAGNER-PL.

RICHARD-WAGNER-PL. Ⓤ

Wilmersdorfer Str.

Pestalozzistr.

STUTTGARTER PL.

CHARLOTTENBURG Ⓢ

LEHNINER PL.

Hochmeister Platz

HOCHMEISTERPL.

Düsseldorfer Str.

Wittenbergische Str.

Kol.-Württemberg

GIERKE- PL.

Goethe Park

Fritschestr.

Lewishamstr.

Droysenstr.

Schustehrus-park

SOPHIE-CHARL.-PL. Ⓤ

Sesenheimstr.

Windscheidstr.

Stuttgarter PL.

Röntgenstr.

Kaiserdamm

Giesebrechtstr.

Christstr.

Fraunhoferstr.

Caprivistr.

Einsteinufer

Dernburgstr.

Salzufer

SCHLOSS CHARLOTTENBURG 🏛

MUSEUM BERGGRUEN / BRÖHANMUSEUM 🏛

Spandauer Damm

Schloßstr.

Danckelmannstr.

Knobelsdorffstr.

Spree

Landwehrkanal

Handelallee

Altonaer Str.

Klopstockstr.

Bachstr.

Flotowstr.

Großer Weg

Hofjägerallee

Tiergartenstr.

Tiergartenstr.

Lützowstr.

Einemstr.

Kleiststr.

An der Urania

Kurfürstenstr.

Nürnberger Str.

Tauentzienstr.

Regensburger Str.

Ansbacher Str.

Meinekestr.

TIERGARTEN Ⓢ

400 yards
400 meters

0
0

258 ℚ www.letsgo.com

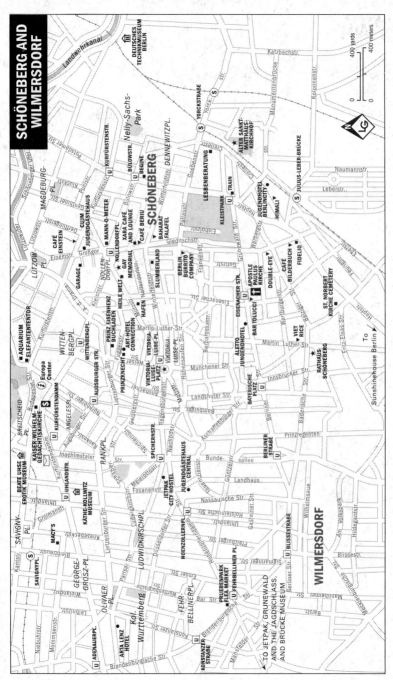

SCHÖNEBERG AND WILMERSDORF

Landwehrkanal

DEUTSCHES TECHNIKMUSEUM BERLIN

Nelly-Sachs-Park

Katzbachstr.

YORCKSTRABE

ALTER SANKT-MATTHÄUS-KIRCHHOF

BÜLOWSTR.

BEGINE

SCHÖNEBERG

LESBENBERATUNG

TRAIN

KLEISTPARK

JUGENDHOTEL BERLINCITY

HIMALI

JULIUS-LEBER-BRÜCKE

Naumannstr.

Leberstr.

CUM JUGENDGASTEHAUS

CAFÉ EINSTEIN

MANN-O-METER

XARA CAFÉ AND LOUNGE

CAFÉ BERLIN

BAHARAT FALAFEL

GARAGE

GAY MEMORIAL

PRINZ EISENHERZ BUCHLADEN

HEILE WELT

HAFEN

SLUMBERLAND

BERLIN BURRITO COMPANY

CAFÉ BILDERBUCH

FIDELIO

DOUBLE EYE

APOSTEL PAULUS KIRCHE

ST. NORBERT KIRCHE CEMETERY

AQUARIUM

ELEFANTENTOR

WITTEN-BERGPL.

WITTENBERGPL.

ART-HOTEL CONNECTION

PRINZKNECHT

VIKTORIA-LUISE-PL.

VIKTORIA

BAR TOLUCCI

VIET RICE

Europa Center

AUGSBURGER STR.

Martin-Luther-Str.

Münchener Str.

ALETO JUGENDHOTEL

VIKTORIA

Höhensaufen Str.

BAYERISCHE PLATZ

RATHAUS SCHÖNEBERG

Innsbrucker Str.

To Sunshinehouse Berlin

BEATE UHSE EROTIK MUSEUM

BREITSCHEID-PL.

KAISER-WILHELM-GEDÄCHTNISKIRCHE

KURFÜRSTENDAMM

ANGELESPL.

UHLANDSTR.

KÄTHE-KOLLWITZ MUSEUM

RANKPL.

SPICHERNSTR.

Landshuter Str.

Landhaus

BERLINER STRABE

Prinzregenten

Bunde-sallee

MACY'S

SAVIGNY-PL.

JETPAK CITY HOSTEL

JUGENDGASTEHAUS CENTRAL

HOHENZOLLERNPL.

Nassauische Str.

WILMERSDORF

ADENAUERPL.

ARTA LENZ HOTEL

Kol. Württemberg

PRUEBENPARK FLEA MARKET

FEHRBELLINER PL.

BLISSESTRABE

Blissestr.

OLIVAER PL.

GEORGE-GROSZ-PL.

LUDWIGKIRCHPL.

FEHR-BELLINERPL.

TO JETPAK, GRUNEWALD AND THE JAGDSCHLASS, AND BRÜCKE MUSEUM

KONSTANZER STRABE

Brandenburgische Str.

400 yards
400 meters

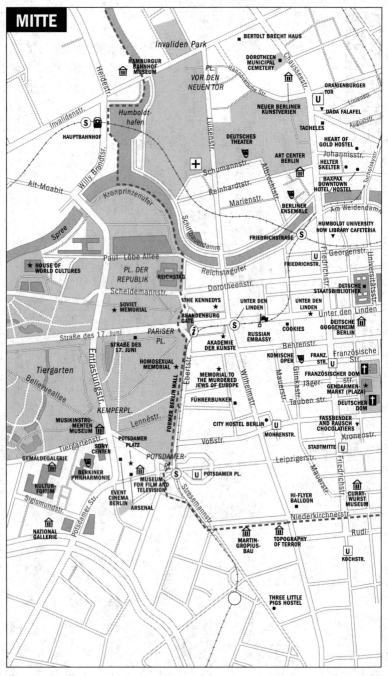

MITTE

Invalidenpark

BERTOLT BRECHT HAUS

HAMBURGUR
BAHNHOF
MUSEUM

DOROTHEEN
MUNICIPAL
CEMETERY

PL.
VOR DEN
NEUEN TOR

ORANIENBURGER
TOR

Heidestr.

Invalidenstr.

NEUER BERLINER KUNSTVERIEN

DADA FALAFEL

TACHELES

Luisenstr.

Hannoversche Str.

Chausseestr.

Humboldt-
hafen

HAUPTBAHNHOF

Willy Brandtstr.

Alt-Moabit

DEUTSCHES
THEATER

HEART OF
GOLD HOSTEL

Johannisstr.

ART CENTER
BERLIN

HELTER
SKELTER

Schumannstr.

BAXPAX
DOWNTOWN
HOTEL/HOSTEL

Reinhardtstr.

Albrechtstr.

Marienstr.

Kronprinzenufer

Am Weidendam

Spree

Schiffbauerdamm

BERLINER
ENSEMBLE

HUMBOLDT UNIVERSITY
NOW LIBRARY CAFETERIA

FRIEDRICHSTRASSE

Reichstagufer

FRIEDRICHSTR.

Georgenstr.

HOUSE OF
WORLD CULTURES

Paul- Löbe Allee

PL. DER
REPUBLIK

REICHSTAD

Scheidemannstr.

Dorotheenstr.

DETSCHE
STAATSBIBLIOTHEK

SOVIET
MEMORIAL

THE KENNEDYS

UNTER DEN
LINDEN

UNTER DEN
LINDEN

Unter den Linden

DEITSCHE
GUGGENHEIM
BERLIN

Straße des 17. Juni

BRANDENBURG
GATE

PARISER
PL.

COOKIES

STRAßE DES
17. JUNI

AKADEMIE
DER KÜNSTE

RUSSIAN
EMBASSY

Ebertstr.

HOMOSEXUAL
MEMORIAL

Behrenstr.

KOMISCHE
OPER

FRANZ.
STR.

Französische
Str.

Tiergarten

MEMORIAL TO
THE MURDERED
JEWS OF EUROPE

Wilhelmstr.

FRANZÖSISCHER DOM

Glinkastr.

Mauerstr.

Jäger-
str.

GENDARMEN-
MARKT (PLAZA)

Bellevueallee

FÜHRERBUNKER

Tauben str.

DEUTSCHER
DOM

Entlastungstr.

KEMPERPL.

Lennéstr.

CITY HOSTEL BERLIN

MOHRENSTR.

FASSBENDER
AND RAUSCH
CHOCOLATIERS

MUSIKINSTRU-
MENTEN
MUSEUM

Voßstr.

STADTMITTE

Kronenstr.

Tiergartenstr.

POTSDAMER
PLATZ

SONY
CENTER

POTSDAMER
PL.

Leipzigerstr.

Mauerstr.

Friedrichstr.

GEMÄLDEGALERIE

BERKINER
PHILHARMONIE

MUSEUM
FOR FILM AND
TELEVISION

POTSDAMER PL.

HI-FLYER
BALLOON

CURRY-
WURST
MUSEUM

KULTUR-
FORUM

EVENT
CINEMA
BERLIN

ARSENAL

Stresemannstr.

Niederkirchnerstr.

Sigismundstr.

Potsdamer Str.

NATIONAL
GALLERIE

MARTIN-
GROPIUS-
BAU

TOPOGRAPHY
OF TERROR

Rudi-

KOCHSTR.

THREE LITTLE
PIGS HOSTEL

berlin

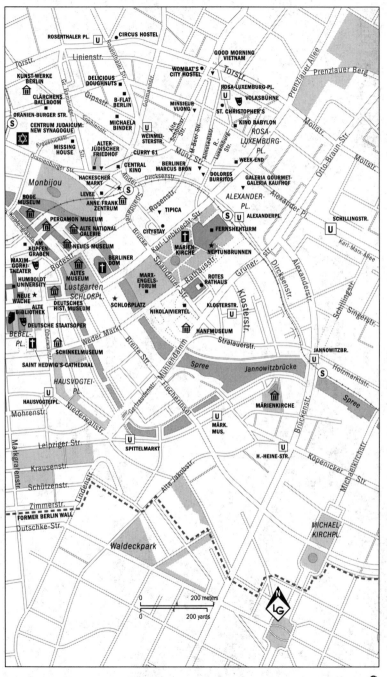

ROSENTHALER PL. 🚇 ● CIRCUS HOSTEL

Torstr.   Linienstr.

GOOD MORNING VIETNAM

Prenzlauer Berg

KUNST-WERKE BERLIN 🏛

WOMBAT'S ● CITY HOSTEL

Torstr.

DELICIOUS DOUGHNUTS

Gipsstr.

ROSA-LUXEMBURG-PL.
🚇 ● VOLKSBÜHNE

Prenzlauer Allee

CLÄRCHENS BALLROOM

DRANIEN-BURGER STR.

B-FLAT BERLIN

MINSIEUR VUONG ▼

ST. CHRISTOPHER'S

Möllstr.

Ⓢ

CENTRUM JUDAICUM: NEW SYNAGOGUE ✡

MICHAELA BINDER

🚇 WEINMEI-STERSTR.

KINO BABYLON

ROSA-LUXEMBURG-PL.

Otto-Braun-Str.

Möllstr.

MISSING HOUSE

ALTER JÜDISCHER FRIEDHOF

CURRY 61

WEEK-END

SCHILLINGSTR.

Oranienburger Str.

Monbijou

CENTRAL KINO

BERLINER MARCUS BRÄU ▼

Dircksenstr.

DOLORES BURRITOS

GALERIA GOURMET: GALERIA KAUFHOF

Ⓤ

BODE MUSEUM 🏛

HACKESCHER MARKT

LEVEE

Ⓢ

ALEXANDER-PL.

Alexander Pl.

SCHILLINGSTR.

Karl-Marx-Allee

ANNE FRANK ZENTRUM 🏛

Rosenstr.

PERGAMON MUSEUM 🏛

TIPICA ▲

Ⓢ 🚇 ALEXANDERPL.

ALTE NATIONAL GALERIE 🏛

CITYSTAY

FERNSEHTURM ■

NEUES MUSEUM 🏛

AM KUPFER-GRABEN

BERLINER DOM

MARIEN-KIRCHE ✝

NEPTUNBRUNNEN ★

MAXIM-GORKI-THEATER

ALTES MUSEUM 🏛

✝

Grüner-

HUMBOLDT UNIVERSITY 🏛

Lustgarten

MARX-ENGELS-FORUM

ROTES RATHAUS

Rathausstr.

Klosterstr.

NEUE ★ WACHE

SCHLOßPL.

SCHLOßPLATZ ★

DEUTSCHES HIST. MUSEUM

NIKOLAIVIERTEL

KLOSTERSTR. 🚇

Dicksenstr.

ALTE BIBLIOTHEK

BEBEL- 🏛 PL.

DEUTSCHE STAATSOPER

Weder Markt

HANFMUSEUM 🏛

Stralauerstr.

JANNOWITZBR. 🚇

SCHINKELMUSEUM 🏛

Breite Str.

Mühlendamm

Fischerinsel

Spree

Jannowitzbrücke

Ⓢ

Holzmarktstr.

SAINT HEDWIG'S CATHEDRAL

HAUSVOGTEI-PL.

Spree

Gertraudenstr.

🚇 HAUSVOGTEIPL.

MÄRIENKIRCHE 🏛

Mohrenstr.

Niederwallstr.

MÄRK. MUS.

Brückenstr.

Köpenicker Str.

Leipziger Str

🚇 SPITTELMARKT

🚇 H.-HEINE-STR.

Michaelkirchstr.

Krausenstr.

Schützenstr.

Zimmerstr.

Lindenstr.

Alte Jakobstr.

Makgrafenstr.

FORMER BERLIN WALL

Dutschke-Str.

MICHAEL-KIRCHPL.

Waldeckpark

0   200 meters

0   200 yards

N

LG

mitte map

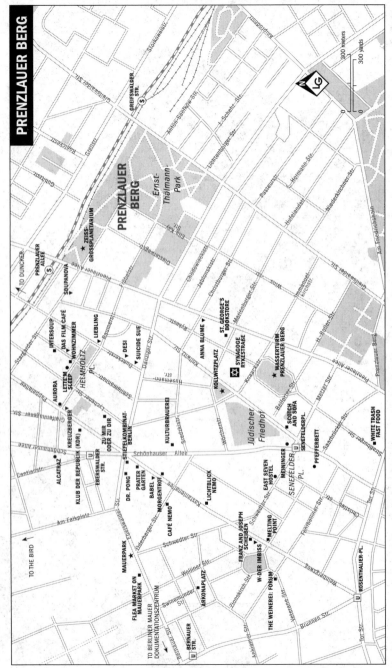

PRENZLAUER BERG

Ernst-Thälmann-Park

ZEISS-GROSSPLANETARIUM

SOUPANOVA

INTERSOUP
DAS FILM CAFÉ
WOHNZIMMER
LIEBLING
AURORA
LETTE'M SLEEP
DESI
SUICIDE SUE
HELMHOLTZ PL.
KREUZBERGER
ZU MIR ODER ZU DIR
ALCATRAZ
SIEFELKOMBINAT-BERLIN
KULTURBRAUEREI
KLUB DER REPUBLIK (KDR)
EBERSWALDER STR.
DR. PONG
PRATER GARTEN
BABEL
MORGENTROT
CAFÉ NEMO
Schönhauser Allee

ANNA BLUME
ST. GEORGE'S BOOKSTORE
SYNAGOGE RYKESTRASSE
KOLLWITZPLATZ
WASSERTURM PRENZLAUER BERG

Jüdischer Friedhof

SCOTCH AND SOFA
SENEFELDERPL.
PFEFFERBETT
WHITE TRASH FAST FOOD
EAST SEVEN HOSTEL
MEININGER
MELTING POINT
LICHTBLICK
NEMO

MAUERPARK
FLEA MARKET ON MAUERPARK
BERLINER MAUER DOKUMENTATIONSZENTRUM
BERNAUER STR.
ARKONAPLATZ
THE WEINEREI: FORUM
FRANZ AND JOSEPH SCHEIBEN
W-DER IMBISS

ROSENTHALER-PL.

TO THE BIRD
TO DUNCKER
PRENZLAUER ALLEE
GREIFSWALDER STR.

300 meters
300 yards
LG

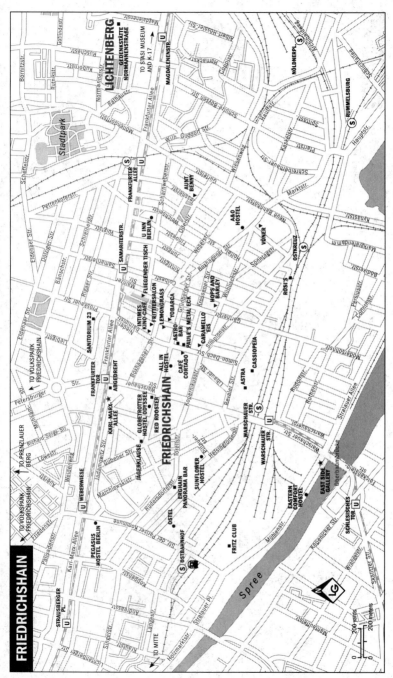

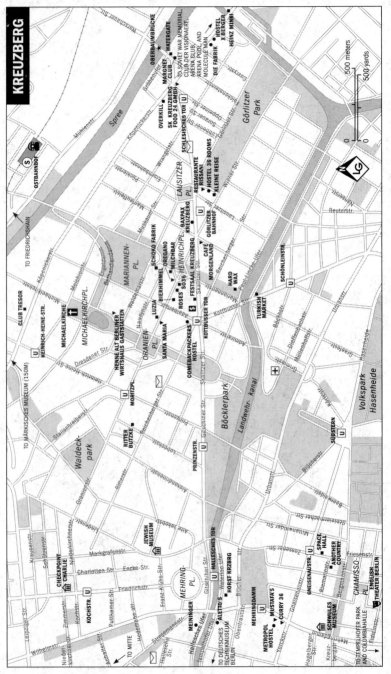

KREUZBERG

berlin

TO FRIEDRICHSHAIN
TO MITTE
TO MÄRKISCHES MUSEUM (150M)
TO DEUTSCHES TECHNIKMUSEUM BERLIN
TO TEMPELHOFER PARK AND COLUMBIAHALLE

OSTBAHNHOF

Spree

OBERBAUMBRÜCKE
WATERGATE
MAGNET CLUB
TO SOVIET WAR MEMORIAL, CLUB DER VISIONAERE, ARENA CLUB, ARENA POOL, AND MOLECULE MAN
DIE FABRIK
HOSTEL X BERGER
HEINZ MINKI

Görlitzer Park

OVERKILL
SK KREUZBERG FOOD 24 GMBH
SCHLESISCHES TOR

LAUSITZER PL.
RESTAURANTE RISSANI
HOSTEL 36 ROOMS
KLEINE REISE

KREUZBERG
GÖRLITZER BAHNHOF
BAXPAX
SCHOKO FABRIK
OREGANO
MILCHBAR
BIERHIMMEL
LUZIA
ROSES S036
HEINRICHPL.
FESTSAAL KREUZBERG
CAFÉ MORGENLAND
HARD WAX
KOTTBUSSER TOR
TURKISH MARKET

CLUB TRESOR
HEINRICH-HEINE-STR.
MICHAELKIRCHE
MICHAELKIRCHPL.
HENNE ALT BERLINER WIRTSHAUS GASTSTÄTTEN
ORANIEN-PL.
SANTA MARIA
COMEBACKPACKERS HOSTEL
MARIANNEN-PL.
MORITZPL.
RITTER BUTZKE
PRINZENSTR.

SCHÖNLEINSTR.

Böcklerpark
Landwehr Kanal

Volkspark Hasenheide

SÜDSTERN

Waldeckpark

JEWISH MUSEUM
MEHRING-PL.
HALLESCHES TOR
HORST KRZBRG
MEININGER
ALETTO'S
MEHRINGDAMM
METROPOL HOSTEL
MUSTAFA'S
CURRY 36
SCHWULES MUSEUM

CHECKPOINT CHARLIE
KOCHSTR.

SPACE HALL
ANOTHER COUNTRY
GNEISENAUSTR.
CHAMISSO
ENGLISH THEATER BERLIN

0   500 meters
0   500 yards

LG

FLORENCE

The Medici. Botticelli. Dante. What do these names, familiar to anyone who has studied history, art, or literature (or a combination of all three), have in common? All of them were natives of Florence, and their presence survives in the city today. As the birthplace of the Italian Renaissance and an epicenter for high culture, Florence has become one of the artistic treasure troves of the world. You can barely walk along the streets and *piazze* without running into famous works (or their replicas), and the myriad museums are rivaled in number by dozens of churches, which house priceless artwork and frescoes all their own. One might think that being a tourist in Florence would get old, once the splendor of walking through yet another museum with yet more artistic landmarks wears off. But this city is so much more than that: you can sip regional Chianti at the many cafes and bars, enjoy traditional Tuscan cuisine in trattorias and *ristoranti,* and view spectacular live performances of everything from music to theater. This is a city of purely Florentine sights, tastes, and customs, and if you allow yourself to embrace that culture, you'll no doubt leave feeling like a true *fiorentino.*

greatest hits

- **LINES BE DAMNED.** There's a reason people wait 4hr. to get into the **Uffizi.** See possibly the world's greatest collection of Renaissance art, and follow our guide to understanding the art and avoiding the lines (p. 281).

- **GELATO GIANTS.** Head to **dei Neri** (p. 303) or **Festival del Gelato** (p. 298) to cool off from the hot sun, or just to appreciate their deliciousness.

- **THE JOYS OF ACCADEMIA. Michelangelo's David** is the centerpiece of this museum in San Marco. There are numerous replicas all over the city (Florentines like to remind you of why they're great), but this is the real thing (p. 288).

- **BRIDGE OVER TROUBLED WATER.** Florence's "old" bridge, **Ponte Vecchio** was the only one the Nazis didn't destroy during their evacuation. Come here today to end up in someone's wedding photos or to land a smooch on your own bride-to-be (p. 284).

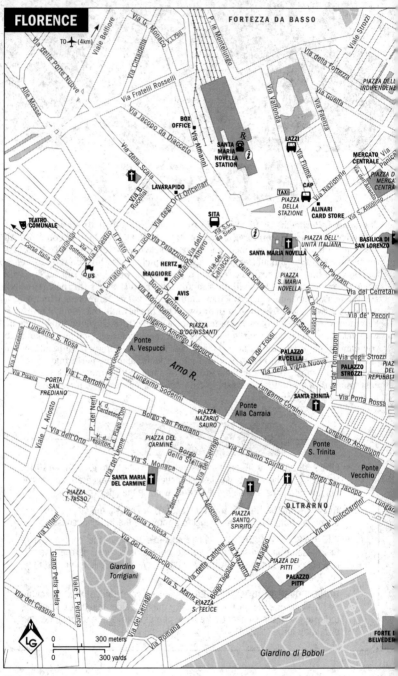

FLORENCE

FORTEZZA DA BASSO

TO ✈ (4km)

Viale Belfiore

Via G. Monaco

P. le Montelungo

Via delle Ponte Nuove

Via della Fortezza

Viale Strozzi

Via della Cittadella

PIAZZA DELL'
INDIPENDENZ

Via della Scala

Via Fratelli Rosselli

Via Valfonda

Via Guelfa

Via Jacopo da Diacceto

Via Almanni

BOX
OFFICE

SANTA
MARIA
NOVELLA
STATION

Via Fiume

LAZZI

Via Faenza

MERCATO
CENTRALE

Via
Panica

PIAZZA D
MERCA
CENTRA

Via della Scala

LAVARAPIDO

Via B.
Rucellai

Via degli Orti Oricellari

SITA

Via S.C.
a Siena

TAXI

PIAZZA
DELLA
STAZIONE

CAP

Via Nazionale

ALINARI
CARD STORE

Via Sant'Antonio

TEATRO
COMUNALE

Corso Italia

Via Garibaldi

Via sottomen

Il Prato

Via Palazzuolo

Via S. Lucia

Via dell'

Via de' Canacci

PIAZZA DELL'
UNITÀ ITALIANA

SANTA MARIA NOVELLA

BASILICA DI
SAN LORENZO

Via de' Panzani

BUS

Via Curtatone

Via Montebello

HERTZ

MAGGIORE

AVIS

Borgo Ognissanti

V. Fniggeria

Via dell'Albero

Via della Scala

PIAZZA
S. MARIA
NOVELLA

Via del Cerretan

Via de' Sole

Via delle Belle Donne

Via de' Pecori

PIAZZA
D'OGNISSANTI

Lungarno Amerigo Vespucci

Via de' Fossi

PALAZZO
RUCELLAI

Via de' Tornabuoni

Via degli Strozzi

PIAZ
DEL
REPUBBLI

Lungarno S. Rosa

Via d. Ancenella

Ponte
A. Vespucci

Arno R.

Via della Vigna Nuova

PALAZZO
STROZZI

Via Porta Rossa

Via Pisana

PORTA
SAN
FREDIANO

Via L. Bartolini

Lungarno Soderini

Lungarno Corsini

SANTA TRINITA

Lungarno Acciaiuoli

Via L. Ariosto

Via dell'Orto

P. del Neri

Via d. Cardatori

Via d. Tessitori

P. Piazza Cirò

Borgo San Frediano

PIAZZA
NAZARIO
SAURO

Ponte
Alla Carraia

Ponte
S. Trinita

Ponte
Vecchio

PIAZZA DEL
CARMINE

Via S. Monaca

Borgo
della Stella

Via de' Serragli

Via di Santo Spirito

Borgo San Jacopo

SANTA MARIA
DEL CARMINE

PIAZZA
T. TASSO

Via della Chiesa

Via dell'Ardiglione

Via S. Agostino

PIAZZA
SANTO
SPIRITO

Via Mazzetta

OLTRARNO

Via de' Guicciardini

Lungar

PIAZZA
Y. Villani

Via del Campuccio

Via delle Caldaie

Borgo Tegolaio

Via Maggio

PIAZZA DEI
PITTI

Giardino
Torrigiani

Via S. Maria

PALAZZO
PITTI

Giano Pretta Bella

Viale F. Petrarca

Via del Serragli

PIAZZA
S. FELICE

FORTE I
BELVEDER

Via del Casone

Via Romana

Giardino di Boboli

N

LG

0 _____ 300 meters
0 _____ 300 yards

florence

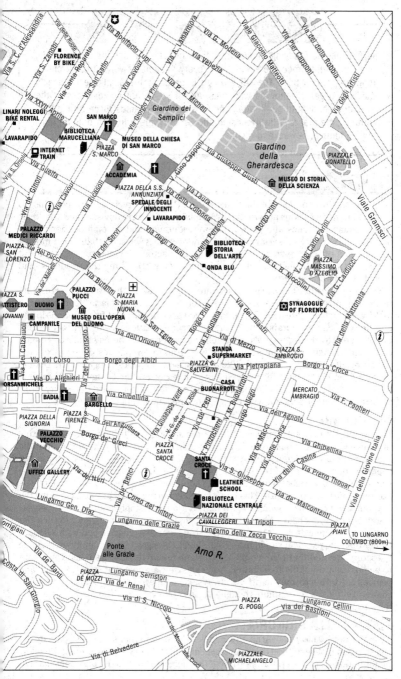

florence overview map

To find people studying things other than the sublime carving of the *David*, head to Santa Croce. Here you'll find every student's favorite things: cheap food and cheap beer. **The Oil Shoppe** is probably the single-best place in the city to get a sandwich with fries. And if you're not up for crossing the Arno and heading to book-laden and foosball-heavy **James Joyce Pub** in East Oltrarno, the *piazze* **Sant'Ambrogio** and **Ghiberti** are your best bets for finding students on a weekend night.

orientation

Welcome to Florence, land of the Renaissance. Painted, carved, and frescoed half to death, Florence's famous art practically bursts out of its ornately sculpted windows. Amid solemn churches and posh palaces, restaurants and accommodations often have to get creative, squeezing into tiny windows, alleyways, or abandoned monasteries. Many of these patterns repeat themselves across the city, so you might not notice that much distinction between neighborhoods. Don't tell the residents that, though: local pride is fierce.

Our coverage of Florence is divided into neighborhoods that roughly correspond to the major church districts. You'll most likely arrive at Santa Maria Novella Station in the western half of the city. This area is not especially different from stations in any other city; cheap restaurants and clustered accommodations await weary travelers. Follow the crowds to the city's geographical focal points: the ostentatious Duomo that dominates the city center and the River Arno that separates the city from the Oltrarno, a greener land that feels like a whole separate world. Between the Duomo and the river, Piazza della Signoria blends seamlessly into the Duomo neighborhood to form a hub for high-end shopping and tourism. The eastern third of the city looks after the student population with cheap pubs and kebab shops.

THE DUOMO

Florence's distinctive Duomo is perhaps the most helpful feature for wandering tourists—it's easy enough to find your way back here, so learn the route from the Duomo to your hostel and you'll never be lost. If you imagine a *piazza*-compass, the **Baptistery** points west and the Duomo points east. The tall tower just south of the Duomo is the **Campanile.** While the streets south off P. del Duomo run straight, the northern ones veer eastward. This huge, bustling *piazza* is full of tourists during the day, but the incredibly diverse crowd makes it a surprisingly cool place to people-watch. As with any heavy tourist zone, though, there are a few things to watch out for. Ignore the fake designer brands on the street, or risk being slapped with a fine far higher than the real deal would have cost. Check the signs before joining the snaking lines, or you could find yourself paying to climb hundreds of stairs when you meant to be poking around the free church. You can safely assume that street vendors and beggars are trying to rip you off. As always, keep an eye out for pickpockets. P. del Duomo isn't just a tourist hub, though—locals come here to drink and mingle once the sun and crowds have gone.

PIAZZA DELLA SIGNORIA

Near the **Uffizi Gallery** and Arno River, this *piazza* is perhaps the best part of the city to wander. Cheap food and accommodations are tucked away among the many ritzier options, but the eastern portion of this neighborhood is the best bet (near the

florence

abominable **Casa di Dante**). Take V. Calimala toward the Mercato Nuovo to observe the daily chalk art creations that are wiped clean by the noisy street-cleaning trucks. Outside the Uffizi, you'll often find human statues and other street performers, while **Piazza della Repubblica** is the place for live music. A block north of the river along Borgo Santi Apostoli, you'll find designer clothing shops with tempting window displays. Along the Arno, you'll primarily find unaffordable hotels, expensive home decor, and fancy leather. Piazza della Signoria is the place to be as the evening cools and the sweaty tourist mobs retreat.

piazza palooza

When looking at a map of must-see places in Florence, the word *piazza* is likely to show up often. The word refers to a paved public area, usually in front of a significant building or shopping area. If the dizzying number of *piazze* is overwhelming, put a pep in your tour-ridden step by asking about the stories behind your favorite square. For example, in 1869, architect Giuseppe Poggi solidified his man crush on Florence's greatest sculptor by erecting a monument in his honor, the Piazzale Michelangelo. Poggi's plan for a museum to accompany the park of statues was vetoed, with the building instead being transformed into a restaurant. This offers yet more proof that Italy's joy lies in not love of man or art, but of food.

SANTA MARIA NOVELLA

The Santa Maria Novella **train station** will likely be your first introduction to Florence, and the decision to venture east or south will color your earliest impressions of the city. To the east of the station you'll find the cheap accommodations and casual food joints that you'd expect near the train station of any major city. To the south, clustered around the church that gives the station its name, you'll find art galleries, modern museums, and a calm stretch of the Arno. Don't bother venturing north or west (unless you're trekking out to the Central Park nightclub) as you'll be leaving Florence's historic center before you've even set foot in it. Stop by in the evening to find happy young Italians smoking outside the entrance to their favorite bar or club.

SAN LORENZO

Just east of the train station lies a land of markets and 99-cent stores. Come for the cheap accommodations on **Via Faenza** and **Via Nazionale;** stay for the food around San Lorenzo's vibrant outdoor market on **Via dell'Aviento** and the adjoining **Mercato Centrale.** If you're only here for a little while, these will be the most memorable sights in San Lorenzo, which is light on museums. Nightlife is more of the relaxed bar variety and a bit removed from the more happening Florentine clubs.

SAN MARCO

By "San Marco," we mean pretty much everything between **Piazza di San Marco** and the northern edge of the old city. The primary draw of this area is the density of museums and bus stops, not to mention the (real!) statue of David in the **Accademia** (which, unfortunately, also comes with a block-long line of tourists). To the east, **Piazza Santissima Annunziata** has its own concentration of sights worth exploring. Late at night, stick to the southern edge of the area or travel with a friend—north of P. di San Marco is one of the quietest parts of the old city and can be unsafe after the buses stop running.

orientation

SANTA CROCE

Santa Croce is Florence's student and nightlife center and a great place to go exploring. The neighborhood spans the area east of the Duomo down to the river and is laced with cheap restaurants. Interspersed between the shops, food stations, and cultural venues, you'll find an exotic synagogue, the remains of many of Italy's greats, Michelangelo's house, and a once-a-year event where a bunch of guys in medieval garb beat each other up before a large audience. As you wander, note the neighborhood's walls—though plaques marking the water line of the 1966 Arno flood can be found all over Florence, the profusion of watermarks here show that Santa Croce was hit the hardest. **Piazza Santa Croce** is filled with clothing and leather shops, and the antique market under **Piazza dei Ciompi's** old arches is worth checking out even if you don't plan on lugging anything home. **Piazza Sant'Ambrogio** is the epitome of Florence's casual, *piazza*-based nightlife scene. If there were cheap accommodations in Santa Croce, it would be the best budget base in the city.

WEST OLTRARNO

This is the cool, artsy half of the Oltrarno, the area on the south side of the Arno. With a concentration of pharmacies, supermarkets, and dogs, it feels more authentic and lived-in than the other side of the river but still has a high density of hostels, museums, and study-abroad students. The main tourist draw is the **Palazzo Pitti** complex, but let the young and trendy vibe take you a few steps further to eat in **Piazza Santo Spirito** and explore the jewelry boutiques, art galleries, and studios nestled in the residential streets.

EAST OLTRARNO

The most common reason to trek to East Oltrarno is for the unbeatable view of Florence from the **Piazzale Michelangelo.** This generally quiet residential area is laced with some of Florence's most active nightlife, which makes crossing the river even more worth your while. We've set the Oltrarnos' dividing line at **Ponte Vecchio,** but you'll find a large residential stretch between the bridge and the lively evening entertainment around **Ponte San Niccolò.**

accommodations

The best way to get your money's worth in Florence is to travel in a small group, so if you're still hesitant to invite that slightly annoying friend with the buckteeth on this trip, remember that he could save you a fair deal of cash. Small groups can score gorgeous rooms in three-star hotels at the same price as a hostel, especially during the low season. Unfortunately, solo travelers with a fear of hostel showers are out of luck—singles in otherwise affordable hostels often cost almost as much as doubles. Those armed with flip flops and ready to brave the showers will find a few reputable hostels to choose from. If you're sticking around a little longer, consider commuting from a hostel outside the city, where you'll find better deals, cleaner air, and other travelers with similar priorities. Whatever you choose, you'll be glad to hear that prices drop significantly during the low season: you can save €10-20 per night when the city is less flooded with out-of-towners seeking beds. In our listings, we've stuck to high-season rates, so those of you traveling to Florence in February can silently gloat every time you read a price estimate and think about how much lower your rate will be.

THE DUOMO

While Florence is quite small, it's still expensive to stay right at its heart. There are a lot of options here, though none are super cheap. **Academy Hostel** is your best bet if you can book in advance. There are also many small hotels east and north of the Duomo that are surprisingly affordable considering their top-notch locations.

ACADEMY HOSTEL — HOSTEL $$

V. Ricasoli 9 — ☎055 23 98 665; www.academyhostels.eu

Don't wait another minute to make a reservation at this hostel—with only 30 beds and the best value in the neighborhood, it's no surprise that Academy doesn't have many last-minute vacancies. The nightly "snack" of pasta and wine brings guests together, though the small plates mean that everyone will know if you're trying to turn this snack into a meal. Academy keeps clean with a lengthy lockout and laminated signs that say things like "We aim to keep this bathroom clean. Gentlemen: your aim will help. Stand closer—it's shorter than you think. Ladies, please remain seated for the entire performance." You'll find everything you need here: a stock of Italy guidebooks, large lockers, beds (not bunked!) with privacy screens, towels, a smoker-friendly balcony, and an awesome complimentary breakfast, which includes the best fruit salad we've ever tasted.

➜ Less than a block north of the Duomo, on the left. ℹ Breakfast included. Free Wi-Fi in reception. Complimentary pasta and wine "snack" 6:30pm. [$] Dorms €29-34. Credit card min. €150. ⏰ Reception 24hr. Lockout 11am-2pm.

HOTEL LOCANDA ORCHIDEA — HOTEL $$

V. Borgo degli Albizi 11 — ☎055 24 80 346; www.hotelorchideaflorence.it

For almost the same price as a bed in a bare-bones dorm elsewhere, you can get a spacious room at Locanda Orchidea. Rooms are adorned with paintings and have large, clean shared bathrooms. Amid the homey charm of tile floors, leather couches, and an overgrown terrace, you'd hardly believe you're just a few blocks from the bustling Duomo.

➜ Take V. Proconsolo at the southeast edge of P. del Duomo and turn left onto Borgo degli Albizi. ℹ Complimentary tea and coffee all day. [$] Singles €30-60; doubles €50-80; triples €65-100; quads €75-120. Slight discount for stays over 2 nights. ⏰ Reception 8am-10pm.

HOTEL DALÍ — HOTEL $$

V. dell'Oriuolo 17 — ☎055 23 40 706; www.hoteldali.com

Located on V. dell'Oriuolo ("The Clock Road"), Hotel Dalí will persist in your memory not for its eccentric mustache but for the ornate wooden headboards on its pale orange beds. Simple rooms with rugs and stenciled walls overlook a small, verdant courtyard. Perhaps most surreal is Dalí's free parking in the middle of the Old City.

➜ About a 5min. walk down V. dell'Oriuolo from the Duomo. [$] Singles €40; doubles €65-70, with bath €80-85. Up to 20% discount on low-season rooms. Special offers listed online. ⏰ Reception 24hr.

HOTEL CASCI — HOTEL $$$

V. Camillo Cavour 13 — ☎055 21 16 86; www.hotelcasci.com

This old Medici palace passed through the hands of composer Gioachino Rossini just a few centuries ago, but now one of the 24 unique rooms can be yours. At Casci you can find fresh fruit, eggs, toast, and homemade cakes, with modern amenities like cable TV and mini-fridges. The family rooms are a great deal for a small group.

➜ Follow V. de' Martelli north of the Duomo to V. Camillo Cavour; Hotel Casci is on the right. ℹ Breakfast and small lockers included. Free Wi-Fi. [$] Singles €60-110; doubles €80-150; triples €110-190; quads €140-230. 10% discount for paying cash. Winter visitors get 1 free museum ticket for stays over 3 nights. ⏰ Reception 24hr.

RESIDENZA DEI PUCCI B AND B $$$$

V. dei Pucci 9 ☎055 28 18 86; www.residenzadeipucci.com

Each of the 12 doubles (and one panoramic suite) of this little bed and breakfast is different, but four-poster beds, glass-fronted armoires, and small balconies are common features. You can even bring the cereal, yogurt, and croissant to your room in hopes that a bribe of breakfast in bed will convince your traveling companions to hold your spot in line in the Duomo while you explore.

 # From north of the Duomo, follow V. Ricasoli and turn left onto V. dei Pucci. i Wi-Fi €10 per day. $ Doubles €80-150, superior €105-170; suite €120-250. €15 discount for single-occupancy doubles. ⏰ Reception 9am-8pm.

PIAZZA DELLA SIGNORIA

This area is the quintessence of convenience, but you'll pay for it with sky-high prices or fewer amenities. That said, it's prime real estate for a short stumble home or a couple nights of pretending you're filthy rich.

✓ **FLORENCE YOUTH HOSTEL** HOSTEL $$

V. della Condotta 4 ☎055 21 44 84; www.florence-youth-hostel.com

Roll out of bed and into the Uffizi—you can't get much more central than this. You may love the location during the day, but you'll be less of a fan at night when drunken student noise rises from the street. Here's what to do: down complimentary tea and coffee, (ET) phone home, and take advantage of the staff's uncommon willingness to give you advice about the city.

 # Coming from V. dei Calzaioli, the building is on the left. Florence Youth Hostel is on the top floor. i Wi-Fi, local calls and some international calls, maps, tea, and coffee included. No elevator. Breakfast M-Sa. $ Dorms €28; twins with bath €45; doubles €90; triples €105. Hot breakfast €2.50. ⏰ Reception 24hr.

HOTEL BRETAGNA HOTEL $$$$

Lungarno Corsini 6 ☎055 28 96 18; www.hotelbretagna.net

Hotel Bretagna floods your senses in class from the moment you step inside with soft classical music, subtle incense, and a postcard-perfect balcony. The feast for the senses continues with a literal feast in the palace-like breakfast room. Dream of ceiling frescoes in an unnecessarily large suite, or if you're frescoed out, the standard room's high ceilings are mercifully blank. Be sure to reserve a room with a corner bathtub or a view of the river.

 # Facing the river, it's 2 blocks right of Ponte Vecchio. i Wi-Fi and breakfast included. Tell reception if you are arriving by car. $ Singles €99-139; doubles €109-119. Prices vary by room and season, so check the website. ⏰ Reception 24hr.

HOSTEL VERONIQUE/ALEKIN HOSTEL HOSTEL $$

V. Porta Rossa 6, 2nd and 4th fl. ☎055 26 08 332

Be ready to explain yourself when you buzz for these two barebone hostels, because owner Alekin won't let just any old passerby into the building. Fewer rooms at Alekin Hostel (2nd fl.) mean less crowded bathrooms than in Hostel Veronique (4th fl.). The rooms here are all private, but what you're paying for a convenient place to crash.

 # Just north of Mercato Nuovo. i Free Wi-Fi. $ Private twins €34; doubles €67; triples €64; quads €78. Cash preferred. ⏰ Reception 24hr.

SANTA MARIA NOVELLA

As in most cities, there are plenty of budget hotels right next to the train station. If you roll into town late and are just looking for somewhere to crash, head straight to **Via Fiume.** The area between the station and the river offers mainly posh options; hostel-seekers should look in neighboring San Lorenzo. Whatever you seek, ignore the monstrous Majestic Hotel that is very visible from the train station—despite the building's valuable real estate, it is abandoned.

PENSIONE LA SCALA — PENSIONE $$$$

V. della Scala 21 ☎055 21 26 29

Bearded owner Gabriel, a stuffed crocodile, frescoed ceilings, and a nifty vintage radio (that sometimes works) set this quirky place apart from the generally yawn-worthy hotels in the area. With your room's abundant floorspace, you'll have space for a workout to burn off all that pasta, and you can shower in the full bath (so no one has to see your sweaty face afterwards).

 # Down from the train station, on the left. Look for the vertical Pensione sign; it's on the 1st floor. i All rooms with bath. $ Doubles €80-90; triples €120-135; quads €160-180. Cash preferred. ⏰ Reception 24hr.

HOTEL CONSIGLI — HOTEL $$$$

Lungarno Amerigo Vespucci 50 ☎055 21 41 72; www.hotelconsigli.com

The few extra steps it takes to get to Hotel Consigli are rewarded by a quieter area and an enormous rooftop terrace that overlooks the river. Small groups can score a 16th-century frescoed suite, though at this point you're probably wondering who doesn't casually offer old, original frescoes. In other news, Tolstoy stayed here, so you know they've done something right. And with the American consulate right next door, you're sure to be first in line for the airlift if Florence is invaded by zombies.

 # Follow the river west, just past the consulate on the right. i A/C. Wi-Fi, luggage storage, and breakfast included. $ Doubles €130-200; triples €170; family suite €130-170. ⏰ Reception 6am-midnight.

DESIREE HOTEL — HOTEL $$$

V. Fiume 20 ☎055 23 82 382; www.desireehotel.com

Stained glass is common for the hotels in this building, but at the Desiree it has broken out like gorgeous colored-window chicken pox. Find your perfect combination of balcony, chandelier, big antique armoires, and floral bathroom tiling. Walking through the Christmas-colored hallways to the sunny mini balcony may confuse your sense of season, but a little holiday cheer never hurt anyone.

 # V. Fiume is parallel to the train station. i A/C. Breakfast and Wi-Fi included. $ Singles €60-70; doubles €75-100; triples €99-125; quads €115-150. ⏰ Reception 24hr.

HOTEL SERENA — HOTEL $$$

V. Fiume 20 ☎055 28 04 47; www.albergoserena.it

Hotel Serena is the standard hotel incarnate, give or take some stained-glass doors. Reasonable prices make this a practical option with no big surprises—the most stressful room choice you'll have to make is along the lines of "tiled floors or hardwood floors?"

 # From the train station, turn left onto V. Nazionale then left onto V. Fiume. i A/C. Breakfast and safes included. All rooms with bath. $ Singles €45-75; doubles €60-110; triples €105; quads €100-175. ⏰ Reception 24hr.

HOTEL STELLA MARY — HOTEL $$$

V. Fiume 17 ☎055 27 41 599; www.hotelstellamary.it

After a dizzying day of art, Hotel Stella Mary's institutional white walls and big windows (don't jump!) may be just what you need. You might have to dodge a crowd of students to get in, though, since the building shares an entrance with an Italian language school. Between the students and its location across from the station, this hotel isn't for the noise-sensitive.

 # Look for the McDonald's when you exit the front of the train station. V. Fiume is 1 street over in that direction, parallel to the station. i Breakfast included. All rooms with bath. Pay for plug-in internet. $ Singles €60-70; doubles €70-83; triples €80-103. ⏰ Reception 24hr.

sexiest artwork alive

Italy has more than its fair share of beautiful people—both real and imaginary. Of course, no one wants to end up creepily falling in love with a statue, but here are *Let's Go*'s picks for the five sexiest artworks in Florence.

5. GIAMBOLOGNA'S MERCURY. He may not have the six-pack abs or bulging biceps of Hercules, but you've got to admit that this is a messenger god with poise. He's got a pretty cute butt, too. Ogle him at the **Bargello.**

4. CRISTOFANO ALLORI'S JUDITH. Judith would be higher up on our list if she wasn't holding a severed head. Still, with her sultry gaze, she's downright sexy. Word has it Allori modeled Judith after his mistress and the head after himself. Ogle her at the **Palazzo Pitti.**

3. VENUS DE' MEDICI. Exiled from Rome by Pope Innocent XI in 1677 (perhaps because her provocative nudity was making him feel less than innocent), this lovely lady has been a famously titillating highlight of European tours ever since. Ogle her at the **Uffizi.**

2. BOTTICELLI'S VENUS. It's hard not to be dazzled by this early bloomer. (Really, who comes out of the womb with hair like that?) Ogle her at the **Uffizi.**

1. MICHELANGELO'S DAVID. This choice is obvious but unavoidable. The symbol of Renaissance humanism, *David* oozes with the kind of charisma only an icon of human perfection can. He beats out Venus for our number one spot thanks to being in three dimensions rather than two. Ogle him at the **Accademia.**

SAN LORENZO

Check out **Via Faenza** for San Lorenzo's primary hostel scene. Proximity to the train station and the cheap food at the **Mercato Centrale** make this neighborhood one of the best places to stay in Florence.

florence

⛨ OSTELLO ARCHI ROSSI
HOSTEL $

V. Faenza 94r ☎055 29 08 04; www.hostelarchirossi.com

You'll have the best of times, you'll have the worst of times. The hostel's staff are sometimes too busy to care about your Wi-Fi difficulties or the miniature lake on your bathroom floor. But when you're strolling through the garden or past the graffitied walls gripping a free cappuccino and snacking on giant portions of pasta for a mere €2.50, your anger will melt away. Choose your room wisely—the lower the floor the better—to avoid the damp, overcrowded bathrooms on the upper floors. Lockers come with keys to keep out nosy roommates, but the luggage area is only under video surveillance. Despite its cons, this is definitely one of the best values in Florence, particularly for solo travelers on a budget.

⚑ *From the train station, take V. Nazionale and turn left onto V. Faenza.* **i** *Breakfast included. Beer sold at desk. Wi-Fi available. Rooms are equipped with computers.* ⑨ *Dorms €21-27; singles €40.* ⏱ *Reception 6:30am-2am. Curfew 2am; some travelers report that if you ring the doorbell, the door will open regardless of the hour.*

⛨ SOGGIORNO ANNAMARIA / KATTI HOUSE
B AND B $$$$

V. Faenza 21 ☎055 21 34 10; www.kattihouse.com

If you're traveling with friends and don't mind sharing queen-sized beds, don't hesitate to stay here. With exposed-beam ceilings, grandfather clocks, and an unusually enthusiastic staff, this bright bed and breakfast—which is split into

Soggiorno Annamaria and Katti House—wants to be your home away from home. Plus, they keep it all in the family: the brother of the titular Annamaria puts his 30 years of culinary experience to use, serving local specialties in the on-site restaurant (*primi* €6-8, *secondi* €4-14; three-course meal €25-30).

*# On V. Faenza, look for the doorway with all the Let's Go stickers. **i** Breakfast of cappuccino, croissant, and biscottini included. A/C. Wi-Fi available only in Katti house, but those staying at Soggiorno Annamaria are welcome to use it. [$] Soggiorno Annamaria singles €65-100. Katti House singles €75; doubles and triples €120-130.*

HOTEL ESTER
HOTEL $$$$

Largo Alinari 15, 2nd fl. ☎055 28 09 52; www.roominflorence.com

Don't let the grimy stairs or flimsy-looking elevator of the building's shared entryway put you off of these clean, colorful rooms near the train station. Your feet will love the cool hardwood after a long day's trek, and the rest of your body will appreciate the kitchen, flatscreen TV, and air-conditioning. Inquire at reception, which is decorated with terrain maps of Italy, about special deals for larger groups.

 # From the train station, turn left at the McDonald's; Hotel Ester is about 1 block down on the right. Luna Rossa is across the street but shares Hotel Ester's reception. [$] Mar-Oct doubles €75, with bath €90; Nov-Feb €55/60.

HOLIDAY ROOMS
HOTEL $$

V. Nazionale 22 ☎055 28 50 84

Three rooms with double windows to keep out the street noise face V. Nazionale, while a fourth faces the courtyard with a view of monuments that casually peek over the back wall. Nothing says "holiday" like sunny-colored walls, flatscreen TVs, and computers (and nothing says "room" like the wooden armoires). You won't even need the communal kitchen thanks to free breakfast and the machine that dispenses hot drinks for only €0.50 each.

*# Finding these aptly named 4 rooms is only slightly less difficult than the quest for the Holy Grail, but we've got you covered. On V. Nazionale, look for Hotel Nazionale on the right when walking away from the train station. Ring the bell to get in and climb the stairs until you see Holiday Rooms on the right. Enter Machia's on your left for reception. **i** A/C. Free Wi-Fi. [$] Singles €40-45; doubles €65-74.*

OSTELLO CENTRALE EURO STUDENTS/HOSTEL CENTRAL
HOSTEL $

V. Faenza 46r ☎055 41 44 54

Beware of cars when following the driveway entrance to this no-frills hostel. The beds are dorm-style without bunks, but what you gain in comfort you lose in floor space. The entrance is plastered with signs that read "No disturbing noise after 11"—you have to wonder if the owners were once the accidental audience to some travelers' tryst. There's something mystifying about this hostel: somehow, the tiny patio with potted plants lined up like a firing squad holds a certain charm.

 # From the train station on V. Nazionale, take a right onto V. Faenza and look for the driveway with flags. [$] Dorms €20-22.

SAN MARCO

Staying in San Marco is convenience at its laziest for the greedy museum-goer. As you go farther north, San Marco gets increasingly quiet and residential, which is great for daytime peace of mind but eerie late at night.

HOSTEL PLUS
HOSTEL $

V. Santa Caterina d'Alessandria 15 ☎055 46 28 934; www.plushostels.com

This chain hostel is better than chain smoking, chain mail, and maybe even daisy chains. The beastly gray building can feel empty without the tourist hordes, but this just means more room for you at the pool table, Turkish-style bath, gym, sauna, and tupperware-sized pool. When the place is crowded, be sure to bring your own lock, as the constant flux of people makes it easy for non-guests to walk in. Special offers include a pasta and wine dinner and all-you-can-eat breakfast combo (€10), day and night bike tours, and wine-tasting trips. Backpackers with a girly side will adore the pink all-female floor and hair straightener rental service. Pop into the rooftop terrace bar or the basement restaurant, where the disco ball doesn't care that no one is dancing.

⇞ Follow V. Nazionale until it changes names. Hostel Plus is the big gray thing on your left soon after P. dell'Indipendenza. i Wi-Fi. $ Dorms €20-25. ⏰ Reception 24hr. Walk-ins, come after noon to check availability.

DAVID INN HOSTEL $$

V. Ricasoli 31 ☎055 21 37 07; www.hostelfirenze.splinder.com

One of the few small hostels in Florence, the three rooms of David Inn sit on the top floor of a residential building and provide you with somewhere to sleep, but not much else. There's no common space except a few squishy couches against an orange wall, and the dorms are your basic bunk-bed situation. But the small hostel scene in town is fairly dire, so if Academy (see **The Duomo** above) is full or too posh for your hosteling tastes, try David Inn.

⇞ About 5min. north of the Duomo, on the right. It's the door with the funny pull knob doorbells. i Luggage storage. Wi-Fi. All-female room available. Cash only. $ Dorms €27. ⏰ Reception 24hr.

OSTELLO GALLO D'ORO HOSTEL $$

V. Camillo Cavour 104 ☎055 55 22 964; www.ostellogallodoro.com

San Marco's other small hostel lies in the quiet northern part of town. Ensuite bathrooms mean you might stand a chance at the shower being free when you want it. A sign at the reception desk reads "No partying on the balcony," as if you could somehow fit both a beer and yourself out there.

⇞ 5min. up V. Camillo Cavour from P. di San Marco, on the right. i Breakfast included. A/C. Wi-Fi. Room cleaning 10am-noon. $ Dorms €26-28; doubles €60; triples €96; quads €120. ⏰ Reception 24hr.

HOTEL GIOIA HOTEL $$$$

V. Camillo Cavour 25 ☎055 28 28 04; www.hotelgioia.it

If you're hopeless at finding hostels tucked discreetly into shared buildings, then this hotel's video-monitored, private entry from the street will be your favorite kind of conspicuous. The 28 rooms here are reminiscent of an American chain hotel—they must've ordered the bedspreads from Holiday Inn's supplier. Four couches make up Gioia's social scene, unless the TV is on.

⇞ Easy to find. It has its own door! i Breakfast included. $ Singles €95; doubles €140. ⏰ Reception 24hr.

HOTEL SAN MARCO HOTEL $$$

V. Camillo Cavour 50 ☎055 28 18 51; www.hotelsanmarcofirenze.it

You pay dearly for location at this small hotel, but at least you get a wooden dining room and a fully equipped kitchen. If you're lucky, you can catch an Italian soap on the common TV.

⇞ Just past the Gran Caffè from the piazza. i A/C. Wi-Fi. $ Singles €50; doubles €80. ⏰ Reception 24hr.

HOTEL BENVENUTI HOTEL $$$

V. Camillo Cavour 112 ☎055 57 21 41; www.benvenutihotel.it

This hotel is nothing exceptional—just plenty of rooms and in the quiet northern part of San Marco. Expect quite a few common sitting rooms, breakfast in a yellow and white dining room, and bedspreads that could get second jobs as tablecloths.

⇞ Walk north from P. di San Marco on V. Camillo Cavour. Pay attention to the doorbells on the right side as you near the end of V. Camillo Cavour. i Breakfast included. $ High-season singles around €64; doubles around €74. ⏰ Reception 24hr.

SANTA CROCE

Looking to minimize the stumble home after a night out? Unfortunately, you're out of luck. Affordable accommodations in Santa Croce are difficult to come by, so you may be better off looking in the adjacent Duomo neighborhood and just walking from there.

HOTEL ARIZONA

HOTEL $$$$

V. Luigi Carlo Farini 2 ☎055 24 53 21; www.arizonahotel.it

If you're studying at the university and your parents come to visit, this is a good place to put them; otherwise, you'll do better in another neighborhood. Rooms feature mini-fridges and often have tables or small balconies overlooking the street.

 # To the right of the synagogue, on the corner. i Free Wi-Fi. [S] Singles from €102; quads €145. Discounts for stays over 4 nights. ⏰ Reception 24hr.

HOTEL ARISTON

HOTEL $$$

V. Fiesolana 40 ☎055 24 76 980; www.hotelaristonfirenze.it

Ariston has two things to offer: space and convenience. Well, that and a mini plaster David (in case you haven't seen enough of that guy around Florence already). If you're desperate for a place to crash in Santa Croce, Ariston will do, but it's not the most affordable option in the city.

 # Look for the neon hotel sign from the intersection with V. Pietrapiana. i Breakfast included. Free Wi-Fi. [S] Singles from €45; high-season doubles €60-70. ⏰ Reception 8am-9pm.

the emperor's new retirement home

You probably don't spend much of your free time visiting retirement homes. So as you flit around Florence, keep in mind that the city was originally established in 59 CE as a retirement home for Caesar and his veteran troops. The average Roman soldier retired around age 40, when the time was just about ripe to buy that shiny new leather tunic and saddle. In their last conquest, these old timers named this city *Conolia Florentice*, or the Flourishing Colony. Though it's questionable how much these early residents flourished after settling here, the city they founded hasn't done too badly for itself.

WEST OLTRARNO

The hostels on this side of the river aren't significantly cheaper than more centrally located ones; they're best if you intend to spend the majority of your time in West Oltrarno.

HOSTEL SANTA MONACA

HOSTEL $

V. Santa Monaca 6 ☎055 26 83 38; www.ostello.it

This former monastery is massive enough to feature a 22-bunk dorm room. Follow the laminated, rainbow WordArt signs to your room. The simple kitchen, small balcony, and picnic-tabled common room are all kept clean during a strict lockout. Perks include free Wi-Fi, a refrigerator, and satellite TV in the common room. If you're not a light packer, don't expect your bag to fit into the lockers. The "kitchen" is poorly equipped and can get overcrowded during meals, but the proximity to P. Santo Spirito means you have plenty of dinner and after-dinner options nearby, as long as you manage to stumble back before the 2am curfew. This place is perfect for people who intend to spend the day without frequent trips back to the hostel.

 # From P. Santo Spirito, turn right onto V. Sant'Agostino and left onto V. Santa Monaca. i Free Wi-Fi. [S] Dorms €18-21. Laundry €6.50 per 6kg. ⏰ Reception 6am-2am. Curfew 2am. Lockout 10am-2pm.

SOGGIORNO PITTI HOSTEL, HOTEL $

Palazzo Pitti 8 ☎055 39 21 483; www.soggiornopitti.com

Soggiorno Pitti is a posh hotel with a hostel alter ego. You won't find their handful of dorm beds on the website—that might scare off customers looking for majestic doubles with a view of the *piazza*, which go for a hefty price. In the affordable range, you may have to deal with tiny stairs and shared bathrooms, but at least you've got the best location in West Oltrano and a big common room TV.

 # Across the street from Palazzo Pitti. $ Dorms €20; singles with bath from €45; doubles with bath €70-100. Cash only. ⏰ Reception 8am-11pm.

YOUTH FIRENZE 2000 BED AND BREAKFAST B AND B $$$

Viale Raffaello Sanzio 16 ☎055 23 06 392; www.cheap-hotel-florence.com

This bed and breakfast is anything but central, and by "breakfast" they mean sweet jam and fruit. It's on a busy road far from the main drag, but if you want to be somewhere more residential, Youth Firenze is about as local as it gets.

 # From Santa Maria Novella train station, board the #12 bus and ask for the 1st stop in Viale Raffaello Sanzio. $ Doubles with bath €60. Credit card €60 min. ⏰ Reception 7am-7:30pm.

EAST OLTRARNO

Unless you have a reason to stay in this neighborhood, you might as well book a room at a nice bed and breakfast a few kilometers away in Bagno a Ripoli. Either way, you'll still have to take a bus to reach the sights.

PLUS CAMPING MICHELANGELO CAMPING $

Viale Michelangelo 80 ☎055 68 11 977; www.camping.it

Camping sure sounds nice, doesn't it? A bit of the great outdoors, some greenery, roughing it a little? Don't be fooled. Whether you're packing a tent or renting a bungalow, this campsite has all the appeal of the neighboring Piazzale Michelangelo—which is to say, of a parking lot. The bungalows sleep two or three in bunk beds. You have to share a key, and there's no locker in the tent, so we don't recommend going halfsies on one with a stranger. The bathroom facility at the top of the hill is akin to the locker room at a large gym, Wi-Fi is expensive and limited, and the cafe is your only option for dinner that doesn't require a good walk. You'll only see Florence from a distance as a stunning view. Still, the low prices and relative isolation mean a crowd of other cheap travelers are always hanging around the outdoor bar, and for a small group the price couldn't get much better.

 # To the left of Piazzale Michelangelo, stay on the left side of the road and look for a small sign with a tent on it next to a steep downward path. Alternatively, take bus #12 to the Camping stop. ℹ Safe deposit boxes for rent at reception. $ 2-bed tents €29; 3-bed €36. ⏰ Reception 24hr.

VILLA ALLE RAMPE B AND B $$$

P. Francesco Ferrucci 6/7 ☎055 68 00 131; www.villaallerampe.com

If you have reason to be staying way over in East Oltrarno, the small and modern Villa Alle Rampe should do just fine. The rooms feel like an Ikea catalogue, there's a small garden, and you're just off the river.

 # Straight ahead from Ponte San Niccolò, across the street from James Joyce Pub. ℹ Wi-Fi included. $ Singles €60-75; doubles €70-100.

sights

This section can be summed up in a single word: Renaissance. Part of being in Florence is reaching the day when you've officially seen more of Jesus's face than your own mother's. You may be surprised by just how few Renaissance artists stray from the biblical theme, but they'll still manage to wow you again and again. If you think the religious theme means paintings of stern guys in robes, check out any rendition of Judgment Day, in which humans are skewered, devoured, or burned according to the horrifically inventive imaginings of the artists' twisted minds. Florence's architecturally masterful churches and fancy palaces attest to an age when the only people making it into the handwritten history books were religious authorities, the absurdly rich, and the artists they commissioned. Because the art collection is so vast, attempting to see too much too quickly will leave you with nothing but a devalued mush of crucifixes and semi-attractive women. It's best to choose a few select spots and take your time. When you've had enough Medici and Michelangelo for one day, there are a handful of unusual spots that aren't rooted in the 16th century. You can also check out www.firenzeturismo.it for information regarding current expositions, festivals, and other events in Florence.

THE DUOMO

The Duomo-related sights (the church and its complex) are pretty much the main event in this neighborhood.

DUOMO — CHURCH

P. del Duomo ☎055 23 02 885; www.operaduomo.firenze.it

Construction of Florence's Duomo began before anyone had come up with a solution to actually build and support the signature red dome that now pokes its head above the city. A man named **Filippo Brunelleschi** claimed he could build the largest and tallest dome ever made, and would do so without scaffolding. Though most called him a lunatic, he won the dome's commission in a contest without ever revealing how he actually planned to build it. Somehow, he came through in one of the greatest triumphs of Renaissance architecture. Just as beautiful as the dome is the shock of pink and green laced into the Duomo's stunning marble facade. Most tourists don't realize, though, that the facade was left unfinished until the 19th century (last Thursday by Florentine standards). The line to enter the free interior advances quite swiftly. Unfortunately, all the Duomo's artwork has been moved to the Museo Opera complex (see below), and to get a real view of the Duomo fresco you'll need to pay for the separate climbing entrance. Still, the 24hr. clock by **Paolo Uccello** that runs counter-clockwise is worth a look, and if you don't mind odd-smelling spaces, you can take the stairs in the middle of the church's floor down to the basement and pay €3 to see the archeological remnants of the Duomo's previous site.

🧭 Come on, you can't miss it. ℹ Audio tour available in English. $ Free. Archeological site €3. Audio tour €5, students and under 18 €3.50. ⏰ Open M-W 10am-5pm, Th 10am-4pm, F-Sa 10am-5pm. Holidays open 1:30-4:45pm. 1st Sa each month open 10am-3:30pm.

CAMPANILE AND DOME — CHURCH

P. del Duomo ☎055 23 02 885; www.operaduomo.firenze.it

Endless lines not tiring enough? Try climbing hundreds of stone steps! The Campanile's 414 steps are steep, not too crowded, and lead to a view of the Duomo's exterior. The Duomo's 463 are less strenuous, wider, and have a separate exit path, but their best feature is that they lead right past the bright Judgment Day fresco inside the dome. (How 16th-century painters Giorgio Vasari and Federico Zuccari managed to paint better 340 ft. above ground than most people can in a luxury studio, we really don't know.) Both climbs offer worthwhile views of

Florence and the surrounding hills. But if you're going to do that corny thing from the movies and meet your lover on top of the Duomo, make sure you settle on whether to meet at the dome or the tower. Otherwise, you might be staging your reunion via shouting and Semaphore flags.

♯ *Enter the dome from the north side of the round part of the Duomo. Enter the Campanile at the base of the big tower.* ⓘ *Not for the out-of-shape.* Ⓢ *Dome €8. Campanile €6. Tour of the dome and the cathedral's terraces €15.* ⏰ *Dome open M-F 8:30am-6:20pm, Sa 8:30am-5pm. Campanile open daily 8:30am-6:50pm.*

what not to wear

See that strip of naked brick around the base of the Duomo? As you might have guessed, plans for the cathedral included decoration that would cover this portion of the structure. In 1506, **Baccio d'Agnolo**, a talented young woodcarver, won the commission to complete this section of the cathedral. Unfortunately, only one side of the dome's octagonal base was covered with his design before Michelangelo dubbed it a "cage for crickets" and shut down construction. At least d'Agnolo was saved the acid comments Mickey G reserved for his own apprentice, **Bartolomeo Ammannati.** Upon viewing the Neptune Fountain Ammannati had constructed for the P. della Signoria, Michelangelo is rumored to have said to his pupil, "What a beautiful piece of marble you have ruined." Who knew *David*'s daddy was the Simon Cowell of the Renaissance?

MUSEO OPERA DI SANTA MARIA DEL FIORE   MUSEUM
P. del Duomo   ☎055 23 02 885; www.operaduomo.firenze.it
If the Duomo seemed a little empty to you, that's because all the art was moved here. Thankfully, this means an escape from the Duomo's crowds and a chance to get up-close and personal with some big-name artwork. Unlike many church museums, this one doesn't fade into a blur of chipped noses and column fragments. Instead, Donatello's *Maddalena* successfully dresses herself using nothing but her own hair, and *Mary of the Glass Eyes* makes up for her lack of pupils with her excessive creepiness. Unfortunately for him (and fortunately for you), you'll also find Michelangelo's *Pietà* here, even though the artist had intended it for his own tomb. Get a good look at Nicodemus—his features are sculpted to resemble the sculptor's own. On the second floor, models and sketches of the Duomo detail the long genesis of its 19th-century facade, displayed alongside the fixed pulleys and hoists used to construct Brunelleschi's dome.

♯ *On the south side of the Duomo.* ⓘ *Most texts in Italian, but the important ones are also in English.* Ⓢ *€6. Audio tour €3.50.* ⏰ *Open M-Sa 9am-6:50pm, Su 9am-1pm.*

BAPTISTERY OF SAN GIOVANNI   MUSEUM
P. del Duomo   ☎055 23 02 885; www.operaduomo.firenze.it
Though there's little else to see besides the Baptistery's magnificent doors, the mosaic ceiling could keep you staring upward until your neck gets stuck that way. Judgment Day scenes separated by columns on a sparkly gold background surround a massive Jesus, whose awkwardly shaped greenish toes dangle over the edge of a decorated circle. Until the 19th century, his stern visage presided over the baptism of Florence's infants, including **Dante.**

♯ *The octagonal building next to the Duomo.* Ⓢ *€4.* ⏰ *Open high season M-W 12:15-6:30pm, Th-Sa 12:15-10:30pm, Su 8:30am-1:30pm; low season M-Sa 12:15-6:30pm, Su 8:30am-1:30pm. 1st Sa of every month open 8:30am-1:30pm.*

florence

PIAZZA DELLA SIGNORIA

Piazza della Signoria is one of the most beautiful parts of Florence. Home to the city's most famous museum, the **Uffizi Gallery**, the area also holds innumerable noteworthy outdoor spaces from the **Ponte Vecchio** to the **Loggia**.

UFFIZI GALLERY

MUSEUM

Piazzale degli Uffizi 6 ☎055 23 88 651; www.firenzemusei.it

Welcome to the Uffizi. The first thing you should know about this museum is that Michelangelo's *David* is not here—he's on the other side of town, in the Accademia. Also, the *Mona Lisa* is in France, and de Nile ain't just a river in Egypt.

You're going to wait in line for what seems like an eternity. Consider passing the time by drawing terribly unflattering portraits of the people around you and trying to sell them for a euro. Alternatively, attempt to recreate Venus's hairstyle, guess the nationality of the others waiting in line, or convince everyone that you are the reincarnation of Botticelli and should be getting in for free.

If you're looking for an art history lesson, don't expect to find one in this listing. You won't find one in the galleries' texts either: although the explanatory panels are in both Italian and English, they're not hugely informative. Your best bet is to take an audio tour (€5.50) or to stick with *Let's Go*. The Uffizi's rooms are numbered; look to the lintel of the doorway to figure out what room you're in.

Start the Uffizi from the top. Don't crumple up your ticket at the bottom of your bag because, after climbing two flights of the Uffizi's grand staircase, you'll be asked to flash your *biglietto* once more. At this point, you're standing in an enormous hallway lined with statues and frescoed within an inch of its life.

Room 1 is on your right, but you can't enter. **Room 2** begins the long parade of Jesuses that you'll be visiting today. **Rooms 3-4** are particularly gilded. In Martini's *Annunciation*, Gabriel literally spits some Latin at Mary, who responds with the mother of all icy stares.

In **Room 6,** take some time with Fra Angelico's fun *Scenes From the Lives of Hermits*. Who knew hermits could be so social? If you're with a friend, try narrating some of the little vignettes or see if you can identify which clusters of hermits match the following made-up titles:

"And if you buy this one now, you'll get a second miniature stone FREE!"
"Not dead yet!"
"It rubs the lotion on its skin."
"The lion sleeps tonight."
"Psychiatric advice, five cents please."
"Questionably Appropriate Activities With Animals"

Room 8 is all about Fra Filippino Lippi. In the center of the room, his two-sided panel of a rather homely couple staring longingly at one another gives confirmation that even ugly people can find love.

Our second big-name artist is in **Room 9.** On your left, the seven virtues—which woman is which?—are lined up like dating show contestants, all painted by Pollaiolo. Well, all except for *Fortitude*, on the left. She is one of the earliest documented works by his student, a fellow by the name of Botticelli.

Rooms 10-14 are the main event. Where there be crowds and benches, there be the postcard works. Not that we need to tell you this, but Botticelli's *The Birth of Venus* is on the left—that's right, behind all those people. Push your way to the front to enjoy all the little details that don't come across in the coffee mug and mousepad reproductions, like the gold trim on the trees; the detail of the fabrics; the luminous, sleepy expression; and the weave Venus stole off Rapunzel. Look to the opposite side of the room for a big triptych with some seriously wonky perspective courtesy of Hugo Van Der Goes.

Room 15 is another example of the student surpassing the teacher. Examine the painting by Andrea del Verrochio across the room on the right. Several of the painting's figures—it is still contested which ones specifically—were painted by his student, Leonardo da Vinci. Maybe you've heard of him? The two paintings to the left are fully Leonardo's.

Odds are, you're going to start speeding up at this point, so to keep pace, you might want to take a break at the **cafeteria**—go out into the main hallway and follow the signs. This is your typical overpriced museum cafe, give or take a balcony view of the Palazzo Vecchio. Take some snacks with you or buy an espresso at the bar (stand outside to avoid the pricey table service) and refresh your brain.

Right then—where were we? **Room 19** has Pietro di Cosimo's depiction of Perseus tackling Andromeda, a monster with a serious under-bite. If you're getting sick of Catholicism, skedaddle to **Room 20** to view a couple rare portraits of Martin Luther. Ninety-five theses, three chins. **Room 22** has an Andrea Mantegna triptych on the right with a curved center panel that makes it seem 3D. **Room 25** proves that Salome knew how to get a head.

There's a seriously ginormous baby in **Room 29's** Parmigianino painting, which is called *Madonna of the Long Neck* for obvious reasons. A painting of a woman bathing hangs on the right wall of **Room 31.** What do you look at first? Don't be shy, we know you're eyeing her luscious breasts. And then you probably look at her legs and thighs, and perhaps the rest of her. And then, if you haven't yet turned away, maybe you will notice King David in the top left corner. The woman is Bathsheba, and Brusasorci's painting is remarkable for making the viewer mimic the intensity of David's ogling gaze.

Leda and the swan have finally gotten a room—**Room 32** to be exact. On the left in **Room 35** is a *Massacre of the Innocents* by Daniele Ricciarelli. Despite the pile of dead babies in this painting, *Let's Go* does not condone the making of dead baby jokes.

Finally, you'll reach the **Room of Niobe,** an impressive palatial space full of statues posed as if frozen in horror. These statues were discovered in the Villa Medici gardens and are supposed to be the unfortunate children of Niobe about to be slain by the gods as revenge for their mother's pride in her progeny.

If you have time and energy left at this point, the last few rooms are refreshingly different 18th-century stuff. If you don't, no one has to know. Congratulations on finishing the Uffizi; now you can go act like a Botticelli expert, even if the only thing you remember is Venus's terrible haircut.

*‡ It's the long narrow part of P. della Signoria. Enter (or stand in line) on the left, reserve tickets on the right. To avoid the lines without paying for a reservation, arrive late in the day, when your time in the museum will be limited by closing. **i** Expect to wait 2-3hr. to enter. $ €10, EU citizens ages 18-25 €5, EU citizens under 18 and over 65 and the disabled free. €4 reservation fee. Audio tour €5.50. ⏰ Open Tu-Su 8:50am-6:35pm.*

THE BARGELLO — MUSEUM

V. del Proconsolo 4 ☎055 23 88 606; www.firenzemusei.it

For a change of pace, the Bargello offers a nice dose of 19th-century eclecticism. Though you'd never know it from the inside, the Bargello was once a brutal prison. The statues here seem to know this—most are mid-kill, mid-struggle, or mid-sprint.

In the **courtyard,** once the site of public executions, be sure to look up. The ceiling frescoes are much more interesting than the old crest collection along the walls. Meanwhile, the meanest-looking fish you've ever seen awaits you to the left of the entrance, and several statues remain from an old fountain in which the three figures compete for who can place their spigot in the most suggestive location. In truly eclectic style, there's also a huge cannon and some Lion Kings from before Disney made them cool.

Pass the (very *Narnia*) lions to find a hall full of pagan (not so *Narnia*) sculptures such as Adonis and Bacchus as well as Musticci's *Madonna and Child.* Of all Florence's renditions, Musticci's is perhaps the most touching, human, and just plain adorable.

The courtyard stairs bring you to some stone fowl and a series of numbered galleries. **Room 4** is evidence of what you can make out of a little elephant tusk and a lot of skill—the minutely carved ivories range from tiny portraits to a giant chessboard. **Room 6** holds a huge collection of Maiolica, an earthenware pottery that is decorated before being glazed. **Room 8** will introduce you to the Ninja Turtle you know the least. This *Salone di Donatello* was designed for the artist's 500th birthday in 1887, and has remained unchanged ever since.

Room 9 contains probably the only Arabic script you'll see in Tuscany. This chamber is devoted to Islamic ceramics and textiles. **Room 10** is a true Victorian *Wunderkammer* (wonder-cabinet). There's the case of pipes, the case of bottles, and the collection of keys and locks. There are even table settings, scientific instruments, metalwork, jewelry, and that 17th-century spork you've been missing. On the third floor, check out the fantastic tiny bronzes in **Room 15. Room 13's** glazed terra cotta in blues, greens, and yellows creates a color scheme that will make you feel as if you've been sucked into a game of *Oregon Trail.*

 # Behind the Palazzo Vecchio. $ €7, EU citizens ages 18-25 €3.50, EU citizens under 18 and over 65 free. Cash only. ⏰ Open daily 8:15am-4:50pm. Last entry 4:20pm. Closed 2nd and 4th M and 1st, 3rd, and 5th Su each month.

cut to the chase

If there's one thing that can ruin the experience of seeing Florence's amazing art, it's long lines. Fortunately, the wait is totally avoidable. Avoid spending your whole trip in a sweaty queue by making a reservation beforehand. You can do so online, over the phone, or in person for both the Uffizi and the Accademia. Booking online is the priciest option since you'll pay at least a €4 reservation fee upfront. If you're staying in a hotel, ask your hotelier to book for you, generally at no extra cost. The best option is to call the Florence Museums telephone booking center at ☎055 29 48 83. With a reservation booking number in hand, you'll be ready to jump the line at both museums—definitely worth the extra €4 you'll pay when you purchase your ticket at the "reservations only" window. And, if it turns out there is no line when you arrive, you won't have paid any upfront reservation fee, so you can buy an unreserved ticket at the normal price.

PIAZZA DELLA SIGNORIA — PIAZZA

P. della Signoria is the place to go if you want to see sculptures without the museum prices. The **Loggia,** a portico full of statues that's as legit as any room in the Uffizi, is free. Don't be fooled by the *David* in front of the **Palazzo Vecchio**—the real deal is in the **Accademia.** The reproduction in the *piazza* stands just as proud as the original did when he was installed in this exact location to celebrate Florence's dominance over Tuscany. The Loggia does one-up the Accademia by being the true home of Giambologna's spiraling **Rape of the Sabine Women.** To the left of the *David* is a giant fountain that Michelangelo despised so much that he called it a waste of perfectly good marble. This bustling daytime *piazza* full of tour groups, art students sketching, and street musicians gets calmer and more pleasant in the evenings as music spills out of the square's restaurants.

⚑ *This is the main piazza north of the Uffizi.*

PONTE VECCHIO   BRIDGE

Looking for El Dorado? Here it is. On the Ponte Vecchio, the streets are paved with gold! And that gold is in the tons of gold shops that line this bustling bridge. It has been called the "old" bridge for, oh, 400 years or so, ever since the Florentines built a second bridge over the Arno and had to find a way to distinguish this one from their new *ponte*. When the Nazis evacuated Florence, Ponte Vecchio was the only bridge they didn't destroy. Come on a weekend afternoon and you are guaranteed to be in the wedding photos of at least half a dozen bridal parties. Visit at night for a romantic view of the river—and of other couples seeking the same.

⚑ *From the Uffizi, walk to the river. It's the one with the shops on it.*

PIAZZA DELLA REPUBBLICA   PIAZZA

For hundreds of years, this was the sight of the walled Jewish Ghetto, but when Florence's Jewish population was finally permitted to live and work elsewhere in 1888, the Ghetto was razed and paved over to create this spacious *piazza*. Now it's just another place to hang out, featuring a carousel (€2) and street performers. The restaurants surrounding the square are pricey, but their live music drifts into the open space for all to enjoy. Head to the northwest corner of the *piazza* where there is a large raised map of the city with streets labeled in Braille. Evenings in P. della Repubblica are more upbeat than in the more subdued P. della Signoria.

⚑ *From P. della Signoria walk north up V. del Calzaioli and turn left on V. Speziali*

PALAZZO VECCHIO   MUSEUM

P. della Signoria   ☎055 27 68 465

The real draw here is that it's the only museum you can visit post-*aperitivo*. As you proceed through the palace, framed paintings on the ceilings and walls might make you feel like you're trapped in a fine-art Rubiks cube, and the fact that the finest paintings are on the ceiling takes a toll on your strained neck. Not that you'll know what you're looking at—explanatory panels are as rare here as tour groups of wallabies. Just enjoy the overall beauty. And keep your eyes peeled for the man with long, droopy whiskers like Jar Jar Binx that appears all over the walls and ceilings throughout the palace. Some of the highlights are the Room of the 500s, which features worryingly aggressive statues for a room that used to hold a political council; a fleur-de-lis room that might as well have belonged to Louis XIV; and a map room walled with yellowing maps of Italy. The palace also has some impressive views: the **Salon of Leo X** provides a great photo op of the city and the surrounding hills, and the **Sala dei Gigli** boasts a spectacular view of the Duomo. Finally, don't forget to call ahead and book a free Renaissance reenactment!

⚑ *The huge building in P. della Signoria.* 𝒊 *Activities and tours with costumed actors available; call for times.* Ⓢ *€6, ages 18-25 and over 65 €4.50. Tours free if requested at time of ticket purchase.* ☒ *Open M-W 9am-midnight, Th 9am-2pm, F-Su 9am-midnight.*

CASA DI DANTE   MUSEUM

V. Santa Margherita 4   ☎055 21 94 16; www.museocasadidante.it

If you want to read about Dante from a wall instead of a book, this is the place for you. It isn't really Dante's house; it's a reconstruction of how Dante's house probably looked in the place his house probably was, with a few artifacts from Dante's time that have no specific connection to him. The slow-paced historical panels are easy to tune out—but if you do, there's really nothing left. If this place

florence

were free, we'd say why not. But we can't in good conscience send you to pay €4 for a kitschy giftshop and a Dante-esque robe.

✚ *On the corner of V. Dante Alighieri and V. Santa Margherita; it's very well marked.* Ⓢ *€4, under 6 free—but they won't get anything from it at all. Cash only.* Ⓔ *Open Apr-Sept daily 10am-6pm; Oct-Mar Tu-Su 10am-5pm.*

SANTA MARIA NOVELLA

Clustered around some notable churches, you'll find a few more modern museum collections here, like photography and shoes. These can provide a much-needed balance to all the Jesuses. For an additional off-beat option, check out the **Farmaceutica di Santa Maria Novella** (see **Shopping**).

▧ MUSEO DI FERRAGAMO   MUSEUM
P. Santa Trinita 5r   ☎055 33 60 456; www.museoferragamo.it

Ferragamo was like the Leonardo da Vinci of shoes: he brought anatomy, chemistry, and engineering into the creation of footwear. The shoe molds of famous people might make you feel like Bigfoot, and Ferragamo's elegant designs may make your own shoes feel clunky and out-of-place. But you don't have to be Carrie Bradshaw to appreciate a fashion and culture exhibit as thoughtfully assembled as this one, which includes video and painting. The gift shop is surprisingly tiny, but check out the real Ferragamo store upstairs to ogle shoes you can't possibly afford.

✚ *Enter at P. Santa Trinita on the side of the building that faces away from the river.* ⓘ *Ticket proceeds fund scholarships for young shoe designers. 1st and 2nd rooms are permanent; the rest of the exhibits change annually.* Ⓢ *€5, under 10 and over 65 free.* Ⓔ *Open M 10am-6pm, W-Su 10am-6pm. Closed Su in Aug.*

PALAZZO STROZZI   MUSEUM, PALAZZO
P. degli Strozzi   ☎055 27 76 461; www.palazzostrozzi.org

While this may seem like yet another old palace, no more impressive than any of the others, it isn't the seen-one-seen-'em-all Renaissance decor that makes Palazzo Strozzi worth visiting. The **Center for Contemporary Culture Strozzina,** which produces recent and contemporary art exhibits in the palace's halls, is the main draw here. To give you an idea, the likes of Dalí, Miró, and Picasso recently graced these halls, as did an exhibition on social media. The programming changes regularly, so check the website or stop by if you want to shake a little 21st century into Florence's 15th-century aesthetic. Free events often take place on Thursday evenings.

✚ *West of P. della Repubblica.* ⓘ *Prices and hours vary; check website for details.*

BASILICA DI SANTA MARIA NOVELLA   CHURCH
P. Santa Maria Novella   ☎055 21 59 18; www.chiesasantamarianovella.it

If you're only going to bother with one of the non-Duomo churches, consider making it this one. Between the checkered floor and plethora of 3D figures, this church could be a giant's chessboard, and in the morning or early evening, sunlight streaming through the stained glass may remind you of last night's disco. Upon entering the church, you'll see a fresco of God doing the *Titanic* pose with Jesus on the cross. Do you notice anything strange about this picture? If God is standing on that back platform, how could he be leaning far enough forward to be touching Jesus in the front? Rather than believe that Masaccio could have made such a salient perspective error, some art historians argue that this is symbolic of God's capacity to be everywhere at once. Cappella Strozzi on the left has a sadly faded fresco of Purgatory (inspired by Dante), where goblins, centaurs, and less familiar mythological figures like the man-dove hide or torture people. If the frescoes are too much for you, check out the giftshop postcards for bite-sized morsels.

✚ *Just south of the train station; you can't miss it. Enter through the P. Santa Maria Novella entrance.* Ⓢ *€3.50; over 65, visitors with disabilities, and priests free. Audio tour €1.* Ⓔ *Open M-Th 9am-5:30pm, F 11am-5:30pm, Sa 9am-5pm, Su and religious holidays 1-5pm.*

5 ways to survive art museums

Woe is you—you've accidentally befriended (or worse, started dating) an artsy type. As they gush and stare riveted at the walls, you're checking your watch for the 56th time. Never fear! Here's a quick list to help you avoid getting crushed by the incredible weight of your own boredom:

1. Frescoes are a race against time to paint everything before the plaster dries—try and guess which area the painter was on when he started running out of time.

2. Pretend to be a statue. Stare uncomfortably intensely at everyone that enters. If reproached, claim you are just trying to relate to the artwork.

3. In museums that allow cameras, take pictures only of one specific thing, like noses.

4. Lay down across the whole span of possible seating and close your eyes. When the museum proctor asks you to stop, open your eyes widely and tell them you just had an art-coma epiphany, and have now attained nirvana. Extra credit if you seamlessly segue into singing "Smells Like Teen Spirit."

5. Walk over to whatever painting your friends are looking at and pretend to be their tour guide. See how many other visitors you can get to eavesdrop on your extensive knowledge of how Leonardo, Raphael, Donatello, and Michelangelo had a secret society with a fighting turtle as its symbol, or how Michelangelo's *David* is actually a self-portrait from the waist down.

MUSEO NAZIONALE ALINARI DELLA FOTOGRAFIA — MUSEUM

P. Santa Maria Novella 14A ☎055 21 63 10; www.alinarifondazione.it

Despite the somewhat ambiguous name, this is not just a museum *of* photography, but a museum *about* photography. This means you can walk a giant roll of film like a red carpet through a hall of cameras from different time periods. Ornate albums accompany a fascinating range of pictures of everything from camels to early 19th-century Florence to an albino sword swallower. Flip through 3D binocular images, or feel the tactile versions of some photographs that have things like wigs attached to render them accessible to the blind. Check if there's a temporary exhibit—we attended one on the history of photographic controversies that was awesomely outrageous.

 # Across the piazza from Santa Maria Novella. ***i*** *Audio tour €4. Braille texts, audio tour, and 3D reproductions of some images available for the blind. Sign language tour guides available on request.* *[$] M €6, Tu €9, Th-Su €9; students and over 65 €7.50.* *⏰ Open M-Tu 10am-6:30pm, Th-Su 10am-6:30pm. Last entry 6pm.*

CHIESA DI SAN SALVATORE A OGNISSANTI — CHURCH

P. Ognissanti 42 ☎055 23 96 802

Stop by this church to pay your respects to **Botticelli,** who probably never imagined his own *St. Augustine* would adorn his final resting place. The solemn mood is set by the monks' chants wafting in from the neighboring monastery—oh wait, no, it's from the speakers on the wall. The church's simple architecture is masked by a great deal of imaginary additions, from the trompe-l'œil molding to a fairly convincing balcony painted on the ceiling. And, of course, the 2D balcony also has a fresco, which presents a ceiling painting of a ceiling painting. Try to wrap your head around that one.

 # 1 block north of the river. *[$] Free.* *⏰ Open daily 7am-12:30pm and 4-8pm.*

SAN LORENZO

PALAZZO MEDICI RICCARDI

MUSEUM

V. Camillo Cavour 1 ☎055 27 60 340; www.palazzo-medici.it

Welcome to the Medici's not-so-humble abode. The tiny chapel is flooded with frescoed Medici faces attending the Adoration of the Magi. Downstairs, motion sensor technology lets you point at a projection of the chapel's frescoes and, without touching anything, cue explanations in Italian, French, or English. If you're excessively tall or short, be prepared to flail unsuccessfully until the guard adjusts the camera. The palace also hosts the current provincial government. The members of this council can zone out during dull meetings to the image of fleshy angels in the **Sala Luca Giordano,** which are more impressive than the modern projection screen, conference table, and rows of plexiglass chairs. *Let's Go* does not condone taking water from the conference room dispenser.

⇟ From San Lorenzo you can see the back of the huge brown palace. Enter from the reverse side on V. Camillo Cavour. $ €7, ages 6-12 €4, people with disabilities and their assistants free. ⏰ Open M-Tu 9am-7pm, Th-Su 9am-7pm.

keeping up with the medici

It's impossible to tour Florence without hearing about the Medici, the family that ran the show here between the 15th and 18th centuries. While the Medici are best known for their banking skills, political prowess, and patronage to the arts and sciences, no family is without its eccentricities. Here's a crib sheet that'll help you keep the multi-faceted Medici men straight:

1. The first Medici to make it big was **Cosimo the Elder.** He was incredibly wealthy due to his father (Giovanni di Bicci) having founded the Medici Bank. He established his family's de facto rule in Florence by appealing to the working class, buying favors, and raising taxes on the wealthy. The players may change, but politics stays the same.

2. Cosimo had a son who was nicknamed **Piero the Gouty** because of the infection in his foot. He found it difficult to rule Florence with a swollen big toe, so he didn't last very long.

3. Despite their power, the Medici weren't always the coolest kids in the cafeteria. Rival families and a priest conspired to "sacrifice" Piero's son **Lorenzo** during a church service. After a brief period of expulsion (it's a long story), the Medici made a comeback in the early 1500s, helping to patronize artists like Leonardo da Vinci and Raphael.

4. Cosimo I de Medici is famous for establishing the Uffizi and Palazzo Pitti, ruling Florence, and patronizing the arts. He also deserves props, though, for embodying the "work hard, play harder" motto. In his free time he managed to father 15 children with four different women.

5. Cosimo II established the Medici family as patrons of science and technology. Cosimo *numero due* was Galileo's sugar daddy, supporting his research, giving him a place to stay, and offering him the chance to schmooze with the upper classes. In return, Galileo dedicated his books to the Medici, named some stars after them, and allowed the family first dibs on his new inventions, like the telescope.

MEDICI CHAPELS
MUSEUM

P. Madonna degli Aldobrandini 6   ☎055 23 88 602; www.firenzemusei.it

Even a dead Medici is bathed in more wealth than most of us will ever touch. The **Cappella Principe,** begun in the 16th century, should be a Guinness World Records runner-up for slowest project of all time—the frescoes weren't painted until the 1870s, and the fancy altar wasn't completed until 1937. Some statues were commissioned by still-living Medicis, while others (the empty slots) they expected their sons to fill for them. The ceiling in here is higher than the sky outside; we started counting how many dozens of us we would need to build a human pyramid to the top. The **New Sacristy** is smaller and less colorful, but we'll forgive its designer, a fellow named Michelangelo. And not to be crude, but goodness, someone should give the statue of *Night* a sweater, because she's clearly finding it a bit nippy, if you know what we mean.

✤ *It's the roundish building to the right of Basilica di San Lorenzo.* ℹ *Likely visit length: 30min. tops.* Ⓢ *€6, EU citizens ages 18-25 €3, EU citizens under 18 and over 65 free.* ⏰ *Open daily 8:15am-4:50pm. Closed 1st, 3rd, 5th M and 2nd and 4th Su each month.*

BASILICA DI SAN LORENZO
CHURCH

P. San Lorenzo   ☎055 26 45 184; www.sanlorenzo.firenze.it

The Basilica di San Lorenzo is just over 1600 years old. Its Old Sacristy has a small cupola painted with gold constellations on a midnight blue background that represent the sky over Florence on July 4th, 1442. You could save your €3.50 and instead peruse the night sky for free every 24hr., but there's no way Filippo Brunelleschi's version of it can be blocked by clouds or tall buildings. If you're determined to not spend any money, you can take advantage of the free private prayer section and sneak glances at the church, but you'll have to deal with your guilt when you then blow your money on a large gelato instead. If you're truly shameless, you could then take that gelato back to the church and eat it in the pleasant, and unusually green, cloister to the left of the basilica.

✤ *In P. San Lorenzo, just a little north of the Duomo.* Ⓢ *€3.50, under 10 free.* ⏰ *Open M-Sa 10am-5pm, Su 1:30-5pm.*

SAN MARCO

Around P. di San Marco, museum density and diversity soar, so choose your own adventure!

🖼 GALLERIA DELL'ACCADEMIA
MUSEUM

V. Ricasoli 60   ☎055 23 88 612; www.firenzemusei.it/accademia

Leonardo da Vinci once said that Michelangelo's figures resemble "a sack full of walnuts," but in a classic size comparison, whose masterpiece comes up a tad short? At an easy 17ft., it's no wonder the *David* can't find any robes in his size. Do you see those veins on his hand? The guy's a beast. Four unfinished statues by Michelangelo share *David*'s hall, trapped in the remaining block of marble like Han Solo encased in carbonite. You may understand on an intellectual level that the master's statues are carved from a single piece of marble, but seeing these unfinished works (who go by *The Slaves*) drives it home. One man. A bunch of chisels. One big rock.

If you've saved room for dessert after staring amorously at the *David*, head to the right of the entrance for a musical instrument gallery. Check out serpents, trumpet marines, and hurdy gurdies, but let someone else try the water spring bowl—same great sound, no need to get grimy hands. In the next room on the left, you may notice the adored gnomish son about to pick his nose, or, we don't know, the enormous *gesso* model of *The Rape of the Sabines.*

Past the *David* gallery on the left is a 19th-century workshop overflowing with sculpted heads and busts. Notice the little black dots freckling the pieces?

In the Accademia's days as an actual academy, the dots served as reference points for students making copies for practice. Upstairs, you'll see Jesus's face more times than you've seen your own mother's.

Tip: It's worth noting that visiting the Accademia generally won't take more than an hour. Bear that in mind when weighing the choice between paying extra for a reservation or waiting in a line that lasts far longer than you'll spend in the actual museum.

Line for entrance is on V. Ricasoli, off of P. di San Marco. ℹ Make reservations at the Museo Archeologico, the Museo di San Marco, or the Museo del'Oficio. The non-reservation line is shortest at the beginning of the day. Try to avoid the midday cruise ship excursion groups. $ €6.50, EU citizens ages 18-25 €3.25, art students EU citizens under 18 or over 65 free. Reservations €4 extra. ⏰ Open Tu-Su 8:15am-6:50pm. Last entry 6:20pm.

will the real david please stand up?

You've heard about the *David*. You've read about the *David*. You've seen coffee mugs and aprons and boxer shorts emblazoned with the *David*. And now you're ready to see the real deal. So you're making your way through Florence and wow! There he is! In all his naked *contrapposto* glory, chilling in the P. della Signoria. Not quite as impressive as the hype made him out to be, but then few tourist traps are. You snap a few pictures, pretend to grab *David*'s well-sculpted posterior, and congratulate yourself—you saw the statue. Your work here is done.

Think again. Do you really believe they'd keep the world's most famous statue outdoors? You can be forgiven for being fooled, though—that replica in the *piazza* rests right where the real statue originally stood before it migrated indoors in the 19th century. The replica is far from the only copy of the *David*—the world is swarming with models of the Michelangelo masterwork. Head up to the Piazzale Michelangelo to see another replica—and you haven't even left Florence yet. There's a replica at Caesar's Palace in Las Vegas and one at Ripley's Believe It or Not in Florida. The campus of California State University, Fullerton, has one whose buttocks are traditionally rubbed by students seeking good luck. At the Victoria and Albert Museum in London, a strategically placed fig leaf was once hung for visits from Queen Victoria and other delicate ladies.

So who needs to see the original, if replicas are a dime a dozen? Head to the **Accademia** and see the difference for yourself. Can't see it? At least you can feel superior to the amateurs who were tricked by the statue outside.

MUSEO DI SAN MARCO — MUSEUM

P. di San Marco 3 — ☎055 23 88 608; www.firenzemusei.it

Florence is hardly lacking in religious artworks, but Museo di San Marco packs in more than most. The themes may become repetitive, but the artistic importance of the works is impressive. The entrance courtyard features barely-there frescoes and some unattractive portraits that only get sadder when you imagine they are probably flattering. Enter the first room on the right for our favorite judgment day portrayal: on the hell side, people are eating what appears to be feces while others chew their own arms and *Lord of the Rings* style orcs string a man who appears quite content. Gold offsets dark paint in dozens of especially apathetic baby Jesuses (maybe Renaissance babies just looked like that), and when he's not an ugly baby or busy suffering for our sins, Jesus even randomly pokes his head into a study of drawing hands. Even Italian *paintings* use lots of hand gestures.

Upstairs, the museum is divided into the former cells of monks, each with its own painting on the wall. Pop inside and imagine spending four decades copying manuscripts by hand in there. Then look at Fra Angelico's famous fresco **The Annunciation** and imagine what it would be like if an angel arrived to announce that you were about to experience an unplanned pregnancy. In the last cloister on the right, note that the guy on Jesus's left doesn't appear to be suffering. This is because, five seconds before dying, he announced that God is his master, and as we all know, God practices the five second rule.

⚓ *The north side of the piazza.* ⓘ *Approximate visit time: 30min.* Ⓢ *€4, EU citizens ages 16-25 €2.* Ⓞ *Open M-F 8:15am-1:50pm, Sa 8:15am-4:50pm, Su 8:15am-7pm. Closed 2nd and 4th M and 1st, 3rd, and 5th Su each month. Last entry 30min. before close.*

BOTANIC GARDENS
GARDENS

V. Micheli 3 ☎055 23 46 70; www.msn.unifi.it

Listen. There are way more impressive botanical gardens in the world. Don't come here to learn about horticulture or to feel transported to a Chinese bamboo forest. Do come to sit somewhere green and relax. It is probably the best-smelling place in historic Florence outside of the Boboli Gardens, especially after it rains. Grab a bench to rest both your feet and your nostrils. Some say the Botanic Gardens are also a fine place to sneak a siesta, if you don't mind getting poked on the shoulder when a guard reluctantly decides to enforce the anti-vagrancy rules.

⚓ *Continue past P. di San Marco; the gardens are on the right (and kind of obvious).* Ⓢ *€6.* Ⓞ *Open Apr-Oct M-Tu 10am-7pm, Th-Su 10am-7pm; Oct-Mar M 10am-5pm, Sa-Su 10am-5pm.*

MUSEO DELL'OPIFICIO DELLE PIETRE DURE
MUSEUM

V. degli Alfani 78 ☎055 26 51 11; www.opificiodellepietredure.it

If the word "mosaic" makes you think of your elementary school walls, you are in for a surprise. Here, mosaics are slabs of stone cut to fit together like colored, unimaginably detailed puzzle pieces. Sure, a lot of the themes are pretty standard. You've got your typical birds, fruit, crests, and flowers—but you've also got LOL (Lots of Lions!), side-by-side paintings and mosaics of the same scene, and countrysides and faces you won't believe are made of stone. Upstairs, you can see the tools and process laid out, in case you thought you might actually recreate these masterpieces. A good look around won't take you more than 30min., but it's a change of pace from the Jesus paintings.

⚓ *From P. di San Marco, head 1 block down Ricasoli then left onto V. degli Alfani.* Ⓢ *€4; EU citizens ages 18-25 €1; EU citizens under 18 and over 65, students and professors of architecture, art, or even literature or philosophy with an inscription certificate free.* Ⓞ *Open M-Sa 8:15am-2pm.*

MUSEO DEGLI INNOCENTI
MUSEUM

P. della Santissima Annunziata 12 ☎055 20 37 323; www.istitutodeglinnocenti.it

In 1251, Florence decided that a guild of silk workers would protect and educate Florence's abandoned children. Foundlings, silk... the connection is obvious, right? This massive, terracotta-adorned hospital, where unwed mothers once served as wet nurses in exchange for being assisted in childbirth there, is now a UNICEF center, so you're bound to see some miniature Italians ushered through the courtyard by their impatient mothers. The museum portion is home to the orphanage's absurdly rich art collection, from standard oversized religious paintings to dioramas that will throw you back to your middle school book report days—including one that shows off the actual bones of St. Marcus. This place has some crazy history, but if your wallet's not feeling it, or for some reason you don't have a burning desire to see the birthplace of artificial nursing, you could always just read about the place. Ask at the desk about temporary exhibits in the cavernous basement which can make the €4 fee less painful.

⚓ *On the right in P. di San Marco. It's the one with the babies on it.* Ⓢ *€4, children and seniors €2.50.* Ⓞ *Open daily 10am-7pm. Last entry 6:30pm.*

MACCHINE DI LEONARDO MUSEUM

V. Camillo Cavour 21 ☎055 29 52 64; www.macchinedileonardo.com

No, these models were not built by Leonardo da Vinci's own hand. Yes, this means you can touch them. The museum is a collection of realized models of Leonardo's many ahead-of-his-time blueprints. Get your money's worth by watching the Italian or English series about the artist's life, which—despite reading the English translations of notebook excerpts in a cheesy Italian accent—reveals lesser-known sides of the artist, from his cooperation with a pillaging lord to his love of autopsies.

 # 5min. up V. Camillo Cavour from the Duomo, on the left. $ €7. ⏰ Open daily 9:30am-7:30pm.

MUSEO ARCHEOLOGICO MUSEUM

P. Santissima Annunziata 9B ☎055 23 575; www.archeotoscana.beniculturali.it

Florence is admittedly a strange place for the Ancient Egyptian knickknacks that begin this exhibit, but if you were impressed by how old the rest of Florence's art was, this place will floor you. Browse sphynxes, mummies, and statuettes displayed on shelves like they were a child's figurine collection. The space is way too large for the number of objects on display, so there's twice as many posters as actual artifacts. If you like eerie rooms with old things and don't care much for background information (or if you know something about archeology), this is the place for you.

 # Facing P. Santissima Annunziata, it's on the right. $ €4, EU citizens ages 18-25 €2, EU citizens under 18 and over 65 free. ⏰ Open Tu-F 8:30am-7pm, Sa-Su 8:30am-2pm.

SANTA CROCE

Santa Croce is a little out of the way of the main attractions, but its scattered sights are some of Florence's most memorable.

SYNAGOGUE OF FLORENCE SYNAGOGUE, MUSEUM

V. Luigi Carlo Farini 4 ☎055 24 52 52

This beautiful building definitely doesn't fade into the surrounding Florentine architecture. Its conspicuousness was a bold choice: when it was built, the Jewish population still lived in a walled ghetto in the city center and most synagogues were designed to blend in to avoid drawing attention to the community. Constructed in 1868, it's young by Florentine standards, but has still managed to have quite a life. The Nazis used it as their headquarters during the occupation of the city, and when they evacuated, they rigged the temple to explode. Somehow, all but one of the bombs failed to detonate, which is why the building is still standing today. The beauty of its exterior is matched by the abstract and colorful geometric patterns of the interior, making it so different from other places of worship in the city that you'll wish you didn't have to leave your camera behind the metal detector at the entrance.

 # From the Basilica di Santa Croce, walk 7 blocks north on V. dei Pepi. Turn right onto V. dei Pilastri and left onto V. Luigi Carlo Farini. i Yarmulkes required and provided. Check bags and cameras at lockers before entering. $ €5, students €3. Cash only. ⏰ Open Apr-Sept M-Th 10am-6pm, F 10am-2pm; Oct-Mar M-Th 10am-3pm, F 10am-2pm. The 1st fl. of the museum is only open during the 2nd half of every hr.

BASILICA DI SANTA CROCE CHURCH

P. Santa Croce 16 ☎055 24 66 105; www.santacroce.firenze.it

This enormous basilica has more celebrities than the Academy Awards. They happen to have been dead for hundreds of years, but no matter. Machiavelli lies in a chilling and understated tomb, Rossini under subtle decoration of treble clefs and violin bridges, and Galileo with a globe and etching of the solar system. Michelangelo's tomb explodes with color and features a painting of the statue he'd intended for his final resting place. Dante's tomb is just gray, but it holds some inordinately large statues. You'll even find Marconi, inventor of the radio. The complex also includes exhibits, cloisters, and gardens, which are full of dead people of the less famous variety. To the right of the entrance through the gift shop, the Santa Croce leather school awaits to instruct you in the ways of leatherworking or to sell you its students' handiwork. *Let's Go* does not recommend cheating Jesus, but some travelers report that it's not difficult to sneak into the basilica through the leather school's entrance at V. San Giuseppe 5r.

 # Take Borgo de' Greci east from P. della Signoria. $ €5, ages 11-17 €3, under 11 and disabled free. Combined ticket with Casa Michelangelo €8. Audio tour €5. ⏰ Open M-F 9:30am-3:30pm, Sa-Su 1-5:30pm.

attention body snatchers

Step into a church in Florence and you'll likely run into a lot of saintly detritus. Thumbs, fingernails, femurs, and forearms are frequently enshrined as relics, often enclosed in carefully crafted and lavishly ornamented displays. Frankly, we don't understand why no one has thought to turn all these beatified bits into one Frankensaint. In case the mad scientist within you wants to run with our idea, here's a list of the relics worth reanimating:

- **AT THE MUSEO OPERA DI SANTA MARIA DEL FIORE:** This peaceful museum contains Donatello's shockingly grim statue of a haggard Mary Magdalene. In a glass case along the wall, find a finger reputed to belong to St. John the Baptist, Florence's patron saint.
- **AT THE MEDICI CHAPELS:** Glass cases of reliquaries are scattered about the entrance lobby, and in the Capella Principe, you'll find a treasure trove of elegantly displayed human odds and ends. Those greedy Medici weren't just content with collecting art masterworks—they wanted human flesh as well.
- **AT THE BASILICA DI SANTA CROCE:** Check out Saint Francis's cowl and girdle. Wouldn't they look great on a Florentine Frankenstein?

CASA BUONARROTI MUSEUM

V. Ghibellina 70 ☎055 24 17 52; www.casabuonarroti.it

When Michelangelo hit it big, he did what any new celebrity would do: bought a bunch of houses and then never lived in them. Unlike the completely fabricated Casa di Dante, Casa Buonarroti is not a reproduction. It was home to several generations of Michelangelo's descendants, and, lucky for you, they were avid art collectors. The museum's collection includes Etruscan archeological fragments, rare sketches, models by Michelangelo himself, and 19th-century Michelangelo-themed kitsch produced during a Victorian burst of Michelmania. The relative lack of tourists means plenty of space to get up close and personal with Michelangelo's work, provided being followed from room to room by the museum staff doesn't put you off. Our favorite curiosity is the small model of the wooden contraption used to transport *David* from P. della Signoria to the Accademia. If you can only visit one Florentine palace, this one's a good bet.

 # From P. Santa Croce, walk 1 block to the left to V. Ghibellina. $ €6.50, students and seniors €4.50. Cash only. ⏰ Open M 10am-5pm, W-Su 10am-5pm.

WEST OLTRARNO

palazzo pitti

The major sights of West Oltrarno are all condensed into the enormous Palazzo Pitti (www.uffizi.firenze.it/palazzopitti). It's not hard to find the complex: just cross Ponte Vecchio and walk until you reach the very obvious *palazzo*. The Palazzo Pitti museums are grouped into two ticket combos. **Ticket One** gets you into Galleria Palatina, Galleria d'Arte Moderna, and Apartamenti Reali. **Ticket Two** is for the Boboli Gardens, Museo degli Argenti, Galleria del Costume, and Museo della Porcellana. Overall, if you're choosing one ticket combo over the other, we recommend Ticket Two.

Ⓢ *Ticket 1 €13, after 4pm €12; EU citizens ages 18-25 €6.50/6; EU citizens under 18 and over 65 free. Ticket 2 €10, EU citizens ages 18-25 €4.50, EU citizens under 18 and over 65 free. Audio tour €5.50, 2 for €8.* ⌚ *Ticket 1 sights open Tu-Su 8:15am-6:50pm. Ticket 2 sights open daily June-Aug 8:15am-7:30pm; Sept 8:15am-6:30pm; Oct 8:15am-5:30pm; Nov-Feb 8:15am-4:30pm; Mar-May 8:15am-6:30pm. Closed 1st and last M of each month.*

🏛 BOBOLI GARDENS

GARDENS

www.uffizi.firenze.it/boboli

The Boboli Gardens feel like a cross between Central Park and Versailles. Imagine you're a 17th-century Medici strolling through your gardens—but don't imagine your way into a corset, ladies, because the gardens are raked at a surprising incline. They're also easily large enough for you to lose yourself for an entire afternoon. Head uphill from the palace for the porcelain museum and a stunning view of the valley where the city's packed red buildings give way to sprawling monasteries and trees. Further garden exploration results in the usual non-functioning fountains and mossy statues, but Boboli also features grottoes that look like drip castles, a sculpture of a fat man riding a turtle, and some colorful striped people added in 2003. As with any gardens, they are most fragrant and lovely right after the rain.

i Ticket 2.

GALLERIA PALATINA

MUSEUM

www.uffizi.florence.it/palatina

Gold, statues, and paintings of gold and statues deck every possible inch of this ridiculously ornate gallery. The permanent collection is housed in rooms named not for the displays, but for the ceiling art of figures like Saturn and Apollo. We are still in a *palazzo*, remember, so the organizational logic is still that of a rich royal wanting to clutter his brocaded walls with all the big-ticket masterpieces he could commission. The quirkiest object in the collection sits alone in a small chamber between the Education of Jupiter and Ulysses rooms. It belonged to Napoleon and proves that great conquerors come in small bathtubs.

i Ticket 1.

GALLERIA DEL COSTUME

MUSEUM

www.uffizi.firenze.it/musei/costume

This fashion collection isn't just Medici-era vintage—it stretches all the way into the modern day. A true Italian knows that clothes are every bit as sacred as paintings of angels, so the couture is presented thematically. Pieces from the collection rotate, but the current exhibit categorizes styles by gimmick—one display includes classically inspired sheath dresses from 1890, 1923, 1971, and 1993. It's fascinating to see the same basic ideas get reinterpreted every other generation, and you can have fun playing the "guess the decade" game before reading the title cards (you'll be surprised how easy it is to confuse the '20s with the '80s). The one permanent display is for the true Medici completist. The actual burial clothes of several dead Medici were torn from their rotting corpses and preserved for your viewing pleasure. You're welcome.

i Ticket 2.

MUSEO DEGLI ARGENTI
MUSEUM

www.uffizi.firenze.it/argenti

This museum is a pirate's dream. There's no getting lost in code or confusing markings: the treasure map is simply a sign that says, "To the Treasure." Visiting Museo degli Argenti is like wandering through a painted jewelry box. Lavish rings, minute ivories, precious jewels, dazzling crowns, and Chinese porcelain abound, and less traditional treasures like tiny shell statues of Arcimboldo's famous fruit people are also featured. Additional loot sometimes appears in temporary exhibits.

ℹ Ticket 2.

APARTAMENTI REALI
MUSEUM

The back end of the Galleria Palatina gets it right by doing away with the pesky art and sticking to the rich people's bedrooms; it's like a live version of MTV's *Cribs*. You can practically see lords nonchalantly strolling ahead of you through the marble columns and chandeliers as they chatter about some fresco or another. By the end, you'll definitely wish these apartments were listed in the Accommodations section.

ℹ Ticket 1.

MUSEO DELLE PORCELLANA
MUSEUM

www.uffizi.firenze.it/musei/porcellane

The top of that hill in the Boboli Gardens is home to a porcelain museum. Sounds dull, right? Turns out, whoever spent centuries amassing this collection of dishware really knew what he or she was doing. Even if you tune out all the floral plate motifs, there are some amazingly intricate painted scenes, including one that depicts lords and ladies milling in the garden in outlandishly fancy getup.

⌖ At the highest point of the Boboli Gardens. Just keep walking up. ℹ Ticket 2.

GALLERIA D'ARTE MODERNA
MUSEUM

Palazzo Pitti Complex ☎055 23 88 616; www.uffizi.firenze.it/musei/artemoderna

Only in Florence could people define "modern art" as stuff that predates the French Revolution. This gallery begins in the 1780s when art was no longer just for dukes, but for nobles, too. Talk about progress! The focus then moves toward 19th-century Naturalism as the motifs shift to motion, countrysides, and social scenes. It's a good palette cleanser to keep you conscious through the gilded palace rooms full of gods and angels—and we promise, you won't see any Madonna and Child renditions here.

ℹ Ticket 1.

other sights

MUSEO DI STORIA NATURALE: ZOOLOGIA LA SPECOLA
MUSEUM

V. Romana 17 ☎055 23 46 760; www.msn.unifi.it

This natural history museum is not for the faint of heart. Preserved specimens of hundreds of species—from lions to walruses to stickbugs—leer audaciously at you from behind glass walls. If you had trouble stomaching giant pinned beetles and hairy spiders in the first rooms, close your eyes when you reach the snakes in vials and run through the rest of the museum. The last five rooms are filled with 17th-century wax models of human innards and nerves, including skinless people, severed legs, and twin fetuses curled up in the womb. There's also a gruesome but anatomically accurate diorama of people dying of the plague. Indulge your inner crow downstairs at the **crystal museum**—it's only a few rooms long, but you've never seen this many sparkly things. Over 500 rare crystals from the world over are assembled here while a video explains how crystals formed along Colorado fault lines and how miners used to swap silver for a pint at the bar.

⌖ Continue a few more min. on the multi-named street that runs in front of Palazzo Pitti. ℹ Ticket office on 2nd fl. Advance booking required for groups of 10 or more. $ €10, ages 6-14 and over 65 €5, under 6 free. Crystal museum only €6/3/free. ⏰ Open June-Sept Tu-Su 10:30am-5:30pm. Last entry 5pm.

EAST OLTRARNO

You haven't seen Florence until you've seen it from the **Piazzale Michelangelo.** You'll find an extensive network of designated jogging routes and a number of small, lesser-known churches and sights amid the area's greenery. Some less typical gems like the Bardini museum await the determined explorer of East Oltrarno's residential area.

◼ PIAZZALE MICHELANGELO   PANORAMIC VIEWS
Piazzale Michelangelo

When you reach the top of your climb and find yourself facing Piazzale Michelangelo, you may wonder if you're in the right place. "I thought this was a famous sight, but all I see is a parking lot, some tourist stalls, and an oxidized *David* reproduction," you may say in disappointment. But then you'll turn around. Suddenly, you won't care how many cars are behind you sharing the same view, as Florence unfolds all around you in stunning clarity. If you stick around for the nighttime city lights, you may even begin to understand why the false *David* likes hanging out here so much.

✴ *From pretty much any bridge, bear east along the river until P. Guiseppe Poggi, where the base of the steps is located. If you're not wearing walking shoes, take bus #12 or 13.* Ⓢ *Free.*

MUSEO STEFANO BARDINI   ANTIQUE MUSEUM
V. dei Renai 37   ☎055 23 42 427

If you can't beat 'em, collect from 'em. When his painting career faltered, Stefano Bardini chose to channel his energies into collecting and dealing antiques. We know what you're thinking: "egad, antiques! The epitome of boring." But Bardini didn't buy 100-year-old desks—the man collected guns, spears, Donatellos, and suits of armor. He took frescoes from walls and ancient archways from build-ings. The guy had taste. And when his business slowed toward the end of his life, he turned his loot into a permanent collection that was donated to the city of Florence. The rooms mix pieces from various time periods, and you may even recognize some of the artists, like the expressive faces of sculptor Nicola Pisano or the blue terra cotta of Luca della Robbia. Also, the endless Donatello Madonna and Child paintings are all placed in one room, so you can compare them, contrast them, or easily skip over all of them.

✴ *Cross over Ponte alle Grazie and continue 2 blocks.* Ⓢ *€5, ages 18-25 and over 65 €4, 4-17 €3, under 4 free.* ⏲ *Open M 11am-5pm, Th 11am-5pm, Sa-Sun 11am-5pm.*

food

Florence's cuisine is typical Tuscan fare: endless combinations of meat, olive oil, truffles, and (of course) pasta. Florence's signature dish is thin slices of extremely rare steak, known as *bistecca alla fiorentina*. Rustic trattorias are ubiquitous, and the good news is that you can't really go wrong with any of them. The only thing to note is the sneaky cover charge for table service, often tucked under a pushpin or typed in tiny font at the bottom of the menu. In casual joints, you can generally escape the cover by standing at the bar—hovering gets less awkward with practice. If predictable trattoria cuisine starts to lose its excitement, hole-in-the-wall panini places, pizzerias, or the international restaurants in Santa Croce provide delicious accents so you can attack your *tagliatelle al pomodoro* with renewed zeal. Food markets are also great for classic Tuscan prosciutto and cheese picnics to take down to the river. Breakfast is an adjustment: we hope you loaded up on bacon before you left home, because all you'll get here is a croissant and coffee. Get your cappuccino or latte macchiato fix before noon—coffee after noon is such a faux pas that some waiters may even refuse to serve it. Finally, as Florence claims to be the birthplace of gelato, it's totally acceptable to eat some every day that you're here, even if you're staying for the next five years.

THE DUOMO

The places in **Piazza del Duomo** offer some great deals, making it a good spot for a bigger meal. If you want quick food, though, skip the square's overpriced snackbars and venture a few blocks further.

👍 VESTRI CIOCCOLATO D'AUTORE — GELATERIA $

Borgo degli Albizi 11r — ☎055 23 40 374; www.vestri.it

While the masses descend upon (admittedly delicious) Grom, head a few blocks east for an artisanal gelato experience. This little shop is the kind of place that can tell you exactly what variety of pistachio they used for your gelato. The flavor list isn't extensive, but with top-notch combinations like the *cioccolato fondente* with mint, you'll neither notice nor care. Alongside the exceptional gelato, the shop also sells homemade chocolates and milkshakes.

➤ From the Duomo, take V. Proconsolo south from the Duomo and turn left onto Borgo degli Albizi. [$] Gelato from €1.80. Cash only. ⏰ Open daily 10:30am-8pm.

👍 MESOPOTAMIA — KEBAB $

P. Salvemini 14 — ☎055 24 37 05

For a cheap and delicious taste of something different, any student will tell you that simple, unobtrusive, and white-tiled Mesopotamia has the best kebabs in the city.

➤ Follow V. dell'Oriuolo from the southeast corner of P. del Duomo. Mesopotamia is on the left when the street opens onto a piazza. [$] Kebabs €4. ⏰ Open daily 11am-late.

CAFFÈ DUOMO — RISTORANTE $$

P. del Duomo 29/30r — ☎055 21 13 48

This trattoria stands out among others under the Duomo for its specials: a light cheese and cold cut platter with a glass of Chianti for lunch (serves two people; €12), or a dinner of bruschetta, salad, spaghetti bolognese or lasagna, and a glass of wine. The young staff have also been known to dance to Justin Bieber when business is slow.

➤ On the north side of P. del Duomo. [$] Bruschetta, salad, entree, and wine €9. ⏰ Open daily noon-11pm.

LITTLE DAVID — RISTORANTE $

V. de' Martelli 14r — ☎055 23 02 695

Little David's crowds are smaller than the big *David*'s, making it a great spot to drop by with your laptop, refuel, and connect to the free Wi-Fi. Be sure to ask about the student special (pizza or pasta and a soft drink; €6), as it's listed separately from the main menu.

➤ Just north of the Duomo, on the right. [$] Primi €4.90-9.40. Pizza €5.50-12. 0.5L wine €4.90. ⏰ Open daily noon-1am.

PIZZERIA DEL DUOMO — PIZZERIA $

P. di San Giovanni 21 — ☎055 21 07 19

For the fastest, cheapest option without leaving the *piazza*, Pizzeria del Duomo gets the job done. They cut a generous slab, so if you're not too hungry, don't feel shy asking for a smaller piece. Downstairs seating comes at no charge if you want to get out of the sun, but otherwise your slice can be taken to go.

➤ Between where Borgo San Lorenzo and V. de' Martelli feed into the piazza. [$] Pizza €1.50-3 per slice. ⏰ Open daily noon-11pm.

BUCA NICCOLINI — RISTORANTE $

V. Ricasoli 5/7r — ☎055 29 21 24; www.bucaniccolini.it

"Make food, not war" proclaim the placemats at this trattoria, and after a big lunch, it's hard to disagree. The restaurant is inches from P. del Duomo, but every inch is another penny saved. The interior features a panoramic picture of

Florence, so you might as well skip the dome's stairs and spend that €8 on beer and pizza instead.

⚒ Immediately north of the Duomo, on the left. Ⓢ Pizza and beer €8. Pasta and beer €9.50. Ⓩ Open daily 11am-3pm and 5pm-midnight.

TRATTORIA LA MADIA
RISTORANTE $$

V. del Giglio 14 ☎055 21 85 63

If you're tired of unsalted Tuscan bread, come here for a welcome dose of sodium. The bruschetta is especially good, as are the seafood specialties, and everything is pleasantly salty compared to the dishes in other identical trattorias.

⚒ Off V. dei Banchi, toward P. Santa Maria Novella. Ⓢ Cover €2. Primi €7-9; secondi €10-18. Ⓩ Open Tu-Su 1-10pm.

GROM
GELATERIA $

V. del Campanile ☎055 21 61 58; www.grom.it

Grom is a high-end *gelateria*, which means it has a posh location right off P. del Duomo, a branch in New York City and Tokyo, and slightly higher prices than the city's other top-notch *gelaterie*. Sure, you'll find it mentioned in every guidebook and, if you catch it at the wrong time, you'll be waiting in line for 15min., but at least your little cup is made with all-natural ingredients.

⚒ Just south of the Duomo. Ⓢ Starting at €2. Ⓩ Open daily Apr-Sept 10:30am-midnight; Oct-Mar 10:30am-11pm.

LE BOTTEGHE DI DONATELLO
RISTORANTE $$

P. del Duomo 27r ☎055 21 66 78

Le Botteghe di Donatello is one of many trattorias in P. del Duomo, but it can be a godsend for those in search of a gluten-free menu. The interior seating is surprisingly extensive, air-conditioned, and rustic, so it's a fine option no matter the weather.

⚒ On the south side of the Duomo. Ⓢ Pizza and pasta €7-12. Ⓩ Open daily 11am-11pm.

PIAZZA DELLA SIGNORIA

Considering that this area teems with tourists of the well-heeled variety, there are still a surprising number of diverse, budget-friendly eateries. Good rule of thumb: the farther north or east of the Uffizi, the better off you are. This is also the place to find the city's best panini.

🏛 DA VINATTIERI
SANDWICHES $

V. Santa Margherita 4r ☎055 29 47 03

Nothing attests to quality quite like the willingness of customers to balance on disarrayed wooden stools under a damp archway. For only €3.50, you can watch your tripe or *lampredotto* panini made to order before your eyes. Step into the tiny shop or just nab a quick bite through the counter window. Choose from the long menu of sandwich suggestions or invent your own—they all cost the same.

⚒ Across the alley from Casa di Dante, so just follow the signs for that attraction. On V. del Corso, take a right just before Lush. Ⓢ Panini €3.50. Tripe €5. Ⓩ Open daily 10am-8pm.

🏛 I FRATELLINI
SANDWICHES, VINERIA $

V. dei Cimatori 38r ☎055 23 96 096; www.iduefratellini.com

This open stall with an overhang and no seating dates to 1875. Yet it still manages to draw crowds thanks to the tantalizing smell of lunchmeat panini, local wines, and the crowd psychology of seeing everyone else outside.

⚒ Come to the junction of V. dei Cimatori and V. dei Calzaioli, and it will be on the left. Ⓢ Sandwiches €2.50. Ⓩ Open Sept-June M-F 9am-8pm.

food

FESTIVAL DEL GELATO

GELATERIA $

V. del Corso 75r ☎055 29 43 86

Festival del Gelato is not what it sounds like (a festival) or what it looks like (an arcade). We had dismissed this tacky, neon-flooded *gelateria* as a certain tourist trap, but when a local recommended it, we caved and gave the disco gelato a try. At our first bite of *cioccolato fondente*, the garish fluorescence melted into warm candlelight and fireflies and a violinist in white tie began to... OK, no, the place still looked ridiculous, but hot damn, that be good gelato.

 # V. del Corso is just east off P. della Repubblica. Look for the neon—you can't miss it. $ Gelato from €1.80. ⏰ Open daily noon-midnight.

O'VESUVIO

PIZZERIA $

V. dei Cimatori 21r ☎055 28 54 87

If you gym, tan, laundry daily and have an "I heart Vinnie" tattoo on your neck, you might need a therapist. But you also won't want to miss the pizzeria where your favorite fist-bumpers worked during the Florence season. For those who couldn't care less about *Jersey Shore*, the place actually dishes up some really great pizza.

 # 1 block west of the Baia on V. dei Cimatori, on the left. $ Pizza €3-9. Calzones €5.50. ⏰ Open daily noon-midnight.

ACQUA AL 2

RISTORANTE $$

V. della Vigna Vecchia 40r ☎055 28 41 70; www.acquaal2.it/Firenze.html

Why restrict plates to live on tables? Acqua al 2 allows plates to follow their true passion: decorating walls. While otherwise a bit pricey, this cloth napkins kind of joint makes a dreamy **blueberry steak**.

 # On the corner of V. della Vigna Vecchia and V. dell'Acqua. $ Primi €7-12; secondi €9-23. Cover charge 10%. ⏰ Open M-Sa noon-11pm.

TRATTORIA GUSTO LEO

PIZZERIA $$

V. del Proconsolo 8-10r ☎055 28 52 17; www.gustoleo.com

This yellow restaurant near the major sights should never have opted for the corny lion theme. But if you can't beat 'em, join 'em: at least the ext-roar-dinarily large calzones, pizzas, and salads provide a real lion's share!

 # Coming from P. della Signoria, it will be on the right. $ Pizzas €5.40-8.90. Calzones €7.60-7.90. ⏰ Open daily 8am-1am.

OSTERIA DEL PORCELLINO

RISTORANTE $$$

V. Val di Lamona 7r ☎055 26 41 48; www.osteriadelporcellino.com

Osteria del Porcellino's wrought-iron tables take up most of the alleyway under a yellow arch just off the Mercato Nuovo. This is the place to savor a glass of wine and a typical Italian meat or pasta dish once the area's tourist freight has calmed. We have no reason to believe that the name is a jab at the owner's appearance.

 # Right off P. di Mercato Nuovo. $ Cover €2. Primi €7-11; secondi €15-26. ⏰ Open daily noon-3pm and 5-11pm.

SANTA MARIA NOVELLA

Pizzerias, cafes, and kebab shops abound near the train station and church. This is a good neighborhood to find a generic, cheap bite to eat, but look elsewhere for a sit-down meal.

TRATTORIA IL CONTADINO

RISTORANTE $$

V. Palazzuolo 69/71r ☎055 23 82 673

Come check the chalkboard to fill up with a *prix-fixe* menu that includes *primo*, *secondo*, veggie, and wine. If you come at lunchtime, you can use the two euro you saved to go pack some gelato into what little stomach space may remain.

 # From P. Santa Maria Novella, take a right onto V. Palazzuolo. $ Prix-fixe menu €11-13. ⏰ Open M-F noon-9:40pm, Sa 11am-3pm and 7pm-midnight.

the cold war

With hot food, hot weather, and hot residents, Florence is a hot place to be. You would think an ice cold drink is the perfect way to relax from all that humidity. But in Florence, this is simply not the case—Florentines have embarked on a cultural crusade against the cold. This doesn't mean that everything is warm (thank goodness for gelato), but be prepared for a few things, including milk, to be served slightly warmer than usual. Most of us have only heard of warm milk in the context of grandmothers and cats, but here it's common practice to leave milk out at room temperature or to give it a quick zap in the microwave.

PIZZERIA CENTOPOVERI
                                                          PIZZERIA $
V. Palazzuolo 31r   ☎055 21 88 46

The two elegant Centopoveri restaurants that straddle punk bar Public House 27 (see **Nightlife**) make for quite the juxtaposition. Go to the right for the younger, cheaper sister: the pizzeria. True, the long dining rooms with curved ceilings may make you feel like you're eating in a tunnel, but the light at the end is the excellent pizza.

✱ Corner of V. della Porcellana, on either side of all the punks smoking outside Public House 27. ⑤ No cover in the pizzeria. Pizza €4.50-9. Primi €7-10; secondi €9-15. ✷ Open daily noon-3pm and 7pm-midnight.

RISTORANTE LA SPADA
                                           RISTORANTE, ROAST MEATS $$
V. della Spada 62r   ☎055 21 87 57; www.laspadaitalia.com

Roasting spits ooze an enticing scent at this to-go or sit-down locale. Meanwhile, slabs of meat and heaps of asparagus call your name from under a glass case.

✱ Near the corner of V. della Spada and V. del Moro. *i* Mention the "free website after-dinner treat." ⑤ Primi €6.50-9. Roast meat from the spit €8.50-14. Grill menu €8-19. Vegetables €4-6.50. Desserts €3-5. ✷ Open daily noon-3pm and 6-11pm.

50 ROSSO
                                                              CAFE $
V. Panzani 50r   ☎055 28 35 85

This is the kind of place you duck into to escape a rainstorm or buy chewing gum. Then you discover it offers a surprising selection. The tiny cafe's eclectic fare includes panini (€2.50), chickwiches (€3), and miniature Tic Tac boxes. And if you're not already a convert, the Nutella crepe (€3) will have you head over heels for the hazelnut spread.

✱ You'll find the start of V. Panzani in the northeast corner of P. Santa Maria Novella, nearer to the train station. ⑤ Cappuccino €1.20. Cash only. ✷ Open daily 6:30am-12:30am.

CAFFÈ GIACOSA
                                                              CAFE $
Inside Palazzo Strozzi   ☎055 42 65 04 86

Backpacking is murder on your lower lumbar, and the curved wooden wall at Caffè Giacosa fits just right in the small of your back. Lean back with a cappuccino and it's as good as Ibuprofen. The prices triple for courtyard seating, but who cares? The nice wooden wall inside the self-serve area is the point of the visit. The pots of tea are made of fancy bagged stuff—a delight for tea-drinkers stranded in coffee country.

✱ Inside Palazzo Strozzi, which is west of P. della Repubblica. There is a 2nd location down the street at V. della Spada 10. ⑤ Cappuccino €1.30. Pot of tea €2. ✷ Open daily 10am-10pm.

LA GROTTA DI LEO
                                                          TRATTORIA $
V. della Scala 41/43r   ☎055 21 92 65

Far from the only lion-themed restaurant around, this brick-walled trattoria is bigger than it looks, with two grotto-esque dining rooms and a couple outdoor

food

tables. It seems Italian lions really like pizza and pasta served in brick buildings, although some say the tiramisu (€4) is the *mane* attraction.

 # From P. Santa Maria Novella, take a right onto V. della Scala. [$] Pizza €5-8. Primi €5.50-8; secondi €5-19. ⏰ Open daily 10am-1am.

SAN LORENZO

The **Mercato Centrale** contains a feast of lunch options, but venturing outside to nearby restaurants is no step down. For dinner, **Via Nazionale** is lined with standard-fare pasta and pizza that isn't the cheapest in the area, but it gets the job done.

👍 TRATTORIA MARIO — RISTORANTE $

V. Rosina 2r — ☎055 21 85 50; www.trattoriamario.com

If you're starting to wonder where all the Italians are hiding, show up for a late lunch at Trattoria Mario. Diners are haphazardly packed into tables with strangers, wherever there's room, which makes for creative combinations. If you're lucky, your tablemates might share their wine with you as you dine on the day's pasta special.

 # Just off Mercato Centrale, on the right. [$] Cover €0.50. Daily specials €6-9. ⏰ Open M-Sa noon-3:30pm, but try to show up a bit earlier to beat the lines.

👍 NERBONE — RISTORANTE $

P. del Mercato Centrale — ☎055 21 99 49

Nerbone is the love child of a garage and a picnic. It has stood in a corner of the Mercato Centrale for over 100 years. Crowd around the counter to order whatever happens to be on offer, take your tray, and squeeze in with some locals to remind yourself how fantastic your Italian isn't. A sign warns that tables are only for eating, so forget those autopsies you were planning on doing over lunch.

 # Enter Mercato Centrale from V. dell'Arte and go all the way to the right. [$] Primi and secondi €2.50-7. House wine €1. Cash only. ⏰ Open M-Sa 7am-2pm.

👍 IL PIRATA — RISTORANTE $

V. de' Ginori 56r — ☎055 21 86 25

Buy homemade food (pasta, meats, or vegetables) priced by the kilogram from a glass case opposite a line of stools and a counter. Refuel your immune system with a plate of vegetables (€5.50) or fill up with a big plate of pasta and side of vegetables (€6.50), but be careful when attempting to pour the self-serve olive oil. If business is slow, the owner may try to guess your nationality.

 # From P. San Lorenzo, walk north up V. de' Ginori for a few minutes. i Takeout available. [$] Lunch specials €5.50-7.50. Buffet €7.50, with wine €10. ⏰ Open daily 11am-11pm.

florence

👍 ANTICA GELATERIA FIORENTINA — GELATERIA $

V. Faenza 2A — ☎388 05 80 399; www.gelateriafiorentina.com

Antica's wide variety of cone sizes splay across the counter, starting at a one-flavor cone for just €1. Snack on classics or check the label stickers for the *gelati speciali*—flavors invented by the owner—such as Bianca (sweet coconut, honey, and yogurt), named after his young daughter.

 # Toward the far end of V. Faenza, on the left. [$] Cones from €1. €15.50 per kg. ⏰ Open daily noon-midnight.

IL BRINCELLO — TUSCAN $

V. Nazionale 110r — ☎055 28 26 45

The battle between convenience and quality is over at last. May we present: 👍**takeout homemade pasta!** And for a reasonable price! The sit-down option is less exciting and more orange.

 # Just down V. Nazionale from the train station on the right. [$] Primi €3.50-10. Takeout pasta €5. ⏰ Open daily noon-3pm and 7-11pm.

BAR CABRAS CAFE $

V. Panzani 12r ☎055 21 20 32

Italy takes regional specialties seriously, so you'd usually be hard pressed to find decent cannoli outside its southern home turf. Yet these cylinders of desire glistening with creamy goodness pose seductively from behind glass until you just can't say no.

 # Just down the street from the train station. $ Cannoli €1.50-2.50. ⏰ Open daily 8am-8pm.

OSTERIA ALL'ANTICO MERCATO RISTORANTE $$

V. Nazionale 78r ☎055 28 41 82; www.anticomercatofirenze.it

The €10 combo meals are the draw here—try the *bruschetta e spaghetti bolognese.* Those sick of carbs will be happy to find that "Big Salads" get their own section of the menu (oh hey, *Seinfeld*) and gluten-free lasagna and pasta are also available. You get the same view whether you dine inside or out: the dining room features a mural of the street outside, minus the noisy cars and mopeds.

 # Slightly south of P. dell'Indipendenza. $ Combo meals €10. ⏰ Open daily noon-11pm.

TRATTORIA ZAZA RISTORANTE $$

P. del Mercato Centrale 26r ☎055 21 54 11; www.trattoriazaza.it

The alfresco seating is typical for a *piazza ristorante*, but the quirky logo on the menu—a naked child being stung on the buttocks by a bee—should give you a clue to the offbeat glamour of the dining rooms inside. Lurid frescoes coat the vaulted ceilings, while staid dead white men in gilded portraits watch you devour fresh pasta. For those not inclined toward the bloody *bistecca alla fiorentina* there are abundant creative salads—try Zaza's, with chicory lettuce, walnuts, brie, and Roquefort dressing.

 # Exit behind the Mercato Centrale and go diagonally right, looking for tents. $ Cover €2.50. Primi €7-18. ⏰ Open daily 11am-11pm.

RISTORANTE LE FONTICINE RISTORANTE $$

V. Nazionale 79r ☎055 28 21 06; www.lefonticine.com

This restaurant will call your name as you wander V. Nazionale looking for a place to eat. Standard pasta awaits you where the walls are packed full of paintings—don't look too closely at the humans with black holes for eyes, or they might try to steal yours. Also beware the exorbitant cover charge and spurious claims that their tap water comes from the river.

 # To the right of the V. Nazionale fountain (hence the name). $ Cover €2.50. Primi €6-13; secondi €8-16. ⏰ Open daily noon-2:30pm and 7-10:30pm.

SAN MARCO

There are lots of self-evidently cheap places near the Accademia if you want to grab something for the botanical gardens. Venture a few blocks further for more pleasant sit-down options.

IL VEGETARIANO VEGETARIAN $

V. delle Ruote 30 ☎055 47 50 30

This unobtrusive establishment will surprise you. Walk beyond the cool, shady front room for a bustling haven of custom salads, glistening cakes, and assorted teas. You won't rue the lack of meat in the lush, flavorful pasta dishes. Here's an itinerary to help you get food with the minimum amount of jostling: grab silverware on the right of the register, order and pay, then pick up a tray and give your order sheet to the guy behind the salad options. Seat yourself—we recommend the peaceful bamboo courtyard.

 # From V. Nazionale it's a subtle wooden sign on the left. i Gluten-free options. $ Primi €5.50-6.50; secondi €6.50-8.50. ⏰ Open Tu-Su 12:30-3pm and 7:30pm-midnight.

RISTORANTE PIZZERIA DA ZEUS PIZZERIA $

V. Santa Reparata 17r ☎328 86 44 704

The student special is as appealing as Zeus was promiscuous—only €5 for pizza and a soda. The large rear dining hall is air-conditioned, and the *prix-fixe* menu (drink, a salad or pizza or *primi*, dessert, and coffee) is one of the cheapest in town.

 # Off V. 27 Aprile. [$] Cover €1. Prix-fixe menu €6.50. ⏰ Open daily noon-11pm.

GRAN CAFFÈ SAN MARCO CAFE $

P. di San Marco 11r ☎055 21 58 33; www.grancaffesanmarco.it

This chintzy but cheap cafe is the chameleon of eateries. Enter from the main *piazza* and it's a *gelateria*. Enter from the side street and it's a pizzeria. Walk further in, and it's a cafeteria meets coffee bar meets garden cafe. Don't be caught off guard by the charge for table service, or the fact that the enormous gooey bowls of lasagna (€4.50) are reheated. This food is good for a quick museum refueling rather than a lingering stay.

 # The south end of the piazza. [$] Panini €3. Secondi €7. ⏰ Open daily 8am-10pm.

beef up

Florence is known for its festivals, which usually include food, wine, and costumes. But there's one festival that's off the beaten track. The Sagra della Bistecca celebrates the region's most popular cuisines: steak. The festival is held in the Gardens of Parterre from August 14-16. Chefs line up to grill steaks *alla fiorentina*, and locals line up to get a taste. If you want some of the best beef around, head on down for some straight-off-the-cow chow.

DIONISO GREEK $$

V. San Gallo 16r ☎055 21 78 82; www.ristorantegrecodionisio-firenze.com

Sick of typical Tuscan cuisine? Have a little baklava! It's your predictable Greek joint, in that predictable shade of blue that seems to be international code for "here be filo dough." The menu's in Italian and Greek only, but we are confident you can recognize the Greek for "souvlaki."

 # Just to the west of P. di San Marco. [$] Souvlaki and gyro plates €12. Baklava €3.50. Ouzo €3. ⏰ Open M-Sa noon-3pm and 7:30pm-midnight, Su 7:30pm-midnight.

VIN OLIO RISTORANTE $$

V. San Zanobi 126r ☎055 48 99 57; www.vinolio.com

Vin Olio is a quiet, grown-up sort of place, with subdued art and fans that slowly whir under the high beamed ceilings. The front room has a small bar serving cocktails (€3) and *grappa* (€1.80). Try the penne with duck meat, if the place is actually open when they claim to be.

 # From P. dell'Indipendenza, take V. 27 Aprile to V. San Zanobi. [$] Antipasti €5-9. Primi €8-9. ⏰ Open daily 11am-midnight.

SANTA CROCE

If you're craving something a little different, look no further than Santa Croce, where cheap and late-night food options abound. There are even a few upscale establishments huddled around the Basilica di Santa Croce. We almost don't want to spoil the fun you'll have discovering this quirky and diverse area on your own—in fact, we're tempted to just give you a world map and send you on a scavenger hunt to check off each country's cuisine. Then again, it never hurts to have some options handy; here are a few spots to get you started.

THE OIL SHOPPE
SANDWICHES $

V. Sant'Egidio 22r ☎055 20 01 092; http://oilshoppe.blogspot.com

Whether it's the student-friendly prices, the warm and filling panini, the fresh salads, or the charm of friendly chef Alberto, something keeps every stool in The Oil Shoppe filled with study-abroaders. If the extensive menu overwhelms you, the meatball and the #24 are deservedly popular.

⇟ From P. del Duomo, take V. dell'Oriuolo, turn right onto V. Folco Portiani then right onto V. Sant'Edigio. [$] Sandwiches €3-4. Fries and drink €2. Cash only. ⏰ Open M-F 11am-6pm.

CIBRÉO TEATRO DEL SALE
RISTORANTE, PERFORMANCE VENUE $$$$

V. de' Macci 111r ☎055 20 01 492; www.cibreo.it

Normally we would never recommend a €30 meal. But this isn't a meal—it's the equivalent of buying infinite glasses of wine, ordering every dish on a fancy restaurant menu, and then buying theater tickets. You won't even need to eat lunch before this food marathon. The chef at Teatro del Sale is one of Italy's most renowned, and a meal at his restaurant across the street (served out of the same kitchen) goes for at least twice the price. Yet here, diners seat and serve themselves in the cozy interior and peer into the kitchen through a glass wall. We're pretty sure that this is the only place in the world where a famous Italian chef with a Santa Claus beard announces dish names in a town crier voice or merrily shouts things like "If I see anyone use a fork for these clams they will be thrown out on the spot!" Then, when you are full beyond your wildest dreams, the tables disappear and the focus shifts to the small stage for a live performance—young and upcoming theater performances, musical acts, dancers, film screenings, and lectures are all frequently on rotation. Membership may be private, but it's not exclusive—a one-year membership costs just €5 if you're foreign or under 26.

*⇟ Just west of P. Sant'Ambrogio. **i** There's no stated dress code, but try not to look like a backpacker. Membership required. [$] 1-year membership €10, foreign and under 26 €5. Breakfast €7. Lunch €20. Dinner buffet €30. A voucher from the previous Sunday's La Repubblica newspaper gets you a 30% discount. ⏰ Club open 9am-11pm. Dinner at 7pm. Performances begin around 9pm.*

GELATERIA DEI NERI
GELATERIA $

V. dei Neri 20/22r ☎055 21 00 34

Being a *Let's Go* researcher requires eating at a different *gelateria* each time in the quest of Florence's very best. So why can't we stop eating at this one? It might have something to do with the mousse-like *semifreddo*—try the tiramisu—or the insanely spicy Mexican chocolate, which we found too intense to finish.

⇟ From Ponte Grazie, head north on V. de' Benci and turn left onto V. dei Neri. [$] Gelato from €1.50. Cash only. ⏰ Open daily 9am-midnight.

LA GHIOTTA
CAFE $

V. Pietrapiana 7r ☎055 24 12 37

Take a number at this student-friendly rotisserie—the line is out the door during lunchtime. Patrons don't seem to mind waiting to pick their meals from platters behind the counter. Order one of the 20 varieties of pizza and cram into the seats in the back. It's even cheaper if you take it to go: you can get half a rotisserie chicken or a giant slab of eggplant *parmigiana* for just a few euro.

⇟ From Borgo Allegri, take a right onto V. Pietrapiana. [$] Primi €5-6; secondi €5-7. Pizza and calzoni €5-7. Wine €6. ⏰ Open Tu-Su noon-5pm and 7-10pm.

RUTH'S

KOSHER, VEGETARIAN $$

V. Luigi Carlo Farini 2A ☎055 24 80 888; www.kosheruth.com

This welcoming restaurant by the synagogue caters to Florence's Jewish community as well as local students. From the visitor drawings in the entryway to the bearded photos on walls, Ruth's has its own unique ambience.

✪ To the right of the synagogue. Ⓢ Primi and secondi €7-10. Falafel platter €9. Entrees €9-18. W night student menu €10-15. ✪ Open M-F 12:30-3pm and 7:30-10:30pm, Su 12:30-3pm and 7:30-10:30pm.

ALL'ANTICO VINAIO

CAFE $

V. dei Neri 65r ☎055 23 82 723

There's something endearing about the way this storefront trusts you to pour your own tiny glass of wine and pay for your self-serve coldcut sandwiches after eating them on the wooden seats out on the street. The prices don't hurt either.

✪ 2 blocks east of the Uffizi. Ⓢ Sandwiches from €1. Student special: sandwich and drink €4. Glass of wine €2. Cash only. ✪ Open daily 8am-9pm.

EBY'S BAR

MEXICAN $

V. dell'Oriuolo 5r ☎055 24 00 27

Heck yes, burrito joint! The food isn't exactly Mexican—it's more of a loose Italian variation—but hey, it's still a hot tortilla full of meat and cheese. This is a place that knows its clientele: a sign on the door proudly heralds the "Late Night Chicken Quesadilla." You can take your €4 burrito to go, munch it in the colorful interior, or head to the covered Volta di San Pietro alleyway. The alleyway also has a kebab place, so there are multiple options for the cheap, drunk, and hungry.

✪ From the Duomo, head east on V. dell'Oriuolo. On the corner of V. dell'Oriuolo and V. dei Pucci. Ⓢ Nachos €3. Burrito €4. Sangria €3. ✪ Open daily 10am-3am.

TRATTORIA ANITA

RISTORANTE $$

V. Parlascio 2r ☎055 21 86 98

Anita is tucked off the major streets, protecting it from the largest tourist waves. Nestle into the homey interior for some home-cooked Tuscan specialties like *ravioli alla gorgonzola*.

✪ Near the Uffizi, on the corner of V. Vinegia and V. Parlascio. Ⓢ Primi €7; secondi €7-12. ✪ Open M-Sa noon-2:30pm and 7-10:15pm.

CAFFÈ PASTICCERIA LA LOGGIA DEGLI ALBIZI

BAKERY $

Borgo degli Albizi 99r ☎055 24 79 574

If for some strange reason you don't feel like eating gelato, the baked goods here will satisfy your sweet tooth. The gorgeous pies are topped with nuts, the macaroons are as big as your face, and there are numerous Italian specialties like *biscotti* and *panforte*. You'll even be able to take your time over them, since, unlike gelato, they won't be melted by the hot summer.

✪ From the Duomo, follow V. del Proconsolo south and turn right onto Borgo degli Albizi. Ⓢ Torrone €4.50. Panforte €4.50. ✪ Open daily 7am-8pm.

THE DINER

DINER $

V. dell'Acqua 2 ☎055 29 07 48; www.theflorencediner.com

Eating local food is one of the best parts of traveling, especially in Italy, but sometimes you just miss home. That's where The Diner comes in—you won't find a more American home-away-from-home in all of Florence. You might forget you're in Italy when you're munching on pancakes and burgers while chatting with friends back home via the free Wi-Fi.

✪ From the Duomo, follow V. del Proconsolo south, turn right onto V. dell'Anguillara and left onto V. dell'Acqua. Ⓢ American coffee free on W. ✪ Open daily 8am-10:30pm.

florence

WEST OLTRARNO

West Oltrarno is teeming with supermarkets and food machines, some of which even sell hot, fresh pasta. The restaurant scene is quirkier than across the river, but keep your eye out for sneaky cover charges.

🔖 DANTE

RISTORANTE $$

P. Nazario Sauro 12r ☎055 21 92 19; www.trattoriadante.net

Dante is an excellent choice for students—with any meal, students get a free bottle of wine. The pizza is the same as anywhere, but, dude, **free wine.** This place also displays lots of images of Dante on the wall, as you'd expect. Free wine!

✦ *A block south of Ponte alla Carraia, on the right.* ⑤ *€3 cover is hidden by pushpins on the outdoor menu. Fish €5-6. Pizza €6-9. Pasta €8-10.* ⌚ *Open daily noon-1am.*

🔖 GUSTAPANINO

SANDWICHES $

V. de' Michelozzi 13r ☎333 92 02 673

Unlike other sandwich places around, this one makes your hot focaccia or *piadine* (wrap) to order, and you can see the ingredients prepared in front of you. The turkey, pesto, tomato, and mozzarella option is to die for. There's also a lewd pig in pink underwear on the counter, which can only be a plus. Gustapanino is perfect for a grab-and-go meal.

✦ *In P. Santo Spirito; facing away from the Santo Spirito church, it's the 2nd building on the left.* ⑤ *Focacce and piadini €3-4.* ⌚ *Open Tu-Su 11:30am-3pm and 7-11pm.*

GELATERIA LA CARRAIA

GELATERIA $

P. Nazario Sauro 25r ☎055 28 06 95; www.lacarraiagroup.eu

An excellent gelato option right across the river, La Carraia serves cones starting at €1. Try the minty After Eight or Nutella yogurt. There's a lot of ambience in the shop, but go stand by the river—it's right outside.

✦ *Right across Ponte alla Carraia.* ⑤ *Gelato from €1.* ⌚ *Open daily 11am-11pm.*

test your gag reflex

Italy is known for its pasta and wine, but there's another side of Italian cuisine that might make your stomach turn.

- **PORK BLOOD CAKE.** Florentines don't like to waste any part of the pig—they've even found a way to use the blood in this daring concoction, which is served warm.

- **CASU MARZU.** Not all the cheese you find in Florence will be palatable. This goat cheese, otherwise known as Maggot Cheese, is filled with fly larvae and must be eaten while the maggots are still alive.

- **CIECHE FRITTEN.** At the end of winter, baby eels born in the Saragasso Sea migrate and colonize the rivers of Italy. In Florence, these creatures are caught and served fried to those looking for a different seafood taste.

- **LAMPREDOTTO.** Give your stomach a taste of stomach with this local specialty. You'll see many stalls selling this gray, rubbery tripe, which comes from cow stomachs. It's usually served with tomato, onion, parsley, and celery on a panini.

food

GUSTA PIZZA
PIZZERIA $

V. Maggio 46r ☎055 28 50 68

Run by the same family as Gustapanino (see above), Gusta Pizza serves Neapolitan-style, thin-crust pizza. Eat on location for that personal service feel—if they really like you, they may even shape your pizza into a heart. Order to go if you want something warm and cheesy to eat by the river.

⇟ On the corner of V. de' Michelozzi and V. Maggio. Facing the Santo Spirito church, turn right. Look for it on the next corner, on the right. [$] Pizza €4.50-8. ⏰ Open Tu-Su 11:30am-3pm and 7-11pm.

OSTERIA SANTO SPIRITO
RISTORANTE $$

P. Santo Spirito 16r ☎055 23 82 383

Delightful wooden tables behind bamboo screens line the street in front of this *osteria*, while the inside has large round tables suffused with a flickering red light. Linger after your pasta for the crème brûlée (€6) and other posh desserts.

⇟ It's at the far end of P. Santo Spirito from the church, on the right. [$] Pizza €6-9. Primi €7-12. Desserts €6. Wine by the bottle from €12. ⏰ Open daily noon-11:30pm.

EAST OLTRARNO

In **Piazza di Santa Felicita** there are a couple serviceable options for pit stops, including **Bibo, Ristorante Celestino,** and **Snack Le Delizie.** The eastern part of East Oltrarno is home to dinner gems frequented by locals, which means a lot less English on the menus.

L'HOSTERIA DEL BRICCO
RISTORANTE $$

V. San Niccolò 8r ☎055 23 45 037; www.osteriadelbricco.it

Behind an unobtrusive entrance, this gorgeous space with brick arches, flowers, and stained glass over the door is well worth the cover. A suit of armor stands casually on the side as L'Hosteria's most steadfast patron. The smell will kick-start your appetite, and meat or pasta from the handwritten menu will indulge all your senses.

⇟ Cross Ponte alla Grazie and turn left onto Lungarno Serristori. After 3 blocks, turn right onto V. Lupo and then left onto V. San Niccolò. [$] Cover €2.50. Primi €7; secondi €12-14. Desserts €4. ⏰ Open daily for lunch from noon and dinner 7:30pm-late.

nightlife

Florence specializes in laid-back nightlife rather than the dance-until-dawn variety. We know this may be hard for under-21s recently unleashed in Europe and looking to booze-cruise, but if you come here with the go-hard-or-go-home mentality, you may end up sorely disappointed. Instead, drink wine and mingle by the river, fall in love with the concept of *aperitivo*, and chill in *piazze* that are full of students. Still, from the hilariously huge selection of Irish pubs to a number of chic venues that turn more club-like as the night goes on, you should be able to find an ambience that suits your intensity level. During major sporting events and festivals, the streets fill with people and spill with wine. If you're really serious about clubbing, you should think about taking a taxi to larger venues outside the city proper.

THE DUOMO

This isn't exactly a traditional nightlife area. You'll find a couple of bars right by the Duomo, but you'll be better of venturing into other neighborhoods. When the weather is beautiful and the town is particularly crowded, people hang out on the Duomo steps all night. Nearby shops like **Mill Wine Shop** (V. Camillo Cavour 32) offer student specials like 10 beers for €10, making an outdoor evening a highly affordable option.

SHOT CAFE

BAR

V. dei Pucci 5 ☎055 28 20 93

Umbrellas, lion paintings, and inner tubes beneath blue Christmas lights make up the aggressively quirky decor of this fun little bar. Those who haven't changed their money yet can pay for drinks in US dollars for the going exchange rate. The music is American "oldies," as long as you define oldies as anything recorded between 1920 and 2005. The TV is usually tuned to MTV—now that's retro.

❖ *A block north of the Duomo.* ℹ *Free Wi-Fi.* Ⓢ *Beer €3; pitchers €10. 10 shots for €19. More expensive in winter.* ❍ *Open daily 5pm-3am. Happy hour daily 5-9pm.*

ASTOR CAFE

BAR

P. del Duomo 20r ☎055 23 99 318; www.astorcafe.com

Astor is a popular stop for locals and tourists just starting their night out. Hip hop and pop videos (and sometimes NFL) light up the walls of the interior, while the outside is a colorful candlelit scene looking up at the Duomo.

❖ *On the northeast side of the piazza.* Ⓢ *Beer €5. Cocktails €7. 1L of whatever's on tap €10.* ❍ *Open daily 8am-3am.*

PIAZZA DELLA SIGNORIA

At night, this area lights up with bars and fills with wandering groups of students. For a range of options in a short stretch, try **Via de' Benci** between P. Santa Croce and the river: Moyo is modern and trendy, the Red Gartello's karaoke entrance looks like the tunnel of love, and pubby Kikuya offers sandwiches and Dragoon Strong Ale. **Piazza della Signoria, Piazza della Repubblica,** and **Ponte Vecchio** are other excellent places to hang out with a beer—get one to go from a local bar for some DIY nightlife. It should also be noted that the Ponte Vecchio is a fine place for a snog and that *Let's Go* does not condone drunk-riding the P. della Repubblica carousel.

MOYO

BAR

V. de' Benci 23r ☎055 24 79 738; www.moyo.it

A sophisticated crowd lounges in Moyo's modern, two-pronged black chairs. Candles and green disco lights that shine through a chandelier give this place a surreal, smoky atmosphere with an undulating beat.

❖ *Just off P. de' Davanzati.* Ⓢ *Wine €6.* ❍ *Open M-Th 8pm-2am, F-Sa 9pm-3am, Su 8pm-2am. Aperitivo sushi W 7-10:30pm.*

AMADEUS

PUB

V. dei Pescioni 3 ☎055 28 17 09

Amadeus fosters a healthy young crowd that, as pubs go, is not too male-heavy. The genre changes nightly between "happy music," house, R and B, reggae, and hip hop.

❖ *Just off P. de' Davanzati.* Ⓢ *Beer €6. 3 drinks for €10.* ❍ *Open daily 7pm-2:30am.*

THE OLD STOVE

IRISH PUB

V. Pellicceria 2r ☎055 29 52 32

Hey look, it's another Irish pub! Which, of course, actually means American, because Irish people know better than to go to Florence to drink. The dive-bar inside pales in comparison to the social outdoor seating. The soccer-match board indicates The Old Stove's rowdy fan days.

❖ *Walk to the side of P. della Repubblica that doesn't have the carousel and look down the street to the left.* ℹ *Dollar Day on W—pay in US$ all day long. Another branch is located by the Duomo.* Ⓢ *Pints €6, happy hour €4. Cocktails €7.* ❍ *Open M-Th noon-2am, F-Sa noon-3am, Su noon-2am. Happy hour M-Th 5-9pm.*

TWICE

CLUB

V. Giuseppe Verdi 57r ☎055 24 76 356

Mostly sweaty guys, half-hearted dancing, and colored lights, Twice is the sort of place for clubbing when you don't feel like making a big production out of it.

This cover-free club is a favorite of drunk students, people with no other club ideas, and Italian men on the prowl. (Unsurprisingly, this was a favorite *Jersey Shore* haunt while they were in Florence.) The weird mix of music should have you giggling every time some forgotten hit from eighth grade plays. There's also a booth in plain view where people get hot and heavy, and a fairly arbitrary VIP area—if you get waved in, just take the free drinks and roll with it.

 # From the Duomo, head east on V. dell'Oriuolo, then right onto V. Giuseppe Verdi. $ Beer €5. Cocktails €9. ⏰ Open daily 9pm-4am.

SLOWLY BAR

V. Porta Rossa 63r ☎055 26 45 354; www.slowlycafe.com

Slowly will drain your bank account quickly. This blend of candlelight, flashing colors, thumping music, and well-dressed clientele leisurely sipping overpriced cocktails could have been imported from Manhattan.

 # Just off P. de' Davanzati. $ Beer €6. Cocktails €8. ⏰ Open daily 7pm-2:30am.

THE BLOB CLUB CLUB

V. Vinegia 21r ☎055 21 12 09; www.blobclub.com

To visit this exclusive club, you have to submit for a membership card (€5) on the Blob website. Some travelers report that this is the choice haunt of bartenders after hours.

 # East of the Palazzo Vecchio, on V. Vinegia. $ Membership €5. ⏰ Live music Su.

top 5 smooch spots

Florence is undeniably romantic, with movie-set side streets and constant streams of wine. If you're inspired to indulge in a Florentine romance, here are some options preferable to hostel bunk beds.

- **PONTE VECCHIO.** It's as cliché as the Eiffel Tower and not remotely private, but no one bats an eye at some smooching along the most famous bridge in town. Hope the constant stream of wedding parties isn't a turn-off, though.
- **PONTE SANTA TRINITA.** Keeping along the Arno, score a little more isolation and an even better view on one of the broad stone triangles over the edge of this less trafficked bridge. Come early (or very late) to find one unoccupied, though–this is prime canoodling real estate.
- **THE DUOMO.** Want to tick blasphemous make-out session off your "Never Have I Ever" list? The steps in front of Florence's most recognizable church are scenic and quiet after midnight, but more daring couples could try climbing the dome or tower. Right before closing, the 300+ steps of winding stairwells will be mostly deserted, and your hearts will already be racing from the climb. If you make it to the top, the view ain't too shabby either.
- **PIAZZALE MICHELANGELO.** It might seem like an obvious choice, but it's a bit too parking lot to really set the mood. Try a corner along the hike up to the *piazzale* or keep going up the hill to find a small park that's far darker, deserted, and every bit as scenic.
- **LEAVE THE CITY.** Take your romance out under the Tuscan sun and head to the hills. Hostels in adjacent towns let you escape the crowds and perhaps snag a private room while staying within a backpacker's budget.

SAN LORENZO

In the evening, the streets of Santa Maria Novella are alive with youth. There are some stellar nightlife options, but in this area it's best to choose a destination and stick to it rather than bar hop due to cover fees, distance, difference of style, or some combination of the three. If you're trekking out to Central Park, be smart: pull a group together and set aside funds for a cab home.

SPACE ELECTRONIC DISCOTHEQUE — CLUB

V. Palazzuolo 37 ☎055 29 30 82; www.spaceelectronic.net

Do you wish you could go clubbing in Epcot? Then join the happy young crowd around the aquarium bar in this conveniently located space-age dance hall. Everyone joins in with whoever's blowing up the small karaoke stage. Meanwhile, the DJ upstairs rains techno down on you like a robot space god. If the bouncer waves you in, don't be fooled into thinking you got a free entrance—you'll pay the steep cover (€16) when you leave. Special events like guest bands and foam parties are extensively advertised on posters around town, so keep an eye out. The club's location means it's one of the few in the area that won't require you to take a cab home.

⇏ From the river, take V. Melegnano to V. Palazzuolo, and turn right. $ Cover €16. Shots €3. Cocktails €6.50. Fine for lost entry cards €50. ⏰ Open daily 10pm-4am.

THE JOSHUA TREE PUB — PUB

V. della Scala 37r www.thejoshuatreepub.com

There's something homey about the worn green paint on this pub's wooden walls. Smaller than similar places in town, the Joshua Tree feels cozier and less deserted in the early evening hours. Launch your evening itinerary here, or chill with the international regulars that often cluster on weeknights.

⇏ On corner of V. Benedetta. $ Pints €5. ⏰ Open daily 4pm-2am. Happy hour 4-9:30pm.

PUBLIC HOUSE 27 — BAR

V. Palazzuolo 27r ☎339 30 22 330; www.publichouse27.com

This punk bar emits a sanguine glow and a cloud of smokers from early in the evening. If you aren't put off by the scary face stuck on the door, brave the red interior for a €3 pint.

⇏ On the corner of V. della Porcellana. $ Pints €3. ⏰ Open M-Sa 5pm-2am, Su 2:30pm-2am.

CENTRAL PARK — CLUB

V. del Fosso Macinate 2 ☎055 35 99 42; www.centralfirenze.it

This enormous, heavily staffed club in the middle of Parco delle Cascine is quite a schlep from the city center, but it's hard not to be at least a little impressed by the beautiful people and differently colored outdoor dance floors that undulate with house and hip hop astride chandelier-lined bars. They provide alcotesters, but save yourself the pocket change: you'll know you're drunk when you mistake the tree in the middle of the dance floor for a sexy lady.

⇏ From the river, go to Ponte della Vittoria, the westernmost bridge of the city center. Follow Viale Fratelli Rosselli north (careful, it's busy), then turn left onto V. Fosso Macinante. Let's Go does not recommend walking through the area at night. $ Cover €20; international visitors before 12:30am €10, after 12:30am €13. Some travelers report negotiating entrance fees when in a large group. All drinks €10. ⏰ Open W 9:30pm-4am, F-Sa 9:30pm-4am. Often doesn't allow non-VIP guests in until at least 11pm.

SAN LORENZO

North American and Australian backpackers are common here due to the proximity of budget hostels. Nightlife is mostly pub-like places to chill and watch the game.

MOSTODOLCE — BAR

V. Nazionale 114r ☎055 23 02 928; www.mostodolce.it

"In wine there is wisdom, in beer there is strength, in water there is bacteria." This is how the Mostodolce menu greets its patrons—in English, by the way, thanks to the influx of American tourists in the summer months. Come to watch a sporting event with big crowds, or just to drink artisanal beers brewed in Prato and ponder the random duck above the bar. Warning: pondering increases with alcohol consumption. If you're around for a while (or drink fast) there's a "10th beer free" punch-card.

⇟ On the corner of V. Guelfa. $ 30cl beer €3.50; 50cl €5. ⏰ Open daily 11am-late. Happy hour from 10:30pm.

DUBLIN PUB — BAR

V. Faenza 27r ☎055 27 41 571; www.dublinpub.it

If men in their 20s and 30s are your calling, they're calling you from Dublin Pub. This little bar is great for some international mingling, but not so popular with women or those under 20 (though, if you're one of those, you can still have a good time). Also, the bar has purse hooks—score! Stick it out, because by the end of the night, an old Italian man could be teaching you how to curse in Italian.

⇟ The far end of V. Faenza. $ Cider €4.40. Guinness €6. Pizza €5. ⏰ Open daily 5pm-2am.

KITSCH THE PUB — BAR

V. San Gallo 22r ☎328 90 39 289; www.kitsch-pub.com

What do you expect from a place called "kitsch" if not red velvet and stained glass? During the low season, try to nab some of the alfresco seating and mix with locals to avoid the TV that blares Gwen Stefani.

⇟ Off V. Camillo Cavour. $ Shots €3.50-4.50. Small Fosters €3.60; medium €6.60. Cocktails €7. ⏰ Open daily 5pm-3am. Aperitivo 6-9:30pm.

THE FISH PUB — BAR

P. del Mercato Centrale 44r ☎055 26 82 90; www.thefishpub.com

While the ads for a "free crazy party" here every weekend night may seem slightly fishy, you might as well print the flier on the website for discounts and a free shot. While you're at it, capitalize on the free champagne glass for students on Thursdays and free champagne on Mondays for women. Once you've looted the area, grab a handy plastic cup from the exit and take your drink to go. As for the bar itself, downstairs is loud and lit up blue, while upstairs features a quieter lounge area, a license plate collection, and a distorted portrait of the queen of England.

⇟ Right out of Mercato Centrale. i Rock music on Tu. Bring your own iPod on W. Latin music on Su. $ 5 shots for €5. Cocktails €7. ⏰ Open daily from 3pm to "late night." Happy hour 3-9pm.

SAN MARCO

San Marco is not the liveliest neighborhood at night. The area north of P. di San Marco is particularly deserted, especially after the buses stop running, and the places that are open serve scattered crowds. But if you're looking for something relaxed or just want to meet a few locals, you might like it here.

THE CLUBHOUSE — BAR

V. de' Ginori 6r ☎055 21 14 27; www.theclubhouse.it

This sports bar serves alcohol from dresser drawers under a chandelier—that is, except for the Absolut, which gets a special glowing shelf like it's the goblet of fire. Plasma TVs and martinis are at your disposal all day to coast toward a relaxed evening.

⇟ Off V. dei Pucci. i Wi-Fi. $ Shots €3. Beer €5.50. Cocktails €6. ⏰ Open daily noon-midnight. Kitchen open until 11pm.

FINNEGAN IRISH PUB IRISH PUB

V. San Gallo 123r ☎055 49 07 94; www.finneganpub.com

Another ★**Irish pub!** This one has outdoor seating, dedicated screenings of soccer and rugby, typical pub booths, and rugby paraphernalia on the walls. Finnegan boasts its international flair with an eclectic collection of currencies stuck behind the bar. You know the drill: good place for casually watching the game, whatever the game may be, and hanging with the regulars. They also advertise dartboard competitions, because sharp objects and alcohol are a fantastic mix.

 # North of P. di San Marco. $ Beer €4-5. Cocktails €6.50. ⏰ Open M-Th 1pm-12:30am, F-Sa 1pm-1am, Su 1pm-12:30am.

WINE BAR NABUCCO WINE BAR

V. 27 Aprile 28r ☎055 47 50 87; www.nabuccowine.com

You could live here from dawn to dusk. Nabucco starts the day with an international breakfast (€1-4.20) followed by a coffee bar (coffee €1; lattes €1.10), lunch, and the *aperitivo* buffet. And of course, the wine bar. Try the frozen Bailey's (€4).

 # On the corner of V. Santa Reparata. i Free Wi-Fi. h Open daily 8am-midnight. Aperitivo 6:30-9:30pm

the secret's out

Ask any Florentine for late-night munchies and they may send you to a generic restaurant or simply shrug their shoulders. But ask them about the ★**secret bakeries**, and they'll suddenly lower their voice to a whisper and, if you're lucky, divulge the location of one of these glorious pastry speakeasies. If you find one, you'll probably just see a small cluster of locals huddled around a non-descript establishment. But the golden glow shining through the glass doors lets you know that something's going on inside. Working hard to supply the daytime pastry shops with fresh treats for when they open in the wee hours, these late-night pastry shops don't mind selling their delicious treats to those looking to chow down before hitting the sack. So, keep a nose out for chocolatey smells wafting from an alleyway, for even *Let's Go*'s best researcher-writers had a hard time finding these places.

SANTA CROCE

Santa Croce is the soul of Florence's nightlife. If the street you're on seems oddly quiet, just keep walking—the lively hotspots show up in unexpected pockets. Try **Via de' Benci** for a rich selection. On nice evenings, join the swarm of young people lounging and drinking in **Piazza Sant'Ambrogio** and **Piazza Lorenzo Ghiberti.**

★ **LAS PALMAS** PIAZZA

Largo Annigoni ☎347 27 60 033; www.laspalmasfirenze.it

What seems like a perfectly ordinary *piazza* by day tranforms into a rowdy beach-themed block party when evening rolls around. We're talking palm trees, seafood, and straw screens right in the middle of Florence's cobblestone streets. Performers grace the enormous stage with theater, dance, music, or some combination, setting the mood for a whole *piazza* of merriment. Groups of students, families, and older folk cram into the scores of tables and pile up on the generous *aperitivo* buffet, and children compete at foosball and table tennis. If you think the place is rowdy on a regular night, wait until you come when they're projecting sporting events on the big screen.

 # Off of P. Lorenzo Ghiberti, in front of the La Nazione building. i Check website for performance and screening schedule. $ Beer €4. Pizza €5-8. Primi €7-10. ⏰ Open May-Sept daily, hours vary. Aperitivo 8:30-9:30pm.

👍 LOCHNESS LOUNGE — BAR

V. de' Benci 19r ☎055 24 14 64

"Get messy with Nessy" alongside a laid-back mix of young locals, students, and visitors. Art and photography exhibits frequently join Warhols on the red walls, while live music or dance hits set the mood for pool and foosball.

➔ From Ponte alle Grazie, follow V. de' Benci north. ℹ Live acoustic music on Tu and Sa. 2-for-the-price-of-1 drinks during aperitivo. 💲 Beer €5. Cocktails €7. ⏰ Open daily 6:30pm-2am. Aperitivo 7-11pm.

👍 CAFFÈ SANT'AMBROGIO — BAR

P. Sant'Ambrogio 7r ☎055 24 77 277

Caffè Sant'Ambrogio's primary role is to seemingly single-handedly serve the young P. Sant'Ambrogio scene. Since everybody and their brother is out drinking in the *piazza*, that's saying something. The bar thinks it's being classy with its tasteful female nude, but it's the *piazza* that drives its business.

➔ The piazza is at the end of V. Pietrapiana. 💲 Wine €4-7. Cocktails €6-7. ⏰ Open M-Sa 8:30am-2am. Aperitivo 6-9pm.

OIBÒ — CAFE, LOUNGE

Borgo de' Greci 1 ☎055 26 38 611; www.oibo.net

Florence's casual chic crowd comes here to sip drinks on the large outdoor patio and dance in the loud stone interior. As the night goes on, the DJ tends to break out the Italian hits, and you might witness a bar full of elegant Italians belting along. This is a great spot for an *aperitivo* on your way to the Teatro Verdi.

➔ On the corner across from the Basilica di Santa Croce. ℹ DJ parties on Th-Sa. 💲 Beer €6. Cocktails €7.50. ⏰ Open Apr-Nov Tu-Su 8am-2am. Aperitivo 6:30-9:30pm.

NAIMA — CAFE, BAR

V. dell'Anguillara 54 ☎055 26 54 098; www.naimafirenze.it

The subtle violet-and-stone bar area of Naima is a great place to start the night, while the lounge has couches and candlelight for an intimate feel. Here you'll find light-hearted internationals and Euro-hipsters taking advantage of the affordable drinks.

➔ From southeast of the Duomo, follow V. del Proconsolo south and turn right onto V. dell'Anguillara. ℹ €1 vodka shots on M and W. €3 vodka lemon shots on Tu. 💲 Pizza and beer special €6. Cocktails from €7. Aperitivo €8. ⏰ Open daily 10pm-2am. Aperitivo 7-9pm.

PLAZ — CAFE, BAR

V. Pietrapiana 36r ☎055 24 20 81

Plaz gets a lot of traffic. The 30-something crowd gathers inside, while the outdoor seating under the *piazza*'s ancient arches draws an equally ancient crowd. You'll find the youngest Plaz visitors standing around the street or under the tents just outside the door, where you can make a pit-stop to watch the drunk university students stumble by.

➔ On P. dei Ciompi at the end of V. Pietrapiana. 💲 Cover €1.50. Aperitivo from €8. ⏰ Open daily 8am-3am.

KITSCH BAR — BAR, CONCERT VENUE

Viale Antonio Gramsci 1/3/5 ☎055 23 43 890; www.kitsch-bar.com

If a summer evening's booze-fueled wanderings take you to this edge of the historic city center, a small outdoor stage that often features local musicians will probably lure you to Kitsch. The purple tablecloths, giant chandeliers, and zebra chairs live up to Kitsch's not-quite-ironic name. The bar's proximity to parking and the edge of the city center attracts locals driving from the parts of Florence they didn't include on your tourist map.

➔ Follow Viale Giovine Italia up from the river, or take Borgo Croce east until you hit the traffic circle. It's on the northwestern corner. 💲 Aperitivo €8. Happy hour beer and cocktails €5. ⏰ Open daily 6:30pm-2am. Aperitivo 6:30-10:30pm. Happy hour 10pm-1am.

BE BOP MUSIC CLUB
CLUB, CONCERT VENUE

V. dei Servi 76r ☎055 29 52 30

This basement club attracts overheated foreigners with its gospel of air-conditioning. The grotto-like space doesn't have optimal acoustics, but for the price of a beer you can sit right by the stage and discover some pretty great cover bands.

⇟ Although the postcards hilariously provide a map all the way from the train station (clear on the other side of town), just walk up V. dei Servi from the Duomo and look for the "A/C" sign. $ Beer €5. Cocktails €6-8. ⏰ Open daily 11am-2am. Concerts start at 9pm.

glbt nightlife

A number of bars and clubs in this area cater to a **[▼]GLBT** clientele—however, they would prefer not to be listed in guidebooks. Many of these establishments are unmarked or tucked down alleys. If you can get yourself in the correct general vicinity, the staff at neighboring bars can usually direct you the rest of the way. For a list of gay-friendly nightlife options, contact the organization Arcigay (www.arcigay.it) or check out www.patroc.com/florence.

TARTAN JOCK
PUB

Corso dei Tintori 41r ☎055 24 78 305

Don't worry, it's not another Irish pub... this one's Scottish! A lively young crowd kicks back in the bright wood interior, which is one of the most casual in the city. If too much Guinness gives you a sudden urge to be classy, cross the street to Gran Tintori. which beckons with an older crowd, occasional live music, black-and-white photographs, and leather seats.

⇟ On the right just off V. de' Benci near Ponte alle Grazie. $ Shots €3. Guinness €5. ⏰ Open daily 8pm-2am.

I VISACCI CAFFÈ
BAR

Borgo degli Albizi 80r ☎055 20 01 956

There are five-shots-for-€5 deals at a few places in town, but it's good to know which ones they are. This is an excellent joint for a pre-game—if you can convince yourself to leave the €5 cocktails and three beers for €10 behind.

⇟ From the Duomo, take a left off V. Proconsolo onto Borgo degli Albizi. ⏰ Open daily 10am-late.

THE WILLIAM
BAR, CONCERT VENUE

V. Antonio Magliabechi 9 ☎055 26 38 357

An enormous railroad car of an English pub, The William features live music many nights and reasonably priced pub food. Belying the customer base, international flags line the comfy side room to the left of the bar.

⇟ To the right of the Basilica di Santa Croce. $ Pints from €5. ⏰ Open M-Th 11:30am-2am, F-Sa 11:30am-3am, Su 11:30am-2am.

WEST OLTRARNO

West Oltrarno has a good concentration of students, making it a lively and diverse evening locale, especially around the P. Santo Spirito. If you want to go dancing, you'll have to look somewhere else.

▨ VOLUME
BAR

P. Santo Spirito 5r ☎055 23 81 460

There's a quirky atmosphere in this *"museo libreria caffè."* Busy and cluttered, Volume is decorated with woodworking tools, mismatched chairs, a jukebox, and a giant old printing press. The place is just as much about gelato and sweets as it is about cocktails, but the gelato is fancy, starting at €2.50.

⚘ *To the right of the Santo Spirito church, sandwiched between 2 larger establishments.* Ⓢ *Cocktails €7. Crepes €4-7.* ⏰ *Open daily 11am-3am.*

▨ DOLCE VITA
WINE BAR

P. del Carmine 6r ☎055 28 45 95; www.dolcevitaflorence.com

Trendy young adults with margarita glasses populate this happening, artsy bar. The bold interior hosts monthly photo shows as well as live Brazilian, jazz, or contemporary music every Wednesday and Thursday night. Travelers on a budget can break out that one nice outfit they brought, nab a spritz, and feast on the *aperitivo* buffet.

⚘ *In P. del Carmine, by the Carmine church.* ℹ *Live music W-Th 7:30-9:30pm.* Ⓢ *Spritz €7.* ⏰ *Open M-Sa 5pm-2:30am. Aperitivo buffet 7:30-9:30pm.*

POP CAFE
BAR

P. Santo Spirito 18 ☎055 21 38 52; www.popcafe.it

This funky, simple setup has a Pinocchio-nosed, one-eyed girl as its symbol, hinting at its draw to the artsy modern crowd. On the happening P. Santo Spirito, Pop Cafe is further enlivened by a DJ and cheap drinks. Carnivores take heed—the *aperitivo* buffet is vegetarian, as is the weekday lunch menu.

⚘ *To the left of the Santo Spirito church.* Ⓢ *Beer, shots, and prosecco €3 at the bar, €4 at tables. Bagel sandwiches €5.* ⏰ *Open daily 11:30am-2am.*

ONE-EYED JACK
BAR

P. Nazario Sauro 2 ☎055 62 88 040

You shouldn't have any trouble finding this Australian-run bar—a big painting of Jack in an eyepatch spans the front shutter. Live bands and international DJs often come by on weekends; other nights you can hit up the jukebox. This is a great spot for a pint and a bite.

⚘ *Across the street from Gelateria La Carraia and Dante.* Ⓢ *Pints €4.50. Cocktails €7. Sandwich €3.50-4.* ⏰ *Open daily 11am-2am. Happy hour daily until 11pm.*

EAST OLTRARNO

Far east of any part of Florence you're likely to visit, East Oltrarno is where the locals go to party. Since they're real people with real jobs, things tend to be most happening here on weekends. Investigate **Piazza Giuseppe Poggi** (at the base of the hill up to Piazzale Michelangelo), **Via San Niccolò**, and **Via dei Renai** to get your game on. In late summer, bars alight along the southern banks of the Arno.

▨ JAMES JOYCE PUB
BAR

Lungarno Benvenuto Cellini 1 ☎055 65 80 856

This enormous, comfortable bar is filled with students for a reason, particularly on weekend evenings. You don't even have to step inside to order another round of drinks—a window in the bar opens onto the patio. There's foosball, literary kitsch on the walls, and a fun local vibe. Unusual offerings include crepes and staff favorite drinks such as the Mint Alexander with white chocolate, brandy, and mint liqueur.

⚘ *On the western side of the traffic circle after the Ponte San Niccolò.* Ⓢ *Shots €3-4. Wine from €4.50. Bottled beer €5.* ⏰ *Open daily until 3am.*

florence

ZOE
BAR

V. dei Renai 13   ☎055 24 31 11; www.zoebar.it

The colorful outdoor seating and zebra decorations give this place an upbeat feel as it floods with 20- and 30-somethings for its renowned *aperitivo*. Take advantage of Zoe's extensive cocktail menu.

⚑ Across the river from V. de' Benci. Cross Ponte alle Grazie, walk 1 block, and turn left onto V. dei Renai. ⑨ Wine €7. ② Open M-W 8pm-2am, F-Su 8pm-2am.

RIFRULLO
BAR

V. San Niccolò 55r   ☎055 23 42 621; www.ilrifrullo.com

This calm, classy restaurant-bar draws a mix of ages. Come for a subdued but busy weekday *aperitivo* in the garden or a weekend DJ dance set, especially on Sunday.

⚑ Cross Ponte alle Grazie and continue 2 blocks. Turn left onto V. San Niccolò and continue walking. It's the place with a barely legible curlicue name. ⑨Aperitivo and drink €8. ② Open May-Sept daily 7:30pm-2am.

NEGRONI
BAR

V. dei Renai 17r   ☎055 24 36 47; www.negronibar.com

Negroni is the other big name on V. dei Renai, where patrons spill out of the official outdoor seating to populate the small green square and the banks of the Arno. The petite interior is hopping when there's a DJ or bad weather.

⚑ Cross over Ponte alle Grazie and turn right onto Lungarno Serristori. The bar is on P. Giuseppe Poggi, to the right. ⑨ Grappa €4. Beer €5.50. Aperitivo €7-11. ② Open M-Sa 8am-2am, Su 6:30pm-2am. Aperitivo 7-11pm.

arts and culture

You may think that all the grand cultural events in Florence happened several hundred years ago during the Renaissance. In reality, those ancient frescoes and palaces now provide a great backdrop for modern culture. Florence's cultural scene is always changing, with lots of new and small venues. Follow the posters and brochures around town to be rewarded with the latest and greatest. Be on the lookout for festivals, which range from music to cinema to our personal favorite, gelato. Florence's lively bars and lounges tend to also be some of its best music and theater venues, and for some reason they don't charge extra for the entertainment. A good starting point on your cultural excursions is the Teatro Verdi, which sells tickets for theatrical, cultural, and sporting events all over the city. You can also check www. informacitta.net to see what shows are on during your stay.

LIBRARY CAFES

Florence's library cafes are the kind of place you could happily live in forever. Who knew nightlife, books, music, culture, and food could fuse so seamlessly into one?

◾ LA CITÉ LIBRERIA CAFE
WEST OLTRARNO

Borgo San Frediano 21   ☎055 21 03 87; www.lacitelibreria.info

Books, sandwiches, comfy couches, and affordable alcohol—this cozy three-room venue's got pretty much everything you need. And that's before you realize they've also got tango lessons, live music, dance, and theatrical performances.

⚑ From Ponte alla Carraia, walk west on Borgo San Frediano. The library cafe spans 3 windows on the right. ⑨ Beer €3.50. Cocktails €5-6. ② Open M 3:30pm-midnight, Tu-Sa 11:30am-midnight, Su 3:30pm-midnight.

BRAC

V. dei Vagellai 18r   ☎055 09 44 877; www.libreriabrac.net/brac

This chameleon of a place is the perfect daytime escape. You can spend a whole afternoon with a book or laptop while sampling delicious pie in the glass-walled courtyard. In the evening, the back room full of books, glass tables, and artsy placemats becomes one of the few quality vegetarian dinner spots in Florence. The front room is also a fully operational bar.

⌗ *From Ponte alle Grazie, walk 2 blocks down V. de' Benci and turn left onto V. dei Vagellai. It's a small, discreet door on the right just before the piazza.* ⓘ *Free Wi-Fi; ask at bar for the code.* ⓢ *Desserts €6.* ⓩ *Open M-Sa 11am-midnight, Su noon-5pm. Closed 2 weeks in Aug.*

---

festival phobia

Florence spices up its streets with a number of festivals throughout the year. However, these apparently benign celebrations threaten the well-being of some sensitive travelers, so we've assembled a helpful calendar of events:

- **DON'T LIKE CREEPY-CRAWLIES?** Steer clear of the Parco delle Cascine on Ascension Day (40 days after Easter). During the Festa del Grillo, thousands of "lucky crickets" are put up for sale in celebration of the arrival of spring. Actually, thanks to animal rights groups, none of the *grilli* are real—since 1999, Florentines have bought cages with electronic replicas instead.

- **HAVE POLLEN ALLERGIES?** Guess you won't see the P. della Signoria when it's carpeted in fragrant blossoms during the city's annual flower display (usually in late-spring or early summer).

- **SUFFER FROM DODGEBALL-INDUCED PTSD?** Save yourself from the testosterone frenzy of Calcio Storico, an annual tournament in which four teams compete in a 16th-century form of football. The tourney takes over P. Santa Croce in late June.

- **PEDOPHOBIC?** Some people find the procession of singing children who carry papier mâché lanterns through Florence's moonlit streets during the Festa della Rificolona charming. Others find it all too *Children of the Corn*. If you belong in the latter category, stay inside the evening of September 7th.

florence

CLASSICAL MUSIC

Florence is typically a visual-arts city, but there's still plenty of music to be found in the world of frescoes. Operas are also sometimes hosted by **Saint Mark's Church** (V. Maggio 16).

CHIESA DI SANTA MARIA DE' RICCI

V. del Corso   ☎055 21 50 44

An unassuming little church with a loud voice, this *chiesa* boasts a pretty spectacular pipe organ. Fortunately for the music-starved traveler, it likes to show it off. The church doors are thrown open every evening for 7pm vespers and again at 9pm for an organ recital. The concert programs are crowd pleasers. If the only organ piece you know is Bach's *Toccata and Fugue*, you're still likely to be in luck, as it's performed frequently.

⌗ *From the Duomo, take V. dei Calzaioli south and turn left onto V. del Corso.* ⓢ *Free.* ⓩ *Vespers daily 7pm. Organ recital daily 9pm.*

TEATRO VERDI SANTA CROCE

V. Ghibellina 99r ☎055 21 23 20; www.teatroverdionline.it

Perhaps Florence's most famous music venue, this grand red-and-gold concert hall lined with box seats swells with concerts from symphonies to modern favorites.

From P. Santa Croce, walk up V. Giovanni da Verazzano. i Credit card required for phone or online reservations. $ Prices vary depending on show and seat. ⏰ Box office open daily 4-7pm during the theater season. Alternative box office at V. delle Vecchie Carceri 1 open M-F 9:30am-7pm, Sa 9:30am-2pm.

ROCK AND JAZZ

The rock and jazz venues in Florence attract lively crowds and tend to cost no more than the price of a drink—and any drink tastes sweeter when sipped to the sound of a sweet serenade. Many of the places we list in **Nightlife** regularly host live music, including West Oltrarno's **Dolce Vita** and **Volume.** Big-name artists have been known to show up anywhere from the **Teatro Verdi** to small cafes, so keep your eyes peeled for posters.

SEI DIVINO SANTA MARIA NOVELLA

Borgo Ognissanti 42r ☎055 21 77 91

Live music fills this *aperitivo* destination every Thursday. On all the other days, you can still count on a strict diet of rock and roll to go with your cocktails and wine. For some reason, the tourist crowds haven't discovered this gem yet, so, for your sake, please don't tell them.

Go northwest on Borgo Ognissanti from Ponte alla Carraia. It's on the right. i Live music on Th. $ Cocktails from €7. ⏰ Open M-Sa noon-2am, Su 3pm-2am.

JAZZ CLUB SANTA CROCE

V. Nuova de' Caccini 3 ☎055 24 79 700; www.jazzclubfirenze.com

Contrary to what you might expect, Jazz Club isn't just about jazz: they also play blues, rock and roll, rock, funk, soul, swing, and world music. Whatever the genre, their live music guarantees a relaxing night out.

Going north on Borgo Pinti, turn left just before V. degli Alfani. Jazz Club is on the left. i Rock and blues on Tu. Jazz on W. $ Cover €5. ⏰ Open Tu-Sa 9pm-late. Concerts 10:15pm.

THEATER

Don't be scared off because you assume performances will be in Italian; theaters are some of the best evening experiences in Florence, and the fact that they're often free is the icing on an already awesome cake. Florentine theater turns up in the most unexpected places, like restaurants and museums. In the summer, the **Bargello** sometimes hosts site-specific productions in its courtyard, while temporary stages in the **Piazza della Signoria** host music and dance acts. If you're here a bit longer, there are some worthy venues just outside town like the **Teatro Puccini,** the **Teatro Sotteraneo,** and the **Saschall.**

TEATRO DELLA PERGOLA SAN MARCO

V. della Pergola 18 ☎055 22 641; www.teatrodellapergola.com

Nowadays, the only opera you hear in this 1656 opera house happens during the *Maggio Musicale Fiorentino* festival. The rest of the time, you can enjoy a selection of about 250 drama productions each year from its plush red seats and gilded galleries.

At the intersection of V. della Colonna and V. Nuova de' Caccini. $ Prices vary by performance. ⏰ Box office open M-F 9:30am-6:45pm, Sa 10am-12:30pm.

CINEMA

Check listings for VO *(versione originale)* to find films that have not been dubbed over in Italian. There's also a trend among Italian cinemas to have 3D screenings of concerts or theater performances happening elsewhere in Italy.

CINEMA TEATRO ODEON — PIAZZA DELLA SIGNORIA

P. degli Strozzi 1r ☎055 21 40 68; www.odeon.intoscana.it

The grand cinema itself will probably outshine whatever film you intend to watch here. Beyond the massive stones and imposing wooden doors, the interior is so ornate that the ticket booth is decked with Doric columns, the columns are decked with golden orbs, and the orbs are decked with golden elephants and 👍**dragons.** The month's schedule of English-language features is posted outside, but you may want to stop in anyway for the fresh, air-conditioned interior.

*➤ From P. della Repubblica, walk up V. degli Strozzi. **i** A/C. Bistro and bar inside. $ Tickets €7.50, students M-F €6. ⏰ Screenings begin in early evening.*

SPECTATOR SPORTS

STADIO ARTEMIO FRANCHI — OUTSKIRTS

Viale Manfredo Fanti 4A ☎055 55 32 803; http://en.violachannel.tv

As is true for most Italian cities, Florence has a soccer team, and that soccer team is one of the primary obsessions of the city's residents. Purple-clad Fiorentina waver on the brink of success but never quite seem to achieve it, making them a great team to support if you're more into roller-coaster rides than easy victories. Catch the games here on Sunday during most of the year. The stadium is largely uncovered, though, so pick a day when it's not raining.

➤ Take bus #7, 17, or 20, or the train from Santa Maria Novella to Firenze Campo di Marte. The bus takes you directly to the stadium; it's a short walk from the train. $ Tickets €14-80. ⏰ Box office open M-F 9:30am-12:30pm and 2:30-6:30pm. Most matches Sept-May Su afternoons.

shopping

Florence may not be Paris or Milan, but it sure has some snazzy window displays—you'll be tempted to stop at nearly every store you pass. For upscale designer shopping, look to Piazza della Signoria, while San Lorenzo and Santa Croce tend to be home to the boutiques. Florence is also brimming with open-air markets where you can find just about anything—if you know where to go. Whatever you do, steer clear of fake merchandise, like knock-off handbags. They're cheap (and for a reason), but they're illegal to buy as well as to sell, and you could face a hefty fine if caught with one.

OPEN-AIR MARKETS

Open-air markets are some of the most authentic experiences Florence has to offer. Of course, you'll have to break through the natural assumption that foreigners are too stupid to bargain. If you need further venues to hone your negotiation techniques, you can also try the enormous food and clothing market in **Parco delle Cascine** (P. Vittorio Veneto ➤ Off Viale Fratelli Rosselli on the western edge of the city. ⏰ Open Tu 7am-1pm.), the flower market in **Piazza della Repubblica** (⏰ Open Th 10am-7pm.), or the antique market at **Giardini Fortezza Firenze.** (➤ Follow V. Faenza north as it becomes V. Dionisi. ⏰ Open Sept-June every 3rd Su of the month.)

👍 MERCATO CENTRALE — SAN LORENZO

P. del Mercato Centrale

This technically isn't an outdoor market, but it's chaotic enough to feel like one. At Mercato Centrale you can find just about anything within the realm of food, from cheeses to spices to singing butchers. To stand out, stalls tack up random items (like a pair of striped purple and white balloon shorts) to their roofs or counters. You can also find unusually shaped pasta casually mixed in with the standard shapes: tortellini, spaghetti, penises, ravioli, striped farfalle... Wait—striped farfale? If all this food ogling is making you hungry, some stalls in the center sell pizza and sandwiches by weight.

✦ It's the huge green-and-red building in the middle of all those sidewalk vendors. ☒ Open spring-fall M-Sa 7am-2pm; winter Sa 7am-2pm.

◼ SAN LORENZO   SAN LORENZO
V. dell'Ariento

San Lorenzo's market spans the entire length of V. dell'Ariento. Vendors actively try to sell you hats, scarves, journals, or souvenirs as you pass, regardless of your apparent interest level. If you've got an eye for quality, this is the place to buy some of that famous Florentine leather. Just walking past, this researcher was offered a 90% discount on anything in an entire leather stall, so don't feel guilty working that price down. Vendors are used to ignorant tourists paying full price, so don't expect to shave more than a few euro off the price except through some hard-line bargaining. Since so many stalls have similar wares, you can always move on to the next one (or pretend you're going to) to get better prices.

✦ Walking away from the station on V. Nazionale, V. dell'Ariento is on your right just across from the fountain. ☒ Open daily 9am-7pm.

SANTO SPIRITO   WEST OLTRARNO
P. Santo Spirito

This *piazza* across the Arno offers a smaller, more local flea market. Shoes, clothes, cosmetics, and plants await every day of the week (particularly on Saturday), but the best time to go is on the second and third Sunday of each month. Artisans and antique vendors flood the square on the second Sunday, while the third Sunday hosts the Fierucola organic foods market. Be careful cutting through the tree-adorned center of the market—locals have been known to convert this fountain space into a neighborhood water fight.

✦ From Ponte Santa Trinita, walk past the bridge, turn right onto V. di Santo Spirito, and turn left onto V. del Presto di San Martino. It's in the piazza at the end of the street. ☒ Open M-Sa 8am-1pm. 2nd and 3rd Su of the month open 9am-7pm.

CLOTHING

The true traveler is a clothing chameleon; here are some shops that can help you blend in. **Piazza della Signoria** and **Santa Maria Novella** are home to department stores and fun display windows, which become increasingly expensive toward the river. For cheap boutiques, hit up **San Lorenzo,** especially along V. Faenza and around the outdoor market, and **Santa Croce,** notably along V. Giuseppe Verdi.

PROMOD   SAN LORENZO
V. de' Cerretani 46-48r   ☎055 21 78 44; www.promod.eu

Akin to H&M or Forever 21, Promod sells relatively disposable women's fashions at bargain prices. When we visited, the "in" thing was bold color motifs and revamped granny flower patterns.

✦ Take V. de' Cerretani west from the Duomo. *i* Women's clothing only. ☒ Open daily 10am-8pm.

GOLDENPOINT   SAN LORENZO
V. de' Cerretani 40r   ☎055 28 42 19; www.goldenpointonline.com

Goldenpoint deals in women's swimsuits and lingerie. It offers few bargains, but there's a bigger selection of swimsuit sizes and styles than elsewhere. Curvy women take note: Italian swimsuits offer far better support than American styles.

✦ Take V. de' Cerretani west from the Duomo. *i* Other locations at V. Panzani 33 (☎055 21 42 96) and V. dei Calzaioli 6 (☎055 27 76 224). ☒ Open daily 10am-7pm.

ARTISAN GOODS

Florence has numerous artisan goods for which it is justly famous. It is particularly renowned for its soft, quality leather. The cheapest place to find it is the **San Lorenzo** market (see above). If you want to learn about the actual craft of leatherworking, stop by the **Scuola del Cuoio** within the Basilica di Santa Croce. Founded by Franciscan friars in the 1930s, this leather school continues to offer courses that last from one day to six months. Classes don't come cheap, though. Visit www.scuoladelcuoio.com for information, or enter their storefront in the basilica via the apse entrance at V. di San Giuseppe 5r. If you're looking for gold, the Ponte Vecchio, lined with numerous goldsmiths and jewelers as well as shady street sellers, is the place for you. There is also a smattering of gold stores around the city, misleadingly called *"Oreficerie.* " Finally, though masks are a bigger deal in Venice, you can still get a sense for the *commedia dell'arte* tradition at Alice Atelier. With any luxury good, we recommend you do background research before making any serious purchases. The listings below are included more because of how fascinating they are to browse than for the likelihood of you actually buying anything from them.

👍 FARMACEUTICA DI SANTA MARIA NOVELLA — SANTA MARIA NOVELLA

V. della Scala 16 — ☎055 21 62 76; www.smnovella.com

You can smell the talcum and perfume before setting foot in this time capsule of a perfumery. The Santa Maria Novella monks have been bottling medicines in this museum-worthy space since the 13th century, but the "modern" pharmacy is straight from the Victorian age. Elixirs, perfumes, juleps, salts, spirits, waters, and protective oils are all available, displayed on shelving and sold in packaging that's been updated little over the course of the past century. As you browse through colored bottles of essence of myrrh under a chandelier, imagine your life as a Victorian aristocrat.

➡ At the corner of V. della Porcellana. Coming from P. Santa Maria Novella, turn right onto V. della Scala. $ Candles €10-50. 500ml liqueurs €50. Dog collars from €30. ⏰ Open daily 10:30am-7:30pm. In Aug, closes on Sa at 1pm.

👍 ALICE ATELIER: THE MASKS OF PROF. AGOSTINO DESSÌ — SAN LORENZO

V. Faenza 72r — ☎055 28 73 70; www.alicemasks.com

Masks aren't just quick and easy Halloween costumes—at Professor Agostino's Dessì's studio, they are a true art form. Here you can find the perfect two-faced mask to express your split personality, or to give to a friend as an elaborate insulting pun set-up. Handmade masks of things you never imagined, from bionic metal-faced creatures to puzzle people, are as good as a museum visit. Highly involved in Florence's art scene, Dessì has been making masks for world exhibitions since the '70s and brought his daughter, Alice, into the family business in 1997. The shop offers mask-making courses and will happily direct you to nearby exhibitions.

➡ From P. della Stazione, take V. Nazionale and turn left onto V. Faenza. ℹ Application form for mask-making courses can be found on the website. $ Masks from €50. 5-session course €500. ⏰ Open M-Sa 9am-1pm and 3:30-7:30pm.

GALLERIA MICHELANGELO — SANTA CROCE

P. Santa Croce 8 — ☎055 24 16 21

This vast, Japanese-run leather emporium is a frequent stop for cruise-ship shore excursions. They often have whole rooms full of items at a 50% discount.

➡ On the left side of the piazza, facing the basilica. $ Bags from €80. ⏰ Open daily 9am-2pm and 2:30-8pm.

BOOKS AND JOURNALS

Florentine leather isn't just to drape on your own body—albums and notebooks can wear it too. Marbelized and leather journals are a big thing in this city. Follow our lead (and check the street markets) to avoid paying €60 for a journal you'll start and probably never finish.

ALBERTO COZZI — SANTA MARIA NOVELLA

V. del Parione 35r — ☎055 29 49 68

You can see right into the workshop of this artisanal paper-goods shop, which has been passed down through four generations. They sell items like glasses cases and bracelets in addition to the standard albums and notebooks. You can get your leather photo album customized with gold etching right before your eyes for no additional cost, and they have demos on Saturday afternoons. A word of warning: if you pet the sweet spaniel, she'll insistently follow you around for the rest of your visit.

From P. Carlo Goldoni, head right onto V. del Parione. $ 5 handmade pens €12. Marbleized leather-bound journals from €18. Refillable leather journals from €35. ⏰ Open daily 9am-1pm and 3-7pm. Workshop demonstrations on Sa afternoons.

MADE IN TUSCANY — SAN MARCO

V. degli Alfani 120r

This is the way to have the artisan experience on a budget. For the same price as the options on the shelf, the owner will make you one with your own selection of leather and cover stamp.

Just south of the Accademia, off V. Ricasoli. ℹ Custom journals usually take overnight to make. $ Custom leather journals from €10. ⏰ Open M 2:30-7pm, Tu-Su 9:30am-2pm and 2:30-7pm.

how they stack up

Paul Newman or Robert Redford? Chocolate or vanilla? Dante or Boccaccio? OK, people may not debate Italian authors the way they do ice cream or attractive cinema stars, but they should. Both writers grew up and spent important parts of their life in Florence, revolutionized literature by writing in vernacular Italian, and are famous for sprawling allegorical works (*The Divine Comedy* and *The Decameron*, respectively). If you're spending any amount of time in Florence, you may find the rich cultural history infecting you with a desire to pick up one of these masterpieces. To help you decide which one, here's a quick summary of how they stack up.

- **ARTISTIC INFLUENCE:** Both are hugely influential, but we've got to give this one to Dante. His work paved the way for Boccaccio and popularized a new conception of heaven and hell. Boccaccio gets points for inspiring Hugh Hefner's attempt to adapt the bawdier stories of *The Decameron* into highfalutin porn.
- **ORIGINALITY:** A tie. Using established biblical and classical themes, Dante crafted an original tale of spiritual discovery. Boccaccio drew on international folktales to fashion his patchwork of plots.
- **PIETY:** Definitely Dante. In the *Inferno,* he depicts heretics punished in flaming tombs. In one of Boccaccio's tales, an abbess has her way with a gardener. Did we mention the porn connection?

essentials

PRACTICALITIES

- **TOURIST OFFICES: Uffici Informazione Turistica** has its primary office at **Via Manzoni 16.** (☎055 23 320 ⏰ Open M-F 9am-1pm.) Other locations include **Piazza della Stazione 4** (☎055 21 22 45 ⏰ Open M-Sa 8:30am-7pm, Su 8:30am-2pm.), **Via Cavour 1r** (☎055 29 08 32 ⏰ Open M-Sa 8:30am-6:30pm, Su 8:30am-1pm.), and **Borgo Santa Croce 29r.** (☎055 23 40 444 ⏰ Open Mar-Oct M-Sa 9am-7pm, Su 9am-2pm; Nov-Feb M-Sa 9am-5pm, Su 9am-2pm.)

- **CURRENCY EXCHANGE: Best and Fast Change** has offices at V. de' Cerretani 47r (☎055 23 99 855) and Borgo Santa Lorenzo 16r. (☎055 28 43 91.)

- **ATMS: BNL** (V. de' Cerretani 6) accepts Visa. **Banca Toscana** (V. dell'Ariento 18) accepts Mastercard.

- **LUGGAGE STORAGE:** At **Stazione Santa Maria Novella.** (⚑ By platform 16. ⓢ 1st 4hr. €4, 5th-12th hr. €0.60 per hr., €0.20 per hr. thereafter. Cash only. ⏰ Open daily 6am-11:50pm.)

- **LAUNDROMATS: Onda Blue.** (V. degli Alfani 24 and V. Guelfa 221r ⏰ Open daily 8am-10pm.)

- **INTERNET: Internet Train** can be found all over the city. For a central location, try **Via de' Benci 36r.** (☎055 26 38 555; www.internettrain.it ⚑ From P. Santa Croce, turn left onto V. de' Benci. ⓢ Wi-Fi €2.50-3 per hr. Internet €3-4.50 per hr. ⏰ Open daily 10am-10:30pm.) Many restaurants and library cafes offer free Wi-Fi. Try **BRAC.** (V. dei Vagellai 18r ☎055 09 44 877 ⏰ Open daily 10am-11pm.)

- **POST OFFICES: Via Pellicceria 3.** (☎055 27 36 481 ⚑ South of P. della Repubblica ⏰ Open M-F 8:15am-7pm, Sa 8:15am-12:30pm.) Other locations include V. de' Barbadori 37r (☎055 28 81 75), V. Pietrapiana 53 (☎055 42 21 850), V. de' Barbadori 37r (☎055 28 81 75), and V. Camillo Cavour 71a. (☎ 055 47 19 10.)

- **POSTAL CODE:** 50100.

EMERGENCY

- **EMERGENCY NUMBER: Ambulance:** ☎118.

- **POLICE: Polizia Municipale.** (☎055 32 85, 24hr. non-emergency helpline ☎055 32 83 333) Help is also available for tourists at the mobile police units parked at V. dei Calzaioli near P. della Signoria and at Borgo Santa Jacopo in the Oltrarno near Ponte Vecchio. The emergency **Carabinieri** number is ☎112.

- **LATE-NIGHT PHARMACIES: Farmacia Comunale.** (Stazione Santa Maria Novella ☎055 21 67 61 ⏰ Open 24hr. Ring the bell 1-4am.) **Farmacia Molteni.** (V. Calzaioli 7r ☎055 28 94 90 ⚑ Just north of P. della Signoria.) **Farmacia All'Insegna del Moro.** (P. San Giovanni 20r ☎055 21 13 43 ⚑ A little east of the Duomo.)

- **HOSPITALS/MEDICAL SERVICES: Arcispedale Santa Maria Nuova** is northeast of the Duomo and has a 24hr. emergency room. (P. Santa Maria Nuova 1 ☎055 27 581) Tourist medical services can be found at **Via Lorenzo II Magnifico 59.** (☎055 47 54 11 ⚑ In the north of the city, near P. della Libertà. ⏰ M-F 11am-noon and 5-6pm, Sa 11am-noon.) **Associazione Volontari Ospedalieri** provides free medical translation. (☎055 42 50 126; www.avofirenze.it ⏰ Open M 4-6pm, Tu 10am-noon, W 4-6pm, Th 10am-noon, F 4-6pm.)

GETTING THERE

How you arrive in Florence will be dictated by where you come from. Florence may have named its Amerigo Vespucci airport after the guy who in turn gave the Americas their name, but that doesn't mean the city has any flights from the USA. Those flying across the Atlantic will have to transfer at another European airport. If flying from within Europe, it will probably be cheaper for you to fly into the budget-airline hub that is Pisa Airport. Buses run regularly from Pisa Airport to Florence; they take just over an hour and cost about €10. If coming from within Italy, you will most likely catch a train, which will bring you into Santa Maria Novella station. If traveling locally, buses may be useful.

by plane

Aeroporto Amerigo Vespucci is Florence's main airport. (V. del Termine 11 ☎055 30 615 main line, 055 30 61 700 for 24hr. automated service; www.aeroporto.firenze.it. ℹ For lost baggage, call ☎055 30 61 302.) From the airport, the city can be reached via the **VolainBus shuttle.** You can pick up the shuttle on the Departures side. (➔ Exit the airport to the right and pass the taxi stand. Drop-off is at Santa Maria Novella station. $ €5. ⏰ 25min., every 30min. 6am-11:30pm.) A cab from the airport to the city center costs about €20.

by train

Santa Maria Novella train station dominates the northwest of the city. (www.grandistazioni.it ⏰ Open daily 6am-midnight.) You can purchase tickets from the fast ticket kiosks or tellers. There are daily trains from: Bologna ($ €25-36. ⏰ 40min., 2 per hr. 7am-11:26pm.); Milan ($ €53. ⏰ 1¾hr., 1 per hr. 7am-9pm.); Rome ($ €45. ⏰ 1½hr., 2 per hr. 8:30am-11:33pm.); Siena ($ €6.30. ⏰ 1½hr., 6 per hr. 5am-9:18pm.); Venice. ($ €43. ⏰ 2hr., 2 per hr. 7:30am-7:30pm.) For precise schedules and prices, check www.trenitalia.com.

by bus

Three major intercity bus companies run out of Florence's bus station. From Santa Maria Novella train station, turn left onto on V. Alamanni—the station is on the left by a long driveway. **SITA** (V. Santa Caterina da Siena 17 ☎800 37 37 60; www.sitabus.it) runs buses to and from Siena, San Gimignano, and other Tuscan destinations. **LAZZI** (P. della Stazione 4/6r ☎055 21 51 55; www.lazzi.it ⏰ For timetable info call ☎055 35 10 61.) buses depart from P. Adua, just east of the train station. Routes connect to Lucca, Pisa, and many other regional towns. **CAP-COPIT** (Largo Fratelli Alinari 10 ☎055 21 46 37; www.capautolinee.it) runs to regional towns. Timetables for all three companies change regularly, so call ahead or check online for schedules.

GETTING AROUND

The main thing that you should know is that Florence is a small city. Most visitors simply walk everywhere without any need for public transportation. This is ideal for the budget traveler, as you won't rack up the Metro and bus fares like you do in many other European cities. And if you're going to venture outside the compact city center, Florence has you covered.

by bus

As the city's only form of public transportation, Florence's tiny orange buses are surprisingly clean, reliable, and organized. Operated by **ATAF** and **LI-NEA,** the extensive bus network includes several night-owl buses that take over regular routes in the late evenings. The schedule for every passing line is posted on the pole of each well-marked bus stop, complete with the direction the bus is going and a list of every stop in order. Most buses originate at P. della Stazione or P. di San Marco. Buses #12 and #13 run to the Piazzale Michelangelo; bus #7 runs to Fiesole. You're unlikely to need to use the buses unless you're leaving the city center. You can buy tickets from most newsstands, ticket vending machines, or the ATAF kiosk in P. della Stazione. (☎800 42 45 00 ⓢ 90min. ticket €1.20, €2 if purchased on board; 24hr. ticket €5; 3-day ticket €12.) Stamp your ticket when you board the bus; you then have the length of time denoted by the ticket to re-use it. Be careful—if you forget to time-stamp your ticket when you board the bus (and can't successfully play the "confused foreigner" card), it's a €50 fine.

by taxi

To call a cab, call **Radio Taxi.** (☎055 4390, 055 4499, 055 4242, or 055 4798) Tell the operator your location and when you want the cab, and the nearest available car will be sent to you. Each cab has a rate card in full view, and the meter displays the running fare, which is based on the distance traveled and any supplements charged. If you're going far or are nervous, it never hurts to ask for an estimate before board- ing. There are surcharges for Sundays, holidays, luggage, and late nights. Unless you have a lot of baggage, you probably won't want to take a taxi during the day, when traffic will make the meter tick up mercilessly. At lunchtime, a 5min. ride from the Duomo to the Oltrarno will cost €7. Nevertheless, cabs are a manageable late-night option if you're outside the city, and especially if you're in a group. Designated cab stands can be found at P. della Stazione, Fortezza da Basso, and P. della Repubblica. Cabs can also often be found at Santa Maria Novella.

by bike

It takes some confidence to bike in the crowded parts of central Florence, but cy- cling is a great way to check out a longer stretch of the Arno's banks or to cover a lot of territory in one day. **Mille E Una Bici** (☎055 65 05 295; www.comune.firenze. it/servizi_pubblici/trasporti/noleggiobici.htm) rents 200 bikes that can be picked up and returned at any of its four locations: P. della Stazione, P. di Santa Croce, P. Ghiberti, and Stazione F.S. Campo Di Marte. **Florence By Bike** (V. San Zanobi 91r and 120/122r ☎055 48 89 92; www.florencebybike.it ⌚ Open Apr-Oct daily 9am-7:30pm; Nov-Mar M-Sa 9am-1pm and 3:30-7:30pm.) is another good resource. Staff will help renters plan routes, whether it's an afternoon or a multi-day trip outside of town.

MONEY

tipping and bargaining

In Italy, a 5% tip is customary, particularly in restaurants (10% if you particularly liked the service). Italian waiters won't cry if you don't leave a tip; just be ready to ignore the pangs of your conscience later on. Taxi drivers expect tips as well, but lucky for alcohol-lovers, it is unusual to tip in bars. Bargaining is appropriate in markets and other informal settings, though in regular shops it is inappropriate. Hotels will often offer lower prices to people looking for a room that night, so you will often be able to find a bed cheaper than what is officially quoted.

SAFETY AND HEALTH

local laws and police

In Italy, you will mainly encounter two types of boys and girls in blue: the *polizia* (☎113) and the *carabinieri* (☎112). The *polizia* are a civil force under the command of the Ministry of the Interior, whereas the *carabinieri* fall under the auspices of the Ministry of Defense and are considered a military force. Both, however, generally serve the same purpose—to maintain security and order in the country. In the case of attack or robbery, both will respond to inquiries or desperate pleas for help.

drugs and alcohol

Needless to say, **illegal drugs** are best avoided altogether, particularly when traveling in a foreign country. In Italy, just like almost everywhere else in the world, drugs including marijuana, cocaine, and heroin are illegal, and possession or other drug-related offenses will be harshly punished.

The legal drinking age in Italy is (drumroll please) 16. Remember to drink responsibly and to **never drink and drive.** Doing so is illegal and can result in a prison sentence, not to mention early death. The legal blood alcohol content (BAC) for driving in Italy is under 0.05%, significantly lower than the US limit of 0.08%.

travelers with disabilities

Travelers in wheelchairs should be aware that travel in Italy will sometimes be extremely difficult. This country predates the wheelchair—sometimes it seems even the wheel—by several centuries and thus poses unique challenges to travelers with disabilities. **Accessible Italy** (☎378 941 111; www.accessibleitaly.com) offers advice to tourists of limited mobility heading to Italy, with tips on subjects ranging from finding accessible accommodations to wheelchair rental.

CLIMATE

You'd think that Italy was balmy and beautiful, bordering the Mediterranean as it does. And you'd be right—for some places, some of the time. Surrounded by hills, Florence has pretty consistently hot summers, and, with very little wind, its inhabitants don't get much respite from the humidity. The winter is a little more bearable, but wetter, with a lot of precipitation in late fall and early winter. Long story short, we at *Let's Go* can't really tell you what the weather is going to be like on your trip, so check the forecast before you go. And then don't trust it, because it's probably wrong anyway.

florence 101

Epicenter of the Italian Renaissance, home to some of history's most noted artists, scientists, and religious leaders, and the place with the world's highest concentration of dudes named David, Florence has a rich culture all its own. Over the years, the former capital of Italy has amassed an incredible collection of art, including Botticelli's luminescent *Primavera* and, of course, Michelangelo's 17 ft. masterpiece (and its rockin' abs). But Florentine history is not only defined by brush strokes and chiseled marble. Once ruled by the Medici family, the banking barons of Renaissance Italy, Florence has a dark past deep with political turmoil and controversy. Nowadays things have calmed down a bit, giving tourists the perfect opportunity to stroll along the *piazza*, explore more churches than they ever thought possible, and quickly sink into a food coma after overdosing on gelato. Offering something for both newcomers and veterans, Florence still has all the pizzazz and flair that it did centuries ago. Read on to learn some of the dos and don'ts of the Florentine lifestyle, how to stay as chic as the locals (it's not as easy as you think), and the best way to burn off those ever-increasing gelato calories.

HISTORY

no country for young men? (59 bce-700 ce)

Florence was founded in 59 BCE by **Julius Caesar** as a retirement center for his veteran military officials. Keeping with the military theme, the city was first designed to mimic a military camp. With its gridded layout, Florence became a metropolitan *tour de force* in Central Italy and attracted both the **Byzantines** and **Goths** after the Roman Empire fizzled out.

In the sixth century, Florence adopted Christianity as its principle religion and built its very first churches, which were dedicated to patron saint San Giovanni. Now a Christian community, Florence was largely under papal control, as the Pope held serious sway over the city's development and governing bodies.

cathedrals and communes (774-1200)

Florence fell under rule of the **Holy Roman Empire** in 774 when Charlemagne conquered the city. Fearful of Hungarian invasions, the city's ruling counts and countesses built walls to protect Florence. Free from foreign attack, the city prospered, growing from a former military community to a center of religious thought. Under the direction of **Pope Victor II,** the city built up its booming collection of churches.

From 1125 until the turn of the 13th century, Florence's ruling military leaders amassed control over surrounding towns in Tuscany. After winning numerous battles, Florence and its newly acquired territories established a constituted **commune,** a medieval allegiance of defense between neighboring communities. During the city's time as a commune, Florentine leaders took advantage of the protection granted by their allies to develop the city's infrastructure and industries.

galloping guelphs and gibillines! (13th century)

By 1215, the city had been divided into two classes: the working class **Guelphs** and the noble **Gibillines.** If you couldn't guess already, the huge gap between the two groups drove the Guelphs to kick some Gibilline butt a la *Braveheart*. With their newfound control of city politics, the Guelphs, who were mostly merchants and artisans, created a new social order that encouraged growth in the agricultural and—you guessed it—arts industries.

The Guelphs' hold on Florence, however, was failing, and the Gibillines took power once again in 1260. After a few more decades of back-and-forth struggle, two new political groups emerged in Florence, the entrepreneurial **Magnati** and laboring **Popolani.** In spite of the political tensions that resulted from the four-way frenzy, Florence continued to develop as one of the most prominent cities in Europe. It was during this time that **Dante Alighieri** began crafting *The Divine Comedy*, a symbol of the booming art scene. And then a few fleas came along.

the mighty medici (1348-1737)

The year 1348 marked the beginning of the **Black Plague,** the only period in history during which the world population actually decreased. As the Plague drew to a close and society began to get back on its feet again, the conniving **Cosimo de'Medici** seized the opportunity to make some major bucks off of Florence's own little baby boom. The wealth he amassed in his surprisingly long life of 75 years established his family as the de facto rulers of Florence and Tuscany for the next three centuries.

Using their newfound power, the Medici began a campaign to jumpstart the city's less than prospering art scene by commissioning sculptors and other artists to recapture the grandeur of classical antiquity. During their reign, Renaissance royalty like **Leonardo da Vinci** and **Michelangelo** revolutionized the fields of art and science. A good deal of the work in the Uffizi Galleries and especially the Pitti Palace (the Medici's former residence) was given to the city of Florence when the last Medici, Gian Gastone de'Medici, died. Also during the Renaissance, famed architect Filippo Brunelleschi designed the **Duomo,** Florence's most recognizable cathedral. The emergence of the Italian High Renaissance might not have begun in Florence, or even have happened at all, without the financial backing of the Medici and their affiliates.

the woes of world wars (1900-today)

As the 20th century dawned on Italy, so did the country's most devastating political turmoil. Madman **Mussolini** took advantage of Europe's post-WWI disrepair to seize control in 1922. In 1940, convinced that his pal Hitler would easily win the war against Britain and France, Mussolini decided to side with the Axis. Once the US entered the war, Italy reaffirmed its alliance with Germany and declared war on America. The decision, though, proved to be extremely unwise, ultimately leading to the worst destruction of Italian cultural property since the Middle Ages.

Florence was occupied by Germany from 1943-44, during which time allied fighters continuously bombed the city. As the Germans realized they were losing control of Europe, though, they commenced a full-scale retreat from Italy. On their way out of Florence, they bombed every bridge leading into the city (except for the **Ponte Vecchio,** which was spared) to spite the allied troops.

In 1945 the occupation ended, ushering in the modern era of Italian politics. The current constitution, instituted in 1948, allows for a democratic republic, with a president, a prime minister, a bicameral parliament, and an independent judiciary. Though the government has changed nearly 60 times since, one element remains consistent: powerful, bold leaders. Self-made tycoon **Silvio Berlusconi** is the latest in this colorful lineup, elected as prime minister in 1999... and 2001... and 2008, with plenty of corruption scandals as well as two resignations in between. Berlusconi's middle-right stance aligned him with American President George Bush and the Iraq war. Though the unpopularity of this decision opened the doors for the more liberal Romano Prodi to move into power, Italians have proven themselves to be more forgiving than the oft-divorced Berlusconi's ex- and estranged wives, as this philanderer now once again serves as Prime Minister of Italy.

CUSTOMS AND ETIQUETTE

Florentines exude the typical boisterousness and sociability of any Italian. Despite the metropolitan atmosphere, Florence isn't New York, so lose the "I'm in a constant rush" mentality: slow down and take in all that the city has to offer. Sure, mealtime conversations with Italians tend to be loud and include many indecipherable hand gestures, but don't interpret this boldness as rudeness. Instead, try to be as expressive as the locals—like the old saying goes, "When in Florence, do as the Florentines do." Or something like that.

save the short shorts

Although most churches don't mind visitors during the day, Catholic parishioners in Florence expect the women in their churches to dress more like Mother Theresa than Lady Gaga. While the more popular Duomo and Santa Croce may provide sheaths to cover your shoulders and legs, smaller churches are unlikely to offer this amenity. Don't be caught off guard and have to hike back to your hostel because your shorts are a bit above fingertip length; plan your outfit ahead of time.

cutting the queue

Kindness is king in Florence, but that doesn't mean the locals don't know how to get what they want, when they want it. Warning: shopping in Florence is a high-energy, competitive activity, suited only for trained professionals and veterans. Unlike in the United States, cutting in front of a line is not at all uncommon for Italian shopaholics. If you're seriously tempted to knock out the cutter's lights, hold yourself back from causing a scene. The last thing you want is a Florentine fashionista giving you a smack down in the middle of Miu Miu. But, if you're in a hurry yourself, give barging a go. The locals may even commend you for your crassness as you leave the store, Versace shoes in tow.

FOOD AND DRINK

Florence is particularly well known for its reliance on rustic, hearty Tuscan staples. As the city has transitioned into the 21st century, chefs have begun to experiment with contemporary haute cuisine, creating dishes that combine the comfort of traditional local foods with innovative ingredients and techniques.

horses and donkeys and sheep, oh my!

Florentines have what some might deem unusual tastes, but you'll discover that shredded horse meat, braised donkey rump, and *trippa* (stewed sheep intestines) aren't really as offensive as they sound. The dishes date back to Roman antiquity, and despite the passing of millennia and ever-changing culinary trends, they remain just as popular among Florentines. If you eat meat, each is worth a try; after all, the

florence 101

sale of horse meat for human consumption is illegal in many countries, so when else will you get the chance?

drink (more than you can actually remember)

There's nothing more calming than a fine bottle of *vino* after a strenuous day hitting the tourist circuit. Because of its prime location in Tuscany, arguably Italy's finest wine-making region, there's never a lack of Jesus juice in Florence. Whether you're looking for a bold Chianti or a mellower white Trebbiano, you're guaranteed an abundance of locally produced options.

ART AND ARCHITECTURE

Florence was the preferred playground of some of Italy's most renowned artists, whose names live on in everyone's favorite crime-fighting amphibians, the Teenage Mutant Ninja Turtles. Leonardo, Michelangelo, Raphael, and Donatello, among others, revolutionized Western art, replacing the austere religious iconography of the Middle Ages with highly idealized representations of both religion and man.

the rockin' renaissance

Florence was the birthplace of the Italian High Renaissance, boasting such artistic big-wigs as **Botticelli** and **Brunelleschi,** in addition to the TMNT crew. Make sure to stop at Florence's major venues for Renaissance art—the Uffizi Galleries, Pitti Palace, and the Galleria dell'Accademia—to see the extensive collections that made these guys famous in the first place. Using newly developed scientific studies of anatomy and physiology, the Renaissance Masters created these sculptures and paintings that accurately represent the human form. Like pre-teen boys discovering their first *Playboy*, the citizens of Florence were fascinated by the explicit nudity of most Renaissance art. Doing what they do best, the Vatican deemed the art morally unsuitable and either castrated statues or covered up their junk with grape leaves.

HOLIDAYS AND FESTIVALS

In keeping with the rest of Italy, most Florentine festivals are religiously oriented, often celebrating some facet of Jesus's life. But don't worry if it's been a while since you last went to confession. Florence's events calendar abounds with traditional cultural holidays, most of which, not unlike college frat parties, involve copious amounts of eating and drinking.

HOLIDAY OR FESTIVAL	DESCRIPTION	DATE
Capodanno	Ringing in the New Year receives the royal treatment in Florence. Revelers party in the streets and set off fireworks over the Arno.	January 1
Easter Sunday (Explosion of the Cart)	To get Easter started off with a blast, a mechanical dove lands on a wire above the Duomo's high altar, setting off a cart of fireworks.	late March or early April
Calcio in Costume	This summer festival's hoards of dancing men dressed in outlandish costumes might remind you of a '90s Cher concert.	late June
Festival of San Giovanni	Enjoy plentiful helpings of pasta during this festival dedicated to the patron saint of Florence.	June 24
Festa della Rificolona	This procession of children through the streets of Florence to commemorate the birth of the Virgin Mary will surely bring a tear to your eye.	September 7
Festival dei Popoli	This film festival, though not as well known as Cannes, gives local artists a chance to showcase their independent works.	late November
Burning of the Tree	In preparation for Christmas, Tuscan revelers throw a massive bonfire of evergreen branches. Kind of like Burning Man, but without all the acid.	December 24

florence

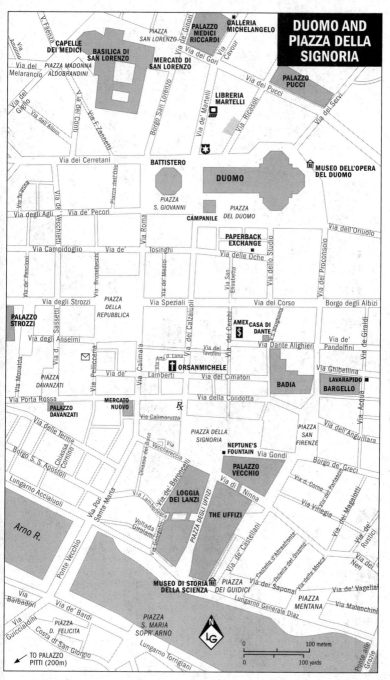

DUOMO AND PIAZZA DELLA SIGNORIA

V. Faenza
V. Ariento
CAPPELLE DEI MEDICI
BASILICA DI SAN LORENZO
PIAZZA SAN LORENZO
PALAZZO MEDICI RICCARDI
GALLERIA MICHELANGELO
Via de' Ginori
Via dei Gori
Via Cavour
Via del Melarancio
PIAZZA MADONNA ALDOBRANDINI
Via del Giglio
Via de' Conti
Via dei Banchi
Via dell'Alloro
Borgo San Lorenzo
Via de' Zanetti
MERCATO DI SAN LORENZO
Via de' Martelli
LIBRERIA MARTELLI
Via Ricasoli
PALAZZO PUCCI
Via dei Pucci
Via dei Servi
Via dei Cerretani
BATTISTERO
Piazza dell'Olio
PIAZZA S. GIOVANNI
DUOMO
PIAZZA DEL DUOMO
MUSEO DELL'OPERA DEL DUOMO
Via de' Vecchietti
Via Teatina
Via degli Agli
Via de' Pecori
CAMPANILE
Via dell'Oriuolo
Via de' Pescioni
Via Campidoglio
Via de'
Via Roma
Via de' Brunelleschi
Tosinghi
PAPERBACK EXCHANGE
Via delle Oche
Via dello Studio
Via San Elisabetta
Via del Proconsolo
Via degli Strozzi
PIAZZA DELLA REPUBBLICA
Via Speziali
Via de' Medici
Via del Corso
Borgo degli Albizi
PALAZZO STROZZI
Via Sassetti
Via degli Anselmi
Via d.
Via del Calzaiuoli
Via de' Cerchi
AMEX CASA DI DANTE
Via Dante Alighieri
Via de' Pandolfini
Via de' Giraldi
Via Monalda
Via Pellicceria
Via de' Lamberti
Via de' Tavolini
Arte d. Lana
ORSANMICHELE
Via dei Cimatori
Via della Condotta
BADIA
Via Ghibellina
LAVARAPIDO
BARGELLO
Via dell'Acqua
PIAZZA DAVANZATI
Via Porta Rossa
PALAZZO DAVANZATI
MERCATO NUOVO
Via Calimaruzza
Calimala
Via della Condotta
PIAZZA SAN FIRENZE
Via dell'Anguillara
Via delle Terme
Chiasso Cornino
Chiasso del Buco
Via Vacchereccia
PIAZZA DELLA SIGNORIA
NEPTUNE'S FOUNTAIN
Via Gondi
Borgo de' Greci
Borgo S. S. Apostoli
Via Pellicceria
PALAZZO VECCHIO
Via d. Corno
Via de' Magalotti
Lungarno Acciaiuoli
Via Lambertesca
Via Por Santa Maria
Via de' Baroncelli
LOGGIA DEI LANZI
Via di Ninna
Via Vinegia
Via de' Rustici
Arno R.
Voltada Girolami
Via de' Bentaccordi
PIAZZA DEGLI UFFIZI
THE UFFIZI
Via de' Castellani
Castellato d'Altrafronte
Chiasso del Gramolo
Borgo dei Greci
Via de' Neri
Ponte Vecchio
Via Barbadori
Via de' Bardi
MUSEO DI STORIA DELLA SCIENZA
PIAZZA DEI GUIDICI
Via dei Saponai
Via della Mosca
PIAZZA MENTANA
Via de' Vagellai
Via Malenchini
Via Guicciardini
PIAZZA D. FELICITA
Costa di San Giorgio
PIAZZA S. MARIA SOPR'ARNO
Lungarno Generale Diaz
Ponte alle Grazie
Lungarno Torrigiani

TO PALAZZO PITTI (200m)

N

0   100 meters
0   100 yards

duomo and piazza della signoria map

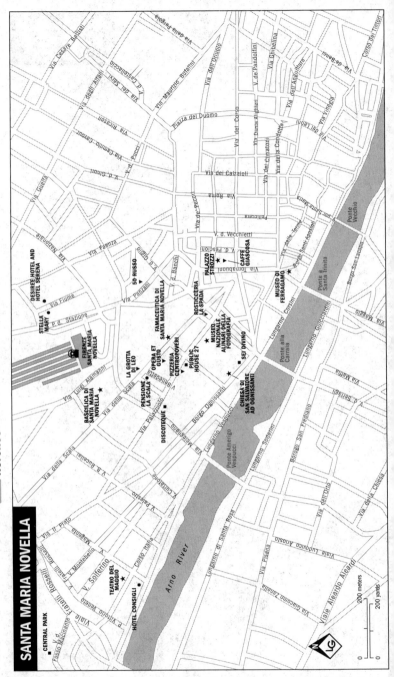

SANTA MARIA NOVELLA

florence

■ CENTRAL PARK

- DESIRÉE HOTEL AND HOTEL SERENA
- STELLE MARY
- FIRENZE SANTA MARIA NOVELLA
- 50 RUSSO
- FAMACEUTICA DI SANTA MARIA NOVELLA
- ROSTICCERIA LA SPADA
- PALAZZO STROZZI
- CAFFÈ GIACOSA
- MUSEO DI FERRAGAMO
- BASILICA DI SANTA MARIA NOVELLA
- LA GROTTA DI LEO
- OPERA ET GUSTO
- PIZZERIA CENTROPOVERI
- PUBLIC HOUSE 27
- MUSEO NAZIONALE ALINARI DELLA FOTOGRAFIA
- SEI DIVINO
- PENSIONE LA SCALA
- DISCOTEQUE
- CHIESA DI SAN SALVATORE AD OGNISSANTI
- TEATRO DEL MAGGIO
- HOTEL CONSIGLI

Via Cesare Battisti
Via della Pergola
Via dell'Alloro
Via degli Aglii
Via Ricasoli
Via Camillo Cavour
Via Guelfa
V. d. Ginori
Via Nazionale
Via dei San Gallo
Via Maurizio Bufalini
Piazza del Duomo
Via dell'Oriuolo
Via dei Pandolfini
Via Ghibellina
Corso dei Tintori
Via de' Benci
Via del Corso
Via Dante Alighieri
Via della Condotta
Via dei Leoni
Via de' Pandolfini
Via dei Calzaioli
Via Roma
Via de' Tornabuoni
Via de' Pecori
Pellicceria
V. d. Vecchietti
V. d. Pescioni
Via de' Tornabuoni
Via delle Terme
Via Santa Margherita
Via Faenza
Via Panzani
Via de' Banchi
V. d. Giglio
Ponte Vecchio
Via delle Terme
Borgo Santissimi Apostoli
Ponte a Santa Trinità
Lungarno Corsini
Lungarno degli Acciaiuoli
Ponte alla Carraia
Borgo San Jacopo
Via Maggio
Via Maffia
Via de' Serragli
P. d. Stazione
Via Luigi Alamanni
Via della Scala
Via Palazzuolo
Via Benedetta
Borgo Ognissanti
Lungarno Vespucci
Ponte Amerigo Vespucci
Via del Moro
Via del Porcellana
Via Maso Finiguerra
Via Montebello
Via della Scala
V. d. Rucellai
V. Curtatone
V. Palestro
Via Il Prato
Via Maso Finiguerra
V. Ceretani
V. Solferino
V. Vittorio Veneto
Viale Fratelli Rosselli
Viale Filippo Strozzi
V. d. Fosso Macinante
Corso Italia
Lungarno di Santa Rosa
Lungarno Soderini
Borgo San Frediano
Via del Drago d'Oro
Via della Chiesa
Via di Camaldoli
Via Pisana
Viale Ludovico Ariosto
Via Giacomo Zanella
Viale Aleardo Aleardi

Arno River

200 meters
200 yards

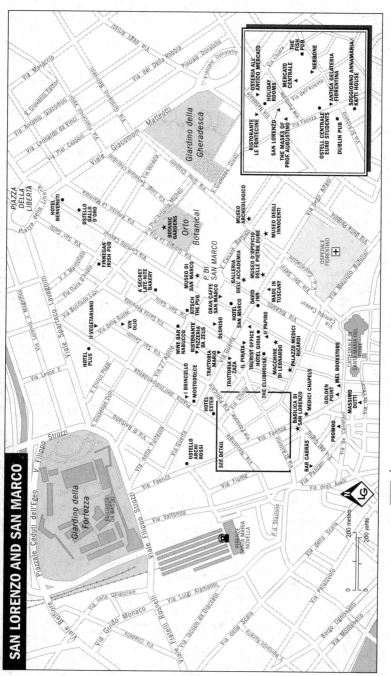

SAN LORENZO AND SAN MARCO

san lorenzo and san marco map

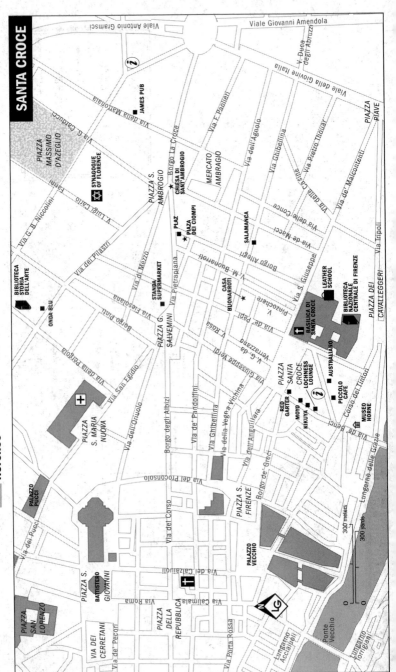

SANTA CROCE

florence

332 www.letsgo.com

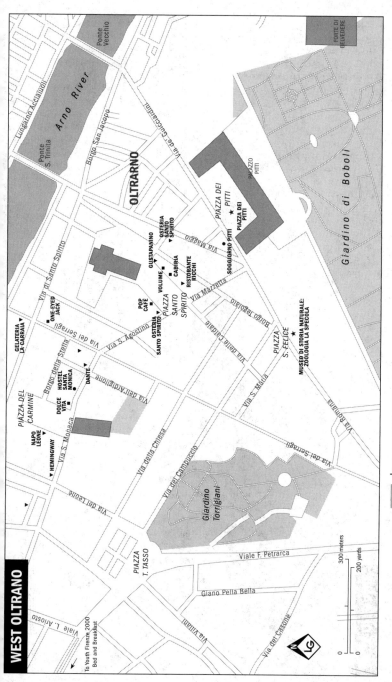

WEST OLTRANO

Arno River

Lungarno Acciaiuoli

Ponte S. Trinita

Ponte Vecchio

Borgo San-Jacopo

OLTRARNO

Via de' Guicciardini

FORTE DI BELVEDERE

Via Maggio

PIAZZA DEI PITTI

PALAZZO PITTI

★ PIAZZA DEI PITTI

Giardino di Boboli

OSTERIA SANTO SPIRITO

GUSTAPANINO

CABIRIA

VOLUME

RISTORANTE RICCHI

POP CAFÉ

PIAZZA SANTO SPIRITO

SOGGIORNO PITTI

Via Mazzetta

Via di Santo Spirito

ONE-EYED JACK

OSTERIA SANTO SPIRITO

Via S. Agostino

Via dei Serragli

GELATERIA LA CARRAIA

Via delle Caldaie

Borgo Tegolaio

PIAZZA S. FELICE

Via S. Maria

MUSEO DI STORIA NATURALE: ZOOLOGIA LA SPECOLA ★

Via Romana

Borgo della Stella

HOSTEL SANTA MONICA

DANTE

DOLCE VITA

Via dell'Ardiglione

PIAZZA DEL CARMINE

NAPOLEONE

HEMINGWAY

Via S. Monaca

Via della Chiesa

Via del Campuccio

Giardino Torrigiani

Via dei Serragli

Via del Leone

PIAZZA T. TASSO

To Youth Firenze 2000 Bed and Breakfast

Viale L. Ariosto

Viale F. Petrarca

Giano Pella Bella

Via Villani

Via del Campuccio

Via del Cassone

300 meters
200 yards

LG

west oltrano map

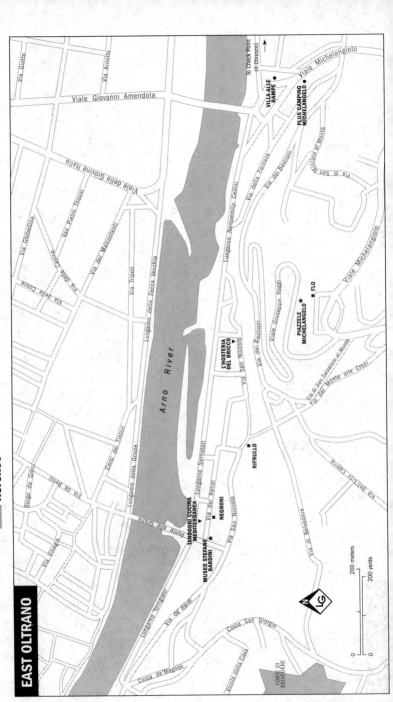

EAST OLTRANO

florence

Arno River

To Check Point (Il Chiesso)

VILLA ALLE RAMPE ●

PLUS CAMPING MICHELANGELO ●

Viale Michelangiolo

Viale Giovanni Amendola

Viale della Giovine Italia

Via Giotto

Via Arnolfo

Via Ghibellina

Via Pietro Thouar

Via dei Malcontenti

Via Tripoli

Lungarno della Zecca Vecchia

Via delle Casine

Via delle Conce

Lungarno delle Grazie

Corso dei Tintori

Borgo de' Greci

Via de' Benci

Via Vinegia

Via de' Bardi

Lungarno Torrigiani

Ponte alle Grazie

Lungarno Serristori

Lungarno Cellini

Lungarno Benvenuto Cellini

Via della Fornace

Via dei Bastioni

Via di San Miniato al Monte

Viale Michelangiolo

Via San Niccolò

■ FLO

PIAZZALE MICHELANGELO ★

Viale Giuseppe Poggi

Via dei Bastioni

Via di San Salvatore al Monte

Via di San Monte alle Croci

Via del Monte alle Croci

L'HOSTERIA DEL BRICO ▷

RIFRULLO ■

TANDOORI CUCINA MEDITERRANEA ▷

NEGRONI ■

Via dei Renai

MUSEO STEFANO BARDINI ★

Via della Caluria

Via di Belvedere

Costa San Giorgio

Costa de' Magnoli

Vicolo della Cava

FORTE DI BELVEDERE

N LG

0 200 meters
0 200 yards

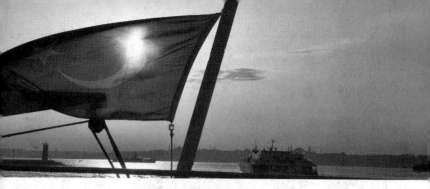

ISTANBUL

"All other cities are doomed, but I imagine that as long as people exist, Constanti-nople will exist." —Petrus Gyllius

Istanbul is a city like no other. Compasses here point east and west at the same time. The only city in the world to straddle two continents, Istanbul is the crossroads of all crossroads. This seriously ancient city has survived for more than 2500 years, during which time it has served as the capital of three empires, been called by at least four names, and been fought over by Greeks and Romans, barbarian tribes and Crusaders, and Byzantines and Ottomans.

The past and the present bump and grind here like they were revelers at one of Beşiktaş's nightclubs. Lean minarets pierce the sky alongside glittering modern skyscrapers, bearded old men nurse *nargiles* on street corners, and fanny-packed tourists pay 10 times too much for carpets. Istanbul is a hectic, crazy mix of cultures, styles, smells, and lifestyles, and it can be a challenge for the uninitiated. Luckily, you've got us to help you navigate the maze of the Grand Bazaar, find your way onto the right Bosphorus ferry, and choose the best hostel in Beyoğlu. Whether you're heading to Istanbul to take in the history, study the culture, or enjoy the hedonism, you're in store for one wild magic-carpet ride. Just remember: if you've got a date in Constantinople, they'll be waiting in Istanbul.

greatest hits

- **MY PLATE FLOWETH OVER.** Istanbul's cuisine will delight you. Get started with *pide* at **Hocapaşa Pidecisi** (p. 361).

- **MOSQUERCIZE.** Istanbul's **mosques** are renowned, and most of them don't even charge any entrance fee (p. 351).

- **LEARN TO HAGGLE.** If you don't try to bargain at the **Grand Bazaar,** the shopkeepers probably won't know what to do with themselves (p. 385).

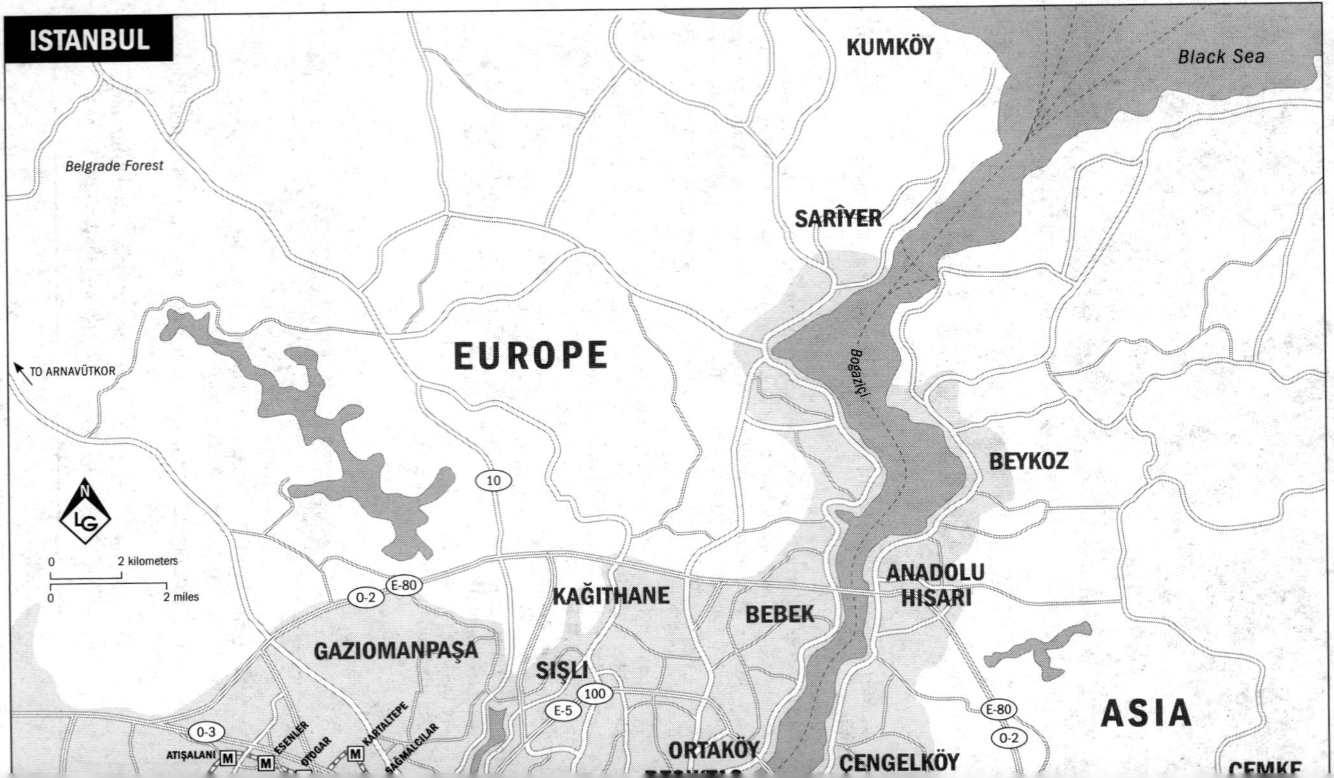

ISTANBUL

Belgrade Forest

TO ARNAVÛTKOR

EUROPE

Black Sea

KUMKÖY

SARÎYER

Bogaziçi

BEYKOZ

ASIA

CEMKE

ANADOLU
HISARI

E-80
O-2

CENGELKÖY

BEBEK

ORTAKÖY

KAĞITHANE

ŞIŞLI

E-5
100

10

E-80

O-2

GAZIOMANPAŞA

BAĞMALLIDILAR

MATRALTEPE

ESENLER

BYOGAR

M

M

ATIŞALANI

M

O-3

0   2 kilometers

0   2 miles

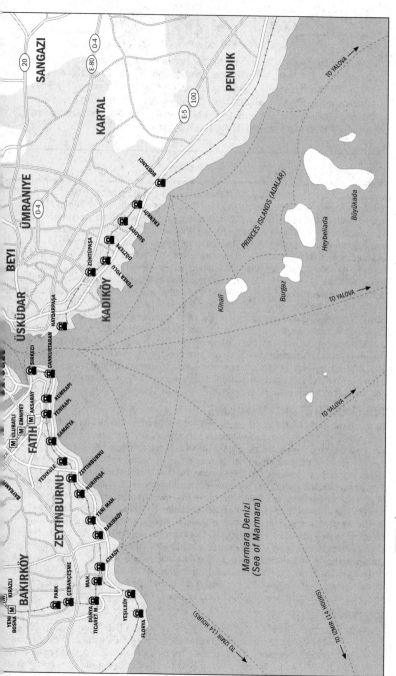

istanbul overview map

Like most things in Istanbul, the demographics in the city are carefully balanced between old and young. While the younger generation in Istanbul isn't as hopping as in, say, Berlin, there is a growing population of students and youth gaining visibility, especially in the Beyoğlu area. Beşiktaş is also a good option because of its proximity to and popularity with nearby university students. These areas also are where most of the worthwhile nightlife is found.

orientation

Istanbul would be nothing without its waters. Acting as barriers, shipping lanes, and passages, they've come to define the city. The Bosphorus links the Sea of Marmara in the south to the Black Sea in the north, marking the border between Europe and Asia. Meanwhile, the Golden Horn (*Haliç*) divides the European side into north and south. Istanbul is a single city, but its components are vibrant and distinct. European Istanbul, which features most of the historic and cultural sights, is the better-looking half (sorry Asia!), although that also means it's crammed with tourists (and those trying to make money off of them). Walk around Sultanahmet for the most famous sights, but cross over to Beyoğlu to find the soul of modern Istanbul. Heading north on the European side, you'll find bustling Beşiktaş and opulent Ortaköy, where Istanbul's glitterati spend and party. On the Asian side, the mostly residential Üsküdar is bordered in the south by Kadıköy, the unofficial center of this half, while farther south, the quiet and comfortable life of Moda might tempt you to move there. With all these neighborhoods stretched between two continents, you'll have a lot to take in. Thankfully, between the city's buses, trains, and trams, you'll never find yourself far from Istanbul's cheap, convenient public transportation network, and the city's ferry service is the cheapest intercontinental cruise you'll ever take.

SULTANAHMET AND ENVIRONS

Home to the **Hagia Sophia** and the other crown jewels of historical Istanbul, Sultanahmet is the first stop for anyone who wants to explore the city. Sultanahmet proper is the area teeming with tourists around the **Blue Mosque,** where many budget accommodations and historical sights can be found. To the north are the **Sirkeci** and **Eminönü** neighborhoods, known for the **Spice Bazaar,** bustling streets, and gorgeous mosques. The **Galata Bridge** above Eminönü connects the historic peninsula with Karaköy, across the **Golden Horn.** You'll find ferry terminals and tram stops on both sides of the bridge. The eastern tip of the peninsula is occupied by **Topkapı Palace** and **Gülhane Park.** To the west of Sultanahmet are **Çemberlitaş** and **Beyazıt Square,** the location of some nice tea houses and cheap restaurants. The tram conveniently connects all of these neighborhoods, though it's also possible to walk. Shopaholics and hardcore hagglers can spend hours in the **Grand Bazaar,** a maze-like warren above Beyazıt. Below Beyazıt is the **Kumkapı** neighborhood, renowned (or infamous) for its overpriced fish restaurants. Come to Sultanahmet for the fabled sights and the full tourist experience, but look elsewhere for a more authentic (and cheaper) vision of the city.

WESTERN FATIH

You will hear two different Fatihs talked about in Istanbul. The municipality of Fatih covers the entire historical peninsula and includes Sultanahmet, Beyazıt, and all the nearby neighborhoods. Fatih proper, on the other hand, is a small neighborhood around **Fatih Mosque** where government officials dwell and fun goes to die. It's more conservative than other neighborhoods, which can be a refreshing change from **İstiklal Caddesi**. One of the liveliest roads here is **Fevzi Paşa Caddesi,** which runs northwest from **Fatih İtfaiye Park**. If you follow the **Valens Aqueduct** from its southern end, you'll find the **Siirt Bazaar**, a square with plenty of small restaurants. A marginally classier cluster of restaurants can be found on **Atpazarı,** a square just a few blocks east of the mosque, but almost no establishment in Fatih serves alcohol. To the north of the Fatih Mosque is **Çarşamba**, which makes Fatih look like a hippie commune.

calling istanbul?

Changing names faster than Facebook statuses, Istanbul has a history of monikers that will give even the snobbiest polyglot a run for his money. Dust off your Greek, brush up on your Latin, and practice your Arabic for a ride through the city's history.

- **SON OF A GOD!** The Greeks called their colony *Byzantium*, after their King Byzas, who, if the myths are true, was the son of the sea-god Poseidon and the grandson of Zeus.

- **VANITY FAIR.** Always the narcissists, the Roman emperors who came next named the city after themselves. *Augusta Antonina* quickly gave way to "New Rome," and then *Constantinople*, after Constantine the Great. This one stuck for the next 16 centuries.

- **THE EMPIRE STRIKES BACK.** When the Ottoman Empire took over, they let *Constantinople* stay, but added their own names to the mix. *Islambol* ("lots of Islam") and *Islambul* ("find Islam") made sure travelers knew who's god was now in charge.

- **GOING POSTAL.** After WWI, the Republic of Turkey ditched Roman and went even more retro, adapting *Istanbul* from the Greek phrase for "to the City." And to make sure that it stuck, the Turkish Post Office since then delivers letters marked only for *Istanbul*. A city by any other name, apparently, only gets lost in the mail.

FENER AND BALAT

Fener and Balat used to be home to the Greek, Jewish, and Armenian minorities of Istanbul, but today they are populated mostly by poor Muslim migrants. It's a very dilapidated area, but it doesn't feel unsafe. Housewives chat across windows and children play while old men sip tea and comb their beards in the streets. Of course, be vigilant, even if tourist traps don't lurk behind every corner here (we're looking at you, Sultanahmet). This is one of the most conservative parts of Istanbul, so you'll never see the words "nightlife" and "Fener and Balat" in the same sentence—except when the sentence is, "The neighborhoods of Fener and Balat have no nightlife."

The fastest way to get here is by bus, but the prettiest is by ferry from Eminönü. Since the street plan is rather confusing, bring a good map and use landmarks to navigate the area. Public transportation sticks mainly to the periphery, so get ready for a rigorous walk. **Vodina Caddesi** runs parallel to the shore between Fener and Balat and is packed with local stores. The impressive red-brick **Phanar Greek Orthodox College** (Özel Fener Rum Lisesi) can be found some 300m inland from the Fener ferry jetty. The **Edirnekapı** neighborhood is a 15min. walk inland, close to the city walls, and home to the mosaic-filled **Chora Church**. You can find **Eyüp Sultan Mosque** and the **Pierre Loti Cafe** in **Eyüp**, a few kilometers north of Balat.

orientation

BEYOĞLU

Beyoğlu is the beating heart of modern Istanbul, brimming with galleries, restaurants, bars, and clubs. Many of these establishments are located off **İstiklal Caddesi**, a throbbing promenade that connects the transportation hub of **Taksim Square** in the north with **Tünel Square** in the south. You'll find brand names, consulates, and an almost constant flow of people on and around İstiklal. Halfway into İstiklal, you can't miss the ornate gates of Istanbul's most prestigious high school, the Galatasaray Lisesi. A bit below Tünel is the **Galata Tower**, the most recognizable point on Istanbul's European skyline. The blocks around it house designer shops, cafes, and a revitalized creative scene. For a calmer, residential feel, head to **Cihangir**, a bohemian neighborhood popular with expats, located south of Taksim Sq. and bordered by **Sıraselviler Caddesi** to the west. The Sultanahmet tram doesn't run to İstiklal; to get there, either get off at Karaköy and take the funicular to Tünel, or go to Kabataş and take the funicular to Taksim.

BEŞIKTAŞ AND ORTAKÖY

Beşiktaş is a village a few kilometers up from Kabataş, with a small pedestrian center that is popular with students. The **eagle statue** near the triangular fish market is a good orientation point. To reach it, head inland from the ferry terminal or the bus station onto Ortabahçe Cad. and take the second right. There are a few expensive places here, but it's **Ortaköy** that's known as Istanbul's leading site of conspicuous consumption. Not much has changed here over the years. Instead of sultans, millionaires now live in the waterside palaces, and you can't swing a Louis Vuitton bag without hitting a BMW. Ortaköy's small center is near the water, around the **Ortaköy Mosque**, where you'll find plenty of shops and pricey eateries. The city's famous clubs are mostly concentrated on **Muallim Naci Caddesi**, which runs from Ortaköy to **Kuruçeşme**. Muallim Naci is part of the main road (at some points Dolmabahçe and Çırağan) that runs along the shore, connecting Kabataş with these neighborhoods. Although you can take one of the many buses, the frequently bad traffic means that you're better off walking and basking in the opulence of your surroundings.

ASIAN ISTANBUL

The Asian side of Istanbul tends to be confusing for travelers, since it isn't laid out like most European cities. However, make your way through this part of town to discover a lively alternative art scene and an abundance of cafes and restaurants free from the mobs of tourists common across the Bosphorus. Window-shoppers might never leave **Bağdat Caddesi**, İstiklal Cad.'s fancier sibling, where high-end luxury stores compete with sexy cars for the greatest glitz. There are a few streets in the historical **Kadıköy** neighborhood to keep in mind: **Söğütlüçeşme Caddesi** runs inland from the ferry terminal and intersects with Kadıköy's important pedestrian street, **Bahariye Caddesi** This intersection is home to a well-known statue of a bull. Parallel to Bahariye Cad. is the neighborhood's "bar street," **Kadife Sokak. Güneşlibahçe Sokak**, which intersects with Söğütlüçeşme Cad. near the ferry terminal, is known for **Kadıköy Market** and many restaurants with live music.

To the south of Kadıköy, you'll find **Moda**, a well-to-do residential area with beaches, perfect for romantic sunset watching. Moda is accessible on foot, but you can take the nostalgic shoebox of a **tram** that follows a circular route around Kadıköy into suburbia. **Üsküdar**, home to over 180 mosques, is a rather sleepy historical neighborhood some kilometers north of Kadıköy. Visit the Mihrimah Sultan, Şemsi Pasha, and Çinili mosques for a sampling of the best. For easy travel between Kadıköy and Üsküdar, take public bus #12 or #12A. Farther into Asia, the suburbs have their own charms and personalities.

istanbul

amazing race

If you're the only city in the world located on two continents, you might as well take advantage of it. One of the many ways Istanbul flaunts its geography is by hosting the world's only Asia to Europe swim race, the annual **Bosphorus Cross-Continetal.** The race, organized by the Turkish Olympic Committee, draws anywhere from 70 to 500 competitors, who swim across the Bosphorus in one of the coolest continent-hopping trips we can imagine. You must be 14 or older, and take a swim test to race.

accommodations

Most of Istanbul's budget accommodations are concentrated in Sultanahmet, but Beyoğlu is becoming more and more popular with travelers looking for cheap rooms. The main advantage to staying in Sultanahmet is being close to the major historical sights, while residing in Beyoğlu brings you closer to the city's culture and nightlife. Accommodations on the Asian side and in the more conservative districts like Fatih and Fener are sparser, less conveniently located, and generally lacking in English fluency. Beşiktaş is home to mostly upscale hotels. Avoid staying in hotels in the Aksaray area, which is the city's seedy red light district, or Tarlabaşı, the run-down neighborhood close to Taksim. Another option is to rent an apartment, especially if you're thinking of staying for a few weeks (or a semester).

The prices of Istanbul's hostels can change faster than you can say "*Çekoslova kyalılaştıramadıklarımızdanmışsınız*" (which, by the way, means "are you one of those whom we couldn't have possibly turned into a Czechoslovak?"). All the prices quoted here were collected during the high season (August to September and around Christmas), but they may be much lower at other times. Not all hostels change their prices at the same time, and some maintain the same prices year-round. The best way to find a bargain is to ask around at multiple hostels, or look for current prices on the internet. Most places accept euro and Turkish lire, and most hostels (and virtually all hotels) accept credit cards, though they may charge a commission fee (usually 3%).

SULTANAHMET AND ENVIRONS

Catering mainly to foreign tourists, Sultanahmet's accommodations range from the Four Seasons to some pretty cheap dorm beds. Boutique hotels and small guesthouses often provide the best value, but they fill up quickly. Many of the hostels and hotels in this area are clustered around **Akbıyık Caddesi,** downhill from the Blue Mosque and Hagia Sophia. To get there, start from the Blue Mosque's north entrance (the one facing Hagia Sophia), turn right, and go downhill. Take the first right and then turn left; Akbıyık Cad. runs through the intersection ahead.

✓ METROPOLIS HOSTEL — HOSTEL $

Terbıyık Sok. 24 — ☎0212 518 1822; www.metropolishostel.com

Though we're skeptical of everything in Sultanahmet that's less than 400 years old, we still found a hostel to wholeheartedly recommend. Metropolis Hostel seems to really know what international travelers need. The rooms are clean, air-conditioned, and welcoming; the beds are comfortable (a rarity in Sultanahmet hostels); and the terrace view beats much of the competition. The hostel has a large DVD collection, but why stay inside when you can be smoking *nargile* on the rooftop bar, bar-hopping in Taksim, or shakin' dat thang on belly-dancing nights.

➡ [M]Sultanahmet. Near İshak Paşa Mosque. From the entrance to Topkapı Palace, go downhill and turn right onto Kutlugün Sok. Take the 1st left, go down 2 blocks, and turn right. The hostel is on the left. ℹ Breakfast included. Free Wi-Fi. $ Co-ed dorms €17-18. Female-only €18; singles €40; doubles €48, with bath €70-80; triples €84; quads €88. 🕐 Reception 24hr.

CORDIAL HOUSE

HOSTEL $

Peykhane Sok. 29

☎0212 518 0576; www.cordialhouse.com

One of the best budget accommodations on the historic peninsula, this big hostel near Çemberlitaş is cheap, close to a tram stop, and near both the Grand Bazaar and Sultanahmet. Since it has so many rooms, you might get a low rate even when other hostels are charging their high-season prices. The shared bathrooms are clean and spacious, and the basement's colorful breakfast and lounge areas feel like they belong in a small American liberal arts college. Good luck trying to cook in the tiny kitchen, though.

✈ Ⓜ️Çemberlitaş. From the tram station, walk toward Vezhiran Cad. and take the 1st right. Cordial House is on the left. *i* Some rooms include free breakfast, otherwise it costs €3. HI members get discounted rates online. Ⓢ Dorms €12; singles €35, with bath €50; doubles €45/60; triples €60/75; quads €80/90. ⏰ Reception 24hr.

TULIP GUESTHOUSE

GUESTHOUSE $

Terbıyık Sok. 15

☎0212 517 6509; www.tulipguesthouse.com

Staying close to the nightlife doesn't mean you have to sleep above the bars. This charming guesthouse is on a quiet street just a block from the busy bar and restaurant street Akbıyık Cad. The staff has tried hard to make Tulip a welcoming place, with well-picked decorations, tapestries to liven up even the dorm room, and occasional community dinners. It feels so homey, we're surprised people haven't started moving in for good.

✈ Ⓜ️Sultanahmet. Near İshak Paşa Mosque. From the entrance to Topkapı Palace, go downhill and turn right onto Kutlugün Sok. Take the 1st left, go down 2 blocks, and turn right. The guesthouse is on the right. *i* Breakfast included. Bathrooms ensuite. Free Wi-Fi. Ⓢ Dorms €15; singles €40; doubles €50-55; triples €60. ⏰ Reception 24hr.

CHEERS HOSTEL

HOSTEL $

Zeynep Sultan Camii Sok. 21

☎0212 526 0200; www.cheershostel.com

Though it's surrounded by expensive accommodations, Cheers Hostel offers great value for your money. The rooms are decorated with objects that could easily be mistaken for Ottoman relics, and the showers are inside glass cubicles (not as common around here as you might think). Start the day off right by eating your fill at the breakfast buffet, and finish it right too, with the cheap beer and killer view of the Hagia Sophia from the terrace. The dorm beds have their own storage containers (most Istanbul hostels only have safety boxes at the reception desk), but the dorms themselves aren't usually locked.

✈ Ⓜ️Gülhane. Continue along the tracks to Sultanahmet. Turn right after Zeynep Sultan Mosque. The hostel is on the right, where the road bends. *i* Breakfast included. Free Wi-Fi. Doubles and triples have ensuite bath. Ⓢ Dorms €15-20; doubles €60; triples €90. Beer 5TL. Cash only. ⏰ Reception 24hr.

NOBEL HOSTEL

HOSTEL $

Mimar Mehmet Ağa Cad. 32

☎0212 516 3177; www.nobelhostel.com

Nobel is yet another good hostel that combines relatively low prices with acceptable quality. A vertigo-inducing staircase leads to a terrace with great views of the Blue Mosque. A less impressive view can be found in the bathroom, which has a rather unappealing brown color scheme. Guests get a 10% discount at the restaurant downstairs, and a beer for just 4TL on the terrace.

✈ Ⓜ️Sultanahmet. From the Blue Mosque's north entrance (the 1 facing Hagia Sophia), turn right and go downhill. Take the 1st right, turn left, and Nobel is on the right. *i* Breakfast included. Some rooms have A/C. Free Wi-Fi. Ⓢ Dorms €10-15; singles €30-45; doubles €40, with bath €47; triples €50/60. ⏰ Reception 24hr.

BIG APPLE HOSTEL

HOSTEL $

Bayram Fırını Sok. 12

☎0212 517 7931; www.hostelbigapple.com

Don't read too much into the name—the closest you'll get to New York is the crowd of American tourists staying here. The Big Apple has a comfortable though not very scenic terrace, and it'll bring the belly dancing to you (on Fridays) and then take you disco-hopping (on Saturdays). The rooms are clean and pleasant, and the spacious showers look like they're out of a much nicer hotel room.

✈ Ⓜ Sultanahmet. *From the Blue Mosque's north entrance (facing Hagia Sophia), turn right and go downhill. Take the 1st right, turn left, and left again onto Akbıyık Cad. Take the 1st right; Big Apple is on the left.* **i** *Breakfast included. Private rooms have ensuite bath. Free Wi-Fi.* Ⓢ *Dorms €12-15; singles €40; doubles €50; triples €75; quads €80.* ☼ *Reception 24hr.*

ORIENT HOSTEL (HI)
HOSTEL $

Akbıyık Cad. 13   ☎0212 517 9493; www.orienthostel.com

One of the biggest hostels in Istanbul, and allegedly the first to open in Turkey, Orient is a safe bet when other hostels are full. The huge size means that it can be a bit impersonal, but the number of other guests creates plenty of opportunities to socialize. A daily happy hour, pub crawls, many common spaces, and a 30-person dorm room add to the community atmosphere. The rooms are small and reasonably clean, even if parts of the hostel are a bit musty. With a capacity of 152 guests, this is a good place to try if you're showing up in Istanbul at 3am with no reservation.

✈ Ⓜ Sultanahmet. *From the entrance to Topkapı behind the Hagia Sophia, walk downhill and take the 2nd right onto Akbıyık Cad. It'll be 2 blocks down on the left.* **i** *Breakfast included. Free Wi-Fi.* Ⓢ *Dorms €10-15; singles €30; doubles €40, with bath €55; suites €60-85. Rates 10% higher for non-HI members.* ☼ *Reception 24hr.*

OCEAN'S 7
BOUTIQUE HOTEL $$$

Amiral Tafdil Sok. 18   ☎0212 458 6669; www.hoteloceans7.com.tr

Let's Go has no idea where the other four went, but you'll feel like you've robbed a casino too after a stay at Ocean's 7. With golden sheets, fluffy rugs, and bouquets of fake roses on each floor, the décor smacks of Vegas, so you may need to climb to the covered terrace to remind yourself that you're still in Istanbul. The kitchen, also on the terrace, is available for guest use, and might be the most scenic place you've ever cooked a hamburger. With prices close to what hostels charge in the high season, you know you've hit the jackpot at Ocean's elev—er, seven.

✈ Ⓜ Sultanahmet. *From the Blue Mosque's north entrance (facing Hagia Sophia), turn right and go downhill. Take the 1st right, turn left, continue to the end of the road, and turn right.* **i** *Breakfast included. All rooms with ensuite bath. A/C. Free Wi-Fi.* Ⓢ *Singles €50; doubles €75; triples €85; family rooms €100.* ☼ *Reception 24hr.*

HOTEL ERENLER
HOSTEL $

Tayahatun Sok. 11   ☎0212 527 3468; www.hotelerenler.com

A great choice for cheapskates who don't want to stay in a dorm, this hostel has single rooms that are half the price and size of regular hostels. The lime green and beige color scheme can be stomach-churning, showers longer than 15min. incur a "bath fee," and the hostel is tucked away on a small street in Sirkeci that looks a bit eerie at night. But hey, you get to stay in your own room for the price of two kebabs. The reception also has a fun sheet of Turkish phrases with a whole section titled "for your lover," but unless you want to pick up the carpet salesmen next door, stick to English for flirting with fellow tourists.

✈ Ⓜ Gülhane. *Follow the tram tracks north along the Gülhane Park walls. When the tram tracks turn left, keep to the right and continue for 2 blocks.* **i** *Free Wi-Fi.* Ⓢ *Dorms €10-15; singles €14; doubles with bath €34.* ☼ *Reception 24hr.*

BEST ISLAND HOSTEL
HOSTEL $

Kutlugün Sok. 5   ☎0212 518 0170; www.bestislandhostel.com

We're not sure which island it refers to, or why it's the best; all we know is that Best Island is one of the cheapest accommodations in Sultanahmet. Well, we also know that it has its share of highs and lows. Among the lows are the occasional

accommodations

peeling paint or hole in the floor, the small shared bathrooms, the basement doubles, and the one-time kitchen fee (5TL). On the high side, the hotel offers a great view of Hagia Sophia. Come here when the other hostels run out of beds. Otherwise, we suggest you splurge a little more for the extra comfort.

✦ ⓂSultanahmet. *Walk down Caferiye Sok. away from Hotel Sultanahmet, past the Hagia Sophia Museum. Turn right onto Kabasakal Cad., left onto Tevkifhane Sok., and left onto Kutlugün Sok.* ⓘ *Breakfast included. Free Wi-Fi.* Ⓢ *Dorms €10-15; singles €30; doubles €30-40.* ⓚ *Reception 24hr.*

WESTERN FATIH

PIANOFORTE HOTEL
HOTEL $$

Feyzullah Efendi Cad. 17 ☎0212 534 2080; www.hotelpianoforte.com

There's nothing musical about this place. In fact, it's quieter than other hotels in the area. The lobby sometimes doubles as luggage storage, but it's not like space is lacking: a spa takes up the whole basement. Aspiring to luxury, the rooms have spacious showers, golden sheets, and imitation wood floors. The hotel is popular with Middle Eastern guests, and the flags outside make it look like an Arab Summit meeting.

✦ *From the Fatih bus stop, go to the end of Fevzi Paşa Cad. and turn right onto Feyzullah Efendi Cad.* ⓘ *Breakfast included. A/C. Free Wi-Fi.* Ⓢ *Singles €30; doubles €45; triples with foldout bed €60.* ⓚ *Reception 24hr.*

OTEL ERCIYES
HOTEL $

Aslanhane Sok. 12 ☎0212 533 0843; www.otelerciyes.com.tr

No frills and no nonsense, Otel Erciyes gives you breakfast, Wi-Fi, and a place to sleep. The rooms are small, and the bathrooms bundle shower, sink, and commode in one space (sorry, no shower curtains for you). There's no elevator, but you should get used to climbing steep inclines anyway if you're staying in Istanbul.

✦ *From the Fatih bus stop, walk south down Fevzi Paşa Cad., past the mosque walls. Take the 1st left, and the hotel is on the right.* ⓘ *Breakfast included. A/C. Free Wi-Fi.* Ⓢ *Singles €20; doubles €40.* ⓚ *Reception 24hr.*

FATIH REŞADIYE HOTEL
HOTEL $$

Büyük Karaman Cad. 6 ☎0212 635 9587; www.fatihresadiyehotel.com

If you think the call to prayer makes a great alarm clock, you'll appreciate this hotel's proximity to the Fatih Mosque. Fatih Reşadiye has spacious, sunny rooms, sparsely decorated with single historical photographs. The rooms are adequate, but the showers are so small you might not have room to scrub yourself. Surprisingly for such a conservative neighborhood, the hotel's bar serves alcohol.

✦ *From the Fatih bus stop, walk south down Fevzi Paşa Cad., past the mosque walls. Take the 1st left, then the 2nd right. The hotel is on the right. It's a straight shot from the mosque's southeastern exit.* ⓘ *Breakfast included. A/C. Free Wi-Fi.* Ⓢ *Singles €33; doubles €48; triples €60.* ⓚ *Reception 24hr.*

HOTEL YEŞILPARK
HOTEL $$

Büyük Karaman Cad. 15 ☎0212 523 0338; www.hotelyesilpark.com

Yeşilpark offers a comfortable, if less-than-stellar, stay at reasonable prices. The dark facade and the lobby's UV-light fishtank may seem a little eerie, but the rooms are spacious and well kept, with pleasant wood furnishings and generous windows. Some even have a balcony facing the park, though the view is mediocre compared to others in Istanbul.

✦ *From the İtfaye bus stop, go up Macar Kardeşler Cad. toward the Fatih Mosque. Turn right at the northern corner of the park and walk 1 block. The hotel is at the corner of the intersection.* ⓘ *Breakfast included. Free Wi-Fi.* Ⓢ *Singles €30; doubles €45; triples €60.* ⓚ *Reception 24hr.*

DAREYN KONAK HOTEL $$$$

Eski Saraçhane Sok. 32 ☎0212 621 9900; www.dareynotel.com

Opened in February 2011, this classy hotel spares no expense, and it won't spare you any either. Marble covers the bathrooms, each bed is paired with a large flat-screen TV, and the elevator features touchscreen buttons. Less impressive are the breakfast and restaurant area (sumptuously decorated but confined to the basement), the rather small singles, and the size of the rooms' windows. If you're really hankering for sunlight, you can still enjoy fresh air and a view of the nearby mosque on the hotel's terrace. This level of sophistication is a bit out of character for the neighborhood, but you won't care when you're lounging in your luxurious room.

⇟ From the Fatih bus stop, walk down Fevzi Paşa Cad. as it turns into Macar Kardeşler Cad., then turn right onto Kıztaşı Cad. The hotel is on the left. ***i*** *Breakfast included. Free Wi-Fi.* [$] *Singles €70; doubles €95; triples €130.* ⏰ *Reception 24hr.*

boom boom boom boom

Are you a morning person? You better be when Ramadan comes around. At around 3:30am every morning, drums boom through the quiet streets of Istanbul, setting off car alarms and interrupting many sweet dreams. What's all the noise about? An Ottoman tradition, the *davul* (drums) wake up Muslims to the pre-dawn breakfast that they take before fasting through the day. The drums wake up Muslims and non-believers indiscriminately, so be prepared to hear them every day for the whole holy month of Ramadan. Some people are so grateful for the wake-up call that they even tip the drummers. Other parts of the city, which have started banning these noisemakers, seem to have discovered a modern alternative: the alarm clock.

FENER AND BALAT

Fener and Balat are mostly residential districts, but that doesn't mean that you should set up shop there as well. The neighborhoods are too far away from most of the city's action for hostels and other cheap accommodations to bother operating here, so if you really want to stay in this quieter locale, you'll have to splurge a bit.

KARIYE OTELI HOTEL $$$

Kariye Camii Sok. 6 ☎0212 534 8414; www.kariyeotel.com

This hotel gives you easy access to Chora Church next door, so it makes up for the neighborhood's relative peace and quiet with the mobs of tourists next door. Take your breakfast free and alfresco at the hotel's outdoor restaurant, (avoid the lunch and dinner, which are much pricier). If you like your urban life throbbing and wild, this place is not for you, but the quieter souls among us might sleep better here.

⇟ Bus to Edirnekapı. As you get off the bus, turn left, then take the nearest right turn and walk for 3 blocks. Just before you reach the city walls, turn right and walk 2 blocks down the slope until you see the Chora Museum, next door to the hotel. ***i*** *Breakfast included. Free Wi-Fi.* [$] *Doubles €50; triples €70.* ⏰ *Reception 24hr.*

HOTEL DAPHNIS HOTEL $$$$

Abdi Subaşi Mah. Dr. Sadık Ahmet Cad. 12 ☎0212 531 4858; www.daphnis.com.tr

A boutique hotel with prices to match, Hotel Daphnis comes as a surprise in a neighborhood filled with car shops and garages. Unfortunately, the prices are also surprisingly high, for its out-of-the-way location and unexceptional amenities. Though it's a long way from the livelier parts of Istanbul, Daphnis is next to a bus stop and a 10min. ride into central Taksim Sq. It makes for comfortable and nicely decorated living, but unless you have the cash to spend or a thing for car mechanics, you're better off finding somewhere closer and cheaper.

✦ *Bus to Fener. From the inland side of Abdülezelpaşa Cad., walk away from the ferry terminal and take the 1st sharp corner onto Dr. Sad Ahmet Cad.* **i** *Breakfast included. Has air-conditioning and a restaurant.* ⓢ *Singles €90; doubles €110.* ⓚ *Reception 24hr.*

BEYOĞLU

▨ RAPUNZEL GUESTHOUSE
HOSTEL $
Bereketzade Camii Sok. 3 ☎0212 292 5034; www.rapunzelistanbul.com

The three charming owners of this house have helpfully compiled a list of museums and events that might interest travelers. The rooms and decor are modestly vintage, with nothing of the leftist ideologies or cartoonish colors typical of other hostels. It's quiet and peaceful, the mattresses are orthopedic, and the location below the Galata Tower is very convenient—the ⓜTünel is just down the hill, although you'll have to climb some steep slopes to reach İstiklal.

✦ ⓜ*Tünel or Karaköy. From the entrance to Galata Tower, head down the hill on Camekan Sok. and take a right turn at the Berekzade Mosque. The hostel is on the right.* **i** *Breakfast included. Free Wi-Fi.* ⓢ *6-bed dorms €18; doubles with bath €60, triples with bath €75.* ⓚ *Reception 24hr.*

NEVERLAND HOSTEL
HOSTEL $
Boğazkesen Cad. 96 ☎0212 243 3177; www.hostelneverland.com

Walking into Neverland is a colorful trip. With hand-painted walls, posters calling for the fall of neoliberalism, a giant yin-and-yang seat, and multicolor sheets, this place would make more sense in *Let's Go Amsterdam*. It's alternative down to the trash—few other places in Istanbul care this much about recycling. The pleasant common spaces and kitchen lack natural light, but the Wi-Fi and complimentary tea and coffee might entice you to stay. Creative folks, get your brushes ready—the hostel will let you paint the walls, but make sure to stick with the anti-capitalist theme.

✦ ⓜ*Tophane. Walk uphill on Boğazkesen Cad. for 5min. The hostel is on the right.* **i** *Breakfast included. Lockers included. Laundry 10TL per load. Wi-Fi in lounges, lobby, and 1st fl. only.* ⓢ *Dorms €9-12; singles €20; doubles €28, with bath €34; triples €39. Cash only.* ⓚ *Reception 24hr.*

CHILL OUT CENGO HOSTEL
HOSTEL $
Halas Sok. 3 ☎0212 251 3148; www.chillouthc.com

Fun, easy-going, and with a love of painting: Chill Out Cengo could make a great boyfriend. The cartoon map of Istanbul and innovative stairs to the attic rooms may not help you get where you're going, but the laid-back staff and colorful rooms will brighten up your stay. It's also close to many bars and restaurants. If this location is full, there are five other Chill Out hostels scattered throughout the neighborhood (from Taksim to Galata). Head to the nearby **Chill Out Lya Hostel** (Toprak Lüle Sok. 1 ☎0212 244 7400) or the **Chill Out Classic Hostel** (Balyoz Sok. 3A ☎0212 249 4784).

✦ *From ⓜTaksim, walk down İstiklal, turn right after the Ağa Camii mosque, and continue down Atif Yilmaz. Take the 2nd left and the hostel's unmarked gate is on the left.* **i** *Breakfast 5TL. Laundry 10TL per load.* ⓢ *Dorms €12; doubles €40, with bath €60.* ⓚ *Reception 24hr.*

INTERNATIONAL HOUSE ISTANBUL
HOSTEL $
Zambak Sok. 5 ☎0212 244 3773; www.ihouseistanbul.com

Among the hostels in Beyoğlu, this is probably the closest to Taksim Sq., so this is an ideal location if you want to move around the city. It's also well positioned for exploring İstiklal's bars. There's not much else that distinguishes it, as the rooms are unmemorable. The lounge is rather small but serves complimentary

istanbul

coffee and tea. There's no breakfast, but the street food and shops around İstiklal make for cheap eats.

⚑ *From Ⓜ Taksim, walk down İstiklal and take the 1st right turn. The hostel entrance is an unmarked black door on the left.* ⓘ *Free Wi-Fi.* Ⓢ *4-bed dorms €14; doubles with bath €45; triples €54.* Ⓒ *Reception 24hr.*

SOHO HOSTEL
Süslü Saksı Sok. 5

HOSTEL $
☎0212 251 5866

It's not the neatest of hostels (there isn't much space and the bathrooms can look a bit unappealing), but there's a sense of free-spiritedness to its color and common room (think a headache-inducing Barney with yellow patches). Soho is one of the cheapest hostels near İstiklal Cad. and is close to all the nightlife, so it can be a good place to sleep and connect with fellow travelers.

⚑ *From Ⓜ Taksim, walk down İstiklal and take the 5th right onto İmam Adnan Sok. Continue to the end and turn left; the hostel is on the left.* ⓘ *Free Wi-Fi. Laundry €6.* Ⓢ *Dorms €7-13; singles €20; doubles €34. Cash only.* Ⓒ *Reception 24hr.*

WORLD HOUSE
Galipdede Cad. 85

HOSTEL $
☎0212 293 5520; www.worldhouseistanbul.com

This is among the better hostels in the Galata area. Galipdede is an especially well-positioned street: two steps north to Tünel, two steps south to the Galata Tower. It's also close to plenty of designer shops and up-and-coming stores. The common spaces don't feel very intimate when employees of the downstairs cafe run to and from the adjoining kitchen, but if all you want is to watch TV, you'll be fine.

⚑ Ⓜ *Tünel.* ⓘ *Breakfast included. Laundry 6TL. Wi-Fi only in the lobby.* Ⓢ *Dorms €12-16; doubles €50; triples €60.* Ⓒ *Reception 24hr.*

GALATALIFE
Galipdede Cad. 75

HOTEL $$$$
☎0212 245 2315; www.galatalifeistanbul.com

It's more expensive than all the nearby hostels in the area, but Galatalife's five rooms come with air-conditioning, and its "family room" quads are huge. On the other hand, the doubles are disproportionately small, and the quad bathrooms feel a bit institutional, with blue plastic doors are straight out of a high school locker room.

⚑ Ⓜ *Tünel.* ⓘ *Breakfast included. Free Wi-Fi.* Ⓢ *Doubles €64; quads €98. 15% discount on cafe downstairs.* Ⓒ *Reception 24hr.*

HOTEL RESIDENCE
Sadri Alışık 19

HOTEL $$$
☎0212 252 7685; www.hotelresidence.com.tr

As the English-speaking staff and the flags outside the lobby attest, this hotel caters to a Western crowd. Its polished and well-lit appearance is a refreshing change from the less appealing hotels on the other side of İstiklal. The rooms fit the bed and not much else, and the bathrooms equally small. Thanks to a club next door and a police station around the corner, the nights can get noisy.

⚑ *From Taksim, go down İstiklal Cad. and turn left at the Ağa Mosque. Residence is on the left.* ⓘ *Breakfast included. Free Wi-Fi.* Ⓢ *Singles €48; doubles €59; triples €78.* Ⓒ *Reception 24hr.*

CHAMBERS OF THE BOHEME
Küçük Parmakkapı Sok. 11/13

HOSTEL $
☎0212 251 0931

Your nana would feel right at home at Chambers of the Boheme, provided she didn't sleep in the 12-person dorm room. The hostel's style is more old-fashioned than alternative, with many private rooms decked out in antique furniture, rugs and frilly purple ornaments. The hostel was given an online "Best Hostel in Turkey" award in 2009, and the management equates this with winning an Oscar—we suggest you remain a bit skeptical.

⚑ *From Ⓜ Taksim, walk down İstiklal and take the 2nd left turn. The hostel is on the left.* ⓘ *Breakfast included. Free Wi-Fi.* Ⓢ *Dorms €15-22; 4-person family room €120.* Ⓒ *Reception 24hr.*

accommodations

BEŞIKTAŞ AND ORTAKÖY

HOTEL ÇIRAĞAN — HOTEL $$

Müvezzi Cad. 1 ☎0212 260 0230; www.ciraganhotel.com

Congratulate yourself for finding one of the rare budget accommodations in Beşiktaş, an area otherwise dominated by international luxury chains. If it weren't for some very tall trees, this hotel would have what qualifies as a "Bosphorus view" (the phrase justifies unreasonably high prices in many establishments in Istanbul). The rooms are lacking in decor and have no air-conditioning, but the windows sometimes let in a cooling Bosphorean breeze. The pleasant restaurant on the sixth floor has a great (read: non-obstructed) view.

🚏 From the Beşiktaş bus station, walk down Çirağan Cad. toward Yıldız Park until you see Müvezzi Cad. on the left, just before the park walls start. The hotel is at the base of Müvezzi Cad. on the left. Alternatively, the hotel is very close to the Çirağan bus stop. ℹ Breakfast 10TL. Wi-Fi available in the lobby and in the restaurant. [$] Singles €30; doubles €41; triples €52. ⏰ Reception 24hr.

OTEL BEŞIKTAŞ — HOTEL $$

Ihlamurdere Cad. 13A ☎0212 261 0346

This locals-oriented hotel is right in the center of Beşiktaş, close to the ferry terminal and the bus station. The cramped rooms mean you'll also be close to your roommate, sleeping toe to toe in doubles, or else close up against the wall in singles. Despite the elevator's elegant granite base, the decor is sparse, and some rooms lack natural light. You'll have to cross the street for breakfast (€3), and there's no air-conditioning.

🚏 From the Beşiktaş bus station, walk inland onto Ortabahçe Cad., which intersects with Dolmabahçe Cad. near the Naval Museum. After a few blocks, the hotel will be on the left. ℹ Free Wi-Fi. No English spoken. [$] Singles €30; doubles €35. ⏰ Reception 24hr.

GOLDEN STREET EXECUTIVE APARTMENTS — APARTMENTS $$$$

Müvezzi Cad. 33 ☎0536 544 4025; www.apartmentinistanbul.co.uk

Make yourself at home, literally. Perched on the hill of a quiet, residential neighborhood, these apartments have none of the hotel feel (or pampering). You can easily walk to Beşiktaş, but going home will be an uphill battle. Most apartments can sleep up to four people, and some have balconies with gorgeous views of the Bosphorus. Of course, these aren't the only apartments in Istanbul for rent—many individuals sublet their places. Consult http://craigslist.com.tr for other offers.

🚏 From the Beşiktaş bus station, walk down Çirağan Cad. toward Yıldız Park until you see Müvezzi Cad. to the left, just before the park walls start. The apartment building is a 4min. walk up a steep hill. Alternatively, the Çirağan bus stop is at the foot of the hill. ℹ A/C. Laundry and kitchen available. No elevator. [$] 2-person studios €100; 4-person apartments €120.

THE HOUSE HOTEL — HOTEL $$$$

Salhane Sok. 1 ☎0212 327 7790; www.thehousehotel.com

Just slightly more affordable than most of the international chain hotels nearby, this local boutique chain recently opened their third Istanbul location in Ortaköy. The marble bathrooms give the feel of an Ottoman hamam, but the treatment here is less royalty and more bourgeoisie. Don't miss breakfast in the upstairs lounge.

🚏 From the ferry dock at Ortaköy, head inland and take the 1st left. The hotel is right next to the House Cafe. ℹ A/C. Free Wi-Fi. [$] Doubles from €300, with sea view from €450; suites €600-800; penthouse €800-1300. Rates are seasonal and vary by availability. ⏰ Reception 24hr.

ASIAN ISTANBUL

👍 HUSH HOSTEL LOUNGE — HOSTEL $

Iskele Sok. 46, Kadıköy ☎0216 450 4363; www.hushhostelistanbul.com

Though the rooms take the word "bare" to new extremes, their size and added perks like cool lounges and alternative music in the lobby make up for it. The staff claims that it's the only hostel in town with a garden, so take advantage and eat your complimentary breakfast there. A terrace on top makes for cramped sunbathing. Sparse pieces of indie art liven up the empty walls, but the angsty photographs in your dorm room might get scary in the dark. The hostel also runs a bar and art gallery. A bit removed from most nightlife and on top of a hill, the location might make for an impossible, drunken climb back up to bed.

From the Kadıköy ferry terminal, cross the street and head north. Turn right onto Iskele Sok. and continue up the hill. HUSH will be on your right. i Sheets provided. Luggage storage available. Free Wi-Fi, kitchen, and TV room. $ Dorms €12-13; singles €31-44; doubles €35-53; triples €46-60; quads €53-71. Rates vary according to A/C and ensuite bathroom availability. ⏰ Reception 24hr.

AS HOTEL HOTEL $$

Yoğurtçu Şükrü Sok. 16, Kadıköy ☎0216 337 0652; www.ashotel.biz

Despite the unfortunate name, this is one of the better options among the cluster of hotels near the ferry terminal, which range from completely unmemorable to unforgettably terrible. Here, the staff speaks some English (or will at least pull up Google Translate when you hit the language barrier), and the rooms have ensuite bathrooms. True, the TVs and the elevator are tiny, but you probably won't be spending enough time in the room to care. This hotel brings you close to the shopping in the Asian side without the overwhelming hustle and bustle.

From the ferry terminal, head up Söğütlüçeşme Cad. Turn left at Osmanağa Mosque, stay left, walk 2 blocks, and turn right. i Breakfast included. Free Wi-Fi. $ Singles €26; doubles €40; triples €53, with extra bed €66. ⏰ Reception 24hr.

ZÜMRÜT OTEL HOTEL $$$$

Rıhtım Cad. Reşitefendi Sok. 5, Kadıköy ☎0216 450 0454; www.kadikoyzumrutotel.com

A little polish goes a long way, especially in this hectic and busy part of Istanbul. The nice lobby, plentiful breakfast spreads, and ensuite bathrooms may hike up the price, but at least you won't have to hike too far to get to the action.

3 streets north from Söğütlüçeşme Cad. The vertical sign is hard to miss. i Breakfast included. $ Singles €57; doubles €84. ⏰ Reception 24hr.

sights

Historical, beautiful, scenic, artsy, quirky: Istanbul has many personalities. Each sight has a history (often a very long one), and as a rule of thumb, the older the building, the more likely it's had at least one makeover. You'll see many mosques, where Muslims covered or destroyed Christian symbols to make way for their own faith. Even contemporary spaces like the Istanbul Modern Art Museum have used the old, an abandoned warehouse, to create something new, a showcase for the country's contemporary art scene. Sometimes, renovation wasn't enough. The sprawling home of the sultans, Topkapı Palace, was abandoned for the more ornate and European-style Dolmabahçe. Go beyond art and architecture, too: you'll find culture and history everywhere, from museums to manuscripts to uncovered mosaics in old churches. Remember to step back and take in the big picture. Revel in the sensation of crossing between continents like it's no big deal, float into the sky on the Turk Balon for an aerial view, or make your way up Çamlıca Hill for a 360-degree panorama. Whether you have your nose pressed against the glass or your neck craned back to take in the magnificence of the Blue Mosque, Istanbul has an incredible number of things to see.

SULTANAHMET AND ENVIRONS

If you came to Istanbul to be dazzled, you'll leave Sultanahmet satisfied. This neighborhood's sights are awe-inspiring in every regard—the architecture, the history, the culture, and (if you're unlucky) the crowds. The magnificent edifices of the Hagia Sophia, the Blue Mosque, and Topkapı Palace are only more spectacular when you see them up close. The collections in the Archaeological Museums will transport you back to the world's earliest civilizations, and public spaces like the Galata Bridge are great spots to rest and take in the bustling city.

HAGIA SOPHIA
MUSEUM

Aya Sofya
☎0212 522 1750; www.ayasofyamuzesi.gov.tr

If you had to sum up Istanbul in one building, this would be it. Built in the sixth century CE under the Byzantine emperor Justinian I, the Hagia Sophia served as a church until the Ottoman conquest of Constantinople in 1453. The Ottomans turned it into a mosque, adding minarets and plastering over the Christian art. In the 1930s, Atatürk ordered that the Hagia Sophia be turned into a museum and opened to all (paying) visitors. And it's worth every lira. As you enter, skim the brief exhibit on the building's history, then climb the ramp to the upper gallery. There, stand in the **Empress's Loge** to get the best view of the **dome,** a massive architectural wonder that seems to float without pillars or other supports. Past the **Marble Door** on the same floor, admire the restored mosaics in the South Gallery, including the 13th-century **Deisis Mosaic,** which depicts Jesus, John the Baptist, and the Virgin Mary. Gazing out from the balcony, you'll see the **calligraphed medallions,** inscribed with the names of Allah, the Prophet Muhammad, the first four caliphs, and two of the Prophet's grandsons. Take the ramp down to the ground floor, where the scale is even more impressive. Religions and centuries overlap here: Archangel Gabriel watches over Mary; baby Jesus; and the *mihrab*, the niche in the wall that points toward Mecca.

✚ ⓜSultanahmet. Walk down Caferiye Sok. away from Hotel Sultanahmet; it's on the left. *i* Arrive early on weekday mornings for the shortest lines. ⓢ 20TL, under 12 free. Audio tours 10TL. ☼ Open Tu-Su in summer 9am-7pm; in winter 9am-5pm. Last entry 1hr. before close. Upper gallery closes 15min. before closing.

ISTANBUL ARCHAEOLOGY MUSEUMS
MUSEUM

İstanbul Arkeoloji Müzeleri
☎0212 520 7740; www.istanbularkeoloji.gov.tr

If you thought simply walking through Istanbul was an overload of history, you'll be blown away by the collections in Istanbul's Archaeology Museums, which display millennia of artistic and cultural achievement. Start near the entrance at the **Museum of the Ancient Orient,** where beasts from the walls of Babylon rear their heads next to mummies and the world's oldest love poem (8th century BCE; our favorite line: "...let me caress you, / My precious caress is more savory than honey."). Farther into the courtyard, the **Tiled Kiosk Museum** houses a modest collection of Seljuk and Ottoman ceramics. The biggest draw is the **Archaeological Museum.** Classicists and collectors of fine Roman marbles can see their favorite legends come to life (well, at least come to stone) in the ground floor's huge sculpture galleries. Beware of the dead: sarcophagi and skeletons fill almost half of the ground floor. Some sarcophagi are so big, they're more like small houses. If you can't make it all the way to Troy, you can at least see some artifacts from the famed city on the second floor. Don't miss the surviving fragments of the Mausoleum of Halicarnassus, one of the Seven Wonders of the Ancient World. The museum's collections span the ancient Mediterranean, gleaned in the days when the Ottomans ruled it all, but the coolest part of this place is seeing the history of Istanbul itself come to life before your eyes.

✚ ⓜSultanahmet. From the Metro, follow the signs. It's in the 1st courtyard of Topkapı Palace. From Topkapı's main entrance behind Hagia Sophia, turn left and go downhill. ⓢ 10TL, under 13 free. Audio tour 10TL. ☼ Open Tu-Su in summer 9am-7pm; in winter 9am-5pm. Last entry 1hr. before close.

istanbul

TOPKAPI PALACE

Topkapı Sarayı

PALACE

☎0212 512 0480; www.topkapisarayi.gov.tr

Perched on the tip of the European peninsula, Topkapı served as the official residence for Ottoman sultans for almost 400 years. The views are great, the buildings are impressive, and the treasures are pretty outrageous. The palace is split between four courtyards. The First Courtyard contains the grounds outside of the Palace, including the Archaeological Museums and **Hagia Eirene.** The Second Courtyard's Imperial Council Hall is where the business of governance was once discussed. To avoid the crowds, you can take a look into the private lives of the palace's inhabitants by touring the **Harem** (15TL). Once home to all the important women in the sultan's life, it's rather empty now, and not different enough from the rest of the palace to be worth the extra cost. If you do visit, look for the **Golden Road,** now an empty and bare passage, where sultans—the rich sugar daddies that they were—used to throw gifts for their concubines to pick up.

The Third Courtyard is the real heart of the Palace. Sultans received foreign dignitaries in the **Privy Chamber,** and the **Chamber of Sacred Relics** displays some of Islam's most valued items: the Prophet Muhammad's sword, a cloak, a tooth, and other belongings. You'll also find the arm of John the Baptist and the saucepan of Abraham (equally well protected, though perhaps more mundane.) Depending on your religion, the shiny collection of thrones, pendants, and gems might be more impressive. Behind the Privy Chamber, the kiosks and pavilions of the Fourth Courtyard have some of the best views, and the **Circumcision Room** is adorned with rare and pretty tiles (though the boys who were brought here were probably too preoccupied to notice). To do justice to this sprawling palace complex, you need to spend at least a few hours exploring.

✦ Ⓜ*Sultanahmet or Gülhane. Enter the grounds down the hill from Hagia Sophia.* Ⓢ *20TL, with harem tour 35TL. Audio tour 10TL.* Ⓓ *Open M 9am-6pm, W-Su 9am-6pm.*

catch them if you can

For obvious reasons, security at the Topkapı palace and the associated museum are pretty tight, but this has not kept thieves from taking valuable pieces of Turkish heritage. According to museum officials, the largest and "scariest" heist occurred in 1999, when thieves broke in and stole a 12th-century Qur'an in the aftermath of a massive earthquake. Although no major robberies have occurred since then, visitors still manage to take little pieces of the palace home with them. Some of the more popular items on the Ministry of Culture's database of "Artefacts Stolen From Topkapı Palace Museum" (sic) include various copies of the Sultan's Monogram, panels, and mysterious shawls. The museum would like both the shawls and the 12th-century Qur'an back, so any information on their whereabouts is valued at a whopping undisclosed amount by the Turkish government.

BLUE MOSQUE (SULTANAHMET MOSQUE)

Sultanahmet Camii

MOSQUE

☎0545 577 1899

While people say Hagia Sophia is less remarkable on the outside than on the inside, the Blue Mosque is often said to be the reverse. Perhaps this is true, but only because the mosque's exterior is quite difficult to match. When the Blue Mosque was built in the early 17th century, its six impressive minarets are said to have caused an uproar, as the Haram Mosque in Mecca was the only place of worship with the same number. In an elaborate bit of damage control, the

sights

sultan sent his architect to Mecca to build a seventh minaret for their mosque. Decorated with the blue Iznik porcelain tiles responsible for the mosque's name, the dome is supported by four "elephant feet," enormous pillars 5m in diameter. Since the Blue Mosque is still in active use, tourists have to enter through a separate entrance, keep to a designated area, and remain outside during prayer times. The mosque is free and popular with families and their kids. If you're not a practicing Muslim, come early or late for a more serene atmosphere.

☩ Ⓜ Sultanahmet. Walk down Atmeydani Cad., away from the park. The mosque is on the left. *i* No shoes or shorts allowed. Women must wear head cover. Ⓢ Free. 🕐 Open in summer M-Th 9am-12:30pm, 2-4:30pm, and 5:45-6:30pm; F 9-11:30am and 2:15-6:30pm; Sa-Su 9am-12:30pm, 2-4:30pm, and 5:45-6:30pm; in winter similar but shorter hours.

SULTANAHMET SQUARE (HIPPODROME)   SQUARE

Sultanahmet Meydanı   ☎ audio guide 444 2648; www.historycalls.com

Very little remains of the old Byzantine Hippodrome, which was a chariot-racing stadium capable of seating 100,000 spectators. Much of what does remain was brought here from other places. Walking from Hagia Sophia, you'll see the **German Fountain** (1901) and its golden mosaic ceiling; the fountain was a gift from Kaiser Wilhelm II intended to symbolize the friendship between the two empires. Down the square, the **Obelisk** (1490 BCE) was built by the Egyptian pharaoh Thutmose III. The hieroglyphs look freshly carved, but the obelisk is actually not intact: what you see is just the top portion of the original, which was three times the current height. The Greek **Serpent Column** (5th century BCE) was made from the melted-down shields of Persian soldiers, in honor of the Greek victory in the Battle of Plataea. In fact, the only monument still around today that was actually constructed here is the **Walled Obelisk,** which now looks pretty decrepit (Crusaders stole all the gilded plates from it in 1204).

☩ Ⓜ Sultanahmet. Go downhill on Divan Yolu and turn right after the Firuz Ağa Mosque. It's the square north of the Blue Mosque. *i* Free Wi-Fi. 🕐 Open 24hr.

GALATA BRIDGE   BRIDGE

You've probably taken a tram across the bridge or a ferry under it, but it's worth the time to walk across and catch your favorite sights of Istanbul, from the distant Çalımca Hill and its antennas to Hagia Sofia and Topkapı Palace. Below, you'll see the spectacle of ferries and boats criss-crossing the Golden Horn, and the lines of fishermen reeling in their catch. On the lower level, waiters reel in tourists to eat at their overpriced seafood restaurants. Stick to the upper level, and if you're hungry, try one of those famous fish sandwiches (*balık ekmek;* 4TL).

☩ Ⓜ Eminönü or Karaköy. You'll see the bridge from either stop.

BASILICA CISTERN   CISTERN

Yerebatan Sarayı, Yerebatan Cad. 13   ☎ 0212 522 1259; www.yerebatan.com

Built more than 1400 years ago under the direction of Emperor Justinian, the same guy responsible for the Hagia Sophia, this underground cistern once stored water for the whole city. Today, the dank, subterranean space makes for a welcome respite from the heat and sun. Walk to the back, where two mysterious medusa heads form the bases of two columns. These craniums were supposedly brought here from pagan Roman temples, but nobody seems to know why they are positioned as they are (upside down and sideways).

☩ Ⓜ Sultanahmet. The entrance is across the street from Hagia Sophia, near the Million Stone. Ⓢ 10TL. Audio tour 5TL. 🕐 Open daily 9am-6:30pm.

SÜLEYMANIYE MOSQUE MOSQUE

Süleymaniye Camii ☎0212 251 8819

With the highest dome in the city, this mosque represents Ottoman architecture at its elegant and innovative best. In order to prevent the build-up of soot from the oil lamps used for heating, the famous Ottoman architect **Mimar Sinan** designed the building's airflow so that the soot collected in one small room. The Süleymaniye Mosque complex is the second largest in Istanbul (after the Fatih Mosque), and, fresh from a recent renovation, its interior's rather subtle and restrained decorations are a sharp contrast to Hagia Sophia and the Blue Mosque. Come here to get away from the crowds of tourists and enjoy reasonably priced food and *nargile* at the restaurants and cafes along the western wall.

⇄ [M]Beyazit. Walk north to the gate of Istanbul University, turn right, and follow its walls all the way up. Alternatively, [M]Eminönü. Exit the Spice Bazaar on Sabuncuhanı Sok., turn left onto Vasit Çinar Cad., and continue up the hill. ⏰ Mosque open daily 5am-8pm. Tombs open daily 9am-5pm.

GREAT PALACE MOSAICS MUSEUM MUSEUM

Büyük Saray Mozaikleri Müzesi ☎0212 518 1205; www.muze.gov.tr/mozaik

These mosaics, which at one stage included 75 million cubes of glass and terra cotta, once decorated the floors of the Byzantine Great Palace of Constantinople. They're now all that remain of the once-expansive palace. Though only a fraction of their former self, they remain unique in size and in breadth of subjects (none of the scenes are religious). The careful use of color and stones produces shading and control that you'd expect to find only in a painting. Despite extensive damage, you can admire astonishing scenes of lions, leopards, their hunters, and mythical creatures like griffins and a Pegasus (well, at least his surviving hind legs).

⇄ From the Hippodrome's Walled Obelisk, turn left, go downhill, and take the 1st left onto Tavukhane Sok. Stay on the road and then take the 1st left. $ 8TL. ⏰ Open Tu-Su in summer 9am-7pm; in winter 9am-5pm.

BEYAZIT SQUARE SQUARE

This square is a good place to relax after finally finding your way out of the Grand Bazaar. Behind the impressive gate of **Istanbul University,** students lounge on shaded lawns with an impressive view of the Süleymaniye Mosque. From the square, you can see the **Beyazıt Tower,** an off-limits structure behind the university walls that was used as a fire tower. There used to be a giant triumphal arch here, but only fragments remain since a 1509 earthquake. Visit the **Beyazıt Mosque** nearby (☎0212 519 3644), one of the oldest mosques in Istanbul. You can also take a look at the **Sahaflar Bazaar** (Old Book Bazaar, east of the mosque), and browse university textbooks and unconvincingly aged replicas of antique books.

⇄ [M]Beyazıt. ⏰ Mosque open daily 5am-11pm.

WESTERN FATIH

[icon] MILLET MANUSCRIPT LIBRARY — LIBRARY, MUSEUM

Millet Yazma Eser Kütüphanesi, Feyzullah Efendi Sok. 1 ☎0212 631 3607; www.milletkutup.gov.tr

"Treasure at every corner" is usually an exaggeration, but that's exactly what you'll find around the corner of Fatih Mosque. The modest Millet Manuscript Library houses an impressive book collection, gathered by the scholar Ali Emiri (1857-1924). Gold-inlaid manuscripts, ornate Ottoman maps, and the world's first Turkish-Arabic dictionary *(Divanü Lugati't-Türk)* shine alongside the poetry of sultans, in their own handwriting. Sure, you might not get the meaning of Suleiman the Magnificent's verses, but you can still admire his delicate, centuries-old calligraphy. If you're hankering to flip the pages of these ancient books, spare yourself a burglary and head to the reading room *(Okuna Salonu)* across the hall to browse the entire collection digitally.

🚏 From Fatih bus stop, head south down Fevzi Paşa Cad. and turn right onto Feyzullah Efendi Sok. The museum is on the left after you enter the complex. ℹ No photography allowed. $ Free. ⏰ Open M-F 8am-5pm.

FATIH MOSQUE — MOSQUE

Fatih Camii ☎0212 631 6723

A few years after the Ottomans conquered Constantinople, Sultan Mehmet the Conqueror demolished the **Church of the Holy Apostles** (an important Byzantine basilica) and built the Fatih Mosque in its place. Unfortunately, what you'll see today is a completely different mosque: the original 15th-century building was destroyed by an earthquake in 1766, and was completely rebuilt by Sultan Mustafa III. Fatih Mosque is undergoing an extensive restoration project, but this shouldn't deter you from visiting—the temporary metal walls inside make the mosque resemble a warehouse, and people still pray here to the sound of drills, hammers, and imams. The **tomb of Sultan Mehmet the Conqueror** just outside the mosque is particularly memorable. Its interior is effusively decorated, a contrast with the bareness of his wife's tomb nearby. A short bio of the Sultan displayed inside states that he was poisoned by a "Jewish doctor" in the service of the Venetians, even though the cause of the Sultan's death remains unknown.

🚏 Take the bus to Fatih. The mosque is behind the tall walls near the bus stop. ℹ Mosque etiquette applies. According to staff, the reconstruction will be complete by 2012. $ Free. ⏰ Open dawn to dusk, closed for prayer times. Tomb open daily 8:30am-5pm.

VALENS AQUEDUCT — RUINS

Bozdoğan Kemeri

Dating back to the fourth century CE, the Valens Aqueduct was completed under the Roman Emperor Valens to keep Constantinople supplied with water. Almost 1km long, this ancient aqueduct is one of Istanbul's most distinctive landmarks. It's not the most interactive historical sight, so unless you're one of the local hoodlums who frequently climb its steep walls, you can really just walk along it. Start at the Şehzade Mosque, which lies at the aqueduct's southeastern end, and continue northwest, crossing the **Atatürk Bulvarı**, a major road that passes right underneath the aqueduct and gives the best view of the structure. Farther up, you'll see the **Siirt Bazaar** on the right, as well as a few cafes with small tables set up against the aqueduct's walls. A few blocks past the end of the aqueduct is the Fatih Mosque.

🚏 Take the bus to Müze or İtfaiye, or take the tram to Aksaray and walk north along Atatürk Bulvarı. $ Free.

FENARI ISA MOSQUE — MOSQUE

Molla Fenari Isa Camii, Halıcılar Cad. 115

Talk about an extreme makeover. Thanks to fire, invasion, and an empress's vanity, the Fenari Isa Mosque has served as two churches, a nunnery, a monastery, and a mausoleum. The complex used to be one church, until Empress Theodora added a second, **the South Church,** to serve as her family's mausoleum in the late 13th century. The Ottomans then turned the whole thing into a mosque, redesigning the interior. However, you can still see some crosses and Christian carvings on parts of the walls and columns in the North Church, a rare example of surviving Byzantine church architecture. Most of the walls are exposed brick, which make for a cooling and quiet break from the busy avenue outside.

🚌 From the Fatih bus stop, go north on Fevzi Paşa Cad. and turn left onto Halıcılar Cad. Go downhill until you reach Adnan Menderes Blvd. The mosque is on the left. $ Free. ⏰ Open dawn-midnight. Closed during prayer times.

prayer time

Six times per day, *muezzins* across the city give the *adhan,* which alerts the faithful that it's time to pray. The *adhan* is delivered in Arabic, and is the same across the Muslim world. However, you don't have to be a devout Muslim to make use of these summons. Keep track of time with these six calls.

- **IMSAK.** Two hours before sunrise. *Imsak* wakes up the early birds and tucks in the night owls.
- **GÜNES.** At dawn, just before sunrise. *Gune* is technically not a prayer itself but marks the end of the first one. Breakfast anyone?
- **ÖGLE.** Midday. A perfect time for a nap to catch up on sleep lost from *imsak.*
- **IKINDI.** Clue: at this time, you're as tall as your shadow's length.
- **AKSAM.** Sundown. When the new day starts in the Islamic calendar.
- **YATSI.** The last rays of light have gone out into the night, and so have you.

FENER AND BALAT

EYÜP SULTAN MOSQUE — MOSQUE

Eyüp Sultan Camii

This is one of the most important pilgrimage sites in Islam. People come to see the grave of Ayyub Al-Ansari (Eyüp Sultan in Turkish), a close friend of the Prophet Muhammad and the standard-bearer of Islam until he died in 674 during the first Muslim siege of Constantinople. This was the first mosque built by the Ottomans after the Conquest (the giant plane tree that grows in the mosque's courtyard was supposedly planted around that time). The **Tomb of Eyüp Sultan** is a wonderfully decorated burial site that's even more beautiful on the inside. Within the tomb, you can find the footprint of the Prophet Muhammad, a strange white object inside a glass display in the wall. The tomb is almost constantly full of pilgrims paying their respects, so make sure to act accordingly. You're also likely to see young boys in curious white costumes visiting the tomb as a part of their *sünnet*—the circumcision ritual that most Turkish boys undergo. The mosque has a separate entrance for women, who generally pray in the upper gallery, but it's usually possible for female tourists to enter through the main entrance, provided that they stick to the usual mosque etiquette. When you're done with the tomb, go for a walk up the hill through the cemetery, all the way to **Pierre Loti Cafe** (see **Food**).

*🚌 Bus or ferry to Eyüp. Cross the road and head inland, toward the visible minaret of Eyüp Mosque. You'll have to pass through a long bazaar street and by a fountain. **i** Standard mosque etiquette applies. $ Free. ⏰ Mosque open daily 5am-11pm. Tomb open daily 9:30am-6:45pm.*

sights

CHORA CHURCH CHURCH, MUSEUM

Kariye Müzesi, Kariye Camii Sok. 29 ☎0212 631 9241

Chora Church requires some serious ceiling-gazing skills—you'll find some of the most beautiful surviving Byzantine art on the domes above your head. The church dates to the fourth century, when Constantinople was so small that this church stood outside the city walls—hence the name *Chora*, meaning "countryside" in Old Greek. However, most of the mosaics date to the early 14th century, when the church was restored following an earthquake. Once you're done craning your neck, make sure to take in the sweeping view of Fener, Balat, and the rest of Istanbul from the back of the museum.

🪧 Bus to Edirnekapı. As you get off the bus, turn left, then take the nearest right turn and walk for 3 blocks. Just before you reach the city walls, turn right and walk 2 blocks down the slope until you see the museum. $ 15TL, under 12 free. ⏰ Open in summer M-Tu 9am-6pm, Th-Su 9am-6pm.

BULGARIAN ST. STEPHEN CHURCH CHURCH

Sveti Stefan Kilisesi ☎0212 635 4432

This church has none of that stone-and-concrete nonsense found in most of Istanbul's houses of worship. St. Stephen is made entirely of iron, assembled from 1893 to 1896 from parts manufactured in Vienna and shipped down the Danube. Iron was in vogue back then (the church is just a few years younger than the Eiffel Tower), and this is one of the few surviving cast-iron churches in the world. You can learn (or review) the story of Jesus from the painted altar and decorations. Stop by if you're in the area, but unless you're a Bulgarian Orthodox Christian or want to marry one, this place isn't really worth a whole pilgrimage.

🪧 Bus or ferry to Fener. The church is located in the park between Fener and Balat ferry jetties. If you're arriving by ferry at Fener, turn right and walk along the shore until you see the church across the road to the left. $ Free. ⏰ Open daily 8am-5pm.

BEYOĞLU

ISTANBUL MUSEUM OF MODERN ART MUSEUM

Liman İşletmeleri Sahası Antrepo 4,
Meclis-i Mebusan Cad. ☎0212 334 7300; www.istanbulmodern.org

Although almost every corner in Beyoğlu has its own gallery, this is the place to get your modern-art fix. The upper floor houses a permanent collection that chronicles the development of modern art in Turkey, while the lower level hosts temporary exhibits by local and international artists. Even the "Stairway to Hell" between the floors is a work of art. The museum sometimes takes the every-picture-worth-a-thousand-words thing a little too seriously; with mini-dissertations accompanying each work, feel free to skip the audio tour. However, don't miss the autoportrait gallery on the upper level or the "False Ceiling" installation next to the library downstairs (it's a layer of books suspended from above, forming an artificial ceiling). The many paintings, video projections, photographs, and installations here show that culture in Istanbul goes beyond the old stuff.

🪧 From [M]Tophane, walk toward Kabataş. After passing the Nusretiye Mosque, turn right and follow the signs. ℹ Free guided tours Th and Su. $ 14TL, students 7TL. Free on Th. Audio tour 4TL, students 3TL. ⏰ Open Tu-W 10am-6pm, Th 10am-8pm, F-Su 10am-6pm. For a schedule of the museum's frequent film screenings (mostly classics and modern Turkish films), check the website.

SANATKARLAR PARK PARK

Sanatkarlar Parkı

Forget those bars and restaurants that make you climb 10 flights of stairs and then overcharge you for drinks with the view: at this public park, you'll get one of European Istanbul's best vantage points for free. The grass is unkempt and the plants are unruly, but locals and expats crowd it on weekend nights—as the morning-after beer caps and cigarette butts can attest. You can settle down in the park itself or on the stairs above it to watch the sunset glow over Topkapı Palace across the water. Steer clear of the back wall, though; since the park has no bathrooms, it's become a popular alternative for those who've had too many beers.

⚡ *From Ⓜ Taksim, walk down Sıraselviler Cad. as it becomes Defterdar Yokuşu. Turn left onto Kasatura Sok. (a block after the Firüzağa Mosque), then right onto Tüfekçi Salih Sok. Go down the road, down the steps, and the park is below.* **i** *Also known as Cihangir Park, even though that name also refers to a different place, without the view.* Ⓢ *Free.* 🕐 *Open 24hr.*

PERA MUSEUM
MUSEUM

Meşrutiyet Cad. 65 ☎0212 334 9900; www.peramuzesi.org.tr

Run by the Suna and İnan Kıraç Foundation, this museum is worth visiting both for its temporary exhibits (which occupy the top three floors and have included works by Picasso, Chagal, and Kurosawa) and its permanent collection. The museum's best-known painting is Osman Hamdi Bey's strangely funny *The Tortoise Trainer*, which the Pera bought for $3.5 million in 2004. It's displayed on the second floor, alongside other Orientalist paintings depicting scenes from life in the Ottoman Empire. The first floor houses collections of Kütahya tiles, ceramics, and—for those of you turned on by girth and length—an extensive collection of measuring instruments.

⚡ Ⓜ *Tünel. Walk up İstiklal until you reach a silver statue resembling a sea urchin (opposite Nuri Ziya Sok.). Turn left into the passage, and at the end turn left. The museum is on the left.* Ⓢ *10TL, students 5TL. Students free on W. Audio tours 4TL.* 🕐 *Open Tu-Sa 10am-7pm, Su noon-6pm.*

QUINCENTENNIAL FOUNDATION JEWISH MUSEUM OF TURKEY
MUSEUM

Perçemli Sok. ☎0212 292 6333; www.muze500.com

When Jews were banished from Spain in 1492, the Ottoman Sultan Bayazid II was the first to welcome the diaspora, and Turkey has hosted a vibrant Jewish community ever since. Did you know that Einstein wrote a letter to Atatürk, asking for Turkey to harbor persecuted Jewish-German scientists? The letter and Atatürk's positive response are just two of the many examples of Turkish-Jewish friendship featured in this museum. The displays all have English translations, and the museum is small and easy to navigate. You'll also find informative tidbits on local landmarks, like the nearby **Banks Street** (Bankalar Cad.) and the Art Nouveau-style **Camondo Stairs** that lead up from it.

⚡ Ⓜ *Karaköy. From the entrance to the Tünel, take the 2nd left and walk uphill to the end of the street.* Ⓢ *10TL, students 3TL.* 🕐 *Open M-Th 10am-4pm, F 10am-2pm, Su 10am-2pm.*

snip snip

You're a six-year-old boy, dressed like a prince. You and your friends ride around in an amusement-park ride with cars shaped like soccer balls while a clown dances on the side. Your family cheers as you strut on stage and give the emcee a high-five. You sit down on a big, plush chair in front of all your family and friends. Then a large man pulls down your pants and reaches for a knife.

Welcome to the **Circumcision Palace!** Since 1964, Kemal Ozkan has built a business helping over 120,000 boys get rid of their foreskins. He's done it everywhere: on a train, on an airplane, on a raft, and of course, on the back of a camel. Continuing a centuries-old Turkish tradition (one sultan held a festival with 52 days of free circumcisions to honor his own son's passage), Mr. Ozkan built his "Disneyland for circumcisions" in a suburb of Istanbul, with music, prayers, clowns, rides, and dancing all included. His sons now do most of the knife work, but you can still catch the "Sultan of Circumcision" cheering with families as their sons shed part of their manhood to become men.

sights

BEŞIKTAŞ AND ORTAKÖY

DOLMABAHÇE PALACE — MUSEUM

Dolmabahçe Sarayı ☎0212 236 9000; www.millisaraylar.gov.tr

Hoping to keep up with the Europeans, Sultan Abdülmecid I commissioned Dolmabahçe in 1856 to replace Topkapı as the sultans' official residence. The palace is an exercise in architectural and decorative overkill (think bear pelts, crystal chandeliers, and man-sized Japanese vases) and has 285 rooms, 68 toilets, 44 halls, and six hamams. The most impressive part is the central **Grand Ceremonial Hall,** which features the heaviest chandelier in Europe (4.5 metric tons) and is still used for special government events. During the separate tour of the **Harem,** you can also see the room where Mustafa Kemal Atatürk died on November 10, 1938 (many clocks in the palace are set to 9:05, the exact time of Atatürk's death). Keep an eye out for the circumcision room, where royal boys shed a bit of their manhood to become men. This is a very popular attraction, and the line for tickets can be very long and very slow. Your best bet is to come on a weekday early in the morning.

⌗ Ⓜ Kabataş. The palace is a short walk northeast, going parallel to the shore past the Dolmabahçe Mosque. From Beşiktaş, walk for approx. 7min. toward Kabataş down Dolmabahçe Cad. i 40min. guided tours in Turkish or English start about every 15min. Separate tour for the Harem 30min. No photos. Ⓢ 20TL, student with ISIC card 1TL. ⏰ Open Apr-Oct Tu-W 9am-5pm, F-Su 9am-5pm; Nov-Mar Tu-W 8:30am-4pm, F-Su 8:30am-4pm.

ORTAKÖY MOSQUE — MOSQUE

Büyük Mecidiye Camii

The Armenian father-son team who built Dolmabahçe Palace also designed this Ortaköy landmark. The style here is also neo-Baroque, though not as outrageously decorated as the palace down the shore. The inside is pretty, but you probably won't spend more than a few minutes there. The mosque is best viewed from the outside. Get a *kumpir* (potato stuffed with cheese and other fillings) from one of the nearby stalls, bask in the sun by the water, and watch Ortaköy's beautiful and well-to-do youth promenade down the Bosphorus. Just avoid sitting under the trees where pigeons roost, or you might get some precipitation on an otherwise sunny day.

⌗ The mosque is right by the sea, to the east of the Ortaköy ferry terminal. Ⓢ Free. ⏰ Open daily 4am-midnight.

ISTANBUL NAVAL MUSEUM — MUSEUM

Deniz Müzesi, Hayrettin Iskelesi Sok. ☎0212 327 4345; www.denizmuzeleri.tsk.tr

For those who retain their childhood interest in model ships, this museum might make for a diverting visit. The top floor has old boat escutcheons (plates bearing the ship's name) and monograms, while the bottom floor holds some relatively modern naval weapons. In the basement, you can learn to tie knots and watch videos of the modern Turkish navy doing cool things like exploding ships, all to the main theme from Michael Bay's film *The Rock*. You can see part of the chain the Byzantines strung across the Bosphorus to keep out Turkish ships during the 1453 seige. Fanboys and fangirls of Atatürk (and in Turkey, who isn't one?) can squee over his death certificate and a copy of his will. The square opposite the museum houses the tomb of Barbaros Hayrettin Paşa (known as Barbarossa), an Ottoman admiral who once dominated the Mediterranean Sea. Don't flaunt your camera too much when entering the museum—the exhibits aren't worth paying extra to immortalize them on film.

⌗ The museum is on the square in front of the Beşiktaş ferry terminal. Ⓢ 4TL, students 1TL. Cameras 8TL. ⏰ Open daily W-F 9am-5pm, Sa-Su 10am-6pm.

YILDIZ ŞALE

MUSEUM

Yıldız Park ☎0212 259 8977; www.millisaraylar.gov.tr

This stuffy guesthouse built by Sultan Abdülhamit II once hosted important state visitors, like Kaiser Wilhelm II and Charles de Gaulle. The building pales in comparison to Dolmabahçe Palace, or to any other interesting place really, but it has some highlights—the carpet in the **ceremonial hall** is 450 sq. m and was rolled into such a huge roll that a hole had to be made in the walls to bring it inside. Gold, crystal, porcelain, and mother-of-pearl adorn nearly every surface. Yıldız Şale isn't the only interesting structure inside the Yıldız Park. There's also the **Malta Köşkü,** now a restaurant, where the paranoid Abdülhamit II once kept his brother Murad V and mother as prisoners. Full of trees, flowers, kitschy animal statues, and innumerable canoodling lovers, the park itself is worth some aimless walking.

🪧 Buses running between Beşiktaş and Ortaköy stop near the entrance to Yıldız Park. Once inside the park, stay on the main asphalt road and follow the signs up the hill. The walk takes about 20min. ℹ Compulsory 20min. guided tours offered every 15min. No photos. $ 4TL; students Tu-W 1TL and F 1TL, Sa-Su 2TL. ⏰ Open Tu-W 9:30am-5pm, F-Su 9:30am-5pm.

PALACE COLLECTIONS MUSEUM

MUSEUM

Saray Koleksiyonları Müzesi, Dolmabahçe Cad. ☎0212 236 9000; www.millisaraylar.gov.tr

The Ottomans may have passed, but they left a lot of stuff behind them. After all, they had to fill up all those huge palaces with something. Housed in the former kitchens of the Dolmabahçe Palace, this museum gives visitors the opportunity to browse through some of the former contents of palaces from all over Istanbul. Items range from delicate blown crystals to an antique dentist's chair to the earliest phonographs, showing how the palace tried to keep up with Western technology. The well-preserved articles make for an intimate, sometimes haunting look into the lives of past dynasties.

🪧 The easternmost part of the Dolmabahçe Palace complex. Go down Dolmabahçe Cad., past the palace proper, and the museum will be on your right. ℹ Most of the displays have English introductions, but descriptions are only in Turkish. $ 2TL, students 1TL. Cash only. ⏰ Open Tu-W 8:30am-4:30pm, F-Su 8:30am-4:30pm.

ASIAN ISTANBUL

👍 ISTANBUL TOY MUSEUM

MUSEUM

Dr. Zeki Zeren Sok. 17, Göztepe ☎0216 359 4550; www.istanbuloyuncakmuzesi.com

Alright, it's no Hagia Sophia, but Istanbul's Toy Museum is unlike any other museum you'll visit in the city. This multi-story villa houses a collection of mostly European and American antique toys, the oldest of which dates back to 1817. Each room is dedicated to different kinds of toys, with music and lighting to complement the theme—for example, the space exploration room looks like the set for a disco dance party set to soaring *Star Wars* symphonies. The museum has its share of kitsch, but there are many memorable exhibits. Come see what are supposedly the first *Micky* Mouse toy (Performo Toy Company, 1926) and the first Mickey Mouse toy (now with an "e"!) standing side-by-side, throwing some suspicion on how Walt Disney was inspired to create his cartoons in 1928. This exhibit proves that running a "toy museum" isn't just a frivolous waste of time, but also provides a fascinating new angle on understanding history. After all, children's toys often reflect adults' dreams.

🪧 Take the suburban train Haydarpaşa-Gebze from Haydarpaşa Train Station to Göztepe (10min.). After you leave the station, cross and walk down the street on the right of the train tracks. After the street turns right, take the nearest left turn and go straight. There are giant giraffe statues in front of the museum. $ 8TL, students 5TL. ⏰ Open Tu-F 9:30am-6pm, Sa-Su 9:30am-7pm.

ÇAMLICA HILL

Çamlıca Tepesi, Büyük Çamlıca

Discover another side (or rather, all the sides) of Istanbul. This hilltop park is a bit out of the way, but it's well worth the climb. Çamlıca is a favorite with locals drawn by the nearly 360-degree view, lush landscaping, and fresh mountain air. Kids play on the scenic terrace while elderly couples stare lovingly at each other over cups of *çay*. A classy restaurant with reasonable prices (part of Çamlıca Sosyal Tesisleri; ☎0212 444 1034) has a monopoly on the view up top, but you can always get food at the booths near the entrance and bring it up to the terrace. Cuddle in the cute marble pavilions, enjoy the restaurant's 1TL tea and Ottoman pleasure-dome atmosphere, or have a picnic and hike around the large pine forest. Sure, radiation from the hill's cell phone antennas might eventually kill you, but what's fun without a little danger?

*Take bus 15C from Üsküdar's ferry terminal to its terminus at Ferah Mahallesi. Go uphill on Çeşme Sok. and take the 2nd left to stay on Çeşme Sok. Keep straight until it becomes Girgin Sok. and follow till the end, then turn right onto Kural Sok. Take a left on Televizyon Sok. and walk to the end. **i** Skip the paid public toilets at the entrance and head for the free ones behind Sosyal Tesisleri. Ⓢ Free.*

MAIDEN'S TOWER

Kız Kulesi, Üsküdar   ☎0216 342 4747; www.kizkulesi.com.tr

On a tiny islet in the Bosphorus near the Asian side, Maiden's Tower is like a mountain—it looks more interesting from afar. The oldest legend surrounding the tower tells the tale of an elderly nun named Hero who used to live here and received secret visits from **Leander,** the love of her life, who would swim to her at night by following the tower's light. One night, a storm blew the light out, Leander got lost and drowned, and a grieving Hero threw herself from the tower. It's a good story, but since the islet is within spitting distance of the Asian side, it's safe to assume that Leander must have had a very poor sense of direction. Legends aside, the Greeks built the first structure here around 400 BCE, but what you see is still standing today thanks to numerous reconstructions. The beautifully lit tower looks best from a ferry after dark. The tiny tower is often claustrophobically crowded and isn't worth a visit unless you're really scraping the bottom of your Istanbul bucket list. Yes, you could bring your date here and splurge at the super-pricey restaurant, but every couple since Byzantine times has already thought of that.

From Üsküdar's ferry terminal, walk around the huge construction site and then follow the shore south until you see the tower (15min.). Shuttle boats run on demand from the pier to the south of the tower. There are hourly shuttle boats from Kabataş as well. Ⓢ Tickets from Üsküdar 5TL; from Kabataş 7TL. 🕐 Shuttle boats run daily 9am-6:45pm. Check the website for evening schedules.

pria-rection

Priapus was a minor Greek god (supposedly born in Turkey) who was the protector of livestock, fruit plants, gardens, and male genitalia. Priapus is known for his permanently erect phallus (an attribute that gave way to the medical term priapism). Statues of this erotic god were commonly placed in gardens, doorways, and crossroads, where travelers would stroke the statue's oversized penis as they passed, in hope of generating good luck. These days, miniature statues are available at souvenir stands throughout Turkey, but think twice before buying one as a souvenir for grandma.

istanbul

TURK BALLOON PANORAMIC VIEWS

Kadıköy ☎0216 347 6703; www.turkbalon.net

Among the meager selection of tourist attractions on the Asian side of Istanbul, this is perhaps the best known. Big enough for 30 people, this balloon rises 140m into the air and allows passengers to experience Istanbul from a rather unusual perspective. The balloon floats at its maximum height for 10min. before descending. The balloon isn't always available, and it wasn't operating at the time of writing—you wouldn't want to risk getting blown away by heavy winds, would you?—however, according to the staff, it should be back up soon. If this sounds like your idea of a good time, look up and search for a big white object in the sky to see if it's in service.

⌖ From the Kadıköy ferry terminal, head west along the shore. The balloon should be on top of a white building that resembles an anemone. [$] 20TL, students 15TL. ⏰ Open daily summer 8am-1am; winter 9am-midnight.

food

Contrary to popular belief, food in Istanbul isn't just kebabs and meatballs. Start your day with a generous Turkish breakfast (usually bread, cheese, olives, eggs, tomatoes, cucumbers) or, even better, with *kaymak* (cream) and honey. If you don't have time to sit down for breakfast, grab a street-side *simit* (Turkish bagel with sesame). For lunch, pop into a *lokanta* to choose from the prepared dishes waiting for workers on their lunch breaks, or go to a restaurant and order a thin *pide*, the so-called "Turkish pizza." To combat your afternoon slump, find a patisserie and have a baklava, or any one of the many similar syrup-soaked pastries the Turks love so much. For dinner, try a fish restaurant or order some mezze (vegetable or seafood appetizers) to share between friends. When late-night fast-food cravings kick in, look for joints that sell *dürüms* (kebab wraps); *tantuni* (diced meat); and, if you're feeling adventurous, *kokoreç* (chopped lamb intestines). Oh, and let's not forget about *çay* (black tea), without which no Turkish meal can be complete. It's amazing that all these things are just the basics. Over time, you'll discover many more options. You probably shouldn't eat all the above in one day, though. It would be delicious, but you might explode, and that would put a real damper on your Istanbul trip.

SULTANAHMET AND ENVIRONS

Eating in Sultanahmet is a tricky affair. Stay too close to the tourist hotspots and you end up paying twice the price of your dorm room. Veer too far, and the menus will be in incomprehensible Turkish. But you can find some local favorites mixed in with the touristy places. The farther you go from Sultanahmet proper, the lower the prices—especially if you're willing to break out the Turkish dictionary. Try the Beyazıt neighborhood and the restaurants along the southwestern wall of Süleymaniye Mosque for some cheap and tasty food.

HOCAPAŞA PIDECISI PIDE $

Hocapaşa Sok. 19 ☎0212 512 0990; www.hocapasa.com.tr

Unlike its neighbors, who prey on overwhelmed tourists, Hocapaşa Pidecisi doesn't have to shove its menu in your face—the sight of fresh *pide* coming out of its oven is enough to tempt anyone to eat here. The all-Turkish menu is only displayed inside, but most of the locals know their orders by heart. Try the *kıymalı* (7TL) for a flavorful blend of meat and spices, or the *peynirli* (7TL), cheese pizza's Turkish cousin. If minced meat and cheese are old hat for you—look at you, you *pide* aficionado—then upgrade your order to *pastirmalı* for a salty taste of air-dried beef (12TL).

⌖ [M]Sirkeci. Go south (up the slope), turn left onto Hocapaşa Sok., and the restaurant is on the left.
i Free Wi-Fi. [$] Pide 7-12TL. ⏰ Open daily noon-9pm.

HAMDI RESTAURANT

TRADITIONAL $$$

Kalçın Sok. 17 ☎0212 528 0390; www.hamdi.com.tr

If you thought the view from Galata Bridge was good, just wait until you sit on this restaurant's terrace—that is, if you're smart enough to make a reservation or early enough to get a table. Good tables are hard to find, even at lunchtime. The food is traditional southeastern Turkish cuisine (kebabs), but everyone comes for the view across the Golden Horn. Without a reservation, you can still end up with scenic seats—just sit one floor below the terrace, where there are fewer people, a great view, and the most potent air-conditioning. You'll want to linger and take in the view, even though the speedy service encourages quick table turnover.

✠ ⓂEminönü. Walk past the New Mosque and take the 1st left after the Spice Bazaar. Turn right and continue until you see Hamdi on the left. Ⓢ Appetizers 7-10TL. Kebabs 19-24TL. ⓒ Open daily noon-midnight.

ALI BABA LOKANTASI

LOKANTA, TRADITIONAL $

Profesör Sıddık Sami Onar Cad. 1 ☎0212 520 7655; www.alibabakanaat.com.tr

Right outside the Süleymaniye Mosque complex, Ali Baba is a favorite of local professionals for its cheap *kuru fasülye*, stewed beans served either by themselves or on top of rice *pilav* (4.5TL). It's not unusual to see everyone ordering the same thing, and you should try it too. The flavorful and slightly spicy taste provides a surprisingly filling lunch, especially with the generous bread basket. You can also order off the menu posted by the door, or go inside and point at your favorite dishes. It's a bit far from the rest of the neighborhood, but if you're visiting the nearby mosque, Ali Baba is a great bet for delicious local flavor.

✠ From the Süleymaniye Mosque, head out of the gate that faces the entrance to the tombs. Ⓢ Beans 4.50TL. Döner kebab 10TL. Köfte 8TL. ⓒ Open daily 7am-8pm.

DOY-DOY

TRADITIONAL $$

Şifa Hamam Sok. 13 ☎0212 517 1588; www.doydoy-restaurant.com

Recommended by perhaps every travel guide writer who has ever passed through this area, Doy-Doy's reasonably priced kebabas and pizzas are on the brink of flipping from underrated to overrated. For some, hearing Ke$ha playing as people dig into their *sütlaç* might take away from the authenticity of the meal. However, Doy-Doy's interior walls are covered with wallpaper and tiles fit for an Ottoman palace, and the view of the Blue Mosque is breathtaking, making this place perfect for those who love Islamic architecture with a side of American pop music.

✠ ⓂSultanahmet. From the walled obelisk in the Hippoddrome, turn left and go downhill. Stay on the road, and Doy-Doy is on the right. ⓘ Free delivery within Sultanahmet. Ⓢ Kebabs 9-19TL. Desserts 4-5TL. ⓒ Open daily 8am-10:30pm.

BAB-I HAYAT

TRADITIONAL $$$

Yeni Cami Cad. 47 ☎0212 520 7878

You, too, can dine like a sultan. Previously used as a stable, a tax collector's office, and a warehouse, this restaurant was renovated by the people who restored Topkapı Palace, tiled walls and hand-painted ceilings included. Bab-ı Hayat serves big and well-arranged portions as well as a popular lunch buffet that includes soup, appetizer, salad, main course, and dessert (30TL). If you still have some lire left over, come after a haggling session in the Egyptian Bazaar to enjoy their selection of classic Ottoman dishes.

✠ ⓂEminönü. Walk straight through the Spice Bazaar and turn left to reach the southeastern gate. The restaurant is on the right, inside the gateway. ⓘ Additional 10% service fee. ⓒ Open daily noon-midnight.

istanbul

YENI YILDIZ
Cankurtaran Meydani 18

TRADITIONAL $$
☎0212 518 1257

Down a crooked cobblestone path from Sultanahmet, this *pide* and kebab restaurant is tourist-friendly but offers better quality and prices than many of the establishments uphill. Originally owned by the late Erol Taş, a popular Turkish actor to whom much of the wall space is now devoted, Yeni Yildiz has expansive and colorful outdoor seating where you can eat, play backgammon, and smoke *nargile* (15TL). As for food, try the vegetarian kebab or the generous plate of grilled and cold mezzes (10TL).

✦ Ⓜ*Sultanahmet. From the entrance to Topkapı Palace (behind Hagia Sofia), go downhill and stay on the road until the train tracks. The restaurant will be ahead on the right, before the bridge.*
i Free Wi-Fi. Ⓢ *Appetizers 4-10TL. Kebabs 10-15TL.* ⏰ *Open daily 9am-midnight.*

PAŞAZADE RESTAURANT
İbn-i Kemal Cad. 5A

TRADITIONAL $$$
☎0212 513 3757; www.pasazade.com

Dine like the Ottomans on dishes that you can't find on the street and that haven't been eaten in ages. Forget grilled kebabs (there's only one on the menu) and admire the artfully arranged plates of boiled and stewed foods, like the *Mahmudiye* (a mix of chicken, mashed potatoes, and fruits; 18TL). This is one of the few places where you can get upscale decor (candles and all) and classy waiters without paying more than they're worth.

✦ Ⓜ*Gülhane. Follow the tracks toward Sirkeci, turn left onto Erdoğan Sok., and then turn right. Paşazade is on the left.* Ⓢ *Entrees 16-23TL. Desserts 6-8.50TL.* ⏰ *Open daily 12:30-11pm.*

eat up the streets

Istanbul is a paradise for street foodies. Though they're one of the tastiest and cheapest ways to eat in town, the multitude of options can be overwhelming. Luckily, we're here to help guide your culinary adventures.

- **PIPING HOT MINI-BURGERS** (really more like sloppy-joe sliders) are mostly concentrated in Taksim Sq., but can be found in other parts of the city as well. Perfect at the end of a night out drinking, or as an afternoon snack.

- **GRILLED FISH SANDWICHES** are best from the vendors along Galata Bridge (who are catching your meal right before you eat it). Although street seafood may seem dubious, they are usually safe and always delicious—just watch out for the occasional bone.

- **BEWARE THE FRIED MUSSELS.** Once you try them, you won't be able to stop. Served three to a stick with a dash of creamy sauce, these are the perfect way to satisfy late-night cravings.

- **KÖFTE.** Wrap it in pita; cover it in tomatoes, parsley, and onions; and eat it anywhere you find it.

ORIENT EXPRESS RESTAURANT
İstasyon Cad. 2

INTERNATIONAL $$$
☎0212 522 2280; www.orientexpressrestaurant.net

Once upon a time, electricity was exciting, people dressed nicely before stepping outside, and killing someone on a train made for a fun story. You can still relive those times by dining at the Orient Express Restaurant, where bow-tied waiters serve dishes like roast lamb shoulder (30TL) under tall ceilings and elegant stained glass, next to a wall dedicated to Ms. Christie and her stories. Or you might want to skip the interior and its distracting fountain for the tables by

food

the tracks featuring an open view of the station. Once you've settled the bill, hop on the next Orient Express—just be sure to watch your back.

➜ ⓂSirkeci. Enter the train station, and the restaurant is on the left by the tracks. $ Entrees 20-35TL. Desserts 10TL. ⏰ Open daily 10am-10pm.

TARIHI SULTANAHMET KÖFTECISI SELIM USTA KÖFTE $$

Divan Yolu Cad. 12 ☎0212 520 0566; www.sultanahmetkoftesi.com

Selim Usta has been making meatballs since 1920, and the frequent long lines outside are a testament to this eatery's fame. It's close to all the main attractions and is a traditional favorite for families breaking their Ramadan fasts, but, unfortunately, the rubbery *köfte* doesn't live up to the hype. Though salad portions are generous, the food is inevitably overpriced, like so many other things in this neighborhood.

➜ ⓂSultanahmet. Walk downhill from the tram stop. Selim Usta is on the left. $ Bean salad 5TL. Köfte 10TL. Cash only. ⏰ Open daily 10:30am-11pm.

WESTERN FATIH

👍 FATIH KARADENIZ PIDECISI PIDE $

Büyük Karaman Cad. 57 ☎0212 635 0509

Snap, crackle, *pide*. This popular lunch spot gets so busy, you'll probably end up sharing a table with the locals. All of the menu's four options are delicious. Meateaters will eye the *kıymalı* (meat) or the *karşılı* (meat and cheese; 9.50TL), while vegetarians can munch on the cheese *peynirli* or the butter-filled *yağlı* (8.50TL). If you're looking to pile on protein, add a freshly cracked egg (0.50TL). The wait can be agonizingly long, but once the food reaches the table, even the businessmen who crowd this place stop checking their smartphones. Plunge the lump of butter straight into the *pide*, or rub it along the crust, but for the sake of your arteries, try not to come here more than twice a day.

➜ From the Fatih bus stop, walk down Fevzi Paşa Cad. as it turns into Macar Kardeşler Cad. Turn left onto Dülgeroğlu Sok. and take the 1st right. The restaurant is on the left. $ Pide 8.50-9.50TL. Drinks 0.50-3TL. ⏰ Open Tu-F 10:30am-10pm.

ESKI KAFA CAFE, ORGANIC $$

Atpazarı Meydanı Sok. 11A ☎0212 533 4296

The cafe's name ("old head"), motto ("eat, drink, think"), and organic menu all emphasize the philosophy of good thinking through good food. Enjoy your cup of hibiscus tea (4TL) in the dark interior, or outside at one of the tables made from concrete blocks. The owner, a children's book author, has eclectically decorated Eski Kafa with records of his thoughts and achievements, so everything you see is a great conversation starter (if you speak Turkish).

➜ From the southeastern exit of the Fatih Mosque grounds, turn left and walk for 3 blocks. Turn right onto Atpazarı Meydanı Sok., and Eski Kafa is on the right. ℹ Free Wi-Fi. $ Gulaş 14TL. Desserts 6-7TL. Tea 1.50-4TL. Cash only. ⏰ Open daily 9:30am-2am.

SUR OCAKBAŞI TRADITIONAL $$

İtfaiye Cad. 27/1 ☎0212 533 8088; www.surocakbasi.net

Apparently, Anthony Bourdain visited this place in 2009, and the food gave him an alleged orgasm—so it's about time tourists started crowding in. The specialty is the *büryan kebab* (12TL): succulent sliced lamb with just the right amount of fat, layered between two pieces of fresh bread. If one regional dish isn't enough for you, down the lamb with *açık ayran* (2.50TL), a savory, yogurt-like drink that tastes like milk for grown-ups. The mascot of this restaurant is a nude, bewildered child standing inside a huge watermelon. Don't ask why.

➜ From the Fatih Mosque, walk southeast until you reach the aqueduct. Walk along it, then turn left into Siirt Bazaar (one street west of Atatürk Bulvari) and go straight. The restaurant is on the left. $ Pide 10TL. Kebabs 10-19TL. ⏰ Open daily 8am-1am.

SELAM — TRADITIONAL, FAST FOOD $$

Fevzi Paşa Cad. 69 — ☎0212 631 2595; www.selam.com.tr

This chameleon of a restaurant offers something different on each of its three floors: sweets in the basement, fast food on the first floor, and kebabs on the second. With English translations and gorgeous pictures, the top floor's menu looks more like a fashion magazine, and the food is as tasty as the photos. Order the *soslu mantı* (10-12TL), a handmade pasta with bits of meat inside. Come at the right time and you'll see it being prepared inside the cubicle near the entrance.

➡ From the Fatih bus stop, walk northwest on Fevzi Paşa Cad. Selam is on the left, close to where the Fatih Mosque's walls end. $ Pide 7-13TL. Kebabs 14-20TL. Pastries 4-7TL. ⏰ Open daily 11am-11pm.

SARAY MUHALLEBICISI — SWEETS $

Fevzi Paşa Cad. 1 — ☎0212 521 0505; www.saraymuhallebicisi.com

If you want to have a substance-induced state of altered consciousness in alcohol-less Fatih, your best bet will be to go for a sugar high. Take the elevator to the terrace on Saray's top floor, where you can feed on *kazandibis*, *muhallebis*, profiteroles, and baklava while taking in a view of the city. Suffering from a sugar hangover? It's also a good spot for breakfast (4.50-8TL). Look for this chain of sweets and dessert shops all over Istanbul.

➡ From the southeastern exit of the Fatih Mosque grounds, turn right and walk to Fevzi Paşa Cad. Saray is on the right, across the road. $ Sandwiches 6-7TL. Desserts 3-7TL. Pastries 3-8TL. Coffee 4TL. ⏰ Open daily 6am-1am.

KÖMÜR LOKANTASI — LOKANTA $$

Fevzi Paşa Cad. 18 — ☎0212 521 9999

Kömür is busy, with a fleet of delivery vans and a lot of waiters running around. All of the food, both raw and cooked, is laid out behind the glass counter, so non-Turkish-speakers can take advantage of the old point-to-order system. Don't expect dazzling culinary excellence, but you'll get efficient service and no surprises. You'll spot Kömür's delivery boys running all around the neighborhood, dressed in neon-yellow vests emblazoned with the restaurant's logo.

➡ If you're walking northwest on Fevzi Paşa Cad., Kömür is on the right, on the 1st corner after the mosque's walls end. $ Pilaf 3-5TL. Kebabs 7-12TL. Desserts 4-5TL. ⏰ Open daily 4am-11pm.

salep it on

Feeling cold? Have a sore throat? Libido not what it used to be? Perk yourself up with a cup of *salep*. Made from the ground-up roots of orchids boiled in water or milk, *salep* has been warming up sultans and soothing sick Turks for centuries. Perhaps because the flower's roots are shaped like a pair of gonads, the drink is also considered a potent 👍**aphrodisiac.** *Salep* has become so popular, with its own flavors of ice cream and pastries, that the Turkish government banned its export to save the orchid from extinction (and perhaps to hog all the benefits). Get yours while you can. And don't forget to dust your *salep* with a bit of cinnamon (also, purportedly, an aphrodisiac) for that extra kick.

FENER AND BALAT

👍 **FINDIK KABUĞUNDA KÖFTE** — KÖFTE $

Mürsel Paşa Cad. 89 — ☎0212 635 3310; www.findikkofte.com

In Balat, it's surprising to find such a tourist-friendly restaurant with such reasonable prices. A clean interior, free Wi-Fi, and a terrace overlooking the

Bulgarian St. Stephen Church and the Golden Horn make this local favorite a great lunch spot. Try one of the three varieties of meatballs, the artichoke, or the saffron-tinged lentil soup. Vegetarians can graze on the mezze sampler (15TL), featuring dishes like smoky grilled eggplant and Turkish potato salad. There's no menu, so point away at the counter.

🚏Bus or ferry to Fener. From the ferry jetty, go inland, cross the road, turn right, and walk until you see the Bulgarian St. Stephen Church on the right. The restaurant is opposite the church. ℹ Free Wi-Fi. [$] Köfte 8TL. Sides and salads 3TL. Desserts 4-7TL. ⏰ Open daily 9am-10:30pm.

PIERRE LOTI CAFE — CAFE $

Gümüşsuyu Balmumcu Sok. 5 — ☎0212 581 2696

You might not know who Pierre Loti is (if you're wondering, it's the pen name of 19th-century French writer Julien Viaud), but this place sure knows how to make money off him. Enjoy an apple tea (2TL) while taking in the view over the Golden Horn. The cigarette burns on the tablecloths, no doubt marks of past intellectual discussions, might even inspire you to light up some of your own (cigarettes and discussions, that is). The souvenir shop aspires to Turkish-French literary greatness, selling books about its namesake and artsy postcards of old Constantinople.

🚏 Bus or ferry to Eyüp. From the Eyüp Sultan Mosque, you can either take a cable car (Piyerloti teleferik, token (jeton) 2 TL; runs 8am-11pm) or walk. It's a 15min. hike up the hill through the cemetery; climb the flight of stairs behind the mosque and follow the path marked "1. Cadde." [$] Tea 2TL. Coffee and soda 4TL. Accepts euro, dollars, and even marks, but no credit cards. ⏰ Open daily 8am-midnight.

NEV-I CAFE — CAFE, NARGILE $

Abdülezelpaşa Cad. 264 — ☎0212 531 8602; www.nevicafe.com

Ease yourself into exploring Fener and Balat with a cup of tea at this roadside cafe. True to its motto, *antik bir keyif* ("an ancient pleasure"), every surface is covered in traditional carpets and tapestries. You'll want to escape the street noises at ground level by going up the steps to the covered terrace. The food selection is sparse (toasts 5TL; salads 10TL), so save your lire for a relaxing puff on the *nargile* (15TL). The cafe has a sibling restaurant down the waterfront in Unkapani (☎0212 621 6456), which serves larger portions of Italian-style fare in a slightly more formal atmosphere.

🚏 Bus to Ayakapı. Cross the main avenue (Abdülezelpaşa Cad.) inland. The cafe is at the intersection. [$] Cold drinks 1-3TL; hot drinks 2.50-5TL. ⏰ Open daily 9am-midnight.

HALIÇ SOSYAL TESISI — TRADITIONAL $$

Kadir Has Üniversitesi Karşısı, Abdülezelpaşa Cad. — ☎0212 621 9075; http://tesislerimiz.ibb.gov.tr

This government-run restaurant exists thanks to the many attempts of local authorities to turn Fener and Balat into a hip, gentrified area like Cihangir. They haven't succeeded (yet), but this restaurant is well done. Clean, spacious, and with reasonable prices, they cook up standard Turkish offerings, served by smartly dressed waiters who speak very little English. Snag a spot by the water to catch the cool breeze off the Golden Horn.

🚏 Bus or ferry to Fener. Head southeast along the shore (toward Sultanahmet), a little past the Yakapı bus stop. The restaurant is right by the water. [$] Köfte 7.50-8.5TL. Fish 9-17TL. Desserts 4-7.50TL. ⏰ Open daily 9am-midnight.

BEYOĞLU

★ MANGAL KEYFI — DÜRÜM $

Öğüt Sok. 8 — ☎0212 245 1534

This charismatic, unpretentious restaurant is filled with young locals, and it's got better *dürüms* than you'll get at any touristy restaurant in Taksim. Try the excellent chicken *tavuk dürüm*, (grilled chicken wrapped with chopped lettuce and tomatoes; 4TL), with a cup of frothy *ayran*. The dark red walls, plethora of posters, and nonstop Western rock music make eating here pleasant, but you could forget you're in Turkey if it wasn't for the food.

From [M]Taksim, walk down İstiklal. Take a right onto Ağa Camii, then take the 2nd right onto Öğüt Sok. The restaurant is on the left. $ Dürüms 4-5TL. Kebabs 9-15TL. Ayran 1.50TL. ⏰ Open daily noon-midnight.

LADES RESTAURANT — MENEMEN $

Sadri Alışık Sok. 14 — ☎0212 251 3203

What do you do when your first restaurant is wildly successful? Build one right across the street, of course. That's the case with Lades and Lades 2. Come here for a fast, no-frills Turkish breakfast. The crowds have died down a bit, but this is still possibly the best *menemen* in European Istanbul. Try the *pastırmalı menemen*, which puts pungent bits of Ottoman-style cured beef in your eggs (7TL). The portions and the bread baskets are generous too, so you can do a proper job and wipe the pan clean. If you want to see them make it, head to Lades 2.

From [M]Taksim, go down İstiklal Cad. and turn left at the Ağa Mosque. The restaurant is a few meters ahead (Lades 2 is on the left). $ Menemen 4-7TL. Cash only. ⏰ Open daily 8am-9pm.

VAN KAHVALTI EVI — BREAKFAST $$

Defterdar Yokuşu 52A — ☎0212 293 6437

Cihangir is the best area in Beyoğlu for a lazy breakfast, probably because most of its inhabitants are a lazy lot (expats, artists, and the like). Van Kahvaltı Evi offers the best deal in the neighborhood, serving up excellent scrambled eggs with cheese and sausage (8TL). Tea is served in big cups, but we recommend the organic fruit juices (4TL). It's a simple place, but on weekend mornings it's hard to find an empty table.

From [M] Taksim, walk down Sıraselviler Cad. Van Kahvaltı Evi is on the left, 1 block after the Firuzağa Mosque. $ Eggs 5-8TL. Breakfast plates 8-15TL. Coffee 3-4TL. ⏰ Open daily 7am-7pm.

ZENCEFIL — VEGETARIAN $$

Kurabiye Sok. 8A — ☎0212 243 8234; www.zencefil.org

If you're a vegetarian sick of navigating the kebab minefield that is Istanbul, you should definitely head over to this hip Taksim eatery. Its "vegetable-oriented" menu changes by season and is a cut above the standard of many meat-focused restaurants. Zencefil cans its own vegetables, makes its own butter and bread, presses its own homemade lemonade, and churns its own ice cream. Even die-hard carnivores will come out wishing they could afford to eat all their meals here.

[M]Taksim. Walk down İstiklal, take the 1st right, the 1st left, then keep going until you see the restaurant on the right. i Free Wi-Fi. $ Full entrees 10.50-15TL; small entrees 8.50-11.50TL. Ice cream 8.50-11.50TL. Lemonade 8TL. ⏰ Open daily 8am-midnight.

KAFE ARA — CAFE $$$

Tosbağa Sok. 2 — ☎0212 245 4105

The cosmopolitan Kafe Ara is owned by Ara Güler, a respected Turkish photographer whose giant black-and-white photographs of Istanbul adorn the walls. If you come in the afternoon, you might even see the old man himself, now in his 80s, hanging in his shrine. If you're hungry, splurge on a pricey entree, but otherwise just drop by for a coffee or herbal tea with a shot of culture. It sure beats the generic Starbucks experience.

[M]Taksim or Tünel. Walk down İstiklal Cad. to Galatasaray Lisesi, then go down Yeni Çarşı and take the 1st right. $ Breakfast buffet 15TL. Entrees 16.50-23.50TL. Desserts 7-10.50TL. Su brunch 28TL. ⏰ Open M-F 7:30am-midnight, Sa 10am-1am, Su 10:30am-midnight.

EMINE ANA SOFRASI
TANTUNI $

Billurcu Sok. 5A ☎0212 292 8430

The stools are of different heights and the tables are short, but you'll be too busy wolfing down one *tantuni dürüm* after another to notice how uncomfortable you are. Made of diced meat, and wrapped with some lettuce and tomatoes, *tantuni* are kebabs' lesser-known, equally tasty cousins. If you get takeout, we dare you to try and finish it before you reach the door.

✚ *From ⓂTaksim, go down İstiklal and turn left on Kücükparmakkapı Sok. Go to the end of the road, turn right, and then left. It's the corner on the left.* Ⓢ *Tantuni dürüm 5TL.* Ⓐ *Open daily 11am-6am.*

CEZAYIR
TRADITIONAL $$$$

Hayriye Cad. 12 ☎0212 245 9980; www.cezayir-istanbul.com

Cezayir is housed in an old Italian building that used to be a school, but is now one of Galatasaray's best-known restaurants. The cuisine is Turkish with a twist—the halloumi cheese with tomato pesto (10TL) and grilled lamb tenderloin (30.50TL) are among the more popular dishes. If this place is too expensive for you, try browsing the Cezayir Sok. nearby, which has plenty of atmospheric and lesser-known, if kitschy, restaurants.

✚ ⓂTaksim *or Tünel. From Galatasaray Lisesi, go down Yeni Çarşı and take the 1st left. The restaurant is on the right.* ⓘ *Reservations recommended.* Ⓢ *Appetizers 11-20TL. Entrees 17-37.50TL. Beer 8-13TL.* Ⓐ *Open daily 9am-2am.*

an ode to manti

Why is it that dumplings are always the most delicious element of any cuisine? We may never know, but the pattern certainly holds true for Turkish food. *Manti* are pasta-dumpling hybrids, fluffy triangles of folded dough, usually filled with a dollop of ground meat. Vegetarians fear not, for meatless *manti* are often available. What really sets this dish apart, however, are the condiments. Traditionally topped with garlic yogurt and tomato oil, diners are free to add sumac, mint, and red pepper flakes to taste. The combination is light, satisfying, and delicious. Look for smaller restaurants where they make them from scratch.

BEŞIKTAŞ AND ORTAKÖY

🖼 CAN CIĞER
LIVER $$

Barbaros Bulvarı 25/4 ☎0212 260 2154

Liver-haters take note: this restaurant will convert you. Here, the cow's most unappreciated organ comes thinly sliced and fried, with each bite starting off crunchy and then quickly melting in your mouth. Since mom always said to eat your vegetables, the plates come with a few redeeming slices of tomatoes, chopped onions, and a whole fried chili pepper. The service is fast, but save yourself from ordering twice (trust us: you will) by getting the double portion at a slight discount.

✚ *From the Beşiktaş ferry terminal, go up Barbaros Bulvarı. The restaurant is on the left.* Ⓢ *½-portion of liver 8TL, full 12TL, 1½ 17TL, double 21.50TL. Salad 4TL. Drinks 1-2.50TL.* Ⓐ *Open daily 9am-9:30pm.*

YEDI-SEKIZ HASANPAŞA FIRINI
BAKERY $

Şehit Asim Cad. 12 ☎0212 261 9766

The smell hits you first—sweet, tinged with something like anise, it lures you from the street into the shop. The windows are lined with baked goodies, but the tables piled high with cookies and bread are even more impressive. The founder named the store "7-8," after the signature of Hasanpaşa, an Ottoman officer who only knew how to write numbers. Thankfully, you don't have to know the Turkish alphabet to enjoy the crumbly, delicious cookies. Pick from orange, pistachio, cherry, chocolate (we could go on for days), or just get one of each for a sampling of the best.

From the eagle statue, walk down Şehit Asim Cad.; the store is on the left. $ Tea cookies (all flavors) 14TL per kg. Coconut-flavored cookies 20TL per kg. Sandwiches 1.50TL. ⏰ Open daily 8am-9:30pm.

SIDIKA SEAFOOD $$$

Şair Nedim Cad. 38 ☎0212 259 7232; www.sidika.com.tr

Many seafood restaurants in Istanbul put candles on their tables and hire some musicians, then think they are entitled to charge a lot for mediocre food. Sıdıka, on the other hand, serves delicious fish in a low-key, stylish environment. The mezze are wonderful, but the house specialties are grilled octopus (12TL) and the grilled bass in grape leaves (18TL). Everything here is small: the chairs, the salt and pepper shakers, the bread basket, and sadly, the portions, too. Don't expect to leave with a full belly.

From the eagle statue, walk down Şehit Asim Cad., cross Ortabahçe Cad., and continue until you get to Şair Nedim Cad. Turn right onto Şair Nedim Cad. and continue up the road until you see the restaurant on the right. i Free Wi-Fi. $ Meze 3-12TL. Fish 8-22TL. Desserts 5-10TL. Rakı 10TL. ⏰ Open M-Sa noon-2am.

PANDO KAYMAK BREAKFAST $

Mumcu Bakkal Sok. 5 ☎0212 258 2616

The jars of honey lining the window are as sweet as the elderly Bulgarian-speaking couple who run this place. Come here for bread with *kaymak* (cream) and honey (5TL), and have a cup of hot milk with it (1TL). Despite the faded decor and cramped interior, Pando Kaymak is a very popular breakfast spot among students and expats. Good luck getting a seat on a weekend morning.

From at the eagle statue, walk away from the fish market. Pando Kaymak will be on the left (above the door, it says, "Kaymaklı kahvaltı burada"). $ Breakfast omelettes 5-6TL. Cash only. ⏰ Open daily 7:30am-7pm.

KARADENIZ PIDE VE DÖNER SALONU PIDE $$

Mumcu Bakkal Sok. 6 ☎0212 261 7693

Even though this part of town is generally associated with expensive dining, it is possible to find cheap, excellent kebabs. Karadeniz doesn't have a varied menu; instead, they have one enormous ball of lamb meat on a spit from which they cut off meat for individual portions. It gets packed around lunchtime, when those who can't find seats crowd around the standing counter. Avoid sitting by the dumbwaiter, or you'll be too busy watching dirty plates to focus on the food.

Karadeniz is near the eagle statue, opposite Pando Kaymak. $ Pide 7-10TL. Döner 12TL. İskender 13TL. ⏰ Open daily 5:30am-7pm.

THE HOUSE CAFE CAFE $$$

Salhane Sok. 1 ☎0212 444 4842; www.thehousecafe.com

The House Cafe has a number of locations throughout the city, but this one is probably the best known. The most Turkish food is the *lahmacun* pizza. Otherwise, the dishes show a Western influence, veering on Italian. Large portions, high prices, and a trendy design (a cross between backyard workshop and sexy lounge) make this a popular hangout for well-to-do local students. The service runs at a leisurely pace, so don't come in a rush. Late at night, the cafe turns into a bar with DJ performances.

The cafe is right by the Ortaköy ferry dock. i Free Wi-Fi. $ Pizza 19.50-32TL. Beer 12-16TL. Desserts 3-14TL. Teas 4-9TL. ⏰ Open daily 9:30am-1am. Kitchen closes earlier.

ASIAN ISTANBUL

ALI USTA — ICE CREAM $

Moda Cad. 264A, Moda ☎0216 414 1880

This small ice cream shop doesn't look like much, but the long line of locals out the door says more than the modest exterior. In fact, this is one of the best, and best-known, ice cream joints in Istanbul. Get a scoop or two, add caramel sauce, chocolate chips, and chopped nuts (for free—something American stores need to emulate) and set out for Moda's beaches. You can even take it home by the kilogram (35TL).

From Kadıköy, get on the nostalgic tram (near the Osman Ağa Mosque) and get off near Moda Cad. Walk down the street, and Ali Usta will be on the right side, close to where Moda Cad. forks. $ Scoops 2TL; 35TL per kg. Open daily 8am-2am.

dukkan the divine

While you probably didn't come to Istanbul for the burgers, there is one you really ought to try before you leave. Enter Dukkan Burger. Initially a gourmet butcher shop, Dukkan branched out and now serves one of the best burgers in the city (and people in Istanbul are actually pretty into burgers these days). Imagine a thick, juicy, perfectly grilled patty on a toasted bun. Add a secret spice blend, and top it with tomato, *peynir* (Turkish cheese), and house-made mayonnaise. Wrap it in paper, and you have a Dukkan cheeseburger. Skip the imitation bacon (it's not the same when it's not made out of pig) and order a side of fries instead. While pricier than your average fast food, it's well worth the splurge. With several locations throughout the city, Dukkan makes it easy to satisfy your craving.

BAYLAN PASTANESI — PASTRY SHOP $$

Muvakkıthane Cad. 9A, Kadıköy ☎0216 346 6350; www.baylangida.com

Top off your shopping spree at Kadıköy Market with a pastry spree at Baylan. A culinary landmark, Baylan is one of the last remaining branches of a pastry shop started by a Greek immigrant named Philip Lenas. Forget the kilograms of European-style sweets and pastries on display and head for the patisserie's most famous creation, the *Kup Griye* (12TL): a foodgasm of vanilla ice cream, caramel sauce, chopped almonds, ground pistachios, Chantilly cream, and a ladyfinger biscuit. If you're greedy for more, browse your table's copy of the store's illustrated history book. The interior can be dark, so try the shaded garden in the back.

From the Kadıköy ferry terminal, head inland to the start of Söğütlüçeşme Cad. Turn right, keeping the park on your right, then turn left at the PTT store. Baylan will be on your left. $ Tea 3.50TL. Coffee 5.50-6.50TL. Open daily 8am-10pm.

MEŞHUR MENEMENCI — MENEMEN $

Pavlonya Sok. 16, Kadıköy ☎0216 336 6308

Preparing almost exclusively *menemen* (a popular scrambled egg dish), this tiny eatery is a great place to start your day. It's mostly populated by locals, but *Let's Go* likes its authenticity. The dishes are custom-made, so you can choose whether you want cheese, sausage, or chili inside your *menemen* (you want it all, by the way). Supersize it *("kebir")* if you're feeling ravenous. And don't forget to use bread to wipe the pan clean—leaving any of it would be an act of barbarism.

From the Kadıköy ferry terminal, walk up Söğütlüçeşme, turn right immediately after Osman Ağa Mosque, and walk up the hill. Meşhur will be on your right. $ Menemen 4-6TL. Cash only. Open daily 7am-8pm.

KANAAT LOKANTASI LOKANTA $$

Selmanipak Cad. 25, Üsküdar ☎0216 553 3791

Although the decor and atmosphere are nothing outstanding, this place makes it easy to eat across all the Turkish food groups. The menu translates the crucial ingredient descriptions, and almost all of the hot, cold, and dessert offerings are on display. The most impressive part of the restaurant is the desserts counter, perfect for those whose eyes are even bigger than their stomachs.

🚏 Take the ferry to Üsküdar. It's quite close to the ferry terminal. Cross the street and keep the mosque to your left, take the 2nd left (before Selmanağa Mosque), and Kanaat will be ahead on your right. [$] Pilaf 4.50TL. Vegetarian entrees 6.50-10TL; meat entrees 7.50-15TL. Desserts 5-7TL. Cash only. ⏰ Open daily 6am-11pm.

MOLA YEMEKEVI TRADITIONAL $

Damacı Sok. 8/3, Kadıköy ☎0216 348 6310

Authentic holes-in-the-wall like this are a good bet for travelers who want to experience what Turkish food is supposed to taste like. Mola Yemekevi has a distinctly domestic feel with its tiny kitchen, handwritten menu, and a vintage Hi-Fi system playing Turkish oldies. Order in the back, then enjoy your meal outside under the enthusiastically sprouting canopy of climbing plants.

🚏 From the Kadıköy ferry terminal, go down Söğütlüçeşme Cad. and turn right just before the Osman Ağa Mosque. Follow the road as it turns into Moda Cad. Shortly before Moda Cad. splits into separate lanes, make a sharp left onto Damacı Sok. The restaurant will be to your right, tucked into a small corner. [$] Soup 3-3.50TL. Entrees 4.50-8TL. Salads 5.50-7.50TL. Köfte 8.50TL. Cash only. ⏰ Open daily 9am-9pm.

PIDE SUN PIDE $

Moda Cad. 67B, Kadıköy ☎0216 347 3155; www.pidesun.com

Pide Sun hits all the important points for an easy meal: cozy, cheap, and tasty. The *pides* here are so thin that even the most devoted pizza aficionados will be forced to swallow their pride and eat them the Turkish way (i.e. with utensils). It's easy to pass by Pide Sun without noticing it, but the food is worth the extra time you'll spend searching for it. The oven tends to make the inside overheated, so take your *pide* to the tables outside.

🚏 From the Kadıköy ferry terminal, go down Söğütlüçeşme Cad. and turn right just before the Osman Ağa Mosque. Follow the road as it becomes Moda Cad. Pide Sun is on your left, very close to a Migros supermarket. [$] Pides 7-12TL. ⏰ Open daily 11am-11pm.

İSKENDER İSKENDECFROĞLU KEBAB $$$

Rıhtım Cad. PTT yanı, Kadıköy ☎0216 336 0777; www.iskender.com.tr

Who would have guessed that the famous İskender kebab was named not after a Turkish village but after a person? A century or so ago, Mehmet Oğlu İskender invented the dish in Bursa, later passing the recipe to his descendants. This restaurant is run by third- and fourth-generation İskenders who take their legacy very seriously. Black-and-white portraits and a wall dedicated to the family tree reflect a Slytherin-esque obsession with genealogy. The kebabs are good—although they cost double what you'd pay elsewhere—but diehard fans of İskender kebabs might want to make the pilgrimage anyway. Next on the list: Mr. Döner and his grandchildren.

🚏 From the Kadıköy ferry terminal, head inland to the start of Söğütlüçeşme Cad. Turn right, keeping the park on your right. Walk past the PTT store on your left. İskender İskenderoğlu will be on your left. [$] Iskender kebabs 21-32TL. Desserts 5-6TL. ⏰ Open daily 11am-10pm.

ÇIYA SOFRASI ANATOLIAN, VEGETARIAN $$

Güneşlibahçe Sok. 43, Kadıköy ☎0216 330 3190; www.ciya.com.tr

Arguably the best-known restaurant on the Asian side, Çiya has three branches right next to each other—two focus on kebabs, while this one has more vegetar-

food

ian dishes. The always changing menu is in English, and vegetarians will delight at the creative starters and entrees (8-12TL). Carnivores can have kebabs delivered from next door. Musa Dağdeviren, Turkey's closest thing to a celebrity chef, reinvents Anatolian cuisine with obscure ingredients and reasonable prices. Get portions half-sized (and half-priced) to sample a wider selection.

⇞ A few blocks from Kadıköy market. From the ferry terminal, go on Söğütlüçeşme and turn right onto Güneşlibahçe Sok. $ Soups 5TL. Meat entrees 11-16TL. Desserts 3.50-7.50TL. ⏰ Open daily noon-10pm.

nightlife

Istanbul's bars and clubs are concentrated around İstiklal Cad., so if you're staying in Sultanahmet, you should prepare yourself for a good amount of commuting. Sultanahmet does have a few bars, but these are generally looked down upon by the locals—that's why we list a handful of *nargile* cafes instead. Another center of night-time activity is Muallim Naci Cad., the road running up from Ortaköy. Here you'll find Kuruçeşme, the city's most prestigious clubs. Note that during summer, many music venues (such as the famous Babylon) close down and move to their summer locations. The English-language *Time Out Magazine* lists current performances, as well as a comprehensive list of GLBT-friendly bars and clubs. If you want to drink rakı, the anise-flavored Turkish national drink, the best place to do so is at a traditional *meyhane.* Whatever you do, don't fall for the night-time scams: if a local speaking perfect English approaches you on the street and invites you for a beer after three lines of uninteresting conversation, he's probably planning a scam (which usually involves a traveler, an exorbitant bill, and a dose of coercion).

hooked on hookah

Bigger than cigarettes and more sophisticated than a bong, the elegant water pipe (a.k.a. *nargile*, hookah, and hubble-bubble) lets you try smoke without the dope. Originally from India and the Middle East, the tall smoking instrument has filled Turkish cafes and lounges for more than five centuries.

You can sample a wide range of tobacco flavors, from mint to cherry to cappuccino. After the waiter sets the pipe with a hot coal and primes the water pipe for you, suck on the end of the hose and inhale gently. The smoke passes above the water at the base of the *nargile,* which filters the smoke and cools it down before you inhale.

Smoking has its rules. If you're sharing, remember to put the pipe down and let the next person pick it up, instead of passing it directly. Turks traditionally drink tea with *nargile* and usually avoid alcohol while smoking. As you puff, save up those white clouds of smoke for your best 🐉**dragon** impression.

SULTANAHMET AND ENVIRONS

Unlike the excitement of the daytime, spending the night out in Sultanahmet is a quieter affair. You won't find clubs blaring loud music or streets crowded with revelers here. Instead, you'll find *nargile* cafes and tourist-targeted bars. Unless you think that a quiet night is a fun night, you should really head to Beyoğlu instead. If you insist on staying in Sultanahmet, however, it would be hard to miss **Akbıyık Caddesi,** conveniently close to most of the hostels and hotels. Like Galata Bridge, it's remarkably bland in its many tourist-catered (read: high-priced) bars and restaurants. Another option is to stay in—many hostels have their own terraces with fantastic views and cheap beer.

SETÜSTÜ ÇAY BAHÇESI   CAFE
Gülhane Park

Perched on a ridge in Gülhane Park, this cafe offers an unbelievable, 180-degree view of Istanbul and the waters that run through it. With row after row of small wooden tables, almost everyone gets Setüstü's best seats. The pot of tea seems pricey, but it's meant to be shared. Confused by the two-part teapot they hand you? Here's a lesson in Turkish *çay:* pour yourself about half a cup or more of the top pot's brew, and fill the rest with the water from the bottom pot. Besides the occasional screech of the railway, the only sounds on a late night are the locals' conversation, the knock of dice on tables, and the tinkling of tea cups being stirred. Tea certainly makes a refreshing change from loud music, hangovers, and regrettable drunken hookups.

♯ Ⓜ*Gülhane. Enter the park and continue on the main road all the way to its back gate, then turn right (uphill) and follow the signs. It will be on your left.* Ⓢ *Tea 6TL. Turkish coffee 6TL. Potato chips 5TL. Ice cream 6TL. Cash only.* ⓘ *Open daily 8am-11pm.*

ERENLER NARGILE   CAFE, NARGILE
Çorlulu Ali Paşa Medresesi 36   ☎0212 511 8853

Çorlulu Ali Paşa Medresesi, a courtyard that formerly belonged to a *madrasa* (theological school), is famous among local students as the perfect place to come for a *nargile.* Erenler is the biggest of three cafes here and supplies visitors with waterpipes (12TL) and non-alcoholic drinks (coffee and juice; 4TL). With plentiful seating and a 24hr. courtyard, the entire place smells of sweet fumes. While there's indoor seating, these rooms seem to be dominated solely by Turkish men playing backgammon.

♯ Ⓜ*Beyazır. Follow the tram tracks in the direction of Hagia Sophia. The entrance to the courtyard is on the left. After you enter, Erenler Nargile is the cafe on the right.* Ⓢ *Nargile 12TL. Cash only.* ⓘ *Open 24hr.*

THE NORTH SHIELD   PUB
Ebusuud Cad. 2   ☎0212 527 0931

Sports fans, you can catch your favorite teams' games along with a pint at this tourist favorite. The signs posted outside advertise upcoming games, which are shown on seven flatscreen TVs. Whether it's the NFL, the NBA, tennis, or the Russian Premier League (CSKA Moscow, anyone?), the North Shield has got you covered. A slightly disconcerting mix of Turkish and Italian food alongside dark wood and dim lighting straight out of an English pub make the North Shield an example of globalization at its finest (or worst, depending on your tastes).

♯ Ⓜ*Gülhane. Exit the tram in the direction of Sultanahmet. The pub is on the right, at the corner of the intersection.* Ⓢ *Beer 8-9TL. Rakı 11TL. Buffalo wings 16.50TL. Additional 10% service charge.* ⓘ *Open daily 11:30am-2am.*

GÜLHANE SUR CAFE   CAFE, NARGILE
Soğukçeşme Sok. 40A   ☎0212 528 0986

Gülhane Sur Cafe, set on a historic cobblestone street between Hagia Sophia and Topkapı Palace, is an excellent place to take a break from sightseeing—the two stone walls on either side of the street are as scenic as this small cafe gets. Have some tea or coffee while watching the other tourists trudge by and eye you enviously. To double their envy, order *nargile* (15TL). The cafe is part of Coşkun Bazaar, a gift shop located right above it. It's popular with foreigners, who leave their creative marks on the owner's guestbook.

♯ Ⓜ*Sultanahmet or Gülhane. Find the small street behind Hagia Sophia and continue down the hill.* Ⓢ *Tea and coffee 2-6TL.* ⓘ *Open daily 10am-1am.*

nightlife

CHEERS BAR
BAR

Akbıyık Cad. 28

One of the many options on Akbıyık Cad., this bar has been around for a while and caters almost exclusively to tourists. If you're staying in Sultanahmet, your hostel is probably just across the street. Unless you'd rather stay on your hostel's terrace (which, frankly, is sometimes a very good option), come here for a beer and a bit of the old, "Oh, you're from Australia? I'm from Austria!" thing. Your experience here really depends on whom you're with, as the bar itself is pretty standard.

 # [M]Sultanahmet. From the entrance to Topkapı Palace behind the Hagia Sophia, walk downhill and take the 2nd right onto Akbıyık Cad. It is 2 blocks down on the right. $ Small beer 6-7TL. Entrees 10-22TL. Nargile 10TL. ⏰ Open daily 11am-2am.

WESTERN FATIH

Ready to rock Western Fatih tonight? Tough luck. Because it's such a conservative area, few places serve alcohol, throw raging parties, or crank out the latest tunes. People stay up late here mostly for *nargile* or to chat at cafes.

ASMALI SOHBET ÇAY EVI
NARGILE

Daruşafaka Cad. 1A
☎0539 223 0009

Although you have to look up to see them, you can puff your night away admiring the domes on the newly restored Fatih Mosque. You might stick out from the middle-aged and elderly local men who come here to lounge and smoke under the vine-covered roof, but there's no better way to experience the (rather quiet) street life in one of Istanbul's most conservative neighborhoods. Plus, the tea is probably the cheapest you'll get in town.

 # To the right of the exit from the mosque complex's northern gate. Or, from the Fatih bus stop, walk north on Fevzi Paşa Cad. to the end of the mosque walls. Turn right onto Islambol Cad., then left onto Fatih Cad., right onto Feraizci Cad., and take the 2nd left. ℹ No English spoken. $ Nargile 10TL. Tea 1TL. ⏰ Open daily 7am-midnight.

DERSAADET NARGILE AND CAFE
NARGILE

Atpazarı Meydanı Sok. 17
☎0212 631 1126

It's no surprise that this place is filled with smoke, given the crowds of men who gather here even before dinner. Overachievers can multi-task at this *nargile* joint by simultaneously eating, smoking, socializing, and even working (thanks, free Wi-Fi!). Others are just happy to spend hours in conversation, lounging in the lawn chairs under the covered terrace. Sports fans can catch a game on the large TV inside. There's not much of a view besides the other *nargile* places next door, but the lively, loud ambience makes for good man-to-man bonding time.

 # From the southeastern exit of the Fatih Mosque grounds, turn left and walk for 3 blocks. Turn right onto Atpazarı Meydanı. Dersaadet is on the right. ℹ No English spoken. $ Nargile 10TL. Tea 1TL. ⏰ Open daily 10am-2am.

BEYOĞLU

Beyoğlu is the capital of Istanbul nightlife. It's normal to walk into an İstiklal building and find a different bar on each floor, yet still have to fight crowds well past midnight. The streets around **Sofyalı Sokak,** just north of Tünel, are full of restaurants, bars, and clubs. Live music venues are a dime a dozen (or rather, tens of lire in cover fees) on the blocks north of İstiklal. Venues like **Araf** and **Eski Beirut** don't charge a cover and are popular with Erasmus exchange students and the locals who chase them. Whether you want to admire the view with an *Efes* beer or dance at the clubs until sunrise—Beyoğlu is the place to do it.

PEYOTE
CONCERT VENUE, BAR
Kameriye Sok. 4 ☎0212 251 4398; www.peyote.com.tr

Peyote has something for everyone. The second floor's live music draws a young, alternative crowd, while, on the third floor's crowded beer terrace, piercings sometimes outnumber people three to one. The bands play mostly Turkish rock, but jazz, reggae, ska, and folk sometimes sneak in as well. Peyote has its own recording label, so you might catch the next big star on the Turkish rock scene. The ground floor, featuring electronic music, stays pretty empty until late in the night.

🎈 Ⓜ*Taksim. Walk to Galatasaray, turn right onto Balık Sok. (after Çiçek Pasajı), take the 2nd right, and then the 1st left. Peyote is on the left.* Ⓢ *Cover varies. Beer 7TL. Shots 8.50-10TL. Sausages 8TL.* 🕐 *Open daily 5pm-3am. Live music starts around 11:30pm; check the website for artists.*

BALKON
BAR
Şehbender Sok. 5, 6th fl. ☎0212 293 2052

When the streets around Sofyalı feel too crowded and tipping street musicians becomes an expensive habit, head upstairs for the lively vibe at Balkon. The two floors play the same music (jazz gradually turns into electronica over the course of the night), but take your date to the top terrace, where the softer volume and flattering lighting can help your game. They even provide blankets for when it gets chilly up top.

🎈 *From* Ⓜ*Tünel, walk north through the passageway across the street and onto Sofyalı Sok. Walk straight and turn left at Şehbender Sok. Balkon is on the left.* Ⓢ *Beer 8-10TL. Shots 6-12TL. Desserts 7-8TL. Pizzas 12-16TL.* 🕐 *Open M-Th 11am-2am, F-Sa 11am-3am, Su 11am-2am.*

MACHINE
CLUB
Balo Sok. 31

This rather clandestine establishment has no phone number or website, and is open only 10hr. per week. If you're into dancing to loud electronic music until the morning, this is for you. The metallic walls feel like the inside of a shipping container, but the flashing lights and the cage that separates the DJs from the dance floor are a perfect fit for the music. Gentlemen, find a lady, or you'll be stuck in line forever.

🎈 Ⓜ*Taksim. Walk down İstiklal toward Galatasaray, then turn right at Halkbank. Machine is downhill, behind an unmarked black gate.* Ⓢ *Beer 9TL. Shots 10TL.* 🕐 *Open F-Sa noon-5am.*

TEKYÖN CLUB
CLUB, GLBT
Sıraselviler Cad. 63 ☎533 377 2393; www.clubtekyon.com

Although it's underground, Tekyön is anything but unknown to Istanbul's gay scene. With a large dance floor, 11 disco balls (at last count), and colorful backlit walls, this is the place to get down with that hamam cutie. The music remixes Western and Turkish beats in equal measure, while special events like the International Bear Festival add some heft and hair to the crowd. This club is for action, not talk, but if you're tired of flirting with your body, head to the back garden for some conversation.

🎈 *From* Ⓜ*Taksim, walk down Sıraselviler Cad. The club is on the left.* Ⓢ *Beer 13TL.* 🕐 *Open M-Th 10pm-4am, F-Sa 10pm-5am, Su 10pm-4am.*

nightlife

more beer for your buck

If you are a beer drinker and spend any time in Istanbul, you will quickly become intimately acquainted with Efes, Budweiser's Turkish cousin. Ubiquitous, cheap, and refreshing, Efes is best enjoyed from a 0.7TL stein while sitting at a rooftop bar overlooking the city.

BEŞİKTAŞ AND ORTAKÖY

ANJELIQUE
CLUB, RESTAURANT

Salhane Sok. 5 ☎0212 327 2844; www.istanbuldoors.com

Sexy and fun, Anjelique is just the right size and has just the right crowd. Women tower in 12 in. heels, one hand on their dates and the other on their designer purses, while guys swagger to the beats of the two DJs (one for each floor). You can lounge indoors or at the two restaurants (Mediterranean and Asian themed), but you'll find all the action out on the decks. If you want to kick it up a notch, schedule a water landing at the club's private dock. The drink prices make up for the lack of a cover charge, but this is still the cheapest way to experience the beautiful life in Ortaköy.

✦ *From the Ortaköy ferry jetty, head inland and take the 1st left; Anjelique is on the left. It's on a small street in the center of Ortaköy, opposite the Jazz Center and near a Hotel Radisson entrance.* *i Men need female company to enter the club. Reservation required for dinner. Dress code (no athletic wear, no shorts) strictly enforced.* Ⓢ *Beer 16TL. Cocktails from 35TL.* ⌚ *Club open Tu-F midnight-4am. Restaurant open daily 6pm-midnight.*

REINA
CLUB, RESTAURANT

Muallim Naci Cad. 44 ☎0212 259 5919; www.reina.com.tr

If you're going to indulge, do it big time. Probably the most famous club in the city, Reina is where local and international social elites come to spend obscene amounts of money. The club has six different restaurants (Chinese, sushi, kebabs, Mediterranean, fish, and international) and a dance floor in the middle, all with the Bosphorus Bridge looming as a backdrop. Reina also owns two boats that will transport you here from your hotel, if you happen to be one of the VIP guests. Not sure if you qualify as a VIP or not? Then you probably don't. The actual VIPs vary from from college kids to middle-aged couples—as long as they can afford to drink Absolut like water and dance on slabs of marble. But come on a weekday and nurse a beer or two so you can enjoy the atmosphere and people-watching without paying like a *paşa*.

✦ *From the Ortaköy bus stop, walk down Muallim Naci Cad. Reina is on the right.* *i Men need female company to enter the club. Reservation required for dinner. Dress code is strictly enforced.* Ⓢ *Cover F-Sa 50TL; includes 1 drink. Beer 10TL. Cocktails 30TL.* ⌚ *Restaurants open daily 6pm-midnight. Club open daily midnight-4am.*

SORTIE
CLUB, RESTAURANT

Muallim Naci Cad. 141 ☎0212 327 8585; www.sortie.com.tr

Like its neighbors, Sortie's many restaurants and bars cater to the elite and those who wish they were the elite. However, its relaxed atmosphere and expansive grounds make it easy to enjoy your night without worrying about rules, nasty bouncers, or unwittingly venturing onto private VIP docks. The decor is unimpressive, but it has the best view of the Bosphorus Bridge among any of the clubs around here. Clubgoers care less about out-dazzling each other and more about having a good time, chatting, dancing, and posing for silly pictures.

✦ *From the Ortaköy bus stop, walk down Muallim Naci Cad. until you see it to the right, just past Reina.* *i Men need female company to enter the club. Reservation required for dinner. No athletic wear or open-toed shoes for men.* Ⓢ *Cover Sa 50TL; includes 1 drink. Beer 15TL. Cocktails from 25TL.* ⌚ *Restaurant open daily 7-11pm. Club open daily 11pm-4am.*

SUPPERCLUB
CLUB, RESTAURANT

Muallim Naci Cad. 65 ☎0212 261 1988; www.supperclub.com

A chain with branches around the world, Supperclub seats you on huge beds covered with white satin. There is no menu—you just tell them if you're vegetarian or not and they bring you a surprise dinner (includes two glasses of wine; 100TL). The experience is hit or miss though. It's smaller than the other clubs, with the dancing section separated from the drinking section by a big glass wall. R and B nights (Thursday and Sunday) are the biggest draw, but you should hit another place when the club plays less popular house music (Tuesday, Wednesday, and Friday). The latest among the Bosphorus's bling establishments, the club stays open until 6am, making it popular even with the competitors' staff.

From the Ortaköy bus stop, walk down Muallim Naci Cad. until you see it on the left. [i] Men need female company to enter the club. Reservation required for dinner and club. Dress code strictly enforced, but athletic wear works on R and B nights. [$] Cover F-Sa 35TL; includes 1 drink. Beer 10TL. Cocktails 25TL. ⏰ Club open 11:30pm-6am. Restaurant open Tu-Su 7-11:30pm.

AŞŞK KAHVE
CAFE

Muallim Naci Cad. 64B ☎0212 265 4734; www.asskkahve.com

Aşşk really ought to mean "love" in Turkish, considering this cafe's romantic atmosphere. Featuring a waterside terrace and plenty of vegetation, Aşşk is popular with stunning young girls and passable young men (the view and the waiters look good too). You can get specialties like the smoked veal tongue sandwich ("Tongue of Aşşk"; 19TL) and homemade burgers, but the cocktails are the true standouts.

It's quite a hike up Muallim Naci Cad. from Ortaköy, so you're better off taking one of the buses that run along the shore to Kuruçeşme. To get to the cafe from the Kuruçeşme bus stop, walk in the direction of the Bosphorus Bridge and go down the unmarked steps right before the Macrocenter. [i] Free Wi-Fi. [$] Beers 12-15TL. Cocktails 25-28TL. Sundaes 14-16TL. Burgers 17-26TL. ⏰ Open daily 9am-1am.

ISTANBUL JAZZ CENTER
JAZZ CLUB

Salhane Sok. 10 ☎0212 327 5050; www.istanbuljazz.com

If you're one of those people whose knees start to shake when you hear names like Mike Stern, Dave Weckl, or Stanley Clarke, you'll enjoy this club. Outside of the summer months, the Jazz Center hosts concerts five days a week, with two sets per night. The names that play here are relatively big, and so is the bill at the end of the night. The small performance room gets crowded, so come early to catch a good spot.

From the Ortaköy ferry dock, head inland and take the 1st left. Jazz Center is on the right. [$] Cover varies based on the performer, but is usually 15-50TL. Beer 15TL. Set menu 60-70TL. Entrees 29-37TL. Required to spend 50TL on top of cover. ⏰ Open M-Sa 7pm-4am. Music 9:30pm-12:30am. Performances less frequent during the summer.

ASIAN ISTANBUL

ARKAODA
BAR

Kadife Sok. 18, Kadıköy ☎0216 418 0277; www.arkaoda.com

With red lighting and three different levels, Arkaoda tries to embody the alternative spirit of Asian Istanbul. Usually playing minimalist techno, ambient drone, or freak folk, Arkaoda also hosts frequent live concerts and DJ nights with internationally acclaimed acts in the summer. If the music doesn't pick you up, try one of their alcoholic coffees (8.50-10TL) to stay buzzed late into the night, or ask for the house's unlisted specialty, a spicy concoction known as Three Monkeys.

Walk south on Bahariye Cad. and take the 1st right after the Opera House. Then take the 2nd left and walk a block. Arkaoda has an unmarked wooden door right next to Karga. [i] Check the website for performances. [$] Tea 4TL. Beer 6.50TL. Rakı 9TL. Whiskey 14-16TL. Cocktails 14-70TL. ⏰ Open M-Th 2pm-2am, F-Sa 2pm-4am, Su 2pm-2am. Live music starts around 8pm; DJs start spinning most nights at 10-11pm.

KARGA
BAR

Kadife Sok. 16, Kadıköy ☎0216 449 1726; www.kargabar.org

One of the best-known bars this side of the Bosphorus, Karga is so cool that it doesn't even need a name on its door. With four stories, a garden, numerous balconies, and a top-floor art gallery, you can choose the decibel of your music and what kind of night you're going to have. The dark interior and rotating playlists of mainly alternative set an edgy mood, but you could easily cuddle up to your date and make it a romantic night thanks to the intimately spaced (read: tiny and cramped) tables.

⚞ *Walk south on Bahariye Cad. and take the 1st right after the Opera House. Take the 2nd left, walk a block, and look for the unmarked wooden door with a raven above it.* ⓘ *Live music Sept-May, but nightly DJs continue through the summer.* Ⓢ *Beer 6TL. Cocktails 6-16TL. Rakı 7.50TL. Food 4-12TL.* ⓘ *Open M-Th 11am-2am, F-Sa 11am-4am, Su 11am-2am. Closes later in the winter.*

BOMONTI CAFE
Sair Nefi Gıkmazı, Moda

GARDEN
☎0216 346 3430

Bomonti is not worth a long trek, but if you're in the area, it's a nice place to sit and unwind. Many tables offer a really nice view of the sea, though a bunch of unruly trees partially block some tables' views. Have some tea or *nargile*, then pursue romance in the tiny park underneath the cafe.

⚞ *Get off the historic tram at the intersection of Cem Sok. and Moda Cad. Go down Moda until the road forks, then take a left. When you see the sea, take another left and continue straight for about 5min. past Moda Teras.* ⓘ *Cash only.* Ⓢ *Tea 1.50TL. Nargile 12.50TL. Food 5-14TL.* ⓘ *Open daily 8am-midnight.*

KÜP CAFE
Caferağa Mah. Güneşlibahçe Sok. 47, Kadıköy

GARDEN CAFE, BAR
☎0216 347 8694

It's difficult to find if you aren't searching for it, but Küp's atmospheric courtyard has everything you need for a quiet night out. There's a jungle of vegetation, mood lighting, and a lot of nooks and corners to sit in. Come here when you're fed up with looking at the skyline, not too excited about people-watching, and just want to have a beer and relaxed conversation.

⚞ *Located toward the end of Güneşlibahçe Sok. From the Kadıköy ferry terminal, go on Söğütlüçeşme Cad., and turn right onto Güneşlibahçe Sok.* Ⓢ *Tea 2-4TL. Beer 5.50TL. Entrees 8.50-15TL.* ⓘ *Open daily 9am-1am.*

check the clock

Gündüz = day. Gece = night. When you take taxis, make sure the driver doesn't turn on the higher night rate before midnight (the meter will flash gündüz or gece depending on what it's been set to).

arts and culture

In Istanbul, you don't just enjoy arts and culture—you live arts and culture. Music is a big deal in the city, whether it's jazz, classical, electronica, or anything. Besides large concerts, the city hosts plenty of festivals that showcase local bands and bring in international stars. Cultural centers sponsored by banks sometimes offer the cheapest entertainment, with student tickets and frequent programming even in the concert low season (summer). Don't forget the bars, nightclubs, and smaller venues, where you can discover rising talents in the Turkish and European music scenes.

While music is for locals and visitors alike, folk and religious dances like the *sema* do great business in the tourist industry. Despite all their marketing and showbiz airs, the dances still offer colorful insights into traditional Turkish culture. Hamams, or bathhouses, are also becoming less of an exclusively local attraction—there's nothing like a traditional bath to refresh your body after a day of sightseeing.

THEATER AND CLASSICAL MUSIC

While most of Istanbul's theater is in Turkish, you'll do just fine with the musical performances—after all, isn't music the universal language? Old classical favorites grace established venues like the CRR Konser Salonu and Süreyya Opera, while you can find more modern and experimental works in the bank-sponsored art centers. Almost all tickets can be purchased through Biletix (www.biletix.com), though it's easier to get student tickets at box offices.

GARAJ İSTANBUL
BEYOĞLU

Kaymakam Reşat Bey Sok. ☎0212 244 4499; www.garajistanbul.org

Many performance venues in Istanbul are housed in restored hamams or ancient cisterns (or fancy things like that), so a restored parking garage seems like a fresh idea. The space is used for contemporary art performances, including theater, music, and dance. You can catch shows ranging from Samuel Beckett's absurdist *Waiting for Godot* to the more light-hearted Istanbul International Puppet Festival. Since Garaj hosts international artists, some of the events are in English or have English subtitles, giving this venue a distinct edge over the small, artsy places.

⚡ ⓜTaksim. Walk down İstiklal and turn left immediately after Yapıkredi near Yeni Çarşi Cad. Turn right, then left, and you'll see it on the left. ⓢ 25TL, students 15TL, art students 10TL. ⚄ Open Sept-June. Consult the online program for performance times.

CEMAL REŞIT REY KONSER SALONU
BEYOĞLU

Gümüs Sok. ☎0212 232 9830; www.crrks.org

The CRR Konser Salonu is the city's leading venue for classical music performances. Its 860-seat concert hall has hosted acts ranging from the Tchaikovsky Symphony Orchestra to Spanish flamenco guitarist Paco de Lucía. There are about 20 concerts per month during the working season. While official programming takes a break during the summer, the space is rented out for other performances. The programs might be written in Turkish, but you'll recognize the tunes.

⚡ ⓜOsmanbey. Go down Cumhuriyet Cad. in the direction of Taksim. Turn left at Tekstilbank, then take the 2nd right. Cross the street, enter the park, and go down the steps. The venue is on the right, behind the Military Museum. Alternatively, hike 1km from Taksim up Cumhuriyet Cad. Turn right after the İstanbul Radyosu Building and then left before the Hilton park lot. The venue is on the right, past the Lütfi Kırdar Convention Center. ⓢ Prices vary. ⚄ Performances Oct-Apr. Box office open daily 10am-8pm. Concerts typically start around 8pm.

AKBANK SANAT
BEYOĞLU

İstiklal Cad. 8 ☎0212 252 3500; www.akbanksanat.com

Don't worry about the commercial branding—corporate-sponsored venues like this host some of the best events around. Akbank Sanat runs weekly concerts and a jazz festival in the fall. The first two floors function as an exhibition space for contemporary art (with six or seven exhibitions per year), while the upper floors hold a music archive, lithography workshops, and a modern dance studio. The 125-person performance space is an intimate setting for concerts and screenings. Many events, especially foreign performances, have English translations, and some are even free.

⚡ ⓜTaksim. The venue is a few meters down İstiklal on the right side. ⓢ See online program for prices. Student discounts available, usually 50%. ⚄ Open Tu-Su 10:30am-7:30pm. Music archive open Tu-Su 2-7pm. For performance times, check the online or printed program.

SÜREYYA OPERASI
ASIAN ISTANBUL

Bahariye Cad. 29 ☎0216 346 1531; www.sureyyaoperasi.org

Home to the IDOB (Istanbul State Opera and Ballet), Süreyya hosts about 20 performances each month from September to June. Not everything involves elaborate costumes and staging, as the venue also presents classical music recitals by the city's local groups and conservatories. If you're an opera fan and are

arts and culture

in Istanbul during the summer (when the venue is closed), you can still catch the International Istanbul Opera Festival, which takes place in eccentric venues like Topkapı Palace and Rumeli Castle each July (see **Music Festivals** below).

⇆ Ferry to Kadıköy. Walk up Söğütlüçeşme Cad., turn right onto Bahariye Cad., and continue until you see the venue on the left. Or, take the nostalgic tram, getting off at the nearby Eyüp stop. Ⓢ Tickets 13-30TL. ⏰ Open Sept-June. Box office open daily 10am-6pm. Performances usually start at 8pm.

SANTRALISTANBUL — EYÜP

Eski Silahtarağa Elektrik Santrali, Kazım Karabekir Cad. 2, Eyüp

☎0212 311 7347; www.santralistanbul.org

An old power station turned into a museum, Santralistanbul now produces art instead of electricity. The **Krek Threatre Company,** headquartered in Gallery 1, puts on plays by Turkish playwright Berkun Oya (☎0212 311 7824; www.krek.net). In the same complex, the space known as Tamirane serves food with a side of fresh music during its "Weekday Session," Saturday's "Morning Indie," and Sunday's "Morning Jazz Sessions." And Santralistanbul is still growing—the place opened its old control room as a venue for the 2011 International Music Festival. Talk about power to the arts.

⇆ Bus to Bilgi University or Silahtar. Free shuttle service from Taksim's Atatürk Culture Center. Ⓢ Prices vary. ⏰ Performances times vary. Tamirane open M-Th 9:30am-midnight, F 9:30am-2am, Sa 10am-2am, Su 10am-9pm. Taksim shuttle M-Sa every 30min. 8am-6:30pm.

play tavla, make friends

The Turkish answer to backgammon, *tavla* is a favorite national pastime. Most cafes and *nargile* bars have sets for patrons to play, and you often see pairs of old men engaged in fierce combat on the street. Simpler than regular backgammon (they don't use that pesky doubling cube), *tavla* can be learned quickly. Chatting over a game can be a great way to meet locals (although your opponent may be a few decades older than you). For a head start, lull yourself to sleep on your flight to Istanbul by playing electronic backgammon on your in-flight TV.

DANCE

HODJAPASHA CULTURE CENTER — SULTANAHMET

Hocapaşa Hamamı Sok. 3B ☎0212 511 4626; www.hodjapasha.com

Sema is a religious ceremony that has become a popular tourist attraction—a fact that few people seem to find strange. The highlight of the event is the activity that so many tourist brochures present as quintessentially Turkish—the **whirling of dervishes.** The dancer's arms, one palm pointing to the sky and the other to the ground, symbolize the channeling of spiritual energy from God to earth. Until the Galata Mevlevihanesi reopens from restoration, the Hodjapasha Center (a former 15th-century hamam) is the easiest place to see a whirling dervishes performance. The ticket price includes a small beverage and Turkish delight service before the performance. Because half of the show is actually a Sufi music concert with no interesting physical movement, we suggest you hit up the coffee stand for the sake of your attention span. The center also hosts Turkish Dance Night, one of the cheaper ways to watch traditional dances without paying for a full meal.

⇆ ⓂSirkeci. After getting off the tram, walk north, away from the water. Take the 1st left after the tram tracks and turn right. There are signs pointing to the venue. ℹ Reserve weeks in advance for the best seats. Ⓢ Sema 40TL, ages 12 and under 30TL. Turkish Dance Night 50TL. ⏰ Semas last 1hr. and start M 7:30pm, W 7:30pm, F-Su 7:30pm. Turkish Dance Night Tu 8pm, Th 8pm, and Sa 9pm. Box office open daily 10am-9pm.

GALATA TOWER

Galata Kulesi　　　　　　　　☎0212 293 8180; www.galatatower.net

Few locals would ever see a traditional Turkish dance performance, so if you're set on seeing **belly dancing**, you're going to have a hard time finding something that's not expensive. Dancing is usually packaged with a set menu into a "Turkish night" that takes a few hours and can be thoroughly entertaining—until you get the bill. However, the 14th-century Galata Tower is a picturesque (and popular) option. And if you don't want to pay for the cultural night, take an elevator up during the day and check out the view, arguably the best in Istanbul. A word of caution though: it gets crowded up there.

⚥ Ⓜ*Tünel. Head southeast down Galipdede Cad. until you see the tower on the right.* ⓢ *"Turkish night" €80 per person; includes a set menu and unlimited local drinks. Entry during the day 11TL, under 6 free. Cash only for entry.* ⌚ *Shows 8pm-midnight. Tower open daily 9am-8pm.*

MUSIC FESTIVALS

The listings below are far from being the only festivals in Istanbul, but they're some of the newest and hottest ones hitting the city. Also check out the **Istanbul Jazz Festival,** the metal **Sonisphere** festival, and the **Club to Club** dance and electronic festival. Keep an eye out for other events advertised on posters, flyers, and billboards across the city.

ROCK'N COKE

Hezarfen Airfield, Demirkapı Sok. 1, Arnavutköy　　　　　　www.rockncoke.com

Turkey's biggest outdoor music festival is also its most branded. If the number of Facebook followers is any indication, it's also its most popular, and with good reason. Held on an airfield, the main stage has hosted artists like Franz Ferdinand, Limp Bizkit, and Linkin Park, while smaller stages specialize in electronic, alternative, and DJ acts. Buy a day pass, which costs just a bit more than the tickets to the major acts. Rock'n Coke lasts for a full 48hr., so get ready to camp out and live off the conveniently marketed caffeinated drinks.

⚥ *Take the Metrobüs to Avcılar and take the festival's shuttles from there. The festival also provides direct transportation from Taksim and other central parts of the city.* *i* *2 day passes available. Buy tickets at www.biletix.com.* ⓢ *Concerts around 60TL. Day pass 90TL, students 60TL; with camping 180/120TL.* ⌚ *Held in July or Aug.*

ISTANBUL MUSIC FESTIVAL

☎0212 334 0700, box office 0212 334 0941; http://muzik.iksv.org

Instead of shopping around the world for the best orchestras and classical music, have them come to you. Now entering its 40th year, the Istanbul Music Festival spans almost the whole month of June and fills up venues like Topkapı Palace's Hagia Irene, the Sürreya Opera House, and the electrifying control room of the old santralistanbul power station. From Bach to Schubert to the premiere of brand-new pieces, the concerts are a great way to discover artists and composers or warm up for July's opera festival.

i *Buy tickets at www.biletix.com. Student tickets only available at IKSV box office.* ⓢ *Prices vary. Students 20TL.* ⌚ *During June. Box office open daily 10am-6pm.*

INTERNATIONAL ISTANBUL OPERA FESTIVAL

☎0212 245 1636; www.istanbuloperafestival.gov.tr

As if opera weren't dramatic enough, this festival stages it in some of the city's most picturesque sights, including Rumeli Fortress, Yıldız Palace, and even Topkapı Palace. Although most of the operas are in German or Italian, the past two seasons have included a bit of local flavor, like the 2011 productions of *Fatih Sultan Mehmet* and *Sultan Murat IV.* Performers are drawn from Turkish and foreign companies, and the historical venues serve as stunning backdrops to

arts and culture

the elaborate costumes and theatrics. If you thought Topkapı was awesome, just wait until you see the sultan sing his way through the palace.

[$] 20-100TL. Student tickets are available for some performances (usually 20TL). ⏰ During late July.

HAMAMS

Steam, sweat, squeeze, and scrub: you can get it all at your local hamam. Once a mainstay of Turkish urban society, the neighborhood hamam is losing its share of the bathing scene thanks to the spread of indoor plumbing and adjustable shower nozzles. These days, hamams are mostly frequented by older men looking to relive the good ol' days and tourists looking for a taste of traditional Turkish culture. If you can get over the fear of getting pummeled while nearly naked, you're in for an invigorating treat.

Hamams vary: you can either wash yourself, or have someone do all the work for you. Everything starts with the shoes—in order to keep the place clean, it's customary to take them off and put on slippers. In the changing rooms, bathers-to-be undress and put on the *peştamal*, a traditional towel that covers those very important parts. Start your journey in the sauna, or *sıcaklık*, where you'll lie on a warm marble slab and feel like every single drop of moisture is being squeezed out of you. When it seems like your body has lost half its weight, cool off by turning on the tap and splashing yourself with the blissfully refreshing water. If you've ordered a massage, the masseur or masseuse will leave almost nowhere on your body untouched. They do leave one or two parts untouched, although it can get uncomfortably close. Next, say *"güle güle"* to the layers of dead skin, as your body is scrubbed, lathered, and washed to baby smoothness. Finally, you'll be handed a towel and dried off, before heading to a cool room to lounge and relax with a cup of tea.

And what about those steamy, bathhouse fantasies? Forget it—most hamams have separate sections, or segregated bathing times, for men and women, and if they don't, both genders wear bathing suits (all of the hamams listed below have separate rooms). Hamams in Istanbul, especially the tourist-oriented ones, provide same-gender attendants for men and women. We recommend trying one of these hamams first, and if you get hooked, branch out and visit a more authentic (and cheaper) bathhouse.

ÇEMBERLITAŞ HAMAMI — SULTANAHMET

Vezirhan Cad. 8 — ☎0212 522 7974; www.cemberlitashamami.com

This is one of best-known hamams in Istanbul, and it's mostly frequented by tourists. Everything here corresponds to that fact: it's clean, aesthetically pleasing, and on the expensive side. Built in 1584 and based on plans created by famed Ottoman architect Mimar Sinan, Çemberlitaş Hamamı gets into spa territory, going beyond the basics of body scrubs and bubble washes to fancy facial masks and head massages. Your experience here depends on the crowds, so try to avoid it during rush hours (4-8pm). If you plan to go to a hamam only once, this place should be one of the top contenders, as it's a reassuring first-time hamam experience.

🧭 [M]Çemberlitaş. The hamam is just across the street from the tram stop and the column. [$] Self-service 39TL. Body scrub and bubble wash 59TL, with oil massage 99TL. Facial mask 12TL. Reflexology 40TL. Indian head massage 40TL. ⏰ Open daily 6am-midnight.

SOFULAR HAMAMI — WESTERN FATİH

Sofular Cad. 28 — ☎0212 521 3759

If a local experience is what you're after, consider going to Sofular Hamamı. Don't expect much English from the staff or too much polish in the small changing rooms, but once you enter the *hararet* (hot room) and lie down under its pleasant dome, such amenities won't matter. Instead of other tourists, there will be old, local men with enormous bellies, and you'll pay about half the price that

istanbul

touristy hamams charge. You could be the only foreigner there, but the locals probably won't care and might even make conversation. Suggested one-liner for the sauna: "*Sıcak!*" (hot!).

⚑ Bus to Fatih. Head southeast down Fevzipaşa Cad. and turn right at Aslanhane. To get on Sofular Cad., turn left and immediately turn right. Continue downhill on that street until you reach the hamam, which is on the left, near the Sofular Mosque. Ⓢ Self-service 20TL. Bath with massage 28TL, with scrub 28TL, with scrub and massage 36TL. Cash only. ◱ Open daily 6am-10:30pm for men, 8am-8pm for women.

TARIHI GALATASARAY HAMAMI
BEYOĞLU

Turnacıbaşı Sok. 24   ☎0212 249 4342 for women, 0212 252 4242 for men; www.galatasarayhamami.com

Tarihi Galatasaray Hamamı is another hamam directed toward tourists. How do we know? Their brochure is filled with pictures of some pretty steamy heterosexual situations, despite the fact that hamams separate by gender. This hamam is one of the priciest of the lot, but in exchange for its price tag, it offers one of the fanciest interiors of any Istanbul hamam. You won't be paying much attention to the decor when you're being massaged, but it's a nice touch.

⚑ Ⓜ Taksim. Walk down İstiklal from Taksim and turn left at Turnacıbaşı, near Halk Bank. It's at the end of the street. Ⓢ Self-service 50TL. Bath with scrub 75TL, with massage 80TL, with scrub and massage 95TL. Full service 125TL. ◱ Open daily 7am-10pm for men, 8am-9pm for women.

BÜYÜK HAMAM
BEYOĞLU

Potinciler Sok. 22   ☎0212 253 4229; www.buyukhamam.net

Serving mostly locals, this is one of the biggest hamams in town (as you probably figured out by your fourth day in Turkey, *büyük* means "big"). Although this hamam isn't full of tourists, it holds historic value similar to that of its more popular brethren—it was built in 1533 and, like Çemberlitaş, was designed by Mimar Sinan. Its walls could use a fresh coat of paint, but the rooftop swimming pool (only for men) and cheap prices make Büyük a decent choice. The catch? It's quite a hike down (and back up) from Taksim, so you'll be sweaty and ready for another bath by the time you hit İstiklal.

⚑ Ⓜ Tünel. Go up İstiklal and turn left onto Asmalı Mescit Cad. Go down the hill, pass the stadium, and follow the road as it turns left onto Çivici Sok. Cross the street, turn right, and walk for 1 block. The hamam is on the left close to Kasimpaşa Mosque. Ⓢ Self-service 18TL. Bath with massage 25TL, with scrub 23TL, with massage and scrub 30TL. Cash only. ◱ Open daily 5:30am-10:30pm for men, 8am-7pm for women.

CAĞALOĞLU HAMAMI
SULTANAHMET

Cağaloğlu Hamamı Sok. 34   ☎0212 522 2424; www.cagalogluhamami.com.tr

For some reason, somebody decided to list Cağaloğlu Hamamı in a book called "1001 Things To Do Before You Die," and it's been unabashedly profiting ever since. With walls covered in photos of celebrities who have stopped by (these include a photo of Atatürk as well as a few of Kate Moss engaging in some softcore posing), these guys certainly know how to self-promote. The facilities and service live up to the hype, but be prepared to pay up, too: Cağaloğlu is almost twice as expensive as other touristy hamams. The "Sultan Mahmut Service" enlists two attendants to massage you simultaneously, but you could get six full-service baths somewhere else for the same cost. Unless it's your last hour in Istanbul and you can't make it to the other hamams, head somewhere cheaper.

⚑ Ⓜ Sultanahmet. It's a few blocks down the street from the entrance of Basilica Cistern, on the right. Ⓢ Self-service 69TL. Bath with scrub 80TL, with massage 92TL, with scrub and massage 115TL. "Sultan Mahmut Service" 253TL. Cash only. ◱ Open daily 8am-10pm for men, 8am-8pm for women.

arts and culture

shopping

Carpets, antiques, clothes, perfumes, Turkish delight, teas, pastries, spices, *nargile*, evil eye beads... we (and you) could go on for days. From weekly street markets to roofed passages, brick-and-mortar stores to covered bazaars, it's not hard to find a place in Istanbul to spend your lire. But since no one wants to overpay, remember the three H's: haggle, haggle, haggle. The prices on the sign are probably too high, and, unless you're talented or lucky, the seller will still make good money even when you finally strike a deal. To get a better idea for the prices, don't just stop by one shop; similar stores usually cluster around each other, so you should visit more than one to compare.

You'll also notice that some things are more expensive in Turkey. Electronics and designer brands are imported, so, unless you come from Zimbabwe, you'll probably enjoy a cheaper price for those back home. Also on the do-not-buy list: antiques. If it's more than 100 years old, it's probably illegal to take it out of the country, and you could face fines or a prison sentence. Carpet stores will usually provide a certificate of non-antique-ness, but be extra careful buying in open markets and antique shops. Another antiques-gone-wrong scenario: that calligraphed poem in Sultan Mehmet's own handwriting. It's probably a fake.

BAZAARS AND MARKETS

With bazaars dedicated to almost every day of the week, you could easily spend your entire stay in Istanbul shopping. Simply walking through them is a treat in its own right and won't cost you a thing (just beware of pickpockets). Don't be taken aback by how aggressively friendly some sellers can be, especially in the larger bazaars. If you're really not interested, a polite *"hayır teşekkürler"* (no, thanks) should do the trick. It's common for stores, especially those selling carpets, to offer tea or other drinks, and accepting them doesn't obligate you to buy anything. Be firm and insistent if you're not looking to buy.

istanbul

if you suck at haggling...

...Pretend you're not American. One of the simplest yet most effective ways to get a better deal in the Grand Bazaar (or anywhere else bargaining is appropriate) is to speak a foreign language—other than English. You will be quoted lower prices, end of story. If you have a little Spanish or French in your repertoire, bust it out. Many of the vendors are multilingual, but most only know the basics of the romance languages so you probably won't get called out on your patchy Italian. The worst you can do is embarrass yourself, but you'd do that by overpaying for your souvenirs anyway.

◼ GRAND BAZAAR

SULTANAHMET

Kapalı Çarşı
☎0212 522 3173; www.kapalicarsi.org.tr

You haven't shopped in Istanbul until you've shopped at the Grand Bazaar. With 21 gates, 66 streets, 3600 shops, and 30,000 employees, you're bound to spend hours in the world's largest open-air market. Arm yourself with your wallet and get ready to haggle. Opened in 1461, the bazaar's streets are named after the trades that were centered there (fez-makers, slipper manufacturers, etc.), although much of that doesn't apply anymore. It helps to have a rough idea of the layout in order to navigate and avoid getting lost. There's a central **bedesten** (market hall, also known as *Cehavir*) where jewelry and antiques are sold. Around it, the streets adhere to a grid pattern. If you're hungry, you'll find overpriced cafes clustered in this area. The gold and jewelry street, **Kalpakçılar Cadddesi,** runs east-west from Nuruosmaniye Gate (1) to Beyazıt Gate (7). Another main street—known variously as Sipahi, Feraceciler, and Yağlıkçılar—connects the southern Çarşı Gate (5) to the northern Örücüler Gate (14). Lined with carpet sellers, **Halıcılar Sokak** runs above the central *bedesten*. Entering from the Nuruosmaniye Gate, you'll find the **Sandal Bedesten,** another place for clothes, souvenirs, and antiques. The streets in the bazaar's west end, closer to Beyazıt, are less regular in layout, and you'll find jeans, leather, and the PTT post and exchange booth there. Try to search online for a map, or pick one up at the director's office near Gate 4, off Kalpakçılar Cad. Try not to go in with any specific shops in mind, though—let your eyes, nose, and thrift (yes, that's a sense) sniff out the best deals.

♯ ⓜBeyazıt. Exit the tram station away from Sultanahmet, turn right before the bus stops, and turn right into Beyazıt Gate (7). The Bazaar is a straight shot from the entrance of the Nuruosmaniye Mosque to Gate 1. *i* The police station is 1 block in from Gate 19 (coming in, turn right). Don't be confused by the bedestens, which have their own gate numbers. Currency exchanges are easy to find. ⌚ Open M-Sa 8:30am-7pm.

SPICE BAZAAR

SULTANAHMET

Mısır Çarşısı
☎0212 513 6597

Also called the Egyptian Bazaar, this market is much easier to navigate than the Grand Bazaar—its layout is brought to you by the letter "L." Completed in 1663, the bazaar was built to generate funds for the upkeep of the New Mosque. The bazaar sells what it's named after (that's spices, not Egyptians), and since prices don't vary much across the city, come here for everything that weighs little but costs a lot: teas, saffron, and caviar. On the other hand, you're better off buying other products (dried fruit, nuts, sweets, and trinkets) elsewhere. Some merchants get more creative than others—you'll come across sticky balls of dried figs and walnuts called "Turkish Viagra." *Let's Go* doesn't give

shopping

medical advice, but after trying one, the only thing that might be hard is trying to win back your friends' respect.

✢ ⓜEminönü. After walking out of the station, you'll see Yeni Cami, the New Mosque. The bazaar is behind the mosque. Its entrance has 3 domes and 3 arches. ✪ Open M-Sa 8am-7:30pm.

ARASTA BAZAAR
SULTANAHMET

Arasta Çarşısı 107   ☎0212 516 0733; www.arastabazaar.com

What's that? Your flight home's in 4hr. and you forgot to buy an "I Love Turkey" T-shirt? Run to Arasta Bazaar, a conveniently located strip of shops right below the Blue Mosque. As well as clothes, you'll find all kinds of souvenirs—fabrics, *nargile*, handmade pipes, tiles, and cheap bric-a-brac of all sorts. Prices are comparable to many tourist shops and the products are the same, but you'll be set to board with your suitcase full and the last of your lire spent.

✢ ⓜSultanahmet. Walk down Atmeydani Cad., away from the park. The Blue Mosque is on the left, and the bazaar is behind that. ✪ Open daily 9:30am-8pm. Some stores stay open later.

SALI PAZARI (TUESDAY MARKET)
ASIAN ISTANBUL

Kent Meydanı, Tarihi Salı Pazarı, Kadıköy   ☎0216 339 9819

Every Tuesday, this enormous marketplace in Kadıköy fills with locals selling and buying cheap clothes and fresh produce. Women outnumber men 10 to one, and the goods on sale reflect that—men might have more fun looking at the veggies (near Gate 2) than the limited apparel selection. Those looking for a snack will find dried fruits and nuts at half the price of those at European-side markets. The Tuesday Market is also open on Fridays, but there are usually fewer sellers. If your clothes have endured some wear and tear during your travels, come here to replenish your supply.

✢ Take the bus or Metrobüs from Kadıköy to Uzun Çayır Metrobüs stop. For the free shuttle, walk down Söğütlüçeşme Cad. away from the ferry terminal past the bull statue, and turn right onto Mahmut Baba Sok. There's a shuttle stop behind Wash Point. ✪ Open Tu 8am-6pm, F 8am-6pm. Shuttle 10min., every 10min.

EKOLOJIK PAZARI
BEYOĞLU

Lala Şahin Sok.   ☎0212 252 5255; www.bugday.org/eng

Organized by the ecological Buğday Association, this organic market has expanded from its first venue in Şişli to a total of four across Greater Istanbul, all offering organic fruit, vegetables, and household products. The Şişli and Kartal markets have recently added organic meat and tofu to their inventory, and the others will soon follow suit. Most of the food is locally sourced, a plus for voracious locavores. The markets also host film screenings and other events, though they're usually in Turkish. Come to Ekolojik Pazarı to enjoy the fresh food and get things like rice and soy milk, which are otherwise difficult to find in Istanbul.

✢ The Şişli location is the easiest to access from historic Istanbul. From ⓜOsmanbey, cross to the other side of the cemetery and continue down Ergenekon Cad. until you reach Lala Şahin Sok. *i* There are 3 other locations in Bakırköy, Beylikdüzü, and Kartal. ✪ Şişli market open Sa 8am-5pm.

▧ TARLABAŞI PAZARI
BEYOĞLU

The streets around Tarlabaşı

Tarlabaşı isn't the safest neighborhood for tourists (some say the police tank parked at its edge is a sign of how bad things are), but Sundays provide the best opportunity to walk the streets of this run-down but historic district. Prices are incredibly low, and the fruits and vegetables are some of the freshest in the city. The place looks quite pleasant when it's bright and sunny out, but it's best to go with someone else and beware of pickpockets. Don't stray too far from the market, and remember that Taksim is just a short uphill climb away. While bargaining isn't encouraged for the edible items, perishable goods are usually half price as night approaches, as sellers try to get rid of their stock. Just don't linger too long when it starts to get dark out.

✠ ⓂTaksim. Walk down İstiklal Cad., turn right onto Ağa Camii, and cross Tarlabaşı Bul. Continue down the hill until you hit the market, which sprawls across many streets. ☒ Open Su 10am-dusk.

SOUVENIRS AND BOOKS

Your friends back home will never forgive you if you don't bring back some good gifts with you, so remember to pick something up from Istanbul's many idiosyncratic stores. If you're looking for some reading material, there's a huge number of bookstores in **Aslıhan Pasajı**, just off İstiklal. (Meşrutiyet Cad. 10 ☒ Open daily 8am-8pm.) Bookstores tend to come in clusters, so you can also try looking in the **Sahaflar Bazaar** (between Beyazıt and the Grand Bazaar) and the **Akmar Pasajı** in Kadıköy (between Mühürdar Cad. and Neşet Ömer Sok.).

KARADENIZ ANTIK   BEYOĞLU
Çukurcuma Cad. 55   ☎0212 251 9605; www.karadenizantik.com
This is a good place to start your search for the kinds of junk that get lumped into the category of antiques. Across its five floors, Karadeniz Antik sells everything from old gramophones and cameras to paintings and furniture. Those with a generous baggage allowance could try lugging them back home. Just make sure you don't buy anything of real value—if it's more than 100 years old, taking it out of the country may be illegal. The shop has other locations inside the Grand Bazaar's central *bedesten* and in the huge Horhor Flea Market.

✠ ⓂTophane. Walk up Boğazkesen Cad. until you reach Çukurcuma, then turn right and continue straight until you see the shop to the right. Alternatively, walk down from Galatasaray on Yeni Çarşı Cad., and take the 3rd left. ☒ Open daily 9am-7pm.

FELT IN LOVE   BEYOĞLU
Camekan Sok. 2   ☎0212 243 7574; www.feltinloveshop.com
Soft, cushy, and cute, Felt in Love makes original souvenirs you can hang, squeeze, and wear. The felt products (get the name now?) range from Christmas-tree ornaments to turbaned finger puppets. The store also carries leather shoes and woven hats (though, sadly, no fezzes) that will add that Turkish flair your wardrobe has been looking for. If you missed the hamam experience, bring home the traditional *peştamal* towel (steam bath and masseur not included). Although the prices might be higher than those of traditional souvenirs, most of the stuff is handmade, and unlike that gaudy ceramic plate covered with evil eye charms, these won't break when your luggage gets tossed around on the trip home.

✠ ⓂTünel. At the corner of the block, near the entrance to Galata Tower. ⓘ Accepts euro and US dollars. Ⓢ Finger puppets and ornaments 15TL. Towels 40TL. Leather shoes 65TL. ☒ Open daily 10am-9pm.

carpet diem

Whether you're at the Grand Bazaar or outside of the Blue Mosque, get ready to be assaulted by a barrage of tongues ("Hello! Merhaba! Bonjour! Nihao?") as carpet salesmen try to lure you into their shops. If you're looking to buy, go ahead, and while you're at it, enjoy an enlightening introduction to oriental carpet-making. But if you'd rather not lug back home the finest in Turkish rugs, you can still pass through unscathed. Smile, say *tesekkür* ("thanks"), and move on. Your luggage (and wallet) will thank you.

shopping

CLOTHING

Beyoğlu is once again the main neighborhood if you're looking to buy some new clothes (and don't feel like braving a bazaar to get them). Hit up the **Atlas** and **Halep** passages (opposite each other, north of Galatasaray), both of which have their share of stores. The **Avrupa** passage right next to the **Aslıhan** book passage (across from Galatasaray) conforms to the "shiny bric-a-brac" category, while the **Aznavur** passage offers clothing, comic books, and CDs.

BY RETRO   BEYOĞLU

Suriye Pasajı 166C   ☎0212 245 6420; www.byretro.com.tr

Outfit your cinematic fantasies at this second-hand vintage and costume shop. Possible screenplay: handsome WWII soldier (army uniforms; 60-700TL) saves gorgeous bride (wedding dresses; 50-200TL) from pink-turbaned sultan (turbans; 50-70TL). You'll also find the usual fur coats and outfits that should probably have stayed in the '60s. Come here to browse, try on some ridiculous stuff, and be amused, but don't get too crazy with the role-playing.

✦ Ⓜ*Tünel. Walk up İstiklal for a few blocks and the Suriye passage is on the left across from the Richmond Hotel. By Retro is in the back of the passage before the barbershop.* ⌚ *Open daily 10am-10pm.*

KANYON LEVENT   BEYOĞLU

Büyükdere Cad. 185   ☎0212 317 5300; www.kanyon.com.tr

Trade your traditional bazaar shopping for another kind of covered market: shopping malls. Their numbers and popularity are growing in Istanbul, and one of the newer arrivals, Kanyon, is worth the Metro ride. Besides 160 shops, its own radio station (99.4FM Virgin Radio), and a multiplex cinema (☎0212 353 0853; www.cinebonus.com.tr), it also won an architecture award for its sexy, truly canyon-like curves. You can find the usual McDonald's and Starbucks here, but try one of the Turkish chains, like the dessert palace Saray Muhallebicisi or the clothing store Vakko. Better yet, just window shop and admire the mall's design for free.

✦ Ⓜ*Levent. It's on the Taksim-4 Levent Metro line. Exit the Metro station at the Gültepe or Kanyon exits, and follow the signs to the mall.* ⌚ *Open daily 10am-10pm.*

AVANTGARDEAST   BEYOĞLU

Galatasaray İş Hanı 12, İstiklal Cad. 120   ☎0212 245 1507; www.avantgardeast.com

Gentlemen disappointed by the gender bias of street bazaars, this one's for you. This store in Galatasaray passage has an extensive collection of jeans (around 55TL), mostly from brands you've never heard of, and a basement outlet section with lower, street-bazaar prices.

✦ *From Galatasaray, walk toward Tünel, and the Galatasaray passage is on the right.* ❦ *Cash only.* ⌚ *Open daily 10am-midnight.*

istanbul

essentials

PRACTICALITIES

- **TOURIST OFFICES:** There are a number of offices in different districts, including **Sultanahmet** (Meydanı 5 and Divan Yolu Cad. 5 ☎0212 518 1803, 0212 518 1802), **Beyoğlu** (Seyran Apt., Mete Cad. 6 ☎0212 233 0592), **Sirkeci Train Station** (☎0212 511 5888), **Atatürk International Airport** (☎0212 465 3151 ⌚ Open daily 9am-10:30pm.), **Sabiha Gökçen International Airport** (☎0216 588 8794) and **Karaköy** (Karaköy Limanı Yolcu Sarayı ☎0212 249 5776). All provide free maps, brochures, and information in English. Unless noted otherwise, they are open daily from mid-June to September 9:30am-6pm; from October to mid-June 9am-5:30pm.

- **CURRENCY EXCHANGE:** Exchange bureaus are called *döviz* and can be found on İstiklal and around Divan Yolu. Among the better ones are **Klas Döviz** (Sıraselviler Cad. 6F ☎0212 249 3550 ⏰ Open daily 8:30am-10pm.) and **Çözüm Döviz.** (İstiklal Cad. 53 ☎0212 244 6271 ⏰ Open daily 9am-10pm.)
- **ATMS:** English-language ATMs *(bankamatik, bankomat)* can be found on almost every corner. If your account is at a foreign bank, cash withdrawal will cost you extra. Most ATMs dispense Turkish lire. If you want to withdraw American dollars or euro, try the banks around Sirkeci Train Station and İstiklal Cad.
- **LUGGAGE STORAGE:** 24hr. luggage storage *(Emanet Bagaj)* is available at **Atatürk International Airport** (☎0212 465 3442 $ 10-20TL per day.) and **Sirkeci Train Station.** (☎0539 885 2105 $ 4-7TL for 4hr., 0.50 TL per hr. thereafter; max. 4 days.)
- **GLBT RESOURCES: Time Out Istanbul** magazine provides a good overview of the city's GLBT establishments. Some other organizations of interest are **Lambda** (Tel Sok. 28/5, 4th fl., Beyoğlu ☎0212 245 7068, advice line 0212 244 5762; www.lambdaistanbul.org ⏰ Open F-Su 3-8pm. Hotline open M-Tu 5-7pm and F-Su 5-7pm.), trans-focused **Istanbul LGBTT** (Atıf Yılmaz Cad. Öğüt Sok. 18/4, Beyoğlu ☎0212 252 1088; www.istanbul-lgbtt.org), and Ankara-based **Kaos GL.** (☎0312 230 0358; http://news.kaosgl.com.)
- **TICKET AGENCIES:** Tickets to most major cultural events are available through **Biletix** (☎0216 556 9800; www.biletix.com).
- **LAUNDROMATS:** Most hostels will do your laundry for a small fee. If you'd prefer a laundromat, try **Beybuz** (Topçekerler Sok. 7A ☎0212 249 5900 $ Wash 3TL per kg. Dry cleaning 10TL. ⏰ Open 24hr.) or **Şık Çamaşır Yıkama.** (Güneşli Sok. 1A ☎0212 245 4375 $ 15TL per load. ⏰ Open M-Sa 8:30am-8pm.)
- **INTERNET: Sultanahmet Square** offers free Wi-Fi. **İstiklal Caddesi** supposedly has free Wi-Fi as well, but coverage is spotty. One of the best internet cafes in town is **Net Club** (Büyükparmakkapı Sok. 8/6, 3rd fl. ➔ Just off Istiklal Cad., a few blocks from Taksim Sq. $ 1.25TL per hr. ⏰ Open 24hr.), but there are many others around İstiklal and a few near the Sultanahmet tram stop. In most cafes, expect to pay about 2TL per hr.
- **POST OFFICES:** You can send letters and make calls at any of the many **PTT booths** around the city. Normal hours are 8:30am-12:30pm and 1:30-5:30pm. There's a central post office in **Eminönü** (Büyük Postahane Cad. 25 ☎0212 511 3818 ⏰ Open daily 8:30am-9pm.), while some other offices are in **Taksim** (Cumhuriyet Cad. 2 ☎0212 292 3650 ⏰ Open M-Sa 8:30am-12:30pm and 1:30-5:30pm.), **Galatasaray** (Tosbağa Sok. 22 ☎0212 243 3343 ⏰ Open M-Sa 8:30am-7pm, Su 8:30-12:30pm and 1:30-5:30pm.), and **Sultanahmet.** (Sultanahmet Meydanı ☎0212 517 4966 ⏰ Open in summer Tu-Su 8:30am-12:30pm and 1:30-5:30pm; in winter daily 8:30am-12:30pm and 1:30-5:30pm.)

EMERGENCY

- **EMERGENCY NUMBER:** ☎112.
- **POLICE:** ☎155. **Tourism Police**, in Turkish *Turizm Şube Müdürlüğü.* (Yerebatan Cad. 6, Sultanahmet ☎0212 527 4503.)
- **LATE-NIGHT PHARMACIES:** Some pharmacies *(eczane)* stay open overnight *(nöbetçi)* on a rotating basis; for a list, go to www.treczane.com. Closed pharmacies will list the nearest open pharmacy on their doors.

- **HOSPITAL/MEDICAL SERVICES:** The best option for international travelers is to use a private hospital. They are clean and efficient, and have 24hr. emergency units and some English-speaking staff. Some of the options are the German Hospital, **Alman Hastanesi** (Sıraselviler Cad. 119 ☎0212 293 2150; www.almanhastanesi.com.tr Ⓢ Consultation 160TL.) and the **American Hospital.** (Güzelbahçe Sok. 20 ☎0212 444 3777, ext. 9; www.americanhospitalistanbul.com Ⓢ Consultation 215TL.) Public hospitals are generally crowded, confusing, and lack English-speaking staff, but they are cheaper. The most conveniently located one is **Taksim Hastanesi.** (Sıraselviler Cad. 112 ☎0212 252 4300; www.taksimhastanesi.gov.tr.)

GETTING THERE

by plane

Istanbul is serviced by **Atatürk International Airport** (☎0212 463 3000; www.ataturkairport.com), which has both international and domestic terminals. The airport serves almost 40 airlines, including Turkish Airlines (☎0212 444 0849), British Airways (☎0212 317 6600), and Air France (☎0212 310 1919). The airport is 28km from central Istanbul. The easiest way to get from the airport to the center is to take the **Metro** (M1) and then the **tram.** At the airport, follow the "M" signs, get on the Metro (Ⓢ Tokens 1.75TL.), and get off at Zeytinburnu. Here, transfer to the tram going to Ⓜ Kabataş, which passes through Ⓜ Sultanahmet. You'll need to buy another 1.75TL token for the tram. You can also get off the Metro at Ⓜ Aksaray, but the transfer to the tram here isn't as convenient. You can also get to and from the airport via the express **Havaş bus** (☎0212 465 4700; www.havas.net Ⓢ 10TL. ☪ 40min., every 30min. 4am-1am.) and **taxis.** (Ⓢ Around 30TL to Sultanahmet, 35TL to Taksim.)

Sabiha Gökçen International Airport (☎0216 585 5000; www.sgairport.com) is located on the Asian side, about 40km from Kadıköy and 50km from Taksim. The best way to get from Sabiha Gökçen to central Istanbul is to take the **Havaş bus** (Ⓢ 14TL. ☪ 1hr.; every 30min. from airport 5am-midnight, from Taksim 4am-1am.) Alternatively, you can take the **public E10 bus** to Kadıköy (Ⓢ 1.75TL. ☪ 90min., every 10min. or 1hr. depending on time of day) and then transfer to a **ferry** to either Eminönü or Karaköy. (Ⓢ 1.75TL. ☪ Around 20min.) **Taxis** are expensive, charging around 80TL for the trip to Taksim.

by bus

Buses are concentrated at the **Büyük İstanbul Otogarı** (☎0212 658 0505; www.otogaristanbul.com), known simply as the Otogar. The Aksaray-Havalimanı Metro line (M1) has a stop here, so to get to the center from the bus station, take the Metro to Aksaray and then walk to the Yusufpaşa tram stop, or take the Metro to Zeytinburnu and switch onto the tram. Many bus companies have free shuttle service *(ücretsiz servis)* between the Otogar and Taksim. Among the major bus companies are **Metro** (☎0212 444 3455; www.metroturizm.com.tr), **Kamil Koç** (☎0212 444 0562, 0212 658 2000; www.kamilkoc.com.tr) and **Ulusoy.** (☎444 1888; www.ulusoy.com.tr) Some of the most frequent bus routes go to: Ankara (Ⓢ From 35TL. ☪ 6-7hr.); Edirne (Ⓢ From 20TL. ☪ 2½ hr.); Çanakkale (Ⓢ From 35TL. ☪ 6hr.); Izmir (Ⓢ From 50TL. ☪ 9hr.), often via Bursa. (Ⓢ From 20TL. ☪ 4hr.)

by train

Sirkeci Train Station (☎0212 520 6575) is the final stop for all trains from Europe. The Bosphorus express connects Istanbul to **Bucharest** (☪ 20½hr.) while the Balkan Express comes from **Sofia** (☪ 12½hr.) and **Belgrade.** (☪ 21½hr.) Trains from the Asian side terminate at **Haydarpaşa Train Station** (☎0216 336 4470). Different trains connect Istanbul with Ankara (Ⓢ Daytime tickets from 16TL, overnight 90TL. ☪ 8hr., 5 per day.) Information about train schedules and routes can be found on www.tcdd.gov.tr or by calling the **Turkish State Railways** (TCDD) at ☎0212 444 8233.

GETTING AROUND

The public transportation network in Istanbul is reliable and easy to navigate. This applies especially to ferries, trams, and trains, because they don't suffer from Istanbul's traffic congestion. Rides on all of the following (apart from the dolmuşes and the Tünel funicular) have a flat rate of 1.75TL, but it's a bit cheaper if you use **Akbil** or a transit pass like the **Istanbulkart.**

Akbil is a keychain-like transit pass that you can get at major transportation hubs like Taksim (they have signs that say Akbil). Though the passes are useful, they are gradually being phased out. Instead, get the Istanbulkart at the same locations (like Taksim, Kabataş, and ticket booths at Metro stops) for 10TL. The card stores value, and you can add money to it as required. The pass is definitely worth it if you're in the city for a week and don't want to buy individual tickets (jetons) for each trip. The card works on buses, ferries (even some to the Princes' Islands), the Metro, and trams.

by tram and funicular

The tram line that runs from Bağcılar through Zeytinburnu and on to Kabataş is a great option for getting around the European side. It runs from 6am-midnight, stopping in Aksaray, Sultanahmet, and Karaköy. There are two nostalgic tram lines (old streetcar lines dating back to the early 20th century). One runs along İstiklal Cad., connecting Tünel and Taksim, while the other follows a circular route in Kadıköy and Moda, on the Asian side.

Istanbul is also connected by underground funiculars. Since there is no direct tram connection between Taksim and Sultanahmet, the funicular connecting Kabataş and Taksim is necessary in order to get between the two. Another funicular connects Karaköy and Tünel. (ⓢ 2.50TL.)

by metro and rail

Istanbul's Metro (☎0212 568 9970; www.istanbul-ulasim.com.tr) has two lines. The M1 runs from Atatürk International Airport (Havalimanı) through Büyük Otogar to Aksaray. Aksaray is a 5min. walk from the Yusufpaşa tram stop (signs point the way). Another Metro line (M2) runs from Şişhane north to Atatürk Oto Sanayi and runs from 6am-midnight. Two suburban trains (www.tcdd.gov.tr) complement the rail service and use the same fare system. One line starts at Sirkeci Train Station and goes west through Kumkapı and Yenikapı (🕒 Around every 20min., 5:45am-midnight.), while the other starts at Haydarpaşa Train Station in Kadıköy and runs east through Göztepe and Bostancı. (🕒 Around every 20min., 5am-midnight.)

by ferry

Commuter ferries are the best way to get to the Asian side and to access some of the more distant neighborhoods. The most useful lines are **Eminönü-Kadıköy, Karaköy-Haydarpaşa-Kadıköy, Kabataş-Üsküdar, Eminönü-Üsküdar, Kadıköy-Beşiktaş, Kabataş-Kadıköy-Princes' Islands,** and the **Golden Horn line** (stops include Üsküdar, Eminönü, Fener, and Eyüp). Ferries usually run every 20min. or so. The two major intra-city ferry companies are **Şehir Hatları** (☎0212 444 1851; www.sehirhatlari.com.tr) and **Turyol.** (☎0212 251 4421, tourism line 0212 512 1287; www.turyol.com.)

by bus

You can get information on the city's many useful bus lines through **IETT** (☎444 1871, Turkish-speaking; www.iett.gov.tr). The **dolmuş** is a shared minibus that runs on set routes, stopping every couple of blocks to pick up and drop off passengers. The system is somewhat chaotic, but destinations are always listed on boards visible through the windows. The **Kadıköy-Taksim** dolmuş (ⓢ 5TL.) is especially useful, as it leaves every 20min., even after ferries stop running.

by taxi

The initial charge for cabs is 2.50TL and every additional kilometer costs 1.40TL. If you're taking a cab across the Bosphorus, you'll have to pay the bridge toll as well. Locals round up on the fare for tip. Beware of common taxi scams like a "broken meter" and roundabout routes.

VISAS

Citizens of Australia, Canada, Ireland, the UK, the US, and most other developed countries are required to get three-month, multiple-entry visas in order to enter Turkey. Visas range from €15-45, depending on your nationality, and usually allow you to spend up to 90 days in Turkey. Visas can be purchased at entry points in Turkey: airports, train stations, and bus terminals. Though they are technically called "tourist visas," most travelers report that they are basically a cash grab, and the officials seem to change the rates at will. Citizens of New Zealand do not need a visa in addition to a valid passport for entrance into Turkey.

MONEY

currency

Turkey's duality does not end with its continental identity crisis. Both the euro and the Turkish lira (TL) are common currency in the city. It's best to be armed with a little bit of both just in case. We find that travelers will usually use euro to pay for accommodations, and TL for everything else. Many restaurants, non-touristy shops, supermarkets, bars, clubs, sights, and utilities only take TL. This is not the case for hotels, most of which quote in euro (with the logical exception of those on the Asian side). Euro prices tend to be slightly marked up, to take advantage of lazy tourists. Only tourist-oriented locales bother to list euro prices. In places intended to rip tourists off, such as shopping venues in Sultanahmet, Istanbul, only euro are accepted. Ultimately, it's just cheaper to pay in lire, so the budget traveler should definitely carry many more lire than euro.

tipping and bargaining

In Turkey, you should tip around 5-10% in fancier restaurants (but make sure they didn't already include a service fee). Tips aren't expected in inexpensive restaurants. It is not customary to tip taxi drivers, but people will often round up the fare. At hamams, attendants will line up to "bid you goodbye" when you leave, meaning that they expect tips—distribute 10-15% of the total cost among them. Porters generally expect a few lire, and generally if anyone ever helps you, they are likely to smile kindly (sometimes creepily) and ask for a *baksheesh*, or tip.

The Turks see bargaining in a street market or bazaar as a life skill, but trying to get a cheaper price in an established shop can be disrespectful. If it's unclear whether bargaining is appropriate in a situation, hang back and watch someone else buy first. Be warned, merchants with any pride in their wares will refuse to sell to someone who has offended them in the negotiations, so don't lowball too much.

taxes

In Turkey, there is an 18% value added tax (VAT), known as the KDV, included in the price of most goods and services (including meals, lodging, and car rentals). Before you buy, check if the KDV is included in the price to avoid paying it twice. Theoretically, the KDV that you pay on your trip can be reclaimed at most points of departure, but this requires much persistence and it's a hassle and a half. You may also encounter an airport tax of $15, which is levied only on international travelers, but it is usually included in the cost of plane tickets.

SAFETY AND HEALTH

unsafe areas

The suburbs are the least safe area of the city, especially at night. Thieves also tend to target known student areas. Nationalist, neo-fascist mobs of students in the Zeytinburnu area have been reported attacking visitors. Another place that locals recommend avoiding at night is Tarlabaşı.

local laws and police

The **General Directorate of Security** (*Emniyet Genel Müdüdlüğü*) is the civilian police force in Turkey. Police officers wear navy-blue uniforms and caps. Police cars are blue and white and have "Polis" written on the side doors and hood. Police violence is a problem in Turkey, especially at protests and demonstrations, so exercise caution when near these events (in fact, try not to be near them at all). According to Human Rights Watch, police routinely use firearms during arrests without exhausting non-violent means and also when there is not an apparent threat of death or injury. Always be respectful and compliant when dealing with the police, and make it clear that you are a tourist.

drugs and alcohol

Turkey is a huge locus of drug trafficking coming from Afghanistan and Iran into Europe. It is estimated that as much as 80% of the heroin in Britain comes through Turkey. In recent years, the Interior Ministry has boasted a 149% increase in seizures of opium and opium derivatives, so the government takes drug trafficking very seriously. The Turkish government has adopted a harsh policy (including fines and jail time) for those caught with drugs. If caught, a meek "I didn't know it was illegal" will not suffice. Remember that you are subject to Turkey's laws while within its borders, not those of your home country.

The official drinking age is 18. **Avoid public drunkenness.** Islam prohibits the consumption of alcohol, even though it is legal in Turkey, so the drinking culture here is very different from what you may be used to. Do not drink during the holy month of Ramadan. At sporting events, the drinking age is 24, but it is not heavily enforced.

natural disasters

In one of the world's most seismically active areas, Turkey experiences frequent and occasionally large **earthquakes.** The most recent serious quake in 1999, whose epicenter was about 70km east of Istanbul, caused nearly 45,000 casualties. Earthquakes are unpredictable and can occur at any time of day. If a strong earthquake does occur, it will probably only last one or two minutes. Protect yourself by moving under a sturdy doorway, table, or desk.

terrorism

Though the threat is lower in Istanbul than elsewhere in the country, terrorism is a persistent problem in Turkey. A number of terrorist groups remain active, mostly in the south east, where the separatist Kurdistan Workers' Party (PKK) regularly attacks national security forces. *Let's Go* does not recommend travel in the southeastern provinces of Hakkari, Sirnak, Siirt, or Tunceli due to the instability and terrorism in these provinces. However, the PKK has in recent years bombed government and civilian targets in Istanbul, Ankara, Izmir, and tourist resorts of the Mediterranean and Aegean. Bombs are normally planted in crowded areas in trash cans, outside banks, or on mini-buses and trains. Bombings occur a few times a year but are generally not deadly and are targeted toward the police and the government. The best thing you can do to be safe is to be aware of your surroundings, especially in crowded areas and tourist sites.

essentials

glbt travelers

Homosexuality is not illegal in Turkey, but it is recommended that GLBT travelers exercise caution when traveling due to the conservative values embedded in Muslim-majority Turkish society.

nationalism

The Turks are very proud of all people, items, and history associated with their nation. Do not insult, profane, or ridicule Mustafa Kemal Atatürk. Never. He is a national legend and is practically untouchable. The joke goes that a Turk will flinch if you insult his mother but will kill you if you insult Kemal. So please, don't even try. You should adopt the same reverent attitude toward the Turkish flag. It's everywhere and it symbolizes patriotic pride. It is best to steer clear of discussing politics (especially around election time) or the Kurdish situation.

contraceptives and feminine hygiene

Turkey is much more conservative than other travel destinations. It's almost impossible to find tampons, due to suspicion that they lead to the deflowering of women. Either bring a supply with you, or stock up on sanitary napkins when you get there. The morning-after pill is illegal without a prescription, as is birth control. Pharmacies and some large supermarkets sell condoms, but women should take care to be discreet with these purchases.

water

In Turkey, be wary of the tap water. Though Istanbul is fairly modernized, the water throughout the city and country still isn't safe to drink. Even the locals don't touch it, and there is no need for you to either, since bottled water is pretty cheap.

istanbul 101

HISTORY

a head start (ancient times)

Our story begins not in the misty shroud of lore and legend, but in the 21st century. A construction worker digging a subway tunnel in 2005 came upon the surprise of a lifetime: peering inside an ancient bag, he found himself face-to-face with the grins of **nine human skulls.** Dating back to the seventh century BCE, these remains, along with some amphorae, shells, and enough horse skulls to make the Godfather proud, are the oldest evidence of human settlement in what is now Istanbul.

to byzantion and beyond! (667-512 bce)

Although the area had been dotted with small settlements for centuries, it wasn't until 667 BCE that it became home to a true city. Legend has it that a Greek named **Byzas** (see where this is going?) wanted to find some prime real estate where he could found his very own metropolis. In the absence of ancient realtors, he paid a visit to the **Oracle at Delphi** for advice. In typical oracular ambiguity, he was told to set up shop "opposite the blind." Not having a clue what the oracle meant, he set off across the Aegean and eventually stopped at the Bosphorus, a narrow strait between the European and Asian continents. The Greek city of Chalcedon occupied the eastern shore, and Byzas decided that its inhabitants must have been totally blind not to notice the fabulous land lying only a half a mile away on the western shore. With one fanciful interpretation of prophecy under his belt, Byzas established a city on this western shore and named it **Byzantion,** after himself.

capture the flag (512 bce-324 ce)

Byzantion's strategic location made it a hub for commerce, as well as an appealing prize for passing conquerors. In 512 BCE, the city was captured by the Persian Emperor Darius, only to fall under Spartan rule 30 years later. Athens soon decided that it wanted in on the action, and ruled until 334 BCE, when **Alexander the Great** rolled into town. After Alexander's death, Roman influence increased, and by 74 CE the region was firmly in the hands of the Roman Empire. In the first of many renamings, the Romans decided that Byzantion would sound way better in Latin and dubbed the city **Byzantium.** Byzantium was almost completely destroyed in 196 CE after siding against the Emperor Severus in a Roman civil war. After actually getting to know Byzantium, Severus decided it wasn't so bad after all, and made up for the whole almost-completely-destroying-you thing by rebuilding the city, complete with fancy new walls.

capital gains (324-600)

Emperor **Constantine I** chose Byzantium as his new capital in 324 CE, just as the Roman Empire began to splinter into eastern and western halves. Like Rome, Byzantium was built on seven hills, and Constantine did his darndest to extend the resemblance by rebuilding the entire city to be Rome 2.0. After his death, the city was renamed **Constantinople** in his honor. When Rome fell in 476 CE, Constantinople became the capital of the surviving Eastern Roman Empire, which later became known as the Byzantine Empire. A bustling port at the nexus of continents, the city flourished as a commercial and cultural center. Byzantine Emperor **Justinian** (527–565 CE) expanded the empire's domain to extend from Egypt to Spain, created an organized legal code, and ordered the construction of the magnificent **Hagia Sophia** church.

time to split (600-1453)

Things took a turn for the worse in the seventh and eighth centuries as Constantinople found itself under siege from Arab armies. A disagreement about the presence of icons in churches later caused the **Great Schism** between Constantinople's **Greek Orthodox Church** and the church in Rome. In 1204, Crusaders passing through the city on their way from Europe to Jerusalem decided to just plunder Constantinople instead (those icons basically made them infidels too, right?). Despite the hardships, Byzantine art continued to flourish during this period, and can still be seen in the city's many exquisite mosaics and magnificent monasteries.

state of the art (1453-1923)

Constantinople fell to the Ottoman Turks in 1453, after a lengthy and tenacious siege led by the aptly nicknamed Sultan Mehmed "the Conqueror." The city was refurbished yet again to become the new capital of the Ottoman Empire. The Hagia Sophia was turned into a mosque (just plaster over the mosaics of Jesus and add minarets!) and the city reached its height as a multicultural center of learning and art. Under Sultan **Suleiman I** (1520–1566), the famous architect Sinan designed numerous grand mosques, and the arts of calligraphy and ceramics flourished. After the 17th century though, Constantinople's fortunes declined, as the Ottoman Empire entered a long period of stagnation and decline, leading to its eventual collapse in 1923.

istanbul, not constantinople (1923-today)

In the wake of the Ottomans' defeat in World War I, the victorious allies jockeyed to take over its remaining territories. A Turkish army officer named **Mustafa Kemal** resisted Western efforts to colonize Constantinople, and created a secular, modern Republic of Turkey out of the heartland of the old Ottoman Empire. Today, Kemal is better known by his nickname, **Atatürk** (Father of Turks). Atatürk ended Istanbul's 1500-year-run as a capital city and moved the seat of the new Turkey to the more centrally located Ankara. In the 1940s, Istanbul began a modernization campaign, with public squares and sweeping boulevards breathing new life into the city. The 1970s were a period of rapid industrialization and population growth as workers flocked to the city to find jobs in factories.

Skyrocketing demand for housing drove the city to swallow up nearby towns and forests. If the urban sprawl seems poorly planned, that's because it wasn't planned—experts estimate that 65% of the city's structures do not meet building codes. In 1985, Istanbul's historic center was designated a UNESCO World Heritage site, and the city was chosen as a European Capital of Culture for 2010.

CUSTOMS AND ETIQUETTE

when in istanbul...

Istanbul is a modern, cosmopolitan city that has adopted many Western social customs, but visitors who've never traveled to a Muslim country before may find certain traditions completely foreign. Public displays of affection are not as common or as widely accepted as in many other European countries, so if you find yourself a Turkish sweetheart (or brought your own with you), keep the public canoodling to a minimum. Turks are very proud of their country, and visitors should be aware that insulting the Turkish nation, national flag, or Atatürk is not only rude, but against the law. Steer clear of touchy subjects: Islam and the Armenian Genocide are not acceptable targets for your latest rant or comedy routine. Turkish culture also places a high value on respect for elders. It is considered proper to make your greetings from eldest to youngest, regardless of how well you know each person.

at the table

Invited to dine at someone's home? Welcome to Istanbul, land of legendary hospitality. Show your gratitude by bringing a small gift, such as flowers or a dessert. Play it safe and don't bring a bottle of wine for your host. Because Turkey is predominantly Muslim, many residents don't drink alcohol. Enjoy your meal, and make sure to let your host know how good it tastes. They'll be sure to keep loading up your plate, so bring a hearty appetite and pants loose enough to accommodate an expanding waistline. If you're invited to dine out at a restaurant, bear in mind that the host always pays, although an offer to pay is customary.

mosque etiquette

Though some mosques are open only to Muslims, most of Istanbul's exquisite mosques welcome all visitors, provided they are courteous and dress appropriately. Remove your shoes before entering and wear modest clothing. Miniskirts, shorts, and tank tops are definite no-nos. Make sure you have your shoulders, upper arms, and thighs completely covered. When entering, women will be provided with a head-scarf to cover their hair—though if you want it to match your outfit, you might want to bring your own. Once inside, remember that this is a place of worship, so keep your voice down and be conscientious if you want to snap a picture. When you hear the call for prayer, clear out to make room for worshippers.

body language

Remember that body language isn't universal. Even something as simple as shaking your head might not mean what you expect. To say "yes," nod your head downward. "No" is nodding your head upward, while shaking your head from side to side means that you don't understand. The hand gesture made by forming an "O" with your thumb and index finger, which means "OK" in the US, is considered very offensive in Turkey. It signifies that someone is a homosexual, and if you like your nose unbroken, we don't recommend making it. When you enter someone's home, take off your shoes and accept slippers if offered. Sitting cross-legged on the floor is common, but pay attention: exposing the bottoms of your feet is offensive, no matter how adorable your toe socks are. Blowing your nose in public is considered rude, so take a quick trip to the bathroom to save yourself from awkward stares.

FOOD AND DRINK

fusion food

With more than 2000 years of culinary history, Istanbul has had plenty of opportunity to refine its palate. Fish, eggplant, fragrant herbs, and fresh olive oil will please your stomach and maintain your waistline. Modern cuisine is a delicious blend of Balkan, Central Asian, and Middle Eastern specialties. *Doner kebabs* (lamb roasted to perfection on an upright spit) are one of the most popular Turkish dishes. Meat-lovers will also enjoy *kofta*, balls of ground beef or lamb mixed with onions and spices.

For lighter fare, there's *dolma*, vine leaves stuffed with anything from spiced rice (*zeytinyagli dolma*) to eggplant (*patlican*) to mussels (*midye*). Another Turkish specialty is *pilav*, known to Westerners as pilaf, a rice dish cooked with an almost infinite variety of spices and ingredients. Carnivores should try *özbek pilav*, made with diced lamb, onions, tomatoes, and carrots, or *hamsili pilav*, cooked with anchovies. Vegetarians can order *domatesli pilav* (tomato pilaf) or *nohutlu pilav* (rice cooked with seasoned chickpeas). Desserts include *sütlaç*, a fresh rice pudding, and flaky pastries like **baklava** and *kadaif*. Turkish sweets are world-renowned and sure to sate even the most die-hard sweet tooths.

istanbul 101

drink up!

Caffeine addicts should try a strong Turkish coffee on for size, then examine the grounds at the bottom to try your hand at *kahve fali*, or coffee-dreg fortune-telling. For less mystery and a stronger kick, sip *rakı*, an anise-flavored liquor, often served with seafood. *Rakı* turns milky-white when diluted with water, as it is usually served—hence its nickname, *aslan sütü* (lion's milk). A common Turkish saying claims that if you want to get to know someone you should either travel or drink rakı together. If you're visiting Istanbul with friends, you can do both, and the effects of this famously strong drink will probably reveal more secrets than the *kahve fali* did earlier. Teetotalers can try another of Turkey's favorite drinks, *ayran*. A unique mix of yogurt, water, and salt, *ayran* is served chilled and is the ideal companion to a steaming kebab.

istanbul

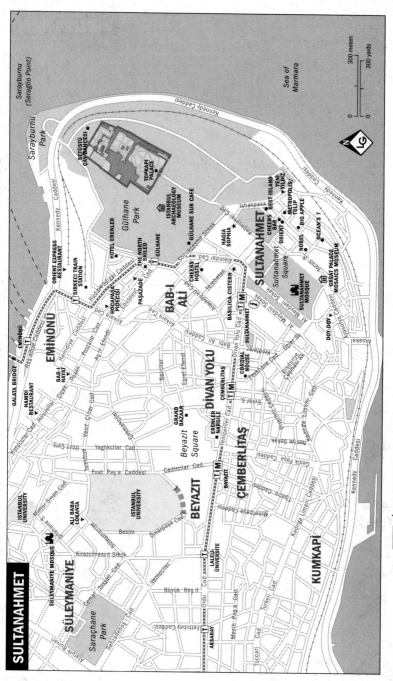

SULTANAHMET

SÜLEYMANIYE

SÜLEYMANIYE MOSQUE

ALI BABA LOKANTA

ISTANBUL UNIVERSITY

Saraçhane Park

Beyazit Square

ISTANBUL UNIVERSITY

BEYAZIT

AKSARAY

Yaglikcilar Cad.

GRAND BAZAR

Büyük Reşit

KUMKAPI

CEMBERLITAS

ERENLER NARGILE

CEMBERLITAS

DIVAN YOLU

CORDIAL HOUSE

BAB-I ALI

PAŞAZADE

HOTEL ERENLER

ORIENT EXPRESS RESTAURANT

SIRKECI TRAIN STATION

EMINÖNÜ

BAB-I HAYAT

HAMDI RESTAURANT

GALATA BRIDGE

THE NORTH SHIELD

CHEERS HOSTEL

BASILICA CISTERN

HAGIA SOPHIA

GÜLHANE SUR CAFE

ISTANBUL ARCHAEOLOGY MUSEUM

SETÜSTÜ ÇAY BAHÇESI

TOPKAPI PALACE

Gülhane Park

SULTANAHMET

Sultanahmet Square

CHEERS BAR

BEST ISLAND

YENI YILDIZ

METROPOLIS TULIP

BIG APPLE

ORIENT

NOBEL

OCEAN'S 7

SULTANAHMET MOSQUE

GREAT PALACE MOSAICS MUSEUM

DOY-DOY

Sea of Marmara

Sarayburnu (Seraglio Point)

Sarayburnu Park

300 meters

300 yards

N

sultanahmet map

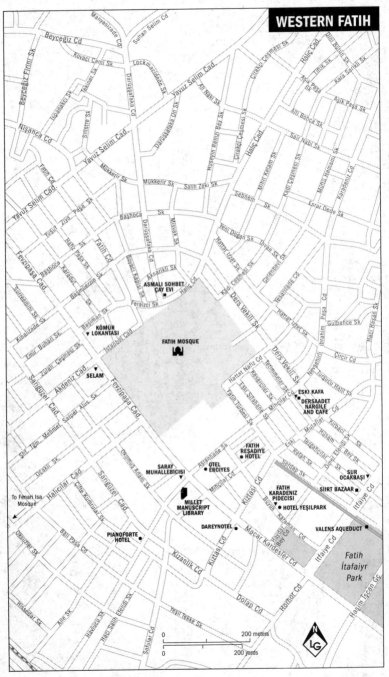

WESTERN FATIH

Manyasizade Cd
Beycegiz Cd
Sultan Selim Cd
Kovaci Cami Sk
Diri Bdrin Sk
Haliç Cad
Tiftik Sk
Kara Sarikli Sk
Beycegiz Firini Sk
Pastaci Sk
Darüşşafaka Cd
Lockmacinade Sk
Çirağci Çeşmesi Sk
Aşik Paşa SK
Espanakçi Sk
Darüşşafaka Dil Sk
Yavuz Selim Cad.
Ali Naki Sk
Alti Boğca Sk
Aşik Paşa Sk
Nisanca Cd
Simsirc Sk
Huseyin Remzi Bey Sk
Çirakçi Çeşmesi Sk
Sair Nabi Sk
Fatih Cd
Yavuz Selim Cad.
Mükkerir Sk
Kadi Çeşmesi Sk
Karadeniz Cd
Yavuz Selim Cad.
Mükkerir Sk
Salih Zeki Sk
Sebnem Sk
Mimar Kemal Sk
Mufti Hamami
Yusuf Ziya Paşa Sk
Baskoca Sk
Darüşşafaka D
Mısbah Sk
Esrar Dede Sk
Fevzi Paşa Cad
Fatih Cd
Yeni Doğan Sk
Ilvan Sk
Baskoca Karakol
Başmuezzin Sk
Akşemsettin Sk
Asmali Sohbet Çay Evi
Haliç Cad
Hattat İzzet Sk
Getemenet Cd
İbrahim Paşa
Gülbahce Sk
Haci Hasan Sk
Ferajci Sk
Kinalizade Sk
Başiman Sk
Kömür Lokantasi
Fatih Mosque
Ders Vekili Sk
Yeşaretpaşa Cd
Zulali Çeşmesi Sk
İstanbol Cad
Emir Buhari Sk
Selam
Akdeniz Cad.
Fevzipaşa Cad
Çırçır Cd
Sahzede Cad
Salper Alus Sk
Hattat Nafız Cd
Yetimoğlu Sk
Ders Vekili Sk
Eski Kafa
Nevşehirli Halil Sk
Sht. Tüm. Mehmet Sk
Ocaklar Sk
Esar Şifahane Sk
Keserciler Sk
Eski Turgucu Halil Sk
Dersaadet Nargile and Cafe
Fatih Türbesi Sk
Mufti Sk
Hüsam Sk
Halicilar Cad
Ayşekadin Sk
Fatih Resadiye Hotel
Mufti Sk
Kirbaci Sk
Saray Muhallebicisi
Otel Erciyes
Refat Sk
Tezgahçilar Sk
Dimet Efendi Bey Sk
Çifte Kumrular Sk
Sangüzel Sk
Okurus Adani Sk
Minciler Cd
Kızilaş Cd
Serdap Sk
Sur Ocakbaşi
Millet Manuscript Library
Fatih Karadeniz Pidecisi
Siirt Bazaar
Balı Paşa Cd
Dareynotel
Hotel Yeşilpark
Pianoforte Hotel
Kızilaş Cd
Macar Kardeşler Cd
Burdur Karaman Cd
Valens Aqueduct
Hordar Bey Cd
Ballı Paşa Cd
Ocaklar Sk
İtfaiye Cd
Oksuzler Sk
Kızilik Cd
İtfaiye Cd
Fatih İtafaiyr Park
To Fenari Isa Mosque
Dolap Cd
Hornor Cd
Hissedar Sk
Alle Sk
Haci Salih Efendi Sk
Haliducu Sk
Yeşil tekke Sk
Sofular Cd
Hasim İşcan Gç

istanbul

0   200 meters
0   200 yards

N
LG

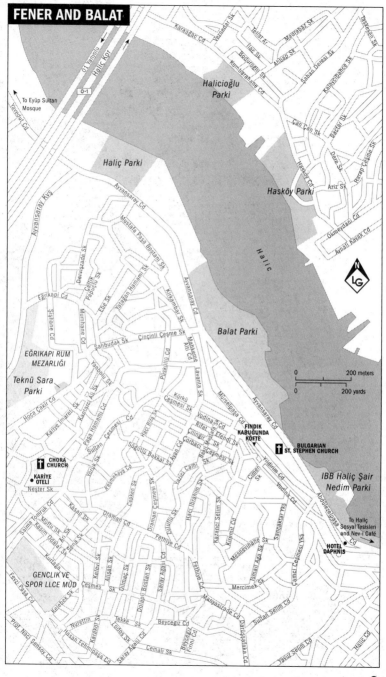

FENER AND BALAT

To Eyüp Sultan Mosque

Haliçioğlu Parki

Haliç Parki

Hasköy Parki

Haliç

Balat Parki

EĞRİKAPI RUM MEZARLIĞI

Teknü Sara Parki

FINDIK KABUĞUNDA KÖFTE

BULGARIAN ST. STEPHEN CHURCH

CHORA CHURCH

KARİYE OTELİ

IBB Haliç Şair Nedim Parki

To Haliç Sosyal Tesisleri and Nev-i Café

HOTEL DAPHNIS

GENÇLIK VE SPOR LLCE MÜD

0   200 meters

0   200 yards

fener and balat map

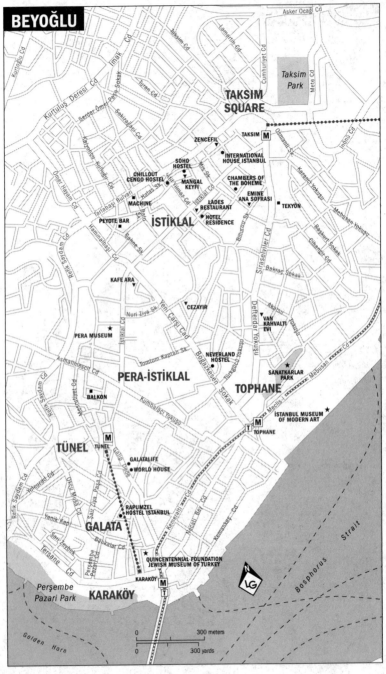

BEYOĞLU

Asker Ocağı Cd

Taksim Cd

Lamartin Cd

Cumhuriyet Cd

Mete Cd

Taksim Park

İmak Cd

Kurtuluş Deresi Cd

Serdar Ömer Paşa Sokak

Turan Cd

Şahkulu Cd

TAKSİM SQUARE

Osman Sk.

İnönü Cd

TAKSİM Ⓜ

Kazancı Yokuşu

Mebusan Yokuşu

ZENCEFİL

Miss Sk.

INTERNATIONAL HOUSE ISTANBUL

SOHO HOSTEL

İstiklal Cd

CHAMBERS OF THE BOHEME

Başkurt Sokak

Ömer Hayam Cd

Manyasızade-Kılıbdağı Cd

Tarlabaşı Bulvarı

CHILLOUT CENGO HOSTEL

MANGAL KEYFİ

Hanas Sk.

Hümar Cd

İstiklal Cd

EMİNE ANA SOFRASI

TEKYÖN

Cihangir Cd

MACHINE

LADES RESTAURANT

Binnaz Sk.

Sıraselviler Cd

PEYOTE BAR

Sehne Sk.

HOTEL RESIDENCE

İSTİKLAL

Hammalbaşı Cd

Refik Saydam Cd

Bakraç Sokak

KAFE ARA

Yeni Çarşı Cad

CEZAYİR

Aksaray Yokuşu

VAN KAHVALTI EVI

Detterdar Yokuşu

Nuri Ziya Sk.

PERA MUSEUM ★

Asmalımescit Cd

İstiklal Cd

Tomtom Kaptan Sk.

PERA-İSTİKLAL

NEVERLAND HOSTEL

Boğazkesen Sokak

Turnacıbaşı Yokuşu

SANATKARLAR PARK

Meşrutiyet Cd

BALKON

Kumbaracı Yokuşu

TOPHANE

Mebusan Cd

Balık Saydam Cd

İstanbul

Meclis-i Mebusan Cd

İSTANBUL MUSEUM OF MODERN ART ★

TÜNEL

TÜNEL Ⓜ

Galip Dede

GALATALIFE

WORLD HOUSE

Ⓜ Ⓣ TOPHANE

Refik Saydam Cd

Yolcuzade Cd

Okçu Musa Cd

Şair Ziya Paşa Cd

RAPUMZEL HOSTEL ISTANBUL

Kemeraltı Cd

Necati Bey Cd

Kemankeş Cd

Bosphorus Strait

Yanık Kapı

Sert Zeybek

GALATA

Bankalar Cd

★

Tersane Cd

Perşembe Pazarı Cd

Perşembe Pazarı Park

QUINCENTENNIAL FOUNDATION JEWISH MUSEUM OF TURKEY

KARAKÖY

KARAKÖY Ⓜ Ⓣ

N Ⓥ Ⓖ

Golden Horn

0   300 meters

0   300 yards

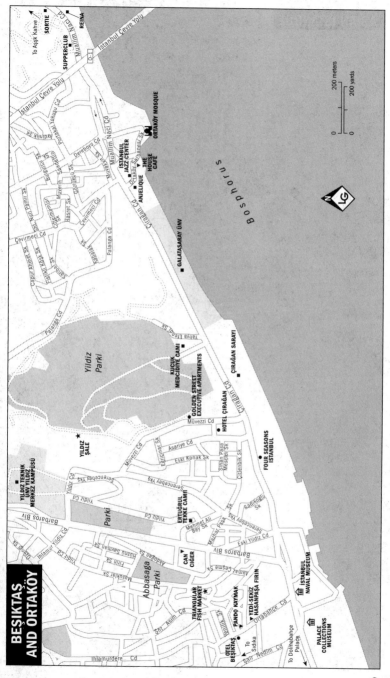

BEŞİKTAŞ AND ORTAKÖY

To Aşyk Kahve

SORTIE

REINA

SUPPERCLUB

Muallim Naci Cd

İstanbul Çevre Yolu

İstanbul Çevre Yolu

Portakal Yokuşu Sk

Derebeyu Cd

Muallim Naci Cd

ORTAKÖY MOSQUE

Dereboyu Cd

İSTANBUL JAZZ CENTER

THE HOUSE CAFÉ

ANJELIQUE

Çilgin Sk

Yıldırım Sk

Bulgurlu Sk

Büyükdere Sk

Hasırcı Sk

Müvezzi Sadullah Sk

Çeşitmen Sk

Çevirmeci Cd

Palanga Cd

Çapur Ahmet Sk

Pestemal Kösk Sk

Kahraman Sk

Müvezzi Cd

Çırağan Cd

Çevirmeci Cd

GALATASARAY ÜNV

B o s p h o r u s

Palanga Cd

Yıldız Parkı

Yahya Efendi Sk

KÜÇÜK MECİDİYE CAMİİ

ÇIRAĞAN SARAYI

GOLDEN STREET EXECUTIVE APARTMENTS

Çırağan Cd

HOTEL ÇIRAĞAN

Müvezzi Cd

Müvezzi Cd

YILDIZ ŞALE

Asariye Cd

Eğlence Sk

Eski Konak Sk

Sinan Paşa Mescidi Sk

FOUR SEASONS İSTANBUL

Çitlenbik Sk

YILDIZ TEKNİK ÜNV YILDIZ MERKEZ KAMPÜSÜ

Yıldız Cd

Serencebey Ykş

Serencebey Ykş

Parkı

Yıldız Cd

ERTUĞRUL TEKKE CAMİİ

Serencebey Ykş

Eski Yıldız Cd

Barbaros Blv

Yıldız Cd

Çırağan

Mehmet Ali Bey Sk

Mabut Paşa

200 meters
200 yards
0
0

N

Orenç Sk

Barbaros Blv

Dereng Sk

Abbasağa Parkı

Masklar Sk

Hüsnü Savman Sk

Akdoğan Sk

CAN CİĞER

Almaz Çeşme Sk

Barbaros Blv

İSTANBUL NAVAL MUSEUM

Firin Sk

TRIANGULAR FISH MARKET

PANDO KAYMAK

YEDİ-SEKİZ HASANPAŞA FIRIN

Ortabahçe Cd

Şht. Asım Cd

Yalıköy Sk

OTEL BEŞİKTAŞ

To Sidika

To Şair Nedim Cd

PALACE COLLECTIONS MUSEUM

İhlamurdere Cd

To Dolmabahçe Palace

ASIAN ISTANBUL

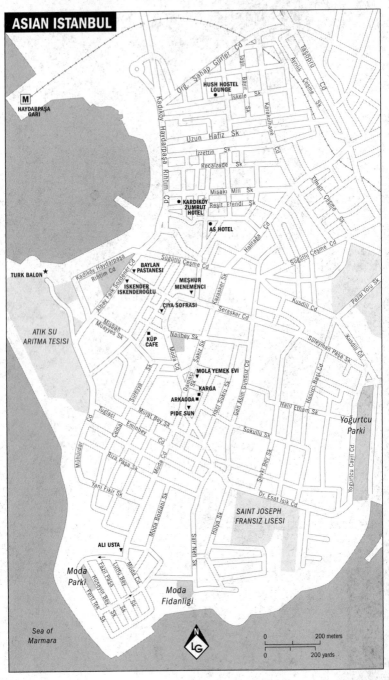

M HAYDARPAŞA GARİ

Org. Şahap Gürler Cd

HUSH HOSTEL LOUNGE

Kadıköy Haydarpaşa Rıhtım Cd

Uzun Hafız Sk

İzzettin Sk

Recaizade Sk

Misakı Mili Sk

Reşit Efendi Sk

KARDIKÖY ZUMRUT HOTEL

AŞ HOTEL

Halitaga Cd

Söğütlü Çeşme Cd

Söğütlü Çeşme Cd

İskele Sk

Bayır Sk

Karakolhane Cd

Aynik Çeşme Sk

Taşüprü

Efnan Çeşme Sk

TURK BALON ★

Kadıköy Haydarpaşa Rıhtım Cd

Albey Faik Sozdener Cd

BAYLAN PASTANESI

İSKENDER İSKENDEROĞLU

MEŞHUR MENEMENCİ

ÇİYA SOFRASI

Misbah Muayyeş Sk

KÜP CAFE

Nailbey Sk

Moda Cd

Şakir Sk

Kazasker Sk

Serasker Cd

Kuşdili Cd

Süleyman Paşa Sk

Kuşdili Cd

Pazar Yolu Sk

ATİK SU ARITMA TESİSİ

MOLA YEMEK EVİ

KARGA

ARKAODA

PIDE SUN

Damacı Sk

Hacı Şükrü Sk

Gen Asım Gündüz Cd

Halit Etham Sk

Haşuç Başa Cd

Yogurtcu Parki

Süreyya Sk

Tuğlacı Cd

Cemal Eminbey Cd

Murat Bey Sk

Moda Cd

Rıza Paşa Sk

Sokullu Sk

Sevil Bey Sk

Dr. Esat Işık Cd

Yoğurtcu Çayrı Cd

istanbul

Mühürdar Cd

Yeni Fikir Sk

Moda Bostanı Sk

Şair Nefi Sk

Hüya Sk

SAINT JOSEPH FRANSIZ LİSESI

ALİ USTA

Moda Parki

Fazıl Paşa Sk

Hüseyin Bey Sk

Ferit Tek Sk

Lütfü Bey Sk

Moda Cd

Moda Fidanliği

Sea of Marmara

N

0   200 meters

0   200 yards

LONDON

Most people have a well-defined idea of "London"—staid tradition, afternoon tea, heavy ales, and cultured accents in tweed. People with this notion of London can easily complete their vacation in 3min. by making their way to the banks of the Thames and staring pointedly at the gilded heights of Big Ben, but this would be to miss the true charm of this expansive, diverse place.

Despite its weighty history, the city today is not all ghost tours, beefeaters, and double-decker buses. Beyond Buckingham Palace and the blinding lights of Piccadilly Circus, London is a living, breathing metropolis, home to more people than any other city in the European Union. Comprised of 32 boroughs along with the City, London can seem at times more like a conglomerate of villages than a unified city, but each part's unique heritage and character contributes to the big picture. Thanks to the feisty independence and diversity of each area, the London "buzz" is continually on the move—every few years a previously disregarded neighborhood explodes into cultural prominence. Wander between immigrant neighborhoods in East London, take part in a political rally in Trafalgar Square, and watch the Olympics return to the city for a third time. Each day in London brings something new, so finish up your pint and Let's Go!

greatest hits

- **MUSEUM MOSEYING.** In a very uncapitalist move, most of London's museums open their doors for free. Our favorites are the **British Museum** (p. 434), **Tate Modern** (p. 428), **National Gallery** (p. 424), and **Victoria and Albert Museum** (p. 430), but there are many more great ones.

- **OLYMPIC FEVER.** Brush up on your modern pentathletes and synchronized swimmers (or just your regulation superstars), as the **Olympics** come to London in 2012 (p. 460).

- **OH MY, WHAT A PIE!** For the best cheap pie in London, we recommend the punny **Pie Minister** (p. 442).

orientation

To say that London is a sizeable city is to adopt the infamous British tendency for understatement. London is bloody massive. The central knot of museums, historical sights, shopping, and entertainment stretches along the Thames from the City of London (yes, a city within a city) through the West End to Westminster. The luxurious residential neighborhoods of Chelsea, Kensington, Notting Hill, and Marylebone lie to the north and west. Add in the university neighborhood of Bloomsbury and the culturally prominent South Bank and you've got the whole of central London in a nice package.

Now for the fun bits. With sky-high rents in the city center, the beating heart of city life has migrated a few miles out from the center. North London is the most upscale, East London is home to the city's hip and artsy, and South and West London are defined by their large immigrant communities (and great ethnic cuisine).

Navigating the sprawl of London can be incredibly frustrating. Fortunately, the ever-obliging Brits plaster the city center with maps, which can be found reliably at bus stops. If you don't want to leave your direction to chance, you can always out shell out for the all-knowing **A-Z** city map.

THE CITY OF LONDON

One of the oldest and most historic parts of London, the City of London, often referred to as "the City," is home to many of London's finest (and most crowded) tourist attractions as well as the city's financial center. The City holds many of London's Roman artifacts, including vestiges of the ancient London Wall. Next to these relics, the spires of famous churches are juxtaposed with the towers of powerful insurance companies. Many old buildings are marked by two of the city's most devastating tragedies: the Great Fire of 1666 (which destroyed 80% of the city in five days) and the German Blitz during WWII. The fantastic architecture that either survived these calamities or replaced the less fortunate buildings now stands as a monument to London's resilient spirit. As you head farther north, the City fades into **Farringdon** and **Clerkenwell,** which provide something of a buffer zone from East London. Here you'll

london

find a mix of the yuppie-gentrified City and the hipster-gentrified East; somehow, this turns out to be a magical combination, producing quirky pubs and terrific food.

THE WEST END

The West End is one of the largest, most exciting parts of London. Its twin hearts are **Soho** and **Covent Garden,** but the neighborhood encompasses the area between Bloomsbury and the Thames, from the edge of Hyde Park to the City of London. Within that expanse are some of the city's best public museums (such as the **National Gallery** and the **National Portrait Gallery**), world-famous theater, interesting restaurants, loads of shopping, and vibrant nightlife. You can find just about anything you're looking for here (except maybe a good curry—Indian culture is strangely absent in this part of London).

Soho, most easily accessible via ⊖**Tottenham Court Road,** is one of the hipper and seedier parts of London. Home to one of the city's most prominent GLBT communities, Soho bursts at the seams with nightlife for gay and straight clubgoers alike. By day, this area (particularly **Chinatown,** located off Gerrard St.) is known for its excellent restaurants. North of Soho, **Oxford Street** is the capital of London shopping streets, with department stores and cavernous flagships of major clothing chains. Smaller boutiques and many salons can also be found in this part of town. To the south and west, the buildings get fancier and the streets are quieter in regal neighborhoods like **St James's.** All in all, the West End feels like one of the most touristy parts of the city, but perhaps that's because it so conveniently encapsulates what London is (deservedly) famous for.

WESTMINSTER

Westminster lays claim to the remainder of London's most famous sights unclaimed by the City of London. Between **Westminster Abbey,** the **Houses of Parliament,** and **Buckingham Palace,** Westminster still feels like the seat of the royal empire. Aside from these sights, though, there isn't much to do here. Nearby ⊖Victoria is a transport hub, surrounded by fast-food restaurants and touristy pubs. South of Victoria lies **Pimlico,** a residential neighborhood offering a few accommodations, many of them on Belgrave Rd. This area is also home to some higher-quality places to eat and drink.

THE SOUTH BANK

This neighborhood is located in the south of Central London on, you guessed it, the south bank of the Thames. Populated with the renovated factories of yore, the South Bank has undergone a renaissance, reinforcing its status as a hub of London entertainment. This reputation didn't spring from nowhere: both the **Rose** and **Shakespeare's Globe Theatre** once stood here. Now, the **Southbank Centre** hosts classical music concerts, films, and more. There are also some of the best museums and galleries in London, including the famous **Tate Modern. Millennium Mile** stretches from the London Eye in the west eastward along the Thames, making for a beautiful walk, especially around sunset. More than just a cultural or aesthetic destination, the area around London Bridge and Borough is full of great pubs and restaurants with an eye on quality, perhaps thanks to the local **Borough Market.**

SOUTH KENSINGTON AND CHELSEA

Kensington and Chelsea—excuse us, the Royal Borough of Kensington and Chelsea—is quite possibly the poshest part of London. And it knows it. The winding avenues and tree-lined side streets are full of mansions, columned townhouses, leafy gardens, and even royal residences. You'll know you're in the right place if you find yourself surrounded by nice suits, pearls, and the smell of money. High-priced restaurants are found alongside swanky cocktail bars and plenty of grand pubs. The shopping is to die for, and the museums are the city's best—and most are free. This is a big neighborhood—its geography almost as intimidating as its prices—extending roughly from Hyde Park Corner south to the river, and west all the way to Earl's Court.

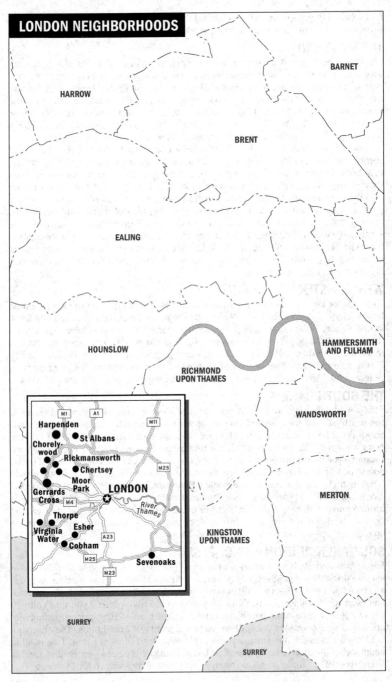

LONDON NEIGHBORHOODS

BARNET

HARROW

BRENT

EALING

HOUNSLOW

HAMMERSMITH
AND FULHAM

RICHMOND
UPON THAMES

WANDSWORTH

MERTON

KINGSTON
UPON THAMES

SURREY

SURREY

M1
A1
M11

Harpenden
St Albans

Chorely-
wood
Rickmansworth
Chertsey
M25

Moor
Park
LONDON
Gerrards
Cross
M4
River
Thames

Thorpe
Virginia
Water
Esher
A23
Cobham
M25
Sevenoaks
M23

london

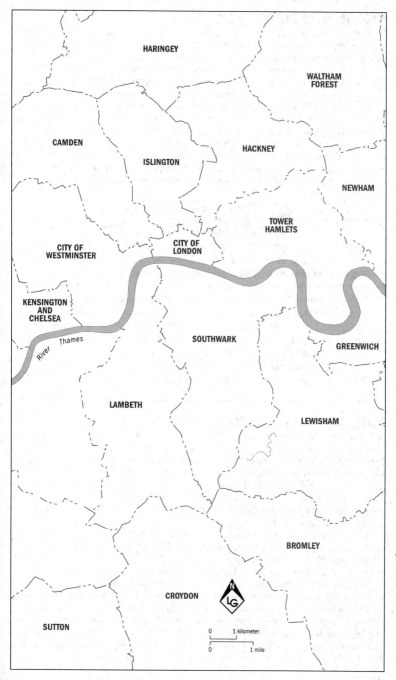

london overview map

HYDE PARK TO NOTTING HILL

Hyde Park is, we promise, actually a park. It's roughly rectangular with a Tube stop at pretty much every corner—**Marble Arch,** the incredibly unhelpfully named **Hyde Park Corner, High Street Kensington,** and **Queensway.** North of the park are a set of neighborhoods that get progressively nicer as you move west. Paddington, Edgware Rd., and Queensway mix fairly fancy houses on their back streets with main roads that have plenty of cheap ethnic eateries, souvenir shops, and stores of questionable legality that can unlock your phone, cash your checks, and wire your money across the world. Notting Hill has the mansions you would imagine, but popping out of the Tube at **Notting Hill Gate** may be a bit of a shock if you're expecting the set from a Julia Roberts movie—it's pretty much dull commercial real estate. Head slightly north, though, and you'll find the villas you were expecting. In the middle of that, **Portobello Road** has a market, antique stores, vintage clothing, and the kind of minimalist, hip cafes and restaurants that seem to appear anywhere you can get a secondhand prom dress or a pair of cowboy boots.

the old smoke

Paris is the City of Light. Rome is the Eternal City. London is the... um... sorry, what?

While other popular destinations proudly brand themselves and emboss glossy advertisements with catchy slogans, it's as difficult to discover London's nickname as it is to see the bottom of the Thames. On a related note, the term "The Old Smoke" is derived from London's notorious environmental issues. As commonplace and exasperating as the Cockney accent, industrialization and coal-burning caused air pollution, which in turn caused smog over the city. After the Great Smog of 1952, the government initiated efforts to clean up their act with the well-named Clean Air Act. Though the environmental outlook has altered, London's nickname hasn't yet. Probably because "The City Formerly Known as the Old Smoke" doesn't sound any better.

MARYLEBONE AND BLOOMSBURY

It doesn't get much more British than Marylebone—from the fact that Sherlock Holmes lived here to its mystifying pronunciation (it's *Mar*-leh-bone). Lush **Regent's Park** is surrounded by gleaming mansions, **Marylebone Lane** is lined with pubs, and the side streets are pocketed with clusters of Indian and Middle Eastern restaurants. The neighborhood stretches from Regent's Park south to Oxford St., and from Edgware Rd. east until it bleeds into Bloomsbury. While Marylebone is fun to poke around in, the prominence of fancy residential areas and spiffy office buildings means that good values here are hard to find.

Bloomsbury, on the other hand, is famous for its bohemian heritage. The namesake Bloomsbury Group included luminaries like Virginia Woolf, John Maynard Keynes, and E.M. Forster. Today, you can feel the continuation of all that cleverness emanating from the **British Library** and **University College London**—though creeping gentrification means there are few affordable garrets left for the burgeoning artist-intellectuals of today. Bloomsbury, centered on **Russell Square,** stretches east to King's Cross Rd., and is bounded on the north and south by Euston Rd. and High Holborn, respectively. The western part is now very high-end, while the eastern and northern bits retain more of the old student vibe. You can find some cheap pubs and restaurants throughout the streets surrounding the university, and the area is packed with good hostels, especially around **King's Cross.**

london

NORTH LONDON

North London is a sprawling expanse of fairly residential, but often quirky, neighborhoods. **Hampstead, Islington,** and **Camden Town** are the most popular draws. On the whole, north London is characterized by its gentrification, which has made the area safer without entirely depriving it of character. Hampstead provides pleasant dining and a proper small-town feel. Camden was once punk central, but it's now full of safety-pin-wearing 16-year-olds pretending that it still is. It also offers the glorious and meandering **Heath,** a must for all nature-lovers. Still worth a visit, Camden contains some underground culture and many upscale restaurants and boutiques. Islington is the easternmost part, quite pretty and residential but still with a bit of East London grit. Check out Upper St., which runs between ⊖Angel and ⊖Highbury and Islington, for great restaurants, bars, and shopping.

EAST LONDON

Once upon a time, East London (and especially the **East End**) was considered a den of poverty and crime due to poor dockworkers and waves of immigrants who settled there over the centuries. You can see traces of the neighborhood's gritty past in the winding old lanes and thriving curry houses of **Brick Lane,** but it has slowly evolved into one of the most interesting parts of the city. The converted warehouse galleries and cutting-edge exhibitions attest to its popularity with artists. The hipsters and students who flocked to the cheap rents and underground cool factor have made it a haven for exciting and alternative nightlife (centered on **Shoreditch** and **Old Street**). The presence of immigrant communities mean that it's packed to the gills with cheap ethnic cuisine, and a new Overground line has made it more accessible than ever.

SOUTH LONDON

South London has long been maligned as one of London's dodgier neighborhoods. While the area has enjoyed something of a renaissance in recent years, it's still not as safe as much of central London. **Clapham** is a good place to find pubs and restaurants full of young professionals. Clapham has also become a cultural hub as the home of the **Battersea Arts Centre,** renowned for its groundbreaking productions. **Brixton** is less quaint, but a bit more fun. Bible-thumpers preach the Apocalypse from convenience store pulpits, and purveyors of goods set up shop at the nearby Afro-Caribbean market, despite the overpowering smell of fish. Brixton is the place to come if you've started missing fast food, though some truly excellent restaurants peek out from between the fried-chicken stands. At night, it's a popular place to hear underground DJs and live reggae shows. The local Underground stations across the south of the city play classical music, thought by many to be a tactic for keeping young people from accumulating in the Tube, *Clockwork Orange*-style.

WEST LONDON

West London is one of the most shape-shifting parts of the city. **Shepherd's Bush** is a hub of ethnic life, evident in the varied restaurants lining Goldhawk Rd., culminating in the veritable World's Fair of Shepherd's Bush Market. Shepherd's Bush is also home to Westfield's, a 43-acre ode to consumerism that makes American strip malls look like rinky-dink corner stores. **Hammersmith,** the neighborhood to the south of Shepherd's Bush, is quieter and more gentrified. It feels more like a seaside resort than London—once you get out of the thriving area surrounding the Tube station, that is. Farther south and west are **Kew** and **Richmond,** which have the luscious greenery of Kew Gardens and Hampton Court, two easily accessible places to escape the urban jungle.

orientation

accommodations

London is an infamously expensive city, and its accommodations are no exception. Standard London hotels almost always come with astronomical price tags (for an exception, see East London's **Hoxton**). But there are many excellent hostels, especially in Earl's Court, the area north of Hyde Park, and Bloomsbury (extra emphasis on Bloomsbury). In most neighborhoods, you can choose between party hostels with late-night bars and organized pub crawls, and quieter ones with more sedate guests. Travelers looking for long-term lodgings should look into renting college dorms during the summer. You can also find short-term rentals online (www.gumtree.com is a good place to start), which can save you precious pounds. Keep in mind that many hostels also offer private rooms. For those unwilling to stay in a hostel, guesthouses and bed and breakfasts are much more reasonable. Many pubs also rent rooms on their upper floors. Though these smaller establishments still aren't exactly cheap, they tend to offer a good value for their high quality.

THE CITY OF LONDON

YHA ST PAUL'S — HOSTEL $

36 Carter Ln. — ☎0845 371 9012; www.yha.org.uk

We don't know how they managed to squeeze a budget hostel into the heart of the City, but somehow they did. This YHA outpost is housed in the former school for St. Paul's choir, a splendid old stone building just across from the cathedral. Rooms are clean and modern with useful amenities, like ensuite washbasins and desks. There's a lounge and dining area available, and although there's no kitchen, an on-site restaurant does serve meals. The staff organize events and tours of the city. Check the list of upcoming concerts on the blackboard by reception.

⇄ ⊖St. Paul's. Go right down New Change, turn at the cathedral onto Cannon St., then take a left onto Carter Ln. ℹ Breakfast available. Laundry facilities available. All dorms single-sex. Wi-Fi available in the lounge and some rooms; £1 per 20min., £5 per day., £9 per week. [$] 4- to 11-bed dorms £15-25; singles £20-35; doubles £41-74.

FOX AND ANCHOR — HOTEL $$$$

115 Charterhouse Sq. — ☎0845 347 0100; www.foxandanchor.com

The six rooms on top of this elegant pub are what a Victorian gentleman's bachelor pad must have looked like (minus the flat-screen TVs, of course). Larger rooms—the "Superior" ones and the suite—have old-fashioned bathtubs right in the bedroom, and all are done up with luxurious fabrics and beautiful prints of the London skyline. With all the amenities of a luxury hotel, but with infinitely more character, Fox and Anchor is pricey, but similar rooms can go for hundreds of pounds more in the City.

⇄ ⊖Barbican. Turn left onto Aldersgate St., left onto Charterhouse St,. then right onto Charterhouse Sq. ℹ Book at least a few weeks in advance for the weekend. Free Wi-Fi. [$] Deluxe rooms M-F £221, Sa-Su £137; Superior rooms £163-243; suite £243-327.

WESTMINSTER

👍 ASTOR'S VICTORIA

HOSTEL $

71 Belgrave Rd. ☎020 7834 3077

This branch of the Astor's family has all the chummy backpacker charm of the other locations, with the added benefit of recently refurbished rooms sporting new carpets and fresh paint. Even the larger dorms don't feel cramped, and those on the upper floors have wonderfully high ceilings. The staff goes out of their way to welcome guests, learning names and hosting pub crawls. Multiple common spaces give you the opportunity to make some friends of your own, too.

 # ⊖Victoria. Upon exiting the station, turn left onto Buckingham Palace Rd., and left onto Belgrave Rd. i Breakfast included. Female-only dorms available. Kitchen available until 10pm. Wi-Fi £1 per 40min., £5 per day. [$] 4- to 8-bed dorms £14-23; doubles £25-35.

VICTOR HOTEL

HOTEL $$$$

51 Belgrave Rd. ☎020 7592 9853; www.victorhotel.co.uk

It's no Mandarin Oriental, but, unlike many of the other townhouse hotels on Belgrave Rd., Victor has enough space for you and your suitcase to fit in the room at the same time. The rooms are basic, with limited decoration and simple furnishings, but they're clean, comfortable, and a good value for the area.

 # ⊖Victoria. Upon exiting the station, turn left onto Buckingham Palace Rd., and left onto Belgrave Rd. i Breakfast included. Free Wi-Fi. [$] Singles £65-85; doubles £85-150; triples £110-160.

THE SOUTH BANK

👍 ST. CHRISTOPHER'S VILLAGE

HOSTEL $

165 Borough High St. ☎020 7939 9710; www.st-christophers.co.uk

This proud party hostel is the perfect place to make camp if you want convenient access to the city center as well as a more local, authentic neighborhood feel. The rooms are remarkably spacious—even the 22-bed dorm has its bunks lining the walls so there is plenty of open, glossy wood floor. St. Christopher's has all the amenities, including a chill-out room with a TV and DVDs to borrow, plus an action-packed bar next door. The hostel hosts karaoke, dance parties, and a 👍**Big Lebowski** night every Thursday, complete with £2 White Russians and a bowling excursion. If you're looking for a bit more peace and quiet, you can stay in the smaller St. Christopher's Inn next door or the female-only Oasis.

 # ⊖London Bridge. Walk down Borough High St. with the bridge at your back. i Breakfast included. Laundry and luggage storage included. Wi-Fi £2 per hr. [$] 4- to 22-bed dorms £12-23.

THE STEAM ENGINE

HOSTEL $

41-42 Cosser St. ☎020 7928 0720; www.bestplaceinns.com

About as British as central London hostels get, the Steam Engine is perched on top of an old-fashioned pub, complete with faded pool table and garishly lit jukebox. Located down a small side street, the bar isn't particularly rowdy, and feels more like a rustic country establishment. The rooms upstairs have simple wooden bunks and not much else, though the beds certainly look comfortable. The downside is that the bunks have three beds, so perish the person who ends up sandwiched in the middle; the space is also probably not ideal for the very tall traveler. Guests get a variety of deals and after-hours access to the pub.

 # ⊖Lambeth North. Exit down Kennington Rd. and turn right onto Cosser St. i Breakfast included. Free Wi-Fi. [$] 9- and 12-bed dorms M-F £12-15, Sa-Su up to £27.

SOUTH KENSINGTON AND CHELSEA

This is not the place to come for budget accommodations. But while you can't walk a block without seeing a five-star luxury hotel, it is possible to find similar comfort at a much more affordable price.

ASTOR HYDE PARK

HOSTEL $

191 Queen's Gate ☎020 7581 0103; www.astorhostels.co.uk

The flagship of the Astor Hostels chain, the Hyde Park location is all high ceilings, comfort, and aged grandeur—relics of its first life as a Victorian mansion. Rooms on the upper floors have massive French windows, and others feature domed glass skylights. The large common room, self-catering kitchen, and dining area make great hangout spaces. The endearing young staff organizes events like pub quizzes and beer Olympics every night.

 # ⊖High St. Kensington. Turn right onto Kensington High St., then right onto Queen's Gate. i Breakfast included. Free Wi-Fi. Laundry available. $ Dorms £15-26.

YHA LONDON HOLLAND PARK

HOSTEL $

20 Holland Walk ☎020 7937 0748; www.yha.org.uk

A patchwork of three buildings (one of which is an old manor house), this is definitely not a typical hostel. The location at the rear of Holland Park makes it feel a bit like a park ranger's office. The tranquil garden, which features a fish-filled fountain and weird duck-like creatures, is particularly peaceful when there's a classical music concert in the park. The hostel is often crowded with school groups, but it still manages to be quieter than its competitors. The rooms are worn but well cleaned, with bunks stacked in Lego-like arrangements. The canteen serves breakfast and dinner, and there's also a kitchen available for guests' use.

 # ⊖High St. Kensington. Turn left onto Kensington High St., then right down Holland Walk in Holland Park. Look for signs for the hostel. i Use night gate at the rear after 10pm when the park closes. All rooms are single sex. Laundry available. Wi-Fi £1 per 20min., £3 per hr., £5 per day, £9 per week. $ 12- to 20-bed dorms £15-23. ⏰ 7-day max. stay.

smooth criminal

London's long history has left behind some pretty absurd laws that never got taken off the books. Here are some you should probably know, as breaking them is very doable. Disclaimer: Let's Go does not endorse violating laws, even the stupid ones.

- **POSTAGE TREASON.** Don't put a stamp upside-down if it's got a picture of the Queen on it, or you might find yourself charged with treason against the crown.
- **CATTLE CALAMITY.** Sorry to break it to you, but you're going to have to wait until the evening to herd your cattle through Piccadilly Circus. One law stipulates that you cannot drive cattle down a road between the hours of 10am and 7pm, unless you've received authorization from the Police Commissioner.
- **ARMOR OFF.** Since 1313, it has been illegal to enter the House of Commons in a full suit of armor. (You have to wonder what incident led to that one being implemented.)
- **SOCKS ON.** Don't dare showcase your carefree spirit by walking barefoot past Buckingham Palace. It's illegal to be sockless within 100 yards of the monarch. We hope Prince Philip gets an exemption.

HYDE PARK TO NOTTING HILL

Given how swanky Notting Hill is, it's actually pretty surprising how many decently priced accommodations you can find here. Around Paddington are scores of simple hotels, but the ones farther south toward Hyde Park tend to offer more quality for comparable prices and convenience. Many of these establishments are tucked away on leafy residential streets, perfect for pretending that you're neighbors with some of the poshest people in London.

ASTOR QUEST

HOSTEL $

45 Queensborough Terr. ☎020 7229 7782; www.astorhostels.com

Astor Quest's rooms are par for the course in hostel-land, though the cherry-red metal bunks add a touch of mod flavor and the windows let in plenty of light and air. Breakfast is included and served in a room by the large kitchen, which is freely available for use (and has a seemingly unlimited supply of bread and peanut butter). You also have the unique experience of dining under Sid Vicious's drugged-out gaze. Be sure to ask the 24hr. reception for deals on clubs.

Bayswater. Take a right onto Queensway, left onto Bayswater Rd., then left onto Queensborough Terr. ***i*** *Ages 18-35 only. Luggage storage included. Laundry facilities available. Wi-Fi £5 per day. 1 female-only room available.* [$] *Dorms £14-23; twins £25-35.*

EQUITY POINT HOSTEL

HOSTEL $$

100-102 Westbourne Terr. ☎020 7087 8001; www.equity-point.com

It's always tempting to stumble out of the train station into the first hostel you see, but if that stumble happens to take you to this hostel's door, then you should consider yourself very lucky indeed. Rooms are decorated in blocks of bright color, with rainbow stripes stretching across the hallways, making the whole place feel cheerful. There's a common room with TV and video games, as well as a bar.

Paddington. Make a right onto Praed St. and a right onto Westbourne Terr. ***i*** *Breakfast included. Wi-Fi available.* [$] *4- to 8-bed dorms £20-34; doubles £92-113; triples £102-114.*

THE PAVILION

HOTEL $$$

34-36 Sussex Gardens ☎020 7262 0905; www.pavilionhoteluk.com

All you really need to know about the Pavilion is that the most popular room is named "Honky Tonk Afro." Besides blaxploitation, other rooms have themes ranging from Middle Eastern casbah to Baroque drawing room. The whole building feels like a drug-enhanced dream of a Victorian townhouse, with intensely colored velvet and stacks of oil paintings in ornate frames. This is definitely a standout among the rows of ordinary hotels lining the road.

Paddington. Take a left onto Praed St., right onto London St., then a left onto Sussex Gardens. ***i*** *Continental breakfast included.* [$] *Small singles £60, large singles £85; doubles £100; triples £120; family rooms (quads) £130. 4% surcharge with credit card.*

HYDE PARK HOSTEL

HOSTEL $

2-6 Inverness Terr. ☎020 7727 9163; www.smartbackpackers.com

Right across from Hyde Park and surrounded by columned mansion entrances, this hostel will make you feel quite posh. Ten-bed dorms have high ceilings with intricate woodwork and lots of open space. While it doesn't seem to be a particularly convivial hostel, the price is excellent for the area.

Bayswater. Take a right onto Queensway, left onto Bayswater, and then a left onto Inverness Terr. ***i*** *16+. Wi-Fi £1 per hr. Lockers £1.50 per day. Linens included.* [$] *4- to 14-bed dorms £10-16.* *Reception 24hr. 2-week max. stay.*

accommodations

MARYLEBONE AND BLOOMSBURY

The northern part of this neighborhood, close to King's Cross, is packed with some of London's best hostels. Here, you can stay at a hostel where you can party all night without stepping outside your door, or somewhere that's more conducive to recovering from jet lag. Given the proximity to the station, there are also a number of nondescript hotels, though you're unlikely to find a good deal at any of them.

👍 CLINK 78 — HOSTEL $

78 King's Cross Rd. ☎020 7183 9400; www.clinkhostels.com

The name of this hostel is not the only cheeky nod to the fact that the building it inhabits was once a courthouse and jail; its expertly renovated interior takes that theme and runs with it. Two common rooms on the main floor (one for internet access, one for TV and chilling out) are former courtrooms. Some of the private rooms are capsule-like "cells," set in what were once prisoners' quarters, and are definitely not for the claustrophobic. The dorms are brightly painted and covered in mod stencils, giving the rooms more character than those in most hostels. In the larger dorms, though, the bunks are packed together like they're in a prison. Downstairs is a self-catering kitchen, lots of picnic-like tables, and a popular bar that hosts events every night, from beer pong to karaoke to live DJs.

➜ ⊖King's Cross St. Paincras. Make a left from the station down Euston Rd. Follow it as it turns into Pentonville Rd., and then make a right onto King's Cross Rd. ℹ Continental breakfast included. Luggage storage included. Laundry facilities available. Wi-Fi £1 per 30min., £5 per day, £15 per week. Female-only dorm available. [$] 4- to 16-bed dorms £10-27; singles, doubles, and triples £40-90.

👍 ASTORS MUSEUM HOSTEL — HOSTEL $

27 Montague St. ☎020 7580 5360; www.astorhostels.com

This is a true backpackers' hostel, quiet but centrally located (the name isn't kidding—it's directly across the street from the British Museum). The staff live on-site and seem to have all the perks you could want at their fingertips: a good song on the reception speakers, an organized pub-crawl, a discount on local sights, and themed parties once per week. Astors is welcoming, comfortable, and exciting all at once. The rooms are spacious and simple, the kitchen is open for guest use, and everything is cleaned at least once daily.

➜ ⊖Russell Sq. Go down Guilford toward Russell Sq., turn left into the square, and follow it around until you reach Montague St., then turn left. ℹ Ages 18-35 only. Continental breakfast included. Luggage storage included. Laundry facilities available. Wi-Fi 40min. free upon arrival, £5 per day, £8 per week. Book 2 weeks in advance, 3 weeks for weekends. Female-only dorm available. [$] 4- to 12-bed dorms £15-26; twins £60-80.

GENERATOR HOSTEL — HOSTEL $

37 Tavistock Pl. ☎020 7388 7666; www.generatorhostels.com

Upon waking up in the Generator Hostel after a night of revelry, you may wonder if you forgot to leave the club. To be fair, you don't even have to leave the building to indulge in debauchery—the downstairs bar is gigantic, has a DJ each night, and serves up every variation of Jagermeister you can think of. Theme parties are organized frequently (some with professional sponsors), and, with 900 beds, the hostel is a popular destination for bachelor and bachelorette parties. Actually want to get some sleep? The simple rooms lack the steel plates and neon lights of the common areas, but all have sinks and lockers. Massively popular and clearly well run, the hostel also has a canteen, travel shop, and cafe.

➜ ⊖Russell Sq. Go down Colonnade away from Russell Sq. and turn left onto Grenville St.; follow it onto Hunter St. and turn left onto Tavistock Pl. ℹ Breakfast included. Luggage storage included. Laundry available. Wi-Fi free for 1hr. Female-only dorms available. [$] 4-to 12-bed dorms £15-30; singles £55-60. Other private rooms £20-30 per person. Check for frequent online deals. 🕐 Bar open 6pm-2am or later. Happy hour 6-9pm.

CLINK 261 HOSTEL $

261-265 Gray's Inn Rd. ☎020 7833 9400; www.clinkhostels.com

The Clink 261 is the sister hostel of Clink 78, but with a more intimate, boutique-y feel and without a bar. If you dream of hostels where every night is movie night (where the film is picked by majority vote and watched from comfortable leather chairs), where cube chairs fill the entry, and where retro plastic coverings blanket every surface, then you've probably dreamed of Clink 261. Particularly notable is the large self-catering kitchen, with plenty of supplies and lots of room to hang out, though the beds themselves are packed together like sardines.

➡ ⊖King's Cross St. Pancras. Turn left onto Euston Rd. and follow it as it curves right into Gray's Inn Rd. ℹ Breakfast included. Luggage storage included. Laundry available. Wi-Fi £1 per 30min., £2 per 2hr. Female-only dorms available. $ Dorms £20-25; private rooms £50-75.

THE GEORGE HOTEL $$$

58-60 Cartwright Gardens ☎020 7387 8777; www.georgehotel.com

The rooms at The George are grandiose in space and furnishings, with a somewhat more inspired decorating scheme (interesting prints on the walls and luxurious bedspreads) than most inexpensive hotels. Tucked away from the main streets of busy Bloomsbury, the George is a quiet and cozy hotel that'll let you sleep, without keeping you too far from the action.

➡ ⊖Russell Sq. Go down Colonnade away from Russell Sq. and turn left onto Grenville St., follow it onto Hunter St., and turn left onto Cartwright Gardens. ℹ Full English breakfast included. Free Wi-Fi. $ Singles £59, with bath £79; doubles £79/97; triples £95/115; quads with bath £109. Discounts for stays longer than 5 nights.

NORTH LONDON

👍 PALMER'S LODGE SWISS COTTAGE HOSTEL $

40 College Crescent ☎020 7483 8470; www.palmerslodge.co.uk

Northwest London may feel like a random place to stay, but this location provides easy access to Hampstead Heath, and public transportation will bring you to the center of town in 10min. What's more, the hostel is consistently one of the highest-rated in London. It's easy to see why: dorms are spacious and feature linen curtains and carved wooden bunks reminiscent of a treehouse. The common spaces are plentiful and comfortable, and the staff is tremendously accommodating. Palmer's Lounge is located in a giant refurbished Victorian house that feels like the school in *X-Men*, except there are backpackers instead of mutants. The bar, with its enclosed terrace and squishy armchairs, is particularly inviting. All the dorms are single-sex.

➡ ⊖Swiss Cottage. Take exit 2 from the station, turn left onto Eton Ave., then right onto College Crescent. ℹ Breakfast included. 18+. Free Wi-Fi. $ Dorms £16-30; doubles from £35.

ST. CHRISTOPHER'S CAMDEN HOSTEL $

50 Camden High St. ☎020 7388 1012; www.st-christophers.co.uk

This outpost of the St. Christopher's hostel chain puts you in the heart of Camden Town, and all the good and bad that entails. The rooms may feel a touch boring (just metal bunks with little other decoration), but each dorm includes an ensuite bathroom. Downstairs is the usual attached pub, with ample drinks and meal specials.

➡ ⊖Camden Town. Turn left onto Camden High St. (walking away from the market). ℹ Breakfast included. Free Wi-Fi. $ Dorms £17-28.

EAST LONDON

👍 THE HOXTON HOTEL $$$

81 Great Eastern St. ☎020 7550 1000; www.hoxtonhotels.com

The Hoxton is a large, elegant hotel that would break the bank if it weren't for their incredible pricing structure. Every room is the same, so there's no confusion about what a "super-deluxe-luxury-magical-suite" entails, and each goes for the same price on a given day. If you book well in advance, you can save up to two-thirds off the price—plus, unlike many London establishments, their rates tend to go down on the weekends. Best of all: four times per year they have a sale where 500 rooms are sold for just £1. The rooms themselves are fantastic: great views, fluffy beds, sleek furniture, and plenty of amenities.

⇄ ⊖Old St. Veer right at the roundabout, go down Old St., and then turn right onto Great Eastern St. ℹ Breakfast included. 1hr. of free international landline calls per day. Free Wi-Fi. [$] Rooms £59-199, depending on when you book.

QUEEN MARY UNIVERSITY CAMPUS ACCOMMODATIONS DORM $$

Mile End Rd. ☎020 7882 8177; www.accommodation.qmul.ac.uk

This East London university opens its dorms to travelers during the summer, roughly from mid-June to mid-September. The rooms are arranged in six- to nine-person flats, and each room has access to a kitchen and living room. You can relive your college days in these simple rooms, with twin beds, standard wardrobes, and desks. The dorms are arranged in a "student village" with laundromat, restaurants, and a convenience store. For long stays, this is one of the best options in London. The location may seem a bit out of the way, but a short walk to the Tube station means you can be in the city center within 20min.

⇄ ⊖Mile End. Turn left down Mile End Rd. The campus will be across the canal, on your right. The accommodations office is at point 4 on the campus map, on the main road. ℹ Breakfast included with B and B prices. Flats cleaned weekly during longer stays. [$] B and B singles £42-49; twins £60-65. Weekly singles £154, with bath £175; additional night £25. Credit card only.

SOUTH LONDON

JOURNEYS LONDON BRIDGE HOSTEL HOSTEL $

204 Manor Pl. ☎020 7735 6581; www.visitjourneys.com

Pretty much the only budget accommodation in South London, this hostel is located in a fairly quiet area just a short distance from the Tube. Journeys has all of the usual hostel amenities, including a bar, common room, and kitchen. The nine- and 12-bed dorms all have three-bed bunks, but each comes with its own curtain and reading lamp. The rooms may feel a bit dark thanks to the subdued color scheme of the carpets and walls.

⇄ ⊖Kennington. Make a left onto Braganza St. and then a left onto Manor Pl. ℹ Breakfast included. Free Wi-Fi. Female-only dorms available. [$] Dorms £10-18.

WEST LONDON

THE MONKEYS IN THE TREES HOSTEL $

49 Becklow Rd. ☎020 8749 9197; www.monkeysinthetrees.co.uk

The Monkeys in the Trees may be a bit far from the city center, but immersing yourself in this residential neighborhood will give you a real feel for the city. Bright, cheery dorms are located above a classic pub. Guests have access to the bar and its garden as well as a TV lounge with movies and board games, plus a kitchen. The three-bed bunks are a bit of a squeeze, but each bed has its own curtain and reading light for a bit of privacy.

⇄ ⊖Shepherd's Bush Market. Cross Uxbridge Rd. and make a right, then a left onto Becklow Rd. It's about a 15min. walk. Alternatively, take bus #207 or 260 to Wormholt Rd. ℹ Breakfast included. Luggage storage included. Free Wi-Fi. [$] Dorms £13-20.

ST. CHRISTOPHER'S HAMMERSMITH HOSTEL $

28 Hammersmith Broadway ☎020 8748 5285; www.st-christophers.co.uk

St. Christopher's is truly on top of the action—the hostel sits over its own busy bar (where guests receive a 10% discount), which is itself right on top of the Hammersmith Tube station. The rooms retain many of the details of the venerable old building, like wooden floors, fireplaces, and elegant windows. The bathrooms, fortunately, are entirely modern. The staff here are always ready to organize events or give tips for a good night out.

🚏 ⊖Hammersmith. It's right above the Tube entrance on Hammersmith Broadway. ***i*** *Breakfast included. Wi-Fi £2 per hr. Female-only dorms available. Ⓢ Dorms £15-25.*

sights

From the time Londinium was a rainy outpost of ancient Rome to the days when it governed a quarter of the world, London has accumulated a few worthwhile sights. A little religion called Christianity came along and led to the elegant churches of Christopher Wren. Centuries of exploration around the world deposited a bounty of treasures into the British Museum. The monarchy's predilection for home improvement scattered palaces across the city. A thriving 20th-century art scene produced some of the best (and strangest) modern art you'll ever see. Don't worry—all this splendor is accessible to travelers on a budget, as most of the city's major museums are free. Trying to see a church? Look for service times, as you can frequently get in free by attending Eucharist or Evensong. Even if you can't afford to visit all of the sights individually, save up to buy a ticket to St. Paul's Golden Gallery—the view from the top is worth every penny.

Don't limit your experience to ticketed sights, either. London's history is everywhere. Whatever path you choose—whether you're strolling down the winding streets of Marylebone or stalking the curry houses of Brick Ln.—your exploration will be rewarded. There's no wrong turn. Unless you're on the Hampstead Heath and you hear a strange growling to your left. In that case, a left turn may be the wrong one.

something old, something blue

If you see a little blue plaque out of the corner of your eye, stop! These little signs mark the sites where famous Londoners have lived. Here are a few highlights:

If you wander the streets around Marylebone, you may come across one of the newest plaques at 34 Montague Sq. Though the plaque is dedicated to John Lennon and Yoko Ono, who had their first London home here, the property was originally bought by Ringo Starr and rented to both Paul McCartney and—sorry, George—Jimi Hendrix.

A short distance away, you can find Hendrix's other London home at 23 Brook St., which is physically connected to George Frederick Handel's place at number 25. Though Lennon's home is not open to the public, both Hendrix's and Handel's abodes have been combined to host the Handel House Museum. (☎020 7495 1685 🚏 ⊖Oxford Circus. Ⓢ £6, concessions £5, under 17 £2. ⏰ Open Tu-W 10am-6pm, Th 10am-8pm, F-Sa 10am-6pm, Su noon-6pm.)

If you're around Bloomsbury, don't miss the plaque dedicated to Charles Dickens at 48 Doughty St. You can even go inside and see his original manuscripts. (☎020 7405 2127 🚏 ⊖Russell Sq. or Farringdon. Ⓢ £7, concessions £5, under 10 free. ⏰ Open daily 10am-5pm.)

THE CITY OF LONDON

Many of London's most popular sights are found here, and they shouldn't be missed—even if you'll be surrounded by camera-dependent tourists with the same idea.

👍 SAINT PAUL'S CATHEDRAL — CHURCH

St. Paul's Churchyard ☎020 7246 8350; www.stpauls.co.uk

It's something of a challenge to enter St. Paul's Cathedral and not take the Lord's name in vain. The church is epically grandiose, whether it's the huge size, ornate ceilings, or glowing stained glass that attract your eyes. This is the fourth cathedral to stand on this site, the first dating back to 604 CE. The third incarnation was destroyed, like so much of London, in the Great Fire of 1666. Architect Christopher Wren rebuilt many of London's churches after the fire, but St. Paul's, consecrated in 1708, is his masterpiece. From the start, Wren fought to include the fantastic dome that is now visible throughout the city, but the Church of England was hesitant to include an architectural feature that was so characteristically Roman Catholic. Ultimately, Wren won. If you're able to pull your eyes away from the dome—one of the highest in the world—look out for the cathedral's other highlights: the terrifyingly huge memorial to the **Duke of Wellington** (on your left in the north aisle as you walk through the nave); William Holman Hunt's *The Light of the World* in the Middlesex Chapel (which is set aside for private prayer); Henry Moore's strikingly modern *Mother and Child* sculpture, and the memorial to American and British servicemen in WWII.

We know what you're really thinking, and, yes, you are allowed to climb to the top of the **dome.** After 257 dizzyingly tight wooden steps, visitors find themselves in the **Whispering Gallery,** a seating area around the inner ring of the dome where, under the right conditions, you can hear a whisper from the other side. Many people try this simultaneously, which makes standing at the rim of the dome feel a bit like one of the scarier whisper segments in *Lost,* but it's worth giving this acoustic novelty a try. The climb is greatly enhanced if you make the journey while a choir sings in the nave; the acoustics in the Whispering Gallery are incredible. After 376 steps, visitors can climb out onto the **Stone Gallery,** which is open-air, low-stress, and thoroughly enjoyable. Then it's another 152 steps to the **Golden Gallery,** which offers an incredible view over the city. During WWII, the army used this gallery to spot German planes up to 10 miles away. Once you've been to the top, descend beneath the cathedral to find a veritable who's who of famous Britons—including Horatio Nelson, Florence Nightingale, the Duke of Wellington, William Blake, Henry Moore, and Christopher Wren—buried in St. Paul's **crypt.** Wren's inconspicuous tomb (to the right of the OBE Chapel) is inscribed *"Lector, si monumentum requiris circumspice,"* meaning, "Reader, if you seek his monument, look around."

🚇 ⊖St. Paul's. Signs outside the station lead you to the cathedral. ℹ 1½hr. free guided tours at 10:45, 11:15am, 1:30, and 2pm. Briefer introductory tours run throughout the day. A handheld multimedia tour is included in the price of admission. [$] £14.50, concessions £13.50, children £5.50. ⏰ Open M-Sa 8:30am-4pm. You can get in for free (though you'll have limited access) during church services. Matins M-Sa 7:30am. Eucharist M-Sa 8am and 12:30pm; Su 8, 11am, and 6pm. Evensong M-Sa 5pm, Su 3:15pm. Free organ recitals Su 4:45-5:15pm. Service times subject to change; check the website or the signs outside the cathedral.

👍 THE TEMPLE — HISTORICAL SITE

Between Essex St. and Temple Ave. ☎020 7427 4820

The Temple is a stunning complex of medieval, Elizabethan, and Victorian buildings, first established by the Knights Templar in 1185 as the English seat for the order (and catapulted into stardom by *The Da Vinci Code*). After the Knights were disbanded at the beginning of the 14th century, the buildings were leased to lawyers, and the site is now devoted to two of London's Inns of Court, legal and parliamentary offices, and training grounds for baby lawyers. The gardens, medieval church, and Middle Temple Hall are occasionally open to the public. Middle Temple Hall (www.middletemple.org.uk) is an excellent example of Elizabethan architecture with its beautiful double hammer beam roof. Originally used as a stable, it is now famous for hosting the premiere of Shakespeare's **Twelfth Night** in 1602. The large gardens are perfectly manicured with lush shrubberies and provide a handy spot for quiet reflection. The church (www.templechurch.com) has phenomenal stained glass windows and a grand vaulted ceiling. Opening hours for the various sites are erratic, but even when things are closed, the labyrinthine paths around the Temple's many buildings are well worth the visit.

Temple. Go to the Victoria Embankment, turn left, and turn left again at Temple Ln. i Book 1hr. tours in advance. You can book to stay for lunch if you're appropriately dressed. $ Church and tours free. Middle Temple Hall open M-F 10am-noon and 3-4pm, except when in use. Hours for church vary, but are posted outside. Services Oct-July Su 11:15am. Organ recitals Oct-July W 1:15-1:45pm. Tours Oct-July Tu-F 11am.

MUSEUM OF LONDON — MUSEUM

150 London Wall ☎020 7001 9844; www.museumoflondon.org.uk

The Museum of London is an exhaustive celebration of the city, tracing its history from the pre-Roman days to the present through timelines, reconstructions, and artifacts. The fascinating pieces of history on display include a replica of a London Saxon house from the mid-11th century, a beautiful model of the original St. Paul's Cathedral, a taxi from 1908, and Beatlemania paraphernalia. Relatively compact for its scope, the Museum of London gives you a sense for the city's development and how it grew into the international metropolis that you see today.

St. Paul's. Go up St. Martins and Aldersgate. $ Free. Open M-F 10am-6pm. 45min. tours at 11am, noon, 3, and 4pm.

COURTAULD GALLERY — MUSEUM

Somerset House, Strand ☎020 7872 0220; www.courtauld.ac.uk

Courtauld Gallery is a very small gallery in a very large house. The famous **KGB** double agent, Anthony Blunt, was director of this gallery for nearly 30 years. The collection includes medieval and Renaissance art from the likes of Botticelli and Rubens, but it's most renowned for its delightful Impressionist and post-Impressionist collection, featuring paintings by Degas, Monet, Manet (including **A Bar at the Folies-Bergère**), Seurat, and van Gogh. Upstairs, you'll find works by Cezanne, Pissarro, Matisse, and Kandinsky.

Temple. Turn right onto Temple Pl., left onto Arundel St., then left onto Strand. $ £6, concessions £4.50. Free on M 10am-2pm. Open daily 10am-6pm.

TOWER BRIDGE — BRIDGE

☎020 7403 3761; www.towerbridge.org.uk

Erected between 1886 and 1894, Tower Bridge was built when London Bridge became too crowded—and, perhaps, as a little insurance in case the bridge they'd been singing about really did fall down. Unlike London Bridge, Tower Bridge does not disappoint on the aesthetic front. It's a bascule bridge, meaning that you might get to see it rise—check the bridge lift times online if you don't want to leave it to chance. The exhibition you can pay to get into is enjoyable, but might not be for those afraid of heights. Hear fun facts and enchanting anecdotes, like the story of a 1952 double-decker bus that accidentally jumped the bridge while it was rising—clearly the driver never heard the phrase "mind the gap." Tower Bridge is less of a tourist trap than the Tower of London, though you can skip the ticket price and just enjoy its stunning architecture for free.

Tower Hill. Follow signs to Tower Bridge. $ £8, concessions £5.60, ages 5-15 £3.40, under 5 free. Open daily Apr-Sept 10am-6:30pm; Oct-Mar 9:30am-6pm. Last entry 1hr. before close.

TOWER OF LONDON HISTORICAL SITE

Between Tower Hill and the Thames ☎0844 482 7777; www.hrp.org.uk/toweroflondon

In its 1000-year history, the Tower of London has been a fortress, a royal palace, a prison, a zoo, a mint, the site of the first royal observatory, and, now, a tourist trap. If tourists were an invading army in the days of William the Conqueror, he would have surrendered instantly. Unusually dressed men and women, known as "Beefeaters," guard and live in the tower as well as give guided tours. Despite its name, there are actually multiple towers in the complex, each with its own myths and anecdotes. **Wakefield Tower** is near the home of six famous ravens—legend claims that if they fly away the white tower will crumble and disaster will befall the monarchy. The **Bloody Tower,** built in 1225, is allegedly where Richard III had the young King Edward V and his brother Richard ("The Princes in the Tower") murdered—what is thought to be their remains were found under a staircase two centuries later. The **White Tower,** built by William the Conqueror in 1078, is the oldest part of the Tower. It was once a royal palace: the top floor was reserved for kings and queens, the floor below housed the servants, and the basement served as a dungeon (and guest house!). The **Jewel House** boasts gemstones with enough glitter to induce a seizure, and it contains the royal family's famous **Crown Jewels.** The jewels are the focal point of many people's visits to the tower, so arrive as early as possible. Inside, you'll see the sovereign's scepter highlighted by a cross featuring the **First Star of Africa** (the largest perfect diamond in the world at 530.2 carats). Outside the Tower lies **Tower Hill,** the execution site where Anne Boleyn lost her head; her ghost is said to haunt the chapel of **St. Peter ad Vincula** (the Tower's chapel), where she's also buried. The last executions to take place here were of prisoners convicted of espionage during WWII.

⇟ ⊖Tower Hill. ℹ Buy tickets at the Tube station or at the Welcome Center, as these places tend to be less crowded. $ £19.80, concessions £17.05, under 5 free. Audio tours £4, students £3. ⏰ Open Mar-Oct M 10am-5:30pm, Tu-Sa 9am-5:30pm, Su 10am-5:30pm; Nov-Feb M 10am-4:30pm, Tu-Sa 9am-5:30pm, Su 10am-4:30pm. Last entry Mar-Oct 5pm; Nov-Feb 4:30pm.

ST STEPHEN WALBROOK CHURCH

39 Walbrook ☎020 7626 9000; www.ststephenwalbrook.net

The marshmallow-like object sitting in the center of the room is actually Henry Moore's controversial idea of what an altar should look like. Rumored to have "the most perfectly proportioned interior in the world," St Stephen Walbrook, a Saxon church built in the seventh century, is yet another beautiful Christopher Wren construction. It's unusually square, with pews arranged in a circle around the aforementioned altar. Offsetting the white walls and large, arched windows is a magnificently carved dark wood pulpit. The church used to be bordered by a river, and the structure slips downward in a continuous battle against gravity. Visit toward the end of a summer day to bask in the light that floods through the glass windows.

⇟ ⊖Mansion House. Turn right onto Cannon St., then left onto Walbrook. $ Free. ⏰ Open M-F 10am-4pm. Organ recitals F 12:30pm. Eucharist M 1pm.

CLOCKMAKERS' MUSEUM MUSEUM

Inside Guildhall Library off Aldermanbury ☎020 7332 1868

The Clockmakers' Museum is sort of like the interior of Doc Brown's house from *Back to the Future,* except with more clocks. Each clock, watch, sundial, and chronometer from the 500-year history of clocks is explained in this one-room museum. For those less inclined to horological technology, the museum has famous watches and clocks, including some of the first mass-produced watches and the watch worn by Sir Edmund Hillary during his 1953 climb of Mount Everest. The museum is worth a brief visit, if only to hear the sound of so many clocks ticking in unison.

⇟ ⊖St. Paul's. Go down Cheapside with your back to St. Paul's Cathedral. Turn left onto King St., left onto Gresham, and right onto Aldermanbury. Enter through the library. $ Free. ⏰ Open M-Sa 9:30am-4:45pm.

THE WEST END

Thanks to the street performers around Convent Garden, enough theaters to make drama-school kids think acting is a promising career, and a generally bustling atmosphere, the West End is something of a sight in itself. The area around **Trafalgar Square** is home to some of the city's most interesting museums and monuments.

NATIONAL GALLERY — MUSEUM

Trafalgar Sq. ☎020 7747 2885; www.nationalgallery.org.uk

The National Gallery presides over Trafalgar Sq. and is perhaps even more impressive than the square itself. Founded in 1824 and moved to its current location in 1838, the gallery encompasses all the major traditions of Western European art from the Middle Ages (housed in the **Sainsbury Wing**) to the early 20th century. Works are arranged chronologically and then geographically, so if you're fascinated by 16th-century Dutch painting, you can make a beeline for Room Five. Some rooms are packed floor to ceiling with Italian masterpieces by Michelangelo and Raphael; if you really want to piss people off, ask them where they're keeping the Donatellos. We have to put in a plug for Room 30, a must-see for any aspiring mustache-growers: see Velázquez's 1656 *Philip IV of Spain* for curl, and Juan Bautista del Mazo's *Don Adrián Pulido Pareja* for volume and under-lip work. When all of the stern portraits, religious iconography, and pastoral allegories get to be too much, move on to the gallery of 18th- to early 20th-century paintings. Here you'll find a number of British artists, including Turner, plus plenty of works by Frenchmen like Manet, Monet, and Cézanne. Many people think that the best way to view an Impressionist work is to squint and back away from it. We share this not to advise you, but rather to explain why people keep crashing into you. If knowing where you are is important to you, don't forget to pick up a map at the entrance (£1)—the museum is just one floor, but it's one huge floor.

*⊖Charing Cross. $ Free. Special exhibits around £10. Audio tours £3.50, students £2.50. ⏰ Open M-Th 10am-6pm, F 10am-9pm, Sa-Su 10am-6pm. 1hr. guided tours daily at 11:30am and 2:30pm; meet at Sainsbury Wing info desk. Additional tour F at 7pm. 10min. talks on individual paintings M-Tu 4pm, F-Su 4pm.*

NATIONAL PORTRAIT GALLERY — MUSEUM

St. Martin's Pl. ☎020 7306 0055; www.npg.org.uk

In London, it's easy to get lost in history. You have to remember names of monarchs, gossip stars, the insanely wealthy, the star-crossed lovers—and we haven't even talked about those outside of the royal family. The National Portrait Gallery is less about the art than it is about the subjects of the portraits and what they meant for England. The gallery presents excellent short histories of the individuals and organizes the rooms to trace British history through its greatest assets: its women and men. It also answers the all-consuming question: which of your favorite British royals, politicians, writers, and scientists were total hotties? There are loads of kings, queens, and plenty of Churchill and other Prime Ministers in the imposing **Statesmen's Gallery,** but there are also rooms devoted to thinkers and popular figures. You can see poets Byron (hottie) and Andrew Marvell (nottie—no wonder he resorted to poetry for seduction); scientists like Charles Darwin and Michael Faraday (no, not the dude from *Lost*); and novelists like Jane Austen and James Joyce. As you get to the contemporary portraits, things get a little bit more experimental and the faces can be less easy to identify. These modern portraits include Marc Quinn's *Self*, much of which is made from the artist's frozen blood (talk about suffering for your art). For the less squeamish, there are photographs of fan favorites like Princes William and Harry, George Michael, and Iman. Each summer, the gallery hosts selections from the BP Portrait Award contest, showing the best international portraits of the past year.

✠ ✆Charing Cross. Walk down Strand to Trafalgar Sq. and turn right. Ⓢ Free. Small special exhibits £5, large exhibitions £10. Audio tours £3. 🕐 Open M-W 10am-6pm, Th-F 10am-9pm, Sa-Su 10am-6pm. Guided tours Tu 3pm, Th 1:15pm, Sa-Su 3pm. Open until 10pm on select nights; check website for details.

TRAFALGAR SQUARE
HISTORICAL SITE

Trafalgar Sq. is one of the many places in central London where oodles of people are packed amid gorgeous architecture. This is arguably the most famous of all those places, and it has some of the best architecture and seemingly almost all of the people. Designed by Sir Charles Barry, who also designed the Houses of Parliament, Trafalgar Sq. commemorates **Admiral Horatio Nelson.** The **National Gallery** stands to the north of the square, and the rest is lined with grand buildings belonging to various international institutions. The central space serves as a meeting point, demonstration area, and the home of an annual Christmas tree (donated by Norway in thanks for service given in WWII). A sandstone statue of Nelson tops the square's most notable feature: the 50m tall **Nelson's Column.** It's a pretty impressive sight, especially against the backdrop of **St Martin-in-the-Fields's** spires at the edge of the plaza. The four panels at the column's base celebrate Nelson's naval victories at St. Vincent (1797), the Nile (1798), Copenhagen (1801), and Trafalgar (1805). A bronze lion rests on each corner of the block supporting the column—children climb all over them and occasionally dangle from their mouths. There are two beautiful fountains in the square, each with teal statues of strange merpeople holding fish. Perhaps even more jarring, the water is an unnatural shade of aquamarine—so blue that it makes the Thames look black, instead of just sickly green.

✠ ✆Charing Cross.

ST MARTIN-IN-THE-FIELDS
CHURCH

Trafalgar Sq. ☎020 7766 1100; www.smitf.org

In the 16th century, Henry VIII significantly renovated the medieval version of this church to keep plague victims away from his palace. The building's current incarnation is a Neoclassical marvel, with a large columned terrace and a beautifully carved arched ceiling. The architecture was originally panned, but it went on to inspire the design of many early American churches. St Martin's is the parish church of the royal family, but it's best known for its strong musical tradition. Every Monday, Tuesday, and Friday at 1pm, the church holds a 45min. "lunchtime concert," a classical recital from students at musical academies and colleges. In the evening, more renowned artists perform in the beautiful space.

✠ ✆Charing Cross. It's on the eastside of Trafalgar Sq. *i* Jazz concerts W 8pm. Ⓢ Free. Lunchtime concerts £3.50 suggested donation. Reserved ticket for jazz £9, unreserved £5.50. 🕐 Open M-Tu 8:30am-1pm and 2-6pm, W 8:30am-1:15pm and 2-5pm, Th 8:30am-1:15pm and 2-6pm, F 8:30am-1pm and 2-6pm, Sa 9:30am-6pm, Su 3:30-5pm. Open at other times for services and concerts.

WESTMINSTER

sights

WESTMINSTER ABBEY
CHURCH, HISTORICAL SITE

Off Parliament Sq. ☎020 7222 5152; www.westminster-abbey.org

London has no shortage of lovely churches steeped in history. But Westminster Abbey stands out as the best combination of historical importance, breathtaking beauty, and a still-vibrant community of worshippers. The kernel (the Romanesque-style center of the church) was built in the mid-11th century by Edward the Confessor. You can trace the development of English architecture through the later additions, from the Gothic nave (the highest in England) to the Lady Chapel, built in the Late English Gothic style, with a ceiling that looks like carved lace. While the vaulted ceilings and glowing stained glass might tempt you to keep your neck craned upward, don't miss the exquisite Cosmati pavement in front of the altar. At its center is the spot where every English sovereign since William the Conqueror has been crowned.

While the Abbey is undeniably a tourist attraction (and an expensive one at that), it is still, first and foremost, a functioning house of worship. Nearly all important British church ceremonies take place here, including last year's royal wedding. Pilgrims come here from across the world, and its daily services are packed with people taking in the atmosphere of a place that's been the scene of prayer for over 1000 years. We recommend visiting for Evensong—not only is it free and less crowded, but seeing the Abbey in action with the sound of the choir is an experience you won't soon forget.

✣ ⊖*Westminster. Walk away from the river. Parliament Sq. and the Abbey will be on your left.* ***i*** *The Abbey vergers offer 1½hr. tours.* Ⓢ *£16, students and seniors £13, ages 11-18 £6, under 11 free. Verger-led tours £3.* Ⓧ *Open M-Tu 9:30am-3:30pm, W 9:30am-6pm, Th-Sa 9:30am-3:30pm. Verger-led tours M-F 10, 10:30, 11am, 2 and 2:30pm; Sa 10, 10:30, and 11am. Services: M-F Matins 7:30am, Holy Communion 8am and 12:30pm, choral Evensong 5pm (spoken on W); Sa 8am Morning Prayer, 9am Holy Communion, 3pm choral Evensong (June-Sept 5pm); Su 8am Holy Communion, 10am Choral Matins, 11:15am Sung Eucharist, 3pm Choral Evensong, 5:45pm organ recital, 6:30pm Evening Prayer.*

▨ CHURCHILL MUSEUM AND CABINET WAR ROOMS   MUSEUM, HISTORICAL SITE
Clive Steps, King Charles St.   ☎020 7930 6961; www.iwm.org.uk/cabinet

The Cabinet War Rooms opened in 1939, just a few days before the outbreak of WWII. They were used as a shelter for important government officers, and Winston Churchill spent almost every day of the war in the windowless, airless subterranean rooms, recreated vividly in this museum. The rooms are tense with wartime anxiety, and the map room, with lights that were never turned off during the war's six years, still burn brightly. Connected to the Cabinet War Rooms is the Churchill Museum. Visitors can step on sensors to hear excerpts from some of his most famous speeches and watch videos detailing the highs and lows of his career. Also on display are his alcohol habits, which included drinks with every meal, and his signature "romper," better known as a onesie. The interactive, touchscreen "lifeline" is phenomenally detailed; be sure to touch his 90th birthday and August 6th, 1945, but be prepared to draw stares from the other museum patrons. It should be noted that, while a lock of Churchill's hair is on display, the heavy security surrounding it makes it impossible to use a voodoo doll or potion to bring the great man back to life.

✣ ⊖*Westminster. Turn right down Parliament St., and left onto King Charles St.* Ⓢ *£16, students and seniors £13, disabled £8, under 16 free.* Ⓧ *Open daily 9:30am-6pm. Last entry 5pm.*

HOUSES OF PARLIAMENT   HISTORICAL SITE
Westminster Palace   www.parliament.uk

The iconic Palace of Westminster is the home of the United Kingdom's two houses of Parliament: the House of Lords and the House of Commons. This super-pointy Gothic structure was built in the mid-19th century, after a fire consumed the earlier complex of buildings that stood on this spot (more recent renovations repaired bomb damage from the Blitz). It's hard to do justice to the sheer majesty of this complex of three towers, 1000 rooms, and three miles of corridor. For the best view of the entire structure, head to the south bank of the Thames—especially at dusk, when the palace is lit up. Besides holding the chambers where the two Houses hold their debates, the Palace is the location of countless Parliamentary offices, committee chambers, and rooms for ceremonial functions (notably Westminster Hall, a relic from the 11th century). The Houses are steeped in countless rumors, stories, and strange practices. Some of our favorites include the tradition that the Yeomen of the Guard check the basement of the Palace whenever Parliament opens (ever since Guy Fawkes's Gunpowder Plot of 1605), and that, though eating and drinking are prohibited in the Commons, the Chancellor of the Exchequer may have an alcoholic drink in hand when giving the budget speech (Disraeli went with brandy and water, while Gladstone preferred sherry with a beaten egg).

There are a number of ways members of the public can visit the Houses of Parliament. Debates in both Houses are generally open to the public; visitors can queue for admission during sitting times, though entrance is not guaranteed. Nor is it guaranteed that anything interesting will be going on—we recommend checking the website to see what bills are on the table. Question Times are livelier, though tickets may only be reserved by UK residents, so foreign visitors can only take the rare leftover spaces. Visitors can also watch committee meetings on more specific topics, like Science and Technology or Foreign Affairs; the weekly schedule of these sessions is posted on the website as well. Finally, tours of the Houses are given throughout the year, but foreign visitors can only attend on Saturdays and during the Summer Recess (August and September).

⊖Westminster. The public entrance is at Cromwell Green, on St. Margaret St., directly across from Westminster Abbey. $ Debates and committee sessions free. Tours £15, concessions £10, children £6. ⏰ When Parliament is in session, House of Commons open M-Tu 2:30-10:30pm, W 11:30am-7:30pm, Th 10:30am-6:30pm, sometimes F 9:30am-3pm; House of Lords open M-Tu 2:30-10pm, W 3-10pm, Th 11am-7:30pm, sometimes F 10am-close of business. Tours leave every 15min. Aug M-Tu 9:15am-4:30pm, W 1:15-4:30pm, Th 9:15-4:30pm; Sept M 9:15am-4:30pm, Tu-Th 1:15-4:30pm, F-Sa 9:15am-4:30pm; Oct-July Sa 9:15am-4:30pm.

for ben the bell tolls

Everybody knows about London's signature timekeeper, Big Ben. But while most people use the name to refer to the 316 ft. tall monster clock tower above the Palace of Westminster, it actually belongs to the huge bell inside of it. The most common theory about the name is that the bell was named for Sir Benjamin Hall, a civil engineer who oversaw the final reconstruction of the Houses of Parliament. Calling our friend Ben merely "big" is like suggesting that the Hulk could get a little cheesed off: the bell has a width of 8 ft. and clocks in at around 13.5 tons. We guess "Humongous Ben" just wouldn't have the same catchy alliteration.

BUCKINGHAM PALACE

PALACE, HISTORICAL SITE

The Mall

☎020 7766 7300; www.royalcollection.org.uk

Cushy though it is, Buckingham Palace wasn't originally built for the royals. George III bought it from the Duke of Buckingham which in 1761 for his wife, Queen Charlotte, who gave birth to 14 out of her 15 children here. The house was expanded by their son, George IV (the one who wasn't born here), who commissioned John Nash to transform the existing building into a palace. In 1837, Queen Victoria moved in, and it has remained a royal residence ever since.

The **Changing of the Guard** takes place here every day at 11:30am from April to late July, and then on alternate days throughout the rest of the year. Forget the dumb American movies where obnoxious tourists try to make the unflinching guards move; they are far enough away that tourists can do no more than whistle every time they move three feet and salute. The entire spectacle lasts 40min.; to see it, you should show up well before 11:30am and stand in front of the palace in view of the morning guards. The middle of the week is the least crowded time to watch.

The interior of the palace is, for the most part, closed to the public—we can't imagine the Queen would be pleased with tourists tramping through her tearoom. From late July to early October, though, the royals head to Scotland and the **State Rooms** are opened to the public. These rooms are used for formal occasions, so they're as sumptuous and royal as you could hope they'd be. They feature fine porcelain, furniture, paintings, and sculptures by famous artists like Rembrandt and Rubens. In addition to the permanent pieces, the rooms often exhibit treasures from the Royal Collection—jewels, Fabergé eggs, and Kate Middleton's wedding dress. The **Royal Mews,** open most of the year, functions as a museum, stable, riding school, and a working carriage house. The carriages are fantastic—especially the "Glass Coach," which carries royal brides to their weddings, and the four-ton Gold State Coach. Unfortunately, the magic pumpkin carriage used to escape from evil step-royals is only visible until midnight, but if you're in the Royal Mews past midnight, you have other problems. Finally, the **Queen's Gallery** is dedicated to temporary exhibitions of jaw-droppingly valuable items from the Royal Collection. Five rooms designed to look like the interior of the palace are filled with glorious artifacts that the Queen holds in trust for the nation. They feature everything from Dutch landscape paintings to photographs of Antarctic expeditions to Leonardo da Vinci's anatomical drawings.

⊖Victoria. Turn right onto Buckingham Palace Rd. and follow it to Buckingham Gate. ***i*** *Audio tour provided for State Rooms.* $ *State Rooms £18, students and seniors £16.50, ages 5-16 £10.25, under 5 free. Royal Mews £8.25/7.50/5.20; Queen's Gallery £9.25/8.50/4.65. Combined ticket to Royal Mews and Queen's Gallery £15.75/14.50/9. Royal Day Out ticket (access to all three) £32/29.25/18.20.* ⏰ *State Rooms open daily late July to Oct daily 9:30am-6:30pm. Last admission 4:15pm. Royal Mews open Apr-Oct daily 10am-5pm; Nov-Dec 22 10am-4pm; Feb-Mar M-Sa 10am-4pm. Last entry Apr-Oct 4:15pm; Nov-Dec 22 and Feb-Mar 3:15pm. Queen's Gallery open daily 10am-5:30pm. Last entry 4:30pm. Open daily late July-Oct.*

THE SOUTH BANK

With its warren of cobblestoned streets and picturesque views of the Tower and Tower Bridge, just strolling through the South Bank is an experience. Much of the neighborhood capitalizes on this feeling, with establishments like the London Dungeon and the Clink Prison Museum ready to take you back in time to the neighborhood's less savory past. And who can forget the **London Eye?** We're not sure if the view is worth £17 (just crane your neck at the window when your plane is landing), but it's certainly a staple of the London tourist experience.

TATE MODERN — MUSEUM, MODERN ART

53 Bankside — ☎020 7887 8008; www.tate.org.uk

It's hard to believe that you can see all this incredible art for free. Located in George Gilbert Scott's old Brutalist Bankside Power Station (the entrance hall is a magnificent example of grand industrial architecture), Tate Modern defies traditional methods, organizing itself thematically rather than chronologically. The permanent collection sits on two floors, with rotating special exhibits sandwiched in the middle. If you're searching for one work in particular, check out the computers on the fifth floor to scan through the entire collection. Level 3 houses the **Material Gestures** gallery, which focuses on post-war European and American art with gritty, textural works by Claude Monet, Francis Bacon, and Jackson Pollock. Sculptures by Giacometti can also be found here. **Poetry and Dream,** meanwhile, presents themes associated with Surrealism, including the fluid art of Dalí and Picasso. On Level 5, **Energy and Process** looks at Arte Povera, the movement from the 1970s in which everyday materials and natural laws were used to create art; other fancily named genres like post-minimalism and anti-form are also included. **States of Flux** focuses on Cubism and Futurism, among other important modern movements, and presents works by Roy Lichtenstein, Robert Frank, Andy Warhol, and Marcel Duchamp.

⊖Southwark. Turn left onto Blackfriars Rd., right onto Southwark St., left onto Sumner, and finally left onto Holland St. $ Free. Tickets for special exhibits vary; often around £15. Multimedia guide £4, concessions £3.50. ⏰ Open M-Th 10am-6pm, F-Sa 10am-10pm, Su 10am-6pm. Free guided tours of each permanent gallery 11am, noon, 2, and 3pm. 10min talks F and Sa 1pm.

IMPERIAL WAR MUSEUM
MUSEUM

Lambeth Rd. ☎020 7416 5000; www.iwm.org.uk

Housed in what was once the infamous Bedlam insane asylum, the Imperial War Museum is mad for history. The exhibits start out with two massive naval guns standing sentinel over the imposing building's entrance. The first room is cluttered with enough war-making machinery to make any general salivate. Highlights include a Polaris A3 Missile, the first submarine-launched missile, a full-size German V2 Rocket, and the shell of a "Little Boy," the type of atomic bomb detonated above Hiroshima. Luckily, the bomb is non-functional, but it's still disconcerting when kids whack the casing. The third floor houses a haunting, expansive Holocaust exhibition, which traces the catastrophic injustice of WWII Nazi atrocities with cartographic precision, its miles of film exploring everything from the rhetoric of the Nazi party to the history of anti-Semitism. If this subject matter is too light for your fancy, take solace in the Crimes Against Humanity video exhibition one floor down. The first floor houses the exciting, if sensational, "Secret War" exhibit of WWII spy gadgetry, which provides a brief history of MI5 and the Special Operations Executive. Art nuts will enjoy the museum's unique art collection, called "Breakthrough." The ground floor is devoted to the World Wars, with artifacts, models, videos, and the popular Blitz Experience and Trench Experience exhibits that recreate the feeling of hiding during an air raid and living in the trenches. Also down here is a section on post-1945 conflicts, sure to make you feel chipper about the state of the world.

⊖Lambeth North. Exit the station and walk down Kennington Rd., left onto Lambeth Rd. $ Free. Special exhibits £6, students £5. Multimedia guides £4.50. ⏰ Open daily 10am-6pm. The Blitz Experience daily schedule is downstairs; it lasts around 10min.

DESIGN MUSEUM
MUSEUM

Shad Thames ☎020 7940 8790; www.designmuseum.org

There's something quietly inspirational about this museum, in that it's full of objects that have been designed to make everyday life a little bit prettier, easier, or more fun. The museum doesn't house a permanent collection but rather fills its two floors with rotating exhibits. These tend to focus on things like retrospectives of particular designer's work or collections of the year's most innovative designs from around the world. If you find the incessant parade of paintings and sculptures at other museums a bit boring, come here to find collections of posters, bikes, chairs, video games, and fashion. The galleries themselves are, of course, also impeccably designed in gleaming whites to offset the bright and quirky pieces.

⊖Tower Hill. Cross Tower Bridge. Turn left onto Queen Elizabeth St., then left onto Shad Thames. $ £11, concessions £10, students £7. ⏰ Open daily 10am-5:45pm. Last entry 5:15pm.

SHAKESPEARE'S GLOBE
THEATER, HISTORICAL SITE

21 New Globe Walk ☎020 7902 1500; www.shakespearesglobe.com

The original Globe Theatre burned down during a performance of *Henry VIII* in 1613—whose idea was it to fire a real cannon toward a thatched roof, anyway? Shakespeare's Globe is a recreation of the unique open-air theater, with numerous exhibits and a tour on the history of Shakespeare and London theater. Though short on actual artifacts, the historical overview is fascinating and well designed, and brings to life the bustle and debauchery of the 16th-century South

Bank. You'll leave here wondering how the area looked back in the days when bear-baiting was people's idea of a good time. Special booths allow visitors to speak lines with automated casts, and others enable visitors to listen to iconic Shakespearean monologues read by famous actors; check out the one devoted to *Hamlet* to see if you prefer Kenneth Branagh's or Peter O'Toole's rendition of "To be or not to be..." For information on productions, see **Arts and Culture.** Tours of the nearby Rose, an excavated archaeological site of an earlier theater, are also available.

 # ⊖Southwark. Turn left onto Blackfriars Rd., right onto Southwark St., left onto Great Guildford, right onto Park St., left onto Emerson St. The entrance faces the river, around the corner from the main entrance to the theater. $ Exhibition and Globe tour £11.50, students and seniors £10. Exhibition and Rose tour £9/7.50. ⏰ Exhibition open daily 10am-5pm. Globe tours Apr-Oct 9am-noon. Rose tours Apr-Oct noon-5pm.

SOUTH KENSINGTON AND CHELSEA

VICTORIA AND ALBERT MUSEUM

MUSEUM

Cromwell Rd. ☎020 7942 2000; www.vam.ac.uk

The V and A is one of the most all-encompassing museums out there, with a truly memorable collection of beautiful things from across time and space. Founded in 1852 to promote different design ideas to the British public, the museum has examples of styles from around the world. Unlike many museums that feature such a global collection, the V and A is as much about the making of things as it is about the artifacts themselves. The Asia gallery features everything from ornate, gold Buddhist shrines to traditional suits of armor; especially popular is the beautiful Iranian Ardabil Carpet (only lit for 10min. per hr.). The Europe gallery features the enormous (11m by 10.5m) Gothic Revival Hereford Screen that depicts Christ's Ascension, while the British galleries showcase the ever-popular Great Bed of Ware, a 16th-century bed big enough to sleep 15 people. The stained-glass collection on the third floor is another highlight. Those looking for education on the arts should visit the Lecture Theatre or the famous National Art Library, which houses some of Charles Dickens's manuscripts and Leonardo da Vinci's sketches. When you enter the main rotunda, don't miss the Rotunda Chandelier by Dale Chihuly right above you.

 # ⊖South Kensington. Turn right onto Thurloe Pl. and left onto Exhibition Rd. The museum is to the right across Cromwell Rd. $ Free. Special exhibitions generally £6-10. ⏰ Open M-Th 10am-5:45pm, F 10am-10pm, Sa-Su 10am-5:45pm. National Art Library open Tu-Th 10am-5:30pm, F 10am-6:30pm, Sa 10am-5:30pm. Free daily tours available; check screens at entrances for times.

coming up roses

Every spring, central London hosts the Chelsea Flower Show, one of the most famous gardening shows in the world. It's impressive even in the likely event that plants aren't really your thing. Stop by to smell the roses in one of the romantic garden pavilions or venture through a tropical wonderland in an expansive rainforest of trumpet trees, yerba mate, and sweet potato plants. The show usually takes place in the last week of May, and you can check the Royal Horticultural Society's website (www.rhs.org.uk) for tickets.

SAATCHI ART GALLERY

ART GALLERY

Duke of York Sq. ☎020 7811 3085; www.saatchigallery.co.uk

It's rare to find a free gallery of this caliber. The rooms are cavernous and bright, providing ample space for each installation. The gallery focuses on contemporary art from Charles Saatchi's collection. Check out the shop, where many of the works are condensed into pocket-sized forms. There are a few shows every year, with pieces like paintings, sculptures, LED light constructions, and frightening plaster people hunched in corners. Most rooms only have one or two pieces, giving you plenty of space to roam and observe the weird art from all angles—because you know the disaffected art students who work as security guards will judge you if you spent less than 10min. staring at each piece.

*⊖Sloane Sq. Go straight out of the Tube and continue onto King's Rd. The square is on the left. $ Free as the wind. ⏰ Open daily 10am-5:45pm.*

ST MARY ABBOTS

CHURCH

High St. Kensington ☎020 7937 5136; www.stmaryabbotschurch.org

This gorgeous and silent church sits on a site where Christians have worshipped for 1000 years. It's quite a shock to step off the busy High St. into its stony calm. Designed in 1873 by Victorian architect Sir George Gilbert, the church is known for its stained glass by Clayton and Bell and the scorch marks of the 1944 bombing that are visible in the pews. Musicians from the Royal Academy of Music perform for free on Fridays from 1-2pm

*⊖High St. Kensington. Turn right onto Kensington High St. and left onto Kensington Church St. $ Free. ⏰ Open M-Tu 8:30am-6pm, W-F 7:10am-6pm, Sa 9:40am-6pm, Su 8am-6pm.*

NATIONAL ARMY MUSEUM

MUSEUM

Royal Hospital Rd. ☎020 7730 0717; www.nam.ac.uk

Yet another museum with far too many plaster-people for its own good, the National Army Museum answers the question on everybody's mind: what are British soldiers wearing? With funny hats galore, the museum is packed with information on British military operations since 1066. It paints a vivid picture of army life and presents a remarkably nuanced treatment of the political issues surrounding each conflict. The true gems are W. Siborn's 420 sq. ft., 172-year-old model of the battle of Waterloo and the skeleton of Marengo, Napoleon's favorite horse. Of course, there's the colo(u)ring station and the guns that you can "load" and "fire," but if you want to see what a real gun is like, you might have to wrestle one off an actual guard.

*⊖Sloane Sq. Turn left onto Lower Sloane St. and right onto Royal Hospital Rd. $ Free. ⏰ Open daily 10am-5:30pm.*

CHELSEA PHYSIC GARDENS

GARDENS

66 Royal Hospital Rd. ☎020 7352 5646; www.chelseaphysicgarden.co.uk

The Physic Gardens are some of the oldest botanic gardens in Europe. Established in 1673 by a society of apothecaries, the gardens contain pharmaceutical and perfumery plant beds, tropical greenhouses, Europe's oldest rock garden, and a total of 5000 different plants. It's nifty to see plants used to treat everything from heart disease to Alzheimer's, but they're worth a visit for their beauty alone. Witchcraft and wizardry nerds should look for the mandrake roots.

*⊖Sloane Sq. Turn left onto Lower Sloane St. and right onto Royal Hospital Rd.* ***i*** *Free guided tours, depending on availability of guides. $ £8, students and children £5, under 5 free. ⏰ Open Apr-Oct W-F noon-5pm, Su noon-6pm.*

CHELSEA OLD CHURCH

CHURCH

64 Cheyne Walk ☎020 7795 1019; www.chelseaoldchurch.org.uk

Though Chelsea Old Church was bombed like so many others in 1941, its rebuilding was slightly different than most; parishioners simply picked up the destroyed plaques and monuments and put them back together, leaving the cracks to serve as delicate reminders of the war. The church has also hosted several celebrity worshippers. Henry VIII is rumored to have married Jane Seymour here; Queen

Elizabeth I, "Bloody" Mary, and Lady Jane Gray worshipped here; and Thomas More prayed in the chapel that is named after him.

Sloane Sq. Turn left onto Lower Sloane St., right onto Royal Hospital Rd., and right onto Cheyne Walk. $ Free. Open Tu-Th 2-4pm, Su for services (Holy Communion 8am and 12:15pm, children's service 10am, Mattins 11am, Evensong 6pm).

BROMPTON ORATORY — CHURCH

Brompton Rd. ☎020 7808 0900; www.bromptonoratory.com

Built between 1880 and 1884, the Brompton Oratory is named after its founders, the Oratorians. Its breathtaking nave is wider than the one in St. Paul's. The marble-packed Catholic church is filled with Baroque flourishes, as well as Soviet secrets: the KGB used it as a drop point for secret messages during the Cold War.

Knightsbridge. Turn left onto Brompton Rd. $ Free. Open daily 6:30am-8pm. Services M-F 7, 8, 10am, 12:30, 6pm (in Latin); Sa 7, 8, 10am, 6pm; Su 8, 9, 10, 11am (Latin), 12:30, 4:30, 7pm.

NATURAL HISTORY MUSEUM — MUSEUM

Cromwell Rd. ☎020 7942 5011; www.nhm.ac.uk

Sure, the museum may be intended for kids—cue the roving school groups—but who doesn't love a moving T-Rex? Known as the "Cathedral of the Animals," the Natural History Museum houses exhibitions on everything from animal anatomy to histories of scientific research. Though the dinosaurs rule, there are also exhibits on every type of animal, plant, and ecosystem—the Darwin Centre features more than 20 million species in jars. The grand Victorian building, with turrets and gargoyles galore, is enough to make the visit worthwhile.

South Kensington. Turn right onto Thurloe Pl. and left onto Exhibition Rd. The museum is to the left across Cromwell Rd. i Book early for tours of Darwin's special collections. $ Free. Special exhibits around £8; students get discounts. Open daily 10am-5:50pm. Last entry 5:30pm.

KENSINGTON PALACE — PALACE

Kensington Palace Gardens ☎0844 482 7777; www.hrp.org.uk/kensingtonpalace

This elegant royal residence was begun in the 17th century and expanded by the legendary architect Sir Christopher Wren. It's long been home to monarchs and other nobility, though it was never the official seat of the court. Queen Victoria and the princes William and Harry grew up here. Even though Will is now taken (he and the Duchess of Cambridge use the palace as their official London residence), princess hopefuls can still catch sight of Harry during his occasional visits. The majority of the palace is closed until construction is completed in 2012, but the State Rooms have been transformed into an "Enchanted Palace" exhibit, which features a story about seven of the legendary princesses who lived here. The exhibit threads through many magnificent galleries and drawing rooms done up in an eerie, fairy-tale style with a soundtrack to match.

High St. Kensington. Turn right leaving the station and head down the road, then enter the park and make for the palace (it's kind of hard to miss). $ £12.50, concessions £11, under 16 £6.25. Open daily 10am-6pm.

HYDE PARK TO NOTTING HILL

It's pretty hard to be in central London and not run into **Hyde Park** at some point—the park is larger than the entire principality of Monaco. The land was first converted into a park by Henry VIII in the 16th century. Since then, it's developed from a royal deer park into open public space. Technically the roughly rectangular area of greenery here comprises both Hyde Park and Kensington Gardens (the latter is the western part, closer to Notting Hill), but you'll barely notice the difference except for the fact that Hyde Park closes at midnight while the other shuts its gates at dusk. The parks are full of winding pathways, open fields, floral gardens, and small clusters of woods. Since Hyde Park has been around for nearly 500 years, there are also a number of interesting historical sites for those who want more than just greenery.

SPEAKERS' CORNER HISTORICAL SITE, PERFORMANCE SPACE

Hyde Park, Park Ln.

This innocuous corner of Hyde Park is the stage for political, religious, and social debates. Speakers present ideas, challenge each other, and take questions from the audience (some regular hecklers hang out in the area). Back in the day, it was used by social revolutionaries like Marx, Lenin, and George Orwell; today you're as likely to find a fundamentalist Christian as a ★**Communist**. There are no set hours, and anyone is welcome to speak, though sometimes the area remains empty. Come watch free speech in action!

➤ ⊖Marble Arch. Go through the arch into the park and the area where most people speak is the paved section between the arch and the beginning of the main grassy area. $ Free. ⏰ Hours vary, but around 9am-10pm in summer.

SERPENTINE BOATING LAKE LAKE BOATING

Hyde Park ☎020 7262 1330; www.theboathouselondon.co.uk

Built from 1727 to 1731 in memory of Queen Caroline, the Serpentine Boating Lake is one of the most beautiful parts of Hyde Park. Rented boats drift lazily across the placid waters as fat waterfowl battle it out for pieces of bread. Boats can be rented and taken out for any amount of time. The water stretches across a large portion of the park; at the Bayswater end is a terraced bit with fountains—refined British landscapery at its best.

➤ ⊖Hyde Park Corner. $ Pedal boats and row boats £8 per person per 30min., £10 per person per hr. ⏰ Open daily Easter-October10am-sundown.

SUBWAY GALLERY GALLERY

Joe Strummer Subway ☎078 1128 6503; www.subwaygallery.com

Bringing a new meaning to the term "underground art" (their joke, not ours), the Subway Gallery features installations from local artists, often dealing with pop culture and music. The main spot is in a tiny kiosk, though pop graffiti adorns the walls of the underpass. Exhibits change monthly. If you're in the area (or a huge fan of the Clash), it's definitely worth stopping by this very cool, quirky venue. At night, though, it might feel deserted and a bit dangerous.

➤ ⊖Edgware Rd. Take a sharp right down Cabbell St., left before the flyover and then go down the stairs into Joe Strummer Subway. $ Free. ⏰ Open M-Sa 11am-7pm.

APSLEY HOUSE HISTORICAL SITE, MUSEUM GALLERY

Hyde Park Corner ☎020 7499 5676; www.english-heritage.org.uk

Named for Baron Apsley, the house later known as "No.1, London" was bought by the Duke of Wellington in 1817 (his heirs still occupy a modest suite on the top floor). The house is a stunning architectural triumph, from the gilded mirrors to the oval spiral staircase. Perhaps the most fantastic of all the valuable collections in the house is Wellington's art collection, much of which he received from grateful European monarchs after he defeated Napoleon at the Battle of Waterloo. One of the most sought-after pieces is Velázquez's beautiful *The Water-Seller of Seville*. Throughout the house, you can find various pretty awesome collectibles, including a silver-gilt dessert plate bearing Napoleon's arms, the key to the city of Pamplona (granted after the Duke captured the city), the death masks of Wellington and Napoleon, and a stunning 6.7m Egyptian service set given by Napoleon to Josephine as a divorce present. Scholars maintain that the dessert service was meant as a mean joke about Josephine's weight—it's huge. Unless you're particularly interested in English history or Portuguese silverwork, though, it may not be worth the price of admission given that so many other museums and galleries in the city are free.

➤ ⊖Hyde Park Corner. ℹ June 18 is Wellington Day, so check for special events. $ £6.30, concessions £5.70, children £3.80. Joint ticket with Wellington Arch £7.90/7.10/4.70. Audio tour free. ⏰ Open Apr-Oct W-Su 11am-5pm, Nov-Mar W-Su 11am-4pm. Last entry 30min. before close.

MARYLEBONE AND BLOOMSBURY

With the **British Museum** and the **British Library** just a 15min. walk from each other, you've got basically the whole empire packed into this one little area (eh, we guess you'd want Buckingham Palace and Westminster in there too if you were going to be really thorough about it). **Regent's Park** is one of the loveliest expanses of green in London, and all the streets surrounding the park have stunning architecture that makes a perfect continuation of your stroll around the verge. **University College London** is located along Gower St.—its main campus and the red-brick Cruciform building (once the old teaching hospital) are worth a gander.

[✓] BRITISH MUSEUM — MUSEUM

Great Russell St. ☎020 7323 8299; www.british-museum.org

Ah, colonialism. It's a bummer about the whole exploitation and oppression thing, but, man, does it make for some awesome souvenirs. Nowhere is this clearer than the British Museum, founded in 1753 as the personal collection of Sir Hans Sloane. Nowadays, the museum juxtaposes Victorian Anglocentricism with more modern, multicultural acceptance, but there's no way you won't be reminded of the fact that back when this place was built, the sun never set on the British Empire. The building itself, in all its Neoclassical splendor, is magnificent. The stunning **Great Court** is the largest covered square in Europe, and has been used as the British Library stacks for the past 150 years. The blue chairs and desks of the **Reading Room,** set under a towering dome of books, have shouldered the weight of research by almost every major British writer, as well as Marx, Lenin, and Trotsky.

The collection is organized by geographic region: Greece and Rome, Egypt and Sudan, the Middle East, Britain and Europe, etc. Most of the extremely famous pieces, like the **Rosetta Stone** and the **Elgin Marbles,** are located on the ground floor. However, don't miss out on the galleries above; the Early Britain collection is particularly fine, with intensely detailed artifacts that are hard to imagine coming from muddy Dark Ages-era England.

Look out for the **King's Library** on the eastern part of the ground floor, which holds artifacts gathered from throughout the world by English explorers during the Enlightenment. Some of the central display cases bear descriptions, but much of the collection is jumbled together without explanation—a curatorial choice meant to recreate the feel of collections from the period. We think it works pretty well. Mixed in with the artifacts are shelves full of books from the House of Commons' library—get your dork on and try to find an 18th-century copy of your favorite Roman poet or Greek historian.

 # ⊖ Tottenham Court Rd., Russell Sq., or Holborn. ℹ Tours by request. $ £4 suggested donation. Prices for events and special exhibitions vary, most £8-12. Excellent color maps with self-guided tours £2. Multimedia guide £5. ⏰ Museum open daily 10am-5:30pm. Select exhibitions M-W 10am-5:30pm, Th-F 10am-8:30pm, Sa-Su 10am-5:30pm.

[✓] BRITISH LIBRARY — LIBRARY

96 Euston Rd. ☎020 7412 7676; www.bl.uk

Though it was castigated during its long construction by traditionalists for being too modern and by modernists for being too traditional, the new British Library building (opened in 1998) now impresses all nay-sayers with its stunning interior. The 65,000 volumes of the King's Library, collected by George III and bequeathed to the nation in 1823 by his less bookish son, George IV, are displayed in a glass cube toward the rear. The sunken plaza out front features an enormous and somewhat strange statue of Newton, and also hosts a series of free concerts and other events. The heart of the library is underground, with 12 million books on 200 miles of shelving. The above-ground brick building is home to cavernous reading rooms and an engrossing museum. Find **Shakespeare's first folio,** Lewis Carroll's handwritten manuscript of *Alice in Wonderland* (donated by Alice

Liddell herself), and Virginia Woolf's handwritten notes for *Mrs. Dalloway* (then called *The Hours*) in the **Literature Corner** of the Sir John Ritblat Gallery. Music-lovers will appreciate Handel's handwritten *Messiah*, Mozart's marriage contract, Beethoven's tuning fork, and a whole display dedicated to the Beatles. The last of these includes the original, handwritten lyrics to "A Hard Day's Night," scrawled on the back of Lennon's son Julian's first birthday card. In the museum, the original copy of the **Magna Carta** has its own room (accompanied by the Papal Bull that Pope Innocent III wrote in response). Leonardo da Vinci's notebooks are in the **Science** section, while one of 50 known **Gutenberg Bibles** can be found in the **Printing** section. Another gallery hosts temporary exhibitions that dig up more gems from the Library's collection, often mixed in with interviews from authors and artists. Even if you don't crack a book during your entire stay in London, you'll still feel at least 10 IQ points smarter just from being around all this knowledge.

✚ ⊖ *Euston Sq. or King's Cross St. Pancras. **i** Free Wi-Fi; the cafe offers lots of seating where you can take advantage of it. To register for use of reading room, bring 2 forms of ID—1 with a signature and 1 with a home address. ⑤ Free. Tours free. Group tour up to 15 people, £85. ⏰ Open M 9:30am-6pm, Tu 9:30am-8pm, W-F 9:30am-6pm, Sa 9:30am-5pm, Su 11am-5pm. Group tours Tu 10:30am and 2:30pm, Th 10:30am and 2:30pm. Call ☎020 7412 7639 to book. Individual tours M, W, F 11am. Call ☎019 3754 6546 to book.*

abbey road

London has numerous pilgrimage sites for music fanatics, but few can compare with six thick stripes in St John's Wood, a little west of Regent's Park. Located near EMI's Abbey Road Studios at 3 Abbey Rd., this zebra crossing was vaulted into iconic status by the Beatles' final album, *Abbey Road*. For the album's cover, John, Ringo, Paul, and George strode across the southeastern edge of the street and onto the to-do list of every tourist who saw them standing there. If you've grown out some happening facial hair and slipped on your hippest pair of bell-bottoms, feel free to pose like it's 1969. But please be quick; busy Londoners driving their cars don't appreciate day trippers on magical mystery tours trying to decide whether or not to do it in the road.

▨ THE REGENT'S PARK

PARK

☎020 7486 7905; www.royalparks.org.uk

In 1811, the Prince Regent commissioned John Nash to design him a private garden; the park was opened to the public in 1841, and the city lives all the better for it. Locals, pigeons, and tourists alike frolic among the 10,000 wild flowers and 50 acres of pitches and courts. **Queen Mary's Garden** houses the national collection of delphiniums and a gorgeous collection of 30,000 roses. It is also home to an interesting strain of pink flower known as **Sexy Rexy**. The park's popular open-air theater is the setting for all kinds of shows (book tickets at www.openairtheatre.com). The **Gardens of St. John's Lodge,** behind one of the park's eight villas, serve as a place for quiet meditation beneath gorgeous latticed archways—a sort of secret garden that also affords a peek into the back of St. John's Lodge. Be aware that security here is tight; the **Winfield House** just off the outer circle is home to the American ambassador. In the northern section of the park is the **London Zoo** (www.zsl.org), home to all sorts of critters and, in summertime, a giant penguin pool.

✚ ⊖*Regent's Park. ⑤ Deck chair £1.50 per hr., £4 per 3hr., £7 per day. Boats £6.50 per 1hr., £4.85 per 1½hr. Zoo £20, concessions £19, children £16. ⏰ Park open daily 5am-dusk. Boating lake open daily Mar-Oct 10:30am-7pm. Zoo open daily 10am-5:30pm.*

sights

NORTH LONDON

HAMPSTEAD HEATH

PARK

Hampstead ☎020 7332 3030

Hampstead Heath was initially much smaller than its present 800 acres. After Sir Thomas Maryon Wilson tried to develop and sell off the Heath in the early 19th century, the public fought to keep the Heath wild; an 1872 Act of Parliament declared it open to the public forever. Now it sprawls gloriously in the heart of Hampstead, feeling much wilder and lusher than the manicured parks of central London. The beautiful, tamer **Hill Gardens** are in the southwest corner of the Heath just off North End Ave., created out of the surrounding landscapes by Lord Leverhulme (of Lever Soap fame). For a stunning sunset view, look through the pergola with Georgian columns and rose-entwined lattice. **Parliament Hill** is one of the highest points in London, offering those willing to climb its deceptively steep sides a glorious reminder that they're only four miles from London proper, not in the middle of rural England. Parliament Hill derives its name from its use as a point of defense for Parliamentarian "Roundheads" during the English Civil War—though legend has it that Guy Fawkes planned to watch Parliament explode from the hill.

➡ Bus #210 will drop you at the north of the Heath. Alternatively, get off at ⊖Hampstead, turn right onto Heath St., go up North End Way, left onto Inverforth Close, and left onto a path to arrive at the hill gardens. Bus #214 allows easy access to Parliament Hill. ⏰ Heath open 24hr. Hill Garden open daily May 24-Aug 1 8:30am-8:30pm; Aug 2-May 23 8:30am-1hr. before sunset.

KENWOOD HOUSE

GALLERY

Hampstead Ln. ☎020 8348 1286; www.english-heritage.org.uk

Lord Iveagh, a barrister and Lord Chief Justice, lived here in the 18th century. Visitors to Kenwood House can now admire his fabulous art collection and see how the 18th-century elite lived. Iveagh's bequest fills the house with paintings that are essentially odes to the London of yore. Views of the city from the Heath, like Crone's *View of London from Highgate*, and an early Turner depict themes common to the bequest—typical British life. Though they aren't British, the stars of the collection are probably Rembrandt's *Portrait of the Artist* and Vermeer's *The Guitar Player*. The Suffolk Collection, composed mainly of portraits, is on semi-permanent exhibition on the first floor. Concerts are held in the grounds during the summer.

➡ Bus #210 stops on Hampstead Ln. at the Kenwood House stop. The park is across the road. [$] Free. Booklets £4. ⏰ Open daily 11:30am-4pm. Last entry 3:50pm.

EAST LONDON

WHITECHAPEL GALLERY

GALLERY

77-82 Whitechapel High St. ☎020 7522 7888; www.whitechapelgallery.org

In business since 1901, the Whitechapel Gallery was originally an effort by hoity-toity uppity-ups to bring art to the culturally deprived inhabitants of the East End. Today, the gallery's atmosphere has changed, but its commitment to excellence remains. Gallery 7 is dedicated to temporary exhibits (which change four times per year), Gallery 2 features year-long commissioned works, and the rest of the gallery is filled with other contemporary works, as well as occasional mid-career retrospectives. Art films run on loop in the cinema space.

➡ ⊖Aldgate East. Turn left on Whitechapel High St. [$] Free. Special exhibits normally under £10, students £2 discount. ⏰ Open Tu-Su 11am-6pm, 1st Th of every month 11am-9pm.

GEFFRYE MUSEUM

MUSEUM

136 Kingsland Rd. ☎020 7739 9893; www.geffrye-museum.org.uk

At first glance, the Geffrye is yet another house-turned-museum, but if the thought of looking at upholstery for an hour has you cringing, think again. The museum consists of several old almshouses arranged around a pretty garden. Inside, walk through a series of 17th- to 21st-century living rooms, whose changing styles do a remarkably good job of eking out social, cultural, and political themes—who knew you could learn so much from a chair? Special exhibits often feature model living spaces from other cultures.

⊖Hoxton. Make a right onto Geffrye St., a left onto Pearson St., and a left onto Kingsland Rd. [$] Free. Special exhibits around £5. ⏰ Open Tu-Sa 10am-5pm, Su noon-5pm.

ROYAL OBSERVATORY HISTORIC SITE, MUSEUM

Blackheath Ave. ☎020 8312 6608; www.nmm.ac.uk

Charles II founded the Royal Observatory in 1675 to "advance navigation and astronomy." Translation: to stop British ships from sinking so frequently. The observatory is at Greenwich, the site of the Prime Meridian (or longitude 0° 0'0"), which demarcates the boundary between the Eastern and Western hemispheres. If your visit to London hasn't yet demonstrated the sheer power of the British Empire, this should—once upon a time, the British got to decide how time worked. Visitors can pose for pictures straddling the red LED strip, thus standing in two hemispheres simultaneously. After seeing this intersection, visitors choose one of two routes. One explores the history of the observatory and its research, while the other focuses on astrology and leads to the popular planetarium.

*⊖Greenwich. Turn left onto Kay Way, right down Straightsmouth to Greenwich High Rd., right onto Stockwell St., left onto Nevada St., then left onto King William Walk. Finally, take a right onto Romney Rd. and walk up the hill. **i** Handicapped tourists should know that, while there is parking on top of the hill, the hill itself is very steep. [$] £10, concessions £7.50. Planetarium shows £6.50/4.50. Audio tour £3.50. Guided tours free. ⏰ Open daily 10am-5pm.*

ripperology

Whether you're a big fan of Wikipedia's list of serial killers or too afraid to watch commercials for *Dexter*, you've probably heard of Jack the Ripper. Believed to have been responsible for at least five and up to 11 murders in the Whitechapel area east of central London, the killer caused quite a splash in the press, thanks in great part to his gruesome methods–he usually slashed the throat, mutilated the face and genitals, and removed the internal organs of his victim. The policemen and various newspapers received letters from people claiming to be responsible, one of which included half a human kidney, and the claim that the writer had "fried and ate" the other half. The name "Jack the Ripper" comes from one of these letters; less catchy nicknames offered at the time include "The Whitechapel Murderer," "Leather Apron," and "Nigel the Ripper."

Of course, the most interesting thing about Jack the Ripper is that he was never caught or even identified. Before you start panicking, remember that these murders took place in 1888–meaning it's really Dexter, not Jack, you should be worried about. If you're still itching to learn more, a number of tour companies (try www.jack-the-ripper-tour.com or www.thejacktherippertour.com) offer tours with no shortage of grisly details.

SOUTH LONDON

SOUTH LONDON GALLERY — ART GALLERY

65 Peckham Rd. ☎020 7703 6120; www.southlondonartgallery.org

This tiny art gallery attracts as many visitors with its lively cafe as it does with its two exhibition spaces. It showcases works by artists of all sorts—established, up-and-coming, British, international, you name it. There are events like talks and film screenings here, and many are free. With so much art in London, the out-of-the-way location means this gallery isn't really a must-see, but, if you're in the area, it's worth stopping by to take a peek at the interesting art and the lovely 19th-century building.

➡ ⊖Peckham Rye. Bus 37 goes from the station to the gallery. $ Free. ⏰ Open Tu 11am-6pm, W 11am-9pm, Th-Su 11am-6pm.

WEST LONDON

👍 HAMPTON COURT PALACE — PALACE

East Molesey, Surrey ☎0844 482 7777; www.hrp.org.uk/hamptoncourtpalace

If you're a fan of the Tudors (either the historical figures or the saucy Showtime television series), the lavish Hampton Court is a must-see. It was originally built by Cardinal Wolsey to be his own palace while he was in the good graces of Henry VIII, but he gave it to the king in a last-ditch effort to prevent his downfall. Henry added vast kitchens and the magnificent Great Hall where he dined in style (and where Shakespeare's theater company later performed). Mary I spent her honeymoon here, and Elizabeth I used the palace as well. Each monarch added his or her own touches, which can be seen in the variety of architectural styles, from medieval gates to faux-Versailles frippery. It remained a royal residence until the early 18th century. Visitors can see many of the royal apartments, grand rooms like the Chapel Royal, and the extensive kitchens (which had to feed 1200 people every day). While the rooms are visually stunning and packed with art, the real draw is that the palace uses interactive exhibits and informative guides to give a genuine feel for what life was like within its walls. Don't be limited by those walls, though, as there are 750 acres of impeccably maintained grounds to stroll. These include the Privy Garden, the Rose Garden, the Exotics Garden, and—if all the perfectly manicured grass and topiaries are driving you crazy—a 20th-century garden done in a more "informal" style. Best of all, there is a world-famous maze that will put your navigational skills to the test.

➡ Trains run from Waterloo to Hampton Court (£5.50). The palace is just across the bridge from the train station. ℹ Audio and guided tours included with admission. $ Gardens £5.30, concessions £5, children free. Maze £3.85, children £2.75. Combined ticket £16, concessions £13, children under 16 £8. ⏰ Open daily 10am-6pm. Last entry to garden 5pm; last entry to maze 5:15pm.

ROYAL BOTANIC GARDENS, KEW — BOTANICAL GARDENS

Richmond, Surrey ☎020 8332 5000; www.kew.org

Kew Gardens make most other botanical gardens look like suburban backyards. This is one of the foremost botanical research facilities in the world, home to thousands of plant species and hundreds of scientists who tend to them. Perhaps more relevant to the casual visitor, it has exquisite gardens, winding paths through leafy forests and rolling lawns, and conservatories with collections of everything from orchids to carnivorous plants. There's even a skywalk that takes you through the tree canopy. If you prefer buildings to shrubberies, you can check out the many interesting architectural specimens: Swiss-style cottages, faux-Chinese pagodas, one of the smaller royal palaces, and several galleries and museums with plant-related art and information.

➡ ⊖Kew Gardens. Exit the station and walk down Litchfield Rd. to the gardens' Victoria Gate. $ £13.90, concessions £11.90, under 17 free. Kew Palace £5.30/4.50/free. ⏰ Open M-F 9:30am-6:30pm, Sa-Su 9:30am-7:30pm. Last entry 30min. before close. Glasshouses and galleries daily 9:30am-5:30pm. Free guided tours leave Victoria Plaza at 11am and 2pm.

food

British food doesn't have a great reputation. Yes, it is bad for you and no, it doesn't have complex flavors, but it is so intrinsically a part of British life that to forego it would be a grave error for any visitor. Fish and chips, bangers and mash, tikka masala (a British invention), and warm ale are all different names for the same thing: comfort food. Neighborhoods like Brixton and Shoreditch serve up a span of ethnic cuisine, from Caribbean to Indian, while gourmet restaurants whip up inventive dishes. "Pub grub" still rules over everything. In case you hadn't noticed, Brits like to operate in certain set ways. There's a reason that old war propaganda line, "Keep Calm and Carry On," is plastered all over the place; there's a reason the Queen still rolls down the Mall every June; there's a reason the Brits always think England will win the Cup; there's a reason fair Albion still uses the pound; and for that same reason, you'll always be able to get a pie and a pint on any corner in London. Now eat your mushy peas—the cod's getting cold.

THE CITY OF LONDON

Many of the culinary offerings in the City are geared toward businessmen (expensive) and tourists (expensive, but not very good). Fortunately, if you know where to look, this neighborhood also holds some of London's best eats. The area around **Clerkenwell** overflows with creative and delicious restaurants, pubs, and cafes.

👍 CITY CÀPHÊ
VIETNAMESE $

17 Ironmonger Ln. www.citycaphe.com

If you want a cheap yet delicious sandwich, try one of the exquisite bánh mì at this simple Vietnamese joint. Slices of pork, chicken, or tofu are served with salad and dressing on baguettes, which are baked using a closely guarded secret recipe. We don't know how a pork sandwich with some salad on a white baguette can be so good, so if you have any ideas, let us know. Pho, rice noodle dishes, and a variety of rolls are also available.

➡ ⊖Bank. Head down Poultry away from the stop, then turn right onto Ironmonger Ln. $ Bánh mì £4. Other dishes £4-6. 🕐 Open M-F 11:30am-3pm.

👍 COACH AND HORSES
PUB $$

26-28 Ray St. ☎020 7278 8990; www.thecoachandhorses.com

"Pub food" often brings soggy pies and oily fish and chips to mind, but this Victorian pub in a seemingly abandoned corner of Clerkenwell upends these expectations with fresh, inventive takes on British fare. Coach and Horses does have mushy peas, fish and chips, burgers, and the like, but it also has beetroot risotto, heirloom tomato salad, and duck confit. A variety of roasts are served on Sunday. You can eat in their enclosed garden, sidewalk patio, or elegant dining rooms.

➡ ⊖Farringdon. Walk north on Farringdon Rd. and turn left onto Ray St. $ Main courses £8-12. 2-course lunch £10. 🕐 Open M-F noon-11pm, Sa 6-11pm, Su 1-5pm. Kitchen open M-F noon-3pm and 6-10pm, Sa 6-10pm, Su 1-4pm.

👍 BAR BATTU
MEDITERRANEAN $$

48 Gresham St. ☎020 7036 6100; www.barbattu.com

Primarily known for their all-natural wines (fewer sulfites, less hangover!), Bar Battu serves up some pretty outstanding food as well. Get a selection of charcuterie or a leek tart or go all out with linguini with borlotti beans in a lemon-caper vinaigrette. Bar Battu is one of London's best values for a gourmet meal, with all the impeccable service and classy atmosphere you'd expect, but lower prices and larger portions.

➡ ⊖Bank. Go down Prince's St. and turn left onto Gresham St. $ Appetizers and small plates £4.50-6.50. Main courses £9.50-14. 2-course meal £16.25; 3-course £20. 🕐 Open M-F 11:30am-11pm.

🍴 THE CLERKENWELL KITCHEN

BRITISH, SEASONAL $$

31 Clerkenwell Close ☎020 7101 9959; www.theclerkenwellkitchen.co.uk

Normally when a restaurant advertises "soft drinks," they mean cola and root beer, but here at the Clerkenwell Kitchen, the term refers to taste-bud-exploding concoctions like their elderflower cordial (£2). Match that with their locally grown ingredients and organic, free-range meat, and you'll have a welcome introduction to the lighter side of British fare. During the summer, bask in the sun outside on the terrace; in the winter, warm up with dishes like slow-roast pork belly with braised lentils, chard, and quince aioli. The menu changes daily based on which fresh, local ingredients they receive, but the high quality of this hidden restaurant is consistent.

⇄ ⊖Farringdon. Turn right onto Cowcross St., right onto Farringdon Rd., right onto Pear Tree Ct., and right onto Clerkenwell Close. Walk straight as if still on Pear Tree Ct. If you see the church, you've gone too far. [$] Main courses £7.50-11. Tea and coffee £1.50-1.85. ⏰ Open M-F 8am-5pm.

child's play

Remember singing "London Bridge is Falling Down" as a kid? If this is your first time in the British capital, you might be interested to see the bridge still standing. That's about where the interest will end, as London Bridge is one of the city's most boring river crossings. But the song's ambiguous history might make up for its subject's aesthetic dullness. One theory, going off the parallel between the song and similar verses in a Norse saga, claims the rhyme refers to Norweigian King Olaf II's 11th-century invasion of London and destruction of London Bridge. A slightly less interesting version says that children simply chanted about the deterioration of London Bridge after the Great Fire of London in 1666. The most bizarre theory is also the goriest: some say the song refers to the burial of children inside the foundations of the bridge due to an ancient belief that bridges would collapse without human sacrifice. Hopefully, the fact the bridge was "falling down" refers to the lack of children buried in it, rather than there simply not being enough.

THE WEST END

🍴 KULU KULU

SUSHI $$

76 Brewer St. ☎020 7734 7316; www.kulukulu.co.uk

Kulu Kulu is a conveyor-belt sushi restaurant—the chefs send a steady stream of fresh dishes around the bar on a little runway. You can see everything before you order it and try lots of little dishes. Different plates indicate different prices; when you're ready to pay, a waiter will come over and add up your plates. Typical choices are nigiri, sashimi, and maki, and some vegetables and non-sushi dishes. It's a no-frills environment, but one of the best values in the area.

⇄ ⊖Piccadilly Circus. Go down Glasshouse St., keep right onto Sherwood St., and turn left onto Brewer St. [$] Dishes £1.50-3.60 (4-5 dishes make a good meal). ⏰ Open M-Sa noon-10pm.

🍴 FREEBIRD BURRITOS

MEXICAN $

Corner of Ruper St. and Brewer St. www.freebirdburritos.com

Just a humble food stand, Freebird has one of London's great rarities: a pretty good burrito. It maybe isn't as good as what you'd find in the US (or Mexico, obviously), but it's cheap and a rare find around here.

⇄ ⊖Piccadilly Circus. Turn right down Shaftesbury Ave. and left onto Rupert St. [$] Burritos £5, with guacamole £5.50. ⏰ Open M-F 11:30am-3pm.

👍 MONMOUTH COFFEE COMPANY

CAFE $

27 Monmouth St. ☎0872 148 1409; www.monmouthcoffee.co.uk

Monmouth makes the best coffee in London (some say the world, but we still have our researchers working to verify that one). Their carefully selected and roasted beans are served at other establishments in the city, but you should come to the flagship store itself. They use amazingly creamy milk from an organic farm in Somerset, so skip the skim this time. Try their pastries and truffles, too. The shop is small, but there's some seating available on the upper floor.

 # ⊖Leicester Sq. Turn right and then left onto Upper St. Martin's Ln., which becomes Monmouth St. $ Coffee £1.20-2.50. ⏰ Open M-Sa 8am-6:30pm.

FORTNUM AND MASON

AFTERNOON TEA, FOOD STORE $$$$

181 Piccadilly ☎020 7734 8040; www.fortnumandmason.com

If you have a bit of extra money to burn and want to experience some classic hoity-toity English elegance, try the afternoon tea at Fortnum and Mason. Not only do you get a whole spread of sandwiches, scones, and cakes, you can sit in luxurious armchairs while being served by a waiter who is too well trained to look askance at your grubby flip-flops (not that we speak from personal experience). If you're going to splurge on one meal in London, it should be at this truly British institution that has been around for over 300 years. If, however, the prices seem a tad too exorbitant, pick up specialty teas, jams, biscuits, and much more at the amazing food store downstairs.

 # ⊖Piccadilly Circus. Turn left down Piccadilly. $ Afternoon tea £34-40. ⏰ Open M-Sa noon-6-:30pm, Su noon-4:30pm. Store open M-Sa 10am-8pm, Su noon-6pm.

WESTMINSTER

👍 POILÂNE

BAKERY $

46 Elizabeth St. ☎020 7808 4910; www.poilane.com

This is the only non-French branch of the famous Parisian bakery chain Poilâne, which means that it's ungodly good by London standards. The commitment to excellence at Poilâne is unparalleled: many of their bakers actually live above the shop, baking the bread all through the night to ensure that it's fresh for the morning crowd. They use the time-honored traditions and techniques when creating their sourdough masterpieces, and the *pain au chocolat* is to die for. Also worth noting, they bake in wood-fired ovens of the type that started the Great Fire of London—good thing the city's not built of wood anymore.

 # ⊖Victoria. Turn left onto Buckingham Palace Rd., then right onto Elizabeth St. $ Pain au chocolat £1.50. Walnut bread £4. Sourdough bread £5. Custard tart £17. ⏰ Open M-F 7:30am-7pm, Sa 7:30am-6pm.

👍 PIMLICO FRESH

CAFE, MEDITERRANEAN $

86 Wilton Rd. ☎020 7932 0030

If you're stumbling off a train at Victoria, we know pretty much any combination of carbohydrates and protein will probably sound like manna from heaven. But if you're by the station (whether for transportation reasons or not), try and hold out until you're a bit farther down the road. You'll be rewarded by this fabulous bakery and restaurant. Try a baked egg with chorizo or salmon and avocado toast for breakfast; the rest of the day, Pimlico serves lasagna, stews with rice, salad, omelettes, and a number of daily specials. They also serve the ever-popular Monmouth coffee.

 # ⊖Victoria. Wilton Rd. runs behind the station, toward Pimlico, away from Buckingham Palace. i Takeaway available. $ Main courses £4.50-7. Coffee from £1.80. ⏰ Open M-F 7:30am-7:30pm, Sa-Su 9am-6pm.

BUMBLES BRITISH $$

16 Buckingham Palace Rd. ☎020 7828 2903; www.bumbles1950.com

Specializing in highbrow British cuisine and the fine art of the affordable *prix-fixe* menu, Bumbles is an incongruously good value for this part of town. It looks unremarkable from the outside, but is surprisingly elegant within, with white leather chairs and wine-red walls. Dishes include truffled toast, Devonshire lamb, and roasted frogs' leg trifle. Try them in an extremely affordable three-course meal from a limited menu, a two- or three-course choice from the full selection, or go crazy and get the eight-course "Taste of Mr. Bumbles." You can also order a la carte, but where's the fun in that?

➥ ⊖Victoria. Exit the station and turn right onto Buckingham Palace Rd. Ⓢ Limited 3-course menu £10; 2 courses £20, 3 courses £23; 8-course menu £39. ⏰ Open M-F noon-3pm and 5-10pm, Sa 5-10pm.

JENNY LO'S TEAHOUSE ASIAN FUSION $$

14 Eccleston St. ☎020 7259 0399; www.jennylo.co.uk

Want to see how people besides the Brits do tea? This unassuming teahouse serves delicious Asian classics like Vietnamese-style vermicelli rice noodles, Thai-style lamb in green curry, and wok noodles. But they also have their own herbalist (Dr. Xu) and a terrific selection of soothing and tasty teas.

➥ ⊖Victoria. Turn left onto Buckingham Palace Rd., then a right onto Eccleston St. ℹ Takeaway and delivery available. Ⓢ Main courses £7.50-9.50. Teas £2-4. Cash only. ⏰ Open M-F noon-3pm and 6-10pm.

THE SOUTH BANK

The South Bank is home to the terrific **Borough Market.** Located just south of London Bridge, it's a tangle of stalls and shops where you can get prime cuts of meat, organic vegetables, and fragrant cheeses. If you want a more structured meal, this is generally a pretty good neighborhood to find a deal, as prices are lower than in the city center.

👍 **PIE MINISTER** PIES $

Gabriel's Wharf, 56 Upper Ground ☎020 7928 5755; www.pieminister.co.uk

Gabriel's Wharf is a little square by the river ringed with cafes and restaurants, of which Pie Minister is by far the best. Their pies are creative twists on classic British dishes; there's steak and kidney, plus the Matador Pie (chorizo, tomatoes, and sherry) and the Thai Chook Pie (chicken green curry). Vegetarians, rejoice! Forget the perennial roasted vegetables option in favor of pies like the Heidi (sweet potato and goat cheese). Round off your all-pie meal with a dessert pie. The store is tiny, so there's no place to sit in winter, but in summer there's plenty of seating on the patio.

➥ ⊖Waterloo. Walk toward the main roundabout and onto Waterloo Rd., then turn right onto Upper Ground. Ⓢ Pies £4.25; with gravy, mashed potatoes, and mushy peas £5.95. ⏰ Open daily 10am-5pm.

TSURU JAPANESE $

4 Canvey St. ☎020 7928 2228; www.tsuru-sushi.co.uk

This simple and efficient sushi spot is the perfect place to grab lunch if you're at the Tate Modern. The sushi comes packaged in containers suspiciously reminiscent of the stuff they serve at Tesco, but it's all freshly made by the chefs, whom you can watch working while you eat. In addition to various sushi combinations, you can order their fabulous *katsu* curry or *katsu bento*, slices of meat or vegetables fried and served on a mound of rice with tasty sauces. Tsuru offers all the ease of a fast-food restaurant with the flavor (and sake!) of a proper Japanese joint.

➥ ⊖Southwark. Walk down Blackfriars Rd. toward the river, turn right onto Southwark Rd., and left onto Canvey St. Ⓢ Sushi boxes £4-6. Katsu £6. ⏰ Open M-F 11am-9pm, Sa noon-7pm.

SOUTH KENSINGTON AND CHELSEA

Most restaurants in these neighborhoods cater to the rich and powerful, but there's also a good selection of delicious mid-range eateries, and the main roads (King's Rd., Old Brompton Rd., High St. Kensington) are packed with more inexpensive options.

BUONA SERA

ITALIAN $$

289A King's Rd. ☎020 7352 8827

If the bunk beds in your hostel haven't made you hate ladders, come to Buona Sera for good eats and even better interior design. The small restaurant manages to fit 14 tables into a tight space by stacking booths on top of each other. It's sort of like Tetris, except with delicious, affordable Italian food.

Sloane Sq. Exit the Tube and head straight down Sloane Sq. Turn onto King's Rd, which slants gently off to the left. Alternatively, take bus #11, 19, 22, 211, or 319. $ Salads £5. Pasta and risotto £9. Meat and fish main courses £14. Open M-F noon-3pm and 6pm-midnight, Sa-Su noon-midnight.

BUMPKIN

BRITISH $$$

109 Brompton Rd. ☎020 7341 0802; www.bumpkinuk.com

Every single thing in this restaurant, except for the olive oil (and we hope the wine) is British. The menu changes daily to accommodate the sustainable, seasonal organic ingredients. If this kind of eco-conscious ethos usually sends you running for the hills, read on—this is just plain ol' British food, done right. Dishes include pork chops with apple chutney, Scottish sea bass filet with pearl barley, and baked macaroni with local cheddar. Leave with your belly full and your carbon footprint light.

South Kensington. Exit down Old Brompton Rd. $ Appetizers £5.50-9. Main courses £12-20. Open daily 11am-11pm.

BORSCHT 'N' TEARS

RUSSIAN $$$

46 Beauchamp Pl. ☎020 7589 5003

Longing for Mother Russia? All the capitalism in South Ken getting you down? Never fear, comrade, this Eastern European enclave has enough vodka to fortify the entire Red Army. Enjoy comfort food just like your *babushka* used to make—dumplings, stroganoff, Chicken Kiev, and yes, borscht. Frequent live music gets the party started, and by the time you leave, you'll be feeling positively Slavic. Indulge your inner Soviet. You know you can't resist.

Knightsbridge. Turn left down Brompton Rd. and left onto Beauchamp Pl. $ Main courses £12-16. Open daily 11am-1am.

THAI SQUARE

THAI $$

19 Exhibition Rd. ☎020 7584 8359; www.thaisquare.net

Thai Square is a solid option for all the usual Thai favorites—spring rolls, curries, noodle dishes—in generous portions and with authentic flavors. One of the calmer restaurants in the museum area, Thai Square's serenity is aided by dark wooden furniture and delicate floral trimmings.

South Kensington. Turn right onto Thurloe St. and left onto Exhibition Rd. $ Appetizers £3-5. Main courses £7-12. Open M-Sa noon-3pm and 6-11pm, Su noon-3pm and 6-10pm.

THE MARKETPLACE

EUROPEAN $$$

125 Sydney St. ☎020 7352 5600; www.marketplacerest.com

Befitting a restaurant located in the Chelsea Farmer's Market, The Marketplace boasts a menu of fresh ingredients and a swath of picnic tables to eat it all on. Heaters keep the place bearable in winter, but if you must sit indoors you'll be welcomed by a similarly bright, farmhouse feel. This is Chelsea, so you're paying quite a bit more than you would back on the ranch, but the food—hummus, pesto linguine, steak, smoked salmon salad, etc.—is tasty and the mood is unfussy. That's a lot more than can be said for many of the neighbors.

Sloane Sq. Walk down King's Rd. and turn right onto Sydney St. $ Main courses £12-20. Open daily 9am-8pm.

PASHA
MOROCCAN $$

1 Gloucester Rd. ☎020 7589 7969; www.pasha-restaurant.co.uk

It's not just the food that's exotic here. The whole restaurant is decked out with low tables, bejeweled curtains, and ornate lamps. Once you're done gawking at your surroundings, choose from a variety of North African delights like lamb tagine, *merguez* couscous, and saffron-stuffed zucchini.

➜ ⊖Gloucester Rd. Turn left when leaving the station. $ Main courses £14-20. ⏰ Open M-W noon-12:30am, Th-Sa noon-1:30am, Su noon-12:30am.

THE ORANGERY
CAFE $$$

Kensington Palace Gardens ☎020 7376 0239

Just across the lawn from Kensington Palace, the Orangery is the place to come to have tea and feel like a princess. The tea menus come with a selection of finger sandwiches, pastries, scones, and even a glass of Champagne. They serve other lunch options too, but who could resist the traditional afternoon tea in this proper English setting? Take it in the grand hall or on the patio outside, and remember to raise your pinky.

➜ ⊖High St. Kensington. Turn right down Kensington High St. and head through the park and toward Kensington Palace. The Orangery is on the far side. $ Tea menus £15-33. ⏰ Open daily Mar-Sept 10am-6pm; Oct-Feb 10am-5pm.

MY OLD DUTCH PANCAKE HOUSE
DUTCH $$

221 King's Rd. ☎020 7376 5650; www.myolddutch.com

The name says it all: this place dishes out delicious Dutch-style pancakes (i.e., crepes). Pick a savory filling, like smoked duck and spring onions or mozzarella and tomato, or go the sweeter route with lemon and sugar or banana, nuts, and chocolate sauce. Or, let's be honest, just get one of each. Top it all off with your favorite from their selection of Dutch beers.

➜ ⊖Sloane Sq. Exit the Tube and go straight down Sloane Sq. The street slanting gently left is King's Rd. $ Savory crepes £8-11, sweet £5.50-8. ⏰ Open M-Sa 10:30am-10:45pm, Su 10:30am-10pm.

HYDE PARK TO NOTTING HILL

Queensway is lined with cheap Chinese, Indian, and Lebanese restaurants, so it's always a surefire place to find a decent and inexpensive, if generic, meal. Notting Hill Gate is packed with chain cafes and little else. Paddington is something of a mix between the two. Portobello Rd. has some quirky and interesting spots, while Westbourne Terrace has quite a few high-quality yet mid-price places mixed in with some exorbitantly expensive ones.

👍 OTTO
PIZZA $

6 Chepstow Rd. ☎020 7792 4088; www.ottopizza.co.uk

Cornmeal-crust pizza? Sounds exactly like the kind of soggy, bland culinary idea Britain is famous for (sorry, Jamie Oliver). But the pizzas at Otto are good enough to make even Italian food purists ask for seconds. The crusts are crisp and hearty, and the fillings are packed on—choose from options like fennel sausage and caramelized onion, or roasted eggplant and bleu cheese. The staff are very encouraging about experimentation, so you can either get a couple of slices to try or go for the chef's taster: a whole pizza where each slice is a different flavor.

➜ ⊖Notting Hill Gate. Make a right down Pembridge Rd., which will turn into Pembridge Villas, and then a left onto Chepstow Rd. ℹ Takeaway available. Gluten-free and vegetarian options always available. $ Slices £3.50; whole pizza (serves 2-3) £18. ⏰ Open M-F 5:30-11pm, Sa noon-11pm, Su noon-10pm.

👍 DURBAR RESTAURANT
INDIAN $

24 Hereford Rd. ☎020 7727 1947; www.durbartandoori.co.uk

It's hard to resist the warm smells from the kitchen of Durbar, where the same family has served up Indian specialties for the last 54 years. This was a popular Indian restaurant before Indian restaurants were popular, and—in a city brimming with Indian food—it still manages to be one of the best values. The menu ranges across India, with a collection of favorites and some unexpected dishes.

⚑ ⊖Bayswater. Left onto Queensway, left onto Moscow Rd., right onto Hereford toward Westbourne Grove. $ Starters £2-5. Main courses £6-9. Lunch special £4.50. ⏰ Open M-Th noon-2:30pm and 5:30-11:30pm, F 5:30-11:30pm, Sa-Su noon-2:30pm and 5:30-11:30pm.

LA BOTTEGA DEL GELATO GELATO $

127 Bayswater Rd. ☎020 7243 2443

La Bottega Del Gelato, deservedly popular, schools the rest of the London ice cream scene with a variety of delicious homemade flavors. Enjoy it outside on Bayswater Rd. in their seating area or across the road in Hyde Park. Even in the heart of the city, this gelato will make you feel like you're on a quiet street in Roma. The Ferrero Rocher is especially good.

⚑ ⊖Bayswater. Right onto Queensway, follow it until you hit Bayswater Rd. i Free Wi-Fi. $ 1 scoop £2; 2 scoops £3.50; 3 scoops £4.50. Milkshakes £3.50. ⏰ Hours change depending on the weather, but the store opens daily at 10:30am.

CHARLIE'S PORTOBELLO ROAD CAFE CAFE $

59A Portobello Rd. ☎020 7221 2422; www.charliesportobelloroadcafe.co.uk

Tucked away in a small alcove off busy Portobello Rd., Charlie's Portobello Road Cafe is a hidden gem in one of London's most trafficked areas. Despite serving classically British sandwiches like ham, cheddar, and chutney, Charlie's has a decidedly continental vibe, with large French windows and rustically worn wood tables. Main courses, salads, soups, and plenty of baked goods are also available.

⚑ ⊖Notting Hill Gate. Take a right onto Pembridge Rd. and then a left onto Portobello Rd. i Free Wi-Fi. $ Sandwiches £4-6. Salads £6-8. Full English breakfast £9.50. ⏰ Open M-Sa 9am5pm, Su noon-3pm.

TINY ROBOT ITALIAN $$

78 Westbourne Grove ☎020 7065 6814; www.tnyrbt.com

This is the sort of kitschy diner/foodie establishment that only hipsters love, but the food is tasty and the decorations are simple (lots of exposed brick, pastel tiles, and chrome). Dining options vary from American bar classics like sliders to sophisticated Italian options like *cotechino* sausage, *arancini*, and *burrata*. At night, the bar serves elegant cocktails, but bites from the menu are available until late. On weekends, brunch is served.

⚑ ⊖Bayswater. Make a left onto Queensway and then a left onto Westbourne Grove. $ Small dishes £2-6. Main courses £6-14. ⏰ Open M-Tu 5pm-midnight, W-F 5pm-2am, Sa 10am-2am, Su 10am-10:30pm.

MARYLEBONE AND BLOOMSBURY

The back streets of Bloomsbury offer some cheap ethnic restaurants and cafes where you can grab a meal that, if not particularly exciting for any culinary reason, will be unlikely to put you back more than 10 quid. Toward Marylebone, the main roads have a surplus of the usual chain restaurants, while Goodge St. has a smattering of more unique and flavorful (though a bit pricier) establishments.

LA FROMAGERIE
CHEESE $

2-6 Moxon St. ☎020 7935 0341; www.lafromagerie.co.uk

Cheese. Hundreds of different kinds of cheese, as far as the eye can see. If this thought delights and excites you, you'll enjoy La Fromagerie, a store that has its very own Cheese Room. Buffalo, goat, cow, sheep, soft, semi-soft, hard... they've got them all. Man cannot live on cheese alone, though (trust us, we've tried), so the store also stocks other gourmet goodies and a rustic cafe where you can get a sandwich, salad, or tart (and try some of the cheeses).

✴ ⊖Baker St. Turn left onto Marylebone Rd., right onto Marylebone High St., and right again onto Moxon St. ⑤ Cheese prices vary wildly. Sandwiches £6. Salads £8 or £16 per kg. Picnic basket for 2 £30. ☑ Open M-F 8am-7:30pm, Sa 9am-7pm, Su 10am-6pm.

NEWMAN ARMS
BRITISH PIES $$

23 Rathbone St. ☎020 7636 1127; www.newmanarms.co.uk

Established in 1730, the Newman Arms has been serving succulent British pies about as long as the Queen's relatives have been on the throne. The menu reads like an ode to comfort food, with pies like beef and Guinness, steak and kidney, and lamb and rosemary. The exceedingly English upstairs dining room fills up fast, so be sure to reserve a table a day in advance during the summer and much further in advance during the winter (sometimes even months). Don't forget to save room for the gooey desserts as well.

✴ ⊖Goodge St. Turn left onto Tottenham Court Rd., left onto Tottenham St., left onto Charlotte St., and right onto Rathbone St. Enter through the corridor next to the entrance to the pub. ⑤ Pies £10. Desserts £4.50. ☑ Open M-F noon-3pm and 6-10pm.

SHIBUYA
JAPANESE $$

2 Acton St. ☎020 7278 3447

Shibuya is a no-fuss Japanese restaurant that strives to use locally sourced and sustainable ingredients. They serve freshly made sushi, but there are plenty of noodle and curry dishes available. The lunch specials are excellent deals (we like the filling vegetable tempura udon soup served with a salmon avocado sushi roll). Given how exorbitantly expensive fresh sushi tends to be in London, this place is a steal. The Zen-like room with delicate blossom wallpaper will only add to your peace of mind.

✴ ⊖King's Cross St. Pancras. Make a left leaving the station, stay on Euston as it turns into Pentonville Rd., then make a right onto King's Cross Rd. The restaurant is on the corner with Acton St. ⑤ Sushi from £2.50. Main courses £7-10. Lunch specials £7.50.

FAIRUZ
LEBANESE $$

3 Blandford St. ☎020 7486 8108; www.fairuz.uk.com

This popular Lebanese spot is a solid neighborhood choice if you want a tasty sit-down meal without shelling out too much cash. Lamb features prominently on the menu; grilled or minced, it's always flavored with exotic spices. Starters include favorites like hummus and *baba ghanoush*. In the summer months, outdoor seating is available.

✴ ⊖Bond St. Left on Oxford St., and right onto James St., which will eventually turn into Thayer St. then make a right onto Blandford St. *i* Takeaway available. ⑤ Starters £4-6. Main courses £12-17. ☑ Open M-Sa noon-11pm, Su noon-10:30pm.

london

ALARA ORGANIC, VEGETARIAN $

58-60 Marchmont St. ☎020 7837 1172; www.alarashop.com

If you're feeling a little overwhelmed by all the pints and pies that London has thrust upon you, come to this health-food store and cafe to cleanse your palate and your conscience. You can pick up all kinds of vegan, organic, or just generally hippie-ish groceries in the shop, while the cafe offers smoothies, frozen yogurt, and a delicious lunch buffet. The dishes are all vegetarian and include moussaka, spinach tortillas, and some magical things made from legumes. Seating is available on a sidewalk patio.

⊖Russell Sq. Veer right when exiting the station and head up Marchmont St. $ Smoothies and frozen yogurt £2-4. Buffet £1.15 per 100g. ⏰ Open M-F 8am-8pm, Sa 10am-6pm, Su 11am-6pm. Buffet available until about 4pm.

gourmet glossary

One of the best parts about going to London is not needing to learn another language. You should be able to understand your waiter—most of the time. But you might want to stash this list under the table in case you run into a phrase you don't recognize:

- **BANGERS** are sausages.
- **BLACK PUDDING** is sausage made from pig's blood and fat.
- **BROWN SAUCE** usually refers to HP sauce, which is made of malt vinegar, tamarind, tomatoes, and dates.
- **BUBBLE AND SQUEAK** means leftover vegetables and potatoes mashed together.
- **BUCKS FIZZ** is a mimosa.
- **FAIRY CAKES** are cupcakes. Fairies are too small to eat whole cakes.
- **JELLY** actually means jello. It's alive!
- **KIPPER** is smoked herring.
- **MASH** means mashed potatoes (most often in "bangers and mash").
- **OFFAL** refers to animal organs and entrails, usually liver and kidney meat.
- **RASHERS** are slices of bacon.
- **PUDDING** refers to all desserts, not just the kind you eat after having your wisdom teeth removed.
- **SOLDIERS** are small pieces of toast.
- **SPOTTED DICK** is a dessert with dried fruit or custard—not any other kind of dick.

NORTH LONDON

LA CRÊPERIE DE HAMPSTEAD CREPERIE, STREET STAND $

Around 77 Hampstead High St. www.hampsteadcreperie.com

Walking down Hampstead High St. from the underground station, you may notice people ravenously eating crepes out of small conical cups. Walk a bit farther and you'll come upon La Crêperie de Hampstead, which has been serving the city's best crepes for over 30 years. The crepes are expertly crafted—a perfect balance of light and doughy—and the ingredients, sweet or savory, are bursting with flavor.

 # ⊖Hampstead. Turn left onto Hampstead High St. ℹ No seating. $ Sweet crepes £3.40-3.90; savory £4.30-4.80. ⏰ Open M-Th 11:45am-11pm, F-Su 11:45am-11:30pm.

✪ LE MERCURY — FRENCH $$

140A Upper St. ☎020 7354 4088; www.lemercury.co.uk

Le Mercury proves that good French food doesn't have to be expensive. Most starters are under £4, and all main courses are under £8. These include dishes as luxurious as *ballotine de foie gras*, lobster ravioli, and pork belly with *celeriac confit*. Enjoy them in the yellow interior by flickering candlelight and you may wonder why they even bothered building the Chunnel.

 # ⊖Angel. Exit and turn right onto Upper St. $ Starters £4. Main courses £8. Desserts £3. ⏰ Open M-Sa noon-1am, Su noon-11:30pm.

MANGO ROOM — CARIBBEAN $$

10-12 Kentish Town Rd. ☎020 7482 5065; www.mangoroom.co.uk

Mango Room offers a pleasant escape from the bustle of nearby Camden Town. The bright paintings, reggae, and delicious Caribbean dishes—like ackee and saltfish, jerk chicken, and curries—will cheer you up on a rainy London afternoon.

 # ⊖Camden High St. Turn left onto Camden High St., left onto Camden Rd., and left onto Kentish Town Rd. $ Lunch main courses £7-8.50. Dinner main courses £10.50-11. Happy hour cocktails £4. ⏰ Open M-Th noon-11pm, F-Sa noon-1am, Su noon-11pm. Kitchen open daily noon-11pm. Happy hour 6-8pm.

GALLIPOLI — TURKISH $$

102 Upper St. ☎020 7359 0630; www.cafegallipoli.com

Bronze lamps, painted plates, and wooden knick-knacks make this restaurant feel like a Turkish bazaar. The food—tangy feta, smoky grilled meats, and delicately spiced pilafs—feels no less authentic. Choose from a selection of mezze, or order a more traditional main course.

 # ⊖Angel. Turn right onto Upper St. $ Mezze £3-5. Main courses £8-12. ⏰ Open M-Th 11am-11pm, F 11am-midnight, Sa 10am-midnight, Su 10am-11pm.

INSPIRAL CAFE — VEGAN, CAFE $$

250 Camden High St. ☎020 7428 5875; www.inspiralled.net

A stupendous view over Camden Lock accompanies Inspiral Cafe's great selection of vegan food. You can choose between curries, lasagnas, breakfast scrambles, and even chocolate truffles.

 # ⊖Camden Town. Turn right onto Camden High St. ℹ Free Wi-Fi. $ Breakfast £3-5. Main courses £7-10. ⏰ Open M-Th 8am-10pm, F 8am-2am, Sa 9am-2am, Su 9am-11:30pm.

EAST LONDON

Most of East London's culinary offerings are packed into the unbeatable **Brick Lane.** If you're looking for curry, you'd have to be blind (not to mention smell-challenged) to miss it. There are other ethnic restaurants of various stripes, as well as the requisite number of cafes for an area this rife with flannel and skinny jeans.

✪ CAFE 1001 — CAFE $

91 Brick Ln. ☎020 7247 9679; www.cafe1001.co.uk

Hip East Enders bask in the British sun's occasional appearances while chatting over coffee from Cafe 1001's year-round outdoor cart. But they serve more than just coffee—the barbeque also grills all sorts of affordable burgers. Inside, patrons kick back in the warehouse-like space, where a variety of sandwiches and light food are served against a backdrop of Brazilian jams. At night, the salad bar turns into a real bar, and the back room becomes a venue for up-and-coming bands and DJs. Bloc Party filmed their video for "The Prayer" here. "East London is a vampire," as the boys would say.

Aldgate East. Turn left onto Whitechapel Rd., left onto Osborn St., then continue onto Brick Ln. ***i*** *Live bands on Tu (rock) and W (folk and jazz). Swing dancing classes Th 11am-5pm. Club night F-Su 7pm-midnight. Free Wi-Fi.* [$] *Cover £3-5 after midnight. Burger and chips £5. Coffee £1.20-2. Credit card min. £4.* ⏰ *Open daily 7am-midnight, often stays open all night F-Su.*

MIEN TAY VIETNAMESE $

122 Kingsland Rd. ☎020 7729 3074; www.mientay.co.uk

What Brick Lane is to Bengali food, this stretch of Kingsland Rd. is to Vietnamese. Mien Tay sets itself above the rest with low prices and high-quality crispy spring rolls, fragrant *pho*, and tasty noodle dishes (try the lemongrass and curry noodles). The service is swift and the dining room is bright and roomy.

Hoxton. Make a left after leaving the station, then a right onto Cremer St., and a left onto Kingsland Rd. [$] *Starters £2-5. Main courses £5-9.* ⏰ *Open M-Th noon-11pm, F-Sa noon-11:30pm, Su noon-11pm.*

SOUTH LONDON

FRANCO MANCA PIZZERIA $

Unit 4, Market Row ☎020 7738 3021; www.francomanca.co.uk

You'd be forgiven for thinking that you've stumbled through a wormhole to Naples when you step into this tiny pizzeria behind the Brixton Tube station. The chefs chatter away in Italian as they flip dough and transform it into one of the six gourmet pizzas on their seasonal menu. Besides the standard, perfectly crisped margherita, you can try pies with toppings like chorizo, organic pecorino cheese, and wild broccolini. Each individual pizza comfortably serves one, and you can wash it down with something from their well-curated selection of beer and wine.

Brixton. Make a left leaving the Tube, a quick left onto Electric Ave., then a right onto Electric Ln. and a left onto Market Row. [$] *Pizzas £4.50-7.* ⏰ *Open M-Sa noon-5pm.*

NEGRIL CARIBBEAN $$

132 Brixton Hill ☎020 8674 8798

Brixton is famous for its Afro-Caribbean food, and Negril is the place to sample some of the best of it. You can try regional specialties like callaloo (a leafy green), saltfish fritters, and goat curry, or go with something more familiar, like roasted chicken or barbeque ribs. Negril's rich, spicy gravy might be the best we've ever tasted. They also have quite a few vegan options, based on the traditional Rastafarian diet. Their weekend brunch is very popular.

Brixton. Make a left leaving the Tube and continue as the road becomes Brixton Hill. ***i*** *Delivery and takeaway available. No alcohol served, but you can BYOB for a £2.50 corkage charge per person.* [$] *Main courses £7-12.* ⏰ *Open M-F 5-10pm, Sa-Su 10am-10pm.*

THE COMMON CAFE $

21 The Pavement ☎020 7622 4944

The Common is a simple French-style cafe across from Clapham Common with some of the cheapest prices in the area. You can grab sandwiches to picnic in the park, or hang out on one of the two levels of seating. At night, they serve bistro-style dishes (steak, pasta, etc.), but they're better known for their abundant breakfast, which includes everything from granola with yogurt and fresh fruit to a full English fry-up.

Clapham Common. Go left from the station and continue along The Pavement toward the park. [$] *Sandwiches £2-4.50. Brunch and breakfast dishes £4-7. Main courses £7-12.* ⏰ *Open daily 7am-10pm.*

WEST LONDON

SUFI — PERSIAN $$

70 Askew Rd. ☎020 8834 4888; www.sufirestaurant.com

A very unassuming corner of West London hides this very unassuming restaurant with what many people swear is the best Persian food in London. It's easy to pass by the nondescript storefront, unless the window plastered with stickers and reviews happens to catch your eye. Inside the elegant dining room, you'll find perfectly charcoal-grilled skewers of meat, exotic stews, and hearty noodle soups, all for very reasonable prices—you can easily get a full meal here for £8.

⊖Shepherd's Bush Market. Make a right down Uxbridge Rd. when leaving the station, then after about 15min. make a left down Askew Rd. You can also take Bus #207 to the beginning of Askew Rd. [$] Starters £2-4. Main courses £7-12. ⏰ Open M-Sa noon-11pm, Su noon-10:30pm.

PATIO — POLISH $$

5 Goldhawk Rd. ☎020 8743 5194

You may not always have been raring to try Polish cuisine, but this restaurant will make you realize what you've been missing. Owned by a former Polish opera singer, Patio is filled with warm carpets and over-stuffed chairs, meant to create a casual but pleasant (read: comforting and grandmotherly) atmosphere. Diners enjoy traditional Polish fare like stuffed pancakes, veal, and cucumber and dill salad. The portions are hearty—even one of the "lighter" dishes can serve as a full meal. There's even a dusty-sounding piano for guests to bang out a tune.

⊖Shepherd's Bush. Cross Uxbridge Rd. and turn right onto Shepherd's Bush Green. Follow it until it becomes Goldhawk Rd. [$] Main courses £8-13. 3-course meal £15. ⏰ Open M-F noon-3pm and 5-11pm, Sa-Su 6-11:30pm.

nightlife

Pubs are the fabric of British life; most are open daily 11am to 11pm. The best ones claim residence in the oldest drinking locations in London, meaning that people have been drunk there since the dawn of time. Be wary of the "George Orwell drank here" line—you'll see those claims everywhere, because not only were many British icons fantastic drunks, they were also prolific walkers.

"But," you say, "how can it be nightlife if it closes down at 11pm?" Good question. If you seek the club scene of say, Barcelona, go to Barcelona. London is less lively than many European cities, and the elitist impulse often rears its head in British club life (especially in South Kensington and Chelsea, where many clubs are "members only"). The West End is full of bar-club hybrids that fill with cocktail-drinkers after work and morph into dance clubs on the weekends. This is also the only neighborhood where you're guaranteed to find something open after midnight on a Monday. Shoreditch is London's other nightlife center, and, though it's less prolific during the week, you'll find better music, cheaper prices, and more plaid than high heels. Speakeasy-style bars focusing on mixology and feeling hip can be found throughout the city. Keep an eye on local listings (in free daily newspapers, posters, and flyers) to find out what's going on after dark.

THE CITY OF LONDON

Pricey pubs filled with business suits are a dime a dozen in the City, but your options improve as you head north toward **Clerkenwell.**

FABRIC — CLUB

77A Charterhouse St. ☎020 7336 8898; www.fabriclondon.com

Despite being one of London's most famous clubs, Fabric has never lost its underground edge. Perhaps that's due to their carefully cultivated soundtrack—you won't hear David Guetta here, just cutting-edge dub, drum 'n bass, and techno. The space, a renovated warehouse full of deconstructed industrial decor, is the perfect place for the club's fun-loving clientele to dance. Look out for hidden quirks and flourishes, like 3D floor maps in the stairwells and a copy of Rubens's *Samson and Delilah* presiding over the smokers' courtyard. Or, entertain yourself by watching the guy with the dilated pupils try to figure out the faucets in the futuristic bathrooms (hint: there are buttons on the floor).

⊖Farringdon. Turn left onto Cowcross St. and continue until you hit Charterhouse St. $ Cover F-Sa £15-20, students £10; Su £10/5. Get discounts by buying tickets in advance. Beer £4.50. ⏰ Open F 10pm-6am, Sa 11pm-8am, Su 11pm-6am.

THE JERUSALEM TAVERN — PUB

55 Britton St. ☎020 7490 4281; www.stpetersbrewery.co.uk

The Jerusalem Tavern is the kind of London pub where you might be convinced you're back in the 18th century. The tavern is as bare as they come: a narrow, wooden interior without even any music playing. It's the only tavern in London to offer all of the St. Peter's ales. These specialized brews—including Golden Ale, Ruby Red Ale Honey Porter, and Cream Stout—are worth trying, though we're not saying you should try all of them at once... that would be irresponsible. Or so we hear.

⊖Farringdon. Turn left onto Cowcross St., left onto Turnmill St., right onto Benjamin St., and left onto Britton St. $ Pints £3.25. ⏰ Open M-F 11am-11pm.

THE SLAUGHTERED LAMB — PUB

34-35 Great Sutton St. ☎020 7253 1516; www.theslaughteredlambpub.com

Don't be put off by this pub's macabre name—it comes from this neighborhood's former career as London's meatpacking district. The Slaughtered Lamb feels a bit like a gigantic old living room with leather couches, comfy armchairs, and framed pictures around a fireplace (though most living rooms don't have this interesting a mix of indie rock and hip hop playing in the background). Downstairs, the music continues with frequent live shows and occasional comedy acts.

⊖Barbican. Turn left onto Goswell Rd. and left onto Great Sutton St. $ Pints from £3.60. ⏰ Open M-Th 11:30am-midnight, F 11:30am-1am, Sa noon-1am, Su 12:30-10:30pm.

THE WEST END

For many people, the West End is synonymous with London nightlife. On the plus side, this is the one part of the city where you're guaranteed to find something to do at 1am on a Monday. But the price for that is a glut of overcrowded and expensive bars and clubs. The truly chic head to private clubs in fancier areas, so the dominant theme in the West End is bar-and-club combos where everyone's trying a little too hard. Don't despair, though. Soho has the highest concentration of GLBT nightlife in the city, and the neighborhood draws crowds looking to have a good time. Mixed in with the bad suits and tourist traps, you'll find one of London's best clubs and a few quality bars.

THE BORDERLINE — CLUB

Orange Yard, off Manette St. ☎020 7734 5547; venues.meanfiddler.com/borderline/home

In the sea of booty-shaking Top 40 that is the West End, The Borderline offers something completely different. Though the club is a bare, dark basement with the same drunken dancing as at any London club, here you'll be moving to the likes of Joy Division, the Smiths, The Kooks, and Vampire Weekend. The crowd is devoted to the music, and you can't help but get into the spirit of things when everyone shouts the lyrics to "Friday I'm in Love." The club also hosts live music (see **Arts and Culture**). Plus, where else in the West End can you get a beer for two quid? (Answer: nowhere.)

➡ ⊖Tottenham Court Rd. Turn right onto Charing Cross Rd. and right onto Manette St. ℹ *Focus on punk on W, Student Night on Th, indie rock and Brit pop on F-Sa.* $ *Cover W-Th £5; F-Sa £7. Frequent £2 drink specials.* ⏰ *Open W-Sa 11pm-4am.*

👍 DIRTY MARTINI — BAR, CLUB

11-12 Russell St. ☎0844 371 2550; www.dirtymartini.uk.com

This bar's martini creations—fruity, chocolatey, fizzy, and everything in between—are impressive enough. But it gets better: drinks are half price during happy hour. As it gets later, the stylish lounge transforms into a dance club. The drink prices may rise, but that's offset by the fact that this is one of the only clubs in the West End that never charges cover. To top it off, Dirty Martini offers something even rarer than a straight man at a Bieber concert: free coat check. So you can get two martinis. Just remember what Dorothy Parker said.

➡ ⊖Covent Garden. Head down James St. to the Covent Garden Piazza, turn left and go around it until you come to the corner of Russell St. $ *Beers £4. Cocktails £8-9.* ⏰ *Open M-W 5pm-1am, Th-Sa 5pm-3am, Su 5-11pm. Happy hour M-Th 5-10pm, F-Sa 5-8pm, Su 5-11pm.*

👍 AIN'T NOTHIN' BUT... — BAR, LIVE MUSIC

20 Kingly St. ☎020 7287 0514; www.aintnothinbut.co.uk

Your woman done left you? Your baby got you down? Come commiserate (or drink away your sorrows) at this excellent blues bar, where there's live music every night of the week. From established bands to open-mic nights to jam sessions, they've got it all. Even when no one's performing, a contingent of grizzled regulars line the bar, nursing double bourbons and enjoying the CD collection.

➡ ⊖Oxford Circus. Head down Regent St., turn right onto Great Marlborough St., and right onto Kingly St. $ *Nominal cover charge F-Sa after 8:30pm. Beers from £3.50. Double bourbon £6.60.* ⏰ *Open M-Th 5pm-1am, F 5pm-2:30am, Sa 3pm-2:30am, Su 3pm-midnight.*

👍 HEAVEN — CLUB, GLBT

Under the Arches, Villiers St. ☎020 7930 2020; www.heavennightclub-london.com

This gigantic, multi-room club is home to a variety of popular GLBT and mixed nights. Mondays have "Popcorn," a student-friendly event with good drink specials and a welcoming door policy; the music varies from hip hop to techno to classic dance tunes. Thursday through Saturday the club is run by G-A-Y, London's biggest GLBT party organization. Friday night brings "Camp Attacks" (with amazingly cheesy disco music) and performances by famous pop stars. Saturdays are usually the most popular night at Heaven.

➡ ⊖Charing Cross. Turn right from the station and head down Villiers St. The club is under the archway about halfway down. $ *Cover £4-5; usually free before midnight or if you sign up on the guest list.* ⏰ *Open M 11pm-6am, Th 11pm-3am, F-Sa 11pm-5am.*

FREUD — BAR

198 Shaftesbury Ave. ☎020 7240 9933

Freud, standing out with a laid-back, bohemian atmosphere, is the West End bar for those trying to pretend they're not in the West End. You won't hear any Beyoncé, but Freud is nowhere near as pretentious as some of the bars in Shoreditch. The drinks are big and strong, but be careful about what you order if you don't want to be psychoanalyzed: the Slippery Nipple and Harvey Wallbanger are crying out for the great man's intervention.

➡ ⊖Piccadilly Circus. Turn right onto Shaftesbury Ave. $ *Beer £3.50. Cocktails £5.50-7.50. Credit card min. £10.* ⏰ *Open M-Th 11am-11pm, F-Sa 11am-1am, Su noon-10:30pm.*

VILLAGE BAR, GLBT

81 Wardour St. ☎020 7478 0530; www.village-soho.co.uk

Early in the evening, Village looks like just another after-work bar (except with slightly nicer suits on slightly better-looking men). As the night wears on, however, it gets more exciting with drag queens, karaoke (Tuesdays and Wednesdays), go-go boys (Saturdays), and more. The slightly carnival-esque decorations and tantalizing cocktail menu only add to the fun.

⊖Piccadilly Circus. Turn right onto Shaftesbury Ave. then left onto Wardour St. $ Cocktails £6-7. ⏰ Open M-Sa 4pm-1am, Su 4-11:30pm.

CANDY BAR BAR, CLUB, GLBT

4 Carlisle St. ☎020 7287 5041; www.candybarsoho.com

Candy Bar is London's premier—and certainly most popular—lesbian bar and club. Ladies flock to the pop-colored bar for drinks, pool, and dancing. Boys are allowed if they bring at least two female friends, but they're barred from the downstairs floor when dancers are performing. DJs spin records Wednesday through Sunday; the music varies from hip hop to chart hits to funk and soul. Check out the ridiculous Monday drink specials.

⊖Tottenham Court Rd. Turn left onto Oxford St., left onto Dean St., and right onto Carlisle St. $ Cover £5 F-Sa after 10pm. Drinks £1.50-6. ⏰ Open M-Th 5pm-3am, F-Sa 4pm-3am, Su 4pm-12:30am.

WESTMINSTER

Westminster isn't an ideal location for nightlife, pubs, or clubs. Enjoy it during the day, and then take the party elsewhere, old sport—unless you're in the market for really good beer.

CASK BEER HEAVEN

6 Charlwood St. ☎020 7630 7225; www.caskpubandkitchen.com

Whether or not you know the difference between a dubbel and a tripel, or that gueuze is the weirdest beer you'll ever taste, Cask has a drink for you. Their beer "menu" is actually a binder full of hundreds upon hundreds of bottled beers from around the world. A couple dozen more are on tap, and they rotate the selection so they can accommodate as many rare and novel brews as possible. Despite being a true aficionado's bar, neophytes will also feel right at home; the staff is always ready to make recommendations, and refrain from snobbery when responding to even the most basic questions and silliest mispronunciations. Ample seating ensures that, despite the bar's popularity, you'll be able to enjoy your pint comfortably.

⊖Pimlico. Turn right onto Tachwood St., Cask is at the corner on the right with Charlwood St. i Free Wi-Fi (as if you needed an excuse to spend more time here). $ Pints start around £3.70, but vary wildly from there. ⏰ Open M 4-11pm, Tu-Su noon-11pm.

BRASS MONKEY PUB

250 Vauxhall Bridge Rd. ☎020 7834 0553; www.brass-monkeybar.co.uk

Unless you're absolutely gasping for a pint the second you leave Victoria station, ignore the tourist trap pubs nearby and walk a few minutes to this significantly more appealing establishment. Brass Monkey has a modest selection of draft beers, two excellent cask ales, and a decent wine list, but the real draw is the atmosphere. It's tasteful and polished, with locals enjoying pints and conversation across its two floors.

⊖Victoria. Turn right onto Vauxhall Bridge Rd. $ Pints £3.65. ⏰ Open M-Sa 11am-11pm.

THE SOUTH BANK

Back in Shakespeare's day, the South Bank was a hotbed of taverns, brothels, and bear-baiting. Things have calmed down a bit since then, but this is still a great place to find a pint or a stiff drink. Plenty of spots are clustered around London Bridge and Borough.

THE HIDE — BAR

39-45 Bermondsey St. ☎020 7403 6655; www.thehidebar.com

You automatically feel a few degrees classier when you step inside this relaxed cocktail bar, without even having to change out of the jeans you've been wearing for a week straight. The Hide has candlelight, plenty of space, leather couches, and crackly jazz—but also a totally unpretentious atmosphere, and a crowd that includes everyone from backpackers to young lovers to old men in suspenders. The focus is on the cocktail menu, with oodles of drinks carefully mixed from apothecary-like glass bottles. Try the Boston Tea Party, which serves two from a porcelain tea pot into tiny little cups.

🚇 London Bridge. Walk toward the bridge and turn right onto Tooley St., then right onto Bermondsey St. $ Most spirits £4. Cocktails £7-8. ⏰ Open Tu 5pm-midnight, W-Th 5pm-1am, F-Sa 5pm-2am, Su 3-10:30pm.

SOUTHWARK TAVERN — PUB

22 Southwark St. ☎020 7403 0257; www.thesouthwarktavern.co.uk

You can go on the gimmicky London Dungeon experience, or you can come here and drink in one of the subterranean cells on the pub's lower floor. This place used to be a prison (it seems like half of the South Bank was), and it retains its original brick-and-iron-bars style. Doing better than bread and water, the pub offers 21 beers on draft, including a number of American imports (Sierra Nevada, Brooklyn Lager) if you're feeling homesick.

🚇 London Bridge. Exit down Borough High St. and the pub is where Southwark St. splits off. ℹ Quiz night on Tu. $ Pints £4. ⏰ Open M-W 11am-midnight, Th-F 11am-1am, Sa 10am-1am, Su noon-midnight.

london skittles

While the majority of Londoners today associate skittles with candy, a few old-timers picture bowling. Imbibing ale instead of tasting the rainbow, participants in this traditional pub game hurl a 10 lb. *fromage*-shaped hunk of wood at a diamond of nine pins, aiming to clear the lane in the least amount of throws. Skittles has been played since Danish sailors brought it up the Thames in the 17th century. Nothing kills a good drinking game quite like a world war, but skittles has been making a comeback in the London drunken debauchery scene. Stop by the Freemasons Arms on Tuesdays 8-11pm or Saturdays 6-9pm for a game. (81-82 Long Acre ☎020 7836 3115 🚇 Covent Garden. ⏰ Open daily 11am-late.)

SOUTH KENSINGTON AND CHELSEA

THE DRAYTON ARMS — PUB

153 Old Brompton Rd. ☎020 7835 2301; www.thedraytonarmssw5.co.uk

The Drayton Arms is a comfortable, well-kept pub that mixes the classiness of its postcode (chandeliers, high ceilings) with laid-back ease (oversize couches, worn wooden tables). Enjoy a fine selection of beers around the fireplace, then see a play or film in the first floor's black-box theater, which features everything from improv comedy to classic foreign films.

🚇 Gloucester Rd. Turn right onto Gloucester Rd. and right onto Old Brompton Rd. $ Pints around £3.80. ⏰ Open M-F 11am-midnight, Sa-Su 10am-midnight.

👍 **THE TROUBADOUR CLUB** LIVE MUSIC, BAR

263-267 Old Brompton Rd. ☎020 7370 1434; www.troubadour.co.uk

Many famous acts have graced the Troubadour's small stage since its founding in 1954. The hanging string lights have illuminated the likes of **Bob Dylan, Jimi Hendrix,** and **Joni Mitchell,** and pictures of these artists cover the tabletops. To this day, The Troubadour is a community of aspiring and acclaimed artists bound together by the intoxicating atmosphere of good drinks and great music. Come here to see some of the city's most exciting acts before they make it big.

🚶 ⊖Gloucester Rd. Turn right onto Gloucester Rd., then turn right onto Old Brompton Rd. ℹ Live music most nights. Poetry night every other M. Friday shows 21+. $ Cover usually £5-10; cash only. ⏰ Open M-W 8pm-midnight, Th-Sa 8pm-2am, Su 8pm-midnight. Happy hour Tu-Su 8-9pm.

👍 **MISS Q'S** CLUB, BAR

180-184 Earl's Court Rd. ☎020 7370 5358; www.missqs.com

This old-school rock 'n' roll bar and club provides enough kitschy Americana to satisfy those still sad they missed the Elvis era. There's diner food on the menu, three classic pool tables, red lights, and black leather. Wednesday has live music, mostly rock and blues, while Thursday through Saturday nights host DJs diverging slightly from the theme by playing a range from classic soul to the latest hip hop. It may feel a bit schizophrenic, but it certainly gets people moving on the dance floor.

🚶 ⊖Earl's Court. Turn left when exiting the station. $ Cover Th-F £5 after 10pm; Sa £5 after 9pm. Pints £4. Cocktails £7-11. ⏰ Open M-W 5pm-midnight, F-Sa 5pm-2am, Su 5pm-midnight. Happy hour M-Th 5-8pm.

THE BLACKBIRD PUB

209 Earl's Court Rd. ☎020 7835 1855

The Blackbird is the quintessential local pub, with a long bar, plenty of booths, and unassuming rock playing softly overhead. It also serves many varieties of the Fuller's brand of (wholesomely British) beer. The food is the usual pies and Sunday roasts. At the edge of Kensington, it's less expensive and more authentic than the other "local English pubs" to the east.

🚶 ⊖Earl's Court. Just across the road from the station, slightly to the right. $ Pints from £3.50. ⏰ Open M-Sa 11am-11pm, Su 11am-10:30pm.

JANET'S BAR BAR

30 Old Brompton Rd. ☎020 7581 3160

Janet's is the closest thing to a dive bar that you'll find in South Kensington. The walls are plastered with photos of regulars and Red Sox and Yankees pennants (closer together than most fans would like). It's still popular with the locals, despite the Americana—there are even rumors of occasional celebrity sightings. If the atmosphere doesn't make you feel welcome, the Beatles sing-alongs will, and it's one of the few bars in the neighborhood open past 11pm.

🚶 ⊖South Kensington. As you exit the station, Old Brompton Rd. is across the street. ℹ Live music Tu-Su after 9:30pm. $ Beer around £4.50. Cocktails £6.50-8.50. Credit card min. £3. ⏰ Open M-W 11:45am-1am, Th 11:45am-1:30am, F 11:45am-2:30am, Sa noon-2:30am, Su 2pm-1am.

HYDE PARK TO NOTTING HILL

For all the bustle around Bayswater during the day, it's pretty deserted at night. Notting Hill is largely residential, and the few nightlife spots it does have are dominated by businesspeople grabbing drinks on their way home from work. However, Portobello Rd. has a sprinkling of good bars that pop up when the shops close, although the long street can feel even longer and more desolate at night.

👍 **NOTTING HILL ARTS CLUB** CLUB

21 Notting Hill Gate ☎020 7460 4459; www.nottinghillartsclub.com

Notting Hill is not a place that makes you think of exuberant dancing, cutting-edge music, and cheap covers. And yet, tucked underground just off the main road lies this exciting den offering all those things and more. One room contains a circular bar with tables and couches set into the wall for lounging; the other has the dance floor and stage. There are virtually no decorations to speak of, so nothing will distract from your gyrations. Each night has a different mix of musical genres: Wednesday is indie and punk; Thursday has a supremely popular offering of hip hop and dub; Friday and Saturday might feature soul and funk, salsa, or who knows what else. The crowd varies from well-dressed young professionals to urban b-boy types who clearly know what this place is about.

⚡ ⊖*Notting Hill Gate. The door isn't well marked, but look for the smoking area and metal fences keeping the entrance line in place.* ⓘ *18+; make sure to bring proof of age. Sign up for the guest list via Facebook for Th nights. Some special events pop up occasionally on other days.* Ⓢ *Cover varies, generally £5-8; free on W. Beer £3. Cocktails from £6.* ⓩ *Open W-Sa usually 8pm-2am.*

▨ PORTOBELLO STAR   BAR
171 Portobello Rd.   ☎020 7229 8016; www.portobellostarbar.co.uk

We can't decide which we like best: the cheeky drink descriptions on the menu or the drinks themselves. Clearly at the forefront of the cocktail revolution, the libations at Portobello Star are creative and made from top-notch ingredients. The overall feeling of the place is that they take their booze (and not much else) seriously. You'll hear your favorite classic rock, indie hits, R and B, soul, and hip hop from the bar or the leather couches in the calmer chill-out room on the first floor. The crowd is in their early 20s to early 30s, clad in everything from dresses and heels to flannel and tattoos—or all four at once. During the day, the pub transforms into a cafe that serves pies made by the famous Ginger Pig butchers.

⚡ ⊖*Notting Hill Gate. Take a right onto Pembridge Rd. and then left onto Portobello Rd.* Ⓢ *Cocktails £7-10.* ⓩ *Open M-Th 10am-midnight, F-Sa 10am-1am, Su 10am-midnight.*

PORTOBELLO GOLD   PUB
95 Portobello Rd.   ☎020 7229 8528; www.portobellogold.com

Portobello Gold is an old-fashioned pub with a crowd that sings along to the classic rock soundtrack. The clientele represents the whole age spectrum—from young hipsters to 70-something locals. Basically, there's a whole lot of plaid. They have a good selection of beers on tap, and a full-service restaurant with pub grub (and famous oysters) in the back. Especially popular on Saturdays after 11pm.

⚡ ⊖*Notting Hill Gate. Take right onto Pembridge Rd. and then left onto Portobello Rd.* ⓘ *Live music Su 6:30-10pm.* Ⓢ *½ pints from £3.60. Wine £4-6. Cuban cigars £10.* ⓩ *Open M-Th 10am-noon, F-Sa 10am-12:30am, Su 10am-11:30pm.*

MARYLEBONE AND BLOOMSBURY

While Bloomsbury is filled with universities, most students only live in the area for their first year (if at all). Student-oriented nightlife is thus limited to a few pubs here and there, while the rest of the area is dominated by the suits of the after-work crowd. However, a few old-fashioned haunts are worth checking out—perhaps more for sightseeing than nightlife purposes—and, since it's London, there's always a club or two to be found.

▨ THE SOCIAL   CLUB, BAR
5 Little Portland St.   ☎020 7636 4992; www.thesocial.com

Though the upstairs, with its exposed light bulbs and bare wood floor, looks like a typical hip bar, the underground space at the Social is where most of the action takes place. A ragingly popular hip-hop karaoke night takes place here every other Thursday, as well as club nights and live performances. Many nights have no cover charge. The Social is a lively contrast to the scores of traditional pubs filled with businessmen that surround the area and is the closest to a club you're likely to find around here.

⚡ ⊖*Oxford Circus. Right onto Regent St., right onto Little Portland St.* ⓘ *DJs on the ground fl.*

london

most nights. $ *Pints around £3.70. Cocktails around £7. Cover £5-7 on club night. Student cards will get you discounts on most covered nights. Credit card min. £10.* ⏰ *Open M 5pm-midnight, Tu-W noon-midnight, Th-F noon-1am, Sa 7pm-1am.*

👍 PURL

BAR

50/54 Blandford St. www.purl-london.co.uk

Designed to look like an old-school speakeasy, Purl would be gimmicky if the theme weren't pulled off so well. From the subterranean darkness to the bartenders' 1920s-style vests, everything is crafted to make Al Capone feel right at home. The crowd, though, tends to be very chic and modern. The drinks are pricey, but they are astounding works of art; some arrive steaming with liquid nitrogen, while others are packaged in a squat bottle complete with its own brown paper bag—and all are delicious and innovative mixtures, and definitely a far cry from a glass of bathtub gin.

🧭 *⊖Bond St. Left onto Oxford St., and right onto James St., which will eventually turn into Thayer St. Right onto Blandford St.* **i** *Reservations recommended for tables; book online through their website.* $ *Cocktails £7.50-10.* ⏰ *Open M-Th 5-11:30pm, F-Sa 5pm-midnight.*

👍 THE GOLDEN EAGLE

PUB

59 Marylebone Ln. ☎020 7935 3228

London is incredibly diverse, but sometimes you just want to experience something that feels truly British. So, what could be more perfect than hanging out with old men boozily belting out their favorite songs? Three nights a week at The Golden Eagle, the bespectacled Tony "Fingers" Pearson rolls out an old upright piano and proceeds to hammer out classics like "La Vie En Rose" and "Just One of Those Things." Between the alcohol-induced golden haze, the music, and the cheery staff, the pub is a living Capra film, and in no way is that a bad thing. Plus, the beer is cheap enough that soon you might be singing along with the crowd.

🧭 *⊖Bond St. Right onto Oxford St., left onto Marylebone Ln.* **i** *Music Tu and Th-F 8:30pm.* $ *Average pint £3.50.* ⏰ *Open M-Th 11am-11pm, F-Sa 11am-midnight, Su noon-7pm.*

THE FITZROY TAVERN

PUB

16A Charlotte St. ☎020 7580 3714

Many pubs try to ensnare tourists by claiming they are the oldest pub in England or telling bizarre perversions of famous stories ("and that penny that Dickens gave to the little boy was spent on whiskey in our pub...") that lend a historical respectability to what is actually just a decrepit pub with bad ale. The Fitzroy Tavern actually has a published book about its history, with artifacts from that history coating its walls. Famous for the charitable program instated by the tavern to send kids on outings to the country and for the authors who frequented the pub—most notably **Dylan Thomas** and **George Orwell**—The Fitzroy Tavern is the real deal. Pints of the many tasty varieties of Sam Smith are cheap, the history's free, and there's a comedy night too.

🧭 *⊖Goodge St. Left onto Tottenham Ct. Rd., left on Tottenham St., left onto Charlotte St.* **i** *Comedy night W 8:30pm.* $ *Pints around £2.50. Credit card min. £10, plus 1.5% surcharge.* ⏰ *Open M-Sa noon-11pm, Su noon-10:30pm.*

SCALA

CLUB

275 Pentonville Rd. ☎020 7833 2022; www.scala-london.co.uk

This multi-level club, just across the road from King's Cross, hosts a diversity of nighttime entertainment. From live bands to indie rock DJ mashups to hip hop to straight up club techno, there's always something loud playing. Scala is very popular with the younger end of the student crowd. Tickets are generally much cheaper in advance or with a flyer, so look online to plan ahead.

🧭 *⊖King's Cross St. Pancras. Head left when leaving the station.* $ *Cover varies, usually £5-12.* ⏰ *Opening hours depend on the event; club nights F-Sa 10pm-4am or later.*

NORTH LONDON

Camden Town and the area around **Angel** come alive at night, but the scene is primarily limited to pubs and bars. Camden is also home to some important live-music venues.

🔲 69 COLEBROOKE ROW
BAR

69 Colebrooke Row　　　　　　　☎07540 528 593; www.69colebrookerow.com

This lounge put a lot more effort into creating swanky atmosphere and inventive cocktail menu than they did their name. Of the cocktails, we like the Serafin (made with tequila, poire liqueur, and ginger beer) and the champagne topped with English rose aromatics. Popular among Islington yuppies and cocktail connoisseurs, the bar's vibe is saved from pretension by the impromptu ditties played by patrons on the upright piano.

✝ ⊖*Angel. Turn right after leaving the station and stay to the right as you pass Islington Green. Then turn right onto Colebrooke Row.* Ⓢ *Cocktails £8.50.* 🕔 *Open M-W 5pm-midnight, Th 5pm-1-am, F-Sa 5pm-2am, Su 5pm-midnight.*

SLIM JIM'S LIQUOR STORE
BAR

112 Upper St.　　　　　　　　　☎020 7354 4364; www.slimjimsliquorstore.com

Not all American-themed establishments in London focus on hamburgers and BBQ; Slim Jim's pays homage in the form of old-school rockabilly and a sterling selection of bourbons. It's dark and divey, just like your favorite Delta honky-tonk. When the music gets going, couples show off their swing-dancing moves. Don't forget to appreciate the impressive collection of bras hanging from the ceiling, and feel free to add your own to the collection.

✝ ⊖*Angel. Turn right and continue up Upper St.* Ⓢ *Bourbon and scotch £3-10. Pints from £3.75.* 🕔 *Open M-W 4pm-2am, Th 4pm-3am, F-Sa noon-3am, Su noon-2am.*

EAST LONDON

🔲 THE BOOK CLUB
BAR, CLUB

100 Leonard St.　　　　　　　　　☎020 7684 8618; www.wearetbc.com

No, this isn't a place where suburban housewives get together to discuss the latest Nicholas Sparks novel. In keeping with the ever-experimental, avant-garde atmosphere of East London, this multi-level former warehouse is a cafe, bar, lecture hall, dance club, art installation space, and more. During the week, there might be a Glam Poetry Slam or one of their signature "Thinking and Drinking" events—lectures on topics from laugh therapy to the connection between scent and memory. Thursday through Saturday are usually reserved for dancing. Thursdays are "Human Juke-box" (the crowd decides the music), while on Fridays and Saturdays they bring in excellent electronic and hip-hop DJs. The Book Club distills all the quirky creative energy of East London into one spot and adds a bar (or two).

✝ ⊖*Shoreditch High St. Make a left after leaving the station, then a right onto Great Eastern St., and a left onto Leonard St.* Ⓢ *Cover varies from free to £12; on most F-Sa, it's £5 after 9pm.* 🕔 *Open M-W 8am-midnight, Th-F 8am-2am, Sa 10am-2am, Su 10am-midnight.*

🔲 STRONGROOM BAR
BAR

120-124 Curtain Rd.　　　　　　　☎020 7426 5103; www.strongroombar.com

It seems like all the "cool" places in Shoreditch are down an alley or through a tunnel. Strongroom is no different, but it makes excellent use of its alleyway real estate with a large, heated patio area. Inside is a pub-like upper level and a downstairs lounge with couches and room for dancing. DJs spin old-school rock and soul, and there are occasionally live performances. They offer a truly stellar beer selection and some well-made cocktails.

✝ ⊖*Shoreditch High St. Make a left after leaving the station, then a right onto Great Eastern St., and a right onto Curtain Rd.* Ⓢ *Pints from £3.50.* 🕔 *Open M 9am-11pm, Tu-W 9am-midnight, Th 9am-1am, F 9am-2am, Sa noon-2am, Su noon-10pm.*

london

SOUTH LONDON

Brixton is teeming with pubs, clubs, and live-music venues. Most of them are clustered around the Tube station, so just wander about until you see something that strikes your fancy. Clapham's nightlife is popular with the yuppier crowd, who troll the cocktail bars up and down Clapham High St.

👍 HOOTENANNY — BAR, CONCERT VENUE

95 Effra Rd. ☎020 7737 7273; www.hootenannybrixton.co.uk

The walk from the Tube takes you through a quiet residential neighborhood, but just as you start thinking you must have gone the wrong way, you come upon Hootenanny's warehouse-and-patio complex. Inside, you'll find a bar with pool tables and couches, plus the real draw of the venue: a concert space that hosts live roots, rock, reggae, and ska almost every night. Outside, there's a barbeque and smokers clustered around the many picnic tables. The cheerful vibe is infectious; it's hard not to groove along when an old Jamaican man is cutting a rug right next to you.

⇞ ⊖Brixton. Make a left as you exit the station and continue on Effra Rd. as it forks off. ℹ 21+. [$] Most shows are free; occasional £5 cover. Beers from £3. ⏰ Hours vary, usually open W-Su 9am-2pm.

THE WHITE HORSE — PUB

94 Brixton Hill ☎020 8678 6666; www.whitehorsebrixton.com

The White Horse is a large, laid-back pub with some curious touches—semi-pornographic bestial artwork, anyone?—that make it a bit more interesting than your average local. During the week, the pub attracts a young professional crowd for no-fuss drinks, while DJs liven things up on the weekends with hip hop, funk, and house. Sunday afternoons host live folk and jazz.

⇞ ⊖Brixton. Make a left leaving the station and stay on the road as it turns into Brixton Hill. [$] Pints from £3. ⏰ Open M-Th 5pm-midnight, F 4pm-3am, Sa noon-3am, Su noon-midnight.

WEST LONDON

👍 THE GOLDHAWK — PUB

122-124 Goldhawk Rd. ☎020 8576 6921

The Goldhawk is just like that kid you know who is always ineffably cool without even trying—yeah, you know the one. Its indie-rock music is just a little bit better than the stuff played at other pubs. The beer selection is just a little bit more interesting—they've got an unusual Belgian brew or two mixed in with a wide selection of British ales. Its underdone-chic lounges and tables are just a little bit more artfully distressed. But, of course, it's totally unpretentious about the whole thing. This makes it one of the best simple hang-out-and-have-a-beer pubs in the city.

⇞ ⊖Goldhawk Rd. Make a left when leaving the station. ℹ Open-mic night Th 8pm. [$] Pints from £3.50. Frequent deals, like 4 beers for £10. ⏰ Open M-W noon-11pm, Th noon-midnight, F-Sa noon-12:30am, Su noon-11pm.

👍 DOVE — PUB

19 Upper Mall ☎020 8748 9474

This stretch of the Thames in Hammersmith feels calm, secluded, and rural, and any of the pubs along it are worthy of a visit. The Dove is probably the most beloved by locals. The taps hold a strong selection of British ales, and the kitchen serves up comforting pub grub. Best of all are the picnic tables, which let you sit right by the river in summer, and the toasty upper rooms, which provide a sheltered view in winter.

⇞ ⊖Ravenscourt Park. Make a left down Ravenscourt Rd., cross King St. onto Rivercourt Rd., and make a left onto Upper Mall. [$] Pints from £3.50. ⏰ Open M-Sa 11am-11pm, Su noon-10:30pm.

arts and culture

From Shakespeare to the Sex Pistols, London has never been behind the times when it comes to the entertaining arts. Every time you take an escalator in a Tube station, the barrage of posters will remind you of the breadth and quality of the city's cultural opportunities. Experience the delights of the stage at a major West End musical, a quirky new production at the Young Vic, an elegant ballet at the Royal Opera House, or that famed British wit at one of the city's comedy clubs. If it's dulcet tones you're looking for, catch chamber music in St Martin-in-the-Fields, or check out an up-and-coming indie band at The Borderline. In the summer, the city explodes with festivals of all shapes and sizes. And for a city as expensive as London, cultural events can be surprisingly cheap. Whatever you need tickets for, make sure to check for deals—student discounts, standby tickets, and officially sanctioned theater passes can save you a lot of money.

THE 2012 OLYMPICS

As great as it always is to travel to London, 2012 is going to be special. Whether you're a sports buff, want to experience one of the world's greatest spectacles, or just dream of meeting Usain Bolt, being in London for the 30th Summer Olympics will be a remarkable experience. If you're going to be in the city between July 27 and August 12, read up on what you can expect to see.

games past and present

HOSTESS WITH THE MOSTEST

Though London will be the first city to host the modern Games three times, the 2012 Olympics are being treated as London's chance to really shine. Both previous times the Olympic torch was lit in London, the city played the role of understudy, stepping in at the last minute. An eruption of Mount Vesuvius put the original 1908 host, Rome, out of commission, and, on short notice, London hosted a characteristically well-organized Olympics, even inaugurating the practice of constructing a new stadium for the Games. In 1948, London showcased British resolve and resilience, reinvigorating the Games after a 12-year hiatus during WWII.

THIRD TIME'S THE CHARM

London won the bid for the 30th Olympiad with a plan for the "greenest" games in history. The games have transformed the once-forgotten hinterlands of northeast London's Stratford neighborhood (not to be confused with Shakespeare's hometown, Stratford-Upon-Avon), from garbage dump to verdant Olympic showpiece. The Games' planners hope to make these Games entirely car-free, send no waste to landfills during the games, and plant more than 4000 trees to fill the Olympic Park and Village.

ICONIC OR MORONIC?

If you've seen the 2012 Olympics logo or mascots, you know that British wits will have many chances to flex their muscles by the time these Games are up. Since it was unveiled in June 2007, the London Olympics logo, a garishly colored, zig-zaggy rendering of the year 2012, has been the subject of controversy. Some think the logo looks uncomfortably like a broken swastika. Iran thinks it spells "Zion" and has threatened to boycott the Games in protest. For many people, though, it looks most like Lisa Simpson performing a certain sex act.

Almost as entertaining as the logo are the mascots. Whereas past Olympic planners drew upon their cities' cultural and biological heritage to design adorable mascots, London organizers were inspired by drops of molten steel from the factory in Bolton where the Olympic Stadium's girders were produced. Maybe that explains why "Wenlock" and "Mandeville" look so ridiculous.

get your game on

The heart of the Olympics will be in the East London district of Stratford. The Olympic Park there contains the 80,000-seat **Olympic Stadium,** the sleek new **Aquatics Centre,** featuring a wave-like roof designed by Iraqi-British architect Zaha Hadid, and the 17,320-bed **Olympic Village.** The recently expanded Stratford Regional station connects the Park to central London by DLR, Underground, and bus.

There will also be plenty going on in the city center and hinterlands of London. Here's a quick guide to some of the other venues.

HORSE GUARDS PARADE

Sand is being trucked in to create a **beach volleyball** court on this parade ground between St. James's Park and a stretch of buildings that includes #10 Downing Street and the Horse Guards. Sadly, the arrangement is only temporary, and neither the Queen nor David Cameron responded to our request for a pick-up game.

HYDE PARK

Triathletes and marathon swimmers will dip into the waters of this famous park's Serpentine Lake. This will certainly be much more pleasant than going for a dip in the Thames.

EARLS COURT

There's no sand in this 1935 conference center in South Kensington and Chelsea, but it will make do with regular volleyball.

EXCEL

You'll be able to catch boxing, fencing, judo, wrestling, and (everyone's favorite) table tennis at this exhibition center in the London Docklands. From the Olympic Park or central London, take the DLR to get here.

GREENWICH PARK

A popular tourist destination even outside of Olympics season thanks to its glorious Old Royal Naval College (among other things), Greenwich Park will be going neigh-val rather than naval when equestrian events get going here. The venue is near Greenwich rail and DLR stations.

O$_2$ ARENA

This North Greenwich arena was originally built for the city's Millennium celebrations, and is now being repurposed as the venue for artistic gymnastics, trampoline, and wheelchair basketball. The venue is best reached by Tube, and there will be a shuttle running from Charlton. Note that, during the Games, it will be called the North Greenwich Arena thanks to the International Olympic Committee's hatred of all sponsors except their own.

WIMBLEDON

This one shouldn't be a surprise: the home of the All England Lawn Tennis and Croquet Club will open its pristine grass courts up to Olympic tennis competition. You can reach it by Tube, rail, or Tramlink (between Croydon and Wimbledon).

WEMBLEY STADIUM

Soccer players will duke it out at Wembley, six miles northwest of the city center. Coming from the north, the stadium can be reached by rail and London Overground; otherwise, you're best taking the Tube.

spectating

You can find the most up-to-date information about purchasing tickets at www. tickets.london2012.com. If you haven't obtained tickets yet, expect slim pickings, but don't despair. You probably won't be able to get (or afford) tickets to the premier events, but you might be able to find some for the less popular ones. The cheapest £20 tickets are mainly for preliminary rounds of events, so you may be paying more for atmosphere than a good look at the competition. All tickets include a Travel Pass good for all London public transportation on the day of competition. Tickets cannot be sold legally without London 2012's permission, so make sure you deal with an official retailer.

Fortunately, there are plenty of opportunities to soak up the spirit of the games without having to buy a ticket. You can catch the cycling portion of the triathlon from Hyde Park. The marathon winds past many of London's famous monuments, including St. Paul's Cathedral and Big Ben—just make sure to claim your spot along the course early enough to get a good view. Our pick for the most absurd Olympic event, walking, as well as the cycling road races can also be viewed courseside without a ticket. Plans for the Olympic Park include "Henman Hills" from which visitors will be better able to view large screens broadcasting the games. Then of course, you can always drop into a pub and watch on the telly with some locals—probably the most authentically British way to experience the Games.

an opening ceremony to remember

With Danny Boyle (director of *Slumdog Millionaire, Trainspotting,* and *28 Days Later*) as Artistic Director and Stephen Daldry (director of *Billy Elliot, The Hours,* and *The Reader*) on board as Executive Creative Producer, the 2012 Opening Ceremony arrives with a fine pedigree. Add to that a few ex-Spice Girls and you've got quite the heady (though perhaps incoherent) mix of talent. Here are our humble suggestions for Messers Boyle and Daldry as they set about designing a ceremony that will highlight all that's great in British culture.

- **TEAM UP** the Spice Girls with Justin Bieber. Yes, he's not exactly British, but get ready to send tween girls into Nirvana.

- **ROYAL FOREVER.** Can you get the royal family involved? We'd love to see the Queen try her hand at archery. Even better, a beach volleyball match-up between William and Kate and Harry and... anyone but Camilla.

- **ANYTHING HARRY POTTER** is golden. Bringing Dumbledore back to life gets you extra points.

- **END IT ALL** with the giant *Monty Python* foot smashing everything.

THEATER

Ah, "theatre" (thee-ya-tah) in London. The city is renowned for its affordable performances—tickets for big musicals on the **West End** can be had for as little as £25, a pittance compared to the $100 tickets sold on Broadway. In the West End, London's main theater district, you'll find big musicals that stay in residence at a single theater for decades. Other theaters put on more cutting-edge works. Many pubs have live performance spaces where theater groups rehearse and perform for audiences that, after a few pints, tend to find the second act more confusing than the first. Some churches, like St. Paul's in Covent Garden, host shows during the summer. Only buy discounted tickets from booths with a circle and check mark symbol that says **STAR** on it; this stands for the Society of Tickets Agents and Retailers, and it vouches for the legitimacy of a discount booth.

▨ ROYAL COURT THEATRE
Sloane Sq.

SOUTH KENSINGTON AND CHELSEA
☎020 7565 5000; www.royalcourttheatre.com

Famous for pushing the theatrical envelope, the Royal Court is the antidote to all the orchestral swoons and faux-opera sweeping through the West End. The Royal Court's 1956 production of John Osborne's *Look Back in Anger* (not to be confused with the Oasis song) is credited with single-handedly launching mod-

london

ern British drama. Royal is known as a writers' theater, purveying high-minded works for audiences that will appreciate them.

🚶 ⊖Sloane Sq. $ Tickets M £10, Tu-Sa £12-28. Student discounts available on day of performance. ⏰ Box office open M-F 10am-6pm or until the doors open, Sa 10am-curtain (if there's a performance).

👍 **NATIONAL THEATRE** THE SOUTH BANK

Belvedere Rd. ☎020 7452 3400; www.nationaltheatre.org.uk

Opened in 1976 by appointment of the Queen, the National Theatre's multiple stages host new and classic British drama, including many premieres, revived lost classics from around the world, and a standard repertoire of Chekhov and Ibsen. Half the seats are sold for £10 at special Travelex discount shows.

🚶 ⊖Waterloo. Turn right onto York Rd. and left onto Waterloo Rd. $ Tickets £10-44. ⏰ Box office open M-Sa 9:30am-8pm, Su noon-6pm.

👍 **THE OLD VIC** SOUTH LONDON

The Cut ☎0844 871 7628; www.oldvictheatre.com

This famous, stately theater was built in 1818 and has hosted the likes of Ralph Richardson and Laurence Olivier. Though showcasing a huge range of styles, the Old Vic focuses on the classics, including star-studded Shakespeare productions. Kevin Spacey has served as artistic director since 2003.

🚶 ⊖Southwark. Turn right onto The Cut. $ Tickets £10-52. 100 tickets for each performance available to those under 25 for £12; call ahead to book. ⏰ Box office open M-Sa 10am-7pm on show days, 10am-6pm on non-show days.

THE YOUNG VIC SOUTH LONDON

66 The Cut ☎020 7922 2922; www.youngvic.org

Formerly the studio space for the Old Vic, the Young Vic now puts on a variety of shows, generally edgier and more exciting than its more decorous parent theater down the road. Between its main stage and two studio spaces, the Young Vic also provides greater flexibility in stagings.

🚶 ⊖Southwark. Turn right onto The Cut. $ Tickets £10-30. ⏰ Box office open M-Sa 10am-6pm.

SHAKESPEARE'S GLOBE THE SOUTH BANK

21 New Globe Walk ☎020 7401 9919; www.shakespearesglobe.org

The original Globe burned down during a performance of *Henry VIII* in 1613, but this accurate reconstruction was opened near the original site in 1997. Much like the original theater, it has an open roof and standing area for "groundlings." Steeped in historical and artistic tradition, the Globe stages works by the Bard, along with two new plays per year. Their season only runs from April to October, but you probably wouldn't want to stand for three hours in the British winter, no matter how good the play.

🚶 ⊖Southwark. Turn left onto Blackfriars Rd., right onto Southwark St., left onto Great Guildford St., right onto Park St., then left onto New Globe Walk. $ Standing £5; seats £15-35, under 18 £12-32. ⏰ Box office open M-Sa 10am-8pm, Su 10am-7pm.

POP AND ROCK

Clubs are expensive, and many pubs close at 11pm. Especially during the current recession, fewer young people are willing to shell out £10-15 to get into a club, especially since beers inside cost a further £4-5. To find the heart of London's nightlife, you have to get beyond the pub-and club surface and head into the darkened basements of bars and seismically loud music clubs. With a history of homegrown musical talent—including **The Rolling Stones, Radiohead,** and **The Clash,** all of the bands from the infamous **"British Invasion,"** and many of the best '90s pop groups—London's fantastic music scene goes way back. Today, it has all of the big name acts you'd expect a major city to draw, in addition to an underground focus on indie rock and a surprisingly ample dose of folk and blues.

[icon] KOKO
NORTH LONDON

1A Camden High St. ☎0870 432 5527; www.koko.uk.com

Koko's isn't a typical rock and roll venue. Originally a theater, then a cinema, then one of the BBC's first broadcasting locations, and then the famous Camden Palace Nightclub, Koko holds its 110-year history within its music-soaked red walls and gilded balconies. Bringing in mostly big-name indie acts, along with some pop and rock acts (they've had everyone from Madonna to Usher to Justice), Koko is one of the premier venues in London. It also hosts an indie night, with DJs and dancing, on Friday.

⊖Mornington Crescent. Turn right onto Hampstead Rd. Koko is on the right. ℹ Tickets sold online. $ Concerts £10-30. Beer £3.50-4. For indie night, the 1st 100 people get in free. Cover £7; students £5 before midnight, £7 after. Cash only for in-person purchases. ⏰ Box office open noon-5pm on gig days. Indie night F 9:30pm-4am.

BORDERLINE
THE WEST END

Orange Yard, off Manette St. ☎020 7734 5547; venues.meanfiddler.com/borderline/home

This simple venue (which is also a fantastic club, see **Nightlife**) lacks the outlandish Art Deco trappings of other London concert halls, but it oozes the spirit of rock and roll from every beer-soaked wall and ear-blowing speaker. Big-name artists often play The Borderline when starting solo careers. Townes Van Zandt played his last show here; Eddie Vedder, Jeff Buckley, and Rilo Kiley have played here; and **Spinal Tap** performed here right after the movie came out. The amps go up to 11, the music's piping hot, and the location is prime.

⊖Tottenham Court Rd. Turn right onto Charing Cross Rd., and right onto Manette St. $ Tickets £6-20. Pints £3.40. ⏰ Doors open daily 7pm. Tickets available at the Jazz Cafe box office M-Sa 10:30am-5:30pm.

HMV APOLLO
WEST LONDON

15 Queen Caroline St. ☎020 8563 3800; www.hmvapollo.com

Like many of the big, architecturally stunning venues in London, the Art Deco HMV Apollo used to be a cinema. It was originally called the Hammersmith Odeon, and was the site of Bruce Springsteen's 1975 concert film. It's also hosted big acts like Oasis, R.E.M., Elton John, the Rolling Stones, and even the Beatles.

⊖Hammersmith. Apollo is opposite the Broadway Shopping Centre. There are plenty of signs leading to it. ℹ Call ☎08448 44 47 48 for tickets. $ Ticket prices vary; check online for more info. ⏰ Box office open on performance days 4pm-start of the show.

CLASSICAL MUSIC

If your tastes run more toward Mozart than the Arctic Monkeys, there's still plenty of music in London for you. For free chamber and classical music, check out London's churches—in particular, St Martin-in-the-Fields—where students from famous music schools often give professional-quality recitals for no charge.

ROYAL OPERA HOUSE
THE WEST END

Bow St. ☎020 7304 4000; www.roh.org.uk

The glorious glass facade of the Royal Opera House makes it look more like a train station than a theater, but that doesn't mean that the opera performed here is anything less than world-class. Tickets go on sale about two months before performances, and it's a good idea to book early. Or you can wait for standby tickets, which are offered four hours before performances for half price, and are only $12 for students. The ROH also sponsors free outdoor film screenings. For information on dance performances at the ROH, see **Dance.**

⊖Covent Garden. Turn right onto Long Acre, then right onto Bow St. $ Tickets £5-150. ⏰ Box office open M-Sa 10am-8pm.

ROYAL ALBERT HALL
SOUTH KENSINGTON AND CHELSEA

Kensington Gore ☎0845 401 5045; www.royalalberthall.com

Deep in the heart of South Kensington, the Royal Albert Hall, commissioned by

mousey mystery

Here's a fun trivia question: what's the longest-running stage show in the world? Agatha Christie's *The Mousetrap*. Here's a more relevant question: where is it playing? London!

After 58 years and over 23,000 performances, the show has involved more than 380 actors, sold over 415 tons of ice cream at intermission, and ironed more than 116 miles of shirts. Don't waste your time at the discount ticket booths in Leicester Sq.–though those are great for other shows, *The Mousetrap* tickets are only on sale at St. Martin's Theatre box office. Because the show runs so often, it's hardly ever sold out, so you can often show up 15min. before curtain and still get a seat. (St. Martin's Theatre, West St. ☎0844 499 1515 🚇 ⊖Covent Garden or Leicester Sq. $ Tickets £16-60. ⏰ Shows M 7:30pm, Tu 3 and 7:30pm, W-F 7:30pm, Sa 4 and 7:30pm. Box office open M-Sa 10am-8pm.)

Prince Albert, has been bringing the arts to London since 1871. The hall hosts some of the city's biggest concerts, including the **BBC Proms** classical festival (see **Festivals**) and a range of other phenomenal musical events. This is a historical and cultural experience that's not to be missed.

🚇 ⊖Knightsbridge. Turn left onto Knightsbridge and continue onto Kensington Rd., which becomes Kensington Gore. $ Tickets from £10. ⏰ Open daily 9am-9pm.

THE LONDON COLISEUM — THE WEST END

33 St. Martin's Ln. ☎0871 472 0600; www.eno.org

Home to the **English National Opera,** the London Coliseum showcases new, cutting-edge ballet and opera. They also perform unique reworkings of classic opera productions, like a version of Donizetti's *L'Elisir d'Amore* set in a 1950s diner.

🚇 ⊖Charing Cross. Walk toward Trafalger Sq. on Duncannon St., turn right at the square onto St. Martin's Pl., and St. Martin's Ln. splits off to the right. ℹ Sometimes students and other concessions can get discounted tickets 3hr. before the performance. $ Tickets £15-90. ⏰ Box office open M-Sa 10am-8pm on performance days, 10am-6pm on non-performance days.

JAZZ

👍 RONNIE SCOTT'S — THE WEST END

47 Frith St. ☎020 7439 0747; www.ronniescotts.co.uk

Ronnie Scott's has been defining "hip" in Soho for the last 51 years. It was the first British club to host American jazz artists—everyone from Chick Corea to Tom Waits (ok, not jazz, but who's complaining?) has played here. The venue is all flickering candlelight and dulcet reds and blues. Black-and-white photos of jazz giants line the walls, and a diverse crowd imbibes cocktail creations like Jazz Medicine (Jägermeister, sloe gin, Dubonnet, fresh blackberries, and angostura bitters). The venue's cool, but the jazz is hot. Stop by if the Soho scene gets overwhelming.

🚇 ⊖Tottenham Court Rd. Turn onto Oxford St. with your back to Tottenham Court Rd., then left onto Soho St., right onto the square, and right onto Frith St. $ Cover £10, more for big acts. Cocktails £8.50-9. ⏰ Open M-F 6pm-3am, Sa 6:30pm-3am, Su noon-4pm and 6:30pm-midnight. Box office open M-F 10am-6pm, Sa noon-5pm.

THE 606 CLUB — WEST LONDON

90 Lots Rd. ☎020 7352 5953; www.606club.co.uk

On quiet Lots Rd., opposite a foreboding abandoned factory, the 606 Club has been quietly hosting the best of the UK music scene since 1969. Properly underground (it's in a basement), the club is candlelit and closely packed. The music may be jazz, Latin, soul, gospel, R and B, and rock, and while the artists may be relatively unknown, they're almost always worth hearing.

Buss #22 from Sloane Sq. to Edith Grove/World's End. Continue walking on Kings Rd., turn left onto Tadema Rd., walk to the end, and turn right onto Lots Rd. i Non-members have to eat in order to drink. Check website for special Su afternoon lunch and show. $ Cover M-Th £10; F-Sa £12; Su lunch £8, evening £10. ⏰ Open M 7-11:30pm, Tu-W 7pm-12:30am, Th 7-11:30pm, F-Sa 8pm-1-:30am, Su 12:30-4pm and 7-11pm.

DANCE

As with everything else in London, the dance scene is diverse, innovative, and first-rate. Come for the famous ballets at older venues like the Royal Opera House or stop by a smaller company for some contemporary dance.

SADLER'S WELLS — NORTH LONDON

Rosebery Ave. ☎0844 412 4300; www.sadlerswells.com

Sadler's Wells is renowned for stunning dance shows, including traditional ballet, contemporary dance, and dazzling Cuban ensembles. With multiple performance spaces, they might even all be on at the same time.

⊖Angel. Turn left onto Upper St., then right onto Rosebery Ave. i Some shows offer student discounts. $ Tickets £10-55. ⏰ Box office open M-Sa 9am-8:30pm.

ROYAL OPERA HOUSE — THE WEST END

Bow St. ☎020 7304 4000; www.roh.org.uk

The Royal Opera House may be opera-oriented in name, but in repertoire, it's split between opera and ballet. See the listing in **Classical Music** for more information.

⊖Covent Garden. Turn right onto Long Acre, then right onto Bow St. $ Tickets £5-150. ⏰ Booking office open M-Sa 10am-8pm.

COMEDY

The English are famous for their dry, sophisticated yet sometimes ridiculous ("We are the knights who say 'Ni!'") sense of humor. This humor thrives in the standup and sketch comedy clubs throughout the city. Check *Time Out* for listings, and be warned that the city virtually empties of comedians come August when it's festival time in Edinburgh.

COMEDY STORE — THE WEST END

1A Oxendon St. ☎0844 871 7699; www.thecomedystore.co.uk

Hands-down the most famous comedy venue in London, the Comedy Store made a name for itself in the '80s as a home for up-and-coming comedians like Jennifer Saunders, Dawn French, and Mike Myers (who was one of the founding members). Nowadays, visiting comics perform Thursday through Saturday, and the resident sketch-comedy team takes the stage on Wednesdays and Sundays. Tuesdays have standup on recent topical events, while the last Monday of the month hosts would-be comedians who are either encouraged or heckled by the audience. Famous comedians like Eddie Izzard have been known to pop in from time to time for impromptu performances.

⊖Piccadilly Circus. Turn left onto Coventry, then right onto Oxendon. $ Tickets £14-20. ⏰ Box office open M-Th 6:30-9:30pm, F-Sa 6:30pm-1:15am, Su 6:30-9:30pm. Doors open daily 6:30pm. Shows usually 8 and 11pm.

HEN AND CHICKENS THEATRE — NORTH LONDON

109 St. Paul's Rd. ☎020 7704 2001; www.unrestrictedview.co.uk

You'll be treated to some of the most hilarious and quirky comedy around in this 50-seat venue, located above an Islington pub. Acts vary from standup to sketch-comedy groups. Past performers have included the Unexpected Items, a group that includes the originator of the sidesplitting "Gap Yah" video. Come in July to see comedians try out the material they're taking up to Edinburgh. Head down to the pub to enjoy a pint with the performers after the show.

⇄ ⊖Highbury and Islington. Turn right and go down the road past the green. $ Tickets £6-8. ⏰ Performances usually at 7:30 or 9:30pm.

CINEMA

London is teeming with traditional cinemas, the most dominant of which are **Cineworld** (www.cineworld.co.uk) and **Odeon** (www.odeon.co.uk). But the best way to enjoy a film is in one of the hip repertory or luxury cinemas. *Time Out* publishes showtimes, as does www.viewlondon.co.uk.

👍 BFI SOUTHBANK — SOUTH BANK

Belvedere Rd. ☎020 7928 3232; www.bfi.org.uk

Hidden under Waterloo Bridge, the BFI Southbank is one of the most exciting repertory cinemas in London. Showcasing everything from current blockbusters to challenging foreign works, the BFI's slate of screenings keeps all cinema-lovers happy. It runs in themed "seasons" that focus on the work of a particular director, cinematographer, or actor. The Mediatheque is free and allows you to privately view films from their archives.

⇄ ⊖Waterloo. $ £9.50, concessions £6.75. Tu £6.50. ⏰ Open daily 11am-11pm. Mediateque open Tu-F noon-8pm, Sa-Su 12:30pm-8pm.

RIVERSIDE STUDIOS — WEST LONDON

Crisp Rd. ☎020 8237 1111; www.riversidestudios.co.uk

Frequently showing films in old-school double features, Riverside Studios specializes in foreign films, art-house flicks, and classics. The building is a hotbed for other culture as well, featuring an exhibition space, live theater performances, a popular cafe, and a bar.

⇄ ⊖Hammersmith. Take the south exit and pass the Hammersmith Apollo. Continue to follow Queen Caroline St. and turn left onto Crisp Rd. i Ethernet access in cafe. $ Tickets £8.50, concessions £7.50. ⏰ Open M-F 8:30am-11pm, Sa 10am-11pm, Su 10am-10:30pm. Box office open daily noon-9pm.

FESTIVALS

Come summer, it seems like every park in London hosts a festival each weekend. There are folk festivals, hard-rock festivals, indie/pop/hip-hop festivals, food festivals... you name it. It's impossible to keep track of them all, so keep an eye out for posters around the city.

👍 BBC PROMS — SOUTH KENSINGTON AND CHELSEA

Kensington Gore ☎0845 401 5045; www.bbc.co.uk/proms

The Proms are a world-famous classical music festival put on by the BBC in the Royal Albert Hall. If you're thinking teenagers in taffeta, think again. "Prom" stands for "Promenade Concert"—a performance at which much of the audience only has standing-room tickets. There's at least one performance every day at the Royal Albert Hall, plus around 70 other events and discussions throughout the city. All the performances are broadcast for free.

⇄ ⊖Knightsbridge. Turn left onto Knightsbridge, then continue onto Kensington Rd., which becomes Kensington Gore. $ Tickets from £10. ⏰ July-Sept.

LONDON LITERARY FESTIVAL — THE SOUTH BANK

Southbank Centre, Belvedere Rd. ☎0844 847 9939; www.londonlitfest.com

Some of the world's most famous poets, novelists, musicians, and scientists (it's quite the interdisciplinary fest) assemble at the South Bank Centre every July for this literary extravaganza. The festival also hosts writing workshops; you can download podcasts of past events on their website.

⇆ ⊖Waterloo. Turn right onto York Rd. and then left onto Waterloo Rd. The festival is held on the embankment before York Bridge. $ Ticket prices free-£15, concessions often ½ off. ⏰ Call daily 9am-8pm. Book through Royal Festival Hall Ticket Office daily 10am-8pm.

like proper english blokes

So you're looking for a reason to party, and you want to do it with a bit of English class? One of the best ways to really experience English life at its poshest is to attend the Henley Royal Regatta, which takes place in Henley-on-Thames (40 mi. west of London) during the first weekend of July. In the wonderful world of rowing, this race is about as important as it gets, and it was even featured in *The Social Network*. But if you're like the rest of us, you can simply use it as an excuse to dress prep-chic (think matching striped jackets and ties), pretend you're sophisticated enough to judge each rower's form, and sip Pimm's by the river.

shopping

London is known as one of the shopping capitals of the world. Knightsbridge's famous department stores fight to keep the tradition of shopping class alive, Soho offers vintage clothing stores and independent record shops, and the East End is filled with fun boutiques. Notting Hill is famous for Portobello Market, but even on off-market days, the road has a host of cute secondhand shops. Chelsea is for those with a bit more money and a serious commitment to shopping. For you literary junkies, John Sandoe's is our favorite bookstore in the city. Shopping is a significant part of London tourism, but if you're broke and have no extra room in your backpack, you can always just browse the day away at Harrods.

BOOKSTORES

📖 JOHN SANDOE BOOKS — SOUTH KENSINGTON AND CHELSEA

10 Blacklands Terr. ☎020 7589 9473; www.johnsandoe.com

The stairs to the second-floor fiction section at John Sandoe reminds visitors of the joy of independent bookstores. There's barely space for peoples' feet, as half of each stair is taken up by piles of carefully selected books. A cracked leather chair presides over bookcases so packed with masterworks and little-known gems that they're layered with moving shelves. The knowledgeable, personable staff is ever-ready to dole out excellent suggestions. Book-lovers beware: it's easy to spend a day (and a pile of cash) in this shop.

⇆ ⊖Sloane Sq. Exit the Tube and go straight down Sloane Sq. Veer left onto King's Rd., and turn right at Blacklands Terr. ⏰ Open M-Tu 9:30am-5:30pm, W 9:30am-7:30pm, Th-Sa 9:30am-5:30pm, Su noon-6pm.

📖 SKOOB — MARLEBONE AND BLOOMSBURY

66 The Brunswick, off Marchmont St. ☎020 7278 8760; www.skoob.com

The Brunswick Center is all white and shiny and full of bougie stores—not the place where you'd expect to find a haven for dusty secondhand books. And yet here is Skoob, a basement shop where most books are £1-4. They come from pretty much any genre you can think of: travel writing (if *Let's Go* has inspired you), fiction, mysteries, history, biographies, you name it. They have over a million more books in their warehouse, thousands of which can be ordered from their website. As if that wasn't enough, they offer a 10% student discount.

⇆ ⊖Russell Sq. Turn right and then left up Marchmont St. Skoob is at the far end of Brunswick, on the right. ⏰ Open M-Sa 10:30am-8pm, Su 10:30am-6pm.

ART

MARCUS CAMPBELL ART BOOKS
THE SOUTH BANK

43 Holland St. ☎020 7261 0111; www.marcuscampbell.co.uk

Close enough in theme and proximity to the Tate Modern to be considered its unofficial bookstore, Marcus Campbell Art Books sells a wide variety of exhibition catalogues (many for £1-2), and rare and expensive art books (up to £3000). A fun store for browsing and shopping alike, with books so beautiful they're works of art in themselves.

⇄ ⊖Southwark. Turn left onto Blackfriars Rd., then right onto Southwark St. Next turn left onto Sumner, and left onto Holland St. ⏰ Open M-Sa 10:30am-6:30pm, Su noon-6pm.

SOUTHBANK PRINTMAKERS
THE SOUTH BANK

Unit 12 Gabriels Wharf, 56 Upper Ground ☎020 7928 8184; www.southbank-printmakers.com

Every 5min., someone in London is sold a cheap work of bad, tourist-trap art. Southbank Printmakers aim to stop this grave injustice. The artist cooperative has been around for 10 years, producing quality lino cuts, wood cuts, etchings, and monoprints at a range of prices. Many of the prints are London-themed, making for original and affordable souvenirs.

⇄ ⊖Southwark. Turn left onto Blackfriars Rd., left onto Stamford St., and right onto Duchy St. ⏰ Open in summer M-F 11:30am-6:30pm, Sa-Su 10am-8pm; in winter M-F 11:30am-5:30pm, Sa-Su 10am-7pm.

MUSIC

👍 MUSIC AND VIDEO EXCHANGE
HYDE PARK TO NOTTING HILL

42 Notting Hill Gate ☎020 7221 2793; www.mgeshops.com

Music and Video Exchange will provide hours (if not days) of entertainment to any audiophile. The staff engage in constant *High Fidelity*-esque conversations and practically ooze musical knowledge, while customers browse through vinyl, CDs, and cassettes in the bargain area. Upstairs in the rarities section, you can find anything from a £12 original vinyl of the Rolling Stones' *Get Yer Ya-Ya's Out!* to the original German sleeve for the Beatles' *Let it Be.* Customers can trade in their own stuff in exchange for cash or—in a move betraying MVE's cold-hearted understanding of a music-lover's brain—twice the cash amount in store vouchers.

⇄ ⊖Notting Hill Gate. Walk out the south entrance of the Tube and go down Notting Hill Gate. ⏰ Open daily 10am-8pm.

👍 SISTER RAY
THE WEST END

34-35 Berwick St. ☎020 7734 3297; www.sisterray.co.uk

An old-school record shop of the best kind, Sister Ray's stellar staff is adept at creating musical matches-made-in-heaven. Hip, cheap books about music line the check-out counter, and listening stations are located throughout the store. The store also buys, so if you want to sell your classic punk records to fund the next leg of your vacation, this is the place for you.

⇄ ⊖Tottenham Court Rd. Turn left onto Oxford St., left onto Wardour St., and left onto Berwick St. ⏰ Open M-Sa 10am-8pm, Su noon-6pm.

THE SCHOTT MUSIC SHOP
THE WEST END

48 Great Marlborough St. ☎020 7292 6090; www.schottmusic.co.uk

Opened in 1857, Schlott is the oldest sheet-music shop in London. This quiet, spacious store sells everything from the Beatles to Bartók. Especially notable to music-starved travelers are the three practice rooms beneath the shop (each with a baby grand Steinway) available to rent by the hour.

⇄ ⊖Oxford Circus. Turn left onto Regent St., and left onto Great Marlborough St. ℹ 10% student discount on print music. $ Practice rooms £10 per hr. before noon, £12 per hr. noon-6pm, £15 per hr. after 6pm. ⏰ Open M-F 10am-6:30pm, Sa 10am-6pm.

(e.t.) phone home

In the highly unlikely case that London's internet connection, cell-phone reception, and mail-carrying owls are all out of commission when you need them, you can always step into one of Britain's iconic red telephone boxes. Though these booths were first deployed in London in 1926 for obvious purposes, they have now become more of a novelty for tourists and are utilized for all kinds of non-telephone purposes. Some of the more interesting ones include:

- **BOOK/MOVIE PROPS.** In the **Harry Potter** series, a red telephone box provides a way into the Ministry of Magic. However, given the strange smell wafting about in many of London's actual telephone booths, floo powder might be a better way to travel.

- **ARTWORK.** In **Kingston upon Thames,** several disused red telephone boxes are lined up, all tipped sideways, in an arrangement resembling falling dominoes. This artwork, called *Out of Order,* was commissioned in 1988, when this sort of wackiness was all the rage.

- **COMMERCIAL PRODUCTS.** Want your very own red telephone booth? You can now order a replica online for prices ranging from your arm and leg to your first-born child.

- **MINI-LIBRARY.** You know Britain has too many cell phones—or too few libraries—when they start to convert telephone kiosks into libraries. Located in **Westbury-sub-Mendip,** this mini literary haven is fairly busy. It's also 150 miles west of London, so probably not worth the daytrip.

MARKETS

BOROUGH MARKET

THE SOUTH BANK

Southwark St.   www.boroughmarket.org.uk

Anyone who bemoans the food scene in London has never been to Borough Market. In a tangle of stalls and shops under a set of railway viaducts, traders sell the best in fresh produce, meat, and artisanal products. Looking for rare Italian sausage, the juiciest English strawberries, or decadent French cheese? Find them here. Or just take a wander and discover things you never knew you needed, like truffled *mortadella* and tiny brioches. The people who work here are incredibly knowledgeable and ready to recommend an item or a recipe. And in addition to the food stands, there are a number of restaurants and cafes that share in the gourmet aura of the market.

♯ ⊖*London Bridge. Exit the Tube and walk down Southwark St. away from the river. The market will be on your right, starting where Southwark St. and Borough High St. split off. ☒ Open Th 11am-5pm, F noon-6pm, Sa 8am-5pm.*

OLD SPITALFIELDS MARKET

EAST LONDON

Commercial St.   www.oldspitalfieldsmarket.com

This is the sort of market that clearly belongs in the East End, selling stylish vintage clothes, quirky antiques, and an array of art. It's a mix of stores and stalls offering everything from a quick manicure to a spicy kebab. They're not all open every day, but Sundays are the busiest and have the best variety of vendors. If you're looking for antiques, Thursday is your day.

♯ ⊖*Shoreditch High St. Make a left down Commercial St. ☒ Opening times vary per vendor, but most are open daily 10am-5pm.*

london

DEPARTMENT STORES

HARRODS — SOUTH KENSINGSTON AND CHELSEA

87-135 Brompton Rd. ☎020 7730 1234; www.harrods.com

An ode to the experience of shopping, Harrods is probably the most famous department store on the planet. Packed with faux-hieroglyphs, a "Room of Luxury" (and its sequel, "Room of Luxury II"), and just about anything you could ever want to buy, Harrods is as much a sight to see as it is a place to shop. The prices and the people who pay, may be the most entertaining part of it all. Be sure to check out the toy section—you'll struggle to contain your inner child. Don't miss the food court's candy section, where they sell chocolate shoes (£84 for a pair). On the bottom floor, they sell "Personalised Classics," which enable you to substitute names for the ones already in a given book. Who needs "Romeo and Juliet" when you could have "Fred and Agnes?" "Fred, Fred, wherefore art thou Fred?" The answer: in shopping heaven.

 # ⊖Knightsbride. Take the Harrods Exit. ⏰ Open M-Sa 10am-8pm, Su 11:30am-6pm.

LIBERTY — THE WEST END

Great Marlborough St. ☎020 7734 1234; www.liberty.co.uk

No, this epic Tudor building isn't a giant pub or a replica of a Shakespearean theater; it's a department store that, since the 19th century, has been presenting the best in art and design to its customers. Back in the day, this meant working in the Art Nouveau and Arts and Crafts styles—they were so successful that in Italy, they're just referred to as *Stile Liberty*. Today, you can buy everything from clothes to plates bearing the store's iconic prints. There are also men's and women's collections from fashion-forward designers like Alexander Wang and Vivienne Westwood. Don't miss the array of ribbons, feathers, and tulle in the haberdashery section.

 # ⊖Oxford Circus. Go down Regent St. and turn left onto Great Marlborough St. ⏰ Open M-Sa 10am-9pm, Su noon-6pm.

essentials

PRACTICALITIES

- **TOURIST OFFICES:** The main central tourist office in London is the **Britain and London Visitor Centre (BLVC).** (1 Regent St.; www.visitbritain.com # ⊖Piccadilly Circus. ⏰ Open Apr-Sept M 9:30am-6pm, Tu-F 9am-6:30pm, Sa-Su 10am-4pm; Oct-Mar M 9:30am-6:30pm, Tu-F 9am-6pm, Sa-Su 10am-4pm.) Also useful is the **London Information Centre.** (Leicester Sq. ☎020 7292 2333; www.londoninformationcentre.com # ⊖Leicester Sq. ⏰ Open daily 8am-midnight.)
- **TOURS: Original London Walks** offers walking tours with themes like "Jack the Ripper" and "Harry Potter." (☎020 7624 9255; www.walks.com $ £8, students and over 65 £6.)
- **CURRENCY EXCHANGE: Thomas Cook.** (30 St James's St. ☎084 5308 9570 ⏰ Open M-Tu 10am-5:30pm, Th-F 10am-5:50pm.)
- **CREDIT CARD SERVICES: American Express** (www.amextravelresources.com) has locations at 78 Brompton Rd. (☎084 4406 0046 # ⊖Knightsbridge. ⏰ Open M-Tu 9am-5:30pm, W 9:30am-5:30pm, Th-F 9am-5:30pm, Sa 9am-4pm.) and 30-31 Haymarket. (☎084 4406 0044 # ⊖Piccadilly Circus. ⏰ Open M-F 9am-5:30pm.)

- **GLBT RESOURCES:** The official **LGBT Tourist office** offers information on everything from saunas to theater discounts. (25 Frith St.; www.gaytouristoffice.co.uk ⊖Leicester Sq.) **Boyz** (www.boyz.co.uk) lists gay events in London as well as an online version of its magazine. **Gingerbeer** (www.gingerbeer.co.uk) is a guide for lesbian and bisexual women with events listings. **Time Out London's** magazine and website (www.timeout.com/london) also provide a good overview of the city's GLBT establishments and the city in general.
- **TICKET OFFICES: Albermarle of London** agency provides official tickets for all major West End theatre productions. Book tickets via web, phone, or visiting the office. (5th fl., Medius House, 63-69 New Oxford St. ☎020 7379 1357; www.albemarle-london.com ⏰ Open M-F 8am-8:30pm, Sa 8:30am-8pm, Su 10am-6pm.)
- **INTERNET:** Wi-Fi abounds in this technologically advanced city. Most cafes provide internet access. Chains like **Starbucks** (www.starbucks.co.uk) and **McDonald's** (www.mcdonalds.co.uk) almost always have free Wi-Fi. Other chains with Wi-Fi include **The Coffee Republic** (www.coffeerepublic.co.uk), **Wetherspoon** (www.jdwetherspoon.co.uk), and **Pret a Manger** (www.pret.com). Public areas also have Wi-Fi. The area between **Upper Street and Holloway Road,** also known as **The Technology Mile** is the longest stretch of free internet in the city.
- **POST OFFICES: Trafalgar Square Post Office.** (24-28 William IV St. ☎020 7484 9305 ⊖Charing Cross. ⏰ Open M 8:30am-6:30pm, Tu 9:15am-6:30pm, W-F 8:30am-6:30pm, Sa 9am-5:30pm.)

EMERGENCY

- **EMERGENCY NUMBER:** ☎999.
- **POLICE: City of London Police.** (☎020 7601 2000) **Metropolitan Police.** (☎030 0123 1212.)
- **RAPE CRISIS CENTER: Solace.** (136 Royal College St. ☎0808 802 5565; www.rapecrisis.org.uk ⊖Camden Rd.)
- **HOSPITALS/MEDICAL SERVICES: St. Thomas' Hospital.** (Westminster Bridge Rd. ☎020 7188 7188 ⊖Westminster.) **Royal Free Hospital.** (Pond St. ☎020 7794 0500 ⊖Hampstead Heath.) **Charing Cross Hospital.** (Fulham Palace Rd. ☎020 3311 1234 ⊖Hammersmith.) **University College Hospital.** (235 Euston Rd. ☎0845 155 5000 ⊖Warren St.)

GETTING THERE

by plane

London's main airport is **Heathrow** (**LHR;** ☎0844 335 1801; www.heathrowairport.com), commonly regarded as one of the world's busiest airports. The cheapest way to get from Heathrow to central London is on the Tube. The two Tube stations servicing Heathrow form a loop at the end of the **Piccadilly** line, which runs to central London. (⏰ 1hr.; every 5min. M-Sa 5am-11:54pm, Su 5:46am-10:37pm) **Heathrow Express** (☎084 5600 1515; www.heathrowexpress.com) runs between Heathrow and Paddington station four times per hour. The trip is significantly shorter (though comparably pricier) than many of the alternatives, clocking in at around 15-20min. ($ £16.50 when purchased online, £18 from station, £23 on board. ⏰ 1st train departs daily around 5:10am.) The **Heathrow Connect** also runs to Paddington but is cheaper and takes longer, since it makes five stops on the way to and from the airport. (⏰ 25 min., 2 per hr.) **Taxis** from the airport to central London cost around £60 and take around 45min. In short, they aren't worth it.

Getting from **Gatwick Airport** (**LGW;** ☎0844 335 1802; www.gatwickairport.com) takes around 30min., making it less convenient than Heathrow but less hectic, too.

The swift and affordable train services that connect Gatwick to the city make the trip a little easier. The **Gatwick Express** train runs non-stop service to Victoria station. You can buy tickets in terminals, at the station, or on the train itself. (☎0845 850 1530; www.gatwickexpress.com $ £15.20. ⏰ 35min., every 15min. 5:50am-12:35am.)

National Express runs buses from the North and South terminals of Gatwick to London. The National Express bus (☎0871 781 8178; www.nationalexpress.com) takes approximately 1½hr., and buses depart for London Victoria every hour. Taxis take about 1hr. to reach central London.

by train

Europeans are far ahead of Americans in terms of train travel, and London offers several ways to easily reach other European destinations. Multiple train companies pass through the city. The biggest are **Eurostar** (☎08432 186 186; www.eurostar.com), which travels to Paris and Brussels, and **National Rail** (☎08457 48 49 50; www.nationalrail.co.uk), which oversees lines running throughout the United Kingdom. Train travel in Britain is generally reliable but can be unreasonably expensive. Booking tickets weeks in advance can lead to large savings, but spur-of-the-moment train trips to northern cities could cost more than £100.

by bus

Bus travel is another, frequently cheaper, option. **Eurolines** (☎08717 818 181; www.eurolines.co.uk ⏰ Open 8am-8pm.) is Europe's largest coach network, servicing 500 destinations throughout Europe. Many buses leave from **Victoria Coach Station,** at the mouth of Elizabeth St. just off of Buckingham Palace Rd. Many coach companies, including **National Express, Eurolines,** and **Megabus,** operate from Victoria Coach. National Express is the only scheduled coach network in Britain and can be used for most intercity travel and for travel to and from various airports. It can also be used to reach Scotland and Wales.

GETTING AROUND

Though there are daily interruptions to Tube service, the controlling network, **Transport for London (TFL),** does a good job of keeping travelers aware of these disruptions to service. Each station will have posters listing interruptions to service, and you can check service online at www.tfl.gov.uk or the 24hr. travel information service (☎0843 222 1234). The website also has a journey planner that can plot your route using any public transport service ("TFL" is a verb here). Memorize that website. Love that website. Though many people in the city stay out into the wee hours, the Tube doesn't have the same sort of stamina. When it closes around midnight, night owls have two choices: cabs or **night buses.** Most nightbus lines are prefixed with an **N** (N13, for instance), and some stops even have 24hr. buses.

travel passes

Travel passes are almost guaranteed to save you money. The passes are priced based on the number of zones they serve (the more zones, the more expensive), but zone one encompasses central London and you'll rarely need to get past zone two. If someone offers you a secondhand ticket, don't take it. There's no real way to verify whether it's valid—plus, it's illegal. Passengers under 16 get free travel on buses, those aged 11-15 enjoy reduced fares on the Tube with an Oyster photocard. Students 18 and older must study full time (at least 15hr. per week over 14 weeks) in London to qualify for the Student Photocard, which enables users to save 30% on adult travel cards and bus passes. It's worth it if you're staying for an extended period of time (study-abroad kids, we're looking at you).

Oyster cards enable you to pay in a variety of ways. Fares come in peak (M-F 6:30-9:30am and 4-7pm) and off-peak varieties and are, again, distinguished by zone. Oysters let you "pay as you go," meaning that you can store credit on an as-needed basis. Using an Oyster card will save you up to 50% off a single ticket. Remember to tap your card both on entering and leaving the station. You can use your card to add Travelcards, which allow unlimited travel on one day. This will only be cost-effective if you plan to use the Tube a lot. They cost £8.20 for anytime travel or £6.60 for off-peak travel. You can top up your Oyster at one of the infinite off-licenses, marked by the Oyster logo, that scatter the city.

Season tickets are weekly, monthly, and annual Travelcards that work on all public transport and can be purchased inside Tube stations. They yield unlimited (within zone) use for their duration. (Ⓢ Weekly rates for zones 1-2 £27.50, monthly £106.)

by underground

Most stations have free pocket Tube maps. The map barely reflects an above-ground scale, though, and should not be used for even the roughest estimation of walking directions (seriously). Many platforms will have a digital panel indicating ETAs for the trains and sometimes type and final destination.

The Tube runs from Monday to Saturday from approximately 5:30am (though it depends on station and line) until around midnight. The Tube runs less frequently on Sunday, with many lines starting service after 6am. Around 6pm on weekdays, many of the trains running out of central London are packed with the after-work crowd. It's best to avoid these lines at this time of day.

You can buy tickets from ticket counters (though these often have lines at bigger stations) or at machines in the stations. You need to swipe your ticket at the beginning of the journey and then again to exit the Tube. Random on-train checks will ask you to present a valid ticket to avoid the £50 penalty fee (reduced to £25 if you pay in under 21 days).

by bus

While slower than the Tube for long journeys (thanks to traffic and more frequent stops), buses are useful for traveling short distances covered by a few stops (and several transfers) on the Tube.

Bus stops frequently post lists of buses servicing the stop as well as route maps and maps of the area indicating nearby stops. These maps are also very helpful for finding your way around a neighborhood. Buses display route numbers.

Every route and stop is different, but buses generally run every 5-15min. beginning around 5:30am and ending around midnight. After day bus routes have closed, **night buses** take over. These typically operate similar routes to their daytime equivalents, and their numbers are usually prefixed with an N. Some buses run 24hr. services. If you're staying out past the Tube's closing time, you should plan your night-bus route or bring cab fare. (Ⓢ Single rides £2.20.)

did you know...?

Though many have GPS systems in their cars, the 21,000 London black-cab drivers all had to pass a very intense test called "The Knowledge." In order to earn a license vaid for the entire city, would-be cabbies must prove they know the best routes for all of the 25,000 streets within a six-mile radius of Charing Cross Station. So, if you're ever lost, seek out a black cab and ask for directions.

london

MONEY

tipping and bargaining

Tips in restaurants are sometimes included in the bill (sometimes as a "service charge"). If gratuity is not included, you should tip your server about 10%. Taxi drivers should receive a 10% tip, and bellhops and chambermaids usually expect £1-3. To the great relief of many budget travelers, tipping is not expected at pubs and bars in Britain (unless you are trying to get jiggy with the bartender). Bargaining is practically unheard of in the upscale shops that overrun London. Don't try it (unless you happen to be at a street market or feel particularly belligerent).

taxes

The UK has a 20% value added tax (VAT), a sales tax applied to everything but food, books, medicine, and children's clothing. The tax is included in the amount indicated on the price tag. The prices stated in *Let's Go* include VAT.

SAFETY AND HEALTH

police

Police are a common presence in London, and there are many police stations scattered throughout the city. There are two types of police officers in Britain: regular officers with full police powers, and police community support officers (PCSO), who have limited police power and focus on community maintenance and safety. The national emergency number is ☎999.

drugs and alcohol

The Brits love to drink, so the presence of alcohol is unavoidable. In trying to keep up with the locals, remember that the Imperial pint is 20 oz., as opposed to the 16oz. US pint. The legal age at which you can buy alcohol in the UK is 18 (16 for buying beer and wine with food at a restaurant).

Despite what you may have seen on *Skins*, use and possession of hard drugs is illegal throughout the United Kingdom. Do not test this—Britain has been cracking down on drug use for young people in particular over the past few years. Smoking is banned in enclosed public spaces in Britain, including pubs and restaurants.

MEASUREMENTS

Britain uses a thoroughly confusing and illogical mix of standard and metric measurement units. Road distances are always measured in miles, and many Brits will be clueless if you give them distances in kilometers. For weights, don't be surprised to see grams and ounces used side-by-side. There's also a measurement called a "stone," equal to 14 pounds, that is regularly used for giving body weights. Paradoxically, meters and centimeters are the most common way to give body heights. How the British ever accomplished anything in this world when they can't settle on a consistent system of measurements we'll never know. If you want to figure out whether you're buying enough pasta for one or for your entire hostel, use the chart below.

london 101

HISTORY

Legend has it that London was founded by Brutus of Troy, a descendant of Aeneas who was banished for accidentally killing his father. He then wandered across Europe, arrived in Britain, defeated the giants who lived there, and renamed the island after himself (Bru-tus, Bri-tain). If that sounds far-fetched, it's because it's a legend. But now you know.

birthday (43-410 CE)

London was actually founded in 43 CE by the Romans (they called it **Londinium** then), just seven years after their conquest of Britain. It was meant to be a civilian town, as opposed to the military outposts the Romans had previously built in this restive northern frontier. Seventeen years later, the Celtic Warrior-Queen **Boudica** burned Londinium to the ground during her campaign to expel the Romans from her island. But the pesky foreigners came back and the town was rebuilt, now with city walls!

(These old Roman walls still demarcate the historic **City of London** at the center of the now-sprawling metropolis.) The town grew in size and importance and became the capital of the Roman province of Britannia.

i want you (she's so london) (410-1215)

In 410, after years of fighting British "barbarians," the Romans cleared out in order to battle other "barbarians" (this time, of the German variety) on their home turf. Once the Romans were gone, Britain fell into a period of flux, with Saxons, Angles, and Vikings fighting over the city—until the Normans arrived in 1066 and showed everyone who was boss. **William the Conqueror,** who demolished his competitors for the crown at the **Battle of Hastings,** treated London with special attention. William transformed the city into his capital by building three new castles (one of which is now known as the **Tower of London**). Westminster, whose enormous abbey was built by Edward the Confessor built just before the Normans took over, became the fiscal and legal center of the nation. London's status as the largest and wealthiest city in England made it a kingmaker in every disputed succession (trust us, there were a lot of these). Prospective monarchs had to make sure that they had London's support, or their heads would most likely end up on a pike.

helter skelter (1215-1666)

But political power doesn't make a city invincible. The city's densely packed population and booming commerce made it highly susceptible to plagues and fires. The **Black Death** hit London in 1369 and killed more than half of the population. In 1665, the **Black Plague** reared its ugly head again and carried off about 100,000 Londoners. Then came the **Great Fire of 1666,** which leveled more than 60% of the city, including the original St. Paul's Cathedral and Royal Exchange. This time, many decided to rebuild in stone.

it's getting better all the time (1667-1900)

In spite of its devastating destruction, the Great Fire helped make London the modern city it is today. Over the next 20 years, streets were widened, new stone houses were built, and the city began to assume the character of a modern metropolis. By the end of the 18th century, Samuel Johnson could say without a hint of irony, "when a man is tired of London, he is tired of life; for there is in London all that life can afford."

Despite losing its North American colonies in 1776, Britain (by now England and Scotland had merged into one country) became the most powerful country in the world. After defeating France in the French-Indian and Napoleonic Wars, it was the ultimate colonial power. The spoils of its worldwide empire all poured back to London. Over the next century, **Big Ben** and the **Houses of Parliament** were built, the **National Gallery** was erected, a police force was established by Sir Robert Peel (hence the nicknames "bobbies and "peelers"), and a sewerage system was put into place to spare Londoners a repeat of the **Greak Stink of 1858** (and prevent the cholera outbreaks that followed the habit of dumping an entire city's raw sewage into the Thames). The **Underground,** the first subterranean rail line in the world, opened in 1863. Within a few months, it was carrying more than 25,000 passengers per day.

The **Industrial Revolution** brought huge numbers of rural peasants to work in factories in the capital. London's population passed one million around 1800, and it remained the largest city in the world for much of the 19th century. By 1900, 6.7 million people called London home.

magical mystery tour (1900-today)

Over the course of the 20th century, London survived two world wars, two Olympics, and Johnny Rotten. During WWII, German planes bombarded London in an eight-month **Blitz,** intended to terrorize Britons into submission. Beginning on September 7, 1940, the Luftwaffe bombed the city for 57 consecutive days. The Blitz destroyed more than a million houses and left an enduring mark on the city.

london

But that didn't stop London from playing host to the world three years after the war ended with the first Olympics since the infamous Berlin games of 1936. In 1951, the Festival of Britain served as another much-needed celebration after the tough years of the war. By the 1960s, the city, in the **Swinging London** period, really had its mojo back. Jean Shrimpton became one of the world's first supermodels, **the Beatles** ensconced themselves in Abbey Road Studios, **The Who's** Pete Townshend smashed up his guitar and shattered conventions, and hipsters were known as mods. It was a good time to be in London.

Since then, the city has only become more multi-ethnic, more artistic, and more tourist-friendly. In 2000, Ken Livingstone—a man who said, "If voting changed anything, they'd abolish it"—became London's first elected mayor. Under his watch, London won its bid to host the 2012 Olympics (see **Arts and Culture**), introduced a motorist fee to cut down on congestion in the city, and gave the Underground a facelift. Now London excitedly prepares for its third Olympics, an honor no city has ever received before.

FOOD AND DRINK

British food often gets a bad rap, probably because of English favorites with names like jellied eel and spotted dick. But many traditional standards are actually quite delicious, and no visit to London is complete without sampling some fish and chips, Yorkshire pudding (fried batter), or bangers and mash (sausage and mashed potatoes).

If you don't feel like sampling British classics, however, London has plenty of other things on offer. After all, one of the advantages of having a global empire was the ability to pick and choose all the best foods the world had to offer. **Chicken tikka masala** has become, by some accounts, the most popular English dish. (Chicken tikka is an Indian dish to which cooks added gravy to satisfy the British desire for meat with gravy. In 2001 the UK's Foreign Secretary, Robin Cook, proclaimed it "a true British national dish.") You're as likely to find yourself eating Vietnamese bánh mì or Middle Eastern falafel as you are a plain old sandwich. South Asian curries, Caribbean roti, Chinese dim sum, Spanish paella, and everything in between can be found on London's streets.

HOLIDAYS AND FESTIVALS

HOLIDAY OR FESTIVAL	DESCRIPTION	DATE
London International Mime Festival	So much silence. But really, it's a gathering of more mimes than you'll see in the rest of your life. Check out the theatres or www.mimefest.co.uk to see what those silent actors have gotten up to.	January 14-29, 2012
St. George's Day	England's national day, celebrating the country's favorite dragon-slaying saint.	April 23
The Queen's Diamond Jubilee	Queen Elizabeth II celebrates 60 years on the throne in this Commonwealth-wide party. Many events are planned, including a concert, street parties, and a boat parade on the Thames.	June 5, 2012 (this year only!)
The Queen's Birthday	Official holiday celebrating the Queen's birthday, even though her real birthday is months earlier. It's the biggest royal event of the year. The parade takes place in Whitehall, accessible from the Tube stop at Westminster.	June 9, 2012
Notting Hill Carnival	Billing itself as "the biggest carnival in Europe," this extravaganza looks to show off the biggest and craziest floats ever when it takes the world stage in 2012, sandwiched in between the Olympics and Paralympics.	August 26-27, 2012
Lord Mayor's Show and Fireworks Display	A HUGE fireworks show that has been put on hold only for the Black Death and the Duke of Wellington's funeral. Otherwise it's been happening annually since 1215.	November 10, 2012
Christmas	You know the deal: Christmas tree, baby Jesus, presents—except here in England they actually eat mincemeat pies and fruitcake.	December 25
Boxing Day	The day after Christmas is the British equivalent of Black Friday. Everybody rushes to the stores and spends their Christmas cash on deeply discounted goodies.	December 26

london 101

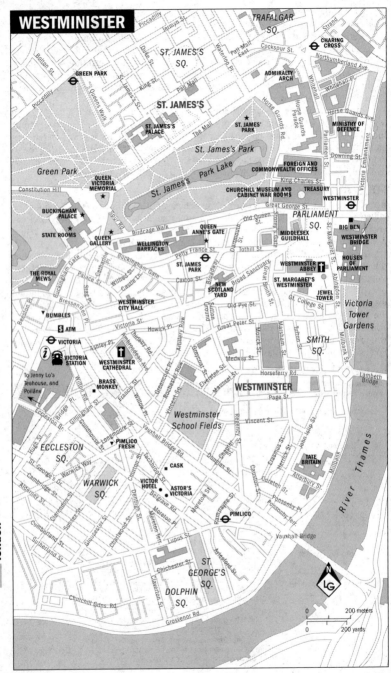

WESTMINISTER

TRAFALGAR SQ.

Piccadilly

Jermyn St.

CHARING CROSS

Cockspur St.

Strand

Northumberland Ave.

ST. JAMES'S SQ.

Duke St.

King St.

Pall Mall East

Waterloo Pl.

Bolton St.

GREEN PARK

St. James's St.

Queens Walk

ADMIRALTY ARCH

Whitehall

Horse Guards Ave.

Horse Guards Pl.

ST. JAMES'S

Pall Mall

The Mall

Horse Guards Rd.

Parliament St.

MINISTRY OF DEFENCE

Piccadilly

ST. JAMES'S PALACE

ST. JAMES' PARK

Downing St.

Green Park

QUEEN VICTORIA MEMORIAL

St. James's Park

St. James's Park Lake

FOREIGN AND COMMONWEALTH OFFICES

King Charles St.

Victoria Embankment

Constitution Hill

Park

CHURCHILL MUSEUM AND CABINET WAR ROOMS

TREASURY

WESTMINSTER

BUCKINGHAM PALACE

QUEEN GALLERY

Birdcage Walk

Great George St.

PARLIAMENT SQ.

BIG BEN

STATE ROOMS

Spur Rd.

QUEEN ANNE'S GATE

Old Queen St.

Storey's Gate

St. Margaret St.

WESTMINSTER BRIDGE

THE ROYAL MEWS

Buckingham Gate

WELLINGTON BARRACKS

Petty France St.

Dartmouth St.

Tothill St.

MIDDLESEX GUILDHALL

WESTMINSTER BRIDGE

Buckingham Gate

Palace St.

Caxton St.

ST. JAMES PARK

Broadway

Broad Sanctuary

Great Smith St.

WESTMINSTER ABBEY

HOUSES OF PARLIAMENT

Bressenden Pl.

State Pl.

Wilfred St.

Castle Ln.

NEW SCOTLAND YARD

ST. MARGARET'S WESTMINSTER

Abingdon St.

BUMBLES

WESTMINSTER CITY HALL

Old Pye St.

Gt. College St.

JEWEL TOWER

ATM

Victoria St.

Sutton Ground

Great Peter St.

Victoria Tower Gardens

Millbank

VICTORIA

Ashley Pl.

Howick Pl.

Thirleby Rd.

Ashley Row

Rochester Row

Gerrard St.

Medway St.

Marsham St.

SMITH SQ.

VICTORIA STATION

WESTMINSTER CATHEDRAL

Greencoat Pl.

Rochester Row

Elverton St.

Horseferry Rd.

WESTMINSTER

To Jenny Lo's Teahouse, and Poilâne

BRASS MONKEY

Francis St.

Wilton Pl.

Vincent St.

Page St.

Eccleston Br.

Gillingham St.

Longmoore St.

Vauxhall Bridge Rd.

Westminster School Fields

Regency St.

Vincent St.

River Thames

High St.

Guildhouse St.

ECCLESTON SQ.

Warwick Way

PIMLICO FRESH

Tachbrook St.

Chapter St.

Erasmus St.

TATE BRITAIN

Lambeth Bridge

St. George's Dr.

Cambridge St.

WARWICK SQ.

Denbigh St.

CASK

Moreton St.

Herrick St.

Atterbury St.

Alderney St.

Clarendon St.

VICTOR HOTEL

Belgrave Rd.

ASTOR'S VICTORIA

Moreton Pl.

Cureton St.

Sussex St.

Ranelagh St.

Ponsonby Pl.

Ponsonby Terr.

Cumberland St.

Gloucester St.

Clarendon St.

PIMLICO

Lupus St.

Vauxhall Bridge

Sutherland St.

Chichester St.

ST. GEORGE'S SQ.

Aylesford St.

Churchill Gdns. Rd.

Claverton St.

DOLPHIN SQ.

Grosvenor Rd.

N

LG

0   200 meters

0   200 yards

london

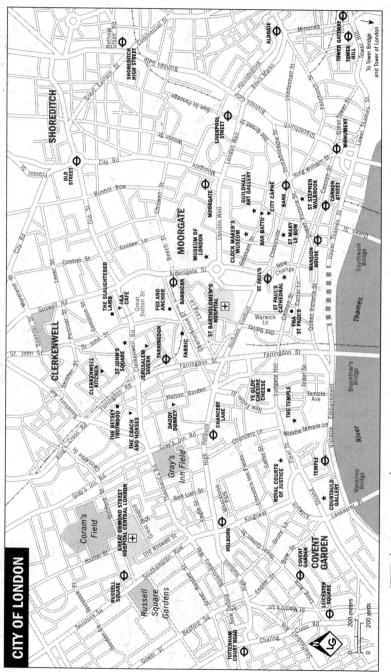

CITY OF LONDON

SHOREDITCH

CLERKENWELL

MOORGATE

COVENT GARDEN

Thames

River

city of london map

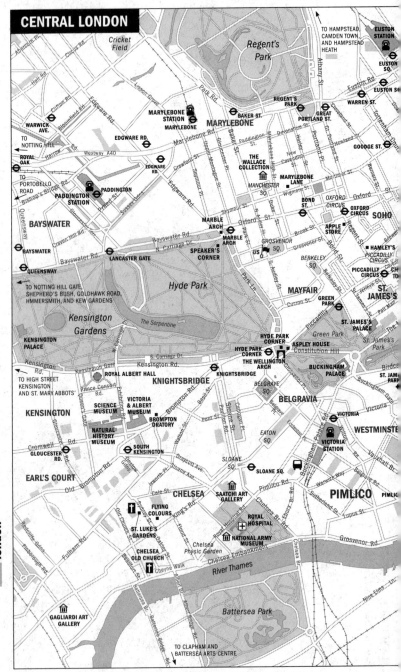

CENTRAL LONDON

Cricket Field

Regent's Park

TO HAMPSTEAD
CAMDEN TOWN,
AND HAMPSTEAD
HEATH

EUSTON STATION

EUSTON SQ.

EUSTON SQ.

WARREN ST.

REGENT'S PARK

GREAT PORTLAND ST.

GOODGE ST.

MARYLEBONE STATION

MARYLEBONE

MARYLEBONE

BAKER ST.

WARWICK AVE.

TO NOTTING HILL

ROYAL OAK

TO PORTOBELLO ROAD

EDGWARE RD.

EDGWARE RD.

Westway A40

THE WALLACE COLLECTION

MARYLEBONE LANE

MANCHESTER SQ.

BOND ST.

OXFORD CIRCUS

OXFORD CIRCUS

SOHO

APPLE STORE

HAMLEY'S

PICCADILLY CIRCUS

PICCADILLY CIRCUS

ST. JAMES'S

PADDINGTON STATION

PADDINGTON

BAYSWATER

BAYSWATER

QUEENSWAY

MARBLE ARCH

MARBLE ARCH

SPEAKER'S CORNER

GROSVENOR SQ.

US

BERKELEY SQ.

MAYFAIR

GREEN PARK

TO NOTTING HILL GATE,
SHEPHERD'S BUSH, GOLDHAWK ROAD,
HMMERSMITH, AND KEW GARDENS

LANCASTER GATE

Bayswater Rd.

N. Carriage Dr.

Hyde Park

Kensington Gardens

The Serpentine

ST. JAMES'S PALACE

St. James's Park

Green Park

KENSINGTON PALACE

HYDE PARK CORNER

HYDE PARK CORNER

THE WELLINGTON ARCH

ASPLEY HOUSE

Constitution Hill

BUCKINGHAM PALACE

ST. JAMES PARK

TO HIGH STREET KENSINGTON AND ST. MARY ABBOTS'

S. Carriage Dr.

Kensington Rd.

ROYAL ALBERT HALL

KNIGHTSBRIDGE

KNIGHTSBRIDGE

BELGRAVE SQ.

BELGRAVIA

SCIENCE MUSEUM

VICTORIA & ALBERT MUSEUM

BROMPTON ORATORY

EATON SQ.

VICTORIA

VICTORIA STATION

WESTMINSTE

KENSINGTON

NATURAL HISTORY MUSEUM

SOUTH KENSINGTON

GLOUCESTER RD.

Cromwell Rd.

EARL'S COURT

SLOANE SQ.

SLOANE SQ.

Pimlico Rd.

PIMLICO

PIMLIC

SAATCHI ART GALLERY

CHELSEA

FLYING COLOURS

ST. LUKE'S GARDENS

ROYAL HOSPITAL

NATIONAL ARMY MUSEUM

Chelsea Physic Garden

Grosvenor Rd.

CHELSEA OLD CHURCH

Cheyne Walk

River Thames

GAGLIARDI ART GALLERY

Battersea Park

TO CLAPHAM AND BATTERSEA ARTS CENTRE

london

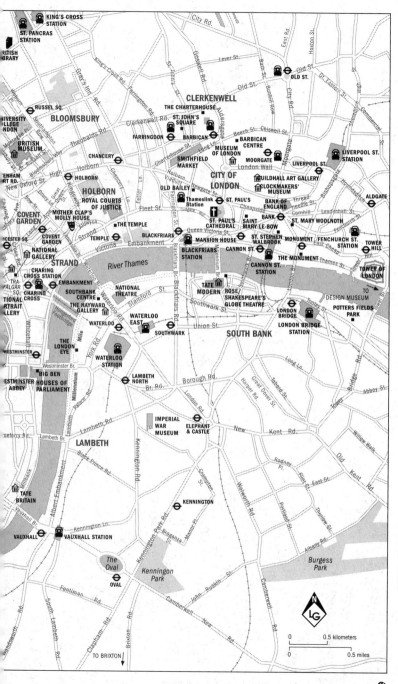

central london map

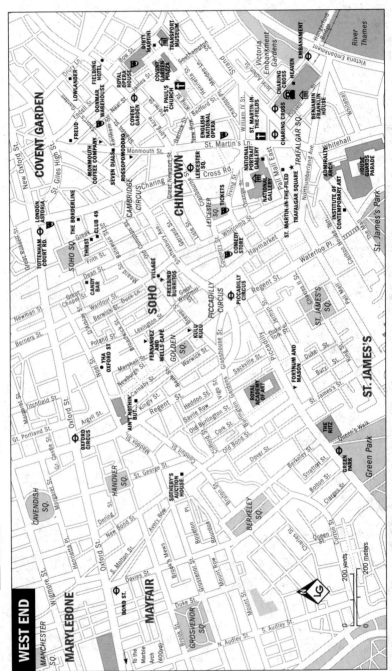

WEST END

MARYLEBONE

MAYFAIR

COVENT GARDEN

SOHO

CHINATOWN

ST. JAMES'S

CAVENDISH SQ.

HANOVER SQ.

BERKELEY SQ.

GROSVENOR SQ.

SOHO SQ.

GOLDEN SQ.

LEICESTER SQ.

TRAFALGAR SQUARE

ST. JAMES'S SQ.

PICCADILLY CIRCUS

OXFORD CIRCUS

CAMBRIDGE CIRCUS

CHARING CROSS

COVENT GARDEN PIAZZA

Green Park

St. James's Park

Victoria Embankment Gardens

River Thames

ROYAL OPERA HOUSE
DONMAR WAREHOUSE
DIRTY MARTINI
FIELDING HOTEL
LONDON'S TRANSPORT MUSEUM
ST. PAUL'S CHURCH
ENGLISH NATIONAL OPERA
ST. MARTIN-IN-THE-FIELDS
CHARING CROSS
HEAVEN
BENJAMIN FRANKLIN HOUSE
ADMIRALTY ARCH
HOUSE GUARDS PARADE
INSTITUTE OF CONTEMPORARY ART
NATIONAL PORTRAIT GALLERY
NATIONAL GALLERY
TICKETS
COMEDY STORE
FREEBIRD BURRITOS
KULU KULU
FERNANDEZ AND WELLS CAFÉ
AIN'T NOTHIN' BUT...
ROYAL ACADEMY OF ART
FORTNUM AND MASON
THE RITZ
SOTHEBY'S AUCTION HOUSE
LONDON ASTORIA
THE BORDERLINE
THIRST
CLUB 49
CANDY BAR
MONMOUTH COFFEE COMPANY
ROESSOPODDROG
SEVEN DIALS
FREUD
LOWLANDER
YHA OXFORD ST.

FREUD
LOWLANDER

200 yards
200 meters

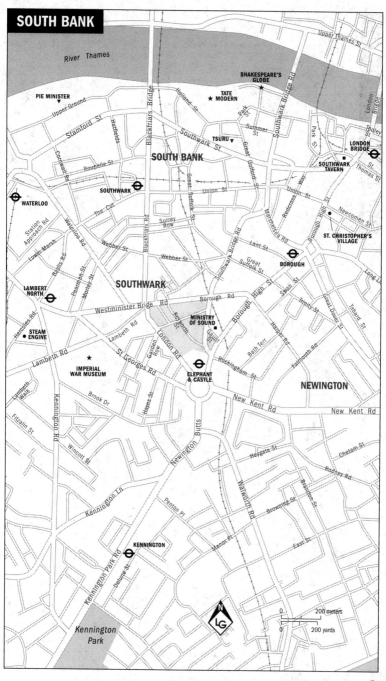

SOUTH BANK

River Thames

Upper Thames St

PIE MINISTER ▼

SHAKESPEARE'S GLOBE ★

TATE MODERN ★

Upper Ground

London Bridge

Stamford St

Blackfriars Bridge

Holland St

Park St

Summer St

Southwark Bridge Rd

Upper Thames St

Tooley St

Park St

LONDON BRIDGE ⊖

Cornwall Rd

Hatfields

Southwark St

TSURU ▼

SOUTH BANK

Great Guildford St

St Thomas St

SOUTHWARK TAVERN ■

Roupelle St

SOUTHWARK ⊖

Union St

Great Suffolk St

Redcross Way

Union St

Borough High St

Newcomen St

WATERLOO ⊖

The Cut

Surrey Row

Marshalsea Rd

ST. CHRISTOPHER'S VILLAGE

Station Approach Rd

Waterloo Rd

Baylis Rd

Webber St

Blackfriars Rd

Webber St

Lant St

Southwark Bridge Rd

Great Suffolk St

BOROUGH ⊖

Long Ln

Lower Marsh

SOUTHWARK

Pocock St

Munton St

Swan St

Trinity St

Great Dover St

Tabard St

LAMBERT NORTH ⊖

Westminster Bridge Rd

Borough Rd

Borough High St

Harper Rd

Hercules Rd

STEAM ENGINE ●

Lambeth Rd

Keyworth St

MINISTRY OF SOUND ■

Bath Terr

Lambeth Walk

Lambeth Rd

St Georges Rd

Garden Row

London Rd

Gaunt St

Rockingham St

Falmouth Rd

IMPERIAL WAR MUSEUM ★

ELEPHANT & CASTLE ⊖

NEWINGTON

Fitralin St

Kennington Rd

Brook Dr

Hayles St

New Kent Rd

New Kent Rd

Wincott St

Newington Butts

Hergate St

Chatam St

Rodney Rd

Kennington Ln

Penton Pl

Walworth Rd

Brandon St

Browning St

Manor Pl

East St

KENNINGTON ⊖

Kennington Park Rd

Dabure St

Kennington Park

N LG

0   200 meters

0   200 yards

south bank map

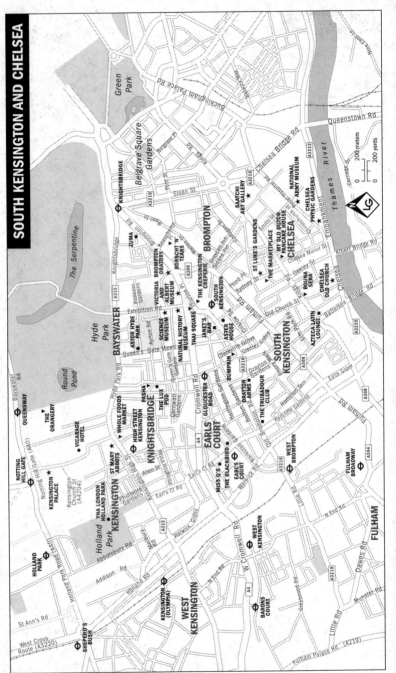

SOUTH KENSINGTON AND CHELSEA

Green Park

Buckingham Palace Rd

Queenstown Rd

Belgrave Square Gardens

KNIGHTSBRIDGE

The Serpentine

Knightsbridge

A315

BAYSWATER

Hyde Park

Round Pond

Bayswater Rd

QUEENSWAY

THE ORANGERY

VICARAGE HOTEL

NOTTING HILL GATE (A40)

Kensington Church St

KENSINGTON PALACE

HOLLAND PARK

Holland Park

YHA LONDON HOLLAND PARK

ST MARY ABBOTS

KENSINGTON

Holland Park Road (A402)

Addison Rd

St Ann's Rd

West Cross Route (A3220)

SHEPERD'S BUSH

Exhibition Rd

VICTORIA AND ALBERT MUSEUM

SCIENCE MUSEUM

NATURAL HISTORY MUSEUM

THAI SQUARE

JANET'S BAR

ASTER HOUSE

Queen's Gate Mews

HIGH STREET KENSINGTON

THE LUX POD

PASHA

WHOLE FOODS MARKET

ASTOR HYDE PARK

KNIGHTSBRIDGE

Cromwell Rd

GLOUCESTER ROAD

EARLS COURT

MISS Q'S

THE BLACKBIRD

EARL'S COURT

Earl's Ct Rd

WARWICK Rd

N Cromwell Rd

W. Cromwell Rd

A4

WEST KENSINGTON

BARONS COURT

FULHAM

Fulham Palace Rd (A219)

Little Rd

Dawes Rd

Munster Rd

KENSINGTON (OLYMPIA)

WEST KENSINGTON

A3218

A4

A4

BROMPTON

SAATCHI ART GALLERY

BROMPTON ORATORY

ZUMA

BORSCHT 'N' TEARS

THE KENSINGTON CREPERIE

SOUTH KENSINGTON

ST LUKE'S GARDENS

THE MARKETPLACE

MY OLD DUTCH PANCAKE HOUSE

CHELSEA PHYSIC GARDENS

NATIONAL ARMY MUSEUM

CHELSEA

BOUNA SERA

CHELSEA OLD CHURCH

Chelsea Bridge Rd

A3216

A3216

Thames River

Embankment

Old Church St

Oakley St

Sydney St

AZTECA LATIN LOUNGE

SOUTH KENSINGTON

A308

BUMPKIN

DRAYTON ARMS

THE TROUBADOUR CLUB

Old Brompton Rd

Bolton Gardens

WEST BROMPTON

A3218

Fulham Rd

A364

FULHAM BROADWAY

A308

A3216

A3220

A3212

0   200 meters
0   200 yards

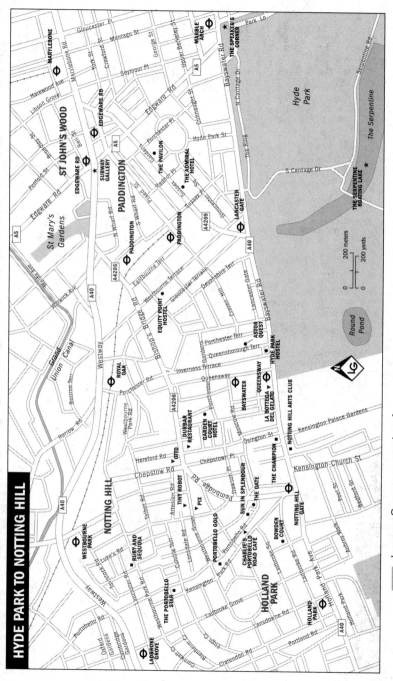

HYDE PARK TO NOTTING HILL

hyde park to notting hill map

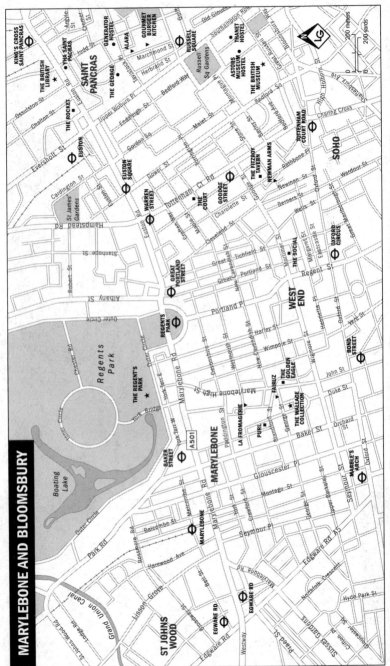

london

MARYLEBONE AND BLOOMSBURY

ST JOHNS WOOD

Regents Park

Boating Lake

THE REGENT'S PARK ★

MARYLEBONE

WEST END

SOHO

SAINT PANCRAS

THE BRITISH MUSEUM ★

RUSSELL SQUARE

Russell Sq Gardens

KING'S CROSS SAINT PANCRAS

THE BRITISH LIBRARY

St James Gardens

GENERATOR HOSTEL ●
ALARA ●
GOURMET BURGER KITCHEN ■

ASTORS MUSEUM HOSTEL ★
THANET HOSTEL ●

THE GEORGE

THE ROCKET ▲

EUSTON

EUSTON SQUARE

WARREN STREET

GREAT PORTLAND STREET

REGENT'S PARK

GOODGE STREET

THE COURT ■

THE FITZROY TAVERN ●
NEWMAN ARMS ▼

TOTTENHAM COURT ROAD

THE SOCIAL ●

OXFORD CIRCUS

THE GOLDEN EAGLE ▼

FAIRUZ ▼
PURL ▲
LA FROMAGERIE ▼

THE WALLACE COLLECTION ★

BOND STREET

BAKER STREET

MARYLEBONE

MARBLE'S ARCH

EDGWARE RD

EDGWARE RD

Grand Union Canal

A501

200 meters
200 yards

486 ♀ www.letsgo.com

MADRID

Welcome to Madrid, where the day starts later, the night ends later, and the locals look like Javier Bardem. Sound good? Well there's more. Much more. Madrid is home to some of the biggest and baddest sights in the world, from museums filled with iconic art to discotheques packed with Spain's most beautiful. From Goya's *The Naked Maya* by day to the (almost) naked *madrileños* at night, Madrid insists that you stay on the move—in only the most laid-back style, of course. When it's time to recuperate, slow down, savor some of the best in Spanish cuisine, and lounge at one of the city's immaculate parks or gardens under the warm Spanish sun. Life is good.

Madrid's plazas, gardens, and monuments tell of the city's rich history. After Philip II made the city the capital of his empire in 1561, Madrid enjoyed centuries of being on top. (Sorry, we couldn't resist.) It served as Spain's artistic hub during the Golden Age, becoming a seat of wealth, culture, and imperial glory, whose legacy can still be felt in literary neighborhoods like Huertas, in the sumptuous interiors of royal estates like the Palacio Real, and in the bad-ass collections of the museums along the Avenida del Arte. So get some rest on the plane, because from here on out it's all dinners at midnight, parties at three, marathon treks through museums the size of small countries by day, and chasing down Javier Bardem at high noon.

greatest hits

- **LIVE LIKE A KING.** No, not the Palacio Real—better! The amenities at the government-run **Albergue Juvenil Municipal Hostel** (p. 498) will make you feel like you're staying in a four-star hotel.

- **ACT THE AFICIONADO. Museo Nacional del Prado** can show only 10% of its gigantic collection at a time (p. 505).

- **ANCIENT EATS. El Sobrino de Botín** is actually the oldest restaurant in the world. (p. 511)

- **SEVENTH HEAVEN. Kapital** offers seven floors of uniquely themed dance fun. (p. 531)

MADRID

500 meters
500 yards

madrid overview map

Ever since Franco's death in 1975, the *madrileños* have been going out like it's going out of style. La Movida, the post-1975 youth countercultural movement, broke all those pesky Franco-era taboos by over-indulging in, well, everything. While the city is less countercultural as it was in the '70s, the student nightlife scene is just as jammin'. Try low-budget live music bars such as **Club Tempo** or the multipurpose **El Círculo de Bellas Artes** to get your fix of youth partying.

orientation

EL CENTRO

Bordered by the beautiful Palacio Real in the west and the relaxing Parque del Retiro in the east, El Centro, the heart of Madrid, encompasses the city's most famous historical sites and modern venues. Clubs and countless tapas restaurants are set beside churches, plazas, and winding cobblestone streets. In the middle is **Puerta del Sol,** the "soul of Madrid," where thousands descend to ring in each New Year. By day, the area around Puerta del Sol is a commercial hub with plenty of name brand stores and fast food chains. The eight streets branching off of Puerta del Sol include C. Mayor, which leads west to **Plaza Mayor,** a vibrant square bordered by restaurants and filled with street performers and vendors. On the western side of Pl. Mayor is **Calle Bailen.** Here you will find El Centro's most famous sights, including **El Palacio Real,** and Madrid's most picturesque formal gardens in **Plaza de Oriente.** While El Centro can be a bit chaotic, it is home to the city's most essential landmarks. El Centro is easily walkable and the Metro provides convenient and reliable access to the rest of the city. The main sights are deceptively close to one another. When in doubt, stick to the main streets **Calle de Alcalá, Calle Mayor, Calle de las Huertas,** and **Calle de Atocha** for adequate restaurants, nightlife, hostels, and cafes.

LA LATINA AND LAVAPIÉS

La Latina and Lavapiés lie just across the southern border of El Centro. These areas are young, hip, and distinctively *madrileño*. While accommodations are limited, these areas provide some of the finest dining and nightlife options in the city. Many unadventurous tourists will stick to the obvious food and drink options surrounding Puerta del Sol and Pl. Mayor, but the *tabernas* of **Calle Cava Baja** and **Calle Alemendro** serve some of the city's best traditional Spanish cuisine. These narrow streets are packed with meal options and one rule is universal: quality matters. While Lavapiés is less active at night, it remains one the best neighborhoods for international cuisine, particularly along **Calle Lavapiés** with its many Indian restaurants. If you are sick of tapas, this is a great place to mix things up. La Latina and Lavapiés are great to explore day and night. If you have the time, try to make it to the Sunday flea market **El Rastro.**

LAS HUERTAS

Las Huertas's walls are etched with quotes from writers like Cervantes and Calderón de la Barca, who lived in this literary neighborhood during its Golden Age. This is its claim to fame, meaning that today it is unmistakably a travelers' haunt, with cafes, bars, pubs, and clubs lining the narrow streets. Unlike El Centro, which is largely commercial and geared toward tourists, Las Huertas feels like a playground for 20-somethings, with small independent shops, cafes, *cervecerías*, bars, and clubs in every direction. **Plaza de Santa Ana** and **Plaza del Ángel** are the vital centers of the area,

madrid

but you will find a greater diversity of food and drink venues as you move outward, especially east down C. de Last Huertas, and to the north up C. de la Cruz. Huertas' northern boundary is C. de Alcalá, the southern is C. de Atocha, and the eastern is Paseo del Prado. Though it is close to the city, Huertas is very much its own world, particularly at night.

AVENIDA DEL ARTE

Bordering the eastern edge of the city, **Parque del Buen Retiro** is Madrid's Central Park. This is where the fast pace of cosmopolitan life breaks down, where *madrileño* families come to spend time together, where tourists can escape their hostel bunk beds. Retiro is its own world of walkways, gardens, fields, and trees, and it is deceptively close to the city center. The Avenida del Arte just west of Retiro is the city's cultural endowment. While the city center is largely commercial (save the odd cathedral or convent), Avenida del Arte protects Spain's most prized cultural artifacts, from Picasso's *Guernica* to Goya's *Second* and *Third of May*. While the **Museo Nacional del Prado**, the **Reina Sofía**, and the **Museo Thyssen** have become famous individually, it is their totality that makes the Avenida del Arte such a powerful display of Spain's culture. The walk along the tree-lined **Paseo del Prado** has become a cultural phenomenon of its own, a celebration of the beauty and sophistication of this city.

GRAN VÍA

Calle Gran Vía is filled with all the stuff that tourists don't need to come to Europe to see: fast-food restaurants, chain stores, and traffic jams. While the main avenue tends to be crowded and commercial, the greater Gran Vía area should not be discounted. Spanning east to west from **Plaza de Cibeles** to **Plaza de España,** Gran Vía has a number of great restaurants, bars, clubs, and live music venues—you just have to look hard. On the southeastern boundary with Chueca, you will find the highest concentration of small restaurants, bars, and boutiques, particularly on **Calle de la Reina** and **Calle de las Infantas.** Calle Gran Vía is nothing glamorous, but as you venture outward, you'll discover plenty of standout venues. They're not always obvious, but they're there.

CHUECA AND MALASAÑA

Once the center of bohemian life in Madrid, and the birthplace of a counterculture movement (La Movida) in the 1970s and early '80s, Malasaña is today somewhat of a caricature of its former self. Within a few decades, Malasaña has become one of the most expensive and image-driven *barrios* of the city, with high-end cafes and international novelty restaurants like creperies and fresh juice stands. It is rumored that somewhere in this *barrio* there is a place that sells "Russian Tapas," which begs the question, "WTF?" (We couldn't find it.) Art supply stores can be found on every other block, meaning that there are either a lot of artists in this neighborhood or a lot of people who like to spend money on expensive paints. For the traveler, Malasaña is a total playground, with the city's best nightlife, live music, and dining. Chueca is no different. Malasaña's historically gay neighbor to the east (bordered by C. Fuencarral) is today a high-end *barrio* with great food and nightlife in every direction. In Chueca you will find plenty of art galleries, yoga studios, and boutique shops, but you will also run into the more insidious signs of the bourgeoisie, such as a yoga studios that rent movies and movie rental places where you can practice yoga. Oh yeah, and a lot of sex shops.

ARGÜELLES AND MONCLOA

Argüelles and Moncloa are quiet residential areas spanning the western edge of the city from the north of Pl. de España to the city's northwest corner at Moncloa. While these areas are less geared towards tourists, they are great areas to explore *madrileño* life in its most simple and unpretentious manner. **Plaza de España, Caso de Campo,** and **Parque del Oeste** provide the city's most expansive green spaces on the west side of Madrid, functioning as both sites of recreation and centers of culture. Outside of the major parks, in these neighborhoods, you will find quiet streets with book stores, small shops, and uninspiring cafes. From Argüelles you can explore the odd and beautiful **Templo de Debod** to the west, and the great restaurants and nightlife options neighboring Malasaña just south. Moncloa is dominated by the presence of Franco's **Arco de la Victoria**, and it is the best outpost from which to explore Parque del Oeste or journey by bus to the palace **El Pardo**. While accommodations are limited in this area, some tourists might find refuge staying in a quiet neighborhood a few stops removed from the chaotic city center.

SALAMANCA

Salamanca is primarily a high-end residential district filled with luxury shopping and fancy restaurants on the side streets of C. del Castellano and C. de Serrano. While this area may seem posh, buried beneath all of the Gucci and Prada is a neighborhood that is very accessible to budget travelers. Salamanca is also deceptively close to city center, just a 5min. walk north up Paseo de la Castellana from el Arco de la Victoria. Here you will find one of Madrid's most beautiful avenues, with a tree-lined promenade running through the center. As you make your way north you will reach the **Biblioteca Nacional,** and, making your way farther north, you will find two of the city's terrific, less visited art museums: the **Museo Sorrola** and the **Museo de Lazaro Galdiano.** A visit to either of these museums will inevitably take you down some of the city's most beautiful residential streets.

words to live by

Four years of high school Spanish will cover the basics, but here is some Madrid-specific slang we bet wasn't on your final exam:

- **MADRILEÑO:** someone from Madrid.
- **CHAO:** no, you didn't get on the wrong flight; *"ciao"* means goodbye in Italy, while *"chao"* means goodbye in Spain.
- **SURFEAR:** to surf the internet.
- **TA-LÓ:** short for *"hasta luego"* ("see you later" for those of you who took French).
- **ME PIRO:** "I'm outta here."
- **PAVOS:** literally "turkeys," though in Madrid it refers to money.
- **GAZPACHO:** unfortunately, not always a tasty tomato soup—a gazpacho is a rough situation you'd rather not be in.
- **DAR LA LATA:** to annoy.
- **BOLI:** short for *bolígrafo,* or "pen."

So the next time a *madrileño* says you owe him 100 pavos, don't bother rounding up 100 turkeys—just say, *"me piro."*

accommodations

Madrid has a range of affordable housing options, from cheap hostels to boutique hotels, in almost every neighborhood. In El Centro, most backpackers' hostels are found close to Puerta del Sol; they offer cheap beds and shared bathrooms, and many have kitchens and common spaces. South of Puerta del Sol, a number of hostels offer slightly pricier private accommodations with ensuite bathrooms. Despite noise and pedestrian traffic, Gran Vía is also a deceptively good place to stay and is home to some of the city's best high-end hostels, where doubles offer some of the best value in the city (€50-70). If you're partying in Chueca and Malasaña, staying in the area at one of the fine private-roomed *hostales* (inexpensive hotels that sometimes offer dorm options) will eliminate the late-night odyssey back to your bed. La Latina and Lavapiés do not offer much in the way of accommodations, while Argüelles and Moncloa have a couple of *hostales*.

EL CENTRO

HOSTAL CERVANTES
HOSTAL $$$

C. de Cervantes, 34 ☎91 429 83 65; www.hostal-cervantes.com

Hostal Cervantes is located in a quiet residential corner of the city center. The rooms are bright, colorful, and somewhat of a relief from the drab accommodations that litter El Centro. The *hostal*'s desirable and affordable rooms have renovated private bathrooms and TVs, but the place is generally booked to capacity. The four rooms with balconies are particularly difficult to reserve in advance.

⚑ *From the Museo Thyssen-Bornemisza, walk toward the Pl. Canovas del Castillo and make a right onto C. de Cervantes.* ⓘ *Free Wi-Fi. Check the website for reservation info.* ⓢ *Singles €40-45; doubles €50-55; triples €65-70.*

HOSTAL IVOR
HOSTAL $$$

C. del Arenal, 24, 2nd fl. ☎91 547 10 54; www.hostal-ivor.com

Hostal Ivor offers clean, comfortable private rooms with flatscreen TVs and ensuite bathrooms away from the most hectic and noisy parts of El Centro. While Hostal Ivor lacks a kitchen and the common space of neighboring *hostales*, it gives the service and quality of a mid-range hotel at a competitive price. Perhaps most importantly, Hostal Ivor has free Wi-Fi everywhere. Enjoy Skyping your friends and family in the privacy of our own bathroom. What? That isn't socially acceptable?

⚑ *From Puerta del Sol, walk down C. del Arenal a little bit past C. de las Hileras.* ⓘ *Free Wi-Fi.* ⓢ *Singles €44; doubles €65.* ⓩ *Reception 24hr.*

LOS AMIGOS HOSTEL
HOSTEL $

C. del Arenal, 26, 4th fl. ☎91 559 24 72; www.losamigoshostel.com

Los Amigos is a classic backpackers' hostel. Located on the top floor, Los Amigos is separated from the madness below and the rooms are surprisingly bright and tranquil. This is one of the city's most affordable options. Guests make use of the hostel's great communal spaces, which include a small TV lounge and a well-stocked kitchen that serves complimentary continental breakfast in the morning. Rooms are clean and comfortable, but, like any backpacker haunt, privacy comes at a price.

⚑ *From Puerta del Sol, walk down C. del Arenal until you pass C. de las Hileras; Los Amigos is on the right.* ⓘ *Breakfast and linens included. Extra large lockers and towels available for a fee. Free Wi-Fi.* ⓢ *Dorms €17, with private bath €19; doubles €45-50.* ⓩ *Reception 8am-midnight.*

HOSTAL RESIDENCIA MARTIN
HOSTAL $$

C. de Atocha, 43 ☎91 429 95 79; www.hostalmartin.com

Hostal Residencia Martin is located between the bars and clubs of Puerta del Sol and the culture and museums of Paseo del Prado. Without any common spaces, it does not provide the social life of a youth hostel, but it does have the comfort and privacy of a small hotel. The rooms are clean, with white tiled floors, geriatric-looking furniture, and floral bedspreads. Though the *hostal*'s location on the major thoroughfare of C. de Atocha may lack glamor, it is within walking distance of all the major attractions in downtown Madrid.

✦ Ⓜ*Antón Martín. Walk down C. de Atocha. The hostel is on the right, before you hit C. de los Ca-ñizares.* ℹ *Safes and towels included. Free Wi-Fi.* Ⓢ *Singles €29; doubles €39; triples €49.*

HOSTAL CENTRO ONE
C. Carmen, 16

HOSTAL $

☎91 523 31 92

Hostal Centro One is a newly renovated backpackers' hangout in the center of the center (two blocks from the center of the Spanish Kingdom). The communal kitchen, living room, and six internet-access computers keep people around well into the day. The *hostal* has hardwood floors, bright lights, new furniture, and a variety of room styles, all of which have clean, shared bathrooms. While the *hostal* is a four-floor walk up an old and tired building, the silver lining is that you are also four floors removed from the madness of C. Carmen.

✦ Ⓜ*Sol. Take C. del Carmen northwest 2 blocks.* ℹ *Kitchen and TV lounge. Free Wi-Fi.* Ⓢ *8-bed dorms €23; 6-bed €25; 4-bed €28. Doubles €30. Towels €1. Luggage storage €2. Cash only.* ⌚ *Reception 9am-10pm.*

LAS HUERTAS

🏨 HOSTAL PLAZA D'ORT
Pl. del Ángel, 13

HOSTAL $$

☎91 429 90 41; www.plazadort.com

Hostal Plaza d'Ort's location on Pl. del Ángel is its biggest attraction. The plaza is a tranquil place to stay, with sophisticated nightlife and none of the chain stores and tasteless bars that swamp so much of El Centro. Hostal d'Ort's private bedrooms are simple and unglamorous. The decor is old-lady-themed. Each room has a flatscreen TV, and some have private bathrooms. The *hostal*'s salon faces the plaza and has a large flatscreen and an espresso bar.

✦ Ⓜ*Sol. Walk south down C. de la Carretas and take a left onto Pl. del Ángel.* ℹ *Safes included. Free Wi-Fi. A/C.* Ⓢ *Singles €35; doubles €55-65; triples €80-110. Cash only.* ⌚ *Reception 9am-10pm.*

🏨 MAD HOSTEL
C. de la Cabeza, 24

HOSTEL $

☎91 506 48 40; www.madhostel.com

From the first-floor bar to the rooftop terrace, Mad Hostel is a temple of fun made for student travelers. While it is located in a traditional Madrid apartment complex, everything about Mad Hostel feels new. The dorm-style rooms with bunk beds are simple, as are the shared bathrooms, but the real appeal here is a renovated bar always alive with travelers and a rooftop terrace that is used as a bar during the summer months. The downstairs bar has a pool table and a small stage where they bring in musical acts for evening parties, and there's even a small weight room available on the top floor.

✦ Ⓜ*Antón Martín. From the Metro, walk down C. de la Magdalena then take the 2nd left onto C. del Olivar. Turn right onto C. de la Cabeza. Look for the Mad Hostel sign on the left.* ℹ *Reservations must be made online ahead of time. Breakfast, safes, and linens included. Towels €5 deposit. Free Wi-Fi. Laundry machines available. €10 key deposit.* Ⓢ *Rooms €16-23.* ⌚ *Reception 24hr.*

🏨 CAT'S HOSTEL
C. de los Cañizares, 6

HOSTEL $

☎91 369 28 07; www.catshostel.com

Cat's Hostel is one of Madrid's most popular backpackers' choices for good reason. Dorms are cheap, clean, and offer the safety of private lockers, but the real appeal here is the hostel's social life. A colorful bar area with beer barrel tables, the "Cat Cave" basement lounge, and a restored Moorish patio, provide guests with plenty of space to mingle. The hostel owners go out of their way to bring guests together through organized events including a complimentary paella dinner for guests each Friday, tapas tours through Las Huertas, and late-night pub crawls. The staff is friendly, but, due to the popularity of the hostel, you might have to wait a bit if checking in during peak hours. While all guests are automatically assigned to the large dorm-style rooms, there are a few double rooms available on request, though these cannot be reserved in advance.

⚑ Ⓜ*Antón Martín. Walk 1 block down C. de la Magdalena and make a right onto C. de los Cañizares. Cat's is on the left.* *i* *Breakfast included. Laundry €5.* Ⓢ *Dorms €17-22; doubles €38-42.* ⧖ *Reception 24hr.*

▨ HOSTAL ASTORIA   HOSTAL $$$

Carrera de San Jeronimo, 32, 5th fl.   ☎91 429 11 88; www.hostal-astoria.com

While slightly more expensive than its neighbors, Hostal Astoria has the best quality rooms in the Carrera de San Jeronimo, 32 building. With hardwood floors, extra pillows, and linen changes available, these rooms are an exceptional value, not just for the neighborhood, but for all of Madrid. All rooms come with ensuite bathrooms, flatscreen TVs, and Wi-Fi. The location on Carrera de San Jeronimo is not picturesque but will offer quieter nights than the center of Las Huertas. As an added bonus, Astoria is on the fifth floor of the building, meaning you will be that much more removed from the stammering drunkards below.

⚑ *From Puerta del Sol, walk 100m east along Carrera de San Jeronimo toward Paseo del Prado.* *i* *Reserve in advance online.* Ⓢ *Singles €40; doubles €60; triples €84. Cash only.* ⧖ *Reception 24hr.*

WAY HOSTEL   HOSTEL $

C. Relatores, 17   ☎91 420 05 83; www.wayhostel.com

Way offers the nicest rooms of all the backpacker hostels listed in this section. While all rooms are shared in four- to 10-bed dorms, the hardwood floors and generous layout sets Way apart. The spacious communal kitchen and large TV room feel like upscale college common rooms—perfect for your next beer.

⚑ Ⓜ*Tirso de Molina. Walk toward the museum district and make a left up C. Relatores. The hostel is on the right.* *i* *Breakfast included. Reserve online.* Ⓢ *Dorms €18-24.* ⧖ *Reception 24hr.*

HOSTAL AGUILAR   HOSTAL $$$

Carrera de San Jeronimo, 32, 2nd fl.   ☎91 429 59 26; www.hostalaguilar.com

With a huge lobby area, swipe access, modern furniture, and private bathrooms, Aguilar is more hotel than *hostal*. Rooms have tiled floors, old TV sets, and light pink bedspreads. The bathrooms are newly renovated. Don't expect the calm of a convent, but, compared to other hostels in the area, you will be paying a good price for a better night of sleep. The availability of four-person rooms is a plus for larger groups.

⚑ *From Puerta del Sol, walk 100m east along Carrera de San Jeronimo toward Paseo del Prado.* Ⓢ *Singles €40; doubles €50; triples €66, quads €84.* ⧖ *Reception 24hr.*

HOSTAL MONTALOYA   HOSTAL $$$

Pl. Tirso de Molina, 20   ☎91 360 03 05; www.hostalmontaloya.blogspot.com

Pricier than dorm-style living, with comfortable beds, TVs, ensuite baths, and even desks in all rooms, Montaloya is more of a small hotel than a youth hostel. Though the employees at the front desk speak only Spanish, the *hostal*'s proximity to restaurants, bars, and stores along the Pl. Tirso de Molina make it a convenient choice. For a weekend stay, ask about interior rooms, as rooms facing the plaza are noisy.

⚑ Ⓜ*Tirso de Molina.* *i* *Call ahead for wheelchair-accessible accommodations.* Ⓢ *Singles €45; doubles €58; triples €80.* ⧖ *Reception 24hr.*

accommodations

INTERNATIONAL YOUTH HOSTEL
HOSTEL $

C. de las Huertas, 21 ☎91 429 55 26; www.posadadehuertas.com

This is one of the best dorm-style hostels in the city. Located right on the drinking hub of C. de las Huertas, International Youth Hostel is ideal for groups of backpackers looking for other people to join their wolf packs. Guests generally take advantage of the great communal facilities: a TV room, a kitchen that serves complimentary breakfast, and free internet in the computer room. Don't expect much privacy, as all rooms are dorm-style with simple bunk beds and storage lockers. The large shared bathrooms are clean and separated by gender. While rooms are bare-bones, cleanliness, and bargain prices are a major draw.

 # [M]Antón Martín. Walk north up C. de León and make a right onto C. de las Huertas. i Single-sex and co-ed rooms available. Luggage storage. Free Wi-Fi. $ Dorms €16-22. ⏰ Reception 24hr.

HOSTAL PERSAL
HOSTAL $$$$

Pl. del Ángel, 12 ☎91 369 46 43; www.hostalpersal.com

This location cannot be beat. Situated on Pl. del Ángel between Pl. Santa Ana and C. de las Huertas, Hostal Persal puts you in the perfect place to discover the best of Madrid's tapas bars and nightlife. The rooms here are of a similar size and decor as other hostels in the area with private rooms, but they are in far better condition. A full continental breakfast, which includes fresh fruit and sandwich fixings, is offered in the downstairs restaurant. With a big lobby, swipe keys, and a friendly and professional staff, this *hostal* is virtually indistinguishable from a medium-sized hotel—and you pay for its identity crisis.

 # [M]Antón Martín. Walk south down C. del Olivar until you see Pl. del Ángel on the right. 2min. from Pl. de Santa Ana. $ Singles €60; doubles €84; triples €125. ⏰ Reception 24hr.

CHIC AND BASIC COLORS
HOTEL $$$$

C. de las Huertas, 14 ☎91 429 69 35; www.chicandbasic.com

This chain hotel looks something like the lovechild of the chic boutique hotel and the conventional European hostel. Each room has a bold color scheme, contemporary furniture, and hardwood floors. This is a great place to stay if you like traveling in style and don't mind paying for it. A simple continental breakfast is available in the small common area, and there are snacks in the fridge, fruit, and an espresso machine. Check the website for various discounts and special offers.

 # [M]Antón Martín. From Pl. del Ángel, walk down C. de las Huertas toward the museum district. Chic and Basic Colors is on the right. i Ensuite bathrooms. Same company has a high-end hotel called Chic and Basic on C. de Atocha, 113. $ Singles €60-70; doubles €80-90. ⏰ Reception 24hr.

HOSTAL LOPEZ
HOSTAL $$

C. de las Huertas, 54 ☎91 429 43 49; www.hostallopez.com

Don't be dismayed by the dreary reception area: Hostal Lopez has some of the best prices for private rooms in Las Huertas. The bedrooms may have cream-colored walls and ugly tiled floors, but they all come with white-tiled ensuite bathrooms. While this isn't much of a backpackers' haunt, the private doubles and triples are relatively affordable, and the location is the biggest draw: Hostal Lopez is close to the nightlife of Las Huertas and just a few minutes walk from Paseo del Prado and Puerta del Sol. Like all *hostales* in Las Huertas, think twice about getting a streetside room, as they're noisy on weekends.

 # [M]Antón Martín. From the Metro, walk north up C. de León and turn right onto C. de las Huertas. $ Singles €35; doubles €45; triples €66 . ⏰ Reception 24hr.

HOSTAL EDREIRA
HOSTAL $$$

C. de Atocha, 75 ☎91 429 01 83; www.hostaledreira.com

Hostal Edreira is located 5min. from the train station between the museum district and the nightlife of Las Huertas. While C. de Atocha is a busy thoroughfare during the daytime, there isn't much heavy pedestrian traffic that will keep you up at night. Rooms are all private, with ensuite bathrooms, hardwood floors, and simple wooden beds, desks, and nightstands. With high ceilings and a generous amount of floor space, the rooms are comfortable and spacious. The *hostal* is often booked, so be sure to check in advance online or by phone.

⚑ Ⓜ*Antón Martín.* ⓘ *Flatscreen TVs. Free Wi-Fi.* ⓢ *Singles €40; doubles €55; triples €70.* ⓩ *Reception 24hr.*

HOSTAL BIANCO III
C. Echegaray, 5

HOSTAL $$

☎91 369 13 32; www.hostalbianco.com

This *hostal* is situated in the middle of the nightlife of central C. Echegaray, between Puerta del Sol and C. de las Huertas. Rooms are all private with ensuite bathrooms and are as clean and simply decorated as they come. The *hostal* was recently renovated, with plenty of fake marble throughout. The rooms come standard with the same understated furniture and uninspired bedspreads. Keep in mind noise levels—interior rooms are certainly preferable to rooms facing the street, particularly for weekend stays.

⚑ Ⓜ*Sol. From the Metro, walk east down Carrera de San Jeronimo and turn right onto C. Echegaray.* ⓘ *Free Wi-Fi.* ⓢ *Singles €35; doubles €44; triples €60.* ⓩ *Reception 24hr.*

HOSTAL NIETO
C. de León, 32

HOSTAL $$

☎91 369 04 20; www.hostalnieto.com

For better or for worse, Nieto feels more like a homestay than a *hostal*, with a small number of singles, doubles, and triples available. Nieto is located just a block away from the center of C. de las Huertas, but it will likely be less noisy than hostels located directly on the busy street. The rooms are simply decorated with white tiled floors, simple wood-framed beds, and clean private bathrooms. Their special "Salon Room" has pink curved walls and garish gold lamps, if you insist on something more decorative.

⚑ Ⓜ*Antón Martín. Walk uphill up C. de Atocha and make a right onto C. de León.* ⓢ *Singles €35; doubles €50; triples €66.* ⓩ *Reception 24hr.*

HOSTAL VETUSTA
C. de las Huertas, 3

HOSTAL $$

☎91 429 64 04; www.hostalvetusta.com

Hostal Vetusta offers some of the cheapest private rooms in Las Huertas. With just a few rooms, this *hostal* is smaller than most, but if you're pinching pennies and want privacy, it might be a good place to look. The location between the nightlife centers of Pl. Santa Ana and C. de las Huertas is great but will inevitably be noisy, so we suggest ear plugs.

⚑ Ⓜ*Antón Martín. Across the street from Pl. del Ángel.* ⓢ *Singles €25-30; doubles €35-45; triples €60.* ⓩ *Reception 24hr.*

GRAN VÍA

HOSTAL ANDORRA
C. Gran Vía, 33, 7th fl.

HOSTAL $$$

☎91 532 31 16; www.hostalandorra.com

Unlike many *hostales* where common spaces are an afterthought, Hostal Andorra does a terrific job with the solarium and breakfast room. High ceilings, hardwood floors, and natural light make for open and inviting common areas. It's actually a pleasant place to catch your breath and read a book. Rooms are spacious, modestly decorated, and come with ensuite bathrooms with clean towels. While €47 is a bit expensive for a single, doubles are a great value.

⚑ Ⓜ*Callao. Walk east down C. Gran Vía.* ⓢ *Singles €47; doubles €62.* ⓩ *Reception 24hr.*

HOSTAL SANTILLAN
C. Gran Vía, 64

HOSTAL $$

☎91 548 23 28; www.hostalsantillan.com

Hostal Santillan offers a great value with simple and sizable rooms, modern furniture, and crisply painted walls. Rooms come with standard wood furniture, refurbished hardwood floors, and clean ensuite bathrooms. This *hostal* has no illusions of grandeur; it just makes sure to do all the little things that will make your stay comfortable. In a neighborhood that is often noisy, expensive, and uncomfortable, Hostal Santillan offers accommodations that are quiet, affordable, and pleasant.

✢ Ⓜ*Plaza de España.* *i* *Laundry service. Ensuite bathrooms and daily room cleaning. Ask about scheduled excursions and complimentary luggage storage.* Ⓢ *Singles €30-35; doubles €50-55; triples €70-75.* Ⓡ *Reception 24hr.*

LA PLATA
HOSTAL $$$
C. Gran Vía, 15 ☎91 521 17 25; www.hostal-laplata.com

The mismatched antique furniture of La Plata makes the decor tough to decipher, but the rooms are pleasant. This family-run *hostal* works hard to keep the rooms clean. Thanks to the incredibly helpful and friendly staff, *Let's Go* recommends this *hostal* out of all the options at C. Gran Vía, 15.

✢ Ⓜ*Gran Vía. Walk east; the building is on the right.* Ⓢ *Singles €45; doubles €60; triples €85.* Ⓡ *Reception 24hr.*

HOSTAL FELIPE V
HOSTAL $$$
C. Gran Vía, 15, 4th fl. ☎91 522 61 43; www.hostalfelipev.com

This *hostal* gets it—you don't book a budget *hostal* to sit in your room and look at the "antiques," you leave that for the Palacio Real. These accommodations are contemporary: rooms all come spacious and standard, with simple furniture, high ceilings, and private bathrooms. At the end of the day, you need a clean and comfortable place to crash, and that is precisely what this *hostal* offers.

✢ Ⓜ*Gran Vía. Walk east; the building is to the right.* *i* *Breakfast €4.50.* Ⓢ *Singles €46; doubles €64; triples €78.* Ⓡ *Reception 24hr.*

HOSTAL SPLENDID
HOSTAL $$
C. Gran Vía, 15, 5th fl. ☎91 522 47 37; www.hostalsplendid.com

If you're pinching euro pennies, Hostal Splendid offers rooms at €5-10 below the standard rate in the building. While most *hostales* in C. Gran Vía offer only suites with ensuite bathrooms, Hostal Splendid has a few individual rooms with shared bathrooms, and a few twin doubles that run smaller and cheaper than the norm. You won't be missing out on any of the basic amenities: Hostal Splendid boasts TV, Wi-Fi, air-conditioning, and clean towels.

✢ Ⓜ*Gran Vía. Walk east; the building is on the right.* Ⓢ *Singles €25-35; doubles €45-60; triples €65-80.* Ⓡ *Reception 24hr.*

HOSTAL AVENIDA
HOSTAL $$$
C. Gran Vía, 15, 4th fl. ☎91 521 27 28; www.hostalavenidamadrid.com

Avenida claims to be within 20min. of over 200 tourist attractions—but, then again, the same can be said for all the hostels within this building complex. With so many options in this neighborhood (and even just in this building), there is nothing special about Avenida, but they do all of the basics: fresh towels, flatscreen TVs, Wi-Fi, and kind employees at the front desk.

✢ Ⓜ*Gran Vía. Walk east; the building is to the right.* Ⓢ *Singles €40; doubles €60.* Ⓡ *Reception 24hr.*

CHUECA AND MALASAÑA

⬛ ALBERGUE JUVENIL MUNICIPAL
HOSTEL $
C. Meija Lequerica, 21 ☎91 593 96 88; www.ajmadrid.es

This is one of only a handful of exciting budget accommodations in the city of Madrid. Albergue Juvenil Municipal is a state-of-the-art youth hostel built by the city government in 2007. The decor is more like that of a four-star city hotel with frosted glass, dark tiled floors, and Ikea-style furniture. Add the pool tables, cafeteria, laundry room, exercise room with stationary bikes, and media room with a computer lab, and you have a true paradise for budget travelers. The layout is spacious enough for you to jump out of bed and rollerblade around the bedroom for a morning workout. Most importantly, the hostel is situated perfectly between the nightlife of Chueca and Malasaña—close to the action but far enough from the busier streets that you're guaranteed a good night's sleep. With the Metro just 2min. away, access to the major sights is a no-brainer, and the English-speaking staff will be happy to give you a free map and point you in the right direction. You may as well be sleeping in the Prado.

♯ [M]Bilbao. Follow C. de Sagasta 3 blocks west to C. Meija Lequerica; the hostel is on the right. i Breakfast included. Laundry €3. Towels €3. 4- to 6-bed co-ed dorms. Book at least 5 days in advance. [$] €27, under age 25 €20, 25-year-olds €22. Cash only. ⏰ Reception 24hr. Inform the staff if you need to check in after 3pm.

HOSTAL LOS ALPES HOSTAL $$

C. de Fuencarral, 17, 3rd and 4th fl. ☎91 531 70 71; www.hostallosalpes.com

Recently renovated, Los Alpes is about as clean, cheap, and comfortable as *hostales* get in Madrid. Rooms in Los Alpes have new hardwood floors, nicely made beds, brightly painted walls, and simple drapes. Unlike many *hostales*, the decor doesn't look like it was selected by dead old people. The look here is refreshingly simple, and all of the rooms come with basic amenities: a tiled bathroom, towels, and TV. While there aren't proper common areas to meet other guests, the reception area is nice and cheery. There's a computer available at no charge and Wi-Fi everywhere. While the *hostal*'s address on C. de Fuencarral, one of Madrid's busiest shopping streets, might be hectic for some, the location just blocks from the centers of Chueca and Malasaña may be too good to pass up.

♯ [M]Gran Vía. Walk north on C. de Fuencarral. [$] Singles €34; doubles €50. ⏰ Reception 24hr.

MALASAÑA TRAVELER'S HOSTEL HOSTEL $

C. Manuela Malasaña, 23 ☎91 591 15 79

With small dorm-style rooms and great common areas, this is a traveler's hostel through and through. The shared bathrooms and bedrooms aren't glamorous, but the private lockers will keep your valuables safe. The common areas are generally in use, particularly the six new computers in the lobby area. The kitchen in back is usually in use by some pajama-clad backpacker cooking up dinner to keep within budget.

♯ [M]Bilbao. Cross C. de Fuencarral to C. Manuela Malasaña and follow it west for 2½ blocks. [$] 12-bed dorms €16-21; 4-bed €19-27; 2-bed €24-36. Cash only. ⏰ Reception 24hr.

HOSTAL AMERICA HOSTAL $$$

C. de Hortaleza, 19, 5th fl. ☎91 522 64 48; www.hostalamerica.net

Located on the top floor, America is the best *hostal* in a building full of accommodation options. Rooms feature big windows, new furniture, spacious bathrooms, and paintings on the wall. Service is friendly, quick, and mostly English-speaking. Be sure to check out the view from the outdoor terrace.

♯ [M]Chueca. Make a right onto C. de Gravina and a right onto C. de Hortaleza. [$] Singles €40-43; doubles €52-55; triples €67-70. ⏰ Reception 24hr.

HOSTAL MARIA LUISA HOSTAL $$$

C. de Hortaleza, 19, 2nd fl. ☎91 521 16 30; www.hostalmarialuisa.com

Nightstands, patterned bed coverings, and wooden wardrobes make this *hostal* feel more like Great Aunt Fanny's upstairs guestroom than the suite of your dreams. The decor might not be Chueca chic, but it's a totally comfortable place to stay. Rooms have hotel-quality amenities like TV, towels, complimentary Wi-Fi, and minibars, all at the standard *hostal* rates. Who needs Chueca? Just stay in your room and drink small nips of alcohol and eat cocktail peanuts and pretend you went out to that club down the block. All things considered, Hostal Maria Luisa does everything that a *hostal* should—it is clean and reasonably priced, particularly if you can swing a double or a triple.

⚑ Ⓜ*Chueca. Make a right onto C. de Gravina and a right onto C. de Hortaleza.* Ⓢ *Singles €39; doubles €50; triples €69; quads €85.* Ⓚ *Reception 24hr.*

HOSTAL PRADA   HOSTAL $$$$
C. de Hortaleza, 19, 3rd fl.   ☎91 521 20 04; www.hostalprada.com

Recently renovated, this *hostal* has a simple aesthetic and squeaky clean bathrooms that make for an enjoyable stay. Equidistant from Gran Vía and Chueca, Hostal Prada provides a great location amid some of the city's best dining and nightlife options.

⚑ Ⓜ*Chueca. Make a right onto C. de Gravina and a right onto C. de Hortaleza.* Ⓢ *Singles €38; doubles €48, triples €69.* Ⓚ *Reception 24hr.*

HOSTAL OXUM   HOSTAL $$$$
C. de Hortaleza, 31   ☎66 472 32 41; www.hostaloxum.com

Oxum feels more like a boutique hotel than a traditional *madrileño hostal*. While the lobby is pretty bare-bones, the rooms offer all the finest amenities: duvets, extra pillows, fine towels, minibars, and even iPod docks and designer clocks. The prices reflect this. If all you care about is a good night's sleep, you might be just as happy saving your money and checking into a nearby family-run *hostal*, but if the little designer touches make a difference, Oxum will be the perfect place to rest your head, dock your pod, and watch the designer clock as the minutes roll by.

⚑ Ⓜ*Chueca. Make a right onto C. de Gravina and a right onto C. de Hortaleza.* Ⓢ *Doubles €65-95; triples €135; quads €175.* Ⓚ *Reception 24hr.*

HOSTAL CAMINO   HOSTAL $$
C. de Hortaleza, 78   ☎91 308 14 95; www.hostalcamino.es

The basic Hostal Camino is ideally located near the best of Chueca shopping and nightlife, but be prepared to climb many flights of stairs for this convenience. Rooms here are on par with other *hostales* of the neighborhood with simple furnishings and the same basic amenities, but tend to be a few euro cheaper. While the staff members speak only Spanish, they go out of their way to make your stay comfortable.

⚑ Ⓜ*Chueca. Make a right onto C. de Gravina and a right onto C. de Hortaleza.* Ⓢ *Singles €30; doubles €50; triples €60.* Ⓚ *Reception 24hr.*

ARGÜELLES AND MONCLOA

ALBERGUE JUVENIL SANTA CRUZ DE MARCENADO (HI)   HOSTEL $
C. de Santa Cruz de Marcendado, 28   ☎91 547 45 32

You'll be hard-pressed to find cheaper accommodations than Santa Cruz de Marcenado's €12 dorms. While rooms are anything but private (guests should be prepared to spend the night on the top bunk), the owners place a premium on cleanliness. The TV lounge and dining areas are simply decorated with modern furniture. Rooms and common areas are also kept relentlessly clean, and secure metal lockers are available for use. Be sure to reserve well in advance, as rooms at this affordable hostel go quickly.

⚑ Ⓜ*Argüelles. Walk 1 block down C. de Alberto Aguilera away from C. de la Princesa, turn right onto C. de Serrano Jover, and then left onto C. de Santa Cruz de Marcenado.* 𝒊 *Free Wi-Fi.* Ⓢ *Dorms €12. Discounts available for HI members.* Ⓚ *Reception 9am-9:45pm. Curfew 1:30am.*

HOSTAL MONCLOA   HOSTAL $$$
C. de Hilarión Eslava, 16   ☎91 544 91 95; www.hostalmoncloa.com

The comfortable rooms at Hostal Moncloa are a bargain. Guests can count on the rooms being nice and quiet, with large ensuite bathrooms, but the lack of natural sunlight might be a moodkiller. This is certainly not a honeymooners' hotel, but it is well kept and well situated in a quiet part of town. Rooms have flatscreen TVs and Wi-Fi.

‡ Ⓜ️Moncloa. Walk south down C. de la Princesa and make a left onto C. de Romero Robledo. Turn left onto C. de Hilarión Eslava. Ⓢ Singles €45; doubles €50; triples €80. ⌚ Reception 24hr.

HOSTAL ANGELINES
HOSTAL $$$

C. de Hilarión Eslava, 12
☎91 543 21 52

If you want to escape the madness of El Centro, this is a great place to do it. Angelines offers simple singles and doubles with private bathrooms and small TVs. While Moncloa might look far from El Centro on the map, it's only a 15min. journey by Metro, and it's within walking distance of Argüelles, Malasaña, and Pl. de España. If you value comfort, sleep, and a clean, private bathroom, Angelines makes for a good refuge.

‡ Ⓜ️Moncloa. Walk south down C. de la Princesa and make a left on C. de Romero Robledo. Turn left onto C. de Hilarión Eslava. *i* Free Wi-Fi. Ⓢ Singles €40; doubles €45. ⌚ Reception 24hr.

sights

The **Avenida del Arte** is reason enough to come to Madrid. A trip down this historic path takes you along Madrid's most picturesque tree-lined avenue, and through the canon of Western art. Other neighborhoods may not have world-class art on every block, but they still pack a punch. El Centro contains some of the city's most iconic sights, like the 18th-century **Plaza Mayor.** Chueca and Malasaña, Madrid's former bohemian centers, provide ample people-watching opportunities, with streets lined with high-end cafes and shops. Argüelles and Moncloa, crucial fighting grounds during the Spanish Civil War, are marked by the **Arco de la Victoria,** erected by General Franco and perhaps the most visible remnant of his haunting legacy. The palace **El Pardo,** just north of Moncloa, offers a view into the dictator's private bunker. Argüelles and Moncloa are also home to the city's most anomalous historical sight, the Egyptian **Templo de Debod.**

EL CENTRO

📷 PALACIO REAL
PALACE

C. de Bailén
☎91 454 88 00; www.patrimonionacional.es

El Palacio Real is the ultimate symbol of the Spanish Empire's wealth and power. The palace was constructed by King Philip V between 1738 and 1755 on the site of a ninth-century Muslim fortress, and one thing is quite clear: the man had a thing for marble. While the palace is the current residence of the Spanish royal family, it is still totally accessible to the general public, and, for a meager entrance fee, you can view the orgy of artistry and craftsmanship of a palace 275 years in the making. The self-guided palace tour (1hr.) takes you through 15 rooms, each of which was curated by a different Spanish royal. The result is an eclectic mix in which artistry and wealth are the only constants. Flemish tapestries, exotic Oriental frescoes, and Persian carpets are thrown together in a maze of opulence, sometimes to gratuitous effect. If you are unconvinced by the end of the tour that the Spanish royal family is actually rich and powerful, rumor has it that they own a condominium in Florida (and a motor boat!). When Carlos IV purchased a set of instruments to be displayed in the Royal Palace, he traveled to Italy and bought the five violins that are displayed in the palace today. And that violin you are looking at ain't just any violin: it was made by Antonio Stradivari, the finest instrument maker the world has ever known. (When the Spanish royal family wants something, they get it.) If you're in town on the first

Wednesday of the month between September and May, check out the changing of the guard ceremony, which takes place at noon.

✈ ⓂOpera. Walk west down C. de Arrieta. Palacio Real is at the end of the road. *i* Come early to avoid long lines. ⓢ €8, with tour €10; ages 5-16, students, and seniors €5. ⌚ Open Apr-Sept M-Sa 9am-6pm, Su 9am-3pm; Oct-Mar M-Sa 9:30am-5pm, Su 9am-2pm.

the real "forbidden fruit"

It's no surprise that the Madrid coat of arms shows a bear climbing up an orange tree. Spain is famous for its bitter oranges, often used to make marmalade, compotes, and orange-flavored liqueurs. One variety, the Bergamot orange, is grown in Italy to produce bergamot oil, and used in perfume and as a flavoring in Early Grey tea. Another closely related variety is the citrus fruit called the "Adam's Apple," thought to have been the forbidden fruit that caused the expulsion of the biblical duo from the Garden of Eden. These fruits were brought to the Iberian peninsula from Asia and the Middle East by Arabs when they moved into Europe. By the 15th century, the exotic citrus was grown throughout Spain where people like Jan van Eyck would have (famously) seen them. In his famous Ghent Altarpiece, van Eyck depicts Eve holding not an apple but a large bumpy thick-skinned citrus.

madrid

PLAZA MAYOR
PLAZA

Today Pl. Mayor is something of a vestigial structure in the bustling cosmopolitan center of Madrid. It may be about as useful as your appendix, but your appendix is probably a lot less awesome looking. While the plaza itself has been around since the reign of Philip III, the buildings of today's plaza date to the late 18th century. During the Inquisition, the plaza was the site of public executions, but today the plaza is best known for the week-long **Fiesta de San Isidor** (May 8-15), during which the city celebrates its patron saint. The buildings around the plaza have become entirely residential; 237 apartment balconies overlook one of the single most important sites in the city's history. While the presence of King Philip III is memorialized at the plaza's center, he doesn't seem to be able to keep the scam artists away. Costumed Elvis and Spiderman wander the plaza daily, looking like they may have both had a few too many *cervezas*. The **tourist office** in the plaza is helpful and offers free maps.

✈ ⓂSol or ⓂOpera. From Puerta del Sol, walk 2min. down C. Mayor toward the Palacio Real. Pl. Mayor is on the left.

PUERTA DEL SOL
PLAZA

Spain's Kilometre Zero, the point from which all distances in Spain are measured, is located in Puerta del Sol. You certainly can't get more *"el centro"* than the center of the Spanish kingdom itself, but Puerta del Sol is something of a cultural wasteland. The plaza, memorialized in Goya's paintings *The Third of May* and *The Second of May* (which hang in the **Prado**), is today overrun by newsstands, billboards, scam artists, and street performers dressed like Mickey Mouse and Spongebob. If these are what brought you to Madrid, you may in fact find Puerta del Sol "soulful," but otherwise it is more of a quick stopping point before you venture farther into the dynamic areas of El Centro, Las Huertas, La Latina, and Lavapiés. With the regional government situated on the southern end of the plaza, the Puerta del Sol has also been the site of major protests and political rallies.

✈ ⓂSol.

CATEDRAL DE LA ALMUDENA
C. de Bailén, 8-10

CATHEDRAL

☎91 542 22 00

Catedral de la Almudena is in many ways a freak of history. While Madrid became the official capital of the Spanish Kingdom during the reign of Philip II, it took many years for the Spanish Catholic Church to recognize the city as a worthy religious center. Favoring the former capital of Toledo, the Church was resistant to the idea of building a new central cathedral in Spain. While Catedral de la Almudena was conceived in the 16th century, construction did not begin until 1879 and was only completed in 1999. Located across from El Palacio Real, this monumental cathedral is little more than a happy accident: the Catholic church's love child with the city of Madrid. The architectural style reflects this precarious past; the roof is painted in bright, bold patterns that resemble the work of Henri Matisse, while the panes of stained glass recall Picasso and the Cubist tradition. In some ways, Catedral de la Almudena may seem like a run-of-the-mill cathedral: you walk into a cavernous space, it looks cool, it feels impressive, you feel insignificant, and then you leave. But if you pay close attention, you will notice that this church is quite peculiar and filled with red herrings. Don't let the exterior fool you—this is a truly modern cathedral.

✣ ⓂOpera. Adjacent to the Palacio Real. ⓈFree. 🕓 Open daily 10am-2pm and 5-8pm.

PLAZA DE ORIENTE

PLAZA

Across the way from the Spanish Royal Palace, Pl. de Oriente is a monument to the empire in its own right. Formal gardens, fountains, and manicured hedges accent the 20 marble statues of Spain's kings and queens. If the Pl. de Oriente can teach us anything, it's that to be a Spanish ruler you need an impressive bone structure, a grizzly beard, or both. Plaza de Oriente is a relaxing retreat where lovers, tourists, sunbathers, and sunbathing-tourist-lovers lounge midday to escape the streets of El Centro. What better place to practice the art of PDA than under the marble gaze of King Philip III?

✣ ⓂOpera. Across from the Palacio Real. ⓈFree.

JARDINES DE SABATINI
C. de Bailén, 9

GARDEN

☎91 588 53 42

If El Palacio Real had a buttcrack, Jardines de Sabatini would be nestled right up next to it. This maze of trees, hedges, and fountains stand on what used to be the stable grounds of El Palacio Real, originally designed by the Italian architect Francisco Sabatini. The immaculately kept trees, fountains, and hedges create a relaxing environment in which to take a break, breathe deep, look up at the palace, and feel helplessly poor and intimidated.

✣ ⓂOpera. Adjacent to the Palacio Real. ⓈFree. 🕓 Open from dawn to dusk.

PLAZA DE LA VILLA

PLAZA

Many of the neighboring plazas in El Centro are bigger, but it isn't size that really matters... right ladies? In any case, Pl. de la Villa is easily overlooked, but very much worth a quick visit. The first major building on the plaza is the Casa de la Villa. (Translation? City Hall.) Plaza de la Villa is also home to El Torre de Los Lujanes, the private family home of the Lujanes that was built in the 15th century. This is not only one of the oldest buildings in the square, but it is also one of city's best remaining examples of Mudéjar, or Islamic-influenced architecture. Unlike Pl. Mayor, Pl. de la Villa is quiet, so you won't find yourself accosted by scam artists.

✣ From the Palacio Real, walk down C. Mayor toward Puerta del Sol; the plaza is on the right. Ⓢ Free.

sights

CONVENTO DE LA ENCARNACIÓN

Pl. de la Encarnación, 1

CONVENT

☎91 454 88 00

Every July 27th, it is said that the blood of St. Panthalon, held in a crystal orb, visibly liquefies. It is not entirely clear that St. Panthalon was in fact a living, breathing (and bleeding) person, but a crystal orb containing his alleged blood is on display at the Convento de la Encarnación. Convents are normally incredibly exclusive: it doesn't matter how hot your friends are, you still aren't getting in. This convent is a little different. While it was founded as an exclusive center of monastic life nearly 400 years ago, today it is accessible to the general public for a small entrance fee. The tour takes you through the formerly secluded chapel filled with artwork by European masters and into the famous reliquary, which contains thousands of Christian relics, most notably the blood-filled crystal orb. Located close to El Palacio Real and Pl. de Oriente, the convent is an easy stop and a great opportunity to get some face time with ancient relics.

✚ ⓂOpera. Take Pl. de Isabel II northwest to C. de Arietta and turn right onto Pl. de la Encarnación. *i* Tours conducted in Spanish every 30min. Ⓢ €3.60. ☾ Open Tu-Th 10:30am-12:30pm and 4-5:30pm, F 10:30am-12:30pm, Sa 10:30am-12:30pm and 4-5:30pm, Su 11am-1:30pm.

LA LATINA AND LAVAPIÉS

BASILICA DE SAN FRANCISCO EL GRANDE

C. de San Buenaventura

CHURCH

☎91 365 38 00

This Roman Catholic Church is one of the most distinctive structures in La Latina. The basilica, designed in a Neoclassical style in the second half of the 18th century, comes to life when lit up at night. The church has three chapels, including the Chapel of San Bernardino de Siena, where Goya's magnificent painting of the chapel's namesake rests. Pay close attention to the picture and you will see that the figure looking down on the right is Goya himself. Don't forget to check out the adjacent gardens, which have spectacular views of western Madrid.

✚ ⓂLa Latina. Walk west down Carrera de San Francisco. Ⓢ Free. Guided tours €3. ☾ Open Tu-F 11am-12:30pm and 4-6:30pm, Sa 11am-noon.

LA IGLESIA DE SAN ANDRÉS

Pl. de San Andrés

CHURCH

One of the oldest parishes in Madrid, La Iglesia de San Andrés used to be *the* go-to church for La Latina local San Isidro Labrador, the patron saint of Madrid. Much of the original interior was destroyed during the Spanish Civil War, but the structure still showcases a Baroque style crafted by designer José de Villarreal. Pay specific attention to the 15th-century cupola stationed above the sanctuary of the San Andrés Chapel.

✚ ⓂLa Latina. Make a left onto C. de la Cava. Ⓢ Free.

LAS HUERTAS

REAL ACADEMIA DE BELLAS ARTES DE SAN FERNANDO

C. de Alcalá, 13

MUSEUM

☎91 524 08 64; rabasf.insde.es

The oldest permanent art institute in Madrid, the Real Academia de Bellas Artes is a short walk away from bustling Puerta del Sol. This is the only museum dedicated exclusively to Spanish artists, and with a collection 1400 paintings, 15,000 drawings, and 600 sculptures, this should be your first stop if you couldn't get enough at El Prado. Particularly notable are the Goya paintings in Room 13, which include two rare self-portraits. The museum also contains notable works by Rubens, Ribera, and Sorolla. The collection is dwarfed by the Prado down the street, but the museum gives a concise tour of art history in Spain from the 17th century through 20th century.

✚ From Puerta del Sol, walk east down C. de Alcalá. Real Academia de Bellas Artes is on the left. Ⓢ €5; groups of 15-25, university students, teachers, under 18, and over 65 free. Free to all W. ☾ Open Tu-Sa 9am-5pm, Su 9am-2:30pm.

madrid

AVENIDA DEL ARTE

✓ MUSEO NACIONAL CENTRO DE ARTE REINA SOFÍA — ART MUSEUM

C. Santa Isabel, 52 — ☎91 774 10 00; www.museoreinasofia.es

Juan Carlos I named the Reina Sofía for his wife and declared it a national museum in 1988. The building itself is a masterpiece: what was once Madrid's general hospital in the 18th century has been gutted and transformed into a temple of 20th-century art. Two glass elevators at either end of the museum ferry visitors between the four floors of the collection. The second and fourth floors are mazes of permanent exhibits that chart the Spanish avant-garde and include galleries dedicated to Juanw Gris, Joan Miró, and Salvador Dalí. The museum's main attraction is Picasso's *Guernica* in Gallery 206. To make the most of your visit, consider investing in an audio guide, which gives a full historical and critical account of the work. The basement and first floor exhibits focus on more contemporary artists.

➜ [M]Atocha. $ €6, ages 17 and under and over 65 free Sa afternoon and Su. Temporary exhibits €3. Audio guides €4, students €3. ⏰ Open M 10am-9pm, W-Sa 10am-9pm, Su 10am-2:30pm.

✓ MUSEO NACIONAL DEL PRADO — MUSEUM

C. Ruiz de Alarcón, 23 — ☎91 330 28 00; www.museodelprado.es

El Prado is one of the greatest art museums in the world. Built from the original collection of the Spanish royal family, El Prado celebrates the entirety of western art from Hellenistic Greek sculpture to Dutch altarpieces to Spanish and Italian Renaissance paintings. The museum requires at least a day-long visit, but if you really can't stay, be sure to put in some face time with the following masterpieces.

Diego Velázquez's ✓**Las Meninas,** one of the most studied pieces of art in the world, captures a studio scene centered on the Infanta Margarita. Velázquez himself stares out from behind his easel on the left side of the painting. It may look like just another picture of wealthy Spaniards and their dwarves, but this piece has been praised as the culmination of Velázquez's career—a meditation on reality, art, illusion, and the power of easel painting. Goya's side-by-side portraits *La Maja Vestida* and *La Maja Desnuda* portray a woman believed to be the Duchess of Alba in different states of undress. (The museum has yet to recover the long-lost third portrait, *La Maja Spread Eagla.*)

The free museum maps offered at the information kiosk will help guide you to the most historically important pieces, while the English audio tour (€3.50) is an invaluable resource for learning about the history of the 1500+ works on display. Evenings are free at the museum, but crowds do gather.

➜ [M]Banco de España and [M]Atocha. From [M]Atocha, walk north up Paseo del Prado; the museum will be on your right, just past the gardens. i Free entry Tu-Sa 6-8pm, Su 5-8pm. Check the website for an up-to-date schedule. $ €8, students €4, under 18 and over 65 free. ⏰ Open Tu-Su 9am-8pm.

✓ MUSEO THYSSEN-BORNEMISZA — MUSEUM

Paseo del Prado, 8 — ☎91 369 01 51; www.museothyssen.org

The Thyssen-Bornemisza has a bit more of an international emphasis than either the Reina Sofía or the Prado. The museum is housed in the 19th-century Palacio de Villahermosa and contains the collection of the late Baron Henrich Thyssen-Bornemisza. Today, the museum is the world's most extensive private showcase. Exhibits range from 14th-century Flemish altarpieces to an impressive collection of German avant-garde canvases from the early 20th century. Take advantage of the spread by checking out its Baroque and Neoclassical collection, which includes pieces by Caravaggio, Riber, and Claude Lorraine. Also, be sure to explore the Impressionist, Fauvist, and early avant-garde pieces that paved the way to modern art as we know it today. There are too many famous artists to name-drop—just come here to be wowed by the gigantic collection.

➜ From the Prado, walk north up Paseo del Prado. The museum is at the corner of Carrera de San Jeronimo and Paseo del Prado. $ €7, children under 12 free. ⏰ Open Tu-Su 10am-7pm.

CAIXAFORUM
MUSEUM

Paseo del Prado, 36   ☎91 389 65 45

The CaixaForum is a visual magnet along Paseo del Prado. The 19th-century factory seems to float on one corner of La Avenida del Arte beside the museum's towering vertical garden. Designed by the same architects as London's Tate Modern, the CaixaForum is an architectural masterpiece and an incredible cultural resource. The interior has two floors of gallery space for art, design, and architecture exhibits, including major retrospectives of internationally renowned architects. The basement auditorium hosts anything and everything cool and relevant, from lectures by architects to dance performances to film screenings. The exterior vertical garden is a marvel of botany and urban design.

✚ ⓜAtocha. From the Metro, walk north up Paseo del Prado; the CaixaForum is on the left. Ⓢ Free. Some special events are ticketed. ◷ Open daily 10am-8pm.

PARQUE DEL BUEN RETIRO
PARK

C. Alfonso XII, 48   ☎91 429 82 40; www.parquedelretiro.es

When a run-of-the-mill millionaire needs a break, he goes to a spa. When a Spanish monarch needs some time off, he builds his own retreat. A former hunting ground, the Parque del Buen Retiro was reconstructed by Felipe IV in the 1630s as his personal retreat. Outfitted with an artificial lake (Estanque Grande) and two palaces (Palacio de Velázquez and Palacio de Cristal), this 300-acre park was certainly a royal getaway. More democratic times have rendered El Retiro a favorite escape of all *madrileños*, who use it for both relaxation and recreation thanks to some modern additions, including a running track and a sports complex. On weekends the promenades fill with musicians, families, and young lovers, amateur rowers go out onto the Estanque Grande, and exhibits and performances are showcased at the palaces. Try to avoid the park after dark if you're alone, as shady characters have been known to hang here at night.

✚ ⓜRetiro. Or, from ⓜAtocha, pass the roundabout north onto Calle de Alfonso XII. The park is on the right. Ⓢ Free. Row boats M-F until 2pm €1.40, Sa-Su and holidays €4.55. ◷ Open daily in summer 6am-midnight; in winter daily 6am-10pm. Estanque pier open July-Aug 10am-11pm; Sept-June 10am-45min. before sunset.

REAL JARDÍN BOTÁNICO
GARDEN

Pl. de Murillo, 2   ☎91 420 30 17; www.rjb.csic.es/jardinbotanico/jardin

The Real Jardín Botánico is not just a garden but a self-proclaimed "museum" of plant life. For our purposes, it's a garden. With beautiful trees, fountains, and exotic plant life, the Real Jardín is the perfect place to reflect on the countless pieces of art you've cranially digested.

✚ Next to the Prado. Ⓢ €2.50, students €1.25, groups €0.50. ◷ Open daily May-Aug 10am-9pm; Sept 10am-8pm; Oct 10am-7pm; Nov-Dec 10am-6pm; Jan-Feb 10am-6pm; Mar 10am-7pm; Apr 10am-8pm.

GRAN VÍA

PLAZA DE ESPAÑA
PLAZA

In a city filled with statues of Spanish royalty and Roman deities, Pl. de España is something of an anomaly. Located on the western edge of Gran Vía, Pl. de España is a monument to the father of Spanish literature, **Miguel de Cervantes.** The stone statue of Cervantes at the center of the plaza is surrounded by characters from his most celebrated work, *Don Quixote.* The bronze statues immediately below Cervantes depict the hero Alonso Quixano and his chubby and slightly less heroic sidekick Sancho Panza. To the right and left are Quixano's two love interests, the peasant lady Aldonza Lorenzo and the woman of his dreams Dulcinea Del Toboso. Like every Spanish plaza, Pl. de España is a prime make-out destination.

✚ ⓜPlaza de España. The western end of C. Gran Vía. Ⓢ Free.

PLAZA DE CIBELES
PLAZA

When Real Madrid fans want to party before a game they come to Pl. de Cibeles and proudly drape their flags on the central fountain. Commissioned by King Charles III, the fountain depicts the Greek goddess of nature, Cibele, on her morning commute, driving a chariot pulled by two lions. The daringly white **Palacio de Comunicaciones** on the edge of the plaza is the headquarters of Madrid's city government. This building is open to the general public, and it's a worthy stop before or after a day in El Retiro or along La Avenida del Arte. The palace's rooftop tower is open to the public and has one of the best free views of the city.

 # [M]Banco de España. From the intersection of C. Gran Vía and C. de Alcalá, walk 1 block east down C. de Alcalá. [$] Free.

TELEFÓNICA BUILDING
ARCHITECTURE

C. Gran Vía, 28

If you want skyscrapers, go to Dubai. If that's why you came to Madrid, you're in the wrong place. That said, the Telefónica Building is Madrid's most iconic 20th-century building. Completed in 1920, this was the first skyscraper in Madrid, and arguably the first in all of Europe. During the Spanish Civil War, the Telefónica Building was used as a lookout by the Republicans to scout Franco's advancing Nationalist troops. It became a target of enemy bombings, and reportedly housed Ernest Hemingway on several occasions. Today the building is used as an office headquarters for the telecom giant, but the lobby is open to the general public and has a free museum of communications technology.

 # [M]Gran Vía.

CHUECA AND MALASAÑA

PALACIO LONGORIA
ARCHITECTURE

C. de Fernando VI, 6

This just might be the ugliest building in the city. Depending on who you are, you will either find Palacio Longoria to be an eyesore or a beautiful relic of *modernista* architecture. Whether you like it or not, you will probably run into it during your time in Chueca, and it is worth noting its peculiarity as the only true example of Catalan *modernisme* (a la Gaudí) in Madrid. Palacio Longoria was built in the early 20th century as a private residence for the banker Javiar González Longoria. In 1950 it was converted into a private office building for the General Society of Spanish Authors and Editors. Unfortunately, the building is rarely open to the public, but its facade is a sight to behold along your way through Chueca.

*# [M]Chueca. Take C. de Gravina 1 block west to C. de Pelayo and follow it 2 blocks north. The building is on the left. **i** The interior is only open to the public during National Architecture Week (2nd week of Oct).*

CONVENTO DE LAS SALESAS REALES
CHURCH

C. de Bárbara de Braganza, 1 ☎91 319 48 11; www.parroquiadesantabarbara.es

Conceived in 1748 by Barbara of Portugal, this monastery continues to function as a church, but for tourists in Chueca it's a great place to slow down, quit eating, and consume some culture instead. Originally designed by Francois Carlier, the church has since suffered a number of fires but still holds King Ferdinand VI and the convent's founder, Barbara of Portugal, in their tombs, which were constructed by Francesco Sabatini and Francisco Gutierrez. The adjacent building of the convent is now the seat of the Supreme Court of Spain, so this would definitely not be the place to go streaking.

 # [M]Colón. From Pl. Colón, go down Paseo de Recoletos and take a right onto C. de Bárbara de Braganza. [$] Free. ⏰ Open M-F 9:30am-1pm and 5:30-8pm, Sa 9:30am-2pm and 5-9pm, Su 9:30am-2pm and 6-9pm. Closed to tourists during mass.

MUSEO DE HISTORIA — MUSEUM

C. Fuencarral, 78 — ☎91 701 18 63; www.munimadrid.es/museodehistoria

This renovated 18th-century building constructed under Philip V now holds a collection of models, illustrations, and documents that showcase the history of Madrid. The building itself is a historical relic as one of Madrid's few lasting examples of Baroque architecture. While it was saved from destruction in 1919 by the Spanish Society of Friends of Art, only recently has the city decided to make this building a tourist destination. The facade is currently being renovated, and upon completion, the museum will have a totally new state-of-the-art facility to exhibit the history and culture of Madrid.

⇄ *[M]Tribunal. Walk north up C. Fuencarral. The large pink building is on the right.* [$] *Free.* ⏰ *Open Tu-Sa 10am-9pm, Su 11am-2:30pm.*

ARGÜELLES AND MONCLOA

👍 TEMPLO DE DEBOD — TEMPLE, PARK

Paseo del Pintor Rosales, 2 — ☎91 366 74 15; www.munimadrid.es/templodebod

On a nice day, this is one of the most beautiful spots in Madrid. In the '60s, the rapid industrialization taking place in Egypt severely threatened its most precious archaeological remains. When the Egyptian government proposed the construction of a hydroelectric dam along the Nile that would have destroyed Egypt's ancient temple complex at Abu Simbel, a team of Spanish archaeologists intervened to rescue the national treasure. In appreciation, the Egyptian government shipped the Templo de Debod to Madrid's Parque de la Montana, where you can now see a small archaeology exhibit inside. The original temple archways are even more impressive at night when lit up and reflected in the adjacent pool. The park surrounding the temple teems with families, runners, tourists, and locals lounging in the afternoon sun. Check out the lookout point behind the temple for one of the most beautiful views of western Madrid.

⇄ *[M]Plaza de España. Walk to the far side of Pl. de España, cross the street, and walk a couple of blocks right; Templo de Debod is on the left.* [$] *Free.* ⏰ *Open Apr-Sept Tu-F 10am-2pm and 6-8pm, Sa-Su 10am-2pm; Oct-Mar Tu-F 9:45am-1:45pm and 4:15-6:15pm, Sa-Su 10am-2pm. Rose garden open daily 10am-8pm.*

👍 EL PARDO — PALACE

C. de Manuel Alonso s/n — ☎91 376 15 00

Originally built in the 15th century as a hunting lodge for Henry IV, El Pardo is today most famous having been the private residence of General Franco during his military dictatorship. While much of the palace seems excessively ornate and unremarkable, the tour (45min.) takes you through Franco's private quarters, which have remained untouched since his death in 1975. His wardrobe, prayer room, personal study, and bedroom (where he kept his most treasured personal possession, a relic of St. Teresa's silver-encrusted petrified arm) are all on display. The tour even takes you into Franco's bathroom, and, yes, he had a bidet. In addition to its function as a museum, El Pardo hosts important state galas and (strangely) functions as the official hotel of foreign dignitaries.

⇄ *[M]Moncloa. Take bus #601 from the underground bus station adjacent to Moncloa.* ℹ *Mandatory 45min. guided tour in Spanish; last tour leaves 45min. before closing.* [$] *€4, students and over 65 €2.30.* ⏰ *Open Apr-Sept M-Sa 10:30am-5:45pm, Su 9:30am-1:30pm; Oct-Mar M-Sa 10:30am-4:45pm, Su 10am-1:30pm.*

CASA DE CAMPO
PARK

Av. de Portugal
Parque de Atracciones ☎91 463 29 00; www.parquedeatracciones.es
Zoo Madrid ☎91 512 37 70; www.zoomadrid.com

Casa de Campo offers many excuses to leave downtown Madrid. While the expansive urban park is a bit removed on the other side of the Mazanares river, Caso de Campo is a totally manageable destination for a morning or afternoon trip out of the city center. Bike trails crisscross the park, and kayaks and canoes are available for rent along the park lagoon. If you are looking for something more than a tranquil afternoon in the park, **Parque de Atracciones** (the amusement park) has rides that will jack your heart rate up without fail. No need to commit yourself to the all-day pass (€24); single and double ride tickets can be purchased on the cheap (single €7; double €12). The park also has Madrid's only **zoo** and **aquarium**, but be prepared to shell out for an entrance pass (€19), and don't expect any particular Castilian flair from the monkeys; they're just regular monkeys. If you plan on visiting these various venues within the park, head to Casa de Campo on quieter weekdays when there aren't long lines.

✚ Ⓜ️Lago, Ⓜ️Batan, and Ⓜ️Casa de Campo are all within the park. Alternatively, take bus #33 or 65 from the city center. **i** Let's Go does not advise walking here after dark. Ⓢ Entrance to the park is free; venues and rentals are ticketed. Ⓩ Parque de Atracciones open M-Sa 9am-7pm. Zoo Madrid open daily, but check website for hours as schedule changes.

ARCO DE LA VICTORIA
LANDMARK

Near Parque del Oeste

This Neoclassical arch at the center of Moncloa was built in 1956 by order of General Franco to commemorate the rebel army's victory in the Spanish Civil War. Looking at the concrete Neoclassical arch at the center of Moncloa, you'd think that Franco and his friends came to power stomping through the country Julius-Caesar-style, but that glorious horse and chariot at the top of the arch is actually a few centuries off the mark. The history of Franco's military dictatorship still touches a nerve with many *madrileños*, who prefer to call the arch Moncloa Gate. Surrounded by traffic, the history of Arco de la Victoria has faded somewhat within the fast pace of cosmopolitan life.

✚ Ⓜ️Moncloa.

PARQUE DEL OESTE
PARK

C. de Francisco y Jacinto Alcântara

Less crowded than the popular Retiro Park, Parque del Oeste is a lush break from the concrete jungle of western Madrid. This vast wooded park, with rolling hills, soaring pine trees, and small lagoons, feels more like a nature reserve than a city park. The dirt paths that cross through the park are great for an afternoon walk or jog, but exercise caution at night, as the park is more deserted after sunset. If you're parched, there are plenty of cafes along the nearby Paseo del Pintor Rosales.

✚ Ⓜ️Moncloa. **i** Let's Go does not advise walking here after dark. Ⓢ Free. Ⓩ Open 24hr.

MUSEO DE AMÉRICA
MUSEUM

Av. de los Reyes Católicos, 6 ☎91 549 26 41; www.museodeamerica.mcu.es

In 1771, Carlos III started a collection that brought together ethnographic objects from scientific expeditions and pieces from the first archaeological excavations carried out in America. Today, the modern Museo de América holds a collection that encompasses American cultures from the tip of South America to the tundra of Alaska. Some of the most interesting artifacts are treasures from the pre-Columbian cultures conquered by Spain, including some Mayan hieroglyphic documents.

✚ Ⓜ️Moncloa. From the Metro, cross the street and make a left. Ⓢ €3; EU citizens €1.50; under 18, over 65, and students free. Ⓩ Open Tu-W 9:30am-3pm, Th 9:30am-3pm and 4-7pm, F-Sa 9:30am-3pm, Su 10am-3pm.

FARO DE MONCLOA
TOWER

Av. de los Reyes Católicos, 0   ☎91 544 81 04; www.elfarodemoncloa.com

This 100m transmission tower, designed by architect Salvador Pérez Arroyo in 1992, originally had an observation deck and restaurant at the top, but the tower has been closed to the public since 2005 because of safety issues. Plans to re-open are still uncertain, but the futuristic architecture still provides an exciting addition to the Madrid skyline.

SALAMANCA

▓ MUSEO SOROLLA
MUSEUM

Paseo General Martínez Campos, 47   ☎91 310 15 84; http://museosorolla.mcu.es/

This museum will surprise you. While the Valencian painter Joaquim Sorolla (1863-1923) is not quite a household name, he is nonetheless one of Spain's greats. The museum, which resides in Sorolla's former palace and studio, is a living monument to the artist. Sorolla's home has a fantastic bohemian vibe, with his studio preserved with simple wooden bookcases filled with rare books and esoteric objects, canvases framed on easels, and paint brushes tucked into ceramic vases around the room. A trip to this museum gives you a sense of Sorolla's importance in art history, and, more importantly, of his spirit.

✠ Ⓜ*Iglesia. Turn right onto Paseo General Martínez Campos.* Ⓢ *€3; free on Su.* ⏰ *Open Tu-Sa 9:30am-8pm, Su 10am-3pm.*

MUSEO LAZARO GALDIANO
MUSEUM

C. Serrano, 122   ☎91 561 60 84; www.fig.es

Museo Lazaro Galdiano holds the personal collections of Spain's great patron of art and literature, Jose Lazaro Galdiano. This 13,000 piece collection, housed in Galdiano's former residence, includes a number of significant works, including Goya's *Witch's Sabbath* and El Greco's *Portrait of St. Francis of Assisi.* While these works are certainly worth seeing, the real appeal of this museum is its assemblage of more esoteric works of art, decorative objects, weapons, jewels, and rare books. Galdiano was an influential board member of the Prado and a publisher of art and literary periodicals, and throughout his life he collected everything from rare jewels and Renaissance paintings to ivory weapons. While the Prado is the obvious stopping point for anyone with even the most fleeting interest in art, Museo Lazaro Galdiano is certainly worthwhile for art lovers interested in visiting one of Madrid's great private collections.

✠ Ⓜ*Gregorio Marañon.* Ⓢ *€4, students €3, EU citizens free.* ⏰ *Open M 10am-4:30pm, W-Su 10am-4:30pm.*

MUSEO DE CIENCIAS NATURALES
MUSEUM

C. de José Gutiérrez Abascal, 2   ☎91 411 13 28; www.mncn.csic.es

You probably went to a natural history museum like this on a fifth-grade field trip, but the great thing about Mother Nature is that she never gets old. This is a particularly great place to go if you enjoy zoos and wild animals but prefer to see them dead. El Museo de Ciencias Naturales, based on the original Cabinet of Curiosities of the Spanish royal family in the 18th century, has today grown into a vast collection of natural specimens, fossils, and minerals. Perhaps the most thrilling room is the public warehouse in the basement, which houses thousands of taxidermied animals in a cramped, dimly lit room. You name it, and you'll likely find it in this room: vultures of every kind, primates, cats, and foxes, all looking at you, ready for the kill. Particularly notable are the preserved 4m African elephant, the giant squid, and the snow leopard (of which there are only 40 living specimens today). This museum is by no means a first stop for tourists, but it is an impressive collection with great historical importance, as it was one of the first state-sponsored collections of natural specimens.

✦ ⓜGregorio Marañon, walk 2 blocks north on Paseo de la Castellana. ⓢ €5, students and ages 4-14 €3, under 4 free. ⌚ Open Jan-June Tu-F 10am-6pm, Sa 10am-8pm, Su 10am-2:30pm; July-Aug Tu-F 10am-6pm, Sa 10am-2:30pm, Su 10am-2:30pm; Sept-Dec Tu-F 10am-6pm, Sa 10am-8pm, Su 10am-2:30pm.

BIBLIOTECA NACIONAL
LIBRARY

Paseo de Recoletos, 20-22   ☎91 883 24 02; www.bne.es

This spartan building on Paseo de Recoletos is the flagship of Spain's national library system. While the main corridors of the library are closed to the public, the building hosts a number of temporary exhibits (usually on literary topics) and cultural performances. For many people, this won't be the most thrilling visit because, let's face it, books are a waste of time (especially guidebooks). Nonetheless, the Biblioteca is a major landmark in the Salamanca area. On your way out of the library, check out the adjacent **Jardines del Descubrimiento,** a grassy public plaza smattered with trees and (expensive) outdoor cafes that spans C. Castellano.

✦ ⓜColón. ⓢ Free. ⌚ Exhibits open Tu-Sa 10am-9pm, Su 10am-2pm.

food

Affordable and delicious food is plentiful in Madrid, but you'll have to dodge the many tourist traps in order to find it. For instance, dining options in El Centro are best for a midday refreshment, and drinks are shockingly cheap, but bottled water and mediocre food come with a hefty price tag. Lavapiés is notable for its reasonably priced international fare and La Latina also has some of the city's best *tabernas.* Las Huertas' central plazas (Pl. Santa Ana and Pl. del Ángel) are packed with contemporary tapas bars, iconic 19th-century *tabernas,* and international restaurants. The southern boundary of Argüelles has spectacular bars, cafes, and *tabernas,* particularly on Calle del Duque de Liria, Calle Conde Duque, and Calle San Bernardino. Chueca and Malasaña are packed with gourmet options that will cost you an arm and a leg. For those on a tight budget, your best bet may be to grab a beer and *bocadillo,* which can cost as little as €2.

EL CENTRO

ⓘ EL SOBRINO DE BOTÍN
TAPAS $$$

C. de los Cuchilleros, 17   ☎ 91 366 42 17; www.botin.es

The world's oldest restaurant, El Sobrino de Botín, reeks of roasted pig and illustrious history: Goya was a waiter here; Hemingway ate here and wrote about it. Step inside and you will quickly realize that this is a truly authentic historical landmark and protector of the *madrileño* culinary tradition. From the gilded oil still life paintings to antique revolvers to porcelain-tiled walls, El Sobrino is what so many restaurants in the barren El Centro restaurant scene aspire to be. As you approach the winding wooden staircase, you will notice *"el horno,"* the nearly 300-year-old wood-fire oven that continues to roast the same traditional dishes. Try the infamous roast suckling pig (€22) that Ernest Hemingway memorialized in the final pages of *The Sun Also Rises.* While the food is not cheap at El Sobrino, even their simple dishes like the *sopa de oja* (garlic soup with egg; €7.90) are far better than what you can expect from neighboring El Centro restaurants. Forget sitting outside in Pl. Mayor and getting accosted by street performers; this restaurant is timeless, if a bit touristy.

✦ ⓜSol. Walk 6 blocks west down C. Mayor to C. Cava de San Miguel to C. de los Cuchilleros. ⓢ Food €6-30. ⌚ Open daily 1-4pm and 8pm-midnight.

CAFÉ DE CÍRCULO DE BELLAS ARTES
CAFE $

C. de Alcalá 42 ☎91 521 69 42; www.circulobellasartes.com

This is Madrid's cafe society at its best—a requisite visit for any connoisseur visiting Madrid. Located on the first floor of the Círculo de Bellas Artes, this cafe is part of an institution. The interior is truly grand with crystal chandeliers, columns stamped with Picasso-like figure drawings, and frescoed ceilings. The wicker chairs on the streetside terrace make for a comfortable place to relax and people-watch amidst the bustle of C. de Alcalá. While the cafe has a full menu, simple things like sangria (€5) and *bocadillos* (€5.80) are excellent and a reasonable price of admission into one of Madrid's finest cafes.

✢ Ⓜ*Sevilla, walk 2 blocks west down C. de Alcalá.* Ⓢ *Coffee drinks €3-6. Wine €3-6. Sandwiches €5-8.* ✪ *Open M-Th 9:30am-1am, F-Sa 9:30am-3am, Su 9:30am-1am.*

MERCADO DE SAN MIGUEL
MARKET $

Pl. de San Miguel, 2 ☎91 542 73 64; www.mercadodesanmiguel.es

This almost-open-air market sells fine meats, cheeses, flowers, and wine. It also contains a number of specialty bodegas, bars, and restaurants. Prices here are reasonable, especially compared to the expensive sit-down dining options in nearby Pl. Mayor. The partial air-conditioning makes it the locals' pit stop for a glass of wine (€2-3), a fresh oyster (€1.50-3), or more traditional tapas (€2-4). Just a few years old, this reinvention of the open-market has already become hugely popular with locals and tourists and is reliably packed night and day. While you can still get traditional market goods like fresh produce, fish, and poultry, the market is more popular as a midday and evening hangout.

✢ *At the Pl. de San Miguel, off the northwest corner of Pl. Mayor, adjacent to the cervecería.* Ⓢ *Prices vary.* ✪ *Open M-W 10am-midnight, Th-Sa 10am-2am, Su 10am-midnight.*

CHOCOLATERÍA SAN GINÉS
CHOCOLATE $

Pl. de San Ginés, 5 ☎91 366 54 31

After spending all day looking at 500-year-old buildings and pretending to care, it's okay to let loose. Sometimes this means treating yourself to a good dinner; sometimes this means ingesting unconscionable amounts of deep fried batter and melted dark chocolate. Since it was founded in 1894, Chocolatería San Ginés has been serving the world's must gluttonous treat: *churros con chocolate* (€4). San Ginés is an institution and an absolute late-night must for clubbers and early risers alike.

✢ *From Puerta del Sol, walk down C. del Arenal until you get to Joy nightclub. Chocolatería San Ginés is tucked in the tiny Pl. de San Ginés.* Ⓢ *Chocolates from €4.* ✪ *Open 24hr.*

MUSEO DEL JAMÓN
TAPAS $$

C. Mayor, 7 ☎91 542 26 32; www.museodeljamon.com

There is something very special about your first *bocadillo* in Madrid. Like the birth of your first child, you probably won't forget it, and you will likely be anxiously snapping pictures to capture the magic of it all. The *bocadillo* is the simplest but most satisfying meal you will have in Madrid, and Museo Del Jamón does right by this tradition: crispy Spanish baguettes, freshly sliced *jamón*, rich Manchego cheese, and dirt cheap prices (€1-2). Vegetarians beware: there is meat everywhere—cured pig legs dangle from the ceilings, and the window display brims with sausages. Museo del Jamón is reliably packed with both locals and tourists. Fanny packs and cameras are plentiful, but nothing can take away from the satisfaction of this authentic and criminally cheap meal. The upstairs dining room also offers more substantial entrees like paella (€12) and full *raciones* (€10-15) of *jamón* and *queso*.

✢ Ⓜ*Sol. Walk 2 blocks west down C. Mayor.* ⓘ *Several locations throughout El Centro.* Ⓢ *Sit-down menu €10-20.* ✪ *Open daily 9am-midnight.*

madrid

EL ANCIANO REY DE LOS VINOS TAPAS $$

C. de Bailén, 19 ☎91 559 53 32; www.elancianoreydelosvinos.es

Right across the street from the Catedral de la Almudena, this is a pit stop for an afternoon drink and snack. Founded in 1909, El Anciano Rey de los Vinos is a granddaddy in the world of tapas bars in El Centro. The cafe has fantastic views, particularly from the terrace tables, but keep in mind the noise and bustle from C. de Bailén. While the menu is not particularly inventive, at a certain point beer is beer and chairs are awesome—especially after a long day of museum-going.

⇆ From the Catedral de la Almudena, walk across the C. de Bailén. [$] Tapas €6-13. Beer €2. Wine €3. ⏰ Open daily 10am-midnight.

CERVECERÍA LA PLAZA TAPAS $$

Pl. de San Miguel, 3 ☎91 548 41 11

If you are looking to avoid the more expensive restaurants in Pl. Mayor, the nearby Cervecería la Plaza is a solid option. Locals and tourists come here to enjoy the simple tapas menu, cheap beer (€2), and pitchers of sangria (€13). With the canopy of trees above and the large canvas umbrellas, Cervecería la Plaza offers one of the best outdoor drinking and dining options in the area, protected from both the sun and the noise of heavy pedestrian traffic in Pl. Mayor.

⇆ From the Palacio Real, walk down C. Mayor toward Puerta del Sol. Pl. de San Miguel is on the right. [$] Entrees and tapas under €10. Beer €3. ⏰ Open daily 7am-midnight.

alterna-big mac

If your siesta lasted a little longer than you expected, you may find yourself with a growling stomach and no place to go, as many restaurants close after lunch and re-open at Madrid's notoriously late dinner hour. Rather than heading to the local McDonald's, pick up a local copy of the global Spanish-language newspaper *El Pais*. The entertainment section, *On Madrid*, will have a listing of restaurants in Madrid open "late" (generally after 5PM) for lunch.

food

FABORIT CAFE, FAST FOOD $

C. de Alcalá, 21 www.faborit.com

The Starbucks of Spain (except with richer coffee), Faborit, with its modern furniture and young, cool vibe, is near almost every major tourist sight in Madrid. Their *shakerettes*, or fresh juice mixes, are delicious. Try the orange and strawberry juice mix or go for an iced coffee frappe. If you can't wait for your next meal, grab a dessert or sandwich (€5).

⇆ Ⓜ Sol. Walk down C. de Alcalá. Faborit is on the left next to Starbucks. ***i*** *Free Wi-Fi at most locations. [$] Juices, coffee drinks, desserts, and sandwiches €3-6. ⏰ Open M-Th 7:30am-10pm, F-Sa 7:30am-midnight, Su 7:30am-10pm.*

LA LATINA AND LAVAPIÉS

ALMENDRO 13 SPANISH $$

C. del Almendro, 13 ☎91 365 42 52

While many *madrileño* restaurants serve pre-made tapas at an uncomfortably lukewarm temperature, everything at Almendro 13 is made hot and fresh to order. Everything comes straight from *la plancha* with enough grease to make your heart murmur "thank you." The restaurant is always packed, with most parties snacking on Almendro's specialty, *huevos rotos* (fried eggs served on top of fries with a variety of toppings; €6-9.50). If this feels gluttonous, just remember that when you split something with a friend, there are no calories. The cold gazpacho (€4) and fresh salads (€7-10) are a welcome vacation from the heavier entrees. While many of the *tabernas* in Latina are cramped and crowded, Almendro 13's setting just off the main drag of C. Cava Baja makes for a quiet and pleasant setting.

✈ Ⓜ*Latina. Walk west on Pl. Cebada 1 block, take a right onto C. del Humilladero, walk 1 block to C. del Almendro, and walk up 1 block.* Ⓢ *Sandwiches, tortillas, and salads €6-8. Entrees €6-9. Beer, wine, and vermouth €3.* Ⓞ *Open daily 1-4pm and 7:30pm-12:30am.*

▨ CAFE BAR MELO'S   BAR, SANDWICHES $
C. Ave María, 44   ☎91 527 50 54

This is an institution in Madrid for good reason. Bread, cheese, and meat, cooked together to perfection. What else do you want in life? A wife? A couple of kids? A home to call your own? Cafe Bar Melo's has mastered the art of the grilled *zapatilla* (grilled pork and cheese sandwich; €3) and subsequently has become a favorite destination for both locals and travelers. Don't expect glamorous decor: Cafe Bar Melo's looks something like a hot dog stand at a major league baseball park after seven innings of play: dirty napkins are littered on the ground, the wraparound wooden bar is covered in half empty beer glasses, and the game blasts on the TV in the corner. This is all part of the magic.

✈ Ⓜ*Lavapiés. Walk up C. Ave María 1 block.* Ⓢ *Sandwiches €2-5. Beer €1-3.* Ⓞ *Open Tu-Sa 9pm-2am.*

▨ TABERNA DE ANTONIO SANCHEZ   TABERNA $$
C. del Mesón de Paredes, 13   ☎91 539 78 26

Founded in 1830 by legendary bullfighter Antonio Sanchez, this *taberna* has had plenty of time to perfect its tapas. The menu hasn't changed much, with the standby matador-worthy favorites like the *morcilla a las pasas* (black pudding and raisins; €9). The interior of this restaurant is every bit as famous as the tapas, with walls covered with original murals by the 19th-century Spanish painter Ignacio Zuloaga and victory trophies from 19th-century bullfights. The dark-wooded interior may not be the most cheery place to spend an afternoon, but it is certainly a chance to step back in time. If all this carnage sounds a little much, they also offer traditional dishes like gazpacho (€4), *sopa de ajo* (garlic soup; €4), and plenty of Manchego cheese and *jamón ibérico* to keep you happy.

✈ Ⓜ*Tirso de Molina. From the Metro, walk past Pl. de Tirso de Molina and take a left onto C. del Mesón de Paredes. The taberna is on the left.* Ⓢ *Entrees €3-15.* Ⓞ *Open M-Sa noon-4pm and 8pm-midnight, Su noon-4pm.*

NUEVO CAFE BARBIERI   CAFE $
C. Ave María, 45   ☎91 527 36 58

Nuevo Cafe Barbieri is nothing short of grand. The high molded ceilings and large windows give the cafe an open and breezy quality. While this may be Lavapiés's finest traditional cafe, it is also a buzzing nightlife hub on weekends. With its Cadillac-sized espresso machine and fine selection of alcohols, Barbieri specializes in mixed drinks like The Barbieri (coffee, Bailey's, and vanilla ice cream; €7.50).

✈ Ⓜ*Lavapiés. Walk up C. Ave María 1 block.* Ⓢ *Desserts €4-7. Coffee drinks €2-5. Tea €2.50.* Ⓞ *Open M-W 4pm-12:30am, Th 4pm-1:30am, F-Su 4pm-2:30am.*

SHAPLA   INDIAN $$
C. de Lavapiés, 42   ☎91 528 15 99

As great as Spanish food is, we get it: it gets fussy. The hearty Indian dishes at Shapla are a welcome relief from picking your way through a bowl of olives and pretending to be full. Shapla serves all of the classics that the world has come to love: *saag paneer* (€7), chicken vindaloo (€7), and freshly baked *naan* (€1.50). In true *madrileño* fashion, Shapla offers a *menú del día* (€7) that lets you sample a few traditional appetizers and entrees at a great value. While the indoor dining is cramped and generally filled to capacity, Shapla has plenty of terrace seating on C. de Lavapiés.

➜ ⓂLavapiés. Walk uphill on C. de Lavapiés. 💲 Meals €8-20. ⏰ Open daily Oct-Aug 10am-1:30am.

SAN SAPORI — CAFE, BAR $

C. Lavapiés, 31 — ☎91 530 89 96

While many of the restaurants in Madrid look worn and tired, San Sapori tries its best to keep things bright and upbeat. The cappuccino drinks, tea, pastries, and 10 rotating flavors of gourmet gelato make this a worthy after-dinner stop on C. Lavapiés.

➜ ⓂLavapiés. Walk uphill on C. Lavapiés. 💲 Coffee €2-5. Gelato €3-6. ⏰ Open daily 11am-midnight.

LAS HUERTAS

👍 **CERVECERÍA LOS GATOS** — TAPAS $$

C. de Jesús, 2 — ☎91 429 30 62

If you took one of the grandfather tapas bars of Las Huertas and gave it a healthy dose of Viagra, it would look and feel something like Cervecería Los Gatos. Sandwiched between the madness of Las Huertas and the quieter museum district, Los Gatos is a local hangout for young *madrileños* that most tourists haven't yet discovered. Los Gatos may be old, but it still has a sense of humor: the ceiling sports a version of Leonardo da Vinci's *The Creation of Man*, in which Adam gracefully holds a beer. The decor is eclectic, with a crystal chandelier hanging from the ceiling across from an antique motorcycle. If ever there's a place to snack on traditional *raciones*, this is it. Try the *jamón ibérico* (€18), Manchego (€11), or the house special *boquerones en vinagre* (anchovies soaked in olive oil, garlic, and vinegar; €10).

➜ ⓂAntón Martín. Take C. de Atocha southeast ½ a block to C. de Moratin. Take C. de Moratin 4 blocks east to C. de Jesús. Turn left (heading north) onto C. de Jesús and walk 2 blocks. 💲 Pinchos €2-4. Raciones €8-18. Cash only. ⏰ Open daily 1:30pm-2am.

👍 **LA BARDEMECILLA DE SANTA ANA** — SPANISH $$

C. Núñez de Arce, 3 — ☎91 521 42 56; www.labardemcilla.com

C. de Augusto Figueroa, 47

If you're wondering what made Javier Bardem the tall, strapping, dazzling Spanish beauty he is today, look no further than La Bardemecilla. The Bardem family restaurant serves only family recipes like *huevos de oro estrellados* (eggs scrambled with *jamón ibérico* and onions; €8.70). With two Madrid locations, Grandma and Grandpa Bardem are getting some long overdue street cred. The food here is traditional, and each dish has a signature touch, like the *chorizo con los días contados* (Spanish sausage cooked in white wine and clove; €9). Just a few blocks from C. de las Huertas, this is a great spot to grab dinner before a big night out.

➜ From Pl. de Santa Ana, take C. de Núñez de Arce on the west side of the plaza north toward Puerta del Sol. Follow C. de Núñez de Arce 1 block. The restaurant is on the right just before C. de la Cruz. 💲 Pinchos €2-4. Entrees €8-10. Cash only. ⏰ Open M-F noon-5:30pm and 8pm-2am, Sa 8pm-2am.

LATERAL — TAPAS $$

Pl. Santa Ana — ☎91 420 15 82; www.cadenalateral.es

Lateral stands apart form the other *cervecerías* on Pl. Santa Ana. If the curators of the Reina Sofía were to make a tapas restaurant, it would look something like this, with its sparse interior, marble bar, and white leather bar stools. The obvious appeal here is that it's located directly on Pl. Santa Ana, but the restaurant delivers much more, with good service, reasonable prices, and a menu full of freshly prepared tapas. Dishes like the lamb crepe (€4.50) and the salmon sashimi with wasabi (€6.50) are a nice break from the traditional oxtails and sweetbreads. While Lateral's menu racks up major points for variety and quality, it doesn't offer substantial entrees, so either order a lot of tapas or have your mother pack you a PB and J.

✚ *If you face the ME Madrid Reina Victoria Hotel in Pl. Santa Ana, Lateral is on the left.* Ⓢ *Tapas €3-8. Combination platters €10-20.* ☒ *Open daily noon-midnight.*

if your mother only knew

Dirty floors may not be the first thing you look for in a restaurant, but in Madrid you may want to give them another shot. It's customary at tapas bars for patrons to throw their trash on the floor after eating to be cleaned up later, and more trash generally means more people have been passing through. So go ahead and toss your garbage—we won't tell your mom.

CASA ALBERTO   TABERNA $$
C. de las Huertas, 18   ☎91 429 93 56; www.casaalberto.es

Founded in 1827, Casa Alberto is one of Madrid's oldest taverns. Once upon a time, bullfighters came here for a "cup of courage" before they entered the bullring. Today it's a tourist favorite and for good reason. The walls are lined with history, with photographs of famous matadors and celebrities who have visited, and the charm hasn't entirely faded. Enter your own bullring of fear by trying tripe: what could be more carnivorous than putting another animal's stomach inside of your stomach? Maybe eating a pig's ear, another dish proudly served here. More popular, less adventurous dishes include Madrid-style veal meatballs, or the house special, *huevos fritos* (fried eggs; €12), served with garlic lamb sweetbreads and roasted potatoes.

✚ *From Pl. del Ángel, walk down C. de las Huertas toward the Prado. Casa Alberto will be on your right.* Ⓢ *Entrees €5-20.* ☒ *Open daily noon-1:30am.*

FATIGAS DEL QUERER   SPANISH $$
C. de la Cruz, 17   ☎91 523 21 31; www.fatigasdelquerer.es

While it doesn't have the institutional status of some of Las Huertas's other tapas bars, Fatigas del Querer still serves great traditional fare. The large open interior is a nice alternative to the cramped elevator-style dining found throughout Madrid. Expect standard, freshly made tapas. The waitstaff is particularly attentive and they keep the turnaround quick. Dishes like the mixed seafood paella (€7) and calamari (€10) are fantastic and won't break the bank, unless, of course, you develop an addiction.

✚ *From Pl. del Ángel, go north up C. Espoz y Mina and bear right. The street becomes C. de la Cruz.* Ⓢ *Tapas €4-12. Cash only.* ☒ *Open M-F 11am-1:30am, Sa-Su 11am-2:30 or 3am. Kitchen open until 1am.*

LA FINCA DE SUSANA RESTAURANT   MEDITERRANEAN $$
C. de Arlabán, 4   ☎91 429 76 78; www.lafinca-restaurant.com

Madrid is not cheap, but La Finca de Susana does its best to offer a gourmet dining experience (think white tablecloths set with silverware and wine glasses) at a reasonable price. Though the look and feel is formal, don't be dismayed: the menu has plenty to offer the budget-conscious. The Mediterranean-inspired menu offers greater variety than you'll find at the traditional *taberna*, with popular dishes like *arroz negro con sepia* (stewed rice with cuttlefish; €11) and *cordera al horno* (roasted lamb; €12). While the setting may feel a bit corporate, the food is far from that: rich in flavor and affordable in price.

✚ Ⓜ*Sol. Follow C. de Alcalá east and take a right (south) onto C. de Sevilla. Follow C. de Sevilla to C. de Arlabán and take a left (heading east).* Ⓢ *Entrees €7-16.* ☒ *Open M-W 1-3:45pm and 8:30-11:30pm, F-Sa 1-3:45pm and 8:30pm-midnight, Su 1-3:45pm and 8:30-11:30pm.*

IL PICCOLINO DELLA FARFALLA ITALIAN $

C. de las Huertas, 6 ☎91 369 43 91

Forget the frou-frou thin crust: this small Italian restaurant serves cheap pizza loaded with cheese and toppings. The obvious choice here is the *pizza a te gusta* (€7.90) served with any two toppings, but staples like the margherita (€6.90) are perfectly satisfying. Split two ways, these pizzas make for a great budget dinner. While Il Piccolino might not be the most authentic Italian food in the city, it is certainly a step up from the pizza-by-the-slice sold throughout Las Huertas. If dessert is in the cards, the Argentine *alfajore* with *dulce de leche* (€4) is gluttonous in the best way possible.

‡ From Pl. del Ángel, take C. de las Huertas east (toward the museum district). Il Piccolino della Farfalla is on the right. [$] Salads €5-7. Pizzas and pastas €6-9. Desserts €3-5. Cash only. ⏰ M-Th 1-4:30pm and 8:30pm-2:30am, F-Su 1pm-2:30am.

VIVA LA VIDA VEGETARIAN $$

C. de las Huertas, 57 ☎91 366 33 49

This mini Whole Foods is a treasure in a city of meat. Everything is vegetarian in this boutique grocery, from the health food products that line the walls to the gourmet buffet in the center. All of the prepared food, including vegan pastries and desserts, are priced by weight. Seating is limited beyond the few stools outside, but the prepared food is great for a picnic in the nearby Parque del Retiro.

‡ On C. de la Huertas between C. de San Jose and C. del Fucar. [$] Buffet €21 per kg. ⏰ Open daily 11am-midnight.

green ears and ham

Some international dishes can be difficult for the unfamiliar traveler to stomach. And some dishes actually contain stomach. Or spleen, intestine, or ears. *Gallinejas* is a popular dish in Madrid that usually contains various sheep entrails such as the pancreas, small intestine, and stomach. Fried in their own fat and served with french fries, *gallinejas* are a cheap street food and can be a wonderful introduction to *madrileño* cuisine.

If you're still hungry, *orejas a la plancha* ("ears of the pig"), is another tasty fried specialty. Or perhaps you're craving some *callos a la madrileña,* a centuries-old dish of chorizo, blood sausage, and the hoof and snout of a cow.

When you can no longer stand even to look at another piece of meat, head to the health food store **Viva La Vida** in Huertas and serve yourself a lunch from the vegetarian buffet.

MIRANDA INTERNATIONAL $$

C. de las Huertas, 29 ☎91 369 10 25

Miranda's burgers, burritos, salads, and other staples make it one of the best budget international menus in the area. While they offer typical bar snacks, items like the Cajun burrito with guacamole (€9.50) or the French burger with chèvre and caramelized onions (€10) are hard to come by in Madrid. While Miranda buzzes through the night, it is particularly popular among travelers for its hearty breakfast menu. The English Breakfast (coffee or juice, eggs, bacon, and toast; €5) is a good alternative to the meager complimentary breakfast at your hostel, and the full brunch (€12 per person) is a major quality-of-life enhancement: fresh orange juice, coffee, eggs, *raciones* of *jamón* and *queso*, and pastries. The walls, covered with portraits of international figures like Jimi

Hendrix, Martin Luther King, Jr., and a silver-encrusted statue of the Buddha hammer home the international theme.

From Pl. de Santa Ana walk down C. de las Huertas toward the museum district. Miranda is on the left. $ Breakfast €4-12. Entrees €8-12. ⏰ Open daily 8am-2am.

LA SOBERBIA TAPAS $$

C. Espoz y Mina, 1 ☎91 531 05 76; www.lasoberbia.es

La Soberbia has struck the happy medium between cramped hole in the wall and expansive contemporary tapas bar. It isn't known for a chic interior or an ironic theme, just for well-priced traditional dishes like paella (€7) and better-than-average *tostados* served on warm baguette (€3-4).

From Pl. de Santa Ana head North on C. Espoz y Mina toward Puerta del Sol. $ Entrees €4-12. Cash only. ⏰ Open M-W 9am-1:30am, Th-Sa 9am-2:30am, Su 10am-1:30am.

GIUSEPPE RICCI GELATO AND CAFFÉ GELATO $

C. de las Huertas, 9 ☎91 429 33 45; www.heladeriaricci.com

This is the best gelato in the area. What better way to enjoy a walk through Las Huertas than with a fistful of calories? Giuseppe Ricci has dozens of flavors. Seasonal fruit flavors like melon and fig are the specialty, but staples like chocolate and hazelnut are hard to beat. They pack plenty of gelato into the small (€2.20) and are very supportive of flavor pairings.

Walk down C. de las Huertas from Pl. del Ángel. Giuseppe Ricci will be immediately on the left. $ Small €2.20; medium €2.70; large €3.20. Cash only. ⏰ Open daily 12:30pm-1:30am.

CAFETERIA MARAZUL SPANISH $

Pl. del Ángel, 11 ☎91 369 19 43

Las Huertas is loaded with places that try really hard; Cafeteria Marazul doesn't seem to give a damn and it's all the better for it. This is a typical *madrileño* cafeteria filled with typical *madrileños* in one of the city's most tourist-heavy plazas. Staples like *patatas bravas* (€6) and *bocadillos* (€4-5) are of standard quality and are served on banged-up steel plates. This is also a great place to pick up a quick-and-dirty breakfast. The Marazul breakfast (€2.40) includes coffee and a plateful of *churros*. Sometimes you need to take off your fancy pants, tame that bougie beast inside of you, and go to a no-nonsense joint like Cafeteria Marazul.

[M]Antón Martín. From the Metro, walk right down C. de Atocha, and make a right onto C. del Olivar. Walk until you see Pl. del Ángel on your left, just before Pl. de Santa Ana. ℹ Expect to be charged extra for terrace seating. $ Meals €4-10. ⏰ Open daily 6:30am-3am.

free tapas

Don't pull out your wallet just yet. Many bars in Madrid will serve you a tapas plate with each drink order at no extra charge. Whether it's olives and cheese or scrambled eggs and sausage, these appetizer-sized portions are a Spanish tradition. Order enough beers and you may even be able to skip dinner and save a few euro for tomorrow night!

EL INTI DE ORO PERUVIAN $$

C. Amour de Dios, 9 ☎91 429 19 58; www.intideoro.com

While plenty of people have tried ceviche in swank gourmet restaurants, few have had authentic Peruvian cuisine. El Inti de Oro is a good place to start, with a menu that is faithful to traditional recipes, using plenty of cilantro, fresh onion, lime, and pepper. Most stick to what they know on the menu, choosing from the selection of ceviches (seafood cooked in lime juice; €11-13), but the waitstaff is very helpful in suggesting other traditional dishes like *arroz con pato norteno* (duck garnished with cilantro, served with rice; €11), or the *seco de corder* (lamb stew; €13). More daring visitors might consider Peruvian cocktails (€4-6), which use the traditional sweet brandy *pisco* mixed with lemon, sugar, and cream. If you're up for dessert, try the homemade fresh fruit gelato (€4.50).

⚑ Ⓜ*Antón Martín. Steps from the Metro, down C. del Amor de Dios.* Ⓢ *Entrees €5-15.* 🕙 *Open daily 1pm-midnight.*

EL BASHA
MIDDLE EASTERN $

C. de las Huertas, 59   ☎91 429 96 10; www.restauranteelbasha.com

El Basha is a tea room, hookah lounge, and Middle Eastern restaurant packed into a single room along C. de las Huertas. Like most Middle Eastern restaurants across town, El Basha sticks to the basics, like kebabs (€4) and falafel (€5), but they also offer full platters of hummus (€5) and *baba ghanoush* (€5). While the interior might seem a bit gloomy for lunch on a bright sunny day, this is a great hangout in the later hours of the evening.

⚑ *Between C. de San José and C. del Fúcar.* 𝒊 *Belly dancing Sa.* Ⓢ *Loose leaf tea €2.50. Hookah €8.* 🕙 *Open M-Th 3pm-1:30am, F-Sa 3pm-2:30am, Su 3pm-1:30am.*

LA NEGRA TOMASA
CUBAN $$

C. de Cádiz, 9   ☎91 523 58 30; www.lanegratomasa.es

La Negra Tomasa is a signature traveler and study-abroad hangout, for better or for worse. Everything at this Cuban restaurant is huge, from the heaping portions of traditional fare to the tall mixed drinks. Live Cuban music dominates the scene as middle-aged couples try to feel young again. Waitresses inside are dressed in colorful traditional garb, and the nighttime bouncer outside is dressed in traditional bouncer attire (head to toe in black). Try one of the main dishes like the *ropa vieja habanera* (shredded flank steak, black beans, and rice; €8-12) or *para picar* (tiny appetizers to share; €3-7).

⚑ *From Puerta del Sol, walk south down C. de Espoz y Mina; the restaurant is on the right.* Ⓢ *Entrees €8-12. Cover €10 after 11:30pm.* 🕙 *Open M-Th noon-3:30am, F-Sa noon-5:30am, Su noon-3:30am.*

AVENIDA DEL ARTE

EL BRILLANTE
TAPAS $

Pl. Emperador Carlos V, 8   ☎91 539 28 06

El Brillante provides quality budget eating in pricey Avenida del Arte. While its claims to have the best *bocadillo de calamares* (fried calamari sandwich; €6) in Madrid have not been substantiated, patrons don't seem to care, and they order the sandwich in abundance. If nothing else, the sandwich is as cheap and flavorful as anything in the immediate area, with the calamari piping hot from the deep-fryer. The restaurant has indoor bar seating and outdoor terrace seating near the Reina Sofía.

⚑ Ⓜ*Atocha.* Ⓢ *Sandwiches €4-8. Cash only.* 🕙 *Open daily 9am-1am.*

LA PLATERIA DEL MUSEO
TAPAS $$

C. de las Huertas, 82   ☎91 429 17 22

This upscale tapas bar has some of the best terrace seating along Paseo del Prado. They offer plenty of staples such as *gazpacho andaluz* (€4.50) and *croqueta de jamon* (€3) that are perfect as a post-museum snack. While entrees and daily specials are generally pricey, regular tapas and refreshments come at a standard price. More than anything, La Plateria del Museo stands out for its exceptional terrace and proximity to the three museums of Avenida del Arte. The wine selection changes daily but the sangria (€3.50) and cocktails (€5) stay the same.

⚑ Ⓜ*Atocha. From the Metro, follow Paseo del Prado 2 blocks and turn left onto C. de las Huertas.* Ⓢ *Appetizers €2.50-8; entrees €8-14. Drinks €2-6.* 🕙 *Open daily 9am-2am.*

🏛 **[H]ARINA** CAFE $$

Pl. de la Independencia, 10 ☎91 522 87 85; www.harinamadrid.com

[H]arina stands out among the many cafes throughout Madrid that feel old and tired. It is one of those places where you will magically feel great after eating a big meal. The menu is made up of all the foods that you likely know and love—fresh salads, sandwiches, and paper-thin-crust pizzas—and the environment is hard to beat. The whitewashed wooden interior makes for a pleasant cafe setting, but the terrace seating overlooking Pl. de la Independencia stands out. Indoor and outdoor seating are both generally packed, particularly on weekends, and many patrons take their food to go from the bakery. The house special lemonade (€3) is made with fresh lemon juice and crushed mint leaves, and keeps people coming back.

✦ Ⓜ*Banco de España. Walk 1 block east to Pl. de la Independencia; the restaurant is on the southwest corner.* Ⓢ *Salads €8. Sandwiches €6. Pizzas €9-11.* *i* *Terrace seating extra €1.* Ⓩ *Open daily 9am-9pm.*

PIZZERÍA CASAVOSTRA ITALIAN $$

C. de las Infantas, 13 ☎91 523 22 07; www.pizzacasavostra.com

Everything on Casavostra's menu is fresh—from the brick-oven pizzas to the traditional appetizers. While many of the restaurants between Gran Vía and Chueca try hard to break out of the tapas mold, Casovostra keeps things simple with a traditional Italian menu. The pizzas (€8.50-14) are fired in the brick oven and topped with ingredients like arugula, fresh mozzarella, and cherry tomatoes. The appetizer salads come in huge portions and are great to share for a first round (€5-10). They also offer a full selection of superb *burrata* (unpasteurized mozzarella) appetizers.

✦ Ⓜ*Gran Vía. Walk east 1 block to C. de Hortaleza and then 2 blocks north to C. de las Infantas.* Ⓢ *Appetizers €4-12; entrees €7-15. Drinks €2-4.* Ⓩ *Open daily 1:30-4pm and 10pm-midnight.*

i smell a rat

The classic Spanish rice dish, paella (the Catalan word for "pan") is traditionally cooked and served in a round shallow pan sometimes also called a *paellera*. In the 18th century, Valencian peasants cooked rice over open-air flames, adding whatever protein they could find. Marsh rat and snail rats were common ingredients, while fishermen added eel, dried cod, and other fish. By the end of the 19th century, living standards had risen and other meats like chicken and rabbit became more common. Today, there are several different styles of paella, including the traditional *paella valenciana* made with chicken or pork, *paella marisco* made with seafood, *paella negra* cooked in squid ink, and even *paella fideus* made with noodles instead of rice. In October 2001, Valencian restaurateur Juan Galbis made what he claims is the world's largest ever paella, feeding approximately 110,000 people.

EL BOCAITO TAPAS $$

C. de la Libertad, 6 ☎91 521 31 98; www.bocaito.com

Ever since Spain's best-known filmmaker, Pedro Almodóvar, cited El Bocaito as one of his favorites in Madrid, it has been all the rage. El Bocaito is as traditional as tapas bars get, from the matador paraphernalia on the walls to the platters of *pinchos*. El Bocaito sticks to tradition and does it well. Its back-to-back bars and four small dining rooms in back are filled nightly with a mix

madrid

of locals and tourists. While drinks (€2-4) and tapas (€2-5) won't cost much, a full sit-down dinner with a bottle of wine and entrees (€12-20) makes for a pretty expensive meal.

 # [M]Gran Vía. Walk east 1 block to C. de Hortaleza, 2 blocks north to C. de la Infantas, and then follow C. de las Infantas 4 blocks west to C. de la Libertad. [$] Appetizers €2-5; entrees €10-20. ⏰ Open Sept-June M-F 1-4:30pm and 8:30pm-midnight, Sa 8:30pm-midnight.

MERCADO DE LA REINA TAPAS $$

C. Gran Vía, 12 ☎91 521 31 98; www.mercadodelareina.es

Mercado de la Reina is one of the few exciting restaurants amid the dearth of options on C. Gran Vía. While the bar snacks are the standard pre-made *pinchos* (€2.50-5) you find elsewhere, the full dinner menu has some great options, including a winning gourmet burger served with a fried-egg (€12). The tables in the back dining area are a bit more quiet and civil than the swarm up front.

 # [M]Gran Vía. Walk east down C. Gran Vía; the restaurant is on the right. [$] Entrees €10-20. ⏰ Open M-Th 9am-midnight, Sa-Su 10am-1am.

RESTAURANTE LA ALHAMBRA DE SANTO DOMINGO MEDITERRANEAN $$

C. de Jacometrezo, 15 ☎91 548 43 31

It's hard to mess up your order at this cheap kebab joint. The menu is full of variety and will please vegetarians and carnivores alike. The kebab platters, salads, and sandwiches are as good as you will find at any fast food Mediterranean joint in Madrid. The lunch special (pita wrap, fries, and drink; €6) is budget-friendly and satisfying.

 # [M]Callao. Walk east down C. de Jacometrezo; the restaurant is on the left. [$] Salads €8. Sandwiches €5. Kebab platters €10.

CHUECA

★ MERCADO DE SAN ANTÓN MARKET $$

C. de Augusto Figueroa, 24 ☎91 330 07 30; www.mercadosananton.com

This is Europe's fierce rebuttal to Whole Foods. What was once an open-air market in the middle of Chueca is now a state-of-the-art building filled with fresh produce vendors, *charcuteriás*, bodegas, and a rooftop restaurant. Along with Mercado de San Miguel, this is a terrific place to get a sweeping tour of Spain's culinary landscape, from traditional delicacies to international fare. Prices might be a bit steep, but, much like at Whole Foods, you can easily sample your way through a meal by visiting a few different shops.

*# [M]Chueca. On the southern end of Pl. de Chueca. **i** For the rooftop terrace, make reservations in advance at ☎91 330 02 94. Visit www.lacocinadesananton.com for more info on the restaurant. [$] Varies greatly, but a full meal at the market costs around €10. Cash only. ⏰ 1st fl. market open M-Sa 10am-10pm. 2nd fl. restaurants and bars open Tu-Su 10am-midnight. Rooftop restaurant open M-Th 10am-midnight, F-Sa 10am-1:30am, Su 10am-midnight.*

★ SAN WISH CHILEAN, SANDWICHES $$

C. de Hortaleza, 78 ☎91 319 17 76; www.san-wish.com

San Wish is a novelty bar and restaurant that looks like it will actually make it in Chueca. The power of their picture menu is magnetic, displaying a lineup of greasy, crispy traditional Chilean sandwiches like the *hamburguesa voladora* (chicken, tomato, lettuce, grilled cucumbers, melon chutney; €6.50) and the *clásica* (grilled steak, sweet pickle, tomato, and lettuce; €6.50). The list goes on, but, true to their name, they don't offer much that doesn't belong between two pieces of bread. This is as trendy as fast food gets, with all sandwiches made on pressed Chilean bread and served alongside traditional cocktails like the Pisco Sour (grape brandy, lemon juice, egg white, syrup, and bitter herbs; €4.50). The young and wealthy *madrileño* crowd can't seem to get enough of it. Seats are nearly impossible to snag, especially during peak weekend hours.

☘ Ⓜ*Chueca. Take C. de Gravina 2 blocks east and turn right onto C. de Hortaleza. The restaurant is on the right.* Ⓢ *Sandwiches €5.50-8.90. Beer €1.50-3.50. Wine €2.50. Cash only.* 🕑 *Open M 8pm-midnight, Tu-Sa 1-4pm and 8pm-midnight, Su 1:30-4pm.*

BAZAAR
MEDITERRANEAN $$

C. de la Libertad, 21 ☎91 523 39 05; www.restaurantbazaar.com

You would expect this restaurant to be prohibitively expensive, but, somehow, it isn't. The expansive two-story restaurant has the look and feel of a high-end place with white tablecloths and wine glasses waiting on the table, but they offer something completely different than dinky *pinchos* and lukewarm a la carte dishes with a menu of fresh pasta (think fettucine with grilled chicken and sundried tomatoes; €7), salads, and meat dishes, with almost everything falling below the €10 mark. The upstairs and downstairs dining rooms are quite large, but partitioned into smaller, more intimate spaces by shelves filled with artisanal food displays. While the food is not necessarily daring, it is fresh, comes in great portions, and can be enjoyed in a relaxed but formal setting.

☘ Ⓜ*Chueca. Make a left onto C. de Augusto Figueroa and a right onto C. de la Libertad.* Ⓢ *Entrees €7-10.* 🕑 *Open M-W 1:15-4pm and 8:30-11:30pm, Th-Sa 1:15-4pm and 8:30-midnight, Su 1:15-4pm and 8:30-11:30pm.*

LO SIGUIENTE
TAPAS $$

C. de Fernando VI, 11 ☎91 319 52 61; www.losiguiente.es

With high bar tables, metal stools, and silver columns, Lo Siguiente has the feel of both a traditional tapas bar and a modern Chueca restaurant. While it may have a cool, polished aesthetic, Lo Siguiente is still an informal restaurant that *madrileños* enjoy for precisely that reason. You can get all of the staples like the classic *huevos rotos* (a fried egg over pan-fried potatoes, garlic, and chorizo; €9.50), but don't be afraid to try the lighter Mediterranean items like tomato and avocado salad and ceviche served atop grilled vegetables. While the food and decor may be slightly more contemporary, the feel of the restaurant is that of a neighborhood *taberna*, with the standard crowd of smirters (smokers and flirters) out front.

☘ Ⓜ*Chueca. Head 2 blocks northeast on C. de San Gregario and take a left onto C. de Fernando VI. Lo Siguiente is on the right.* Ⓢ *Meals €10-15. Cash only.* 🕑 *Open M-Th 8:30am-1:30am, F-Sa 8:30am-2:30am, Su 8:30am-1:30am.*

MAGASAND
CAFE, SMOOTHIES $$

Travesía de San Mateo, 16 ☎91 319 68 25; www.magasand.com

True to its motto, this place serves "incredible sandwiches" and "impossible magazines." The long list of gourmet sandwiches makes the traditional *bocadillo* pale in embarrassment and inadequacy, and the upstairs dining area/library has every pretentious magazine you could imagine. All of the sandwiches are served on fresh bread, with greens, fancy condiments, and a wide selection of meat beyond *jamón*. For a bougie afternoon, order the *el rollito de Luisa* (tuna carpaccio, arugula, and bread pressed with tomatoes; €4), and then pick up the latest edition of *Monocle* upstairs. Magasand also serves fresh salads and a spectacular Saturday brunch (a selection of fresh-fruit smoothies, coffee, pastries, fried eggs, sandwiches, and crepes; €16).

☘ Ⓜ*Chueca. Make a right onto C. de Augusto Figueroa, and another right onto C. de Hortaleza. Turn right onto Travesía de San Mateo (a sign on C. de Hortaleza points you in the right direction).* Ⓢ *Sandwiches €5-8. Salads €4-7.* 🕑 *Open M-F 9:30am-10pm, Sa noon-5pm.*

IL PIZZAIOLO
ITALIAN $$

C. de Hortaleza, 84   ☎91 319 29 64; www.pizzaiolo.es

The appeal of Il Pizzaiolo is pretty clear: it's the cheap gourmet pizzas, made to order and baked super thin. The menu is full of simple crowd-pleasers, including Italian salads, antipasti, pizza, and pasta. The brightly painted murals of Italian landmarks on the walls are an afterthought. The *diavola* (tomato, mozzarella, spicy chorizo; €9.90) is a favorite on the long list.

✦ Ⓜ*Chueca. Make a right on C. de Gravina and a right on C. de Hortaleza. The restaurant is on the right.* Ⓢ *Pizzas €8-10.* ☺ *Open M-Th 1:30pm-midnight, F-Sa 1:30pm-12:30am.*

STOP MADRID
TABERNA $$

C. de Hortaleza, 11   ☎91 521 88 87; www.stopmadrid.es

Founded in 1929, this old-school tapas bar is one of the best in Chueca. *Taberna* fare like *raciones* of *queso, jamón ibérico*, and seafood are of exceptional quality. They serve only *Ibérico de la Belota* (€21), the best quality *jamón* in the world, and the cured Manchego (€10) is richer than most versions in Madrid. But what really sets Stop Madrid apart is its extensive wine list. All of its dozens of wines are available by the glass. For better or worse, this old *taberna* feels a bit out of place in Chueca's clutter of posh cafes and shops selling "XXXleatherXXX."

✦ Ⓜ*Gran Vía. Walk up C. de Hortaleza.* Ⓢ *Entrees €5-10.* ☺ *Open daily noon-2am.*

RESTAURANT VIVARES
SPANISH $$

C. de Hortaleza, 52   ☎91 531 58 13; www.restaurantesvivares.com

Restaurant Vivares may be the best meal in Chueca. The interior of the restaurant is unassuming, with a typical bar up front and tables in back, but during peak hours it's packed with locals. While the traditional tapas of stewed and grilled meats are very popular, we also like the burgers: try the classic (with bacon, fried egg and cheddar; €7) or the chicken burger (with cheddar, lettuce, and tomato; €7). They not only offer a *menú del día* (entree, drink, bread, and dessert; €12), but they also offer a *menú de la noche* (burger, drink, bread, and dessert; €9.60). There's no gimmick here, no catchy decor or fancy menu items, but the nightly crowds don't seem to mind. For a more contemporary menu of salads, pasta, and vegetarian options, they have recently opened an annex restaurant, **Vivares 37**, across the street.

✦ Ⓜ*Chueca. Head 1 block south on C. de Pelayo, make a right onto C. de Augusto Figueroa, and left onto C. de Hortaleza.* Ⓢ *Entrees €5-12.* ☺ *Open daily 12:30-5:30pm and 8:30pm-1:30am.*

DIURNO
CAFE, VIDEO RENTAL $

C. de San Marcos, 37   ☎91 522 00 09; www.diurno.com

This combination cafe, gourmet shop, and DVD store is something of a novelty. At last, Spaniards seem to have figured out that eating a sandwich (try the chicken with pesto and mozzarella; €2.30) is that much better when you get the added pleasure of unwrapping it like a present. Diurno is open through the day for sandwiches and fresh smoothies (€2.50) and serves cocktails (€2-5) in the evening. Browse the DVD rentals on the way out.

✦ Ⓜ*Chueca. Make a left onto C. de Augusto Figueroa and a right onto C. de la Libertad. Diurno is across from Bazaar.* Ⓢ *Salads €5-7. Sandwiches €2-4. Pasta €5-7. Coffee €1-2. Cocktails €2-5.* ☺ *Open M-Th 10am-noon, F-Sa 10am-1am, Su 11am-midnight.*

COCINA DEL DESIERTO
MIDDLE EASTERN $$

C. Barbieri, 1   ☎91 523 11 42

Cocina del Desierto is a cave accessible by a rickety wooden door on C. Barbieri. Like many Middle Eastern restaurants, they use an assemblage of cushions, tapestries, and lanterns to evoke some distant vaguely Middle Eastern land. Are we in Morocco? Israel? Iran? We're not sure exactly sure, but the food is great, and far better than what you'll get in touristy hookah lounges. In addition to staples

food

like hummus, tabouleh, and *baba ghanoush* (€4.20), Cocina Del Desierto offers specialty couscous dishes like lamb and grilled vegetables (€8.50). The *tayin de cordero con circuelas* (lamb stewed with plums; €7.80) is another clear winner. Dishes are served with fresh lemon, parsley, chopped onion, and other Middle Eastern garnishes. If you are looking for wine, the €7.80 bottle of house wine is a pretty great way to start off a long evening.

‡ [M]Chueca. From the Pl. de Chueca, follow C. Barbieri south 3 blocks. The restaurant is on the right across from the restaurant Empatbelas. [S] Entrees €4-10. Cash only. ⏰ Open daily 1:30-4pm and 9:30pm-midnight.

LABONATA ICE CREAM $

Pl. de Chueca, 8 ☎91 523 70 29; www.labonata.eu

If you are going to get ice cream or dessert in Chueca, this is the place to do it. Labonata sells 22 flavors of homemade Italian gelato that will make you feel better about yourself and the world, while padding your hips in preparation for a long winter. The best flavors are the simple ones like vanilla, coffee, and chocolate, or the fresh fruit flavors like strawberry, banana, and coconut. They also make mean smoothies and milkshakes.

‡ [M]Chueca. On the east side of Pl. de Chueca. [S] Ice cream €2.80-3.90. Smoothies €3.90-4.50. Shakes €3.30-4. Cash only. ⏰ Open daily noon-2am.

MALASAÑA

✎ LA DOMINGA TABERNA $$

C. del Espíritu Santo, 15 ☎91 523 38 09; www.ladominga.com

Now with two locations (one in Chueca, one in Malasaña), La Dominga is making a name for itself as one of the best family-run *tabernas* in Madrid. Known primarily for traditional dishes like *rabo de toro* (oxtail stew; €14), it also caters to a younger clientele with plenty of contemporary dishes. Dishes like the beef carpaccio (served with parmesan and arugula; €13) are more refined than the heavier stewed and grilled meats that dominate traditional Spanish cuisine. The decor here is equally mixed, with high ceilings that make it feel more like a modern Malasaña restaurant than an old-time *taberna*. Reservations are a must for prime weekend nights (10pm-1am), but many choose to forgo the sit-down menu in favor of the tapas, which include a platter of *croquettas* (fried stuffed bread; €9.70) that critics have called the best in the city.

‡ [M]Tribunal. Go west on C. de San Vincente Ferrer, make a left onto C. del Barco, and make a right onto C. del Espíritu Santo. [S] Entrees €10-15. ⏰ Open daily 1-4:30pm and 8:30pm-midnight.

✎ LAMUCCA INTERNATIONAL $

Pl. Carlos Carbonero, 4 ☎91 521 00 00; www.lamucca.es

Lamucca covers the globe on its menu, and it does it quite well. While appetizers like cheese fondue and "Nachos de le Tek" might raise some eyebrows, these along with many other international dishes at Lamucca are executed with great sophistication. Dishes like Thai curried chicken with jasmine rice (€11) share the menu with Italian pizza and pasta as well as contemporary Spanish dishes like beef carpaccio (€13). Lamucca has certainly stuck to the trends with exposed brick, mismatched furniture, and chalkboard menus, but, the food here is daring and covers plenty of terrain (from Texas to Switzerland). With a loyal nightly following, Lamucca is well on the way to becoming a neighborhood institution.

‡ [M]Tribunal. Head south on C. de Fuencarral a few meters and take a right (west) onto C. de la Palma, then turn left on C. de San Pablo and follow for 2 blocks. Take a right on C. de Don Felipe and a quick left onto C. del Molino de Viento. Follow C. del Molino de Viento until you reach Pl. Carlos Carbonero. The restaurant is on the right. [S] Appetizers €5-12; entrees €12-20. Pizza €10-15. Cash only. ⏰ Open Tu-F 1:30pm-2am, Sa-Su 12:30pm-2:30am.

HOME BURGER BAR

BURGERS $$

C. del Espíritu Santo, 12

☎91 522 97 28; www.homeburgerbar.com

Other locations: C. San Marcos, 25 and C. Silva, 25

Home Burger Bar is one of many restaurants catching on to the fancy burger craze. This retro diner has dimly lit brown leather booths, plays American doowop and soul, and serves American-style burgers with fries. Portions here are large, but the emphasis is on quality, and all the meat is organic. Burgers come either classic (with lettuce and tomato) or dressed up with add-ons like thickcut bacon, cheddar, avocado, and spinach. They also serve a number of grilled chicken and vegetable club sandwiches, including a hugely popular *hamburguesa caprese* (sun-dried tomatoes, parmesan, and arugula; €14).

✚ ⓂTribunal. Go west on C. de San Vincente Ferrer, make a left onto C. del Barco, and make a right onto C. del Espíritu Santo. Ⓢ Burgers €10-13. Sandwiches €8-15. ☒ Open M-Sa 1:30-4pm and 8:30pm-midnight, Su 1-4pm and 8:30-11pm.

CAFÉ MAHÓN

INTERNATIONAL $$

Pl. del 2 de Mayo, 4

☎91 448 90 02

With a combination of international favorites, Mediterranean-inspired salads, and traditional entrees, Café Mahón is a great budget option on Malasaña's most tranquil plaza. Brightly colored metal chairs and odd tables make for a kooky setup, and the menu of international comfort foods is equally eclectic. Try the nachos with cheese and guacamole (€7), the hummus appetizer (€6), or the moussaka (€8). A menu of specialty teas (€2-3.50) and coffees keeps people coming throughout the day to enjoy the beautiful terrace seating (next to the local jungle gym), and the bar inside gets active post-dinner with locals enjoying cocktails and *chupitos* (shots; €3-4).

✚ ⓂTribunal. Head west on C. de la Palma 2 blocks west to to C. de San Andrés, take a right and follow until you reach the plaza. Café Mahón is at the northeast corner. Ⓢ Salads €7. Appetizers €6-9; entrees €7-12. ☒ Open daily July-Aug 3pm-2am; Sept-June noon-2am. Terrace open daily July-Aug 3pm-1am; Sept-June noon-1am.

food

suck it up

With Chupa Chups, Spain's most popular lollipops! The brand was invented in 1958 by Spaniard Eric Bernat and since then the lollipops have been loved by Spaniards—and Spice Girls—the world over. These suckers (*chupar* means "to suck") boast quite the Surrealist logo, designed by artist Salvador Dalí in 1969. So next time you get a boo-boo in Madrid, buy yourself a Chupa Chups and suck it up.

BANZAI

JAPANESE $$

C. del Espíritu Santo, 16

☎91 521 70 81

Banzai is clearly a Malasaña take on Japanese food, with 1950s bebop playing in the background and rolls named after great American cities. Really? Albequerque? Whatever—the hip picturebook menu with black etchings of all the dishes reveals great variety beyond standard sushi (€9-11). Dishes like the ground *ibérico* burger (marinated in wasabi; €8.50) are unmistakably of Spanish influence, but they also have a selection of miso soups (€5), *gyoza* (dumplings; €7.50-9.50) and sautees (€6-13). While it's easy to rack up a big bill at Banzai, the generous *menú del día* (sushi, salads, and hot appetizers; €11) is a steal.

✚ ⓂTribunal. Go west on C. de San Vincente Ferrer, make a left onto C. del Barco, and make a right onto C. del Espíritu Santo. Ⓢ Meals €10-20. ☒ Open Tu-Su 1-4:30pm and 8:30pm-midnight.

EL RINCÓN
CAFE $$

C. del Espíritu Santo, 26 ☎91 522 19 86

El Rincón seems like a perfect caricature of bohemian Malasaña with its mismatched decor, baby-blue walls, and chalkboard menu. In truth, it's a thoughtfully put-together cafe, from the simple five-item menu to the tasteful interior. With basic wooden tables and small Asian prints on the walls, the decor is sparse compared to the kitschy messes throughout the neighborhood. The large awning shades the terrace seating, which is one of the prime people-watching spots in Malasaña, thanks to its location on the edge of the plaza.

✈ ⓜTribunal. Go west on C. de San Vincente Ferrer, make a left onto C. del Barco, and make a right onto C. del Espíritu Santo. Ⓢ Sandwiches €5. Entrees €10. Cocktails €5-7. Wine €2.50. Coffee €2-3. ⌚ Open daily 11am-2am.

LOLINA VINTAGE CAFE
CAFE $

C. del Espíritu Santo, 9 ☎66 720 11 69; www.lolinacafe.com

Filled with '50s memorabilia like album covers and movie stills, mismatched armchairs, and vintage lamps, Lolina looks like it was assembled from a shopping spree at a Brooklyn thrift store, but it fits perfectly in trendy Malasaña. The intimate space attracts people at all times of day, whether for morning tea or late-night cocktails. The food offerings are limited, with a selection of salads (€8), bratwurst sandwiches (€5), and open faced *tostas* like the Sobrasada (sausage, brie, and honey; €4). These dishes are simple, satisfying, and good for those who don't want to leave Malasaña with empty wallets.

✈ ⓜTribunal. Go west on C. de San Vincente Ferrer, make a left onto C. del Barco, then make a right onto C. del Espíritu Santo. Ⓢ Salads €8. Cocktails €6. Coffee and tea €2-5. ⌚ Open M-Tu 9:30am-1am, W-Th 9:30am-2am, F-Sa 9:30am-2:30am, Su 9:30-1am.

OLOKUN
CUBAN $$

C. de Fuencarral, 105 ☎91 445 69 16

Olokun might not have the quirky decor and garage-sale aesthetic of its Malasaña neighbors, but it has its own appeal with a menu of hearty Cuban dishes. While plenty of restaurants in the neighborhood try to fake different kinds of international cuisine, everything is actually Cuban at Olokun, right down to the dark mojito (made with black rum; €7). Traditional platters like Mi Vieja Havana (pork, fried plantains, black beans; €14) and *soroa* (chili, fried plantains, rice; €15) all come in large portions. With dark walls covered in the etched signatures of customers and a foosball table in the basement, it's pretty clear that Olokun doesn't take itself quite as seriously as many Malasaña restaurants, bars, and cafes. Sometimes that's a really good thing.

✈ ⓜTribunal. Walk north up C. de Fuencarral. The restaurant is on the left. Ⓢ Entrees €10-15. ⌚ Open daily noon-5pm and 9pm-2am.

HAPPY DAY
BAKERY $

C. del Espíritu Santo, 11 ☎66 720 11 69

Andy Warhol would be proud. With walls of Pepperidge Farm Cookies, Betty Crocker Cake Mix, Aunt Jemima Syrup, and Goober Peanut Butter, this is much more than an American bakery—it's a museum of America's best traditions. (Try not to confuse it with the neighboring store, Sad Day, which sells polluted water, handguns, and junk mortgages). While the cupcakes (€2), muffins (€2), and slices of cake (€3) all look great, what are more intriguing are the overpriced American imports, including bags of marshmallows (€4.50). This is definitely a novelty experience, but they do offer a good selection of American desserts and Spanish gelato.

✈ ⓜTribunal. Go west on C. de San Vincente Ferrer, then make a left onto C. del Barco and a right on C. del Espíritu Santo. Ⓢ Pastries €2-4. Ice cream €2-3. Packaged goods €2-6. ⌚ Open daily 9am-11:30pm.

CREPERIE LA RUE

CREPERIE $

C. del Espíritu Santo, 18

☎91 189 70 87

Creperie La Rue's small shop is filled with murals of Parisian street scenes, French music, and, most importantly, the aroma of crepes. Sweet and savory offerings here are fairly standard for a small creperie: goat cheese and grilled vegetables, *jamón* and Emmental, and sweet crepes like the *limon cointreau* (lemon, liqueur, and cinnamon) and chocolate and orange. Sweet crepes are large enough to share as a dessert, and savory crepes make a good late-night fix. All crepes are served on paper plates, as there are only a few seats in shop.

✦ ⓂTribunal. Go west on C. de San Vincente Ferrer, make a left onto C. del Barco, and make a right onto C. del Espíritu Santo. Ⓢ Crepes €4-8. ⌚ Open daily 11:30am-midnight.

LA VITA È BELLA

ITALIAN $

Pl. de San Ildefonso, 5

☎91 521 41 08; www.lavitaebella.com.es

La Vita è Bella looks and feels like a college-town pizza joint. With limited seating, most people order cheap and greasy Sicilian-style pizza by the slice (€2.50) or the calzones (ham, mozzarella, and mushroom; €3.50). This joint also bakes personal thin-crust pizzas made to order like the Malasaña (tomato, mozzarella, bacon, egg, and parmesan; €8.50) and the La Vita è Bella (tomato, buffalo mozzarella, and basil; €8.50). While the slices are fine for a quick fix, the personal pizzas are a bit more authentic and still a solid budget option.

✦ ⓂTribunal. Go west on C. de San Vincente Ferrer, make a left onto C. del Barco, and make a right onto C. del Espíritu Santo. Ⓢ Entrees €2.50-5. ⌚ Open daily noon-2am.

ARGÜELLES AND MONCLOA

▨ LA TABERNA DE LIRIA

SPANISH $$$

C. del Duque de Liria, 9

☎91 541 45 19; www.latabernadeliria.com

Most of the items on the menu of Taberna de Liria have been staples for years. Head Chef Miguel Lopez Castanier is an authority on traditional Mediterranean cuisine, and has led Taberna de Liria through a very successful 22 years in Madrid and published a cookbook. Dishes are simple and sophisticated, and the house specialty is the menu of foie gras appetizers (€11-14). While this is not a budget restaurant, it offers excellent food and a romantic setting for a special night in Madrid. Call ahead to make reservations, particularly on weekends.

✦ ⓂVentura Rodríguez. Head left at the fork in the road onto C. de San Bernardino. Ⓢ Appetizers €8-15; entrees €17-25. Tasting menu €50. ⌚ Open M-Sa 2-4pm and 9-11:45pm.

EL JARDÍN SECRETO

CAFE $

C. de Conde Duque, 2

☎91 541 80 23

Tucked away in a tiny street close to C. de la Princesa, El Jardín Secreto is, appropriately, Argüelles's best-kept secret. Walk into this eclectic cafe filled with beaded window coverings, wooden ceiling canopies, and crystal-ball table lamps to enjoy one of their dozens of coffees, hot chocolates, and snacks. For a real taste of what Secreto has to offer, try the *chocolate El Jardín*, served with chocolate Teddy Grahams and dark chocolate at the bottom of your cup (€6), or the George Clooney cocktail with *horchata*, crème de cacao, and Cointreau (€7.25).

✦ ⓂVentura Rodríguez. Take the left fork in the road onto C. San Bernardino. Ⓢ Desserts €4.20. Coffee and tea €3-6. Cocktails €7.25. ⌚ Open M-Th 6:30pm-1:30am, F-Sa 6:30pm-2:30am, Su 6:30pm-1:30am.

EL REY DE TALLARINES

ASIAN $$

C. de San Bernardino, 2

☎91 542 68 97; www.reydetallarines.com

El Rey de Tallarines is a great option for noodles and dumplings in a land of tortillas and *tostados;* it has built a reputation as one of the best options for budget Asian food in Madrid. The specialty here is La Mian, the ancient art of the hand-pulled noodle. Every day at 1 and 9pm the cooks prepare fresh noodles from scratch at the main bar of the restaurant. Dishes like La Mian with chicken and vegetables (€6) do not disappoint. The menu also has a number of meat dishes like the crunchy roast duck (€14), and the assorted dim sum (eight pieces; €9) is particularly popular for sharing with a small group.

🚏 [M]Ventura Rodríguez. Take the left fork in the road onto C. San Bernardino. $ Entrees €8-15. 🕐 Open daily 12:30-5pm and 7:30pm-midnight.

paella day

Known simply as "Thursday" to the rest of us, in Madrid it's often paella day at many restaurants with *menús del día.* Restaurants in Madrid frequently offer lunch specials in which €10 buys an appetizer, entree, dessert, and—if you're lucky—some *vino.* Legends on the origin of this tradition range from an official order by General Franco to Thursday being the cook's day off.

LAS CUEVAS DEL DUQUE SPANISH $$$

C. de la Princesa, 16 ☎91 559 50 37; www.cuevasdelduque.galeon.com

What distinguishes Las Cuevas del Duque is its selection of big-game dishes like the stewed deer with mixed vegetables (€14). They offer a great selection of steaks and grilled fish; the filet mignon (€20) is a particularly popular choice. The basement location makes the restaurant feel a bit like a cave, but eating meat underground has its own appeal.

🚏 [M]Ventura Rodríguez. Take the left fork in the road onto C. San Bernardino; the restaurant is on a tiny street to the right. $ Entrees €15-30. 🕐 Open daily 7-11pm.

KULTO AL PLATO SPANISH $$

C. de Serrano Jover, 1 ☎91 758 59 46; www.kultoalplato.com

Kulto al Plato serves contemporary tapas in an upscale setting. While its location between El Corte Inglés and the neighboring hotel isn't thrilling, it's one of the best dining options near [M]Argüelles. Tapas dishes have a modern take, such as the mushroom ravioli with foie gras sauce (€13). The fish and meat entrees are grilled fresh. The roasted duck with seasoned pear is a house specialty (€16).

🚏 [M]Argüelles. Walk south down C. de la Princesa to C. de Serrano Jover. $ Meals €12-20. 🕐 Open M-Th 8:30-11:30pm, F-Sa noon-1am, Su 8:30-11:30pm.

CASCARAS SPANISH $

C. de Ventura Rodríguez, 7 ☎91 542 83 36; www.restaurantecascaras.com

While the decorations at Cascaras may confuse you, the food is straightforward and convenient for a snack after an afternoon around Pl. de España. Cascaras has a number of good vegetarian options, such as the baked eggplant appetizer (€10). Though it won't change your life, Cascara is perfectly fine for drinks or a casual dinner.

🚏 [M]Ventura Rodríguez. Walk south down C. de la Princesa and make a right onto C. de Ventura Rodríguez. $ Meals €5-15. 🕐 Open M-F 7:30am-1am, Sa-Su 7:30am-2am.

SALAMANCA

LA ÚRSULA TAPAS $$

C. López de Hoyos, 17 ☎91 564 23 79; www.laursula.com

Across the street from the Museo Lazaro Galdiano, La Úrsula is an upscale tapas bar with terrace seating on a quiet side street off C. Serrano. The setting is fantastic and attracts a steady crowd of wealthy *madrileños.* La Úrsula offers particularly great lunch deals, including one of the city's best hamburger specials (€8)—a large burger with three tasty toppings of your choice (fried egg, Manchego, sauteed peppers, etc.) and served with fries, a drink, and coffee or dessert.

✦ ⓂGregorio Marañon. *Cross Paseo de la Castellana on C. de Maria de Molina. Follow C. de Maria de Molina for 3 blocks until you reach C. de Serrano.* ⓈMenú del día €7-11. Meals €14-20. Cash only. ⚄ Open daily 8am-midnight.

MUMBAI MASSALA
INDIAN $$

C. de Recoletos, 14   ☎91 435 71 94; www.mumbaimassala.com

Gourmet Mumbai Massala is not exactly a bargain. Rather than the heaping portions you find at many Indian places, taste and quality are the focus of Mumbai Massala, which garnishes dishes with lemon, fresh parsley, and chopped onion. It has the typical stewed meat and vegetable dishes like tikka masala and *saag gosht*, and the traditional tandoor turns out spectacular charcoal-grilled entrees like Peshwari *gosht tikka* (lamb marinated in yogurt and spices; €14). While the *menú del día* (€15) is a bit expensive for lunch, it's a good deal if you plan on ordering more than one dish.

✦ ⓂColón. *Walk 2 blocks south down Paseo de Recoletos. Turn left (east) onto C. de Recoletos and follow for 1 block.* ⓈAppetizers €8-12; entrees €10-16. Menú del día €15. Menú de la noche €25. Cash only. ⚄ Open daily 1:30-4:30pm and 9pm-midnight.

nightlife

If you came to Europe for the nightlife, you've chosen the right city. Not only does Madrid offer every type of nightlife experience known to man, but thanks to the youth culture of *el botellón*, it offers one experience known only to sleepless teenaged zombies. La Latina and Lavapiés are home to some internationally recognized clubs, a spectrum of bars, *tabernas*, and late-night cafes. Meanwhile, the streets of Las Huertas are packed with *discotecas* that would have the old literati of the neighborhood pondering the great moral dilemma of the dance floor makeout. In Chueca and Malasaña, the nightlife scene is chameleon-like, with clubs and bars opening and closing at a rapid pace. Other neighborhoods, like Argüelles and Moncloa, are more laid-back and offer some great live music venues. So pick your poison, get crazy, and stay hydrated.

EL CENTRO

PALACIO GAVIRIA
CLUB

C. del Arenal, 9   ☎91 526 60 69; www.palaciogaviria.com

Built in 1850 and inspired by the Italian Renaissance, Palacio Gaviria is a beautiful palace turned nightlife hotspot. Make your royal entrance by heading down the grand marble staircase onto the dance floor, which is powered by techno beats and electric dance moves. Be on the lookout for promoters of Palacio Gaviria in Puerta del Sol, as they will often have vouchers for free entry or drinks.

✦ *From Puerta del Sol, walk down C. del Arenal.* ⓈCover M-Th €10, F-Sa €15, Su €10. ⚄ Open daily 11pm-late.

CAFE DEL PRÍNCIPE
BAR

Pl. de Canalejas, 5   ☎91 531 81 83

A 2min. walk from Puerta del Sol, this bar and restaurant offers the "best mojitos in Madrid" as well as a variety of entrees and beverages. Come to take a tranquil break from the noisy Sol without venturing too far from all the clubs.

✦ *At the corner of C. de la Cruz and C. del Príncipe.* ⓈMixed drinks €5-15. ⚄ Open M-Th 9:30am-2am, F-Sa 9:30-2:30am, Su 9:30am-2am. Kitchen open daily 9:30am-4pm and 8pm-2am.

JOY ESLAVA CLUB

C. del Arenal, 11 ☎91 366 37 33; www.joy-eslava.com

An old standby, this converted theater has stayed strong amid Madrid's rapidly changing nightlife scene. Number one among study-abroad students and travelers, Joy Eslava plays an eclectic mix of music and features scantily clad models (of both genders) dancing on the theater stage. Balloons and confetti periodically fall New-Year's-Eve-style from the ceiling.

‡ From Puerta del Sol, walk down C. del Arenal. $ Cover M-W €12, Th €15, F-Su €18. ⏰ Open M-Th 11:30pm-5:30am, F-Sa 11:30pm-6am, Su 11:30pm-5:30am.

late night munchies

After a long night of bars and *discotecas*, join the natives for the Spanish munchie of hot chocolate (the thick, pudding-like kind) and *churros*, sticks of fried dough coated in sugar. To make it look like you do this all the time, daintily dip one end of the *churro* in the chocolate before devouring the double sweetness. At 6am, only a few things warrant your consciousness, and a plate of *churros con chocolate* is definitely one of them.

LA LATINA AND LAVAPIÉS

👍 **CASA LUCAS** BAR, TAPAS

C. Cava Baja, 30 ☎91 365 08 04; www.casalucas.es

Props to Casa Lucas for making life seem simple and delicious. On a long block of successful restaurants, bars, and *tabernas* that thrive on gimmicks, Casa Lucas stands out by sticking to the basics: freshly prepared tapas and a premium wine list. The interior of the restaurant is bright, comfortable, and packed with locals. The tapas here are a notch above what you will find elsewhere. Dishes like calamari (€14) are cooked fresh, which is something of a rarity in Madrid. The *secreto ibérico* is one the most popular dishes, garnished with fresh greens and mustard vinaigrette (€14). The chalkboard menu of wines changes nightly, and nearly everything is offered by the bottle or the glass.

‡ ⓂLa Latina. Walk west down Pl. de la Cebada. Make a right onto C. de Humilladero and continue right on C. Cava Baja. $ Wine by the glass €2-4, by the bottle €16-25. Raciones €7-15. ⏰ Open M-Th 8pm-midnight, F-Sa 8pm-1am, Su 8pm-midnight.

LA PEREJILA BAR, TAPAS

C. Cava Baja, 25 ☎91 364 28 55

La Perejila feels a bit like the world's most inviting shoebox. The interior is filled with beautiful antiques from the golden age of flamenco, vintage photographs, gold-leafed paintings, and vases of flowers that make this place come alive. Live parakeets greet you at the door. While grabbing a table is tricky, patrons are happy to stick around anyway to enjoy some of C. Cava Baja's freshest *taberna* food. The most popular dish is the namesake La Perejila (veal meatballs served in a clay plot; €9). *Tostados* like the *queso manchego* (€5) are made fresh to order and come piping hot. The wine selection changes daily.

‡ ⓂLa Latina. Walk west down Pl. de la Cebada. Make a right onto C. del Humilladero and continue right on C. Cava Baja. $ Cocktails €5-10. Tostados €5-7. Entrees €9-12. ⏰ Open daily 1-4pm and 8:15pm-12:30am.

ANGELIKA COCKTAIL BAR BAR

C. Cava Baja, 24 ☎91 364 55 31; www.angelika.es

Vintage DVD posters line the walls, projectors screen international films, and the walls are lined with DVDs for rent. Angelika has over 3000 titles available to borrow from their library, and they also serve a mean mojito. We can't decide if this is the most cinema-friendly bar in Madrid, or the world's bougiest Blockbuster. Sure, it's a gimmick, but sometimes gimmicks are fun. While they certainly try hard to impress with their cool alternative theme, the well-mixed cocktails and hip environment are what make Angelika a worthy stop on a pub crawl down C. Cava Baja.

*[M]La Latina. Walk west down Pl. de la Cebada. Make a right onto C. de Humilladero and continue right on C. Cava Baja. $ Cocktails €5-10. ⏰ Open daily 3pm-1am.*

EL BONANNO

BAR

Pl. del Humilladero, 4 ☎91 366 68 86; www.elbonanno.com

Located at the southern end of the bustling C. Cava Baja, El Bonanno makes a great first stop of the evening or last-minute drink before you hit the club. Plaza del Humilladero comes alive late at night, and El Bonanno is close to the action of El botellón. Because space is limited in the bar, people take their drinks to the sidewalk. El Bonanno serves the requisite tapas, but the cramped interior makes it better suited for a quick drink.

*[M]La Latina. Walk 1 block west down Pl. de la Cabeza. Take a left onto Pl. del Humilladero. $ Cocktails €3-10. ⏰ Open daily 12:30pm-2:30am.*

AROCA XI

BAR, SPANISH

Pl. de los Carros ☎91 366 54 75; www.grupoaroca.com

Aroca XI is painfully posh. And the drinks are objectively great. Fresh fruit makes everything better. The cocktail menu is more like a cocktail bible, with six fresh-fruit mojitos alone. Unlike the many cramped bars that line C. Cava Baja, Aroca XI has plenty of space and the only terrace seating in Pl. del Humilladero; it's the only place to sit among the gathering storm of El botellón in the plaza.

*[M]La Latina. Walk west down C. del Humilladero until you see Iglesia San Andrés on the right. As you face the church, Aroca XI is on the left. $ Cocktails €6-8. Entrees €5-15. ⏰ Open daily noon-midnight.*

SHOKO

DISCOTECA

C. de Toledo, 86 ☎91 354 16 91; www.shokomadrid.com

With massive "bamboo" shoots that reach to the ceiling, a huge stage featuring internationally acclaimed acts, and a swanky VIP section that *Let's Go* wishes we could live in, Shoko is an Asian-inspired *discoteca* that violates every last rule of feng shui. Shoko is the big leagues of nightlife in La Latina.

*[M]La Latina. Head south down C. de Toledo. $ Cover €10-15. ⏰ Open daily 11:30pm-late.*

LAS HUERTAS

KAPITAL

CLUB

C. de Atocha, 125 ☎91 420 29 06; www.grupo-kapital.com/kapital

This is the mothership of Madrid nightlife. Built in a gutted theater, Kapital is a seven-story temple of trashy fun. The first floor, which blasts house music, is where most of the action happens, but it keeps going, with separate dance floors for hip hop, reggae, and Spanish pop on the stories above. There is a little bit for everybody here: the third floor has a karaoke bar; the sixth floor screens movies; the seventh floor terrace has hookahs, pool tables, and killer views; and finally, on the yet-to-be-completed eighth floor, they hold live reenactments of the American Civil War (BYOB: bring your own beard). The good people of Kapital are rumored to be expanding upward at a rapid pace all the way to heaven itself. If you plan on making the pilgrimage, whatever you do, wear nice clothes—no sneakers or shorts. While Kapital doesn't get busy until around 2am, arriving early dressed in something nice will let you avoid the long wait.

*2min. walk up C. de Atocha from [M]Atocha. $ Cover €15; includes 1 drink. Drinks €10-15. ⏰ Open Th-Su 11:30pm-5:30am.*

SOL Y SOMBRA
CLUB
C. de Echegaray, 18 ☎91 542 81 93; www.solysombra.name

With thousands of LED lights on every last surface, Sol y Sombra might be the most high-tech thing ever to hit Madrid. Unlike the monster warehouse-style *discotecas* around the city, Sol y Sombra is surprisingly intimate. The walls shift in color to accent the bold patterns, while the music shifts between techno, jazz, funk, and hip hop. This is not a sloppy Eurotrash *discoteca;* it's a cool and innovative club. While you should expect a line out the door during prime weekend hours (midnight-3am), you won't be endlessly stranded: people tend to move in and out pretty quickly on their way to bigger *discotecas.*

☖ Ⓜ*Sol. From the Metro, walk toward the museum district on Carrera de San Jeronimo and make a right onto C. de Echegaray.* Ⓢ *Cover €10. Beer €5. Cocktails €7.* ☖ *Open Tu-Sa 10pm-3:30am.*

CAFE LA FIDULA
JAZZ CLUB
C. de las Huertas, 57 ☎91 429 29 47; www.myspace.com/lafidula

This jazz bar has been on the Las Huertas strip since long before the tourists started showing up. For more than 30 years, La Fidula has attracted some of the city's best jazz and blues musicians. While it's every bit as famous as Cafe Central and Cafe Populart (see **Arts and Culture: Music**), the setting is more intimate: built inside a 19th-century grocery store, the small stage encircled by tables puts you within spitting distance of the performers. While La Fidula isn't normally packed, this is precisely its appeal—a setting apart from the ebb and flow of Las Huertas where you can enjoy some of the city's most talented musicians. The performance schedule shifts nightly, with a combination of sets in the early evening from 8 to 10pm and jam sessions that carry on until the early hours of the morning.

☖ Ⓜ*Antón Martín. Take C. León north to C. Las Huertas.* 𝒊 *Visit the MySpace page for an up-to-date schedule, or call to inquire about late night performances.* Ⓢ *Coffee €3-4. Beer €2-4. Cocktails €5-8. Cash only.* ☖ *Open M-Th 7pm-3am, F-Sa 7pm-4am, Su 7pm-3am.*

EL IMPERFECTO
BAR
Pl. de Matute, 2 ☎91 366 72 11

El Imperfecto is unapologetically kitschy with walls plastered with images from American film, music, and art, and decorations straight from the garage sale (would it be a crime if two stools matched?). This shoebox interior is always fun and upbeat with people sipping cocktails (€6-10) and milkshakes (€4-6). Ice-blended drinks are reasonably priced for Madrid (€7) and much better than anything you'd find at a major club. Expect a crowd, and, on weekend nights, plenty of American study-abroaders, some friendly German accents, and some fanny packs. El Imperfecto is packed during weekend dinner hours (11pm-1am), so expect to stand at the bar.

☖ Ⓜ*Antón Martín. Walk uphill to Pl. de Matute and make a right toward C. de las Huertas. El Imperfecto is on the right.* Ⓢ *Drinks €4-10. Sangria €2 per glass; pitchers €11.* ☖ *Open daily 3pm-2:30am.*

EL SECRETO DE RITA
BAR
C. de Echegaray, 10

El Secreto de Rita is a small bar that holds its own on a long block of *discotecas.* Dim lighting, soul revival music, and cheap cocktails are the major draw. While many bars need a critical mass to keep the energy alive, El Secreto de Rita is still fun even when it isn't packed. If conversation, eye contact, and interpersonal connection are things you value in life, you'll find El Secreto a good alternative to the flashing lights, onerous covers, and mind-numbing sound systems of so many clubs in the area. Bonus points to anyone who can figure out what's up with Rita... why is she always holding back? What's her deal?

☖ *From Pl. de Santa Ana, walk north up C. de Echegaray toward Puerta del Sol. Rita's on your left.* Ⓢ *Drinks €3-10.* ☖ *Open M-W 6pm-2am, F-Sa 6pm-2:30am.*

VIVA MADRID
BAR

C. de Manuel Fernández y González, 7   ☎91 429 36 40

Viva Madrid has long been a favorite celebrity haunt; it's rumored that Ava Gardner and the bullfighter Manolete got handsy here in the '50s. While this might have once been an artists' hangout, today it's been adopted by young *madrileños* and internationals. The front terrace is in the thick of the pedestrian traffic of Las Huertas nightlife, but the interior feels dramatically removed, with a wood-carved ceiling and velvet drapes straight out of El Palacio Real.

✛ Ⓜ️Sol. *Walk toward the museum district on Carrera de San Jeronimo and turn right onto C. de Manuel Fernández y González.* Ⓢ *Beer €2.50-4. Cocktails €6-10.* ☼ *Open daily noon-2am.*

IREAL
BAR

C. de Echegaray, 16

Gaga gets old. When you tire of American dance music, iReal is a good place to educate yourself in the latest Spanish discopop. Expect flashing lasers, disco balls, and pulsing Spanish pop brought to you by lyricists that make Rebecca Black sound like T.S. Eliot. Jump on the dance floor and get lost in the fun, or sit on the sidelines in ironic detachment. Drinks run a bit pricey with €5 beers and mixed drinks from €6. iReal doesn't have a cover so at the very least it's a good stop on the way to bigger and badder clubs on Las Huertas.

✛ *From Pl. de Santa Ana walk up C. de Echegaray toward Puerta del Sol.* Ⓢ *Drinks €5-8.* ☼ *Open daily 11pm-3am.*

MIDNIGHT ROSE
BAR

Pl. de Santa Ana, 14   ☎91 701 60 20; www.midnightrose.es

Swanky, bougie, euro-yuppy—these are all words that apply to Pl. de Santa Ana's top-dollar cocktail lounge in the ME Madrid Reina Victoria Hotel. Cocktails are expensive (€12-14), lights are dim, and the young and wealthy European clientele is predictably beautiful. The leather-cushioned penthouse terrace is a total fantasyland, if you can make it up there. It's open to the proletariat but charges a steep cover (€15) on weekend nights when the crowds arrive. The line can be long, so your best bet is to go for an early drink (7-10pm) when there's neither cover nor line.

✛ *It's the most prominent building on Pl. de Santa Ana (lit purple at night).* Ⓢ *Cover for penthouse terrace €15 Th-Su. Cocktails €5-15. Cash only.* ☼ *Downstairs lounge open daily 1:30-4pm and 10pm-2:30am. Penthouse terrace open daily 7pm-2:30am.*

words to know

Go shopping with Spanish girls and you will immediately hear them giddily exclaiming with two words: *"guay"* and *"mono."* You really don't need any other Spanish language skills to enter the world of shopping. *"Guay"* means "cool," and can be used to describe anything or anyone you think is a G. *"Mono"* means cute, and is mostly used to describe adorable children and the latest in fashion. Another word that might stun you is the verb *"coger"* (pronounced co-hehr), which means "to get" or "to take." You might have learned in Spanish class that coger in other countries means to, well, fornicate, but the Spanish use this word frequently in its more innocent connotation.

DUBLINERS BAR

C. de Espoz y Mina, 7 ☎91 522 75 09

How many *pequeñas cervezas* does it take to get drunk? A lot. This is just one reason why so many come to Dubliners, a traditional Irish pub with traditional Irish pints (€3). It's dark and loud with a fun international vibe, and gets packed and crazy during major sports games. Ever seen grown men from around the world attempt their own drunken rendition of "We Are the Champions"? This is a great place to make friends, taunt enemies, and, when it's all said and done, come back the next morning for the Dubliner's Irish Breakfast (€5.70).

⇆ From Puerta del Sol, walk south down C. de Espoz y Mina. The bar is on the left. $ Beers €2-4. Cocktails €6-10. ⏰ Open M-Th 11am-3am, F-Sa 11am-3:30am, Su 11am-3am.

VINOTECA BARBECHERA BAR, TAPAS

C. del Príncipe, 27 ☎91 420 04 78; www.vinoteca-barbechera.com

Vinoteca Barbechera is a nationally successful chain that delivers premium Spanish and imported wines. Nearly everything on the menu is available by the glass. While Vinoteca Barbechera also offers a range of tapas and *pinchos* (€3-6), the appeal here is clearly the wine list. With over 300 domestic brands, this is a great place to test your palate or your bullshitting skills. The waitstaff can help you find a glass that suits your tastes, and the terrace seating on Pl. de Santa Ana can't be beat.

⇆ Pl. de Santa Ana. $ Wine €2-8. Cocktails €5-15. ⏰ Open M-Th noon-1am, F-Su noon-2am.

SWEET FUNK CLUB CLUB

C. del Doctor Cortezo, 1 ☎91 869 40 38; www.myspace.com/sweetfunkclub

Suspended cages, disco balls, and a daringly clad clientele are staples of this hot club. Sweet is a self-proclaimed funk club that plays American auto-tuned hip hop to a primarily *madrileño* crowd. By 4am on weekends, the dance floor here is usually packed, and women with very little clothing keep things steamy with suggestive dances on the small circular stages throughout the club.

⇆ [M]Antón Martín. From the Metro, walk uphill on C. de Atocha and make a left on C. del Doctor Cortezo. $ Cover €10-14; includes 1 drink. Beer €5. Cocktails €7. ⏰ Open F-Sa 11pm-sunrise.

GRAN VÍA

REINABRUJA CLUB

C. Jacometrezo, 6 ☎91 542 81 93; www.reinabruja.com

Reinabruja is not just a club, it's a futuristic fantasyland. Here, the internationally renowned industrial designer Tomas Alia has created a world of endless light and sound. Every surface—including the toilet seats—changes color using cutting-edge LED technology. Reinabruja is Madrid nightlife at its most creative and over-the-top. This subterranean world of phosphorescent lighting and stenciled pillars is hugely popular with tourists but hasn't lost its edge in the *madrileño* scene.

⇆ [M]Callao. $ Cover €12; includes 1 drink. Wine €7. Mixed drinks €9. ⏰ Open Th-Sa 11pm-6am.

EL TIGRE BAR

C. de las Infantas, 30 ☎91 532 00 72

The motto of El Tigre might as well be "dont f*@% with Spain." On a block with fusion restaurants, contemporary cuisine, and fancy cocktail lounges, El Tigre keeps everything Spanish with beer, mojitos, and sangria in towering glasses and taxidermied bulls on the wall. We can only imagine the interior decorator's philosophy was "put the head on the wall and serve everything else as tapas." Drinks are served with a plate of greasy fries, pork loin, and chorizo. This place is absolutely packed; it can be hard to make your way through the door. While the noise and crowds may be a turn-off for some, this is definitely a place where you can start your night off cheap, drunk, and greasy.

✤ ⓂGran Vía. Walk north up C. de Hortaleza, then make a right onto C. de las Infantas. Ⓢ Drinks €2-5. ⏰ Open daily 10:30am-1:30am.

EL PLAZA JAZZ CLUB
JAZZ CLUB
C. de Martín de los Heros, 3   ☎91 548 84 88; www.elplazacopas.com

The nightly program of live sets at El Plaza is one of the best in the city for jazz, particularly the Wednesday night Dixie Jam. The typically *madrileño* crowd comes here to drink, socialize, and lounge on comfortable couches, not just to listen to saxophone solos and pretend to understand every last note. El Plaza also screens films and hosts open mic nights and the occasional comedy performance.

✤ ⓂPlaza de España. Walk 1 block west to C. de Martín de los Heros. Ⓢ Most events are free; some ticketed shows €5. Drinks €3-6. Cash only. ⏰ Open daily 7:30pm-2:30am.

EL BERLIN
MUSIC VENUE
C. de Jacometrezo, 4   ☎91 521 57 52; www.nuevocafeberlinmadrid.webgarden.es

This is one of the best-known jazz clubs in all of Madrid. El Berlin attracts the city's most talented artists in jazz, blues, funk, and soul for its nightly sets and is most famous for its Tuesday Jam Sessions (10pm). The crowd is generally more middle-aged and the intimate venue isn't always packed, but El Berlin is a popular alternative to fussy and expensive clubs.

✤ Next to ⓂCallao. Ⓢ Drinks €3-7. ⏰ Opens daily at 9pm. Sets begin at 10pm.

DEL DIEGO COCKTAIL BAR
BAR
C. de la Reina, 12   ☎91 523 31 06

Del Diego is an upscale one-room cocktail lounge that is quiet and spacious and has served the same classic cocktails for 20 years. Drinks are expensive, but Del Diego is one of the nicest cocktail lounges in the area and a better place for conversation than many of the standing-room-only tapas bars.

✤ ⓂGran Vía. Walk north up C. de Hortaleza and make a right onto C. de la Reina. Ⓢ Cocktails €10. ⏰ Open daily 7pm-3am.

POUSSE
BAR
C. de las Infantas, 19   ☎91 521 63 01

With refurbished antique furniture and music from every decade, the ambience at Pousse is self-consciously eclectic. The cardboard and fingerpaint art on the walls was made by either avant-garde artists or kindergarteners. The drink menu is every bit as mixed as the decor, with everything from all-natural fresh fruit milkshakes (€6) to gourmet cocktails made with premium liqueurs (€9-13). Each cocktail has its own full-page entry in the lengthy drink menu and specials like Meet Johnny Black (Black Label whiskey, fresh OJ, sugar, and lemon; €12) are all made with fresh juices and top-dollar booze. Pousse attracts a loyal crowd of locals, but the tourists have caught on.

✤ ⓂGran Vía. Walk north up C. de Hortaleza and turn right onto C. de las Infantas. Ⓢ Drinks €6-13. ⏰ Open M-Sa 10pm-2am.

LOLA
BAR
C. de la Reina, 25   ☎91 522 34 83; www.lola-bar.com

Lola Bar is a cool but unpretentious cocktail bar. Groups of 20-something professional *madrileños* come here for their first drink of the night on a pub crawl through Gran Vía and Chueca. While this bar doesn't pack full, groups arrive as soon as work gets out around 7pm. Lola serves plenty of American favorites such as Coito a la Playa (Sex on the Beach), but they also keep things simple with Spanish wines by the glass (€2-4) and beer on tap (€3).

✤ ⓂGran Vía. Walk north up C. de Hortaleza and turn right onto C. de la Reina. Ⓢ Cocktails €9-10. ⏰ Open M-Th noon-2am, F-Sa noon-2:30am.

nightlife

MUSEO CHICOTE

C. Gran Vía, 12 ☎91 532 67 37; www.museo-chicote.com

A longtime favorite of artists and writers, this retro-chic cocktail bar maintains its original 1930s design. During the Spanish Civil War, the foreign press came here to wait out the various battles, and during the late Franco era it became a haven for prostitutes. Today Museo Chicote offers one of the best happy hours on C. Gran Vía (cocktails €5; 5-11pm), but things shift pretty quickly at midnight when the nightly DJ set starts. Well-known DJs play everything from '80s American pop to European house. Located directly on C. Gran Vía, this isn't the most adventurous place, but it's a Madrid institution with a steady crowd.

✠ ⓜGran Vía. Walk east. Museo Chicote is on the left. Ⓢ Cocktails €7-9. ☼ Open daily 8am-3am.

CHUECA

🔲 BOGUI JAZZ CLUB

JAZZ CLUB

C. del Barquillo, 29 ☎91 521 15 68; www.boguijazz.com

Bogui is one of Madrid's premier jazz venues and most happening weekend clubs. Nightly sets of live jazz (9 and 11pm) are a fantastic way to get plugged into the local music scene, and during weekend DJ sets (Th-Sa 1am), Bogui brings in some of Madrid's best-known jazz, funk, and soul DJs from Sala Barco. Bogui also caters to a Chueca crowd that likes to dance. The Wednesday midnight set (otherwise known as La Descarga or "The Dump") is when musicians from around the city convene for a late-night jam session after a long night of gigs.

✠ ⓜChueca. Take C. de Gravina 2 blocks west to C. del Barquillo. The club is on the left. Ⓢ DJ sets Th-Sa free; concerts €10. Beer €4. Cocktails €7. €1 surcharge for all beverages Th-Su. ☼ Open M-Sa 10pm-5:30am.

AREIA

BAR, TAPAS

C. de Hortaleza, 92 ☎91 310 03 07; www.areiachillout.com

Areia calls itself a "chillout zone," which must sound cool to native Spanish speakers. While to Americans this slogan seems to fit better in your teen rec center, this is one of the hippest spots in Chueca. The Moroccan-themed bar and lounge has a crimson-draped ceiling, low-lying tables, large cushion seats, and embroidered pillows where people snack on international tapas like pad thai (€6) and tandoori chicken (€6) as well as traditional Moroccan dishes like *tayin de cordero* (stewed lamb). Things stay pretty laid-back, even during the weekend DJ sets (11pm-late). Cocktails are set at standard prices (€6-8) and come served with fresh fruit. Music ranges from house to reggae.

✠ ⓜChueca. Make a right onto C. de Augusto Figueroa, then a right on C. de Hortaleza; Areia is on the right. Ⓢ Cocktails €6-9. ☼ Open daily 1pm-3am.

DAME UN MOTIVO

BAR

C. de Pelayo, 58 ☎91 319 74 98

Dame un Motivo is a one-room bar with an outlook on nightlife that's refreshing in Chueca: strip it down to its essentials (good music, cheap drinks, and sparse decor). The idea here is to do away with all of the excess of Chueca nightlife—cover charges, overpriced sugary drinks, flashing lights, and loud music—and offer an alternative environment for people to hang out and converse. That Dame un Motivo is busy on the weekends with a primarily local crowd is a testament to its success. During the week, people come to enjoy the film and book library.

✠ ⓜChueca. Take C. Gravina 1 block west to C. de Pelayo and follow north ½ a block. The bar is on the right. ⓘ Check out Dame un Motivo's Facebook page for event listings. Ⓢ Beers €1.30-2.50. Cocktails €5.50. ☼ Open W-Th 6pm-2am, F-Sa 4pm-2:30am, Su 4pm-2am.

LA SUECA

BAR

C. de Hortaleza, 67

☎91 319 04 87

The drag queen beauties behind the bar are a huge presence in this small cocktail lounge. They joyously shake martinis and mix fruit daquiris for a young and beautiful *madrileño* crowd. Like many bars on the block, La Sueca is small, but it has enough white leather lounge seating to accommodate larger groups. The crystal chandeliers are a nice touch, but nothing out of the ordinary for Madrid's most flamboyant *barrio*.

 # [M]Chueca. Make a right onto C. de Augusto Figueroa and a right onto C. de Hortaleza. $ Beer €3.50. Cocktails €8. ⏰ Open daily 8pm-3am.

STUDIO 54

DISCOTECA

C. de Barbieri, 7

☎61 512 68 07; www.studio54madrid.com

You're going to see a lot of six packs at Studio 54, and we're not talking beer. With pulsing Spanish pop and sculpted bartenders wearing nothing but bow ties, Studio 54 tends to attract a crowd of predominantly gay *madrileños* and American and European tourists. If you haven't spent a night dancing to ridiculous Spanish pop music yet, this is the place to do it, with crystal chandeliers and disco balls hanging above a violet dance floor, surrounded by mirrors and etched silhouettes of curvy women.

 # [M]Chueca. Walk south down C. de Barbieri toward C. Gran Vía. The discoteca is on the right. $ Cover €10 after 1am. Cocktails €8. ⏰ Open Th-Sa 11:30pm-3:30am.

EL51

BAR

C. de Hortaleza, 51

☎91 521 25 64

EL51 is a posh single-room cocktail lounge with white leather chairs, crystal chandeliers, and mirrors lit with violet bulbs. Just steps from the center of Chueca's nightlife, it tends to pack people in during prime hours (midnight-2am), but also attracts a steady crowd with a two-for-one happy hour that includes mojitos, caipirinhas, martinis, and cosmopolitans. Spanish pop plays in the background, but, unlike other bars, they keep the volume low enough that you can still hold a conversation (if you're still sober enough, that is).

 # [M]Chueca. Make a right on C. de Augusto Figueroa, then a right onto C. de Hortaleza. $ Cocktails €8-10. ⏰ Open daily 6pm-3am. Happy hour F-Sa 6-11pm, Su 6pm-3am.

LONG PLAY

DISCOTECA

Pl. de Vázquez de Mella, 2

☎91 532 20 66; www.discotecalongplay.net

Clubs in Chueca come and go, but Long Play has been around to see it all. Once a venue of the early 1970s *madrileño* counterculture, today Long Play attracts a crowd of gay *madrileños*, European tourists, and American study abroaders. Things tend to start late at Long Play with the crowds descending en masse around 3am. The downstairs DJ plays a variety of international pop, and things get pretty sweaty on the upstairs dance floor, which plays strictly European house.

 # [M]Gran Vía. Head north up C. de Hortaleza, make a right onto C. de las Infantas, and a left to Pl. de Vázquez de Mella. $ Cover €10 Th-F after 1:30am (includes 1 drink), all night Sa. Drinks €8. ⏰ Open daily midnight-7am.

'bares versus 'tecas

No, it's not Madrid's *West Side Story* rivalry. But it can be an epic struggle for the Madrid nightlife n00b to try to go to a famous *discoteca* at 11pm on your first night in the city. Instead, hop around *discobares:* rock, dance, and salsa music bars that are common in Madrid. Even better, take part in *el botellón* and pregame on the cheap. Then, grab your friends and head to a *discoteca.* Just don't go before midnight—*discotecas* usually don't get going until at least 1am.

MALASAÑA

LA VÍA LÁCTEA — BAR

C. de Velarde, 18 ☎91 446 75 81; www.lavialactea.net

La Vía Láctea is a Spanish temple dedicated to rock, grunge, and everything '70s counterculture. It was founded in the early years of Movida Madrileña, the youth-propelled revolution of art, music, fashion, and literature. Today it's more a relic of this past than a continuing force of change, with pop music memorabilia covering the walls from floor to ceiling and a fine perfume of stale beer lingering in the air. The sentimentality of La Vía Láctea is unashamed and seems to draw crowds of loyal *madrileños* and international tourists night after night. Music spans Elvis to Prince and the pool tables are popular.

⇞ [M]Tribunal. Walk north up C. de Fuencarral and make a left onto C. de Velarde. $ Cover €10 after 1am; includes 1 drink. Beer €3-5. Cocktails €5-7. ⏰ Open daily 7:30pm-3:30am.

CLUB NASTI — DISCOTECA

C. de San Vicente Ferrer, 33 ☎91 521 76 05; www.nasti.es

Come to Club Nasti on Saturday nights for a hipster heaven of synth pop, electro beats, and punk jams. For a lighter touch, try Friday nights, when house DJs spin indie rock like The Strokes and The Arctic Monkeys. Now in its 11th year, Nasti is a neighborhood institution that remains hugely popular among locals. The small dance floor gets packed as the night progresses, and you might end up shimmying out of your sweaty plaid shirt to dance in your nevernudes. Don't say we didn't warn you: there's no PBR.

⇞ [M]Tribunal. Walk south down C. de Fuencarral and make a right onto C. de San Vicente Ferrer. $ Cover €10 after 2am; includes 1 drink. Beer €4-5. Cocktails €8-9. ⏰ Open Th 2-5am, F 1-6am, Sa 2-6am.

BARCO — MUSIC, DISCOTECA

C. del Barco, 34 ☎91 521 24 47; www.barcobar.com

With a full program of nightly concerts, late-night DJ sessions, and weekly jam sessions, this small venue covers plenty of musical terrain. While many bars and clubs in the area try to attract international bands, BarCo has made its name as a stalwart venue for local acts, with most bands drawing heavily on funk, soul, rock, and jazz. While the concert schedule is continually changing, the nightly DJ sets are given to a handful of veteran European DJs who have been spinning in Madrid for years. For those more interested in live music, the Sunday night jam session brings in some of the city's best contemporary jazz musicians. The cover charge changes with the act, so check online for updates.

⇞ [M]Tribunal. Head south on C. de Fuencarral 3 blocks. Take a right onto C. Corredara Baja de San Pablo, walk 2 blocks, and take a left (south) onto C. del Barco. The bar is on the right. $ Cover €5-10. Beer €4. Cocktails €7. F-Sa €1 drink surcharge. Cash only. ⏰ Open M-Th 10pm-5:30am, F-Sa 10pm-6am, Su 10pm-5:30am.

CAFE-BOTILLERIA MANUELA

C. de San Vicente Ferrer, 29

CAFE, BAR

☎91 531 70 37

Dark wood shelves filled with liquor, a white marble bar, and gilded columns make CAFE-Botilleria feel like a five-star hotel lobby in miniature. The list of cocktails is standard for the late-night *madrileño* cafe, and so are the prices. Most people choose to imbibe rather than caffeinate, and many take advantage of the cafe's selection of board games. The small tables and red-cushioned booths are nearly always full. CAFE-Botilleria Manuela is one of the best venues to avoid the here-today-gone-tomorrow side of Malasaña nightlife.

✇ Ⓜ*Tribunal. Walk south down C. de Fuencarral and make a right onto C. de San Vicente Ferrer.* Ⓢ *Wine €2.50-3.50. Beer €1.50-3.50. Cocktails €8-12.* ⌚ *Open daily June-Aug 6pm-2am; Sept-May 4pm-2am.*

CAFE COMERCIAL

Glorieta de Bilbao, 7

BAR, TAPAS

☎91 521 56 55

Founded in 1887, Cafe Comercial remains a Malasaña institution. Once a meeting point for the anti-Franco Republican army during the Spanish Civil War, today it remains a place for informal gatherings of tourists and locals of all ages. The downstairs dining room, with dark wood pillars, marble tables, and mirrored walls, makes the setting a bit less intimate than smaller tapas bars or *cervecerías* in the area, but that doesn't keep it from being packed. More than anything, it is convenience that keeps people coming to CAFE Comercial: it's a great place to park for a few cheap drinks before pub crawling through the more contemporary bars. There is a surcharge for table service (€0.25-1 per item), but it's small enough that most people don't seem to care.

✇ Ⓜ*Bilbao.* Ⓢ *Beer €1-3. Wine €2-3. Cocktails €5-7. Internet access €1 per hr. Tapas €3-7.* ⌚ *Open M-W 7:30am-midnight, Th 7:30am-1am, F 7:30am-2am, Sa 8:30am-2am, Su 9am-midnight.*

ARGÜELLES AND MONCLOA

▨ TEMPO CLUB

C. del Duque de Osuna 8

LIVE MUSIC

☎91 547 75 18; www.tempoclub.net

International or local, jazz or soul, Tempo Club does not discriminate so long as a rhythm section and horns are involved. Tempo is one of the premier spots in Madrid to catch great live funk, soul, rock, and hip hop, with all of their acts accompanied by a full live band. Even when the DJ takes over for the late night set, the rhythm section often sticks around. While Tempo thrives on rich instrumentals, most of their acts involve talented vocalists. The venue is divided between a street-level cafe and cocktail area and the downstairs concert hall. This is a great alternative to large clubs and *discotecas* where lines are rampant and cover charges are onerous.

✇ Ⓜ*Ventura Rodríguez. From C. Princesa follow C. del Duque de Liria and turn left onto C. del Duque de Osuna.* 𝒊 *Live performances Th-Sa.* Ⓢ *No cover. Cocktails €5-8. Cash only.* ⌚ *Open daily 6pm-late.*

CAFE LA PALMA

C. de la Palma 62

LIVE MUSIC

☎91 522 50 31; www.cafelapalma.com

Cafe la Palma is in many ways a typical Malasaña rock club even though it is just outside of the *barrio*. Like many clubs in the area, La Palma strives for a lot—a cafe that people can enjoy during the day, a cocktail lounge at night, a concert venue in the late night, and a full club with a live DJ set in the early morning. The music acts La Palma attracts are every bit as eclectic as the venue itself. While they try to accomplish a lot within the three small rooms of the cafe, they don't spread themselves too thin. There is a drink minimum (€6) for some live sets, but this is a great alternative to forking over a fat cover charge.

✇ Ⓜ*Plaza de España. Follow C. de los Reyes northeast 2 blocks, take a left onto C. Amaniel, and walk 2 blocks to C. de la Palma.* Ⓢ *Drink minimum for some events €6; check website for more info. Cocktails €6. Cash only.* ⌚ *Open M-Th 4pm-3am, F-Su 4pm-4am.*

nightlife

ORANGE CAFE

BAR, CLUB

C. de Serrano Jover, 5 ☎91 542 28 17; www.soyorangecafe.com

Orange Cafe is a venue for local rock acts in the evening and a packed dance club later at night. If you are more interested in finding a local *madrileño* venue, this club might not be for you, as it normally fills with tourists and travelers looking for American pop music. Women can take advantage of free drinks and free entry Wednesday nights (11:30pm-12:30am). Check the website for a list of concerts and cover charges.

♯ ⑩Argüelles. Ⓢ Cover €10-15. ⌚ Open F-Sa 11:30pm-6am.

EL CHAPANDAZ

BAR

C. de Fernando, 77 ☎91 549 29 68; www.chapandaz.com

This place is ridiculous. Not only is it designed to look like a cave, but it is a fully functional, lactating cave with stalactites hanging from the ceiling that periodically drip milk into glass pitchers. The house drink, Leche de Pantera (panther's milk), is a combination of rum, cinnamon, and that special milk that drips from the ceiling. If you are suspicious (for perfectly good reasons), it also offers standard fare and a full menu of sweet, fruity, and colorful drinks. The bar is generally quiet until 11pm but fills up with a mostly international study-abroad crowd who stop in for the novelty before they head out clubbing.

♯ ⑩Moncloa. Walk down C. de la Princesa and turn left (east) onto C. de Fernando "El Católico."
i International night Tu. Ⓢ Drinks €10. ⌚ Open daily 10pm-3am.

madrid

12 angry bulls

For an adrenaline rush like no other, try running away from a dozen angry bulls in a huge crowd of similarly terrified people on a narrow street where you could be trampled or gored at any second. Although it may appear to be just a large group of men running like chickens with their heads cut off as huge beasts charge behind them, the running of the bulls *(encierro)* serves a practical purpose. The bulls must be transported from the corrals where they spend the night to the bullring where they will be killed the next evening. According to Spanish folklore, this tradition began in the early 14th century in northeastern Spain. Men would attempt to get the bulls to market faster by provoking them, and over time this evolved into a competition where young men would try to race in front of the bulls to the pens without being overtaken.

Nowadays, the event starts off with runners gathering in a blockaded street. All hell breaks looses when the police move out of the way and the runners dash pell-mell in front of the oncoming bulls and their pointy horns. The race covers a mere 903 yards in only four minutes, but a surprising amount of chaos can ensue in that time. During the race in San Fermín, 200-300 people are injured each year, mostly minor injuries as a result of falling down and tripping over other people. In late summer every year, the Madrid suburb San Sebastián de los Reyes sponsors a smaller version of the running. Adrenaline junkies in Madrid can have the same experience with a smaller chance of being trampled by other runners, although if you are sane (or slow), the sidelines are a safer option.

arts and culture

With some of the best art museums, public festivals, and performing arts groups in the world, Madrid's arts and culture scene is thriving. From street performers in Parque del Buen Retiro to Broadway musicals, you can find anything you're looking for in this metropolis.

CORRIDAS DE TOROS
Bullfights

Whether you view it as animal cruelty or national sport, the spectacle of *la corrida* (bullfighting) is a cherished Spanish tradition. Although it has its origins in earlier Roman and Moorish practices, today bullfighting is considered Spain's sport, and some of the top *toreros* (bullfighters) are national celebrities. The sport has been subject to continuing protest in recent years by animal rights activists, and it's common to see demonstrations outside of stadiums, but many tourists observe the tradition nonetheless.

If you choose to go, it is important to know a little bit about the rituals of the sport. The bullfight has three stages. First, the *picadores*, lancers on horseback, pierce the bull's neck muscles. Then, assistants thrust decorated darts called *banderillas* into the bull's back to injure and fatigue it. Finally, the matador kills his large opponent with a sword between the bull's shoulder blades, killing it instantly. Animal rights activists call the rituals savage and cruel, but aficionados call it an art that requires quick thinking, great kill, and an enormous amount of skill.

The best place to see bullfighting in Madrid is at the country's biggest arena, **Plaza de las Ventas,** where you can buy tickets in *sol* (sun) or *sombra* (shade) sections. Get your tickets at the arena the Friday or Saturday leading up to the bullfight. (C. de Alcalá 237 ☎91 356 22 00; www.las-ventas.com ✚ ⓂVentas. ☑ Ticket office open 10am-2pm and 5-8pm.) You'll pay more to sit in the shade, but either way you'll have a good view of the feverish crowds, who cheer on the matador and wave white handkerchiefs called *pañuelos* after a particularly good fight. Rent a seat cushion at the stadium or bring your own for the stone seats. Bullfights are held Sundays and holidays throughout most of the year. During the **Fiesta de San Isidro** in May, fights are held almost every day, and the top bullfighters come face to face with the fiercest bulls. People across Spain are bitterly divided about the future of the sport, so visitors should approach the topic with sensitivity.

MUSIC

By 10pm, bars across Madrid are filled with live music. For visitors unfamiliar with local bands and venues, this can seem daunting and difficult to navigate. The best way to tame this beast is to check out the citywide program *Madrid En Vivo* (www.madridenvivo.es; paper copy available at most bars). The calendar is organized by neighborhood, venue, and musical style. Most events require a cover of €5-10, which usually includes a drink.

EL CÍRCULO DE BELLAS ARTES DE MADRID
EL CENTRO

C. de Alcalá, 42 ☎91 360 54 00; www.circulobellasartes.com

El Círculo de Bellas Artes is a factory of culture. This Art Deco tower on the periphery of the city center provides first-rate facilities to support the visual and performing arts and is accessible to the general public. Located on the pulsing C. de Alcalá, this hub of innovation fiercely rejects the idea that art and culture are made in kitschy shops on winding, romantic European roads. The seven floors provide facilities for temporary visual arts exhibits, performing arts exhibitions, and film screenings. The building both celebrates Spain's rich cultural traditions and provides institutional support for emerging artists. Make sure to leave enough time to visit the rooftop terrace, which provides stunning panoramic views of the city. Also check out the streetside cafe—it's one of Madrid's finest. This is where serious art happens in Madrid, and it's not to be missed. ‡ ⓂSevilla. Walk 1 block northwest to the intersection of C. Gran Vía. ⓲ Check the website for ticket prices and event schedules. Free Wi-Fi. Ⓢ Rooftop access €2. ⓄOpen M 11am-2pm, Tu-Sa 11am-2pm and 5-8pm, Su 11am-2pm. Cafe open M-Th 9am-midnight, F-Sa 9am-3am.

madrid

CAFE CENTRAL
LAS HUERTAS
Pl. del Ángel, 10   ☎91 369 32 26; www.cafecentralmadrid.com
Since 1982, Cafe Central has been a premier venue for live jazz in Madrid. While plenty of cafes and bars of a similar breed have cropped up since then, Cafe Central continues to attract the best groups in the city. With its signature red facade along Pl. del Ángel and cool Art Deco interior, it stands out from the pack. Nightly concerts last from 10pm until midnight and feature primarily instrumental groups and the occasional vocalist. Check online for an up-to-date schedule. ‡ ⓂAntón Martín. From the Metro, take C. de León 1 block north to C. de las Huertas, and follow for 3 blocks until it ends at Pl. del Ángel. The cafe is on the left. Ⓢ Cover €8-12. ⓄOpen M-Th 1:30pm-2:30am, F-Sa 1:30pm-3:30am, Su 1:30pm-2:30am.

CLAMORES
MALASAÑA
C. de Albuquerque, 14   ☎91 445 79 38; www.salaclamores.com
Located just north of Malasaña, Clamores attracts a following of madrileños committed to the city's live music scene. While Clamores calls itself a jazz venue, it pushes the envelope with a program of pop, soul, funk, rock, and everything in between. Unlike some of the smaller jazz bars and cafes around Madrid, Clamores has a proper stage and better acoustics, which allows for more dynamic programming across musical genres. Clamores has been around for 25 years, but the program is fresh and new, so be sure to check the website for an up-to-date calendar. ‡ ⓂBilbao. Walk north up C. de Fuencarral and make a right on C. de Albuquerque. Ⓢ Cover €5-12. Beer €3-5. Cocktails €6-8. ⓄMost shows 9, 9:30, or 10:30pm. Check the schedule online.

CAFÉ JAZZ POPULART
LAS HUERTAS
C. de las Huertas, 22   ☎91 429 84 07; www.populart.es
Café Jazz Populart has a mixed program of American jazz, blues, and country for its nightly sets. While many jazz clubs in Madrid stick to traditional instrumental trios, quartets, and quintets, Café Populart features more vocalists and rowdier

juan belmonte

Known as the "greatest matador of all time," Juan Belmonte revolutionized the art of bullfighting. Although he was born in 1892 with slightly deformed legs and could not run and jump, that did not stop him from becoming a matador. Unlike the other matadors of his time who jumped and twirled around the bull like circus performers, Belmonte stood still and forced the bull to move around him. Within inches of the bull, he stood his ground, while other matadors stayed well out of range. In 1919, he set a record by fighting in 109 corridas (bullfights) in a single year, despite being frequently gored as a result of his daredevil style. He sustained one of his most serious injuries in a 1927 bullfight, when he was impaled through the chest and pinned against a wall by a bull. After lifelong injuries and trauma, his doctors informed him in 1962 that he could no longer smoke cigars, ride horses, drink wine, or have sex. In a last act of Tarantino-style defiance, he did all four and then took a pistol to his head, claiming "if I can't live like a man, I might as well die like one."

groups that get people out of their seats. The small room, styled like an old school *madrileño* cafe with musicians cramped onto a tiny stage, creates the setting for one of the city's most enjoyable live music venues.

✈ Ⓜ*Antón Martín. Walk north up C. de León and make a left onto C. de las Huertas. Ⓢ Cover €5; includes 1 drink. ☖ Open M-Th 6pm-2:30am, F-Sa 6pm-3:30am, Su 6pm-2:30am. Sets daily 10:15, 11:30pm.*

HONKY TONK

SALAMANCA

C. de Covarrubias, 24 ☏91 445 68 86; www.clubhonky.com

Honky Tonk is where nostalgic *madrileños* come to hear cover bands play The Rolling Stones, The Beatles, and other classic '60s rock and roll. While Honky Tonk is open throughout the week and has live sets most nights, given its location in the quieter neighborhood of Chamberí (near Salamanca), things can be pretty quiet early in the evening. Honky Tonk is best on weekends, especially when the cover bands take the stage at 12:30pm.

✈ Ⓜ*Alonso Martinez. Go north up C. de Santa Engracia. Make a left onto C. de Nicasio Gallego and a right onto C. de Covarrubias. Ⓢ Cover €10; includes 1 drink. Beer €3-5. Cocktails €9. ☖ Open M-Th 9:30pm-5am, F-Sa 9:30pm-5:30am. Concerts M-Sa 12:30am.*

FLAMENCO

Flamenco is a gypsy art dating back to 18th-century Andalucía that has become a 21st-century business in Madrid. Many flamenco clubs offer overpriced dinners combined with overdone music and dance spectaculars geared toward tourists. There are some clubs in Madrid that offer more traditional and soulful flamenco. You'll still pay a decent amount to see it, but it's a great way to learn about the art form that is often described as Europe's counterpart to the blues.

arts and culture

flamenco

Flamenco, an exotic dance involving flowing skirts, castanets, and quick steps, originated with gypsies in southern Spain. Spain first ridiculed the dance, like everything cool done by the gypsies, but gradually accepted and transformed it into a beloved—and lucrative—art. Those gypsies were onto something. In November 2010, UNESCO named flamenco a globally treasured art form. Although Madrid is not the birthplace of flamenco, it does have some great venues. Various restaurants have flamenco performance nights, and you may be able to find clubs offering flamenco lessons.

▨ CASA PATAS

LAS HUERTAS

C. de los Cañizares, 10 ☏91 369 04 96; www.casapatas.com

While Casa Patas certainly caters to tourists, it remains one of Madrid's best venues for traditional flamenco. Though it offers dinner, the real attraction is the flamenco stage in back, where some of Madrid's finest dancers perform for packed tourist audiences. Tickets aren't cheap, but they're worth every penny. Shows sell out night after night, particularly in the summer months. The restaurant and tapas bar up front serve the usual suspects: platters of *jamón y queso* (€19), fried squid (€13), and *albondigas de la abuela* (grandma's meatballs; €3). Who could turn down grandma's meatballs?

✈ Ⓜ*Antón Martín. From the Metro, walk up C. de Atocha and turn left onto C. del Olivar. Casa Patas is on the right. Ⓢ Tickets €32; includes 1 drink. Entrees €10-25. ☖ Open M-Th 1-4pm and 8pm-midnight, F-Sa 7:30pm-2am. Flamenco M-Th 8:30pm, F-Sa 9pm and midnight.*

CARDAMOMO
LAS HUERTAS

C. de Echegaray, 15 ☎91 369 07 57; www.cardamomo.es

Cardamomo offers traditional flamenco that has a raw improvisational quality to it. The focus is more on rhythm and movement and less on the kitschy costumes that are usually synonymous with flamenco. You can expect to hear syncopated guitars and soulful old men crooning flamenco verse, and to see swift choreography. The nightly sets are short but intense (50min.) and a good way of seeing flamenco without dedicating an entire evening to it.

*[M]Sol. Walk east toward Pl. de las Cortes and make a right onto C. de Echegaray. $ Tickets €25; includes 1 drink. Check with your hostel for discounts. ⏰ Shows daily 10:30pm.*

LAS TABLAS
GRAN VÍA

Pl. de España, 9 ☎91 542 05 20; www.lastablasmadrid.com

This newly renovated tapas bar just west of Pl. de España features a fine ensemble of soulful old guys and fit leading men and women. While the space is more comfortable than the smaller flamenco venues around the city, the intensity of the rhythm and movement doesn't hold up quite as well in the renovated space. Reservations are definitely recommended, as this is one of the more popular tourist venues for flamenco. Arrive early to get a seat up front—it will make a world of difference.

*[M]Plaza de España. Head to the far end of the plaza. $ Tickets €25; includes 1 drink. ⏰ Shows M-Th 10pm; F-Sa 8, 10pm; Su 10pm.*

THEATER

The obvious consideration for those interested in seeing live theater in Madrid is the language barrier. Madrid has a thriving theater scene, but much of it is inaccessible to those who don't speak Spanish. Madrid does host a number of international musicals like *Mamma Mia!* that are written in the universal language of glee. Many theaters also host concerts, dance productions, and flamenco spectacles that don't require any language skills.

👍 TEATRO COLISEUM
GRAN VÍA

C. Gran Vía, 78 ☎91 542 30 35

Since C. Gran Vía is often referred to as the Broadway of Madrid, it makes sense that the sprawling Teatro Coliseum, home (at time of research) to the smash hit *Chicago, El Musical*, is located there. One of the largest theaters in the city, Teatro Coliseum has hosted some of Broadway's biggest international hits, like *Beauty and the Beast* and *Mamma Mia!* Tickets can be purchased online at www.arteria.com or at the box office. Teatro Coliseum also hosts concerts featuring Spanish and international pop musicians.

*[M]Pl. de España. From the plaza walk east down C. Gran Vía. The theater is on the left. $ Tickets €10-40. ⏰ Box office open M-Th noon-8:30pm, F-Sa noon-10pm, Su noon-7pm. Check online for showtimes.*

TEATRO ESPAÑOL
LAS HUERTAS

C. del Principe, 25 ☎91 360 14 84

Funded by Madrid's municipal government, the Teatro Español features a range of classic Spanish plays and performances. This is Madrid's oldest stage; it dates back to a 16th-century open-air theater. Though the building has since been reconstructed many times, it has consistently played a critical role in the development of dramatic literature in Spain. The present building, which dates to the mid-1800s, has premiered works by Spain's most notable writers, including Benito Galdós and Antonio Vallejo, and played a critical role in the development of the literary culture of Las Huertas. Tickets can be purchased online at www.telentrada.com, by telephone, or at the box office.

*[M]Antón Martín. Walk uphill on C. de Atocha. Make a right at the 1st light and head north until*

you see Pl. de Santa Ana. The theater is on the east side of the plaza. $ Tickets €3-20; ½-price on W. ⏰ Box office open Tu-Su 11:30am-1:30pm and 5pm-curtain.

TEATRO HÄAGEN-DAZS CALDERÓN LAS HUERTAS

C. de Atocha, 18 ☎90 200 66 17; www.teatrohaagen-dazs.es

Named for its recent takeover by Häagen-Dazs, this theater has a seating capacity of 2000 and features musical, dance, and theaterical performances, with a focus on local Spanish musicals. Tickets can be purchased online at www.arteriaentradas.com, by telephone, or at the box office. Check online for up-to-date box office hours and showtimes.

 # [M]Tirso de Molina. From the Metro, walk north up C. del Doctor Cortezo. $ Tickets €25-60. ⏰ Shows begin most evenings at 8pm.

TEATRO BELLAS ARTES EL CENTRO

C. del Marqués de Casa Riera, 2 ☎91 532 44 37; www.teatrobellasartes.es

Founded in 1961 by Jose Tamayo, the former director of the Teatro Español, this avant-garde theater was originally created to expose audiences to America's great playwrights of the 1950s, such as Arthur Miller and Tennessee Williams. Today Teatro Bellas Artes has a more diverse program with a mix of original Spanish productions and adaptations and translations of famous international works.

 # [M]Banco de España. Walk west down C. de Alcalá and make a left onto C. del Marqués de Casa Riera. $ Tickets €16-25. ⏰ Box office open Tu-Su 11:30am-1:30pm and 5pm-curtain.

FÚTBOL

You might see churches every city you go to in Spain, but the official national religion is fútbol. Matches are a beloved spectacle everywhere in the country, but particularly in Madrid, which is home to **Real Madrid,** arguably the greatest soccer club the world has ever known. On game days, from the end of August through the end of May, locals line the streets and pack bars to watch the match. Celebrations after games are common in public plazas and squares, probably helped by the fact that most matches fall on Saturdays. For Real Madrid, the victory party always takes place in **Plaza Cibeles,** just outside of town hall. The other two major teams in Madrid are **Atlético** and **Getafe.**

fútbol fail

After 18 years of disappointing losses, Madrid's soccer team, Real Madrid, finally won back the Copa del Rey trophy in 2011. But within a few hours of defeating archrival Barcelona, Real Madrid lost the trophy again—under the wheels of a bus. In the raucous post-game celebration on the bus back to the city, Sergio Ramos dropped the 33-pound cup on the ground and the team bus ran it over. This generated plenty of smart-assery—"apparently the weight of the win was too much for the team to handle," etc. Needless to say, the cup was a bit squished, and team officials hastened to pick up the broken pieces and get the cup repaired. Sixty thousand fans gathered at Cibeles, the fountain where Real Madrid celebrates its victories, to catch a glimpse of the shiny trophy, but the shattered pieces were hidden from sight. Madrid went wild anyway—even a broken trophy couldn't put a dent in their celebrations.

Seeing a game live with 80,000 other fans can be an incredible experience, but often difficult logistically. Tickets are expensive and hard to come by. All teams sell a number of tickets through their stadium box offices and release a limited number online through their club website. If you are intent on going to a game, research ticket availability at least two weeks in advance. Tickets are also available from vendors outside the stadium, but these are often counterfeited or marked up well above face value. Tickets for Atlético and Getafe tend to be cheaper and more available than tickets for Real Madrid. And if you don't make it to the stadium, it's worth going to a local tapas bar to watch.

▧ ESTADIO SANTIAGO BERNABÉU   NORTH OF CITY CENTER

Av. de Concha Espina, 1   ☎91 464 22 34; www.santiagobernabeu.com, www.realmadrid.com

Site of the 2010 European Final Cup, Estadio Santiago Bernabéu is also home to Real Madrid, named the greatest club of the 20th century by FIFA. Come watch a match and feel the tumultuous energy of the crowd as it cheers on its beloved home team. Tours of the stadium are also available and take you to its most hallowed grounds: from the trophy room to the visitors' dressing room to the pitch itself. Tickets to European club soccer games are notoriously difficult to come by, and Real Madrid is no exception. Most tickets go to season ticket holders, and a limited number of tickets are released at the central stadium box office at Gate 40 located next to tower A. Advance tickets can also be purchased at www.servicaixa.com, and remaining tickets are released on the club website at 11am the Monday before each game.

✦ Ⓜ*Santiago Bernabéu. The stadium is across the street from the Metro.* Ⓢ *Tickets €30-300. Tours €16, under 14 €10.* 🕑 *Season runs from the beginning of Sept through the end of May. Check online for game schedules and tour times.*

get real

You're bound to come across a couple of Real Madrid fans in Madrid. Officially the most popular team in the world with over 228 million supporters, Real Madrid has enjoyed the love of *madrileños* and fans the world over, and the team has the track record to keep it. Real Madrid's biggest rival is Barcelona, against whom they face off twice a year. If you do manage to nab a ticket for a match (whether it's to watch soccer or just ogle attractive men running across a field) during the *fútbol* season, remember to cheer *"Hala Madrid!"*—or else feel the wrath of a stadium full of raucous *madrileños*.

ESTADIO VICENTE CALDERÓN   SOUTH OF CITY CENTER

Paseo de la Virgen del Puerto, 67   ☎91 364 22 34; www.clubatleticodemadrid.com

Estadio Vicente Calderón is home to the Atlético *fútbol* club (red and white stripes). With a storied past that includes European Cups and international recognition, this Madrid-based club participates in the esteemed Primera División of La Liga. While they've had some big wins in the past, they are the perennial underdogs in the city rivalry with Real Madrid. While this stadium may not be the city's biggest stage for soccer, it's a good place to take part in the *madrileño* tradition. Tickets can be purchased at www.servicaixa.com or on the club website.

✦ Ⓜ*Pirámides. From the Metro, head west 1 block to C. de Toledo and follow it 1 block south to Paseo de los Melancólicos. The stadium is on the left.* Ⓢ *Prices vary.* 🕑 *Check the website for schedule.*

COLISEUM ALFONSO PÉREZ   SOUTH OF CITY CENTER

Av. Teresa de Calcuta   ☎91 695 97 71; www.getafecf.com

Coliseum Alfonso Pérez is home to the Getafe *fútbol* club. The club was founded in 1946 and merged with another local club in 1983. This club offers spectators some great soccer, but it pales in comparison to local rivals. Tickets can be purchased in person at the stadium box office or online from www. entrada.com.

♯ Ⓜ*Villaverde Alto. Stop is 1hr. from Puerta del Sol on the number 3 Metro. From the Metro, walk 1 block east to Av. Real de Pinto. Take Av. Real de Pinto 4 blocks through the highway underpass and turn left on Av. Teresa de Calcuta. The stadium is on the left.* Ⓢ *Tickets €40-80.* 🕐 *Check the website for a schedule.*

FESTIVALS

THREE KINGS PROCESSION   EL CENTRO

The one day Spaniards don't party too hard is Christmas. So they instead celebrate the Epiphany, the day when the three kings arrived to Bethlehem to view baby Jesus. During the Three Kings Procession, three Santa-like men parade through the downtown with 30 carriages filled with 7000kg of sweets, making a pathway from from Parque del Buen Retiro to Pl. Mayor via Puerta del Sol. The kings and their helpers (not elves) shower sweets on the huge crowd in the streets, and local establishments host events for children.

♯ Ⓜ*Sol.* 🕐 *Jan 5.*

---

el gordo

What better way to get in the Christmas spirit than by gambling away your savings in a huge, country-wide lottery? Each year on December 22nd, tickets are drawn for the largest prize of any lottery in the world, El Gordo. Starting around mid-September, 85,000 different numbers are sold in a complicated system that involves buying a tenth of a ticket, or *decima*. Tickets are €20 apiece, culminating in a €3 billion prize pot. Of course, like any good European government, the Spanish administration takes 30% off the top, leaving a still ridiculously large pot of €2.142 billion. There are thousands of different prizes, but the coveted first prize is a whopping €3 million. Drawing the tickets is an elaborate ritual that begins on the morning of December 22nd. In the Lotería Nacional Hall of Madrid, one ball from a large cage is drawn bearing the winning number and another ball is drawn from a different cage representing the prize. Life in Spain comes to a halt while children from San Ildefonso school sing out the numbers as they are drawn. With 1787 prizes to award, the whole lottery process takes about three hours, but don't worry about the children—they sing in shifts. When the top prize is drawn, you can almost hear Spain's collective sigh of disappointment (minus the winner, of course, who is busy with a heart attack).

MADRID CARNIVAL   CITYWIDE
http://carnaval.esmadrid.com/

The week before Lent, Madrid celebrates with a citywide festival of theater, dance, and music, culminating in a grand parade on Saturday evening. The parade starts in Parque del Buen Retiro and travels to Pl. de Cibeles before ending at Pl. de Colón. There's also a tradition called "The Burial of the Sardine," in which participants decked out in black cloaks and hats walk through the streets with a coffin containing an effigy of a dead sardine. Don't understand? Neither do we, but it's cool. You can download a full program of events at the festival website.

🕐 *Mar 4-9. Grand Parade Sa 7pm.*

arts and culture

MADRID EN DANZA CITYWIDE

www.madrid.org/madridendanza

From mid-March to late April, Madrid plays host to a flurry of dance performances from around the world. From ballet to modern, there's something for everyone at this festival that celebrates movement, not Tony Danza.

i Consult the festival website for a performance schedule. $ Tickets €5-20. Most tickets sold online at www.entrada.com. ⏰ Mar-Apr.

DOS DE MAYO MALASAÑA

On May 2, 1808, the people of Madrid rose up against Joseph Bonaparte, Napoleon's brother, to fight for freedom from French rule. Among the mobs was Manuela Malasaña, a 17-year-old seamstress who died a brutal death defending Spain. Today she and the many other victims of the attacks are honored in Malasaña's biggest party. The center of the festivities is the Pl. del Dos de Mayo, a major site of the uprisings. The gathering of young people in the plaza is one of the most infamous festival events of the calendar year, and the party carries on well into the night in the area's bars, cafes, restaurants, and clubs.

✢ [M]Tribunal. From the Metro, take C. de la Palma 2 blocks west to C. de San Andrés. Turn right and head north 1 block.

FIESTAS DE SAN ISIDORE CITYWIDE

www.esmadrid.com/sanisidro

This week-long festival takes over the city's streets and plazas to celebrate Madrid's patron saint Isidore the Laborer. The primary stage is Pl. Mayor, where street performers, parades, and vendors selling *barquillos* (ice cream cones) take over. There are dance, theater, and music performances throughout the city, and fireworks along the banks of the Mazanares near San Isidore's home. The festivities culminate on May 15 with a large procession across the Mazanares and a mass at the Basilica of San Isidore. While the festival is filled with pomp and circumstance, many *madrileños* celebrate more informally with picnics in Parque del Buen Retiro and parties at bars, cafes, and clubs around the city. For bullfighting enthusiasts, this festival marks the beginning of a month of nightly bullfights at La Plaza de las Ventas, which features the world's best fighters and most vicious bulls. Tickets for these bullfights are difficult to get; check the stadium website www.las-ventas.com for schedules and availability.

✢ [M]Sol. i Consult the festival website for details on concerts and performances around the city. ⏰ May 8-15.

BOLLYMADRID LAVAPIÉS

www.bollymadrid.com

During the first week of June, Lavapiés features Bollywood dance performances, movies, and amazingly cheap Indian food. Get that henna facial tattoo you always wanted, grab a few samosas, and check out the mighty Sharukh Kahn in one of the open-air film screenings. Check online for an updated schedule of performances.

✢ [M]Lavapiés. $ Performances free. Food €1-5. ⏰ 1st week of June.

DÍA DE LA MÚSICA SOUTH OF CITY CENTER

Paseo de la Chopera, 14 ☎91 517 95 56; www.diadelamusica.com

What was once the city's largest slaughterhouse is now home to one of Madrid's biggest music festivals. Within a few years, Matadero Madrid, with help from the city government, has been converted from an industrial wasteland into a vast multipurpose community art center with art installations, exhibition halls, and bandshells. This music festival brings in big name international artists like Janelle Monae and Lykke Li. Día de la Música is one of Matadero Madrid's biggest annual events, with great music and the latest in contemporary art and design.

♯ ⓂLegazpi. *From the Metro station, walk 1 block northwest up Paseo de la Chopera. Matadero is on the left. i Tickets can be purchased online at www.entradas.com or in person. Ⓢ €15-24. ⓐ Mid-June. Concerts M-Tu 8pm-1am, Sa-Su 11am-1am.*

ORGULLO GAY
CHUECA
www.orgullogay.org

During Orgullo Gay, one of the biggest Pride parades in Europe, Madrid explodes with GLBT celebrations, parades, parties, and more. Chueca, Madrid's gay district, is packed, particularly on the last Saturday of the festival when the parade takes over the neighborhood.

♯ ⓂChueca. ⓐ *Last week of June.*

PHOTOESPAÑA
EL CENTRO
☎91 298 55 23; www.phe.es/festival

PhotoEspaña is a public photography exhibition that takes over the city center in early summer. From exhibits in the Reina Sofía to sidewalk installations, PhotoEspaña seeks to showcase the latest developments in still photography and video art. Each year the festival exhibits work of a common theme by dozens of artists from around the world. Plans of the exhibition are available at various public info points or online.

i Public info points at Real Jardín Botánico; Pl. de Murillo, 2; and Teatro Fernan Gomez Centro de Arte, Pl. de Colon, 4. Ⓢ Free. Exhibits in ticketed museums subject to normal admission fees. ⓐ June-July.

FIESTAS DE LA LATINA AND LAVAPIÉS
LA LATINA AND LAVAPIÉS

This triumvirate of festivals in La Latina and Lavapiés celebrates the neighborhoods' respective patron saints. These days are typically a hot sweaty mess of tradition, with *madrileños* dressed in unseasonably warm 19th-century clothing and drinking sangria to cool off. The first festival takes place around August 7th, and celebrates San Cayetano in and around Pl. de Cascorro. The second festival (Aug 10), celebrates San Lorenzo near Pl. de Lavapiés. The final festival day (Aug 15) features a parade in which the city firemen carry an image of the Virgin of Paloma between the two neighborhoods as locals sing her praises.

♯ ⓂLavapiés or ⓂLa Latina. ⓐ *2nd week of Aug.*

too many grapes

On New Year's Eve, thousands gather in Puerta del Sol in the center of Madrid to ring in the New Year. As the clock strikes 12, a strange thing happens—everyone starts eating grapes. For each of the 12 chimes of the clock, each person eats one grape, symbolizing one month of good luck. All the grapes must be finished by the last chime to ensure a year of good fortune, but many people can't eat the grapes fast enough and end up ringing in the New Year looking like chipmunks. This tradition dates back to 1909, when the grape growers of Alicante had a huge grape surplus. One smart fellow decided to invent a new tradition to convince his neighbors to help eat the extras. With everyone in Spain eating grapes on the New Year, the Alicante grape growers will likely be in business for a long time.

arts and culture

To ring in the new year, thousands of *madrileños* gather at the city's version of Times Square, Puerta del Sol, to watch the ball drop from the clock tower. Instead of counting down, the clock chimes 12 times to represent the 12 upcoming months of the year, ending with a fireworks display. According to tradition, you're supposed to eat a grape at every toll and drink at midnight for good fortune.

✚ Ⓜ*Sol.* ☏ *Dec 31.*

shopping

While areas like Puerta del Sol, Pl. Mayor, and Gran Vía are filled with name-brand chains, there are plenty of local boutiques, marketplaces, and flea markets that sell products unique to Madrid. **El Rastro** is undoubtedly the biggest shopping event in Madrid. This flea market, which takes place on Sundays in La Latina and Lavapiés, was once where thieves went to pawn goods. Today it offers antiques, clothes, books, and more. In the neighborhoods of Chueca and Malasaña you'll find the city's best upscale **boutiques,** many of which are prohibitively expensive for the budget traveler but always worth it for the window shopping. Salamanca is home to high-end European designers like Gucci and Prada. There, socks cost as much as a suit, and a suit costs more than a single family home.

Generally speaking, buying clothes in Europe isn't easy, it's often expensive, and it's not feasible for the budget traveler. If you're shopping more out of necessity than impulse, **department stores** like H&M and El Corte Inglés offer the cheapest clothes on the continent. There are also a number of good Spanish **chain stores** like Zara that offer quality products at reasonable prices.

the royal family

Like many in the EU, Spain's royal family retains little of the power wielded by their ancestors. Nonetheless, they are still important national symbols. One royal couple that gets particular media attention is heir apparent Prince Felipe and his lovely (OK, hot) wife Letizia. Formerly a journalist, the princess is known for her fashion flare and for dressing up her two gorgeous daughters in Spanish brands like Mango and Zara. Just when you thought she couldn't get more patriotic, she loyally wears Spanish brands as she conducts her royal activities.

RETAIL STORES

ABC SERRANO   SALAMANCA
C. de Serrano, 61   ☎91 577 50 31; www.abcserrano.com

Located in the refurbished publishing headquarters of the ABC Newspaper, this complex houses upscale chains that sell everything from jewelry and cosmetics to art, housewares, and electronics. The location in the middle of Salamanca's high-end shopping district tends to attract *madrileños* from nearby. There's a rooftop terrace as well as a few cafes and dining options for when you need a quick break. While ABC Serrano might not be the most glamorous way to spend an afternoon in Madrid, it does conveniently bring all your errand destinations together under one roof.

✚ Ⓜ*Rubén Dario. From the Metro, walk 2 blocks east down C. de Juan de Bravo (crossing C. de Castelló) and turn right onto C. de Serrano. The complex in on the left.* ☏ *Open M-Sa 10am-9pm, Su noon-8pm.*

madrid

EL CORTE INGLÉS EL CENTRO

C. de Preciados, 3 ☎91 379 80 00; www.elcorteingles.es

Many other locations around the city

Steps away from Puerta del Sol, El Corte Inglés is the most conveniently located department store in the city. Located in multiple buildings around the central plaza, El Corte Inglés sells clothing, cosmetics, shoes, books, and electronics. Some staff members speak English.

 # [M]Sol. C. de Preciados is to the left of the fountain as you face north. ⏰ Open M-Sa 10am-10pm.

ZARA SALAMANCA

C. de la Princesa, 45 ☎91 541 09 02; www.zara.es

Other major locations: C. de la Princesa, 58; C. de las Infantas, 5; C. de Preciados, 18.

There is at least one Zara in every major shopping district in Madrid. Much like Banana Republic in the United States, Zara offers professional attire as well as sportswear at reasonable prices. Men's and women's pants cost anywhere from €20 to 60, suits can be purchased for as little as €90, and women's dresses cost €20-60. Zara is a cheaper yet reliable alternative to boutique shopping.

 # [M]Argüelles. ⏰ Open M-Sa 10am-8:30pm.

CAMPER GRAN VÍA

C. Gran Vía, 54 ☎91 547 52 23; www.camper.es

Other major locations: C. de Serrano, 24; C. de Preciados, 23; C. de Fuencarral, 45.

Camper promises that "Imagination Walks," and delivers with high-fashion leather, suede, and canvas shoes. Over the last 35+ years, Camper has developed into a signature Spanish brand.

 # [M]Santo Domingo. [$] Leather shoes €100-200. Sneakers and sandals €50-100. ⏰ Open M-Sa 9:30am-8:30pm.

EL RASTRO

El Rastro is the biggest thing in Madrid on Sundays. This open-air flea market takes over La Latina beginning at **Plaza de Cascorro** off C. de Toledo and ending at the bottom of **Calle Ribera de Curtidores,** with rows of stalls set in the middle of the road between the city's infamous streetside pawnshops. Modern art, American comics, and Art Deco furniture can all be found throughout the market. Bargains are possible if you keep your eyes peeled and haggle. While El Rastro is hugely popular with tourists, it's still typical for local families to head to the market together and go out to brunch afterward in La Latina or Lavapiés. El Rastro starts at 9am sharp and ends at 3pm, with many of the better shops closing earlier. While El Rastro is generally safe, the large crowds tend to attract pickpockets, so use common sense and be aware of your surroundings.

BOUTIQUES

YUBE MADRID CHUECA

C. de Fernando VI, 23 ☎91 319 76 73; www.yubemadrid.com

European boutique shopping is unfortunately expensive and Yube is no exception. The carefully curated store in the middle of Chueca sells beautiful garments from international and local designers that are financial eons beyond reach for budget travelers. Menswear from designers like Paul Smith and women's blouses and dresses from French designer ba&sh are the very pinnacle of European style. While justifying the purchase might be difficult, this is a great place to check out the latest European trends.

 # [M]Alonso Martínez. From the Metro, take Pl. de Santa Bárbara south 2 blocks to C. de Mejía Lequerica. Follow C. de Mejía Lequerica 2 blocks southeast until it becomes C. de Fernando VI. ℹ Check the website for info on seasonal sales. [$] Men's shirts €100-200. Women's dresses €100-300. ⏰ Open M-Sa 9am-6pm.

POÈTE
C. de Castelló, 32   ☎91 577 60 62; www.tiendapoete.com

Poète is one of Spain's finest boutique chains specializing in women's apparel. Originally started in Madrid, Poète has now expanded to 14 locations across the country. Poète models itself on the traditional French boutique, offering simple-patterned dresses and blouses. Poète also has more reasonable prices than other *madrileño* boutiques.

✝ Ⓜ*Velázquez. Head east on C. de Goya 1 block and make a left onto C. de Castelló. Ⓢ Dresses and blouses €80-120. Shoes €100. Accessories €10-20.*

MINI
ARGÜELLES
C. del Limón, 24   ☎91 548 08 35; www.gruposportivo.com

Mini offers a collection of high-end menswear primarily from American upscale brands like Band of Outsiders, Universal Works, and Levi's Vintage, in addition to British brands like Fred Perry and Oliver Spencer. Mini's small boutique shop on C. del Limón is complemented by two sibling shops owned by Group Sportivo: **Duke,** which specializes in high-end shoes, and **Sportivo,** which focuses on American vintage. You can expect fairly standard European boutique prices at all three stores, with jeans and long-sleeved cotton shirts starting at €100.

✝ Ⓜ*Ventura Rodríguez. From the Metro, head southeast on C. del Duque de Liria 2 blocks (just past El Jardin Secreto) and take a left onto C. del Limón. i Sportivo located at C. del Conde Duque, 20. Duke located at C. del Conde Duque, 18. Ⓢ Shirts €50-150. Pants €50-150. Shoes €100-200. ☉ Open daily 10am-9pm.*

MADRID IN LOVE
CITYWIDE
☎63 989 15 18; www.madridinloveindustrial.com

Modeled on a concept that has taken Paris by storm, Madrid in Love is bringing the novelty of the "pop-up store" to Spain. Rather than owning a set retail space, Madrid in Love showcases a gallery of vintage decorative objects in various industrial spaces around the city. The company's owners travel through Europe carefully collecting, and every three to four months announce a two-week sale that attracts the city's most style-conscious. Though you may not have the chance to see this pop-up store in action, it's worth checking the website to see if there's an event while you're in town.

i *Location changes; consult the website for latest events. Exhibitions and sales last 2 weeks and take place every 3-4 months.*

OHMYGOD
SALAMANCA
C. de Serrano, 70   ☎34 914 354 412; www.ohmygod.com.es

Come to OhmyGOd boutique in upscale Salamanca for funky, chunky, one-of-a-kind jewelry. While you may not be able to take your eyes off these fancy baubles, keep in mind that they're about three times as much as a backpacker's daily budget.

✝ Ⓜ*Serrano. Walk 4 blocks north up C. de Serrano. Ⓢ Items start at €100. ☉ Open M-Sa 10am-8:30pm.*

BOOKS

Finding English books in Madrid can be very difficult. If you're looking for an English title, the best bet is to head to mega-chain stores like **El Corte Inglés** or **Casa del Libro** that sell whatever is on the bestseller list in addition to a small library of classic literature. If you're just browsing, Madrid has plenty of small bookstores that sell secondhand paperbacks and art books. You'll find many of these types of stores in Malasaña on **Calle de la Palma** and in Las Huertas on **Calle de las Huertas.** **Cuesta de Mayona** marketplace along the southern end of Parque del Buen Retiro has interesting offerings every Sunday, though be prepared to dig around to find something in English.

CASA DEL LIBRO

C. Gran Vía, 29
☎90 202 64 02; www.casadellibro.com

Other locations C. de Fuencarral, 119 and C. de Alcalá, 96

This is the city's best bet for English titles. This Spanish equivalent of Barnes and Noble has three locations in Madrid, and many more across the country, each offering as substantial a foreign literature section as you will find. The location on C. Gran Vía has an entire floor of books in English and French where you can find everything from *Harry Potter* to Proust. They carry most bestsellers in English, and prices are reasonable, with paperbacks starting around €12.

✠ ⓜGran Vía. Walk west down C. Gran Vía. ⓢ Paperbacks €8-15. Hardcovers €20-30. ⓩ Open M-Sa 9:30am-9:30pm, Su 11am-9pm.

ARREBATO LIBROS

C. de la Palma, 21
☎91 282 11 11; www.arrebatolibros.com

Arrebato Libros is a typical Malasaña bookshop featuring esoteric books of poetry, philosophy, art, and graphic novels. This two-room shop has plenty of titles in Spanish and a modest English selection, but they are best known for their collections of rare books salvaged from fairs around the city. Secondhand paperbacks run exceptionally cheap (€3-6), and rare secondhand books and art books tend to be more expensive (€20). The shop is also involved in the local literary community, hosting weekly readings and lectures. Check the website for a schedule of upcoming events.

✠ ⓜTribunal. From the Metro, head west down C. de la Palma. ⓩ Open M-Sa 10:30am-2pm and 5-8:30pm.

BERKANA LIBRERÍA GAY Y LESBIANA

C. de Hortaleza, 64
☎91 522 55 99; www.libreriaberkana.com

This Chueca bookstore features a large selection of books related to GLBT issues, from novels by famous gay writers like Truman Capote, Allen Ginsberg, and Tennessee Williams to comics like *El Kamasutra Gay*. It also has a wide collection of books about adolescence, education, religion, and philosophy. Prices here tend to be a bit higher than at most bookstores. Berkana keeps a table of flyers and pamphlets about the latest GLBT happenings in and around the *barrio*.

✠ ⓜChueca. From the Metro, turn around, make a right on C. de Augusto Figueroa, and make another right onto C. de Hortaleza. ⓢ Paperbacks €10-25. DVDs €10-15. ⓩ Open M-F 10am-9pm, Sa 11:30am-9pm, Su noon-2pm and 5-9pm.

ALTAÏR

C. de Gaztambide, 31
☎91 543 53 00; www.altair.es

Altaïr specializes in all books related to travel. They offer an extensive collection of English-language city and country guides as well as handy books of maps, photography, and travel writing. Altaïr's location in Argüelles won't be accessible by foot for most visitors to Madrid, but if you are need of anything travel-related, this is your best bet, as most bookstores in Madrid have very limited travel sections and mostly carry Spanish titles.

✠ ⓜArgüelles. Walk north up C. de Hilarión Eslava, then make a right onto C. de Meléndez Valdés and a left onto C. de Gaztambide. ⓩ Open M-F 10am-2pm and 4:30-8:30pm, Sa 10:30am-2:30pm.

CUESTA DE MOYANO

If you're looking for Spanish books, head to Cuesta de Moyano, the book marketplace on the southern edge of Parque del Buen Retiro. Around 30 stalls set up shop every Sunday to sell secondhand finds and antique books. Come and browse the stalls to find some Spanish first editions before heading to an afternoon picnic in the park.

✠ ⓜAtocha. Cross Paseo del Prado and walk uphill. The market is on the edge of the park on the right. ⓩ Open Su 10:30am-sunset.

essentials

PRACTICALITIES

- **TOURIST OFFICES:** The **Madrid Tourism Centre** in Pl. Mayor (☎91 588 16 36; www.esmadrid.com) is a good place to start. You'll find city and transit maps as well as suggestions for activities, food, and accommodations. English is spoken at most tourist offices. There are additional tourist offices and stands throughout the city; look for large orange stands with exclamation marks: **Calle del Duque de Medinaceli 2** (☎91 429 49 51 ☒ Open M-Sa 9:30am-8:30pm, Su and holidays 9:30am-2pm.), **Estación de Atocha** (☎91 528 46 30 ☒ Open M-Sa 9:30am-8:30pm, Su and holidays 9:30am-2pm.), and **Madrid-Barajas Airport Terminal 1** (☎91 305 86 56).

- **TOURS:** Themed tours leave regularly from the Madrid Tourism Centre. For dates, times, and more info, visit **www.esmadrid.com.** Many youth hostels host tapas tours, pub crawls, and walking tours for reasonable prices. Check out **www.toursnonstop. com** (⑤ €10 tapas and pub tours). **LeTango Tours** (☎91 369 47 52; www.letango. com) is run by a Spanish-American husband-wife team, with tours that take you to local bars, give fun city facts, and explain Spanish traditions. Run by historian and writer Stephen Drake-Jones, the **Wellington Society** (☎60 914 32 03; www.wellsoc. org) offers themed tours of Madrid and daytrips to Toledo and Segovia.

- **POST OFFICES:** Buy **stamps** (*sellos*) from post offices or tobacco stands. Madrid's **central post office** is at Pl. de Cibeles. (☎91 523 06 94; 90 219 71 97 ☒ Open M-F 8:30am-9:30pm.) Mailboxes are usually yellow with one slot for "Madrid" and another for everywhere else.

- **POSTAL CODE:** 28008.

EMERGENCY

- **EMERGENCY NUMBERS:** In case of a **medical emergency**, dial ☎061 or ☎112. For non-emergency medical concerns, go to **Unidad Medica Angloamericana,** which has English-speaking personnel on duty by appointment. (C. del Conde de Aranda, 1, 1st fl. ☎91 435 18 23 ☒ Open M-F 9am-8pm, Sa 10am-1pm.)

- **POLICE: Servicio de Atención al Turista Extranjero (SATE)** are police who deal exclusively with tourists and help with contacting embassies, reporting crimes, and canceling credit cards. (C. Legantos, 19 ☎91 548 85 27; 90 210 21 12 ☒ Open daily 9am-midnight.)

GETTING THERE

by plane

All flights come in through the **Aeropuerto Internacional de Barajas** (☎90 240 47 04; www. aena.es). The **Barajas** Metro stop connects the airport to the rest of Madrid (⑤ €2). To take the Metro into the city center, take #8 toward Nuevo Ministerios, transfer to the #10 toward Puerta del Sur, get off at ⓂTribunal (3 stops), transfer to the #1 toward Valdecarros, and get off at ⓂSol. The journey should take 45-60min. By bus, the **Bus-Aeropuerto 200** leaves from the national terminal T2 and runs to the city center through ⓂAvenida de América. (☎90 250 78 50 ☒ Every 15min. 5:20am-11:30pm.) **Taxis** (⑤ €35. ☒ 30min.) are readily available outside of the airport. For more info on ground transport, visit **www.metromadrid.es.**

by train

Trains (☎90 224 02 02; www.renfe.es) from northern Europe and France arrive on the north side of the city at Chamartín. Trains to and from the south of Spain and Portugal use Atocha. Buy tickets at the station or online. There is a **RENFE** information office at the main terminal. (☎90 224 02 02 🕗 Open daily 7am-7pm.) **AVE** trains offer high-speed service throughout Spain, including Barcelona, Salamanca, Segovia, Sevilla, and Toledo. (Estación Chamartín, C. de Agustin de Foxá ☎91 300 69 69; 91 506 63 29.) Be sure to keep your ticket, or you won't be able to pass the turnstiles. Call RENFE for both international destinations and domestic travel. (☎90 224 34 02 for international destinations; ☎90 224 02 02 for domestic.) Ticket windows are open daily 6:30am-9pm; when they're closed, you can buy tickets at vending machines.

by bus

If you prefer four wheels, many private bus companies run through Madrid, and most pass through **Estación Sur de Autobuses.** (C. de Méndez Álvaro ☎91 468 42 00; www.estacionautobusesmadrid.com 🕗 Info booth open daily 6:30am-1am.) National destinations include Algeciras, Alicante, Oviedo, and Toledo. Inquire at the station, online, or by phone for specific information on routes and schedules.

the tortoise and the train

Do you have some time to kill at Atocha? Wander over to the tropical garden in the center of the station and see if you can spot a few turtles sunbathing near the pond. The turtles have been added to the park over time by local residents. Abandoned by their owners or donated out of good will, the turtles have become a fixture at the station.

GETTING AROUND

by metro

The Madrid Metro system is by far the easiest, cheapest way to get almost anywhere you need to go in the city. It is clean, safe, and recently renovated. Service begins Monday through Saturday at 6am—Sunday at 7am—and ends daily around 1:30am. Try to avoid rush hours (8-10am, 1-2pm, and 4-6pm). You can buy a one-way ticket (€1), or, if you're making multiple trips, you can save by purchasing a combined **10-in-one metrobus ticket** (€9.30). Trains run frequently, and green timers above most platforms show approaching train times. Be sure to grab a free Metro map (available at any ticket booth or tourist office). **Abonos mensuales,** or monthly passes, grant unlimited travel within the city proper for €47.60, while **abonos turísticos** (tourist passes) come in various denominations (1, 2, 3, 4, or 7 days) and cost €6-25 at the Metro stations or online. For Metro information, visit **www.metromadrid.es** or call ☎90 244 44 03.

by bus

Buses cover areas that are inaccessible by the Metro and are a great way to see the city. The pamphlet "Visiting the Downtown on Public Transport" lists routes and stops. ($ Free at any tourist office or downloadable at www.madrid.org.) Tickets for the bus and Metro are interchangeable. The Búho (night bus; literally "owl"), or night bus, travels from Pl. de Cibeles and other marked routes along the outskirts of the city. (🕗 M-Th every 30min. midnight-3am, every hr. 3-6am; F-Sa every 20min. midnight-6am; Su every 30 min. midnight-3am.) These buses, marked on the essential Red de Autobuses Nocturnos (available at any tourist office), run along 26 lines covering regular daytime routes. For info, call **Empresa Municipal de Transportes** (☎90 250 78 50; www.emtmadrid.es). Estación

Sur (C. de Méndez Álvaro ☎91 468 42 00) covers mainly southern and southeastern destinations outside Madrid such as Granada, Málaga, Sevilla, and Valencia. Visit **www. avanzabus.com** for timetables and routes.

LOCAL LAWS AND POLICE

Travelers are not likely to break major laws unintentionally while visiting Spain. You can contact your embassy if arrested, although they often cannot do much to assist you beyond finding legal counsel. You should feel comfortable approaching the police, although few officers speak English. There are three types of police in Spain. The **policía nacional** wear blue or black uniforms and white shirts; they guard government buildings, protect dignitaries, and deal with crime investigation (including theft). The **policía local** wear blue uniforms, deal more with local issues, and report to the mayor or town hall in each municipality. The **guardia civil** wear olive-green uniforms and are responsible for issues more relevant to travelers: customs, crowd control, and national security.

drugs and alcohol

Recreational drugs are illegal in Spain, and police take these laws seriously. The legal **drinking age** is 18. Spain has the highest road mortality rate and one of the highest rates of drunk driving deaths in Europe. Recently, Spanish officials have started setting up checkpoints on roads to test drivers' blood alcohol levels (BAC). Do not drive while intoxicated, and be cautious on the road.

PHRASEBOOK

ENGLISH	SPANISH	PRONUNCIATION
Hello!/Hi!	¡Hola!	Oh-lah!
Goodbye!	¡Adiós!	Aw-dee-ose!
Yes.	Sí.	See.
No.	No.	samesies
Please.	Por favor.	pohr fa-VOHR.
Sorry!/Excuse me!	¡Perdón!	pehrd-OWN!
Good morning.	Buenos días.	BWEH-nos DEE-as.
Good evening.	Buenas noches.	BWEH-nas DEE-as.
How are you?	Cómo estás?	CO-mo ays-TAS?
I'm fine, thanks, and you?	Bién, gracias, ¿y tú?	Bee-AYN, GRA-thi-as, ee too?
What time is it?	¿Qué hora es?	Kay ora es?
It's 5 o'clock.	Son las cinco.	Sown las SEEN-ko.
Wait!	¡Espera!	Ace-PEHR-a!
EMERGENCY		
Go away!	¡Vete!	VAY-tay!
Help!	¡Socorro!	So-CO-ro!
Call the police!	¡Llama a la policía!	YA-ma ah la po-lee-SEE-a!
Get a doctor!	¡Llama al médico!	YA-ma ahl MAY-dee-co!
FOOD AND DRINK		
Waiter/waitress	camarero/a	Cama-RAY-roh/rah
I'd like...	Me gustaría...	May goost-er-EE-a...
Is there meat in this dish?	¿Tiene carne este plato?	Tee-YEN-ay CAR-nay ES-tay plah-to?
salad	ensalada	en-sa-LAHD-a
wine (sherry)	vino (jerez)	VEE-no (hay-rayth)
shots	chupitos	choo-PEE-tos
Spanish cured ham	jamon serrano	ha-MONE serr-AH-no
Can I buy you a drink?	¿Te compro una copa?	Tay COM-pro OO-na CO-pa?
Is the bread free?	¿Está gratis el pan?	Es-TAH GRA-tees el pan?
How much does it cost?	¿Cuánto cuesta?	KWAHN-to KWEH-stah?

madrid

FOR KICKS		
I believe that David Bowie is my soulmate.	Creo que David Bowie es mi alma gemela.	CRAY-o kay David Bowie es mi AL-ma HEH-meh-la.
Do you have anything a little sexier?	¿Tienes algo un poco mas sexy?	Tee-YEN-ays AL-go un PO-co mas SEH-xy?
These grapes taste funny.	Estas uvas tienen un sabor raro.	AYS-tas OO-bas tee-YEN-en OO-na sah-BOOR RAH-ro.
Will you marry me?	¿Te casarás conmigo?	TAY cah-sah-RAHS con-MEE-go?
I would like eight kilograms of french fries, please.	Póngame ocho kilos de patatas fritas, por favor.	POHN-gah-may OH-cho KEE-lohs day pah-TAH-tahs FREE-tahs, por fah-VOOR.

madrid 101

HISTORY

ain't no there there (big bang–939 CE)

It's hard to imagine while exploring today's Madrid, but there was a time when the land on which the capital sits was an empty plain, sparsely inhabited by livestock, Neanderthals, Romans, and dinosaurs, though not necessarily in that order. The eighth century saw the invasion of Moorish armies from North Africa, who conquered nearly all of the Iberian Peninsula. The **Moors** brought the region an era of enlightenment and relative religious tolerance, which the Christian armies to the north found wholly unacceptable. At the time, Madrid was but a small village in the shadow of a ninth-century fortress erected by **Muhammad I** of Córdoba. The city of Madrid takes its name from the locale's Arabic name, **Majerit**.

munchies against drunk driving

Tapas refers to any of the hot or cold appetizers that that are a staple of Spanish cuisine. They were first conceived in the 13th century to feed stagecoach drivers when they stopped off at taverns en route. Because of drunk driving accidents, the government passed a law forcing drivers to eat a snack, usually a piece of bread with *jamón*, as they drank. They would rest these snacks on top of the glass, earning them the name tapas, which means "tops" or "lids." Today, tapas have become far more elaborate, but cured meats like chorizo and *jamón serrano* remain among the most popular. To wash down your tapas, order a *caña* (0.3L) or a *caña grande* (0.5L) of beer.

this land is your land, this land is my land (939–1469)

As the first millennium drew to a close, the various Christian kingdoms of the Iberian north began the nearly 800-year-long campaign to push their Moorish neighbors back across the Strait of Gibraltar. This gradual wave of **Reconquista** (Reconquest) arrived at Majerit's doorstep in 939, when Don Ramiro II of León razed the town. The fortress and humble town sat near the frontier between the warring groups and was attacked several times until **Alfonso VI** of León and Castile finally took the city in 1085 on his way to the Moors' stronghold at **Toledo.**

Madrid obtained its charter in 1200 and became a favorite retreat of Castilian royals, who used it as a hunting ground. But the town remained more rustic-backwater-with-big-castle than metropolis. That all changed when a sudden need for a cosmopolitan capital with an even bigger castle arose.

age of empires (1469–1561)

Until the marriage of **Isabella of Castile** and **Ferdinand of Aragón** in 1469, the Iberian Peninsula was a collection of many kingdoms, united only by their shared enthusiasm for crusades. Isabella and Ferdinand's marriage brought the two most powerful kingdoms under the same crown, laying the foundations for a dominant state that controlled much of the peninsula and nearly all of its center. By 1500 the Moors were gone, the New World was being conquered and its riches plundered for the crown, and the Inquisition was going strong, uniting the peninsula in religion as well as political dominion. All those Spanish royals needed was a capital to call their own. In 1524, **Charles V** came to Madrid to recover from a fever (the cure, oddly enough, was more cowbell), and in 1561 his son, **Philip II,** declared Madrid his capital and moved his court there from Toledo. The rationale was that the new capital was not associated with any one former kingdom but could instead serve as a neutral center of a new, unified nation.

capital gains (1561–1650)

Except for four wild years when **Philip III** moved the capital to Valladolid, Madrid remained the seat of Spanish power and flourished. The old Moorish fortress was replaced with the **Palácio Real,** luxurious churches and convents were put up all over the city, and literature and the arts thrived. Wealth poured into the city from the farthest reaches of the vast and still-expanding empire, but the prosperity was short-lived.

it's a mad, mad, mad madrid (1650–1759)

Financial mismanagement and massive foreign debts caused much of the silver and gold of Nuevo España to pass straight through Spain and into the coffers of other European powers and creditors. This age of decadence saw poverty across the nation, and Madrid went through a period of starvation, destitution, and lawlessness. The shift from Austrian to Bourbon rulership in 1700 began the revitalization of the state and the city, and this comeback culminated in the rule of Charles III.

one borbón, one scotch, one beer (1760–1808)

Though he was king of one of the largest empires the world has ever known, **Charles III** focused most of his energy on the city of Madrid. The "best mayor of Madrid" was an enlightened ruler with liberal policies, to whom Madrid owes dozens of schools, colleges, parks, promenades, public buildings, and museums, including the **Museo del Prado.** One of his most celebrated actions was urging the citizens of Madrid to stop throwing their waste out their windows; passersby remain grateful to this day.

war, war, and more war (1808-1939)

The salad days of the Bourbons ended with the **Peninsular Wars,** the violent French invasion of Spain in 1808. **Napoleon's** ruthless troops took Madrid in May 1808, and the city's citizens revolted, which didn't end so well for them (cf. Goya's *Dos de Mayo, 1808* and *Tres de Mayo, 1808,* both in the Prado). Spain regained its independence from France in 1814 and restored its monarchy, but three wars over royal succession in the 19th century tore the nation apart, and the 1898 Spanish-American War left Spain at an all-time low. Spain stayed neutral during WWI, but another war of its own was not far off.

At the start of the 1930s, leftists saw huge gains, but—surprise, surprise—the anarcho-syndicalists did not govern very effectively. In 1934, a conservative government was established, and revolts broke out in Oviedo, Gijón, and Barcelona. These outbreaks were quelled by the army, led by **General Francisco Franco.** In 1936, a coalition of Republicans narrowly won parliamentary elections, and Franco led an insurgency in a **Civil War** that lasted three years. Madrid stayed loyal to the Republic until it fell to Franco's forces in March 1939.

generalísimo francisco franco... (1939–75)

As under previous absolutist rulers of Spain, Madrid was Generalísimo Franco's seat of power. Before the 20th century, Madrid had served mainly as a bureaucratic hub, but Franco's regime brought about much **internal migration** and the capital grew in population and socio-economic diversity. Intense **industrialization** characterized Madrid under Franco's often brutal rule. Today the Franco era continues to divide Spaniards who lived through it and their descendants; it should probably be avoided as a topic of conversation.

...is still dead (1975–today)

After Franco's death in 1975, Spain transitioned to a democratic government, and the modernizing city of Madrid benefited from the ensuing economic prosperity. Today, Madrid is a cultural and tourist center of Europe, a gleaming city of parks, fountains, and some of the best professional *fútbol* the world has ever seen.

CUSTOMS AND ETIQUETTE

greetings and addresses

When meeting for the first time, two men usually shake hands, two women usually exchange a kiss on each cheek, and a man and woman will, well, you know. (Just kidding—depending on circumstances and age range, either the handshake or double-kiss is appropriate, though a handshake is safer.) Acquaintances will generally greet each other with a double-kiss, hug, or "man-hug." It is polite to address men as *señor* and women as *señora* (if married) or *señorita* (if unmarried). *Usted* ("you") is only used in very formal situations or when speaking to someone from an older generation; the informal *tú* ("you") is much more common. If you find the *tú-usted* duality a source of confusion, don't worry: many young Spaniards do too.

madrid 101

schedule

The Spanish schedule tends to confuse visitors, so here's a quick run-down. The workday usually starts around 9am—so far, so good. Around 1 or 2pm, most Spaniards will go home for lunch and a **siesta,** and stores and businesses usually close from around 2-5pm. Everything (except banks) reopens around 8pm. Dinner usually starts between 9pm and midnight, with trendy *madrileños* dining on the later side.

touchy subjects

There are a few topics of discussion that can be rather delicate in Spain. The **Franco** era remains the elephant in the nation, and it's unwise to discuss it unless you know what you're talking about and know your audience agrees. **Bullfighting** is another divisive issue: some view it as a longstanding tradition that is a rich part of Spain's cultural heritage, while others see it as barbaric bloodsport. Finally, be careful when discussing certain regions' **separatist movements.** If you read the **History** section, you know that the unified nation of Spain is a relatively recent construct; regional identities are still very strong. The Basque Country (País Vasco) has been trying for decades to gain independence from Spain, with the militant group ETA using terrorist tactics to try to reach this goal. The region of Catalonia (Catalunya), which includes Barcelona, also has a strong independence movement.

that's bull

Bullfights have a long history in Spain. One of the oldest representations of bullfighting, or tauromachy, is a prehistoric cave painting called *"El toro de hachos,"* in the Altamira caves in northern Spain. When the Moors conquered Andalucía in 711 CE, they brought an elaborate bullfighting ritual in which trained horsemen confronted and killed bulls on certain feast days. As the ritual became more widespread, the assistants, who remained on foot and used their capes to draw the bulls into the proper position for the horsemen, became a crowd favorite. The modern *corrida* took shape in the early 18th century, when Francisco Romero enhanced the showmanship aspects by adding the sword *(estoque)* and the *muleta,* the small cape used at the end of the fight. Today, many say that the sport is dying out, but if you're curious, bullfights still take place on Sunday evenings in the summer at Madrid's two arenas, **Vista Alegre** and **Las Ventas.**

ART AND ARCHITECTURE

the big three

The traditional view of premodern Spanish art focuses almost exclusively on El Greco, Velázquez, and Goya, and with good reason. Yes, **Zurbarán** did some striking still lifes, **Murillo** could paint a rosy-cheeked Virgin like nobody's business, and **Ribera's** use of light might have grabbed even Caravaggio's attention, but the works of the three masters are a level above. **El Greco** (born Domenikos Theotokopoulous; 1541-1614) was born in Crete, trained in Venice, opened up shop in Rome, and spent the rest of his life in **Toledo.** His vivid colors, heavy shadows, and expressively elongated figures are often seen as precursors to Cubism and Expressionism. El Greco never achieved the favor of the royals, but **Diego Velázquez** (1599-1660) was beloved at court in Madrid. Many of his paintings are of members of the court, from the King and Queen to the dwarves and jesters. His most famous work, on display in the **Prado,** is *Las Meninas*, an enigmatic group portrait of the princess and her ladies-in-waiting, with the King and Queen reflected in the mirror and the artist himself at the easel on the left. Velázquez is also celebrated for his marvelous ability to capture various textures and surfaces, such as the ceramics in *The Water Carrier of Seville*. **Francisco de Goya** (1746-1828) also spent much of his career painting royals and courtiers in Madrid, but exhibited an impressive range of subjects and styles. Many of his works are quite playful and humorous, while others, such as his Black Paintings, are downright nightmarish.

the new guys

The 20th century saw a new crop of celebrated Spanish artists; few hailed from the capital, and nearly all spent a good part of their careers abroad, but many of their works now permanently reside in Madrid. The most famous is **Pablo Picasso** (1881-1973), illustrious pioneer of **Cubism** and **womanizing**. His manifesto *Guernica*, an enormous, emotional protest against the bombing of civilians during the Spanish Civil War, can now be seen in the **Reina Sofía** after a long stay at MoMA in New York City. Other modern Spanish artists include the Catalan **Joan Miró** (1893-1983), whose works are beautifully child-like; Madrid native and skillful cubist painter **Juan Gris** (1887-1927); and darkly zany Surrealist **Salvador Dalí** (1904-89), perhaps best known for his unique moustache and pet anteater.

five famous *madrileños*

Convince locals you're serious about their city by brushing up on these five famous figures with ties to Madrid:

- **MIGUEL DE CERVANTES (1547-1616).** Renowned author of Spain's Golden Age, Cervantes is best known for burdening Spanish lit students forever with the first modern novel—*Don Quixote de la Mancha*.

- **SALVADOR DALÍ (1904-89).** An eccentric Surrealist artist, Dalí is known for his melting clocks in the painting *The Persistence of Memory*.

- **ERNEST HEMINGWAY (1899-1961).** Hemingway, literary giant and tortured writer, set several of his works in Spain, including *The Sun Also Rises* and *For Whom the Bell Tolls*.

- **PENÉLOPE CRUZ (1974-).** Originally a dancer and Spanish soap opera star, Cruz is now a big-time actress and Hollywood superstar in movies as diverse as *Volver* and *Pirates of the Caribbean: On Stranger Tides*.

- **JULIO IGLESIAS (1943-):** internationally renowned singer-songwriter, Iglesias has sold over 300 million records worldwide, and his son, Enrique, is as well-known in the younger generation the world over for such gems as "Tonight I'm [Ahem] Loving You."

madrid 101

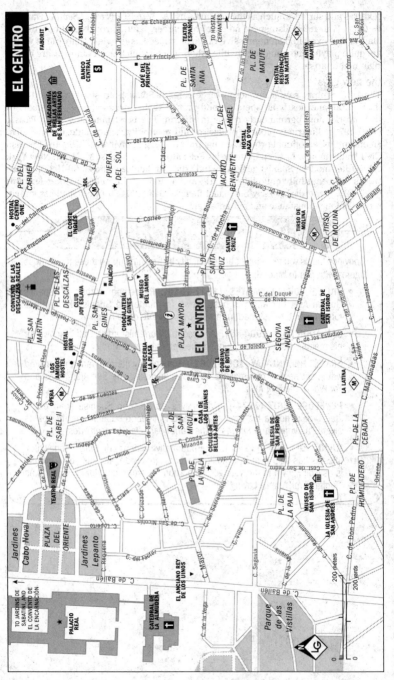

madrid

EL CENTRO

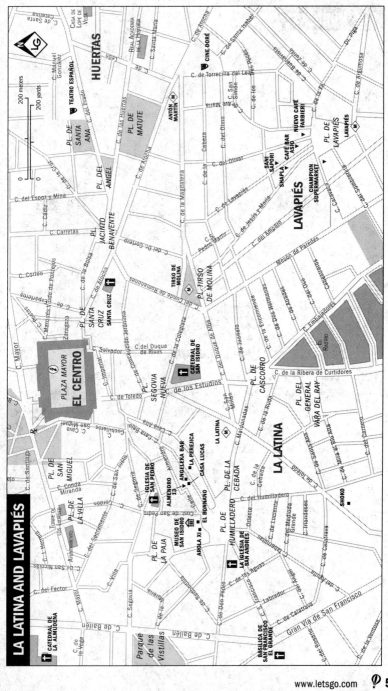

la latina and lavapiés map

LAS HUERTAS

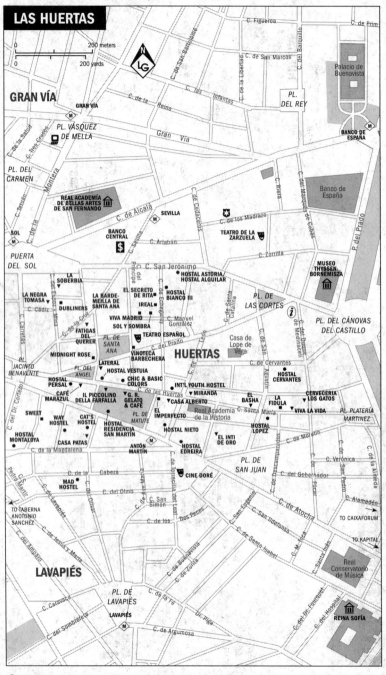

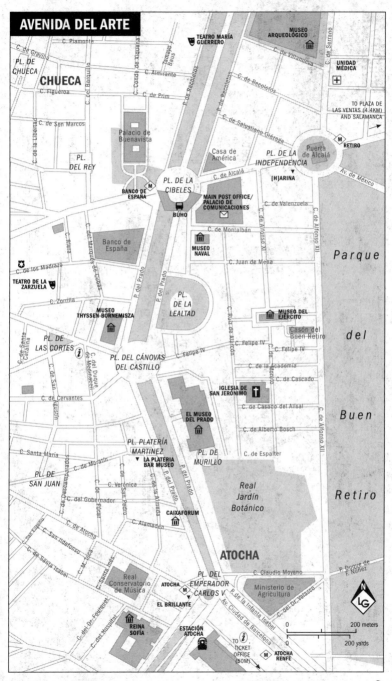

AVENIDA DEL ARTE

C. Piamonte
C. de Gravina
PL. DE CHUECA
CHUECA
C. Figueroa
C. de San Marcos
C. del Barquillo
C. de Almirante
TEATRO MARÍA GUERRERO
C. de Recoletos
MUSEO ARQUEOLÓGICO
C. de Villanueva
C. de Serrano
UNIDAD MEDICA
TO PLAZA DE LAS VENTAS (4.4KM) AND SALAMANCA
C. de Prim
P. de Recoletos
P. de la Recoletos
C. de Salustiano Olózaga
PL. DEL REY
Palacio de Buenavista
Casa de América
PL. DE LA INDEPENDENCIA
Puerta de Alcalá
RETIRO
Av. de México
BANCO DE ESPAÑA
C. de Alcalá
[H]ARINA
Banco de España
C. de los Madrazo
MAIN POST OFFICE/ PALACIO DE COMUNICACIONES
BÚHO
C. de Valenzuela
C. de Montalbán
C. de Alfonso XI
C. de Alfonso XII
Parque
C. del Marqués de Cubas
MUSEO NAVAL
C. Juan de Mena
TEATRO DE LA ZARZUELA
C. Zorrilla
P. del Prado
P. del Prado
PL. DE LA LEALTAD
del
MUSEO THYSSEN-BORNEMISZA
C. Ruiz de Alarcón
MUSEO DEL EJÉRCITO
Casón del Buen Retiro
PL. DE LAS CORTES
C. del Duque de Medinaceli
PL. DEL CÁNOVAS DEL CASTILLO
C. Felipe IV
C. Felipe IV
C. Felipe IV
C. de Santa Catalina
C. de San Agustín
C. de la academia
C. de Cascado
Buen
PL. DEL CÁNOVAS DEL CASTILLO
C. de Cervantes
C. del Moreto
IGLESIA DE SAN JERÓNIMO
EL MUSEO DEL PRADO
C. de Casado del Alisal
C. de Alberto Bosch
C. de Alfonso XII
C. Santa María
PL. PLATERÍA MARTÍNEZ
LA PLATERÍA BAR MUSEO
PL. DE MURILLO
C. de Espalter
Retiro
PL. DE SAN JUAN
C. del Moratín
C. Verónica
C. de la Almeda
P. del Prado
P. del Prado
C. del Gobernador
Real Jardín Botánico
C. de San Eugenio
C. de San Ildefonso
C. de Atocha
C. Alameda
CAIXAFORUM
C. de Santa Isabel
ATOCHA
Real Conservatorio de Música
PL. DEL EMPERADOR CARLOS V
ATOCHA
C. Claudio Moyano
P. Duque de F. Núñez
Ministerio de Agricultura
N
C. del Dr-Fourquet
C. del Hospital
EL BRILLANTE
P. de la Infanta Isabel
C. del Dr-Velasco
200 meters
200 yards
REINA SOFÍA
ESTACIÓN ATOCHA
Av. Ciudad de Barcelona
TO TICKET OFFICE (50M)
ATOCHA RENFE

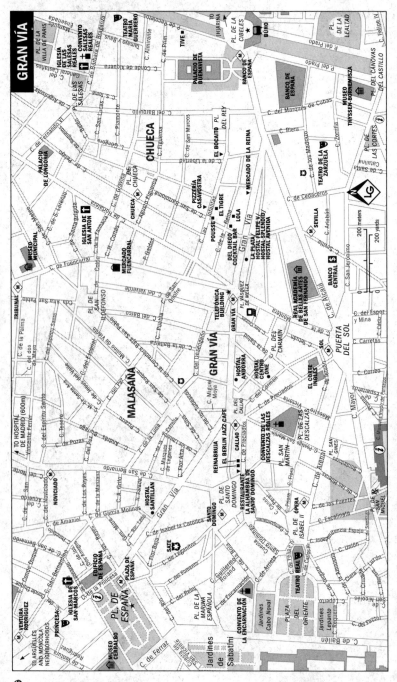

GRAN VÍA

madrid

CHUECA AND MALASAÑA

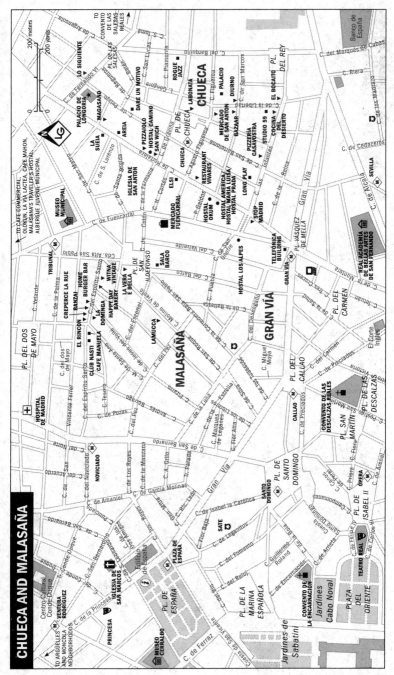

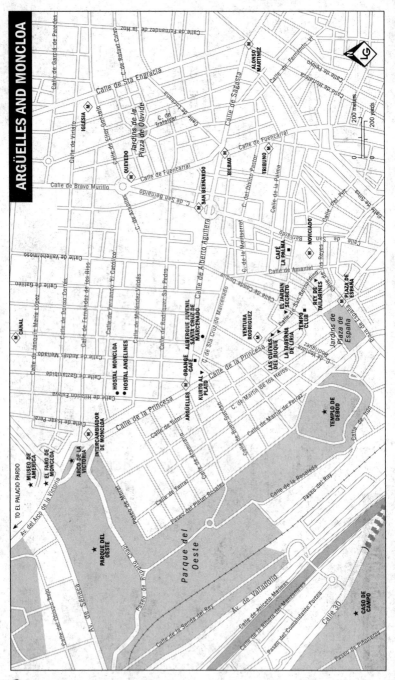

ARGÜELLES AND MONCLOA

madrid

PARIS

Paris leaves an impression on everyone, from students perfecting their *langue française* to tourists who wonder why the French don't pronounce half the consonants in each word. This city has been home to countless films, revolutions, and kings named Louis, and, in case you hadn't heard, it's a really big deal. Nearly everyone in the world idealizes Paris, whether it's for the Eiffel Tower, the Grands Boulevards, or the fact that there are more miles in the Louvre than in many towns. Don't let yourself be content with ideals. If you want to know the danger of that, do some research on Paris Syndrome. This city can be rough, and, yes, the waiters are judging you. When you get Englished for the first time (when someone responds to your mangled-French inquiry with an English response), you'll realize that you maybe weren't prepared for all this. But Paris and its people pull through spectacularly for those who can appreciate the sensory experiences around every corner—the sweet tastes to be found in a patisserie, the resonating bells of Notre Dame, the springtime greens in the Jardin des Tuileries. This city will charm and bitchslap you with equal gusto, but don't get too *le tired*—by your third or fourth sincere attempt at *s'il vous plaît*, even those waiters will soften up.

greatest hits

- **"METAL ASPARAGUS" INDEED.** Lord knows the **Eiffel Tower** wasn't popular at first, but it's done pretty well for itself since then (p. 595).

- **SIXTH SENSE.** If you're looking to see some famous dead people, **Cimetière du Père Lachaise** won't let you down (p. 605).

- **STUFF YOUR FACE.** Foodies and gluttons alike shouldn't miss the Martiniquais fare at **Chez Lucie.** Don't forget to try the *ti' ponch!* (p. 613).

- **VD.** Known as "Le VD" to the locals, **Le Violin Dingue** has some of the cheapest happy hour drinks, and it's open until 5am. Don't worry—this place won't give you an STI, but you may end up with a pounding headache the next morning (p. 626).

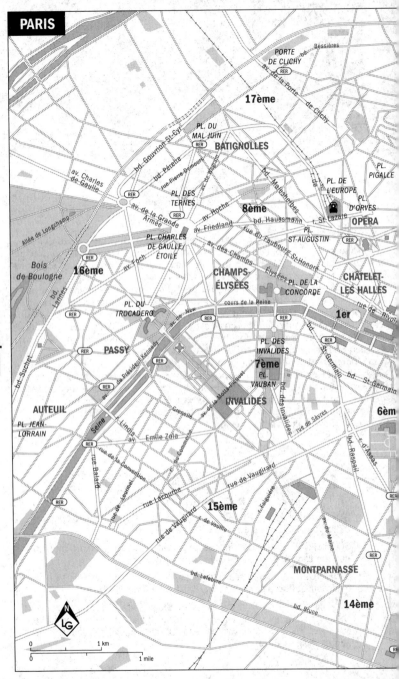

PARIS

Bessières
PORTE DE CLICHY
17ème
PL. DU MAL JUIN
BATIGNOLLES
bd. Gouvion-St-Cyr
av. Charles de Gaulle
bd. Péreire
rue Pierre Demours
PL. DES TERNES
PL. PIGALLE
PL. DE L'EUROPE
PL. D'ORVES
bd. Malesherbes
8ème
av. Hoche
bd. Haussmann
r. St-Lazare
OPÉRA
av. de la Grande Armée
av. Friedland
rue du Faubourg St-Honoré
PL. ST-AUGUSTIN
Allée de Longchamp
PL. CHARLES DE GAULLE/ ÉTOILE
av. Foch
av. des Champs-Élysées
CHÂTELET-LES HALLES
Bois de Boulogne
16ème
CHAMPS-ÉLYSÉES
PL. DE LA CONCORDE
bd. Lannes
PL. DU TROCADÉRO
cours de la Reine
rue de Rivoli
1er
bd. St-Germain
av. de New
PASSY
bd. Suchet
av. du Président Kennedy
PL. DES INVALIDES
7ème
PL. VAUBAN
bd. des Invalides
6èm
Grenelle
av. de la Motte-Picquet
INVALIDES
rue de Sèvres
AUTEUIL
PL. JEAN LORRAIN
Seine
r. Linois
av. Émile Zola
bd. de Grenelle
bd. Raspail
bd. de Courcelles
r. d'Assas
bd. Exelmans
rue de la Convention
rue de Vaugirard
15ème
rue Lacourbe
r. de Vouillé
bd. Lefebvre
MONTPARNASSE
14ème
bd. Brune

N
LG

0   1 km
0   1 mile

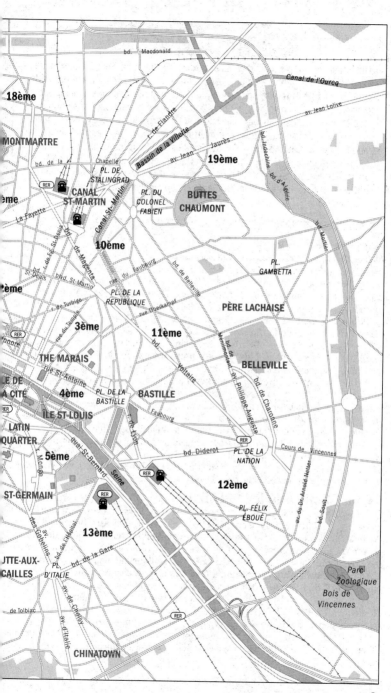

18ème

MONTMARTRE

bd. de la

Chapelle

PL. DE
STALINGRAD

CANAL
ST-MARTIN

La Fayette

bd. de St-Louis

St-Denis

blvd. St-Martin

r. de Turbigo

PL. DE LA
RÉPUBLIQUE

THE MARAIS

rue St-Antoine

LE DE
A CITÉ

ÎLE ST-LOUIS

LATIN
QUARTER

ST-GERMAIN

des Gobelins

de Tolbiac

JTTE-AUX-
CAILLES

PL.
D'ITALIE

CHINATOWN

Canal de l'Ourcq

bd. Macdonald

r. de Flandre

Bassin de la Villette

av. Jean Jaurès

19ème

PL. DU
COLONEL
FABIEN

BUTTES
CHAUMONT

10ème

rue du Faubourg

bd. de Belleville

av. Jean Lolive

bd. Indochine

bd. d'Algérie

bd. Mortier

PL.
GAMBETTA

PÈRE LACHAISE

3ème

11ème

rue Oberkampf

bd.

Voltaire

bd. de Ménilmontant

BELLEVILLE

bd. de Charonne

4ème

PL. DE LA
BASTILLE

BASTILLE

Faubourg

r. de Lyon

bd. Philippe-Auguste

5ème

Monge

Quai St-Bernard

Seine

bd. Diderot

PL. DE LA
NATION

Cours de Vincennes

12ème

PL. FÉLIX
EBOUÉ

av.-du-Dr.-Arnold-Netter

bd.-Soult

13ème

av. de l'Hôpital

bd. de la Gare

av. de Choisy

av. d'Italie

Parc
Zoologique
Bois de
Vincennes

paris overview map

www.letsgo.com φ 571

Other tourists may proclaim that Paris is expensive, but we at *Let's Go* know better. Paris is teeming with universities, especially on the Left Bank around the **Latin Quarter and St-Germain,** and with universities come student deals. Many of the cheap bars sprinkled throughout the Latin Quarter offer student happy hours or English trivia nights. Although you might not be staying in the area, you might just find yourself stumbling back at night from rue Mouffetard and admiring the student graffiti that line the walls. Students fleeing from the tourist-heavy areas of the Champs-Élysées and Châtelet-Les Halles can also be found in the cheap brasseries and restaurants of Montparnasse and Southern Paris. And when the sun sets, the Seine and Canal St-Martin fill up with young Frenchies clutching bottles of wine.

orientation

Despite all the invasions, revolutions, and riots throughout French history, Paris was still meticulously planned. The Seine River flows from east to west through the middle of the city, splitting it into two sections. The *Rive Gauche* (Left Bank) to the south is known as the intellectual heart of Paris, while the *Rive Droite* (Right Bank) to the north is famous for banking and commerce. The two islands in the middle of the Seine, the Île de la Cité and Île St-Louis, are the geographical and historical center of the city. The rest of Paris is divided into 20 arrondissements (districts) that spiral outward from the islands. The arrondissements are numbered; for example, the Eiffel Tower is located in *le septième* (the seventh), abbreviated 7ème.

If this description sounds too good to be true, it is. Neighborhoods frequently spread over multiple arrondissements and are often referred to by name rather than number. (The Marais, for example, is in both the 3ème and the 4ème.) Neighborhood names are based on major connecting hubs of the Metro or train (Montparnasse, Bastille), or major landmarks and roads (Champs-Élysées, Invalides). Streets are marked on every corner, and numerous signs point toward train stations, landmarks, and certain *triomphant* roundabouts. You can try to walk through it all, but the size of the city is deceiving. When your feet start to fall off, buses go almost everywhere in the city, and your hostel is just a ride away.

ÎLE DE LA CITÉ AND ÎLE ST-LOUIS

Situated in the physical center of Paris, these two islands are where the French monarchy (and the country itself) grew up, sheltered by the easily defendable Seine. Some 2000 years later, after the monarchy was politely asked to step down from power, the symbolic presence still remains. Île de la Cité is the larger island, where the French officially marked *kilomètre zéro*, a circular sundial in front of **Notre Dame,** as the point from which all distances in France are measured. This island is also where you'll find the seat of government and the judicial palace. The smaller Île St-Louis is a little more laid-back and is home to cafes and restaurants that aren't choked with tourists. We were hard pressed to find a non-uniformed French person on these islands, unless you count gypsies. You can't blame them for hanging out in this area, since the high prices guarantee that tourists will be carrying a lot of cash. When you're exploring Île St-Louis, keep one eye on the sights and the other on your wallet.

paris

CHÂTELET-LES HALLES (1ER, 2ÈME)

Châtelet-Les Halles is famous for the **Louvre** and the marketplace at **Les Halles.** Due to these time-honored tourist traditions, the 1er and 2ème swell beyond carrying capacity during the day. Châtelet is also the central hub of all bus and most Metro lines, but when they stop for the night the area can get a little derelict. It's often difficult to distinguish between genuinely good deals and tourist traps. The area between **rue des Halles** and **Forum des Halles** has lots of cheap brasseries that won't rip you off. The easiest way to navigate the area is to find **rue de Rivoli,** which runs parallel to the Seine and past the **Hôtel de Ville.**

THE MARAIS (3ÈME, 4ÈME)

The Marais embodies the ultimate ugly duckling tale. Originally a bog—*marais* means "marsh"—the area became livable in the 13th century when monks drained the land to build the **Right Bank.** When Henri IV constructed the glorious **place des Vosges** in the early 17th century, the area suddenly became the city's center of fashionable living, with luxury and scandal taking hold. Royal haunts gave way to slums and tenements during the Revolution, and many of the grand *hôtels particuliers* fell into ruin or disrepair. In the 1950s, the Marais was revived and declared a historic neighborhood; since then, decades of gentrification and renovation have restored the Marais to its pre-Revolutionary glory. Once-palatial mansions have become exquisite museums, and the tiny twisting streets are covered with hip bars, avant-garde galleries, and one-of-a-kind boutiques. **Rue des Rosiers,** in the heart of the 4ème, is the center of Paris's Jewish population, though the steady influx of hyper-hip clothing stores threatens its identity. Superb kosher delicatessens neighbor Middle Eastern and Eastern European restaurants, and the Marais remains livelier on Sundays than the rest of the city. The Marais is unquestionably the GLBT center of Paris, with the community's hub at the intersection of **rue Sainte-Croix de la Brettonerie** and **rue Vieille du Temple.** Though the steady stream of tourists has begun to wear on the Marais's eclectic personality, the district continues to be a distinctive mix of old and new, queer and straight, cheap and chic.

LATIN QUARTER AND ST-GERMAIN (5ÈME, 6ÈME)

The Latin Quarter and St-Germain are two of Paris's primary tourist neighborhoods, playing into the hands of those who expect the romantic Paris of yesteryear. The intellectual heart of Paris, these neighborhoods are home to the **Sorbonne,** various high schools, and *les Grandes Écoles,* and they are very student- and budget-friendly. The main road that divides the 5ème and 6ème is the **boulevard Saint-Michel,** which runs along the eastern border of the **Jardins de Luxembourg.** As tempted as you may be to explore St-Germain-des-Prés, your wallet will thank you as if you head to the 5ème and roam **rue Monge** and **rue Mouffetard** for food, nightlife, and accommodations.

INVALIDES (7ÈME)

With tourist attractions and museums on every corner, it can be difficult to find a deal in the 7ème. This neighborhood is spread out, so orienting yourself isn't always easy. At the center are **Tour Eiffel** and **Invalides,** each with a large grassy lawn in front, **Champ de Mars** and **Espalande des Invalides** respectively. Rue de l'Université and the quais run parallel along the Seine throughout the neighborhood, while the main roads in and out of the center are av. de Bourdonnais, which leads to quai Branly, and av. Bosquet, which leads to **Musée d'Orsay.** Travelers should take advantage of metro lines 6, 8, and 13.

CHAMPS-ÉLYSÉES (8ÈME)

If the Champs-Élysées were a supermodel, it would have been forced to retire for being well past its prime. This arrondissement was synonymous with fashion throughout the 19th century, and many boulevards are still lined with the vast mansions, expensive shops, and grandiose monuments that brought in tourists. But that old sense of sophistication has since been juxtaposed with charmless boutiques, office buildings, and car dealerships. Only the **Champs-Élysées** itself bustles late into the night, thanks to its unparalleled nightclubs and droves of tourists. A stroll along **avenue Montaigne, rue du Faubourg Saint-Honoré,** or around the **Madeleine** will give you a taste of excessively rich life in Paris. There are fewer tourists in the northern part of the neighborhood, near the **Parc Monceau.**

OPÉRA (9ÈME) AND CANAL ST-MARTIN (10ÈME)

The 9ème and the 10ème are the more difficult neighborhoods to wander due to their lack of tall landmarks (as opposed to, for example, the 7ème's Eiffel Tower, or the 18ème's Sacré-Cœur). Criss-crossing the 9ème are the main roads **rue la Fayette** and **rue Fontaine,** with the famous **Opéra Garnier** sitting in the southeast corner next to its appropriately named Metro stop. This is a neighborhood of extremes: the northern boundary is just before the red light district of **Pigalle,** the southern is marked by the chic shopping districts on the **Grands Boulevards,** and there is enough residential area in between to make it feel less touristy.

Right next to the 9ème, the 10ème is known (and named for) the **Canal Saint-Martin,** which runs along the eastern border of the arrondissement. Stray too far from this "mini-Seine" (i.e., anywhere west of bd de Magenta) and you'll find yourself smack in the middle of the sketchy area that surrounds the **Gare du Nord** and **Gare de l'Est.** If the gun armories and cash-for-gold stores didn't give you a hint, we'll tell you to stay clear of this area at night.

BASTILLE (11ÈME, 12ÈME)

The Bastille area is famous for housing the prison where the French Revolution kicked off on July 14, 1789. Hundreds of years later, Parisians still storm this neighborhood nightly in search of the latest cocktails, culinary innovations, and up-and-coming musicians. Five Metro lines converge at Ⓜ**République** and three lines at Ⓜ**Bastille,** making this district a busy transport hub. The 1989 opening of the glassy **Opéra Bastille** on the bicentennial of the Revolution was supposed to breathe new cultural life into the area, but the party atmosphere has yet to give way to galleries and string quartets. Today, with numerous bars along **rue de Lappe,** manifold dining options on **rue de la Roquette** and **rue Jean-Pierre Timbaud,** and young designer boutiques, the Bastille is a great area for unwinding after a day at the museums.

MONTPARNASSE AND SOUTHERN PARIS (13ÈME, 14ÈME, 15ÈME)

These three arrondissements, which make up nearly one-sixth of Paris, lack the photo ops and famous sights that attract tourists elsewhere in the city. However, they do portray the local side of Paris: more laid-back, cheaper, and friendlier. The 13ème has a strange combination of characters thanks to **Chinatown,** around rue de Tolbiac, and the small hippie enclave surrounding **rue de la Butte-aux-Cailles,** which avoids the capitalist drive to overcharge for meals or entertainment. The main hub of the 13ème is **Place d'Italie,** where you can find brasseries and a huge mall. Montparnasse is more homogeneous than the 13ème and is similar to the St-Germain of the 1920s. Here you'll find bohemian Parisians whose souls have yet to harden. Markets, cemeteries, and major boulevards cater to the locals. On the border between the 14ème and 15ème, the domineering **Tour de Montparnasse** gives a point of reference and access to transport almost anywhere in the city, while **boulevard de Rennes** and **boulevard Raspail** lead to St-Germain. The 15ème is quiet and even more residential than the 13ème and 14ème; most travelers don't make it farther south than bd de Grenelle.

slight redistricting

Paris wasn't always divided into 20 arrondissements; strange references to *anciens* arrondissements on old churches and random street corners come from the city's old organization. While his uncle controlled most of Europe, Napoleon III conquered the internal structure of Paris, doubling the area of the city and subsequently reorganizing it all. It's no surprise Napoleon I remains the more famous of the two: as great as sensible municipal organization is, it's no match for continental domination.

WESTERN PARIS (16ÈME, 17ÈME)

These two arrondissements are almost devoid of tourists. More residential, these neighborhoods are home to ladies who lunch, their beautiful children, and their overworked husbands. The 16ème is frequented by Parisian elites who have money and are willing to spend it in the expensive boutiques and cafe lounges lining the main roads around **Trocadéro. Avenue Georges Mandel** cuts the neighborhood in two, and **avenue Kléber** will take you straight to the Arc de Triomphe in the 8ème.

The 17ème is way more relaxed in terms of residents and prices. Its sheer size and lack of notable sights make this area a retreat for the working class and overly earnest teenagers who take leisurely strolls or sit in the many cafes. Around Ⓜ**Ternes,** you'll find smaller boutique hotels and older tourists, whereas on the opposite side, around Ⓜ**Rome,** you'll get a sense of the community that exists next to Montmartre. Running through the center and connecting these two areas is **boulevard de Courcelles,** which turns into **boulevard des Batignolles.**

MONTMARTRE (18ÈME)

Montmartre may just be the most eccentric of Paris's arrondissements, featuring scenic vistas at the **Basilique du Sacré-Cœur,** historic cabarets, the **Butte vineyard,** and the unsurprisingly skin-toned establishments in the **Red Light District** on the southern border. Hiking the 130m hill can be a challenge. The 18ème has recently exploded with youth hostels that keep bars full at night while simultaneously giving pickpockets an easy target.

EASTERN PARIS (19ÈME, 20ÈME)

This is a huge area. The lack of visible landmarks make it difficult to navigate on foot, so it's better to take the Metro during the day and a taxi at night (if for some reason you end up there after dark—trust us, you don't want to). The main places worth visiting are the **Parc des Buttes-Chaumont** (Ⓜ Buttes Chaumont, Botzaris, or Laumière) and **Cimetière du Père Lachaise** (Ⓜ Père Lachaise, Gambetta, or Philippe Auguste). Running along the northern edge of the 19ème is **avenue Jean-Jaurès,** which leads straight to the Museum of Science. From av. Jean-Jaurès any turn up the hill leads to the park. **boulevard de Belleville** connects the two arrondissements and has some of the best (and cheapest) African and Asian restaurants in the city. But as soon as the sun sets, this place turns into a Parisian mini-Marseille, and that's not where you want to be.

orientation

accommodations

Budget accommodations (or budget anything, for that matter) can be difficult to find in Paris. Hostels and hotels generally get cheaper as you journey out of the center into the less trafficked arrondissements. Once you get to the 17ème, though, you're looking at a pretty long Metro ride, and an inconvenient location doesn't always translate into a decent price. But there are still deals for savvy travelers who know where to look. Both Châtelet-Les Halles and Bastille are home to youth hostels with rock-bottom prices that are ridiculously close to Paris's main attractions. When it comes to hotels, be on the lookout for exceptionally good two-stars, especially in the 5ème and 6ème. Expect to pay about €40-60 for the best budget hotels, which can be very quirky or forgettable but are always clean and more peaceful than the alternatives. Free Wi-Fi and cheap breakfasts are almost always provided, and it's not uncommon for hotels and hostels to have adjoining bars. But if you're doing Paris on the cheap, be warned that you can't always count on having your own bathroom or shower, even if you shell out for a single. What better way is there to get to know your neighbors?

CHÂTELET-LES HALLES

While affordable hotels in this trendy neighborhood are usually hard to come by, there are a few high-quality budget locations that are worth checking out. Be sure to make reservations far in advance; cheap spots in such a central location fill up quickly year-round. Also, be vigilant around Châtelet, where passersby won't stick up for you (or even tell you) when a pickpocket or mugger is about to strike.

CENTRE INTERNATIONALE DE PARIS (BVJ): PARIS LOUVRE   HOSTEL $$
20 rue Jean-Jacques Rousseau   ☎01 53 00 90 90; www.bvjhotel.com
This monstrous 200-bed hostel has clean rooms. (Even the lofts are clean—they must have high-reaching dusters.) In the summer, it's packed with international youths and backpackers. Despite the hostel's location next to the old Parisian stock market, you won't pay much for a huge entry, glass ceiling foyer, and the free language lessons you get when conversing with your bunkmates.

✦ ⓂLouvre-Rivoli. Walk north on rue du Louvre and turn left onto rue St-Honoré. Turn right onto rue Jean-Jacques Rousseau. *i* Breakfast included. Lockers €2. Wi-Fi in dining hall €2 per hr., €3 per 2hr. Reservations can be made no more than 2 months in advance Jul-Aug, no more than 15 days in advance Sept-June. Ⓢ Dorms €29; doubles €70. Cash only. 🕑 Reception 24hr. 3-night max. stay; extensions can be arranged on arrival.

HOTEL TIQUETONNE   HOTEL $$
6 rue Tiquetonne   ☎01 42 36 94 58; www.hoteltiquetonne.fr
Extremely close to the center of the 1er, Hotel Tiquetonne is a very confused one-star budget hotel: it serves breakfast in your room, but charges €6 for shower tokens if you are in a single *sans-douche.*

✦ ⓂÉtienne Marcel. Walk against the traffic on rue de Turbigo and turn left onto rue Tiquetonne. *i* Breakfast €6. Hall showers €6. Must reserve in advance. Parking available. Ⓢ Singles €40, with bath €50; doubles with bath €60. 🕑 Reception 24hr.

HÔTEL MONTPENSIER   HOTEL $$$
12 rue de Richelieu   ☎01 42 96 28 50; www.hotelmontpensierparis.com
One of few affordable hotels in the area, Hôtel Montpensier doesn't skimp on amenities, offering marble bathrooms and large beds. It has a convenient location up the street from the Place du Palais Royal, and the rooms will remind you of the Belle Époque.

✦ ⓂPalais Royal-Musée du Louvre. Facing la Comédie Française, turn left and walk up rue de Richelieu. The hotel is 1½ blocks up on the right. *i* Breakfast €9. Free Wi-Fi. Ⓢ Singles €60, with bath €70; doubles with shower €99, with full bath €100; triples €149; quads €159. 🕑 Reception 24hr.

HÔTEL DES BOULEVARDS

HOTEL $$$

10 rue de la ville Neuve   ☎01 42 36 02 29; www.hoteldesboulevards.com

Hôtel des Boulevards is a simple hotel that clearly couldn't afford a decorator. If you aren't looking for more than clean, cheap rooms and complimentary breakfast, then you won't be disappointed. Rooms cost the same if you're solo or traveling with someone else, so find a friend and split the cost.

✠ Ⓜ*Bonne Nouvelle. Walk 2½ blocks down rue de la ville Neuve. The hotel is on the right.* ⓘ *Breakfast included. Free Wi-Fi.* Ⓢ *Singles and doubles €55, with toilet €63, with full bath €68.*

bike it out

You may notice a number of gray bikes scattered around the city. These are part of a city-wide bike-sharing program called **Vélib**. If you're going to be in Paris for a while and have a credit card with an EMV-chip (few US cards currently have them; most European ones do), it may be worth getting a subscription. Bikes are €1 per day and you can take unlimited 30min. trips. Longer rides face extra charges, but, as long as you're staying in the central part of Paris, you'll rarely need it for more than half an hour.

THE MARAIS

The Marais provides budget accommodations with a bit of flair in the center of Paris's action. The trendy, down-to-earth 4ème is home to some of the best deals and most worthwhile splurges in the city.

⬙ LE FAUCONNIER

HOSTEL $$

11 rue du Fauconnier   ☎01 42 74 23 45; www.mije.com

Le Fauconnier is an ivy-covered, sun-drenched building just steps from the Seine and Île St-Louis. Clean rooms have beds arranged in every possible way: lofts, bunks, and even Tetris-inspired arrangements. But don't worry, you'll get to know your neighbors after soaking in the sun on the terrace.

✠ Ⓜ*Pont Marie. Walk east on quai des Célestins and turn left onto rue du Fauconnier.* ⓘ *Breakfast included. Lockers €1 deposit. MIJE membership required. Reserve 45 days before arrival online or 1 week ahead if by phone. Ages 18-30 only. Internet €0.50 initial connection fee, €0.10 per min. thereafter.* Ⓢ *Dorms €30; singles €49; doubles €72; triples €96. MIJE membership €2.50.* ☒ *Curfew 1am; notify in advance if returning later. Lockout noon-3pm. 1-week max. stay.*

⬙ MAUBUISSON

HOSTEL $$

12 rue des Barres   ☎01 42 74 23 45; www.mije.com

Run by the same company as Le Fauconnier, Maubuisson is in a former 17th-century convent on a quiet street by the St-Gervais monastery. In a move that would make Mother Superior nervous, the hostel only accommodates individual travelers between the ages of 18 and 30, but the quality of the hostel benefits from the lack of foot traffic.

✠ Ⓜ*St-Paul. Walk against traffic on rue François Miron for several blocks and turn right onto rue des Barres.* ⓘ *Breakfast included. Lockers €1 deposit. Internet €0.50 initial connection fee, €0.10 per min. thereafter. MIJE membership required. Reserve 45 days before arrival online or 1 week ahead if by phone. Ages 18-30 only.* Ⓢ *Dorms €30; singles €49; doubles €72; triples €96. MIJE membership €2.50.* ☒ *Lockout noon-3pm. Curfew 1am; notify in advance if returning later. 1 week max. stay.*

HOTEL DE LA HERSE D'OR

HOTEL $$$

20 rue St-Antoine   ☎01 48 87 84 09; www.parishotelherseor.com

Quiet, peaceful rooms can be difficult to find in the Marais. The Hotel de la Herse d'Or, though, provides a tranquil place to crash just a block from the pl. des

Vosges. Though not the best budget option for a couple nights' stay, the lavish doubles and apartment-sized triples create a bohemian escape that can be affordable for stays over one week.

✦ Ⓜ*Bastille. Walk toward the Marais on rue St-Antoine for 1½ blocks.* ⓘ *Discounts up to 20% for stays of 1 week or longer.* Ⓢ *Singles €69; doubles €79, with bath €109; triples with bath €139.*

HÔTEL SÉVIGNÉ
HOTEL $$$$

2 rue Malher ☎01 42 72 76 17; www.le-sevigne.com

Everyone knows that the French are skinny, but even Twiggy would have a hard time squeezing around this hotel. The air-conditioned rooms are more spacious than the cramped staircase and come with full baths. The rooms have small balconies that overlook rue de Rivoli, and with such a central location, you probably won't come back except for a quick nap after a meal in the Marais.

✦ Ⓜ*St-Paul. Walk against traffic on rue de Rivoli for 1 block and turn left onto rue Malher.* ⓘ *Breakfast €8.* Ⓢ *Singles €71-81; doubles €88-98; quads €140.*

HÔTEL DU SÉJOUR
HOTEL $$$$

36 rue du Grenier St-Lazare ☎01 48 87 40 36; www.hoteldusejour.com

Bringing the spirit of minimalism to the hotel industry (read: no TV or air-conditioning), Hôtel du Séjour features 20 basic rooms decorated with Pop Art of Parisian landmarks and colorful stripes. It's a little loud, but worth the price for the ideal location one block away from Les Halles and the Centre Pompidou.

✦ Ⓜ*Étienne Marcel. Walk 3 blocks down rue aux Ours, turn left onto rue St-Martin, and right onto rue du Grenier St-Lazare.* ⓘ *Reserve 2-3 weeks in advance.* Ⓢ *Singles €82; doubles €87, with shower and toilet €97.* 🕐 *Reception 7:30am-10:30pm.*

LATIN QUARTER AND ST-GERMAIN

Hotels in these neighborhoods are generally a bit overpriced due to their central locations. Even with this handicap, secret gems that are accessible to budget travelers are usually located down quiet alleys right around the corner from some of the most popular nightlife spots.

YOUNG AND HAPPY HOSTEL
HOSTEL $$

80 rue Mouffetard ☎01 47 07 47 07; www.youngandhappy.fr

A funky, lively hostel with 21 clean (if basic) rooms, some with showers and toilets, Young and Happy Hostel is where you want to stay in the 5ème. It's a great option if you're young, fun, and on a budget, as it's on the rue Mouffetard and in the center of the cheapest student watering holes in Paris. While impromptu, their reception doubles as a bar and serves drinks if you ask for them.

✦ Ⓜ*Place Monge. From rue Monge, walk behind the pl. Monge on rue Ortolan and turn left onto rue Mouffetard. The hostel is on the right.* ⓘ *Breakfast included. Internet €2 per 30min.* Ⓢ *High-season dorms €28-45.*

HÔTEL DE NESLE
HOTEL $$$

7 rue de Nesle ☎01 43 54 62 41; www.hoteldenesleparis.com

Hôtel de Nesle is a phenomenal place to stay. Each room is unique and represents a particular time period or locale. The Molière room is ideal for the comically minded, and a Colonial room is available for undying proponents of the good ol' days of the Scramble for Africa (don't let that be you). Reserve in advance, because space fills up quickly, especially in the summer.

✦ Ⓜ*Odéon. Walk toward the church on bd St-Germain and turn right onto rue Mazarine. Turn right onto rue Dauphine and head toward the river. Rue de Nesle is the 1st street on the left.* ⓘ *Laundry facilities on-site as well as a Turkish bath (Le Hammam).* Ⓢ *Singles €55-65; doubles €75-100. Extra bed €12.*

HÔTEL STELLA

HOTEL $$

41 rue Monsieur-le-Prince ☎01 40 51 00 25; http://site.voila.fr/hotel-stella

Designed in the style of Old World Paris, Hôtel Stella has no place for TVs or even an elevator. The rooms are huge and boast high ceilings, exposed beams, the occasional piano, and oriental rugs. With a location down the street from the Jardin de Luxembourg, Hôtel Stella could charge twice as much for their rooms, so thank God they don't.

 # [M]Odéon. Walk up rue Danton in the direction of traffic past Université René Descartes Paris V and turn left onto rue Monsieur-le-Prince. The hotel is just past the intersection with rue Racine. [$] Singles €30-50; doubles €60; triples €80; quads €100.

DELHY'S HÔTEL

HOTEL $$$

22 rue de l'Hirondelle ☎01 43 26 58 25; www.delhyshotel.com

This might be the easiest hotel to find in the Latin Quarter. It's close to pl. St-Michel and the Seine, yet tucked away from the hustle and bustle down a quiet cobblestone alleyway. Cheaper rooms have just a sink, but we would advise against bathing in the St-Michel fountain.

*# [M]St-Michel. Facing the St-Michel fountain, turn to your right and walk through the passage to the left of La Rive Gauche cafe. The hotel is on the right. **i** Breakfast included. Check website for promotions. [$] Singles €58, with shower €73; doubles €76/83; triples €119. Extra bed €15.*

INVALIDES

Budget travel isn't exactly synonymous with the elegant 7ème. Outside the touristy areas, you will find many expensive apartments. If you absolutely must stay here, there are a couple of options that are easy to get to and affordable, by local standards. You have been warned.

HÔTEL DE TURENNE

HOTEL $$$

20 av. de Tourville ☎01 47 05 99 92; www.france-hotel-guide.com/h75007turenne.htm

Centrally located Hôtel du Turenne offers little more than what you would expect from every forgettable hotel you've ever stayed at. What you do get is the much sought-after air-conditioning, full bath, and satellite TV in every room.

*# [M]École Militaire. Exit the metro facing away from the Tour Eiffel and walk down av. de Tourville. Hotel is at the intersection of av. de Tourville and rue Chevert. **i** Breakfast €9. [$] Singles €69; doubles €85-100; twins €105; triples €140.*

CHAMPS-ÉLYSÉES

If you are staying for more than a month, you can stay in the 8ème. If not, there are very few places that are affordable, especially for solo travelers.

WOODSTOCK HOSTEL

HOSTEL $

48 rue Rodier ☎01 48 78 87 76; www.woodstock.fr

Woodstock's reception instills an intimate vibe, with a back wall covered in stickers (the backpacker's version of a guestbook) and a Beatles-decorated VW bug that pays homage to the hippies of old. Rooms are basic but clean, and the quiet inner courtyard terrace comes complete with odd vagabonds reading or chilling with a cigarette.

*# [M]Anvers. Facing away from the metro, walk down the right side of pl. d'Anvers and turn right onto rue Rodier. The hostel is 1½ blocks down on the left. **i** Wi-Fi included. Computers €2 per 30min. Towels €1. [$] High-season dorms M-F €25, Sa-Su €28; doubles M-F €56, Sa-Su €62. Low-season dorms M-F €22, Sa-Su €25; doubles M-F €50, Sa-Su €56. ⏰ Lockout 11am-3pm. Curfew 2am.*

PERFECT HOSTEL

HOSTEL $$$

39 rue Rodier ☎01 42 81 18 86

Perfect Hostel actually claims to be a "Hotel-Hostel," which probably just gives it an excuse to have lockout hours, a shared kitchen, and private rooms with maid service. While the decor is not the most original, the real deal here is that the apartments have full kitchens (oven, microwave, coffee maker, and fridge) and cost the same as a simple room. You can't get more perfect than that.

✻ ⓂAnvers. *With your back to the Metro, walk down the right side of the pl. d'Anvers and make a right onto rue Rodier. The hotel is 1½ blocks down on the right.* ⓘ *Breakfast included. Reserve 2 months ahead—there are only 10 rooms, and with these prices, the hotel fills up weeks in advance during the summer.* Ⓢ *Singles €52; doubles €52-72, double apartments €72; triples and triple apartments €87.*

money-making decision

When Disney proposed the construction of its multi-million dollar theme park in Paris, many locals scoffed at the idea. They called it "cowboy colonialism" saying that the park would threaten French culture. But when the French government realized how much revenue the park could rake in, it gave Disney the green light. Thus began the era of **Disneyland Paris,** whose 15 million annual visitors make it the most popular tourist attraction in France. Sorry to disappoint you, Walt, but money has a lot more pull than Mickey Mouse.

OPÉRA AND CANAL ST-MARTIN

You should know better than to stay in a hotel close to the **Gare du Nord.** Whether its because you're coming in late and don't want to go far or you're only in Paris for a night (shame on you), resist the urge to park yourself there. Instead, hop on the Metro to the canal, which is more central, cheaper, and infinitely more scenic (not to mention less sketchy).

🏨 HÔTEL PALACE   HOTEL $$
9 rue Bouchardon   ☎01 40 40 09 45

Try as we might, we cannot figure out why this newly renovated (as of November 2011) hotel has such low prices. Its quiet location and brand new breakfast terrace in the inner courtyard make this a hard place to leave, even with the Metro stop less than two blocks from this wannabe-Art Deco hotel. People are catching on to this deal, so book well in advance.

✻ ⓂStrasbourg-St-Denis. *Exit Metro and walk east on bd St-Martin for 1 block. Walk through the roundabout and turn left onto rue René Boulanger. Rue Bouchardon is the 1st left. The hotel is on the left.* ⓘ *Breakfast €4. Free Wi-Fi.* Ⓢ *Singles €23-35; doubles €28-45; triples €60; quads €70. Prices increase with each additional bathroom accoutrement (sink, sink and toilet, full bath).*

PEACE AND LOVE HOSTEL   HOSTEL $
245 rue la Fayette   ☎01 46 07 65 11; www.paris-hostels.com

This is one of the only hostels in this neighborhood, but the low prices come with some drawbacks. The reception doubles as a bar and stays open until 2am serving the cheapest pints (€3.80) around for mostly Anglo-backpackers. But the limited hours for Wi-Fi, cash-only policy, and strict adherence to check-in times (read: they will give away your bed if you are more than 3hr. late) make this a hostel for those who can stick to a schedule. That's what backpacking, peace, and love are all about, right?

✻ ⓂJuarès. *Like, right there. Or from Gare du Nord, it's a 10min. walk up rue la Fayette, and the hostel is on the left.* ⓘ *Wi-Fi 8am-6pm only. Ages 18-35 only. Cash only.* Ⓢ *High-season dorms €23; private rooms €30. Low-season dorms €18; private rooms €26.*

BASTILLE

The 11ème is littered with hotels (among other things) and offers something for everybody, including many quality budget hotels. The neighboring 12ème offers relatively inexpensive and simple accommodations, which work hard to make up for being more remote. The best options cluster around the **Gare de Lyon.**

AUBERGE DE JEUNESSE "JULES FERRY" (HI)   HOSTEL $$
8 bd Jules Ferry   ☎01 43 57 55 60; www.fuaj.org/Paris-Jules-Ferry

Located on the Seine in the 11ème, Jules Ferry provides the perfect location for Bastille bar hopping. The hostel's colorful rooms with sinks, mirrors, and tiled floors match the carefree atmosphere.

✦ Ⓜ*République. Walk down av. de la République, cross over Canal St-Martin, and turn left onto bd Jules Ferry.* ⓘ *Breakfast included. Wi-Fi €5 per 2hr. Kitchen available for guest use.* Ⓢ *Dorms from €25.* ⓩ *Reception 2pm-10:30am. Lockout 10:30am-2pm.*

PARIS ABSOLUTE   HOSTEL $$
1 rue de la Fontaine au Roi   ☎01 47 00 47 00; www.absolute-paris.com

Paris Absolute is made popular by its location a few blocks from the party center of Oberkampf. Clean, lime green dorms will welcome you after a long night out, when you'll be grateful there's no curfew.

✦ Ⓜ*République. Walk toward Canal St-Martin on rue du Temple and cross the canal. The hostel is on the right.* ⓘ *Breakfast included.* Ⓢ *Dorms €29; doubles €75-85.*

HÔTEL DES ARTS BASTILLE   HOTEL $$$
2 rue Godefroy Cavaignac   ☎01 43 79 72 57; www.paris-hotel-desarts.com

If you're traveling in a small group, this hotel can be cheaper than a hostel. Bright rooms with large windows light up the already arresting orange color scheme. Reserve online for almost 60% off listed prices; take an additional €10 off if you book a three-night stay.

✦ Ⓜ*Charonne. Walk down bd Voltaire away from the* Ⓜ*Voltaire and turn right onto rue de Charonne. Walk for 200m and turn right onto rue Godefroy Cavaignac.* Ⓢ *If booking online, singles €55; doubles €55; twins €60; quads €89. By phone or in person, singles €90; doubles €99; twins €109; quads €130.*

AUBERGE INTERNATIONALE DES JEUNES (AIJ)   HOSTEL $
10 rue Trousseau   ☎01 47 00 62 00; www.aijparis.com

The AIJ attracts a steady stream of 20-somethings with what it claims are the cheapest dorms in Paris (we believe them). Clean bathrooms are located in the hallways, and vending machines provide late-night snacks for those sober enough to sort through their coins. Guests really just get the basic amenities, but AIJ does throw in a free map of Paris, which has to be worth something.

✦ Ⓜ*Ledru-Rollin. Walk 3 blocks away from Bastille down rue du Faubourg St-Antoine and turn left onto rue Trousseau. AIJ is on the right.* ⓘ *Breakfast included. Under 30 only.* Ⓢ *Dorms €18; doubles €40.* ⓩ *Lockout 11am-4pm.*

MONTPARNASSE AND SOUTHERN PARIS

This area is calmer than others in Paris, so you won't pay as much for more comfort. Stay close to public transport, as this area is large and hard to navigate at night.

🔖 OOPS!   HOSTEL $$
50 av. des Gobelins   ☎01 47 07 47 00; www.oops-paris.com

Why it's named Oops!, we have no idea. Maybe it's the creative use of bright colors and patterns that vary by room (and sometimes by wall). Both private rooms and dorms are remarkably clean and have balconies that overlook av. d'Italie. Book well in advance for the summer months, as Oops! is very popular among young backpackers.

✦ Ⓜ*Les Gobelins. Walk south on av. des Gobelins toward pl. d'Italie. The hostel is 3 blocks from the Metro, on the right.* ⓘ *Breakfast included. Reserve online.* Ⓢ *High-season dorms €30; private rooms €70. Low-season dorms €23; private rooms €60.*

FIAP JEAN-MONNET

HOTEL $$$

30 rue Cabanis ☎01 43 13 17 00; www.fiap.asso.fr

With a bar, two restaurants, an outdoor terrace, and regular parties on Wednesdays and Fridays, this student-friendly hotel definitely has a vibrant social scene. The rooms match the '60s-meets-modern-art-museum feel. This is one of the only hotels we've ever heard of that allows six people in one room, although they don't have air-conditioning and have to check out at the ungodly hour of 9am.

 # [M]Glacière. Walk down bd Auguste Blancqui and turn left onto rue Dareau. Walk 2 blocks, turn left onto rue Broussais, and then left onto rue Cabanis. i Lockers €3 per day. Reserve at least 1 month in advance. [$] Singles €59; doubles €79; triples €105; quads €140; 5- and 6-person rooms €136-162. ⏰ Reception 24hr.

THREE DUCKS HOSTEL

HOSTEL $

6 pl. Étienne Pernet ☎01 48 42 04 05; www.3ducks.fr

It's always happy hour at the Three Ducks Hostel: the concierge desk doubles as a bar. They're so laid-back that they haven't gotten around to painting the walls or trimming the plants in the garden recently. If the frequency of people coming and going makes you feel more uneasy than social, you can ask to store your belongings in the safe at reception.

 # [M]Félix Faure. Exit the Metro across from St-Jean-Baptiste de Grenelle Church and follow the street to the left. i Reserve at least 1-2 months in advance. Free Wi-Fi and computer. [$] High-season dorms €23; doubles €52. Low-season dorms €18; doubles €46. Beer €2.20-7. ⏰ Reception 24hr.

HÔTEL DE BLOIS

HOTEL $$$

5 rue des Plantes ☎01 45 40 99 48; www.hoteldeblois.com

Those who get a thrill from finding a bargain should try their hand at the website for this 25-room boutique hotel. Prices vary between €65 and €200—it takes a bargain hunter's will and determination to nab one of the cheaper rooms. The pastel-colored rooms are in good shape and the neighborhood is peaceful.

 # [M]Alésia. Walk 2 blocks toward the Tour Montparnasse on rue du Maine and turn left onto rue de la Sablière. Turn right onto rue des Plantes. i Breakfast €12. Reserve at least 1 month in advance. [$] Prices vary depending on availability; check the website for current prices. ⏰ Reception 7am-10:30pm.

ALOHA HOSTEL

HOSTEL $$

1 rue Borromée ☎01 42 73 03 03; www.aloha.fr

Although Aloha serves cheap cocktails, the lockout and 2am curfew might put a damper on your wild side. Then again, it does ensure that you don't have to take a taxi back, since the Metro will still be open, and the bar stays open late enough for you to get your nightcap on. There's free computer access, and the dorms and bathrooms are nothing to quibble with.

 # [M]Volontaires. Walk with traffic on rue des Volontaires. Turn left onto rue Blomet and walk 2 blocks to the corner of rue Blomet and rue Borromée. i Breakfast included. Reserve a few weeks in advance. [$] Dorms €28; doubles €64. Reserve with a credit card; pay in cash. ⏰ Curfew 2am. Lockout 11am-5pm.

WESTERN PARIS

Don't say we didn't warn you about this posh area. In the 16ème you'll find some "budget" areas by parental standards, whereas the 17ème has slightly more affordable options. But really, if you're staying in the 17ème, cancel your booking and go next door to the 18ème where hostels abound and budget hotels (the kind that don't rent by the hour) line the red light district and surround the Sacré-Cœur.

HÔTEL CHAMPERRET HÉLIOPOLIS

HOTEL $$$$

13 rue d'Héliopolis ☎01 47 64 92 56; www.champerret-heliopolis-paris-hotel.com

This brightly lit boutique hotel with a quiet, flowery (as in full of flowers) inner courtyard and private wooden balconies is perfect for grandparents or those who appreciate the "homey" feel. Just make sure you can speak French, since the reception doesn't speak English.

✦ ⓜPorte de Champarret. ⓢ Singles €77; doubles €90, with bath €96; twin €96; triples with bath €120.

HÔTEL DE L'EUROPE
HOTEL $$$

67 rue de Moins ☎01 53 31 01 20; hotel.europe75@gmail.com

Close to the 18ème, this Art Deco hotel explodes with random colors and patterns and has a room to suit just about anyone, from a long backpacker's single with just a sink to a large room with a kitchenette and bathroom for families or friends. Not to worry if you prefer to rough it: there are shared toilets on every floor and a shared kitchen on the ground floor.

✦ ⓜBrochant. With your back to the post office, walk 1 small block and turn left onto rue de Moins. The hotel is ½ a block down on the left. ⓢ Singles €55, with shower €65, with full bath €75; doubles €65/75/88. Email reservations for triples and quads with kitchenette and bathroom; prices vary with availability and season but hover around €20-30 per person.

don't get stuck

If you need a break from hectic city life, visit rue du Chat-qui-Pêche, the narrowest street in Paris. Built in 1540, the road contains only a few windows and no doors. The street's name, "Street of the Fishing Cat," comes from an ancient tale about a cat who fished in the flooded cellars of houses during monsoon season before the harbor was built on the Seine. A word of caution to prospective visitors: walking through the 1.8m wide street is not for the claustrophobic or faint of heart—it wasn't named for the stealthiest and most flexible of mammals for nothing.

MONTMARTRE

◼ PLUG-INN BOUTIQUE HOSTEL
HOSTEL $

7 rue Aristide Bruant ☎01 42 58 42 58; www.plug-inn.fr

Recently opened, this hostel is named for the unlimited free Wi-Fi and computer use. The brand new rooms and untouched bathrooms make you feel slightly cleaner after being in the cabaret- and sex-shop-infused neighborhood, and the views of Paris from the roof are stunning. Check out their blog for details on *soirées* and various discounts.

✦ ⓜBlanche Sarl. Face the Moulin Rouge and walk 5 blocks up rue Lepic. Turn right onto rue des Abbesses. Rue Aristide Bruant is the 1st right. *i* Breakfast included. Free Wi-Fi and computer use. ⓢ Dorms €25; doubles €60; triples €90. ⌚ Lockout 10am-3pm.

LE MONTCLAIR HOSTEL
HOSTEL $$

62 rue Ramey ☎01 46 06 46 07; www.montclair-hostel.com

Complete with funky striped walls, a foosball table, and vending machines, Le Montclair is a standard young and hip hostel. Clean dormitories have shared bathrooms, but Montclair offers doubles with either a shower or full bath for those looking for more privacy.

✦ ⓜJules Joffrin. Follow rue Ordener and turn right onto rue Hermel and rue Ramney is the 1st left. *i* Breakfast included. Computer €1.50 per 30min., €2.50 per hr. ⓢ Dorms €29, with full bath €35; doubles €76, with toilet €80, with full bath €88. ⌚ Lockout 10am-3pm.

EASTERN PARIS

This area is devoid of tourist accommodations, and its not a place you want to be stumbling home to after bar hopping. The places below are decent, but be sure to call a cab if you indulge too much on your night out. You shouldn't stay this far out unless you want to be near the **Gare Routière International.**

AUBERGE DE JEUNESSE "LE D'ARTAGNAN"

HOSTEL $

80 rue Vitruve ☎01 40 32 34 56; www.fuaj.org

A healthy walk from the Metro and a stone's throw from the Cimetière du Père Lachaise, this is everything you'd expect from FUAJ: clean rooms (around 440 beds), a bar, a majority of French or non-anglophone clients, and a totally relaxed atmosphere. Mingle with French transients and pregame at the bar before heading out.

✦ ⓜPorte de Bagnolet. Exit onto bd Davout and take the first right onto rue Vitruve. The hostel is on the left. *i* Breakfast included. Lockers €2-4 per day. Wi-Fi €2 per hr. Reserve online. ⓢ Beds from €27. Discounts for International Youth Hostels Association members. ⓩ Lockout noon-3pm. Max. stay 4 nights.

sights

For those who aren't *Let's Go* researchers, seeing everything in Paris is exhausting if not impossible (even we struggled a bit). For a short trip, visiting the main attractions can mean waiting in lines, feeling the urge to add the annoying couple in front of you to the body count at the Catacombs, and becoming completely desensitized to some of mankind's greatest feats of engineering and art. Give yourself a break. Before heading off to see something because you saw it on a postcard, check this section for what's really worth it. Some of Paris's most interesting sights are devoid of tourists. To save money and give yourself a more authentic Parisian experience, picnic in a park that once housed a palace; go to a less famous museum when the line for the Louvre is more than the flight time to CDG; and realize that some of the best (and cheapest) history lessons are found in the city's churches, squares, and public landmarks. When you can appreciate the small things, the Louvre and the Eiffel Tower will be even more awe-inspiring.

ÎLE DE LA CITÉ AND ÎLE ST-LOUIS

Île de la Cité is a pressure cooker of tourists and sights. It's home to two of Paris's oldest and most famous churches and its oldest-running hospital, where you can stroll the gardens for free. On the smaller Île St-Louis, the sights and tourists thin out, but it's still worth a stroll to check out the art galleries, ice cream parlors, and some eateries where you can find locals who have been there since before WWII.

🏛 NOTRE DAME

CATHEDRAL

Île de la Cité ☎01 53 10 07 00

Centuries before it witnessed Quasimodo's attempts to rescue Esmeralda, Notre Dame was the site of a Roman temple to Jupiter. Having decided that a pagan temple would be a good place for some Catholic infusion, Rome began building churches, the last of which was Notre Dame in 1163. Taking a liking to the high Gothic ceilings and explosion of color from the large stained-glass windows, the French nobility claimed it for most of their weddings (we can only assume Maui was booked at the time.) Among those who took their vows were François II to Mary Queen of Scots and Henri of Navarre to Marguerite de Valois. On the other side of the happiness spectrum, this is also where **Joan of Arc** was tried for heresy. She was only 19 at the time of her trial and subsequent barbecue. To make up for that tiny injustice, she was made a patron saint of France (after almost 500 years) and has her own shrine next to the Treasury.

The revolution had the same effect on Paris, and especially Notre Dame, as a drunken weekend in Vegas has on the individual. Everyone woke up five years later to discover that Notre Dame had been renamed the Temple of Reason and covered with a Neoclassical facade. It was later reconsecrated and served as the site of **Napoleon's** famed coronation in 1804. However, the building fell into disrepair, and for two decades it was used to shelter livestock. **Victor Hugo** cleared away the donkeys and pigs when he wrote his famed novel *The Hunchback of Notre Dame* in 1831, which revived the cathedral's popularity and inspired Disney to introduce the French idea of "gypsycide" to children all over the world. Restorations (read: major changes) by **Eugène Viollet-le-Duc** included a third tower, gargoyles, and a statue of himself admiring his work. Most of the 20th century included more praying against German invasion (we know how that ended up) and famous masses for the funerals of both Charles de Gaulle and François Mitterrand.

If you've read this far, stay with us for a little longer. Here is what you need to see and do when visiting Notre Dame. First, as you enter, notice the headless figures above the doors. Revolutionaries thought that the King of Judah was somehow related to the French monarch (he's not) and decapitated him. From the entrance, you'll see massive crowds. Keep to the right and follow the arrows past Joan of Arc to the Treasury, where you can see Napoleon's sweet emperor cloak as well as relics like St. Louis's tunic. Jesus's thorny crown rests here too, but it's only revealed on the first Friday of the month at 3pm. Round the church and get a good look of the stained-glass window in the back and the altar from the priest's point of view. For the towers, you'll have to brave a line that only lets in 20 people at a time and a 422-step climb to the bell towers to take in the views of the Latin Quarter and the Marais. The *crème de la crème* is the 13-ton bell in the South Tower that requires eight men—or one hunchback—to ring.

✚ ⓂCité. Ⓢ Free. Audio tour €5, includes treasury visit. Treasury €3, ages 12-25 €2, 5-11 €1. ⓩ *Cathedral open daily 7:45am-6:45pm. Towers open daily 10am-5:30pm, last entry 4:45pm. Free tours in French M-F 2 and 3pm; English W-Th 2pm, Sa 2:30pm. Treasury open M-Sa 9:30am-6pm, Su 1:30-5:30pm; last entry 15min. before close. Su mass 8:30am (French), 10am (Gregorian Chants), 11:45am (international i.e. easy French with some English thrown in), 12:45pm, and 6:30pm.*

🏛 SAINTE-CHAPELLE

CHURCH

6 bd du Palais   ☎01 53 40 60 97; www.monuments-nationaux.fr

Everybody needs the occasional diversion to get through a service. Take the 13th-century equivalent of TVs in church: the stunning floor-to-ceiling stained-glass windows in the **Upper Chapel** of Sainte-Chapelle, illuminating dreamscapes of no fewer than 1113 individual Biblical stories. They really tried, but you just can't squeeze that many depictions onto stained glass and make it understandable without a priest (or tour guide) explaining each one. The easiest to make out is the Passion of the Christ, located at the apex of the Chapel. Originally designed to house the Crown of Thorns and an actual piece of the crucifix, Sainte-Chapelle has a good reason for its smaller size: most of the budget was blown on the crown itself, purchased for the ungodly sum of UKE135,000 (adjust that puppy for about 800 years of inflation). They lost out anyway, since the crown now resides in Notre Dame. The **Lower Chapel** has a blue vaulted ceiling dotted with the golden symbol of the French monarchy, the *fleurs-de-lis*, and contains a few "treasures"—platter-sized portraits of saints. This was where mortals served God, while royalty got to get a little closer in the Upper Chapel.

✚ ⓂCité. Within Palais de la Cité. Ⓢ €8, ages 18-25 €5, under 18 free. Twin ticket with Conciergerie €11, ages 18-25 €7.50, under 18 free. ⓩ Open daily Mar-Oct 9:30am-6pm; Nov-Feb 9am-5pm. Last entry 30min. before close. Guided tours in French 11am, 3, and 4:40pm; in English 3:30pm.

sights

HÔTEL-DIEU

BUILDING, HOSPITAL

1 pl. Parvis Notre-Dame   ☎01 42 34 82 34

Upon realizing that it might be helpful to save actual people in addition to their Christian souls (this was the Dark Ages, it was a pretty revolutionary idea), Bishop St. Landry built this hospital in 651 CE. If you're wondering why you want to visit a hospital, we would probably share your skepticism. However, the open-air colonnade and impeccably kept gardens are open to the public and are worth a look for multiple examples of irony, including memorial plaques to Louis Pasteur (in a country that doesn't pasteurize most of its milk and cheese) or doctors and nurses using the garden as a smoking lounge.

⚤ ⓜCité. Ⓢ Free. ☼ Open M-F 8am-8pm, Sa-Su 10am-5pm.

MÉMORIAL DES MARTYRS DE LA DÉPORTATION

HOLOCAUST MEMORIAL

Hidden away at the east end of the Île de la Cité, this small, concrete, incredibly depressing monument pays tribute to the French citizens deported to concentration camps during WWII. A flight of narrow concrete stairs leads you to a sunken platform, from which the high, spiked gates resemble those of the concentration camps. Inside the memorial, you see a long tunnel of 200,000 lit quartz pebbles, that represent each of the French citizens killed. Famous quotes are carved into the walls of the memorial, the most arresting of which is at the exit: *"Pardonne. N'oublie Pas"* ("Forgive. Do Not Forget").

⚤ ⓜCité. At the eastern tip of the Île de la Cité, on quai de l'Archevêché. A 5min. walk from the back of Notre Dame cathedral and down a narrow flight of steps. Ⓢ Free. ☼ Open Tu-Su 10am-noon and 2-7pm. Last entry 11:45am and 6:30pm.

PALAIS DE JUSTICE

COURTHOUSE

4 bd du Palais   ☎01 44 32 51 51

The Palais has witnessed the German spy Mata Hari's death sentence, Sarah Bernhardt's divorce from the Comédie Française, and Alfred Dreyfus's guilty verdict and subsequent declaration of innocence. Learning from the Joan of Arc mistake of the past, the court managed to declare Dreyfus innocent while he was still alive, but only after 12 years of solitary confinement on the hard-labor penal colony Devil's Island. While the courtrooms and legal consultants are open to the public, "public" does not mean foreigners. For those without an EU passport, you'll have to settle for the massive 1760 sq. m colonnade **Conciergerie,** through which every prisoner with a death sentence was marched (when they still did that). You can gain entry through a joint ticket with Sainte-Chapelle.

⚤ ⓜCité. Within Palais de la Cité. Ⓢ Conciergerie and Sainte-Chapelle €11, ages 18-25 €7.50, under 18 free. ☼ Open daily Mar-Oct 9:30am-6pm; Nov-Feb 9am-5pm. Last entry 30min. before close.

PONT NEUF

BRIDGE

Though its name might suggest otherwise, the bridge cutting through the western tip of Île de la Cité is the oldest in Paris. Completed in 1607, it would have been the busiest street in Paris for tourists in the 17th century. Today the bridge is lined with lip-locked lovers, seated in the many romantic enclaves overlooking the Seine. That's about it, though: youthful romance and the occasional gargoyle (which you can find at just about every Gothic building in Paris) are all that Point Neuf has to offer nowadays.

⚤ ⓜPont Neuf.

CHÂTELET-LES HALLES

Châtelet-Les Halles is perhaps Paris's densest tourist area, and that's saying something. From the commercial indulgence of the pl. Vendôme to the mind-numbing grandeur of the Louvre to the bizarre trends on display at the Musée des Arts Décoratifs, the 1er and 2ème have it all.

🏛 MUSÉE DU LOUVRE   MUSEUM
rue de Rivoli   ☎01 40 20 53 17; www.louvre.fr

Try as you might, it's impossible to see everything in the Louvre. The museum's miles (yes, miles) of galleries stretch seemingly without end, and their collections span thousands of years, six continents, countless artistic styles, and a vast range of media. It's no wonder that the Louvre sees an average 8.5 million visitors per year. Like most of Paris's spectacular sights, the Louvre was initially commissioned by kings and intended as a tribute to... themselves. Thinking that those tributes should be shared with everyone, revolutionaries made the museum permanent after kindly asking the monarchy to leave. Napoleon filled the Louvre with plundered goods from just about everywhere he went, and its massive bankroll has allowed the museum to continue acquiring pieces that make Jean Paul Getty look like a stamp collector. Successful trips to the Louvre require two things: a good sense of direction and a great plan of attack. If you're looking for detailed tours, the Louvre's website describes several thematic trails you can follow.

The museum sprawls four floors and three main wings: **Sully, Richelieu,** and **Denon.** To make this easier for you, we'll give you the breakdown of the floors, as the wings really have nothing in common other than to tell you where you are. The basement is where you'll be shuffled to buy tickets and make the daunting selection of which wing to enter first. Here you'll see the medieval foundations of the Louvre as well as its history, which reads like a European History 101 textbook. Appropriately, this is where some of the Louvre's oldest pieces are stored, which include sculptures from the 10th and 11th centuries and the first items from the Egyptian collection.

The **ground floor** houses some of the works that people flock to Paris to see. The *Venus de Milo* is in room 16 in the Sully wing, while the *Law Code of Hammurabi* is stored with the Near Eastern Antiquities in Room 3 of Richelieu. You can find the full extent of the Egyptian collection as well as Greek and Roman sculpture sprawled out on this level.

The biggest crowds are located on the **first floor,** and rightfully so. The most impressive halls of the museum are rooms 77 and 75 in the Denon wing, which house Théodore Géricault's *Raft of the Medusa,* Eugène Delacroix's *Liberty Leading the People,* Jacques-Louis David's *Coronation of Napoleon,* and Paolo Veronese's *The Wedding at Cana.* These paintings are all gigantic, which makes the crowds seem less of a hassle, as everyone can get a good view. We wish we could say the same for Leonardo's **Mona Lisa** (*La Jaconde* for those of you who like to sound lofty and enlightened). The tiny painting has an entire wall to itself, and there is almost always a crowd surrounding it. In the Richelieu wing, the museum has more Jesus-inspired paintings from the Renaissance as well as Napoleon III's fully furnished apartments.

On the **second floor,** only Sully and Richelieu are accessible. In Sully, all of the rooms are filled with French paintings that typically require some background study in art history to fully appreciate. Richelieu is filled with student groups and more obscure tours checking out the remaining Belgian, Dutch, German, Russian, and Scandinavian paintings. These are pretty to look at, but you may be better off spending a little more time getting friendly with your favorites from earlier. At the Louvre, unless you're planning on bunking up next to the *Venus de*

Milo, seeing everything is impossible. Just getting a glimpse of what's in front of you, though, is a pretty good start.

⚓ Ⓜ*Palais Royal–Musée du Louvre.* *i* The Carte Louvre Jeunes entitles the owner to 1 year unlimited access without waiting in line and free access for the owner and a guest W and F after 6pm. Ⓢ €10, under 18 and EU citizens ages 18-25 free. Special exhibits €11. Combined ticket €14. Carte Louvre Jeunes ages 18-25 €15, 26-29 €30. 1st Su of every month (does not include special exhibits) free. F after 6pm free for under 26 of all nationalities. Audio tour €6, under 18 €2. ☒ Open M 9am-6pm, W 9am-10pm, Th 9am-6pm, F 9am-10pm, Sa-Su 9am-6pm. Last entry 45min. before close; rooms begin to close 30min. before museum. "Discovery trails" tours in English, French, or Spanish daily 11am, 2, and 3:45pm; sign up at the info desk.

poor francis

Francis I wasn't the most successful king. He faied to become the Holy Roman Emperor, lost a series of wars in Italy, and was captured by the actual Holy Roman Emperor. He was held in Madrid until he agreed to sign over all claims to Milan and Naples and hand over his two sons as payment for the ransom. Having done this, he returned to his comfy Palais du Louvre, only to invade Italy again and again until he ran out of money. Perhaps his only success was picking up a portrait for the palace during his conquests: The *Mona Lisa.* You win some, you (mostly) lose some.

🏛 JARDIN DES TUILERIES   GARDEN
pl. de la Concorde, rue de Rivoli

Covering the distance from the Louvre to the pl. de la Concorde, the Tuileries are a favorite of tourists during the summer and Parisians when there aren't too many tourists to scare them off (read: annoy them). In the tradition of matching garden size to house size, the Tuileries are a massive complex of hedges, trees, and a very large fountain. Originally built for Catherine de' Medici, the garden was modeled after her native Florence to make her feel more at home—or to take her mind off the fact that her husband, Henry II, was much more infatuated with his mistress. The gardens grew as each successive king added something to call his own. Today, the Tuileries are filled with food stands, merry-go-rounds, and a huge ferris wheel near the rue de Rivoli entrance, quite different from the Tuscan sanctuary Henry imagined.

⚓ Ⓜ*Tuileries.* Ⓢ Free. ☒ Open daily June-Aug 7am-11pm; Sept 7am-9pm; Oct-Mar 7:30am-7:30pm; Apr-May 7am-9pm. Amusement park open June to mid-Aug.

🏛 ÉGLISE SAINT-EUSTACHE   CHURCH
2 rue du Jour   ☎01 42 36 31 05; www.saint-eustache.org

What do Cardinal Richelieu, Molière, Louis XIV, and Mme. de Pompadour have in common? Église St-Eustache is where each of them was baptised. As a result of some poor fundraising (surprising, since their marketing plan was to tax baskets of fish from the market at Les Halles), the church took over a century to build. You can still see the impact of this dearth of funds on its two towers, one of which is complete while the other is nothing more than a stump. The interior houses a pipe organ larger than that of Notre Dame, paintings by Peter Paul Rubens, and a silver sculpture dedicated to the victims of the AIDS epidemic. Église St-Eustache sees few tourists, allowing the intrepid few to enjoy the silence and grandeur of the 34m vaulted Gothic ceilings.

⚓ Ⓜ*Les Halles.* *i* Audio tours available in English, ID required. Ⓢ Free. Audio tour suggested donation €3. ☒ Open M-F 9:30am-7pm, Sa 10am-7pm, Su 9am-7pm. Mass Sa 6pm; Su 9:30, 11am, 6pm.

MUSÉE DE L'ORANGERIE

MUSEUM

Jardin des Tuileries

☎01 44 77 80 07; www.musee-orangerie.fr

Once the greenhouse of the Jardin des Tuileries, l'Orangerie opened as a museum in 1927. Today, it displays works by Impressionist and post-Impressionist painters including Monet, Matisse, Picasso, and Renoir. Since its conversion into a museum, L'Orangerie has become home to Monet's *Water Lilies* and received the collection of renowned art collector Paul Guillaume in the 1960s. This impressive list probably explains why it's impossible to enter the museum without waiting in line, even on weekdays. On weekends the wait can last up to 2hr. Show up at 9am or on Free Sunday (the first Sunday of every month) if you don't want to roast in the sun for most of the day. If you're okay with a quick visit, the admission fee is reduced for the last hour it's open.

⇄ Ⓜ︎Concorde. $ €7.50, students and after 5pm €5. Combined ticket with Musée d'Orsay €13. Free 1st Su every month. ⏰ Open M 9am-6pm, W-Su 9am-6pm.

MUSÉE DES ARTS DÉCORATIFS

MUSEUM

107 rue de Rivoli

☎01 44 55 57 50; www.lesartsdecoratifs.fr

Fashion-conscious Francophiles could easily spend a full day perusing the Musée des Arts Decoratifs. The complex is comprised of three different museums in addition to many smaller exhibits. **Arts Décoratifs** (Interior Design), **Mode et Textile** (Fashion and Fabric), and **Publicité** (Advertisement) are all dedicated to *haute couture* designs that the average tourist has probably never experienced. In the Arts Décoratifs, you'll find sheep-shaped chairs, elephant-shaped fountains, and chairs whittled into birds. The Mode et Textile has exhibits on the evolution of fashion from the '70s to the '90s and features small exhibits on prominent fashion designers, including Yves Saint Laurent. The jewelry collection, **Galerie des Bijoux,** will make anyone's engagement ring look embarrassing.

⇄ Ⓜ︎Palais Royal-Musée du Louvre. $ All 3 museums €9, ages 18-25 €7.50, under 18 and EU citizens 18-25 free. ⏰ Open Tu-W 11am-6pm, Th 11am-9pm, F-Su 11am-6pm. Last entry 30min. before close.

PALAIS-ROYAL

PALACE

25 rue de Valois

☎01 49 27 09 09

This palace has a history plagued with death, bad luck, and low funding. Cardinal Richelieu, who commissioned it, died the same year it was completed. Queen of England Henrietta Maria called the palace home after being kicked out of her own country for being Catholic. (The French reaction to her showing up was apparently "You're Catholic? Move into this palace!") Finally, in 1781, the broke Duke of Orléans had to rent out the space to raise money. It's a place to wander and window-shop, while the interior is occupied by government offices.

⇄ Ⓜ︎Palais Royal-Musée du Louvre. $ Free. ⏰ Fountain, galleries, and garden open daily June-Aug 7am-11pm; Sept 7am-9:30pm; Oct-Mar 7:30am-8:30pm; Apr-May 7am-10:15pm.

THE MARAIS

You'll see more here than just strolling rabbis and strutting fashionistas. The eastern section of the arrondissement is a labyrinth of old, quaint streets dotted with churches and some of Paris's most beautiful mansions (particularly around the **place des Vosges**). The **Centre Pompidou,** the Marais's main attraction, breaks up the beige monotony in the western half (or maybe it's just a tourist eyesore—ask any Frenchman). Though the Pompidou, quite like a spoiled child, steals the show, there are a number of other museums that are just as entertaining. If you aren't the museum-going type, **rue Vieille du Temple** and **rue des Rosiers** are great streets to explore.

✪ CENTRE POMPIDOU

MUSEUM, LIBRARY

pl. Georges Pompidou, rue Beaubourg

☎01 44 78 12 33; www.centrepompidou.fr

Though describing the exterior of the Pompidou in words is almost impossible, we'll give it a shot: the exterior of the Pompidou features a network of yellow electrical tubes, green water pipes, and blue ventilation ducts. You have to see it to really get it. The center's functions are as varied as its colors: it serves as a sort of cultural theme park of ultra-modern exhibition, performance, and research space. It is home to the famous **Musée National d'Art Moderne**, whose collection spans the 20th century. TVs display what can be characterized as Andy Warhol's drug-induced visions alongside amorphous tie-dye colored statues, a giant mushroom, and a wall of globes with layered tape to represent the cancerous growth of wars and violence. The second floor features pre-1960s art with less provocative pieces but just as famous names: Duchamp, Picasso, and Miró. Temporary exhibits on international modern art fill the top floors. Other parts of the complex to explore include **Salle Garance,** which runs an adventurous film series; **Bibliothèque Publique d'Information,** a free, noncirculating library; **Institut de la Recherche de la Coordination Acoustique/Musique (IRCAM),** an institute and laboratory for the development of new technology; and the rooftop restaurant, **Georges.**

✠ ⓂRambuteau or Hôtel de Ville. Ⓢ Museum €12, under 26 €9, under 18 and EU citizens ages 18-25 free. Library and forum free. ☼ Center open M 11am-9pm, W-Su 11am-9pm. Museum open M 11am-8:50pm, W 11am-8:50pm, Th 11am-11pm, F-Su 11am-8:50pm. Last entry 1hr. before close. Library open M noon-10pm, W-F noon-10pm, Sa-Su 11am-10pm.

🎨 MUSÉE CARNAVALET   MUSEUM
23 rue de Sévigné   ☎01 44 59 58 58; www.carnavalet.paris.fr

Located in Mme. de Sévigné's beautiful 16th-century *hôtel particulier* and the neighboring Hôtel Le Peletier de St-Fargeau, this meticulously arranged and engaging museum traces Paris's history from its origins to Napoleon III. The city's urban development is conveyed through paintings, furniture, and sculptural fragments. Highlights include Marcel Proust's fully reconstructed bedroom and a piece of the Bastille prison wall. (We tried, but shouting *"Vive la Revolution!"* doesn't entitle you to touch it.)

✠ ⓂChemin Vert. Take rue St-Gilles, which becomes rue du Parc Royal, and turn left onto rue de Sévigné. Ⓢ Free. ☼ Open Tu-Su 10am-6pm. Last entry 5:15pm.

🎨 MUSÉE DE LA CHASSE ET DE LA NATURE   MUSEUM
62 rue des Archives   ☎01 48 87 40 36; www.chassenature.org

The collection may be quirky, but it's sure to elicit some sort of response—whether it's fascination or disgust. The museum displays hunting-themed art, weaponry, and stuffed animals from several continents in lavish, elegantly arranged rooms that would bring a tear to Allan Quatermain's eye. While the Trophy Room is the most impressive section of the museum, it's basically a what's what of endangered species, the most arresting of which are a polar bear on its hind legs and a pair of cheetahs in a glass case.

✠ ⓂRambuteau. Walk against traffic on rue Beaubourg, turn right onto rue Michel le Comte, and left onto rue des Archives. Ⓢ €6, ages 18-25 and seniors €4.50, under 18 free. 1st Su of each month free. ☼ Open Tu-Su 11am-6pm.

🎨 PLACE DES VOSGES   PARK
Paris's oldest and perhaps snootiest public square has served many generations of residents, from the knights who clashed swords in medieval tournaments to the hipsters who swap bottles during picnics today. All 36 buildings that line the square were constructed by Baptiste du Cerceau in the same architectural style; look for pink brick, slate roofs, and street-level arcades. The quaint atmosphere attracted **Cardinal Richelieu** (who lived at no. 21 when he wasn't busy mad-dogging musketeers), writer **Alphonse Daudet** (who lived at no. 8), and **Victor Hugo** (no. 6). It was also the venue for one of seven-year-old prodigy **Mozart's** concerts, inspiring every "My Child is an Honor Student" bumper sticker. Come here to people-watch, nap in the grass, and wish you were friends with Molière or Voltaire.

✠ ⓂSt-Paul or Bastille. Follow rue St-Antoine and turn onto rue de Birague.

MAISON DE VICTOR HUGO

MUSEUM

6 pl. des Vosges　　　　　　　　☎01 42 72 10 16; www.musee-hugo.paris.fr

Dedicated to the father of French Romanticism and housed in the building where he lived from 1832 to 1848, the museum displays memorabilia from his pre-exile, exile, and post-exile days, including his family's little-known paintings and the desk where he wrote standing up. On the first floor, the collection reveals paintings of scenes from *Les Misérables* and other works. Upstairs, you'll find Hugo's apartments; a recreation of the bedroom where he died; and the *chambre chinoise*, which reveals his flamboyant interior decorating skills and just how romantic he really was.

✠ ⓂSt-Paul or Bastille. Follow rue St-Antoine and turn onto rue de Birague. Ⓢ Free. Special exhibits €7-8, seniors €5, under 26 €3.50-4. Audio tour €5. ◷ Open Tu-Su 10am-6pm. Last entry 5:40pm.

MUSÉE D'ART ET D'HISTOIRE DU JUDAÏSME

MUSEUM

71 rue Vieille du Temple　　　　　　☎01 53 01 86 53; www.mahj.org

Displaying a very select portion of Jewish history in Europe and North Africa, with a focus on community traditions throughout the Diaspora, the Musée d'Art et d'Histoire du Judaïsme begins with the cut-and-dry aspect of circumcision (apparently Abraham did it to himself at the age of 99—that's commitment). Modern testimonials on Jewish identity are interspersed with exquisite ancient relics. While they have extensive collections of art and relics looted by the Nazis from Jewish homes, don't expect to learn anything about the horror of the Vélodrome d'hiver. History buffs, prepare to be appalled.

✠ ⓂRambuteau. From the Metro, turn right onto rue Rambuteau, and then left onto rue Vieille du Temple. Ⓢ €6.80, ages 18-26 €4.50, under 18 and art students free. Special exhibits €5.50, ages 18-26 €4. Combined ticket €8.50/6. Guided tours €9/6.50. ◷ Open M-F 11am-6pm, Su 10am-6pm. Last entry 5:30pm.

sights

you say you want a revolution?

Paris was the center of one of the most violent and bloody revolutions in history. Here are some key revolutionary sites that can still (sort of) be seen today.

- **CAFE DE FOY:** Appropriately located in front of the Palais-Royal in the center of the city, this was where Camille Desmoulins supposedly sparked the first revolt, ending a speech against Louis XVI with the call "Aux armes!" If only your valedictorian speech stirred up that much commotion.

- **BASTILLE:** Thanks to its storming and subsequent destruction, the infamous fortress isn't there anymore. If you're lucky, there might be a carnival in the open *place* where the mighty armory once stood, where rioting Parisians freed a grand total of seven innocent civilians from tyrannical and unjust imprisonment in 1789.

- **TUILERIES:** This palace was also destroyed, but not by angry peasants. It was purposefully burned down in 1871 during the suppression of the Paris Commune. In its place is a huge garden where you can try to picture Marie Antoinette crying after she was forced here from the Palais du Versailles.

LATIN QUARTER AND ST-GERMAIN

Sights, sights, and more sights. There's more to see in the 5ème and 6ème than there is time to do it in. If you're only in Paris for a short while, there are a few things you can't miss. The **Jardin du Luxembourg** is magnificent and, alongside the Tuileries, one of the best relaxation spots in Paris. If you want museums with more than just paintings and sculptures, the **Musée National du Moyen Âge** and the massive **Museum of Natural History** are two of Paris's most important collections. If you're the artsy type, don't miss the slew of galleries in the **Odéon/Mabillon** area. And if you're in the mood to walk in the footsteps of Jean-Paul Sartre, Simone de Beauvoir, and Ernest Hemingway, make sure to visit **Saint-Germain-des-Prés** and **Shakespeare and Co. Bookstore.**

[✓] PANTHÉON — HISTORIC MONUMENT, CRYPT

pl. du Panthéon ☎01 44 32 18 04; http://pantheon.monuments-nationaux.fr

If there's one building that doesn't know the meaning of antidisestablishmentarianism, it's the Panthéon. Because the Neoclassical building went back and forth between a church and a "secular mausoleum" over the years, it contains some surprising gravemates. Within the crypt, tombs alternate between Christian heroes such as St. Louis and Enlightenment thinkers like Voltaire, who would probably object to being placed so close to icons of church dogma. What's worse, both Foucault's pendulum and revolutionary statues lie above the remains of Joan of Arc and St. Geneviève. The trip up the dome has three stops with 360-degree views of the Marais and Latin Quarter, and you can meander the colonnade at the top for the allotted 10min. before being herded back down.

*‡ Ⓜ Cardinal Lemoine. Head away from the river on rue du Cardinal Lemoine and turn right onto rue Clovis. Walk until you reach pl. du Panthéon. **i** Dome visits Apr-Oct in Dutch, English, French, German, Russian, and Spanish. $ €8, ages 18-25 €5, under 18 free. Oct-Mar 1st Su of each month free. 🕐 Open daily Apr-Sept 10am-6:30pm; Oct-Mar 10am-6pm. Last entry 45min. before close.*

[✓] LE JARDIN DU LUXEMBOURG — GARDEN

Main entrance on bd St-Michel

As with most ornate things in Paris, these gardens used to be exclusively for royalty. When the great expropriation occurred around 1789, the fountains, statues, rose gardens, and well-kept hedges were opened to the public, ensuring a quick picnic spot for every student in the Latin Quarter and St-Germain. The Palais is still off-limits, but the best and most sought-after spot in the garden is the **Fontaine des Médicis,** a vine-covered grotto east of the Palais complete with a murky fish pond and Baroque fountain sculptures.

*‡ Ⓜ Odéon or RER B: Luxembourg. **i** Guided tours in French Apr-Oct 1st W of each month 9:30am. Tours start at pl. André Honnorat behind the observatory. $ Free. 🕐 Open daily in summer from 7am to 1hr. before sunset; in winter from 8am to 1hr. before sunset.*

MUSÉE NATIONAL DU MOYEN ÂGE (MUSÉE DE CLUNY) — MUSEUM

6 pl. Paul Painlevé ☎01 53 73 78 00; www.musee-moyenage.fr

Originally occupied by Gallo-Roman baths and then by the 15th-century Hotel of the Abbots of Cluny, the Musée National du Moyen Âge sits on one of the prime pieces of historic real estate in Paris. The main attraction, *La Dame à la Licorne*, is a collection of tapestries featuring every little girl's dream pet: the unicorn. The horned animal paradoxically represented both a Christ figure and a profane abomination, depending on how it was depicted through the ages. In addition to making you nostalgic for My Little Pony, the museum hosts many exhibitions, including one on medieval sword fighting.

*‡ Ⓜ Cluny-La Sorbonne. Walk up bd St-Michel and turn left onto rue du Cluny. **i** Audio tour included. $ €8, ages 18-25 €6, EU citizens under 26 free. 1st Su of the month free. 🕐 Open M 9:15am-5:45pm, W-Su 9:15am-5:45pm. Last entry 5:15pm.*

JARDIN DES PLANTES — GARDEN, MUSEUM, ZOO

57 rue Cuvier ☎01 40 79 30 00; www.mnhn.fr

This one is a doozy. Within the Jardin des Plantes, you can find a whopping five museums, a garden, and a zoo. The **Museum of Natural History,** divided into three separate institutions, is housed here. Of its constituent parts, the four-floor

Grande Galerie d'Évolution is the best; while not striking in and of itself, it looks better alongside its positively horrible comrades. The exhibit illustrates evolution with a series of stuffed animals (Curious George not included) and numerous multimedia tools. Next door, the **Musée de Minéralogie** displays rubies, sapphires, and other minerals. The **Galeries d'Anatomie Comparée et de Paléontologie** are at the other end of the garden. Inside is a ghastly cavalcade of femurs, ribcages, and vertebrae from prehistoric animals (all the ingredients to create your own Frankenstein). Despite some snazzy new placards, the place doesn't seem to have changed much since it opened in 1898; it's almost more notable as a museum of 19th-century grotesquerie than as a catalogue of anatomy. The largest part of the garden is taken up by the **menagerie,** which houses an impressive reptile terrarium as well as a huge ape house with orangutans.

✠ Ⓜ*Jussieu.* Ⓢ *Musée de Minéralogie €8, students under 26 €6. Galeries d'Anatomie Comparée et de Paléontologie €7, under 26 free. Grande Galerie de l'Évolution €7, students under 26 free. 2-day passes for the 3 museums and the menagerie €25.* 🕐 *Museums open W-Su 10am-5pm. Last entry for all museums 4:15pm.*

SHAKESPEARE AND CO. BOOKSTORE
BOOKSTORE

37 rue de la Bûcherie   ☎01 43 25 40 93; www.shakespeareandcompany.com

Sylvia Beach's original Shakespeare and Co. at 8 rue Dupuytren (later at 12 rue de l'Odéon) is legendary among Parisian Anglophones and American literature nerds alike. An alcoholic expat crew of writers gathered here in the '20s; Hemingway described the bookstore in *A Moveable Feast.* After closing during WWII, George Whitman—no relation to Walt—opened the current ragtag bookstore on the shores of the Seine in 1951, dubbing it "a socialist utopia masquerading as a bookstore." You're free to grab a book off the shelves, camp out, and start reading. This isn't your run-of-the-mill, money-machine bookstore; they're in it for the love of the game.

✠ Ⓜ*St-Michel. Take quai de Montebello toward Notre Dame and turn right onto rue St-Jacques. Rue de la Bûcherie is on the left.* 🕐 *Open daily 10am-11pm.*

ÉGLISE SAINT-GERMAIN-DES-PRÉS
CHURCH

3 pl. St-Germain-des-Prés   ☎01 55 42 81 33; www.eglise-sgp.org

The Église St-Germain-des-Prés is the oldest church in Paris, and it shows. A popular place to store loot from the Holy Land, this church was sacked by the Normans and was the trial run for revolutionaries looking to hone their storming abilities before the Bastille. Apparently this didn't send a strong enough message the first time, so the revolutionaries returned in 1792 to kill 186 priests (it probably wasn't fairest fight). The abuse continued after, with someone missing the "No Smoking" sign next to 15 tons of gunpowder in 1794, and the church suffered complete devastation when urban planner Georges-Eugène Haussmann extended rue des Rennes in the 1850s, tearing down what was left of the abbey. It has since been refurbished with frescoes, mosaics, and, oddly enough, the interred heart of René Descartes.

✠ Ⓜ*St-Germain-des-Prés.* Ⓢ *Free.* 🕐 *Open daily 8am-7:45pm. Information office open M 2:30-6:45pm, Tu-F 10:30am-noon and 2:30-6:45pm, Sa 3-6:45pm.*

RUE MOUFFETARD
HISTORICAL NEIGHBORHOOD

The 5ème's rue Mouffetard hosts one of Paris's oldest and liveliest street markets in addition to stretches of food vendors. Local English-speaking students lovingly refer to a night on rue Mouffetard as "getting Mouffe-tarded"—it's good to see that the *bon vivant* lifestyle of Hemingway (who used to live nearby) continues today. With endless alternating kebab stands and cheap bars, you can keep drinking until you wake up where you never had plans to sleep.

✠ Ⓜ*Cardinal Lemoine, Place Monge, or Censier-Daubenton.* 𝒊 *Market open Tu-Su in the morning.*

LA FONTAINE DE SAINT-SULPICE

HISTORIC MONUMENT

pl. St-Sulpice

Situated adjacent to the church in the middle of the pl. St-Sulpice, this fountain by sculptor Louis Visconti is often known as *La Fountaine des Quatre Points Cardinaux*. The rather bitter nickname is to deride the four ambitious bishops—Bossuet, Fénelon, Massillon, and Fléchier—who grace its four sides. None of these men ever became cardinals. How hard you choose to mock them should be based on whether you think becoming a cardinal or being enshrined on a monumental fountain is a bigger achievement.

✠ ⓂSt-Sulpice.

found underground

Paris is a city of appearances, and this extends to the aesthetic effort that the city has put into decorating its Metro stations. With artful posters and complimentary graffiti, certain stops are tourist destinations themselves.

- **ABBESSES.** This Montmartre station has a winding staircase that lets the athletically inclined trek seven stories to the exit. Although there's an elevator, take the stairs to appreciate the mural depicting abstract scenes of Paris.

- **SAINT-GERMAIN-DES-PRÉS.** This station holds a collection of famous poetry books in glass cases. Not only that, projectors blow up quotes from French poets onto the walls, making for some higher quality reading during the morning commute than the usual tabloids.

- **CONCORDE.** This one's for people who love both history and Scrabble. The station has what looks like a gigantic word search, and the letters spell out the Declaration of the Rights of Man penned during the French Revolution.

- **ARTS ET MÉTIERS.** Redesigned in 1994 with inspiration from the Conservatory of Arts and Crafts Museum above, this stop looks like a submarine, complete with metallic walls and portholes. Don't forget your oxygen tank.

MUSÉE DELACROIX

MUSEUM

6 rue de Furstemberg   ☎01 44 41 86 50; www.musee-delacroix.fr

If you really like the Romantic era, you'll have a blast here. Painter Eugène Delacroix, the artistic master behind the famous *Liberty Leading the People* (which is actually housed in the Louvre), lived in this three-room apartment. It has since been turned into a museum filled with his watercolors, engravings, letters to Théophile Gautier and George Sand, sketches for his work in the Église St-Sulpice, and souvenirs from his journey to Morocco.

✠ ⓂSt-Germain-des-Prés. Walk toward Odéon and turn left onto rue Cardinale. The museum is straight ahead as the street bends left. *i* Free same-day entry with a Louvre ticket. ⑤ €5, students and under 18 free. ⏱ Open June-Aug M 9:30am-5pm, W-Su 9:30am-5:30pm; Sept-May M 9:30am-5pm, W-Su 9:30am-5pm. Last entry 30min. before close.

GRANDE MOSQUÉE DE PARIS

MUSEUM, MOSQUE

39 rue Geoffroy-St-Hilaire   ☎01 43 31 38 20; www.mosquees-de-paris.net

The Grande Mosquée de Paris was built in 1920 to honor the contributions of North African countries during WWI. Given the nature of the times, the North Africans had to build it themselves, but the French did at least finance the construction. While prayer and worship spaces are closed to the public, all visitors are welcome to wonder at the 33m minaret, sweat it out in the hammam's marble steam baths, and sip mint tea in the cafe.

paris

♯ Ⓜ*Censier-Daubenton.* Ⓢ *Guided tour €3, students €2. Hammam (steam bath), 10min. massage, and black tea €38.* ♨ *Cafe open daily 9am-11:30pm. Restaurant open daily noon-evening. Hammam open for women M 10am-9pm, W-Th 10am-9pm, F 2pm-9am, Sa 10am-9pm; open for men Tu 2-9pm, Su 10am-9pm.*

CAFE DE FLORE
172 bd St-Germain

HISTORIC CAFE
☎01 45 48 55 26

Legend has it that when Jean-Paul Sartre dined here, he and his friends (with benefits, if we're talking Simone de Beauvoir) sat opposite from communist Marguerite Duras and company. If the coffee at Fouquet's on the Champs-Élysées was too rich for your taste, you can get the Left Bank's version for almost half the cost and feel just as spiffy and a little bit more intellectual.

♯ Ⓜ*St-Germain-des-Prés.* Ⓢ *Coffee €4.10. Cocktail "Le Flore" €15.* ♨ *Open daily 7:30am-1:30am.*

LES DEUX MAGOTS
6 pl. St-Germain-des-Prés

HISTORIC CAFE
☎01 45 48 55 25

Attracting intellectuals and those who just like to be seen, Les Deux Magots was a lot cheaper back when Hemingway, Camus, and Picasso visited, which may have been why it almost went bankrupt in 1913. Today it's far from broke, although the coffee is 10 cents cheaper than at neighboring Le Café de Flore.

♯ Ⓜ*St-Germain-des-Prés.* Ⓢ *Coffee €4. Cocktails €13.* ♨ *Open daily 7:30am-1am.*

INVALIDES

Visit this arrondissement more than once if you can. Unsurprisingly, the Tour Eiffel towers over all of the 7ème attractions, but the posh neighborhood also hosts the French national government, a number of embassies, and an astonishing concentration of famous museums. Be sure to stop by the Musée Rodin and Musée d'Orsay.

▨ EIFFEL TOWER
Champs de Mars, closest to the Seine

TOWER
☎01 44 11 23 23; www.tour-eiffel.fr

In 1937, Gustave Eiffel said, "I ought to be jealous of that tower; she is more famous than I am." The city of Paris as a whole could share the same lament, especially since the Eiffel Tower has come to stand for Paris itself. Gustave Eiffel designed it to be the tallest structure in the world, intended to surpass the ancient Egyptian pyramids in size and notoriety. Apparently hard to impress, Parisian society continues to shrug in disappointment; the response they'll give is usually, "*c'est honteux*" (it's shameful). Despite the national love-hate relationship, over 150 million Parisians and (mostly) tourists have made it the most visited paid monument in the world, proving once again the French ability to make a fuss and do nothing about it.

Still, at 324m—just a tad shorter than New York City's Chrysler Building—the tower is a tremendous feat of design and engineering, though wind does cause it to occasionally sway 6 to 7cm (nobody's perfect). The unparalleled view from the top floor deserves a visit. The cheapest way to ascend the tower is by burning off those *pain au chocolat* calories on the world's tallest stairmaster, although the third floor is only accessible by elevator. Waiting until nightfall to make your ascent cuts down the line and ups the glamour. At the top, captioned aerial photographs help you locate other famous landmarks; on a clear day it is possible to see Chartres, 88km away. From dusk until 2am (Sept-May 1am) the tower sparkles with light for 10min. on the hour.

♯ Ⓜ*Bir-Hakeim or Trocadéro.* Ⓢ *Elevator to 2nd fl. €8.20, ages 12-24 €6.60, 4-11 and handicapped €4.10, under 4 free; elevator to top €13.40/11.80/9.30/free; stair entrance to 2nd fl. €4.70/3.70/3.20/free. Buy your ticket online and pick your time to climb and cut down the wait. Champagne bar on top, €10 per glass (don't say we didn't warn you).* ♨ *Elevator open daily June 17-Aug 28 9am-12:45pm; Aug 29-June 16 9:30am-11:45pm; last entry 45min. before close. Stairs open daily June 17-Aug 28 9am-12:45pm, last entry at midnight; Aug 29-June 16 9:30am-6:30pm, last entry 6pm.*

top 5 views in paris

- **EIFFEL TOWER:** You can see many of the city's famous landmarks from its deck. Buy a postcard and send it to your jealous friends from the post office on the first level of the Tower.

- **ARC DE TRIOMPHE:** See the perfect symmetry of av. des Champs-Élysées, the chaotic Paris traffic, and the majestic Eiffel Tower from the viewing platform on the top of the arch. This ancient monument has no elevator, so be prepared to climb more than 280 steps.

- **MONTMARTRE:** Walk or ride the funicular to the top of Montmartre for a panoramic view of Paris, the highest hill in the city. Try to visit at night to catch a view of Paris glowing in light.

- **TOUR MONTPARNASSE:** Take Europe's fastest elevator to the 56th floor of this modern skyscraper, where you will get an amazing view of the city through floor-to-ceiling windows. You can also walk three more floors for outdoor viewing on the roof.

- **NOTRE DAME DE PARIS:** Walking up nearly 400 steps to the top may be a challenge for the unfit, but the breathtaking view of the Seine and the Latin Quarter, as well as a closer look at the gargoyles, is sure to relieve the pain in your calves. No pain, no gain, right?

CHAMPS DE MARS   PARK

Lined with more lovers than trees, the expansive lawn that stretches from the École Militaire to the Eiffel Tower is called Champs de Mars (Field of Mars). Close to the neighborhood's military monuments and museums, it has historically lived up to the Roman god of war for whom it was named. The open field has been used for military boot camp and as a convenient place for violent demonstrations, including but not limited to civilian massacres during the Revolution. At the end toward the Military School is the "Wall of Peace," a glass structure that has 32 languages worth of the word "peace" in an attempt to make up for the field's bloody past.

☩ Ⓜ*La Motte-Picquet-Grenelle or École Militaire.*

MUSÉE RODIN   MUSEUM
79 rue de Varenne   ☎01 44 18 61 10; www.musee-rodin.fr

According to Parisians in the know, this is one of the city's museums. During his lifetime, Auguste Rodin (1840-1917) was among the country's most controversial artists and was considered to be the sculptor of Impressionism. Today, the art world considers him the father of modern sculpture and applauds him for imbuing stone with a downright groovy level of "psychological complexity." While most of his lesser known sculptures are inside the former Hôtel Biron, the 18th-century building where he lived and worked, the two museum must-sees are *Le Penseur (The Thinker)*, and *La Porte de L'Enfer (The Gates of Hell)*. These two are rightfully displayed side by side: *The Thinker* is Dante contemplating the *Divine Comedy*, which is portrayed in the *Gates of Hell*, a bronze mess of lustful pairs swirling in the violent turbulence of the second ring of Hell.

☩ Ⓜ*Varenne. i Temporary exhibits housed in the chapel, to the right as you enter. Touch tours for the blind and educational tours available (☎01 44 18 61 24). Ⓢ Museum €6, ages 18-25 €5, under 18 and EU citizens under 26 free. Joint ticket with Musée d'Orsay €12. Garden €1/1/free/ free. 1st Su of the month free. Audio tours in 7 languages €4 each for permanent and temporary exhibits, combined ticket €6. Ⓩ Open Tu-Su 10am-5:45pm; last entry 5:15pm.*

🏷 MUSÉE D'ORSAY

MUSEUM

62 rue de Lille ☎01 40 49 48 14; www.musee-orsay.com

Aesthetic taste is fickle. When a handful of artists were rejected from the Louvre salon in the 19th century, they opened an exhibition across the way, prompting both the scorn of stick-up-their-arses *académiciens* and the rise of Impressionism. Today, people line up at the Musée d'Orsay to see this collection of groundbreaking rejects. Originally built as a train station, the Musée d'Orsay opened as President Mitterrand's gift to France. It gathered works from the Louvre, Jeu de Paume, Palais de Tokyo, Musée de Luxembourg, provincial museums, and private collections to add to the original collection the Louvre had refused. On the ground floor, you can see the pre-Impressionist paintings, and it only gets weirder as you go up. In the back sits a model of the Parisian Opera cut in two to reveal the inside. Despite our best efforts, we were unable to find the elusive Phantom. The top floor includes all the big names in Impressionist and Post-Impressionist art: Degas, Manet, Monet, Seurat, and Van Gogh. Degas's famed "dancers" are a particular highlight.

⇄ Ⓜ Solférino. Access to visitors at entrance A off the square at 1 rue de la Légion d'Honneur. $ €8, ages 18-25 €5.50, under 18 and EU citizens 18-26 free. ⏰ Open Tu-W 9:30am-6pm, Th 9:30am-9:45pm, F-Su 9:30am-6pm. Visitors asked to leave starting at 5:30pm (Th 9:15pm).

INVALIDES

MUSEUM

Esplanade des Invalides ☎08 10 11 33 99; www.invalides.org

For the history buff, this is a must see. A comprehensive collection of all things war-like and French (yes, including the defeats), this building is more than just a pretty gold dome. Although you have to pay to enter the various military museums, as well as **Napoleon's tomb,** the majority of the complex is accessible for 🏷**free,** including the inner courtyard (tip: it's about 15 degrees cooler in the shade), upper walkway, and the St-Louis des Invalides Chapel, all of which have samples of what's inside the museums, including a battery of 60 cannons. Also check out the Charles de Gaulle *Historial* (film), which outlines the famed president/general's efforts during the Nazi resistance. There are also a number of rotating exhibitions that highlight particular times in French military history, from Louis XI, "The Spider King," to the wars in Indochina.

⇄ Ⓜ Invalides. $ €9, under 18 and EU citizens 18-25 free. ⏰ Open Apr-Sept M 10am-6pm, Tu 10am-9pm, W-Su 10am-6pm; Oct-Mar daily 10am-5pm. Closed 1st M each month. Charles de Gaulle Historial closed M. Films show every 30min. Dome open Jul-Aug until 7pm.

MUSÉE DU QUAI BRANLY

MUSEUM

37 quai Branly ☎01 56 61 71 72; www.quaibranly.fr

A gift to the French people from Jacques Chirac, this adventure/time machine/museum sucks you in with its overgrown gardens of exotic plants under the shade of the raised modern building. Don't let the architecture fool you: this museum houses a huge collection of ancient artifacts from tribal cultures around the world. Organized into four areas (Africa, Asia, Americas, and Oceania), the museum has anticipated your impending boredom and made the museum as visually and auditorily stimulating as possible. Timothy Leary would be so proud. In case you can't tell the difference between a Nepalese tunic and an African one, look at the floor: the color under your feet corresponds to what section of the world you are in. Be sure to sit in one of the many hidden sound caves to take in some tribal noises in solitude, but beware of local high school students using the dark spaces as personal make-out rooms.

⇄ Ⓜ Alma-Marceau. Cross Pont de l'Alma and follow quai Branly toward the Eiffel Tower. $ €8.50, under 18 and EU citizens 18-25 free. ⏰ Open Tu-W 11am-7pm, Th-Sa 11am-9pm, Su 11am-7pm.

CHAMPS-ÉLYSÉES

There's a reason that the 8ème has remained popular with tourists long after the Champs-Élysées ceased to be posh. The neighborhood harbors more architectural beauty, historical significance, and shopping opportunities than almost any other in the city and remains an exhilarating—if hectic—place to spend a day. Champs-Élysées is also home to a variety of art museums in its northern corners; they are often located in *hôtels particuliers*, where they were once part of private collections.

🏛 ARC DE TRIOMPHE   HISTORIC MONUMENT
pl. Charles de Gaulle-Étoile   www.arc-de-triomphe.monuments-nationaux.fr

Probably the second most iconic image in the whole city, the Arc de Triomphe dominates the Champs-Élysées and remains strikingly powerful even when viewed from a distance. The original architect imagined an unparalleled tribute to France's military prowess in the form of a giant, bejeweled elephant. Fortunately, Napoleon had the more restrained idea of building an arch. You could probably pull together an exhibition of French history since the arch's 1836 completion based purely on photos of the Arc's use in ceremonial celebrations. It stands both as a tribute to French military triumphs and as a memorial to those who have fallen in battle. The Tomb of the Unknown Soldier, added in 1920, lies under the arch. The Arc is spectacular to look at, and it returns the favor by being spectacular to look from. The observation deck offers a brilliant view of the Historic Axis, which stretches from the Louvre to the Grande Arche de la Défense.

   � ⓂCharles de Gaulle-Étoile. You will die (and face a hefty fine) if you try to dodge the 10-lane merry-go-round of cars around the arch, so use the pedestrian underpass on the right side of the Champs-Élysées facing the arch. ⓲ Expect long waits, although you can escape the crowds if you go before noon. Buy tickets in the pedestrian underpass. ⑨ €9.50, ages 18-25 €6, under 18 and EU citizens 18-25 free. ⌚ Open daily Apr-Sept 10am-11pm; Oct-Mar 10am-10:30pm. Last entry 30min. before close.

AVENUE DES CHAMPS-ÉLYSÉES   SHOPPING DISTRICT
From pl. Charles de Gaulle-Étoile to pl. de la Concorde

There's a reason we included it here and not in **Shopping**: you can't afford it. The Champs-Élysées seems to be a magnificent celebration of the elite's pomp and fortuitous circumstance, but it's mostly filled with flashy cars, expensive cafes filled with rich foreigners, and kitschy shops. On the plus side, it does have some of the best people-watching in Europe. The avenue also hosts most major French events: on **Bastille Day,** the largest parade in Europe takes place here, as does the final stretch of the **Tour de France.** While the Champs itself may be deteriorating in class (with the invasion of chain stores), many of its side streets, like **avenue Montaigne,** have picked up the slack and ooze sophistication.

   ✦ ⓂCharles de Gaulle-Étoile.

GRAND PALAIS   PALACE
3 av. du Général Eisenhower   ☎01 44 13 17 17; www.grandpalais.fr

Designed for the 1900 World's Fair, the Grand Palais and the accompanying Petit Palais across the street were lauded as exemplary works of Art Nouveau architecture. Since the novelty of a then-modern building has worn off in the past century, most of the Grand Palais houses a 20th-century fine art exhibit and a children's science museum, **Palais de la Découverte** (see below). Most of the building's beauty can be admired outside for free, especially at night when its 6000 metric ton glass ceiling glows, lighting up the French flag that flies above it.

   ✦ ⓂChamps-Élysées-Clemenceau. ⑨ €11.50, students €8. For special exhibits, admission varies; expect €8-16, students €6-9, art students free. ⌚ Open M-Tu 10am-8pm, W 10am-10pm, Th-Su 10am-8pm. Last entry 45min. before close.

paris

PETIT PALAIS
MUSEUM

av. Winston Churchill ☎01 53 43 40 00; www.petitpalais.paris.fr

The Petit Palais showcases a hodgepodge of European art from Christian orthodoxy to 20th-century Parisian artists. If you are really into obscure works by famous artists, go for it. Otherwise you might be burnt out after d'Orsay and the Louvre. But hey, the Petit Palais is free for the permanent collection, so it's got that going for it.

✦ ⓂChamps-Élysées-Clemenceau or Franklin D. Roosevelt. Follow av. Winston Churchill toward the river. The museum is on the left. Ⓢ Permanent collection free. Special exhibits €5-11, ages 14-27 half price, under 13 free. Audio tour €4. Credit card min. €15. 🕐 Open Tu-Su 10am-6pm. Special exhibits open Tu-W 10am-6pm, Th 10am-8pm, F-Su 10am-6pm. Last entry 1hr. before close.

MADELEINE
CHURCH

pl. de la Madeleine ☎01 44 51 69 00; www.eglise-lamadeleine.com

While this famous church is worth a visit to admire its immensity and large sculpture of Mary Magdalene, there isn't much else to see, though there are frequent chamber and music concerts. Today, pricey clothing and food shops line the square surrounding Madeleine, including the famous macaroon boutique, Ladurée (see **Food**).

✦ ⓂMadeleine. 🕐 Open daily 9am-7pm. Regular organ and chamber concerts; contact church for schedule and tickets. Mass M-F 12:30 and 6:30pm at the nearby chapel; Sa 6pm; Su 9:30, 11am, and 7pm with organ and choir.

PALAIS DE LA DÉCOUVERTE
MUSEUM

av. Franklin D. Roosevelt, in the Grand Palais ☎01 56 43 20 20; www.palais-decouverte.fr

Children tear around the interactive science exhibits in the Palais de la Découverte, and it may be hard not to join them—nothing brings out your inner child like buttons that start model comets on their celestial trajectories, spinning seats that demonstrate angular motion, and displays of creepy-crawlies. What's more, both adults and children are likely to learn a surprising amount about physics, chemistry, astronomy, geology, and biology. The temporary exhibits (four per year) are usually crowd-pleasers; the most recent, entitled "Dinosaur Diet," featured real-sized animated dinosaurs. The planetarium has four shows per day; arrive early during school vacation periods.

✦ ⓂFranklin D. Roosevelt or Champs-Élysées-Clemenceau. Ⓢ €7; students, seniors, and ages 5-17 €4.50; under 5 free. Planetarium €3.50. 🕐 Open Tu-Sa 9:30am-6pm, Su 10am-7pm. Last entry 30min. before close. Planetarium shows 11:30am, 2, 3:15, 4:30pm.

OPÉRA AND CANAL ST-MARTIN

While the 9ème and 10ème don't offer much in the way of landmarks or museums, there are a few sights that you might want to quickly check out. **Le Marché Saint-Quentin** could be worth a longer perusal.

OPÉRA GARNIER
THEATER

pl. de l'Opéra ☎08 92 89 90 90; www.operadeparis.fr

Formerly known as the Opéra National de Paris before the creation of the Opéra Bastille in 1989, the Opéra Garnier became world famous when its main six-ton chandelier crashed to the ground in 1896, killing one person. This incident inspired the longest running musical on Broadway and a weird sex idol for drama kids everywhere. Yes, we're talking about the *Phantom of the Opera*, and its songs may run through your head throughout your visit. Today, visit the Opéra (when it's not sporadically closed due to preformances) and see the grand staircase, grand foyer, and stage—all decorated with frescoes and ornate stone and marble designs that often leave visitors speechless.

✦ ⓂOpéra. ⓘ Tickets usually available 2 weeks before the show. Rush tickets go on sale 1hr. before show. Ⓢ Tickets generally €7-160. Tours €9, under 25 €5. Guided tour €12, over 60 €10, students €9, under 13 €6. 🕐 Open daily 10am-4:30pm. Box office open M-Sa 10:30am-6:30pm.

sights

LE MARCHÉ SAINT-QUENTIN   MARKET
Corner of rue de Chabrol and bd de Magenta

The largest covered market in Paris, Le Marché St-Quentin is an overwhelming combination of the finest cheeses, fish, and meats. Even if you're not shopping, come just to experience the mix of aromas and mingle with veteran foodies who spend their days browsing for the perfect Camembert. There's a bistro in the middle of the market for those who can't wait until they get home to chow down on their produce.

☆ ⓂGare de l'Est. ⧖ Open M-Sa 8:30am-1pm and 4-7:30pm, Su 8:30am-1pm.

BASTILLE

Aside from the **place de la Bastille,** there are few monumental sights left in this neighborhood. Still, the symbolic historical value remains, and this lively area provides many contemporary diversions. The 12ème boasts monoliths of modern architecture like the **Opéra Bastille.** The formerly working-class neighborhood is now mostly commercialized, but a bit of idiosyncratic charm can be seen in the funky **rue de la Roquette,** where clubs and bars sit alongside boutiques and cafes.

PLACE DE LA BASTILLE   SQUARE

Though the revolutionary spirit has faded, a similar fervor still manifests itself nightly in fits of drunken revelry, most marked on **Bastille Day**. At the center of the square, a monument of winged Mercury holding a torch of freedom symbolizes France's movement (albeit a slow one) from monarchy to democracy.

☆ ⓂBastille.

BASTILLE PRISON   HISTORIC LANDMARK

Visitors to the prison subsist on symbolic value alone—it's one of the most popular sights in Paris that doesn't actually exist. On July 14, 1789, an angry Parisian mob stormed this bastion of royal tyranny, sparking the French Revolution. They only liberated seven prisoners, but who's counting? Two days later, the Assemblée Nationale ordered the prison demolished. Today all that remains is the fortress's ground plan, still visible as a line of paving stones in the pl. de la Bastille. But it was hardly the hell hole that the Revolutionaries who tore it down imagined it to be. The Bastille's elite inmates were allowed to furnish their suites, use fresh linens, bring their own servants, and receive guests; the Cardinal de Rohan famously held a dinner party for 20 in his cell. Notable prisoners included the ⧗**Man in the Iron Mask** (made famous by writer Alexandre Dumas), the Comte de Mirabeau, Voltaire (twice), and the Marquis de Sade. The anniversary of the storming is July 14th, which (much like a certain celebration 10 days earlier across the Atlantic) is a time of glorious fireworks and copious amounts of alcohol, with festivities concentrated around pl. de la Bastille.

☆ ⓂBastille.

OPÉRA BASTILLE   PERFORMANCE HALL
130 rue de Lyon   ☎08 92 89 90 90; www.operadeparis.fr

The "People's Opera" has been not-so-fondly referred to as ugly, an airport, and a huge toilet, due to its uncanny resemblance to the coin-operated *pissoirs* on the streets of Paris. Yet the opera has not struck a completely sour note, as it helped renew local interest in the arts. The guided tours offer a behind-the-scenes view of the colossal theater. The modern granite and glass auditorium, which seats 2723, comprises only 5% of the building's surface area. The rest of the structure houses exact replicas of the stage (for rehearsal purposes) and workshops for both the Bastille and Garnier operas.

☆ ⓂBastille. Look for the box office (billetterie). ⓘ Tickets can be purchased online, by mail, by phone, or in person. Rush tickets 15min. before show for students under 25 and seniors. Call in advance to arrange English tour. Ⓢ Tickets €5-180. Tours €11, students and over 60 €9, under 18 €6. ⧖ Box office open M-Sa 10:30am-6:30pm. 1hr. guided tours in French fall-spring daily at 1 and 5pm.

paris

JULY COLUMN
MONUMENT

Towering above the constantly busy pl. de la Bastille, this light-catching column commemorates many groups of French freedom fighters—though, somewhat illogically, not the ones who stormed the Bastille. It celebrates the *Trois Glorieuses*, the "three glorious" days that toppled Charles X's monarchy in favor of a free republic... just kidding, it was another monarch, Louis-Philippe, who took over. When Louis-Philippe was in turn deposed in 1848, the column was rededicated to those fighters as well, and 200 additional bodies were buried under it. Apparently thinking it was a revolutionary good luck trinket, the Communards used the tower as a rallying point for their 1871 uprising, but, after three successful months, the French army came in and deported nearly 7500 and executed 20,000. Sheer numbers prevented any additional burials under the column.

✦ ⓂBastille. In the center of pl. de la Bastille.

CITÉ NATIONALE DE L'HISTOIRE DE L'IMMIGRATION
MUSEUM

293 av. Daumesnil　　　　　　　　　　　☎01 53 59 58 60; www.histoire-immigration.fr

It's both appropriate and ironic that this recently opened museum on immigration is housed in the Palais de la Porte Dorée, which was built during France's colonial expansion and thus features not-so-politically-correct friezes of "native culture" on its walls. Presented chronologically, the permanent collection traces the arrival and subsequent attempts at integration of immigrants from all over the world. The message is driven home with stories of Algerians seperated from families and a model of a six-person bunk bed. After seeing this, you'll definitely have to stop complaining about how cramped your hostel room is.

✦ ⓂPorte Dorée. In the Palais de la Porte Dorée, on the western edge of the Bois de Vincennes.
Ⓢ €5, ages 18-26 €3.50, under 18 and EU citizens ages 18-26 free. 1st Su of every month free.
� Open Tu-F 10am-5:30pm, Sa-Su 10am-7pm. Last entry 45min. before close.

MONTPARNASSE AND SOUTHERN PARIS

There are few monuments in Montparnasse and Southern Paris. Diverse, residential, and pleasantly odd, these neighborhoods remain uninterrupted by the troops of pear-shaped tourists in matching fanny packs that plague the more pristine arrondissements. Though short on medieval cathedrals, hidden gems from Paris's recent waves of immigration and perturbed Bo-Bos (Bohemian Bourgeoisie) are scattered throughout the area.

▧ CATACOMBS
HISTORIC LANDMARK

1 av. du Colonel Henri Roi-Tanguy　　　　☎01 43 22 47 63; www.catacombes-de-paris.fr

The Catacombs were the original site of Paris's quarries, but were converted into an ossuary in 1785 to help alleviate the stench rising from overcrowded cemeteries (perfume only goes so far). Not for the claustrophobic or faint of heart, this 45min. excursion leads visitors down a winding spiral staircase to a welcoming sign: "Stop! Here is the Empire of Death." Stacks of skulls and femurs line the walls, and the remains of six million people make you feel quite insignificant in the grand scheme of things. Try to arrive before the opening at 10am; hordes of tourists form extremely long lines hoping to escape the beating sun. The visitors' passage is well marked, so don't worry about getting lost. Try trailing behind the group a little for the ultimate creepy experience—you won't be disappointed.

✦ ⓂDenfert-Rochereau. Cross av. du Colonel Henri Roi-Tanguy with the lion on your left. Ⓢ €8, over 60 €6, ages 14-26 €4, under 14 free. Ⓐ Open Tu-Su 10am-5pm. Last entry 4pm.

TOUR MONTPARNASSE
TOWER

33 av. du Maine　　　　　　　　　　　　　　　　　☎01 45 38 52 56

Built in 1969, this modern tower stands 196m tall and makes Paris look like a miniature model. The elevator is allegedly the fastest in Europe (moving at 5.12m per sec.—not a lot of time to clear the pressure in your ears) and spits you out to a mandatory photo line on the 56th floor. After being shoved in front of a fake city skyline and forced to smile for a picture that you probably don't want, you're finally allowed up to the 59th floor to take in the beauty and meticulous planning of Paris's historic streets. Thankfully, the city ruled that similar eyesores could not be constructed in Paris's downtown shortly after this one was built.

✣ ⓂMontparnasse-Bienvenüe. Entrance on rue de l'Arrivée. ⓈЄ10, students Є7. ◷ Open M-Th 9:30am-10:30pm, F-Sa 9:30am-11pm, Su 9:30am-10:30pm. Last entry 30min. before close.

CIMETIÈRE DU MONTPARNASSE
CEMETERY
3 bd Edgar Quinet
☎01 44 10 86 50

Paris certainly has a lot of cemeteries. Despite the repetitiveness of buried celebrities, there are some unique features that make Montparnasse worth visiting. Because it's secluded from the main tourist areas, this cemetery is more of a local park during the day, but one where you can stroll past Jean-Paul Sartre and Simone de Beauvoir (the two are buried together—how cute). Watch out for older kids from the *banlieues* bumming cigarettes off tourists and the occasional homeless drunk. Nonetheless, the cemetery showcases some delightful architecture and an impressive list of tenants.

✣ ⓂEdgar Quinet, opposite Sq. Delambre. Ⓢ Free. ◷ High season open M-F 8am-6pm, Sa 8:30am-6pm, Su 9am-6pm; low season open M-F 8am-5:30pm, Sa 8:30am-5:30pm, Su 9am-5:30pm.

QUARTIER DE LA BUTTE-AUX-CAILLES
NEIGHBORHOOD
Intersection of rue de la Butte-aux-Cailles and rue des 5 Diamants

Traces of the district's original counterculture from the 1968 riots are alive and well here: dreadlocks are the hairstyle of choice, the walls are covered in graffiti, and the fashionably unaffected are armed with guitars at all times. Here you can find some of the cheapest cafes and restaurants, which (as expected) only accept cash. Basically, this neighborhood makes Haight-Ashbury look like Silicon Valley, and provides a good chance for you to get cheap eats and free entertainment from carefree hippies.

✣ ⓂPlace d'Italie. Take rue Bobillot south a few blocks and turn right onto rue de la Butte-aux-Cailles.

QUARTIER CHINOIS
NEIGHBORHOOD
Just south of rue de Tolbiac

Spread out over four Metro stops just south of rue de Tolbiac, Paris's Chinatown should really be called Paris's Indo-Chinatown. Thanks to years of colonialism, some of the most authentic and talented chefs have flocked to this region from Cambodia, Laos, Vietnam, and Thailand to provide super cheap food. A walk here (especially in the sweltering summers) will transport you to Ho Chi Minh City.

✣ ⓂTolbiac, Maison Blanche, Porte de Choisy, or Porte d'Ivry.

WESTERN PARIS

Fortunately for tourists, all of these museums are within walking distance of each other. To keep your sanity, please don't go to all of them at once, even though you might be tempted to cross the road and continue knocking them off your to-do list. We suggest you head to the wine museum first, get a buzz going, then hike up the road to **Trocadéro**.

🖾 MUSÉE DU VIN
MUSEUM
rue des Eaux
☎01 45 25 70 89; www.museeduvinparis.com

Formerly a 15th-century monastery, the Musée du Vin's underground tunnels and vaults take visitors through the history of wine production, including the tools that till the soil, the harvesting techniques in different regions of France, and how they make champagne. The exhibits integrate history with models of Louis

Pasteur, who cured wine disease by heating the wine in a vacuum, and Napoleon, who cut his wine with water (you know, to stay sharp on the battlefield). The tour ends with a tasting of one of three types of wine (rosé, white, or red—we recommend the last one), but only after a thorough explanation of where each came from. Be patient, and for goodness's sake let them pour it for you.

✝ ⓂPassy. Go down the stairs, turn right onto pl. Albioni, and then right onto rue des Eaux; the museum is tucked away at the end of the street. ⓈSelf-guided tour and 1 glass of wine €12; students, seniors, and visitors with disabilities €9.70. 🕐 Open Tu-Su 10am-6pm.

CIMETIÈRE DE PASSY
CEMETERY

2 rue du Commandant-Schloesing ☎01 53 70 40 80

Opened in 1820, this cemetery is home to some of Paris's most notable deceased, including the fashionable Givenchy family, composer Claude Debussy, Impressionist Berthe Morisot, and painter Édouard Manet. The idiosyncrasies and enduring rivalries of these figures continue even in death: the graves here look more like miniature mansions than tombstones. The tomb of the Russian artist Marie Bashkirtseff is a recreation of her studio and stands at an impressive 40 ft. tall. Morisot and Manet are buried in a more modest tomb together; we suspect that Morisot's husband would not have approved. Well-groomed and quiet, the graveyard is more like a shadowy garden, with a wonderful view of the Eiffel Tower.

✝ ⓂTrocadéro. Follow av. Paul Doumer right. The cemetery is on the right. ⓈFree. 🕐 Open Mar 16-Nov 5 M-F 8am-6pm, Sa 8:30am-6pm, Su and public holidays 9am-6pm; Nov 6-Mar 15 M-F 8am-5:30pm, Sa 8:30am-5:30pm, Su and public holidays 9am-5:30pm. Last entry 30min. before close. Conservation office open M-F 8:30am-12:30pm and 2-5pm.

JARDINS DU TROCADÉRO
GARDEN

The ultimate tourist hub, the gardens provide the perfect "I've been to Paris" photo op, with one of the clearest views of the Eiffel Tower. The fountain and sprawling, sloping lawns are great for a picnic or watching the many street performers working for your spare change.

✝ ⓂTrocadéro.

MUSÉE MARMOTTAN MONET
MUSEUM

2 rue Louis Boilly ☎01 44 96 50 33; www.marmottan.com

Even for the artistically challenged, this is worth a visit. Less crowded than any other popular museum in Paris, the gold-detailed, ornately decorated museum brings you back to the Belle Époque. Housing Monet's water lilies as well as Berthe Morisot's works of the same Impressionist genre, this museum also throws a bone to the iconography of the Middle Ages.

✝ ⓂLa Muette. Walk through the Jardin de Ranelagh on av. Jardin de Ranelagh. The museum is on the right on rue Louis-Boilly. Ⓢ€10, under 25 €5. 🕐 Open Tu-W 11am-6pm, Th 11am-10pm, F-Su 11am-6pm. Last entry 30min. before close.

MONTMARTRE

Just because the sights in Montmartre aren't captured on postcards doesn't mean they don't exist. While most people come to see the **Moulin Rouge** or **Sacré-Cœur,** you can learn just as much about Paris by grabbing a coffee along the Pigalle while watching seedy crowds roam the streets and gullible tourists fall for souvenir tourist traps. It's more important here than anywhere in Paris to blend in—tourists are frequent targets for pickpockets and scammers, so for Lady Marmalade's sake, don't go wandering around these sights at night.

▨ BASILIQUE DU SACRÉ-CŒUR
CHURCH

35 rue du Chevalier-de-la-Barre ☎01 53 41 89 00; www.sacre-coeur-montmartre.fr

Situated 129m above sea level, this splendid basilica was first planned in 1870. Its purpose? To serve as a spiritual bulwark for France and the Catholic Church, which

sights

were under the weight of an imminent military defeat and German occupation. The basilica was commissioned by the National Assembly and was initially meant to be an assertion of conservative Catholic power, but the only people that assert themselves on the steps today are the scammers offering "free" bracelets, so beware. The basilica sees over 10 million visitors per year and offers a free, spectacular view of the city. On a spring day, grab some ice cream and marvel at the view.

⚑ Ⓜ Lamarck-Caulaincourt. Take rue Caulaincourt and turn right onto rue Lamrack. Follow rue Lamrack until you reach the basilica. Ⓢ Free. Ⓩ Basilica open daily 6am-10:30pm. Dome open daily Mar-Nov 9am-7pm; Dec-Feb 9am-6pm. Mass M-F 11:15am, 6:30, 10pm; Sa 10pm; Su 11am, 6, 10pm.

HALLE SAINT-PIERRE   MUSEUM
2 rue Ronsard   ☎01 42 58 72 89; www.hallesaintpierre.org

Halle St-Pierre is a one-of-a-kind (read: weird) abstract art museum located right down the street from the Sacré-Cœur. Exhibits change constantly, so the museum is hard to pin down. In general, the art tends to be a bit far out. The most recent exhibition, on display until March 4, 2012, is on "Modern Art and Pop Culture," and displays paintings such as Mickey Mouse smoking a cigarette and (to the dismay of Chistendom) three pumas being crucified.

⚑ Ⓜ Anvers. Follow rue de Steinkerque up the hill and turn right onto pl. St-Pierre. Walk 1 block and turn left onto rue Ronsard. Ⓢ €7.50, students €6. Ⓩ Open Sept-July daily 10am-6pm; Aug M-F noon-6pm.

CIMETIÈRE DE MONTMARTRE   CEMETERY
20 av. Rachel   ☎01 53 42 36 30

The vast Cimetière de Montmartre, stretching across a significant proportion of the 18éme, lies below street level on the site of a former quarry. It is the resting place of multiple acclaimed artists: writer Émile Zola, painter Edgar Degas, saxophone inventor Adolphe Sax, and ballet dancer Marie Taglioni are among the long-term residents. If you have an extra pair in your backpack, you can leave pointe shoes on Taglioni's grave. The other dead celebs prefer coins on their gravestones. One of the most infamous killers in French history is also buried here: Charles Henri Sanson, Royal Executioner, who executed nearly 3000 people, including Louis XVI himself.

⚑ Ⓜ Place de Clichy. Head up bd de Clichy, which becomes rue Caulaincourt. The entrance is at the intersection of rue Caulaincourt and av. Rachel. Ⓢ Free. Ⓩ Open May 16-Nov 5 M-F 8am-6pm, Sa 8:30am-6pm, Su 9am-6pm; Nov 6-May 15 M-F 8am-5:30pm, Sa 8:30am-5:30pm, Su 9am-5:30pm.

PIGALLE   NEIGHBORHOOD

This famous, seedy neighborhood has a bad reputation for a reason. Home to strip clubs, sex shops, and fake designer clothing and handbags, Pigalle turns a dark corner at night. Travelers report that you shouldn't take the Metro at night around here; instead, opt for a taxi. Now that the disclaimer is out of the way, the **Moulin Rouge** (82 bd de Clichy ☎01 53 09 82 82; www.moulinrouge.fr) cabaret show is definitely worth the €90 you have lying around, as it's the classiest titty show you'll ever see. The neighborhood is improving as young bohemians take advantage of the low rent rates, so there is a growing rock and hip-hop scene, especially at **Elysée Montmartre** (72 bd de Rochechouart ☎01 44 92 45 36; www.elyseemontmartre.com).

⚑ Ⓜ Pigalle.

EASTERN PARIS

▨ PARC DES BUTTES-CHAUMONT   PARK

Not your average Parisian park, the Buttes-Chaumont was modeled after Hyde Park in London, but it seems more like Pandora from *Avatar*. Despite the barrier of trees around the park and walkways, there is more than enough sun for a picnic or laying out on the steep grassy slopes that overlook the high cliff. Bridges lead over the surrounding lake to the top, where designer Adolphe

Alphand decided (why? we don't know) to build a small Roman Temple. In the 13th century, this area was the site of a gibbet (an iron cage filled with the rotting corpses of criminals), a dumping ground for dead horses, a haven for worms, and a gypsum quarry (the origin of the term "plaster of Paris"). Thankfully, it's come a long way since then.

✢ ⓂButtes Chaumont. ⑤ Free. 🕐 Open daily May-Sept 7am-10:15pm; Oct-Apr 7am-8:15pm.

▨ CIMETIÈRE DU PÈRE LACHAISE
CEMETERY

16 rue du Repos
☎01 55 25 82 10

After Pasteur and his germ theory totally messed with the zoning regulations of the Cimetière des Innocents (right next to the Les Halles food market), Père Lachaise was opened as a place to bury the dead. Parisians have buried over one million bodies here, despite there being only 100,000 graves. Highlights include elbowing your way past leather-studded jackets at Jim Morrison's grave, where people have taken to "madly loving" their rock/drug idol; kissing Oscar Wilde's grave (we passed on that one); or just getting utterly lost in the maze of head-stones, Tim Burton-esque mausoleums, and cobblestone paths.

✢ ⓂPère Lachaise or Gambetta. 𝒊 Free maps at the Bureau de Conservation near Porte du Repos; ask for directions at guard booths near the main entrances. For more info on "theme" tours, call ☎01 49 57 94 37. ⑤ Free. 🕐 Open from mid-Mar to early Nov M-F 8am-6pm, Sa 8:30am-6pm, Su 9am-6pm; from Nov to mid-Mar M-F 8am-5:30pm, Sa 8:30am-5:30pm, Su 9am-5:30pm. Last entry 15min. before close. Free 2½hr. guided tour from Apr to mid-Nov Sa 2:30pm.

the kiss of death

The word "romantic" may not be the right adjective to describe a stroll through a cemetery. But Cimetière du Père Lachaise, the world's most visited cemetery, is a favorite spot for couples to smooch in front of graves and tombstones of famous people like Oscar Wilde or Frédéric Chopin. Not ghoulish at all, right?

When the cemetery first opened in 1804, it was unpopular thanks to its dis-tance from the heart of the city. The cemetery's reputation changed when Honoré de Balzac's novels featured characters buried in Père Lachaise. People infatuated with the story quickly began to flock to the city to visit the gravesites of fictional heroes and heroines.

Today, Jim Morrison's grave is the most visited. His grave was unmarked for many years, but that didn't stop crazy fans from having drug-fueled orgies over his dead body, hoping that Jim's spirit would join them in their outlandish hooligan-ism. The cemetery officials eventually placed a stone block over his resting place to prevent fans from unearthing the body.

▨ CITÉ DES SCIENCES ET DE L'INDUSTRIE
MUSEUM

30 av. Corentin Cariou
☎01 40 05 12 12; www.cite-sciences.fr

If art isn't your cup of tea and you have a passion for the sciences, welcome to your Louvre. This massive complex has anything that would make Bill Nye giggle like a school girl. Permanent exhibits on energy use, optical illusions, and human genetics all have videos and interactive games to make those subjects palatable for those who couldn't stay awake in biology class, and the constantly rotating temporary exhibits keep up with what's interesting in scientific news. Recent exhibits have tackled climate change, the ocean, and new transport technology (complete with a flight simulator). Carl Sagan would cry tears of joy

sights

while watching their planetarium show on the history of the universe, projected onto a nearly 11,000 sq. ft. dome. If you're low on cash, the aquarium is free.

♯ ⓂPorte de la Villette. *i* Free access to job placement assistance, health information center (for medical document consult and translating), and multimedia library. Ⓢ €8-20. Admission price depends on what exhibits you want to see. ◰ Open Tu-Sa 10am-6pm, Su 10am-7pm. Health info center open Tu-Su noon-6pm.

food

Say goodbye to foot-long subs and that sticky pre-sliced cheese they sell at Costco; you're not in Kansas anymore. Food is an integral part of French life—while world-famous chefs and their three-star prices are valued Parisian institutions, you don't have to break the bank for excellent cuisine, especially if you come at lunch (when prices are nearly half what they are at dinner). Brasseries are even more casual and foster a lively and irreverent atmosphere. The least expensive option is usually a creperie, which specialize in thin Breton pancakes filled with meat, vegetables, cheeses, chocolate, or fruits. Creperies might conjure images of yuppie brunches and awkward first dates for Americans, but here in Paris you can often eat a crepe for less than you'd pay at the great Golden Arches. Specialty food shops, including *boulangeries* (bakeries), patisseries (pastry shops), and *chocolatiers* (chocolate shops), provide delicious and inexpensive picnic supplies. A number of cheap kebab and falafel stands around town also serve quick, cheap fare. *Bon appétit!*

ÎLE DE LA CITÉ AND ÎLE ST-LOUIS

The islands are expensive. Forage all you want, but the cheapest meal you can put together is a crepe and maybe some ice cream. If you want an actual meal, head to Île St-Louis where the tourist crowds (and the prices) tend to diminish. Of course, if you do happen to be loaded, there are a lot of dimly lit, intimate (read: expensive) restaurants where you will pay for the privilege of eating in the true center of Paris.

⬚ MA SALLE À MANGER
RESTAURANT, COCKTAIL BAR $$

26 Passage Dauphine ☎01 43 29 52 34

This cafe in the quiet pl. Dauphine gains curb appeal from its funky explosion of color. The establishment is a quirky combo of Corsican posters, old movies, and old French adverts. Think of a French hippie's garage sale, but throw in cheap lamb, *moules-frites*, and a selection of (relatively) affordable cocktails for an early start to the night.

♯ ⓂCité or Pont Neuf. Ⓢ Entrées €6-10. Menu du jour (entrée and plat, or plat and dessert) from €13. Cocktails €8. ◰ Open M-F 11am-3:30pm and 7-10:30pm, Sa-Su 11am-10:30pm.

CAFÉ MED
RESTAURANT, CREPERIE $$

77 rue St-Louis-en-l'Île ☎01 43 29 73 17

Come here for a fix of Moulin Rouge, where the Red Windmill is the central theme of this usually packed cafe. The most affordable meal is a traditional Bretagne crepe/cider combo, but for a healthy dose of carbs, go for the lunch or dinner menu, where most of the main dishes are pasta with *herbes de Provence*.

♯ ⓂPont Marie. Ⓢ Galette/crepe/cider combo €10.50. Lunch menu €12. Dinner menu €18. ◰ Open M-F 11am-3:30pm and 7-10:30pm, Sa-Su 11am-10:30pm.

BERTHILLON
ICE CREAM $

31 rue St-Louis-en-l'Île ☎01 43 54 31 61; www.www.berthillon.fr

If you are the ice cream aficionado who has made pilgrimages to the Ben and Jerry's or Blue Bell factories, this should probably be on your bucket list. While it may not offer the tours or free samples of larger factories, one similarity remains: the ice cream is phenomenal. The sweet dessert is served (mixed with fresh fruit on demand) minutes after it's made in the old parlor room.

✿ ⓜPont Neuf. ⓢ 1 scoop €2.50; 2 scoops €3.50; 3 scoops €5. ⏰ Open from Sept to mid-July W-Su 10am-8pm. Closed 2 weeks in Feb and Apr.

CHÂTELET-LES HALLES

Food in Châtelet caters to tourists and is unabashedly overpriced. While you can get a lot of bang for your buck in the many pizza and pasta places in the center of the area, once you go farther up **rue Saint-Honoré** or past Les Halles you'll find quirkier places that aren't crowded with hungry shoppers and tourists.

☒ LE JIP'S   FUSION $$
41 rue St-Denis   ☎01 42 21 33 93

Le Jip's has some of the cheapest and most authentic Cuban/African/Brazilian food in Paris (wrap your head around those flavor combos). You could spend the whole day chowing on chicken creole in coconut milk, melt-in-your-mouth lamb, and desserts like *crème de citron vert* (lime green custard) and caramelized pineapple. Tapas platters and mojitos with a choice of four kinds of rum can warm you up until the bar explodes with salsa dancing until 2am.

✿ ⓜChâtelet. *i* Salsa dancing Su 3-5pm; call ahead to reserve. ⓢ Tapas platters €12. Lunch menu €15. Mojitos €10. Salsa dancing €10; includes 1 drink. ⏰ Open daily 11am-2am.

FLAM'S   CAFE $
62 rue des Lombards   ☎01 42 21 10 30; www.flams.fr

Flam's is a basic cafe chain that has taken the Alsatian recipe for *flammkueche* ("cake baked in flames"; a thin pizza topped with cheese and cream) and made it available for next to nothing. The bright orange exterior makes it easy to find, and the cheap beer and cocktails make it hard to leave. While this isn't the chain's only location in Paris, it's most attractive here thanks to being one of the cheapest places around.

✿ ⓜChâtelet. ⓢ Flammekueche €5.50-8. Prix-fixe menu €17. Beer €2.50-3.50. Cocktails €4.50-7. ⏰ Open M-Th 11:45am-midnight, F-Sa 11:45am-11:30pm, Su 11:45am-midnight.

LE STADO   BASQUE $$
150 rue St-Honoré   ☎01 42 60 29 75; www.lestado.com

Don't let the rugby jerseys or Olympic photos make you think Le Stado is a sports bar, because it's almost the opposite. The upscale Basque restaurant serves *canard*, *salade paysanne*, and regional cakes. Come here for a three-course lunch on a weekday, as it's difficult to afford the dinner menu (€28).

✿ ⓜLouvre-Rivoli. ⓢ Salads €8-11. Plats €10-25. Lunch menu €13. Dinner menu €26. ⏰ Open daily 11:30am-2:30pm and 7-11pm.

RIZ QUI RIT   KOREAN, VEGETARIAN $$
142 rue St-Denis   ☎01 40 13 04 56; www.rizquirit.wordpress.com

This hip Korean restaurant will maintain your Zen (or at least try to explain to you what Zen is) with their eco-friendly meat dishes and vegetarian options. Bento Zen lunch boxes combine a whole meal into one partitioned tray and can be taken to go for those in a hurry.

✿ ⓜÉtienne Marcel. Walk against traffic on rue de Turbigo and turn left onto rue St-Denis. ⓢ Bento Zen lunch box €12. Vegetable and meat dishes €8-16. ⏰ Open daily 9am-7pm.

1979   TRADITIONAL $$
49 rue Berger   ☎01 40 41 08 78

Appropriately decorated with Pop Art, mardi gras masks, and the odd faux polar bear mounted on the wall, 1979 serves traditional French foods with a twist, like clams, prawns, and smoked salmon combined with *ravettes de foie gras*.

✿ ⓜLouvre-Rivoli. Take rue du Louvre north and turn right onto rue Berger. ⓢ Prix-fixe menus €9-16. ⏰ Open M-Th noon-2:30pm and 8-10:30pm, F noon-2:30pm and 8-11pm, Sa 8-11pm.

food

CHEZ MÉMÉ TRADITIONAL $$

124 rue St-Denis ☎01 40 28 43 20

Decorated like an aviary, Chez Mémé serves traditional dishes in a funky, jazz-filled environment with tables topped by fake birds in cages. Chalkboards with messages from past patrons advise you what to order.

⇟ [M]Étienne Marcel. Walk against traffic down rue de Turbigo and turn left onto rue St-Denis. [$] Plats €8-15. Salads €9-11. ⏰ Open M-Sa noon-2:30pm and 7-10pm.

THE MARAIS

Though it sometimes feels like dining in the 4ème is less about food and more about how you look eating it, there are a number of quality restaurants here that specialize in everything from regional French cuisine to New Age fusion. This is not the cheapest area, but if you're ready for a bit of a splurge, your appetite will be more than satiated, especially by affordable lunch menus or the falafel on **rue des Rosiers.** If you decide on dinner, make sure to make a reservation at the more popular restaurants. Dozens of charming bistros line **rue Saint-Martin,** and kosher establishments are common on **rue du Vertbois** and **rue Volta.**

👍 **L'AS DU FALAFEL** FALAFEL $

34 rue des Rosiers ☎01 48 87 63 60

L'As du Falafel has become a landmark, and with good reason. Get a view into the kitchen and you'll see giant tubs of freshly cut veggies and the chef frying falafel as fast as it's ordered. Patrons line up outside for the famous "falafel special"—we saw it as more of a magic trick, because we still don't know how they managed to fit everything into that pita. Seriously, it's huge, especially for only €5.

⇟ [M]St-Paul. Take rue Pavée and turn left onto rue des Rosiers. [$] Falafel special €5. Shawarma €7.50. ⏰ Open high season M-Th noon-midnight, F noon-7pm, Su noon-midnight; low season M-Th noon-midnight, F noon-5pm, Su noon-midnight.

👍 **CHEZ JANOU** BISTRO $$

2 rue Roger Verlomme ☎01 42 72 28 41; www.chezjanou.com

Tucked into a quiet corner of the 3ème, this Provençal bistro serves affordable ambrosia to a crowd of enthusiasts. The duck practically melts in your mouth, and the chocolate mousse (€6.60) comes in an enormous self-serve bowl, though Parisians count on self-control. For those without it, the choice of more pastis (over 80 varieties) than food items will have you channeling your inner Fitzgerald—just don't drive home.

⇟ [M]Chemin-Vert. Follow rue des Tournelles south until the intersection with rue Roger Verlomme. ℹ Reservations recommended, as this local favorite is packed every night of the week. [$] Plats from €14. Prix-fixe menu €14. ⏰ Open daily noon-midnight. Kitchen open M-F noon-3pm and 7:45pm-midnight, Sa-Su noon-4pm and 7:45pm-midnight.

MICKY'S DELI KOSHER $$

23 bis rue des Rosiers ☎01 48 04 79 31

Thanks to Rabbi Rottenberg, every slice of meat and beef patty at this deli is pure to the standards of the Torah. One of the last traditional holdouts of the 3ème, Micky's Deli gets a lot of traffic, so head in early or toward closing to get a hold of its monster-sized hot pastrami or burger, or go for the famous Micky's Burger, which blasphemously combines the two.

⇟ [M]St-Paul. Take rue Pavée and turn left onto rue des Rosiers. [$] Burger and fries with drink €7. Deli sandwiches €11-17. ⏰ Open M-Th 11:30am-3pm and 7-11pm, F 11:30am-3pm, Sa 8pm-midnight, Su noon-11pm.

ROBERT ET LOUISE
FRENCH $$$

64 rue Vieille du Temple ☎01 42 78 55 89; www.robertetlouise.com

Defined by a firm belief that chicken is for pansies (let's not even talk about vegetarians), Robert et Louise offers a menu that's wholeheartedly carnivorous—we're talking veal kidneys, steak, prime rib, and lamb chops. The only concession to white meat is the *confit de canard*. There's a definite homey vibe here; you'll feel like you've been taken in by a generous French family who found you abandoned and shivering on their way home from a hunt.

✚ Ⓜ*St-Paul. Follow the traffic on rue de Rivoli and turn right onto rue Vieille du Temple. i Reservations recommended.* Ⓢ *Entrées €5.60-8. Plats €12-63. Lunch menu €12. Desserts €5.60-6.* ☼ *Open Tu-Su noon-2:30pm and 7-11pm.*

BREAKFAST IN AMERICA
DINER $$

4 rue Malher ☎01 42 72 40 21; www.breakfast-in-america.com

BIA promises to be one thing: "an American diner in Paris." It sure delivers—from the shiny red booths to the delicious fries, shakes, bottomless mugs o' joe, and the expected post-meal tips, it doesn't get more American than this.

✚ Ⓜ*St-Paul.* Ⓢ *Burgers and sandwiches €9-12. Student menu (burger, fries, and drink) €8. All-you-can-eat-brunch Su €20. Milkshakes €5.* ☼ *Open daily 8:30am-11pm.*

PAGE 35
CREPERIE $$

4 rue du Parc Royal ☎01 44 54 35 35; www.restaurant-page35.com

Instead of picking which type of French restaurant to go to, check out this hip, modern-art gallery/restaurant/creperie that serves anything under the red, white, and blue banner. Page 35 sums up the spirit of the Marais with its extensive menu of sirloin, tartare, *confit de canard*, poached egg on foie gras, and pasta with *herbes de Provence*. For those who haven't tried them yet, they also serve traditional buckwheat crepes from Brittany. Come toward the end of lunch to avoid the heavy crowds.

✚ Ⓜ*St-Paul. Take rue de Sévigné to the intersection with rue du Parc Royal.* Ⓢ *Flash your Let's Go guide for a free Kir.* Ⓢ *Lunch menu €13. Dinner menu €24.* ☼ *Open Tu-F 11:30am-3pm and 7-11pm, Sa-Su 11:30am-11pm.*

LE LOIRE DANS LA THÉIÈRE
PATISSERIE, CAFE $$

3 rue des Rosiers ☎01 42 72 90 61

If we were to rename this cafe, we'd call it "Just Desserts"—and not in the bad-karma sense. Almost like a hip cafe in New York's SoHo, Le Loire dans la Théière serves pies, cakes, tartes, and meringue with a tea for under €10. It's so popular that it closes at 7pm. The walls are covered with ads for jazz and rock concerts, and they serve omelettes at Sunday brunch with mint and goat cheese.

✚ Ⓜ*St-Paul. Take rue Pavée and turn right onto rue des Rosiers.* Ⓢ *Pot of tea and dessert €9.50.* ☼ *Open daily 10am-7pm.*

MARCHÉ DES ENFANTS ROUGES
MARKET $

39 rue de Bretagne

Paris's oldest covered market is a foodie's paradise of hidden restaurants and chaotic stands where you can grab a meal for under €10. Parisians often stop by for lunch at the wooden tables or heated patios. Since you can find French *boulangeries*, *fromageries*, and patisseries almost anywhere, your best bet is to go for the more exotic (like Moroccan *tagines* or Japanese sushi bento boxes), since they are much cheaper here than in specialty restaurants.

✚ Ⓜ*Filles du Calvaire. Turn left onto rue Froissart, which becomes rue de Bretagne.* ☼ *Open Tu-Th 9am-2pm and 4-8pm, F-Sa 9am-8pm, Su 9am-2pm.*

food

LA PAS-SAGE OBLIGÉ

VEGETARIAN $$

29 rue du Bourg Tibourg ☎01 40 41 95 03; www.lepassageoblige.com

Seemingly defying French culture, this restaurant manages to present traditional dishes without meat. The general VG burger (pronounced VEH-jee) and the more authentic *terrine de champignons* are both satisfying, and carnivores are kept happy with *entrecôte* and tartare.

✚ Ⓜ*Hôtel de Ville. Walk against traffic on rue de Rivoli and turn left onto rue du Bourg Tibourg.* Ⓢ *Plats €11-15. Su brunch buffet €19.* ⌚ *Open daily noon-2pm and 7-10:30pm.*

LE TRÉSOR

TRADITIONAL $$$

5/9 rue du Trésor ☎01 42 71 35 17; www.restaurantletresor.com

If you want to experience swanky side of the Marais (without blowing a hole in your wallet), come here and deliberate between the veal and the bread-encrusted salmon. You might miss it altogether, though, as the restaurant's exterior is hidden by plants and flowers.

✚ Ⓜ*St-Paul. Walk with traffic on rue de Rivoli, turn left onto rue Vieille du Temple, and turn right onto rue du Trésor.* Ⓢ *Lunch menu €13. Dinner menu €24.* ⌚ *Open daily noon-2am.*

LATIN QUARTER AND ST-GERMAIN

These neighborhoods are deceptive. What look like cute French restaurants can be total tourist traps where the waitstaff will rush you out as fast as you eat. Yet you can also find food from all over France at a reasonable cost. As a general rule, restaurants between the Seine and bd St-Germain are not as authentic as those south of St-Germain. **Rue Mouffetard** has some smaller, cheaper options that are popular with students and budget travelers.

SAVANNAH CAFÉ

LEBANESE $$

27 rue Descartes ☎01 43 29 45 77; www.savannahcafe.fr

A contradictory mix of Lebanese cuisine and French flavors makes Savannah all the rage with Parisian restaurateurs. One of the best deals is the mix of six Lebanese appetizers for €17. The bright yellow interior is covered with stuffed toy zebras, photos of the Middle East, and framed recommendations.

✚ Ⓜ*Cardinal Lemoine. Walk uphill on rue du Cardinal Lemoine and turn right onto rue Clovis. Walk 1 block and turn left onto rue Descartes. The cafe is on the left.* Ⓢ *Entrées €7-14. Plats €14-16. Desserts €6-7.50.* ⌚ *Open M-Sa 7-11pm.*

CRÊPERIE DES CANETTES

CREPERIE $

10 rue des Canettes ☎01 43 26 27 65; www.pancakesquare.com

Creperies are ubiquitous; however, this one uniquely prepares affordable crepes in the traditional way—square and crispy, not round and soft. The goat cheese and walnut crepes (€7) are a good choice, as is the "Typhoon" (salmon, crème fraiche, and lemon; €9), which appropriately goes with the sailing theme.

✚ Ⓜ*Mabillon. Walk down rue de Four and turn left onto rue des Canettes.* Ⓢ *Crepes €3.50-9. Lunch and dinner menus €12.* ⌚ *Open M-Sa noon-11pm.*

LA METHODE

PROVENÇAL $$

2 rue Descartes ☎01 43 54 22 43

This Provençal restaurant takes French dishes and gives them a southern flair, creating an upscale meal that won't leave you broke. One of the best starters is the artichoke salad and foie gras, or, for the less adventurous, the salmon and ratatouille *entrée* is pretty damn good. The most difficult decision will be where to sit: the terrace overlooks the small plaza while the converted wine cave from the 17th century is perfect for a glass of wine.

✚ Ⓜ*Cardinal Lemoine. Walk uphill on rue du Cardinal Lemoine and turn right onto rue Clovis. Walk 1 block and turn right onto rue Descartes. The restaurant is on the left in the square.* Ⓢ *Plats €11-14. Lunch menu €14. Dinner menu €15.* ⌚ *Open Oct-Aug M-Sa noon-2pm and 7-10pm, Su noon-10pm.*

snack attack

Parisians prefer traditional patisseries, *boulangeries,* and *fromageries* to supermarket chains that sell pre-packaged cheese and baguettes. But Paris's supermarkets still treat taste buds better than their equivalents in most other cities. Hop into any Carrefour, Monoprix, or Franprix to get ahold of these unique snacks.

- **SPECULOOS BISCUITS.** Based with a Nutella-like spread, this alternative to graham crackers was featured on pastry chef David Lebovitz's famous Parisian food blog.
- **PIMM'S COOKIES.** These crunchy treats based on the British drink are filled with orange or raspberry jelly. Though they won't give you a buzz, the sugar high might make up for your sobriety.
- **KINDER BARS.** This Italian candy bar is highly popular in France. Try a Bueno bar for its wafery goodness with a tongue-numbing hazelnut cream filling. The Duplo bar is a classier alternative with nougat cream, whole walnuts, and milk chocolate. A word of caution: avoid the candy aisle after schools let out, or you'll be duking it out with hungry French children for these treats.
- **FLAVORED YOGURT.** The French love being daring with dairy, so take advantage of the interesting yogurt varieties sold in most grocery stores. Among the unique flavors are citrus *(citron)* and hazelnut *(noisette).* Quality (read: expensive) brands come in glass jars.

CAVE LA BOURGOGNE BRASSERIE $$

144 rue Mouffetard ☎01 47 07 82 80

Whether you go for beer or a full meal, this brasserie's terrace is usually packed (even on Sunday), and its location in the middle of a roundabout makes it great for people-watching. If you don't want to wait for outside seating, the interior is decorated with wine barrels and empty wine bottles that clue you into what should be paired with your affordable steak tartar (€15).

[M]Censier-Daubenton. Walk down rue Monge and turn right onto rue Censier. Walk until you reach Sq. St-Médard. It's on the other side of the roundabout. [$] Salads €7-10. Meat dishes €14-18. ⏰ Open daily noon-3pm and 7:30-11pm.

LE VIEUX BISTRO BISTRO $$

54 rue Mouffetard

Visit Le Vieux Bistro for one of the cheapest three-course meals in the 5ème, served by a staff that won't rush you. The bistro serves traditional Savoy faire with *escargot,* onion soup, and tenderloin that melts in your mouth. The local youth make Le Vieux their hangout spot, despite the somewhat cheesy baskets, pots, and spices that hang from the ceiling.

[M]Place Monge. Walk down rue Monge and turn right onto pl. Monge. Keep going as it turns into rue Ortolan and turn right onto rue Mouffetard. The restaurant is on the left. [$] 3-cheese fondue €14. Lunch menu €10. Dinner menu €16. ⏰ Open daily noon-3pm and 6pm-midnight.

DANS LES LANDES

TAPAS $$

119 bis rue Monge

☎01 45 87 06 00

This bistro will have you thinking it's Spanish with their tapas happy hour (cocktail and choice of *tapa*; €8). The terrace is tempting, but the inside draws you in with its curvy stone-finish walls, Southern European wine that doubles as decoration, and huge shared tables that encourage chatting with your neighbors.

✦ Ⓜ*Censier-Daubenton. Walk down rue Monge. The restaurant is on the left.* Ⓢ *Plats €7-21. Happy hour special €8.* Ⓩ *Open daily noon-11pm. Happy hour 5-7:30pm.*

LE BISTROT D'HENRI

TRADITIONAL $$

16 rue Princesse

☎01 46 33 51 12

For a really impressive meal—or to impress your date—this Old World bistro serves some reasonably priced traditional French food. The chef recommends the lamb, which is expertly marinated in prune juice for 7hr. (this may strike you as over the top, but he's an artist), or the duck breast covered in honey. Landing a table at this Art Deco joint can be difficult, so call ahead for reservations or hop on La Fourchette (www.lafourchette.com) to nab a table and get discounts on *entrées* or drinks.

✦ Ⓜ*Mabillon. Walk down rue du Four and turn left onto rue Princesse.* Ⓢ *Entrées €7-11. Plats €14-23.* Ⓩ *Open M-Sa noon-2:30pm and 7-11:30pm.*

BOTEQUIM

BRAZILIAN $$

1 rue Berthollet

☎01 43 37 98 46

If you're looking for an escape from traditional Parisian cuisine, enter Botequim and be transported to Brazil. Statues of Catholic saints stand alongside tribal boa headdresses on the shelves. Without a knowledge of Portuguese, it will be a little hard to navigate the menu. Never fear: go for anything, from the coconut shrimp to the *salade tropicale* (hearts of palm, shrimp, cashews, and pineapple) or the salmon with mango sauce. Just be prepared for the culture shock when you leave and discover you're back in France.

✦ Ⓜ*Censier-Daubenton. Walk down rue Monge and turn right onto rue Claude Bernard. The restaurant is at the corner with rue Berthollet.* Ⓢ *Entrées €8-9. Plats €15-17.* Ⓩ *Open M-Sa noon-3:30pm and 8pm-2am.*

L'ASSIETTE AUX FROMAGES

FONDUE $$

25 rue Mouffetard

☎01 43 36 91 59; www.lassietteauxfromages.com

This Swiss establishment is the answer to your authentic-fondue prayers. The smiling cow in the window hints at the wide variety of French cheeses you can order to accompany any salad or melon and ham dish. Choose between the two *formules* (one more expensive than the other) that include *confit de canard* or lamb with rosemary.

✦ Ⓜ*Place Monge. Walk down rue Monge and turn right onto pl. Monge. Keep going as it turns into rue Ortolan and turn right onto rue Mouffetard. The restaurant is 1½ blocks down on the right.* Ⓢ *Fondues €15-17. Formules €16 or €26.* Ⓩ *Open daily noon-2:30pm and 6:30-11:30pm.*

AUX DOUX RAISINS

BISTRO $$

29 rue Descartes

☎ 01 43 29 31 13

While most of the items on the menu of this winery-inspired bistro may be as basic as you'd pack for a picnic in the Jardin du Luxembourg, they do serve popular dishes that would be familiar to any French farmer: *bœuf bourguignon*, foie gras, and *confit de canard* (€13-14). For an impressive spread of meats and cheeses for two, split the *planche doux raisins* (€13).

✦ Ⓜ*Cardinal Lemoine. Walk uphill on rue du Cardinal Lemoine and turn right onto rue Clovis. Walk 1 block and turn left onto rue Descartes.* Ⓢ *Entrées €7-8.50. Plats €13-14. Desserts €7-8.* Ⓩ *Open daily 11:30am-1am.*

INVALIDES

The chic 7ème is low on budget options, but there are a number of quality restaurants that are worth the extra euro. **Rue Saint-Dominique, rue Cler,** and **rue de Grenelle** feature some of the best gourmet bakeries in Paris. The steaming baguettes and pastries make for an ideal picnic by the nearby Eiffel Tower.

CHEZ LUCIE
CREOLE, STUFF YOUR FACE $$

15 rue Augereau ☎01 45 55 08 74

Specializing in dishes from Martinique, this Creole hole in the wall will make you abandon your Eurotrip for a sailboat in the French Antilles. The owner prides himself on his conversation skills; he shoots the breeze with customers and will even show you pictures of his wife while you dine on gumbo, spicy catfish, or—for the more adventurous—shark. The portions are enormous for such a low price, and the *ti' ponch* (rum punch) will knock you on your ass.

♯ ⓂÉcole Militaire. Walk toward the Eiffel Tower on av. de la Bourdonnais, turn right onto rue de Grenelle, and then take an immediate left onto rue Augereau. The restaurant is on the right (with a bright yellow awning). ⓈEntrées €7. Plats €10-30. 3-course lunch special €16. Dinner special €16-25. ⏰Open daily noon-2pm and 7-11pm.

LES COCOTTES
RESTAURANT $$

135 rue St-Dominique ☎01 45 50 10 31; www.maisonconstant.com

Christian Constant, a famed Parisian chef, realized that not everyone wants to pay an arm and a leg for a good meal. He then opened Les Cocottes and began serving quick gourmet salads (poached egg and dried meat on greens with vinaigrette) and dishes cooked in the famed metal kettles (like caramelized potatoes with pork) for up-and-coming, business-casual French as well as intrepid tourists.

♯ ⓂÉcole Militaire. Walk toward the Eiffel Tower on av. de la Bourdonnais, turn right onto rue de Grenelle, followed by an immediate left onto rue Augereau. Walk to St-Dominique and turn right. The restaurant is on the right. ⓈMousseline d'artichaut €16. Salads €10-12. Mousse au chocolat €7. ⏰Open M-Sa noon-4pm and 7-11pm.

LE SAC À DOS
TRADITIONAL $$$

47 rue de Bourgogne ☎01 45 55 15 35; www.le-sac-a-dos.fr

This hidden gem makes up for generic French fare with personality that will make you blush. Or was that because the sun-bleached owner's shirt is unbuttoned to his navel? Choose from one of the main dishes written on chalkboards, and make room for the *mousse au chocolat* that is served in a cookie bowl.

♯ ⓂVarenne. Walk away from Pont d'Alexandre III on bd des Invalides, turning left on rue de Varenne. Walk 1 block, past the Musée-Rodin, to rue de Bourgogne and turn left. The restaurant is on the right. ⓈPlats €17. Desserts €6. ⏰Open M-Sa 11am-2:30pm and 6:30-11pm.

CHAMPS-ÉLYSÉES

Once the center of Paris's glamorous dining scene, the 8ème's culinary importance is on the decline, but its prices are not. We don't recommend eating on the Champs-Élysées, but we do suggest visiting the bakeries, *épiceries*, and cafes below for a small (but expensive) treat. Thabthim Siam is a total exception: eat there. There are also cheaper establishments around **rue la Boétie, rue des Colisées,** and **place de Dublin.**

THABTHIM SIAM
THAI $$

28 rue de Moscou ☎01 43 87 62 56

Thabthim Siam is where locals come to get their curry fix. The changing menu allows patrons to sample a wide range of Thai cuisine. Linguistically challenged customers beware: authentic Thai names only have French translations, so if those aren't in your repertoire, just point to a neighboring table and order what they're eating—it's most likely delicious.

♯ ⓂRome. ⓈEntrées €8. Plats €13-17. 2-course lunch menu with drink €15. ⏰Open M-Sa noon-2pm and 7-10:30pm.

LADURÉE
TEA HOUSE $

18 rue Royale ☎01 49 60 21 79; www.laduree.com

Opened in 1862, Ladurée started off as a modest bakery. It has since become so famous that a *Gossip Girl* employee was flown here to buy macaroons so Chuck could offer his heart to Blair properly. On a more typical day the Rococo decor of this tea salon—the original location of a franchise that now extends to 13 countries—attracts a jarring mix of well-groomed shoppers and tourists in sneakers. Along with the infamous mini macaroons arranged in pyramids in the window (beware: the rose flavor tastes like bathroom freshener), most items will induce a diabetic coma. Dine in the salon or queue up an orgasm to go.

✠ ⓂConcorde. ⓈMacaroons €1.70. ⏱ Open M-Th 8:30am-7:30pm, F-Sa 8:30am-8pm, Su 10am-7pm. Other locations at 75 av. des Champs-Élysées, 21 rue Bonaparte, and 64 bd Haussmann.

white is the new yellow

The McDonald's on av. des Champs-Élysées is not your typical grab-and-go fast food. While taking a bite of your *Croque McDo* (grilled ham and cheese sandwich) and sipping a can of Kronenbourg 1664 in the spacious restaurant, you'll notice that the famous golden arches in front of the store look unusually pale. Apparently, Parisians considered the traditional Mickey D's yellow to be too tacky—the city enforces a regulation that requires shops on this posh avenue to flaunt classy white signs only.

MOOD
ASIAN, BURGER BAR $$

114 av. des Champs-Élysées and 1 rue Washington ☎01 42 89 98 89; www.mood-paris.fr

Like the Asian woman's nipple that greets you at the door (don't get too excited; it's only a photograph), Mood is a matter of personal taste, and you may or may not think the restaurant warrants all the fuss. The sensuous melange of Western decor and delicate Japanese accents reflects the fusion cuisine that revisits the classic American hamburger. The *prix-fixe* lunch (€17-21) might be the only affordable way to finagle your way into the beige upper dining room.

✠ ⓂGeorge V. ⓈEntrées €10-19. Plats €17-35. Cocktails €15. ⏱ Restaurant open M noon-2::30pm, Tu-F noon-2:30pm and 7pm-1am, Sa 7pm-1am, Su noon-2:30pm and 7pm-1am. Bar open daily 5pm-1am. Happy hour daily 5-8pm.

FOUQUET'S
CAFE $$$$

99 av. des Champs-Élysées ☎01 47 23 50 00

Restaurants can only dream of this kind of fame. This sumptuous, red velvet-covered cafe once welcomed the likes of Chaplin, Churchill, Roosevelt, and Jackie Onassis. While Fouquet's past its glory days, the people-watching on the Champs-Élysées alone is worth the €8 coffee. Just so you know, you're paying to sit among the rich, not for your beverage. Still, it's an experience of quintessential old-time Parisian glamour, easy on the eyes and devastating for the bank account (*entrées* start at €30).

✠ ⓂGeorge V. ⓈPlats €20-55. ⏱ Cafe open daily 8am-2am. Restaurant open daily 7:30-10am, noon-3pm, and 7pm-midnight.

FAUCHON
FOOD STORE $$$

26-30 pl. de la Madeleine ☎01 47 42 60 11; www.fauchon.com

If you didn't blow all your euro at Ladurée, then you might be able to afford this pricey and equally upper-class *épicerie*. Splurge on nougat (€8-13) or *pâte de fruit* (fruit paste; €6.50) to add some class to your picnic, or buy teas and chocolates (€10-145) as a gift for your connoisseur friend.

⯑ [M]Madeleine. ⏰ Épicerie and confiserie open M-Sa 9am-8pm. Boulangerie open 8am-9pm, eat-in 8am-6pm. Traiteur and patisserie open 8am-9pm. Tea room open 9am-7pm.

TY YANN — CREPERIE $

10 rue de Constantinople — ☎01 40 08 00 17

The ever-smiling Breton chef and owner, M. Yann, cheerfully prepares outstanding and relatively inexpensive *galettes* (€7.50-11) and crepes in a tiny, unassuming restaurant—the walls are decorated with his mother's pastoral paintings. Creative concoctions include La Vannetaise (sausage sautéed in cognac, Emmental cheese, and onions; €10). Create your own crepe (€6.40-7.20) for lunch.

⯑ [M]Europe. [$] Crepes €7.50-11. Credit card min. €12. ⏰ Open M-F noon-2:30pm and 7:30-10:30pm, Sa 7:30-10:30pm.

OPÉRA AND CANAL ST-MARTIN

It's not a challenge for the average tourist to find the famous places in the 9ème, most of which are located around **rue Saint-Georges.** Here, we're throwing out some harder-to-find but equally good restaurants in price and quality. The unknown secret is the 10ème, which easily outshines the 9ème in terms of quaint, cheap establishments, especially around the canal area. Passage Brady, two blocks north of [M]Strasbourg-St-Denis, has a wealth of Indian and Pakistani restaurants serving the best cheap curries in Paris.

✎ BOB'S JUICE BAR — SMOOTHIES, BAGELS $

15 rue Lucien Sampaix — ☎09 50 06 36 18

This small hippie, eco-conscious smoothie and bagel shack is usually filled with backpackers sharing long tables and snacking on homemade baked goods (€1-3) and bottomless coffee brewed all day.

⯑ [M]Jacques Bonsergent. Walk up bd de Magenta toward Gare du Nord, and turn right onto rue Lucien Sampaix. Juice Bar is ½ a block up on the left. [$] Smoothies €5-6. Bagel sandwiches €5.50. ⏰ Open M-F 8am-3pm.

food

✎ CHEZ MAURICE — BISTRO $$

26 rue des Vinaigriers — ☎01 46 07 07 91

Finally, a real French meal for dirt cheap. If the old-fashioned interior doesn't transport you to the turn of the century, a carafe of wine from the tap will help. Hold out for dessert, where it will be hard to choose between crème brûlée or chocolate fondue, even after stuffing yourself with *escargot* or steak tartare.

⯑ [M]Jacques Bonsergent. Walk up bd de Magenta toward Gare du Nord, and turn right onto rue Lucien Sampaix. Walk 1 block to rue des Vinaigriers and turn right. The restaurant is on the right. [$] Menu €11-16. Cash only. ⏰ Open M-F noon-3pm, Sa 6:30-11pm.

NO STRESS CAFE — TAPAS, CAFE $$

24 rue Clauzel — ☎01 48 78 00 27

The huge terrace and quiet plaza give this funky cafe its namesake vibe. While you can skip most of the food, No Stress has a killer happy hour (Tu-Th 6-8pm) with cheap cocktails (€5) and tapas (€3.50) that draw a young crowd that quickly evaporates once the deal ends, only to reappear again before closing.

⯑ [M]St-Georges. Walk up rue Notre Dame de Lorette in the direction of traffic until you reach rue H. Monnier. Turn left and the cafe is in the pl. Gustave Toudouze. [$] Lunch menu €13. Plats €14-€18. Woks €15-18. Salads €14-€16. Desserts €7.50-€8.50. ⏰ Open Tu-Su 11am-2am.

QUAI GOURMAND — PASTA, CAFE $

79 quai de Valmy — ☎01 40 40 72 84

This super cheap, albeit tacky, cafe serves the type of food that you could probably prepare yourself in a hostel kitchen. But its location right on the canal and tempting selection of Magnum Bars for dessert will help you withstand the bright pink and green interior and NRJ pop music soundtrack.

✠ ⓂRépublique. Walk toward the canal on rue de Faubourg (the one that bisects pl. de la République). Turn left once you get to the canal and walk 3 blocks. The cafe is on the left. Ⓢ Sandwiches €4.50. Lunch menu (until 3:30pm) €8. To-go pasta bowls €6. Crepes €3, additional ingredients €1. ☼ Open daily 10am-8pm.

URFA DURUM   KURDISH $

58 rue Faubourg St-Denis   ☎01 48 24 12 84

In a city full of kebabs and faux Middle Eastern fast food, Urfa Durum stays true to its Kurdish roots. Cheap lamb sandwiches are served in bread baked to order. Top off the experience by eating at the traditional (read: miniature) wooden tables and stools outside the shop.

✠ ⓂChâteau d'Eau. Exit onto bd Stasbourg. Facing the Gare de l'Est at the intersection of bd Stasbourg and rue du Château d'Eau, walk left and take the 1st left onto rue Faubourg St-Denis. Ⓢ Sandwiches €6. ☼ Open daily noon-8pm.

LE CAMBODGE   CAMBODIAN $$

10 av. Richerand   ☎01 44 84 37 70; www.lecambodge.fr

If you can't manage to get a seat because of the obscene crowds, this traditional Cambodian restaurant does takeout. Cambodge prides itself on spicy mixes of herbs, curry, and meats. Specialties include caramelized pork and citronella beef, which can be washed down with (slightly off-theme) Chinese Tsing-Tao beer. Yes, the beer is also available to go.

✠ ⓂRépublique. Walk toward the canal on rue de Faubourg (the one that bisects pl. de la République). Cross the canal, and turn left onto quai de Jemmapes. Walk 2 blocks to av. Richerand; the restaurant is on the right. Ⓢ Entrées €3-11. Plats €8.50-13. Desserts €4.50-5.50. ☼ Open M-Sa noon-2:30pm and 8-11:30pm.

BASTILLE

Bastille swells with fast-food joints, so you can choose which of the kebab stands grosses you out the least. But the diverse neighborhood also boasts a number of upscale ethnic restaurants, many of which are cheaper than those in the central arrondissements. The most popular haunts line the bustling **rue de Charonne, rue Keller, rue de Lappe,** and **rue Oberkampf.** The 12ème is generally affordable, with casual establishments that serve a variety of cuisines, from North African to Middle Eastern to traditional French. The best places are found on the side streets, while **Viaduc des Arts** hosts a few terrace cafes that are popular with designers.

🄰 AUGUSTE   SANDWICHES $

10 rue St-Sabin   ☎01 47 00 77 84; www.augusteparis.com

A tiny hole in the wall whose clientele look like throwbacks to the days of the Paris Commune, this *sandwicherie* is packed at lunchtime with students and penny-pinchers looking to get at simple—but huge—sandwiches like the salmon and avocado or goat cheese and honey.

✠ ⓂBréguet-Sabin. Cross Canal St-Martin on rue Sedaine and turn right onto rue St-Sabin. Ⓢ Sandwiches €2-4. Soups €3-5. Cash only. ☼ Open M-Sa 11am-4pm.

KATMANDOU CAFE   INDIAN $$

14 rue de Bréguet   ☎01 48 05 36 36; www.katmandou.fr

Specializing in everything spicy, this Indian restaurant has six types of naan and curry for those who want their taste buds slowly singed off. To wash it down, order a lassi with mint, banana, or rose and mango.

✠ ⓂBréguet-Sabin. Cross Canal St-Martin on rue Sedaine, turn left onto bd Richard Lenoir, and turn right onto rue de Bréguet. Ⓢ Plats €9.50-13. Prix-fixe menu €12. 10% discount for takeout. ☼ Open M-Sa noon-2:30pm and 7-11:30pm, Su 7-11:30pm.

paris

MORRY'S BAGELS AND TOASTS
BAGELS $

1 rue de Charonne
☎01 48 07 03 03

Those who miss the towering *grattes-ciel* of NYC should stop at Morry's for heated bagels topped with pastrami, cream cheese, avocado, or salmon. While the young clientele probably don't recognize the picture of a young Bob Dylan, they do know budget eats when they see them.

✝ Ⓜ*Bastille. Walk down rue du Faubourg St-Antoine and turn left onto rue de Charonne.* Ⓢ *Bagels €3-5.90. Desserts €1.50-3.40.* 🕐 *Open M-Sa 8:30am-7:30pm.*

BARBERSHOP
BISTRO $$

68 av. de la République
☎01 47 00 12 85

For a Parisian restaurant, Barbershop manages the rather impressive task of making French food seem out of place, since everything else here seems to have come straight from Jamaica. Enjoy your beef in Roquefort sauce or roasted Camembert while pictures of Bob Marley watch over you. DJs take the theme further by spinning soul and reggae tunes during dinner.

✝ Ⓜ*Rue St-Maur.* Ⓢ *Plats €10-18. Prix-fixe menu €13.* 🕐 *Open M-Sa noon-3pm and 8-11pm, Su noon-4pm.*

LE DALLERY
BISTRO $$

6 Passage Charles Dallery
☎01 47 00 11 72

"French" and "hole in the wall" don't always go together, but this bistro combines them perfectly with express menus of grilled beef, lamb, or *salade paysanne* (€11) with dessert and coffee. The smell alone is enough to make you wander in from the main street.

✝ Ⓜ*Ledru-Rollin. Take av. Ledru-Rollin north, turn right onto rue de Charonne, and then left onto Passage Charles Dallery.* Ⓢ *Express menu €11. Regular menu €12.* 🕐 *Open M-Sa noon-8pm.*

PAUSE CAFE
CAFE $$

41 rue de Charonne
☎01 48 06 80 33

Hipster glasses are an unofficial pre-req for working here. People climb over themselves to get a seat on the large outdoor terrace and peruse the basic menu of salads, beer, tartare, and honey-glazed duck breast. It's run-down chic, but it was cool enough to be featured in the film *Chacun Cherche Son Chat*, which we suspect is the main reason people come here.

✝ Ⓜ*Ledru-Rollin. Take av. Ledru-Rollin north and turn left onto rue de Charonne.* Ⓢ *Plats €8-11.* 🕐 *Open M-Sa 8am-2am, Su 9:30am-9pm. Kitchen open M-Sa noon-midnight, Su noon-5pm.*

LE TOUAREG
AFRICAN $$

228 rue de Charenton
☎01 43 07 69 49

Le Touareg will throw you across the Mediterranean before you realize what you ordered—unless you're familiar with Moroccan cuisine, you won't notice. The *couscous méchoui* piles up with *merguez*, vegetables, and lamb, while their bowls of *chakchouka* (a spicy vegetable and egg dish) are big enough to bathe in. But these spicy dishes might make you sweat, so we suggest having pitchers of water handy.

✝ Ⓜ*Dugommier.* Ⓢ *Lunch menu €12. Plats €12-17.* 🕐 *Open M-Sa noon-3pm and 7pm-midnight.*

LE BAR À SOUPES
SOUP BAR $

33 rue de Charonne
☎01 43 57 53 79; www.lebarasoupes.com

This soup bar offers a pick-me-up for anyone feeling under the weather or a little homesick. Their lunch menu has basic soups like lentil and, for those whose hearts flutter when they hear "mmm mmm good," tomato soup. Giant paintings of vegetables match the equally large portions of soup. The rotating menu ensures that no two days are exactly the same.

✝ Ⓜ*Ledru-Rollin. Take av. Ledru-Rollin north and turn left onto rue de Charonne.* Ⓢ *Soups €5-6. Lunch menu €9.80.* 🕐 *Open M-Sa noon-3pm and 6:30-11pm.*

food

BODEGA BAY

SOUTH AMERICAN $$

116 rue Amelot   ☎01 47 00 13 53; www.bodega-bay.fr

Bodega Bay might seem like a cheesy throwback to TexMex and gringos, but you can skip over the nachos and fajitas for the more authentic grilled swordfish and bitter chocolate cake. If you're wondering why there's a large mural of a space invasion, we couldn't figure it out either.

✠ ⓂOberkampf. Follow the traffic on rue de Crussol and turn left onto rue Amelot. Ⓢ Plats €13-14. Prix-fixe menu €12. ☒ Open M-F noon-3pm and 6pm-midnight, Sa 6pm-midnight.

CAFE DE L'INDUSTRIE

CAFE $$

16 rue St-Sabin   ☎01 47 00 13 53

Though the coffee is one of the major draws here, the cafe expands its repertoire to include traditional French dishes (*plat du jour*; €10), including a selection of sliced meats and *tartines* if you just want to nibble as you down cheap wine. If the Cubist artwork starts to morph, we suggest slowing down on the wine.

✠ ⓂBréguet-Sabin. Ⓢ Plats €9-13. Desserts €2.50-6. ☒ Open daily 10am-2am. Kitchen closes at 12:30am.

MONTPARNASSE AND SOUTHERN PARIS

More relaxed than the areas constantly full of tourists and the pickpockets that follow them, Montparnasse and southern Paris offer restaurants that are refreshingly affordable. Neighborhoods around the lower half of **boulevard Raspail** in the 14ème serve more traditional French cuisine, while the **Quartier de la Butte-aux-Cailles** and **Chinatown** in the 13ème serve obscure foreign dishes for next to nothing.

🏚 CHEZ GLADINES

BASQUE $

30 rue des 5 Diamants   ☎01 45 80 70 10

What Chez Gladines lacks in decoration (beyond a prominent Basque flag) it makes up for by sticking to its separatist roots. Customers constantly line up to enjoy *cassoulets* and *piperade* (scrambled eggs with vegetables).

✠ ⓂPlace d'Italie. Take bd Auguste Blanqui away from pl. d'Italie and turn left onto rue des 5 Diamants. Ⓢ Assiettes €4-7.90. Plats €8.90-12. Cash only. ☒ Open daily noon-3pm and 7-10:30pm.

🏚 AU BRETZEL

ALSATIAN $$

1 rue Léopold Robert   ☎01 40 47 82 37

This is a more upscale Alsatian restaurant that still serves affordable *flammekeuche* (a kind of thin pizza). Come here to settle down in the carved wood chairs next to murals of German and French towns. The huge *flammekeuche* can be shared and are some of the most traditional in Paris, despite decor that feels like the inside of a cuckoo clock.

✠ ⓂVavin. Walk down bd du Montparnasse away from the tower and turn right onto rue Léopold Robert. Ⓢ Flammekeuche €8.50-10. Prix-fixe menu €18. ☒ Open M 7:30-10:30pm, Tu-Sa noon-2pm and 7:30-10:30pm.

🏚 PHO 14

VIETNAMESE $

129 av. de Choisy   ☎01 45 83 61 15

If you only eat in one place in Chinatown, make it Pho 14. A local favorite that draws starving students and penny-pinching barmen, Pho 14 (not to be confused with Pho 13 next door) serves huge bowls of *pho* beef (flank steak in spicy soup with rice) for next to nothing. This restaurant usually has a line out the door at night, so try to arrive on the early or late side of dinner.

✠ ⓂTolbiac. Walk east on rue de Tolbiac and turn left onto av. de Choisy. Ⓢ Pho €6-10. ☒ Open daily 9am-11pm.

food in the fast lane

Even Paris, a city filled with fine dining, isn't immune to the fast-food invasion. If *escargots* are a little too slow for you, get in the fast lane to some of these cheap joints.

- **QUICK BURGER.** Although it's a clear rip-off of McDonald's, Parisians prefer it to the original, even if they can't get a *Royale* with cheese.

- **FLUNCH.** The chain was named after a *portmanteau* between "fast food" and "lunch," which is now French slang meaning "to eat on the go" *(fluncher)*. The food is cooked in minutes at the grill, including the steak, green beans, and potatoes meal. We're not sure if that gives the cook enough time to determine whether the steak is *"rosé"* or *"à point,"* so dine at your own risk.

- **BRIOCHE DORÉE.** This chain patisserie sells all the usual tarts, morning croissants, and lunchtime baguettes. Located in some Metro stations, these identical shops mass manufacture pastries and are only redeemed by their gleaming glass cases and over-the-top gilded signs. After all, presentation is everything.

CHEZ PAPA 14
6 rue Gassendi

TRADITIONAL $$
☎01 43 22 41 19

Specializing in cuisine from the wine production regions of southwestern France, Chez Papa serves cheap foie gras, salads, and *cassoulets*. Don't let the low-hanging peppers, grapes, and spices hit you in in the head as you're being seated.

✚ Ⓜ*Denfert-Rouchereau. Walk toward Cimetière Montparnasse on rue Froidevaux. The restaurant is at the intersection of rue Froidevaux and rue Gassendi.* Ⓢ *Entrées €5-7. Plats €9-12. Prix-fixe menu €12.* Ⓩ *Open daily noon-3pm and 6pm-midnight.*

MUSSUWAM
33 bd Arago

AFRICAN $$
☎01 45 35 93 67; http://mussuwam.fr

Mussuwam serves traditional Senegalese food that provides a spicy break from the creamy and cheesy fare of French establishments. Some of the dishes are listed in a strange dialect that makes us wonder if Senegalese is its own language. Dinner is too pricey to bother, but if you keep an open mind, their lunch menu changes daily and costs a fraction of the regular prices.

✚ Ⓜ*Les Gobelins.* 𝒊 *Lunch menu Tu-F.* Ⓢ *Lunch menu €16. Dinner and weekend menu €25.* Ⓩ *Open Tu-Th noon-3pm and 7-10:30pm, F-Sa noon-10:30pm*

LES TONTONS
3 rue des Gobelins

BISTRO $$
☎08 99 69 76 21

Designed after an old-style bistro with mirrors to make it appear larger than it is, Les Tontons specializes in steak and tartare. You can even order bone marrow. If steak isn't your thing, choose from desserts like tiramisu with strawberry tagada or simple Nutella cake.

✚ Ⓜ*Les Gobelins.* Ⓢ *Lunch menu €13. Dinner menu €16.* Ⓩ *Open M-Sa noon-2:30pm and 7-10:30pm.*

LES TEMPS DES CERISES
18 rue de la Butte-aux-Cailles

TRADITIONAL $$
☎01 45 89 69 48

One of several outrageous menu options at Les Temps des Cerises is a *pot-au-feu* with a mix of pig cheek and duck. Waiters joke with each other and clients and are happy to point you in the direction of more obscure French dishes.

✚ Ⓜ*Place d'Italie.* Ⓢ *Entrées €7.50-11. Plats €10-17. Lunch menu €9.20.* Ⓩ *Open M-F 11:45am-2:10pm and 7:15-11:45pm, Sa 7:15-11:45pm.*

WESTERN PARIS

These two arrondissements are kind of a challenge. On one side, the 16ème has the upscale restaurants that often charge just for the privilege of breathing in their establishment. Then you have the 17ème, where attitudes and prices are much more relaxed, and the locals are more than willing to befriend you or go out of their way to add an extra table to their terrace to accommodate you.

LA VILLA PASSY — CAFE $$

4 Impasse des Carrières — ☎01 45 27 68 76

Tucked away from the main roads in the 16ème, this cafe allows you and your date to swoon under the ivy-covered seating on pink-and-white cushioned benches. Or you can get the same theme inside, since the plants and fountains make the interior look like an outdoor courtyard. La Villa Passy is a bit more expensive than most restaurants, but if you're looking for the 16ème at its best, your search is over.

 # [M]La Muette. Walk in the direction of traffic (toward the Seine) down rue de Passy. Impasse des Carrières is the 5th street on the left, and the restaurant is at the end of the alley. [$] Plats (like salad and steak tartare) €15-19. Su brunch (salad, omelette, croissants, and coffee) €25. ⏰ Open Tu-F noon-3pm and 7-11pm; Sa noon-4pm and 7-11pm; Su noon-4pm.

CAFÉ DES PETITS FRÈRES DES PAUVRES — CAFE $

47 rue des Batignolles — ☎01 42 93 25 80

It's not so impressive in the food department, but this cafe is among the most affordable around: the €1.50 breakfast includes croissants, jam, and coffee. If that doesn't do it, some of the **cheapest coffee in Paris** (€0.45) will surely make you fall in love. The older regulars and staff are quick to chat and welcome you into their artsy community. In the afternoon, stop by to see local performances by poets, singers, and bands, plus the occasional movie showing.

 # [M]Place de Clichy. With your back to Montmartre, walk down bd des Batignolles 3 blocks and turn right onto rue des Batignolles. The cafe is 3 blocks down on the left. ⏰ Open M 9am-12:30pm and 2-6pm, Tu 9am-12:30pm, W-Th 9am-12:30pm and 2-6pm, F 9am-12:30pm and 2-5pm, 1st and 3rd Sa each month 9am-12:30pm.

LES FILAOS — AFRICAN $$$

5 rue Guy de Maupassant — ☎01 45 04 94 53; www.lesfilaos.com

The first joint in Paris to specialize in Mauritian cuisine, Les Filaos provides an ethnic touch to the 16ème restaurant scene. *Ti' ponches* (rum punches; €5) are made fresh behind the straw hut bar. Curries (€15-16) can be made as spicy as you like, and be sure to save room for the coconut tarts. Saturday night *soirées* feature live Mauritian dancers.

 # [M]Rue de la Pompe. Walk toward the RER station Henri Martin, and turn left onto bd Emilie Augier. Walk 1 block and turn left onto rue Guy de Maupassant. The restaurant is on the left. [$] Prix-fixe lunch €20; dinner €35. ⏰ Open Tu-F noon-2pm and 7-10pm, Sa 7-10:30pm.

LE MANOIR — BRASSERIE $$

7 rue des Moines — ☎01 46 27 54 51

A local favorite (if the packed terrace of chattering Parisians didn't give it away), this restaurant and cafe attracts laid-back 17ème residents. To keep up with high demand in the summer months, the owner makes a habit of expanding his outdoor seating well into the public sidewalk.

 # [M]Brochant. With your back to the post office, walk down av. de Clichy 1 block and turn right onto rue des Moines. The restaurant is 3 blocks down and on the left. i Wi-Fi. [$] Plats €10-20. 2-course lunch €12. Su brunch €20. ⏰ Open daily 7:30am-2am.

MONTMARTRE

Montmartre has bistros from the turn of the last century, creative chefs looking for new ways to do the same thing, and a host of nicer internationally influenced establishments. The upscale options are in **Clichy** and **Jules Joffrin.**

LE REFLET DU MIROIR — CREPERIE, INTERNATIONAL $

161 rue Ordener — ☎01 42 62 23 97; www.lerefletdumiroir.fr

If you stare into the mirrors that decorate this "creperie," you'll probably have a confused look on your face. These aren't your average crepes, and it's not your average creperie. Drawing inspiration from around the world, Le Reflet du Miroir uses chutney from London or shredded parmesan from Italy and puts them in French wrapping. Apparently beside themselves with what to do with American cuisine, they gave up and served plain ol' burgers (€11).

[M]Jules Joffrin. With your back to the church, walk to the left of the triangular building and up rue Ordener. [$] Crepes €8-10; deluxe crepes €11. Plats €4-12. ⏰ Open Tu-F 7-10pm, Sa noon-10pm, Su 7-10pm.

LE PERROQUET VERT — BISTRO $$$

7 rue Cavallotti — ☎01 45 22 49 16; www.perroquet-vert.com

This French bistro is named after a book by Marthe Bibesco, a scandalous writer from the 1920s (don't worry, we had to Wikipedia her too). While we can't promise artistic talent after eating here, we can promise one of the oldest bistros in Montmartre with traditional French fare like veal and market fish with chorizo sauce. Enjoy your food while sitting in red velvet chairs and waiting for an epiphany. Try to dine here during the week, as the weekend selection is pricey.

[M]Place de Clichy. Walk up av. de Clichy for 3 blocks. Turn right onto rue Capron, walk 1 block, and turn left onto rue Cavallotti. [$] Entrées €8. Plats €16-17. Weekday lunch menu €14; weekend €29. ⏰ Open M-Sa 12:15-2:30pm and 7:30-10:30pm.

parisian bistro?

Think that bistros are a French invention? Think again. The word "bistro" originated during the occupation of Paris by the Russian army. In the 1814 Montmartre neighborhood, Cossack Russians set up a cafe that aimed to serve food quickly, or быстро (Russian for "quickly," pronounced "BEE-struh"). French linguists, however, dismiss this claim and say "bistro" is a shortening of the word *bistrouille*, meaning brandy and coffee.

RESTAURANT SEÇ — TURKISH $$

165 rue Ordener — ☎01 42 51 18 46; http://restaurant-sec.com

This upscale Turkish restaurant serves one hell of a lunch menu, with choices like stuffed peppers, kebabs, and grilled meatballs. But be sure not to miss the the Middle Eastern take on yogurt and honey—after all, it is the region that invented it.

[M]Jules Joffrin. With your back to the church, walk to the left of the triangular building and walk up rue Ordener. The restaurant is on the left. [$] Entrées €4-7. Plats €10-14. Lunch menu €15. ⏰ Open M-Sa 11:30am-3:30pm and 6:30pm-midnight.

EASTERN PARIS

This neighborhood has some of the best international food in the city. **Rue de Belleville** has the cheapest options, but be careful walking around this area after dusk.

🍴 MASSAI MARA — AFRICAN $

66 rue Armand Carrel — ☎01 42 08 00 65; www.massaimara.fr

For students, €5 at lunch gets you whatever the chef whips up, a drink, and a seat in one of the low leather-backed chairs. Fried plantains, rice, and white fish topped with some spicy sauce are some of the staples.

➡ ⓂJuarès. $ Plats €8-13. Student lunch menu €5. ⏰ Open daily noon-3pm and 7-11pm.

🍴 LAO SIAM — VIETNAMESE $$

48 rue de Belleville — ☎01 40 40 09 68

While most of the dishes here are cheap, Lao Siam sneaks a few more euro from your wallet by charging separately for rice (€2.20). The decor is nothing fancy, and paper napkins leave no room for pretension. But the food speaks louder than the decor, and the place is generally packed. The *filet du poisson* with "hip-hop sauce" (€8.80) is not to be missed. They also feature very tasty and salty duck selections.

➡ ⓂBelleville. $ Entrées €7-11. Plats €6.80-22. Beer €3.50. Wine by the bottle €11-55. ⏰ Open daily noon-3pm and 7-11pm.

nightlife

You may have told your parents, professors, and prospective employers that you've traveled to Paris to compare the works of Monet and Manet (hint: its not just one letter), but after 52 years in the business, we at *Let's Go* know it isn't just art that draws the young and the restless to Europe. If you're traveling to drink and mingle, Paris will not disappoint you. Nightlife here is debaucherous, and there's something for everyone. Bars are either chic cafes bursting with people-watching potential, party joints all about rock and teen angst, or laid-back local spots that double as havens for English-speakers. Clubbing in Paris is less about hip DJs and cutting-edge beats than it is about dressing up and being seen. Drinks are expensive, so Parisians usually stick to the ones included with the cover. Many clubs accept reservations, which means there's no available seating on busy nights. It's best to be confident (but not aggressive) about getting in. Bars in the 5ème and 6ème draw international students, while Châtelet-Les Halles attracts a slightly older set. The Marais is the center of Parisian GLBT nightlife.

ÎLE DE LA CITÉ AND ÎLE ST-LOUIS

Far from a party spot, the islands are a bit of a nightlife wasteland. Still, there are a few overpriced brasseries that are worth a stop. The bars are a lot more fun and a lot less expensive on either side of the bank in the neighboring 4ème and 5ème.

🍸 LE LOUIS IX — CAFE, BRASSERIE

25 rue des Deux-Ponts — ☎01 43 54 23 89

The islands are quiet. And so is the rough-looking bearded man in the corner who's working on his third or fourth *pastis* at this local bar. While the clientele may be the kind that go to bed at 8:30pm, its a good place to debate whether to go to the Latin Quarter or Marais over a pint of blond beer.

➡ ⓂPont Marie. $ Wine €3.50-4.60. Beer €3.80-5. Apéritifs €3.80-4.50. ⏰ Open daily 7:30am-8:30pm.

CHÂTELET-LES HALLES

The bars in Châtelet are close together and easy to find. This neighborhood has its fair share of GLBT bars (though it's no Marais) and small bars that are packed until dawn. Watch yourself around Les Halles, since the area is a prominent location for pickpockets.

◪ BANANA CAFÉ   BAR, CLUB, GLBT

13 rue de la Ferronerie   ☎01 42 33 35 31; www.bananacafeparis.com

Situated in the heart of Châtelet, Banana Café proclaims itself the most popular GLBT bar in the 1er, and rightly so. The club suits a wide range of clientele that range from the somewhat reticent patrons who occupy the terrace, to the erotic dancers/strippers stationed outside. Head downstairs after midnight for a piano bar and more dance space. There are weekly theme nights like "Go-Go Boys," which takes place Thursday through Saturday from midnight to dawn.

☂ ⓂChâtelet. Walk 3 blocks down rue St-Denis and turn right onto rue de la Ferronerie. Ⓢ Cover F-Sa €10; includes 1 drink. Beer €5.50. Cocktails €11. Happy hour pints €3; cocktails €4. ☼ Open daily 5:30pm-6am. Happy hour 6-11pm.

BAR N'IMPORTE QUOI   BAR

16 rue du Roule   ☎01 40 26 29 71; www.nimportequoi.fr

Almost anything goes at this bar that's normally packed on the weekends. Bras hang above the bar, possibly as a result of the "le boob shot" policy (flash the bartender for a free shot; women only). The downstairs doubles the size of the bar, alleviating some of the crowds. American sports are shown on Sunday nights, and early in the week draft beer is €5 all night—anything to keep people knocking 'em back.

☂ ⓂLouvre-Rivoli. Walk against traffic on rue de Rivoli and turn left onto rue du Roule. Ⓢ Shots €3. Beer €7-8. Cocktails €8.50. Happy hour cocktails €5.50. ☼ Open M-W 6pm-4:30am, Th-Sa 6pm-5:30am, Su 6pm-4:30am. Happy hour 6-8pm.

LE CLUB 18   CLUB, GLBT

18 rue Beaujolais   ☎01 42 97 52 13; www.club18.fr

Flashing lights and pop, house, and dance beats make for a wild night in this intimate (read: tiny), almost exclusively gay bar. Couches and mirrors line the walls, which means getting cozy with your neighbor is guaranteed. Younger crowds don't show up until after 1 or 2am.

☂ ⓂPalais Royal-Musée du Louvre. Follow rue de Richelieu and turn right onto rue de Montpensier. Follow rue de Montpensier around the Jardin du Palais Royal until rue Beaujolais. Ⓢ Cover €10; includes 1 drink. Cocktails €6-9. ☼ Open W midnight-6am, F-Sa midnight-6am.

nightlife

bare it all

Don't be surprised to find statues or advertisements of topless, bottomless, or completely nude people on the streets of Paris. At Fontaine de l'Observatoire, visitors will find three fully disrobed statues of women atop the fountain. On Paris billboards, Yves Saint Laurent created a new ad for M7, a cologne for men, that featured a full-frontal naked model. In this city, the human body is seen as art rather than a promiscuous eyesore, so don't snicker, giggle, or react in typical *American Pie* fashion.

LA CHAMPMESLÉ CLUB, GLBT

4 rue Chabanais ☎01 42 96 85 20; www.lachampmesle.com

This welcoming lesbian bar is Paris's oldest and most famous. Head under the rainbow for discussions on art, books, and current events. Josy, the owner, still works the bar, knows almost every customer by name, and enthusiastically promotes the bar's late-night spectacles (which, when they happen, are at 2am). The crowd is friendly; straight folk are warmly welcomed. The club hosts weekly cabaret shows and monthly art exhibits.

 # [M]Pyramides. Walk up av. de l'Opéra and turn right onto rue des Petits Champs. After a few blocks, turn left onto rue Chabanais. ***i*** *Cabaret shows Sa 10pm.* $ *Beer before 10pm €5, after €7. Cocktails €8-10.* ⏰ *Open M-Sa 4pm-3am.*

LE BAISER SALÉ JAZZ BAR

58 rue des Lombards ☎01 42 33 37 71; www.lebaisersale.com

This jazz bar is not the stereotypically hip, pretentious place you imagine. Housing African jazz and local alternative bands, Le Baiser Salé offers a quieter night for the partying type, with people intensely dancing in the packed upstairs lounge. Le Baiser Salé will please hipsters and their mainstream friends alike.

 # [M]Châtelet. Take rue St-Denis 2 blocks and turn left onto rue des Lombards. ***i*** *Tickets available at FNAC stores and online. Free jam sessions M at 10pm, 1-drink min.* $ *Cover €12-22. Beer €6.50. Cocktails €9.70. Happy hour beer €4-5; mojitos €4.50; cocktails €7. After 10pm, €1.30 increase on all drink prices.* ⏰ *Open daily 5pm-6am. Happy hour 5:30-8pm.*

THE MARAIS

There are about as many bars and clubs in the Marais as people. Paris's GLBT nightlife scene and other fashionable bars and clubs crowd **rue Sainte-Croix de la Bretonnerie.** Trendy establishments with outdoor seating are piled on top of one another on **rue Vieille du Temple** and between **rue des Francs Bourgeois** and **rue de Rivoli.** The places on **rue des Lombards** are more rough and convivial, though they're often filled with tourists. The 3ème is more laid-back for the most part, so women (and men) can leave the stilettos at home. There are a number of GLBT bars on and around **rue Saint-Martin,** and casual bars host live music, especially around the Pompidou.

RAIDD BAR BAR, CLUB, GLBT

23 rue Vieille du Temple ☎01 42 77 04 88

If you want a penis or just want to see one, come here. Sparkling disco balls light up Raidd Bar, as do the muscular, tank-topped torsos of the sexy male bartenders. After 11pm, performers strip down in the glass shower built into the wall (yes, they take it all off). There's a notoriously strict door policy: women aren't allowed unless they are outnumbered by (gorgeous) men.

 # [M]Hôtel de Ville. $ *Beer €6.50. Cocktails €10. Happy hour beer €4.20; cocktails €4.50.* ⏰ *Open M-Th 5pm-4am, F-Sa 5pm-5am, Su 5pm-4am. Happy hour 5-11pm.*

STOLLY'S BAR

16 rue Cloche Percé ☎01 42 76 06 76; www.cheapblonde.com

This small Anglophone hangout takes the sketchy out of the dive bar, but leaves the attitude. The pitchers of cheap blonde beer (€14) ensure that the bar lives up to its motto: "Hangovers installed and serviced here." Come inside, have a pint, and shout at the TV with the decidedly non-trendy, tattoo-covered crowd.

 # [M]St-Paul. From the Metro, turn right onto rue Pavée and then left onto rue du Roi de Sicile. Turn left onto rue Cloche Percé. $ *Beer pints €5-6; 1.5L €13. Cocktails €6.50-8. Happy hour pints and cocktails €5.* ⏰ *Open M-F 4:30pm-2am, Sa-Su 3pm-2am. Happy hour 5-8pm. Terrace open until midnight.*

ANDY WAHLOO
BAR

69 rue des Gravilliers   ☎01 42 71 20 38; www.andywahloo-bar.com

The walls may be covered with pictures of African women, but the clientele certainly dresses less conservatively. Andy Wahloo, which means, "I have nothing" in a certain Moroccan dialect, serves ambitious mint cocktails with chutney and banana liqueur (€10-14). DJs on Wednesdays start the weekend early with a mix of '90s rap, dance, and some salsa.

✠ ⓂArts et Métiers. Follow rue Beaubourg for 2 blocks and turn left onto rue des Gravilliers. Ⓢ *Cocktails €9-13.* ☼ *Open Tu-Sa 5pm-2am.*

O'SULLIVAN'S REBEL BAR
BAR

10 rue des Lombards   ☎01 42 71 42 72; http://chatelet.osullivans-pubs.com

A tattooed take on an Irish bar, O'Sullivan's Rebel Bar makes Paris's chain bars look like classy English tea rooms. The bartenders serve drinks so quickly that they sometimes use the water gun to cool off (or to squirt shots directly into their mouths). Come on the weekends when the music is loud and the crowd is rowdy.

✠ ⓂHôtel de Ville. Walk up rue du Renard and turn left onto rue de la Verrerie, which becomes rue des Lombards. Ⓢ *Pints €4-5.30. Cocktails €7-9; cocktail of the evening €5.* ☼ *Open M-Th 5pm-2-am, F-Sa 5pm-5am, Su 5pm-1am. Happy hour 5-9pm.*

OPEN CAFÉ
BAR, GLBT

17 rue des Archives   ☎01 42 72 26 18; www.opencafe.fr

Popular almost to the point of absurdity, this GLBT-friendly bar draws a large crowd of loyal, mostly older male customers. Though women are welcome, they will slowly find themselves outnumbered as the ever-expanding sea of Y-chromosomes grows later in the evening.

✠ ⓂHôtel de Ville. *i* ½-price beer 6-10pm. ½-price champagne 10pm-close. Ⓢ Beer €3.80. *Cocktails €7.90.* ☼ *Open M-Th 11am-2am, F-Sa 11am-4am.*

LE KOMPTOIR
BAR

27 rue Quincampoix   ☎01 42 77 75 35; www.lekomptoir.fr

Head to this tapas bar for the cheapest happy hour pints and cocktails in the Marais. Le Komptoir's distinctive backward "K" in its name hints at its backward behavior of cheap drinks, free entry to Thursday and Fridays concerts, and catering to the businessmen who come for afternoon shakes.

✠ ⓂHôtel de Ville. In the pl. Michelet. Walk up rue du Renard, turn right onto rue St-Merri and then left onto rue Quincampoix. *i* Jazz concerts Th 9pm. Pop rock concerts F 9pm. Ⓢ Beer €6.60. *Cocktails €8. Happy hour beer €4, cocktails 2 for 1. Concerts free.* ☼ *Open Tu-Su 10am-2am. Happy hour 6-8:30pm.*

LE DÉPÔT
CLUB, GLBT

10 rue aux Ours   ☎01 44 54 96 96; www.ledepot.com

Le Dépôt is a gay club that revolves around sex—literally. Winding passages lead to dance floors that shoot off into private rooms. Meanwhile, porn stars get off on mounted TVs. A steady stream of men and boys filter in at all hours, hoping for success in the designated "cruising" area. Women, as a rule, are not allowed.

✠ ⓂÉtienne Marcel. Follow the traffic on rue Étienne Marcel, which becomes rue aux Ours. Ⓢ *Cover M-Sa before 9pm and Su before 4pm €8.50; increases incrementally after that.* ☼ *Open daily 2pm-8am.*

LATIN QUARTER AND ST-GERMAIN

This neighborhood is awesome. **Rue Mouffetard** has the cheapest bars in Paris. At night they flood with students and backpackers. You should definitely wander down **rue de la Montagne Sainte-Geneviève** for the English-speaking bars.

👍 LE VIOLIN DINGUE — BAR, CLUB

46 rue de la Montagne Ste-Geneviève ☎01 43 25 79 93

Known as "le VD" to locals, this bar has some of the cheapest happy hour drinks, and it's open the latest. Upstairs feels like a pub with a strong American influence (they show American football, after all). After 1am, though, it floods with young French locals who swarm to get into the huge downstairs club, where the latest pop blasts against the vaulted stone ceilings until 5am.

➡ Ⓜ Cardinal Lemoine. Walk uphill on rue du Cardinal Lemoine and turn right onto rue Clovis. Walk 1 block and turn right onto rue Descartes. When you hit the plaza, the bar is on the left. $ Beer €6. Cocktails €7-10. Happy hour beer €3. Happy hour cocktails €4. Prices increase €1.50 after 1:30am. ⏰ Open daily 8pm-5am. Happy hour 8-10pm.

👍 LE FIFTH BAR — BAR

55 rue Mouffetard ☎01 43 37 09 09

The prized possession of rue Mouffetard, this bar is frequented by students and international travelers—the popularity shows on the scratched-up bar and stools. The drinks are cheap, and there is a sitting area in the back and a small dance floor downstairs that you might confuse with a sweatbox.

➡ Ⓜ Place Monge. Walk down rue Monge and turn right onto pl. Monge. Keep going as it turns into rue Ortolan and turn right onto rue Mouffetard. The bar is on the left. $ Shots €4. Beer €5.50. Cocktails €7-10. Happy hour specials €1-3 cheaper. ⏰ Open M-Th 4pm-2am, F-Sa 4pm-6am. Happy hour 4-10pm.

LA POMME D'EVE — BAR, CLUB

1 rue Laplace ☎01 43 25 86 18; www.lapommedeve.com

The only South African bar in Paris, La Pomme d'Eve is a night owl's hangout that explodes around 2am when the rest of the bars close. Ask George to make you a "Springbuck" (Amarula and Get 27; €5), then mingle under the zebra skin with local bartenders (French and international) who flock here after work.

➡ Ⓜ Cardinal Lemoine. Walk uphill on rue du Cardinal Lemoine and turn right onto rue Clovis. Walk 1 block and turn right onto rue Descartes. Walk until the plaza, turn uphill, walk 1 block, and take the 1st right. The bar is on the left. $ Beer €6.50. Cocktails €7-12. Happy hour beer and cocktails €5. ⏰ Open Tu-Su 8pm-5am. Happy Hour 6-9:30pm.

THE BOMBARDIER — PUB

2 pl. du Panthéon ☎01 43 54 79 22; www.bombardierpub.fr

This laid-back traditional British pub has one of the best locations in Paris, right behind the Panthéon between rue Mouffetard and rue Ste-Geneviève. Come for the cask ale, hang out with expats, and see where the night takes you. The Bombardier is not recommended for the faint of heart—everyone at this pub goes hard, especially the bartenders after closing.

➡ Ⓜ Cardinal Lemoine. Walk uphill on rue du Cardinal Lemoine and turn right onto rue Clovis. Walk 2 blocks and turn right onto pl. du Panthéon. ℹ Student happy hour night on M. Trivia Su 9pm. $ Beer €5.50-6; happy hour €4.50-5. Cocktails €8; happy hour €7. ⏰ Open daily noon-2am. Happy hour 5-9pm.

INVALIDES

While there aren't a lot of hopping clubs and bars in this area, there are a few gems that are geared toward the thinky-artsy types and the more party-hardy travelers. Most of the brasseries stay open until 8 or 9pm in this area (especially in summer when it stays light past 10pm). Find them around rue St-Dominique. For some free hanging out, head to the **Champs de Mars,** but some travelers report that despite seeing droves of youths drinking in public, it is illegal and police will pick up on any non-French behavior and pick off oblivious tourists.

LE CONCORDE ATLANTIQUE CLUB

23 quai Anatole France ☎01 40 56 02 82; www.bateauconcordeatlantique.com

Take a three-story club with themed *soirées*, add copious amounts of booze deals, and stick it right on the Seine. You have just imagined Le Concorde Atlantique. This boat/nightclub keeps going until 4 or 5am. *Soirées* are shamelessly promoted, often with cover charges that include free drinks, and the occasional ladies' night. The deals don't end there: the website **www.parisbouge.com** is an invaluable resource, giving out cheap tickets and drink passes to save travelers as much as 50%.

 # [M]Assemblée Nationale, right on the Seine in between Pont de la Concorde and walking bridge Solférino. $ Cover from €10-20, includes (sometimes up to 5) free drinks. Some nights men pay extra €5-10 and must pay online before. ⏰ Open Tu-Sa 8pm-4am (unless its a special soirée, which occur occasionally on Su).

CLUB DES POÈTES LOUNGE, RESTAURANT

30 rue de Bourgogne ☎01 47 05 06 03; www.poesie.net

If you want to drink and feel cultured, this restaurant-by-day and poetry-club-by-night is exactly what you're looking for. It brings together an intimate community of literati for supper and sonnets as local actors and singers take to the stage for improv poetry readings from around the world. Despite giving off a slightly intimidating hipster vibe, the crowd is well versed in English and welcomes visitors and travelers to cram in next to them on the long L-shaped table.

 # [M]Varenne. Walk towards Pont d'Alexandre III on bd des Invalides, turning right onto rue de Grenelle. Walk 1 block to rue de Bourgogne and turn left. The club is on your right. ℹ Poetry readings M-Sa 10pm. $ Prix-fixe entrée-plat or plat-dessert €10-25. Wine €6 per glass. ⏰ Open for lunch M-F noon-3pm. In the evening arrive between 8-10pm for dinner or drinks. Kitchen open until 10pm. No entry after 10pm.

CHAMPS-ÉLYSÉES

Glam is the name of the game at the trendy, expensive bars and clubs of the 8ème. Dress up, bring some atractive friends, and a fat wallet.

✓ LE QUEEN CLUB

102 av. des Champs-Élysées ☎01 53 89 08 90; www.queen.fr

A renowned Parisian institution where drag queens, superstars, tourists, and go-go boys get down and dirty to the mainstream rhythms of a 10,000-gigawatt sound system. Open all night, every night, Le Queen has *soirées* for just about every party demographic you can think of, as long as you can make it past the bouncer. Be prepared to show ID to gain entrance to this flashy disco with a light-up dance floor, which features theme nights that includes the occasional gay *soirée*.

 # [M]Georges V. ℹ Disco Night on M. Ladies Night on W; no cover for women 11:30pm-1am. Live DJ on F. $ Cover €20; includes 1 drink. Drinks €10. ⏰ Open daily 11:30pm-6am.

LE SHOWCASE CLUB

Under Pont Alexandre III, Port des Champs-Élysées ☎01 45 61 25 43; www.showcase.fr

One of the most popular clubs with the bohemian bourgeoisie in Paris (a.k.a. kids with money), Le Showcase's limited operation days and even more limited entrance make it nearly impossible to get in without some good-looking friends. To be sure you'll make it in, get on the "guest list" by registering your name for free online, then dance 'til dawn in this dungeon-esque club.

 # [M]Champs-Élysées-Clemenceau. ℹ Entrance typically free before midnight. Register for free on their website or Facebook page to be added to the guest list. $ Cover €10-15. Beer €9. Cocktails €15. ⏰ Open F-Sa 11pm-dawn.

THE BOWLER
BAR, RESTAURANT

13 rue d'Artois ☎01 45 61 16 60; www.thebowler.fr

The Bowler's upscale clientele will make you rethink the stereotypical British pub. With (relatively) cheap drinks in the heart of the 8ème it's hard to say no, especially to the weekly Quiz Night or live music. The large interior bar plays sports (tennis, cricket, rugby, and, of course, soccer are the popular ones) as patrons debate whether they are going to continue their night elsewhere or camp out and relax here.

＃ Ⓜ St-Philippe du Roule. Walk down rue de la Boétie toward the Champs and turn right onto rue d'Artois. The Bowler is on the left. *i* Live music M 7pm. Quiz Night on Su. Ⓢ Beer €6-9. Cocktails €9-12. Happy hour beer and cocktails €5. Brunch €10. ⌚ Open M-F noon-2am, Sa-Su 1pm-2am. Happy hour M-F 5-7pm, Sa-Su 1pm-2am. Brunch Sa-Su 1-3:30pm.

THE FREEDOM
BAR

8 rue de Berri ☎01 53 75 25 50

The Freedom might not have the decor or class of the rest of the neighborhood, but it makes up for it in sheer party spirit (we mean both kinds of "spirit"). Student Night has the cheapest shooters in all of Paris.

＃ Ⓜ George V. Walk away from the Arc de Triomphe and turn left down rue de Berri. *i* Student Night on Th. Ladies night F-Sa 11pm-5am. Ⓢ Shots €5. Beer €6. Cocktails €8-9. Student Night shots €2.50; beer €4. Ladies Night cocktail and shot €6. ⌚ Open M-Th 5pm-2am, F-Sa 5pm-5am, and Su 5pm-2am.

OPÉRA AND CANAL ST-MARTIN

Stay on major streets and avoid heading to the Metro on back alleys in the 10ème late at night. Pickpockets, muggers, and general scumbags abound.

LE PACHYDERME
BAR, RESTAURANT

2 bis bd St-Martin ☎01 42 06 32 56

More of a lounge bar than a party spot, this African-themed joint has statues of elephants and black leather love seats inside and a huge heated terrace outside. We would make some jokes about low lighting and elephants, but it's mean to pick on the overweight.

＃ Ⓜ Strasbourg-St-Denis. 3 blocks toward pl. de la République, on the left. Ⓢ Beer €6.80. Cocktails €9.70; "Cocktail of the moment" €7. Entrées €14-19. Plats €17-25. ⌚ Open daily noon-1:30am.

ECLIPSE CAFE
BAR, CLUB

12 rue du Château d'Eau ☎01 42 00 15 41

The party here depends on the size of the crowd. On a calm night, it's just some local youth drinking on the terrace with the bartenders and listening to music. When it gets packed, tables are moved and dancing gets going, aided by the cheap pints and cocktails.

＃ Ⓜ Jacques Bonsergent. Walk down bd de Magenta toward pl. de la République, turn right onto rue de Lancry, and then left onto rue du Château d'Eau. The bar is on the left. Ⓢ Pints and cocktails €5. ⌚ Open daily 6pm-2am.

LE VERRE VOLÉ
RESTAURANT, BAR

67 rue Lancry ☎01 48 03 17 34

You'll need a reservation to dine here, but not if you just want to drink. While you won't hang out here all night, this great location on the canal is the perfect spot to mingle with young Parisian hipsters over a glass of one of the restaurant's many wines.

＃ Ⓜ Jacques Bonsergent. Walk down bd de Magenta and turn left onto rue de Lancry; it's just before the canal. Ⓢ Wine from €5. Beer €5.50. Entrées €5-6. Plats €10-11. ⌚ Open Tu-Su noon-3:30pm and 6:30-11:30pm.

paris

L'ATMOSPHÈRE
BAR

49 rue Lucien Sampaix
☎01 40 38 09 25

L'Atmosphère has the cheapest beer in the 10ème—or at least the cheapest you can find at 1:30am. An older, laid-back crowd sits on the raised terrace overlooking the canal. When they thin out around 1am, 20-somethings flood the place for beer and cocktails and take up the everlasting effort to keep the bar open past closing time.

✦ ⓂJacques Bonsergent. Walk down bd de Magenta and turn left onto rue Lancry. When you get to the canal, turn left and walk 2-3 blocks; the bar is on the left. *i* Live music some nights. Ⓢ Beer €2.50-5. 🕐 Open Tu-F 10am-2am, Sa 2pm-2am, Su 2-9:30pm.

BASTILLE

Nightlife in the 11ème has long consisted of Anglophones who drink too much and the French who hide from them. With a few exceptions, **rue de Lappe** and its neighbors offer a big, raucous night on the town dominated by expats and tourists, while **rue Oberkampf, rue Amelot,** and **rue Thaillandiers** are more eclectic, low-key, and local. All four streets are worth your time, even if you have only one night in the area. **Rue Faubourg St-Antoine** is a world of its own, dominated by enormous clubs who only let in the well dressed.

FAVELA CHIC
BAR, CLUB

18 rue du Faubourg du Temple
☎01 40 21 38 14; www.favelachic.com

A Franco-Brazilian joint, Favela Chic is light on the Franco and heavy on the brassy Brazilian. Wildly popular with locals, this restaurant-bar-club is covered in palm trees, Mardi Gras masks, and sweaty gyrating bodies.

✦ ⓂRépublique. Walk down rue du Faubourg du Temple and turn right into the main rd at no. 18; the club is on the left. Ⓢ Cover F-Sa €10; includes 1 drink. Beer €5.50-6. Cocktails €9-10. 🕐 Open Tu-Th 8pm-2am, F-Sa 8pm-4am.

LE POP-IN
BAR, ROCK CLUB

105 rue Amelot
☎01 48 05 56 11; www.popin.fr

Le Pop-In takes the pretension out of hipster and replaces it with booze. Hosting (almost) nightly concerts and open-mic nights, this mix of punk rock, Swedish metal, and British pop attracts the dreadlocked and skinny-jeaned.

✦ ⓂSt-Sébastien-Froissart. *i* Open-mic night on Su. Check website for concerts. Ⓢ Beer €2.80-5.50. 🕐 Open daily 6:30pm-1:30am. Happy hour 6:30-9pm.

LE KITSCH
BAR

10 rue Oberkampf
☎01 40 21 94 41

This might be the most random collection of objects that we've ever seen on a single wall—particularly the garden gnome next to the tie-dyed porcelain cow next to the Virgin Mary. It is Le Kitsch, after all. Priding itself on the nonsense factor, this bar named its signature drink, a mojito-cum-slushy, Shrek (€7.50). The bar attracts a more laid-back local crowd—or as laid-back as they can be in this weird establishment.

✦ ⓂOberkampf. Ⓢ Beer €3. Cocktails €7.50; happy hour cocktails €5. 🕐 Open daily 5:30pm-2-am. Happy hour 5:30-9pm.

BARRIO LATINO
CLUB

46/48 rue du Faubourg St-Antoine
☎01 55 78 84 75; www.buddha-bar.com

Barrio Latino reminds us of a modern remake of *Scarface:* well-dressed clientele, Latin music broken up with house and techno, and tables filled with G-men watching over a raging five-story party. Enthusiastic and aspiring salsa dancers shake it in various corners and on tables (despite security's best efforts to dissuade them). The giant dance floor heats up around 11pm, but you'll pay a lot to get buzzed enough to fit in.

✦ ⓂBastille. Ⓢ Cover Th-Sa €20. Beer €6.50-9. Cocktails €12-14. Shooters €6.50. 🕐 Open daily noon-2am.

nightlife

SOME GIRLS BAR BAR

43 rue de Lappe ☎01 48 06 40 33

No, it's not a strip joint. It's actually a rock-themed bar that proudly plays the Rolling Stones and other bands from the '60s-'90s in a thoroughly confused, kitschy setting of neon lights, leopard skins, and palm trees. Take advantage of the happy hour that lasts until 10pm, then make your way out before another favorite song convinces you to stay.

⇞ [M]Bastille. Walk down rue de la Roquette and turn left onto rue de Lappe. $ Pints €5. Cocktails €7-9. Happy hour cocktails €5. ⏰ Open M-Sa 9pm-2am. Happy hour 7-10pm.

WAX CLUB

15 rue Daval ☎01 40 21 16 16

Wax is a rare Parisian miracle—a place that is actually fun to dance in and almost free (you have to buy at least one drink to stay, though). Housed in a concrete bunker, the club is packed on the weekends with young locals and tourists. On Tuesdays they host a "soirée groove," making them some of the only people in the world who use the word "groove" unironically.

⇞ [M]Bastille. Take bd Richard Lenoir and turn right onto rue Daval. ℹ Mandatory coat check F-Sa €1.50. "Soirée groove" on Tu. House and techno on Sa-Su. $ Beer €4-6. Cocktails €10. ⏰ Open W-Th 5pm-2am, F-Sa 5pm-5am.

LES DISQUAIRES BAR, CONCERT VENUE

6 rue des Taillandiers ☎01 40 21 94 60; www.lesdisquaires.com

Early in the week, Les Disquaires is a laid-back jazz venue. Come Thursday, it turns into a packed club with DJs mixing pop rock tunes while patrons carve their initials into the wax-coated tables—that is, after they spill drinks on them.

⇞ [M]Bastille. Take rue de la Roquette and turn right onto rue des Taillandiers. ℹ Live concerts daily at 8pm. Club W-Sa. $ Beer €3-4. Wine €3.50. Shots €4. ⏰ Open daily 6pm-2am.

LE CHINA JAZZ BAR, RESTAURANT

50 rue Charenton ☎01 43 46 08 09; www.lechina.eu

Le China could be a clone from the lounges in the 16ème: it's dark, sophisticated, and the prices aim at the well-to-do. Leather couches line the walls as people chat, sip their drinks, and jam to piano tunes. Downstairs in Club Chin Chin, things get a little more energetic (especially on the weekends) but stay classy with red velvet and dimmed lighting.

⇞ [M]Bastille. ℹ Piano bar M and Su 8pm-midnight. Concerts daily 8:30pm. $ Cocktails €9-15. ⏰ Open M-F noon-2am, Sa-Su 5pm-2am.

frenchism

If you hear a few familiar words while in Paris, even though you don't speak French, don't be alarmed; the adoption of English words here is both a common and controversial phenomenon. *Le hamburger, le jogging,* and *le weekend* are all words that French-speakers use regularly. As the digital age introduced words like "podcast," "email," and "Wi-Fi," French has struggled to keep up with English in the creation of new terminology. Most French people find it easiest to simply say "podcast" or "Wi-Fi" (pronounced *"wee-fee"*), but French cultural purists feel that this is an outrage. Enlisting French linguists at the Académie Française, nationalists associated with the stubborn Ministry of Culture have started a movement to invent new French words for the influx of new terms. Podcast becomes "*diffusion pour baladeur,*" and Wi-Fi is "*accès sans fil à l'internet.*" It's a valiant crusade, but Wi-Fi is just so much easier to say.

MONTPARNASSE AND SOUTHERN PARIS

Clubs and Anglophone bars are clustered in Montparnasse near the tower and the train station, while there are some laid-back bars and clubs floating on the Seine near Chinatown. Butte-aux-Cailles has super cheap hippie bars, but they close early due to whiney neighbors. The absolute highlight for anyone between the ages of 18 and 70 is Cafe OZ.

✉ CAFE OZ
BAR

3 pl. Denfert-Rochereau ☎01 47 38 76 77; www.cafe-oz.com

Opened in May 2011, the newest and largest iteration of this Australian chain is rumored to have the largest terraces in Paris. After midnight, the older crowd vacates and the massive interior becomes packed with young bodies dancing on tables, stairs, or wherever there is room. Things are kept cool by the drafty 30 ft. ceilings. Despite OZ's size, the palm fronds above the bar and walls covered in boomerangs still make you feel like you're in a packed hut on the beach of Queensland.

✦ ⓂDenfert-Rochereau, behind the RER station. *i* Snacks served until midnight. ⓈShooters €5. Beer €7-8. Cocktails €10. Happy hour cocktails €6. ⌚ Open M-Tu noon-2am, W noon-3am, Th noon-4am, F-Sa noon-5am, Su noon-2am. Happy hour 5-8pm.

LA FOLIE EN TÊTE
BAR

33 rue de la Butte-aux-Cailles ☎01 45 80 65 99; www.lafolieentete.blogspot.com

Decorated with musical instruments, street signs, and newspaper clippings announcing Bob Marley concerts, this reggae bar has one of the cheapest happy hours in the neighborhood. Hipsters, poets, and broke students keep it packed until closing.

✦ ⓂPlace d'Italie. From pl. d'Italie, follow rue Bobillot. Turn right onto rue de la Butte-aux-Cailles and follow it as it turns right. ⓈBeer €5-6. Cocktails €7. Happy hour cocktails €5. ⌚ Open M-Sa 5pm-2am, Su 6pm-midnight. Happy hour 5-8pm.

WESTERN PARIS

Usually there is a direct correlation between the spice of the nightlife and the prices of drinks, but in the 16ème, bars are pricey, and people rarely leave their lounge chairs. The 17ème has a few gems and lower-priced lounges and bars, but if you want the lounge scene and don't mind spending the big bucks to feel important, stick around the Arc de Triomphe.

THE HONEST LAWYER
BAR

176 rue de la Pompe ☎01 45 05 14 23; www.honest-lawyer.com

The happy hour packs this bar, a throwback from the American Prohibition era and the fleet of alcoholic expats it sent to Paris. Cram into the small round tables with your friends if you're not feeling pretentious enough for the rest of the neighborhood.

✦ ⓂVictor Hugo. Walk down av. Victor Hugo away from the Arc de Triomphe and turn left at rue de Longchamp. Go 1 block and turn right onto rue de Pompe; the bar is at the corner with av. de Montespan. ⓈBeer €5.50. Happy hour cocktails €6. ⌚ Open M-F 7:30am-2am, Sa 10am-2am, Su 7:30am-2am. Happy hour daily 5:30-8:30pm.

LA GARE
BAR

19 Chaussée de la Muette ☎01 42 15 15 31; www.restaurantlagare.com

Once a train station, La Gare is now a trendy bar and favored hang-out spot of the wealthy young locals. Try the heated terrace seating over the old train platforms or warm up by the fire in the inner lounge. If you still have your youth, head out to cheaper, more fun places before midnight (or even 11pm).

✦ ⓂLa Muette. ⓈWine €5.50. Martinis €5.50. ⌚ Open daily noon-2am.

DUPLEX

2 bis av. Foch ☎01 45 00 45 00; www.leduplex.com

Stories of this late-night disco make their way around Paris, and we mean that in an infamous way. The three-story subterranean club plays mostly R and B and hip hop and stays packed until dawn with young people looking to hook up.

✇ ⓂCharles de Gaulle-Étoile. *i* Women enter free before midnight on F. Ⓢ Cover (includes 1 drink) Tu-Th €15, F-Sa €20, Su €15. Drinks M €8, Tu-Th €9, F-Sa €11, Su €9. ☼ Open Tu-Su midnight to dawn.

MONTMARTRE

As we've said, Pigalle is pretty sketchy. But that doesn't mean there aren't decent areas to go at night in Montmartre. The areas around **place de Clichy** and ⓂAbbesses have fewer tourists at night, and therefore have fewer pickpockets hanging around. Still, if you go to Montmartre, don't make yourself a target: take a taxi or the Noctilien home.

▨ LE RENDEZ-VOUS DES AMIS
BAR

23 rue Gabrielle ☎01 46 06 01 60; www.rdvdesamis.com

You know you're in for a night of debauchery when the owners and bartenders drink more than the customers, pounding shots and beers at random. The customers have the advantage of drinking from "giraffes," which are 3 ft. tall, 3L cylinders from which you pour your own beer. Patrons rock out to house music and occasional live guitar jams. Cigarettes are sold out front on an informal basis, but don't bring your drink outside—the burly but friendly bouncer will have words for you. Don't arrive too drunk, either: the subsequent hike from ⓂAbbesses is slightly less challenging than Everest.

✇ ⓂAbbesses. Exit the Metro and walk up rue la Vieuville and follow it as it curves right and then left. Continue (literally) up rue Drevet until you reach rue Gabrielle. Ⓢ Beers €2.30-7; pitchers €7. Giraffes €20. Cocktails €6. Tapas and snacks €7. ☼ Open daily 8am-2am.

▨ L'ESCALE
BAR

32 bis rue des 3 Frères ☎01 46 06 12 38

Young folk cram around the small tables of this tiny bar, and the owner proudly proclaims on their Facebook page that L'Escale and its strong drinks—for example the pint-sized mojitos (€4.50)—are the number-one enemy of the police. There's generally a guest DJ playing house music on Sunday nights (and you thought Sunday was boring).

✇ ⓂAbbesses. Exit the Metro and walk up rue la Vieuville and follow it as it curves right and then left. The bar is straight ahead at the intersection with rue des 3 Frères. Ⓢ Cocktails €4.50. ☼ Open daily 2pm-2am. Happy hour 4-10pm.

HÉLICE BAR
BAR

50 rue d'Orsel ☎01 46 06 24 70

This bar has more of an indie rock scene than most bars in Paris, and is famous for its super cheap beer. The bartenders provide snacks to keep patrons from falling over too fast as they jam to local bands on Thursday nights.

✇ ⓂAbbesses. Walk downhill on rue des Abbesses until you get to rue des Martyrs. Though this is not a straight intersection, keep going as straight as you can onto rue d'Orsel. The bar is on the left. Ⓢ Beer pints €3.50-5. Cocktails €5. ☼ Open Tu-Sa 6pm-2am.

EASTERN PARIS

Bars will try to lure you out here with cheap drinks, but you really shouldn't be wandering this area at night.

▨ ROSA BONHEUR
BAR, GLBT

2 av. de la Cascade ☎01 42 00 00 45; www.rosabonheur.fr

If there is one place in the neighborhood that we recommend you start your night, it's Rosa Bonheur. This bistro bar is located within the confines of the Parc

Buttes-Chaumont, and is right near the Metro. Now that we have security out of the way (thank you, bouncers), it's also in an adorable, almost colonial-style building that emerges from the trees of the park. Rosa hosts lots of community service and charity events for GLBT rights and environmental awareness as well as Paris's *Silence de Danse*, where you put on headphones, dance, and look really funny.

✦ ⓂBotzaris. Ⓢ Shots €4. Beer €5. Cocktails €9. ⌚ Open W-Su noon-midnight. Last entry 11pm.

OURCQ
BAR, TEA HOUSE
68 quai de la Loire
☎01 42 40 12 26

Adjust your sense of "nightlife" to more of a "happy hour" and come here during the day (after a visit to the Cité des Sciences et de L'Industrie, for example). The drinks are cheap and the brasserie doubles as a tea house with books and board games.

✦ ⓂLaumière. Ⓢ Wine €2-3. Beer €2.50-4. Cocktails €5. ⌚ Open W-Th 3pm-midnight, F-Sa 3pm-2am, Su 3-10pm.

a whole new world down there

Every street in Paris has an equivalent address in the underground sewer system, equipped with more than 1300 mi. of tunnels, pipelines, and waterways. All the corners within the sewers have street signs that mirror the ones on the surface—perhaps Parisians were preparing for a sunless, underground lifestyle on the off chance they all turned into vampires.

In actuality, the layout is thanks to architect Eugène Belgrand's efforts to reduce waste in the growing city. He enlarged the size of the drains, increased the sewer system, and built pipelines that, if stretched out, would run from Paris to Istanbul. Unfortunately, with one stinky problem solved, another arose. Since its construction, several robbers—affectionately nicknamed the "termite gangs"—have attempted to break into banks and shops after digging their way from the sewers into the buildings above.

arts and culture

A trip to the Opéra Garnier, comic relief at the Odéon Théâtre, or late-night wining and dining at the Moulin Rouge are all possibilities for total cultural immersion, and will leave you with more memories than that one night on the Mouffetard. If this sounds boring to you (hopefully it doesn't, but we cater to all tastes), you'll be pleased to know that Paris's concerts get just as rowdy as its clubs. Whether you have a solid grasp of French or are a novice who just laughs because everyone else is, you'll definitely leave feeling a bit more *je ne sais quoi*.

THEATER
▨ **ODÉON THÉÂTRE DE L'EUROPE**
LATIN QUARTER AND ST-GERMAIN
2 rue Corneille
☎01 44 85 40 40; www.theatre-odeon.fr

The Odéon is a classically beautiful theater: gold lines the mezzanine and muted red upholstery cover the chairs. Many plays are performed in foreign languages with French translation shown above on a screen. Despite the fact that this is the mecca of Parisian theater, the prices are stunningly reasonable and standing

tickets are dirt cheap. The under-26 crowd can score the luxury of a seat for the same price, so save your young legs—watching foreign performances of *Measure for Measure* or *La Casa de Fuerza* takes enough energy already.
➔ ⓂOdéon. ℹ Limited number of rush tickets available night of the show. $ Shows €10-32, under 26 €6-16. Rush tickets €6. ⏰ Performances generally M-Sa 8pm, Su 3pm.

👍 THÉÂTRE DE LA VILLE — CHÂTELET-LES HALLES

2 pl. du Châtelet — ☎01 42 74 22 77; www.theatredelaville-paris.com

Since the '80s, the Théâtre de la Ville has become a major outlet for avant-garde dance, and it's been attracting art students ever since. One recent show was entitled "Walking next to our shoes… intoxicated by strawberries and cream, we enter continents without knocking." An open mind is a must.
➔ ⓂChâtelet. Walk down rue de Rivoli toward Hôtel de Ville. $ Tickets €24, under 30 €13. ⏰ Box office open M 11am-7pm, Tu-Sa 11am-8pm.

CABARET

👍 LE LAPIN AGILE — MONTMARTRE

22 rue des Saules — ☎01 46 06 85 87; www.au-lapin-agile.com

Halfway up a steep, cobblestoned hill that American tourists describe as "just like San Francisco," Le Lapin Agile has been providing savvy Parisians and tourists with music, dance, and theater since the late 19th century. The tiny theater was a hotspot of the 20th-century bohemian art scene—Picasso and Max Jacob are on the list of people who cabareted here.
➔ ⓂLamarck-Coulaincourt. Follow rue St-Vincen to rue des Saules. $ Tickets €24, students under 26 €17; includes 1 drink. Drinks €6-7. ⏰ Shows Tu-Su 9pm-2am.

BAL DU MOULIN ROUGE — MONTMARTRE

82 bd de Clichy — ☎01 53 09 82 82; www.moulin-rouge.com

Ever since Christina and Co.'s music video, the only thing people associate with the Moulin Rouge is that universal question, *"Voulez-vous coucher avec moi?"* But the world-famous home of the can-can isn't just about sex; it's also about glam and glitz. Since its opening in 1889, the Moulin Rouge has hosted international superstars like Ella Fitzgerald and Johnny Rey, and it now welcomes a fair crowd of tourists for an evening of sequins, tassels, and skin. The shows remain risqué, and the tickets prohibitively expensive. The late show is cheaper, but be prepared to stand if it's a busy night.
➔ ⓂBlanche Sarl. ℹ Elegant attire required; no shorts, sneakers, or sportswear. $ 9pm show €102, 11pm show €92; includes ½-bottle of champagne. 7pm dinner and 9pm show €150-180. Occasional lunch shows €100-130; call for more info. ⏰ Dinner daily 7pm. Shows daily 9 and 11pm.

CINEMA

The French love movies. They go to the cinema almost every week, and conversations are peppered with references to local art films and box-office hits. Angolophone movie-goers should look for "VO" when selecting English-language films, as they are in *version originale*.

👍 L'ARLEQUIN — LATIN QUARTER AND ST-GERMAIN

76 rue de Rennes — ☎01 45 44 28 80

A proud revival theater, L'Arlequin mixes modern French films with selections from a pool of international award-winners. Three films are featured each week, undoubtedly decreasing the prevalence of adolescent movie-hopping. Some films are in English, but the vast majority are in French.
➔ ⓂSt-Sulpice. $ Full price €9.50; M-Th students, under 18, and over 60 €7; F-Su under 18 €7.

CINÉMATHÈQUE FRANÇAISE BASTILLE

51 rue de Bercy ☎01 71 19 33 33; www.cinematheque.fr

Though it's had some problems settling down (it's moved over five times, most recently in 2005), the Cinémathèque Française is committed to sustaining film culture. A must-see for film buffs, the theater screens four to five classics, near-classics, or soon-to-be classics per day; foreign selections are usually subtitled. The cinema also features multiple movie-related exhibits, which include over 1000 costumes and objects from the past and present world of film.

 # Ⓜ Bercy. $ €7, ages 18-26 and seniors €5, under 18 €4. ⏰ Ticket window open M from noon to last showing, W-Sa from noon to last showing, Su from 10am to last showing. Exhibits open M noon-7pm, W-Sa noon-7pm, Su 10am-8pm.

on location

Many films have been shot on location in Paris over the years. If you're a movie buff, head to these locations to see in real life what you saw on screen:

- **THE LOUVRE:** *Funny Face* (1957), *The Age of Innocence* (1993), *The Da Vinci Code* (2006)
- **QUAI SAINT BERNARD:** *The Bourne Identity* (2002)
- **MONTMARTRE:** *Amélie* (2001), *Moulin Rouge!* (2001)
- **BANKS OF THE SEINE:** *Everyone Says I Love You* (1996)
- **PONT DE BIR-HAKEIM:** *Last Tango in Paris* (1972)
- **122 AVENUE DES CHAMPS ELYSÉES:** *The Accidental Tourist* (1988)
- **THEATRE VRAI GUIGNOLET:** *Charade* (1963)
- **PONT NEUF:** *An American in Paris* (1951)
- **TROCADÉRO:** *The Dreamers* (2003)

MUSIC

You can find live music in almost any bar, club, or boat on the Seine, but for true venues that make the House of Blues look tame, head to the party centers of Montmartre and Bastille.

ELYSÉE MONTMARTRE MONTMARTRE

72 bd Rochechouart ☎01 44 92 45 36; www.elyseemontmartre.com

Following a worryingly common trend among Montmartre venues, this concert hall burned down in March 2011. It plans to reopen in early 2012. Famous since 1807 and known to Anglophones for the Roots's song *You Got Me*, this concert hall has hosted the likes of David Bowie, Counting Crows (they recorded their debut album here), and Pendulum. Boxing matches are also held here when the rockers aren't around.

 # Ⓜ Anvers. $ Tickets €14-45. ⏰ Opens at 11:30pm for all shows.

LE BATACLAN BASTILLE

50 bd Voltaire ☎01 43 14 00 30; www.le-bataclan.com

In French, *bataclan* is slang for "stuff" or "junk." In French music culture, Bataclan means a packed 1500-person Chinese pagoda that hosts alternative rock bands like Oasis, Blur, Jeff Buckley, and MGMT. The craziest venue in Bastille, Le Bataclan attracts a more local crowd since, for some reason, the French fall in love with more obscure bands (who are usually cheaper than those playing at Elysée Montmartre).

 # Ⓜ Oberkampf. $ Tickets start at €15. ⏰ Open Sept-July.

shopping

"Shopping" and "Paris" are almost synonymous. But the excessive wealth of Champs-Élysées and Île St-Louis are not for the faint of heart—they're for the rich. The many antiques, rare books, and tempting tourist trappings you find across the city could easily empty pockets. No one likes credit card debt, so we recommend the vintage shops and quirky boutiques in the youthful Marais and Bastille.

BOOKS

The French love reading almost as much as they love film, museums, and art. Some of the best insight into why the French put autodidacts on a pedestal can be seen in these stores. Be sure to check out the most famous of the city's bookstores, **Shakespeare and Co.**

▧ ABBEY BOOKSHOP   LATIN QUARTER AND ST-GERMAIN

29 rue de la Parcheminerie   ☎01 46 33 16 24; www.alevdesign.com/abbey

Clear your afternoon if you're going to Abbey Bookshop—you'll need the time. Set in a back alley, the sheer number of books is a bit overwhelming, whether they're shelved or stacked on the floor. This Canadian-owned shop probably has what you're looking for, and if not, they'll order it for you. Plus, they carry *Let's Go*—they've obviously got the right idea.

⚡ ⓂCluny-La Sorbonne. Follow rue Boutebrie and take a left onto rue de la Parcheminerie. *i* Books in English and other languages available. 🕐 Open M-Sa 10am-7pm.

▧ GIBERT JEUNE   LATIN QUARTER AND ST-GERMAIN

pl. St-Michel   ☎01 56 81 22 22; www.gibertjeune.fr

If you're studying abroad in Paris, this is probably where you'll want to buy your textbooks—Gibert Jeune carries over 300,000 titles. By the time you're through shopping here, you'll look like a real *savant parisien*. And it's air-conditioned, which can be a welcome change during the Parisian summer.

⚡ ⓂSt-Michel. 🕐 Open M-Sa 9:30am-7:30pm.

LADY LONG SOLO   BASTILLE

38 rue Keller   ☎09 52 73 81 53; www.ladylongsolo.com

Offering an assortment of counter-cultural books that range from anti-colonial diatribes to **The Communist Manifesto,** Lady Long Solo stocks all form of left-leaning print, including guides to the wonders of medical marijuana. Thank Marx and his ideas of price controls, since books here are some of the cheapest in the city.

⚡ ⓂBastille. Follow rue de la Roquette until rue Keller. Ⓢ Books as low as €2. 🕐 Open daily 2-7pm.

LES MOTS À LA BOUCHE   THE MARAIS

6 rue Ste-Croix de la Bretonnerie   ☎01 42 78 88 30; www.motsbouche.com

Logically located in the Marais, this two-story bookstore offers mostly GLBT literature, photography, magazines, and art, with everything from Proust to guides on lesbian lovemaking. Straight guys could probably learn a few pointers from that last one, too. The international DVD collection is somewhat hidden in the corner of the bottom level (€7-25); titles range from the artistic to the pornographic.

⚡ ⓂHôtel de Ville. Take a left onto rue Vieille du Temple and a left onto rue Ste-Croix de la Bretonnerie. 🕐 Open M-Sa 11am-11pm, Su 1-9pm.

CLOTHING

Parisians know how to dress well. It's in their blood. If you want to dress like them, you don't have to drain your bank account, or as they say in French, *"fais chauffer ta carte bleu"* (heat up your credit card). **Galeries Lafayette** is the French equivalent of

Macy's and will save you time and money, and for everything vintage, head to the Marais or Châtelet-Les Halles.

▨ FREE 'P' STAR
THE MARAIS

8 rue Ste-Croix de la Bretonnerie   ☎01 42 76 03 72; www.freepstar.com

Enter as Plain Jane and leave a star—from the '80s or '90s, that is. Choose from a wide selection of vintage dresses (€20), velvet blazers (€40), boots (€30), and military-style jackets (€5) that all seem like a good idea when surrounded by other antiquated pieces but require some balls to be worn out in the open. Dig around the €10 jean pile and €3 bin for ripped jeans that died out with Kurt Cobain.

⚏ Ⓜ️Hôtel de Ville. Follow rue de Renard and turn right onto rue St-Merri, which becomes rue Ste-Croix de la Bretonnerie. *i* There are 2 other locations at 61 rue de la Verrerie (☎01 42 78 076) and 20 rue de Rivoli. Ⓢ Credit card min. €20. 🕐 Open daily noon-10pm.

▨ MAMIE BLUE
OPÉRA AND CANAL ST-MARTIN

69 rue de Rochechouart   ☎01 42 81 10 42; www.mamie-vintage.com

This vintage store does more than sell old clothes at reduced prices—it transports shoppers back through the decades. Old French music plays in the background to keep you expecting a giant hug for liberating the city circa 1945. Mamie Blue specializes in clothing from the '20s-'70s, and we're thinking the prices might be a little over-adjusted for inflation.

⚏ Ⓜ️Anvers. Walk toward Ⓜ️Barbès-Rochechouart and take the 1st left. The store is 2 blocks down on the right. Ⓢ Dresses €40-175. 🕐 Open M 2:30-7:30pm, Tu-Sa 11:30am-1:30pm and 2:30-7:30pm.

six ways to dress french

Although Paris is known to be the world's most fashion-conscious city, individuality rarely rears its head. Blending in with the locals means keeping your day-glo American Apparel tights at home and doing as the Parisians do.

- **THE FUR COAT.** The concept of animal cruelty seems to be ignored in Parisian fashion; practically everyone wears a woodland creature at some point during the winter season.

- **THE SCARF.** It's unclear whether Parisians use the *écharpe* as a mere fashion statement, or if they're just morbidly afraid of wind.

- **THE WEDGE HEELS.** Called *escarpin,* the pump isn't just for 30-something cougars dressing too young for their age. High heels are a defining staple in a woman's daily outfit, and even prepubescent Parisian Lolitas sport them.

- **THE NONDESCRIPT LEATHER BAG.** If your forearm isn't raised and your fingers aren't ready to snap at a moment's notice, get out of town.

- **OXFORD LACE-UP SHOES.** In the city where Hemingway began *A Farewell to Arms*, it's not really surprising that the choice of footwear would be equally intellectual.

- **THE PERPETUAL FROWN.** Because being happy is *très* tacky.

GALERIES LAFAYETTE

MONTPARNASSE AND SOUTHERN PARIS

40 bd Haussmann

☎01 42 82 34 56; www.galerieslafayette.com

While Galeries Lafayette has your acronymic clothing brands for men and women, their own brand sells for nearly 60% of the price. For guys who can't quite rock deep V-necks and three-quarter length pants, come here for more subdued button-ups.

✦ ⓜChaussée d'Antin-La Fayette. ⏰ Open M-W 9:30am-8pm, Th 9:30am-9pm, F-Sa 9:30am-8pm.

PRINTEMPS HAUSSMANN

OPÉRA AND CANAL ST-MARTIN

64 bd Haussmann

☎01 42 82 50 00; www.printemps.com

Founded in 1865, this *grand magasin* has over 44,000 sq. m of space and brands from bargain basement to luxury. While the prices are slightly higher than other malls, you get the added benefit of shopping in a historical site and being seen among semi-fashion conscious Parisians.

✦ ⓜHavre-Caumartin. ⏰ Open M-W 9:35am-8pm, Th 9:35am-10pm, F-Sa 9:35am-8pm.

MUSIC

For vinyl collectors, there are two "Croco" music places in the Latin Quarter specializing in soul, rock, and jazz. We have listed CrocoDisc for all your soul and funk needs; CrocoJazz (64 rue de Montaigne Ste-Geneviève) has every type of jazz under the sun, but is probably too cool for you.

⬛ CROCODISC

LATIN QUARTER AND ST-GERMAIN

40/42 rue des Écoles

☎01 43 54 33 22; www.crocodisc.com

Specializing in soul and funk, with its second store next door selling contemporary rock and electro, Crocodisc has everything you might need on disc and vinyl. With the faint smell of slow-burning cigars and stacks of old records, Crocodisc sets the mood just right.

✦ ⓜMaubert-Mutualité. Ⓢ CDs €1-15. Records €2-18. ⏰ Open Tu-Sa 11am-1pm and 2-7pm.

SPECIALTY

For everything else that you can't wear, read, or listen to, we give you this category. Buying these is more for the experience than for utility.

⬛ PYLÔNES

ÎLE DE LA CITÉ AND ÎLE ST-LOUIS

57 rue St-Louis en l'Île

☎01 46 34 05 02; www.pylones.com

A colorful collection of amorphous shapes and colors, Pylônes is the store version of the Pompidou. It sells things you'll impulsively buy, never need, but always marvel at, like cheese graters topped with doll heads (€18). More useful (but just as fun) items include cigarette cases (€12) and espresso cups (€6). The artful objects are fun to look at even if you don't buy anything.

✦ ⓜPont Marie. *i* 5 other locations around the city. Ⓢ Cups €6. Wallets €24. ⏰ Open daily 10:30am-7:30pm.

⬛ LA GRANDE ÉPICERIE DE PARIS

INVALIDES

38 rue de Sèvres

☎01 44 39 81 00; www.lagrandeepicerie.fr

If a Parisian supermodel took on the form of an *épicerie* (supermarket), she'd be this one. Snooty Invalides women saunter up and down the aisles for the best (or most expensive) cheeses, wines, and Nespresso coffee makers. There is an aisle of American candy and products, but it exists mainly for the locals to cluck their tongues as they walk down. La Grande Épicerie de Paris is better for picking up a bottle of wine and some chocolate than a whole list of groceries, as the prices are as out of reach as the model.

✦ ⓜVaneau. ⏰ Open M-Sa 8:30am-9pm.

paris

essentials

PRACTICALITIES

- **TOURIST OFFICES: Bureau Central d'accueil** provides maps and tour information and books accommodations. (25 rue des Pyramides ☎01 49 52 42 63; www.parisinfo.com ✦ ⓂPyramides. ⌚ Open daily May-Oct 9am-7pm; Nov-Apr 10am-7pm.) Other locations at Gare du Nord (☎01 45 26 94 82), Gare de Lyon (☎08 92 68 30 00), and Montmartre. (21 pl. du Tertre ☎01 42 62 21 21 ⌚ Open daily 10am-7pm.)

- **INTERNET: American Library in Paris.** (10 rue du Général Camou ☎01 53 59 12 60; www.americanlibraryinparis.org ✦ ⓂÉcole Militaire. ⌚ Open Tu-Sa 10am-7pm.) There is also free Wi-Fi at **Centre Pompidou** and in its **Bibliothèque Publique d'Information.** (pl. Georges Pompidou, rue Beaubourg ✦ ⓂRambuteau or Hôtel de Ville. ⌚ Center open M 11am-9pm, W-Su 11am-9pm. Library open M noon-10pm, W-F noon-10pm, Sa-Su 11am-10pm.)

- **POST OFFICES: La Poste.** There are many post offices in Paris; the most centrally located are in St-Germain (118 bd St-Germain ✦ ⓂOdéon. ⌚ Open M-F 8am-8pm, Sa 9am-5pm.) and Châtelet-Les Halles. (1 rue Pierre Lescot ✦ ⓂLes-Halles. ⌚ Open M-F 8am-6:30pm, Sa 9am-1pm.)

EMERGENCY

- **EMERGENCY NUMBERS:** Ambulance (SAMU): ☎15. Fire: ☎18. Police: ☎17.

- **POLICE: Préfecture de Police.** (9 bd Palais ☎01 58 80 80 80 ✦ ⓂCité. Across the street from the Palais de Justice. ⌚ Open 24hr.)

- **LATE-NIGHT PHARMACIES: Pharmacie Les Champs.** (84 av. des Champs-Élysées ☎01 45 62 02 41 ✦ ⓂFranklin Roosevelt.) **Pharmacie européenne.** (6 pl. de Clichy ☎01 48 74 65 18 ✦ ⓂPlace de Clichy.)

- **HOSPITALS/MEDICAL SERVICES: American Hospital of Paris.** (63 bd Victor Hugo ☎01 46 41 25 25; www.american-hospital.org ✦ ⓂPort Maillot then bus #82, or take bus #82 from Jardin du Luxembourg to its terminus.)

GETTING THERE

by plane

PARIS-CHARLES DE GAULLE (CDG)

In Roissy-en-France, 23km northeast of Paris   ☎01 48 62 22 80; www.adp.fr

Most transatlantic flights land at Aéroport Paris-CDG. The two cheapest and fastest ways to get into the city from Paris-CDG are by RER and by bus. The RER B (Ⓢ €8.70, which includes Metro transport.) leaves from Terminal 2. The **Roissybus** (☎01 49 25 61 87 Ⓢ €10. ⌚ 35min.; every 15min. during day, every 20min. at night.) stops at every terminal. If you're taking the bus back to the airport, you can catch it at the corner of rue Scribe and rue Auber at pl. de l'Opéra.

ORLY (ORY)

In Orly, 18km south of Paris   ☎01 49 75 15 15; www.adp.fr

Aéroport d'Orly is used by charters and many continental flights. From the Pont de Rungis/Aéroport d'Orly train station, board the RER C to Paris. The RATP **Orlybus** (☎08 36 68 77 14 Ⓢ €6.90. ⌚ 30min., every 12-20min.) runs between Metro and RER stop Denfert-Rochereau and Orly's south terminal. You can also board the Orlybus at Dareau-St-Jacques, Glacière-Tolbiac, and Porte de Gentilly. RATP also runs **Orlyval** (☎01 69 93 53 00 Ⓢ VAL ticket €8.30 or VAL-RER ticket €11.), which is the fastest way to get to the city. The VAL shuttle goes from Antony (RER B) to Orly Ouest and Sud. Buy tickets at any RATP booth in the city, or from the Orlyval agencies at Orly Ouest, Orly Sud, and Antony.

BEAUVAIS (BVA)

In Tillé, 85km north of Paris   ☎08 92 68 20 66; www.aeroportbeauvais.com
Beauvais serves **Ryanair, EasyJet,** and other budget airlines. The **Shuttle Bus** leaves from Paris-Beauvais and goes to Porte Maillot in Paris. (☎03 44 11 46 86; www. aeroportbeauvais.com Ⓢ €15. Cash only. Must be purchased in arrival lounge. Ⓒ Every 20 min. after flight arrivals.)

by train

SNCF (www.sncf.fr) sells train tickets for travel within France and offers *la Carte 12-25*, which, for a one-time €49 fee, guarantees reduced prices if you want to hop around France. If you're traveling to France from another country, check out **Rail Europe** (www.raileurope.com). **Gare du Nord** is the arrival point for trains from northern France and Germany, as well as Amsterdam (Ⓢ €130. Ⓒ 3½hr.), Brussels (Ⓢ €90. Ⓒ 1hr.), and London. (Ⓢ €50-120. Ⓒ 2½hr.) **Gare de l'Est** receives trains from eastern France, southern Germany, Austria, Hungary, Munich (Ⓢ €125-163. Ⓒ 9-10½hr.), and Prague. (Ⓢ €118-172. Ⓒ 12-15hr.) **Gare de Lyon** has trains from: Florence (Ⓢ €135-170. Ⓒ 9-12hr.); Lyon (Ⓢ €60-70. Ⓒ 2hr.); Marseille (Ⓢ €45-70. Ⓒ 3-4hr.); Nice (Ⓢ €100. Ⓒ 5½hr.); Rome. (Ⓢ €177-200. Ⓒ 12-15hr.) **Gare d'Austerlitz** services the Loire Valley and the Iberian peninsula, including Barcelona (Ⓢ €135-170. Ⓒ 7-12hr.) and Madrid. (Ⓢ €220-300. Ⓒ 12-13hr.) **Gare St-Lazare** will welcome you from northern France, while **Gare Montparnasse** is for trains from northeastern and southwestern France.

GETTING AROUND

by metro

In general, the Metro is easy to navigate, and trains run swiftly and frequently. The earliest trains start running around 5:30am, and the last ones leave the end-of-the-line stations at about 12:15am during the week (2:15am on Friday and Saturday). Transfers are free if made within a station. Tickets cost €1.70 per journey, although it's much more useful to buy a *carnet* of 10 tickets for €12.

how to metro

You'll hear it a thousand times: keep your Metro ticket until you exit. If you don't, you may well be caught and, according to French punishment, be horribly shamed in public as well as having to pay a fine. Here are some other Metro tips to be aware of.

- **NO SMOKING:** But that doesn't mean people won't light up while on the exit escalator.

- **MONEY ISSUES:** Unless you have a European credit card, bring coins. Change machines are notoriously hard to find, and shops are not quick to change your €10 note. We've seen many a tear over this problem in the early morning when the red eye from JFK comes in.

- **CONNECTIONS:** The Metro is designed so you only need to make one transfer to get anywhere in the city. But don't be silly—following this rule might mean traveling halfway across the city in the wrong direction just to change just to change lines.. Instead, brush up on your pronunciation of "*correspondence,*" swallow your obsession with efficiency, and take the multiple connections in significantly less time.

by rer

The RER *(Réseau Express Régional)* is the RATP's suburban train system, which passes through central Paris. Within central Paris, the RER works exactly the same as the Metro, requiring the same ticket at the same price. Trips to the suburbs require more expensive tickets. You must know what zone you're going to in order to buy the proper ticket. You'll need your ticket to exit the RER station. Insert your ticket just as you did to enter, and pass through. Like the Metro, the RER runs 5:30am-12:30am on weekdays and until 2:30am on weekends.

by bus

Bus tickets are the same as those used for the Metro and can be purchased in Metro stations or from the bus driver (€1.70). When you want to get off, press the red button so the *arrêt demandé* (stop requested) sign lights up. Most buses run daily 7am-8:30pm, although those marked **Autobus du nuit** continue until 1:30am. Still others, named **Noctilien,** run all night (M-Th approximately every 30min., F-Sa approximately every 15min., Su approximately every 30min.). Check out www.noctilien.fr, or inquire at a major Metro station or at Gare de l'Est for more information on Noctilien buses. Noctilien #2 runs to all the major train stations along the periphery of Paris, while #12 and #13 run between Châtelet and Gare de Montparnasse.

by taxi

A typical taxi ride lasting 20min. will cost €6-10, and a long ride of nearly 40min. will be as much as €20-30. Taxis are easily hailed from any major boulevard or avenue, but stands are often outside major Metro intersections. From the airport, prices skyrocket to around €80-100.

MONEY

tipping

By law in France, a service charge is added to bills in bars and restaurants, called *"service compris."* Most people do, however, leave some change (up to €2) for sit-down services, and in nicer restaurants it is not uncommon to leave 5% of the bill. For other services, like taxis and hairdressers, a 10-15% tip is acceptable.

SAFETY AND HEALTH

drugs and alcohol

Although mention of France often conjures images of black-clad smokers in berets, France no longer allows smoking in public as of 2008. The government has no official policy on berets. Possession of illegal drugs (including marijuana) in France can result in a substantial jail sentence or fine. Police may arbitrarily stop and search anyone on the street.

There is no drinking age in Paris, but restaurants will not serve anyone under the age of 16, and to purchase alcohol you must be at least 18 years old. Though there is no law prohibiting open containers, drinking on the street is considered uncouth. The legal blood-alcohol level for driving in France is 0.05%, which is less than it is in the US, UK, New Zealand, and Ireland, so exercise appropriate caution if operating a vehicle in France.

disabled and glbt travelers

Fear not—Paris loves you. **L'Association des Paralysés de France, Délégation de Paris** is an organization devoted to helping the disabled in Paris. In addition to promoting disabled individuals' fundamental rights to state compensation, public transportation, and handicapped-conscious jobs, the association also organizes international vacations. (17 bd Auguste Blanqui ☎01 53 80 92 97.)

Le Centre Lesbien, Gai, Bi et Trans de Paris et Île-de-France functions both as a counseling agency in and of itself, offering counseling and reception services for limited times during the week, and as the umbrella organization and formal location for many other GLBT resource organizations in Paris. (63 rue Beaubourg ☎01 43 57 21 47 ⚧ ⓂRambuteau or ⓂLes Halles. ♿ Administrative reception open M 1-8pm, T 10am-1pm and 2-6pm, W 1pm-7m, Th-F 1pm-6pm.)

KEEPING IN TOUCH

cellular phones

In France, mobile pay-as-you-go phones are the way to go. The two largest carriers are **SFR** and **Orange,** and they are so readily available that even supermarkets sell them. Cell-phone calls and texts can be paid for without signing a contract with a **Mobicarte** prepaid card, available at Orange and SFR stores, as well as tabacs. You can often buy phones for €20-40, which includes various amounts of minutes and 100 texts. Calling the US from one of these phones is around €0.80 a minute, with texts coming in at around €0.50.

CLIMATE

As pleasantly romantic as it is to think of springtime in Paris, *le printemps* doesn't last forever. Paris has a temperate climate with four seasons. The Northern Atlantic current keeps weather from approaching any extremes. Winters in Paris can be cold, but heavy snow is not characteristic of the City of Lights. Springtime in Paris is definitely a lovely time of year, even if it does come kind of late. Flowers bloom, trees grow leaves—it's everything you've read about. Summers are comfortable for the most part, though some days in August will have you wishing you had picked a city closer to a beach. Fall is brisk but enjoyable as the city's foliage changes before your eyes.

paris 101

You don't need to understand French—or speak with an affected accent—to know that Paris is a big deal (and that Parisians think so too). The allure of visiting the City of Light will never fade. Whether it be for romance, food, or fashion, Paris is at the top of practically everyone's list of desired vacation spots. It's a fashionista's one true love and a culinary enthusiast's heaven, yes, but the city has more to offer than Coco Chanel and croissants. The history and environment of Paris's culture have influenced almost every aspect of Western life: politics, art, and rapidly growing obesity rates, to name a few. *C'est la vie* after all—when in Paris, Parisian life seems like the one most want to live. But come on, do you really want to be that tourist, the one who gawks and fawns over every Parisian you see, adamantly proclaiming your wish to be one of them, when all you're really doing is screaming, "Look at me! I'm a foreigner!"? Didn't think so. Read on to see Paris's rises and falls over the years, because even this idealized European sanctuary has had its low points. Then sit back, pour yourself a glass of wine (or three), and peruse our advice on how to walk, talk, and act like you've lived in Paris all your life.

HISTORY

très, très long ago (250 bce-52 ce)

Paris is more than 2000 years old; the first inhabitants of the area hit the scene around 250 BCE. *Au début* (that's fancy talk for "in the beginning"), a tribe called the **Parisii of Gaul** formed a small fishing village beside the Seine River, naming their town **Lutetia.** Besides its location, Lutetia shared little with modern Paris. But not everything about the town has dissolved with time: while Lutetia was founded on the left bank of the Seine, the right was left abandoned due to a flourishing marsh, or marais—hence the neighborhood name today.

roman glory (52-250)

The people of Lutetia weren't walking around with clubs, though: they were civilized. They even created their own currency. But, alas, sovereignty was not to be. **Julius Caesar,** along with his army of overambitious Romans, set his sights on the city in 52 CE. The Parisii put up a valiant fight under Vercingétorix, their determined leader, but were ultimately defeated at the Battle of Alesia, setting a trend that would later prove unbreakable. To honor the Gauls' effort, Napoleon III had a 7m statue of Vercingétroix built in Alesia in 1865. A French inscription on the larger-than-life statue reads, "The Gauls united, forming a single nation animated by the same spirit, can defy the universe." As history has shown, this is a lie.

Under Caesar, however, the city grew larger and became an important center of the Roman Empire. Paris's first churches were built in the third century as **Saint Denis,** the city's first bishop, attempted to Christianize the city. Although Christianization was a success, St. Denis was abruptly decapitated (another trend, perhaps?) in 250.

hometown heroes (451-1000)

Always a group of active people (especially in war), Parisians took a hands-on approach to protect their city from renowned sweetheart **Attila the Hun** in 451: prayer. Remarkably the prayers led by Saint Geneviève repelled Attila from the city, or so the story goes. Geneviève was then named a patron saint of the city for making Parisians believe they could defend themselves without really doing much at all.

In 800, the Pope crowned **Charlemagne,** King of the Frankish people, as Holy Roman Emperor after he expanded the empire. Around two centuries later, Hugh Capet, the count of Paris, became King of France, and Paris was soon after renamed the capital of the country, generating an eternity of Parisian pride.

french toast (1000-1643)

Under the leader **Étienne Marcel,** Paris became an independent commune in 1358. With the Holy Roman Emperor out of their hair, Frenchmen were now left to sort out their own problems during times of great political and religious conflict. This was a daunting task, since dealing with issues was not exactly a Parisian forte. Perhaps sensing a dangerous future for the country's capital, in 1180, King Philippe Auguste built a highly protected castle known today as the **Louvre.** Later kings held significantly weaker grips on the city. In 1407, civil war swept Paris, and in 1430, the English won control of the city for the following six years of the **Hundred Years' War.** In 1537, around 10,000 Protestants were murdered in the **Saint Bartholomew's Day Massacre**—the worst moment of the long period of religious conflict brought on by the Reformation.

you say you want a revolution (1643-1799)

Unfortunately for the French aristocracy, this was not the end of unrest in Paris. Perhaps due to **Louis XIV's** obscenely luxurious lifestyle during his rule from 1643-1715, and also to the suggestion of his grandson's wife (a young Austrian by the name of Marie Antoinette) that those short on bread should just eat cake, the dregs of French society decided it was time to do something. Storming the Bastille prison seemed like a good idea, and that's just what they did on July 14, 1789. Three years later, the monarchy crumbled. These would be seen as the calm years of the revolution once **Robespierre** and his Committee of Public Safety decided in 1793 to ensure the safety of Louis XVI, Marie Antoinette, and around 3000 others by politely offing their heads.

shorty breaks it down (1799-1914)

Fed up with Robespierre's unhealthy relationship with the guillotine and the ineffectiveness of those who followed him, **Napoleon Bonaparte** overthrew the revolutionary government in 1799. Rewriting the constitution and issuing his own standardized "Napoleonic Code," Napoleon had ambitions that were larger than he was. In 1804, he somehow managed to convince people that naming himself Emperor was totally consistent with the ideals of the revolution. Though his domain at one point stretched from Spain to Russia, the 1815 Battle of **Waterloo** put a damper on his plans. Defeated, Napoleon was exiled to the tropical island of Saint Helena, setting a precedent that the punishment for trying to take over the world is to be forced to chill out in paradise for the rest of your life.

The next hundred years witnessed steady growth in technology, infrastructure, and culture, as well as a healthy smattering of further revolutions. Napoleon's nephew even showed up for a while and defied both republicanism and the rules of counting by ruling for 18 years as **Napoleon III.**

check out these guns (1914-present)

While the stalemate on the Western Front prevented the German forces from reaching Paris in WWI, the second time around the French were not so lucky. Hitler's forces occupied the city from 1940-44. Most of Paris's historical buildings and monuments were spared from the destruction of the war. Over half a million French citizens were not as lucky.

In 1958, undaunted by the failure of the first four, France embarked on the Fifth Republic. This nearly fell in May 1968 when student demonstrations took over the streets of Paris and eventually escalated into a nationwide general strike. The crisis passed, however, and since then, the French government has demonstrated an uncharacteristic stability.

Since taking office in 2007, President **Nicolas Sarkozy** has personally maintained the city's reputation for elegance through his refined eye for accessories, such as third wife Carla Bruni. In Paris, the position of mayor has been held since 2001 by Bertrand Delanoë, an openly gay socialist, proving once again that France is nothing like America.

CUSTOMS AND ETIQUETTE

how to win friends

Everyone knows the stereotype of the unfriendly, pretentious Parisian, but, if you exhibit basic manners, most will simply label you as a foreigner and remain civil. It is important to greet everyone that you interact with as *monsieur* or *madame*. Meeting friends, it is common to kiss once on each cheek, but upon first introductions, a handshake is acceptable. Simply saying please *(s'il vous plaît)* and thank you *(merci,* optional *beaucoup)* will earn you respect. Along those lines, Parisians will appreciate any attempts at speaking French; *bonjour, bonsoir,* and *pardon* are your three favorite words starting now.

table manners for dummies

Simply staying nourished in Paris may be the most difficult task of all. When repeating proper table manners for the third time, at the third meal of the day, your mother was just plain old annoying. "No one's going to terminate a friendship over the occasional elbow on the table," you thought. Well, in Paris they just might. At a meal, don't think about eating before someone says, *"Bon appétit!".* Resist the temptation to fill wine glasses up to the top, no matter how delicious the wine. Although knives and forks are used to eat almost everything (even fruit) don't think about touching a knife to your salad leaves, since to all with some common sense it is inexcusably offensive. And while the French generally abhor finger food, do not cut a baguette on the table—tear it. You may (rightfully) insist that these customs are peculiar, prissy, or pompous, to which we can only bid thee good luck.

FOOD AND DRINK

filet mignon with a side of snails, s'il vous plaît

Whether you sit down at a bistro, bar, or sidewalk cafe, you won't run out of different dishes to enjoy. For breakfast, try a croissant, or a chocolate-filled **pain au chocolat.** Parisians typically sit down to lunch anywhere from noon to 2pm. Meals typically consist of simple salads, sandwiches on baguettes, crepes, croques monsieur (a fancy-pants version of a grilled ham and cheese), or heavier meat dishes. Dinner may include a few fishy options: **bouillabaisse** is a popular traditional soup made from many different types of fish, and *escargots* are available at elegant restaurants for those who dare to try cooked snails. Perhaps the best part of dinner is dessert—from éclairs to chocolate mousse to crème brûlée, you'll find you have much to gain, and some bigger clothes to buy.

drink (read: wine)

Okay, the header is a slight exaggeration—Parisians appreciate a good espresso in the morning and the occasional coffee after dessert. But while in Paris, it may be worthwhile to do as the Parisians do, by which we mean drink wine and lots of it. Just don't be intimidated by the inordinate selection; the wine menu might look more like a textbook. If worse comes to worst, ask the waiter for a cup of the house best.

ART AND ARCHITECTURE

just a few paintings

The **Louvre,** a little museum you may have heard of, holds over 35,000 works of art, one of which is the **Mona Lisa.** Moving forward in time from Leonardo, many famous artists from more recent movements were born in or spent time in Paris, from Impressionists like **Édouard Manet** to Fauvist **Henri Matisse.** If you're interested in modern and contemporary art, the **Centre Pompidou** is devoted entirely to just that.

paris 101

a history in the streets

Paris's history is laid out on its streets, with buildings and monuments still standing from various architectural periods. Back in ancient times, Roman rulers built various religious buildings in their favorite style: their own. During the Medieval period, the Gothic style developed, with flying buttresses suspending intricate stained glass windows and pointed arches. For an example of this, look no further than **Notre Dame.** During the Renaissance, proportion and balance were all the rage. This developed into the Baroque period and culminated in the flamboyance of the **Palace of Versailles.** In the 19th century, Napoleon III had Baron Georges-Eugène Haussmann renovate the streets of Paris: the wider boulevards and balconied apartment buildings that make up the city are all his work. The Industrial Revolution sparked a new form of Art Nouveau architecture that took its designs from patterns in the natural world. For an example, look up and wave hello to the **Eiffel Tower.**

FASHION

Parisians, even when dressed casually, are very put together, and dressing fashionably does not always mean showing it all off—keep it classy. Remember that the gods of fashion reside in the area and are judging you. You can always stroll down the Champs-Élysées or hit up fashion week for inspiration, but you don't have to completely trash your current wardrobe. Jeans are acceptable in most places, but never wear sneakers to a nice restaurant.

HOLIDAYS AND FESTIVALS

HOLIDAY OR FESTIVAL	DESCRIPTION	DATE
Fashion Week	A week of fashion shows complete with new styles by the world's most famous designer labels.	usually in late January
Carnaval de Paris	Over 500 years old, this city carnival gives residents an excuse (as if you need one) to wear masks and parade through the streets.	March 4
VE Day	A celebration of the Allied victory over Germany in WWII. Festivities include a parade on the Champs-Élysées.	May 8
Fête de la Musique	This is pretty self-explanatory; free concerts and performances are given throughout the entire city. All types of music are performed.	June 21
Gay Pride Parade	Parades and presentations celebrating Paris's GLBT life.	mid-June
Bastille Day	This national holiday commemorates the storming of the Bastille in 1789. Kick it off with the *Bal du 14 Juillet*, a giant dance party the previous evening, and end with fireworks over the Eiffel Tower.	July 14
Beaujolais Nouveau Wine Festival	A nationwide celebration of the release of Beaujolais Nouveau wine; bar-hopping and drinking ensue.	November 15

paris

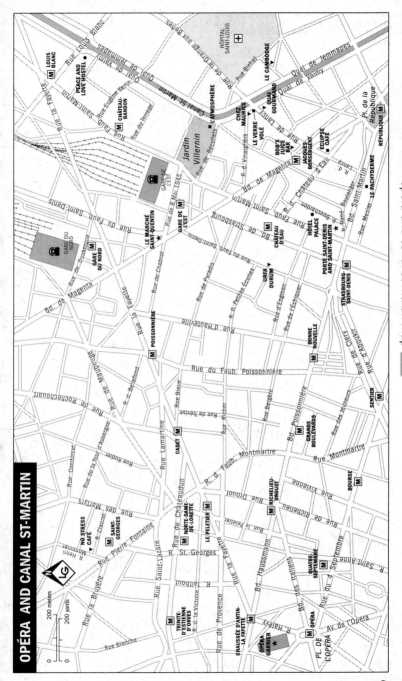

OPÉRA AND CANAL ST-MARTIN

200 meters
200 yards

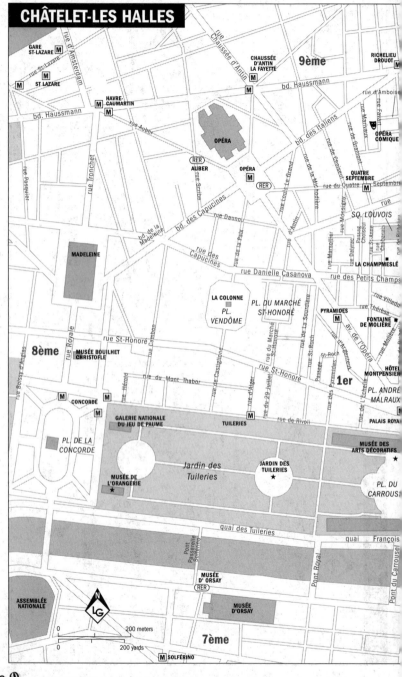

CHÂTELET-LES HALLES

GARE ST-LAZARE

rue d'Amsterdam

rue St-Lazare

ST-LAZARE

HAVRE-CAUMARTIN

bd. Haussmann

rue Auber

rue Tronchet

rue Pasquier

CHAUSSÉE D'ANTIN LA FAYETTE

9ème

RICHELIEU DROUOT

bd. Haussmann

rue d'Amboise

bd. des Italiens

rue Favart

OPÉRA COMIQUE

OPÉRA

rue de Gramont

rue de la Michodière

RER AUBER

OPÉRA

RER

QUATRE SEPTEMBRE

rue du Quatre Septembre

rue de Choiseul

bd. des Capucines

rue Daunou

rue Louis-le-Grand

rue Monsigny

SQ. LOUVOIS

bd. de la Madeleine

rue des Capucines

rue Danielle Casanova

rue de la Paix

rue d'Antin

rue de Richelieu

Passage Choiseul

rue St-Anne

rue Chabanais

LA CHAMPMESLÉ

MADELEINE

rue des Petits Champs

rue Marsollier

rue Ventadour

LA COLONNE

PL. VENDÔME

PL. DU MARCHÉ ST-HONORÉ

PYRAMIDES

rue Villedo

rue Thérèse

FONTAINE DE MOLIÈRE

av. de l'Opéra

rue Molière

rue Royale

rue St-Honoré

8ème

MUSÉE BOUILHET CHRISTOFLE

rue du Marché St-Honoré

rue de la Sourdière

rue St-Roch

HÔTEL MONTPENSIER

rue de Castiglione

rue du Mont Thabor

rue d'Alger

rue du 29 Juillet

rue St-Honoré

St-Roch

Passage

rue des Pyramides

PL. ANDRÉ MALRAUX

1er

rue de l'Échelle

rue de l'Échelle

CONCORDE

rue Boissy d'Anglas

rue St-Florentin

GALERIE NATIONALE DU JEU DE PAUME

TUILERIES

rue de Rivoli

PALAIS ROYAL

PL. DE LA CONCORDE

MUSÉE DE L'ORANGERIE ★

Jardin des Tuileries

JARDIN DES TUILERIES ★

MUSÉE DES ARTS DÉCORATIFS ★

PL. DU CARROUSEL

quai des Tuileries

quai François

Pont Passerelle Solférino

MUSÉE D'ORSAY

RER

Pont Royal

Pont du Carrousel

ASSEMBLÉE NATIONALE

N

LG

MUSÉE D'ORSAY

0   200 meters

0   200 yards

7ème

SOLFÉRINO

paris

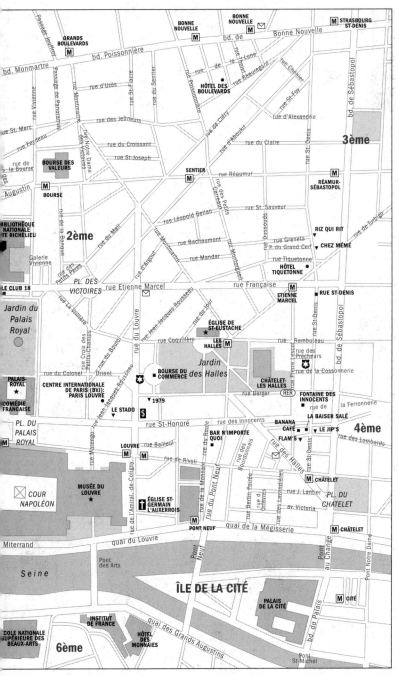

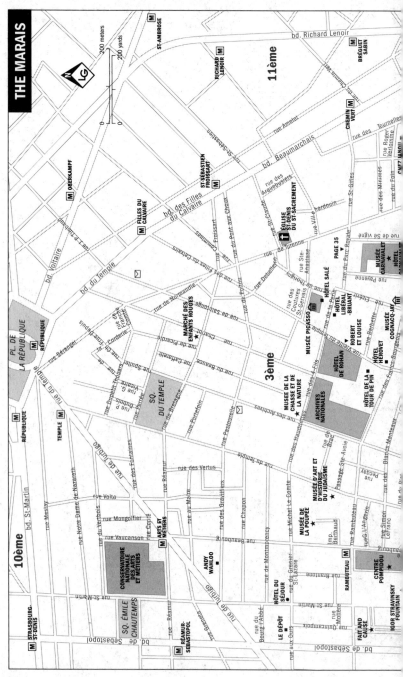

200 meters
200 yards

N

ST-AMBROSE M

bd. Richard Lenoir

M **RICHARD LENOIR**

M **BRÉGUET SABIN**

11ème

M **CHEMIN VERT**

rue des Tournelles

CHEZ MNOU

rue Roger Verlomme

ST-SÉBASTIEN FROISSART M

bd. Beaumarchais

rue des Arquebusiers

bd. des Filles du Calvaire

M **FILLES DU CALVAIRE**

rue St-Claude

rue de Sévigné

rue des Minimes

rue du Foin

rue Ste-Gilles

ÉGLISE ST-DENIS DU ST-SACREMENT ✝

rue Ville hardouin

OBERKAMPF M

MUSÉE CARNAVALET ★ HÔTEL

rue Payenne

rue Ste-Anastase

bd. Voltaire

PAGE 35

rue du Parc Royale

rue de Turenne

rue du Temple

rue de Normandie

rue de la Franche Comté

rue du Pont aux Choux

rue de Saintonge

HÔTEL SALÉ

MUSÉE PICASSO 🏛

rue des Coutures St-Gervais

HÔTEL LIBÉRAL BRUANT

rue de la Perle

MUSÉE COGNACQ-JAY 🏛

rue Elzévir

ROBERT ET LOUISE

HÔTEL HÉROUET

rue de la Barbette

rue des Francs-Bourgeois

MARCHÉ DES ENFANTS ROUGES ★

rue Charlot

rue de Bretagne

rue de Picardie

rue Commines

rue du Perche

rue de Poitou

rue de Béarn

PL. DE LA RÉPUBLIQUE

M **RÉPUBLIQUE**

rue du Temple

M **RÉPUBLIQUE**

rue Béranger

rue de Turbigo

M **TEMPLE**

rue du Temple

rue Dupetit Thouars

SQ. DU TEMPLE

rue de Bretagne

rue Charlot

rue Pastourelle

rue des Archives

3ème

MUSÉE DE LA CHASSE ET DE LA NATURE ★

ARCHIVES NATIONALES

HÔTEL DE ROHAN

HÔTEL DE LA TOUR DE PIN

HÔTEL DE LA PIN ■

rue des Quatre Fils

rue Vieille du Temple

rue des Blancs Manteaux

rue Pecquay

10ème

bd. St-Martin

rue Meslay

rue Notre-Dame-de-Nazareth

rue Volta

M **RÉAUMUR-SÉBASTOPOL**

rue au Maire

rue des Gravilliers

rue Réaumur

rue des Vertus

rue des Fontaines

rue du Temple

rue Chapon

rue Michel-Le-Comte

MUSÉE D'ART ET D'HISTOIRE DU JUDAÏSME ★

rue des Haudriettes

rue Rambuteau

rue de Braque

Passage Ste-Avoie

rue des Francs-Bourgeois

rue du Temple

rue du Grenier St-Lazare

M **ARTS ET MÉTIERS**

rue de Turbigo

rue Mongolfier

rue Vaucanson

rue Conté

CONSERVATOIRE NATIONALE DES ARTS ET MÉTIERS

rue St-Martin

ANDY WAHLOO ▲

HÔTEL DU SÉJOUR

MUSÉE DE LA POUPÉE ★

Imp. Berthaud

rue Beaubourg

rue de Montmorency

rue du Bourg-l'Abbé

M **RAMBUTEAU**

rue Simon LeFranc

rue Pierre-au-Lard

rue Brantôme

CENTRE POMPIDOU ★

STRASBOURG-ST-DENIS M

bd. de Sébastopol

SQ. ÉMILE CHAUTEMPS

rue St-Martin

rue Réaumur

rue aux Ours

RÉAUMUR-SÉBASTOPOL M

rue du Bourg-l'Abbé

LE DÉPÔT ■

rue du Grenier St-Lazare

rue Quincampoix

rue Aubry-le-Boucher

FAT AND CRAZE ■

rue Molière

bd. de Sébastopol

IGOR STRAVINSKY FOUNTAIN

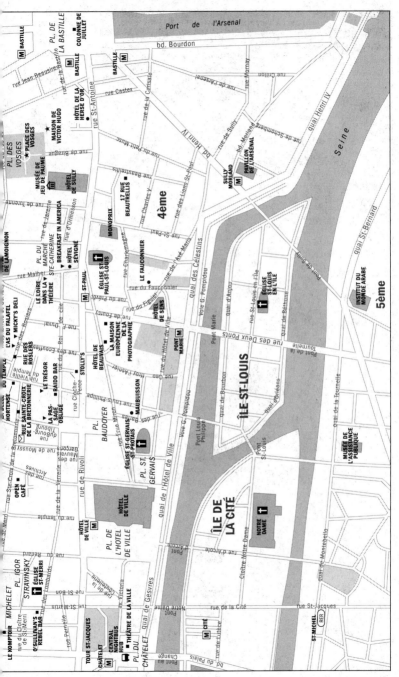

the marais map

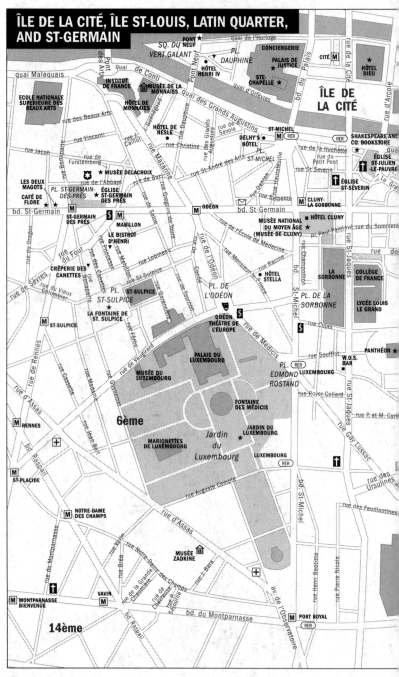

ÎLE DE LA CITÉ, ÎLE ST-LOUIS, LATIN QUARTER, AND ST-GERMAIN

paris

ÎLE DE LA CITÉ

SQ. DU PONT NEUF ★
PONT ★
VERT GALANT
quai de l'Horloge
CONCIERGERIE
CITÉ M
quai des Orfèvres
PL. DAUPHINE
PALAIS DE JUSTICE
HÔTEL HENRI IV
STE-CHAPELLE ★
HÔTEL DIEU ★

quai Malaquais
quai de Conti
Pont des Arts
INSTITUT DE FRANCE
MUSÉE DE LA MONNAIES
quai des Grands Augustins

ECOLE NATIONALE SUPÉRIEURE DES BEAUX ARTS
HÔTEL DE MONNAIES
rue des Beaux Arts
HÔTEL DE NESLE
SHAKESPEARE AND CO. BOOKSTORE ★
ÉGLISE ST-JULIEN-LE-PAUVRE ✝
rue d'Arcole

rue Visconti
rue Jacob
rue de Furstemberg
rue J. Callot
rue Christine
rue de Savoie
rue St-André des Arts
DELHY'S HÔTEL
PL. ST-MICHEL
ST-MICHEL M RER
RER
rue de la Huchette
rue du Petit Pont
rue St-Séverin
ÉGLISE ST-SÉVERIN ✝

MUSÉE DELACROIX ★
rue de l'Abbaye
PL. ST-GERMAIN-DES-PRÉS ★
ÉGLISE ST-GERMAIN DES PRÉS ★
rue de Buci
rue Grégoire de Tours
rue St-Séverin
rue Serpente
CLUNY-LA SORBONNE M

LES DEUX MAGOTS
CAFÉ DE FLORE ★
ST-GERMAIN DES PRÉS M
bd. St-Germain
ODÉON M
bd. St-Germain

MABILLON M
MUSÉE NATIONAL DU MOYEN ÂGE (MUSÉE DE CLUNY)
HÔTEL CLUNY ■
rue du Sommer
rue de

LE BISTROT D'HENRI ●
rue de Seine
rue de l'École de Médecine
pl. Paul Painlevé
rue St-Jacques

CRÊPERIE DES CANETTES
rue des Canettes
rue Princesse
rue Guisarde
rue Mabillon
rue St-Sulpice
rue de l'Odéon
rue Monsieur le Prince
rue Racine
HÔTEL STELLA ●
LA SORBONNE
COLLÈGE DE FRANCE

PL. ST-SULPICE
ST-SULPICE
LA FONTAINE DE ST. SULPICE
PL. DE L'ODÉON
ODÉON THÉÂTRE DE L'EUROPE ⬚
PL. DE LA SORBONNE
LYCÉE LOUIS LE GRAND

ST-SULPICE M
rue du Vieux Colombier
rue de Rennes
rue de Tournon
rue de Condé
rue de Médicis
rue Cujas
$

RENNES M
rue de Vaugirard
PALAIS DU LUXEMBOURG
PL. EDMOND ROSTAND
LUXEMBOURG RER
W.O.S. BAR ■
PANTHÉON ★
rue Soufflot

rue d'Assas
rue Cassette
rue Madame
rue Bonaparte
MUSÉE DU LUXEMBOURG
FONTAINE DES MÉDICIS
rue Royer Collard
rue P. et M. Curie

bd. Raspail
rue Jean-Bart
6ème
Jardin du Luxembourg
JARDIN DU LUXEMBOURG ★
MARIONETTES DE LUXEMBOURG
LUXEMBOURG RER
rue Gay Lussac

ST-PLACIDE M
NOTRE-DAME DES CHAMPS M
rue d'Assas
rue Auguste Compte
bd. St-Michel
rue des Ursulines
rue des Feuillantines

rue Vavin
MUSÉE ZADKINE 🏛
rue Notre-Dame des Champs
rue de la Grande Chaumière
rue Bréa
rue J. Barr
rue Henri-Baptiste
rue Pierre-Nicole

MONTPARNASSE BIENVENUE M ✝
VAVIN M
14ème
bd. du Montparnasse
PORT ROYAL M RER
av. de l'Observatoire
bd. Raspail

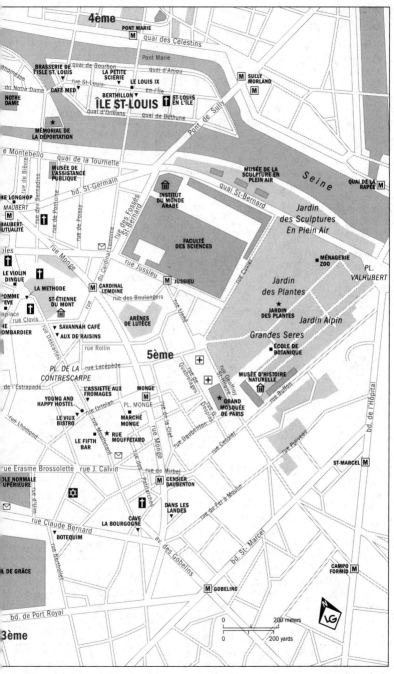

4ème

PONT MARIE M

quai des Célestins

Pont Marie

quai de Bourbon

quai d'Anjou

BRASSERIE DE
L'ISLE ST. LOUIS

rue St-Louis

LA PETITE
SCIERIE

SULLY
MORLAND M

CAFÉ MED

LE LOUIS IX

ÎLE ST-LOUIS

BERTHILLON

en-l'île

ST-LOUIS
EN L'ÎLE

M

NOTRE
DAME

quai d'Orléans

quai de Béthune

MÉMORIAL DE
LA DÉPORTATION

Pont de Sully

QUAI DE LA
RAPÉE M

e Montebello

quai de la Tournelle

MUSÉE DE
L'ASSISTANCE
PUBLIQUE

MUSÉE DE LA
SCULPTURE EN
PLEIN AIR

Seine

rue de Bièvre

rue des Bernardins

bd. St-Germain

quai St-Bernard

NE LONGHOP

MAUBERT M

INSTITUT
DU MONDE
ARABE

Jardin
des Sculptures
En Plein Air

MAUBERT-
UTUALITÉ

rue de Poissy

rue des Fossés St-Bernard

FACULTÉ
DES SCIENCES

MÉNAGERIE
ZOO

PL.
VALHUBERT

les

LE VIOLIN
DINGUE

rue Monge

rue du Cardinal-Lemoine

rue Jussieu

JUSSIEU M

Jardin
des Plantes

OMME
EVE

LA METHODE

CARDINAL
LEMOINE M

rue des Boulangers

JARDIN
DES PLANTES

OMBARDIER

aplace

rue Clovis

ST-ÉTIENNE
DU MONT

ARÈNES
DE LUTÈCE

rue Cuvier

Jardin Alpin

rue des Descartes

SAVANNAH CAFÉ

AUX DE RAISINS

Grandes Serres

ÉCOLE DE
BOTANIQUE

rue Rollin

PL. DE LA
CONTRESCARPE

rue Lacépède

5ème

rue de Quatrefages

MUSÉE D'HISTOIRE
NATURELLE

rue Geoffroy St-Hilaire

de l'Estrapade

L'ASSIETTE AUX
FROMAGES

MONGE

YOUNG AND
HAPPY HOSTEL

rue Ortolan

MONGE M

PL. MONGE

GRAND
MOSQUÉE
DE PARIS

rue Daubenton

rue Gracieuse

rue de la Clef

LE VIEUX
BISTRO

MARCHÉ
MONGE

rue Lhomond

LE FIFTH
BAR

RUE
MOUFFETARD

rue Censier

rue de Mirbel

ue Erasme Brossolette

rue J. Calvin

CENSIER
DAUBENTON M

rue Buffon

ST-MARCEL M

rue Poliveau

OLE NORMALE
UPÉRIEURE

rue d'Ulm

DANS LES
LANDES

bd. de l'Hôpital

rue Claude Bernard

CAVE
LA BOURGOGNE

rue du Fer à Moulin

BOTEQUIM

rue Berthollet

av. des Gobelins

bd. St. Marcel

CAMPO
FORMID M

L DE GRÂCE

bd. de Port Royal

GOBELINS M

0   200 meters

0   200 yards

3ème

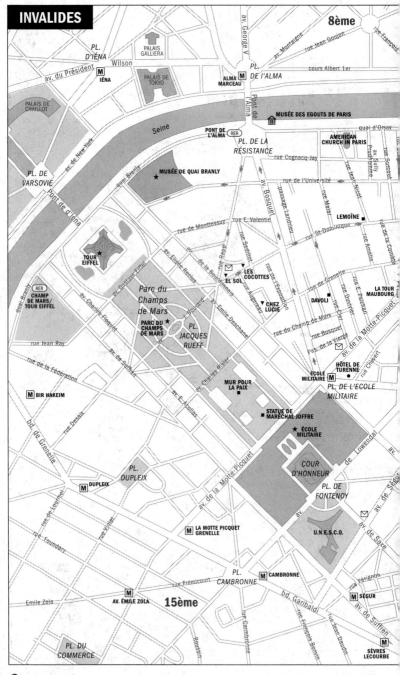

INVALIDES

8ème

PL. D'IÉNA

PALAIS GALLIERA

av. du Président Wilson

M IÉNA

PALAIS DE TOKYO

av. Montaigne

rue Jean-Goujon

rue François

PL. DE l'ALMA

M DE l'ALMA

ALMA MARCEAU

cours Albert 1er

PALAIS DE CHAILLOT

Pont de l'Alma

Seine

MUSÉE DES EGOUTS DE PARIS

av. de New-York

PONT DE L'ALMA **RER**

quai d'Orsay

AMERICAN CHURCH IN PARIS

rue Cognacq-jay

av. Sully Prud'homme

rue Surcouf

PL. DE LA RÉSISTANCE

quai Branly

av. Bosquet

rue de l'Université

PL. DE VARSOVIE

Pont de d'Iéna

★ MUSÉE DE QUAI BRANLY

rue Jean-Nicot

rue de la Comète

rue de Monttessuy

rue E. Valentin

rue St-Dominique

LEMOÎNE ■

rue de l'Amélie

TOUR EIFFEL ★

av. Élysée-Reclus

av. Gustave-Eiffel

rue Sédillot

rue de l'Exposition

rue St-Dominique

Parc du Champs de Mars

rue de Grenelle

rue E. Pichard

LA TOUR MAUBOURG

RER CHAMP DE MARS/ TOUR EIFFEL

av. Charles-Floquet

✉ ★ LES COCOTTES

EL SOL ▼

rue Augereau

DAVOLI ■

rue de la Motte-Picquet

av. de la Bourdonnais

rue Amélie

av. de Suffren

Boulevard

av. Emile-Deschanel

■ CHEZ LUCIE

rue du Champ-de-Mars

rue Bosquet

Pas.-de-la-Vierge

quai Branly

rue Jean Ray

PARC DU CHAMPS DE MARS ★

PL. JACQUES RUEFF

ÉCOLE MILITAIRE **M**

HÔTEL DE TURENNE ● ✉

rue Chevert

rue de la Fédération

av. de Suffren

av. Charles-Risler

MUR POUR LA PAIX ■

PL. DE L'ECOLE MILITAIRE

M BIR HAKEIM

rue Desaix

av. F-Apollais

STATUE DE MARÉCHAL JOFFRE ■

★ ÉCOLE MILITAIRE

PL. DUPLEIX

av. de la Motte-Picquet

COUR D'HONNEUR

de Lowendal

av. de Ségur

M DUPLEIX

PL. DE FONTENOY

rue Letellier

rue Violet

rue du Commerce

M LA MOTTE PICQUET GRENELLE

U.N.E.S.C.O.

av. de Saxe

rue Fondary

rue de la Motte-Picquet

bd. de Grenelle

PL. CAMBRONNE

M CAMBRONNE

rue Frémicourt

bd. Garibaldi

rue Pétignon

M SÉGUR

Emile Zola

M AV. ÉMILE ZOLA

15ème

av. de Suffren

rue Cambronne

rue François Bonvin

PL. DU COMMERCE

rue Jean Daudin

M SÈVRES LECOURBE

paris

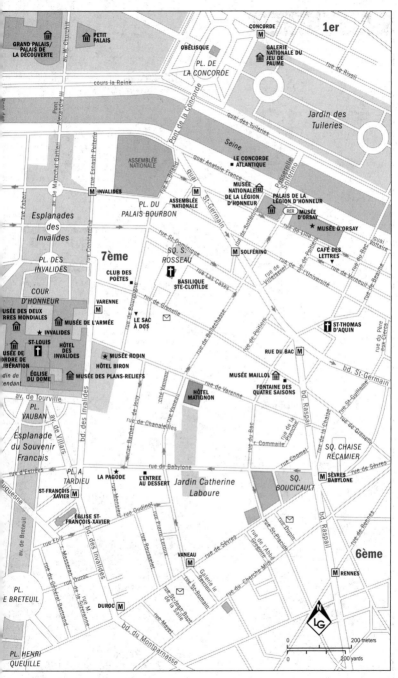

1er

GRAND PALAIS/
PALAIS DE
LA DÉCOUVERTE

PETIT
PALAIS

CONCORDE Ⓜ

OBÉLISQUE

GALERIE DU
JEU DE
PAUME

PL. DE
LA CONCORDE

cours la Reine

Jardin des
Tuileries

quai des Tuileries

Seine

quai Anatole France

ASSEMBLÉE
NATIONALE

LE CONCORDE
■ ATLANTIQUE

Passerelle Solférino

MUSÉE
NATIONALE Ⓜ
DE LA LÉGION
D'HONNEUR

PALAIS DE LA
LÉGION D'HONNEUR

Ⓜ INVALIDES

PL. DU
PALAIS BOURBON

ASSEMBLÉE
NATIONALE

(RER) MUSÉE
D'ORSAY

★ MUSÉE D'ORSAY

Esplanades
des
Invalides

7ème

rue St-Dominique

SQ.
ROSSEAU

Ⓜ SOLFÉRINO

CAFÉ DES
LETTRES
▼

PL. DES
INVALIDES

CLUB DES
POÈTES ■

rue Las Casas

BASILIQUE
STE-CLOTILDE

rue de Villersexel

COUR
D'HONNEUR

VARENNE
Ⓜ

rue de Grenelle

USÉE DES DEUX
RRES MONDIALES

▼ LE SAC
À DOS

✉

ST-THOMAS
D'AQUIN

Ⓜ MUSÉE DE L'ARMÉE

★ INVALIDES

RUE DU BAC Ⓜ

ST-LOUIS

HÔTEL
DES
INVALIDES

USÉE DE
ORDRE DE
IBÉRATION

★ MUSÉE RODIN

HÔTEL BIRON

MUSÉE MAILLOL Ⓜ

FONTAINE DES
QUATRE SAISONS

din de
endant

ÉGLISE
DU DÔME

Ⓜ MUSÉE DES PLANS-RELIEFS

rue de Varenne

bd. St-Germain

HÔTEL
MATIGNON

av. de Tourville

PL.
VAUBAN

bd. des Invalides

rue de Chanaleilles

SQ. CHAISE
RÉCAMIER

Esplanade
du Souvenir
Français

rue de Babylone

SQ.
BOUCICAULT

Ⓜ SÈVRES
BABYLONE

rue de Sèvres

PL. A.
TARDIEU

★ LA PAGODE

L'ENTRÉE
AU DESSERT

Jardin Catherine
Laboure

bd. Raspail

ST-FRANÇOIS-
XAVIER Ⓜ

ÉGLISE ST-
FRANÇOIS-XAVIER

6ème

VANEAU
Ⓜ

rue de Sèvres

bd. Raspail

Ⓜ RENNES

PL.
E BRETEUIL

DUROC Ⓜ

bd. du Montparnasse

N

LG

PL. HENRI
QUEUILLE

0   200 meters

0   200 yards

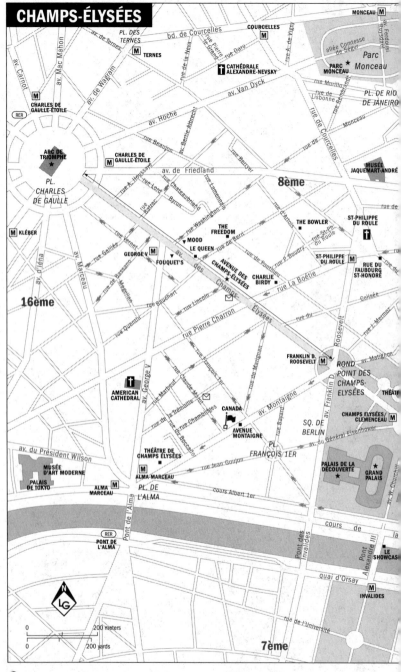

CHAMPS-ÉLYSÉES

MONCEAU Ⓜ

bd. de Courcelles

COURCELLES Ⓜ

PL. DES TERNES

TERNES Ⓜ

av. de Ternes

av. de la Néra

rue Pierre le Grand

rue Daru

av. de Wagram

CATHÉDRALE ALEXANDRE-NEVSKY

av. Van Dyck

av. A. de Vigny

allée Comtesse de Ségur

Parc Monceau

PARC MONCEAU ★

rue Murillo

rue de Lisbonne

PL. DE RIO DE JANEIRO

av. Carnot

av. Mac Mahon

CHARLES DE GAULLE-ETOILE Ⓜ
RER

av. Hoche

rue de Courcelles

rue de Monceau

ARC DE TRIOMPHE ★

PL. CHARLES DE GAULLE

CHARLES DE GAULLE Ⓜ

rue Beaujon

av. Bertie Albrecht

rue Balzac

av. de Friedland

8ème

MUSÉE JAQUEMART-ANDRÉ ★

rue de

KLÉBER Ⓜ

rue Lord Byron

rue A. Houssaye

rue de Chateaubriand

rue de Tilsitt

rue Lamennais

rue d'Artois

THE BOWLER ■

ST-PHILIPPE DU ROULE

av. d'Iéna

av. Marceau

rue Vernet

rue Galilée

rue Washington

THE FREEDOM

rue de Berri

rue de Ponthieu

rue J. Boutry

rue St-Ph-du Roule

ST-PHILIPPE DU ROULE Ⓜ

RUE DU FAUBOURG ST-HONORÉ ★

16ème

rue de Bassano

rue de Magellan

GEORGE V Ⓜ

FOUQUET'S ★

AVENUE DES CHAMPS-ÉLYSÉES ★

MOOD
LE QUEEN

CHARLIE BIRDY ■

rue La Boétie

Colisée

rue Beauchet

rue Lincoln

rue Quentin

rue Pierre Charron

Champs. Élysées

rue du

rue J. Mermoz

av. George V

rue Marbeuf

rue Pierre Charron

rue François 1er

FRANKLIN D. ROOSEVELT Ⓜ

av. Matignon

rue Franklin D. Roosevelt

ROND POINT DES CHAMPS-ELYSÉES

THÉÂT

AMERICAN CATHEDRAL

rue Clément Marot

rue de la Trémoille

av. Montaigne

CANADA

AVENUE MONTAIGNE ★

rue de Chambiges

rue du Boccador

rue Bayard

SQ. DE BERLIN

CHAMPS ELYSÉES/ CLEMENCEAU Ⓜ

av. du Président Wilson

THÉÂTRE DE CHAMPS ELYSÉES Ⓜ

ALMA-MARCEAU

rue Jean Goujon

PL. FRANÇOIS 1ER

av. du Général Eisenhower

PALAIS DE LA DÉCOUVERTE ★

GRAND PALAIS ★

av. W. Churchill

MUSÉE D'ART MODERNE

PALAIS DE TOKYO

ALMA MARCEAU Ⓜ

PL. DE L'ALMA

cours Albert 1er

cours de la

RER
PONT DE L'ALMA

Pont de l'Alma

Pont des Invalides

Pont Alexandre III

LE SHOWCAS

quai d'Orsay

INVALIDES Ⓜ

N

rue de l'Université

0   200 meters
0   200 yards

7ème

paris

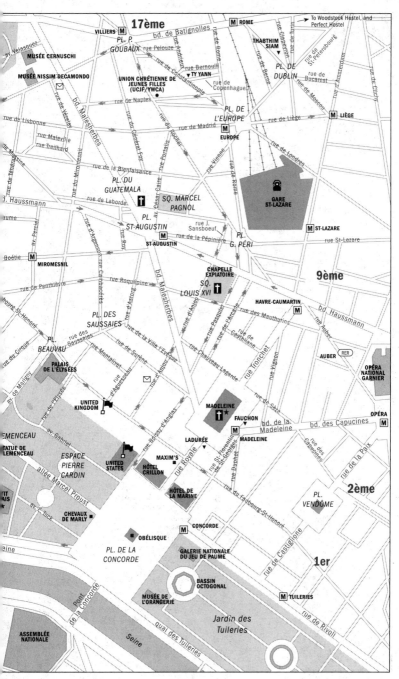

17ème

VILLIERS M

PL. P. GOUBAUX

bd. de Batignolles

M ROME

To Woodstock Hostel, and Perfect Hostel

THABTHIM SIAM ▼

MUSÉE CERNUSCHI

rue Pelouze

rue Andrieux

rue de Rome

rue de Turin

rue Clapeyron

rue de St-Petersbourg

rue de Chigny

rue Bernouilli

rue de Naples

UNION CHRÉTIENNE DE JEUNES FILLES (UCJF/YWCA) ✉

rue de Copenhague

PL. DE DUBLIN

rue de Berne

rue de Bucarest

rue de Moscou

rue d'Amsterdam

MUSÉE NISSIM DECAMONDO

TY YANN ▼

bd. Malesherbes

rue du Général Foy

rue de Lisbonne

rue de Madrid

PL. DE L'EUROPE

rue de Liège

LIÈGE M

rue de Vienne

rue de Rome

rue de Londres

rue de Lisbonne

rue Maleville

rue Treilhard

rue de la Bienfaisance

EUROPE

J. Haussmann

César Caire

rue de Laborde

PL. DU GUATEMALA

SQ. MARCEL PAGNOL ✝

aume

av. Percier

Boétie M

MIROMESNIL

rue de Penthièvre

PL. ST-AUGUSTIN

M ST-AUGUSTIN

rue de la Pépinière

rue J. Sansboeuf

PL. G. PÉRI

GARE ST-LAZARE 🏠

ST-LAZARE M

rue St-Lazare

CHAPELLE EXPIATOIRE

SQ. LOUIS XVI ✝

rue d'Astorg

bd. Malesherbes

rue Roquepine

rue de la Ville l'Evêque

rue d'Anjou

rue de l'Arcade

rue des Mathurins

HAVRE-CAUMARTIN M

bd. Haussmann

rue Auber

9ème

rue de Penthièvre

rue de Cambacérès

rue de Suresne

rue Pasquier

rue de Castellane

rue Tronchet

rue Vignon

AUBER RER

OPÉRA NATIONAL GARNIER

PL. DES SAUSSAIES

rue des Saussaies

rue Montalivet

rue d'Aguesseau

rue du Cirque

PL. BEAUVAU

PALAIS DE L'ÉLYSÉE

av. de Marigny

rue de l'Élysée

rue du Faubourg St-Honoré

UNITED KINGDOM ⚑ ✉

rue d'Anjou

rue du Chevau-Lagarde

rue de Sèze

rue Boissy-d'Anglas

av. Gabriel

EMENCEAU

TATUE DE LEMENCEAU

ESPACE PIERRE CARDIN

allée Marcel Proust

UNITED STATES ⚑

MAXIM'S

HÔTEL CRILLON

rue Royale

MADELEINE ✝★

LADURÉE ▼

FAUCHON ▼

MADELEINE M

bd. de la Madeleine

rue St-Florentin

rue St-Honoré

rue Duphot

bd. des Capucines

rue des Capucines

rue de la Paix

OPÉRA M

2ème

TIT AIS ★

CHEVAUX DE MARLY ▪

HÔTEL DE LA MARINE

av. C. Track

OBÉLISQUE ◆

CONCORDE M

rue du Faubourg-St-Honoré

PL. VENDÔME

1er

eine

PL. DE LA CONCORDE

GALERIE NATIONALE DU JEU DE PAUME

BASSIN OCTOGONAL

rue de Castiglione

Pont de la Concorde

MUSÉE DE L'ORANGERIE

TUILERIES M

rue de Rivoli

ASSEMBLÉE NATIONALE

Seine

quai des Tuileries

Jardin des Tuileries

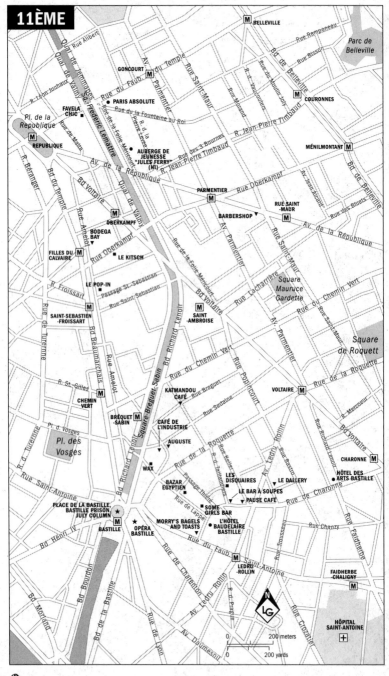

11ÈME

M BELLEVILLE

Rue Ramponeau

Parc de Belleville

Quai de Jemmapes
Quai de Valmy
Rue Aliber
Sq. Frédéric Lemaître

R. Léon Jamhuat

GONCOURT

Rue du Faub. du Temple

Rue Saint-Maur

Bd de Belleville

Rue Bisson

Rue du Moulin Joly

R. Varonneurs

M COURONNES

FAVELA CHIC

● PARIS ABSOLUTE

Rue du Fontaine au Roi

Pl. de la République

R. de Malte

R. d. la Folie Méricourt
Petit Lang

Rue Morand

R. Jean-Pierre Timbaud

MÉNILMONTANT M

M REPUBLIQUE

R. Béranger

Bd du Temple

Av. de la République

Bd Voltaire

AUBERGE DE JEUNESSE "JULES FERRY" (HI)

R. Jean-Pierre Timbaud

Bus 3-Bournes

Rue Oberkampf

PARMENTIER M

Rue Oberkampf

Av. de la République

Quai de Valmy

M OBERKAMPF

BODEGA BAY ▼

● BARBERSHOP

RUE SAINT-MAUR

Rue Saint-Maur

Av. Jean-Aicard

Rue des Bluets

FILLES DU CALVAIRE

● LE KITSCH

Rue Oberkampf

R. Amelot

Av. Parmentier

Bd Beaumarchais

LE POP-IN

Passage St-Sebastien

Rue Saint-Sebastien

Bd Voltaire

Rue de la Folie Méricourt

Rue Lacharrière

Av. Parmentier

Square Maurice Gardette

Rue Saint-Maur

R. Froissart

Rue de Turenne

SAINT-SEBASTIEN -FROISSART

Bd Richard Lenoir

SAINT -AMBROISE

Rue du Chemin Vert

Square de Roquett

R. St-Gilles

CHEMIN VERT

Rue Amelot

Rue du Chemin Vert

Rue Popincourt

VOLTAIRE M

Rue de la Roquette

Bd Voltaire

R. Mercœur

Pr. d. Vosges

Pl. des Vosges

R. de Turenne

BRÉQUET -SABIN

Square Bréguet-Sabin M

KATMANDOU CAFÉ

CAFÉ DE L'INDUSTRIE

Rue Bréguet

Rue Sedaine

Av. Ledru-Rollin

Rue Basfroi

CHARONNE M

Bd Voltaire

Rue Saint-Antoine

Bd Richard Lenoir

AUGUSTE ▼

WAX ▼

BAZAR EGYPTIEN ▼

Rue de la Roquette

Passage Thiéré

R. de la Forge Royale

R. de Lappe

Passage Josset

LES DISQUAIRES

● LE DALLERY

HÔTEL DES ARTS BASTILLE

Rue de Charonne

Rue Richard Lenoir

Rue Faidherbe

PLACE DE LA BASTILLE, BASTILLE PRISON, JULY COLUMN ★

M BASTILLE

★ OPÉRA BASTILLE

MORRY'S BAGELS AND TOASTS ▼

LE BAR À SOUPES ▼
PAUSE CAFÉ ▼

SOME GIRLS BAR ▼

L'HÔTEL BAUDELAIRE BASTILLE ●

Rue Chanzy

Bd Henri IV

Bd Bourdon

Bd Morland

Rue de la Bastille

Rue de Lyon

Rue de Charenton

Av. Ledru-Rollin

R. de Prague

Rue de Charenton

Av. Daumesnil

Rue du Faub. Saint-Antoine

LEDRU -ROLLIN M

Rue de Charonne

Rue Crozatier

Rue Faidherbe

FAIDHERBE CHALIGNY M

HÔPITAL SAINT-ANTOINE ✚

N LG

0 ___ 200 meters
0 ___ 200 yards

paris

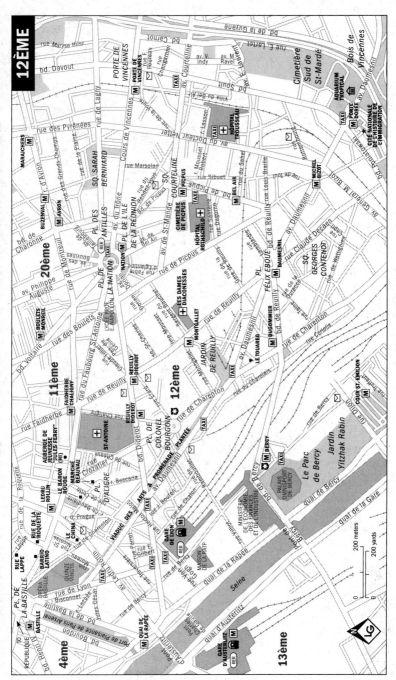

12ème map

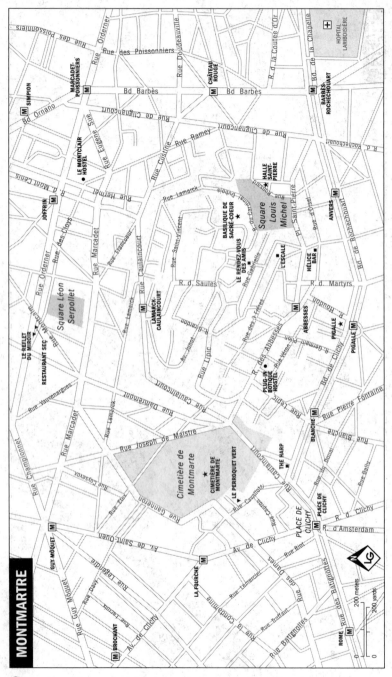

paris

MONTMARTRE

RUE des Poissonniers

Rue Ordener

Rue des Poissonniers

Rue Doudeauville

R. de la Goutte d'Or

Rue de la Chapelle

Bd de la Chapelle

HÔPITAL LARIBOISIÈRE

MARCADET-POISSONNIERS M

SIMPLON M

CHÂTEAU ROUGE M

Bd Barbès

Bd Barbès M

BARBÈS-ROCHECHOUART

Bd Ornano M

Rue de Clignancourt

Rue de Clignancourt

R. de Rochechouart

Rue Eugène Sue

Rue Custine

Rue Ramey

LE MONTCLAIR HOSTEL

Rue Hermel

R. du Mont Cenis

Rue Lamarck

Rue du Chevalier de la Barre

HALLE SAINT-PIERRE ★

Rue Paul Albert

Square Louis Michel

Pl. Saint-Pierre

JOFFRIN M

Rue des Cloys

Rue Marcadet

Rue Francoeur

BASILIQUE DE SACRÉ-COEUR ★

ANVERS M

Rue Caulaincourt

Rue Saint-Vincent

LE RENDEZ-VOUS DES AMIS

Rue Gabrielle

L'ESCALE ●

Bd de Rochechouart

Rue Ordener

R. d. Saules

HÉLICE BAR

Square Léon Serpollet

Rue Lamarck

Rue Girardon

LAMARCK-CAULAINCOURT M

R. d. Martyrs

Av. Junot

ABBESSES M

R. Houdon

LE REFLET DU MIROIR

Rue du Mont Cenis

Rue Lepic

Rue des Abbesses

Rue des 3 Frères

PIGALLE ★

PIGALLE M

RESTAURANT SEC

Rue des Abbesses

Rue Germain Pilon

Bd de Clichy

Rue Yvonnet

PLUG-IN BOUTIQUE HOSTEL ●

Rue Lepic

Rue Pierre Fontaine

Rue Vanvenargues

Rue Damrémont

Rue Caulaincourt

BLANCHE M

Rue Blanche

Rue Marcadet

Rue Lamarck

Rue Joseph de Maistre

Cimetière de Montmartre

CIMETIÈRE DE MONTMARTRE ★

LE PERROQUET VERT ●

THE HARP ▼

Rue Caulaincourt

Rue du Dome

Rue Ballu

Rue Championnet

Rue Cavaillotti

PLACE DE CLICHY

PLACE DE CLICHY M

Rue Coysevox

Rue Cardinal

Rue Ganneron

Rue Capron

R. d. Clichy

R. d'Amsterdam

GUY MÔQUET M

Av. de Saint-Ouen

Av. de Clichy M

Rue Biot

PLACE DE CLICHY

BROCHANT M

Rue Lécluse

LA FOURCHE M

Rue La Condamine

Rue Lacroix

Rue Truffaut

Rue des Batignolles

Rue Guy Môquet

Rue Davy

Rue Lamy

Av. de Clichy

Rue des Dames

Rue Legendre

Rue Nollet

Rue Truffaut

ROME M

Rue des Batignolles

LG Ⓜ

200 meters
0

200 yards
0

PRAGUE

Prague is a city of magic. No, really, it is. Skip the tourist traps and everything that claims to be "authentic Czech culture," and open yourself up to one of the most enchanting cities you'll ever experience. Prague is neither sterile West European capital nor Eastern European post-Communist wreck—it's caught somewhere in between daily reality and the realm of mortal legends. These cobblestone streets were once walked upon by Franz Kafka, the famous brooding author, and planned out by Charles IV, the ambitious Czech king, who dreamed up Prague the way it looks today (aside from the fast food restaurants, of course). And then there's the more recent specter of Communism, which left the entire country with a semi-permanent hangover and some peculiar sights, like a Malá Strana tower where the Communist secret police spied on foreign ambassadors and Czech citizens with hilariously out-dated equipment. But time moves forward, as indicated by the giant metronome that ticks away where an enormous Stalin statue once stood. All this, and the hundreds of spires piercing the air, the roofs merging into one big sea of red, and the glistening Vltava River create the magic. Well, that and the beer that's cheaper than water, the hip cafes, and the art, from the subtlest of jazz melodies to the heaviest of modern sculptures. Sometimes all you will see are masses of tourists, but Prague's magic undoubtedly remains.

greatest hits

- **RADICAL ROOMS. Sir Toby's Hostel** provides more than space with beer tastings, quiz tournaments, and Crepe and Cartoon Sundays (p. 677).
- **POSTCARDS GALORE.** The **Charles Bridge,** probably the most photo-graphed sight in Prague, is beautiful by day or night (p. 682).
- **A MISNOMER.** The food at **Bar Bar** in Malá Strana is reason enough to go (p. 708).
- **CROSS THE LINE.** Get lost in the labyrinthine wonderland that is **Cross Club** in Holešovice (p. 726).

Prague's university is Univerzita Karlova v Praze (Charles University), founded in 1348. Its campus is spread across the city, but you're bound to run into students if you frequent the right bars, such as **Bunkr Parukářka** or **Matrix.** If you're looking to find the study-abroad crowd, **Roxy** is a good club option and is always packed with foreign youth. And if you're just dying to be in an indie film, snoop around **FAMU: Filmová a televizní fakulta Akademie múzických umění v Praze,** a film school located in Nové Město that is known to bring all the alternative boys to its yard.

orientation

NOVÉ MĚSTO

Founded by Charles IV in 1348, Nové Město is not exactly "new." Its historical sights are a bit less known than those of the Old Town, but there's still a lot to see: the **New Town Hall** (where the Hussites famously chucked several town councilors out the window), **Our Lady of the Snow** (a dream cathedral whose construction was interrupted by the Hussite Wars), and **Saint Wenceslas Statue** (where Czechoslovak independence was proclaimed). Less touristy than the Old Town, Nové Město is home to nightlife and affordable restaurants as well as some of the most conveniently located hostels in the entire city. If you're skeptical of Staré Město's artificial charms, this is the perfect neighborhood to start searching for more authentic experiences.

The New Town is dominated by two enormous squares. **Wenceslas Square** (Václavské náměstí), a former horse market, is now occupied by Western-style shops, sausage hawkers, and the equestrian statue of St. Wenceslas, while **Charles Square** (Karlovo náměstí), a former cattle market, is today covered by a somewhat-unkempt park. **Národní třída** is a major street that separates the Old Town from the New; here you'll find the impressive **National Theater.** Fast-food joints litter **I.P. Pavlova,** a square on the border of Nové Město and Vinohrady.

STARÉ MĚSTO

No matter where you look, Staré Město is postcard material. Historical buildings are beautifully renovated, the pedestrian streets are covered in cobblestone, and churches appear around every corner. The downside? Foreigners flock by the hundreds of thousands, bringing out the ugly side of tourism: high prices, omnipresent tourist traps, and false claims of "authenticity." It is up to you—with help from *Let's Go*—to navigate the line between the beautiful and the fake, but don't take this task too seriously: after all, elbowing the crowds on Charles Bridge is pretty authentically Prague.

Old Town Square (Staroměstské náměstí) is the heart of Staré Město. Some of Prague's most famous landmarks—the **Astronomical Clock** and **Church of Our Lady Before Týn**—are located here. To the west is the iconic **Charles Bridge,** while the streets to the east lead to **Municipal House** and Ⓜ Náměstí Míru. To the north is Josefov, a small historic Jewish neighborhood completely enveloped by the river and Staré Město. Finally, streets to the south (Melantrichova, Jilská) connect Old Town Sq. with **Wenceslas Square** and **Národní Třída,** which mark the beginning of Nové Město. Trams and the Metro don't go directly through Staré Město but rather skirt its edges; walking is the preferred mode of transportation.

orientation

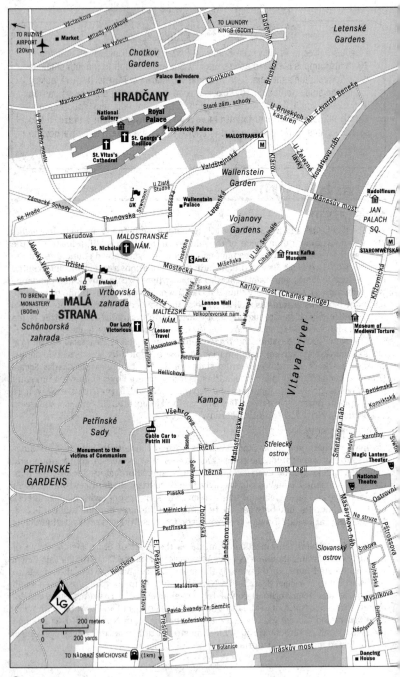

TO RUZYNĚ AIRPORT (20km)

■ Market

Václavkova

Milady Horákové

Na Valech

Chotkov Gardens

Badeního

TO LAUNDRY KINGS (600m)

Letenské Gardens

Mariánské hradby

Palace Belvedere

Chotkova

Staré zám. schody

U Prašného mostu

HRADČANY

National Gallery

Royal Palace

Lobkovický Palace

St. George's Basilica

St. Vitus's Cathedral

U Bruských kasáren

náb. Edvarda Beneše

Bruskov

MALOSTRANSKÁ

Ⓜ

Klárov

U Železné lávky

Kosárkovo náb.

Zámecké Schody

Ke Hradu

Thunovská

Nerudova

UK

Sněmovní

U Zlaté Studně

Valdštejnská

Wallenstein Garden

Wallenstein Palace

Letenská

Tomašská

Vojanovy Gardens

Mánesův most

Rudolfinum

JAN PALACH SQ.

Tržiště

MALOSTRANSKÉ NÁM.

St. Nicholas

Josefská

Jánský Vršek

Vlašská

US

Ireland

Vrtbovská zahrada

MALÁ STRANA

TO BŘENOV MONASTERY (800m)

Schönborská zahrada

Prokopská

MALTÉZSKÉ NÁM.

Our Lady Victorious

Lesser Travel

Mostecká

Josefská

Ⓢ AmEx

Mišeňská

U Luž. Semináře

Cihelná

Franz Kafka Museum

Saská

Lázeňská

Lennon Wall

Velkopřevorské nám.

Na Kampě

Karmelitská

Harantova

Pelclova

Hellichova

Nosticova

STAROMĚSTSKÁ

Ⓜ

Křižovnická

Karlův most (Charles Bridge)

Vltava River

Museum of Medieval Torture

Betlémská

Konviktská

Kampa

Maltezské nám.

Maltézské nám.

Petřínské Sady

Monument to the victims of Communism

PETŘÍNSKÉ GARDENS

Všehrdova

Cable Car to Petřín Hill

Říční

Vítězná

most Legií

Újezd

Šeříková

Zborovská

Plaská

Mělnická

Petřínská

Vodní

Malátova

Pavla Švandy Ze Semčic

Kořenského

V Botanice

Holečkova

El. Peškové

Štefánikova

Preslova

Masarykovo náb.

Střelecký ostrov

Slovanský ostrov

Magic Lantern Theater

National Theatre

Divadelní

Karolíny Světlé

Ostrovní

Na struze

Pštrossova

Sítkova

Vojtěšská

Myslíkova

Dittrichova

Náplavní

Jiráskův most

Dancing House

TO NÁDRAŽÍ SMÍCHOVSKÉ (1km)

N LG

0   200 meters
0   200 yards

prague

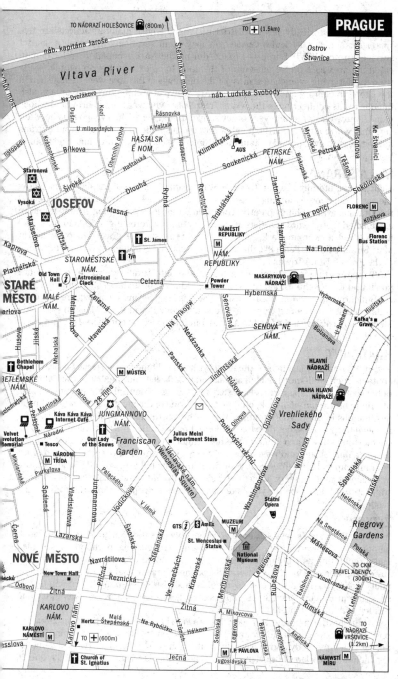

TO NÁDRAŽÍ HOLEŠOVICE (800m)

TO ✚ (1.5km)

náb. kapitána Jaroše

Vltava River

Ostrov
Štvanice

Na Dvořákovo

náb. Ludvíka Svobody

Kozí

Rásnovka

Dušní

U Obecního dvora

K Haštala

**HAŠTALSKÉ
NÁM.**

Klimentská

AUS

**PETRSKÉ
NÁM.**

Bílkova

Haštalská

Soukenická

Biskupská

Petrská

Mlynská

Staronová

Široká

Hradební

Revoluční

Zlatnická

Sokolovská

Maiselova

Dlouhá

Rybná

Truhlářská

Na poříčí

FLORENC Ⓜ

Vysoká

JOSEFOV

Masná

Havlíčkova

Kaprova

Pařížská

Na Florenci

**Florenc
Bus Station**

Platnéřská

St. James

**NÁMĚSTÍ
REPUBLIKY**
Ⓜ

Křižíkova

**STAROMĚSTSKÉ
NÁM.**

Tyn

**NÁM.
REPUBLIKY**

Old Town
Hall ⓘ

Astronomical
Clock

Celetná

Powder
Tower

**MASARYKOVO
NÁDRAŽÍ**

Hybernská

Hybernská

Kafka's
Grave

Husitská

**STARÉ
MĚSTO**

**MALÉ
NÁM.**

Železná

Senovážná

**SENOVÁŽNÉ
NÁM.**

Bolzanova

U Bulhara

Karlova

Melantrichova

Havelská

Na Příkopě

Nekázanka

**HLAVNÍ
NÁDRAŽÍ**
Ⓜ

Hlišká

Michalská

Panská

Jindřišská

Rížová

Bethlehem
Chapel

Ⓜ **MŮSTEK**

Razová

**PRAHA HLAVNÍ
NÁDRAŽÍ**

**BETLÉMSKÉ
NÁM.**

Perlová

28. října

Politických věznů

Opletalova

**Vrehliekého
Sady**

Martinská

**JUNGMANNOVO
NÁM.**

Kolovská

Na Perštíně

Káva Káva Káva
Internet Café

Julius Meinl
Department Store

**Velvet
Revolution
Memorial**

Národní

Our Lady
of the Snows

**Franciscan
Garden**

Tesco

**NÁRODNÍ
TŘÍDA** Ⓜ

Palackého

Václavské nám.
(Wenceslas Square)

Washingtonova

Wilsonova

Purkyňova

Jungmannova

Vodičkova

V jámě

Státní
Opera

Spálená

Vladislavova

Na Smetance

**Riegrovy
Gardens**

Černá

Lazarská

Školská

GTS ⓘ AmEx

MUZEUM
Ⓜ

Helénská

Italská

Španělská

Mánesova

NOVÉ MĚSTO

Navrátilova

Štěpánská

St. Wenceslas
Statue

**National
Museum**

Legerova

Polská

TO CKM
TRAVEL AGENCY
(300m)

New Town Hall

Příčná

Řeznická

Ve Smečkách

Krakovská

Mezibranská

Rubešova

Balbínova

Vinohradská

Odborů

Žitná

A. Mikovcova

Rimská

Anny Letenské

**KARLOVO
NÁM.**

Malá
Štwpánská

Na Rybníčku

Hálkova

Sokolská

Legerova

Bělehradská

Londýnská

Anglická

**KARLOVO
NÁMĚSTÍ** Ⓜ

Hertz

Karlovo nám.

TO ✚ (600m)

Žitná

Ⓜ **I.P. PAVLOVA**

TO
NÁDRAŽÍ
VRŠOVICE
(1.2km)

Eslova

Church of
St. Ignatius

Ječná

Jugoslávská

**NÁMWSTÍ
MÍRU** Ⓜ

Štefánikův most

Hlávkův most

Ke štvanici

Wilsonova

Na pštrosce

Mysliková

Petrská

Na poříčí

náb. kapitána Jaroše

JOSEFOV

Josefov is a historically Jewish district of Prague whose main attractions are five **synagogues** and the **Old Jewish Cemetery**. It may seem surprising that such a district survives in post-WWII Europe—in fact, during the Nazi occupation Hitler demarcated the area as a future museum of the soon-to-be extinct Jewish people. Aside from the surviving synagogues, most of the buildings in the area were demolished in the late 19th century and replaced with Art Nouveau architecture. The area is also famous for its connection to the writer **Franz Kafka,** who was born nearby, and whose name is now plastered on every other souvenir sold here. The synagogues here are certainly worth a visit, but the neighborhood is also one of the biggest tourist traps in Prague, with over-priced restaurants (think mussels and lobster), high-end fashion boutiques, and souvenir peddlers.

MALÁ STRANA

Malá Strana, literally "Lesser Town," got the name because of its placement below the castle, but we see nothing "lesser" about it. Squeezed between Prague Castle and the Vltava, and stretching up Petřín Hill, Malá Strana is the stomping ground for more established, better-known artists. The area is full of interesting cafes and bars, and **Kampa Island,** a riverside park, calls out for you to lie on the grass. The other ace in Malá Strana's hole is **Petřín Hill,** the sprawling park that is home to Prague's fat cousin of the French Eiffel Tower.

To the north, Malá Strana merges smoothly into Hradčany, while to the south you'll find the neighborhood of **Smíchov,** best known for its large shopping mall and the Smíchov train station. **Malostranské náměstí** is Malá Strana's main square and **Újezd** is its main street, snaking from north to south along Petřín Park. Malá Strana's only Metro stop is **Malostranská** (on the A line), but it can also be conquered on foot or by **tram** (12, 20, 22).

HRADČANY

A visit to Hradčany is a must—the neighborhood is home to the **Prague Castle,** which contains such well-known sights as **Saint Vitus Cathedral** and the **Golden Lane.** Outside of the castle, don't miss **Strahov Monastery's** collection of natural oddities (the remains of a dodo bird, a narwhal tusk, etc.) and **Loreta,** one of the most important pilgrimage destinations in the Czech Republic. Most of the surrounding establishments are unabashed tourist traps, but this doesn't detract from Hradčany's real charms—sloping cobblestone streets and some of the best panoramic views of Prague. Located just north of Malá Strana and west of **Letenské sady,** Hradčany is also a good place to start your hike up to Petřín Tower, or your dive down the hill toward Malá Strana's more affordable establishments. To get to Hradčany, take Metro A to **Malostranská** and then walk up the hill, or, better yet, take **tram 22,** which drops you off right above the castle.

ŽIŽKOV

In Žižkov there's no street that doesn't slope, no wall safe from graffiti, and no block without a pub or a bar. Known historically as a rough neighborhood, Žižkov also had a reputation as a bohemian (get it?) district, home to such writers as Jaroslav Hašek (author of *The Good Soldier Švejk*) and Jaroslav Seifert (a Nobel-winning poet). Today, the neighborhood's symbol is the **Žižkov TV Tower,** the tallest and ugliest structure in Prague. Though it's being slowly gentrified, Žižkov remains gritty and bustles with local nightlife.

At the northern border of Žižkov there's **Vítkov Hill** and the **statue of Jan Žižka,** the one-eyed Hussite general for whom the neighborhood is named. To the south Žižkov borders Riegrovy sady and Vinohrady, while to the east it includes two big cemeteries, including **New Jewish Cemetery,** where Franz Kafka is buried. **Trams** 5, 9, 11, and 26 are the best way of getting to and from Žižkov, as the nearest Metro station, **Jiřího z Poděbrad,** is in neighboring Vinohrady.

VINOHRADY

Originally called Královské Vinohrady (Royal Vineyards) to commemorate King Charles IV's contribution to the founding of local viticulture, this relaxed residential neighborhood is a favorite among expats, students, and Prague's gay community. Aside from reigning over an abundance of parks and green spaces, Vinohrady is close to the **Vyšehrad** cultural monument, one of Prague's best known landmarks. You will also find the **Church of Saint Peter and Saint Paul** and the **Vyšehrad cemetery,** where some of the most prominent Czech artists are buried.

The western border of Vinohrady is roughly denoted by Ⓜ**I.P. Pavlova.** The neighborhood then stretches east along **Vinohradská,** all the way to Ⓜ**Želivského. Náměstí Míru** is located just a few blocks away from I.P. Pavlova, while **Jiřího z Poděbrad** is close to Žižkov. **Riegrovy sady** and Žižkov border Vinohrady to the north and **Havlíčkovy sady** is to the south. **Vyšehrad** is a separate district, just one Metro stop southwest of I.P. Pavlova. Walking in Vinohrady is an option, but if you want to save time, you can take advantage of the frequent tram service.

HOLEŠOVICE

Holešovice used to be an industrial suburb, but today, thanks to steady gentrification, it's turning into one of Prague's most exciting neighborhoods. The industrial scale of the buildings here has lent itself well to arts spaces like **DOX** and **Veletržní Palác,** nightclubs like **Cross Club** and **SaSaZu,** and even hostels like **Prague Plus Hostel.** Home to other sprawling complexes such as the **Prague Market, Exhibition Ground,** and **Letenské sady,** Holešovice is the perfect escape from the cramped streets of Staré Město.

Situated north of Staré Město at a bend in the Vltava, Holešovice is split in two by railroad tracks. It's not as pedestrian-friendly a neighborhood as many others in Prague, so we recommend **trams** 1, 3, 5, 12, 14, 17, and 25 to get around. The two closest Metro stations are on the C line: **Vltavská** and **Nádraží Holešovice.**

DEJVICE

There are few tourist sights in Dejvice and consequently, few tourists. This lively locals-only neighborhood has its own charms, and those spending more than a week or two in Prague should definitely take a walk around. Dejvice is organized around an enormous roundabout **(Vítězné náměstí),** and, in addition to being home to a university complex and two famous theaters (**Divadlo Semafor** and **Divadlo Spejbla & Hurvínka,** both on Dejvická), it has plenty of restaurants that won't charge you extra for being a foreigner. The neighborhood is close to both Letenské sady and Hradčany. Northwest of Dejvice, the sprawling natural reserve **Divoká Šárka** is Prague's best refuge for those tired of cobblestone.

SMÍCHOV

Just across the river from Nové Město and Vyšehrad, Smíchov is not as appealing to tourists as the others—there are no old churches or historical buildings to speak of. Instead, it veers toward the modern: the area around Ⓜ**Anděl** is home to the mall **Nový Smíchov,** a few big bookstores, and two multiplex cinemas. To the south, you'll find **Smíchovské nádraží,** a train station that serves most Germany-bound trains and that is home to many a sketchy character. There is also some sightseeing to do—including the free contemporary art gallery, **MeetFactory** and the **Staropramen Brewery.** Metro B and numerous tram lines go to Smíchov.

orientation

traffic win or traffic fail?

We at *Let's Go* certainly love to pull readers' legs from time to time, but this story falls into the "You Can't Make This Stuff Up" category. In December 2010, in an effort to improve traffic safety (we still don't quite follow their logic on that one) while reducing costs, Prague and nearby towns placed cardboard cut-outs of female police officers along certain roads in lieu of costly traffic lights or even more expensive real people. Though cardboard, these officers are most certainly not flat, and they sport heels and miniskirts, no matter how cold the Prague winter gets. The plan quickly backfired, though: only two weeks after the "officers" were installed, their distracting presence had already led to an alleged doubling of the rate of accidents.

accommodations

Prague has accommodations to suit every budget. Thanks to the opening of some new "chic" hostels throughout the city (Mosaic House, Sir Toby's, Miss Sophie's, Czech Inn), travelers willing to pay a bit extra can find digs that almost feel like hotels, some with in-house restaurants and free Wi-Fi. There are many earthier options throughout the city, including a handful of cheaper party hostels. In general, Staré Město costs more and offers less, while Nové Město costs less and offers more. There are several great hostels in Holešovice, Vinohrady, and Malá Strana, but these may require a Metro or a tram ride to visit sights, which might be a bit out of the way for those staying only a few days in Prague. In addition to hostels, there's a network of student dorms that function as hostels during the summer (www.czechcampus.com). These may not give you the traditional hostel experience, but they tend to be cheaper than most hostels.

Finally, a note on prices: the prices included in this guide are approximate. Most Prague hostels price with an algorithm that takes into account the time of year, the day of the week, and hostel vacancy. No matter when you visit, the system rewards those who book in advance.

NOVÉ MĚSTO

Nové Město might be the best part of town to stay in. There's a cluster of reasonably-priced hostels around **Myslíkova.** Many mid-level hotels are also concentrated around **I.P. Pavlova,** but, if you're going to stay in Nové Město, we'd recommend staying a little closer to the center of town.

MOSAIC HOUSE — HOTEL, HOSTEL $$

Odborů 4 — ☎246 008 324; www.mosaichouse.com

Staying at Mosaic House might be even more environmentally friendly than pitching a tent somewhere in Wenceslas Sq. The first of its kind in the Czech Republic, the hostel uses electricity solely from renewable sources and has a graywater recycling system. But the real difference between this and sleeping in a tent? The comfort. The four-star hotel rooms have a spillover effect on the sleek and private dorms. Another major plus is the restaurant downstairs; Belushi's has live music, comedy nights, and other events, in addition to serving generous portions of American food. (*Let's Go* does not recommend camping in Wenceslas Sq.)

 # B: Karlovo náměstí. From the station, head north along the western edge of the square. Take a left at Odborů at the northwest corner. ℹ Breakfast 150Kč. Towels included for hotel guests, with dorms 30Kč. Lockers included. Computer use 50Kč per hr. Women's dorm available. $ Dorms 300-625Kč; doubles 1440Kč. ⏰ Reception 24hr.

DOWNTOWN HOSTEL

HOSTEL $$

Národní třída 19 ☎224 240 570; www.hostel-downtown.cz

One of the best-located hostels in the city, Downtown Hostel straddles the border between Old and New Town, and is within spitting distance from tram and Metro stops. Among the hostel's highlights are its daily social events, which include cooking nights and free sightseeing tours. The rooms are simple and clean—if you're lucky, yours will have unusually tall windows that face the enormous anti-war graffiti across the street. The common room features a piano, and there's a guitar to borrow at reception—a jam session with other hostel guests is at your fingertips.

*🚏 B: Národní třída. From the Metro walk up on Spálená, then turn left on Národní třída. The hostel is on the right. **i** Breakfast 70Kč. Linens and towels included. Laundry 50Kč. Free Wi-Fi. $ Dorms 300-500Kč; doubles 1000-1800Kč. 10% discount for HI members. ⏰ Reception 24hr.*

AZ HOSTEL

HOSTEL $

Jindřišská 5 ☎224 241 664; www.hostel-az.cz

Well-located and quite cheap, AZ is best suited to those who don't ask for too much in terms of hostel culture. The common room may be forgettable, and there may not be that many extra perks (with the exception of complimentary tea and coffee), but the rooms are neatly painted and without bunk beds. Since the hostel lies just off Wenceslas Sq., staying here will afford you the additional pleasure of interacting with the sketchy men trying to lure you into their erotic clubs at night. (Always a perk.)

*🚏 A or B: Můstek. From the station, walk up the square toward the National Museum, then make a left on Jindřišská. The hostel is on the left, inside a courtyard. **i** Linens, towels, and lockers included. Laundry service 190Kč. Computer use 20Kč per 10min. Free Wi-Fi. Women-only dorm available. $ Dorms 320Kč; singles 950Kč; doubles 1000Kč. 10% discount for stays over 1 week. ⏰ Reception 24hr.*

MISS SOPHIE'S

HOSTEL, HOTEL $$

Melounová 3 ☎293 303 530; www.miss-sophies.com

Miss Sophie's is a bit out of the way and on the pricier side, but it's not entirely out of the budget traveler's reach. Genuinely cool modern designs (including mural-sized original artwork) line the newly painted walls and the steel and glass showers are classier than what you'll find in most hotels. The polished wood floors, black bed frames, and intimate brick cellar (where one of Prague's most impressive hostel breakfasts is served) may be worth the few extra crowns and the tram ride to I.P. Pavlova.

*🚏 C: I.P. Pavlova. From the Metro, walk west on Ječná, then take the 2nd left onto Melounová. **i** Breakfast 170Kč. Towels 30Kč. Free Wi-Fi. 2 computers available. $ Dorms 410-600Kč; private rooms 1150-2200Kč. 5% ISIC discount for online reservations. ⏰ Reception 24hr.*

CHILI HOSTEL

HOSTEL $

Pštrossova 7 ☎603 119 113; www.chili.dj

Judging by the phone-book-length list of damage fines posted at the reception, this place can get rowdy. With its army of bunk beds and enormous underground lounge (with both pool and foosball tables), Chili is a real party hostel. Don't expect any luxury (the dorm rooms have barely any furniture); do expect international pregames in the common spaces.

*🚏 B: Národní třída. From the Metro, walk west on Ostrovní and make a left on Pštrossova. The hostel is on the right on a street corner. **i** Linens, towels, and lockers included. Laundry 190Kč; free for stays of 5 days or more. Free Wi-Fi. Computers available. $ Dorms 200-480Kč; doubles 600-700Kč per person. ⏰ Reception 24hr.*

HOSTEL PRAGUE LION
HOSTEL $$

Na Zbořenci 6 ☎731 487 936; www.prague-lion.com

This little hostel may be called the lion, but roaring won't get you very far; with no common spaces, it's ideal for those who want quiet. The hostel is small and tends to fill up, so book at least a week in advance. If you're lucky enough to get a bed, you'll be able to enjoy the spacious, well-equipped rooms, some of which even have their own kitchen counters.

🚇 B: Karlovo náměstí. From the Metro, head down Resslova, then take the 1st right on Na Zderaze and another right on Na Zbořenci. [i] Linens and towels included. Free Wi-Fi and 1 computer available. Fridges and microwaves in all rooms. [$] Doubles 1350-2200Kč; quads 1850-2700Kč. 4% fee for credit card payment. ⏰ Reception 24hr.

HOSTEL U BUBENÍČKŮ
GUESTHOUSE $

Myslíkova 8 ☎224 922 357; www.ububenicku.com

This isn't your typical hostel—the only reception desk you'll find is the bar of the U Bubeníčků restaurant. Located above the restaurant, the fourth-floor hostel offers 38 budget beds and some apartments. Many of the typical hostel facilities are absent—no computers, no common room—but the place combines low rates and pleasant decor. The smells of roast pork and sauerkraut downstairs are free of charge—should you decide to pursue them further, guests get a 10% discount at the restaurant.

🚇 B: Karlovo náměstí. From the Metro, take Resslova toward the river and take a right on Na Zderaze and a left on Myslíková. The guesthouse is on the left. [i] Breakfast 50-90Kč. Linens and lockers included. Towels 50Kč. [$] Dorms 300Kč; doubles 490Kč per person. ⏰ Reception 9am-midnight.

THE WELCOME PRAGUECENTER HOSTEL
GUESTHOUSE $

Žitná 17 ☎224 320 202; www.bed.cz

Possibly the worst-named hostel in the city, Welcome Praguecenter provides reasonably comfortable private rooms for dorm prices. Located on the second floor of an apartment building, this guesthouse has nine rooms featuring king-size beds, refrigerators, and safes. The lack of a common space or kitchen is the only downfall. Well, that and a lame name.

🚇 B: Karlovo náměstí. From the station, head away from the river down Žitná. The guesthouse is on the left. [i] Linens and towels included. Free Wi-Fi; computer use 20Kč per 10min. Reserve in advance. [$] Private rooms 250-450Kč per person. ⏰ Reception open 8am-8pm.

HOSTEL CENTRE
HOSTEL $$

Sokolská 29 ☎224 247 412; www.hostel-centre.eu

Even though the name is more wishful thinking than reality, Hostel Centre still offers acceptable rooms at decent prices. The carpeting adds a level of hominess, and you can use the hostel's Playstation, for €2 per hour. Tram 22 or the Metro line C will take you wherever you need to go.

🚇 C: I.P. Pavlova. From the Metro, head 1 block toward the river on Jugoslávská and turn left on Sokolská. The hostel is on the right. [i] Breakfast 56Kč. Linens and towels included. Free Wi-Fi and computers available. [$] Dorms 420-700Kč; doubles 750Kč. ⏰ Reception 24hr.

STARÉ MĚSTO

Surprisingly, there's only a handful of hostels in Staré Město. The main draw of staying here is the location—roll out of bed in the morning and you'll land on the historic cobblestones. The Old Town is great for those staying in Prague for a day or two and who won't have time to explore the outer neighborhoods much.

OLD PRAGUE HOSTEL
HOSTEL $$

Benediktská 2 ☎224 829 058; www.oldpraguehostel.com

Old Prague and its sister hostel, Prague Square, are perhaps the only hostels in Staré Město that really roll Western-style, despite the old-school buildings they occupy. Common rooms have flatscreen TVs and comfy couches, light breakfast (sandwiches, cereal) is included in the price, and receptionists tend to be young expats. Old Prague Hostel is marginally the better of the two—it feels more welcoming, thanks to some cheerful drawings on the walls. It's also a bit farther away from the rumble of the crowds in Old Town Sq., but still really close to everything in Staré Město.

✠ B: Náměstí Republiky. From the station, walk down to Powder Tower, then turn right on Celetná. Turn right at an underpass that leads to Templová and take the first left on Štupartská. The hostel will be on the right. *i* Non-smoking. Breakfast, towels, linens, lockers, and adapters included. Wi-Fi available on the mezzanine and in the common area; free computer access. Key deposit 100Kč. Ⓢ 8-bed dorms 270-450Kč; 4-bed 350-550Kč. Doubles 500-650Kč. Cash only. ⓩ Reception 24hr.

PRAGUE SQUARE HOSTEL
HOSTEL $$

Melantrichova 10   ☎224 240 859; www.praguesquarehostel.com

In terms of services, Prague Square Hostel is identical to its twin, Old Prague Hostel. The only real difference is in location: the advantage of Prague Square Hostel is that it's right in the stream of people between Old Town and Wenceslas Squares, a bit closer to Nové Město. If you're bothered by the ruckus outside, the reception offers free earplugs.

✠ A or B: Můstek. From the station, head north on na Můstku and continue on it as it turns into Melantrichova. The hostel will be on your right. *i* Non-smoking. Breakfast, adapters, towels, linens, and lockers included. Free computer access and Wi-Fi in common spaces. Ⓢ 8-bed dorms 270-450Kč; 4-bed 350-550Kč. Doubles 500-650Kč. Cash only. ⓩ Reception 24hr.

HOSTEL TÝN
HOSTEL $

Týnská 19   ☎224 828 519; www.hosteltyn.com

Finding this hostel in the maze of Týn-related streets behind Church of Our Lady Before Týn can take a while, but it's worth it. The dorms are bunk-free, which offsets the lack of free breakfast. The underground common room and kitchen are virtually pleasant (helped by the fake window with LED tubes imitating sunlight) and a good place to socialize. The bad news is that the downstairs closes at 2am; the good news is that, depending on your charm, this time may be negotiable.

✠ B: Náměstí Republiky. From the station, head south to Powder Tower and continue on Celetná. Continue towards the river, then take a right at Štupartská and a left onto Týnská. Follow Týnská as it winds around. The hotel is in a courtyard on your right. *i* Non-smoking. Towels and lockers included. Free Wi-Fi in common spaces; free computer access. Ⓢ Dorms 300-400Kč; doubles 900-1200Kč; triples 1000-1400Kč. Cash only. ⓩ Reception 24hr.

PENSION TARA
PENSION $

Havelská 15   ☎224 228 083; www.pensiontara.net

If you're lucky, you'll score this pension's sole dorm, which features six beds in three separate rooms. You can also ask for one of their attic rooms, which are quiet and fun (and by fun we mean you have to step over wooden beams). It's not a hostel, so there's no kitchen, breakfast, or Wi-Fi, but as far as the whole sleeping thing goes, the rooms are nice enough.

✠ A or B: Můstek. From the station, head north on na Můstku and continue on it as it turns into Melantrichova, then take a left on Havelská. The pension will be on your right. *i* Linens and towels included. No Wi-Fi, but the reception has 1 Wi-Fi USB key that they lend to guests. Ⓢ Large dorms 300-400Kč; 4-bed rooms 450-550Kč; doubles 600-850Kč. ⓩ Reception 9am-8pm.

RITCHIE'S HOTEL AND HOSTEL
HOSTEL $$

Karlova 13   ☎222 221 229; www.ritchieshostel.cz

Full of hidden steps, low ceilings, and staircases that twist and creak, this hostel is a bit like one of those colorful adventure playgrounds for kids. You might need to walk out on the balcony to go to the bathroom or to take a shower, or you might end up in a room with a 175cm (5 ft., 10 in.) ceiling. The upside: you're on Karlova, one of the busiest pedestrian streets in Prague, smack dab in the center of everything.

⚐ A: Staroměstské. From the station, head down Křižovnická directly along the river. At the Charles bridge, turn left on Karlova. The hostel will be on the left, through a small gallery. [i] Lockers 30Kč per day. Breakfast 90Kč. Linens and towels included. Laundry 140Kč per load; no dryer. Women's dorms available. $ Large dorms 300-450Kč; 3-bed dorms 450-525Kč. Doubles 600-675Kč. ISIC holders get a 5% discount. Credit card use 3% fee. ⏰ Reception 24hr. Kitchen open 8am-1am.

TRAVELLER'S HOSTEL — HOSTEL $

Dlouhá 33 — ☎224 826 662; www.travellers.cz

It's a bit cheaper than other hostels in Staré Město, and we can see why—the walls could use a new paint job, the dorms have between 10 and 16 beds, bathrooms tend to be humid, and the third floor is a bit claustrophobic. The highlight is the big upstairs bar, where the foosball is free. If you stay for a week you get the seventh night free, but we'll leave it up to you to decide whether you really want to stay here for a week.

⚐ C: Náměstí Republiky. From the station, walk north along Revoluční. Take a left at Dlouhá. The hostel will be on your right. [i] Smoking permitted only in dining room. Breakfast included. Absinthe bar 3rd fl. Computer access available in the front lobby. Free Wi-Fi on the 3rd floor. Key deposit 200Kč. $ Large dorms 270-350Kč; 4-bed dorms 330-500Kč. Singles 700-1390Kč. Doubles 400-800Kč. ISIC/IYHF card holders recieve 40Kč per night discount. ⏰ Reception 24hr.

JOSEFOV

Most accommodations in Josefov are the more-stars-than-through-a-telescope sort. There are no traditional hostels with dorms, but there are a few apartment-turned-hostels that are worth considering if you want to stay here on a budget.

HOSTEL FRANZ KAFKA — HOSTEL $$$

Kaprova 13 — ☎222 316 800; www.czechhostelfranzkafka.com

With a magnificent total of four rooms, Franz Kafka Hostel may be one of the smallest hostels you'll come across in Prague. There are no dorms and the bigger rooms (up to eight bunk beds) are rented out only to groups. Bathrooms are shared. Longer stays are preferred; the minimum is three days.

⚐ B: Staroměstská. From Old Town Sq. walk to St. Nicholas Church and turn left. Walk for a few meters down Kaprova; the hostel is on the right. [i] Free Wi-Fi. Linens and towels included. 3-day min. stay. $ Singles 800Kč; doubles 1100-1300Kč; quads 1560-1960Kč per person. Cash only. ⏰ Reception 9am-6pm, but times vary.

HOSTEL CONDOR I — HOSTEL $$$

Kozí 7 — ☎603 438 943; www.praguecondor.cz

A lot of things at this 12-room hostel are done on an unofficial basis. Reception is rarely open. If you have a small laundry load, they may do it for you for free. The owners of the building prohibit the use of the kitchen, so you can't cook, but you can order a 100Kč breakfast. The rooms are on the smaller side and rather bare, but the great location comes at a decent price. Confirm your arrival ahead of time.

⚐ B: Staroměstská. From Old Town Sq. walk past the Jan Hus statue on Dlouhá. At the roundabout, keep going straight on Kozí; the hostel is to the left. [i] Laundry 50Kč. No Wi-Fi, but internet cable available. Bike rental possible. $ Singles 600-800Kč; doubles 1200-1400Kč. Cash only. ⏰ Call ahead to arrange check-in and check-out.

accommodations

MALÁ STRANA

Not many people stay in Malá Strana, but those who do are rewarded by being farther from the drunken noise of Old Town and closer to Malá Strana's artsy cafes and green spaces.

LITTLE TOWN BUDGET HOTEL — HOTEL, HOSTEL $$

Malostranské náměstí 11 — ☎242 406 965; www.littletownhotel.cz

Officially a "budget hotel," Little Town still has dorms at manageable rates but adds in ensuite bathrooms and attached kitchens. This is perhaps the best-located budget accommodation this side of the Vltava—a short walk across the Charles Bridge lands you right in the Old Town. Plus, it's not the musty apartment building you're likely to find on the other bank, but a real Malá Strana house, with wood floors and a cobblestone courtyard.

⚐ A: Malostranská. From the Metro, walk down Letenská until you reach Malostranské náměstí. The hostel is in the southwest corner of the square, behind the church. ℹ Linens and towels included. Free Wi-Fi; computers available. $ Dorms 450Kč; singles 1500Kč; doubles 1600Kč. ⏰ Reception 24hr.

HOSTEL SOKOL — HOSTEL $

Nosticova 2 — ☎257 007 397; www.hostelsokol.cz

Yet another unfortunate triumph of socialist architecture, Hostel Sokol serves primarily as housing for athletic teams in Prague for competitions but it will happily accommodate tourists when there's space. Their signature barracks-like 12-bed dorm has sparse white beds and linoleum floors, but the prices are some of the lowest in Prague. If you were hoping to get with well-toned jocks, this is the place.

⚐ A: Malostranská. From the Metro, walk south or take tram 12, 20, or 22 to Hellichova. Turn left on Hellichova and continue to the end of the street as it curves left. Continue north on Nosticova, following signs for Hostel Sokol, and turn right into the courtyard. ℹ Linens and towels included. Free Wi-Fi. $ Dorms 300-350Kč. Cash only. ⏰ Reception 24hr.

ARPACAY HOSTEL — HOSTEL $

Radlická 76 — ☎251 552 297; www.arpacayhostel.com

Not technically in Malá Strana, Arpacay is close to Smíchovské nádraží, which serves Germany-bound trains. For a hostel so close to the train station, Arpacay does a much better job than many of its competitors in the center. The dorms are spacious and neat, with noise-muffling double windows. Watch out for last-minute deals: if you book one or two weeks in advance, you can often save 20%. If you're worried about the length of the commute, tram 7 will get you to Karlovo náměstí in about 10min.

⚐ B: Smíchovské nádraží. From the train station, turn left and walk until you reach a small park. Go into the park and turn left, walk up the stairs, and cross the train tracks. At the intersection, keep walking straight, and go up the hill on Radlická. Look for the Arpacay sign on the right. Alternatively, take tram 7, 12, 13, 14, or 20. ℹ Breakfast, linens, towels, and locks included. Free Wi-Fi; computers available. $ Dorms 250-390Kč; doubles 430-650Kč. ⏰ Reception 7am-midnight.

HRADČANY

Few budget travelers stay overnight in this hilly neighborhood, but where there's a will, there's a way. If you do stay here, you'll be close to Prague Castle, Malá Strana, and parks such as Letenské sady and Petřín.

LITTLE QUARTER — HOSTEL $

Nerudova 21 — ☎257 212 029; www.littlequarter.com

This is a hostel that you wouldn't expect to find in Hradčany—it's well-run and reasonably cheap. The dorms have no bunk beds. There's not much in the way of common spaces (just a small terrace and the reception room), but it's a great place to stay if you want to spend most of your time exploring the city. Tram 22, which stops down the road, can take you across the Vltava in a matter of minutes.

🧭 A: Malostranská. From the Metro, walk toward the bridge and take the first right onto Letenská. Continue as it curves, becomes Malostranské square, and then becomes Nerudova. The hostel is to the left. Trams 12, 20, and 22 stop nearby. ℹ Breakfast 80Kč. Free Wi-Fi and computer use. Linens and lockers included. $ 10-bed dorms 240-290Kč; 5-bed 340-430Kč. Doubles 1300-1580Kč. ⏰ Reception 24hr.

PENSION POHÁDKA
PENSION $$$$

Valdštejnská 288/4a ☎257 286 320; www.pensionpohadka.eu

If split between two romantically linked people, a room at this atmospheric little pension can be affordable. The five rooms have names like "President" or "Senator," and are equipped with air conditioning, luxurious beds, and, sometimes, a second floor. We recommend Pension Pohádka for couples on romantic retreats.

🧭 A: Malostranská. From the Metro, walk through the courtyard. The pension is across the street. ℹ Breafast 100Kč. Free Wi-Fi. Mini-fridges in all rooms. $ 1 person 1162-1912Kč; 2 people 1550-2550Kč. Discounts for stays over 5 days. ⏰ Reception 8am-10pm.

KOLEJ KOMENSKÉHO
DORMITORY $$

Parléřova 6 ☎220 388 400; www.kam.cuni.cz

Kolej Komenského is home to university students during the year and transforms into a hostel in the summer. While the summer rates might seem outrageous to Czech students, they run pretty much the going rate of hostel accommodations—single rooms are 550Kč. The more touristy area is just 5min. away by foot, and Kolej Komenského is close to tram 22. The facilities are adequate and popular with foreign students.

🧭 Tram 22: Pohořelec or 36: Hládkov. From the 22, walk past the Brahe/Kepler statue on Parléřova. Take the 2nd right, cross the tram tracks, and you'll arrive at the dorm. $ Singles 550Kč; doubles 880Kč. Cash only. ⏰ Hostel reception M-F 7am-4pm. Building reception 24hr.

ŽIŽKOV

Predictably for the neighborhood, Žižkov's hostels are alternative, reasonably priced, and a bit wild. Staying here allows you to experience one of Prague's more authentic neighborhoods, just a tram ride away from Staré Město.

👍 HOSTEL ONE PRAGUE
HOSTEL $$

Cimburkova 8 ☎222 221 423; www.hosteloneprague.cz

This cool hostel resides in a former residential building, so each room has its own bathroom, fridge, and kitchen counter (only the sinks are functional). Private rooms feel almost like little apartments (especially if they happen to have one of the 10 balconies), while the bigger dorms still offer some privacy. The cascading garden is a good place to grill. Every night, the staff organizes trips (no, not pub crawls—these trips are free) to some of Prague's best nightlife spots.

🧭 Trams 5, 9, or 26: Lipanská. Walk uphill on Seifertova past the big church, then turn right on Cimburkova. The hostel is on the right. ℹ Linens included. Laundry 200Kč. Towels 20Kč. Free Wi-Fi. 8 computers available for use. $ Dorms 250-590Kč; private rooms 590-790Kč per person. ⏰ Reception 7:30am-12:30am. Garden closes at 10pm.

HOSTEL ELF

HOSTEL $

Husitská 11 ☎222 540 963; www.hostelelf.com

A true backpacker's hostel, Elf's walls are covered with all sorts of drawings and stenciled graffiti, supposedly the work of the staff. The common room and the bathrooms are on the smaller side, but all spatial constraints are made up for by Elf's colorful spirit. The staff grills three times per week, providing dinner to the guests at no extra charge.

*Trams 5, 9, or 26: Husinecká. From the tram stop, follow Husinecká until you reach the square, then make a left at Orebitská, which will run into Husitská right in front of the hostel. **i** Credit card surcharge 3%. Breakfast, linens, and towels included. Free Wi-Fi, and computer use. Laundry 200Kč. $ Dorms 260-390Kč; doubles 380-730Kč. 5% student discounts for dorms. ⏰ Reception 24hr.*

CLOWN AND BARD HOSTEL

HOSTEL $

Bořivojova 102 ☎222 716 453; www.clownandbard.com

This party hostel is not for the squeamish—its interior can get very rough around the edges, with rusty stoves and scribbles on walls. But if you're here to party, this could be a place for you. The reception could easily be mistaken for a bar—there's foosball, plenty of wooden tables, and songs like "Keep on Rocking in the Free World" blast from the speakers. Plus it's right on Bořivojova, a street known in Žižkov for its bars.

*Trams 5, 9, or 26: Husinecká. Walk uphill and take the 1st left on Krašová. Continue for 2 blocks, then turn right on Bořivojova. Enter through an underground bar. **i** Breakfast 50Kč. Linen and towels included. Free Wi-Fi and computer use. $ Dorms 250-300Kč; doubles 340-600Kč. Cash only. ⏰ Reception 24hr. Garden closes at 10pm.*

VINOHRADY

There are many hotels scattered around [M]**I.P. Pavlova,** but Vinohrady remains fairly residential otherwise. The walk from here to Staré Město can take quite a while (25min. from [M]Náměstí Míru to Old Town Sq.); the Metro and frequent trams can save you some time.

prague

CZECH INN

HOSTEL $$

Francouzská 76 ☎267 267 600; www.czech-inn.com

Billing itself as a "designer hostel," Czech Inn tries hard to distinguish itself from the sweaty hostel world: it's clean, chic, and asks you to join its "social networks." The lobby and bar serve double duty as an art gallery, and every few weeks the hostel changes up the display and throws a gallery opening. Such appreciation for detail extends to the rooms, which have sleek single-sheet glass showers with polished concrete floors. To take advantage of all this elegance for little money, stay here during the week. Bonus points: if you end up staying here, make at least one joke about "Czeching Inn."

*A: Náměstí Míru, or trams 4 or 22: Krymská. From the station, walk southeast along Francouzská. The hostel is on the right. **i** Breakfast 120Kč. Towels 30Kč with a 100Kč deposit. Wi-Fi and lockers included. Computer use 50Kč per hr. Non-smoking. $ Prices fluctuate wildly on a daily basis. Dorms from 285Kč; private rooms from 990Kč. Expect to pay more on weekends. ⏰ Reception 24hr.*

ADVANTAGE HOSTEL

HOSTEL $

Sokolská 11 ☎224 914 062; www.advantagehostel.cz

The recently renovated Hostel Advantage has no major flaws, nor does it provide any particular thrills. Whether it's worth staying here or not depends mostly on the rates—visit the website to calculate the daily rate and then decide whether it will make a difference to stay this far from Old Town.

*C: I.P. Pavlova. From the station, head 1 block toward the river on Jugoslávská, then turn left on Sokolská. The hostel is on the right. **i** Breakfast, towels, linens, lockers included. Free WiFi and computer use. Women's dorms available. HI member. $ Dorms 300-450Kč; singles 1000-2200Kč; doubles 1300-2200Kč. ⏰ Reception 24hr.*

HOLEŠOVICE

Holešovice is not the most central or pedestrian-friendly part of the town, so you'll probably need to use the tram or the Metro to get to the historic sights. On the other hand, staying in Holešovice will put you within walking distance of some of Prague's best nightlife.

⬛ SIR TOBY'S HOSTEL

HOSTEL $$

Dělnická 24   ☎246 032 610; www.sirtobys.com

From rooms with outlandish names instead of numbers to events like Quiz Mondays, beer tastings, and Crepe and Cartoon Sundays, Sir Toby's does everything with a dose of personality. There's a pub in the brick cellar next to a modern kitchen and a few common rooms where you can cook, watch Czech movies, or have a home-cooked dinner of Czech and Afghan cuisine. The garden, which has a grill, is a good place to hang out on a sunny day. Before heading out, grab one of Sir Toby's custom maps of the area.

🚲 *C: Vltavská. From the Metro, take tram 1, 3, 5, or 25 or walk along the tram tracks for 3 stops to Dělnická. Turn left onto Dělnická; the hostel is on the left.* ℹ *Breakfast 100Kč. Dinner 90-110Kč. Lockers included. Towels 15Kč with a 200Kč deposit; included with private rooms. Laundry 100Kč. Free Wi-Fi and computer use.* Ⓢ *Dorms 150-600Kč; doubles 700-1000Kč. 5% discount for ISIC holders who reserve online.* 🕐 *Reception 24hr.*

PLUS PRAGUE

HOSTEL $$

Přívozní 1   ☎220 510 046; www.plusprague.com

The reception area of this enormous hostel feels like an aiport—people arrive and depart, and things happen efficiently. All rooms have ensuite bathrooms, and one wing is women-only. A separate building houses the hostel's restaurant, which seems geared more toward larger groups, but in which even the solo traveler can enjoy a pool table, foosball, and a full-service bar and grill. Plus Prague is also one of the few hostels in Prague with a sauna and swimming pool. Before you leave the lobby, say hello to Boris the turtle, who isn't dead—"just sleeping."

🚲 *C: Nadraží Holešovice. From the station, take tram 5 or 12, or walk along tram tracks on Plynární for 1 stop, to Ortenovo náměstí. At Hotel Plaza Alta take a left onto Přívozní. The hostel is on the left.* ℹ *Washer 70Kč, dryer 100Kč. Towels 50 Kč. Full breakfast 100 Kč, cold breakfast 70Kč. Linens and lockers included. Free Wi-Fi and computers in the lobby.* Ⓢ *Dorms 190-500Kč, private rooms 400-700Kč per person.* 🕐 *Reception 24hr. Sauna open 8-10am and 4-10pm. Pool open 8am-10pm.*

HOTEL EXTOL INN

HOTEL $$$

Přístavní 2   ☎220 876 541; www.extolinn.cz

If you are set on staying in a private room, Extol Inn offers economy rooms for prices comparable to those you'll find at hostels. We're not going to extol the economical amenities—you'll be barred from most of the free services that are offered to guests in more expensive rooms, including wheelchair access, and you might share a bathroom with one other room—but the set rates mean that staying here might be cheaper than a hostel during the high season.

🚲 *C: Vltavská. From the station, take tram 1, 3, 5, 25 or walk along the tram tracks for 3 stops to Dělnická. Keep walking an additional block, then take a left onto Přístavní.* ℹ *Breakfast included. Free Wi-Fi. Computer use 2Kč per min.* Ⓢ *Singles 820Kč; doubles 1400Kč; triples 1900Kč.* 🕐 *Reception 24hr.*

A&O HOSTEL

HOSTEL $$

U Výstaviště 1   ☎220 870 252; www.aohostels.com

This hostel may not be as generous with its facilities as others (linens aren't included, and there are no laundry facilities or lockers), but it's very close to the Holešovice train station. On the upside, all rooms have tiny TVs, and there's

accommodations

a dungeon-like bar downstairs where you can buy drinks and play with the Wii. We're still deciding whether the strip club that's located right behind this hostel is a good or a bad thing.

🚇 C: Nadraží Holešovice. From the station, walk along tram tracks on Vrbenského and Partyzánska in the direction of Výstaviště (Prague Exhibition Ground); the hostel is on a raised street behind the overpass. ℹ Breakfast 100Kč. Linens 80Kč. Safes available at the front desk. Wi-Fi and computer use available. $ Dorms 250-500Kč; private rooms 450-800Kč per person. 10% discount for ISIC card holders. ⏰ Reception 24hr.

dirty mouth?

You may be surprised to be walking through the historic streets of Prague, overwhelmed by your romantic European notions, only to hear people saying "f*** you" to each other. But don't worry, the city isn't filled with crude or angry Czechs, just a bunch of tourists, like you, who don't know the language. What the natives are really saying is *"fakt jo,"* pronounced fahkt yo. It's a common phrase that means "really?" or "for real?" The Bohemians are pretty nice after all.

sights

If you visit Prague during the summer months, you will be viewing the historical sights around Prague Castle and Old Town Sq. with thousands of other people trying to cram into the same tightly packed spaces as you. The tours of many of the historic buildings are often long and dry. It will be loud. It will be unpleasant. You might get your wallet stolen. It doesn't have to be like this. You'll miss the crowds and save a lot of money if you do your Old Town sightseeing at night. You won't get to see the interiors of the buildings, but for most part that's no great loss. The entire Old Town, and especially the Charles Bridge—virtually impassable during the day—are lit up beautifully at night. Once you get away from Old Town Sq., your options start to open up. Žižkov has its share of large structures, including the TV Tower and the Jan Žižka Statue. In Malá Strana, a panoramic view of the city awaits from the top of Petřín Tower.

Aside from historic sights, it's worth spending a little extra to visit Prague's art museums, which are some of its best treasures. The largest art museum around is the fantastic Veletržní Palác in Holešovice. For more contemporary art, head a little further into Holešovice to DOX. If you need another reason to hit this hip 'hood, Letenské sady (Letná Park) is a great place to relax, and the Metronome has one of the best (free) views of the city.

NOVÉ MĚSTO

✔ ALFONS MUCHA MUSEUM — MUSEUM

Panská 7 — ☎224 216 415; www.mucha.cz

A national hero, artist Alfons Mucha rose to fame overnight when he designed a poster on short notice for the French actress Sarah Bernhardt. These days, you can find copies of his work anywhere (you know, semi-nude women in flowing robes, surrounded by flowers and such), but the Alfons Mucha Museum offers a more in-depth look at Mucha's career. From original banknotes that Mucha designed for the First Czechoslovak Republic to photos of the painter Paul Gaugin playing Mucha's piano to Mucha's childhood drawings, the exhibits paint an intimate portrait of the artist. Don't miss his sketch of a window design for St. Vitus Cathedral (then see the window for yourself in Hradčany). The souvenir shop sells all kinds of reproductions (300-500Kč), so you can take home some Mucha of your very own.

A or B: Můstek. Walk up Wenceslas Sq. toward the St. Wenceslas statue. Turn left on Jindřišská and left again on Panská. $ 90Kč, students 60Kč. ⏰ Open daily 10am-6pm.

good square wenceslas

You wouldn't know it from the traffic, McDonalds, and souvenir shops, but enormous **Wenceslas Square** has quite an eventful history. Here are just some of the square's noteworthy events:

1348: Holy Roman Emperor Charles IV founds the New Town of Prague, including this, the "Horse Market" square.

1680: An equestrian statue of St. Wenceslas (not the statue that is there now) is erected in the middle of the Horse Market square; the saint informally lends his name to the square.

JUNE 12, 1848: A mass is held in protest of the Hapsburgs' military response to calls for liberal constitutional reform. A week of fighting in the streets ensues.

1848: To commemorate the unsuccessful revolutionary uprisings, the square is officially renamed for Wenceslas, the 10th-century duke and patron saint of Bohemia.

1912: The currently standing equestrian statue of St. Wenceslas is installed. Nationalism follows. Other sculptures in the square include a stack of cars and Superman flying face-first into the pavement.

OCTOBER 28, 1918: The First Czechoslovak Republic declares itself an independent nation. Independence is brief.

JANUARY 16, 1969: Student Jan Palach protests the Soviet invasion of Czechoslovakia by lighting himself on fire. Today, a monument commemorates the heroic act.

MARCH 28, 1969: Czechoslovakia defeats its Soviet occupiers in ice hockey. And there is much rejoicing (in Wenceslas Sq., of course).

NOVEMBER 17-DECEMBER 19, 1989: "Velvet Revolution" demonstrations fill the square. Neither the Czechs nor the velvet is crushed—a turning point in the history of each.

TODAY: Make your own history! (No tanks or fires, though, please.)

WENCESLAS SQUARE (VÁCLAVSKÉ NÁMĚSTÍ) SQUARE

Once a horse market, Václavské náměstí now sells everything but. American-style department stores and historic hotels compete for attention with vendors peddling up to six different types of sausage. The square is dominated by the **National Museum,** which closed for a five-year renovation in July 2011, and which will hopefully be less of a snoozefest when it reopens. Some of the exhibits have been moved to the modern building next door (Vinohradská 1, www.nm.cz $ 100Kč, students 70Kč.), so, if you're intent on looking at Czech archaeological finds, rock samples, and stuffed animals, they're all yours. Don't miss the **statue** of St. Wenceslas, where the proclamation of Czechoslovakia's independence was read in 1918. Artist David Černý's hilarious parody of this statue can be found inside the Lucerna complex on Vodičková.

A or B: Můstek; A or C: Muzeum.

DANCING HOUSE — LANDMARK

Rašínovo nábřeží 80

Now in its mid-teens, the Dancing House is one of Prague's most recognizable buildings. Designed by Frank Gehry and Vlado Milunić, it was originally dubbed "Fred and Ginger" after the famous dancing duo. The Dancing House was built in an empty lot left after the Bombing of Prague—an aerial raid by the US Army Air Forces in 1945 that was supposedly the result of a navigational error. It doesn't quite fit in with the crusty Baroque and Art Nouveau crowd nearby, and its construction sparked a heated debate about architecture in Prague. The top floor of the Dancing House is home to an upscale French restaurant, but you can get in for the price of a drink when the restaurant closes to let in customers from the downstairs cafe (4-6pm).

B: Karlovo náměstí. From the Metro, walk down Resslova toward the river. The building is on the left. $ Coffee 45-70Kč. Beer 40-90Kč.

SAINT HENRY TOWER (JINDŘIŠSKÁ VĚŽ) — TOWER

Jindřišská ulice ☎224 232 429; www.jindrisskavez.cz

Dating back to 1455, this tower was ingeniously converted so that most of its floors serve different roles—from the bottom up: whiskey bar (fl. 0-1), gallery (fl. 2-4), toilets (fl. 5), museum (fl. 6), restaurant (fl. 7-9), and observation deck (fl. 10). The price of a ticket allows you to see everything inside, so take the elevator to the top and then descend. The view from the top is rather average, the gallery space is encroached upon by a liquor store, and the exhibition on Prague's 120 towers takes itself a little too seriously, but it's worth peeking inside the posh restaurant, where patrons compete for space with the tower's scaffolding system and a 16th-century bell.

A or B: Můstek. From the Metro, walk up Wenceslas Sq. toward the St. Wenceslas statue. Turn left on Jindřišská and continue to the end of the street. $ 80Kč, students 55Kč. Cash only. ⏰ Open daily Apr-Sept 10am-7pm. Oct-Mar 10am-6pm.

NEW TOWN HALL (NOVOMĚSTSKÁ RADNICE) — LANDMARK

Karlovo náměstí 1/23 ☎224 948 225; www.nrpraha.cz

This town hall is more interesting for its history than its architecture—it was here that the First Defenestration of Prague took place in 1419, when a mob of Hussites stormed the town hall and tossed some 15 councilors and other dignitaries out the window. Later on, the building functioned as a prison, and executions took place in the town hall's courtyard as recently as during the Nazi occupation. Today you can climb the tower's 221 steps to the top and check out photo exhibits as you go.

B: Karlovo náměstí. From the Metro, look for the giant tower on the northern end of the square. $ 30Kč. Cash only. ⏰ Open Apr-Oct Tu-Su 10am-6pm.

OUR LADY OF THE SNOW (KOSTEL PANNY MARIE SNĚŽNÉ) — CHURCH

Jungmannovo náměstí 18 www.pms.ofm.cz

Our Lady of the Snow is one of the most oddly shaped churches in Central Europe. Charles IV commissioned it the day after his coronation, hoping to end up with a monster cathedral that would overshadow even St. Vitus. Unfortunately, the Hussite Wars interrupted construction, and the church was severely damaged. When Dominican monks reconstructed it, they had to abandon the original design. Only one nave and the impressively large ceilings remained from Charles IV's plan. Before you leave, check out the tiny St. Michael's chapel (on the right when you enter), where services take place in winter, since the disproportionately tall church isn't heated.

A or B: Můstek. From the Metro, walk down 28. října, then turn left on Jungmannovo náměstí. The entrance to the church is behind the statue of the poet J. Jungmann. ⏰ Open daily 6:30am-7pm. Services Su 9, 10:15, 11:30am, 6pm.

FRANCISCAN GARDENS
GARDEN

With clipped evergreen hedges and plenty of trees, this hidden oasis between Our Lady of the Snow and bustling Wenceslas Sq. may surprise if you happen upon it by chance. Massive, strange, lightbulb-like street lamps line the walk, but, unfortunately, the park closes before you can see them in their full glory. The picturesque cottage in the middle of the roses is actually a secondhand clothing store.

✢ A or B: Můstek. Enter through the arch to the left of Jungmannova and Národní, behind the statue. ⌚ Open daily Apr-Aug 7am-10pm; Sept-Oct 7am-8pm; Oct-Apr 8am-7pm.

EMAUZY MONASTERY
MONASTERY

Vyšehradská 49 ☎324 917 662; www.emauzy.cz

Founded by (who else?) Charles IV, Emauzy Monastery avoided being burned down by the Hussites thanks to its connection to the martyr Jan Hus, who studied here. Instead, it was turned into the first and only Hussite monastery, which lasted long after the Hussite Wars ended. Some centuries later, the monastery served as home to Johannes Kepler, the scientist who explained planetary motion. If you don't want to pay for a ticket, you can come see the impressive chapel during mass (daily 10am and 6pm). Outside of religious services, Emauzy is your typical monastery—empty, decrepit, and echoing.

✢ B: Karlovo náměstí. From the park, follow the signs to the monastery down Vyšehradská. Ⓢ 50kč. ⌚ Open M-F 11am-5pm, closes earlier in winter. Mass daily 10am, 6pm.

prague's quirkiest museums

When you tire of castles, churches, and pretty houses, check out some of these funky Czech museums:

- **MUSEUM OF COMMUNISM.** The best things about this museum are its promotional posters, featuring a fanged but otherwise adorable matryoshka doll.

- **SEX MACHINES MUSEUM.** The name says it all. The collection (Melantrichova 18) covers the gamut from 16th-century chastity belts to pornographic films allegedly made for King Alfonso XIII of Spain.

- **KEPLER MUSEUM.** Rumor has it that the people in charge of this bizarre, clearly counterfactual museum (Karlova 4) of untruth believe the Earth revolves around the sun!

- **FRANZ KAFKA MUSEUM.** If the authorities decide to allow you to visit this museum, you will wake up one morning to find two men in your hotel room who will let you know when you are scheduled to arrive. **Do not be late.**

sights

MUSEUM OF COMMUNISM
MUSEUM

Na Příkopě 10 ☎224 212 966; www.museumofcommunism.com

If your understanding of communism is limited to Borat's "my sister is number four prostitute in all of Kazakhstan," this is a good opportunity to branch out. Recreations of some of the typical architectural spaces (a grocery store, an interrogation room, etc.) and a number of artifacts from the communist era make this museum amusing for some and terrifying for others. The only gripe on our side is the disproportionately high admission price, but hey, it's capitalism.

✢ A or B: Můstek. From the Metro, head down Na Příkopě, then turn right inside a courtyard. Enter through a casino door. The museum is on the 2nd floor. Ⓢ 180Kč, students 140Kč. ⌚ Open daily 9am-9pm.

ANTONÍN DVOŘÁK MUSEUM

MUSEUM

Ke Karlovu 20 ☎224 918 013; www.nm.cz

Also called "Michnův Letohrádek", this nobleman's villa served as a restaurant and a cattle market before becoming the museum that it is today. The exhibit is on the smaller side, but contains quite a few of Antonín Dvořák's worldly possessions, which range from his graduation gown from Cambridge University (he received an honorary degree) to his musical instruments to his flask and eyeglasses. The upper floor's walls are covered with 18th-century paintings, the only remaining feature of the villa's original decor.

🚇 C: I.P. Pavlova. From the station, head west on Ječná and take the 1st left onto Kateřinská. Then take the 1st left on Ke Karlovu; the museum is on the left. $ 50Kč, students 25Kč. Concerts 575Kč. Cash only. ⏰ Open Tu-W 10am-1:30pm and 2-5pm, Th 11am-1:30pm and 2-7pm, F-Su 10am-1:30pm and 2-5pm.

CHARLES UNIVERSITY BOTANICAL GARDENS

GARDEN

Na Slupi 16 ☎221 951 879; www.bz-uk.cz

Founded in 1898, the Charles University Botanical Gardens contain some 3000 species of plants in a several-acre garden. Admission to the garden is free, but you'll need a ticket to enter the greenhouses, which house temporary plant exhibitions (cacti, orchids, etc.) and a few caged parrots.

🚇 B: Karlovo náměstí. From the Metro, follow Vyšehradská south until it becomes Na Slupi. Alternatively, take tram 18 or 24 to Botanická záhrada. $ 50Kč, students 25Kč. ⏰ Gardens open daily Apr-Aug 10am-7:30pm; Sept-Oct 10am-6pm; Nov-Jan 10am-4pm; Feb-Mar 10am-5pm. Greenhouses close 1hr. earlier.

CHURCH OF SAINT IGNATIUS

CHURCH

Ječná 2 ☎221 990 200; www.jesuit.cz

Notice the figure of St. Ignatius on the peak of this Baroque Jesuit church—in its heyday, it was considered semi-heretical, as clerical rules stated that a full-body halo could only be used for Christ himself. The Jesuit order was so strong, though, that it could afford to break this rule without consequence. The church is the third largest Jesuit complex in all of Europe. The sculptures on the altar are the work of Matěj Václav Jäckel, who is best known for the statues on the Charles Bridge.

🚇 B: Karlovo náměstí. From the Metro, head away from the river toward Ječná. The church is on the corner. ⏰ Open daily 6am-noon and 3:30-6:30pm. Services daily 6:15, 7:30am, 5:30pm. Mass Su 7, 9, 11am, 5:30pm.

STARÉ MĚSTO

★ CHARLES BRIDGE

BRIDGE

Probably the most famous sight in all of Prague, Charles Bridge is always packed, and for good reasons. Charles IV commissioned the bridge (if you haven't figured it out already, Charles IV is responsible for everything cool in Prague), and he laid the first stone on July 9, 1357 at exactly 5:31am. Can you guess why? (See answer below.) Although the bridge was originally decorated with a single crucifix, 30 statues were added between 1600 and 1800, including such shady characters as St. Augustine and Lamenting Christ. Weather damage forced the city to remove the original statues, which are now displayed at the National Gallery (see **Holešovice**) and Vyšehrad (see **Vinohrady**). The bridge also features the **Old Town Bridge Tower** *(Staroměstská mostecká věž)*, which offers a bird's eye view of the city below. If you don't cross the bridge around sunset at least once, you haven't really been to Prague.

🚇 A: Malostranská or Staroměstská. ℹ Here's the answer: if you write down the date and time of when the first stone was laid, you get the chiasmus 1-3-5-7-9-7-5-3-1. (A Dan Brown novel is waiting to be written.) $ Tower 70Kč, students 50Kč. ⏰ Open daily Nov-Dec 10am-8pm; Apr-Oct 10am-10pm; Dec-Mar 10am-6pm.

ASTRONOMICAL CLOCK TOWER AND OLD TOWN HALL (STAROMĚSTSKÁ RADNICE) LANDMARK

Staroměstské náměstí ☎724 911 556; www.praguetowers.com

It is said that after the city council hired the clockmaker Hanuš to build this world-famous clock, they gouged out his eyes so he could never repeat his work (talk about worker's comp issues). In reality, Hanuš wasn't even the builder—the astronomical clock was the work of another clockmaker, Mikuláš of Kadaň. At the ripe age of 600 years (the big birthday bash was in 2010), this mysterious machine still tracks movements of the sun, the moon, and much, much more. On the hour, there's always a little show: 12 apostles poke their heads out, a rooster crows, and the crowd of tourists below goes bananas. If you want to go all meta, take a photo of all the gaping tourists; if you want to go meta-meta, take a photo of people taking photos of people... the possibilities are endless. For an amazing view of the city, head to the top of the tower. There's also a tour of the Old Town Hall, which includes a behind-the-scenes view of the apostle clock (if you come on the hour, you'll see the apostles move) and a walk through the original Romanesque basement. The basement served as the original ground floor before the king raised the level of Old Town by some 5m to protect it from flooding.

🚇 A: Staroměstská. Southwest corner of Old Town Sq. $ Exhibition hall 100Kč, students 80Kč. Tower 100Kč/50Kč. Cash only. 🕐 Hall open M 11am-6pm, Tu-Su 9am-6pm (last tour at 5pm). Tower open M 11am-10pm, Tu-Su 9am-10pm.

CHURCH OF OUR LADY BEFORE TÝN (MATKY BOŽÍ PŘED TÝNEM) CHURCH

Staroměstské náměstí www.tyn.cz

Our Lady Before Týn dominates the skyline of Old Town Sq. with two enormous spires sticking out among the surrounding Baroque buildings. This 14th-century church contains the remains of the astronomer **Tycho Brahe,** who revolutionized the way the movement of planets was understood and who allegedly peed himself to death: as the popular story goes, in 1601 Brahe was at Emperor Rudolf's for dinner, and, in the name of decorum, he refused to leave the dinner table to relieve himself, until his bladder burst. Today, science suggests that the real reason for his death might have been mercury poisoning, but who cares about science? Maybe we'll know for sure when the results of the latest analysis come in—in 2010, scientists closed the church down, opened Brahe's tomb, and studied his remains.

🚇 A: Staroměstská. It's the giant twin towers in Old Town Sq. $ Free. 🕐 Open Tu-Sa 10am-1pm and 3-5pm, Su 10:30am-noon.

MUNICIPAL HOUSE (OBECNÍ DŮM) CONCERT HALL

Naměstí Republiky 5 ☎222 002 101; www.obecnidum.cz

Standing on the grounds where Czech kings used to reside, Municipal House is the site of two important events in Czech history. It was here that Czechoslovakia declared independence in 1918 and that the Communist Party held the first meetings with Václav Havel and other leaders of *Občanské fórum* (Civic forum, a pro-democracy movement) in 1989. But Municipal House is not only historically significant—it's also beautiful. Built in the Art Nouveau style in 1912, this state house features works from more than 20 of the country's top artists; every detail, from the shape of the door handles to the patterns on the banisters, is the careful work of some Art Noveau master. Daily guided tours take visitors through **Smetana Hall,** where the Czech Philharmonic plays, and the **Mayor's Hall,** decorated by Czech artist Alfons Mucha. There's also a separate exhibition that features just one object: a replica (!) of the Crown of St. Wenceslas, a jewel-studded national treasure (the original is locked away in St. Vitus Cathedral). If you don't feel like paying for a tour, you can stop by **Kavárna Obecní Dům** located on the ground floor. It's a bit expensive, but ordering a coffee (58Kč) will allow you to linger under its eight enormous chandeliers in the impressive Art Nouveau interior.

B: Náměstí Republiky. From Old Town Sq., walk east on Celetná all the way to Náměstí Republiky; Municipal House is on the left. ***i*** *Tours in Czech and English. Tickets must be purchased on the day of your visit at the ticket office located in the basement of the Municipal House.* $ *Guided tours 270Kč, students 230Kč. Crown of St. Wenceslas (Svatováclavská Koruna) exhibit 120Kč, students 60Kč.* ⏰ *Open daily 10am-7pm. Tour times vary by week and month; check the online calendar for details.*

SAINT JAMES CATHEDRAL (KOSTOL SVATÉHO JAKUBA VĚTŠÍHO) CHURCH

Malá Štupartská 6

This spectacular church is the subject of several gory legends. According to one, a thief tried to steal the necklace off of a Virgin Mary statue. As you can imagine, the statue came to life, grabbed the thief's arm, and refused to let go. He had to cut off his arm and, to this day, a mummified arm hangs in the church. Another one: during the funeral of Václav Vratislav z Mitrovic, a nobleman and writer, the body was placed into one of the cathedral's most beautiful tombs. For days after he was buried, terrible noises sounded from the tomb, so the priests sprinkled holy water on it. After some time, the noises subsided. It was only years later, during the burial of Vratislav's son, that the tomb was reopened and the coffin discovered to be broken with scratch marks everywhere. Coincidentally, a few years before his death, Vratislav had dreamt that he would be buried alive.

From Old Town Sq. head down Týnska (pass Our Lady Before Týn on the left), continuing straight through the courtyards as it turns into Týn. The courtyard lets out at Malá Štupartská, where you should take a left. $ *Free.* ⏰ *Open M-Th 9:30am-noon, F 2-4pm, Sa 9:30am-noon and 2-4pm, Su 2-4pm.*

ESTATES THEATER (STAVOVSKÉ DIVADLO) THEATER

Železná 11 ☎224 228 503; www.stavovskedivadlo.cz

The Estates Theater is famous for its connection with Wolfgang Amadeus Mozart. It was here that Mozart's *Marriage of Figaro* first became a smash success following a rather lukewarm premiere in Vienna. Perhaps thanks to this turnaround, Mozart premiered his next opera, *Don Giovanni,* in this same theater in 1787—be sure to check out the haunting statue commemorating the premiere outside the theater. More recently, the Oscar-winning film *Amadeus* (directed by Czech emigré Miloš Forman in 1984) features a scene in which Mozart conducts inside the Estates Theater. But Mozart isn't the theater's only claim to fame—it was here that the song *"Kde Domov Můj?"* first played publicly as part of the opera *Fidlovačka.* Why is that important, you ask? It happens to be the anthem of the Czech Republic. Popular ballets, dramas, and operas still play nightly in the Estates, and since the theater offers no public tours, the moderate ticket price is definitely worth the experience.

A or B: Můstek. From Old Town Sq., walk south on Železná. The theater is on the left. $ *Tickets 300-1200Kč.* ⏰ *Performances usually at 7pm.*

THE BLACK MADONNA HOUSE (DŮM ČERNÉ MATKY BOŽÍ) MUSEUM

Ovocný trh 19 ☎224 301 003; www.ngprague.cz

The Black Madonna House is the best standing example of Cubist architecture—a uniquely Czech trend that tried to apply the rules of Cubism to the third dimension. Designed by Josef Gočár, one of the godfathers of Cubist architecture, the building now contains a permanent exhibit devoted to this Bohemian movement. The paintings can be a bit underwhelming for the layman, but one might find some appreciation for the displays of Cubist furniture. Consumers will also enjoy the gift shop downstairs. Finally, check out the fully restored Cubist **Grand Café Orient** (see **Food**) located on the second floor.

B: Náměstí Republiky. From Old Town Sq., walk east on Celetná. The museum is on the left, where Celetná forks with Ovocný trh. $ *100Kč, students 50Kč.* ⏰ *Open Tu-Su 10am-6pm.*

POWDER GATE (PRAŠNÁ BRÁNA) TOWER

Na Příkopě www.praguetowers.com

Six hundred years ago, *Horská brána* or "Mountain Tower" stood on this site, protecting the city and marking the start of royal coronation ceremonies. When New Town (Nové Město) became a part of the city proper, the tower lost its function and became known as the "Shabby Tower." The tower was torn down and in its place an essentially symbolic monument, the Powder Gate, was erected. While the tower served as a gunpowder storage center for a while, these days it just kind of chills and lets cars tickle its belly as they drive underneath. Climb to the top for a great view of the city and a small exhibit.

B: Naměstí Republiky. From Old Town Sq., walk east on Celetná until you reach the tower. $ 70Kč, students 50Kč. ⏰ Open daily Apr-Sept 10am-10pm, Oct 10am-8pm, Nov-Feb 10am-6pm, Mar 10am-8pm.

SAINT NICHOLAS CHURCH (KOSTOL SVATÉHO MIKULÁŠE) CHURCH

Staroměstské náměstí ☎224 190 994

Saint Nicholas Church (not to be confused with the far more impressive church of the same name in Malá Strana) might not be the most famous of the lot, but the "chandelier" hanging in its center might be the city's coolest. Given as a gift to Prague in 1787 by Tsar Nicholas II, this ornament is an enormous replica of the royal crown worn by Russian tsars. The church was under the control of Benedictine monks for most of its existence, and a plaque on the former Benedictine monastery attached to the building marks the site of Franz Kafka's birth. Today, you can enjoy classical music concerts here, if that's the kind of thing you enjoy.

A: Staroměstká. Northwest corner of Old Town Sq. $ Entry free. Concerts 350-490Kč, students 200-300Kč. Cash only. ⏰ Open Tu-Sa 10am-4pm, Su noon-4pm. Concerts daily 5 and 8pm.

JOSEFOV

A **joint ticket** grants admission to all synagogues (aside from Staronová Synagoga) and the Old Jewish Cemetery. (ℹ Audio tours for the entire circuit can be purchased inside Pinkas Synagogue for 250Kč, students 200Kč. $ 300Kč, students 200Kč. ⏰ Open in summer M-F 9am-6pm, Su 9am-6pm; in winter M-F 9am-4:30pm, Su 9am-4:30pm.) There are at least five ticket offices, so if a particular line seems to be advancing at a glacial pace, skip to the next one. (The least busy and fastest location seems to be inside the antique shop at Maiselova 15.) Aside from the Jewish sites, there are some other places worth visiting: Rudolfinum, Klášter Sv. Anežky České, and the Franz Kafka statue.

PINKAS SYNAGOGUE (PINKASOVA SYNAGOGA) SYNAGOGUE

Široká 23/3 ☎222 317 191; www.jewishmuseum.cz

The walls of this otherwise bare 500-year-old synagogue are covered with the names, birth dates, and death dates of almost 80,000 Czech Jews who were murdered at Terezín and other concentration camps during the Holocaust. The names were originally added in the 1950s, but, following the Seven-Day War in 1967, the Communist regime closed the synagogue under the pretext of prolonged renovation and had the walls whitewashed. It was only after Václav Havel was elected president that the names could be painstakingly reinscribed between 1992 and 1996. The second floor contains the haunting drawings and collages done by children during their time in Terezín, all made under the guidance of an imprisoned drawing teacher.

B: Staroměstská. 1 block north of the Metro at the southern border of the Old Jewish Cemetery.

OLD JEWISH CEMETERY (STARÝ ŽIDOVSKÝ HŘBITOV) CEMETERY

U starého hřbitova 243/3a ☎222 317 191; www.jewishmuseum.cz

This cemetery may remind one of a shark's mouth—the eroded and broken tombstones jut out at unexpected angles, one over another. Between the 14th and 18th centuries, the graves were dug in layers, and over time the earth settled so that stones from the lower layers were pushed to the surface, forcing many of the newer stones out of position. Rabbi Loew, the supposed creator of the mythical **Golem,** is buried by the wall opposite the exit. Notice the little stones on the tombstones—traditionally, these are used instead of flowers. Outside the exit is the **Ceremonial Hall,** a two-floor museum on the history of Jewish burials.

Enter through Pinkas Synagogue. $ Camera permit 40Kč.

the makings of a monster

Derived from Jewish lore, one traditional Prague legend is the mysterious golem, a strange, human-like monster. Sorry, *LOTR* fans, this golem isn't a manic 500-year old hobbit searching for the precious ring. Rather, according to legend, rabbis attempted to create golems in order to protect Jews.

As the tale goes, conjuring a golem was not as simple as making morning coffee. The rabbi had to dress in white to show his pureness, and get his hands on soil which no man had ever dug in before, usually from the banks of a river. While kneading the soil with spring water and imagining his creation, he had to meditate, utter complex Hebrew incantations, and say the ancient 42-letter name of God—all without mispronouncing anything, which would result in the speaker's instant death.

One of the most famous golem stories takes place in Prague. The story goes that Rabbi Loew created the last successful golem during WWII to protect the Jews from persecution—a noble effort, but instead the creature became increasingly powerful and began destroying the city. Rabbi Loew put his monster to sleep, and it is said that he still slumbers in Prague's Old New Synagogue. Visitors may still worship, but the attic stairs are inaccessible—they probably don't want anyone getting any bright ideas and waking up the ol' mud monster.

SPANISH SYNAGOGUE (ŠPANĚLSKÁ SYNAGOGA) SYNAGOGUE

Vězeňská 141/1 ☎222 317 191; www.jewishmuseum.cz

The Spanish Synagogue is the most richly decorated of the synagogues in Josefov. Built in the Moorish-Byzantine style, the synagogue is covered from floor to ceiling with elaborate geometric patterns in red, green, and gold, and topped off with a cupola. The synagogue houses an interesting exhibit on the history of the Czech Jews from the Jewish Enlightenment onward, chronicling their attempts at full emancipation (before the rule of Joseph II, Jews had to pay special taxes for their "protection," wear yellow hats and Stars of David, and live in the ghetto). There's also an impressive set of silver Torah crowns and pointers. The synagogue also hosts classical music concerts throughout the year.

On the corner of Široká and Dušní, close to the statue of Franz Kafka.

KLAUSEN SYNAGOGUE (KLAUSOVÁ SYNAGOGA) SYNAGOGUE

U starého hřbitova 243/3a ☎222 317 191; www.jewishmuseum.cz

The Klausen Synagogue was originally built in 1573, burned down a while later, rebuilt in 1604, and then reconstructed in the 1880s. The exhibits inside are dedicated to the cultural aspects of Jewish life, with artifacts like Torah pointers, skull caps, menorahs, and velvet valances. Don't miss the special Halizah shoe on the second floor—according to the Old Testament, a widow had to marry a brother of her dead husband if her marriage was childless. The only way to get out of that obligation was to take this shoe off the brother's foot in front of witnesses.

Adjacent to the Old Jewish Cemetery.

MAISEL SYNAGOGUE (MAISELOVA SYNAGOGA) SYNAGOGUE

Maiselova 63/10 ☎222 317 191; www.jewishmuseum.cz

Like most old things in Prague, the Maisel Synagogue has been partially destroyed and subsequently rebuilt several times. Today it contains artifacts from the history of Judaism in Bohemia and Moravia up until the Jewish Enlightenment. Some of the more interesting objects include the tombstone of Avigdor Kara as well as the robes of a 16th-century Jewish martyr who was burned at the stake by the Inquisition.

On Maiselova, 1 block south of Široká.

OLD-NEW SYNAGOGUE (STARONOVÁ SYNAGOGA) SYNAGOGUE

Maiselova ☎222 318 664; www.synagogue.cz

This is the oldest operating synagogue in all of Europe and one of the earliest Gothic structures in Prague. The usual explanation for its oxymoronic name is that it was called the "New" synagogue when it was built in 1270, then took its present name when newer synagogues were built. Yet, a rumor persists that the name "Old-New" *(Alt-Neu)* is a mistranslation of the Hebrew "Al-Tenai," meaning "on condition," implying that the stones would be returned when the temple in Jerusalem was rebuilt. There are a few legends attached to the place. First, the remains of Golem are said to be hidden in the synagogue's attic. Second, the synagogue is supposedly protected from fire by angels (this would account for its longevity). Unfortunately, it doesn't seem to have been protected from water—a line drawn on a wall inside shows how high the water was during floods in 2002. Inside there's also a replica of the flag flown by the congregation in 1496, when Ladislaus Jagiellon first allowed the Jews to fly their own city flag. The Old-New Synagogue is still the center of Prague's Jewish community. Just south of the Old-New synagogue is the **Jewish Town Hall,** which is not accessible to the public, but whose clock tower has a clock that ticks counter-clockwise.

Between Maiselova and Pařížská, north of the cemetery. **i** *Men must cover their heads. Yarmulkes free. Services reserved for practicing members of the Jewish community.* $ *200Kč, students 140Kč.* ⏰ *Open Apri-Oct M-F 9:30am-6pm, Su 9:30am-6pm; Nov-Mar M-F 9:30am-5pm, Su 9:30am-5pm.*

sights

if i could turn back time

If a clock turns counterclockwise, is it still, in a sense, going clockwise? This question is posed, if not answered, by a clock on Prague's **Jewish Town Hall,** next to the Old New Synagogue. There are two clocks on this building: the higher one's face has Roman numerals and turns clockwise; the lower's has Hebrew numerals (the digits are indicated by letters of the Hebrew alphabet) and turns counterclockwise, since Hebrew is read from right to left. But unless you're used to calculating minutes past hours, it'll probably be easier to stick to the conventional clock above.

STATUE OF FRANZ KAFKA — STATUE

Dušní

One of the more original sculptures from among Prague's lot, the statue portrays Franz Kafka sitting astride an enormous suit. Loosely alluding to Kafka's early story "Description of a Struggle," the statue has become a local landmark. For more Kafka-related places, check out the plaque close to St. Nicholas's Church that marks the building where Kafka was born, the blue house at Golden Lane 22 where Kafka lived for a year, and any souvenir shop, where Kafka lives on as an integral symbol of Prague's tourism industry.

➔ On the square where Široká and Dušní intersect, close to the Spanish Synagogue.

GALERIE RUDOLFINUM — GALLERY, CONCERT HALL

Alšovo nábřeží 12 — ☎227 059 205; www.galerierudolfinum.cz

The Neo-Renaissance Rudolfinum hosts both classical musical concerts (it's the home of the Czech Philharmonic Orchestra) and fascinating contemporary art exhibitions. The likes of Damien Hirst and Cindy Sherman have exhibited here in the past, and there's more to come. Rudolfinum is located at **Náměstí Jana Palacha,** named after a student who set himself on fire in 1969 in protest of the Soviet occupation of Czechoslovakia. Also notice the statue of **Antonín Dvořák,** the famous Czech composer who conducted the first concert at Rudolfinum.

➔ B: Staroměstská. It's the imposing building dominating the square near the Metro. The gallery entrance is on the left side of the building. $ Ticket 50-190Kč. Cash only. ⏰ Open Tu-W 10am-6pm, Th 10am-8pm, F-Su 10am-6pm.

MALÁ STRANA

👍 PETŘÍN TOWER (PETŘÍNSKÁ ROZHLEDNA) — TOWER

Petřín Hill

If the Petřín lookout tower seems like a shameless knockoff of the Eiffel Tower, that's because it is. The Eiffel Tower debuted at the 1889 World's Fair, and this shorter, fatter cousin popped up two years later at the Czech Jubilee Exposition. It's at the top of **Petřín Hill,** and, from the lookout 299 steps up, you can see a 360-degree panorama of the Czech countryside. If you're lazy and have money, you can pay extra to take the elevator (50Kč). Even if you don't go up on the tower, be sure to stop in at the free **Jára Cimrman museum** that's in the basement. Cimrman was a brilliant inventor, dramatist, composer, philosopher, and self-taught midwife. Oh, also, he didn't exist. Invented by two playwrights, Cimrman's life is the biggest inside joke of Czech culture. The objects in the museum might not strike foreigners as outrageously funny, but approach them with an open mind, and you'll learn something about the Czech sense of humor.

➔ Walk up Petřín hill or take the funicular from Újezd (26Kč). After getting off the funicular, turn right and continue along the wall until you see the tower. There's also a path that leads here from Strahov Monastery. $ 100Kč, students 50Kč. Lift 50Kč. Museum free. Cash only. ⏰ Open daily 10am-10pm.

PETŘÍN AREA — OBSERVATORY, MAZE, MONUMENT

Petřín Hill

The hilltop has a number of sites worth checking out. Housed in a tiny château near the tower, the **mirror labyrinth** (built for the 1891 Jubilee Exposition) must have been all the rage back in the day, but it's a little underwhelming in our cynical age. The **gardens** have hundreds of varieties of roses and merit a brief stroll. The **observatory** behind the funicular station houses three telescopes and temporary exhibits on space exploration. On your way down, check out the medieval **Hunger Wall,** the perpendicular wall going from the base to the top of the hill. Built by Charles IV, it could just have easily been named "useless public project" (it is said Charles had it built to give work to the city's poor). When you get back down, stop by the **Memorial to the Victims of Communism,** a haunting monument near the Újezd tram station.

⇟ A: Malostranská. Walk southwest toward the hill. Or, take the funicular from Újezd. The alpine tram runs daily every 10-15min. 9am-11:30pm and accepts standard 26Kč public transportation tickets. $ Observatory 55Kč, students 40Kč. Mirror labyrinth 70Kč, students 50Kč. Cash only. ⏰ Observatory open Apr-Aug Tu-F 2-7pm and 9-11pm, Sa-Su 11am-7pm and 9-11pm; shorter hours in winter. Mirror labyrinth open daily 10am-10pm.

CHURCH OF SAINT NICHOLAS — CHURCH

Malostranské náměstí 1 — ☎257 534 215; www.psalterium.cz

If you've spent any time in Europe, you've likely seen a church or two (or 50) by now. But this ain't no ordinary house of the Lord. Boldly colored celestial scenes play out on an enormous fresco that spans the length of the towering ceiling. Floating above it all, like the magical cherry on this holy sundae, sits the behemoth dome. Built by a father-son team in the 17th century, St. Nicholas is considered to be the most beautiful example of High Baroque architecture in Central Europe and was influential in defining the style throughout the continent. Don't forget to climb upstairs and see the 19th-century graffiti on the wooden handrail.

⇟ A: Malostranská. Follow Letenská to Malostranské náměstí. $ 70Kč, students 35Kč. Free entry for prayer daily 8:30-9am. Cash only. ⏰ Open daily Apr-Oct 9am-4:45pm; Nov-Mar 9am-3:45pm.

JOHN LENNON WALL — MONUMENT

Velkopřevorské náměstí

Western songs were banned during the Communist years, so when someone painted John Lennon's face on this wall after the iconic singer was shot in 1980, it was an act of defiance against the regime. Since then, the wall has been an ever-changing community work of art—graffiti is layered over more graffiti, almost all celebrating peace, freedom, and other things Mr. Lennon stands for. The original drawing is long gone, but there will always be at least one Lennon face for you to pose with. Better yet, draw your own.

⇟ From the Charles Bridge, take a left on Lázeňská soon after the bridge ends. Stay on it as it curves around into Velkopřevorské náměstí. $ Free. ⏰ Open 24hr.

CHURCH OF OUR LADY VICTORIOUS — CHURCH

Karmelitská 14 — ☎237 532 018

This place might seem insigificant when you first enter, but there's more to it than meets the eye. On the right side, notice the wax figurine of the infant Jesus, which is said to have protected the church during the 30 Years' War and which supposedly possesses healing powers. This figurine is known internationally, and a small museum behind the altar displays costumes made for the figurine by friends from around the world, including Empress Maria Theresa. Continue wandering in the area near the souvenir shop, and you'll discover a startling collection of African wood sculptures, brought back from the Carmelite Order's missions. Every week, there are masses in five languages.

⇟ A: Malostranská. Follow Letenská through Malostranské náměstí and continue south onto Karmelitská. The church will be on the right. $ Free. ⏰ Church open daily 8:30am-7pm. Museum open M-Sa 9:30am-5:30pm, Su 1-6pm. English mass Th 5pm, Su noon.

WALLENSTEIN PALACE AND GARDENS — PALACE

Valdštejnské náměstí 4 — ☎257 075 707; www.senat.cz

Originally built in 1626 as a castle for nobleman Albrecht Wallenstein, this immaculate compound now serves as the seat of the Czech Senate. Keep your eyes peeled for live peacocks wandering among the hedge rows and reflecting pools. And don't worry: that albino peacock isn't possessed by Satan, he was just born

that way. Some sad-looking owls chill in the aviary next to the "stalactite wall," where a disorienting array of concrete affects the interior of a cavern. If the statues of Hercules killing all manner of mythical beasts aren't enough to impress you, come back on the weekends, when the castle's interior is open to tourists.
A: Malostranská. $ Free. ⏰ Gardens open June-Sept M-F 7:30am-7pm, Sa-Su 10am-7pm; Oct M-F 7:30am-6pm, Sa-Su 10am-6pm; Apr-May M-F 7:30am-6pm, Sa-Su 10am-6pm. Palace open Sa-Su 10am-5pm.

FRANZ KAFKA MUSEUM MUSEUM

Cihelná 2b ☎221 451 400; www.kafkamuseum.cz

In an attempt to be as disorienting as Kafka's writing, this museum goes crazy with shadowy video projections, sounds of dripping water, and dramatic lighting. There are spiderweb tunnels, rooms of mirrors, and, to be fair, at least one cool staircase. We can't decide whether the whole thing is kitschy or powerful—we'll leave it up to you to judge. The actual exhibit is a bit less dramatic; it's mostly facsimiles of Kafka's written documents and some old photographs. If you want to fuel the Kafka souvenir industry even more, buy a map that marks 34 places in Prague that have something to do with the man—seems like Mr. K was all over the place. Note David Černý's sculpture of pissing statues near the entrance to the museum. Recognize the shape of that pool? It's the Czech Republic.
A: Malostranská. Go down Klárov along the river, veering left at the fork between U Lužické Semináře and Cihelná. The museum is on the left. $ 180Kč, students 120Kč. ⏰ Open daily 10am-6pm.

SAINT NICHOLAS TOWER TOWER

Malostranské náměstí 29 ☎724 323 375; www.abl.cz

During Communist rule, the secret police used the belfry of this tower to spy on Western diplomats and targeted Czechs. Today, said spy work is the subject of a mildly interesting exhibit, which includes old newspaper clippings (seems like the secret police loved soccer) and the TV that helped the agents pass time. (Their office was 299 steps up, so they probably didn't have much fun otherwise.) The climb up is lined by an exhibit on the tower, which was used as a fire tower before it burned down. In the days of yore, the bell was rung on cloudy days—the sound was believed to prevent rain.
A: Malostranská. Follow Letenská to Malostranské náměstí. The tower entrance is at the back of the church. $ 100Kč, students 50Kč. Cash only. ⏰ Open daily Apr-Sept 10am-10pm; Oct 10am-8pm; Nov-Feb 10am-6pm; Mar 10am-8pm.

MUSEUM KAMPA MUSEUM

U Sovových mlýnů 2 ☎257 286 147; www.museumkampa.cz

The cost of admission may be a bit high, but modern art enthusiasts should not miss this riverside museum. The collection focuses on sculptures and paintings by Central European artists, most of whom were persecuted under Communism. At the end, climb the stairs to the observation deck, which has a great view over the Vltava (and feels as though it's about to keel over into it).
A: Malostranská. From the Metro, walk south along the river to Kampa Island. The museum is on the east side of the island at the edge of the river. Look for a giant chair or 3 enormous black babies. $ 280Kč, students 140Kč. ⏰ Open daily 10am-6pm.

HRADČANY

around prague castle

The following sights are only a small sampling of what the castle complex has to offer. **Saint George's Basilica** dates back to 920 CE and is also part of a **short tour** of the area. Next door, **Saint George's Convent** now functions as a museum of 19th-century Bohemian art and sculpture. The **Powder Tower** houses a small exhibit on the castle guards. Admission to the latter two comes with the **long tour** ticket.

[icon] PRAGUE CASTLE (PRAŽSKÝ HRAD) — CASTLE

☎224 372 423; www.hrad.cz

One of the largest castles in the world, Prague Castle has been the seat of the Bohemian government since its construction over a millennium ago. It was home to such legendary kings as Charles IV and Rudolph II as well as the first Czechoslovak president, Tomáš Garrigue Masaryk. During WWII, Reinhard Heydrich, the Nazi-appointed protector of the city and notorious "Butcher of Prague," used the castle as his headquarters. It is said that whoever unlawfully wore the crown jewels would die within a year—Heydrich supposedly wore the jewels and, as predicted, was assassinated less than a year later. Arrive on the hour to catch the changing of the guard—the ceremony at noon also includes fanfare. Bonus points: make one of the guards on duty move without breaking the law. We can't seem to do it, but there must be a way.

⇟ Tram 22: Pražský hrad. From the stop, go down U Prašného Mostu past the Royal Gardens and into the Second Courtyard. Alternatively, hike up Nerudova. ℹ Ticket office and info center located opposite St. Vitus Cathedral, inside the castle walls. "Short tour" covers admission to everything important, "long tour" includes other–rather uninteresting–sights. These are not guided tours. Tickets are valid for 2 consecutive days. $ Short tour 250Kč, students 125Kč. Long tour 350Kč, students 175 Kč. ⏰ Ticket office and historical monuments open daily Apr-Oct 9am-5pm; Nov-Mar 9am-4pm. Castle grounds open daily Apr-Oct 5am-midnight; Nov-Mar 6am-11pm.

[icon] SAINT VITUS CATHEDRAL (KATEDRÁLA SV. VÍTA) — CHURCH

Saint Vitus Cathedral is an architectural masterpiece, complete with three magnificent towers and more flying buttresses than it knows what to do with (no wonder it took almost 600 years to complete). Part of the cathedral is accessible without a ticket, but the inner part is cordoned off for ticket holders. Don't miss the Wenceslas Chapel (Svatováclavská kaple), which has walls lined with precious stones and paintings. Despite their old look, the window mosaics were all made in the 1940s, and some even contain sponsorship messages (including those for an insurance company). Some of the most important Czech kings are buried here, including Charles IV (plus his four wives), Jiří z Poděbrad, and Wenceslas IV. The silver tomb next to the altar belongs to St. John Nepomuk, who supposedly had his tongue torn out and was then thrown off the Charles Bridge because he refused to tell Wenceslas IV what his wife had confessed. The Bohemian crown jewels are kept in a room with seven locks, the keys to which are kept in the hands of seven different Czech leaders, both secular and religious. There's also a reliquary (not accessible to the public) that contains the skulls of various saints and some brain matter of John Nepomuk. For a great view, climb the 287 steps of the Great South Tower.

⇟ Enter the Great South Tower from outside the cathedral. $ Tower 150Kč.

OLD ROYAL PALACE (STARÝ KRÁLOVSKÝ PALÁC) — PALACE

The Old Royal Palace, to the right of the cathedral, is one of the few Czech castles where visitors can wander largely unattended—probably because it's mostly empty. The lengthy Vladislav Hall is the largest Gothic hall in the Czech Republic; it once hosted coronations and indoor jousting competitions. Upstairs is the Chancellery of Bohemia, in which a Protestant assembly found two Catholic governors guilty of religious persecution and threw them out the window in the **Second Defenestration of Prague** in 1618.

GOLDEN LANE AND DALIBOR TOWER — STREET, TOWER

The authorities' decision to make the formerly free Golden Lane accessible only with a paid ticket caused an uproar among Czech citizens a few years ago. This legendary street with hobbit-size houses once belonged to the castle's artillerymen and artisans. Franz Kafka spent a year living in the blue house (#22); today it's a disappointing gift shop. Other highlights include the former house of a psychic (killed by the Gestapo for predicting "an early end to the war") and a few houses showcasing traditional crafts. At the end of the street you'll come to the base of Dalibor Tower, a former prison whose most famous resident was the knight Dalibor. Dalibor is the subject of the imprecise Czech adage "Necessity taught Dalibor how to play the fiddle"—indeed, the only "fiddle" that Dalibor encountered in the prison was the torture instrument designed to get prisoners to confess, by stretching them like horsehair on a fiddle bow. The tower exhibits a variety of torture and execution implements, including cages, "Spanish boots" (designed to crush legs and feet), and an executioner's axe.

To the right of the Basilica, follow Jiřská halfway down and take a left on Zlatá ulička, or "Golden Lane."

spooky stories

Prague is all fairy-tale charm by day, but at night (especially with your beer goggles on), the city transforms into a land of demons, ghosts, and nagging ghost wives. Learn which nooks and crannies to avoid (or perhaps seek out) so you don't accidentally come across any ghouls, witches, or ghosts.

- **OLD TOWN SQUARE.** Look for the 27 crosses on the ground commemorating the rebel leaders executed in Prague in 1621 as part of the 30 Years' War. The rebels are said to haunt the square, coming out annually to check that all is well with the astronomical clock.
- **LILIOVÁ STREET.** If you are on Liliová St. between midnight and 1am, strain your ears to block out the sounds of clanking beer mugs and rowdy Czech drinking songs from the surrounding taverns and you might just hear the pleas of the horse rider of Templar. Only the brave attempt to release him from his ghostly prison. Only the bravest attempt to look him in the eye, as he holds his head casually at his side in a saddle bag.
- **PRAGUE CASTLE.** If you just can't get enough of family bickering, head to the royal crypt of Prague Castle, where the four wives of Emperor Charles IV are buried. Late at night, it is said they rise from their graves to quibble over Charles' body, who evidently remains a studmuffin, even at the age of 700.
- **THE VLTAVA.** The Vltava is thought to be inhabited by water nymphs who appear in the form of tiny men with coats and pipes. They pop up at night to offer advice to passersby, but don't be fooled by their impish cuteness: these nymphs will trick you into crashing your boat and sinking to the murky depths.

ROYAL SUMMER PALACE AND ROYAL GARDENS PALACE, GARDENS

The Italian-designed palace was built in the 16th century to provide entertainment for royals. Near the summer palace, the Singing Fountain uses a vibrating bronze plate to create its rhythmic, enchanting sound, though you have to squat down awkwardly to actually hear it. The surrounding Royal Gardens contain dozens of species of trees and shrubbery and make for a relaxing stroll. The garden is also home to an assortment of birds of prey that a falconer displays daily, usually between noon and 5pm.

The gardens are located outside the castle complex. Exit through the 2nd courtyard, walk across the moat, and turn right. $ Free. ⏰ Open daily June-July 10am-9pm; Aug 10am-8pm; Sept 10am-7pm; Oct 10am-6pm; Apr 10am-6pm; May 10am-7pm.

other sights

[icon] STRAHOV MONASTERY (STRAHOVSKÝ KLÁŠTER) MONASTERY

Strahovské nádvoří 1 ☎233 107 711; www.strahovskyklaster.cz

There are two ticketed parts of the monastery: the gallery and the library. We like the library more—it contains thousands of volumes of philosophical, astronomical, mathematical, and historical knowledge, though your admission only entitles you to look from behind a barrier. Even more interesting is the library's antechamber, home to an 18th-century cabinet of curiosities, the predecessor of the modern museum. There you'll find a dried hammerhead shark, two elephant trunks (or dried whale penises, depending on whom you ask), a crocodile, a narwhal tusk (originally people believed this came from a unicorn), a Tatar bow, Hussite weaponry, bucketloads of boring shells, and the grotesque remains of a dodo bird. Compared to this, the gallery section may seem a bit boring, with its exhibit related to the history of Strahov Monastery and another floor dedicated to Czech paintings from between the 14th and 19th centuries. The remains of St. Norbert can be seen here in a glass coffin.

🚋 Tram 22: Pohořelec. From the tram, walk south and up the street, then take a sharp left onto Strahovské nádvoří. $ Library 80Kč, students 50Kč. Gallery 80Kč, students 40Kč. Photo or video permit 100Kč. Cash only. ⏰ Library open daily 9am-noon and 1-5pm. Gallery open daily 9am-noon and 12:30-5pm.

LORETA CHAPEL

Loretánské náměsti 7 ☎220 516 740; www.loreta.cz

Loreta is one of the most important Christian sites in the Czech Republic and is the traditional starting point of pilgrimages. The central Santa Casa contains a statue of the Lady of Loreta, holding what is purported to be a piece of Mary's house at Bethlehem. Perhaps the most impressive part is the collection of treasures on the second floor, which includes diamond and pearl mitres, coral-decorated bowls, jewel-encrusted religious texts, and some astonishing monstrances.

🚋 Tram 22: Pohořelec. From the tram stop, walk south, turn left on Pohořelec, then left on Loretánské náměsti. $ 110Kč, students 90Kč. Photo permit 100Kč. Audio tour 150Kč. Cash only. ⏰ Open daily in summer 9am-12:15pm and 1-5pm; in winter 9am-12:15pm and 1-4pm.

ŽIŽKOV

[icon] JAN ŽIŽKA STATUE AND VÍTKOV HILL MONUMENT, MUSEUM

U Památniku 1900 ☎224 497 111; www.nm.cz

On top of the hill, you'll find the statue of **Jan Žižka,** the one-eyed Hussite general who gave Žižkov its name. Appropriate to Žižka's stellar reputation (he was a brilliant tactician who supposedly never lost a battle), the statue is the largest equestrian statue in the world. The monument also honors those who fell in WWI and WWII—behind the statue you can find a hall dedicated to the memory of "the unknown soldier" (which is actually two soldiers who died in 1917 and 1944). After 1948, the monument became an important meeting place for the Communist Party and also the mausoleum of Klement Gottwald, the first Czechoslovak socialist president. A ticket to the **museum** allows you to see the presidential salon, mosaics by Max Švabinský, the view from the roof, and the eerie underground laboratory where the Communist leader's preserved body was kept for seven years before it started to go black and had to be cremated. On your way down from the monument, stop by the **Army Museum,** which features artifacts from WWII as well as a stuffed Rottweiler.

🚋 Tram 5, 9, or 26: Husinecká. From the tram, follow Husinecká until you reach the square, then make a left at Orebitská, which will merge into Husitská. Walk down Husitská, then make a sharp right and climb the hill. $ 110Kč, students 60Kč. Camera 80Kč. Army Museum free. Cash only. ⏰ Open W-Su 10am-6pm. Army Museum open Tu-Su 10am-6pm.

ŽIŽKOV TELEVISION TOWER — TOWER

Mahlerovy sady 1 ☎724 251 286; www.praguerocket.com

From a distance, the Žižkov TV Tower looks like a Soviet launch missile that never left Earth. The tower was initially met with some hostility during its construction in the mid-1980s, in part because some feared that the tower would hurt infants living around the area with its radio transmissions. After more than 20 years, the tower remains an eyesore, but it's become one of Prague's best-known landmarks. In 2000, controversial Czech artist David Černý cast nine figures of babies—perhaps in reference to that earlier paranoia—and attached them to the tower, where they've been ever since. The tower hosts a restaurant and three observation decks, allowing for impressive views of the city (don't worry, there's an elevator). In the square next to the tower, there's a historic **Jewish cemetery** that was partly destroyed by the tower's construction.

A: Jiřího z Poděbrad. From the Metro, cross diagonally through the park and then take Milešovská toward the tower. $ 120Kč, students 90Kč. Cemetery 60Kč. Cash only. ⏰ Observation deck open daily 10am-10pm. Cemetery open M and W 11am-3pm, F 9am-1pm.

CHURCH OF SAINT PROCOPIUS — CHURCH

Čajkovského 36 ☎775 609 952

In 1881, Žižkov became an independent city. Amid jubilation over their newfound autonomy, the residents of Žižkov realized that they did not have a Catholic place of worship big enough to accommodate the population of the new city. This neo-Gothic church was completed 13 years later.

Trams 5, 9, or 26, Lipanská. Head west 2 blocks on Seifertova.

VINOHRADY

Aside from Vyšehrad, Vinohrady is also home to some of Prague's nicer parks and greenery. **Riegrovy sady** is a hilly park north of Náměstí Míru with grassy slopes from which you can see the Castle and much of Prague. Do as the young locals do: buy a plastic cup of beer from one of the nearby beer gardens, sit on the grass, and take in the view. The vine-covered **Havlíčkovy sady,** to the southeast of Náměstí Míru, is a posher setting: visit its wine bar, **Viniční Altán,** where you can sample many varieties of wine. (www.vinicni-altan.cz $ Wine from 30Kč. ⏰ Open daily 11am-11pm.)

VYŠEHRAD — MONUMENT

V Pevnosti 5B ☎241 410 348; www.praha-vysehrad.cz

Overlooking the beautiful Vltava, Vyšehrad served as the royal residence of Czech kings until 1140, when they moved to Hradčany. It was supposedly founded by Princess Libuše, who foresaw the greatness of Prague before it became, well, great. Today, the complex contains a number of interesting sites. There's the towering **Church of Saint Peter and Saint Paul,** whose two spires can be seen from much of Prague. Next to the church is the beautiful **Vyšehrad cemetery,** where some of the most prominent Czech artists—writers, painters, poets—are buried. Among those in attendance are writer Karel Čapek (who coined the term "robot"), painter Alphonse Mucha (the pioneer of Art Nouveau), and composer Antonín Dvořák. There's also a snoozefest of an archeological exhibition in the **Gothic Cellar,** while the **Vyšehrad Gallery** exhibits work by Czech painters. If you're interested in seeing six of the statues that were originally part of the Charles Bridge, you can go on a short guided tour of **casemates and Gorlice.** Finally, make sure you check out the view of the city from Vyšehrad's fortifications—it's one of the best in Prague.

C: Vyšehrad. From the Metro, head toward "Kongresové Centrum" and walk across this conference complex, keeping right. At the end turn right and head down a staircase, then turn left and cross a parking lot. To your right you'll see a cobblestone road that leads to Vyšehrad. i Guided tours of the casemate leave every hr. 10am-5pm. $ Park admission free. English map and guide

35Kč. Church of St. Peter and St. Paul 30Kč. Casemate 50Kč. Vyšehrad gallery 20Kč. Gothic cellar 50Kč. Cash only. ⏰ Exhibitions open daily Nov-Mar 9:30am-5pm; Apr-Oct 9:30am-6pm. St. Peter and St. Paul open Tu-Th 9am-noon and 1-5pm, F 9am-noon.

HOLEŠOVICE

DOX — MUSEUM

Poupětova 1 — ☎774 145 434; www.doxprague.org

Along with NOD (an art space affiliated with the Roxy club in Staré Město), DOX is at the leading edge of Prague's contemporary art scene. With exhibits of both domestic and international artists, DOX houses up to eight exhibitions at a time. For about a year, it was home to David Černý's controversial *Entropa*, which depicted each member country of the EU as a stereotype of itself (ire came mostly from Bulgaria, shown as a squatting toilet). We can't predict what show will be up when you visit, but it's sure to be crazy interesting.

🚇 C: Nádraží Holešovice. Take tram 5 or 12 or walk along the tram tracks to Ortenovo náměstí. From there, continue along the tracks on Komunardů and take the 1st right. DOX is to the right. $ 180Kč; students 90Kč; art history, art, design, or architecture students 40Kč. ⏰ Open M 10am-6-pm, W-F 11am-7pm, Sa-Su 10am-6pm.

LETENSKÉ SADY — PARK

A stroll through this sprawling, wooded park with unparalleled views of Vltava will make your day. Don't miss the gigantic **Metronome** that overlooks the city—it was installed in 1991, on the spot where a statue of Joseph Stalin once stood. Today the area is full of skaters doing things their moms probably wouldn't approve of. Toward the east side of the park you can find a sometimes-functioning carousel, the oldest in Europe. There are also a few cheap beer gardens where you can enjoy a cold one while looking over Prague's rooftops. Finally, there's the famous **Hanavský Pavilon** (Letenské sady 173 ☎233 323 641; www.hanavskypavilon.cz $ Small beer 60Kč.), an expensive restaurant in a beautiful Art Nouveau château that was constructed for the Jubilee Exhibition in 1891.

🚇 B: Hradčanská. From the station, walk to the other side of the building, and head southeast. You'll run into the enormous park. Or take Metro C to Vltavská and head west.

VELETRŽNÍ PALÁC / NATIONAL GALLERY (NÁRODNÍ GALERIE) — MUSEUM

Dukelských hrdinů 47 — ☎224 301 111; www.ngprague.cz

One of the coolest National Galleries (the others house mostly older art), Veletržní Palác is Prague's MoMA: there are five enormous floors packed with modern art, both Czech and international. The permanent collection contains the likes of Gustav Klimt, Edvard Munch, Vincent van Gogh, Pablo Picasso, Alfons Mucha, and many more.

🚇 C: Nádraží Holešovice. From the station take tram 12, 14, or 17 or walk along the tram tracks (passing the Exhibition Ground) for 2 stops, to Veletržní. The museum is at the tram stop. $ 250Kč, students 120Kč. Audio tour 30Kč. ⏰ Open Tu-Su 10am-6pm.

PRAGUE EXHIBITION GROUND — LANDMARK

Unless there's a big concert or an exhibition going on, visiting this place feels like going to an abandoned amusement park. It was built for the 1891 Jubilee Exhibition and still contains some of the "modern" wonders exhibited there. There's the ghostly Art Nouveau **Exhibition Palace,** whose left wing burned down some years ago and was replaced by a temporary replica. Behind the palace is the reconstructed **Křížiková Fontána** (☎723 665 694; www.krizikovafontana.cz ⏰ Ticket counter open daily 7:15-10:15pm, performances usually start at 8pm.), a fountain that combines light shows with popular tunes ranging from opera to Metallica. In front of the palace, the **Lapidary of National Museum** ($ 50Kč. ⏰ Open W 10am-4pm, Th-Su noon-6pm.) houses some of the original statues from the Charles Bridge, along with other historical exhibits. Officially, the **Marold's Pan-**

orama ($25Kč. ⏰ Open Tu-F 1-5pm, Sa-Su 10am-5pm.) is the biggest panoramic painting in Central Europe, but unofficially it looks like the interior of some bird pavilion in a zoo. East of the Exhibition Ground, **Stromovka,** a bigger park than Letenské sady, is great for some unstructured lolling around.

✣ C: Nádraží Holešovice. From the Metro, take tram 5, 12, 14, or 17 or walk along the tracks to the next stop, Výstaviště.

PRAGUE ZOO — ZOO

U Trojského Zámku 3 — ☎296 112 111; www.zoopraha.cz

Looking at exotic animals might not seem like the thing to do in Prague, but, in fact, Prague's leafy zoo is a popular refuge for many locals. Among the zoo's highlights are the critically endangered Przewalski's horse and Komodo 👍**dragons.** Before you enter, check out the "walk of fame" near the entrance—star-shaped tiles contain footprints of rhinos, chimps, tigers, and other tenants.

✣ C: Nádraží Holešovice. From the Metro, take bus #112. The zoo is a 10min. ride. $ 150Kč, students 100Kč. ⏰ Open daily Jun-Aug 9am-7pm; Sept-Oct 9am-6pm; Nov-Jan 9am-4pm; Feb-Mar 9am-5pm; Apr-May 9am-6pm.

DEJVICE

THE BÁBA RUIN (ZŘÍCENINA BÁBA) — RUIN

Nad Paťankou

Bába looks like a significant ruin, but it isn't. It's the remnant of an 18th-century wine press (or a chapel, nobody knows for sure) that was renovated to look like a castle ruin in 1858. Nevertheless, the hill where it's located offers a great view of the Vltava and Dejvice, which is perhaps the reason for Bába's popularity as a wedding site. The Bába Ruin remains undiscovered by tourists, so if you're done with all the traditional sightseeing, it might make for a short and refreshing hike.

✣ A: Dejvická. There are many ways to get here. On foot, it's 3km north from the Dejvice roundabout. Public transport can take you closer—buses #116 and #160 leave from the roundabout (get off at Ve Struhách, and then follow Pod Paťankou, Paťanka, and Nad Paťankou up the hill; the whole trip is about 2km), while bus #131 leaves from ⓂHradčanská and stops much closer to the ruin. From the bus stop, walk down the stairs and continue to the end of Nad Paťankou.

DIVOKÁ ŠÁRKA — PARK

This beautiful nature reserve is where Prague's locals take a break from people like you. Spread over some 25 hectares, it's the largest green area in the city, occupying the valley of the Šárka river. The reserve boasts an abundance of forest paths, grassy fields, steep hills, and a **swimming pool** (☎603 723 501; www.koupaliste-sarka.webnode.cz), which is 10min. from the tram stop by foot.

✣ Take trams 8 or 36 to the final stop, Divoká Šárka, which is about 5km west of the Dejvice roundabout. $ Pool 60Kč. ⏰ Open in summer daily 10am-6pm.

SMÍCHOV

MEETFACTORY — GALLERY

Ke Sklárně 15 — ☎251 551 796; www.meetfactory.cz

If you enjoyed any of David Černý's works around Prague (Žižkov babies, Lucerna horse, pissing statues at Kafka Museum), you might be interested in visiting his pet project, MeetFactory. Founded in 2001 as a space for cultural dialogue, this converted glass factory hosts all kinds of events, from concerts to exhibitions to film screenings. It's a bit out of the way, down below the Smíchov train station, but it's just 'cause it's alt.

✣ B: Anděl. From the Metro, take tram 12, 14, or 20 5 stops to Lihovar. Continue walking south along the tram tracks and cross the bridge over the railroad tracks. Turn right and continue until you reach MeetFactory. $ Exhibits free. Theater 150Kč, students 100Kč. Film screenings 60Kč, in summer free. Concert tickets vary. Cash only. ⏰ Hours depend on events; generally open M-F 1-8pm, Sa-Su 3-8pm.

STAROPRAMEN BREWERY BREWERY

Nádražní 84 ☎257 191 111; www.pivovary-staropramen.cz

Staropramen is the second largest beer producer in the Czech Republic and this brewery, established in 1868, churns out hundreds of thousands bottles every day. The tour, which includes a beer tasting, guides you through a few of the giant copper vats that process malt and introduces visitors to the brewing process.

⇄ B: Anděl. Exit the Metro station and take a right. The brewery is a few blocks down Nádražní on the left. $ Tour and tasting 199Kč. Cash only. ⏰ At the time of writing, the tours were being redesigned and put on hold, but they should be back up in 2012.

let there be beer

When they say that beer is sacred to the Czech people, they mean it almost literally. The first documented beer in the Czech Republic was brewed by the Benedictine monks in the Brevnov Monastery in the year 993 CE (they may have been preparing kegs for a huge millennium rager). The beer was fermented in huge caves underneath the monastery and then served to those notoriously fun-loving monk bros in the main abbey. The Czech people clearly liked the taste, and since 993 CE beer has evolved to be the much loved drink of the entire country. To this day, many monasteries in the Czech Republic brew their own ale; one popular lager, Klaster, translates to "monastery." It seems God may be on this liquid's side.

BERTRAMKA MUSEUM

Mozartova 69 www.mozartovaobec.cz

Wolfgang Amadeus Mozart once lived in this villa, and it was here that he finished writing his famous opera, *Don Giovanni.* The exhibition inside is small and rather boring—you'll probably learn more about the ownership struggles that have plagued this little house for decades than about Mozart himself. Here's the shortened version: during the early years of Communism, the state took the house from its original owner (Mozartova Obec), and didn't return it until 2009. But the house was empty when it was returned—the original exhibits were taken to the National Museum in Malá Strana, which is why Bertramka now exhibits mostly borrowed artifacts.

⇄ B: Anděl. Exit the Metro station and turn left. Then take the 1st left onto Plzeňská. Continue past the overpass and take the 1st left onto Mozartova. Bertramka is up a small hill at the end of Mozartova. $ 50Kč. Cash only. ⏰ Open daily 10am-6pm.

food

Czech food tends to be simple, hearty, and meat-heavy. Ironically, the most iconic Czech meal is the fried cheese (*hermelín* or *eidam*), which rose to prominence thanks to Communism, when meat was in short supply. Among other staples are pork knee, goulash with dumplings, and schnitzel (basically a chicken fried steak). Consistent deliciousness comes at the price of variety. Most restaurants share practically the same menu; after a while you'll probably be looking to diversify. American and Mexican food is common, especially in bars and expat restaurants, while Chinese and Thai restaurants are also pretty easy to come by. The cheapest way to eat in Prague is to buy your own groceries. For groceries, head to chain supermarkets (Albert, Billa, Tesco) or small, usually Vietnamese-run corner stores.

No explanation of Czech cuisine is complete without a description of beer, the only liquid substance Czechs seem to consume. Czechs drink beer with every meal, and in restaurants, it's cheaper than non-alcoholic beverages (including water). There's a whole army of dishes that are eaten mainly with beer, including pickled sausages, cheese, or cabbage; "head cheese" (meat in aspic); and deep-fried bread. If you need a break from beer, try Kofola, the Communist answer to Coca Cola.

The best deals in town are the daily lunch menus, which are usually served between 11am-3pm, and cost somewhere between 80-110Kč. The menus are often in Czech, but since they serve the same dishes in most Czech restaurants, it shouldn't be hard to learn the words for the basic dishes. The locals eat small breakfasts, usually just some cheese and bread, but the abundance of tourists has made English and American breakfasts a standard option. Dinner with a mug of beer should come in at below 200Kč, though some items (steaks, pork knees) will generally cost you more.

In addition to restaurants, Prague boasts hundreds of cafe-bars, small atmospheric establishments that serve double duty as cafes during the day and bars at night. They usually have extensive coffee options as well as a full bar and a small food menu.

NOVÉ MĚSTO

The food in Nové Město is generally more affordable than in the Old Town to the north. The best place to buy groceries is **Tesco** on Národní Třída.

👍 POTREFENÁ HUSA — CZECH $$

Resslova 1 — ☎224 918 691; www.staropramen.cz/husa

Launched by the Staropramen brewery to "improve the beer culture in Czech Republic" (which is kind of like somebody aiming to improve the cocaine culture in Colombia), Potrefená Husa is a classy chain restaurant where locals come if they want an above-average meal. The barbecued ribs (185Kč) are an unforgettable experience, especially when paired with a garlic baguette. From the designer flourishes that adorn the brick cellar to the music on the stereo to the food itself, everything is slightly more interesting here than at a typical Czech restaurant.

🚇 B: Karlovo náměstí. From the station, head down Resslova, toward the river. The restaurant will be on the right. $ Entrees 145-285Kč. Desserts 35-89Kč. Beer 25-37Kč. ⏰ Open M-W 11am-midnight, Th-Sa 11am-1am, Su 11am-11pm.

👍 LIBEŘSKÉ LAHŮDKY — BAKERY $

Vodičkova 9 — ☎222 540 828; www.liberskelahudky.cz

With its amazing variety of small sandwiches, cakes, cold salads, baguettes, donuts, and more, Libeřské Lahůdky is the perfect place to get your breakfast or midday snack. The *chlebíčky* (open-faced sandwiches) are artistic creations that come in many variations, all at surprisingly low prices (16-19Kč). If you're unsure about which one of the traditional Czech cakes you'd like, there are also bite-sized versions (8Kč) that allow you to make an informed decision. There's no seating, but you can eat your food standing at the counters or take it with you to the streets.

🚇 B: Karlovo náměstí. From the Metro, head north past the New Town Hall, staying right on Vodičkova when it forks. The restaurant is on the left. $ Baguettes 35-45Kč. Cakes 12-36Kč. Cash only. ⏰ Open M-F 7am-7pm, Sa-Su 8am-6pm.

RESTAURACE V CÍPU — CZECH $$

V Cípu — ☎607 177 107; www.restauracevcipu.cz

Even though it's right in the center of the city, this little restaurant remains a secret to most foreigners. With wooden benches and some rustic decorations, V Cípu feels unpretentious and inviting. Locals come here for cheap Czech classics and for Zlatopramen tank beer, which you can't get anywhere else in the country. Try the excellent fried cheese (75-80Kč) or the duck (94Kč).

🚇 A or B: Můstek. From the Metro, walk northeast on Na Příkopě and take the 1st right onto Panská. Take the 1st right onto V Cípu, opposite the Alfons Mucha Museum. $ Meat entrees 118-153Kč. Lunch menu 73-94Kč. Beer 18-32Kč. ⏰ Open M-Sa 11am-midnight, Su 11am-11pm.

GLOBE CAFÉ AMERICAN $$

Pštrossova 6 ☎224 934 203; www.globebookstore.cz

Part bookstore, part cafe, part cultural center, Globe is one of the best-known American outposts in Prague. Even though the American expat community has dwindled considerably in recent years and the clientele is starting to lean toward locals, Globe still offers some cultural comfort: up to 10,000 English-language books, refillable drip coffee (45Kč), and a menu of burgers, sandwiches, and other Western food. Cultural events (free film screenings, author readings, live music) take place almost every night, and, during happy hour (daily 5-7pm), chicken wings go for 7Kč a piece.

🚇 B: Karlovo náměstí. From the Metro, take Resslova toward the river and then turn right on Na Zderaze, which becomes Pštrossova; the cafe is on the right. $ Sandwiches and burgers 140-180Kč. Desserts 65-80Kč. Beer 20-40Kč. Internet access 60Kč per hr. ⏰ Open M-Th 9:30am-midnight, F-Sa 9:30am-1am (or later), Su 9:30am-midnight. Bookstore open daily 9:30am-11pm.

PIZZERIA KMOTRA PIZZA $$

V Jirchářích 12 ☎224 934 100; www.kmotra.cz

Kmotra ("the godmother") is known for its quality pizza and low prices. Supposedly the oldest pizzeria in Prague, Kmotra sports a cozy downstairs cellar with floating lamps and wooden tables. There are 36 kinds of pizza, all of which come with thin crusts and generous toppings. If you're after slightly less traditional toppings, try Špenátová II, which is topped with spinach, bacon, and a sizzling egg.

🚇 B: Národní třída. From the Metro, head down Ostrovní towards the river. Take the 2nd left at Voršilská. $ Pizzas 109-155Kč. Pasta 89-150Kč. ⏰ Open daily 11am-midnight.

czech these out

Looking for a quick snack before heading to one of Prague's historic sites or a night on the town? Don't overlook this delectable street fare:

- **TRDELNÍK ROLLED PASTRIES:** These pastries are sold fresh all over Prague in Staré Město and Malá Strana. They're hot, fluffy, and sprinkled with sugar—perfect for those seeking a sugar high.
- **SVAŘENÉ VÍNO:** This cold-weather beverage is made from red wine mixed with mulling spices. Sweeten it with sugar or honey.
- **SAUSAGES:** You'll find plenty of sausage carts in areas like Wenceslas Sq. Much like the hot dog, an American favorite, these snacks are filling and easy to take on-the-go.
- **FRIED CHEESE SANDWICH:** This delicious treat may look like a chickwich, but those are actually thick slices of cheese that have been breaded and fried in that bun. The sandwich is usually topped with mayonnaise.

CAFÉ SLAVIA CAFE $$

Smetanovo nábřeží 2 ☎224 218 493; www.cafeslavia.cz

Perhaps the best-known cafe in all of Prague, Slavia was historically the haunt of artists, intellectuals, and dissidents, including Václav Havel. Today it's a bustling tourist attraction, but completely worth the slightly above-average prices. In a prime people-watching and Vltava-gazing setting, Slavia sends you back in time with nightly piano music, an Art Deco interior, and waiters in bowties. And the biggest surprise? The food is actually great. Try something from the seasonal menus built around a single ingredient (asparagus, strawberries, etc.).

⇆ B: Národní třída. From the Metro, walk north on Spálená and then turn left on Národní. The restaurant is at the end of the street, across from the National Theater. $ Czech dishes 139-189Kč. Desserts 45-109Kč. Coffee 39-70Kč. ⏰ Open M-F 8am-midnight, Sa-Su 9am-midnight.

MAMACOFFEE COFFEE $

Vodičkova 6 ☎773 337 309; www.mamacoffee.cz

Mamacoffee is the best coffee place in Prague. In fact, if you're not satisfied, this *Let's Go* researcher will eat a paper coffee cup. The organic, fair trade beans come from all corners of the world and the entire process (from three spoonfuls of coffee beans to a steaming cup) takes place before your eyes. Have your cup to go, or enjoy it while checking your email using the Wi-Fi upstairs.

⇆ B: Karlovo náměstí. From the Metro, head north past the New Town Hall. Stay to the right on Vodičkova when it forks; the cafe is on the right. ℹ 2nd location in Vinohrady. $ Coffee 35-67Kč. ⏰ Open M-F 8am-10pm, Sa-Su 10am-10pm.

LEMON LEAF THAI $$

Myslíkova 14 ☎224 919 056; www.lemon.cz

Classy Lemon Leaf serves delicious Thai food at affordable prices, especially on weekdays during lunchtime (11am-3pm) and during happy hours (3:30-6pm, 20% discount on all meals). If you approve of these, you might also be interested in coming for the weekend all-you-can-eat brunch (noon-3:30pm), which at 249Kč is a bit more costly but gives you a choice of several appetizers and entrees. The spacious interiors and the tables outside are equally alluring.

⇆ B: Karlovo náměstí. From the square, take Resslova toward the river and make a right onto Na Zderaze. Continue to the intersection of Na Zderaze and Myslíkova. $ Curries 159-189Kč. Entrees 139-199Kč. Lunch menu 89-149Kč. ⏰ Open M-Th 11am-11pm, F 11am-midnight, Sa noon-midnight, Su noon-11pm.

ANGELATO ICE CREAM $

Rytířská 27 ☎224 235 123; www.angelato.cz

Word on the street is that this is the best ice cream place in all of Prague. We're inclined to agree—the taste is smooth, creamy, and downright surprising. Intrigued? Then don't take our word for it; go find out for yourself. Ice cream heaven is only 30Kč away.

⇆ A or B: Můstek. From the Metro, walk up Na Můstku toward the Old Town. The shop is on the left. $ 1 scoop 30Kč; 2 scoops 55Kč. Cash only. ⏰ Open daily 11am-10pm.

PIVOVARSKÝ DŮM CZECH $$$

Ječná 15 ☎296 216 666; www.gastroinfo.cz/pivodum

Sure, it's a touristy place, but for good reason. To begin with, there's a microbrewery that makes eight different kinds of flavored beers (among them nettle, cherry, coffee, and banana) which you can drink individually (40Kč) or in a sampler (130Kč). Beer comes in regular sizes as well as in 4L towers that dominate the dining rooms. Food is served in enormous portions, and the football-sized pork knee (205Kč per kg) could be hazardous if it fell from any kind of height. Look for little beer icons on the menu—they denote dishes made with beer.

⇆ B: Karlovo náměstí. From the Metro, take Ječná east away from the river; Pivovarský Dům is on

the right at the corner of Ječná and Štěpánská. $ Czech dishes 155-295Kč. Entrees 105-385Kč. Small beer 40Kč. ⏰ Open daily 11am-11:30pm.

LEICA GALLERY PRAGUE CAFE $

Školská 28 ☎222 211 567; www.lgp.cz

Artsy travelers should stop in to this photography-themed gallery and cafe. The gallery in the back exhibits the work of international and local photographers and offers a new show every month. The cafe itself displays photographs, too, in addition to selling an impressive variety of monographs and magazines. As for food, the selection is small—three kinds of sandwiches and some quick bites. Try one of the exotic lemonades, which come in nettle, hemp, rooibos, and elderberry flavors.

🚇 B: Karlovo náměstí. From the Metro, head away from the river down Žitná. Školská is the 2nd left. $ Soup 38Kč. Sandwiches 59-67Kč. Coffee 39-50Kč. Gallery admission varies, but usually 70Kč, students 40Kč, and art students 30Kč. Cash only. ⏰ Open M-F 11am-9pm, Sa-Su 2-10pm.

POD KŘÍDLEM NOCI CZECH $$$

Národní 10 ☎224 951 741; www.podkridlemnoci.cz

This innovative restaurant has two faces: the modern, green-chaired cafe that's visible to the outside world and the hidden second room, where people gather to eat in absolute darkness two times per week. Should you choose the second option, you'll need a reservation, and you'll have to remove all light-producing objects before you enter. The entire experience costs 790Kč, and includes one of the four set menus and a live performance (all in total darkness). This option is recommended for ugly dates. If, on the other hand, you actually find your date attractive, dine in the properly lit cafe downstairs, which serves a handful of meat entrees and some old-school Czech desserts at surprisingly reasonable prices.

🚇 B: Národní třída. From the Metro, walk north on Spálená, turn left on Národní, and head toward the river. Take the 3rd left onto Voršilská. The restaurant is on the left (despite its address on Národní). $ Entrees 129-245Kč. Set menu 790Kč. ⏰ Open M 11am-4pm, Tu-F 11am-11pm.

CAFÉ RYBKA CAFE $

Opatovická 7 ☎224 931 265; rybkapub.cz

Antique typewriters hang on the book-lined walls of this smoky, cheap cafe. You'll have to compete for table space with Czech hipsters (both young and middle-aged), who'll be feeding on toast (25-45Kč), or, more likely, on beer and cigarettes. When the cafe closes at 10pm, patrons usually move to the cafe's sister; just down the street, the bar Malá Ryba offers everything at the same prices, and stays open 'til 2am.

🚇 B: Národní třída. From the Metro, walk down Ostrovní toward the river. Take the 1st left at Opatovická and follow it around the curve. The cafe is on the right. $ Breakfast 40-45Kč. Coffee 28-40Kč. Beer 17-35Kč. Cash only. ⏰ Open M-F 9:15am-10pm, Sa-Su 10am-10pm.

U MATĚJÍČKŮ CZECH $$

Náplavní 5 ☎224 917 136; www.umatejicku.cz

U Matějíčků does solid Czech favorites right. For an introduction to Czech beer pairings, go for the "Big Board full of Goodies" (199Kč), which includes spicy sausage, head cheese, smoked pork neck, hot peppers, pickled onions, and Hermelin, Edam, and *olomoucké tvarůžky* cheeses. The lunch menu (79-99Kč) is also cheap and filling.

🚇 B: Karlovo náměstí. From the Metro, head toward Resslova. Take the 2nd right onto Dittrichova; the restaurant is on the left at the fork. $ Entrees 109-249Kč. Beer 15-32Kč. ⏰ Open daily 11am-11pm.

CAFÉ LOUVRE CAFE $$

Národní třída 22 ☎224 930 949; www.cafelouvre.cz

This smart Parisian bistro has brought French sophistication to Prague since 1902, serving figures like Kafka, Einstein, and Karel Čapek. It had too much class for its own good, though: during the Communist coup in 1948 its furniture was flung out the windows (defenestrated!). The cafe wasn't renovated until after the '89 revolution. Welcome back, capitalism. Stop by for a breakfast plate (109-149Kč), or for something small later in the day (quiche 129Kč). Any of the mouthwatering cakes on display (46-69Kč) will go well with Louvre's coffee and the view overlooking Národní třída.

🚇 B: Národní třída. From the Metro, head north on Spálená and turn left onto Národní třída. The cafe is to the left. $ Entrees 129-319Kč. Coffee 39-55Kč. ⏰ Open M-F 8am-11:30pm, Sa-Su 9am-11:30pm.

ZVONICE FRENCH $$$$

Jindřišská věž ☎224 220 009; www.restaurantzvonice.cz

Visitors to this intimate restaurant inside historic St. Henry Tower have to share space with the tower's wooden scaffolding and an old bell. It's definitely a splurge, but the setting is unparalleled—perfect for a candlelit dinner, interrupted only by the shaking of the tower when the bells chime. The entrees feature mostly venison and other meat, all prepared in expensive-sounding ways (450-790Kč). If you'd like to make alcohol the focus of your night, try the downstairs **Whiskeria,** which offers some 400 kinds of whiskey at prices that are both student- and billionaire-friendly, depending on what you choose from the enormous menu.

🚇 A or B: Můstek. From Wenceslas Sq., walk down Jindřišská. Zvonice is the giant tower at the end of the street. ℹ Reservations recommended. Dress to impress. Whiskeria ☎224 248 645; www.whiskeria.cz. $ Expect to pay 1000Kč for the full dinner experience. Lunch menu 290Kč. ⏰ Open daily 11:30am-midnight. Kitchen closes 10pm. Whiskeria open daily 10am-midnight.

RESTAURACE U ZPĚVÁČKŮ CZECH, ITALIAN $$

Na struze 7 ☎224 930 493; www.restauraceuzpevacku.com

This place has been a hangout of opera singers, a meeting place for political dissidents, and a drug lair (not all at once). Today, it's an unpretentious restaurant that serves Czech and Italian dishes. The fried cheese with fries and tartar sauce (122Kč) is always a safe bet, while the big selection of spaghetti, risotto, and gnocchi will do if it's Italian cuisine you're after.

🚇 B: Národní třída. Head toward the river down Ostrovní. Turn left onto Pštrossova and then take the 1st slight right. The restaurant is on the right. $ Entrees 124-198Kč. Beer 21-68Kč. ⏰ Open M-F 10am-2am, Sa-Su 11am-2am.

RESTAURACE U ŽALUDŮ CZECH $

Na Zbořenci 5 ☎776 327 118; www.lunchtime.cz/u-zaludu

Don't search for this restaurant in any other travel guide—it's the kind of place where old Czech men hang out, drink beer, smoke cigarettes, and turn and stare if somebody unknown shows up. We are listing it as an interesting cultural experience, so if you're feeling too pampered by the tourist establishments, stop by. The ridiculously cheap food is served only at lunch, but the ridiculously cheap beer flows non-stop.

🚇 B: Karlovo náměstí. From the station, head toward Resslova. Take the 1st right onto Na Zderaze and right onto Na Zbořenci. ℹ Czech menus only. $ Meals 69-79Kč. Beer 14-24Kč. Shots 25-50Kč. Cash only. ⏰ Open M-F 10:30am-11pm, Sa-Su 11am-11pm.

DYNAMO FUSION $$

Pštrossova 29 ☎224 932 020; www.dynamorestaurace.cz

Dynamo prides itself on being the kind of restaurant where you can't get fried cheese—the menu aims to surprise with such combinations as quesadilla with aubergine chutney, or spaghetti with arugula and anchovies. There are only three traditional Czech meals on the menu, and their price tags (190-225Kč) make the other cuisines more appealing. The lime-green interior may have been edgy back in '99 when the restaurant opened; today it comes off as a bit run-down. The walls sport some Andy Warhol pieces, one of them signed.

🚇 B: Národní třída. From the Metro, walk down Ostrovní toward the river and take the 3rd left on Pštrossova; Dynamo is on the right. $ Entrees 150-255Kč. Desserts 60-135Kč. Beer 37Kč. ⏰ Open daily 11:30am-midnight.

CAFÉ ROYAL — CAFE $$

Myslíkova 24 — ☎224 913 037; www.lunchtime.cz/royal-cafe

The real deal at this vaguely colonial cafe is the lunch specials (84-105Kč). There are always five options to choose from, all with a daily soup (which may arrive before you order, if you come here often enough). Coffee and an apple strudel with vanilla ice cream can be added to your lunch for just 55Kč. The lunch menus are in Czech, but the waitresses will happily translate. On sunny days, the terrace is a great place to lounge and watch passersby.

🚇 B: Karlovo náměstí. From the Metro, walk north and turn left onto Odborů. Continue until it runs into Myslíkova. The cafe is on the right. $ Chicken dishes 109-145Kč. Desserts 25-65Kč. ⏰ Open M-F 11am-midnight, Sa-Su noon-midnight. Lunch M-F 11am-3pm.

STARÉ MĚSTO

The rule of thumb for dining out in Staré Město is to follow the locals. Due to the density of tourism, there are a lot of tourist traps more than willing to serve food for twice the price you'd pay in a more residential neighborhood. There are a few grocery stores (Žabka, Albert), but the best place to shop for food is **Tesco MY** (Národní 26 ⏰ Open M-Sa 8am-9pm, Su 9am-8pm.), which has low prices and a large selection.

👍 HAVELSKÁ KORUNA — CZECH $

Havelská 21 — ☎224 228 769

As authentic as anything you might find in Staré Město, Havelská Koruna may be a bit intimidating at first: if you're standing in the lunch line, you'd better have your order from the Czech-language menu ready. But it's hard to go wrong; this is real food for real people. If you're in the market for an enormous dessert, try one of their sweet meals, like *šišky s mákem* (potato dumplings with poppy seeds) or *buchtičky s krémem* (buns in custard). The seating area is very cozy; during lunch hour you may even need to share space with some new friends.

🚇 A or B: Můstek. From the station, head north on na Můstku and continue as it turns into Melantrichova. Take a right on Havelská. The restaurant will be on the left. $ Sides 13-26Kč. Soups 21-33Kč. Entrees 35-79Kč. Cash only. ⏰ Open daily 10am-8pm.

👍 GRAND CAFÉ ORIENT — CAFE $$

Ovocný trh 19 — ☎224 224 240; www.grandcafeorient.cz

Grand Café Orient is supposedly the world's only Cubist cafe. It is located on the second floor of **Black Madonna House** (see **Sights**), and it originally closed after just 10 years in business when the winds of fashion changed. Luckily, the cafe reopened 80 years later when the taste for Cubist architecture returned. Come here after your visit to the Cubist museum (or skip the museum portion altogether) and have a delicious spinach crepe (95Kč) or one of the other light meals on the menu. Bonus points: guess the shape of their special dessert, "cubist cake."

🚇 B: Náměstí Republiky. From Old Town Sq., walk toward Church of Our Lady Before Týn. Keep the church on your right and continue down Celetná. The cafe is at the fork of Celetná and Ovocný trh, on the 2nd floor, through the museum entrance. $ Crepes 95-140Kč. Desserts 25-60Kč. Coffee 45-85Kč. Cash only. ⏰ Open M-F 9am-10pm, Sa-Su 10am-10pm.

BEAS VEGETARIAN DHABA INDIAN, VEGETARIAN $

Týnská 19 ☎608 035 727; www.beas-dhaba.cz

This vegetarian buffet is about as good a deal as you can get in the Old Town. It's cheap, tasty, and while most restaurants here try to rip you off on your teeny-tiny beverage, the water at Beas is free. The selection changes daily, but you can always count on basmati rice, two kinds of *daal*, samosas, and a daily special.

 # B: Náměstí Republiky. From Old Town Sq., walk toward Church of Our Lady Before Týn, pass it on the left, and continue down Týnska. After you pass the church, keep to the left on Týnska—don't go straight. Turn left into a small courtyard; Beas Vegetarian Dhaba is next to Hostel Týn. i Other locations at Vlastislavova 24 ([M]Národní Třída), Sokolovská 93 ([M]Křížikova), Bělehradská 90 ([M]I.P. Pavlova). [$] Self-service food 16Kč per 100g. Lassi 22Kč. Coffee 24-32Kč. ⏰ Open M-F 11am-8pm, Sa noon-8pm, Su noon-6pm.

LOKÁL CZECH $$

Dlouhá 33 ☎222 316 265; www.ambi.cz

Let this place be your introduction to a uniquely Czech way of treating beer—the "tank system." The beer skips pasteurization and is instead stored in giant tanks—not kegs—where it remains cut off from oxygen. The beer's first meeting with air is when it's poured. The menu, which changes daily, comprises traditional Czech dishes served inside a single arched hallway that's as long as a street block and echoes with conversation. Lokál is packed with locals, so it's a good idea to make a reservation.

 # B: Náměstí Republiky. From Old Town Sq., head northeast past the Jan Hus statue, and continue on Dlouhá. Lokál is on the left. [$] Sides 35-45Kč. Buffet appetizers 39-89Kč. Entrees 99-159Kč. Beer 29-39Kč. ⏰ Open M-F 11am-1am, Sa noon-1am, Su noon-10pm. Kitchen open M-F 11am-9:45pm, Sa noon-9:45pm, Su noon-8:45pm.

LEHKÁ HLAVA VEGETARIAN $$

Boršov 2 ☎222 220 665; www.lehkahlava.cz

Even alpha-wolf carnivores should consider this cozy restaurant whose name means "Clear Mind." The interior was created by a number of Czech designers, and each room has a different feel (there's one that looks like a starry night sky), but the atmosphere remains relaxed throughout. Unlike many vegetarian restaurants, this one delivers big plates of great food: try the eggplant quesadilla (145Kč), a blasphemy by Mexican standards but tasty nevertheless. For dessert, go for millet carrot cake covered in chocolate (70Kč), or, if you're low on energy, have some of the Brazilian guarana juice, which has three times the caffeine of coffee (50-75Kč).

 # A: Staroměstská. From Old Town Sq., head west and turn left at the river. Continue on Křižovnické as it becomes Smetanovo nábřeží, then make a quick left fork onto Karoliny Světlé. Then, make a left onto Boršov (it's a tiny street). i Reservations recommended. [$] Sides 25-45Kč. Salads 125-145Kč. Entrees 140-175Kč. Desserts 70-80Kč. ⏰ Open M-F 11:30am-11:30pm, Sa-Su noon-11:30pm. Lunch menu until 3:30pm. Between 3:30-5pm, only drinks, cold appetizers, and desserts. Brunch served 1st Su of the month 10:30am-2pm.

DUENDE CAFE, BAR $

Karolíny Světlé 30 ☎775 186 077; www.barduende.cz

One of the many small bars that cluster around this area, Duende has plenty of personality—so much that it could be mistaken for a junk shop. Buoys hang next to leaping tigers, old guitars, and Christian posters...you get the picture. The small round tables are perfect for friendly conversations—if you have nobody to talk to, try to engage one of the artsy student types brooding over her diary. Drinks are cheap, and there's a small menu of snacks (35-99Kč).

 # B: Národní třída. Walk up on Spálená and turn left on Národní třída. Turn right at Karolíny Světlé, and continue as it curves to the left and to the right. Duende is on the right after the street narrows. [$] Beer 20-35Kč. Coffee 30-55Kč. Cash only. ⏰ Open M-F 1pm-midnight, Sa 3pm-midnight, Su 4pm-midnight.

KRÁSNÝ ZTRÁTY

CAFE $

Náprstkova 10 ☎775 755 142

"Beautiful Losses" is where it's at, at least if you ask local art students, intellectuals, and similar loafers. You'll rarely see someone over 40 here, and the place is clearly geared toward the younger crowds. Photography exhibits hang on the walls and the cafe frequently hosts cultural events. Food is light and reasonably cheap. Try the chicken quesadilla (95Kč), or if you happen to be around late at night, get the "midnight Hermelín" cheese (35-69Kč). If it's a busy night and you want to be really cool, grab some chairs from inside and sit outside, smoke heavily, and perch your beer on the windowsill.

🚇 A: Staroměstská. From Old Town Sq., set out in the direction of Charles Bridge, but continue south on Jilská. When you reach the intersection with Skořepka, take a right and continue to Betlémské Náměstí. Continue as it turns into Náprstkova. The cafe is on the left. [$] Breakfast 85-95Kč. Coffee 29-66Kč. Beer 20-39Kč. ⏰ Open M-F 9am-1am. Sa-Su noon-1am.

CHOCO CAFÉ

CHOCOLATE $

Liliová 4 ☎222 222 519; www.choco-cafe.cz

As the name implies, these guys take their chocolate seriously. Hot chocolate is made on the spot using melted chocolate chips instead of some packaged mixture. Choose from an array of flavors that includes ginger, sea salt, and chili, or get the evening started by spiking your chocolate with rum, egg nog, or whiskey. We also highly recommend their desserts; the tiramisu (60Kč) is massive. This space was a postcard museum before Choco Café came along—be sure to scope out the hilariously old-fashioned collection on the walls.

🚇 A: Staroměstská. From Old Town Sq., set out in the direction of Charles Bridge, but continue south on Jilská. When you reach the intersection with Skořepka, take a right, and continue to Betlémské Náměstí. Pass the church and take a right on Liliová. The cafe is on the right. [$] Bruschetta 78-93Kč. Cakes 60Kč. Hot chocolate 55-75Kč. ⏰ Open M-Sa 10am-10pm, Su 10am-8pm.

APETIT

CAFETERIA $

Dlouhá 23 ☎222 329 853; www.apetitpraha.cz

Apetit embodies the way Czechs and tourists are seen as two different species by most restaurants in Staré Město. There are actually two parts of Apetit: a no-nonsense eatery serving hungry locals upstairs and a gussied-up restaurant downstairs, serving dishes that contain shark, swordfish, and the like at exorbitant prices. Choose the former, which may be one of the cheapest places to eat in Staré Město. Grab a tray, take some silverware, wait in the cafeteria-style lunch line, and use sign language to indicate which of the traditional Czech meals you'd like. It's normal to sit at the same table with strangers in the cramped dining area: just say *dobrý den* (hello) as you join and *na shledanou* (goodbye) when you leave.

🚇 B: Náměstí Republiky. From Old Town Sq., head northeast past the Jan Hus statue, and continue on Dlouhá. Apetit is on the left. [$] Lunch menu 72Kč. Entrees with soda 89-92Kč. Beer 17-25Kč. Cash only. ⏰ Open M-F 9am-8pm, Sa-Su 10am-8pm.

BOHEMIA BAGEL

AMERICAN $

Masná 2 ☎224 812 560; www.bohemiabagel.cz

Other (less touristy) locations at Lázeňská 19, Dukelských Hrdinu 48

Designed for homesick Americans, the Bohemia Bagel chain brings bagels, free coffee refills (49Kč), Ben & Jerry's ice cream, democracy, and more to the Old Continent. Breakfast is served all day, but the restaurant delivers solid lunch options too: burgers, sandwiches, and grilled meat. And, if you need to send an email home or tweet about how *crazy* Europe is, Bohemia Bagel also serves internet.

🚇 A: Staroměstská. From Old Town Sq., head northeast past the Jan Hus statue, and continue on Dlouhá. At the roundabout, take a right on Masná. [$] Bagels 25-80Kč. Sandwiches 95-130Kč. Coffee 35-50Kč. Computers 2Kč per min. Wi-Fi 1Kč per min. Cash only. ⏰ Open daily 8am-9:30pm.

LA CASA BLŮ LATIN AMERICAN $$

Kozí 15 ☎221 818 270; www.lacasablu.cz

Burritos and quesadillas are on the menu, but calling La Casa Blů a Mexican restaurant would do this cool hang-out an injustice. The Latin American chefs also prepare South American sandwiches, plus there's Chilean wine on the menu. A generous happy hour until 6pm includes some cheap meals (tacos 116Kč) and drinks (beer 19-26Kč). La Casa Blů also serves as the local ambassador for Latin culture: the walls are covered with the work of Latin artists, and Latin musicians perform here regularly. La Casa Blů was also the filming site for parts of the Czech cult film Samotáři (*Loners*, 2000)—you can't get much cooler.

🚇 B: Náměstí Republiky. From Old Town Sq., head northeast and continue on Dlouhá. At the roundabout, take a left on Kozí. $ Burritos 168Kč. Quesadillas 148-168Kč. Beer 21-43Kč. ⏰ Open M-F 11am-midnight or later, Su 2pm-late.

KLUB ARCHITEKTŮ INTERNATIONAL $$

Betlémské náměstí 5A ☎224 248 878; www.klubarchitektu.com

If you're in the market for a candlelit dinner in a cavernous setting, this is the place. The cuisine bills itself as "international," but don't expect anything too exotic—it's mostly good old Czech pub entrees in fancier sauces. Given the sophisticated ambiance, the prices are surprisingly reasonable; there's many a dump that will try to sell you this fare for the same price. Oh, and if the ridiculously low-hanging lamp happens to be poking your "beef medallion with apples in cream sauce and mashed potatoes" (185Kč), just ask the waiter to raise the light fixture.

🚇 B: Národní třída. From Old Town Sq., set out in the direction of Charles Bridge, but stay south on Jilská. Take a right at the intersection with Skořepka, continue to Betlémské náměstí, and then turn right into a courtyard (it's next to Betlémska Church). The restaurant is down a staircase. $ Sides 30-40Kč. Entrees 145-185Kč. Desserts 55-80Kč. ⏰ Open daily 11:30am-midnight.

ZAHRÁDKA U KRISTIÁNA BEER GARDEN $

Smetanovo nábřeží 5

This bare-bones assemblage of tables and sunshades has only about three items on the menu: sausage (65Kč), Hermelín (80Kč), and "chicken steak" (180Kč), all grilled on a tiny grill in plain sight. If this sounds tempting, walk down the steps to the river, sit on one of the benches, and enjoy the view. (The view goes well with a beer.)

🚇 A: Staroměstská. From Old Town Sq., head toward the river and when you reach it, turn left on Křižovnická. Continue as it becomes Smetanovo nábřeží. The outdoor terrace will be close to the river on your right, close to the river, down some stairs. $ Food 65-180Kč. Beer 32-42Kč. Cash only. ⏰ Officially open Apr-Sept daily 11am-10pm, but closing time depends on demand and weather.

PIVNICE U RUDOLFINA CZECH $$

Křižovnická 10 ☎222 328 758

You need to know what you're looking for to find it, because the tiny street-level floor doesn't hint at the size of this smoky underground pub. It's quintessentially Czech—there are no English menus and waiters aren't very well-equipped linguistically—but you'll do good to pop in for a traditional Czech meal or for a beer (served from the tank).

🚇 A: Staroměstská. From Old Town Sq., head toward the river and, when you reach it, turn right on Křižovnická. $ Meat entrees 99-199Kč. Beer 25-38Kč. Cash only. ⏰ Open daily 10:30am-11pm. Lunch menu until 2pm.

JOSEFOV

Josefov is full of tourist traps that are to be avoided at all costs. If you do find yourself sightseeing around lunchtime, there are some very cheap lunch menus, even at the more expensive restaurants. Ask about these deals before you sit down.

[✓] KOLKOVNA — CZECH $$$

V Kolkovně 8 ☎224 819 701; www.kolkovna-restaurant.cz

If there's one restaurant in Josefov that's worth the price, it's Kolkovna—not that it's very expensive in the first place. The focus is on grilled meat and skewers, but chances are that whatever dish you order will be tasty and generously portioned. Locals come here for the tank beer, and you should consider yourself lucky if you're able to get a table without a reservation at dinner time. Try the lunch menu first (95Kč)—even lunches here tend to be more creative than elsewhere.

⇟ B: Staroměstská. In the square with the Franz Kafka statue. To get here from Old Town Sq., head north on Dlouhá and turn left on Dušní. $ Czech specialties 169-345Kč. Beer 36-43Kč. ⏰ Open daily 11am-midnight.

LE COURT CAFÉ/GALERIE — CAFE $

Haštalská 1

There's no food served at Le Court, unless we're talking about food for the soul, in which case there's plenty—the indoor part of the cafe serves as a gallery that hosts a new contemporary art exhibit every month. The real place to be, however, is the courtyard, with its wobbly wooden tables and cozy nooks. Decorated with rampant ivy and other greenery, the courtyard is a great place to discuss anything and everything over a beer, coffee, or hot chocolate.

⇟ A: Staroměstská. From Old Town Sq., walk up Dlouhá and, after the roundabout, continue straight on Kozí. The cafe is inside a courtyard in the building that says "Galerie." $ Beer 35-40Kč. Coffee 35-50Kč. Cash only. ⏰ Open daily 10am-10pm.

LA BODEGUITA DEL MEDIO — CUBAN $$$

Kaprova 5 ☎224 813 922; www.bodeguita.cz

Few places in the neighborhood are as hopping as this Cuban restaurant-bar (it doesn't hurt La Bodeguita's odds that most of the neighborhood is a cemetery). Live Latin music flows as freely as the mojitos and margaritas. While most of the meat entrees are on the pricier side, it's possible to keep within the budget by getting one of their soups (85Kč) and perhaps combining it with an appetizer. This is also the place to buy Cuban cigars.

⇟ A: Staroměstská. About 25m east of the Metro on Kaprova. ℹ Latin music and dancing most nights. $ Creole dishes 250-380Kč. Grilled meat dishes 310-440Kč. Beer 60-95Kč. ⏰ Open M 9am-2am, Tu-Sa 9am-4am, Su 9am-2am.

PIVNICE U PIVRNCE — CZECH $

Maiselova 3 ☎222 329 404; www.upivrnce.cz

This could well be the cheapest place in Josefov, offering ordinary, unadorned Czech cuisine. U Pivrnce seems to compete with all the classy tourist traps of the neighborhood by doing the exact opposite—by which we mean not having any class at all. The walls are decorated with vulgar, misogynistic cartoons by a well-known local cartoonist. But even this is Czech authenticity—far more so than what you'd find in the prettied up establishments nearby.

⇟ A: Staroměstská. From the Old Town Sq., walk past the Church of St. Nicholas and onto Maiselova. U Pivrnce is on the left. $ Czech entrees 95-114Kč. Desserts 35-75Kč. Beer 15-35Kč. ⏰ Open daily 11am-midnight.

MALÁ STRANA

Restaurants in Malá Strana tend to be pricey, but there are a few good finds. Thanks to the high proportion of artistic types, the neighborhood has plenty of marvelous cafes. There are no supermarkets in Malá Strana because the neighborhood's aesthetic is under official protection, but to the south there's **Nový Smíchov,** a big shopping mall near [M]Anděl.

👍 BAR BAR — INTERNATIONAL, BAR $$

Všehrdova 17 — ☎257 312 246; www.bar-bar.cz

Bar Bar's blend of local flavor and exotic influences, and its balance of excitement and comfort, would make it a find in any neighborhood. Hiding just off the main street in Malá Strana, this gem has an original menu featuring mostly international dishes, such as souvlaki (174Kč) and fried, cheese-filled jalapeños (79Kč). But the house specialty is the crepes, both sweet (79-85Kč) and savory (125-139Kč). Bar Bar is also—surprise!—a bar, so don't hesitate to come by at night for drinks, all in the company of brooding poets and painters.

➤ A: Malostranská. From the station, walk south or take a tram 12, 20, or 22 to Hellichova. Continue walking south on Újezd, then turn left on Všehrdova. The restaurant is on the right. [S] Entrees 139-195Kč. Desserts 95-125Kč. Beer 23-38Kč. Cocktails 90-175Kč. ⏰ Open M-Th noon-midnight, F-Sa noon-2am, Su noon-midnight.

DOBRÁ TRAFIKA — CAFE, WINE BAR $

Újezd 37 — ☎257 320 188; www.dobratrafika.cz

If you go through the unremarkable store in front, you'll discover an excellent cafe, popular with artists, musicians, and other tea-drinking types. Speaking of tea, this place has a four-page menu dedicated to the stuff, in addition to coffee from 20 different countries and the rare Primátor beer on tap. If you're hungry, try the weirdest pita bread you've ever seen: fillings range from banana (29Kč) to Georgian eggplant (78Kč). There's also a small wine bar downstairs.

➤ A: Malostranská. From the Metro, walk south or take tram 12, 20, or 22 to Hellichova. Continue walking south on Újezd; the specialty store is to the right. [S] Pitas 29-78Kč. Coffee 35Kč. Beer 29-32Kč. Cash only. ⏰ Open M-F 7:30am-11pm, Sa-Su 9am-11pm.

TLUSTÁ MYŠ — CZECH $$

Všehrdova 19 — ☎605 282 506; www.tlustamys.cz

Tlustá Myš ("Fat Mouse"), next door to Bar Bar, has similarly awesome food and prices. The main difference between the two is that Fat Mouse focuses on Czech cuisine and feels down-to-earth, with wooden tables and brick walls. Grilled sausages (55Kč) are cheaper here than at a street vendor, and can be ordered from a menu decorated with cute mice drawings (the real reason to come here). We recommend the steak California (chicken cutlet with cheese and peaches), which, name aside, is a traditional Czech meal.

➤ A: Malostranská. From the Metro, walk south or take tram 12, 20, or 22 to Hellichova. Continue walking south on Újezd and turn left onto Všehrdova. The restaurant is on the right. [S] Entrees 119-165Kč. Desserts 49-59Kč. Beer 20-34Kč. 20% discount daily noon-2pm. Cash only. ⏰ Open M-Sa noon-midnight, Su noon-10pm.

POD PETŘÍNEM — CZECH $$

Hellichova 5 — ☎257 224 408; www.pivnicepodpetrinem.cz

This low-key Czech pub is as cheap as it looks. There are just a few menu items: goulash (85Kč), chicken with rice (95Kč), and pork knee (165Kč), in addition to a set of alternating lunch dishes. There's no English menu, but the staff will kindly translate. Frankly, we were surprised to find such a no-nonsense pub in the middle of Malá Strana.

➤ A: Malostranská. From the Metro, walk south or take tram 12, 20, or 22 to Hellichova. The restaurant is at the intersection of Újezd and Hellichova. [S] Entrees 85-165Kč. Lunch menu 99Kč. Beer 16-36Kč. ⏰ Open daily 11am-12:30am.

LOKÁL U BÍLÉ KUŽELKY   CZECH $$

Míšeňská 12   ☎257 212 014; www.ambi.cz

Decorated like its Old Town cousin, Lokál changes its menu of reasonably priced Czech dishes daily. Aside from normal beer, Lokál also offers *šnyt*, a sort of half beer—most of the glass is occupied by beer foam, which keeps the liquid below fresh and unoxidized. It's the perfect lunchtime solution to the age-old dilemma "have another beer or not?"

✇ A: Malostranská. From the Metro, head south along the river on Klárov past the Kafka Museum. Take a right at Míšeňská; the restaurant is on the right. Ⓢ Lunch menu 89-115Kč. Dinner entrees 159-205Kč. Beer 29-38Kč. Ⓩ Open daily 11:30am-midnight.

MLÝNSKÁ KAVÁRNA   CAFE $

Všehrdova 14   ☎608 444 490

Students love this watermill cafe on Kampa Island, with a functioning water wheel and a terrace that's perfect for sunny days. The food pickings are rather slim, but the daily soup and one of the beer pairings will stave hunger off.

✇ A: Malostranská. From the Metro, head south along the river to Kampa. The cafe is at the south-west corner of the island; look for a giant water wheel. The cafe's address is on Všehrdova, but the entrance is from Kampa Island. Ⓢ Food 24-59Kč. Beer 21-36Kč. Coffee 34-74Kč. Cash only. Ⓩ Open daily noon-midnight.

PÁTÝ PŘES DEVÁTÝ (5/9 CAFÉ)   CAFE, BAR $

Nosticova 8   ☎736 425 011; www.59cafebar.cz

This new cafe is rapidly ascending the popularity ladder among Malá Strana locals. The best feature is the cozy terrace, which sits right above the Vltava (or rather, above the tiny rivulet that separates Kampa from Malá Strana). There are toasts and other snacks, but the drinks are the main event.

✇ A: Malostranská. From the Metro, head south along the river, all the way to Kampa. When you reach the island's park, take the 1st right just after the small statue. The cafe is behind the bridge. Ⓢ Toasts 59Kč. Beer 18-37Kč. Coffee 39-60Kč. Ⓩ Open daily 11am-11pm.

WIGWAM   INTERNATIONAL $$

Zborovská 54   ☎257 311 707; www.cafebarwigwam.cz

The menu at the ambiguously ethnic Wigwam oscillates between Czech experiments, like the pork neck burger (149Kč); American non-experiments, like the classic hamburger (149Kč); and curveball Asian dishes, like the *mat saman* curry (170Kč). The blue cheese nachos (90Kč) are enough to start any party—any cheese party, that is.

✇ A: Malostranská. From the Metro, walk south or take tram 12, 20, or 22 to Újezd. From the tram stop, walk toward the river until you reach Zborovská and turn right. The restaurant is on the left. Ⓢ Entrees 80-195Kč. Beer 20-40Kč. Cocktails 60-90Kč. Ⓩ Open M-F 11am-1am, Sa noon-1am, Su noon-10pm.

CAFE KAFÍČKO   CAFE $

Míšeňská 10   ☎724 151 795

A quiet stop in the middle of tourist town, Cafe Kafíčko is also one of the first nonsmoking cafes in all of Prague. Its coffee comes from 12 different countries, is made from whole beans on the spot, and is *not* served in a paper cup (due to some principled belief about how coffee deserves time and attention). Other than a selection of breakfast items, food is mostly limited to dessert (15-55Kč).

✇ A: Malostranská. From the Metro, head south along the river on Klárov past the Kafka Museum. Take a right at Míšeňská; the restaurant is on the right. Ⓢ Coffee 42-68Kč. Cash only. Ⓩ Open daily 10am-10pm.

KAVÁRNA ČAS   SNACKS $

Míšeňská 2   ☎721 959 903

Kavárna Čas wouldn't be very remarkable if it didn't offer delicious and cheap snacks in this overpriced neighborhood. Toasted cheese sandwiches (45Kč) come with

food

ketchup, and strudel pastries (40-65Kč) are filled with bologna, sausage, or cabbage. The menu has photos of the "Golden Voice of Prague," Karel Gott, visiting the cafe. If you don't know who Karel Gott is, that's one more thing to YouTube tonight.

 # A: Malostranská. From the Metro, head south along the river on Klárov past the Kafka Museum. Take a right at Míšeňská; the restaurant is on the right. $ Toasts 30-60Kč. Beer 20-30Kč. Coffee 20-50Kč. Cash only. ⏰ Open daily 10am-8pm.

HRADČANY

When it comes to most restaurants in Hradčany, we'll quote Admiral Ackbar: "It's a (tourist) trap!" For a cheap bite to eat, try the fast food hole-in-the-wall near the intersection of Pohořelec and Úvoz ($ Hot dogs 25Kč. Cheeseburgers 50Kč.), or the **Žabka** market across the street.

👍 U ZAVĚŠENÝHO KAFE — CZECH $$

Úvoz 6 ☎605 294 595; www.uzavesenyhokafe.com

Unlike so many of the touristy establishments nearby, this restaurant has a strong base of local patrons—in fact, an entire wall is covered by snapshots of customers wearing "U Zavěšenýho Kafe" T-shirts in exotic travel destinations. The portions are huge, and the cozy dining area is segmented into a number of smaller rooms. The inner courtyard is a great place to sit on both sunny and rainy days. Check out the abacus counter near the entrance—it shows the number of coffees that have been purchased in advance by local patrons for the benefit of people without the money to pay. Please don't abuse the honor system.

 # Tram 22: Malostranské náměstí. From the tram stop, walk uphill on Nerudova and continue as it becomes Úvoz. The restaurant is on the right. $ Entrees 85-175Kč. Desserts 22-65Kč. Cash only. ⏰ Open daily 10am-11pm.

ČESKÝ BANÁT — CZECH, ROMANIAN $$

Nerudova 21 ☎721 029 205; http://czrestaurace.ceskybanat.cz

Probably the cheapest restaurant on the block, Český Banát is bare but neat and very welcoming. The owner is Romanian, and it's one of the few places in Prague where you can try cuisine from that corner of the world. To get started, try the *čorba* soup with meat dumplings (55Kč). On your way out, pick up some of the traditional, sugar-covered pastries sold at the entrance.

 # Tram 22: Malostranské náměstí. From the stop, walk uphill on Nerudova. The restaurant is on the left side, next to Little Quarter hostel. $ Entrees 89-129Kč. Sweets 69-115Kč. Lunch menus 89-109Kč. Cash only. ⏰ Open M-Th 9am-9pm, F-Sa 9am-2am, Su 9am-9pm.

BELLAVISTA — CZECH $$$

Strahovské nádvoří 1 ☎220 517 274; www.bella-vista.cz

It doesn't take a genius to figure out that the reason people come here is the *bella vista* (pretty view). The restaurant's wooden tables have some of the best panoramic views of the city, and the prices have been set accordingly. If you want the view for cheap, order a beer or coffee; if you want the view for free, walk down one level to the area full of tourists.

 # The restaurant is below Strahov Monastery. Facing the monastery, turn left and continue until you reach a sloping path leading to the restaurant. $ Czech specials 255Kč. Desserts 120-135Kč. Small beer 65-69Kč. ⏰ Open daily 11am-midnight.

KLÁŠTERNÍ PIVOVAR AND ST. NORBERT RESTAURANT — CZECH $$$

Strahovské nádvoří 301 ☎233 353 155; www.klasterni-pivovar.cz

Turns out Strahov has not only a restaurant, but also a microbrewery with its own signature beer—named after a saint with the somewhat uncommon name, "Norbert." The food isn't necessarily the best thing to happen since St. Norbert was around, but you can enjoy a cool glass of the beer right before going to see the saint's remains, also in glass, at the monastery's gallery. Oh boy!

 # Opposite the Strahov Monastery. i Book tours of the brewery in advance. $ Appetizers 79Kč;

entrees 150-390Kč. St. Norbert beer 35-64Kč. Brewery tours 120Kč; includes 3 small beers. ⏰
Open daily 10am-10pm.

ŽIŽKOV

U SADU
CZECH $$

Škroupovo náměstí 5 ☎222 727 072; www.usadu.cz

This may be one of Žižkov's best-known restaurants. Choose between the patio seating or the dining room, where an entire antique shop dangles from the ceiling. But the coolest part of the restaurant is U Sadu's smoky cellar: behind the gambling machines, a spiral staircase leads to a foosball table and several small rooms filled with young people. Some of the most popular dishes are fried ribs with mustard and horseradish (155Kč) or roasted pork knee (195Kč).

🍴 *A: Jiřího z Poděbrad. From the Metro, cross diagonally through the park (pass in front of the church) and then walk north on Laubova. U Sadu is at the northern side of the square with the roundabout.* Ⓢ *Snacks 55-95Kč. Meat entrees 125-195Kč. Beer 28-33Kč.* ⏰ *Open M-W 9am-2am, Th-Sa 9am-4am, Su 9am-2am. Kitchen open until 2am.*

U VYSTRELENÝHO VOKA
PUB $

U Božích bojovníků 3 ☎222 540 465; www.uvoka.cz

The title of this place means "at the shot-out eye" and over the last 19 years it has become something of a cult establishment. The menu is the opposite of fussy—the only two categories you can choose from are "cold food" and "warm food." Try the inexpensive Danube sausage (35Kč), or, if you want to splurge, the fried cheese (80Kč). The cascading terraces above the pub actually belong to a different establishment, **Kavárna U Voka** (Ⓢ Beer 26-33Kč ⏰ Open M-F 3-10pm, Sa-Su 2-10pm), which is an equally great place to grab a drink. Oh, and if you ask the staff what the name means, you'll get a 30min. lecture on the history of Žižkov. Short answer: it refers to the one-eyed Jan Žižka, the famous Hussite general.

🍴 *Tram 5, 9, or 26: Husinecká. Walk uphill on Seifertova, then turn left on Blahníkova and continue as it turns into Jeronýmova. When you reach Husitská, take a right and then the 1st left into a little alley marked U Božích bojovníků.* Ⓢ *Cold food 30-44Kč. Hot food 35-89Kč.* ⏰ *Open daily 4:30pm-1am.*

AMORES PERROS
MEXICAN $$

Kubelíkova 33 ☎222 733 980; www.amoresperros.cz

The chefs may be Czech and the interior overcompensates (think sombreros and cactuses), but Amores Perros is still known as one of the better Mexican places in Prague (and the only one in Žižkov). Sizzling enchiladas (109Kč) smothered in heart-stopping sauce are the way to go. Come here for lunch, as the menu deals (79Kč) are filling and superb.

🍴 *Tram 5, 9, or 26: Olšanské náměstí. From the stop, walk 2 blocks west on Kubelíkova.* Ⓢ *Salads 84-114Kč. Burritos 164-199Kč.* ⏰ *Open M-Th 11am-midnight, F 11am-1am, Sa 11am-midnight, Su 12:30pm-midnight.*

U MARIÁNSKEHO OBRAZU
CZECH $$

Kubelíkova 26 ☎222 722 007; www.umarianskehoobrazu.cz

This down-to-earth Czech restaurant serves Pilsner from the tank and offers steaks from young cows, along with other, more traditional fare. If you haven't yet, try the Slovak specialty *bryndzové halušky* (115Kč)—the rough translation is sheep's cheese dumplings with bacon, but there's no precise translation for the goodness they entail.

🍴 *A: Jiřího z Poděbrad. From the Metro, cross diagonally through the park and then take Milešovská; Kubelíkova is on the other side of the Žižkov tower park.* Ⓢ *Meals 115-155Kč. Steaks 210-360Kč. Beer 19-35Kč. Cash only.* ⏰ *Open daily 11am-midnight.*

food

ZELENÁ KUCHYNĚ — VEGETARIAN $$

Milíčova 5 ☎222 220 114; www.zelenakuchyne.cz

Clean, fresh, wholesome ingredients combine to make any vegetarian orgasm. Check out the grilled tomatoes with goat cheese and blackberry dressing...you should really get a room. Top off the pleasurable experience with a little dessert: savor cinnamon pancakes made from oatmeal and apples and topped with ice cream and blueberry sauce.

⇒ Trams 5, 9, or 26: Lipanská. From the stop, walk west on Seifertova and turn right at Milíčova. The restaurant is on the left. [$] Menus from 90Kč. Entrees 110-290Kč. Cash only. ⏰ Open M-F 11am-8pm.

VINOHRADY

Almost every street in Vinohrady has a small restaurant or hidden cafe known and frequented by locals; the opportunities for exploration are unlimited. For groceries, there's a **Tesco** near I.P. Pavlova (Vocelova 11 ☎222 212 645 ⏰ Open daily 6am-10pm.) and an **Albert** near Jiřího z Poděbrad. (Vinohradská 50 ☎800 402 402 ⏰ Open daily 8am-9pm.)

> **sweet dreams**
>
> If you're looking for an after-dinner treat but want something a bit more exotic than a hot fudge sundae, try the Czech bakery favorite: honey cake. The delectable creation combines the sweetness of honey with multiple layers of cake-and-cream-filled paradise. Just one taste may be enough to convince you to move to Prague permanently.

★ VINÁRNA U PALEČKA — CZECH $$

Nitranská 22 ☎224 250 626; www.vinarnaupalecka.cz

The rustic interior may look unassuming, but if you're after some great traditional Czech cuisine, this is the place. The menu is longer and more varied than in most Czech restaurants—it even makes a few attempts at Mexican cuisine—but we suggest sticking to the tried and true. The *svíčková* (beef in sour cream sauce; 139Kč) comes with whipped cream and cranberry jam. The lunch menu items are a steal at just 75Kč.

⇒ A: Jiřího z Poděbrad. From the station, head south on Nitranská; the restaurant is on the left. [$] Entrees 80-230Kč. Beer 25-35Kč. Cash only. ⏰ Open daily 11am-midnight. Lunch menu 11am-4pm.

CAFÉ ŠLÁGR — CAFE $

Francouzská 72 ☎607 277 688; www.kavarnaslagr.cz

True to the spirit of the First Czechoslovak Republic (1918-38), a sign on the wall of this traditional cafe prohibits "all left-wing political discussions." So skip the politics and enjoy the desserts: they are homemade and beautiful. If you're unfamiliar with Czech sweets, the overflowing *věterník* (29Kč) is a good place to start, or perhaps you'd like the cream-filled *kremrole* (15Kč). Coffee (42-75Kč) comes with cow-shaped vessels for milk and is a great complement to the desserts.

⇒ A: Náměstí Míru, or tram 4 or 22: Krymská. From the station, walk southeast along Francouzská. The cafe is on the right. [$] Baked goods 17-40Kč. Breakfast 49-79Kč. Cash only. ⏰ Open M-F 8am-10pm, Sa-Su 10am-10pm. Breakfast served 8am-2pm.

LAS ADELITAS MEXICAN $$

Americká 8 ☎222 542 031; www.lasadelitas.cz

There are several would-be Mexican restaurants in Prague, but Las Adelitas is on top of the food chain when it comes to authenticity. The chefs and owners are from Mexico, and the music is Mexican. Try the *sopa Azteca* (49Kč), a soup with croutons, cheese, sour cream sauce, chili, and avocado; you can be sure you won't get this thing anywhere else around here. Thirsty *amigos* might appreciate a Corona (72Kč); frugal *amigos* will probably stick with a Staropramen (18Kč).

A: Náměstí Míru. From the station, walk down Americká. The restaurant is on the left, past the square with the dinosaur fountain. $ Burritos 145Kč. Enchiladas 169-179Kč. Beer 18-39Kč. Cash only. Open M-F 11am-11pm, Sa-Su 2-11pm. Kitchen open until 10pm.

MAMACOFFEE COFFEE $

Londýnska 49 ☎773 263 333; www.mamacoffee.cz

Find more Mamacoffee outposts at Korunní 46 (Náměstí Míru) or Vodičkova 6 (Charles Square).

Coffee lovers, beware: these people take coffee even more seriously than you do. A staunch adherent of fair trade, organic coffee, Mamacoffee even has its own fair trade roasting facility. There are around 10 kinds of coffee waiting for you to try, and they can be made in all kinds of ways. The only gripe one might have is that there's no Wi-Fi, but this isn't the kind of place where you loaf around all day writing your long-postponed novel anyway.

A: Náměstí Míru. From the station, walk down Rumunská, then take a left at Londýnska. The cafe is on the right. $ Desserts 15-35Kč. Coffee 29-67Kč. Cash only. Open M-F 8:30am-8pm, Sa-Su 10:30am-8pm.

student munchies

If you crave pizza, but want to save money and have an ISIC, we have a nearby alternative for you: **Pizzeria Einstein** (Rumunská 25; www.pizza-einstein.cz $ Pizza 106-159Kč Open 11am-11pm). The ambience might not be up to par with nearby Grosseto's, but if you present your ISIC card in advance and order a pizza, you can get a second for **free** (just be careful not to get ripped off on drinks). Few foreigners know about this trick, as the special red menu that advertises the deal is in Czech.

PIZZERIA GROSSETO ITALIAN $$

Francouzská 2 ☎224 252 778; www.grosseto.cz

Popular with locals and tourists, this Italian chain brings a degree of style to Czech pizzerias, which otherwise tend to be rather unassuming. Made from predominantly Italian ingredients, Grosseto's pizzas are generous, and there are almost 30 kinds to choose from. If you snag a table upstairs, you'll be able to eat with a good view of the St. Ludmila Church.

A: Náměstí Míru. Grosseto is directly across the street from the Metro exit. $ Pizza 125-219Kč. Desserts 85-95Kč. Open daily 11:30am-11pm.

RADOST FX VEGETARIAN $$

Bělehradská 120 ☎603 19 37 11; www.radostfx.cz

Before the club downstairs starts thrumming, head to Radost FX for their vegetarian specialties. You can eat in either the quieter, artsier cafe or the lounge, where mirror tiles, poison-green chandeliers, and red sofas combine for a slight hallucinogenic effect. A menu staple is the heavy "Popeye Burger" (180Kč), which replaces meat with—you guessed it—spinach! But there are many more culinary experiments to try, including the "White Trash Hot Artichoke Dip" (155Kč) and the "Crack Slaw Salad" (90Kč).

C: I.P. Pavlova. From the station, walk east on Jugoslávská. Take a left on Bělehradská. The cafe is on the right. $ Entrées 130-210Kč. Cash only. Open M-Th 11am-midnight, F-Sa 11am-1am, Su 10:30am-midnight.

SOKOLOVNA CZECH $$

Slezská 22 ☎222 524 525; www.restaurantsokolovna.cz

Sokolovna is a notch above your traditional Czech restaurant: it's cleaner, more spacious, and the staff is less grumpy. The walls of this former *sokolovna* (gym) are almost completely covered by old newspapers, but the decoration remains understated. The locals keep coming back for the tank beer and hearty meals. The tourists haven't caught on yet; be a good hipster and get in before it gets mainstream.

A: Náměstí Míru. From the station, head down Slezská. The restaurant is on the right. $ Entrees 139-265Kč. Desserts 77-115Kč. Beer 22-37Kč. Open daily 11am-midnight.

KAVÁRNA ZANZIBAR CAFE $

Americká 15 ☎222 520 315; www.kavarnazanzibar.cz

The wicker chairs outside this cafe make for very relaxed seating; it's no wonder this place has become a local hangout. But there's food too! In addition to breakfast sets (79-149Kč), which are served all day, there's a sizeable selection of croque monsieurs, crepes, omelettes, burritos, and more. The local specialty is the "beer cocktail," a mixtures of beer and either Coke, Sprite, or fruit syrup. Yikes.

A: Náměstí Míru. From the station, walk down Americká. The cafe is on the right at the square with the dinosaur fountain. $ Croques monsieur 65-95Kč. Coffee 36-76Kč. Beer 26-45Kč. Open M-Th 8am-11pm, F 8am-late, Sa 10am-late, Su 10am-11pm. Kitchen closes at 10pm.

BANDITOS MEXICAN $$

Melounová 2 ☎224 941 096; www.banditosrestaurant.cz

Nominally Mexican, Banditos seems to be more concerned with appealing to American expats and tourists than nailing the whole Mexico thing. That's not necessarily a bad thing—in addition to tacos, you also get sandwiches and burgers (including "Coronary Bypass" with fried egg, bacon, cheese, and mayo; 255Kč). The best time to come is the happy hour, which offers some really good deals: tacos for 30Kč, nachos for 50Kč, or ribs for 50Kč.

C: I.P. Pavlova. From the station, head left down Ječná. Fork left at Kateřinská, then take the 1st right onto Melounová. i Free Wi-Fi. $ Sandwiches and burgers 170-215Kč. Mexican dishes 165-270Kč. Open daily 9am-1am. Happy hour 4:30-6:30pm.

U BULÍNŮ CZECH $$

Budečská 2 ☎224 254 676; www.ubulinu.cz

Following the quintessentially Czech tradition of fabricated history, this restaurant has a story of its own. The gist is that the original owners made a deal with Satan to be able to make devilishly good food, after which they grew horns. If you're not in the mood for local food, try the popular cheeseburger, made from Uruguay beef (169Kč). There's also very little smoke in this place: it's one of the few restaurants in Prague that has banned smoking.

A: Náměstí Míru. From the station, walk southeast down Francouzská. The restaurant is 3 blocks down on the corner. $ Czech entrees 130-250Kč. Lunch menu 89Kč. Open daily 11am-11pm.

HOLEŠOVICE

There are no big supermarkets in Holešovice, but there's a grocery on every other corner. For cheap Vietnamese food, try the **Prague Market** (see **Shopping: Markets**).

OUKY DOUKY
CAFE $

Janovského 14 ☎266 711 531; www.oukydouky.cz

A favorite of expats, Ouky Douky is a one-stop shop—restaurant, used book store, internet cafe, and Cuban cigars (20-300Kč). Sit down and get one of their crunchy baguettes, or just browse through the English-language section (it's no Barnes & Noble, but there might be one or two good finds).

☀ C: Vltavská. From the Metro, take tram 1 or 25 or walk along the tracks on Bubenské for 1 stop to Strossmayerovo náměstí. Facing the church, take a left onto Janovského. The cafe is to the right.
Ⓢ Breakfast 98-148Kč. Sandwiches 86-126Kč. Coffee 29-39Kč. Internet 65Kč per hr. Cash only.
Ⓩ Open daily 8am-midnight.

LA CRÊPERIE
CREPERIE $

Janovského 4 ☎220 878 040; www.lacreperie.cz

Many cafes in Prague will fix you a crepe, but they are the specialty at this French-owned joint. Come for almost 50 kinds of savory galettes and sweet crepes, or design your own crepe-monster from the list of ingredients. French music plays in its underground rooms and the walls are covered with black and white photos, but La Crêperie is cozy and unpretentious.

☀ C: Vltavská. From the Metro, take tram 1 or 25 or walk along the tracks for 1 stop, to Strossmayerovo náměstí. Turn left just past St. Antonín Church and walk past the tea shop. La Crêperie will be to the left. Ⓢ Crepes 35-85Kč. Galettes 40-100Kč. Cash only. Ⓩ Open daily 9am-11pm.

ZLATÁ KOVADLINA
CZECH, BOWLING $$

Komunardů 36 ☎246 005 313; www.zlatakovadlina.com

Bowling and eating, two pastimes of the wise and lazy man, are ingeniously combined in this underground restaurant. The cuisine is traditional Czech, so you can nibble on your pork fillet or whatnot while taking advantage of one of the four bowling lanes. If you don't plan on bowling, another traditional Czech restaurant, friendly **Korbel**, is just a few meters down the street. (Komunardů 30 ☎222 986 095; www.restauracekorbel.cz).

☀ C: Vltavská. From the station, take tram 1, 3, 5, or 25 or walk along the tram tracks for 3 stops to Dělnická. Continue for 1½ blocks; the restaurant is on the right. Ⓢ Entrees 79-199Kč. Beer 17-32Kč. Bowling 260-360Kč per person per hr. Ⓩ Open M-Th 11am-11pm, F 11am-midnight, Sa noon-midnight, Su noon-10pm. Lanes open daily 2pm-midnight.

LONG TALE CAFÉ
CAFE $

Osadní 35 ☎266 310 701; www.longtalecafe.cz

A frequent haunt of architects and people returning from DOX (see **Sights**), this cafe manages to hover somewhere on the border between industrial and domestic. Housed in a building that used to be a ham factory (we couldn't make this stuff up), Long Tale now serves mostly bagels, baguettes, and panini, but you can also try their homemade ginger lemonade (55Kč). If you're coming from DOX and you're not tired of art, check out either of the two galleries that share the courtyard with Long Tale.

☀ C: Vltavská. From the station, take tram 1, 3, 5, or 25 or walk along the tram tracks for 3 stops to Dělnická. Take a left onto Dělnická and a right at Osadní. The cafe is inside the courtyard to the left. Ⓢ Breakfast 35-55Kč. Baguettes and panini 70-79Kč. Coffee 35-50Kč. Cash only. Ⓩ Open M-F 9am-6pm.

food

MOLO 22 INTERNATIONAL $$

U Průhonu 22 ☎220 563 348; www.molo22.cz

One of the classier joints in this part of town, Molo 22 has a menu that might surprise: you'll probably see something pedestrian like *svíčková na smotaně* (sirloin in cream) alongside such exotic dishes as jumbo tiger prawns. The offerings change every three months, and the restaurant does not commit to any particular cuisine, so when it comes to the menu during your visit, your guess is as good as ours. The interior is chic, and it's a good place to enjoy a glass of wine.

🚶 C: Vltavská. From the station, take tram 1, 3, 5, or 25 or walk along the tram tracks for 3 stops to Dělnická. Continue down Komunardů, then turn left on U Průhonu; the restaurant is on the left. $ Entrees 159-297Kč. Desserts 79-95Kč. Cocktails 99-145Kč. ⏰ Open M-F 8am-midnight, Sa-Su 9am-midnight.

LUCKY LUCIANO II ITALIAN $$

Dělnická 28 ☎220 875 900; www.luckyluciano.cz

Named after the father of modern organized crime, this Czech-owned pizzeria is a solid joint geared toward the locals. On a sunny day, not a soul sits in Lucky Luciano—they're all outside under the giant covered patio. Pizzas are large enough for two but delicious enough for more, so keep leftovers close enough that you can slap away would-be scavengers. If you come during the happy hour (3-5pm), you can take advantage of the 30% discount on all pizzas. Lucky Luciano also offers some heavyweight steaks.

🚶 C: Vltavská. From the station, take tram 1, 3, 5, or 25 or walk along the tram tracks for 3 stops to Dělnická. Turn left onto Dělnická, the pizzeria is to the left. $ Pizza 105-150Kč. Pasta 115-145Kč. Beer 23-35Kč. ⏰ Open M-F 11am-11pm, Sa-Su 11:30am-11pm. Garden open M-F 11am-10pm, Sa-Su 11:30am-10pm.

DEJVICE

Even though it's not very touristy, Dejvice has its share of Western fast-food chains and exotic restaurants. Don't expect rural prices, but there are a few good deals that can't be found closer to the center.

KULAŤÁK CZECH $$

Vítězné náměstí 12 ☎773 973 037; www.kulatak.cz

This young restaurant has already managed to earn the affection of Czech superman Václav Havel, who has a table reserved in the back of the non-smoking section. We recommend the cheap lunch menus (75-99Kč) and the tank beer.

🚶 A: Dejvická. The restaurant is on the eastern side of the large roundabout. $ Entrees 149-249Kč. Desserts 65-89Kč. Beer 24-39Kč. ⏰ Open daily 11am-midnight.

CAFÉ TECHNIKA CAFE $

Technická 6 ☎777 568 658; www.cafe-technika.cz

Housed in the futuristic National Technical Library, this university cafe has an industrial, modern feel. When you come here, take advantage of the cheap Kofola (24Kč), the socialist replacement for Coca Cola that's outrageously overpriced in most restaurants in Prague today. Indian lunches, Mamacoffee coffee, and outdoor seating make this a student favorite.

🚶 A: Dejvická. From the roundabout, walk northwest through the park that's opposite Dejvická. Continue up Technická until you reach the National Technical Library. ℹ DJs and live music Th-Sa. $ Lunch 80-115Kč. Coffee 29-61Kč. Beer 21-34Kč. ⏰ Open daily 9am-11pm.

VEGETKA VEGETARIAN, ASIAN $

Kafkova 16 ☎773 588 518

Vegetka is a Buddhist vegetarian restaurant that serves Chinese, Vietnamese, and Thai dishes (this last category proved too spicy for Czech customers and had to be watered down). It'll be hard not to like tofu after you've eaten here.

The "special soup" is especially noteworthy and stocked with noodles, mushrooms, and coriander, along with some secret ingredients.

A: Dejvická. From the roundabout, walk southeast on Dejvická, take the 1st right onto Kafkova, then take the 1st left. The restaurant is on the left. $ Entrees 60-140Kč. Cash only. ⏰ Open M-F 10:30am-9pm, Sa 11am-9pm.

DEJVICKÁ ČAJOVNA — TEA, HOOKAH $

V.P. Čkalova 12 — ☎776 792 701; www.dejvicka-cajovna.cz

Since you're already so far off the tourist track, we'll have you do something that only locals tend to do—go to a tea room. A favorite among young people who don't need alcohol to have fun, Dejvická Čajovna has candlelit rooms, soft cushions, and teas from around the world. The menu is only in Czech, but the staff will help you choose. The interior tries to look oriental but still has a bit of the socialist, run-down thing going on—the best way to get over it is to become absorbed in a long conversation with friends.

A: Dejvická. From the roundabout, walk southeast on Dejvická, then take the 3rd left onto V.P. Čkalova. The tea room is on the right. $ Tea 55-115Kč. Hookah 89-139Kč. Cash only. ⏰ Open M-F noon-11:30pm, Sa-Su noon-2am.

PERPETUUM — DUCK $$$

Na Hutích 9 — ☎233 323 429; www.restauraceperpetuum.cz

As the duck statues scattered around the interior indicate, this high-end restaurant serves only dishes made from home-bred duck. (Desserts, thankfully, are an exception.) Specialties include foie gras (250Kč) and duck stuffed with pomegranate paste (310Kč). If you came to enjoy duck meat in Czech Republic and have some spending power, Perpetuum is an interesting place to go.

A: Dejvická. From the roundabout, walk on Dejvická and turn left onto Na Hutích. $ Appetizers 130-250Kč; entrees 230-390Kč. ⏰ Open daily 11:30am-11pm.

nightlife

Although Prague has one of the greatest clubs in Europe (Cross Club) and a few genuinely amazing bars, most of the nightlife centers on the *hospoda* (pub) scene. On a typical night, locals head out for dinner at a pub or a cafe bar and just stay there the entire night, drinking beer and chain smoking. Pubs stay open late (W until midnight, Th-Sa until 2-4am, Su until midnight), while clubs stay open until 4am or later. All outdoor terraces have to close at 10pm, after which most guests head indoors. In general, nights out start earlier than in the US, and it's not uncommon for everything to be over by midnight. This doesn't apply to clubbing, which doesn't usually get started before 11pm.

Don't leave Prague without trying the local fire waters: Fernet tastes like a less-syrupy Jagermeister, Becherovka tastes like Christmas in your mouth, and plum vodka tastes—well, the taste isn't the point with plum vodka. There's also the mythical absinthe, a green mouth-burner with a 70% alcohol content.

Alcohol in Prague is cheaper than what most Westerners are used to. On some nights, you can come home completely wasted having spent under 200Kč. But drink responsibly—drunk foreigners are an easy targets for pickpockets and a nuisance for everyone else.

NOVÉ MĚSTO

Most tourists head to Staré Město for nightlife, but Nové Město can get pretty lively, too, especially around **Národní třída** and **Wenceslas Square.** Speaking of "nightlife," Nové Město is also one of Prague's seedier districts at night, with some dubious establishments sprinkled around Wenceslas and Charles Squares.

👍 O2 BAR

BAR

Karlovo náměstí ☎608 144 344; www.o2bar.cz

Located in a former public toilet, the inside of this bar fits only three tables. Quarters are so tight that DJs set up their equipment on top of a foosball table. Even the disco ball above the counter is tiny. The crowds tend to spill out into the park and onto the terrace, which offers a surreal view of the lit-up New Town Hall. Since they also somehow managed to find space to store food (yikes), you can enjoy something called "ethno-sandwiches" (53Kč), which are inspired by Afghani, Armenian, Iranian, and Georgian cuisines. O2 bar is currently waging a war against the city authorities, which are planning to shut the place down and reconstruct the entire square. Sign the online petition if you want, and, while you're at it, check out the live webcam stream from inside the bar.

 # B: Karlovo náměstí, on the northwestern edge of the square. $ Beer 19-34Kč. Vodka 45-85Kč. ⏰ Open daily noon-2am.

U SUDU

BAR

Vodičkova 10 ☎222 232 207; www.usudu.cz

From the street, U Sudu might look pretty tame—four tables and a bar. But head inside and you'll become Alice in Wonderland, at least for a while. The stairs lead down into a large underground room, and then a tunnel to a different room, rinse, repeat: U Sudu's cellar is a labyrinth of drinking spaces, all with a slightly different ambience. There's a room for watching sports and one for foosball and still another with live DJs. Aside from regular drinks, U Sudu also has the 18-proof Master beer on tap.

 # B: Karlovo náměstí. From the Metro, head north on Vodičkova past New Town Hall. The bar is on the right. i DJs play W-Sa 10pm-close. $ Snacks 10-55Kč. Beer 23-38Kč. Cash only. ⏰ Open M-Th 9am-4am, F 9am-5am, Sa 10am-5am, Su 10am-3am.

ROCK CAFÉ

CLUB, MUSIC VENUE

Národní 20 ☎224 933 947; www.rockcafe.cz

Loud and raw, with about equal amounts of beer in the plastic cups and on the floor, Rock Café remains one of Prague's best known music venues. Aside from live music, Rock Café also hosts film screenings and plays. Tuesdays are "Free Zone," which means you get a concert and 15min. of free internet use. (Oh boy!) The bands that play here tend to have weird, unfamiliar names, so if you feel like listening to something you actually know, head across the street to **Vagon** (Národní třída 25 ☎733 737 301; www.vagon.cz), another popular music club,which hosts revival bands every Friday and Saturday.

 # B: Národní třída. From the Metro, walk north on Spálená and then turn left on Národní. The music club is on the left. $ Cover 50-150Kč; Tu free. Beer 27-33Kč. Liquor 30-50Kč. Cash only. ⏰ M-F 10am-3am, Sa 5pm-3am, Su 5pm-1am.

JÁMA (THE HOLLOW)

PUB

V Jámě 7 ☎224 222 383; www.jamapub.cz

Whether you buy its self-styled Americanness or not, Jáma's lively atmosphere makes it a great place to grab a beer in the evening. Pick one of the 11 kinds on offer, and take it to the leafy garden, or to a wooden table inside. The walls are covered with a hodgepodge of posters from American pop culture, but it seems to work—Jáma is quite popular with English-speaking foreigners.

 # A or B: Můstek. From the Metro, walk down Wenceslas Sq. and then turn right onto Vodičkova. Take the 1st left on V jámě; the pub is on the left. $ Tex-Mex meals 99-265Kč. Beer 29-45Kč. ⏰ Open daily 11am-1am.

K*STAR KARAOKE KARAOKE BAR

Legerova 78 ☎720 365 044; kstarkaraoke.com

The first bar to bring Asian-style karaoke to Prague (that is, it's got private karaoke rooms, as opposed to a karaoke stage), K*Star works like this—you come in with your crew, rent a room, and then embarrass yourselves with help from adult beverages. The rooms are elegant and high-tech (you can even order drinks with a touchscreen). Come between 6 and 8pm to get half off the room rental.

🚇 C: I.P. Pavlova. From the station, head north on Legerova. The club is on the right. ℹ 10 languages. Reserve ahead F-Su. $ 800-1500Kč per hr. Bottled beer 45Kč. Cocktails 90Kč. ⏰ Open M-Th 6pm-2am, F-Sa 6pm-5am.

REDUTA JAZZ CLUB JAZZ CLUB

Národní 20 ☎224 933 487; www.redutajazzclub.cz

Founded in 1958, Prague's first jazz club has jazz on the menu every night. Hosting almost exclusively Czech jazz musicians, Reduta nevertheless has quite a reputation—even Bill Clinton visited (twice!). On one of his visits, Clinton hopped on stage and jammed with the band, an event that was recorded and released on CD. What a guy. Check out the "saxophone bar" downstairs, where tap beer is pumped out of a saxophone-shaped spigot. We leave the ensuing Clinton innuendo here to you.

🚇 B: Národní třída. From the Metro, walk north on Spálená and turn left onto Národní. Reduta is on the left. $ Cover 285Kč, students 185Kč. Beer 30-50Kč. Wine 50Kč. Liquor 50-100Kč. ⏰ Open 7pm-midnight. Music 9:30pm-midnight.

LUCERNA MUSIC BAR

Vodičkova 36 ☎224 215 957; www.musicbar.cz

Lucerna is one of the most well-attended music venues in Nové Město. Two or three concerts happen here every week, but on Fridays and Saturdays live music gives way to famous '80s- and '90s-themed dance parties (Cover 100Kč). On your way out, check out the David Černý sculpture hanging inside the Lucerna complex.

🚇 A or B: Můstek. From the Metro, walk up Wenceslas Sq. toward the statue of St. Wenceslas and turn right onto Vodičkova. Lucerna is on the left. $ Cover 100-700Kč. Beer 24-40Kč. Shots 40-95Kč. Cash only. ⏰ Ticket office open daily 10am-7pm. Bar open daily 8pm-3am. Concerts 9pm.

ROCKY O'REILLYS IRISH PUB

Štěpánská 32 ☎222 231 060; www.rockyoreillys.cz

If you're the kind of person who'd go to an Irish pub in Prague—such people must exist—then you might enjoy visiting Rocky O'Reillys. Expect steep prices, rabid decor, and big screens tuned to sports. Perhaps the most interesting aspect of the pub is the hanging poster of "Rocky's Ten Commandments," which aims to educate travelers on the basics of not getting their wallet stolen or themselves arrested. The takeaway? Prague is full of small girls who are after your wallet. Also, if somebody says he is a "currency inspector" and wants to see your money, walk away.

🚇 A or B: Můstek. From the Metro, walk down Wenceslas Sq. and take a right onto Štěpánská. The pub is on the left. $ Entrees 245-295Kč. Beer 40-100Kč. ⏰ Bar open daily 10am-1am. Kitchen open 10am-11pm.

STARÉ MĚSTO

At night, Staré Město is besieged with stag partiers, pub crawlers, and all sorts of revelers. Most places here are geared toward tourists, but it doesn't hurt to try them out before heading to hipper pastures in other neighborhoods.

CHAPEAU ROUGE — BAR, CLUB

Jakubská 2 ☎222 316 328; www.chapeaurouge.cz

For a place established in 1919, Chapeau Rouge is young at heart: the interior decoration tends to be edgy and dark. It's a tourist trap par excellence, but it's still worth the experience. The bar on the street level still maintains some decorum, while the underground dance floor is smokier, darker, and louder. Some people say that this could be a place to go if you're in the market for some weed, but remember that buying drugs in touristy places is generally a bad idea.

⇟ B: Náměstí Republiky. From Old Town Sq., walk toward Church of Our Lady Before Týn and pass it on the right. Bear left on Štupartská and take a left on Malá Štupartská. $ Downstairs is often free; if not, cover may be 50-100Kč 10pm-2am. Beer 28-40Kč. Shots 60-90Kč. Cash only. ⏰ Open M-F noon-3am, Sa-Su 4pm-4am. Dance club open M-Th 9pm-4am, F-Sa 9pm-6am, Su 9pm-4am.

PROPAGANDA PUB (AKA IRON CURTAIN) — PUB

Michalská 12 ☎776 858 333; www.propagandapub.cz

Brought to you by the entrepreneurial mind who also created Bohemia Bagel and the Museum of Communism, Propaganda Pub is one of the newer additions to Prague's nightlife scene. With over 200 original artifacts from the Communist era, Propaganda feels almost like a fun museum that serves drinks. Local bands provide live music four times per week and there's a DJ twice a week, but this underground place is large and can easily accommodate a quiet conversation (especially in the Red Library, a cozy section with a collection of socialist literature). If you're hungry, walk over to the restaurant section and order something from the grill. Oh, and is it a Monday? The first 100 beers are just 12Kč.

⇟ A or B: Můstek. From Old Town Sq., pass the Astronomical Clock and go south on Melantrichova. Take the 1st right and continue until the street becomes Michalská. ℹ Not to be confused with Propaganda Café on Pštrossova 29. $ Beer 25-35Kč. Grilled Hermelín 85Kč. ⏰ Open daily 6pm-late.

sobering up

So you've had a few too many drinks at one of the local bars and you're not sure whether you should head back to your hostel and sleep it off or get some help. Well, Prague has the perfect place for you: a sobering-up station. In the United States, if you're intoxicated in public, the police will take you into custody; in the Czech Republic they'll take you to one of these venues.

Staffed by nurses and doctors, the facilities allow inebriated locals and travelers to sleep off a night of binge drinking under the careful supervision of a medical team. In the morning, when you're sober, you're free to leave. With all of the beer, travelers certainly take advantage of this service.

ROXY

CLUB

Dlouhá 33

www.roxy.cz

Something of a local institution, Roxy is enormous and has a vaguely industrial feel. Locals come here for the concerts (both Czech and international performers; Mondays are free and feature new local bands) and the nightly dance parties. Chill-out sections on the side let you awkwardly watch the revelers below, while the shining circular bars supply reasonably priced drinks.

⇞ B: Náměstí Republiky. From Old Town Sq., pass the Jan Hus statue and continue north on Dlouhá. $ No cover, but concerts are ticketed. Beer 39Kč. Shots 39-70Kč. Cocktails 85-189Kč. Cash only. ⏰ Open M-Sa 10pm-late.

K4 KLUB & GALERIE

BAR

Celetná 20

☎224 491 930; www.k4klub.org

This underground art space is almost exclusively a student hangout, run by and for students from Charles University. Events like concerts, screenings, and gallery openings take place almost every day, and the walls are always covered with art. There's little to do on the weekends; the space is at its liveliest during the week when students are in town. Drinks come at rock-bottom student-friendly prices. This might not be a place to visit if you're in town for only five days, but if you're here for five months, definitely check it out.

⇞ B: Náměstí Republiky. From Old Town Sq., pass the Týn church on the right as you walk down Celetná. At Celetná 20 turn right inside the courtyard, then head down a flight of stairs. $ Beer 19-23Kč. Coffee 26-39Kč. Cuba Libre 39Kč. Cash only. ⏰ Open M-F 10am-midnight, Sa-Su 4pm-midnight.

what would you do?

Wandering Prague's Karlova Street is the ghost of the Mad Barber—or so says a Czech legend. Under Rudolph II, the Barber was successful, but wanted more money. He turned to magical alchemy to make gold at home, but it was never enough. Despite his family's warnings, he let his greed destroy him and spent his family's fortune. After that he sold his house, his three daughters were forced into prostitution, and his wife committed suicide. The Barber was so crazed by his poverty that he began slashing the throats of passersby on the street—Johnny Depp-style—until one night a group of soldiers beat him to death. Now his ghost roams the streets, waiting to be set free. Brave enough to help? Allow him to give you a shave, and his spirit will finally be able to move on.

BUDDHA BAR

BAR

Jakubská 8

☎221 776 300; www.buddhabarhotelprague.com

Pricey and classy, this concept club can be affordable if you keep yourself in check. If you don't, you may end up paying 1600Kč for the set dinner menu. The upper floor is all cozy red sofas and intimate nooks, where you can exchange winks with an enormous, two-story Buddha statue. The music combines Western and Eastern influences, but this isn't where people come to dance—it's more of a pregame destination.

⇞ B: Náměstí Republiky. From Old Town Sq., pass the Týn church on the left and go straight through the underpass. Continue as Týn becomes Jakubská; the bar is on the right. $ Beer 80Kč. Cocktails 160-190Kč. Sushi 95-125Kč per piece. ⏰ Open daily 6pm-late.

KARLOVY LÁZNĚ   CLUB
Smetanovo nábřeží 198   ☎222 220 502; www.karlovylazne.cz

A colossal five-story club with some impressive lighting and dance floor effects,
Karlovy Lázně can be hit-or-miss. Either you spend the night dancing away,
fascinated by the design choices (there's a torso that shoots lasers, a neon cage
containing a half-naked dancer, a kaleidoscope room), or you get a depressive
episode induced by the place's overall ugliness and all the men with popped col-
lars (on some nights, Karlovy Lázně would make for a wonderful gay club, given
the gender ratio). Each floor plays a different kind of music: disco, oldies, dance,
chill-out, and something called "black music." Most pub crawls end here.

☕ *A: Staroměstskà. From the station, head toward the river then south on Křižovnické. Club is
directly past the Charles Bridge, through the tunnel of tourist shops.* ℹ *No dress code. Free computers on the 1st floor.* Ⓢ *Cover 120Kč. Beer 45Kč. Cash only.* ⌚ *Open daily 9pm-5am.*

MALÁ STRANA
Malá Strana has some vigorous nightlife, with many smaller music venues and artsy
dive bars. In addition, many cafes and restaurants serve double duty as bars, staying
open past midnight.

🎵 JAZZ DOCK   JAZZ CLUB
Janáčkovo nábřeží 2   ☎774 058 838; www.jazzdock.cz

This new jazz club has been making waves—and not just because it's on the
water. Jazz Dock swings hard during live performances every night of the week.
The gig here is serious; there are double shows five days per week, children's
theater on Saturday, and a Dixieland program on Sunday. Due to its genius design, live music can play until 4am without prompting noise complaints.

☕ *B: Anděl. From the Metro, head toward the river on Lidická. At the river, take a left and continue for
6 blocks. Jazz Dock is down some stairs on the right.* ℹ *Jam session Sa 1am. Guests who visit the club
3 times are entitled to a 10% discount on future club transactions.* Ⓢ *Cover 120-450Kč, under 25 or
over 65 90Kč. Beer 23-43Kč. Cocktails 135-155Kč. Meals 125-225Kč.* ⌚ *Open M-Th 3pm-4am, F-Sa
1pm-4am, Su 1pm-2am. Concerts daily Jan-June 7, 10pm; Jul-Aug 10pm; Sept-Dec 7, 10pm.*

KLUB ÚJEZD   BAR
Újezd 18   ☎251 510 873; www.klubujezd.cz

The only thing wilder than Klub Újezd's guests is its decor: bathroom doors show
monsters doing their business and a giant leviathan snaps above the bar. The clientele isn't exactly monstrous, but the three floors cater to three very different
scenes. The upstairs cafe is secluded and smoky, the basement is dungeon-like
with a DJ spinning on a mini-stage for the 20 people who can squeeze in, and the
main bar is filled with artists—or people who wish they were.

☕ *A: Malostranská. From the Metro, walk south or take tram 12, 20, or 22 to Újezd.* Ⓢ *Beer 20-
39Kč. Cocktails 59-149Kč. Cash only.* ⌚ *Bar open daily 2pm-4am. Cafe open daily 6pm-4am. Club
open daily 8pm-4am.*

BLUE LIGHT BAR   BAR
Josefská 1   ☎257 533 126; www.bluelightbar.cz

There might not be a better place to go stargazing in Prague than this intimate
bar. It's a well-known hangout for Czech politicians, artists, and singers, and it's
a frequent location for film crews' wrap parties. If Czech heavyweights don't
impress you, check out Daniel Craig's signature right above the bar. While the
odds that you'll brush shoulders with Johnny Depp are slim, you can still pretend
your life is glamorous.

☕ *A: Malostranská. From the Metro, head down Letenská toward Malostranské náměstí. Turn left
into Josefská before you reach the square. The bar is on the right.* Ⓢ *Beer 35-85Kč. Cocktails 105-
175Kč. Coffee 55-100Kč. Cash only.* ⌚ *Open daily 6pm-3am.*

U MALÉHO GLENA JAZZ AND BLUES CLUB JAZZ CLUB

Karmelitská 23 ☎257 531 717; www.malyglen.cz

This tiny jazz spot brings in big talent for small audiences—the pleasurably cramped space has an underground-New-York vibe. The American food here and in the pub upstairs deserves special mention—this is one of the few places in town with chili fries (150Kč). There's Guinness on tap and Staropramen's Velvet. Every Saturday there's a jam session, so if you happen to be a jazz enthusiast and are carrying your instrument around, it may be time to unleash the beast.

🚆 A: Malostranská. From the Metro, walk to Malostranské náměstí and continue south on Karmelitská, which becomes Újezd. The club is on the right. $ Cover 100-200Kč. Beer 30-70Kč. Food 65-189Kč. Cocktails 79-129Kč. ⏰ Club open daily 8pm-2am. Jazz 9:30pm-12:30am. Pub open daily 11am-2am.

POPOCAFEPETL MUSIC CLUB MUSIC CLUB

Újezd 19 ☎739 110 021; popocafepetl.cz

This small music club in a brick cellar captures the essence of cool. PopoCafePetl hosts live music concerts almost every night. Genres vary wildly, with jazz concerts on some nights, art folk on others, and even some hip hop. On Fridays, a DJ spins from the colorfully lit stage. Hoegaarden on tap also comes as a relief to those who've had enough Pilsner.

🚆 A: Malostranská. From the Metro, walk or take tram 12, 20, or 22 to Hellichova and continue south on Újezd; the club is on the right. $ Cover 30-100Kč; some nights free. Beer 24-45Kč. Cocktails 70-110Kč. Cash only. ⏰ Open daily 6pm-2am.

DIVADLO NA PRÁDLE CAFE, THEATER

Besední 3 ☎257 320 42; www.napradle.cz

During the summer, this cafe is merely a hangout for artsy winos, but it gets livelier during the regular season, when all kinds of plays enliven the performance space upstairs. The theater has been around since 1863 and is still a landmark. We recommend the wine, but there's also Bernard beer on tap.

🚆 A: Malostranská. From the Metro, walk south or take tram 12, 20, or 22 to Újezd. Backtrack up Újezd, take the 1st right at Říční, and then a left onto Besední. $ Wine 28Kč. Beer 18-35Kč. Student discounts available for plays. Cash only. ⏰ Open M-F 11:30am-midnight, Sa-Su 3pm-midnight.

ŽIŽKOV

The nightlife in Žižkov is very lively and, for the most part, tourist-free. Go forth and party, brave *Let's Go* reader.

👍 BIG LEBOWSKI BAR

Slavíkova 16 ☎774 722 276; www.biglebowski.cz

There aren't many places in the world where you can come in, order a drink, and then pay whatever price you want. This is such a place. Mr. Lebowski (no relation), the owner and sole employee of this unique bar, decided to dispose with price tags because he "likes freedom." The bar seems small at first, but this is deceptive—there's a surprisingly spacious upper level with walls covered in snapshots from cult films. Oh, and if you're in the mood for chess, there's one more reason to come by—Mr. L will play with anyone who expresses the slightest interest in the chessboard resting on his bar.

🚆 A: Jiřího z Poděbrad. From the Metro, walk north on Slavíkova. The bar is to the right. $ It's all up to you. ⏰ Open M-F 6-11pm (or later).

BUKOWSKI'S BAR

Bořivojova 86

Famous for having some of the best cocktails in Žižkov, Bukowski's is a designer bar popular with intellectuals and expats. It may take some time for you to realize what's strange about this bar, so we'll help you—it's the carpeting! The floor is fully carpeted. Anyway, in true spirit of its patron saint/writer/drunkard, the bar adds a literary flourish here and there (with cocktails like The Dorian Gray and The Naked Lunch), while retaining a certain blunt edge (bathrooms are marked in an unprintable way).

🚊 Trams 5, 9, or 26: Husinecká. From the tram, take Seifertova east, make a right onto Víta Nejedlého, and another right onto Bořivojova. $ Beer 30-45Kč. Cocktails 85-130Kč. Cash only. ⏰ Open daily 7pm-3am.

PALÁC AKROPOLIS CAFE, CLUB

Kubelíková 27 ☎296 330 912; www.palacakropolis.cz

Situated in a pre-WWII theater, Palác Akropolis has become something of a Žižkov landmark. The complex consists of a restaurant, a cafe, a theater, and two downstairs bars with nightly DJs.

🚊 A: Jiřího z Poděbrad. From the Metro, cross diagonally through the park and then take Milešovská. Kubelíkova is on the other side of the Žižkov tower park. $ Cover F-Sa 30-60Kč. Some concerts cost more; check online before you go. Beer 18-30Kč. Cash only. ⏰ Cafe open daily 10am-midnight. Club open daily 7pm-5am.

BUNKR PARUKÁŘKA CLUB, MUSIC VENUE

Parukářka Park ☎774 451 091; www.parukarka.eu

Now here's a novelty for you: a concert venue inside an underground nuclear bunker. It takes a while to descend down the long spiraling staircase, but, once you get there, you're not only ready to listen to some alternative music, you're also 100% safe in the event of nuclear war. The place is rough around the edges, with primitive drawings on its walls and all sorts of decay in the interior, but that only makes a concert here all the more enjoyable. There is no regular events schedule, so check online before you go.

🚊 Trams 5, 9, or 26: Olšanské náměstí. From the square, walk up on Prokopova (toward the overpass) on the right side of the street. Walk past the RIAPS building and up a flight of stairs toward the park. Bunkr is the door to the right. ℹ Wheelchair-accessible through the cargo entrance. $ Beer 20-26Kč. Shots 30-60Kč. Cash only. ⏰ Open only for shows, usually 8pm-late.

MATRIX CLUB, MUSIC VENUE

Koněvova 13 ☎777 254 959; www.matrixklub.cz

This black-and-green-themed dance club has the privilege of playing music as loud as it wants for as long as it wants, since it's acoustically isolated from its upstairs neighbors. It's open to all sorts of music events but is best known for its underground concerts and Techno Fridays. Those disinclined to dance may enjoy playing on one of the many foosball tables (the rare kind designed for only two players).

🚊 Tram 5, 9, or 26: Lipanská. Turn onto Chlumova and walk all the way to Husitská, then take a right. The club is on the left, through a courtyard and above a bowling alley. $ Beer 29-39Kč. Shots 35-75Kč. Cash only. ⏰ Hours depend on concerts, usually 8pm-late.

sweet becherovka

Absinthe may pack a serious alcoholic punch, but the well-known green fairy is so last *fin-de-siècle*. Becherovka, though, is nearly as potent, has medicinal properties (allegedly), and is brewed just outside Prague. The herbal liqueur, concocted in the hot-spring-rich town of Karlovy Vary, is known as the nearby spa city's "13th spring." The closely guarded recipe involves some 35 herbs and spices—putting it two dozen ahead of KFC—and its alcohol content is 38%.

VINOHRADY

Vinohrady is full of small bars and clubs and is home to Prague's gay nightlife.

RADOST FX — CLUB

Bělehradská 120 ☎224 254 776; www.radostfx.cz

The painted Coke bottles seem symbolic: Radost FX opened in 1992 and was among the first to bring Western-style clubbing to the newly democratic country. Not that you care; you're here to dance. Needless to say, you're in the right place. Zebra-print couches and weird chandeliers add up to an edgy atmosphere (to stay fresh, the interior design in Radost FX changes every year), and one of the more advanced light rigs in Prague takes care of the dance floor. When you tire of dancing, head upstairs to the lounge and soak up the alcohol with pricey vegetarian food. You must try one of the following drinks: Cosmic Granny, Lesbian Joy, or Sex with an Alien (just don't combine them).

C: I.P. Pavlova. From the station, head east on Jugoslávská for a little more than 1 block. When you reach Bělehradská, the club is on the left. [i] Hip hop Th. House F. R and B Sa. $ Cover 100-150Kč; women free 10pm-midnight. Beer 35-95Kč. Cocktails 110-145Kč. ⏰ Open Th-Sa 10pm-5am.

ON — CLUB, GLBT

Vinohradská 40 ☎222 520 630; www.club-valentino.cz

Formerly "Valentino," ON is the largest gay club in Prague. On weekends, the caterpillar blooms into a butterfly, and the club adds two additional dance floors to its bar and disco in the basement.

A: Náměstí Míru. From the station, walk east on Korunní, then turn left onto Sázavská and left onto Vinohradská. [i] Women are regularly in attendance; straight gentlemen, not so much. $ Beer 22-35Kč. Shots 45-75Kč. ⏰ Cafe open daily 11am-5am. Disco open daily 9pm-5am. Dance club open Th-Sa 11pm-6am.

SOKOOL — BAR

Polská 1 ☎222 210 528; www.sokool.cz

Housed in an amusingly ugly Communist-era building, the bar's name actually comes from the *sokolovna* (gym) next door. One can tell just by looking that SoKool is a place beloved by young locals: it's got plenty of wooden benches, it serves beer in 1L glasses *(tupláky)*, and it's right next to Riegrovy sady (a popular student hangout—grab a plastic cup of beer and sit on the grassy slope that overlooks the city). Don't expect any dancing; SoKool is more about drinking and bonding.

A: Náměstí Míru. From the station, walk east on Korunní and turn left onto Budečská. Continue to the end and up the stairs. $ Beer 17-64Kč. Shots 30-60Kč. Cash only. ⏰ Open M-F 11am-midnight, Sa noon-midnight, Su noon-11pm.

PIANO BAR — BAR, GLBT

Milešovská 10 ☎775 727 496; www.pianobar.sweb.cz

This low-key gay bar is unlike other local bars. There's no dance floor and no light rigs—just a jukebox. Also, if you play the piano, you might end up being "live music" for the night. The prices are very friendly, and there are two old computers for patrons to use at no cost.

A: Jiřího z Poděbrad. From the station, head east on Vinohradská and take a left onto Milešovská. $ Beer 19-30Kč. Shots 37-57Kč. Cash only. ⏰ Open daily 5pm-5am.

VINÁRNA VÍNEČKO — WINE BAR

Londynská 29 ☎222 511 035; www.vineckopraha.cz

A local wine bar that errs on the side of adult, Vinárna Vínečko is the perfect place to spend a relaxed evening discussing how delightfully well your houseplants have been doing lately. The front garden, with its metal chairs and small hedge, isn't the coziest place ever, but ordering a delicious dessert may solve the problem. If you're lucky enough to be spending the evening with yourself, bring your laptop for the free Wi-Fi and treat yourself to a nice glass of *víno*. No buts—you deserve this.

A: Náměstí Míru. From the station, head west down Rumunská, then take a left down Londynská. The bar is actually to the right on Bruselská where it meets Lodynská. $ Wine 30-38Kč. Beer 23-35Kč. Desserts 35-64Kč. ⏰ Open M-F noon-midnight, Sa 2pm-midnight, Su 2-10:30pm.

LATIMERIE CLUB BAR

Slezská 74 ☎224 252 049; www.latimerieclub.cz

This vaguely nautical gay bar brings together a group of hip locals and fun foreigners. There's a small dance floor and some minor colorful lights flashing, but that's apparently enough to please. This is not to say that the club doesn't get wild—no printed closing time means that party goes as late as you can stand.

A: Jiřího z Poděbrad. From the station, head south down Nidranská. Slezská will be on your left. $ Beer 30-50Kč. Mixed drinks 50-180Kč. Cash only. ⏰ Open M-F 4pm-late, Sa-Su 6pm-late.

HOLEŠOVICE

Holešovice's clubs and bars tend to be huge and far apart. They are among the city's best.

CROSS CLUB CLUB

Plynární 23 ☎736 535 010; www.crossclub.cz

This is about the coolest club you'll ever set foot in. Affectionately dubbed "Optimus Prime's ass" by some, the place is decorated with the most amazing assortment of neon-lit industrial steel you'll find anywhere outside a junk yard, or, well, anywhere at all. Cross exists on five levels, with a three-floor outdoor patio and a maze of a rooms downstairs. There are two sections: the upstairs cafe and patio are free for everyone, while access to the underground club may require a cover. The descent into the club is surreal, as each room has its own quirks: one is only tall enough to sit in, while another has lamps made from car engines. The upstairs cafe hosts cultural events, such as free film screenings on Wednesdays that showcase works by young Czech filmmakers as well as established directors.

C: Nádraží Holešovice. From the Metro, walk east on Plynární, past the bus bay and parallel to the tram tracks. Cross Club is the tall yellow building with metal sculptures out front. $ Cover 40-270Kč. Beer 19-37Kč. Cash only. ⏰ Cafe open daily 2pm-2am. Club open 6pm-late.

SASAZU CLUB, RESTAURANT

Bubenské nábřeží 306 ☎284 097 444; www.sasazu.com

One of the newest and hottest additions to Prague's nightlife scene, SaSaZu has an enormous dance floor flanked by six bars. The DJ's saucer-shaped outpost hovers—sometimes quite literally—over the dancing crowds. Housed in a former slaughterhouse, SaSaZu also contains an über-stylish restaurant that serves Southeast Asian cuisine. Wait for a good event and then pounce—this place is worth checking out at least once.

C: Vltavská. From the Metro, take tram 1, 3, 5, or 25 or walk along the tracks on Bubenské nábřeží for 1 stop to Pražská Tržnice (Prague Market), and enter the Prague Market grounds. SaSa-Zu is to the left, in front of a big parking lot. ℹ No open-toed shoes for men. $ Cover 100-200Kč; no cover for women before midnight. Cocktails 145-185Kč. Beer 49-75Kč. Entrees 130-485Kč. ⏰ Restaurant open daily noon-midnight. Club hours depend on events; check the website.

CLUB MECCA CLUB

U Průhonu 3 ☎602 711 225; www.mecca.cz

If a club's quality can be judged by the number of disco balls hanging above its dance floor, then Mecca's score is around 40. Open only three nights per week, Mecca has hosted some big names and continues to do so twice per month, when it invites well-known international performers. You may appreciate the fact that there's no cover on Wednesdays and that vodka shots cost 39Kč, but if you have money to burn, consider getting a VIP ticket to the upstairs lounge, which will cost either a drinks tab of 1000Kč per person, or the purchase one bottle per two people. If you want to take a break from house music, there's a chill-out lounge downstairs.

⚑ C: Vltavská. *From the station, take tram 1, 3, 5, or 25 or walk along the tram tracks for 3 stops to Dělnická. Continue down Komunardů, then turn left on U Průhonu. The club is on the right.* ⓘ *No shorts or sandals.* ⓢ *Cover F-Sa 190-290Kč. Small beer 39-47Kč. Cocktails 109-219Kč.* ⏰ *Open W 11-5am F-Sa 11pm-5am (or later).*

FRAKTAL
                                                            BAR, RESTAURANT
Šmeralova 1   ☎777 794 094; www.fraktalbar.cz

At night, Fraktal, a favorite local restaurant, functions as one of the more colorful local bars. The cavernous underground features childlike drawings and eccentric seating (one table in the corner is clearly meant for hobbits). Come for drunk food, such as burgers, nachos, or quesadillas, and for the opportunity to peek inside the kitchen through a poster's cut-out eyes.

⚑ C: Vltavská. *From the station, take tram 25 or walk along the tram tracks on Milady Horákové for 3 stops to Letenské náměstí. The bar is on the right.* ⓘ *Wheelchair-accessible on patio only.* ⓢ *Beer 22-37Kč. Nachos 80-120Kč. Burgers 185-250Kč. Cash only.* ⏰ *Open daily 11am-midnight. Kitchen open M-Th 11am-11pm, F-Su 4-11pm.*

arts and culture

While Prague has incredible shows, art, and concerts, there are also tons of God-awful tourist shows that cost inexcusable sums. Use this rule of thumb: if it costs more than 200Kč after a student discount, it's probably not worth the money. Some of the best art can be had for little money: Prague's opera is available to students for the cost of a sausage from a street vendor. The same thing applies to classical music at the Rudolfinum. Prague has at least three world-class symphony orchestras and three opera stages as well as a number of private galleries all around the city.

Travelers interested in seeing English-language theater should visit www.expats.cz or the "English Theatre in Prague" Facebook group for extensive listings. **Prague Playhouse** (www.pragueplayhouse.cz) has been producing English-language plays since 2003, while **Blood, Love, and Rhetoric** (www.blrtheatre.com) is an up-and-coming company. The **Prague Shakespeare Festival** (www.pragueshakespeare.org) puts on several Shakespeare plays each year.

Daily film listings at movie theaters can be found at www.prague.tv. The artsy **Kino Světozor** (www.kinosvetozor.cz) off Wenceslas Sq. shows three or four films every day, many of them indie favorites. **Palace Cinemas** (www.palacecinemas.cz) and **CineStar Anděl** (www.cinestar.cz) are two multiplexes across the street from each other in Smíchov that show Hollywood's latest.

OPERA AND THEATER

NATIONAL THEATER (NÁRODNÍ DIVADLO)   NOVÉ MĚSTO
Národní třída 4   ☎224 901 638; www.narodni-divadlo.cz

Producing a program of ballet, opera, and Czech-language drama, the National Theater is considered one of the most important cultural institutions in the Czech Republic. The theater opened in 1881, though various fires and other setbacks have caused alterations since then. The venue closes for the summer, but smaller, open-air productions often grace its inner courtyard.

⚑ B: Národní třída. *From the station, walk north to Národní třída and turn left toward the river.* ⓢ *Tickets 300-1200Kč.* ⏰ *Open M-F 9am-6pm, Sa-Su 10am-6pm. Evening box office opens 45min. before curtain.*

STATE OPERA (STÁTNÍ OPERA PRAHA)
NOVÉ MĚSTO

Legerova 75   ☎296 117 111; www.opera.cz

Thanks to the State Opera's student-rush program, travelers can see a fully staged opera for less than the price of a sausage at the nearby Wenceslas Sq. Presenting more than a dozen operas every month, the State Opera sticks with favorites; works by Tchaikovsky, Mozart, Puccini, and Verdi are most frequently produced, with some other names occasionally mixed in.

⚡ *A or C: Muzeum. From the station, head past the National Museum.* ℹ *Operas have Czech and English supertitles. Formal attire encouraged.* Ⓢ *Tickets 100-1500Kč. Up to 50% student discounts.* ☒ *Open M-F 10am-5:30pm, Sa-Su 10am-noon and 1-5:30pm. Evening box office opens 1hr. before curtain.*

some strings attached

Puppet theater dates back 600 years in the Czech capital, beginning with Biblical plays and progressing to satirical allegories about Hitler and Nazi occupation—what better way to make fun of Europe's puppet master than through marionettes, right? After the Iron Curtain came tumblin' down, puppet culture declined in scope, although you can still find plays performed in this classic form.

But it's the puppets themselves that make the plays more interesting—and maybe a little bit creepy, too. The puppets are traditionally carved from lime wood, and woodcarvers strive to achieve contradictory goals: they want them to look as human as possible, but strive to craft them with overly neutral expressions. This results in miniature, jagged-featured people who stare blankly into the distance as strings manipulate their otherwise lifeless arms and legs. You might think it's impossible to make puppets seem real, but once you've seen one performing an aria from *Don Giovanni* at the **National Marionette Theatre,** you'll start to forget that he's made of wood.

ESTATES THEATER
STARÉ MĚSTO

Železná 11   ☎224 228 503; www.stavovskedivadlo.cz

If it's not enough for you to walk by the famous theater where Mozart premiered *Don Giovanni*, buy a ticket to one of the performances. These days, the tourist-friendly Estates puts on a few plays as well as operatic hits like *Carmen, The Marriage of Figaro,* and—you guessed it—*Don Giovanni.*

⚡ *A or B: Můstek. From Old Town Sq., walk south on Železná; the theater is on the left.* Ⓢ *Tickets 300-1200Kč.* ☒ *Open M-F 10am-5:30pm, Sa-Su 10am-12:30pm and 1-5:30pm. Evening box office opens 1hr. before curtain. Performances usually at 7pm.*

MUSIC

RUDOLFINUM
JOSEFOV

Alšovo nábřeží 12   ☎227 059 227; www.ceskafilharmonie.cz

Home of the Czech Philharmonic Orchestra since 1896, Rudolfinum is Prague's premiere venue for classical music. The first concert in this building was conducted by none other than the composer Antonín Dvořák, who was the Orchestra's first conductor. The matinees and afternoon concerts tend to be cheaper than those in the evening, and with a student discount on top of that, hearing the Czech Republic's top symphony orchestra will cost practically nothing.

⚡ *B: Staroměstská. From the Metro, walk toward the river. Rudolfinum is the big building to the right. The box office is on the side facing away from the river.* Ⓢ *Tickets 110-600Kč. 50% student discount.* ☒ *Box office open M-F 10am-6pm. Closed in summer.*

MUNICIPAL HOUSE (OBECNÍ DUM) NOVÉ MĚSTO

Náměstí Republiky 5 ☎222 002 101; www.obecni-dum.cz

Home to the Czech National Symphony Orchestra (est. 1993), Municipal House is more tourist-oriented than Rudolfinum—it stays open during the summer and ticket prices tend to be higher. On the upside, many interesting music festivals take place here, so check the schedule online.

B: Náměstí Republiky. From Old Town Sq., walk east on Celetná all the way to Náměstí Republiky; Municipal House is on the left. $ Tickets 500-1000Kč. ⏰ Box office open daily 10am-7pm.

FESTIVALS

There's always some kind of festival happening in Prague. We've listed a few here, but the tourist information website (www.praguewelcome.cz) also has a solid list of festivals and cultural events.

FEBIOFEST CITYWIDE

Růžová 13 ☎221 101 111; www.febiofest.cz

It may not be as high-profile as the festival in Karlovy Vary, but Febiofest is Central Europe's largest film event, screening over 4000 films of all genres. During the festival, Prague comes alive with film, and screenings take place in other Czech towns and in Slovakia as well.

$ Ticket prices vary. ⏰ Mar. Check website for specific dates.

PRAGUE WRITERS' FESTIVAL CITYWIDE

Revoluční 28 ☎224 241 312; www.pwf.cz

An exciting five-day celebration of writers from around the world, the Prague Writers' Festival prides itself on bringing in the best of the craft. In 2011, the festival hosted such names as Don DeLillo, Junot Díaz, and the Iraqi poet Saadi Yousef. Events include readings, signings, galas, and question-and-answer sessions.

$ Tickets 100-300Kč. 50% student discount. ⏰ Mid-Apr. Check website for specific dates.

moviegoer mecca

For film lovers traveling in the Czech Republic in March, **Febiofest** is an event not to be missed. No, it's not a weekend devoted to worshipping the muscular model. Febiofest is a week-long extravaganza that combines the best films and documentaries of the past year, drawing attention from movie buffs worldwide. Started in 1993, the event began as a small gathering for some film-loving friends. Today the festival screens films from nearly 60 countries at 12 locations, including three theaters in Prague. In fact, Febiofest is so big that the country can't handle it on its own: once the Czech event ends, Febiofest moves to neighboring Slovakia for another trip around the world through film.

Think it couldn't get any cooler? When the sun sets, Febiofest turns into the **Febiofest Music Festival,** bringing the night to life with music from around the globe. Jazz, blues, rock, you name it: bands of all genres flock to Febiofest to showcase their world-class talent. In 2010 there was even an Open Stage for groups that didn't make the cut, turning into a "Battle of the Bands" to become the next crowd favorite. To top it off, the music performances are free, and the bands rock on 'til the wee hours of the morning. High cinematic art by day, moshpits by night: Febiofest has it all.

PRAGUE BIENNALE

OUTSKIRTS

Československého exilu 4 ☎244 401 894; www.praguebiennale.org

Prague's Biennale, which takes place on odd-numbered years, is the city's biggest and baddest showcase of international contemporary art. If you're lucky enough to be in town during the three days that the exhibition is on, you have to go.

Ⓢ *150Kč, students 75Kč.* Ⓩ *May. Check website for specific dates. Next festival scheduled for summer 2013.*

PRAGUE SPRING MUSIC FESTIVAL (PRAŽSKÉ JARO)

CITYWIDE

Hellichova 18 ☎257 312 547; www.festival.cz

The enormous, month-long festival features some 50 performances by the world's top soloists, small ensembles, symphony orchestras, and conductors. The festival helps launch the careers of talented musicians by hosting soloist competitions in different instrument categories.

i Check website for specific dates. Ⓢ *Ticket prices range from free to exorbitant. 20% student discount on most concerts.* Ⓩ *From early May to early June.*

KARLOVY VARY INTERNATIONAL FILM FESTIVAL

OUTSIDE THE CITY

Karlovy Vary ☎359 001 111; www.kviff.com

Some 130km west of Prague, Karlovy Vary hosts the country's most prestigious film festival. Screening over 180 feature films, this Czech Cannes has been a launching pad for many European hits, including *Amélie*, *Ma Vie En Rose*, and *The Chorus*. It's a bit of a ride from Prague, but it's a must-see for film enthusiasts who happen to be around in July. The ticket prices are much more reasonable than those at big festivals in Western Europe.

♯ *From Prague's Main Train Station (Hlavní nádraží), trains to Karlovy Vary take just over 3hr. and cost 600Kč.* Ⓢ *Tickets 60Kč, students 50Kč. 1-day pass 200Kč, students 150Kč; 3-day 500/350Kč.* Ⓩ *Early July. Check website for specific dates.*

shopping

Prague may not exactly be a shopping destination, but rare items and great deals await. Staré Město is a bastion of touristy shops selling overpriced Bohemian crystal, marionettes, and all sorts of souvenirs. This is where you can pick up one of those cheesy "Czech Drinking Team" T-shirts, the obligatory uniform of many a foreign tourist. Wenceslas Sq. is home to huge international chain stores, while **Pařížská**, which connects Josefov and Staré Město, is the most expensive street in Prague, famous for its high-end designer shops. Handmade clothes and accessories from Czech designers can be found in a few stores around the center, while some of the more residential areas hold rare communist artifacts and other antiques. There's a handful of Western-style malls; the closest ones are in Staré Město and Smíchov. There are also plenty of good bookstores, and even the lesser-known ones tend to be well stocked with English-language classics from big-name Czech authors like Hašek, Hrabal, Kafka, and Kundera. Then there are the quirky places, like a witch store near Náměstí Míru or the hat shop in Malá Strana. And let's not forget about the Prague Market in Holešovice, the city's largest marketplace, where you can get everything from cheap clothes to swords.

CLOTHING

☒ PARAZIT

STARÉ MĚSTO

Karlova 25 ☎603 561 776; www.parazit.cz

An amazing find in any city, Parazit has more outrageous, one-of-a-kind wardrobe pieces than a Tim Burton nightmare. Every item is handmade by Czech

prague

and Slovak designers and design students. There are definitely more options for women, but men can find a few original T-shirts. If you don't want to spend much, take a look at the huge selection of accessories, diaries, and other bric-a-brac that are sold alongside the clothes.

🚇 A: Staroměstská. From Old Town Sq., head toward Charles Bridge on Karlova. The shop is in a courtyard on the right. $ Shirts 420-1000Kč. Dresses from 1500Kč. Bags from 500Kč. Cash only. ⏰ Open M-Sa 11am-8pm.

JULIUS FASHION — NOVÉ MĚSTO

Ostrovní 20 — ☎731 419 953; www.juliusfashion.com

Julius is very similar to Parazit in that it sells original handmade items by local designers, but the wares here tend to be a bit less crazy and more conventionally elegant. Nevertheless, you'll still find a few outlandish items (handbags made from LPs, for instance). Check out the store's online shop to get a sense of its wares.

🚇 B: Národní třída. Walk on Ostrovní toward the river. The shop is on the left. $ Accessories 100-500Kč. T-shirts 500-690Kč. Dresses 700-3000Kč. ⏰ Open M-F 11am-7pm, Sa 11am-6pm.

PALLADIUM — STARÉ MĚSTO

Náměstí Republiky 1 — ☎225 770 250; www.palladiumpraha.cz

Enter this enormous Western-style mall, and you're not in Old Town anymore—you could be anywhere. There's a food court and plenty of stores selling clothing, books, electronics, beauty products, eyeglasses, and everything else you'd expect from a mall.

🚇 B: Náměstí Republiky. The mall is near the Metro exit. ⏰ Shops open M-W 9am-9pm, Th-Sa 9am-10pm, Su 9am-9pm. Supermarket open M-F 7am-10pm, Sa-Su 8am-10pm.

OBCHODNÍ CENTRUM NOVÝ SMÍCHOV — SMÍCHOV

Plzeňská 8 — ☎251 101 061; www.novysmichov.eu

This giant mall boasts a Tesco, a Palace Cinemas multiplex (☎840 200 240; www.palacecinemas.cz), several coffee shops, clothing stores, a sporting-goods shop, and a food court. Much of downtown Smíchov is organized around this area. The mall may be a bit out of the way, but it's very popular with locals.

🚇 C: Anděl. 1 block north of the Metro. To get here from Malá Strana, walk or take tram 12 or 20. ⏰ Shops open daily 9am-9pm. Tesco open daily 7am-midnight.

ŠATNA (THE CLOAKROOM) — STARÉ MĚSTO

Konviktská 13 — ☎777 030 415

Šatna is a tiny boutique with a large supply of secondhand leather jackets and men's jeans in good condition as well as a few men's shirts, shoes, and some blouses. It may not be exactly a bargain (especially for a secondhand store), but Šatna is definitely the pick of the litter.

🚇 B: Národní třída. From the station, head north on Spálená and continue as it becomes Na Perštýně. Curve around to the left and move onto Konviktská. $ Shirts 100-300Kč. Pants 200-500Kč. Jackets 300-400Kč. Cash only. ⏰ Open M-F 11am-7pm, Sa 11am-6pm.

BOOKS

👍 SHAKESPEARE & SONS — MALÁ STRANA

U lužického semináře 10 — ☎257 531 894; www.shakes.cz

Shakespeare & Sons is our favorite bookstore in Prague, and not just because it sells *Let's Go.* The bookstore boasts an impressive collection of fiction, comics, and social science books (mostly in English), as well as a cozy downstairs cellar that's perfect for browsing, and tons of cheap used books. If you're searching for your obligatory Kundera paperback, start here.

🚇 A: Malostranská. From the Metro, walk south parallel to the river and bear right on U lužického semináře. The store is on the right. ⏰ Open daily 11am-7pm.

GLOBE BOOKSTORE — NOVÉ MĚSTO

Pštrossova 6 ☎224 934 203; www.globebookstore.cz

Attached to a cafe with the same name, the Globe caters specifically to American and British expats looking for literary enlightenment in Prague. The store features an expansive collection of English-language literature, travel guides, and general-interest books, while the cafe hosts cultural events, such as readings or film screenings.

B: Karlovo náměstí. From the Metro, take Resslova toward the river and then turn right on Na Zderaze, which becomes Pštrossova; the cafe is on the right. Open daily 9:30am-11pm.

BIG BEN BOOKSTORE — STARÉ MĚSTO

Malá Štupartská 5 ☎224 826 559; www.bigbenbookshop.com

This cute little bookshop, located across from St. James Cathedral, offers travelers a solid literary outlet in the middle of the Old Town. Despite its small size, Big Ben has enough literature and travel guides to warrant a look. Stop by in June during the Prague Writers' Festival (see **Arts and Culture: Festivals**) for book signings by visiting authors.

From Old Town Sq., take Týnska east, continuing straight through the courtyard as it turns into Týn. Take a left when the courtyard lets out at Malá Štupartská. Open M-Sa 9:30am-8pm, Su 11am-7pm.

ANTIQUES

BAZAR — HOLEŠOVICE

Přístavní 18

Antique shopping in Prague isn't the expensive hipster affair that it is in the States, but there are a bunch of places where you can pick up your First Republic-era bottle opener or Communist-era hat. Bazar is a great place to start your hunt for such objects—the one large room has enough objects to satisfy your inner hoarder. The wares here include war knives, old pocket watches, Art Deco relics, and much more. Look carefully in the store window too—some of the best stuff is not visible from inside the store.

C: Vltavská. From the Metro, take tram 1, 3, 5, or 25 or walk along the tram tracks 3 stops to Dělnická. After 1 more block, Bazar will be on the corner to the left. $ Prices negotiable. Cash only. Open M-F 11am-12:30pm and 1:30-4:30pm.

VETEŠNICTVÍ — MALÁ STRANA

Vítězná 16 ☎257 310 611

Walking around Vetešnictví feels like snooping through somebody's attic, with many strangely personal, flimsy, and useless objects, but here and there you'll discover an actual hidden gem. Even if you don't intend to buy anything, take a few minutes to wander around—it's strangely educational.

A: Malostranská. From the Metro, walk or take tram 12, 20, or 22 to Újezd. Walk toward the river on Vítězná. $ Antiques 10-10,000Kč. Cash only. Open M-F 10am-6pm, Sa 10am-noon.

MARKETS

HOLEŠOVICKÁ TRŽNICE (PRAGUE MARKET) — HOLEŠOVICE

Bubenské nábřeží ☎220 800 592; www.holesovickatrznice.cz

Dozens of clothes vendors, furniture salesmen, food peddlers, and other entrepreneurial-minded gentlemen and women call this market home. Housed in a warehouse complex on the bank of the Vltava, Prague Market is the largest market in town and the perfect place to hunt for bargains on manufactured goods. A sampling of what's for sale: clothes, bags, toys, smokeless cigarettes, swords, ice cream. Bargaining languages are Czech, English, and Vietnamese.

C: Vltavská. From the station, take tram 1, 3, 5, or 25 or walk along the tracks on Bubenské nábřeží for 1 stop to Pražská Tržnice (Prague Market). $ Prices negotiable. Hours vary by vendor, roughly 7am-9pm.

'tis the season

In the last weeks of November, the people of Prague begin to bask in festivity and holiday cheer as the annual Christmas markets roll in. The markets are open from morning until late evening, seven days a week. Don't expect any extraordinary seasonal products, though: there are some nifty stocking stuffers like candles, toys, and ornaments, but those can be bought year-round. The tradition is more about the atmosphere than the actual shopping. If you visit Old Town Sq. or Wenceslas Sq. in the city center, a dazzling spectacle of dozens of street shops, glimmering Christmas lights, and a bustling crowd will surely get you into the holiday spirit. Throw in some traditional Czech cuisine and a glass of mulled wine *(svařené víno)* and you'll want to spend every Christmas in Prague.

FARMERS' MARKETS   NOVÉ MĚSTO, JOSEFOV
Locations vary   www.farmarsketrziste.cz

On most days of the week, there's a farmers' market happening in some part of Prague, selling not only local fruits and vegetables, but also fish, smoked meat, mushrooms, baskets, ceramics, flowers, beer, wine, and more. Some of the locations are a bit out of the way, but two are located on embankments not far from tourist areas—on Saturdays, there are markets at Rašínovo nábřeží (near the bridge connecting New Town with Smíchov), and on Thursdays, there are markets in Josefov, on the river bank between Hotel Intercontinental and a hospital. The markets are a great place to discover what the Czech countryside has to offer.

✈ *To get to Kubánské náměstí, take trams 6, 7, 19, 22, or 24: Kubánské náměstí. To get to Náměstí Jiřího z Poděbrad, take Metro A or trams 10 or 16: Náměstí Jiřího z Poděbrad. To get to Rašínovo nábřeží, take Metro B to Karlovo náměstí and walk toward the river. Dvořákovo nábřeží is just above Hotel Intercontinental in Josefov.* ⏰ *Kubánské náměstí market open Tu 8am-6pm, Th 8am-6pm, Sa 8am-2pm. Náměstí Jiřího z Poděbrad market open W 8am-6pm, Sa 8am-2pm. Rašínovo nábřeží market open Sa 8am-2pm. Dvořákovo nábřeží market open Th 8am-6pm.*

HAVELSKÉ TRŽIŠTĚ   STARÉ MĚSTO
Havelská

Just in case you haven't noticed yet, there's an open-air market in the city center, between Wenceslas and Old Town Squares. It sells fresh produce and, along with the much bigger Pražská Tržnice, is one of the only permanent marketplaces around central Prague.

✈ *A or B: Můstek. From Wenceslas Sq. walk on Na Můstku as it becomes Melantrichova.* ⏰ *Generally open daily 7am-7pm.*

essentials

PRACTICALITIES

- **TOURIST OFFICES: Prague Information Service.** (Staroměstské náměstí 1 ☎221 714 444; www.praguewelcome.cz ✈ On the ground floor of Old Town Hall, to the left of the Astronomical Clock. ⏰ Open daily Apr-Oct 9am-8pm; Nov-Mar 9am-7pm.) Other branches: Rytířská 31, Malostranská mostecká věž (Malá Strana Bridge Tower), Hlavní nádraží (main train station), and Letiště Praha Ruzyně (Prague airport, terminal 2).

- **TOURS: New Europe Tours** offers free tours of the city center. (www.newpraguetours. com ✈ Tours depart the Starbucks in Old Town Sq. 🕐 3hr.; 11am, 2pm.) **Prague Royal Walk** offers walking tours of the city center. (www.discover-prague.com Ⓢ Free. 🕐 2½hr.; 11am, 2pm.)

- **LUGGAGE STORAGE:** At the **main train station** (Hlavní nádraží) in either self-service lockers (☎777 082 226 *i* Max. 24hr Ⓢ 60-90Kč per day 🕐 Open daily 3:10am-12:50am) or in the storage room (*i* Max. 30 days Ⓢ 60-100Kč per day 🕐 Open daily 6am-11pm). **Florenc bus station.** (Ⓢ 35Kč per day. 🕐 Open daily 5am-midnight.)

- **POST OFFICE:** Jindřišská 14. ☎221 131 111; www.ceskaposta.cz. ✈ ⓂMůstek. 🕐 Open daily 7:30am-8pm.

- **POSTAL CODE:** 110 00.

EMERGENCY

- **EMERGENCY NUMBERS:** ☎112 (operators speak Czech, English, and German). **Medical Emergencies** ☎155. **Fire** ☎150.

- **PHARMACIES: Lékárna Palackého.** (Palackého 5 ☎224 946 982 ✈ ⓂMůstek. 🕐 Open 24hr.) **Lékárna u Svaté Ludmily.** (Belgická 37 ☎222 519 731 ✈ ⓂNáměstí Míru. 🕐 Open 24hr.)

- **MEDICAL SERVICES: Na Homolce.** (Roentgenova 2 ☎257 272 144; www.homolka. cz ✈ Tram 22 or 36 to Vypich. 🕐 Emergency room open 24hr. Foreign department open M-F 7:30am-4:30pm, but foreigners can get help any time.) **Doctor Health Centre Prague.** (Vodičkova 28 ☎603 433 833; www.doctor-prague.cz. ✈ ⓂMůstek 🕐 Open M-F 8am-4:30pm. Hotline 24hr.)

SPECIFIC CONCERNS

petty crime and scams

Scams and petty theft are unfortunately common in Prague. An especially common scam in bars and nightclubs involves a local woman inviting a traveler to buy her drinks, which end up costing exorbitant prices; the proprietors of the establishment (in cahoots with the scam artist) may then use force to ensure that the bill is paid. Travelers should always check the prices of drinks before ordering. Another common scam involves a team of con artists posing as metro clerks and demanding that you pay large fines because your ticket is invalid. Credit card fraud is also common Eastern Europe. Travelers who have lost credit cards or fear that the security of their accounts has been compromised should contact their credit card companies immediately.

Con artists often work in groups and may involve children. Beware of certain classics: sob stories that require money, rolls of bills "found" on the street, mustard spilled (or saliva spit) onto your shoulder to distract you while they snatch your bag. **Never let your passport or your bags out of your sight.** Hostel workers will sometimes stand at bus and train arrival points to recruit tired and disoriented travelers to their hostel; never believe strangers who tell you that theirs is the only hostel open. Beware of **pickpockets** in large crowds, especially on public transportation.

Visitors to Prague should never enter a taxicab containing anyone in addition to the driver and should never split rides with strangers. When traveling by train, it may be preferable to travel in cheaper "cattle-car" type seating arrangements; the large number of witnesses makes such carriages safer than seating in individual compartments. Travelers should avoid riding on night buses or trains, where the risk of robbery or assault is particularly high. *Let's Go* discourages hitchhiking and picking up hitchhikers.

GETTING THERE

by plane

Ruzyně Airport (☎220 111 888; www.prg.aero) is some 10km west of the city center. The cheapest way to get to the center is to take bus **#119** to Ⓜ️Dejvická (Ⓢ 26Kč 🕐 24min.) or **#110** to Ⓜ️Zličín (Ⓢ 26Kč. 🕐 18min.) and then change to the Metro. **Airport Express** buses go directly to the main train station. (Hlavní nádraží Ⓢ 50Kč. 🕐 35min., every 30min. 6:30am-10pm.) **Student Agency** go to Florenc bus station. (Ⓢ 60Kč. 🕐 Every hr. 6am-9pm.)

by train

Prague has three major train stations: the main one is **Hlavní nádraží** in Prague 2, the others are **Smíchovské nádraží** in Smíchov, and **Nádraží Holešovice** in Holešovice. Trains are operated by **Česká Doprava** (☎840 112 113; www.cd.cz). International destinations include: Berlin, DEU (Ⓢ 1425Kč. 🕐 5hr., 8 per day.); Bratislava, SLK (Ⓢ 643Kč. 🕐 4hr., 8 per day.); Budapest, HUN (Ⓢ 1430Kč. 🕐 7hr., 6 per day.); Krakow, POL (Ⓢ 1025Kč. 🕐 8hr., 3 per day.); Moscow, RUS (Ⓢ 3628Kč. 🕐 33hr., 1 per day.); Munich, DEU (Ⓢ 1385Kč. 🕐 6hr., 4 per day.); Vienna, AUS (Ⓢ 1010Kč. 🕐 5hr., 8 per day.); and Warsaw, POL. (Ⓢ 1300Kč. 🕐 9-12hr., 3 per day.)

by bus

Florenc ÚAN (☎900 144 444) is Prague's main bus terminal. To search bus schedules, visit www.jizdnirady.idnes.cz/autobusy/spojeni. **Eurolines** (☎245 005 245; www.eurolines.cz) runs international buses to some 20 European countries and a few domestic destinations. **Student Agency** (☎841 101 101; www.studentagency. cz) runs domestic and international buses with discounted prices for ISIC holders and travelers under 26.

GETTING AROUND

by public transportation

Prague's tram system alone could sufficiently serve this pocket-sized city, but Prague also has a Metro, a bus system, a horde of taxis, a funicular, and some ferries. **Dopravní Podnik Prahy** (☎296 191 817; www.dpp.cz) runs the public transportation system. Tickets can be used for trams, the Metro, buses, the funicular, and some ferries. The **limited ticket** (18Kč) is valid for 20min. or five Metro stations, while the **basic ticket** (26Kč) is valid for 75min. and unlimited transfers. One-, three-, and five-day tickets are also available (100/330/500Kč), while a **monthly pass** (670Kč) can be purchased only at certain DPP centers. Tickets are available at ticket machines and convenience stores, and must be validated when you enter a vehicle or the Metro platform; unstamped tickets are not valid. **Ticket inspections** are more frequent in the Metro than on trams and buses; the fine for not having a validated ticket is 800Kč. There are three Metro lines (A is green, B is yellow, C is red); they run Monday through Thursday from 5am to midnight, Friday and Saturday from 5am to 1am, and Sunday from 5am to midnight. Aside from walking, trams are probably the best way to get around the city. **Tram #22** connects some of the most important parts of Prague. Travelers should beware of pickpockets on crowded vehicles. It is customary to let seniors sit in your seat if there are no empty seats. Locals are nearly silent on public transportation—don't make an ass of yourself.

essentials

PHRASEBOOK

ENGLISH	CZECH	PRONUNCIATION
Hello	Dobrý den *(formal)*	DOH-bree dehn
Yes/No	Ano/ne	AH-noh/neh
Please	Prosím	PROH-seem
Thank You	Děkuji	DYEH-koo-yee
Goodbye	Nashledanou	NAS-kleh-dah-noh
Good morning	Dobré ráno	DOH-breh RAH-noh
Good evening	Dobrý večer	DOH-breh VEH-chehr
Good night	Dobrou noc	DOH-broh NOHTS
Sorry/excuse me	Promiňte	PROH-meen-teh
Do you speak English?	Mluvíte anglicky?	MLOO-veet-eh ahng-GLEET-skee
I don't speak Czech.	Nemluvím Česky.	NEH-mloo-veem CHESS-kee
I don't understand.	Nerozumím.	NEH-rohz-oo-meem
When?	Kdy?	gdee

OUT TO LUNCH		
breakfast	snídaně	SNEE-dahn-yeh
lunch	oběd	OHB-yed
dinner	večeře	VEH-cher-zheh
grocery	potraviny	POH-trah-vee-nee
I would like...	Chtěl bych...	khtyel bikh
bread	chléb	khlep
vegetables	zelenina	ZEH-leh-nee-nah
meat	maso	MAH-soh
coffee	káva	KAH-vah
hot	horký	HOR-kee
cold	studený	STOO-deh-nee
Cheers!	Na zdraví!	nahz-DRAH-vee
I don't eat...	Nejím...	NEH-yeem
I'm allergic.	Jsem alergický.	ysehm AH-lehr-gits-kee
Check, please.	Paragon, prosím.	PAH-rah-gohn proh-SEEM

EMERGENCY		
Help!	Pomoc!	POH-mots
Please leave.	Prosím odejděte.	pro-SEEM ODEH-dyeh-teh
police	policie	POH-leets-ee-yeh
doctor	doktor	DOHK-tohr
hospital	nemocnice	NEH-mots-nee-tseh

THE UNIVERSAL LANGUAGE		
I love you.	Mám tě rád.	MAHM tyeh RAHD

CARDINAL NUMBERS		
one	jedna	YEHD-na
two	dvě	dvye
three	tři	trzhee
four	čtyři	CHTEER-zhee
five	pět	pyet
six	šest	shest
seven	sedm	SEH-dom
eight	osm	OH-suhm
nine	devět	DE-vyet
ten	deset	DE-set

prague

prague 101

HISTORY

from spade to trade (500 BCE-1300 CE)

Prague might not technically be the "mother of cities," as the nickname goes, but it certainly has been around long enough. The Celts settled the **Vltava River** basin around 200 BCE, but legend has it that the city was actually founded in the eighth century CE by a Slavic power couple named **Libuse and Přemysl.** This semi-mythical pair founded the Přemyslid dynasty, which ruled the city until 1306. The oldest evidence of the Přemyslids is **Prague Castle,** built on a hill overlooking the Vltava around 870. Prague soon became the seat of the Kings of Bohemia, a region of the Holy Roman Empire. The city kept growing thanks to the trade routes that crossed it. A busy market settlement turned into **Old Town** (Stare Město) on one side of the river, while the other bank saw **Lesser Town** (Malá Strana) grow out of the foot of Prague Castle.

Prague's big break came in the 14th century, when the Bohemian king and Holy Roman Emperor **Charles IV** made it his capital. His reign laid the foundations for **"New" Town** (Nové Město), the aptly named **Charles University** (the first of its kind in Central Europe), and a major bridge over the Vltava, which was then named—you guessed it—Charles.

defenestration: the new reformation (1402-1700)

Prague's prosperity was wounded by the viral Reformation bug spreading across Europe in 1402. The passionate sermons of scholar **Jan Hus** turned Czech parishioners against Catholicism, until the church fought back with fire...and burned Hus at the stake. In response, his followers took the whole "overthrow the Church" thing a bit literally and threw several city councilors out the window in the **First Defenestration** (spoiler: there's another one coming up).

Riding on popular sentiment, Prague and the rest of Bohemia became peacefully Protestant and remained so for the next 200 years. But the rise of the Catholic **Hapsburg Dynasty** to the head of the Holy Roman Empire brought new enemies to Protestantism. Returning to tried and true methods, Praguers sent the Catholic-friendly regents of Bohemia flying out the window in the **Second Defenestration** of 1618. Despite the effort, the Protestant Czechs fell to the Hapsburgs and saw Prague lose its prestige and status as a capital city. Smelling fresh blood (and closed windows), Saxons, Swedes, and two bouts of the plague all invaded Prague by the end of the 17th century.

nationalism czechs in (1784-1945)

Perhaps tired of remembering four names for one city, Emperor Joseph II united Prague's four sections (Old, New, and Lesser Towns, and the Castle District) into a single provincial capital. Later, the Industrial Revolution brought Prague its first suburb, its first railway, and its first replica of the Eiffel Tower **(Petřín Lookout Tower).** In 1848, workers and students took to the streets against their Austrian overlords. In the next decades, Prague fought off Imperialism with liberal politics and cultural cachet, creating the **National Theatre** (Národní divadlo), the **Czech Philharmonic,** and the **National Museum** (Národní muzeum). This Nationalism peaked when Prague became capital of the newly independent Czechoslovakia in 1918. Hungry for more land, the city gobbled up nearby neighborhoods and villages to become a metropolis just shy of one million inhabitants.

Nazi Germany cut this growth short, first by stripping land from Czechoslovakia in the **Munich Agreement** and then by invading the region and the city in 1939. Prague fought back hard. Czech assassins bombed and shot the Nazi Reichsprotektor Reinhard Heydrich in 1942, and the national resistance, with the help of the Soviet Red Army, evicted the Germans and restored the fomer Czechoslovak president in the 1945 **Prague Uprising.**

velvet underground (1948-90)

Riding on popular support for the Soviet Union, the Communist Party came to power and imposed Stalinism in 1948. Economic troubles and student riots, however, pressured the party to adopt the more liberal **Prague Spring** reforms in 1968. Feeling threatened, the Soviet Union led Warsaw Pact countries in a military invasion. Despite the best efforts of city dwellers, who tore down street signs so that the invaders would get lost, Prague was dragged back to Moscow-friendly politics for another 20 years.

In 1989, democratic reformers faced off against the Communist apparatchiks in the **Velvet Revolution.** Half a million people held strikes and marched through Prague, giving Party leaders such a headache that they resigned before the end of the year.

you're up europe (1990-today)

After Czechoslovakia split in 1993, Prague became the capital city of the Czech Republic (Slovakia had dibs on Bratislava). And while it increasingly embraces Western European culture, the city still remembers its history, building memorials to the victims of Communism (such as the one in Malá Strana). The international community honored the city's more distant past, making its medieval center a UNESCO World Heritage Site and later naming Prague a European City of Culture, four years before the Czechs joined the European Union in 2004.

CUSTOMS AND ETIQUETTE

Czechs aren't exactly known for their generous warmth toward foreigners, but you probably wouldn't be either if your city was a favorite of stag parties and tourists looking for cheap beer (yes, we're looking at you). Czechs tend to smile only when genuinely pleased, so don't be surprised at their indifference to your witticisms. Keep in mind that a serious demeanor is a show of respect. It's polite to say hello *(dobrý den)* and goodbye *(na shledanou)* to people you meet, even complete strangers. If you find yourself invited to someone's home, remember to remove your shoes. Finally, shouting, drunkenly singing, or even just speaking to your friends on the subway or tram is a surefire way to identify yourself as a foreigner: you'll notice that natives are positively silent on their commutes.

hospoda-hopping

Pivo (beer) is basically a national treasure. Patrons are expected to sit next to strangers at the **hospoda** (pub). A standard drink is a half liter (16 oz.), which may, for some, require a couple weeks of preseason training. Always finish your beer, and never mix it with anything else, even the leftover beer from a previous drink. It's just rude. **Víno** (wine), on the other hand, is fine to dilute (in the summer try *střík,* a 50-50 mix of white wine and soda). In late summer and early fall, wine shops and pubs throughout the city peddle **burčák,** a partially fermented "young wine" that tastes something like adult Orangina and is best enjoyed in the out of doors. When you're out *hospoda-*hopping, remember that tips aren't expected, and neither is buying rounds for the table.

FOOD AND DRINK

Although Czech writer Pavel Eisner once described his country's food as "quite deleterious to the soul," Prague's heavy **meat and potatoes** diet is a good way to line your stomach for a night of *pivo.* For Czechs, *oběd* (lunch) is traditionally the main meal of the day. In urban Prague they're more likely to go for a quick fix of *klobása* (smoked sausage), from stands such as those that line Wenceslas Sq.

variations on a theme of dumplings

Vepřo-knedlo-zelo, pork-dumpling-cabbage goes the refrain, and you'll easily find these Czech staples around the city. For those with carnivorous urges, menus are conveniently organized by category of meat. Pork, the most popular, comes in sausages, goulash, and, for the more adventurous, pig offal. As for vegetarians, the joke goes that there are two vegetarian options—green cabbage and red cabbage. Although somewhat of an exaggeration (there's often frozen spinach!), traditional non-meat dishes extend little beyond *salat* (salad), *smažený sýr* (fried cheese), and *bramboráky* (potato pancakes). Filling *knedlíky* (dumplings) come as side dishes or desserts, in an uninspiring set of flavors: potato, fruit, and yes, even bread. (If visions of pierogi or Chinese dumplings are dancing in your head, think again: these guys are more like matzah meal rolled into a loaf and sliced.)

lager is for lovers

In the Czech Republic beer is known as "liquid bread," and indeed it is a dietary staple. Educate yourself on this national beverage, and whip out your knowledge for some street cred in the pubs (and even more street cred if you can remember these facts four pints in):

- **WE'RE NUMBER ONE!** The average Czech citizen drinks about 160L of beer per year—that makes the Czech Republic the number one beer-drinking nation per capita in the world. Move over, Ireland.

- **DRINK ON THE CHEAP.** At just 14Kč a pint, Czech beer is cheaper than bottled water.

- **KNOW YOUR NUMBERS.** The number on the side of a Czech bottle of beer refers not to its alcohol content, but rather to the beer's "degree." A higher degree indicates a stronger beer with a fuller taste.

- **L'CHAIM!** Drinking beer, according to many Czechs, reduces the amount of aluminum in the body, helping to prevent Alzheimer's disease and many symptoms of aging.

drinkin' beerz, beerz, beerz

If you don't immediately take to Czech cuisine, fear not: almost everything tastes better with beer (or at least after you've had a few). Czechs are some of the world's heaviest beer drinkers, with each person knocking back five half liters in an average sitting, which computes to a stunning average of 287 pints per person per year. Even under Communist rule, beer was subsidized. The Czechs recognize only two types of beer: **světlé** (light) and **černé** (dark). Darker beers are rich and taste like cake. The local degree system tells you how much malt extract was used in brewing: the higher the degree, the more malt and the greater the alcohol content. Twelve-degree beer is about four- to five-percent alcohol, and most taverns serve 10- or 12-degree beer. The most common Czech beer is Pilsner, named after the town Plzen outside of Prague.

If beer is too tame for you, absinthe and clove-flavored **Becherovka** pack a heavier punch. And if you prefer to stay sober and watch your friends make fools of themselves, power through the night with Turkish coffee (hot water poured directly onto the grounds). Don't expect a to-go cup, though, because they don't exist. Only the silliest of tourists totes a $5 Starbucks through Old Town.

ART AND ARCHITECTURE

With museums and galleries galore and 2000 officially registered monuments it's hard to miss all the art and architecture in Prague. If it's Modern and contemporary art you're after, head to **Museum Kampa** or **DOX**. Even the National Gallery, preserver of all things historic, sponsors the **NG333 competition,** for the best and brightest in

prague 101

young Czech art. Perhaps the best—and certainly the cheapest—way to experience the history of Czech art and architecture is just to walk around and look up.

building excitement

Prague first became know for its **Romanesque** churches and monasteries, with huge rotundas, single-aisle churches, and triple-aisle basilicas. As the power of the Catholic Church rose higher, so did the religious buildings, with the twin spires of St. Vitus Cathedral eventually reaching 318 ft. (a big step in the 1300s!). The cathedral was heralded in the **High Gothic** period, which dressed up Charles University, several churches, and the entire New Town, and gave Prague Castle a 14th-century makeover.

The Hapsburgs brought the bigger-than-life **Baroque** trend, and the Czechs turned to bigger palaces, supersized church buildings, and gaudy interior design. Emperor Joseph II, an ardent Catholic, bulldozed old Protestant churches and buildings to make way for these projects. Meanwhile, Prague Castle was reconstructed (again).

Not content with just waging revolution and forming political parties, Czech Nationalism took up the Neo-Renaissance style in a construction boom that brought the National Theatre and other national treasures. In the 20th century, Czechs looked to Vienna to find the curves of the **Art Nouveau** movement. After WWII, Communism sadly squashed architectural innovation for its own bland brand of Socialist Realism. After the Velvet Revolution, Prague regained architectural freedom and did a celebratory jig in the form of the **Dancing House.**

MUSIC

Prague's music history dates back to the 19th-century Nationalist movement, when Czech composers did their part to help carve out a Czech identity. **Classical** music buffs should check out the **Prague Spring International Music Festival** (☎257 312 547; www.prague-spring.net), which brings some of the best European artists and conductors to the city each year.

Jazz aficionados will be happy to know that the Communists considered jazz a peaceful (read: non-rebellious) type of music and allowed its survival under their regime. These days, festivals like **Strings of Autumn** (☎224 901 247; www.strunypodzimu.cz) let jazz artists jam alongside avant-garde and classical performers from around the world.

The city also has a soft spot for **hard rock.** Under Communism, censors blacklisted Frank Zappa's album *Absolutely Free.* That didn't stop smugglers from bringing the sounds of America to oppressed city dwellers, and Zappa quickly became the hottest thing to hit Prague since Nationalist drinking songs. When the Communist regime collapsed, president Vaclav Havel personally invited Zappa to Prague and even made him a "special ambassador." Although noise regulations have pushed most rock clubs out to the suburbs, you can still catch Zappa's legacy at places like **Rock Café** or **Bunkr Parukářka.**

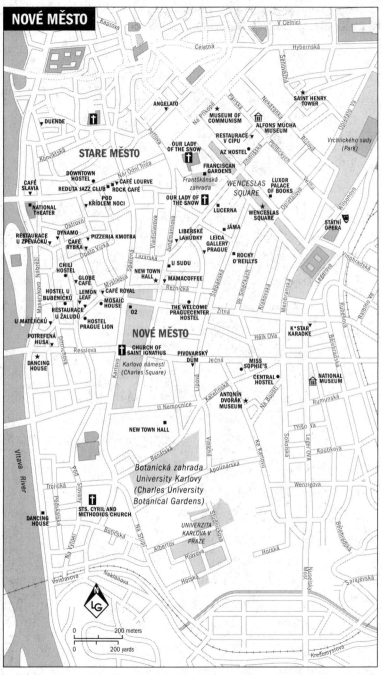

NOVÉ MĚSTO

STARE MĚSTO

WENCESLAS SQUARE

NOVÉ MĚSTO

ANGELATO

DUENDE

MUSEUM OF COMMUNISM

SAINT HENRY TOWER

ALFONS MUCHA MUSEUM

RESTAURACE V CIPU

OUR LADY OF THE SNOW

AZ HOSTEL

Vrchlického sady (Park)

FRANCISCAN GARDENS

Frantškánská zahrada

LUXOR PALACE OF BOOKS

CAFÉ SLAVIA

DOWNTOWN HOSTEL

REDUTA JAZZ CLUB

CAFÉ LOURVE

ROCK CAFÉ

POD KŘÍDLEM NOCI

OUR LADY OF THE SNOW

LUCERNA

WENCESLAS SQUARE

NATIONAL THEATER

STÁTNÍ OPERA

RESTAURACE U ZPĚVÁČKŮ

DYNAMO

CAFÉ RYBKA

PIZZERIA KMOTRA

JÁMA

LIBERSKÉ LAHŮDKY

LEICA GALLERY PRAGUE

CHILI HOSTEL

U SUDU

ROCKY O'REILLYS

GLOBE CAFÉ

NEW TOWN HALL

MAMACOFFEE

HOSTEL U BUBENÍČKŮ

LEMON LEAF

CAFÉ ROYAL

MOSAIC HOUSE

RESTAURACE U ŽALUDŮ

02

THE WELCOME PRAGUECENTER HOSTEL

U MATĚJÍČKŮ

HOSTEL PRAGUE LION

POTREFENÁ HUSA

CHURCH OF SAINT IGNATIUS

PIVOVARSKÝ DŮM

K•STAR KARAOKE

DANCING HOUSE

Karlovo náměstí (Charles Square)

MISS SOPHIE'S

CENTRAL HOSTEL

NATIONAL MUSEUM

ANTONÍN DVOŘÁK MUSEUM

NEW TOWN HALL

Botanická zahrada University Karlovy (Charles University Botanical Gardens)

Vltava River

STS. CYRIL AND METHODIUS CHURCH

DANCING HOUSE

UNIVERZITA KARLOVA V PRAZE

N LG

0   200 meters

0   200 yards

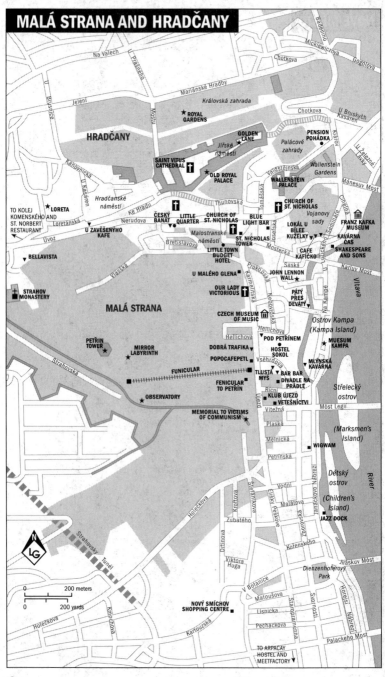

MALÁ STRANA AND HRADČANY

Na Valech

U Prašného

Mariánské Hradby

Královská zahrada

★ ROYAL
GARDENS

Chotkova

Jelení

Na Valech

U Brusnice

Mostu

GOLDEN
LANE

Jiřské
náměstí

HRADČANY

PENSION
POHÁDKA

Palácové
zahrady

U Bruských
Kasáren

Chotkova

SAINT VITUS
CATHEDRAL ✝

★ OLD ROYAL
PALACE

Valdštejnská

Wallenstein
Gardens

Mánesův Most

Kanovnická

U Kasáren

Hradčanské
náměstí

Loretánská

Ke Hradu

Thunovská

Tomášská

WALLENSTEIN
PALACE

Chřtěná

TO KOLEJ
KOMENSKÉHO AND
ST. NORBERT
RESTAURANT

★ LORETA

Nerudova

ČESKÝ
BANÁT

LITTLE
QUARTER

CHURCH OF
ST. NICHOLAS

BLUE
LIGHT BAR

CHURCH OF
ST. NICHOLAS ✝

Vojanovy
sady

FRANZ KAFKA
MUSEUM 🏛

▼ U ZAVĚŠENÝHO
KAFE

Úvoz

Malostranské
náměstí

Bretislavova

ST. NICHOLAS
TOWER

LOKÁL U
BÍLEE
KUZELKY ▼

Josefská

Seminář

KAVÁRNA
ČAS

▼ BELLAVISTA

LITTLE TOWN
BUDGET
HOTEL

Saská

CAFE
KAFÍČKO

SHAKESPEARE
AND SONS

✝ STRAHOV
MONASTERY

Vlašská

U MALÉHO GLENA ▼

Prokopská

JOHN LENNON
WALL ★

Na Kampě

Karlův Most

Vltava

MALÁ STRANA

OUR LADY
VICTORIOUS ✝

Karmelitská

PÁTÝ
PRES
DEVÁTÝ ▼

Nebovidská

CZECH MUSEUM
OF MUSIC 🏛

Ostrov Kampa
(Kampa Island)

PETŘÍN
TOWER

MIRROR
LABYRINTH

Hellichova

Hellichova

▼ POD PETŘÍNEM

MUSEUM
KAMPA ★

Strahovská

DOBRÁ TRAFIKA ▼

HOSTEL
SOKOL ★

POPOCAFEPETL ▼

Vševdova

MLÝNSKÁ
KAVÁRNA ▼

FUNICULAR

TLUSTÁ
MYS ▼

BAR BAR ▼

DIVADLO NA
PRÁDLE ■

**Střelecký
ostrov**

FENICULAR
TO PETŘÍN ▼

Říční

KLUB ÚJEZD ■

Most Legií

★ OBSERVATORY

Újezd

VETEŠNÍCTVI ■

Vitézná

MEMORIAL TO VICTIMS
OF COMMUNISM ★

Plaská

**(Marksmen's
Island)**

Melnická

Petřínská

■ WIGWAM

Štefánkova

Vodní

**Dětský
ostrov**

Konírova

Elišky Peškové

Malátova

Zborovská

Janáčkovo Nábřeží

Matěškovo Nábřeží

River

Drtinova

**(Children's
Island)**

Zubatého

■ JAZZ DOCK

Viktora
Huga

Kořenského

Jiráskuv Most

N
LG

Dienzenhoferovy
Park

Holečkova

Strahovský Tunél

0   200 meters
0   200 yards

Matoušova

Lisnická

V Botanice

NOVÝ SMÍCHOV
SHOPPING CENTRE ■

Karfourzka

Pechackova

Palackeho Most

Horejsi Nábřeží

Vltavská

Staropramenná

Zlíchovská

TO ARPACAY
HOSTEL AND
MEETFACTORY ▼

prague

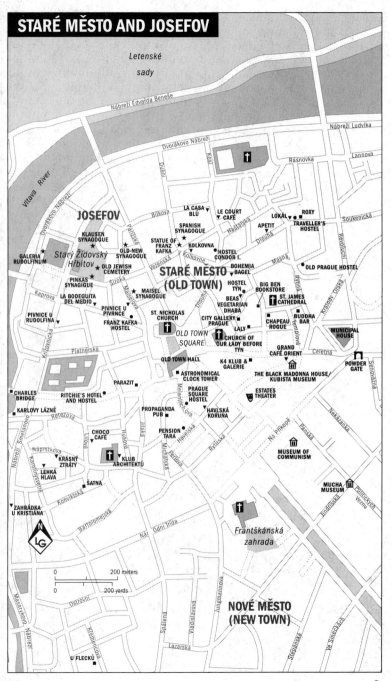

STARÉ MĚSTO AND JOSEFOV

Letenské sady

Nábřeží Edvarda Beneše

Vltava River

Dvořákovo Nábřeží

Nábřeží Ludvíka

Dušní

Kosí

Rásnovka

Lannova

JOSEFOV

Bilkova

LA CASA
BLÚ

LE COURT
CAFÉ

LOKÁL

ROXY

SPANISH
SYNAGOGUE

Hastalská

APETIT

TRAVELLER'S
HOSTEL

Soukenická

KLAUSEN
SYNAGOGUE

Pařížská

STATUE OF
FRANZ
KAFKA

Veřejná

KOLKOVNA

Dlouhá

Revoluční

Starý Židovský
Hřbitov

OLD-NEW
SYNAGOGUE

V Kolkovně

HOSTEL
CONDOR I.

Masná

OLD PRAGUE HOSTEL

GALERIA
RUDOLFINUM

OLD JEWISH
CEMETERY

BOHEMIA
BAGEL

**STARÉ MĚSTO
(OLD TOWN)**

HOSTEL
TÝN

BIG BEN
BOOKSTORE

Rybná

Králodvorská

PINKAS
SYNAGOGUE

Široká

MAISEL
SYNAGOGUE

Dlouhá

BEAS
VEGETARIAN
DHABA

ST. JAMES
CATHEDRAL

Kaprova

LA BODEGUITA
DEL MEDIO

Masařská

BUDDHA
BAR

PIVNICE U
RUDOLFINA

PIVNICE U
PIVRNCE

ST. NICHOLAS
CHURCH

CITY GALLERY
PRAGUE

CHAPEAU
ROGUE

Templová

MUNICIPAL
HOUSE

FRANZ KAFKA
HOSTEL

*OLD TOWN
SQUARE*

LALY

Křižovnická

Platnérská

CHURCH OF
OUR LADY BEFORE
TÝN

GRAND
CAFÉ ORIENT

Celetná

Senovážná

OLD TOWN HALL

K4 KLUB &
GALERIE

POWDER
GATE

CHARLES
BRIDGE

PARAZIT

ASTRONOMICAL
CLOCK TOWER

Melantrichova

THE BLACK MADONNA HOUSE/
KUBISTA MUSEUM

Nekázanka

RITCHIE'S HOTEL
AND HOSTEL

PRAGUE
SQUARE
HOSTEL

ESTATES
THEATER

KARLOVY LÁZNĚ

Retezová

PROPAGANDA
PUB

Na Příkopě

Panská

Iljská

Husova

HAVLSKÁ
KORUNA

CHOCO
CAFÉ

PENSION
TARA

Havelská

Michalská

Rytířská

Náprstkova

MUSEUM OF
COMMUNISM

Karoliny Světlé

Nábřeží Smetanovo

KRÁSNÝ
ZTRÁTY

KLUB
ARCHITEKTÚ

Bartolomějská

MUCHA
MUSEUM

Jindřišská

Politických Vernu

LEHKÁ
HLAVA

ŠATNA

Konviktská

ZAHRÁDKA
U KRISTIANA

N
LG

*Frantškánská
zahrada*

Nár. Odní Třída

0   200 meters

0   200 yards

Ostrovní

**NOVÉ MĚSTO
(NEW TOWN)**

Masarykovo
Nábřeží

Spálená

Vladislavova

Jungmannova

Štěpánská

Ve Smečkách

Lazarská

Křemencova

U FLECKÚ

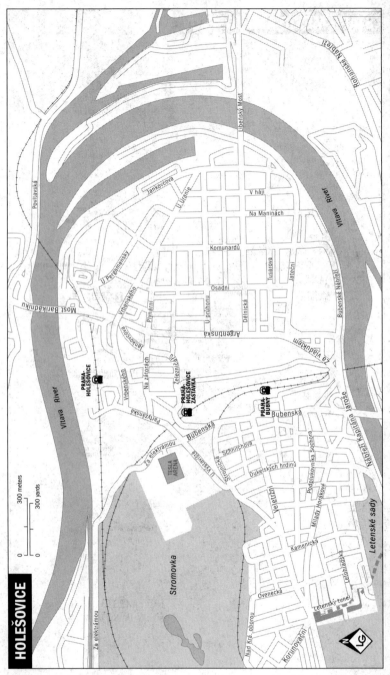

HOLEŠOVICE

Vltava River

Za elektrárnou

Stromovka

TESLA ARENA

Most Barikádníků

Za elektrárnou

U vísárni

Strojnická

Ovenecká

Nad Kró. oborou

Korunovační

Povltavská

Jankovcova

U Uranie

V háji

Na Maninách

U Pergamenský

Vrbenského

Jankovcova

Plynární

Komunardů

Tusarova

Jateční

Osadní

U průhonu

Dělnická

PRAHA-
HOLEŠOVICE

Na zátorách

Železniční

Argentinská

Bubenské Nábřeží

Za viaduktem

PRAHA-
HOLEŠOVICE
ZASTÁVKA

Partyzánská

Vrbenského

Bubenská

PRAHA-
BUBNY

Bubenská

Schnirchova

Dukelských hrdinů

Podplukovníka Sochora

Nábřeží Kapitána Jaroše

Vltava River

Těšnovský Most

Rohanské Nábřeží

Veletržní

Milady Horákové

Kamenická

Letohradská

Letohradská

Letenské sady

Letenský tunel

0   300 meters
0   300 yards

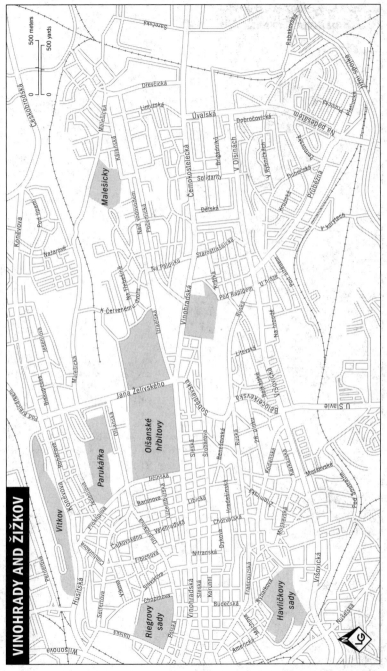

VINOHRADY AND ŽIŽKOV

vinohrady and žižkov map

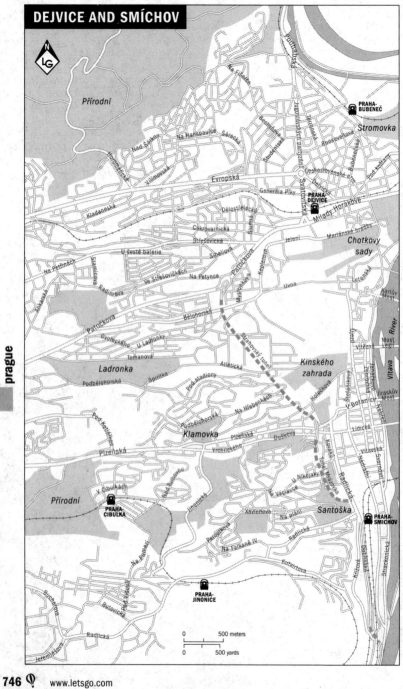

DEJVICE AND SMÍCHOV

Přírodní

Stromovka

PRAHA-BUBENEČ

Nad Šárkou

Na Hanspaulce

Sárecká

Jugoslávských partyzánů

Soudmitská

Roosveltova

Bubenská

Bubenečská

Pod Kaštan.

Hradnická

Vilímovská

Kladanská

Evropská

Československé arm.

PRAHA-DEJVICE

Milady Horákové

Generála Plky

Dělostřelecká

Cikrovarnická

Svatská

Jelení

Mariánské hradby

Chotkovy sady

Střešovická

Ve Střešovičkách

Na Petynce

U šesté Galerie

Patočkova

Koplerova

Na Petřinách

Sibeliova

Letenská

Stamicová

Radiniova

Úvoz

Karlův Most

Vltava River

Linhartská

Patočkova

Bělohorská

Střešovická

Dvoreckého

U Ladronky

Tomanová

Atletická

Myslbekova

Střahovský tunel

Kinského zahrada

Most Legii

Vítězná

Ladronka

Spitka

Podbělohorská

Pod stadiony

Na Hřebenkách

Holečkova

Štefánikova

Zborovská

Matoušova

Jiraskův Most

V Botanice

Podbělohorská

Pilzeňská

Duškova

Lidická

Vrchlického

Vltavská

Svornosti

Klamovka

Pilzeňská

Nádražní

Přírodní

V Cibulkách

PRAHA-CIBULKA

Nad Bučkovou

Jinonická

Na Václavce

U Nikoláky

Kartouz

Nádražní

Radlická

Santoška

PRAHA-SMÍCHOV

Na baních

Petřínová

Xavierlova

Na pláni

Butovická

Na Farkáně IV

Radlická

Kutvirtová

Buchlová

Radlická

PRAHA-JINONICE

Na baních

Pod Kesnerkou

Strakonická

Křížová

Na baních

Jeremiášova

Na Farkáně

Pod Kelimendou

prague

0   500 meters
0   500 yards

ROME

Rome: the epitome of Italy, and its biggest enigma. It condenses every stereotype that plagues the country into one sprawling metropolis... and then rambles on another few kilometers and centuries to reverse them all. With neighborhoods off the map and streets too small to be mapped, this is a city as expansive as it is walkable, as global as it is local. And here's the biggest paradox of all: it's as young as it is old. And that doesn't mean Rome averages out to some middle-aged soccer mom.

People come to this city for many reasons: for history, for artistic enlightenment, or to eat so much pasta and pizza that they won't leave until someone rolls them out. Nowhere else in the world could you view the immaculate ceiling of the Sistine Chapel after exploring the dilapidated remains of ancient settlements, and still dance the night away once the sun has set. Rome brings every Italian experience together but remains truly unique, and you can't expect to conquer it all (Carthage tried with an entire army and failed.) Sometimes, like the speeding Vespas that only stop when you walk in front of them, Rome requires that you stand up to it. Are you ready for the challenge?

greatest hits

- **BUY ONE COUNTRY, GET ONE FREE.** Fed up with Italy? The **Vatican City,** small but magnificent, is still doing pretty well for itself (p. 772).

- **HOSTEL HEAVEN.** Rolling into **Termini Station,** you're on the brink of one of Europe's highest concentrations of cheap beds (p. 760).

- **ANCIENT ANTIQUES.** The **Colosseum** is just the beginning of Ancient Rome's gifts to the modern city (p. 764).

- **CHEEZE-N-PEPA. Cacio e Pepe** in the Vatican City will have your tastebuds singing "Oooh, baby, baby" (p. 790).

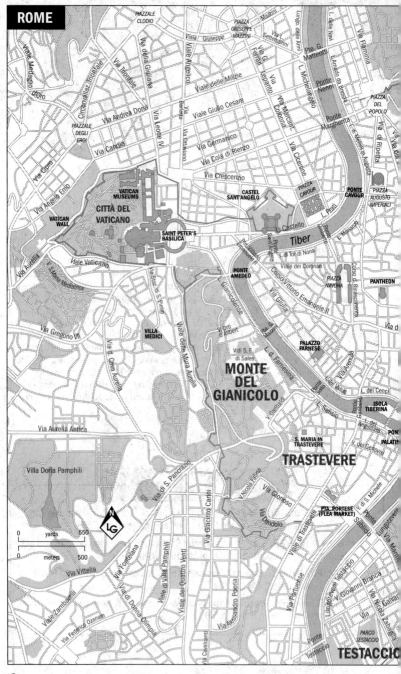

ROME

rome

GALLERIA NAZIONALE D'ARTE MODERNE

VILLA BORGHESE

V. del Muro Torto

Via Salaria

Viale Regina Margherita

V. Dalmazia

VILLA TORLONIA

Via Po

V.Isonzo

Via Nizza

Via Nomentana

Corso d'Italia

PIAZZA FIUME

Via Piave

PORTA PIA

PIAZZA DELLA CROCE ROSA

POLICLINICO UNIVERSITA

Via dei Monti

Via V. Veneto

Via Boncompagni

Viale Regina Elena

SPANISH STEPS

V. Ludovisi

XX Settembre

BIBLIOTECA NAZIONALE

SALARIO

Via dell'Università

PIAZZA

Via Sistina

Via Barberini

MUSEO NAZIONALE ROMANO

Via Palestro

Via dei Castro Pretorio

Via del Tritone

PIAZZA BARBERINI

V. d. Quattro Fontane

PIAZZA DELLA REPUBBLICA

PIAZZA DEL CINQUECENTO

ENJOY ROME

PALAZZO DEL QUIRINALE

PIAZZA VENEZIA

STAZIONE TERMINI

Via Marsala

TREVI FOUNTAIN

Via del Quirinale

Via Nazionale

Via Giovanni Giolitti

Via Tiburtina

Via Panisperna

Via Cavour

PIAZZA SANTA MARIA MAGGIORE

Via Giovanni Lanza

Via Merulana

PIAZZA VITTORIO EMANUELE

Via dei Fori Imperiali

Via Cavour

MPIDOGLIO

PIAZZA DEL COLOSSEO

Via Machiavelli

Via Emanuele Filiberto

Viale Manzoni

V. S. Croce in Gerusalemme

V. Statilia

PIAZZA DI PIA MAGGIORE

FORUM

RO CELLO

TEMPIO DELLA FORTUNA VIRILE

COLOSSEUM

Via Labicana

VILLA WOLKONSKI

TEMPIO DI VESTA

MONTE PALATINO

Via di S. Gregorio

Via Claudia

PARCO DEL CELIO

P. DI SAN GIOVANNI IN LATERANO

PALAZZO LATERANENSE

CIRCO MASSIMO (CIRCUS MAXIMUS)

Via del Cerchi

Via di S. Stefano Rotondo

SAN STEFANO ROTONDO

SAN GIOVANNI IN LATERANO

Via dei Circo Massimo

CELIO

Via dell'Amba Aradam

Via Magna Grecia

Via Appia

Via di S. Prisca

Via delle Terme

Via Druso

Via d. Laterani

Via Cerveteri

P. DEI RE DI ROMA

AVENTINO

Viale Aventino

Viale Aventina

V. Antoniana

Via Galilia

Via Etruria

Nuova

TERME DI CARACALLA

Via di Terme di Caracalla

Viale Metronio

Via di Porta Latina

Via Satrico

Via Concordia

Via Sinta

Viale Giotto

Viale Guido Baccelli

Via di Porta Sebastiano

Via Vetulonia

Via Acaia

Via Marco Polo

It's not only archaeology students who'll find something of interest in Rome. For a destination with such a prominent Ancient City, Rome is shockingly young, and its culture is strongly influenced by its students and 20-something residents. The 147,000 students of Rome's **Sapienza University** give the city one of Europe's largest student bodies. Sapienza is based in the San Lorenzo neighborhood a little to the east of Termini Station. By a convenient coincidence, that puts it right next to tourists' main entrance point and the city's highest concentration of budget accommodations. If you're wondering where the young people stay, this area is it. In a remarkably unsurprising development, the combination of students and student travelers in Termini makes this area into one of the city's biggest nighttime destinations, with bars and clubs crowding the streets. Be aware that students aren't the only people around after dark: pickpockets love to operate here.

As much as Termini and San Lorenzo are the central student destinations, they're just the beginning in this diverse city. The **Centro Storico** may be full of ancient *piazze* and grand temples to the dead, but it also features extremely accessible bars that serve great *aperitivo* buffets each night. Try Drunken Ship if you've been away from a beer pong table for a little too long. To find international students, head across the Tiber to **Trastevere,** home of an American liberal arts college, John Cabot University. This is a favorite haunt of study-abroad students, so come here and relax in Cafe Friends anytime between 7am and 2am and enjoy a 15% discount with a student ID. The southern neighborhoods of **Testaccio and Ostiense** are other great options. In Rome, there's so much going on in the present, you just might forget to appreciate what the city is most famous for: its past.

orientation

rome

Rome is easily navigable on foot—every time you think you're lost, another monument pops up and you're back on track. The best way to think of Rome is as a body: a few major arteries (some with significant blockage problems) will take you from region to region, while countless capillaries branch off into compact neighborhoods. P. Venezia is not really the heart of Rome, but it's where the city's main thoroughfares convene. V. Cavour and V. Nazionale are the legs leading down to Rome's foot: Termini, the city's main transportation hub. The arm of the V. dei Fori Imperiali takes you back in time, passing the Roman Forum and the Colosseum. The other arm, the V. del Corso, heads into the very commercial present, as it's filled with shops and the crowds that go with them. This then becomes the V. Flaminia, which navigates around the Villa Borghese. Rome's "neck" is the Centro Storico, a mass of winding streets where navigation by map is much more difficult than navigation by monument. The Corso Vittorio Emanuele II is a useful throughway which leads across the Tiber River into Rome's slightly less crazy head, home to Trastevere and not-technically-part-of-Rome-but-we're-still-including-it-for-obvious-reasons Vatican City.

ANCIENT CITY

With one of the highest camera-to-square-inch-of-sidewalk ratios in Rome, the Ancient City doesn't exactly feel "ancient." This vast stretch of tourist heaven, whose sights are the reason that many people come to Italy, is a stunning mix of old and new—for every ruin you'll see (and there are plenty), there's probably a plastic replica to match. The **Via dei Fori Imperiali** is the main thoroughfare for ruin-seekers, passing the **Colosseum** and **Roman Forum** before reaching **Piazza Venezia,** where the road ends with the classical pastiche that is the Vittorio Emanuele II Monument. Around the P. Venezia, even more Roman ruins await at **Via del Teatro di Marcello,** although these are less famous (but only moderately less impressive). **Via Cavour** leads from the Roman Forum to the pleasant Monti area and Esquiline Hill, full of narrow, picturesque streets that aren't clogged with tourist traps. Perhaps it's the feeling of time travel as you survey the remains of an extinct civilization (or maybe it's the mouth-watering aroma of fresh-baked pizza that does it), but tourist travails pale in comparison to the pleasures of the Ancient City.

CENTRO STORICO

To the traveler who has paid one too many euro after waiting in one too many 4hr. lines, the Centro Storico offers a reprieve: nearly all of the churches, monuments, and *piazze* are free of charge, and the only lines you'll be waiting in are for overpriced gelato. With most of the main attractions clustered on either side of **Corso Vittorio Emanuele II,** this tangled web of streets is manageable in size, though not the easiest to navigate. Expect to get lost as *vie* suddenly split into numerous *vicoli.* Use Corso Vittorio Emanuele II as a departure point and the vibrant urban living rooms of **Campo dei Fiori** and **Piazza Navona** as your major landmarks. Letting yourself get lost might be the best approach, though: you'll find yourself effortlessly arriving at unassuming churches and monuments, only to realize they're famous landmarks. The entire region seems to be in a constant state of entropy, with tourists bumping into each other as they dart from one photo op to another in a part of town that stays high-energy late into the night.

PIAZZA DI SPAGNA

Nestled between the Tiber River and the grounds of the Villa Borghese, the area around the P. di Spagna is Rome's answer to 5th Ave., the Champs-Élysées, and the West End. From the **Piazza del Popolo,** the neighborhood branches off into three main roads: the quieter **Via della Ripetta,** the overbearing **Via del Corso,** and the **Via del Babuino.** The last of these leads to the **Spanish Steps.** The fashion-obsessed will love **Via dei Condotti,** home to the shops of some of the most exclusive Italian designers. Sightseers on a budget will not be disappointed, either, as many landmarks (like the **Trevi Fountain**) are free to the public. To avoid the capitalist onslaught, take a stroll on the elevated **Viale di Trinita dei Monti,** which offers the best view of P. di Spagna and its artistic marvels.

JEWISH GHETTO

Just across from Trastevere is the small area known as the Jewish Ghetto, the first of its kind in Western Europe. Bordering the **Lungotevere dei Cenci** is the impressive **Great Synagogue,** the spiritual and physical center of the area. It's a small, residential neighborhood that is renowned for delicious Kosher food, especially ⬛**carciofi alla giudia** (insanely delicious fried artichokes) found mainly in the restaurants of the **Via del Portico d'Ottavia.** Friday evenings and Saturdays are not, of course, the times to visit, as residents will be at home observing the Sabbath. The tiny Jewish Ghetto is pretty and peaceful, a welcome break from the many tourists next door in Centro Storico.

VATICAN CITY

The people-to-square-foot ratio is significantly cockeyed in this part of the city: the madhouse of tourists in the Vatican contrasts sharply with the empty boulevards in the surrounding region of **Prati.** That's actually a good thing—after forging through crowds to pay a visit to the pope, you'll be able to wander effortlessly down tree-

orientation

lined streets visited only by dog walkers and the occasional lost tourist looking for a big dome (a.k.a. **Saint Peter's Basilica**). If the plastic souvenirs, bright flags, and English menus aren't enough to indicate which region you're in, the brick wall that physically separates Vatican City from Prati should give you a clue. On the Prati side, you'll find surprisingly affordable hotels and casual trattorias scattered among modern, pastel residential buildings. For all this talk about crowds in Vatican City, even when you make your way back toward the pope's digs, the throng of people is more manageable than what you'll find in central Rome. Maybe it's the gargantuan size of St. Peter's and its *piazza*, or perhaps peoples' religious consciences keeping them away, but somehow the tourist crush is more diluted than you'd expect.

TRASTEVERE

Trastevere is to Rome as Brooklyn is to New York: overlooked by tourists, loved by locals, and removed from the metropolitan center while still being in the thick of things. There aren't any Metro stops nearby, but you can play choose-your-own-adventure by crossing one of the three main bridges into different parts of town. The **Ponte Fabricio** and the **Isola Tiberina** open into the quieter, right side of the neighborhood where there are plenty of restaurants and laid-back bars. The **Ponte Garibaldi** leads into **Piazza G. Belli** and the less-than-beautiful **Viale Trastevere.** Finally, the **Ponte Sisto** brings you right into the **Piazza Trilussa** and the heart of Trastevere's extensive night-life. While you probably won't end up sleeping here, as there are few budget-friendly accommodations, the excellent bar and club scene and unpretentious, homegrown restaurants make this a good bet for evenings, and daytime strolls provide plenty of photo ops. If you've had enough of monuments and ruins, take a walk in the lush gardens and open spaces of **Gianicolo Hill,** but be prepared for a steep hike.

TERMINI AND SAN LORENZO

Ask people if they saw the Vatican, the Colosseum, or any other number of famous sights on their last trip to Rome, and they'll most likely answer no to at least one of them; with so much to take in, something's got to give. It's ironic, then, that everyone passes through Termini, as mundane and unromantic as it is. It's the city's transportation hub—and it's got the blocks of hostels to prove it. Instead of a scenic vista or renowned Roman ruins, prepare yourself for a stifling stream of merchants, restaurants, dives, and—did we mention?—hostels. **Via Giovanni Giolitti,** which runs alongside Termini, and the streets surrounding **Piazza Indipendenza** are lined with budget accommodations. If you haven't made a reservation, you can probably find a last-minute budget option here, but even those who plan ahead often pick this bustling spot to be their home away from home. With prime access to the Metro, major bus lines, great nightlife (read: international student mania), and even a few sights of its own, no other part of Rome matches Termini's convenience. Our only advice: try to arrive by daylight. With a backpack or an unwieldy suitcase, and a long plane ride behind you, trekking through the maze of people and advertisements can provide not only a disheartening first impression of Rome, but a somewhat dangerous one as well.

NORTHERN ROME

Unlike the city center, Northern Rome offers visitors more contemporary sights (at least in Italian terms) and residential areas. Villas from the 17th and 18th centuries are scattered throughout the area, most notably the expansive **Villa Borghese** and the more modest **Villa Torlonia.** You could easily spend a day wandering these villas, but there are also great museums if you're into not-ancient art. Practically every *piazza* and museum features a sculptural or architectural work of the great Gian Lorenzo Bernini; if you're hoping to find something even more recent, Rome's modern and contemporary art museums are nearby. The **Piazza del Popolo,** originally an important entry point into the city, is now at the top of a shopping district and right next to the grounds of the Villa Borghese. To the east, the **Porta Pia** marks the beginning of the beautiful and primarily residential (or ambassadorial) **Via Nomentana.** Inexpensive food can be hard to come by, so take advantage of the many open spaces for picnics and leisurely strolls.

spqr sightings

Look out for the omnipresent letters SPQR just about everywhere in Rome. The acronym, standing for "Senatus Populusque Romanus," ("The Senate and People of Rome"), dates back to the founding of the Roman Republic. Italian cartoonists have re-outfitted the saying as *"sono pazzi questi Romani"* ("these Romans are crazy"). During WWII, Mussolini emblazoned the acronym on manholes and public buildings in an attempt to promote his dictatorship over a new Roman Empire. The fact that the symbol is written on every sewage drain cover in the city probably says something about the quality of Mussolini's reign.

TESTACCIO AND OSTIENSE

Located south of the Colosseum, Testaccio and Ostiense are left off most tourist itineraries and are literally off Rome's central map. ⓂB toward **Piramide** leads to **Piazzale Ostiense,** from which radiate a number of large streets: **Via Marmorata** crosses the river into Trastevere and **Via Ostiense** is the area's main thoroughfare. Composed of newer, residential housing and paved streets, these uncongested neighborhoods let you put away the guidebook for an afternoon (though studies have shown that copies of *Let's Go* double their lifespan if exposed to ample sunlight, so consider keeping yours out), but make sure to save energy for the pulsing clubs. They may have long lines and be far from the center of Rome, but they offer some of the best nightlife in the city. You might not come here with high expectations, but the culinary, cultural, and clubbing surprises are sure to charm you.

SOUTHERN ROME

Just because it's off the tourist map doesn't mean Southern Rome isn't worth at least a day of exploring sans itinerary. This stretch of the city is home to residential streets, enough churches to convert you to Catholicism, and, yes, more ruins. The churches are along the **Via Labicana** and near the **Piazza di San Giovanni in Laterano,** so keep an eye out for towers, nuns, and priests to orient yourself. The **Appian Way** has enough sights to demand its own day-long visit, and is marked at every bend in the road by ruined aqueducts, entrances to catacombs, and fragments of statues. Less touristed than central Rome, this area is a great place to view some amazing Christian monuments without waiting in Vatican-sized lines.

accommodations

Everything from cheap hostels to swanky four-star hotels are available in Rome, making the selection process somewhat daunting. Smaller (and often cheaper) *pensioni* and bed and breakfasts are starting to compete by providing large hotels with amenities like air-conditioning, kitchens, and free Wi-Fi. Even the better hostels seem bent on improving, but you'll still probably have to sleep in a bunk bed if you choose a dorm. Low season starts around November and lasts until early March, when prices pick up considerably. April through October is considered high season, although prices dip a bit in August. For rentals of one to six months, check out the *Porta*

accommodations

Portese newspaper (www.portaportese.it), sold at all *tabaccherie* for €1. Libraries, universities, and even local cafes often post fliers advertising short-term rooms in shared apartments. In terms of convenience, residential feel, and cost, Trastevere, Testaccio and Ostiense, and San Giovanni (south of Termini) are ideal places to find your home-away-from-home. Termini is the best place to find last-minute and conveniently located accommodations, especially for travelers arriving by train. Just be wary of hotel scouts who advertise overpriced rooms late in the evening.

ANCIENT CITY

The Ancient City is not the cheapest place to plant yourself during a visit to Rome, though if you're willing to shell out at least €100 a night, you'll have plenty of four-star options to choose from. A few bed and breakfasts and *pensioni* are more affordable if you'd rather spend your euro on pictures with the Colosseum's gladiators.

▧ CASA SANTA PUDENZIANA   CONVENT $
V. Urbana 158   ☎06 48 80 056; www.santapudenziana.it

Women who don't mind a 10:30pm curfew (midnight on Saturday) may find the quiet and spacious grounds of Casa Santa Pudenziana a welcome relief from the more crowded (and pricier) hostels nearby. This convent's six-bed dorm and few other rooms make for a small community of guests, who often run into each other at meals in the peaceful courtyard. While there are no lockers or keys, don't fear for the safety of your things, since the staff acts as doorkeepers, as well.

✦ Ⓜ B: Cavour. From V. Cavour, turn onto V. Urbana. *i* Breakfast included. Dinner €10. Women only. Ⓢ 6-bed dorms €22; singles €40, with bath €50; doubles €52; triples €78. Inquire about discounts for longer stays. Cash only. ◲ Reception 7am until curfew. Curfew M-F 10:30pm, Sa midnight, Su 10:30pm.

HOTEL SAN DANIELE BUNDÌ   HOTEL $$$
V. Cavour 295   ☎06 48 75 295; www.hotelsandanielebundi.it

Neighboring establishments recommend Hotel Bundì for its simple rooms and accommodating staff. Although the hotel is small, its central location, (relatively) reasonable prices, and surprising tranquility make it a good bet.

✦ Ⓜ A: Colosseum. From V. dei Fori Imperiali, turn right onto V. Cavour. Buzz at the doors and take Scala B to the 3rd fl. *i* Breakfast included. All rooms with bath. A/C. Free Wi-Fi. Ⓢ Singles €55-65; doubles €75-85. ◲ Reception until 8pm.

PENSIONE ROSETTA   PENSIONE $$$
V. Cavour 295   ☎06 47 82 30 69; www.rosettahotel.com

A friendly staff and clean rooms make Pensione Rosetta a convenient option for those who hope to roll out of bed and check out the Colosseum in their pajamas. Each of Rosetta's 20 rooms has a private bathroom, TV, and air-conditioning; free Wi-Fi is available in most rooms and public areas. The central courtyard provides a welcome respite from busy V. Cavour.

✦ Ⓜ A: Colosseum. From V. dei Fori Imperiali, turn right onto V. Cavour. Buzz for entry and take Scala B to the 1st fl. Ⓢ Singles €65; doubles €90; triples €105; quads €120.

CESARE BALBO INN   HOTEL $$$$
V. Cesare Balbo 43   ☎06 98 38 60 81; www.cesarebalboinn.com

Conveniently located entirely on the first floor, Cesare Balbo Inn is perfect for those too lazy to climb a flight of stairs or walk more than a mile to Rome's ancient sights. Rooms here are big, colorful, and sunny. Great restaurants and bars on V. dei Serpenti and V. Cavour are just a few streets away. In spite of the hopping places nearby, Cesare Balbo still manages to remain peaceful.

✦ Ⓜ B: Cavour. Walk down V. Cavour and turn left onto V. Panisperna, walk 2 blocks, and turn right onto V. Cesare Balbo. Ⓢ Doubles €55-99; triples €69-105; quads €90-130. ◲ Reception 24hr.

peek-a-boo

If your mission is to find the greatest views of Rome, you should stop by what is known as the "magic keyhole." Journey to the P. dei Cavalieri di Malta and two guards will show you to the Priory of the Knights of Malta. There you'll find a keyhole. Look through, Mary, and you'll be sure to find a secret garden. At the end of the pathway you'll see shrubs perfectly framing St. Peter's Basilica. The view is spectacular, but don't try to photograph it; many a *Let's Go* Researcher has tried and failed extraordinarily. Perhaps in this adventure a picture won't last longer.

CENTRO STORICO

The Centro Storico is not the cheapest place to stay, but hotels here tend to have more character and better amenities than those found elsewhere. Reserve rooms well in advance, and don't expect them to be cheap.

👍 ALBERGO DEL SOLE — HOTEL $$$$

V. del Biscione 76 — ☎06 68 80 68 73; www.solealbiscione.it

With real metal room keys hanging from wall pegs and antique wooden furniture, the Albergo del Sole feels like a hotel from an earlier era. The conveniences are modern, though, and after a long day of sightseeing in the Centro, you'll appreciate checking your email on the garden terrace or in one of the neatly furnished common areas. While not exactly a bargain, it offers the expected comforts of hotels in this neighborhood, but looks much prettier doing it.

➡ Exit P. di Fiori onto V. del Biscione. ℹ Most rooms A/C. Wi-Fi €1.50 per hr. $ Singles €75, with bath €100-130; doubles €100-110/125-160. Cash only. ⏰ Reception 24hr.

CITY'S HOUSE B AND B — B AND B $$$$

V. della Maddalena 51 — ☎06 45 43 31 75; www.cityhouserome.com

The rooms at City's House are somewhat bigger than others in the area, but the decor is more knock-off Martha Stewart than authentic Roman charm. Prices are a little lower here, though, and the website offers specials for booking online.

➡ From P. Navona, take V. Santa Giovanna d'Arco to P. Maddalena. Buzz for entry. ℹ A/C. $ Singles €60-100; doubles €80-150. Cash only.

ALBERGO POMEZIA — HOTEL $$$$

V. dei Chiavari 13 — ☎06 68 61 371; www.hotelpomezia.it

The rooms are small, which is typical in this jam-packed part of Rome, but free Wi-Fi can at least broaden your digital horizons. As with all of the hotels in the Centro, location is the main draw, so you'll probably spend most of your time outside of your unremarkable room anyway, rightfully avoiding the cheesy *Roman Holiday* paraphernalia.

➡ From Campo dei Fiori, walk down V. dei Giubbonari and turn left onto V. dei Chiavari. ℹ Free Wi-Fi. All rooms with bath. $ Singles €80-130; doubles €90-150. Weekends tend to be more expensive.

CASA BANZO — HOTEL $$$$

P. del Monte di Pietà 30 — ☎06 68 33 909; www.casabanzo.it

Frescoed walls, potted plants, and stained-glass windows at the reception desk hint at the beauty of the rooms and mini-apartments in this converted 15th-century *palazzo*. Some rooms have kitchens and balconies overlooking the central courtyard, while others are so small they fit only a bed and a dresser.

➡ From Campo dei Fiori, walk down V. dei Giubbonari, turn left onto V. della Pietà, and walk into P. del Monte di Pietà. Buzz for entry. ℹ Breakfast €7. Free Wi-Fi. All rooms with bath. $ Standard rooms €120; apartments €120-180. ⏰ Reception 8:30am-1pm and 4pm-midnight; call about arrival time. Guests get a key to enter.

PIAZZA DI SPAGNA

Staying in Piazza di Spagna is a pricey affair, and though you might be getting newer accommodations and slightly better services, you'll be surrounded by more crowds than in the Ancient City or Centro Storico. If your heart is set on staying near the Trevi Fountain, just know that the extra cost might leave you with no coins to throw in it.

🏨 HOTEL PANDA
V. della Croce 35

HOTEL $$$

☎06 67 80 179; www.hotelpanda.it

Though there are no panda bears around, you'll feel as warm and fuzzy as a bamboo-chomping cutie at this small, family-run hotel. Simply decorated rooms come with air-conditioning, Wi-Fi, and TV at a better price than at the spiffier hotels down the street. The rooms with shared bathrooms really only have room for the bed and your legs getting out of it, so if you need more space, opt for a bigger room with an ensuite. While by no means a truly cheap option, Panda's about as close as you'll get to one in this part of town.

🚇 ⓂA: Spagna. From the Spanish Steps, take V. dei Condotti, turn right onto V. Belsiana and right onto V. della Croce. Hotel Panda is on the 2nd fl. ⓈSingles €55-68, with bath €65-80; doubles €68-78/85-108; triples €120-140. 5% discount for cash payment. ⌚Reception 24hr.

OKAPI ROOMS
V. della Penna 57

HOTEL $$$

☎06 32 60 98 15; www.okapirooms.it

Owned by the same people who run Hotel Panda, Okapi is a newer and slightly nicer option. Unfortunately, this also means the prices are higher, but in return you get bigger rooms with ensuite bathrooms on a quiet street near the P. del Popolo. Some rooms have terraces, and common areas on every floor add to the spaciousness. The owners' apparent penchant for exotic animals is not, however, reflected in the decor. Instead, rooms are decorated in soft colors with simple prints of Roman sights, so the closest you'll get to wildlife here is a pigeon on a windowsill.

🚇 ⓂA: Flaminio-Piazza del Popolo. From the piazza, veer right onto V. Ripetta and take an immediate right onto V. della Penna d'Oca, which becomes V. della Penna. 𝒊 A/C. Free Wi-Fi. ⓈDoubles as singles €65-110; doubles €85-160; triples €110-160. ⌚Reception 24hr.

DOMUS JULIA
V. Rasella 32

HOTEL $$$$

☎06 47 45 765; www.domusjulia.it

The excited hotel dog greets guests at Domus Julia, a slightly less expensive addition to the Hotel Julia that's next door. The hotel's 18th-century building retains its historic look but adds modern comforts like free internet. If you've gotten a bit bored of staring at ruins, rent one of the free bikes or hang out in the large breakfast room or bar of the hotel next door.

🚇 ⓂA: Barberini. From P. Barberini, take V. del Tritone, turn left onto V. Boccaccio and then left onto V. Rasella. 𝒊 Breakfast included. All rooms with bath. ⓈSingles €70-140; doubles €78-180; triples €89-210. ⌚Reception 24hr.

VATICAN CITY

When it comes to hotels, the area around the Vatican is as overpriced as the pizza and souvenirs. However, the quiet streets closer to the river and Prati offer many affordable options, mainly small hotels in residential buildings. The area is close to the sights and removed from nightlife, so it provides a quiet escape.

🏨 COLORS
V. Boezio 31

HOTEL, HOSTEL $

☎06 68 74 030; www.colorshotel.com

There's no mystery to this hotel-hostel's name: the walls are brightly painted and adorned with abstract paintings. With common spaces on two floors and spacious terraces for mid-afternoon wine breaks, you'll be sure to meet fellow

travelers, although they might not be as rowdy as the backpackers in other hostels. Free Wi-Fi and air-conditioning in all rooms (even the dorms) give Colors even more of an edge. If you're traveling in a group, save a few euro by booking a three- to six-bed dorm instead of shelling out the extra cash for doubles.

 # [M]A: Ottaviano. Walk down V. Ottaviano and turn left onto V. Cola di Rienzo and right onto V. Terenzio. Colors is at the intersection with V. Boezio. i Breakfast included in hotel; €7 in dorm. [$] Dorms €20-30; singles €40-70, with bath €50-80; doubles €52-100; triples €70-100. Cash preferred. ⏰ Reception 24hr.

HOTEL AL SAN PIETRINO HOTEL $$$

V. Giovanni Bettolo 43 ☎06 37 00 132; www.sanpietrino.it

Small green frogs (don't worry, they're ceramic) and the smell of flowers greet guests at this small hotel, just 5min. from the Vatican Museums. Though the rooms aren't particularly large, free Wi-Fi and air-conditioning make it a better deal than nearby alternatives. Breakfast isn't included, but there's an organic grocery store down the street.

 # [M]A: Ottaviano. Exit onto V. Barletta and turn left onto V. Giovanni Bettolo. [$] Singles €50-65; doubles with bath €70-89; triples with bath €120. ⏰ Reception 24hr.

HOTEL NAUTILUS PENSIONE $$$

V. Germanico 198, 3rd fl. ☎06 32 42 118; www.hotelnautilusroma.it

Big, recently renovated rooms are the main draw here, especially if the crowds at St. Peter's have you longing for some room to breathe. If the Vatican has inspired you, turn your stay here into a monastic experiment: no internet access means it'll be easy to devote yourself to a life of reflection. Hotel Nautilus is a comfortable place to stay if you don't need many amenities and want some quiet.

 # [M]A: Lepanto. Walk down V. Ezio and turn right onto V. Germanico. i Breakfast included. [$] Singles €40-55; doubles €65-90; quads €90-130. ⏰ Reception 24hr. Call to arrange arrival time.

PENSIONE PARADISE PENSIONE $$$

Vle. Giulio Cesare 47, 3rd fl. ☎06 36 00 43 31; www.pensioneparadise.com

The rooms at Pensione Paradise come at good prices but offer less charm than older establishments and fewer amenities than newer ones. Narrow halls match the small rooms, though both are welcoming with warm lighting and old stone floors. Free Wi-Fi in public areas wins it major brownie points, but you're on your own for breakfast. The lack of air-conditioning means this might be a better choice during the non-summer months, or for those who are OK with a tropical atmosphere.

 # [M]A: Lepanto. [$] Singles €50-75, with bath €60-85; doubles with bath €60-98. ⏰ Reception 24hr.

HOTEL LADY PENSIONE $$$

V. Germanico 198, 5th fl. ☎06 32 42 112; www.hotelladyroma.it

Aesthetics trump amenities here: the old-fashioned charm of this former monastery is unfortunately accompanied by a lack of air-conditioning and Wi-Fi. Still, the exposed-beam ceilings and amber stained-glass windows create a feeling of comfort that most modern hotels can't replicate. Rooms without bathrooms may be less convenient but are significantly larger.

 # [M]A: Lepanto. Walk down V. Ezio and turn right onto V. Germanico. [$] Singles €55-70; doubles €70-100, with bath €85-120; triples €100-130. ⏰ Reception 24hr. Call to arrange arrival time.

TRASTEVERE

Chances are you'll spend far more time awake in Trastevere than asleep. There are no hostels in this part of town, and the bed and breakfasts and hotels are pricier because people are, understandably, willing to pay for Trastevere's cobblestone charm.

prego

Prego. The word is like pizza: Italians have somehow found a way to top or dress it with anything; to have it in any context, at any time of day; and to make it hot, cold, or even lukewarm to match the occasion. Whatever the situation, it all flies:

- **"PREGO?"** The first thing you'll hear as you walk into a *pasticceria*. Translation: "How can I help you?" or "What do you want?" And they expect you to know, immediately. (Standing around asking prices doesn't work too well.)

- **"PREGO!"** A favorite of the Sistine Chapel guards. Amid the clamor of docents shushing people and telling them not to take pictures, you hear the word muttered sternly, more like a reprimand than anything else. Translation: "Geez... thanks for being quiet after the 15th time I've told you to turn off your camera and shut your trap!"

- **"PREGO."** The sweetest version of them all, when it's just a simple statement, often following *"grazie."* After you buy a gelato or compliment someone, the recipient of your cash or flattery will often acknowledge his or her thanks by calmly uttering the word. Translation: "You're welcome" or "I'm honored."

- **"PREGO" (WITH OPTIONAL "!")** Actually used as the verb it is, this *prego* can mean "I pray." Now, Italians pray for all kinds of things—in religious contexts, in which case the exclamation mark probably isn't necessary, but also in more mundane or demanding contexts. It's often a favorite of cleaning ladies. Walking into a room full of strewn backpack contents, you might catch a despairing *"Pre-e-g-o-ooooo."*

accommodations

ROMA TRASTEVERINA
B AND B $$$

V. Luigi Santini 21 ☎06 17 37 54; www.romatrasteverina.com

Set off the P. San Cosimato, this three-room bed and breakfast is a small oasis in the heart of Trastevere. Private bathrooms and air-conditioning mean it's also a non-desert oasis. If you get sick of the quiet, never fear: *piazze* aplenty are only steps away, where you can enjoy a drink (or four) and silently gloat over the fact that your walk (or stumble) home is much shorter than everyone else's.

⚑ *From P. San Cosimato, take V. Luigi Santini toward V. Goffredi Mameli. Roma Trasteverina is on the right; buzz and proceed to 2nd fl.* ℹ *Breakfast and Wi-Fi included. Call in advance to set up arrival time.* Ⓢ *Singles €40-75; doubles €60-120; triples €120-180.*

B AND B CHIMERA
B AND B $$$

V. Antonio Pacinotti 13 ☎06 55 30 15 27

Sadly there are no animal-human hybrids at the Chimera, maybe because they all choose to stay closer to central Trastevere. Somewhat far from the maddening crowd, this B and B is in a more residential neighborhood, and so a little knowledge of Italian is helpful for grabbing a late-night kebab on your way back from drinking. If you've met a special someone between glasses of wine, be prepared to sleep *I Love Lucy*-style in two twin beds. Still, the distance makes it cheaper, and the owner lives on-site if you need to know the fastest way to the nightlife. (Spoiler: it's tram #8 from Trastevere Station.)

⚑ *From Trastevere Station, take a right onto V. Portuense and continue under the bridge where the road will turn into V. Giovanni Volpato. Turn left onto V. Antonio Pacinotti; buzz and proceed to the 3rd fl.* ℹ *Free Wi-Fi. Call in advance to set up an arrival time.* Ⓢ *Doubles €64.*

B AND B DANILO

B AND B $$$$

Vle. di Trastevere 60   ☎06 64 56 22 36; www.bebdaniloroma.com

Run by Danilo and his father, the four-room B and B Danilo may not be in the prettiest part of Trastevere, but it's close to all the places you'll want to visit. Its residential location might also keep out some of the noise of late-night revelers, so you can enjoy a nighttime read on your room's balcony when you need a break from mojitos and flaming shots.

☘ *Walk down Vle. Aventino from P. Giuseppe Gioacchino Belli. Danilo is on the right; buzz and proceed to the 3rd fl.* ⓘ *A/C. Free Wi-Fi in some rooms. Call in advance to set up an arrival time.* Ⓢ *Singles with bath €50-90; doubles with bath €70-130; triples €110-150; quads €120-180.*

CALISTO 6

B and B $$$$

P. San Calisto 6   ☎06 99 34 41 09; www.bbintrastevere.com

Arriving at Calisto 6 feels like entering a speakeasy as you press the buzzer of an inconspicuous door tucked between a bar and a restaurant on the small P. San Calisto. The 15th-century building is steps away from Santa Maria di Trastevere and has amazing wood floors and inlaid marble. The windows to the *piazza* below make for dramatic morning greetings and shouted warnings to the sometimes-rowdy barflies next door. Breakfast is served at the bar because, as the owner explains, the bar's espresso is much better than anything he could serve.

☘ *Follow V. San Cosimato from P. Santa Maria di Trastevere to the small P. San Calisto. Located between a bar and a restaurant; buzz for entry and proceed to 2nd fl.* ⓘ *A/C. Free Wi-Fi. Call ahead to set up arrival time.* Ⓢ *Doubles €60-105.*

ancient aphrodisiac

While in Rome you may be tempted to hop into bed with an Italian stallion, but just hope he's not using the aphrodisiacs of his ancestors. Asses' Milk and Spanish Fly were common aphrodisiacs—but only for the wealthy.

Asses' Milk was said to stimulate women and increase male virility. Rumor has it that Nero's wife used to bathe in Asses' Milk for the stimulating effects it had. (Guess Nero wasn't too great in the sack.)

Spanish Fly contained a potentially lethal substance, but the Romans would do anything for love, or at least a good romp in the hay. The fly was crushed up and eaten in order to increase libido. Unfortunately, it also made the genitals swell, itch, and discrete bloody discharge. Not quite the Viagra we know and love.

Moral of the story: stick to strawberries and chocolate.

TERMINI AND SAN LORENZO

Termini is filled with hotels, hostels, bed and breakfasts, and *pensioni.* There's roughly a one-to-one ratio of extremely cheap to extremely overpriced options, so research beforehand and try to book at least one week in advance, especially during the summer. Although the proximity to Termini station makes staying here convenient, it's not the safest area at night. Be wary of pickpockets and avoid walking alone after dark.

🏠 M & J PLACE HOSTEL

HOSTEL $$

V. Solferino 9   ☎06 44 62 802; www.mejplacehostel.com

If a bed is available at this inexpensive social hostel, take it. Great common spaces (kitchen, balcony, and TV lounge) add a lively touch without making M & J Place too loud or crazy—head next door to the hostel's restaurant, bar, and

rome

club for that. Private rooms with air-conditioning, computers, TV, mini-kitchen, and towels are more like hotel accommodations. The reception desk posts weekly events in the city, lends books, and has public computers.

✈ ⓜTermini. *Walk down V. Marsala away from the station and turn right onto V. Solferino.* **i** *Breakfast included in some packages, otherwise €3. Lockers included. Free luggage storage until 9pm. Women-only dorms available. Wi-Fi €2 per hr., €5 per 4hr.* ⓢ *High-season dorms €25-38; low-season dorms €12-20. Singles €75; doubles €80-100; triples €135; quads €160. Cash only.* ⓩ *Reception 24hr.*

🏠 ALESSANDRO DOWNTOWN   HOSTEL $
V. Carlo Cattaneo 23   ☎06 44 34 01 47; www.hostelsalessandro.com

This conveniently located hostel is a bit less party-hardy than its sister, the Palace (see below), but it offers great services to backpackers and students, including daily tours. Large common spaces, communal kitchen, and dorms make it less cramped than nearby hostels, although bunk beds in the larger dorms can take down the comfort level. Great amenities, including a laundry room and free pizza (M-F 7:30pm) make it worth the inconvenience of the long lockout.

✈ ⓜTermini. *Take V. Giovanni Giolitti and turn left onto V. Carlo Cattaneo.* **i** *Breakfast and ensuite lockers included. Free luggage storage before 2pm. Book online 1 week in advance Apr-Aug. 30min. free Wi-Fi per day; €1 per hr. thereafter. Computer room available.* ⓢ *Dorms €17-45; doubles with bath €58-110.* ⓩ *Reception 24hr. Lockout 11am-3pm.*

🏠 ALESSANDRO PALACE   HOSTEL $$
V. Vicenza 42   ☎06 44 61 958; www.hostelsalessandro.com

This historically decorated bar (check out the "frescoed" ceiling) turned modern hostel (check out the speakers and TV) is one of the most social accommodations around. While the nightly pizza giveaway goes fast, great happy hours and drink specials keep guests around all evening. Air-conditioning keeps the rooms bearable in the summer heat, though big dorms—and late-night drinkers downstairs—can make restful sleep difficult.

✈ ⓜTermini. *Walk up V. Marsala away from the station and turn right onto V. Vicenza.* **i** *Breakfast included. Free luggage storage before 3pm. Reserve online at least 1 week in advance during high season. Free Wi-Fi up to 1hr.; €1 per hr. thereafter. Free pizza daily Apr-July 8:30pm.* ⓢ *Dorms €19-45; doubles €60-130, with bath €70-130; triples €78-147/85-147.* ⓩ *Reception 24hr.*

🏠 THE YELLOW   HOSTEL $
V. Palestro 44   ☎06 49 38 26 82; www.the-yellow.com

This hostel isn't called The Yellow because it's scared—it's 'cause it's so darn happy. The perfect place for social butterflies, it boasts a full bar (customers will likely spend more time there than in their small rooms), over five floors of dorms, and colorful hallways. Skype headsets, locks, and even laptops and iPads are available to rent at the reception desk. Come here for fun—especially if your idea of fun is 3am dance parties.

✈ ⓜTermini. *Take V. Milazzo away from the station and turn left onto V. Palestro.* **i** *Breakfast €2-10 at the bar next door. Ensuite lockers included. Free luggage storage before 1:30pm. Towel deposit €10. Free Wi-Fi in public areas; free internet on public computers 30min. per day.* ⓢ *12-bed dorms €18-24; 7-bed €20-26; 6-bed €22-34; 4-bed €24-35. Credit card surcharge €5.* ⓩ *Reception 24hr.*

accommodations

CASA OLMATA HOSTEL $

V. dell'Olmata 36 ☎06 48 30 19; www.casaolmata.com

This quiet, well-kept hostel is in a nice area and is perfect for budget-minded travelers seeking comfort and privacy. The dorms and private rooms are a bit small but come with great amenities like TVs and private bathrooms. Downstairs, a new kitchen and bar area for breakfast, pasta dinners, and evening drinks creates a social atmosphere, although quiet hours after midnight mean you'll have to seek other late-night spots for partying with your new friends.

 # [M]Termini. Walk toward P. Santa Maggiore and down V. Paolina. Turn left onto V. dei Quattro Cantoni and left onto V. Olmata. i Breakfast included. Lockers available. Free Wi-Fi. [$] Dorms €18-20; singles €38; doubles €56-58. Inquire about discounts for longer stays. Cash only. ⏰ Reception 8am-2pm and 4pm-midnight.

FREEDOM TRAVELLER HOSTEL $$

V. Gaeta 23 ☎06 48 91 39 10; www.freedom-traveller.it

Freedom Traveller is a friendly and slightly less crowded hostel with the same great perks you typically find in Termini. Its sunny reception and common spaces immediately make you feel welcome. The first-floor location and proximity to Termini make it especially convenient for weary travelers.

 # [M]Termini. Take V. Marsala away from the station and turn right onto V. Gaeta. i Luggage storage included. Women-only dorms available. Free Wi-Fi. [$] 4- and 6-bed dorms €15-35; doubles €45-80; triples €60-115; quads €90-130. ⏰ Reception 24hr. Lockout 10:30am-2pm (except for private rooms). Quiet hours 11pm-8am.

HOTEL PAPA GERMANO HOTEL $

V. Calatafimi 14A ☎06 48 69 19; www.hotelpapagermano.com

There's nothing particularly inviting about the decor at Hotel Papa Germano, but the rooms are large, and you'll be spending most of the day exploring the city, anyway. You have Wi-Fi, TV, and air-conditioning to keep you comfortable when you are here. Although Papa Germano offers many private rooms, the more economical choice is a dorm, which compares well with the dorms in other hostels.

 # [M]Termini. Take V. Marsala away from the train station, proceed straight as it becomes V. Volturno, and turn right onto the small V. Calatafimi. i Breakfast included. 3 public computers available. [$] Dorms €15-30; singles €30-60; doubles €40-95, with bath €50-120; triples €50-100/60-140; quads €70-130/80-150. ⏰ Reception 7am-midnight.

LEGENDS HOSTEL HOSTEL $$

V. Curtatone 12 ☎06 83 39 32 97; www.legendshostel.com

This cramped but well-equipped hostel brings in a mixed crowd of backpackers and older folk. There's little common space, and rooms are fairly distant from each other (some in a separate building). However, the small kitchen provides a sense of community, especially during breakfast and pasta dinners. Shared bathrooms can be a bit messy, but at least they come with soap. There are better (and cheaper) options in the area, but this isn't a bad choice if you're in a pinch.

 # [M]Termini. Walk up V. Marsala away from the station. Turn right onto V. Gaeta and right onto V. Curtatone. Buzz and walk to the 1st fl. i Breakfast and ensuite lockers included. Free Wi-Fi 5hr. per day, €1 per hr. thereafter. Free pasta M-F 7pm. [$] 4-bed dorms €30-44; doubles €82-142; triples €144-153. ⏰ Reception 24hr.

IVANHOE HOSTEL HOSTEL $

V. Urbana 50 ☎06 48 91 33 39

A bit removed from Termini (which isn't necessarily a bad thing), this small hostel is a real find. Free Wi-Fi and a communal kitchen are particularly convenient and will save you a few euro (but you'll spend them on breakfast since it's not included). Modern, bright hallways lead to eight comfortably sized dorms with large windows. Unfortunately, the long lockout means no siesta.

⚑ Ⓜ B: Cavour. Head down the stairs and walk up V. Urbana. Not to be confused with Hotel Ivanhoe across the street. **i** Breakfast €2. Book online at www.hostelworld.com. Ages 18-35 only. Free Wi-Fi. Ⓢ 12-bed dorms €15-29; 8-bed €16-30; 6-bed €18-30, with bath €20-35. ⌚ Reception 24hr. Lockout 11am-4pm.

HOTEL CERVIA   HOTEL $$
V. Palestro 55   ☎06 49 10 57; www.hotelcerviaroma.com

Open since 1947, this is a well-kept historic hotel for travelers tired of the hostel scene. The friendly owner keeps the small, high-ceilinged rooms clean. Air-conditioning, TV, and Wi-Fi in the downstairs dining area make it better than a hostel, but the location on V. Palestro means you'll be right near the hostel crowd.

⚑ Ⓜ Termini. Take V. Milazzo away from the station and turn left onto V. Palestro. **i** Free luggage storage. Ⓢ Singles €40, with bath and breakfast €70; doubles €65/90. ⌚ Reception 24hr. Call to arrange arrival time.

NORTHERN ROME

The neighbors in this part of Rome are mainly embassies, so it's definitely quieter than nearby Termini. Of course, this also means that party hostels aren't a regular feature, so accommodations are perfect for an early bedtime after a day of sightseeing.

🏠 LA CONTRORA HOSTEL   HOSTEL $$
V. Umbria 7   ☎06 98 93 73 66

La Controra's minimalist white walls and colorblock design make it an appealing place to stay. While there are only 14 beds, a common area and free breakfast mean you'll meet your fellow travelers and maybe even cook a meal together. There's a sister hostel in Naples where artists and musicians perform, and they're hoping to bring this tradition to Rome, so be sure to ask about upcoming events.

⚑ Ⓜ A: Barberini. Walk down V. di San Nicola da Tolentino and then take a left at V. Umbria. It's on the right; buzz for entry. **i** A/C. Breakfast included. Free Wi-Fi. Kitchen available for use. Key deposit €10. Ⓢ Dorms €30-36. ⌚ Reception 8am-midnight.

MOSAIC HOSTEL   HOSTEL $$
V. Cernaia 39B   ☎06 98 93 71 79; www.hostelmosaic.com

Catering mostly to young travelers and backpackers, Mosaic Hostel has clean and simple two- and four-bed dormitories in a five-story building (so keep your hiking boots on if your room is near the top). The lockers are small, but 24hr. reception means that only guests can enter the premises. Since the hostel is near the B line of the Metro and just a 20min. walk from Villa Borghese, it's a convenient spot for access to central Rome and its sights.

⚑ Ⓜ B: Castro Pretorio. Take V. San Martino della Battaglia and then take a right onto V. Castelfidardo. Turn left onto V. Cernaia; it is on the left. Buzz for entry. **i** A/C. Breakfast included. Free Wi-Fi. Booking must be done online. Ⓢ Dorms €33-40. ⌚ Reception 24hr.

TESTACCIO AND OSTIENSE

🏠 A TESTACCIO DA MAX   B AND B $$$
V. Orazio Antinori 7   ☎06 63 81 040; www.domusmax.it

The eponymous Max will greet you when you arrive at this three-room bed and breakfast conveniently located near the Metro and a short walk from Trastevere. While he doesn't live on the premises, he knows a lot about Testaccio and loves to recommend restaurants and sights when he comes by in the morning. The rooms are quite large by Roman standards, and the elevator means you won't have to hike to the fifth floor every day.

⚑ Ⓜ B: Piramide. Follow Vle. delle Cave Ardeatine and veer left onto V. Marmorata. Walk for about 15min., turn left onto V. Amerigo Vespucci, and right onto V. Orazio Antinori. Buzz for entry. **i** A/C. Free Wi-Fi. Ⓢ Single-occupancy doubles €50-60; doubles €70-80. Cash only.

accommodations

BED AND BREAKFAST TESTACCIO B AND B $$

P. di Santa Maria Liberatrice 4 ☎06 57 28 95 62; www.bebtestaccio.it

Right across from a daily market, Bed and Breakfast Testaccio makes you feel like a real Roman. Elena, the proprietor, offers tips for guests, whether they want to explore Testaccio or elsewhere in Italy. Its location away from the clubs on a residential street ensures guests a restful stay.

 # [M]B: Piramide. Follow Vle. delle Cave Ardeatine and veer left onto V. Marmorata. Turn left onto P. di Santa Maria Liberatrice. Buzz for entry. i Breakfast included. A/C. Free Wi-Fi. [$] Singles €40, with bath €55; doubles €55-80/70-90. ⏰ Call to set up an arrival time.

sights

Do the sights of Rome even require an introduction? Like the extrovert who will shake your hand before you take your coat off, Rome's famous destinations have no trouble making themselves known. Interrupting, side-tracking, and dragging out your itinerary before you even get started, these sights seem to beckon from every street corner and *piazza*. If they were anything less than spectacular, the gargantuan number of must-sees in Rome would feel burdensome. Luckily, they're as good as advertised, and fairly concentrated within the city. You'll run into about half of them without even trying. On your way to get gelato, for example, you might turn a corner to find the Colosseum looming ahead, or crowds of people throwing as many coins as they can into the Trevi Fountain. Dominated by ancient ruins (why hello, Roman Forum) and church-related sights (even though the Vatican isn't technically in Rome), the city shows evidence of its historic past at every turn. Our suggestion: take at least one day without the guidebook and see where you end up. Chances are you'll hit a lot of the big names and stumble upon 10 other sights that are just as wonderful.

ANCIENT CITY

The sights of the Ancient City are probably one of the main reasons you came to Rome. The Colosseum pops into view at the end of almost every street, and it's hard to walk anywhere without passing some kind of cordoned-off excavation site. All the while, modern Rome zooms around its past, getting wedding pictures in front of the Arco di Constantine or jogging through the Circus Maximus. The crowds of tourists are formidable, to be sure, but even 60-person tour groups can't detract from the sheer awesomeness (in both senses of the word) of what the ancient Romans left behind.

COLOSSEUM ANCIENT ROME

Bordered by V. di San Gregorio, V. Celio Vibenna, and V. Nicola Salvi

☎06 39 96 77 00; www.pierreci.it

You certainly don't have to pay to see the Colosseum—you'll glimpse it on magnets, postcards, and every vista throughout the city. Still, paying for a walk through the interior is worth it to truly appreciate the structure for what it was: an ancient (and gorier) equivalent to Fenway Park. With numbered sections and several entryways, thousands of Romans would pour in on game days, making their way to seats assigned by social class. For the best view of the arena, make like the wealthy ancients and climb to the upper tiers. In the central area of the stadium are the remains of covered passageways through which gladiators, lions, tigers, bears (oh my), and even the emperor (in his own private corridor, naturally) passed. After taking in the view of the interior, look outward to the Arch of Constantine, the Roman Forum, and Palatine Hill beyond. The upper level also has exhibitions with everything you ever wanted to know about gladiatorial combat but couldn't glean from the Russell Crowe film. Tickets to the

Colosseum can be purchased at the Palatine Hill/Roman Forum entrance on V. San Gregorio. Head there in the afternoon, after the morning frenzy, to avoid waiting in a 2hr. line.

🚇 Ⓜ️B: Colosseo or Termini, then bus #75. *i* Tickets are purchased for entrance to the Colosseum, Palatine Hill, and Roman Forum. They allow 1 entrance per sight over the course of 2 days. Ⓢ €12, EU students ages 18-24 €7.50, EU citizens under 18 and over 65 free. Guided tour €5. Audio tour €5.50. Cash only. 🕐 Open daily from 8:30am to 1hr. before sunset.

fresh facts about an old favorite

Everybody knows about the gory battles and games that took place in the Colosseum, but here are some lesser-known tidbits about the iconic landmark.

- **CAPITAL PUNISHMENT.** In a campaign against capital punishment, whenever an execution is commuted or a government abolishes the death penalty, the lights surrounding the Colosseum are lit for two days.

- **LORD BYRON.** The author once wrote, "While stands the Coliseum [sic], Rome shall stand. When falls the Coliseum, Rome shall fall. And when Rome falls, the world."

- **BLINDFOLDS.** Certain fighters, called *andabatae*, were forced to fight each other blindfolded. They were pushed closer and closer together until one killed the other.

- **MALTA.** There's actually another (manufactured) Colosseum on this Mediterranean island; Ridley Scott didn't think the original was big enough for *Gladiator*.

🏛 ARCO DI CONSTANTINE
ANCIENT ROME, MONUMENT

V. San Gregorio, south of the Colosseum near the Palatine Hill entrance

Although most people only pass the Arch of Constantine on the way to the Colosseum or the Roman Forum across the street, its size and beauty are reason enough to seek it out. Plus, you may be able to snap a photo of a dude in a gladiator costume in the background without giving him €5. The arch was built to commemorate Constantine's victory over Maxentius at the Battle of the Milvian Bridge in 312 CE and is decorated with scenes of the emperor's victories—imperial egotism at its finest. The Romans, who seem awfully good at "borrowing" things (check out the torn-away marble sections of the Colosseum), continued the tradition here, decorating the side of the arch with medallions stolen from other monuments nearby. Guess there's something to be said for kleptomania after all.

🚇 Ⓜ️B: Colosseo or Termini, then bus #75. Walk down V. San Gregorio from the Colosseum. Ⓢ Free.

ROMAN FORUM
ANCIENT ROME

A walk through the Roman Forum provides a pleasant (though somewhat bumpy) 1hr. respite from the busy city outside its gates, even if you don't know a bit of its history or haven't read a single plaque. If you don't feel like getting your shoes dusty (or paying €12), the surrounding roads provide great views of the Forum, but the trip inside really is worth it. Walking in, you'll see a stunning view of the Forum, a plot of land used as a marketplace by the Greeks and Etruscans of the seventh and eighth centuries CE. Today, the area consists mostly of grassy and gravel paths, crumbling temples, and a few reconstructed sites that contain most of the area's history. The scanty remains of the **Basilica Fulvia-Aemilia** are on the right past the entrance, although this basilica was all about justice rather than religion.

sights

Just ahead, a hut dedicated to Julius Caesar has been covered with flowers by modern-day imperial devotees. Turning right from here leads to the **Curia,** originally the meeting place of the Senate and now home to a museum-like display of coins, columns, and recovered friezes, as well as the **Arch of Septimus Severus.** To the left, the **House of the Vestal Virgins** is the prettiest part of this otherwise dusty, brown-and-gray area. Now a green space bordered with flowers and headless statues of the eponymous virgins, it was once a sacred area of the city overseen by the only women allowed to officially participate in Roman religion. These women were important, but that meant they had to stay virgins. No one can have both sex and power (except men, obviously). Straight ahead you'll find the **Tempio di Romolo,** with its massive green door, and the **Tempio di Antonino e Faustina,** with beautiful pink and white columns guarding the entrance. Beyond that is the **Arch of Titus,** built in 81 CE by Emperor Domitian to commemorate his brother Titus's victory over Jerusalem. Check out a carving of the Romans carting off an especially large menorah. From here, continue on to the Palatine Hill beyond, or exit to the Colosseum.

➜ ⓂB: Colosseo or Termini, then bus #75. Enter at V. San Gregorio (near the Arch of Constantine), V. dei Fori Imperiali (halfway between Trajan's column and the Colosseum), or directly opposite the Colosseum. ℹ The entrance to the Forum is joint with the Palatine Hill. Tickets are purchased for entrance to the Colosseum, Palatine Hill, and Roman Forum. They allow 1 entrance per sight over the course of 2 days. $ €12, EU students ages 18-24 €7.50, EU citizens under 18 and over 65 free. Audio tour €5, combined with the Palatine €7; available in English. Cash only. ⏰ Open daily from 8:30am to 1hr. before sunset.

PALATINE HILL

ANCIENT ROME

A trip to Palatine Hill is Rome's answer to the Hollywood celebrities' house tour—if you were in the Roman elite, this was the place to live. Instead of giant swimming pools and seven-car garages, though, ruins of fountains, rooms, private entertainment stadiums, and marble floors are all that remain. Look down to get a good view of the **Circus Maximus,** once home to chariot races and now to free summer concerts. The ascent up the hill is a bit steep and winding, but the convenient steps make getting to the top much quicker. Sprawling ruins of ancient mansions await. The small **Palatine Museum** displays some of the household items excavated in the area. Next, make your way to the beautiful **Farnese Gardens,** which offer an unparalleled vista of the Roman Forum, the Colosseum, and Capitoline Hill. Descend the stairs to check out the **Nymphaeum of the Rain,** a small cave with running water.

➜ ⓂB: Colosseo or Termini, then bus #75. Enter at V. San Gregorio (near the Arch of Constantine), V. dei Fori Imperiali (halfway between Trajan's column and the Colosseum), or directly opposite the Colosseum. ℹ Tickets are purchased for entrance to the Colosseum, Palatine Hill, and Roman Forum. They allow 1 entrance per sight over the course of 2 days. $ €12, EU students ages 18-24 €7.50, EU citizens under 18 and over 65 free. Audio tour €5, combined with the Forum €7; available in English. Cash only. ⏰ Open daily from 8:30am to 1hr. before sunset. Palatine Museum open daily 8am-4pm; 30 people per floor, 20min. at a time.

FORI IMPERIALI

ANCIENT ROME

V. dei Fori Imperiali ☎06 67 97 702

Walking down V. dei Fori Imperiali, it's impossible to miss—you guessed it—the Imperial Fora. These four fora were once the business district of Rome, and thankfully survived Mussolini's somewhat merciless "re-landscaping" during the construction of the Vittorio Emanuele II Monument. The **Forum of Trajan,** the largest of the fora, is marked off by a big column decorated with a spiraling narrative of all of his victories (and, of course, none of the defeats). Unfortunately, the grounds themselves are closed to the public, but plenty can be seen from the sidewalk as you wander past on your way to the Roman Forum.

➜ From the Colosseum, walk down V. dei Fori Imperiali; the ruins are on the right. $ Free. ⏰ Exhibition and info center open daily 9:30am-6:30pm.

CHIESA DI SAN PIETRO IN VINCOLI CHURCH

P. di San Pietro in Vincoli, 4A ☎06 48 82 865

Sitting atop a small hill just off V. Cavour, this fourth-century church houses Michelangelo's famous statue of Moses. The two small protrusions on top of his head are based on a completely un-PC Renaissance Christian belief that Jews did, in fact, have horns. Under the altar of the elaborately frescoed apse are the chains supposedly used to bind St. Peter. It's a bit of an uphill climb to the church, but it's worth it for Michelangelo fans, or those in search of a non-ruined building in the Ancient City.

#From V. Cavour, turn onto V. di San Francisco di Paola and walk up the stairs to the piazza in front of the church. ***i*** *Modest dress required.* $ *Free.* ⏰ *Open daily 8am-12:30pm and 3-6pm.*

THE VELABRUM ANCIENT ROME

Amid all the nearby monuments boasting elevated views of the city, the Velabrum may feel a bit subterranean, but don't let that turn you off. You can approach the Velabrum from the waterfront (Ponte Palatino practically leads straight into it) or on V. Petroselli coming from the **Teatro di Marcello,** a round structure that looks remarkably like the Colosseum (perhaps because it was the model for Rome's most famous ruin). Beyond several other temples and a forum, the real star of the square is the medieval **Chiesa di Santa Maria in Cosmedin,** whose facade holds the famous **Bocca della Verità.** According to legend (and Gregory Peck in *Roman Holiday*), he who places his hand in the stone mouth will have it bitten off if he is a liar. Watch as dozens of people line up to prove their honesty—or perhaps just have their picture taken.

#From the Circus Maximus, walk down V. dei Cerchi until you reach P. di Sant'Anastasia. The Velabrum and its sights are in the flat region at the base of the hill. $ *Suggested donation for picture €0.50.* ⏰ *Church open daily 9:30am-5:50pm.*

CAPITOLINE HILL PIAZZA, MUSEUM

Marcus Aurelius may be dead, but his statue in the **Piazza del Campidoglio** is still a highly photographed attraction. The *piazza* itself, designed by Michelangelo, is at the top of the hill; two naked guys with horses greet you as you arrive (fortunately or unfortunately, they're just sculptures). Rome's small capital is a must-see for enthusiasts of Greek and Roman sculpture, as the *piazza* is surrounded by the impressive **Capitoline Museums** (www.museicapitolini.org), the oldest public collection of ancient art in the world.

#From V. dei Fori Imperiali, veer left toward the Vittorio Emanuele II Monument. Turn onto V. Teatro Marcello and head uphill. $ *Capitoline Museums €12, EU students ages 18-25 €10, EU citizens under 18 and over 65 free. Combined ticket with Centrale Montemartini €14, EU students 18-25 €12. Audio tour €5; available in English.* ⏰ *Capitoline Museums open Tu-Su 9am-8pm. Last entry 7pm.*

CENTRO STORICO

The Centro Storico abounds with sights that are as quintessentially Roman as pasta is Italian. Luckily, you won't have to pay or wait in line to see many of them, and their close proximity to one another makes it possible to visit all these sights in one rewarding afternoon.

PANTHEON ANCIENT ROME

P. della Rotunda ☎06 68 30 02 30

Stepping inside the Pantheon feels like entering a giant eyeball. Its perfectly round dome, pierced with a pupil-like aperture, towers above, and people below strain their own eyeballs to take in the sheer magnitude. Sure, there are cool photos of the Pantheon in almost any book about Rome, but actually standing there and watching the sky through the ceiling is a totally unique experience. The sun's beam is the only source of light in the interior, illuminating (or hiding) things as the day moves on—conspiracy theorists can make of this what they will. Once

sights

you've got a sufficient crick in your neck, head under the giant-columned portico to the **Piazza della Rotunda,** have a seat by the Egyptian obelisk-topped fountain, and enjoy the monument (and the tourists) from the outside.

From P. Navona, follow the signs for the Pantheon toward V. della Dogana Vecchia. $ Free. Audio tour €5, students €3.50. ⏰ Open M-Sa 8:30am-7:30pm, Su 9am-6pm.

liar, liar

What's even more exciting than having your pants set on fire? Having your hand chopped off, of course. According to a legend dating back to the Middle Ages, the Mouth of Truth (or *Bocca della Verità*) at the Chiesa di Santa Maria in Cosmedin discerns between the honest and the insincere. If you tell a lie with your hand in the mouth of the sculpted face, the vicious marble figure will bite it off. The story goes that a man who had rightfully accused his wife of infidelity demanded her to put her hand into the Mouth of Truth to prove his accusation. To avoid the discomfort of losing her hand, the woman arranged for her lover to kiss her in front of the portico, acting as though she didn't know him. She then stuck her hand into the face, asserting that her husband and the stranger were the only two men she had ever kissed. With this small twist of words, her hand–and faithful character–was miraculously saved.

PIAZZA NAVONA PIAZZA

Surrounded by V. di Santa Maria dell'Anima and Corso del Rinascimento

Originally a stadium built by Domitian in 86 CE, the only gladiatorial action P. Navona sees now are the inevitable skirmishes between knock-off bag vendors and Roman authorities. If you can overlook the trite watercolors for sale in just about every inch of space, it is truly a beautiful *piazza.* Weave your way through the crowds—grab a seat if you can—to take a closer look at Bernini's magnificent **Fontana dei Quattro Fiumi,** a massive stone sculpture that depicts four river gods, each representing a continent. While the restaurants and bars surrounding this area are expensive, it could be worth a few extra euro to enjoy a glass of wine and take in the full view of Rome's most famous *piazza.* Or you could just grab a beer from a side street cafe and photobomb the fountain pictures of unsuspecting tourists.

Entrances at Palazzo Braschi, V. Agonale, V. di Sant'Agnese di Agone, and Corsia Agonale.

CHIESA DI SAN LUIGI DEI FRANCESI CHURCH

P. San Luigi dei Francesi 5 ☎06 68 82 71

From the exterior, this 16th-century church could easily be overlooked—the French facade is pretty unimpressive by Roman standards. Consequently, the surprise inside is even sweeter. Three of Caravaggio's most impressive works—**The Calling of Saint Matthew, Saint Matthew and the Angel,** and **The Crucifixion**—grace the Contarelli Chapels in the back on the left. Due to French frugality or (more likely) in order to protect the art, the paintings aren't always lit up, so deposit €1 to see them in their full *chiaroscuro* glory. Better yet, stand craftily to the side and let someone else pony up, and then enjoy your free culture for the day.

From P. Navona, exit onto Corsia Agonale, turn left onto Corso del Rinascimento and right onto V. Santa Giovanna d'Arco. $ Free. ⏰ Open M-W 10am-12:30pm and 4-7pm, Th 10am-12:30pm, F-Su 10am-12:30pm and 4-7pm.

VITTORIO EMANUELE II MONUMENT   MONUMENT, MUSEUM

P. Venezia   ☎06 67 80 664, museum 06 67 93 526; www.risorgimento.it

The view of this monument—affectionately (and mockingly) known as "The Wedding Cake"— is inescapable in the streets of Rome. The area, created when Mussolini razed many medieval and Renaissance neighborhoods (including Michelangelo's house), is packed with tourists, scooters, cars, and buses dodging each other. The gigantic building and equally giant flags are a theatrical statement of national pride centered around the equestrian statue of Vittorio Emanuele II himself, whose mustache is—trivia time—over 1m long. The monument is best seen from P. Venezia or even from a few blocks away, but if you venture up its mighty steps, you'll find the **Museo Nazionale Emigrazione Italiana** and the **Museo del Risorgimento.** These museums are filled with slightly dull (and extremely dark) collections of artifacts tracing the flight of Italians from Italy and Italian unification, respectively. Though the museums are free, the view from outside is brighter and more worth your time.

✦ *In P. Venezia.* Ⓢ *Free.* 🕐 *Monument open M-Th 9:30am-6:30pm, F-Su 9:30am-7:30pm. Museum open daily 9:30am-6:30pm.*

PALAZZO VENEZIA   PALAZZO

V. del Plebiscito 118   ☎06 32 810

The Palazzo Venezia is one of the few Renaissance buildings to survive Mussolini's reconstruction of the area in favor of the gaudy-even-in-comparison Vittorio Emanuele II Monument. Its Renaissance staircase leads to a bigger-than-expected and not very busy museum featuring Italian art from the 14th to the 18th centuries, so if, like us, you have a particular fondness for Quattrocento panel paintings, the €4 entry fee is entirely reasonable. Unfortunately for both you and the art, there's no air-conditioning, but at least you'll be safe from the crazy traffic circle outside.

✦ *Across the way from the Vittorio Emanuele II Monument, in P. Venezia.* Ⓢ *€4, EU citizens ages 18-25 €2, EU citizens under 18 and over 65 free. English audio tour free.* 🕐 *Open Tu-Su 8:30am-7:30pm. Last entry 6:30pm.*

aristocatty

Hundreds of years have passed since Roman emperors monopolized power, but today an elite class still remains: street cats. Originally entering Rome from Egyptian ships, today the ancient kitties account for over 800 estimated "colonies" across the city. But these aren't your average strays—these fancy felines have laws to protect them.

Rome defined cats as part of the city's "bio-cultural heritage" in 1991. Killing stray cats is illegal; the city instead tries to neuter them. A 2005 law bans construction on sites that are home to cats, and the city even provides cats shelter at the temple where Brutus killed Caesar. Now the cats occupy this house of the divine, the Torre Argentina Cat Sanctuary. Women working at the sanctuary, called *gattare,* or cat ladies, work to provide them with food and vaccinations. With this kind of treatment, it's no wonder the feline population is thriving.

sights

AREA SACRA ARGENTINA — ANCIENT ROME

Bordered by V. di Torre Argentina, V. Florida, and Largo di Torre Argentina

As is often the case in Rome, chances are you'll stumble upon this holy area on your way somewhere else. Four Republican temples were uncovered here in 1927 during roadwork, as was the **Theatre of Pompey,** where Julius Caesar met his untimely end. Excavations are ongoing, so unless you're one of the ruin-roaming cats from the no-kill shelter Torre Argentina, you'll have to dramatically cry out, *"Et tu, Brute?"* from behind railings above.

Go up V. Arenula and take a right on V. Florida. The entrance to the shelter is on the corner. i To find out about volunteering at the shelter, call ☎06 45 42 52 40 or email torreargentina@tiscali.it. $ Free. Shelter open daily noon-6pm.

FONDAZIONE ROMA MUSEO — MUSEUM

V. del Corso 320 — ☎06 67 86 209; www.fondazioneromamuseo.it

Founded in 1999, this small museum is a place to remember due to its excellent selection of temporary art exhibits, lectures, and performances devoted to specific artists and periods in art history. The curators at Fondazione definitely have an eye for design, exchanging bare white walls for extra information or complementary colors. Most recently, an exhibition on Rome and Milan in the 1960s incorporated interactive artwork and wall text in both English and Italian. Past shows have included retrospectives on subjects as diverse as the Surrealist painter Max Ernst and Japanese landscape artist Hiroshige, so check the website for upcoming exhibits and events. While not the cheapest museum in Rome, it's definitely one of best curated.

From Palazzo Venezia, walk up V. del Corso for 7min. $ €10, under 26 and over 65 €8, under 6 free. Open Tu-Su 10am-8pm. Ticket office closes 7pm. Hours vary depending on the exhibit.

PIAZZA DI SPAGNA

PIAZZA DEL POPOLO — PIAZZA

At the end of V. del Corso

From the center of P. del Popolo, you can see the magnificent Vittorio Emanuele II Monument glowing in the distance. Likewise, from the monument, a straight shot up V. del Corso has you gazing at this gigantic *piazza*, the "people's square." Despite the *corso*'s noise and crowds, it's the best way to arrive at and get a sense for the openness of P. del Popolo. For being so famous, the *piazza* is surprisingly uncongested. At the center, the **Obelisk of Pharaoh Ramses II** stands triumphantly, attracting a few tourists to sit at its base, and many more tourists to climb on top of the water-spewing lions. The **Santa Maria del Popolo** church is worth a visit, as it contains two Caravaggio masterpieces (*The Conversion of St. Paul* and *The Crucifixion of St. Peter*) as well as works by other artistic bigwigs like Bernini, Pinturicchio, and Raphael.

[M]A: Flaminio-Piazza del Popolo. $ Free. Church open M-Sa 7am-noon and 4-7pm, Su 8am-1:30pm and 4:30-7pm.

MUSEO DELL'ARA PACIS — MUSEUM

At intersection of Lungotevere in Augusta and P. Porto di Ripetta — www.arapacis.it

Enclosed in a modern white building is the famous **Ara Pacis,** a monument built to commemorate Augustus's victories throughout Spain and Gaul. Visitors can walk inside the structure for a closer look at elaborate sculptural friezes on the walls, which were originally a kaleidoscope of colors. The lower level of the museum has extensive information on both the monument and the modern building that houses it, which some people may consider the highlight of this visit. Commissioned from the American architect Richard Meier in 1996, it didn't open until 2006 due to numerous controversies over its design. The museum is a perfect example of the Eternal City's eternal dilemma: how can the past best coexist with the present?

✢ Ⓜ A: Spagna. Take V. delle Carrozze toward V. del Corso and proceed into P. Augusto Imperiale. Ⓢ €6.50, EU students 18-25 €4.50, EU citizens under 18 and over 65 free. Audio tour in English €3.50. ⏰ Open Tu-Su 9am-7pm. Last entry 6pm.

FONTANA DI TREVI   FOUNTAIN
Beyond P. dell'Accademia di San Luca

The best time to see the Trevi Fountain is at 4:30am, because it's probably the only hour where you'll be able to sit on one of the stone ledges without hearing vendors selling overpriced trinkets and tourists snapping picture-perfect shots in the background. That's certainly the hour when actress Anita Ekberg came by to take a dip in the fountain's gushing waters in Fellini's *La Dolce Vita*. While you can make a late-night visit, don't follow her lead or you'll risk a steep fine. Even if you don't make it during this empty hour, Nicola Salvi's mix of masterfully cut rock and stone is phenomenal. Neptune, surrounded by the goddesses of abundance and good health as well as two brawny horsemen, is carved with exacting detail, while the environment in which he sits is realistic because it's been left untouched. As good as gelato might be, save your coins for the fountain: one ensures a prompt return to Rome, two will bring you love in the Eternal City, and three will bring about your wedding.

✢ Ⓜ A: Barberini. Proceed down V. del Tritone and turn left onto V. della Stamperia.

trevi treasures

Just about every tourist who travels to the Eternal City stops at the Trevi Fountain to toss in a coin and wish that he someday returns to Rome. According to the city authorities, nearly €700,000 are thrown into the fountain each year. There are regular attempts to steal coins from the fountain, but such a crime is punishable by jail time. The municipal government donates the collected coins to Caritas, an international Catholic charity dedicated to helping the poor.

PIAZZA DI SPAGNA AND THE SPANISH STEPS   MONUMENT, PIAZZA
Piazza di Spagna is a conglomeration of international roots—not only does it draw a global tourist crowd to its sandy-colored steps, but its history encompasses the Italians (who designed it), the British (who occupied it), the French (who financed it), and, oh yeah, the Spanish (who gave it a name and not much else). Built in 1723 as a way to connect the *piazza* with the new **Trinità dei Monti** church above it, the magnificent steps are mostly a hangout for tired shoppers, gelato eaters, and youth looking to avoid the expensive bar scene around here. The best view is actually from the church's steps directly above, where you can get a better sense of their Spanish companions' size while avoiding the cluster of people below. When you make your way down, check out the **Fontana della Barcaccia,** which was built by Bernini the Elder before the steps were even constructed. The absurdly pink house and its two palm trees might remind you of leisurely beach life, but they actually commemorate the death of John Keats, who died there in 1821.

✢ Ⓜ A: Spagna.

TRINITÀ DEI MONTI   CHURCH
At the top of the Spanish Steps, at the intersection of V. Sistina and P. Trinità dei Monti

All roads lead to Rome, and at the ends of those roads are steps leading to churches. The unlucky Trinità dei Monti, pillaged dozens of times since its construction in 1502, sits at the top of the Spanish Steps. While almost all of its original pieces are now lost, famous frescoes decorate the aisle chapels. Daniele da Volterra's *Descent from the Cross* was especially lauded by the French painter Nicolas Poussin—despite several restorations, it still brings a lot of color to the building's otherwise bleak walls. The *piazza* outside the church provides the best view of the Spanish Steps below.

⇟ [M]A: Spagna. Walk up the steps. ℹ Modest dress required. $ Free. ⏰ Open daily 7am-noon and 4-7pm.

JEWISH GHETTO

The Jewish Ghetto consists of a few blocks just north of **Isola Tiberina.** Come here for great food and a look back at one of the first Jewish communities in Western Europe.

☆ THE GREAT SYNAGOGUE — SYNAGOGUE

Corner of Lungotevere dei Cenci and V. del Tempio

While not a part of the original Jewish Ghetto, the synagogue's huge dome, visible next to St. Peter's from a distance, makes a bold statement about the Roman Jews. There has been a Jewish community in Rome since 161 BCE, and while the Great Synagogue was built two millennia later in 1904, it continues the tradition by incorporating furnishings from the *Cinque Scole* (Five Synagogues) of the ghetto period. It's also architecturally impressive in its own right, with Art Nouveau influences and impressive modern stained glass, and not a figural representation in sight (which might be a welcome change for a weary tourist in Rome). Unless you want to go for services, take advantage of the tour in English included with admission to the Museo Ebraico.

⇟ At the corner of Lungotevere dei Cenci and V. del Tempio. ℹ Open for services or with a tour from the Museo Ebraico. $ Free.

MUSEO EBRAICO — MUSEUM

Corner of V. del Portico d'Ottavia and V. Catalana ☎06 68 40 06 61; www.museoebraico.roma.it

Before entering a food coma from feasting on the Ghetto's fried artichokes, pay a visit to Museo Ebraico to learn more about this tenacious and vibrant community. The collection, which includes textiles, silver, ancient texts, and stone engravings, is also a "living" one, since many of the objects on display are still used today on special occasions.

⇟ From Ponte Garibaldi, turn right onto Lungotevere dei Cenci and take a left onto V. del Portico d'Ottavia to reach the museum entrance. $ €10, over 65 €7.50, EU students €4, under 10 and the disabled free. Free guided tours of the Great Synagogue and the Spanish Synagogue available in English at ¼ past every hr. ⏰ Open June 16-Sept 15 M-Th 10am-6:15pm, F 10am-3:15pm, Su 10am-6:15pm; Sept 16-June 15 M-Th 10am-4:15pm, F 9am-1:15pm, Su 10am-4:15pm.

VATICAN CITY

Unsurprisingly, the sights in Vatican City are all about the long, complex, and often beautiful history of Catholicism. **Saint Peter's Basilica,** home to the masses led by the Pope, actually contains quite a few sights within and around its massive wall. Long lines at the nearby **Vatican Museums** are well worth the wait.

saint peter's basilica and environs

☆ PIAZZA DI SAN PIETRO — PIAZZA

At the end of V. della Conciliazione ☎06 69 88 16 62; www.vaticanstate.va

There's no way to escape the arms of St. Peter's—from the start of V. della Conciliazione they beckon pedestrians into the *piazza*, and, once you've made your way inside, their embrace is enough to silence even the chattiest tourists. If Bernini had seen this effect more than 400 years after the square's construction, he would have smiled—the artist intended the colonnade to symbolize the welcoming arms of the Catholic Church and to greet tired pilgrims after a long trek through the city. Nowadays, those welcoming arms hug tourists snapping photos in front of the giant church or waiting in long security lines to enter the basilica.

➜ Bus #23, 34, 40, 271, or 982 to P. Pia or bus #62 down V. della Conciliazione. ℹ Pilgrim Tourist Office, to the left of the basilica, has a multilingual staff, a gift shop, free bathrooms, a first-aid station, brochures, maps, currency exchange, and Vatican post boxes inside or nearby. $ Free. ⏰ Piazza open 24hr. Tourist Office open M-Sa 8:30am-6:15pm.

👍 SAINT PETER'S BASILICA — CHURCH

At the end of V. della Conciliazione ☎06 69 88 16 62; www.vaticanstate.va

If the Vatican's special post boxes aren't enough to remind you that you've entered another jurisdiction, perhaps the airport-like security at the basilica's entrance will be. Once you've cleared the metal detectors, head inside and be prepared to feel very tiny indeed. Depending on the time of day, the church's interior appears in incredibly different illumination—the ceilings are so high that the small windows near the top of the basilica do little to light the nave on gloomy days. Immediately to the right, look for Michelangelo's 👍**Pietà,** one of the most moving renderings of Mary and Jesus ever created, despite being somewhat obscured behind bulletproof glass. Though it's hard to pinpoint the church's crowning element, Michelangelo's dome at least wins in size—at a spectacular 138m high and 42m wide, it remains the largest in the world. The twisty, ornately decorated *baldacchino* (canopy) marks the pope's altar and is about as whimsical as Baroque Catholicism gets (note the sculpted bumblebees). The supposed tomb of St. Peter sits immediately below the altar. To the right of the *baldacchino* is the famous statue of St. Peter, whose well-rubbed foot is a testament to the masses of pilgrims who touch it for good luck. The statue gets dressed in papal regalia every June 29 for his feast day. Though most people come to the church as tourists, and the flash of cameras is nearly constant, consider participating in mass, which is conducted before Bernini's bronze **Cathedra Petri** and lit by glowing alabaster windows. Not only will you be going to mass in the most famous church in the world, you'll also get to sit in an area closed off to the tourists behind you.

ℹ Free guided tours in English leave from the Pilgrim Tourist Information Center. No shorts, miniskirts, or tank tops. $ Free. ⏰ Basilica open daily Apr-Sept 7am-7pm; Oct-Mar 7am-6:30pm. Tours Tu 9:45am, Th-F 9:45am. Mass M-F 8:30, 10, 11am, noon, and 5pm; Su and holidays 9, 10:30, 11:30am, 12:15, 1, 4, and 5:45pm. Vespers daily 5pm.

SAINT PETER'S GRAVE (PRE-CONSTANTINIAN NECROPOLIS) — TOMB

Office left of the basilica, tombs below Scavi Office ☎06 69 88 53 18; www.vaticanstate.va

The beauty of St. Peter's Basilica draws crowds to its doors, but the mystery of the first pope's tomb has people flocking to the internet—the only way to pay his alleged remains a visit is to book a tour online well in advance. If you finally get a spot, expect a claustrophobic walk through the tombs accompanied by explanations of the site's historical and religious significance. The discovery of ancient ruins and a number of bones in 1939 had the pope claiming that St. Peter's remains did in fact exist under the original altar. Though successive popes have affirmed the presence of the holy remains, many believe that the bones were removed during the Saracen pillaging of Rome in 849 CE. Don't expect to play Sherlock during the tour—just enjoy the sarcophagi, mosaics, and funerary inscriptions along the way.

➜ In the piazza. Instead of entering the Basilica, veer left and look for Swiss Guards dressed in stripes who will grant you access to the courtyard. The Scavi Office is on the courtyard's right side. ℹ The necropolis can only be seen on a guided tour organized by the Scavi Office. Reservations must be made at least 1 day ahead (but should be made as early as possible, as much as 90 days).

Pick up a reservation form at the office and hand deliver it or email scavi@fsp.va with name, number of attendees, tour language, desired dates, and address and telephone number of where you are staying. Fully covered attire required. No backpacks or bulky items. $ €12. ⏰ Scavi Office open M-Sa 9am-5pm. Tours last 1½hr.

CUPOLA AND GROTTE VATICANE — CHURCH, PANORAMIC VIEW

To the right of the basilica — www.vaticanstate.va

If you haven't seen enough of Rome's sky or soil, consider the ascent up to St. Peter's Cupola or the descent into its grottoes. If you head skyward, get ready to be swept away. Lose your breath climbing the 551 steps (320 with the elevator) to the top, then have it stolen by the gasp-inducing view—one of the city's most spectacular panoramas and the only one in which St. Peter's doesn't steal the show. The first 231 steps are actually the easiest, so if you're feeling up to it, save the €2 elevator fee and spend it on a well-earned gelato instead. A walk through the cramped tombs is eerie rather than breathtaking: a seemingly endless collection of sarcophagi (including those of the last four popes) lines the stone passageways. Petri Apostoli's *sepolcro*, guarded by stone lions and protected behind glass, attracts the most attention, but don't miss the gold mosaics crowning Pius XI's final resting place.

⇟ Walk to the last door on the right of the basilica. The entrance to the cupola is on the right in the courtyard. $ Cupola €5, with elevator €7. Grottoes free. Cash only. ⏰ Cupola open daily Apr-Sept 8am-6pm, Oct-Mar 8am-5pm. Last entry 1hr. before close for non-elevator visitors. Grottoes open daily 8am-4pm.

TREASURY — MUSEUM

In the basilica, to the left — www.vaticanstate.va

If the basilica's gold decorations aren't enough to dazzle you, pay a visit to the treasury, a small museum containing gifts bestowed upon the great pope's tomb. Ogle the gold-and-silver-plated, gem-encrusted papal tiara; the intricate gold and silver embroidery on the Dalmatic of Charlemagne; and the diamond, emerald, and ruby rings that are placed on St. Peter's statue to commemorate Saints Peter and Paul Day (June 29th).

⇟ Walk to the last door on the right of the basilica. The entrance to the Treasury is on the left in the courtyard. ℹ No photography. $ €6, under 12 €4. ⏰ Treasury open daily Apr-Sept 8am-6:10pm; Oct-Mar 8am-5:40pm.

other sights

🖼 VATICAN MUSEUMS — MUSEUM

Vle. Vaticano 97 — ☎06 69 88 38 60; www.museivaticani.va

After waiting in a 4hr. line, we hope you spend at least half as much time in the galleries themselves. Unfortunately, the lure of the Sistine Chapel (and frequent arrows pointing the way) pull people onward, creating a human stream with a very strong current. But don't be a fish! Jump out and admire some of the more obscure treasures that are not only on display but comprise the building itself: stunning frescoes, floor mosaics, and even a bronze double-helix ramp.

While the masses will veer left upon entering, take the time to visit the **Pinacoteca** to the right, home to some of the best Italian art from the 12th-17th centuries by artists like Giotto, Fra Angelico, Raphael, and Caravaggio. Next, head to the **Museo Pio-Clemetino,** which contains the world's greatest collection of antique sculptures, including the famous **Laocoön** in an octagonal courtyard. The sculpture, depicting a violent struggle between Laocoön and sea serpents as his sons try to rescue him, is an Ancient Greek masterpiece that awed even Michelangelo. Pass through the **Sala Rotonda,** a small room with unbelievable mosaics on the floor and a domed roof recalling the Pantheon's coffered ceiling and oculus. Upstairs, the **Candelabra Gallery** and dimly lit **Tapestry Gallery** are often treated as thoroughfares, while the **Map Gallery** is worth a stop. Huge frescoed maps of Italy line the walls and provide an eye into the country's diverse geographical regions. Instead of heading to the Sistine Chapel from here, meander through the **Stanze di Rafaele.** These four rooms, originally Julius II's apartments, were decorated by the great Raphael, and include the **School of Athens** fresco on one wall.

In no other collection would all the aforementioned works be considered a precursor to the main show. But you're in the Vatican Museums, and it's time for the main course. The ⭐**Sistine Chapel** is undoubtedly the most crowded and monumental part of the museum. Every few minutes, the guards shush the mass of people, reminding them not to take photos and ushering them onward. Minutes later, the chatter builds again and flashes go off once more. Even those not versed in art history will recognize the famous **Creation of Adam,** one of nine panels depicting scenes from the story of Genesis. Occupying the entirety of the altar wall, the **Last Judgment** can be viewed with much less physical contortion. A forceful, monumental work, it originally depicted the characters fully nude, which was met by a great deal of opposition from the prudish Cardinal Carafa. While Michelangelo finally capitulated to the demands for modesty, it looks like he got the last laugh: the poor schmuck getting his bathing-suit area chomped on by a snake in the bottom right corner is a less-than-flattering portrait of Carafa.

✦ ⓂA: Ottaviano. Head down V. Ottaviano, turn right onto V. dei Bastioni di Michelangelo, and follow the wall until you see the end of the line for the museums. The entrance is on Vle. Vaticano. ⓢ €15, ages 6-18 and EU citizens 18-26 €8, under 6 free. Free last Su of each month. Special viewings €4. Entrance with guided tour €31, ages 6-18 and EU citizens 18-26 €25. Audio tours with map €7. ⓐ Open M-Sa 9am-6pm. Open last Su of each month 9am-2pm. Last entry 2hr. before close. Open Apr-July F 7-11pm for special viewing only; online reservation required. Check the website for hours as there may be additional closings.

MUSEO NAZIONALE DI CASTEL SANT'ANGELO   CASTLE, MUSEUM
Lungotevere Castello 50   ☎06 68 19 111; www.castelsantangelo.com
If you thought Rome was all basilicas and ruins, think again: that circular brick structure on the river is a castle, complete with a moat (okay, it's dried up) and torches (fine, they're electric). Originally built in the first century CE as a mausoleum for Hadrian and his family, it has since been converted from a tomb to a palace, castle, prison, and—finally—museum. While it contains some neat art off the main courtyard and ornately frescoed papal apartments, the real draw is the view from the terrace. The panorama of Rome is one of the best in the city, perfect for capturing St. Peter's Basilica and the statue-lined Ponte Sant'Angelo below.

✦ Bus #23, 34, 40, 271, or 982 to P. Pia. The castle is at the end of V. della Conciliazione at the intersection with Ponte Sant'Angelo. ⓢ €8.50, EU citizens ages 18-25 €6, EU citizens under 18 and over 65 free. Audio tour €4. ⓐ Open Tu-Su 9am-7pm. Last entry 6:30pm.

TRASTEVERE

Really, the main sight in Trastevere is... Trastevere. Down every *vicolo*, in every *piazza*, by every fountain, there's a photo waiting to happen. No one will blame you if you fill your camera's memory card on the kind of rustic charm you thought only existed in movies. Don't be afraid to get a little lost—chances are you'll eventually stumble back into a familiar place like the **Piazza di Santa Maria in Trastevere,** or even better (but much less likely), you'll just have to stay lost in Trastevere indefinitely.

⭐ SANTA MARIA IN TRASTEVERE   CHURCH
P. di Santa Maria in Trastevere   ☎06 58 14 802
The first church in Rome to be built exclusively for the Virgin Mary, Santa Maria in Trastevere is a favorite of tourists—and, apparently, the authors of all art history books. The 12th-century apse mosaic in shimmering golds and blues

depicts Mary being tenderly touched by Jesus, the prototypical boy who loves his *mamma*. And, just as the *mamma* watches over her *ragazzino*, Mary's eyes seem to follow you as you move about the church. After you've managed to escape (or at least ignore) her gaze, look down at the inlaid marble floors and up at the elaborately coffered ceilings. Outside, the fountain is a popular meeting spot for tour groups, but can also be a good place to sit and consult *Let's Go* for your next stop.

⊕ From Vle. Trastevere, turn right onto V. San Francesco a Ripa and walk 5min. until you get to the piazza. $ Free. ⏰ Open M-F 9am-5:30pm.

ISOLA TIBERINA OPEN SPACE

The prettiest way to get to Trastevere is through the Isola Tiberina. Cross the tiny **Ponte Fabricio** (a.k.a. the Ponte dei Quattro Capi), which, in case you couldn't tell by its name, bears pillars with four stone heads, allegedly those of the architects who once restored the bridge. You'll find yourself standing on Isola Tiberina, a small plot of land that, according to legend, is actually composed of the silt-covered remains of Tarquin, an Etruscan ruler who was thrown in the river for raping the beautiful Lucretia. The island is mainly home to the **Fatebenefratelli Hospital** and the **Basilica San Bartolomeo,** so it's a one-stop shop for spiritual and physical healing. Or you can take healing into your own hands and use the expanse on the river as a site for your neo-Victorian rest cure, joining the locals fishing or lying in the sun on the closest thing Rome has to a beach.

⊕ From V. del Teatro Marcello, walk toward the water and onto Lungotevere dei Pierleoni. Turn right to reach Ponte Fabricio. $ Free.

GIANICOLO HILL OPEN SPACE, PANORAMIC VIEW

For a great view and an escape from the urban sprawl of Rome, follow the winding (and steep) V. Garibaldi up Gianicolo Hill, the highest peak in this part of the city. The way up is pretty picturesque, too, passing the 15th-century **San Pietro in Montorio** church, the **Fonte Acqua Paola,** and the surrounding landscape. Continuing upward, you can either go straight to the **Porta San Pancrazio** and the American Academy of Rome or veer right to the **Piazzale Giuseppe Garibaldi,** which offers another great vista. If you venture to the side of the *piazzale* behind the behind of Garibaldi's horse, the dome of St. Peter's is visible. On the road below, numerous graffitied declarations of love will tug your heartstrings (or maybe that's the exercise-induced asthma kicking in).

⊕ From the P. San Egidio, turn left onto Vicolo del Cedro, climb the stairs, and take a left onto V. Garibaldi. $ Free.

BOTANICAL GARDENS GARDENS

Largo Cristina di Svezia 23A ☎06 49 91 71 07

The Botanical Gardens are an oasis of green that make it easy to forget that they border bustling Trastevere. Huge trees from all over the world provide ample shade for those who want to sit and read, and there are plenty of sunny spots to work toward the elusive city-tan. The terrace of roses, some of which have been growing since the Baroque period, is a charming jumble of crumbling steps and rogue branches. As the gardens climb the side of Gianicolo Hill, views of Rome poke through the greenery, creating opportunities for that artistic "nature frames the urban" photograph that every Facebook album needs.

⊕ Walk to the end of V. Corsini until you reach Largo Cristina di Svezia. $ €4, ages 6-11 and over 59 €2, under 6 free. ⏰ Open Mar-Oct Tu-Su 9:30am-6:30pm.

TERMINI AND SAN LORENZO

☑ BASILICA DI SANTA MARIA MAGGIORE — CHURCH

In P. dell'Esquilino ☎06 69 88 68 17

It's a good thing this basilica is so close to Termini, or a slew of cheap food and hostels might be all visitors saw on their first day in Rome. Just a 5min. walk from the station, this fifth-century church is a stunning combination of Baroque and classic Roman design. Even though its design was supposedly modeled on a miraculous snowfall sent by the Virgin herself, the main color palette isn't white but gold, gold, and more gold. If you're around on August 5, white rose petals are scattered in the interior of the church in commemoration of Mary's wintry surprise. Adjoining the basilica is a small museum containing artifacts and artwork relating to the church's history, even though the basilica itself offers plenty to see at no cost.

⇟ [M]Termini. Turn right onto V. Giovanni Giolitti and walk down V. Cavour. ℹ Modest dress required. $ Basilica free. Museum €4, EU students and over 65 €2. Loggia €5/3. Audio tour (available in English) €4. ⏰ Basilica open daily 7am-7pm. Museum open daily 9am-6pm.

CHIESA DI SANTA MARIA DEGLI ANGELI — CHURCH

P. della Repubblica ☎06 48 80 812; www.santamariadegliangeliroma.it

The facade of this Michelangelo-designed *chiesa* is a far cry from the usual Baroque look of Roman churches, as it was adapted from the ruins of the Baths of Diocletian. The especially open interior is more reminiscent of the Pantheon than traditional basilicas. Check out the meridian line that runs from the east transept to the altar; it also acts as a sundial. Inlaid marble designs of the zodiac figures offer birthday-related photo ops. You can also kill two Roman-monument birds with one church-entry stone: the church's sacristy contains the ruins of the baths next door.

⇟ [M]Termini. Walk into the P. dei Cinquecento and veer left toward V. Viminale. ℹ Sundial viewing schedule posted in the church. Reserve sundial demonstrations 2 days in advance, June 15-Sept 15. Call ☎06 48 70 749 for more information. $ Free. ⏰ Open M-F 7am-6:30pm, Sa-Su 7am-7:30pm.

BATHS OF DIOCLETIAN — MUSEUM

V. Enrico de Nicola 79 ☎06 39 96 77 00; www.archeoroma.beniculturali.it

In the heart of busy Termini, the Baths of Diocletian have weathered the city grime. They shelter various Roman artifacts, including two perfectly preserved necropolises found in the early 20th century during roadwork. For the price of entry you can also visit the **Museo Nazionale di Roma,** which is a must for Roman history buffs but a definite pass for anyone else. The ticket is also valid at three other museums for three days, which are worth the trip only if your idea of the perfect day is examining Roman coins and pottery shards.

⇟ [M]Termini. Walk into P. dei Cinquecento; enter on V. Volturno. ℹ Part of the Museo Nazionale Romano group, which also includes the Palazzo Massimo across the street, the Palazzo Altemps near the P. Navona, and the Crypta Balbi near the Largo Argentina. Buy 1 ticket for entrance to all 4 sights over 3 days. $ €7, EU students €3.50, EU citizens under 18 and over 65 free. ⏰ Open Tu-Su 9am-7:45pm. Last entry 6:45pm.

NORTHERN ROME

Northern Rome is home not only to embassies (boring), but also a ton of museums, parks, and historic *piazze* (exciting!). Set away from the ancient ruins, expect to find more recent monuments, at least in Roman terms: 17th-century villas, Bernini's sculptural masterpieces, and modern and contemporary art all reside here.

(really) public restrooms

Ancient Rome took pride in its lavish public bath system. In fact, bathing areas were so pleasant that they became a meeting place for the elite. The large baths were essentially pools of water of different temperatures. A bather first passed through a *caldarium* (hot bath), then a *tepidarium* (warm), and finally a *frigidarium* of cold water. But, instead of using soap, Romans simply covered themselves in scented oil and then removed it with a *stirgil,* a metal scraper, to leave the skin clean and smooth.

Roman baths also housed marble toilets—but don't be fooled, luxury did not mean privacy. The toilets resembled large benches with no dividers between different seats, allowing for personal conversation (so Romans were able to do two types of business at once). Running water underneath the benches carried away the waste; Romans, after all, recognized the importance of sanitation and cleanliness. After a bather had relieved himself, he would clean himself with a shared community sponge (so as to not undo the effects of the bath), provided it was not already in use by his neighbor. He would then, with proper etiquette, rinse the sponge and return it for further public use.

GALLERIA BORGHESE — MUSEUM

Piazzale del Museo Borghese 5 ☎06 84 16 542; www.galleriaborghese.it

If you think the Villa Borghese gardens are beautiful and impressive, be prepared for total sensory overload upon entering the Galleria Borghese itself. Every inch of the 17th-century building's interior is masterfully decorated: marble floors, ancient Roman mosaics, sculptures by Bernini, and the stunning canvases of Caravaggio are guaranteed to leave you as open-mouthed as Goliath's head in Caravaggio's sculpture. Because everyone enters at once, try visiting the Pinacoteca on the top floor first, and then heading down to the Bernini and Caravaggio rooms to avoid the crowds.

 # Enter on V. Pinciana, near V. Isonzo. Proceed up Vle. dell'Uccelleria for about 5min. i Reservations are required but tend to fill up quickly; call ☎06 32 810 or visit www.ticketeria.it. $ €8.50, EU citizens ages 18-25 €5.25, EU citizens under 18 and over 65 €2. Tours €6.50, under 10 free. ⏰ Open Tu-Su 9am-7pm. Last entry 6:30pm.

VILLA BORGHESE — GARDENS

Bordered by Vle. Trinità dei Monti and V. Porta Pinciana ☎06 32 16 564

The Villa Borghese sits north of Termini and provides a needed respite from the busy city. Pathways cut through gardens, lawns, and various museums, making this a public park unlike most others. As you wander through, don't be surprised to stumble suddenly upon neo-Grecian or imitation Egyptian structures as well as statues of decidedly non-Roman figures (who knew the Italians had a soft spot for Gogol?). Bring a picnic lunch and take a stroll, or rent a bike at one of the numerous stands at the entrance near the Galleria Borghese.

 # [M]A: Spagna or Flaminio-Piazza del Popolo. There are multiple entrances to the park: Porta Pinciana, Piazzale Flaminio, Vle. Belle Arti, V. Mercadante, and V. Pinciana. $ Gardens free. Bike rental €4 per hr., €15 per day. Visit www.ascolbike.com for more information. ⏰ Gardens open daily Apr-Aug 7am-9pm; Sept 7am-8pm; Oct-Feb 7am-6pm; Mar 7am-8pm.

CAPUCHIN CRYPT — CHURCH

V. Veneto 27 ☎06 48 71 185; www.cappucciniviaveneto.it

No matter how hot the summer heat, count on getting chills while in this awesome ossuary. Begun by the Capuchins in 1631, each room looks like a traditional

Baroque chapel until you notice that all the tracery and designs are made of human bones. The sheer inventiveness of the decorations is worth the trip: who but 17th-century friars would have thought pelvic bones made great angel wings, and femurs the perfect supports for lanterns? The placard at the front says it all: "What you are now, we were; what we are now, you will be."

🏃 Ⓜ A: Barberini. Follow V. Veneto uphill; the church is on the right. To enter, take the stairs on the right. 𝒊 There is a strict dress code, so avoid low-cut or sleeveless shirts and short skirts or shorts, or bring something to cover up. Ⓢ Min. donation €1. 🕿 Open M-W 9am-noon and 3-6pm, F-Su 9am-noon and 3-6pm.

GALLERIA NAZIONALE D'ARTE MODERNA   MUSEUM
Vle. delle Belle Arti 131   ☎06 32 29 81; www.gnam.arti.beniculturali.it

Just outside of the parks of Villa Borghese, the beautiful Galleria Nazionale d'Arte Moderna displays Marcel Duchamp's *Fountain* and the Futurists' misguided enthusiasm for Fascism. The museum focuses on Italian artists but also contains works by heavyweights like Van Gogh, Miró, Klimt, and Mondrian. A collection of Duchamp's readymades includes the infamous urinal (a.k.a. *Fountain*), a testimony to the truly immortal and universal power of bathroom humor.

🏃 From Vle. del Giardino in the Villa Borghese, veer right and exit the park onto Vle. delle Belle Arti. The museum is on the right. Ⓢ €8, with special exhibition €12; EU students ages 18-25 €4/10; under 18 and over 65 free. 🕿 Open Tu-Su 8:30am-7:30pm. Left half of the building (19th-century Italian paintings) open Tu-Su 12:30-7:30pm. Last entry 6:45pm.

PALAZZO BARBERINI   MUSEUM
V. delle Quattro Fontane 13   ☎06 48 24 184; www.galleriabarberini.beniculturali.it

Caravaggio might be a star of the Galleria Borghese, but he's also here at the Palazzo Barberini, in the company of such greats as Giotto, Lippi, and El Greco. Much less busy than most museums with such masterpieces, it's easy to stroll through the sumptuous rooms and imagine yourself as a guest of Pope Urban VIII. Even if you don't venture inside the Bernini-designed *palazzo* itself, the gardens tucked behind the main building transport you far from the busy streets of the **Piazza Barberini,** which is home to yet another of Bernini's works, the *Fontana del Tritone.*

🏃 Ⓜ A: Barberini. Take a left onto V. delle Quattro Fontane; the entrance is on the left. Ⓢ €5, EU students ages 18-25 €2.50, EU citizens under 18 and over 65 free. English audio tour €2.50. 🕿 Open Tu-Su 8:30am-7:30pm. Last entry 6:30pm.

VILLA TORLONIA   MUSEUM, GARDENS
V. Nomentana 70   ☎06 82 05 91 27; www.museivillatorlonia.it

The Villa Torlonia is a beautiful complex of buildings and parks that served as Mussolini's wartime hideout, complete with underground bunker (sadly closed to the public today). The museums on the property are delightful architectural fantasies, like the Swiss-farm-turned-medieval-hamlet-turned-Art-Deco-showpiece Casina delle Civette and the ornately decorated Casino Nobile. The gardens themselves are the site of ruined 18th-century pleasure gazebos, contemporary sculpture installations, and occasional fashion shoots. If you don't want to pay for the museums, pack a lunch or grab some food in the cafe and enjoy a picnic, but keep an eye out for children playing soccer.

🏃 From Piazzale Porta Pia, walk about 10min. down V. Nomentana. 𝒊 For tickets or reservations call ☎06 06 08 from 9am-7pm. Ⓢ Casina delle Civette €3, EU students ages 18-25 €1.50, EU citizens under 18 and over 65 free. Casino Nobile and show €7/5/free. Casino Nobile, Casina della Civette, Casino dei Principi, and show €9/5.50/free. 🕿 Open daily Apr-Sept 9am-7pm; Oct 9am-5::30pm; Nov-Feb 9am-4:30pm; Mar 9am-5:30pm. Last entry 45min. before close.

sights

QUARTIERE COPPEDÈ NEIGHBORHOOD

Entry arch at intersection of V. Dora and V. Tagliamento

If *Sunset Boulevard* were an Italian film, it would have been shot here (it also would have been called *Quartiere Coppedè*, obviously). Designed by the architect Gino Coppedè in the 1920s, this neighborhood around P. Mincio is full of whimsical Art Deco creations, perfect for an Italian Blanche (Bianca?) Deveraux's delusions of grandeur. After entering under the ornate archway of V. Dora, the **Villini delle Fate** at P. Mincio 3 is covered with frescoes and curlicue ironwork. To its right is the **Palazzo del Ragno,** named for its prominent spider decorations. While the buildings are not open to the public, no one's stopping you from imagining yourself as their proud (and eccentric) owner.

 # Walk up V. Nomentana from Porta Pia and take a left onto Vle. Regina Margherita, then turn left onto V. Tanaro. $ Free.

MAUSOLEUM OF COSTANZA CHURCH

V. Nomentana 349 ☎06 86 20 54 56

Enjoy the walk or bus ride up the picturesque V. Nomentana to the small but famous Mausoleum of Costanza. Connected to the Church of Sant'Agnese Fuori le Mure, this small round building is one of the oldest surviving Christian structures anywhere in the world—it was built around 350 CE. The fourth-century mosaics are truly masterpieces of elaborate vegetal and animal designs combined with charming scenes of wine-guzzling *putti* and ox-drawn carts. If you have money to spare, the third- and fourth-century Catacombs of Sant'Agnese are worth a visit.

 # [M]Termini. Either walk 2km down V. Nomentana or take the #36 bus. $ Mausoleum free. Catacombs €8, under 15 €5. ⏰ Open M 9am-noon, Tu-Sa 9am-noon and 4-6pm, Su 4-6pm.

TESTACCIO AND OSTIENSE

✓ BASILICA DI SAN PAOLO FUORI LE MURA CHURCH

Piazzale San Paolo 1 ☎06 69 88 08 00; www.basilicasanpaolo.org

Although the church's namesake walls now lie in ruins, San Paolo Fuori le Mura ("Saint Paul Outside the Walls") still seems pretty out of the way. This just means that after the trek down the mostly modern V. Ostiense, the church's imposing presence is even more impressive. The basilica is covered inside and out with 19th-century gold mosaics, but expect to see nuns and priests go about their business. Or play "Who's Who: Papal Edition" with the over 200 mosaic portraits of popes along the church's perimeter. You can also pay a visit to the **cloister,** but, honestly, the other cloisters in Rome are cheaper, and they all look the same. While San Paolo Fuori le Mura may be the second largest church in Rome, space appears to be running out, so either the Second Coming needs to hurry up or an expansion will be due.

*# [M]B: Basilica San Paolo, or bus #23 to Ostiense/LGT San Paolo stop. **i** Modest dress required. 1hr. guided visits available; reserve online. $ Basilica free. Cloister €4. ⏰ Basilica open daily 7am-6:30pm. Cloister open daily 8am-6:15pm.*

✓ CENTRALE MONTEMARTINI MUSEUM

V. Ostiense 106 ☎06 06 06 08; www.centralemontemartini.org

Satisfy your inner mechanic and Roman history nerd at Centrale Montemartini, where ancient Roman marbles are displayed alongside heavy black machinery in Rome's first electricity plant. A relatively new addition to the **Musei Capitolini** family, this museum has as much information about electricity at the turn of the 20th century as it does about mosaics of hunting scenes and frolicking nymphs. Somehow, both the sculptures and the 15m boilers benefit from this juxtaposition, creating a welcome change of pace from the more traditional Capitoline Museum displays.

 # [M]B: Ostiense. The museum is a 10min. walk down V. Ostiense. $ €5.50, EU citizens ages 18-25 €4.50. Combined ticket with Musei Capitolini €11/8.50 (valid for 1 week). Cash only. ⏰ Open Tu-Su 9am-7pm. Last entry 6:30pm.

rome

CIMITERO ACATTOLICO — CEMETERY

Cimitero Acattolico at V. Caio Cestio 6 ☎06 57 41 900; www.protestantcemetery.it

With graves marked by everything from faux-Gothic spires to columned mausoleums, the Cimitero Acattolico is a trip down memorials lane. Reserved for non-Roman, non-Catholics who died in Rome, it is inhabited by an eclectic mix of artists, 19th-century youths who sought rest cures, poets like Keats and Shelley, and international diplomats. It seems as though every language and nationality is represented on the beautiful gravestones, a testament to the enduring draw of the Eternal City. Across the street, the smaller and impeccably landscaped War Cemetery is dedicated to soldiers who died in WWII.

⇄ Ⓜ B: Piramide. Walk through the Porta San Paolo and veer left onto V. Marmorata. Take a left onto V. Caio Cestio to reach the Cimitero Acattolico. To get to the War Cemetery, continue on V. Caio Cestio and turn left onto V. Nicola Zabaglia; the entrance is on the right. $ Cimitero Acattolico €2 suggested donation. War Cemetery free. ⏰ Cimitero Acattolico open M-Sa 9am-5pm, Su 9am-1pm. War Cemetery open M-F 8am-3pm. Last entry to both cemeteries 30min. before close.

SOUTHERN ROME

👍 THE APPIAN WAY — ANCIENT ROME

V. Appia Antica ☎06 51 35 316; www.parcoappiaantica.it

When you've had your way with Rome's busy *corsi*, it might be time to try the Appian on for size. Stretching 16km from Porta San Sebastiano to Frattocchie, it's a bit large for most people to handle: walking tours generally end around the **Tomb of Cecilia Metella,** though the road extends another 8-10km. In the third century CE, the Appian Way served as the burial ground for important Romans and early Christians, who were forbidden to keep their tombs within the city walls. Legends who actually walked the road include **Virgil, Saint Peter,** and **Spartacus,** each of whom left a trail of history behind him—and, in the case of Spartacus, a trail of bodies. Don't expect the first stretch to be dirt roads surrounded by fields and crumbling aqueducts, either. Since it was paved over, the Appian Way has become, unfortunately, a modern-day reincarnation of its ancient self: a very busy road. That means cars are constantly driving by, the cobblestone ground practically shakes from buses and scooters, and there's little shoulder reserved for pedestrians. Try to visit on a Sunday when most of the road is closed to traffic. As the road merges into V. Appia Antica, the din doesn't stop until you reach the tourist office, where you'll need to make a decision about which roads to take. For the most scenic path, head up the slightly inclined road leading to San Callisto (closed on Wednesdays), where you can see countryside and bushes of pink flowers. The main attractions on the initial strip are the third-century **catacombs,** underground passageways full of bodies, sarcophagi, and paintings. For the more nature-inclined traveler, the true attractions will not start until after Cecilia Metella, where you can walk on the road's original paving stones and gaze at miles of unsullied land. If you don't want to wander that far south, consider walking down V. della Caffarella (to the left of V. Appia Antica) instead of hitting the catacombs. There are plenty of Roman ruins off of this road, too, but the paths are hilly and rocky. Either way, pack a picnic lunch to avoid the overpriced restaurants along the way.

⇄ Ⓜ A: San Giovanni. Head through Porta San Giovanni into the piazza. Take bus #218; to reach the info office, push the button to request a stop after you turn left onto V. Appia Antica. The bus continues up V. Ardeatina and drops you off near the Santa Domitilla and San Callisto Catacombs. Alternatively, take Ⓜ B: Circo Massimo or Ⓜ B: Piramide. Take bus #118, which runs along V. Appia Antica to the San Sebastiano Catacombs. If you want to walk, head down Vle. delle Terme di Caracalla from the Circus Maximus. At Piazzale Numa Pompilio, veer right onto V. di Porta San Sebastiano through the city wall and onto V. Appia Antica. ℹ Info office at V. Appia Antica 60 offers bike rental, free maps, brochures, a bus ticket machine, and suggestions for activities along the

way. For info on Archeobus tours leaving from Termini, call ☎800 281 281 or visit www.trambuso-pen.com. Ⓢ *Road and park free. Bike rental €3 per hr., €15 per day. Archeobus with audio tour €10.* 🕒 *Info office open May-July M-Sa 9:30am-1:30pm and 2-5:30pm, Su 9:30am-6:30pm; Aug M-Sa 9:30am-1:30pm and 2-5:30pm, Su 9:30am-5:30pm; Sept-Apr M-Sa 9:30am-1:30pm and 2-4:30pm, Su 9:30am-4:30pm. Archeobus tours daily every 30min. 9:30am-4pm.*

how to be a gladiator

If you're like the rest of us, you're traveling to Rome with aspirations of becoming one of the most glorious and badass fighters of the ancient world. You are a destruction machine, and you want to take names. But before you do anything too rash, read these tips to gain some street cred.

- **BE ENSLAVED.** Most gladiators were actually slaves or condemned prisoners forced to fight as part of their sentences. The best became popular, at times attracting a large fan base. (A warning: popular gladiators were few and far between—mainly because they tended to, you know, die.)

- **SWEAT, A LOT.** The most celebrated gladiators sold their sweat in bottles to their fans. The more sweat you can collect after a fight, the more fame you'll acquire. You could try to sell bottled blood as well—you'll have lots of it to spare—but real gladiators don't cry, so save your tears.

- **DON'T STOP FIGHTING.** Gladiators fight to the death. While you may value your life, your title is more important. Full commitment is key.

- **BE A LEFTY (OR FAKE IT).** Left-handed gladiators had an upper hand in battles with right-handed opponents. They were so uncommon that they were even advertised before battles. Remember: being unique will help you stand out in a crowd of hundreds of aspiring gladiators.

- **PRACTICE GOOD MORALS.** Gladiators were regarded as models of good ethics by demonstrating their bravery, pride, and skill, all values that were extremely important in Rome. So as you're ripping your combatant to shreds, remember to keep your strong morals in mind.

rome

🏛 CHIESA DI SAN CLEMENTE
CHURCH

V. Labicana 95   ☎06 77 40 021; www.basilicasanclemente.com

With a breathtaking apse mosaic and the Chapel of Santa Caterina decorated by Masolino, this small church is well worth a visit. Next to the chapel, there's even the original *sinopia* (a rough sketch put on the plaster before painting) from one of the frescoes—even artistic geniuses need some guidance. Once you've ogled these artistic masterpieces, consider a trip downstairs to the remains and ongoing excavations of the original fourth-century CE basilica. Wander freely through the labyrinthine passageways, where frescoes from as early as the eighth century CE lurk in niches and around corners. Also lurking down there is a second-century CE mithraeum (pagan temple) if you're getting tired of all the Christian stuff.

🚶 Ⓜ*B: Colosseo or bus #85 or 87. Walk up V. Labicana and turn right at P. San Clemente.* Ⓢ *Basilica free. Lower level €5, students under 26 €3.50. Cash only.* 🕒 *Basilica open M-Sa 9am-12:30pm and 3-6pm, Su 10am-12:30pm and 3-6pm. Lower level and excavation area open M-Sa 9am-12:30pm and 3-6pm, Su noon-6pm. Last entry 20min. before close.*

👍 CHIESA DEI SANTI QUATTRO CORONATI — CHURCH

V. dei Santi Quattro 20

While no longer the designated refuge for popes as it was 800 years ago, there's still an air of secrecy in this small church. From the austere courtyard, turn right to visit the **chapel,** which features amazing 13th-century frescoes depicting the life of St. Sylvester. You can't just walk in, though, and this is where the secrecy begins: ring a bell and wait for a nun to take your €1 donation and let you in. This clandestine entrance ritual is repeated for entry to the **cloister,** just off the left side of the church. You might not stumble upon hiding popes, but the trek up the steep hill is definitely worth it for the secret-society-style visit.

🧭 [M]B: Colosseo. Head up V. Labicana, turn right onto P. San Clemente, and turn left up the steep hill of V. dei Santi Quattro. The church is on the right. Ⓢ Basilica free. Cloister and chapel requested donation €1 each. ⏰ Basilica and cloister open M-Sa 6:15am-8pm, Su 6:45am-12:30pm and 3-7:30pm. Chapel open M-Sa 9am-noon and 4:30-6pm, Su 9-10:40am and 4-5:45pm. Crypt open M-F; ask at cloister for entry.

CATACOMBE DI SAN SEBASTIANO — ANCIENT ROME

V. Appia Antica 136 — ☎06 78 50 350; www.catacombe.org

Even surrounded by fellow travelers, a trip through San Sebastiano's catacombs can feel like a solo trip back in time. Ancient paintings and carvings are the only navigation tools in the dark passageways lined with thousands of tombs, so you'll be glad you have a guide. Fortunately (or unfortunately, depending on how macabre you are), the bodies have all been moved to other levels out of respect, but the empty tombs are reminder enough of where you are. Keep an eye out for early Christian symbols like fish, doves, and anchors, which were used subtly to mark the tombs of loved ones. Non-Christians were buried here too, and a set of three second-century CE pagan mausoleums owe their well-preserved state to Christians who sealed them off (and then forgot about them). Pictures are not allowed, but the eerie feelings the catacombs inevitably produce stick with you. The guided tour ends in the 17th-century **Basilica di San Sebastiano,** famous for the sculpture of **Jesus Christ the Redeemer,** Bernini's last work at the age of 82.

*🧭 Take bus #218 to stop near San Callisto and Santa Domitilla. Walk down V. della Sette Chiese to V. Appia Antica and turn right. **i** Catacombs accessible only on guided tours (available in English). Ⓢ €8, ages 6-15 €5. Basilica free. Cash only. ⏰ Open Dec 21-Nov 21 M-Sa 9am-noon and 2-5pm. Basilica open daily 8am-6pm. Tours leave every 30min. from the ticket office.*

CATACOMBE DI SAN CALLISTO — ANCIENT ROME

V. Appia Antica 110/126 — ☎06 51 30 15 80; www.sdb.org

More brightly lit than the Catacombe di San Sebastiano, these underground passageways are a better bet for anyone who gets claustrophobic (although this makes it a little less exciting). The real draw here, apart from the now empty tombs of dozens of martyrs and popes, are the incredible wall frescoes. Depicting scenes of the Last Supper, Jonah and the whale, and paradise, it's clear that early Christians weren't concerned about being stuck 25m below ground for too long. Stick with the guide, and you'll be out soon enough, too.

*🧭 From P. di San Giovanni in Laterano, take bus #218 to Fosse Ardeatine. From Circus Maximus or Ostiense, take bus #118 to Catacombe di San Callisto. **i** Catacombs accessible via guided tour (available in English). Ⓢ €8, ages 6-15 €5, under 6 free. ⏰ Open Mar-Jan M-Tu 9am-noon and 2-5pm, Th-Su 9am-noon and 2-5pm. Tours leave every 30min. from the ticket office.*

BASILICA DI SAN GIOVANNI IN LATERANO — CHURCH

P. San Giovanni in Laterano 4 — ☎06 69 88 63 34

San Giovanni in Laterano follows the unwritten rule that churches on the outskirts of Rome must be huge. The massive front doors from the Roman Senate House and a frescoed portico on V. Merulana testify to the basilica's importance—it was home to the papacy before the construction of St. Peter's. Inside, circle the impressive *baldacchino* (canopy) at the front of the church, decorated with a blue- and gold-starred canopy and figures of saints by **Giotto**. A visit to the 13th-century cloister with its sculpture and inscription fragments makes for a more intimate experience—that is, until you're joined by a tour group or two.

✚ ⓂA: San Giovanni or bus #16 from Termini. Ⓢ Basilica free. Cloister €2, students €1. Museo della Basilica €1. Audio tour €5. ⌚ Basilica open daily 7am-6:30pm. Cloister open daily 9am-6pm. Museo della Basilica open M-F 9:30am-6:15pm, Sa 9:30am-6pm.

food

Trattoria, caffè, osteria, ristorante, pizzeria, gelateria—these are all Italian words for one thing: food. It's inescapable in Rome, and much of it is fresh, delicious, and homemade. There are, of course, plenty of tourist traps, so steer clear of places immediately surrounding famous sights or those with "tourist menus" that claim to be the best deal around. For meals on the go, cafes and pizzerias are the best option, offering panini and thin-crust pizza in numerous varieties. Sit-down meals are a social and time-consuming affair in Rome, so don't expect to see many solo diners—or to be done with your meal in under an hour (or even two). You'll also have to acclimate to late dinners: most places don't open until 7:30pm or later, and they don't get busy until well after 9pm. Expect added fees for table service and bread, and, while water spews freely out of the myriad fountains in Rome, restaurants refuse to give out free tap water. Tipping isn't usually expected, but this also means that servers are considerably less attentive than you might be used to; you'll need to be aggressive if you want another glass of wine or the check. Instead of sticking to a schedule, let the homemade pasta, intoxicating wine, strong espresso, and rich tiramisu do their post-sights, pre-nightlife, always-rejuvenating work.

ANCIENT CITY

It's a shame that eating is necessary. Well, not really, but since everyone has to do it—and nearly everyone in Rome comes to the Ancient City—restaurants here are often overcrowded and overpriced. For the best deals, avoid the options closest to the sights and meander down quieter streets.

🔖 PIZZERIA DA MILVIO   PIZZERIA $
V. dei Serpenti 7   ☎06 48 93 01 45

Hanging above this pizzeria's bright red walls, a sign reads, "40 Types of *Pizze e Pane*," a little reminder that this is the spot for variety, convenience, and flavor. Architecture students crowd the casual stools in the back for simple *primi*, like *pomodoro con riso*, and *secondi* served from hot trays. Up front, servers cut dozens of thin-crust pizzas into slices sold by the ounce. Be ready to eat on the go at lunch, but there's generally an open seat somewhere after the midday crowd clears out.

✚ ⓂA: Cavour. From V. Cavour, turn onto V. dei Serpenti and walk 2min. Ⓢ Primi €5; secondi €6. Pizza €0.80-1.40 per etto. Cash only. ⌚ Open daily 7am-midnight.

🔖 LA CUCCUMA   RISTORANTE, PIZZERIA $
V. Merulana 221   ☎06 77 20 13 61

Even when you're not sitting outside, La Cuccuma's yellow walls, arched ceilings, and airy interior make you feel like you're in the warm Roman sun. The huge portions of the €9 *prix-fixe* meal (*primi, secondi, contorni*, and bread) as hard to beat and have become a real draw for locals. If you haven't exhausted your pizza cravings in Rome, they also sell thin-crust pizza loaded with toppings, and *pizze tonde* in the evening for those seeking the pleasure of a pizza fresh from the oven.

✚ ⓂA: Vittorio Emanuele. Walk down V. dello Statuto and turn right onto V. Merulana. Ⓢ Primi €4-5; secondi €5-6. Pizza €8-16 per kg. Pizze tonde (after 7pm) €4-8.50. ⌚ Open daily 10am-11pm.

LA TAVERNA DA TONINO E LUCIA

RISTORANTE $$

V. Madonna dei Monti 79 ☎06 47 45 325

You'll feel like you're in some Italian *mamma*'s home as soon as you walk into this local favorite. Mouthwatering aromas, a view into the kitchen, and a cork-lined wall full of pictures and lights give Tonino e Lucia its cozy feel. Tight quarters may have you becoming *amici* with your neighbors at the next table, but that's par for the course here, as most of the regulars already know each other. The small menu's limited selection is actually a blessing in disguise—the dishes are so good that more options might make choosing impossible. Try the veal rolls with tomato sauce or the specially recommended *paglia ai funghi*.

☩ ⓂB: Cavour. Walk down V. Cavour toward the Fori Imperiali, turn right onto V. dei Serpenti, and left onto V. Madonna dei Monti. ⓈPrimi €8; secondi €9-14. Cash only. 🕐 Open M-Sa 12:30-2:30pm and 7-10:30pm.

LA CARBONARA

OSTERIA $$

V. Panisperna 214 ☎06 48 25 176; www.lacarbonara.it

The wall of handwritten comments and the massive collection of wine corks are a testament to this *osteria*'s long history. At 106 years old, La Carbonara has remained well priced and down to earth. Do some light reading of the rave reviews on the walls while you gobble down classics like *carciofi alla giudia* (fried artichoke) and *cacio e pepe* (cheese and peppers). If you like what you get (and you surely will), don't hesitate to scribble your own sweet nothings to add to the collection, but good luck finding something that rhymes with "carbonara."

☩ From Basilica di Santa Maria Maggiore, walk down V. di Santa Maria Maggiore which becomes V. Panisperna. ⓈPrimi €6-9; secondi €9-15. 🕐 Open M-Sa 12:30pm-2:30pm and 7-11pm.

LA TAVERNA DEI FORI IMPERIALI

RISTORANTE $$$

V. della Madonna dei Monti 9 ☎06 67 98 643; www.latavernadeiforiimperiali.com

The interior is typical of Roman *osterie*, but when you look closely you'll see that those framed photos are of the chef and owner, Alessio, with celebrities like Al Pacino. Family-run for four generations, the cozy restaurant has perfected classic Roman dishes like *pappardelle alla carbonara* (€9) and veal *scaloppini* (€12). After finishing a great meal with a perfect espresso, take a stroll around the Fori Imperiali, just outside the restaurant's walls.

☩ ⓂB: Colosseo. Take V. del Colosseo away from the Colosseum and turn left on V. Cavour. Continue straight onto V. della Madonna dei Monti. ⓈPrimi €9; secondi €12-16. 🕐 Open M 12:30-3pm and 7-10:30pm, W-Su 12:30-3pm and 7-10:30pm.

IL GELATONE

GELATERIA $

V. dei Serpenti 28 ☎06 48 20 187

The name Il Gelatone is fitting: the suffix *"one,"* which means "big," translates to plentiful scoops and an expansive selection of flavors. Twenty-eight types of sorbet (who knew there were even that many kinds of fruit?), more than 30 creamy *gelati*, and four flavors of yogurt make ordering difficult—it's a good thing even small cones (€2) come with a choice of up to three flavors. To make matters better (or worse), toppings include meringue, pistachio, fresh fruit, whipped cream, chocolate, and too many others to list.

☩ From the Fori Imperiali, walk up V. Cavour and make a left onto V. dei Serpenti. ⓈCones or cups €2-4. Cash only. 🕐 Open daily 10am-1am.

CENTRO STORICO

Catering to hungry tourists, food in the Centro Storico tends to be overpriced. Your best bet for a quick meal is to head to a *panificio* (bakery), *pasticceria* (confectionery), or pizzeria and eat your grub in a nearby *piazza*. For a sit-down meal, wander down narrow, out-of-the-way streets rather than central ones.

food

caffei-nation

Italians take their coffee very seriously. So seriously, in fact, that there are unwritten rules about what's offered, when it's offered, and how it's offered. There won't be any grandes or ventis (or trentas for those who actually drink those) in Rome; instead, you'll get yelled at if you don't order properly, and don't even think about asking for a "tall iced soy caramel macchiato with whip." Stick to these few simple rules and you'll get your caffeine fix without hassle.

- **UN CAFFÈ** is an espresso (and "espresso" is an American word, so don't go asking for one or you'll look like a fool).
- **CAPPUCCINOS** are not served after noon, which is annoying when it's all you want at 1pm after rolling out of bed post-clubbing.
- **CAFFÈ FREDDO** is theoretically an iced coffee, but the *freddo* part is more a slightly-cooler-than-room-temperature *freddo* than a brrr-I'm-cold *freddo*.
- **SUGAR** is available, but not many places serve pre-sweetened coffee. Those looking for their *zucchero* substitutes should bring their own Splenda.
- **GRANITA** is the Coffee God's gift to the Italians. With its coffee-infused ice shavings and (un)healthy amounts of whipped cream, anyone looking for a sugar-related caffeine rush and subsequent crash shouldn't pass one up. For a divine granita, try Sant'Eustachio Il Caffè near the Pantheon.

🍴 DAR FILETTARO A SANTA BARBARA — FISH $

Largo dei Librari 88 — ☎06 68 64 018

In the back of this restaurant, you'll find two vats of oil constantly bubbling as cod fillet after cod fillet get tossed in and fried to golden perfection. Despite its fame and hordes of customers—families and fancily clad couples alike—Dar Filettaro a Santa Barbara has remained excellent. It isn't hard to order: the one-sheet menu features only salad, *antipasti*, and the classic fried cod fillet. Plus, with all menu items hovering near €5, this is a chance to enjoy the charms of sit-down service without the extra charge.

 # From Campo dei Fiori, walk down V. dei Giubbonari and turn left onto the tiny Largo dei Librari. [$] Salads, antipasti, and fried fish €5. Desserts €0.50-3.50. Beer €2.50-4.50. Cash only. ⏰ Open M-Sa 5:30-11:30pm.

🍴 FORNO MARCO ROSCIOLI — BAKERY $$

V. dei Chiavari 34 — ☎06 68 64 045; www.salumeriaroscioli.com

If you spot an empty stool at this bakery, grocery, and fresh food deli, grab it or be prepared to eat standing at one of the beer barrel tables outside (which frankly, isn't such a bad option). Most people have a slice of something to go—a strip of thin-crust pizza or *kranz*, a flaky, twisted roll with almonds and raisins. But the best deals are Forno Marco's fresh *primi*, like the cold rice salad and hot tomato gnocchi. At only €5-7 a plate, Forno's prices beat those of any restaurant around.

 # From Campo dei Fiori, walk down V. dei Giubbonari and turn left onto V. dei Chiavari. [$] Primi €5-7. Pizza €9.50-18 per kg. ⏰ Open M-Sa 7am-8pm.

🍴 GELATERIA DEL TEATRO — GELATERIA $

V. di San Simone 70 — ☎06 45 47 880; www.gelateriadelteatro.it

Ever wondered what makes Italian gelato so darn good? Well, much like Willy Wonka, the friendly owners at Gelateria del Teatro offer customers a peek into the magic makings of their product—and it really is a *teatro*-tastic experience watching fruit and milk get churned into creamy perfection. Thankfully it's not just a world of pure imagination, and you can get a taste of one of over 40 flavors of unique gelato. Varieties like lemon cheesecake and garden sage with raspberry are made by people, not enslaved orange-tinted workers, but the taste is truly otherworldly.

✈ *From P. Navona, turn left onto V. dei Coronari and look for the tiny V. di San Simone on the left.* **i** *Free tours offered for groups; call to reserve a spot.* Ⓢ *Cones and cups €2-10. Credit card min. €20.* ⏰ *Open daily in high season 11am-1am; in low season 11am-midnight.*

PIZZERIA DA BAFFETTO   PIZZERIA $$
V. del Governo Vecchio 114   ☎06 68 61 617; www.pizzeriabaffetto.it

Dinner at 9pm may be the norm in Rome, but even the locals get here at 6:30pm to avoid ever-mounting lines. This isn't just another pizza place—it's arguably the best pizza in Rome. Any pie you get will be as delicious as the service is brusque, so save yourself from the exasperated eye rolls and frustrated shouts of "What do you want? Tell me now!" by choosing quickly.

✈ *From P. Navona, exit onto P. Pasquino and continue as it becomes V. del Governo Vecchio.* Ⓢ *Pizza €5-9. Cash only.* ⏰ *Open M 6:30pm-12:30am, W-F 6:30pm-12:30am, Sa-Su 12:30-3:30pm and 6:30pm-12:30am.*

CUL DE SAC   RISTORANTE $$
P. Pasquino 73   ☎06 68 80 10 94; www.enotecaculdesac.com

Cul de Sac definitely emphasizes wine and the foods that go best with it: fresh *salumi*, local cheeses, and homemade pâté. Bottles of wine are just about the only decoration, and with over 1500 kinds on offer, this is both a practical and chic move. For a heartier meal, there are plenty of Roman classics as well as international dishes like *escargots alla bourguignonne* (€6.60) and *baba ghanoush* (€6.20). Whether for lunch or dinner, the place is filled with Italians (or Americans, Frenchmen, and Spaniards, who all can find menus in their native languages) sipping glasses of wine outside the busy P. Navona.

✈ *From P. Navona, walk onto P. Pasquino.* Ⓢ *Primi €7.30-9; secondi €6.60-10. Desserts €4.30.* ⏰ *Open daily noon-4pm and 6pm-12:30am.*

PIZZERIA TAVOLA CALDA   PIZZERIA $
Corso Vittorio Emanuele II 186/188   ☎06 68 80 62 29

Either Coca-Cola has an arrangement with this pizzeria or they just really like vintage Coke memorabilia, but the end result is a relaxed atmosphere to eat really good pizza. Though it's also sold by the slice, the best deal is to order a *pizza tonda* and cheap beer. Classic *primi*, which change daily, are served from behind the counter. With more tables than most pizzerias, it's a great place to refuel before diving back into the crazy pace of Centro Storico.

✈ *From Campo dei Fiori, head toward Corso Vittorio Emanuele II.* Ⓢ *Pizza tonda €3.50-6, slices €9-14 per kg. Primi and secondi €5.50-18 per kg. Beer €2-3.* ⏰ *Open daily 10am-10pm.*

PIZZERIA FLORIDA   PIZZERIA $
V. Florida 25   ☎06 68 80 32 36

On your way to the Area Sacra Argentina (see **Sights**), stop by this small shop for cheap, fresh pizza and even cheaper drinks. It's one of the few places in Rome (other than a supermarket) to get €1 soda, and the beer (€2-3) is hard to pass up. There's not much seating inside, so sit on the long bench outdoors, or perch by the Area Sacra and attempt to woo the austere stray cats that frequent the ruins with little bits of mozzarella or sausage. They may not be impressed, but that just means more pizza for you.

✈ *From the river, go up V. Arenula and take a right onto V. Florida.* Ⓢ *Pizza €8-16 per kg. Bottled water €0.70. Cash only.* ⏰ *Open M-Sa 10am-10:30pm.*

SANT'EUSTACHIO IL CAFFÈ CAFE $

P. Sant'Eustachio 82 ☎06 68 80 20 48; www.santeustachioilcaffe.it

The coffee in Italy is, of course, far better than what Starbucks has to offer, but Sant'Eustachio's is suberb even by Italian standards. Served sweet (request unsweetened if you don't want sugar), the drinks here come in decadent varieties such as *mousse al caffè* (€2.70-6.50) or *granita al caffè* (€4-6.50). While you probably won't make it like they do, they sell their beans by the kilogram if you want to pull your own shot. Drink your joe while standing at the bar—there are tables, but you'll have to cough up at least €2 for the pleasure.

 # From the Pantheon, head onto Salita dei Crescenzi and turn left onto V. Sant'Eustachio, which opens onto P. Sant'Eustachio. Ⓢ Cappuccino or coffee at the bar €2.40, at table €4.90. Coffee beans €24-26 per kg. Cash only. ⏰ Open M-Th 8:30am-1am, F 8:30am-1:30am, Sa 8:30am-2am, Su 8:30am-1am.

PIAZZA DI SPAGNA

Between Prada, the Spanish Steps, and the teems of tourists heading to both, it might be hard to find a tasty and economical midday bite. For lunch, order takeout at one of the *panifici* (bakeries) or pizzerias then eat on the *piazza*. For dinner, avoid the large places with views of P. del Popolo or the Trevi Fountain and veer onto smaller streets for better quality and service. Be warned, though: this is pretty much the most expensive neighborhood in Rome.

FRASCHETTERIA BRUNETTI RISTORANTE $$

V. Angelo Brunetti 25B ☎06 32 14 103; www.fraschetteriabrunetti.it

Save your messiness for a melting gelato after dinner—there'll be no greasy pizza fingers or spaghetti mishaps here. Instead, Fraschetteria Brunetti focuses on baked pasta, including 11 types of lasagna in varieties that you won't find anywhere else, like the rich gorgonzola and walnut. Covered in handwritten notes from loyal patrons, this *ristorante* doesn't let proximity to the sights lead to jacked-up prices or watered-down cuisine.

 # ⓂA: Flaminio-Piazza del Popolo. From P. del Popolo, exit onto V. di Ripetta and turn right onto V. Angelo Brunetti. Ⓢ Panini €3.50. Primi €10. Prix-fixe lunch of entree, coffee, and drink €9. Cocktails €4. ⏰ Open M-Sa 11am-2am, but may close earlier or later depending on the crowd.

CAMBI PIZZERIA, BAKERY $

V. del Leoncino 30 ☎06 68 78 081

The smell of homemade pizza, bread, and pastries wafting down the street attracts customers to Cambi long before the daily lunch rush. If you've reached your pizza quota for the trip, never fear—tons of freshly made panini (€3.50) and *tramezzini* (€2) offer enough variety to please even the pickiest eaters. Unleavened bread is a house specialty and a good option to pair with some cheeses and *salumi*, which are on sale in the small grocery area. Satisfy your sweet tooth with *crostata* (cookies filled with chocolate or fruit) as you savor the knowledge that tourists are paying three times as much down the street.

 # From Ara Pacis/Mausoleo di Augusto, walk down V. Tomacelli and turn right onto V. Leoncino. i No seating. Ⓢ Cookies €0.80, €33 per kg. Panini €3.50. Pizza €8-15 per kg. Crostatine €11 per kg. Cash only. ⏰ Open M-Sa 8am-8pm.

BAR SAN MARCELLO CAFE $

V. di San Marcello 37/8 ☎06 69 92 33 15

This little *tavola calda* is an oasis of Italians just beyond the international chatter surrounding the Trevi Fountain. While chowing down on inexpensive *primi* and panini, local workers talk and gesticulate in that typically Italian way, a welcome reminder that Rome isn't all tourists and cameras. Pasta salads and grilled fish or chicken are lighter than what's offered at sit-down places, so you can get the energy boost you need without the food coma.

🍴 *From P. Venezia, take V. del Corso; turn right onto V. dei Santi Apostoli and left onto V. di San Marcello.* **i** *Takeout available. Limited seating.* 💲 *Panini €3.50-4. Primi €4-5.* 🕐 *Open daily 6am-5:30pm.*

FIASCHETTERIA BELTRAMME
RISTORANTE $$$
V. della Croce 39

When a restaurant has managed to limit its menu to one page and survive for over a century without a phone, you know it's doing something right. Expect classic dishes made with family love rather than creative culinary concoctions. The *cacio e pepe* is some of the best in the neighborhood, and locals will tell you so when you sit next to them in the restaurant's close quarters. We're glad that, despite the modern fashion flash surrounding it, this traditional standby hasn't changed.

🍴 Ⓜ*A: Spagna. From the Spanish Steps, take V. dei Condotti, turn right onto V. Belsiana, and right onto V. delle Croce.* 💲 *Vegetables and sides €6-10. Primi €10; secondi €15-23. Cash only.* 🕐 *Open M-Sa noon-2:30pm and 7-10:30pm.*

NATURIST CLUB
RISTORANTE, VEGETARIAN $$$
V. della Vite 14, 4th fl.
☎06 67 92 509

Like its street name, this restaurant is all about *"la vita"*—that is, saving a few *vite* by serving up an entirely macrobiotic menu. Climb up four well-worn flights of stairs (which might be part of the health kick) to enjoy totally atypical Roman fare like ravioli stuffed with creamy tofu and pesto (€8) or seitan escalope with grilled vegetables (€9). Despite the exotic twists, the dishes taste like they were made in a traditional trattoria. If you're skeptical of macrobiotic cuisine, Naturist Club may just change your mind.

🍴 *Directly off V. del Corso around P. di San Lorenzo in Lucina; turn right onto V. della Vite from V. del Corso and look for #14. Buzz and walk to 4th fl.* 💲 *Primi €8-9; secondi €9-11. Lunch combo €8-10. Fixed vegetarian dinner €16. Dinner combo €20-25. Organic wine €12-16 per bottle.* 🕐 *Open M-F 12:30-3pm and 7:30-10:30pm, Sa 7:30-10:30pm.*

crazy for candy

In Ancient Rome, lead was used as both a preservative for perishable foods and a sweetener for treats. Thankfully, Italians have wised up to the metal's not-so-sweet side effects (probably after Nero went a little nuts after having too much gelato) and Roman sweets no longer taste like plumbing.

JEWISH GHETTO

Most restaurants in this neighborhood are on **Via del Portico d'Ottavia,** and while not exactly cheap, they're a great alternative to classic Italian fare. Most restaurants are kosher and close early Friday and Saturday.

⬛ ANTICO FORNO DEL GHETTO
BAKERY, GROCERY $
P. Costaguti 31
☎06 68 80 30 12

You don't have to resort to pizza to avoid overpriced dishes at Roman restaurants: grab a loaf of to-die-for bread, a few slices of smoked meat, and a hunk of cheese at this family-run neighborhood staple instead. Locals flock to Antico Forno to buy anything from fresh pasta to hot *focaccia* topped with veggies. Be quick—the bread goes fast.

🍴 *From Ponte Garibaldi, walk down V. Arenula, turn right onto V. di Santa Maria del Pianto and into P. Costaguti.* **i** *Only pizza and bread guaranteed kosher.* 💲 *Pizza and focaccia €1.20-2 per slice, €7.70-9.70 per kg. Cash only.* 🕐 *Open M-F 8am-2:30pm and 5-8pm, Sa-Su 8am-1pm.*

food

LA TAVERNA DEL GHETTO   KOSHER $$$

V. del Portico d'Ottavia 8   ☎06 68 80 97 71; www.latavernadelghetto.com

The small dining area out front might have you thinking this is an intimate cafe with Middle Eastern music and delicious food. But head around the block and you'll see that this popular spot opens into an expansive dining and party space. The first kosher restaurant in Rome, La Taverna del Ghetto is an expert in the classics: *baccalà* (fried fish), *fiori di zucca* (zucchini flowers), and any variation of artichoke. Save some room for soy-based desserts like ricotta pies, a light finish to a hearty meal.

⌖ *From Teatro Marcello, walk down V. del Piscaro and veer right as it becomes V. del Portico d'Ottavia.* ⓢ *Primi €12-14; secondi €16-25.* 🕑 *Open M-Th noon-11pm, F noon-4pm, Sa 9-11pm, Su noon-11pm.*

KOSHER BISTROT CAFE   CAFE, KOSHER $$$

V. Santa Maria del Pianto 68/69   ☎06 68 64 398

The Kosher Bistrot Cafe offers Kosher food and Jewish Roman classics, but it's a bit more casual and modern than its neighbors. Picnic-like wooden tables are often full of locals drinking wine and enjoying plates like curry chicken with zucchini or massive plates of *salumi*. The modern interior has a full bar and shelves with packaged food for sale, including tantalizing picnic baskets—though, at €40-60 each, it may be a better idea to dine in.

⌖ *From Ponte Garibaldi, walk up V. Arenula and turn right onto V. Santa Maria del Pianto.* ⓢ *Primi €9-11; secondi €8-9. Beer and wine €6-7. Cocktails €7-8.* 🕑 *Open M-Th 9am-9pm, F 9am-sundown, Su 9am-9pm. Aperitivo 5-9pm.*

PASTICCERIA BOCCIONE LIMENTANI   BAKERY $$

V. del Portico d'Ottavia 1   ☎06 68 78 637

The exterior of this *pasticceria* gives little indication of just how delicious the pastries are. Trays of freshly baked morsels are brought out by the women behind the counter, so choose quickly while they're still warm. Fresh tortes sell out quickly in the mornings, but *biscottini* studded with nuts and fruits and biscotti of all kinds keep customers happy into the afternoon.

⌖ *Take a right on the corner of V. del Portico d'Ottavia; look at the numbers, as it's practically unmarked.* ⓢ *Cookies €18 per kg. Tortes €18-22 each. Cash only.* 🕑 *Open M-Th 7:30am-7:30pm, F 7:30am-3:30pm, Su 7:30am-7:30pm.*

NONNA BETTA CUCINA KOSHER   KOSHER $$

V. del Portico d'Ottavia 16   ☎06 68 80 62 63; www.nonnabetta.it

Yes, the owner of this restaurant actually has a grandmother *(nonna)* named Betta, and it shows in the cooking. Famous for its fine selection of Roman kosher food, this restaurant is popular with locals and tourists seeking a sit-down meal in the Ghetto. There are many vegetarian plates like baked artichokes with mozzarella—in fact, there are artichokes in nearly every dish (look for *carciofi alla giudia*).

⌖ *From Teatro Marcello, walk down V. del Piscaro and veer right as it becomes V. del Portico d'Ottavia.* ⓢ *Primi €8-11; secondi €10-18.* 🕑 *Open M-Th 10am-3:30pm and 6:30-11:30pm, F 10:30am-3:30pm, Su 10am-3:30pm and 6:30-11:30pm.*

VATICAN CITY

The longest lines in Rome eventually become hungry crowds. The selection of neighborhood trattorias and small stores that lines the quiet streets outside the Vatican won't disappoint, but the bright English menus and beckoning waiters closer to the museums will.

🖾 CACIO E PEPE   RISTORANTE $$

V. Giuseppe Avezzana 11   ☎06 32 17 268; www.cacioepeperistorante.com

If you can only afford to eat one sit-down dinner while in Rome, make it at Cacio e Pepe. While removed from the main sights in the area, it will be well worth your time to trek to this true trattoria. Although it's always busy, the welcoming owner Gianni will personally seat you and make sure your *cacio e pepe* (fresh egg pasta topped with oil, grated cheese, and black pepper) is the best pasta you've ever had. Its popularity with locals instead of tourists has kept the vibe casual and the service as good as the food—and that's saying a lot.

⚑ Ⓜ*A: Lepanto. From the Metro, walk up V. Lepanto (away from the Vatican), turn right onto Vle. delle Milizie, and left onto V. Giuseppe Avezzana.* Ⓢ *Primi €8; secondi €9-10. Cash only.* ⌚ *Open M-F 12:30-3pm and 7:30-11:30pm, Sa 12:30-3pm.*

▨ OLD BRIDGE GELATERIA   GELATERIA $
Vle. dei Bastioni di Michelangelo 5   ☎06 38 72 30 26

The gelato here is so sinfully good you might need to visit the Vatican to confess. Despite being practically on the doorstep of the most tourist-heavy sight in the city, this tiny, unadorned *gelateria* has somehow remained a true hole in the wall. Beware: lines may rival those of the Vatican, but the size of your order (huge) will make the wait worthwhile.

⚑ *Off P. Risorgimento and across the street from the line to the Vatican Museums.* Ⓢ *Gelato €1.50-5. Frappes €2. Cash only.* ⌚ *Open M-Sa 8am-2am, Su 3pm-2am.*

FA BIO   CAFE, ORGANIC $
V. Germanico 43   ☎06 64 52 58 10

The name refers to organic produce rather than a certain bare-chested, seagull-hating romance novel heartthrob, but the food will still leave you swooning. In a city of bread, pasta, cheese, and more bread, Fa Bio will be your Eden. Organic pie (€1.50) and bread that is, for once, not white are enough to sustain you through a heavy afternoon of sightseeing. If you still need a pick-me-up after the 4hr. waits, try the *"energizzante,"* a potent shake of milk, pear, ginger, and cacao.

⚑ Ⓜ*A: Ottaviano. Walk down V. Ottaviano and turn left onto V. Germanico.* Ⓢ *Panini €4. Salads €4.50. Cookies €0.50-1. Fruit juices and smoothies €3.50. Cash only.* ⌚ *Open M-Sa in summer 9am-8pm; in winter 9am-5pm.*

FABBRICA MARRONS GLACES GIULIANI   CIOCCOLATERIA $$
V. Paolo Emilio 67   ☎06 32 43 548; www.marronglaces.it

This is the kind of place you visit first for yourself, second to do some gift-shopping for friends back home, and third for yourself again. The shop's old-school '40s feel adds to the delight of ordering sweet confections from the family owners. Their specialties—*marrons glacés* (candied chestnuts) and chocolate—are the perfect combination of sweet and rich. They make great gifts for your folks, but you'll be hard-pressed to bring them all the way home without stealing a few more for yourself.

⚑ Ⓜ*A: Lepanto. Take Vle. Giulio Cesare toward the Vatican and turn left onto V. Paolo Emilio.* Ⓢ *Marron Glacés, candied fruit, and chocolates €4.70 per etto.* ⌚ *Open in summer M-Sa 8:30am-1pm and 3:30-7:30pm; in winter M-Sa 8:30am-8pm, Su 9am-1pm.*

FORNO TACITO   BAKERY $
V. Tacito 20   ☎06 32 35 133

If you're looking for an alternative to gelato (or you're looking for a sweet supplement), try a warm pastry from this local bakery and grocer. Their waffle-shaped *ferratelle* cookies (€15 per kg) are mild and crispy, while their flaky *fiocchetti* twists (€0.85) are a lighter alternative to the standard croissant. To slow the sugar rush, their excellent pizza (less greasy and better priced than at most places) and bread are great hot or cold.

⚑ Ⓜ*A: Lepanto. Walk down V. Ezio and continue straight as it becomes V. Tacito.* *i* *Also sells basic groceries. No seating.* Ⓢ *Pizza €7-13 per kg. Cookies €9.50 per kg. Fruit and cream tarts €1.50 each. Cash only.* ⌚ *Open M-Sa 8-2:30pm and 4:30-8pm.*

food

MONDO ARANCINA

CAFE $

V. Marcantonio Colonna 38   ☎06 97 61 92 13; www.mondoarancina.it

Diverge from the standard pizza lunch and try this bright orange restaurant's namesake product, the *arancino*, a fried rice ball stuffed with mozzarella, meat, or vegetables. Named for their resemblance to oranges (*arance*), these rich spheres are a small but filling meal. For the adventurous, the *vulcano* is a savory blend of black cuttlefish pasta and fresh tomatoes.

  ✢ Ⓜ A: Lepanto. Walk down V. Marcantonio Colonna. Ⓢ Arancine €2.40. Pizza €9-16 per kg; pizze tonde €4-8.50. Calzones €2.50. Cash only. ☉ Open daily 8am-12:30am.

TRASTEVERE

There are plenty of dining options in Trastevere, whether you want a luxurious sit-down meal, a bite on the go, or something in between. While the *piazze* are full of great choices, explore smaller side streets for some diamonds in the rough.

▨ LA RENELLA

PIZZERIA, BAKERY $

V. del Moro 15/16   ☎06 58 17 265

La Renella is as close to a true neighborhood eatery as you're likely to find, with locals coming at all hours of the day for everything from morning bread to lunchtime pizza to after-dinner cookies. The handwritten menu looks like it hasn't changed for years, but with Roman classics like the *fiori di zucchini* (huge orange petals topped with anchovies and cheese), why should it? The walls are covered in flyers for local events, apartments for rent, and job offer-ings, so if you're not in the mood to eat, at least come in to browse through the neighborhood happenings. You may not walk away with a new apartment, but in all likelihood, you'll have succumbed to the tempting call of La Renella's marmalade-and-chocolate *fagotini* cookies (€14 per kg).

  ✢ From P. Trilussa, walk down V. della Renella. There's also a back entrance on V. del Politeama. Ⓢ Pizza €5-15 per kg. Sweet tortes and crostate €11-18 per kg. Biscotti €11-20 per kg. ☉ Open daily 7am-2am.

▨ LE FATE

RISTORANTE $$

Vle. Trastevere 130/134   ☎06 58 00 971; www.lefaterestaurant.it

Inspired by the fable of Princess Aurora, this festive restaurant has taken on the themes of love and solidarity in both its ambience and the quality of its food. All ingredients come from Lazio, so you can expect especially fresh plates; the homemade gnocchi with steak, cream, spinach, and ricotta is as rich in flavor as Aurora was in gold. Students who aren't blessed with riches like the fairytale heroine can take advantage of the €10 meal, complete with bruschetta, pasta, dessert, and a glass of wine. Just say the magic word (or show your student ID).

  ✢ About 15min. down Vle. Trastevere from P. Giuseppe Gioacchino Belli. 𝒊 Free Wi-Fi. Inquire about cooking classes and apartment rentals for students. Ⓢ Primi €9-13; secondi €9-18. Cash only. ☉ Open daily 6-11pm.

SIVEN

PIZZERIA, DELI $

V. San Francesco a Ripa 137   ☎06 58 97 110

The roasting chickens at the entrance and the brick arch behind the counter make Siven feel like the inside of a wood-burning oven, and the delicious pizza and *primi* are sold by weight. The lunch rush is fierce, as tons of locals push in and out for lasagna, gnocchi, eggplant *parmigiano*, and calzones, and especially for a few slices of thin-crust pizza with zucchini, potatoes, mushrooms, or steak. There's nowhere to sit and the service is fast, so be ready to eat on the go.

  ✢ From Vle. Trastevere, turn right onto V. San Francesco a Ripa. Ⓢ Pasta and primi €9-22 per kg. Calzones €3. Pizza €1-1.50 per etto. ☉ Open M-Sa 9am-10pm.

PIZZERIA DA SIMONE

V. Giacinto Carini 50

PIZZERIA, DELI $

☎06 58 14 980

After a long trek up to Ponte Acqua Paola and the surrounding gardens, there's no better way to replenish yourself than with a hot slice of Da Simone's pizza. Pies are topped with anything from shrimp to the classic sun-dried tomatoes and *mozzarella di bufala*. Down the counter, you'll find freshly made pasta, steamed vegetables, and huge chicken legs (€3) that are filling enough to be a complete dinner. If there's room, you can eat at a small banquette, but most likely you'll go back to the summit of Gianicolo Hill to eat while gazing at the city below.

✠ *From the Porta San Pancrazio on Gianicolo Hill, walk downhill on V. Garibaldi and then take a left and follow V. Giacinto Carini for about 7min.* ⑨ *Pizza €1.50-4 per slice, €7-17 per kg. Vegetables €12-17 per kg. Pasta €13-17 per kg. Cash only.* ⌚ *Open M-Sa 7am-8:30pm.*

CASETTA DI TRASTEVERE

P. de Renzi 31/32

RISTORANTE $$

☎06 58 00 158

With the cheapest pizza in town (and as one of the few places that serves it at lunch), Casetta is a great place to rest your feet. Trastevere's picturesque alleyways are clearly the inspiration for the interior decor, although eating under faux clotheslines and painted windows with balconies might get "It's A Small World" stuck in your head. Nevertheless, reasonable prices mean full tables at both lunch and dinner, with large banquet tables upstairs for larger groups. Eating earlier than what is fashionable in Italy (i.e., before 1pm for lunch and before 9pm for dinner) might save you some waiting.

✠ *From P. Santa Maria in Trastevere, walk down V. di Piede until you hit V. della Pelliccia. P. de Renzi is just beyond.* ⑨ *Pizza €3-6. Primi €5-8; secondi €5-16. Desserts €3-5. Cash only.* ⌚ *Open daily noon-11:30pm.*

BISCOTTIFICIO ARTIGIANO

V. della Luce 21

BAKERY $

☎06 58 03 926

Tucked away from the restaurant-lined V. della Lungaretta, Biscottificio Artigiano draws you into its humble interior thanks to the large window displays of Cookie Monster's most sublime dreams. Try the paper-thin *stracetti*, slightly sweet cookies made from a variety of nuts and eggs, or indulge your inner kid-in-a-cookie-store and simply ask for a small sampler bag to munch as you roam the streets. Family-run for over a century, this bakery uses recipes that are like no one else's in Rome.

✠ *From P. Giuseppe Gioacchino Belli, take a left onto V. della Lungaretta and then turn right on V. della Luce.* ⑨ *Most cookies €7.50-16 per kg. Rustic and fruit tortes €15.* ⌚ *Open M-Sa 8am-8pm, Su 9:30am-2pm.*

HOSTARIA DAR BUTTERO

V. della Lungaretta 156

RISTORANTE $$$

☎06 58 00 517

Authenticity is a tricky thing, but Hostaria dar Buttero (whose name is in the old Roman dialect) does an excellent job of convincing you that recreating the past is possible. Serving classic Roman dishes like *cacio e pepe* and *pasta all'amatriciana* in rooms decorated with hanging tools, framed sketches and paintings, dangling lamps, and Polaroid snapshots, it's easy to pretend that you and your dining companions are living in a Fellini film. Seating in an ivy-covered indoor garden continues the fantasy, so if you're looking for a nice dinner that's quintessentially Roman, order some *rigatoni alla buttero* (pancetta, mushrooms, tomatoes, parmesan, and butter; €8) and dream away.

✠ *From P. San Sonnino, turn left onto V. della Lungaretta.* ⑨ *Pizza €5-7. Primi €6-10; secondi €8-18.* ⌚ *Open M-Sa noon-3pm and 7-11pm.*

food

TERMINI AND SAN LORENZO

Termini and San Lorenzo are dominated by restaurants representing both extremes of the price range: cheap eats and overpriced tourist menus. Avoid restaurants near the station and head to the side streets for better options. Hostel dwellers with kitchen access should befriend the huge **SMA** grocery store on P. dell'Esquilino. (⏰ Open M-Sa 8am-9pm, Su 8:30am-8:30pm.)

👍 ANTICA PIZZERIA DE ROMA — PIZZERIA $

V. XX Settembre 41 — ☎06 48 74 624

Businessmen may take home a big paycheck, but that doesn't mean they don't know bargains when they see them; at midday, this tiny pizzeria is full of men in suits munching some of the best-priced and freshest pizza in the neighborhood. While Antica offers standard pizza sold by weight, the workers have cutting, weighing, and serving up fresh pies down to a science, and can whip out an individual one in less than 10min.

➡ From P. della Repubblica, walk down V. Vittorio Emanuele Orlando and turn right onto V. XX Settembre. [$] Individual pizzas €2.20-5.50, €0.70-2 per etto. Cash only. ⏰ Open M-Sa 9:30am-9:30pm.

PASTICCERIA STRABBIONI ROMA — CAFE, BAKERY $

V. Servio Tullio 2 — ☎06 48 72 027; www.strabbioni.it

Not much has changed at Strabbioni since it opened in 1888: not the hand-painted flowers gracing the ceiling, not the old-fashioned lamps, and definitely not the excellent service and food. The second-oldest bar of its type still in Rome, this is the place where locals come for a cheap sandwich, freshly baked pastry, or afternoon cocktail. At only €3.50-4 a drink, how can you resist? Enjoy specialties like the *budino di riso*, a small rice pudding cake, in the casual seating outside or at the wooden bar while you chat with the staff. While *Let's Go* might not have been around in 1888, we're pretty sure this place would have merited a listing in *Let's Go Europe 1889*.

➡ From Porta Pia, walk down V. XX Settembre and turn right onto V. Servio Tullio. ℹ There is also a sit-down restaurant down the street at V. Servio Tullio 8/10. [$] Panini €3-5. Pastries €0.80-3. Cash only. ⏰ Open M-Sa 7am-8pm.

FASSINO — CAFE, GELATERIA $

V. Bergamo 24 — ☎06 85 49 117

The folks at Fassino will have you know gelato isn't just a summer treat. The famous *Brivido Caldo* reinvents the favorite frozen treat, sticking a cookie in the middle and turning it into a hot delight topped with whipped cream. In the winter, try their richest flavor, the *cioccolato* with brandy and cream. In summer, the original *cioccarancio* (dark chocolate and orange) is just the right combination of rich and refreshing. After the sugar rush (or before, if you're one of those people who's been brainwashed into the dessert-after-dinner rule), settle down for a savory crepe. Their fixed lunch meal (a crepe, drink, dessert, and coffee; €8.50) is a steal if you're looking for something more substantial.

➡ From the end of V. XX Settembre, turn left onto V. Piave and walk until you hit P. Fiume. Turn right onto V. Bergamo. [$] Gelato €1.80-3. Brivido Caldo €3 (winter only). Cocktails €4.50-5. Cash only. ⏰ Open M-F 8am-midnight, Sa-Su 4:30pm-1am.

RISTORANTE DA GIOVANNI — RISTORANTE $$

V. Antonio Salandra 1A — ☎06 48 59 50

A hand-written menu, shelf of old typewriters, and hanging carcass greet customers at this subterranean trattoria. Don't worry: the meat is dangling in the kitchen, ensuring that your entree will be fresh. With only a few windows near the ceiling and a wood-lined interior, this family-run Roman restaurant oozes with dark warmth that matches its classic dishes. You've seen it written dozens of times at numerous establishments, but you'll never get tired of da Giovanni's *cacio e pepe,* which they've been making for over 50 years.

➡ From P. della Repubblica, walk up V. Vittorio Emanuele Orlando, turn right onto V. XX Settembre, and left onto V. Antonio Salandra. [$] Primi €6-7; secondi €5-14. ⏰ Open M-Sa noon-3pm and 7-10:30pm.

RISTORANTE AFRICA

AFRICAN $$

V. Gaeta 26/28

☎06 49 41 077

The area around Termini abounds with cheap, international dives, but this African restaurant distinguishes itself with better quality food at reasonable prices. The friendly staff will be happy to recommend dishes to customers who are new to African cuisine (or Italian), but English translations provide ample assistance. Vegetarians can finally feast on something other than pasta: the *aliccia* is a healthful dish of puréed vegetables simmered in onion and herb sauce and served with traditional African bread (€9). Bright orange walls, carved wooden seats, and African sculptures bring you out of Italy, at least for one meal.

➡ ⓂTermini. Walk through P. dei Cinquecento and onto V. Gaeta; follow it as it curves to the right. [$] Appetizers €3-5. Entrees €9-13. ⏰ Open M-Sa 8am-midnight.

PIZZERIA DEL SECOLO

PIZZERIA $

V. Palestro 62

☎06 44 57 606

A favorite among nearby hostel dwellers, this corner pizzeria serves 27 varieties of thin-crust and stuffed pizza, including one loaded with Nutella. Grab a slice or a cheap *primo* before ordering a few rounds of even cheaper Peroni (€2.50).

➡ ⓂTermini. Walk 4 blocks down V. Milazzo and turn left onto V. Palestro. [$] Pizza €0.70-1.10 per etto; whole pizzas €4.50-6. Primi €5-7. Cash only. ⏰ Open daily 8am-midnight.

NORTHERN ROME

Because Northern Rome is primarily residential, dining out tends to be pricey. Your best bet is to pack a picnic and eat it in one of the lovely gardens.

STAROCIA LUNCH BAR

CAFE $

V. Sicilia 121

☎06 48 84 986

Pop into this modern cafe after a stroll in the Villa Borghese. Black-and-white decor and faux-crystal chandeliers distinguish it from other cafes that offer the same, standard fare. Fresh (and huge) panini, pasta, cocktails, and coffee are surprisingly well priced given Starocia's hip vibe. It's especially popular with the lunch crowd, though its evening buffet-only happy hour means you'll probably make it your dinner spot.

➡ Walking south on V. Po (away from the Villa Borghese), make a right onto V. Sicilia. [$] Tramezzini and panini €1.60-3.50. Pasta and secondi €4-7. Coffee €0.80-2. Cocktails €5-6. Happy hour buffet €4, with wine €6. Cash only. ⏰ Open M-Sa 5:15am-9:30pm. Happy hour M-Sa 6pm.

TREE BAR

CAFE $$

V. Flaminia 226

☎06 32 65 27 54

More modern Swedish than traditional Italian, Tree Bar's light wood decor and polished white floors make it a relaxing place to savor reasonably priced snacks and entrees. Behind the bar, a glass door displays the many *salumi* and cheeses on offer, and the menu is written on a chalkboard column in the center of the room. Tree is definitely a local spot—check out the small board near the bar for neighborhood news as you sip wine or nibble cheese far from P. del Popolo (even though it's just a tram ride away).

➡ ⓂA: Flaminio-Piazza del Popolo. Walk about 25min. up V. Flaminia, or take tram #2 to Belle Arti. [$] Primi and secondi €4-15. Beer €3-5. Wine €5-7. ⏰ Open M 6pm-2am, Tu-Su 10:30am-2am.

IL MARGUTTA RISTORARTE
VEGETARIAN $$

V. Margutta 118 ☎06 32 65 05 77; www.ilmargutta.it

Vegetarians, rejoice! Even vegans can let out a shout of joy. The expansive interior of this meat-free restaurant, accented by tall potted plants to match the green cuisine, creates a surprisingly sophisticated feel. Those tired of white pasta can feast on refreshing plates like buckwheat noodles with strawberries, asparagus, and gorgonzola. For a protein kick, try the tofu-based seitan escalope with lemon and Prosecco sauce. The lunch buffet served Monday through Friday offers myriad vegetarian soups, salads, and pastas (€12), and the Sunday version features an even larger buffet and live music (€25).

✠ ⓂA: Flaminio. From Piazzale Flaminia, walk into P. del Popolo and veer left onto V. del Babuino. Walk 5min. and turn left onto the small alley street, V. Margutta. ⓈPrimi €10-12; secondi €10-15. ☑ Open daily 12:30-3:30pm and 7-11:30pm.

BUBI'S
RISTORANTE $$

V. Giovanni Vincenzo Gravina 7/9 ☎06 32 60 05 10; www.bubis.it

The small menu of this elegant restaurant caters to those seeking something a little different from the heavy, cream-based dishes of Lazio. Terrace seating behind a wall of leaves is great for more intimate meals and makes you feel far removed from the busy V. Flaminia. *Primi* and *secondi* prominently feature vegetables and seafood, and entrees like *straccetti di pollo* with curry and Canadian rice and a range of gourmet hamburgers add a bit of international flare.

✠ ⓂA: Flaminio or tram #19 to Belle Arti. From the Metro, walk up V. Flaminio for about 5min. and turn left onto V. Giovanni Vincenzo Gravina. Ⓢ Panini €10-14. Primi €11-14; secondi €12-20. ☑ Open M-Sa 1-3pm and 8-11pm.

RISTORANTE AL BORGHETTO
RISTORANTE $$$

V. Flaminia 77 ☎06 32 02 397

A quality alternative to some fancier spots nearby, this modest restaurant serves delicious and original takes on Roman classics. A great variety of vegetarian plates includes the *orecchiette* with eggplant, mint, ricotta, and walnuts. Fish lovers will appreciate the pesto *taglioni* with octopus for a little variation on standard *primi*. The small, yellow- and scarlet-accented interior creates a welcoming atmosphere for a mostly local crowd relaxing and chatting with friends.

✠ ⓂA: Flaminio. Walk 5min. up V. Flaminia. Ⓢ Primi €7-14; secondi €14-19. ☑ Open M-Sa 12:30-3pm and 7:30pm-midnight.

TESTACCIO AND OSTIENSE

Testaccio is known among Roman residents as one of the city's best spots for high-quality, reasonably priced food. Its location farther from the sights means fewer tourists have caught on. Whether you want an upscale restaurant or a cheap trattoria, you'll have no trouble finding it here.

🏛 IL NOVECENTO
RISTORANTE $$$

V. dei Conciatori 10 ☎06 57 25 04 45; www.9cento.com

Fresh, homemade, family-run—you've heard these adjectives used all too often to describe Italian cuisine, but here, they actually come to life. Watch the owner's son roll out pasta dough, cut it into *tagliatelle*, and dump it into boiling water before it ends up on your plate topped with homemade pesto (€10). If pasta isn't your thing, then how about pizza or roasted meat—again, you can see both sliced and diced minutes before you eat them. Though the wood-paneled rooms up front are especially cozy, try to grab a table in the huge dining room in back to take in all the kitchen action.

✠ ⓂB: Piramide. Walk down V. Ostiense and make a right onto V. dei Conciatori. Ⓢ Pizzas €5-9. Primi €9-10; secondi €12-18. ☑ Open M-F 12:30-2:30pm and 7:30-11pm, Sa-Su 7:30-11pm.

FARINANDO

PIZZERIA, BAKERY $

V. Lucca della Robbia 30 ☎06 57 50 674

Farinando posts a list of the kinds of flour they use on the wall, so it's obvious that they take their pizzas, cookies, and pastries seriously. The pizzas are loaded with every topping imaginable and come straight from the wood-burning oven visible through a glass window in the shop. An extensive seating area and no charge for table service means you can stay put in case that first cookie didn't quite satisfy your sweet tooth.

✦ ⓂB: Piramide. Walk left onto V. Galvani and right onto V. Lucca della Robbia. Ⓢ Calzones €3. Pizza tonda €4-6, €7-16 per kg. Pastries €16-22 per kg. ☒ Open M-F 8am-2:10pm and 4:30-8:30pm, Sa 5-9pm.

LA MAISON DE L'ENTRECÔTE

RISTORANTE, ENOTECA $$$

P. Gazometro 1 ☎06 57 43 091; www.lamaisondelentrecote.it

You don't need a plane ride or a time machine if you want to return to bohemian Paris—just retreat to Le Maison's dim downstairs dining room, where stained-glass lamps and slow music put you at ease. Pair classic French dishes like cheesy onion soup (€7) with Italian staples, and finish it off with a transnational dessert like the *crema* gelato topped with Grand Marnier. Check out the antique mirror with the 10% discounted menu scribbled atop it, then check yourself out to see if your cheeks are *rouge* from the wine you've been sipping.

✦ ⓂB: Ostiense. Walk down V. Marmorata away from Piramide for 5min. and turn right onto P. Gazometro. Ⓢ Salads €5-7. Primi €8-10. Meats €7-15. Beer €4. Cocktails €6. Wine by the bottle €12-16. Cash only. ☒ Open Tu-Th 1-3pm and 8pm-midnight, F-Sa 8pm-midnight.

OSTERIA DEGLI AMICI

RISTORANTE $$$

V. Nicola Zabaglia 25 ☎06 57 81 466; www.osteriadegliamici.info

Aside from the excellent cheese-topped pasta dishes, there's nothing cheesy about Osteria degli Amici. Enjoy hot saffron risotto sprinkled with smoked Scamorza cheese and drizzled in balsamic vinegar while downing a glass of their stellar wine (whose cork might get added to the gigantic collection up front). If the relaxed setting makes you want to linger, split a spicy chocolate souffle—almost as hot as the entrees—with your *amico*, who's hopefully bringing the heat as well.

✦ ⓂB: Piramide. Walk up V. Marmorata, turn right onto V. Luigi Vanvitelli, and turn left onto V. Nicola Zabaglia. Ⓢ Primi €7-9; secondi €12-18. ☒ Open W-Su 12:30-3pm and 7:30pm-midnight.

L'OASI DELLA BIRRA

RISTORANTE $$

P. Testaccio 40 ☎06 57 46 122

Most drink menus round off their selection at a few pages, but this two-floor mecca of food and liquor has six pages devoted to Belgian beer alone. It requires an entire book to list the rest of their international collection, which also includes wine, *grappa*, rum, and whiskey. The best way to tackle the menu is to order a bottle of wine for the table (probably not one that costs €200) and pair it with a few six- or eight-variety plates of *salumi*, cheese, or bruschetta, which come in nearly as many varieties as the alcohol. If you're bad at making decisions, drop in during happy hour when you can sample the goods to your heart's content for just €10 at the *aperitivo* buffet.

✦ ⓂB: Piramide. Walk up V. Marmorata and turn left onto P. Testaccio. Ⓢ Bruschetta €8. Salumi and formaggi plates of 6-8 types €16-19. Draft beer €4-10. Wine starting at €12 per bottle. ☒ Open M-Sa 4:30pm-12:30am, Su 7:30pm-12:30am. Happy hour daily 5-8:30pm.

food

not your average lasagna

The Romans weren't always known for delectable pasta and pastries. In fact, the diet of ancient Romans was quite different and included delicacies like stuffed dormouse, stewed snails, sow's uterus, newborn rabbit, and roasted peacock. We doubt the Ancient Romans would fare well with PETA.

SOUTHERN ROME

👍 LI RIONI — PIZZERIA $$

V. dei Santi Quattro 24 ☎06 70 45 06 05

A *rione* is an old word for a Roman neighborhood, and here at Li Rioni they do the past justice. Open only for dinner, the pizzeria's wood-fired pizza and traditional *fritti* (fried dishes) will fill you up while photographs of 19th-century Rome transport you to a different era. Try the *prato fiorito* (flowery meadow) pizza, which (as its name suggests) is blooming with fresh mozzarella, mushrooms, peas, sausage, egg, and olives.

 # [M]B: Colosseo. Take V. Nicola Salvi to V. Labicana. Turn right at P. San Clemente and walk to V. dei Santi Quattro. $ Pizza €4.80-8. ⏰ Open M 7:30pm-midnight, W-Su 7:30pm-midnight.

OSTERIA IL BOCCONCINO — RISTORANTE $$$

V. Ostilia 23 ☎06 77 07 91 75; www.ilbocconcino.com

With an emphasis on seasonal ingredients and daily specials, Il Bocconcino attempts to bring back some of the more rustic elements of Roman cooking—which is a nice way of saying they would really like you to try the tripe. Even if you prefer your innards to stay inward, reasonably priced classics like *rigatoni alla carbonara* (€8.50) and *polpette con sedano e cannella* (meatballs with celeriac and cinnamon; €11) should fill up your own stomach just fine.

 # [M]B: Colosseo. Follow P. del Colosseo around to V. di San Giovanni in Laterano and turn right onto V. Ostilia. $ Primi €8-12; secondi €11-14. ⏰ Open M-Tu 12:30-3:30pm and 7:30-11:30pm, Th-Su 12:30-3:30pm and 7:30-11:30pm.

L'ARCHEOLOGIA — RISTORANTE $$$$

V. Appia Antica 139 ☎06 78 80 494; www.larcheologia.it

The Appian Way is not the place to look for budget eats, but L'Archeologia is a good choice if you feel like you've earned a nice meal after a long day of trekking. Housed in a former rest stop for travelers of the ancient road, it also sits beside the ruins of a mausoleum and on top of a hypogeum (ancient wine cellar). There's no need to stop sightseeing just because it's lunchtime.

 # Take bus #118 to the San Sebastiano stop. L'Archeologia is on the corner of V. Appia Antica and Vicolo della Basilica. $ Primi €13-16; secondi €15-28. ⏰ Open M 12:30-3pm and 8-11pm, W-Su 12:30-3pm and 8-11pm.

nightlife

Don't spend all your money and energy at the museums—Rome's nightlife is varied and vast, giving you a whole separate itinerary to attack after the guards go home and the cats come out to prowl the ruins. *Enoteche* (wine bars, often with *aperitivi*), which cater to those seeking high-quality drinks and low-key conversation, are especially prevalent in the Ancient City and Centro Storico. Irish pubs and American-style bars populate Trastevere, busy *corsi*, and the areas surrounding Termini. Upscale lounges are common around Piazza di Spagna, while anyone looking to rage should head to the discos in Testaccio. If the weather is warm, it's easy to avoid cover fees and pricey cocktails by simply heading to the many busy *piazze*. In fact, since alcohol by the bottle is surprisingly cheap at the supermarket and drinking outside is as common as smoking, most indoor spots are pretty empty in the spring and summer. Head to Campo dei Fiori, P. Trilussa in Trastevere, P. Colonna (outside the Pantheon), or the Spanish Steps for a large crowd making their own nightlife. But note that drinking outside after 11pm has recently been made illegal, although many Italians seem to ignore this new rule.

ANCIENT CITY

The Ancient Romans might have been known for bacchanalian orgies, but these days the wine bars that crowd the streets of Ancient City are Bacchus's only heirs. These upscale places rarely reach orgiastic levels, but Irish pubs provide rowdier options. Small cafes stay open late as well, so the area is a good choice on a night when dinner turns into a few late-night bottles of wine. If you're looking for young, pumping clubs, though, head south to Testaccio.

⬛ LIBRERIA CAFFÈ BOHEMIEN   CAFE

V. degli Zingari 36   ☎33 97 22 46 22

The name says it all: here you'll find books, wine, and a bohemian feel. Check out the coffered ceiling of the stone "den" downstairs if you want to get cozy on couches. The smooth tunes in the background will feel even smoother after a glass of one of the 47 varieties of wine (€5). This is a place for trading opinions on Karl Marx and Victor Hugo rather than phone numbers with Italian club-goers, so sit back, relax, and let your inner starving artist take over for the night.

⚑ ⓜB: Cavour. From V. Cavour, turn right onto P. degli Zingari and left onto V. degli Zingari. ⓢ Beer €3-5. Cocktails €5-6. Appetizers €6-10. Aperitivo buffet €8; with drink purchase €3. ⌚ Open M 6pm-2am, W-Su 6pm-2am. Aperitivo buffet 7-9pm.

SCHOLAR'S LOUNGE   IRISH PUB

V. del Plebiscito 101B   ☎06 69 20 22 08; www.scholarsloungerome.com

You won't find any scholars reading here—with nine TVs (including two that are over 5 ft. wide) and over 250 kinds of whiskey (the biggest collection in Italy, they say), they'll probably be dancing on the table. Don't bother bringing your Italian phrasebook, either—with a huge Irish flag hanging over the bar, and a steady stream of Irish dishes, Scholar's Lounge is a bit of Dublin on the Tiber. Although you can keep it cheap at only €4 for a pint, those looking for a splurge should check out the whiskey list: a shot of Jameson Rarest Vintage Reserve goes for a whopping €134. Ask to see the private collection, which might as well be a museum.

⚑ From P. Venezia, follow V. del Plebiscito to the intersection with V. del Corso. **i** Karaoke on Tu and Su. Live music on Th-F. ⓢ Pints €4-6. Cocktails €8-10; during the day €5; student cocktails €5. Student shots €1. ⌚ Open daily 11am-3:30am. Happy hour until 8pm.

CAVOUR 313   ENOTECA

V. Cavour 313   ☎06 67 54 96; www.cavour313.it

The savory plates, over 100 varieties of wine, and numerous awards make Cavour 313 a great spot for those looking for an evening of fine food and even finer wine. These wines hail from all over Italy, as do dishes like the Calabrian—a mix of hot salami, sun-dried tomatoes with herbs, and olives. To offset the salty offerings, try a bit of gorgonzola cheese with honey and sweet Marsala wine (€8). Cozy wooden booths make your dining experience private and less noisy.

⚑ Halfway up V. Cavour coming from V. dei Fori Imperiali. ⓢ Wine €3.50-8. Mixed cheese plates €8-12, meat plates €8-10. ⌚ Open M-Sa 12:30-3:30pm and 7pm-midnight.

competition outside the colosseum

Valeria Messalina was Emperor Claudius's third wife, but she was far from a proper Roman empress. You may have thought only gladiators duked it out for fame, but Messalina challenged a prostitute to an all-night sex competition, with an impressive 25 partners—the empress won.

But her sexcapades didn't stop there. Messalina had an affair with Senator Gaius Silius and convinced him to divorce his wife. Together they plotted to kill (gasp!) her very own husband, Claudius. As you can see, even ancient civilization appreciated a good soap opera. Unlucky for the murderous duo, their plans were foiled and they were both summarily executed.

CENTRO STORICO

The Centro Storico might be old, but it packs in a young crowd at night. One of the best places to find bars and clubs, this area remains busy into the early hours of the morning. If you don't feel like heading inside, spend the evening in the **Campo dei Fiori.**

MOOD
CLUB

Corso Vittorio Emanuele II 205 ☎06 68 80 86 19

If you're in the mood to drink and dance, this place is right for you. Most clubs in Rome seem to assume that once you start dancing, you'll be so thirsty you'll pay anything for a drink, which is not exactly cost-effective. Before 1am at Mood, though, drink specials—especially for students—abound, so by the time people start moving to Top 40 and hip hop you'll be good to go until morning.

*# From Campo dei Fiori, take the P. della Cancelleria to the Corso Vittorio Emanuele II and turn left; Mood is on the right. **i** Americans get in free. For student specials, show ID. $ Beer €5. Cocktails €10. 2 drinks for €10 or open bar €15 until 1am. Shots for women €2. ⏰ Open Tu-Su 11pm-4am.*

SALOTTO 42
BAR

P. di Pietra 42 ☎06 67 85 804; www.salotto42.it

The folks at the swanky Salotto 42 have it right: combine ancient pillars with refined, modern decor and a splash of wine, and you can't go wrong. The classy late 20s crowd that convenes here may bump shoulders inside, but the real place to see—and be seen—is the *piazza*. There you can sip drinks alfresco under the ancient facade of Hadrian's Temple.

 # From the Pantheon, turn right onto V. di Pastini and veer left towards the Tempio Adriano. $ Beer €6. Cocktails €10. Free buffet with drink purchase during aperitivo. ⏰ Open M-Sa 10am-2am, Su 10am-midnight. Aperitivo daily 7:30-9pm.

DRUNKEN SHIP
BAR, CLUB

Campo dei Fiori 20/21 ☎06 68 30 05 35; www.drunkenship.com

Wait, is this the Campo or the campus? Walking into Drunken Ship, you might think you're back in college, as it comes complete with nightly beer pong, TVs airing sports games, a DJ spinning Top 40, and a raucous crowd of students ready to enjoy it all. Great weekly specials, including Wednesday night power hours and Pitcher Night Thursdays (€10), make this one of the most popular spots for young internationals aching for some university-style fun.

***i** Student discounts nightly. ½-price drinks for women M-Th until 11pm. Buy 1 drink get 1 free Tu until 11pm. $ Shots €3-6. Long drinks €6. Cocktails €7. Happy hour pint of wine with free buffet €4. ⏰ Open M-Th 3pm-2am, F-Sa 10am-2am, Su 3pm-2am. Happy hour M-F 4-8pm.*

ABBEY THEATRE

IRISH PUB

V. del Governo Vecchio 51/53 ☎06 68 61 341; www.abbey-rome.com

If the kind of homesickness you're feeling is for a pub rather than a frat party, the Abbey Theatre offers bar food, sports from around the world, and great drinks—try a "mixed beer" special like the hard cider and grenadine (€5.50). The wooden interior is huge but fills up quickly during big games and on weekends. People shout at the bar in one room, listen to live music in another, and chat in the (somewhat) quieter rooms upstairs. Drink specials are offered almost every night of the week for students, from half-price cocktails on Wednesdays after 8pm, to free shots for women on Thursday nights.

➡ From P. Navona, exit onto P. Pasquino and continue as it becomes V. del Governo Vecchio. ℹ Check the website for weekly specials. $ Shots €4-5. Beer €4-6.50. Cocktails €7-8. ⏰ Open daily noon-2am. Happy hour daily 3-8pm.

ARISTOCAMPO

BAR

Campo dei Fiori

On the doorstep of Campo dei Fiori, Aristocampo gets crowded early thanks to the large *aperitivo* buffet. Music pulses from the small bar inside, but most of the action is on the patio, where nearly every stool is occupied by laughing Italian and international students. Great panini—good for carni-, herbi-, and omnivores—satisfy the late night cravings wrought by yet another cocktail.

$ Beer €5-6. Cocktails €7. Panini €5. Salads €8. Aperitivo drink and buffet €7. ⏰ Open daily noon-2am. Aperitivo daily 6-8:30pm.

ANIMA

BAR, CLUB

V. di Santa Maria dell'Anima 57 ☎06 68 64 021

To get into Anima, you'll have to pass through a red velvet rope, but don't worry, the inside is (slightly) less cheesy—or at least it seems that way in the low lighting. Lounge music plays in the early evening as a mixed crowd of students and 20-somethings wander in, but things don't pick up until midnight when dance music starts. The club gets really packed after that, so head up the tiny spiral staircase if you want to take a breather, or to seek out the most attractive Italian dance partner from above.

➡ From P. Navona, turn left onto V. di Santa Maria dell'Anima. ℹ Ladies' night 2-for-1 drinks on M. Open bar on Th and Su. $ Beer €4-5. Cocktails €6, after midnight €10. Happy hour beer €2.50; cocktails €4.50. ⏰ Open daily 7pm-4am. Happy hour daily 6-10pm.

FLUID

BAR, CLUB

V. del Governo Vecchio 46 ☎06 68 32 361; www.fluideventi.com

Fluid seems to be working a natural theme—though the fake tree branches, caged rocks, and faux ice cube stools suggest "sale at the craft store" rather than "crunchy granola." With a lounge early in the evening and an upbeat DJ later in the night, this is the place to come for post-dinner drinks and good company. The drink menu, which is essentially a book of cocktails, features unorthodox mixes like the cinnamon red: a smoothie of *cannella rossa* liqueur, yogurt, *crema di limone*, and whipped cream (€7.50).

➡ From P. Navona, exit onto P. Pasquino and continue as it becomes V. del Governo Vecchio. $ Beer €5-6. Cocktails €7.50. Aperitivo drink and buffet €7.50. ⏰ Open daily 6pm-2am. Aperitivo daily 6-10pm.

PIAZZA DI SPAGNA

There's a reason the Spanish Steps are so popular at night, and it's not their beauty. Young travelers seeking nightlife in this neighborhood are wise to lounge on the steps rather than pay €15 for drinks and music at the nearby lounges. The few options here will all do damage to your bank account, so unless you've just hit it big in Monaco, try another neighborhood for nighttime entertainment.

ANTICA ENOTECA DI VIA DELLA CROCE

ENOTECA

V. della Croce 76B ☎06 67 90 896

Escape the pretension of the surrounding bars and head to this old-fashioned *enoteca* for a glass of wine and some cheese or *salumi*. Tall ceilings, rustic arches, and background jazz create a refreshingly airy feel compared to that of nearby places. Most patrons pass the evening with a bottle of wine and some quiet conversation.

🚶 Ⓜ*A: Spagna. From the Spanish Steps, walk down V. della Croce.* Ⓢ *Wine €4-10 per glass. Beer €5. Cocktails €8. Antipasti platters €14-16. Primi €9-10; secondi €12-24. Pizza €9-12.* ⏰ *Open daily 11am-1am.*

HIGHLANDER PUB

IRISH PUB

Vicolo di San Biagio 9 ☎06 68 80 53 68; www.highlanderome.com

Romans seem to love Irish pubs, and even the city's poshest neighborhood has an Emerald Isle representative. As you'd expect, there are dozens of beers on tap: ciders like Magners or Strongbow, the requisite Guinness, and even the Italian beer Poretti. International students nibble traditional Irish grub, while nightly specials make it a rowdy place to get a little (or a lot) drunk.

🚶 Ⓜ*A: Spagna. From the Spanish Steps, walk down V. dei Condotti, which becomes V. Fontanella di Borghese. When it becomes Largo Fontanella di Borghese, turn left onto V. della Lupa. Highlander is on the corner with Vicolo di San Biagio.* *i* *Offers free tours of Rome daily at 5pm. Ladies' Night on Tu. College Night on Th.* Ⓢ *Draft beer €4-6. Wine €5-8. Cocktails €6-7. Cash only.* ⏰ *Open M-Th 5pm-2am, F-Sa 12:30pm-2am, Su 5pm-2am.*

TRASTEVERE

Trastevere is home to some of the best nightlife in the city. American college kids, people inexplicably walking dogs at midnight, Italian teens, and connected-at-the-mouth couples intermingle in the streets in warmer weather, with no apparent destinations. With so many great places to choose from, why make a plan? The **Piazza Trilussa,** right over the Ponte Sisto, is a great starting point, and many of the listings below are only steps away. Whether you want bar-hopping, dancing, chatting, or shouting, make the trek over the river and get ready for a late night.

🏛 FRENI E FRIZIONI

BAR

V. del Politeama 4/6 ☎06 45 49 74 99; www.frenifrizioni.com

To find this place, don't look for a street number: turn your head skyward until you spy people lining railings and a jam-packed bar. Located just up the stairs on V. del Politeama, Freni e Frizioni has essentially created its own *piazza*. The white interior, decorated with artwork and bookshelves, feels like the living room of your mechanic-turned-graphic-designer friend from college. (Thus the name: brakes and shocks.) The extensive bar is only a precursor to the *aperitivo* room, where fresh entrees are served directly from the pot. Check out the "shelf" of wooden drawers filled with international dips like tzatziki and *salsa tonnata*. In the summer, the *piazza* acts as your mechanic-artist friend's impossibly large balcony, perfect for literally looking down on the world.

🚶 *From P. Trilussa, head down the tiny V. del Politeama and look for the steps (and the crowd) on the left.* Ⓢ *Wine €6. Cocktails €7-8. Aperitivo drinks €6-10.* ⏰ *Open daily 6:30pm-2am. Aperitivo daily 6:30-10:30pm.*

CAFE FRIENDS

BAR, CLUB

P. Trilussa 34 ☎06 58 16 111; www.cafefriends.it

Locals and international students crowd this hip cafe-lounge at all hours of the night. Fully decked out with a swanky silver bar, stylish cartooned walls, and spacious indoor and patio seating, Cafe Friends caters to more American tastes: a full breakfast is served daily from 8:30am-12:30pm. But abandon those early-morning ways for the more typically Italian *aperitivo* cocktail buffet, which draws the biggest crowd. The special Friends drinks, like the "Zombie" (rum, Jamaicano, cherry brandy, orange juice, and lime; €8) will keep you going to music that blasts all the way into the early morning.

⚐ From Ponte Sisto, head into P. Trilussa. *i* Free Wi-Fi. Ⓢ Beer €4-5.50. Cocktails €8. Aperitivo drinks €6-8. 15% discount for international students with ID. Ⓣ Open M-Sa 7am-2am, Su 6pm-2am. Aperitivo daily 7-9pm.

BACCANALE
BAR

V. della Lungaretta 81 ☎06 45 44 82 68

While many places may be classier none can approach Baccanale's prices or spirit. Bacchus would be proud. The promotional alcohol paraphernalia and international currency donated by students who have visited are testimony to the undeniable appeal of a well-priced pitcher of mojitos (€15) or Peroni (€18). Pop and R and B during the evening bring in young crowds, and the prices keep them coming back.

⚐ From Vle. Trastevere, turn right onto V. della Lungaretta. Ⓢ Beer €3-5. Cocktails €5-7. Ⓣ Open Tu-Su 11am-2am.

bad romans

Chances are you've seen plenty of cheesy romance movies where the man carries the woman over the threshold. Perhaps you've even wondered where that practice originated. Well, it comes from the Ancient Romans. Back in the day, it was customary for a Roman bride to be carried over the threshold saying the words "Ubi tu Gaius, ego Gaia," meaning something like "Where you are John, I am Jane." Romantic, isn't it? Unless your gladiator was more scrawny than brawny and tripped over—then your marriage was doomed. But hey, divorce in Rome was easy—all you had to do was say, "Tuas res tibi habeto," or "Keep what's yours for yourself." No need for pre-nups, court, or custody battles. The children stayed with the father, and the dowry was returned to the woman. There'd be a lot fewer gold diggers if we did romance like the Romans.

nightlife

DJ BAR
BAR, CLUB

Vicolo del Cinque 60 ☎338 85 98 578

Who ever said size matters? Although the upstairs barely occupies a street corner, DJ Bar pulls a big punch with its loud music, colored lights, and over 100 types of mixed drink. The close quarters mean even the rhythmically challenged will move (or be moved) to the beat. Cool black-and-white wallpaper provides a blacklit backdrop as the DJ blares hip hop and R and B to pump up the crowd. The swanky green bar with lit-up Red Bulls gets busy around 10pm, while the bigger arena downstairs gets crowded with dancers around midnight.

⚐ From P. Santa Maria in Trastevere, veer into P. San Egidio and turn right onto Vicolo del Cinque. Ⓢ Shots €3. Beer €5. Cocktails €7-8. Cash only. Ⓣ Open daily 5pm-2am. Happy hour F-Sa 7-10pm.

GOOD
CAFE, BAR

V. di Santa Dorotea 8/9 ☎06 97 27 79 79

Bookshelves of wine and liquor, quirkily elaborate light fixtures, dark wood banquettes, and comfortable chairs and stools make this place relaxing. At night, a definitely post-grad crowd shows up to chat over drinks, listen to live jazz and blues on Monday and Thursday, and dance to DJ sets on weekends.

⚐ From P. San Giovanni de Matha, take V. di Santa Dorotea as it veers left. *i* Free Wi-Fi. Ⓢ Beer €5-8. Cocktails €9; happy hour €8. Happy hour wine €5. Ⓣ Open M-Sa 8am-2am, Su 8:30am-2-am. Happy hour daily 6:30-9:30pm.

MA CHE SIETE VENUTI A FÀ
BAR

V. Benedetta 25

Cocktails? Wine? Forget it. Ma Che Siete Venuti A Fà's 16 taps and keg-lined interior will make you fall in love with beer—and only beer—all over again. Even the lamps are made from recycled beer bottles. Customers can either retreat to what is essentially a wooden box in the back or spill out onto the street as crowds accumulate in the early evening. Quiet music and tight quarters make casual conversation with *amici* about the only thing possible.

‡ From P. Trilussa, turn right onto V. Benedetta. $ Bottled beer €3.50-5; draft €4-6. Cash only. ⏰ Open daily 3pm-2am.

BEIGE
BAR

V. del Politeama 13/14 ☎06 58 33 06 86; www.beigeroma.com

Somehow swanky black and white decor equals... Beige? Distinguishing itself from some of the more low-key establishments nearby with its plush stools, modern black arches, and dark green lounge, Beige caters to an older, dressed-up crowd. Its 12-page menu, organized solely into pre- and post-dinner beverages, gives a drink to match nearly every hour until 2am. Mellow music and plenty of seating mean you can rest your feet as you sip cocktails with friends.

‡ From Ponte Sisto, turn left onto Lungotevere Raffaello Sanzio, head down the stairs into the piazza on the right, and turn left. $ Cocktails €8. Cash only. ⏰ Open M 7pm-2am, W-Su 7pm-2am.

M8 BAR
BAR

V. Benedetta 17 ☎06 58 33 16 45; www.m8bar.com

A human-sized beer bottle towers over the entrance of M8, a brick-lined bar and lounge that feels a little bit like a cave. Upstairs, DJs spin house and commercial tunes while local and international students sip sweet and reasonably priced specials like the "Mate" (vodka, sambuca, aperol, grenadine, and an orange). For a quieter and more intimate setting, descend the steep staircase to two curtain-enclosed lounges.

‡ From P. San Malva, turn left onto V. Benedetta. i Free Wi-Fi. $ Shots €3. Draft beer €3.50-5. Cocktails €7. Buffet €5; with 1 drink €7. ⏰ Open daily 5:30pm-2am. Buffet daily 6:30-9:30pm.

still kicking?

If you're looking to party, make sure you're in town on April 21st, when the entire city comes together to celebrate the birth of Rome in 753 BCE. The absurd amount of history (2700 years and counting) gives the city the ultimate excuse to party hard. Think of a birthday party that gets more extravagant the older you get. The city holds festivals, shows, and even special gladiator performances near the Roman Forum. At night, fireworks explode over the Tiber River, perhaps the only part of Rome that has remained truly unchanged over the years.

TERMINI AND SAN LORENZO

Termini and San Lorenzo have two very different nightlife scenes. Dozens of bars near Termini's hostels cater primarily to international travelers with drink specials and loud dance music. There are also quite a few Irish pubs for those who'd rather spend the night watching sports over a pint. San Lorenzo, on the other hand, is near the university and thus popular with artsy 20-something Italians. Late-night bookstores, laid-back bars, and pulsing clubs litter the otherwise quiet neighborhood, so the best tactic is to follow the people until you find a place that looks interesting. Stick with a group if you're out late in either neighborhood, as areas near a big train station can be somewhat unsafe.

👍 AI TRE SCALINI

CAFE, ENOTECA

V. Panisperna 251 ☎06 48 90 74 95; www.aitrescalini.org

Look down V. Panisperna and you'll see two things: a hanging curtain of vines and a crowd of people. The smiling, primarily local customers at this socially conscious *enoteca* spill out onto the street, wine glasses in hand. Inside, the giant blackboard menu features only locally grown and seasonally harvested products as post-wine snacks. The beverage selection is just as sustainable and includes organic wines. Blues in the background, frescoed walls, tiny tables, and dim lights make this the perfect spot for the kind of intimate conversations copious amounts of wine seem to induce. Before leaving, check out the *piscina* (male toilet), where vintage photos of nude women tastefully decorate the wall. (Don't ask how *Let's Go*'s female researcher learned about these.)

➡ From the intersection of V. XXIV Maggio and V. Nazionale (near Trajan's column), walk up V. Panisperna. ℹ Free Wi-Fi. 10% discount at lunch. $ Beer €3-5. Wine €4.50-6 per glass; €12-70 per bottle. Sfizi (bite-sized appetizers) €2.50-3. Primi €6-13. ⏰ Open M-F noon-1am, Sa-Su 6pm-1am. Aperitivo 6-9pm.

👍 SOLEA CLUB

BAR

V. dei Latini 51 ☎328 92 52 925

Filled with mismatched couches, stools, and wingback chairs, Solea Club feels like a run-down but still chic living room. The clientele, mostly from the nearby university, adds to the artistic feel. Enjoy some awesome music—everything from Bowie to Cat Power—while sipping a delicious cocktail. The Hemingway Special (€5.50), a combination of rum, lime, and grapefruit, will really get you in the Lost Generation mood.

➡ Tram #3 or 19. Or ⓂTermini. Follow traffic down V. Marsala and turn left onto V. dei Ramni. Turn right onto V. dei Luceri and then right onto V. dei Sabelli; Solea Club is on the corner of V. dei Sabelli and V. dei Latini. $ Beer €3-5. Wine €4.50. Cocktails and shots €5.50. Cash only. ⏰ Open daily 9pm-3am.

7SETTE CL.

BAR, CLUB

V. degli Aurunci 35 ☎06 97 61 24 28; www.7cl.it

In the evening, this place is filled with people taking advantage of the extra long *aperitivo* (6-10pm; buffet free with drink purchase), but as the night gets going it morphs into a crowded dance spot with DJs and live music. The university crowd seeks respite from moving bodies in the first room, where low couches and lights that aren't flashing provide space for drinking and (shouted) conversation.

➡ Tram #3 or 19, or ⓂTermini. Follow traffic down V. Marsala and turn left onto V. dei Ramni. Turn right onto V. dei Luceri and then left onto V. dei Sabelli. Continue into the piazza and, with the church behind you, turn right onto V. degli Aurunci. ℹ Art and cinema night on M. Theme night on Tu. Live music on W and Th. DJ on F and Sa. Salsa and swing on Su. $ Beer €3-5. Wine €4-5. Cocktails and shots €5-7. Cash only. ⏰ Open M-Th 3pm-2am, F-Sa 3pm-4am, Su 3pm-2am.

YELLOW BAR

V. Palestro 40

CAFE, BAR

☎06 49 38 26 82; www.the-yellow.com

Feeling a bit homesick for college, or perhaps just your home country? Whatever locale you have a hankering for, the international folks at Yellow Bar are sure to cure your case of the blues. Next door to its hopping hostel, this bar caters to a crowd of travelers and students who come for cheap drinks, relaxed music, and good company. Order one of their special cocktails like the ⚑**Chuck Norris Roundhouse Kick to the Face Crazy Shot** (don't ask what's in it... just drink up) before heading downstairs to the beer pong room, fully equipped with two regulation-size tables and an official list of house rules. After the long night (or, shall we say, early morning), their full American breakfast will get your day going, or perhaps prepare you for a nap.

✈ ⓂTermini. From V. Marsala, near track 1, walk down V. Marghera and turn left onto V. Palestro. *i* Pub quiz on W €5. Open bar on F €15. Ⓢ Cocktails €8. Pitchers €15. Happy hour spirits €2.50; wine €1.50. ☒ Open daily 7:30am-2am. Kitchen open 7:30am-noon. Happy hour 3-9pm.

THE FIDDLER'S ELBOW

V. dell'Olmata 43

IRISH PUB

☎06 48 72 110; www.thefiddlerselbow.com

So, what exactly is a "fiddler's elbow"? A musician would claim it's a sore elbow caused by fiddle playing, but a good Irishman will tell you it's from raising a beer flask so often that the elbow stiffens. They're more prone to the latter injury here at the oldest Irish pub in Rome, which has been liquoring up The Eternal City since 1976. Renowned in the neighborhood for its family history, congenial company, and great drinks, this pub brings in everyone from the backpacker to the neighborhood expat to the sophisticated businessman stopping in after a day's work. The wooden interior is speckled with objects from the Emerald Isle and full of loud conversation.

✈ ⓂTermini. Walk down V. Cavour, and after V. di Santa Maria Maggiore turn left onto V. dei Quattro Cantoni, then left onto V. dell'Olmata. *i* Open mic Th 10pm. Pool and dart room in back. Ⓢ Beer €5-5.50. Cocktails €6. Happy hour beer €4-4.50 ☒ Open M-F 5pm-2am, Sa-Su 3pm-2am. Happy hour 5-8:30pm.

CHARITY CAFE JAZZ CLUB

V. Panisperna 68

BAR, JAZZ CLUB

☎06 47 82 58 81; www.charitycafe.it

Though the long black benches are lined up like pews, you won't hear any classical choir here—only exceptional live jazz, all night, every night. The terracotta walls are covered with pictures of famed musicians as well as scribbles from past customers singing their praise. Well-priced drinks during happy hour make the jazz sound even smoother.

✈ From the intersection of V. XXIV Maggio and V. Nazionale (near Trajan's column), walk up V. Panisperna. Ⓢ Beer €6-7. Cocktails €8. Happy hour beer €3.50-4.50; cocktails €4.50. ☒ Open in summer M-Sa 6pm-2am; in winter daily 6pm-2am. Happy hour 6-9pm.

TRIMANI WINE BAR

V. Cernaia 37B

ENOTECA

☎06 44 69 661; www.trimani.com

In the nest of mediocre trattorias and pubs that crowd Termini, this slightly upscale wine bar comes as a welcome surprise—especially considering the not-so-upscale prices. The list (or rather book) of wine consists primarily of bottles to be split among the table, though the first page features 20 varieties sold by the glass and organized according to the "four Cs": cult, chic, classic, and casual (one to match every mood?). Delicious platters of cheese, *salumi*, and meats are great for satisfying a post-drink appetite. The two-for-one happy hour special is a great chance to get your drink on and feel classy before a long night of sloppy fun at nearby bars.

✈ From P. Indipendenza, walk up V. Goito and turn right onto V. Cernaia. *i* Buy 1 glass get 1 free during happy hour. Ⓢ Wine €3.50-23 per glass; also sold by the bottle. Cocktails €9. Primi, secondi, and appetizers €7-14. ☒ Open M-Sa 11:30am-3pm and 5pm-12:30am. Happy hour 11:30am-12:30pm and 5-7pm.

rome

NORTHERN ROME

Near the cluster of hostels around Termini, **Via Nomentana** is a great option for those who want to venture a bit farther from their hostel. Good bars and *discoteche* are always popping up. Bars are the best year-round option.

NEW AGE CAFE — CAFE, BAR

V. Nizza 23

In an area without many bars, the New Age Cafe is a great spot to drink or grab breakfast, lunch, or *aperitivi*. Lounge on the outdoor patio, climb the spiral staircase to the mini balcony up top, or grab a stool at the bar while you sip your mixed drink or cappuccino. This little island in the middle of the city is made for chilling at midday or drinking at midnight. Even if the caffeine doesn't pick you up, the upbeat, commercial tunes and TVs showing music videos certainly will.

➔ From P. Fiume, walk down V. Nizza $ Shots €3. Draft beer €5-6. Cocktails €7. Lunch panini and primi €4-6. Cash only. ⏰ Open daily 7am-2am. Aperitivo 6:30-9:30pm.

BOEME — CLUB

V. Velletri 14 — ☎06 84 12 212; www.boeme.it

The black-and-white, barcode-like walls and floors of Boeme might make you dizzy, or maybe your head is spinning from the *Alice-in-Wonderland*-style chairs and bright pink and floral accents. But the high prices here mean any lightheadedness probably isn't due to alcohol consumption. Dancing to Top 40 hits at this club picks up after midnight, but the fact that this isn't a clubbing area means Boeme is less crowded than you'd be in club-heavy Testaccio—and that's a good thing.

➔ From P. Fiume, walk up V. Nizza and turn left onto V. Velletri. $ Cover €15-20; includes drink. Drinks €10. ⏰ Open F-Sa 11pm-5am.

TESTACCIO AND OSTIENSE

Locals who've sought out the best clubs (and savvy tourists who've sought out the best locals) head to Testaccio and Ostiense for big nights out. The strip of clubs, restaurants, and lounges surrounding **Via di Monte Testaccio** begs to be explored, though long lines make it harder to gain admission later in the evening. The streets closer to the train station tend to have smaller, low-key establishments that stay open late and are a good option if you don't feel like heavy-duty clubbing.

👍 AKAB — CLUB

V. di Monte Testaccio 69 — ☎06 57 25 05 85; www.akabcave.com

Dancing is the primary concern for most people at Akab, so make sure you haven't tired yourself out at V. di Monte Testaccio's other clubs before you arrive here. Live bands warm up the crowd, but when the DJ starts, the ramps and flashing lights galore will make you feel like you're in a psychedelic amusement park for adults. Though the cover and drinks cost a pretty penny, you'll be paying for one of Testaccio's hottest clubs.

➔ [M]B: Piramide. Walk up V. Marmorata toward the river, turn left onto V. Galvani, and veer left onto V. di Monte Testaccio. ℹ Electronic music on Tu. House on Th. Rock on F. Commercial and house on Sa. $ Cover F-Sa €10-20; includes 1 drink. Generally no cover Tu or Th. Cocktails and beer €10. ⏰ Open Tu 11:30pm-4:30am, Th-Sa 11:30pm-4:30am.

👍 COYOTE — BAR, CLUB

V. di Monte Testaccio 48B — ☎340 24 45 874; www.coyotebar.it

Cowboys might ride off into the sinking western sun, but visitors at Coyote will wander home as the sun rises in the east. Get here early to avoid lines as long as the Colosseum's and an entrance fee to match. Once the clock strikes midnight, what started out as a casual cocktail bar becomes a full-fledged disco that spins house, Latin, and Top 40. If you're sober enough before heading downstairs for a snack at Top Five, check out the trail of American license plates lining the wall—last time we checked, the Eastern Seaboard was heavily outweighed by the Wild West and the sultry south. New Yorkers, donate a plate?

✱ ⓂB: Piramide. Walk up V. Marmorata toward the river, turn left onto V. Galvani, and veer left onto V. di Monte Testaccio. ⓈCover F-Sa after midnight €10. Beer and wine €5. Cocktails €8. ⓉOpen daily 9pm-5am.

hun-ny i'm home!

Attila the Hun may have been good at war, but he was not smooth with the ladies. In 450 CE, Honoria, sister of Emperor Valentinian III, sent Attila her engagement ring in a desperate attempt to escape an arranged marriage to a Roman senator. She intended it as a plea for help, but he took it as a marriage proposal and demanded Rome as his dowry. When the emperor found out about the misunderstanding, he exiled Honoria and tried to explain the situation to Attila, who was hell bent on claiming what he thought was his. Denied his woman, Attila invaded Italy. After ravaging towns and cities, Attila eventually consented to a negotiated peace. But he never did get his bride.

TOP FIVE   RISTORANTE, BAR
V. di Monte Testaccio 48   ☎06 57 45 453; www.topfivebar.it

When your stomach starts to growl after a night of clubbing, Top Five will be your top priority. It's also a great place to get some cheap drinks and line your stomach before hitting Coyote upstairs. This bright American restaurant-bar satisfies late-night pizza cravings, very early morning breakfast calls, and happy hour drink specials. Kick back like a cowpoke beside an old American movie poster while enjoying pizza or panini (€2), and maybe another cocktail—at these prices, another stiff one is hard to turn down, even if your liver is begging you to stop.

✱ ⓂB: Piramide. Walk up V. Marmorata toward the river, turn left onto V. Galvani, and veer left onto V. di Monte Testaccio. ⓈBeer €4-6. Cocktails €8. Happy hour shots and beer pints €4; cocktails €6. Food €2-8. ⓉOpen Tu-Su 8pm-5am. Happy hour 8:30-11pm.

ON THE ROX   BAR
V. Galvani 54   ☎06 45 49 29 75

The lively crowd at this huge lounge still "rox" out big time, even if it isn't technically a club. The decor is Flintstones-meets-sweet-16-party, with a faux-cave ceiling, brightly colored plastic chandeliers, giant inflatable beer bottles, and neon lights. The bartenders toss glasses around as they make drinks, and great specials mean you can afford to see them do so.

✱ ⓂB: Piramide. Walk up V. Marmorata toward the river and turn left onto V. Galvani. ⓲ Pitchers €10 on M. Buy 1 get 1 free on W. Ladies' night 2-for-1 cocktails on Th. ⓈShots €2.50. Beer €4. Cocktails €6. Student special long drinks €5. Food €6-8. Happy hour buffet €7. ⓉOpen M-W 6pm-4am, Th-Su 6pm-5am. Happy hour daily 6-10pm.

LA CASA DELLA PACE

V. di Monte Testaccio 22

CULTURAL CENTER, CONCERT VENUE

☎329 54 66 296; www.casadellapace.com

More than just a nightlife haven for artsy and intellectual folk, the "House of Peace" holds art exhibits and musical performances throughout the year. In the evening, live music from reggae to electro-funk plays on the dance floor, bringing in a different crowd every night. Drop by Friday or Saturday for La Casa's "Big Bang" nights or check online for a schedule of upcoming events. Be sure to try out the ◼mosaic-tiled bathroom, which rivals some of Rome's greatest.

♿ ⓂB: Piramide. Walk up V. Marmorata toward the river, turn left onto V. Galvani, and veer left onto V. di Monte Testaccio. *i* Membership card required to enter; buy at the desk and reuse it for all events. Ⓢ Membership card €7. Shots €3. Beer €3.50-5. Cocktails €7. Cash only. ⌚ Open M-Th 3-10pm, F-Sa 10pm-5am, Su 3-10pm.

CONTE STACCIO

V. di Monte Testaccio 65B

BAR, CONCERT VENUE

☎06 57 28 97 12

If bumping and grinding to the DJ isn't your thing, you'll probably love Conte Staccio. Indie rock, electro-funk, and everything in between draws a mixed crowd of internationals and not-so-mainstream students and locals. Two rooms—one with a stage, the other with tables for late-night nibbles—give you the option to enjoy the music from afar or rock out up close. Powerful stereos might blow your ears out no matter which room you're in, though, so head to the outdoor steps if you need a break.

♿ ⓂB: Piramide. Walk up V. Marmorata toward the river, turn left onto V. Galvani, and veer left onto V. di Monte Testaccio. Ⓢ Beer €2.50-5. Wine €3-5. Cocktails €6-7. ⌚ Open daily 8am-5pm. Music 11pm-5am.

eternal graffiti

Given the amount of art in Rome, it's no surprise the city's residents have been inspired to add their own, even those whose only tool is a spray can. Graffiti, after all, is an Italian word, deriving from *graffiare*, which means to scratch or scribble. Whether it's vandalism or creative release, Romans have been keeping this Italian tradition alive and well. Here are some examples of the city's best graffiti, in roughly chronological order:

- **SET IN STONE.** In contrast to its modern form, ancient graffiti often displayed phrases of love declarations, political rhetoric, and simple words of thought. There are examples of this throughout Rome, but some of the most well-kept scribbles can be found in the ruins of Pompeii, where some rumored examples include a prostitute's street address and a phallus accompanied by the text *"mansueta tene"* ("handle with care").

- **CARVE A NICHE.** The Mausoleum of Santa Costanza, a fourth-century church in Northern Rome, has outstanding mosaics and equally outstanding graffiti carved into its walls, which date back to 1667.

- **SACRED VANDALISM.** As if there weren't enough art referencing the Virgin Mary all around Rome, you'll occasionally run into wheatpaste versions of the Madonna around town.

- **UFOS.** Even the internationally recognized French urban artist Invader has made his mark planting his "Space Invaders" throughout Trastevere.

nightlife

arts and culture

"Arts and culture," you ask, "isn't that Rome *itself*?" Well, yes—Renaissance paintings, archaeological ruins, and Catholic churches do count. But aside from these antiquated lures, Rome offers entertainment that makes it much more than a city of yore. Soccer games might not quite compare to man-fights-lion spectacles, but with hundreds of screaming Italians around, it comes close. If you need more ideas, check Rome's city website (www.060608.it) for a schedule of upcoming events ranging from live music to festivals. *Roma C'è* (www.romace.it) and www.aguestinrome. com are also good resources. Or just wander the streets scouting out advertisements and flyers, which are nearly as common as ruins. In Rome, it's definitely possible to experience culture in places where an alarm won't go off when you get too close.

JAZZ

Unfortunately, most jazz places close during the summer months, either heading outdoors or waiting to reopen in September. **Alexanderplatz Jazz Club** was, for a time, the only place to hear jazz in the city; luckily, times have changed. Some places, like Termini's **Charity Cafe Jazz Club** (see **Nightlife**), offer indoor jazz even in the summer months. For a schedule of jazz events at various venues check out www.romace.it, www.romajazz.com, or www.casajazz.it.

ALEXANDERPLATZ JAZZ CLUB   VATICAN CITY, ANCIENT CITY
V. Ostia 9 and Villa Celimontana   ☎06 39 74 21 71; www.alexanderplatz.it
One of Rome's most popular jazz clubs and Italy's oldest, the Alexanderplatz Jazz Club operates in a hideout-like basement in the winter. Host to many famous musicians, enjoy the jazz as you decipher the scrawled notes (of the textual kind) they've left behind on the walls. In June the music moves outside to the beautiful Villa Celimontana in the Ancient City.
≇ Ⓜ️A: Ottaviano. Exit on V. Barletta and turn right onto Vle. delle Milizie, then turn left onto V. Tolemaide. Turn right onto V. Ostia. For summer concerts at Villa Celi, Ⓜ️B: Colosseo. Follow V. Nicola Salvi and veer right onto Vle. del Parco del Celio. Then veer left onto V. Claudia, which becomes V. Navicella. Ⓢ Membership €15 per month, €45 per year. ☒ Open daily 8pm-2am. Shows M-Th 9:45pm, F-Sa 10:30pm, Su 9:45pm. Happy hour 7-8:30pm.

FONCLEA   VATICAN CITY, TRASTEVERE
V. Crescenzio 82a and Lungotevere degli Anguillara   ☎06 68 96 302; www.fonclea.it
Crowds linger on the street and trickle down the steps into this den of live jazz and food. Amid hanging skis and teapots, nightly performers pay homage to anything from swing to The Beatles. Munch on chips and guacamole during the *aperitivo* while trumpeters and saxophonists warm up their lips. The drinks and food are a bit overpriced, but with music this good, who's thinking of eating?
≇ Ⓜ️A: Ottaviano. From P. Risorgimento, head away from the Vatican on V. Crescenzio. Ⓢ Cover F-Sa €6. Beer €7. Cocktails €10. ☒ Open from mid-Sept to mid-June M-Th 7pm-2am, F-Sa 7pm-3-am, Su 7pm-2am. Music at 9:30pm. Aperitivo buffet 7-8:30pm. Concerts in June at the Lungotevere degli Anguillara in Trastevere; see website for schedule.

BIG MAMA   TRASTEVERE
Vicolo San Francesco a Ripa 18   ☎06 58 12 551; www.bigmama.it
The titular mama may be big, but the venue isn't, so show up early to get a seat at this popular jazz and blues club. Nightly concerts by aspiring and well-known performers including guitarist Scott Henderson and rock singer-songwriter Elliott Murphy make this self-proclaimed "House of Blues" a place for all kinds of musical fare.
≇ Bus #75 or 170 or tram #8. From P. Garibaldi, walk down Vle. Trastevere, turn left onto V. San Francesco a Ripa, and veer right onto the tiny vicolo. Ⓢ Year-long membership card (€14) or monthly (€8) membership grants admission to most shows. A few big shows require an additional ticket fee. ☒ Open late Sept-late May daily 9pm-1:30am. Music daily 10:30pm.

CLASSICAL MUSIC AND OPERA

TEATRO NAZIONALE

TERMINI AND SAN LORENZO

V. del Viminale 51 ☎06 48 161 or 06 48 17 003; www.operaroma.it

With state-of-the-art acoustics but without old-school charm, the operas and ballets held at the Nazionale allow you to catch some culture for about the same price as a nice meal. If you're more interested in chandeliers, frescoes, and the glamour of the glory days of opera, you might want to consider shelling out the extra euro for **Teatro dell'Opera** (P. Beniamino Gigli 7) down the street. From June 30 to early fall, additional (and more expensive) performances are held outdoors at the **Baths of Caracalla** *(Terme di Caracalla)*.

⇟ [M]A: Repubblica. Walk down V. Nazionale, then turn left onto V. Firenze and left onto V. del Viminale. i Tickets can also be purchased online at www.amitsrl.it. $ Opera €33. Ballet €23. Outdoor performances at the Baths of Caracalla €25-135. Students and over 65 receive 25% discount; 10% discount for Baths of Caracalla shows. Check website for last-minute tickets with 25% discount. ⏰ Box office open Tu-Sa 9am-5pm, Su 9am-1:30pm, and from 1hr. before performance to 15min. after its start. Box office for Baths of Caracalla open Tu-Sa 10am-4pm, Su 9am-1:30pm.

ACCADEMIA NAZIONALE DI SANTA CECILIA

NORTHERN ROME

Vle. Pietro de Coubertin 30 ☎06 80 82 058, for tickets 06 89 29 82; www.santacecilia.it

Founded as a conservatory in 1585, the Accademia is now both a training ground for musicians and a professional symphony orchestra. Concerts are held in three massive halls located in the Parco della Musica near Flaminio, and (very) past conductors have included **Debussy, Strauss, Stravinsky,** and **Toscanini.** For the 2011-12 season, concerts include Liszt, Mahler, Mozart, and Stravinsky.

⇟ [M]A: Flaminio and then tram #2 to P. Euclide. Or take the special line "M" from Termini (every 15min. starting at 5pm) to Auditorium. Last bus after last performance. i Box office at Vle. Pietro de Coubertin 34. $ Tickets €18-50. Under 30 receive 25% discount purchasing from the box office. ⏰ Box office open daily 11am-8pm and 1hr. before a concert.

TEATRO FLAIANO

CENTRO STORICO

V. Santo Stefano del Cacco 15 ☎06 67 96 496; www.piccolalirica.com

Contemporary takes on traditional opera give this small theater a definite edge. Shows are kept short—around 1½hr.—and highlight particularly melodramatic moments of already melodramatic works, including *Tosca* and *Carmen* in recent seasons. While tickets cost more here than for full-length operas elsewhere, you're paying for the envelope-pushing stagings.

⇟ Tram #8. From Corso Vittorio Emanuele II, turn left onto V. del Gesù and right onto V. Santo Stefano del Cacco. $ Tickets €45-60. ⏰ Box office open Tu-Sa 3-7pm. General office open Tu-Sa 11am-7pm. Shows at 8pm.

ROCK AND POP

ROMA INCONTRA IL MONDO

NORTHERN ROME

Villa Ada at V. di Ponte Salario ☎06 41 73 47 12; www.villaada.org

This venue hosts an eclectic mix of rock, reggae, folk, and ethnic music at the large outdoor grounds of Villa Ada, near the Villa Borghese. Dancing or bobbing crowds cluster near the stage while a plethora of tables and beer and food stalls near the back offer a place to refresh post-mosh. Most of the acts are international performers on tour, from as nearby (if you can call it that) as Africa to as far away as Australia. Recent groups include Mulato Astatke (Ethiopia), Yann Tiersen (France), and Caribou (Canada).

⇟ [M]A: Flaminio, then Ferrovie Urbane bound for Civitacastellana; get off at Campi Sportivi. Enter the park at Vle. della Moschea and veer right down the winding V. di Ponte Salario. $ Tickets €5-15. ⏰ Concerts from mid-June to early Aug. Venue opens at 8pm; concerts start at 10pm and usually last until 2am.

FIESTA

SOUTHERN ROME

Ippodrome delle Capanelle, V. Appia Nuova 1245 ☎06 66 18 37 92; www.fiesta.it

This huge concert venue complete with restaurant, bar, disco, and lounge area features popular Latin performers most nights of the week. The fiesta wouldn't be complete without crowds in the thousands and so much dancing that your hips will start to feel like an 80-year-old's. Big name performers include Don Omar, La India, Los 4, and the legendary Ricky Martin.

⇏ Take bus #664 to Colli Albani or [M]A: Cinecittà and then bus #654 down V. delle Capanelle. i Buy tickets online at www.greenticket.it or www.ticketone.it or in person at concert venue. $ Tickets €10-35. Weekday performances usually cheaper than weekends. ⏰ Concerts June-Aug at 9:30pm. Concert venue open for ticket sale M-Th 8:30pm-1am, F-Sa 8:30pm-2am, Su 8:30pm-1am.

SOCCER

STADIO OLIMPICO

OUTSKIRTS

V. del Foro Italico 1 www.asroma.it, www.sslazio.it

While the battles here don't usually end in death for people or animals, as was the case at the Colosseum, this soccer stadium is still a site of epic battles complete with heartrending defeat and triumphant comebacks. These days, the main event is any game between **A.S. Roma** and **S.S. Lazio,** distinguishable by their colors: red and sky blue, respectively. Tickets aren't easy to come by; check the spots below or ask around.

⇏ [M]A: Ottaviano. Then take bus #32 to Piazzale della Farnesina. i Tickets can be purchased at the stadium, online at sites like www.listicket.it, or at various ticketing spots around the city such as Lazio Point (V. Farini 34/36 ☎06 48 26 688). $ Tickets €10-195. ⏰ Most matches Sept-May Su afternoons. Lazio Point box office open daily 9pm-1am and 2:30-6pm.

shopping

When it comes to shopping, it would be significantly easier to make a list of what Rome doesn't have. Fashionista, artista, or "intelligentista," you won't leave Rome unsatisfied, though your pocketbook might be significantly lighter. Those with a taste for high fashion should head to the Piazza di Spagna, Rome's equivalent of Fifth Ave., which is home to the regular gamut of designer stores. Smaller (though no less costly) boutiques dominate the Centro Storico. Major thoroughfares like V. del Corso, V. Nazionale, and V. Cola di Rienzo abound with European chains like United Colors of Benetton, Zara, Mango, and H&M. You can find these places in the US, too, but the offerings are usually pretty different for the European market. There are also plenty of cheap clothing stores touting a similar collection of tight, teeny-bopper glitz and fare that comes unattached to a brand name. The regions around Termini, Vle. Trastevere, and the Vatican contain a fair number of street vendors selling shoes, lingerie, dresses, and sunglasses for under €15. If this is what you're after, though, hit up the established open-air markets for a bigger selection than you could ever need.

DEPARTMENT STORES

Everyone needs a department store that stocks the basics, whether that means Gucci underwear at discounted prices or jeans and a sweater to cover up at the Vatican. Other than Italian prices (and confusing Italian sizes), these stores will probably seem just like home, from the Saks Fifth Avenue-esque La Rinascente to Oviesse, which is more reminiscent of Kohl's. Expect to find everything from makeup to household products to entire wardrobes (both the cabinets and the clothes with which you could easily fill them).

LA RINASCENTE

P. Colonna 195/199   ☎06 67 84 209; www.rinascente.it

Glamorous, big, and well-stocked, La Rinascente will save you a couple euro by offering discounted rates on coveted brands from the designer stores around the block on V. dei Condotti. You can also try on things you would never actually buy without disapproving glances from salespeople, which is really the best part of any fancy department store. With the designer selection of lingerie, you can spend three times the money on one third of the material.

✚ *Bus #116.* ☒ *Open daily 10am-9pm.*

COIN

V. Cola di Rienzo 173   ☎06 36 00 42 98; www.coin.it

With a generous selection of everything you might need in both designer and basic varieties, Coin is a good place to come for hours of rack-sorting, bargain-hunting, euro-dropping, and (if that line at the Vatican has left you in need) pee-ing. While offering fewer name brands than La Rinascente, the clothes for men, women, and children are still well made and stylish, and the home goods section offers a wide range to suit any budget.

✚ *Ⓜ A: Ottaviano. Head down V. Ottaviano and turn onto V. Cola di Rienzo from P. Risorgimento.* ☒ *Open M-Sa 10am-8pm, Su 10:30am-8pm.*

UPIM

V. Gioberti 64   ☎06 44 65 579; www.upim.it

UPIM's well-priced selection of furniture, cookware, bedding, and toys outdoes its basic clothing, most of which is seasonal. Still, it's a good place to buy inexpensive yet fashionable clothes if gelato stains have ruined your wardrobe. Dress up the store's simple garments with some makeup, which has taken over the first floor in full force.

✚ *Near Termini, across from Basilica di Santa Maria Maggiore.* ☒ *Open M-Sa 9am-8:30pm, Su 10am-8:30pm.*

OVIESSE

Vle. Trastevere 62   ☎06 58 33 36 33; www.oviesse.com

Oviesse stocks a somewhat small collection of inexpensive clothes for women and men—it's nothing special, but hey, you're wearing something, right? That something might be covered in sparkles and useless zippers, though. You might smell better than you look; the adjoining *perfumerie*'s collection is of comparable size. There are also plenty of clothes for children and babies in case their fashion is more important than yours.

✚ *Take tram #8 down Vle. Trastevere.* ***i*** *Huge BILLA supermarket downstairs with great prices.* ☒ *Open M-Sa 8:30am-8pm, Su 9:30am-1:30pm and 4-8pm.*

OPEN-AIR MARKETS

One of the few things that tourists and locals appreciate with equal enthusiasm are Rome's open-air markets. You can find real bargains if you're willing to rifle through the crowds. With early opening and closing hours, make sure you set that alarm. It's best to stick to official markets rather than take on merchants who set up shop individually. Watch out: the fine for buying fake designer products rests on the buyer, not the seller, and can reach into the hundreds of thousands of euro.

PORTA PORTESE

From P. Porta Portese to P. Ippolito Nievo   www.portaportesemarket.it

The legs of this U-shaped market seem to extend forever—the longer V. Portuense is occupied by vendors selling the same cheap garments, toiletries, furniture, plastic jewelry, and shoes found on most streets in Rome. We're talking 2m stacks of €2 clothes. If you're not exhausted by the madhouse (which rivals

shopping

the crowds of the Vatican Museums), head to the antiques section where cooler treasures reside: old comic books, records, jewelry, and furniture.

 # Take bus #40 to Largo Argentina and tram #8. $ Cash only. ⏰ Open Su 7am-2:30pm.

how to pick up a roman

Men in Rome are notoriously uninhibited about approaching just about any female with legs. If (for some reason) you want to learn to be more like them, here are a few pickup lines to try out:

- **"SEI UN FAVOLA."** You're a fable, or a dream. Romans dig that fantasy stuff.
- **"MI FAI IMPAZZIRE."** Shouting this alerts your target that he or she makes you crazy (in the romantic sense, of course).
- **"MI FAI MORIRE."** You make me die—of pleasure, presumably, but for allure you can leave it to your subject to fill in the blanks. If he or she is confused, it is, at the very least, an interesting conversation starter.
- **"DAMMI UN BACIO."** If you want to be even more forward, use this phrase to demand a kiss. Your street-smart pick-up lines are sure to impress, so it's not entirely out of the question.

MERCATO DI VIA SANNIO SOUTHERN ROME

V. Sannio

Like the market at Porta Portese, cheap used clothing and various trinkets make up the majority of V. Sannio's goods. Still, for those willing to delve deep into the maze-like covered market, vintage clothes and cheap leather goods await. Just be prepared for a fair amount of cajoling if you show any interest in an item or stall.

 # [M]A: San Giovanni. $ Cash only. ⏰ Open M-Sa 9am-1:30pm.

CAMPO DEI FIORI CENTRO STORICO

Thank God there's a place to buy fresh fruit and vegetables in the middle of all the overpriced trattorias. The lively square makes a great snack spot if you don't mind the crowds. Sample sauces, *limoncello*, and colorful pasta from eager vendors as you browse—it might not be enough for a meal, but it's a cheap start. Adding as much flavor to the *piazza* during the day as the bars do at night, the market's open stalls sell cheap clothing, produce, fish, and even alcohol—no need to head to San Marino to pick up some absinthe.

 # Bus #116 or tram #8. $ Cash only. ⏰ Open M-Sa 7am-2:30pm.

BOOKSTORES

Independent bookstores in Italy (as in the rest of the world) are facing tough times with the rise of giant chains and online vendors, so do the bibliophile community a favor and check out some of the places below to supplement your travel library. If, however, you just need the latest copy of *People* or the new Britney CD, **La Feltrinelli** (www.lafeltrinelli.it) will indeed be your best bet. The indie bookstore **Arion** (www.libreriearion.it) offers more unique finds and hosts literary events. Each branch has a specialty (and limited selections in English), so check the website to find a shop to match your interests.

LIBRERIA DEL VIAGGIATORE CENTRO STORICO

V. del Pellegrino 78 ☎06 68 80 10 48; www.libreriadelviaggiatore.com

Rome may be an amazing place, but after browsing this shop you'll probably be ready to pack up and head out on an adventure. The shelves of this bookstore, arranged by country, are crammed with old and new copies of travel guides, memoirs, and novels. While most books are in Italian, guidebooks and some novels are available in English; part of the fun, though, is wandering the shelves, which becomes a voyage all its own.

➹ From Campo dei Fiori, walk up V. Pellegrino. $ Cash only. ⏰ Open M 4-8pm, Tu-Sa 10am-2pm and 4-8pm.

📚 LION BOOKSHOP — NORTHERN ROME

V. dei Greci 33 — ☎06 32 65 40 07

The oldest English-language bookstore in Rome, the Lion is a welcome sight for Italian-weary eyes. Out front, paperbacks (€3-5) offer cheap beach reads, while inside there's an extensive collection of fiction, classics, poetry, sci-fi, fantasy, and even theory for those who miss college lectures. It's also one of the few bookstores in Italy to stock English translations of Italian authors, in case your love of Italian culture exceeds your linguistic abilities. The children's and young adult section is also quite impressive.

➹ [M]A: Flaminio. From P. del Popolo, take V. del Corso and turn left onto V. dei Greci. ℹ To place a book order, email orders@thelionbookshop.com. ⏰ Open daily 9:45am-7:15pm.

MERCATO DELLE STAMPE — PIAZZA DI SPAGNA

P. Borghese

The small *piazza* and academic assortment of goods make this market more manageable than others in Rome—after all, how rowdy can it get around a stack of books? Older crowds weave through the stalls, where you can find a wide selection of used books, old prints, and other dusty articles. Some English books are hidden in the mix, but the real pleasure is browsing rather than buying.

➹ Take bus #224 or 913 to P. Imperatore or bus #492, 116, or 81. Turn left onto V. della Fontanella di Borghese and continue straight into the piazza. $ Cash only. ⏰ Open M-Sa 7am-1pm.

ALMOST CORNER BOOKSHOP — TRASTEVERE

V. del Moro 45 — ☎06 58 36 942

English-language bestsellers and a wide range of books dealing with Italy and Rome are crammed into this small shop. The British owner is happy to take orders for his primarily expat customers or to chat about purchases.

➹ From P. Giuseppe Gioacchino Belli, follow V. della Renella and turn left onto V. della Pelliccia. Turn right onto V. del Moro. ⏰ Open Sept-July M-Sa 10am-1:30pm and 3:30-8pm, Su 11am-1-:30pm and 3:30-8pm; Aug M-Sa 10am-1:30pm and 3:30-8pm.

essentials

PRACTICALITIES

- **TOURIST OFFICES: Comune di Roma** is Rome's official source for tourist information. Green **PIT Info booths,** located at most major sights, have English-speaking staff and sell bus and Metro maps and the **Roma Pass.** (V. Giovanni Giolitti 34 in Termini, P. Sidney Sonnino in Trastevere, and V. dei Fori Imperiali ☎06 06 08; www.turismoroma.it, www.060608.it ⏰ Most locations open daily 9:30am-7pm; Termini location open daily 8am-8:30pm.) **Enjoy Rome** provides tour bookings, information on bike and scooter rental, and city maps. (V. Marghera 8A; 2nd office in P. San Pietro ☎06 44 51 843; www.enjoyrome.com ➹ [M]Termini. Walk down V. Marghera. ⏰ Both locations open M-F 8:30am-6pm, Sa 8:30am-2pm.)
- **LUGGAGE STORAGE: Termini Luggage Deposit.** (☎06 47 44 777; www.grandistazioni.it ➹ Below Track 24 in the Ala Termini wing. ℹ Storage for bags up to 20kg.

Max. 5 days. Ⓢ 1st 5hr. €4, €0.60 per hr. for 6th-12th hr., €0.20 per hr. thereafter. After 1st day, €5 per day. Cash only. ⌚ Open daily 6am-11:50pm.)

- **LOST PROPERTY: La Polizia Municipale** holds property for a few days after it's found. Property lost on Ⓜ**A lines** is held in an office on P. dei Cinquecento. (☎06 48 74 309 ⌚ Open M 9:30am-12:30pm, W 9:30am-12:30pm, F 9:30am-12:30pm.) For Ⓜ**B lines,** the office is at Circonvallazione Ostiense 191. (☎06 67 69 32 14 ⌚ Open M-F 9am-1pm.) To retrieve an item, you must present a valid form of ID, a statement describing the lost item, and a cash payment of €3.

- **GLBT RESOURCES:** The Comune di Roma publishes a free guide to gay life in Rome, *AZ Gay*. Pick one up at any PIT Info booth. **ARCI-GAY** offers medical, legal, and psychological counseling as well as free courses and general advice. (V. Zabaglia 14 ☎06 64 50 11 02, helpline 800 71 37 13; www.arcigayroma.it ⚸ Ⓜ B: Piramide. Walk up V. Marmorata and turn right onto V. Alessandro Volta; it's at the intersection with V. Zabaglia. *i* ARCI-GAY cards allow access to all events and services run by the program throughout Italy. Ⓢ 3-month card €8; 1 year €15. ⌚ Open M-Sa 4-8pm. Helpline operates M 4-8pm, W-Th 4-8pm, Sa 4-8pm.)

- **POST OFFICES: Poste Italiane** are located throughout the city. (☎800 160 000; www.poste.it) The main office is located at **Piazza San Silvestro 19.** (☎06 67 98 495 ⌚ Open M-F 8:30am-6:30pm, Sa 8:30am-1pm.)

EMERGENCY

- **POLICE: Police Headquarters.** (V. di San Vitale 15 ☎06 46 86 ⚸ Ⓜ A: Repubblica.) **Carabinieri** have offices at V. Mentana 6 (☎06 44 74 19 00 ⚸ Near Termini.) and at P. Venezia. (☎06 67 58 28 00) **City Police.** (P. del Collegio Romano 3 ☎06 69 01 21.)

- **CRISIS LINES: Telefono Rosa** provides legal, psychological, and medical counseling for women. (Vle. Giuseppe Mazzini 73 ☎06 37 51 82 82; www.telefonorosa.it ⌚ Operates 24hr.) **Samaritans** provides psychological counseling in many languages; call for in-person guidance. (☎800 86 00 22; www.samaritansonlus.org ⌚ Operates daily 1-10pm.)

- **LATE-NIGHT PHARMACIES:** The following pharmacies are open 24hr.: **Farmacia della Stazione.** (P. dei Cinquecento 49/51 ☎06 48 80 019) **Farmacia Internazionale.** (P. Barberini 49 ☎06 48 25 456 ⚸ Ⓜ A: Barberini.) **Farmacia Doricchi.** (V. XX Settembre 47 ☎06 48 73 880) **Brienza.** (P. del Risorgimento 44 ☎06 39 73 81 86.)

- **HOSPITALS/MEDICAL SERVICES: Policlinico Umberto I.** (Vle. del Policlinico 155 ☎06 49 97 95 14 or 06 49 97 95 15; www.policlinicoumberto1.it ⚸ Ⓜ B: Policlinico or bus #649 to Policlinico. Ⓢ Emergency treatment free. Non-emergencies €25-50. ⌚ Open 24hr.) **International Medical Center** is a private hospital and clinic. (V. Firenze 47 ☎06 48 82 371; www.imc84.com ⚸ Ⓜ A: Repubblica. *i* Call ahead for appointments. ⌚ Open M-F 9am-8pm.) **Rome-American Hospital.** (V. Emilio Longoni 69 ☎06 22 551 for emergencies, 06 22 55 290 for appointments; www.rah.it ⚸ Well to the east of the city; consider taking a cab. To get a little closer, take bus #409 from Tiburtina to Piazzale Prenestina or tram #14 from Termini. *i* English-speaking. Private emergency and laboratory services, including HIV testing. ⌚ Open M-F 8am-8pm, Sa 8am-2pm. 24hr. emergency care.)

GETTING THERE

If you're traveling to Rome from an international destination, you'll probably arrive at Da Vinci International Airport and take a train into the center of Rome. Trains from the airport arrive at Termini Station during the day, although if you're traveling by night you may have to transfer to a bus. For travelers on a budget, Rome Ciampino Airport is the closest budget airport, although getting to Rome will be a bit slower, as no trains run from here to the city center. If you're heading to Rome from elsewhere in Italy, take advantage of the train network that runs throughout the country.

by plane

DA VINCI INTERNATIONAL AIRPORT (FIUMICINO; FCO)

30km southwest of the city ☎06 65 951; www.adr.it/fiumicino

Commonly known as Fiumicino, Da Vinci International Airport oversees most international flights. To get from the airport, which is located right on the Mediterranean coast, to central Rome, take the **Leonardo Express** train to Termini Station. After leaving the airport's customs, follow signs to the Stazione Trenitalia/Railway Station, where you can buy a train ticket at an automated machine or from the ticket office. ($ €14. ⏰ 32min., every 30min. 6:47am-11:37pm.) The **Sabina-Fiumicino Line (FR1)** will take you to Trastevere Station and other Roman suburbs. (www.trenitalia.it $ €8. ⏰ 20-45min., every 15min. 5:57am-11:27pm.) Don't buy a ticket from individuals who approach you, as they may be scammers. If you arrive after 8:30pm, you'll have to use an automated machine. Before boarding the train, make sure to validate the ticket in a yellow box on the platform; failure to do so may result in a fine of €50-100. To get to or from Fiumicino before 6:30am or after 11:30pm, the easiest option is to catch a **taxi.** ($ €40 flat rate for central Rome, including baggage and up to 4 passengers.)

ROME CIAMPINO AIRPORT (CIA)

15km southeast of the city ☎06 65 951; www.adr.it/ciampino

Ciampino is a rapidly growing airport that serve budget airlines like Ryanair and EasyJet. There are no trains connecting the airport to the city center, but there are some buses. The **SIT Bus Shuttle** (☎06 59 23 507; www.sitbusshuttle.it $ €4. ⏰ 40min., every 30-60min. 7:15am-11:30pm.) and **Terravision Shuttle** (☎06 97 61 06 32; www.terravision.eu $ €4. ⏰ 40min., every 20-60min. 8:15am-12:15am.) run from the airport to V. Marsala, outside Termini Station. For easy and cheap access to the Metro, the **COTRAL bus** runs to [M]A: Anagnina. ($ €1.20. ⏰ 30min., every 40min. 6:30am-11:10pm.)

by train

Trenitalia (www.trenitalia.com) trains run through Termini Station, central Rome's main transport hub. International and overnight trains also run to Termini. City buses #C2, H, M, 36, 38, 40, 64, 86, 90, 92, 105, 170, 175, 217, 310, 714, and 910 stop outside in the P. del Cinquecento, so you definitely aren't short on options for the next leg of your journey. The station is open 4:30am-1:30am; if you arrive in Rome outside of this time frame, you will likely arrive in Stazione Tiburtina or Stazione Ostiense, both of which connect to Termini by the night bus #175. Trains run from: Bologna ($ €26-59. ⏰ 2-5hr., 42 per day 6:15am-12:47am.); Florence ($ €18-45. ⏰ 1½-4hr., 52 per day 5:58am-10:36pm.); Naples ($ €11-45. ⏰ 1-3hr., 50 per day 4:52am-9:50pm.); Venice ($ €46-76. ⏰ 4-7hr., 17 per day 6:45am-10:36pm.); Milan. ($ €46-89. ⏰ 3-8½ hr., 33 per day 6am-12:47am.)

GETTING AROUND

Rome's public transportation system is run by **ATAC.** (☎06 57 003; www.atac.roma.it ⏰ Open M-Sa 8am-8pm.) It consists of the Metro, buses, and trams, which serve the city center and outskirts, as well as various **Ferrovie urbane** and **Ferrovie metropolitane,** which serve more distant suburbs, including Ostia. Transit tickets are valid for any of these lines and can be bought at *tabaccherie*, at some bars, and from self-service machines or ticket windows at major stations including Termini, Ostiense, and Trastevere. A **BIT** (integrated time ticket; €1) is valid for 1¼hr. after validation and allows unlimited bus travel plus one Metro ride within that time frame; it is generally the most economical choice. A **BIG** (integrated daily ticket; €4) is valid until midnight on the day of validation and allows unlimited bus and Metro use. The **BTI** (integrated tourist ticket; €11) grants unrestricted access for three days after validation. The **CIS** (integrated weekly ticket; €16) grants unrestricted access for seven days after validation. These longer-term tickets can save you money, but only if you know you'll be using public transportation a lot. Tickets must be validated at Metro station turnstiles and stamping machines on buses and trams.

by bus

The best way to get around the city other than walking is by bus. Dozens of routes cover the entire city center as well as the outskirts. Bus stops are marked by yellow poles and display a route map for all lines that pass through the stop.

by metro

Rome's Metro system consists of two lines: [M]A, which runs from Battistini to Anagnina (hitting P. di Spagna), and [M]B, which runs from Laurentina to Rebibbida (hitting the Colosseum, Ostiense, and southern Rome). The lines intersect at **Termini Station.** While the Metro is fast, it doesn't reach many regions and is best for getting across long distances. Stations are marked by poles with a red square and white M. Tickets are validated at turnstiles upon entering the station. The Metro usually operates 5:30am-11:30pm and until 1:30am on Saturdays. However, due to construction of a third line, [M]A will be closing at 9:30pm on all days except Saturday until May 2012.

by tram

Trams make many stops but are still an efficient means of getting around. A few useful lines include **#3** (Trastevere, Piramide, Aventine, P. San Giovanni, Villa Borghese, P. Thorwaldsen), **#8** (Trastevere to Largo Argentina), and **#19** (Ottaviano, Villa Borghese, San Lorenzo, Prenestina, P. dei Gerani).

by bike

ATAC runs **Bikesharing.** Purchase a card at any ATAC ticket office. (☎06 57 03 [M]A: Anagnina, Spagna, Lepanto, Ottaviano, Cornelia, or Battistini, or [M]B: Termini, Laurentina, EUR Fermi, or Ponte Mammolo. *i* Bikes can be parked at 19 stations around the city. Cards are rechargeable. $ €5 initial charge, €0.50 per 30min. thereafter. ⏰ Open M-Sa 7am-8pm, Su 8am-8pm. Bikes available for max. 24hr. at a time.) Plenty of other companies also rent bikes, including **Bici and Baci** and **Eco Move Rent** (see below).

rome

by scooter

Rome is truly a city of scooters. Depending on the vehicle, prices range from €19-95 per day. A helmet (required by law) and insurance are usually included. **Bici and Baci** rents bikes and scooters. (V. del Viminale 5 ☎06 48 28 443; www.bicibaci.com ⏰ Open daily 8am-7pm.) **Treno e Scooter Rent** also rents scooters with a lock and chain included. (Stazione Roma Termini ☎06 48 90 58 23; www.trenoescooter.com ⏰ Open daily 9am-2pm and 4-7pm.) **Eco Move Rent** rents scooters, Vespas, and bikes, with a lock included. (V. Varese 48/50 ☎06 44 70 45 18; www.ecomoverent.com ⏰ Open daily 8:30am-7:30pm.)

by taxi

Given the scope of Rome's bus system, taxis should only be reserved for desperate or time-sensitive affairs. Legally, you may not hail a cab on the street—either call **RadioTaxi** (☎06 35 70; www.3570.it) or head to a cab stand (near most major sights). Ride only in yellow or white cars and look for a meter or settle on a price before the ride. Fares start at €2.33 for rides 7am-10pm and €4.91 for 10pm-7am, and are then calculated per kilometer. Sunday and holiday daytime fares start at €3.36. **Rate 1** is charged for rides within the center. ($ €0.78 per km.) **Rate 2** is applied to rides outside. ($ €1.29 per km.) Though it's hard to tell what rate is being applied, write down the license number if the cost seems especially high. Tips are not expected.

MONEY

tipping and bargaining

In Italy, a 5% tip is customary, particularly in restaurants (10% if you particularly liked the service). Italian waiters won't cry if you don't leave a tip; just be ready to ignore the pangs of your conscience later on. Taxi drivers expect tips as well, but lucky for alcohol lovers, it is unusual to tip in bars. Bargaining is appropriate in markets and other informal settings, though in regular shops it is inappropriate. Hotels will often offer lower prices to people looking for a room that night, so you will often be able to find a bed cheaper than what is officially quoted.

SAFETY AND HEALTH

local laws and police

In Italy, you will mainly encounter two types of boys and girls in blue: the *polizia* (☎113) and the *carabinieri* (☎112). The *polizia* are a civil force under the command of the Ministry of the Interior, whereas the *carabinieri* fall under the auspices of the Ministry of Defense and are considered a military force. Both, however, generally serve the same purpose—to maintain security and order in the country. In the case of attack or robbery, both will respond to inquiries or desperate pleas for help.

drugs and alcohol

Needless to say, **illegal drugs** are best avoided altogether, particularly when traveling in a foreign country. In Italy, just like almost everywhere else in the world, drugs including marijuana, cocaine, and heroin are illegal, and possession or other drug-related offenses will be harshly punished.

The legal drinking age in Italy is (drumroll please) 16. Remember to drink responsibly and to **never drink and drive.** Doing so is illegal and can result in a prison sentence, not to mention early death. The legal blood alcohol content (BAC) for driving in Italy is under 0.05%, significantly lower than the US limit of 0.08%.

travelers with disabilities

Travelers in wheelchairs should be aware that travel in Italy will sometimes be extremely difficult. This country predates the wheelchair—sometimes it seems even the wheel—by several centuries and thus poses unique challenges to travelers with disabilities. **Accessible Italy** (☎378 941 111; www.accessibleitaly.com) offers advice to tourists of limited mobility heading to Italy, with tips on subjects ranging from finding accessible accommodations to wheelchair rental.

CLIMATE

Luckily for you, Rome typically enjoys the renowned balmy and beautiful Mediterranean climate. The summer season, lasting from May until October, is generally pleasant, with temperatures only reaching a level of discomfort in July and August. Romans often vacation in August to escape the heat, and, unfortunately for you, it *is* necessary to wear more than a bikini to the Sistine Chapel. Travelers say the best time to visit is in September and October when the summer is rounded out by the *ottobrate romane*—the sunny, beautiful days in October. Despite occasional snowfall in December, January, and February, the winters in Rome are pretty mild.

rome 101

Congratulations! You now hold in your hands an all-access pass to the city to which all roads lead, the land of artwork, terrible drivers, and the oh-so-satisfying carbohydrate/gelato diet. But wait, this popular tourist destination didn't spring up out of nowhere; Rome is also the home of all things ancient and gladiatory, and it has the ruins to prove it. Not only that—as the center of Roman Catholicism (come on, it's even in the name), your stay in the Eternal City will undoubtedly include more churches, basilicas, and Madonna and Child renditions than you can even attempt to count. But don't worry; we at *Let's Go* are here not only to enrich you with the city's history, but to also verse you in Roman custom so you can walk and talk like a local. From the wolf brothers who started it all to the soccer fans who cheer in the subway, this is Rome 101, here to help you do as the Romans do.

HISTORY

feral beginnings (753-700 bce)

Rome, known today as the Eternal City, has been raging since 753 BCE—talk about stamina. As founding stories go, Rome's is pretty wild. The war god Mars fathered the notoriously quarrelsome twins, **Romulus and Remus,** who were raised by a she-wolf who was, we're sorry to say, presumably not Shakira. Eventually the brothers knew it was time to venture from the pack and found a city of their own. Romulus wanted to build the city on one hill; Remus preferred another. Fighting and confusion ensued and, since boys will be boys, Romulus killed Remus. Then, in a fit of humility traditional to Roman leaders, Romulus named his city Rome, after himself.

Not long afterward, Romulus watched the new city's population swell with male outlaws and refugees. But with Roman testosterone levels reaching critical, Romulus realized that the city was in dire need of some ladies. He went to war with the **Sabines** and brought in some well-deserved estrogen. With all those raging hormones, the population inevitably began to rise, the city expanded, and the **Roman Empire** was born. Romulus ruled the Empire as king before disappearing into the annals of ancient lore.

democracy demo (500 bce-14 ce)

Kings maintained the supreme power in Rome until 500 BCE, when the king's son raped **Lucretia** and sparked the overthrow of the monarchy. In its place, the revolutionaries founded the **Roman Republic,** which was cloaked as the foundation of democracy, but was really an excuse for free, rich, white men to vote in strangely comfortable white sheets that they dubbed "togas." Under Republican rule, Roman

---

facts and figures

- **POPULATION:** 2.8 million
- **ANNUAL VISITORS TO THE VATICAN MUSEUMS:** 4.2 million
- **ANIMALS KILLED IN THE COLOSSEUM:** Over 1 million
- **MINUTES FOR 70,000 SPECTATORS TO EXIT THE COLOSSEUM:** 3
- **NUMBER OF STEPS IN THE SPANISH STEPS:** 138
- **NUMBER OF OUTLETS IN THE FIRST-EVER MALL:** 150
- **PERCENT OF SOLDIERS KILLED IN ANCIENT ROMAN ARMY:** 10

power steadily grew until the Roman army could take down almost anyone who challenged its supreme power.

When Gaul came a-knockin' in 58 BCE, there was only one man for the job—**Julius Caesar.** He drove out the Gauls (known today as "the French") and ruled Rome for four glorious years before that fiasco that brought us the phrase "stabbed in the back." Brutus and Cassius, two of Caesar's murderers, didn't quite get the power they thought they would. Instead, Caesar's adopted son, **Octavian,** defeated them and ruled the Roman Empire under the title **Augustus** for the next five decades.

romans ain't weebles (14-1453 ce)

The Roman Empire reached its height of power around 117 CE, when it controlled all of southern Europe, Britain, Asia Minor, Syria, Egypt, and North Africa. It regulated trade; collected taxes; created highways, aqueducts, and sewers; and killed Christians by the dozen. Emperors ruled Rome for hundreds of years, turning the city into the largest empire in world history. Sadly, something was rotten in the state of Italia and, as people began to revolt against empiric rule, emperors got scared and ran.

When **Constantine** became Emperor in 312 CE, he moved the capital to Byzantium (though, to continue the humility of Rome's leaders, he soon changed the name to Constantinople). In an ill-fated attempt to stop the persecution of Christians, he officially converted the empire to Christianity. This stripped the Roman Senate of any real power and reduced the men to a toga-wearing fraternity unfit for **John Belushi.**

While Constantine was busy baptizing everyone he met, the Bishop of Rome was fitted with a shiny new title: **Pope.** The Western Roman Empire met its demise in 476, and the Church used its ever increasing power to transform it into the Holy Roman Empire, naming **Charlemagne** its emperor in 800.

Catholic issues reached new heights during the 1300s when some indecisive cardinals declared two simultaneous popes in 1378, thrusting the Church into the **Western Schism.** Half of the Catholic world looked to Pope Clement VII in Avignon, France; some stayed loyal to good ol' Rome with Urban VI. Finally the Church officials got their act together and ended the conflict in 1414, reestablishing Rome's title as the center of the Catholic Church.

Through all of this religious mess, the Eastern Roman Empire was still holding on in Constantinople. But all good things must come to an end, and the remaining half of the Empire fell to the **Ottoman Turks** in 1453. Although Rome lived on, its status as an empire (and almost all traces of ancient rule) faded into history.

popes and paintings (1453-1527)

After losing most of its power, Rome spent the following centuries rebuilding its reputation as a cultural and political stronghold. Without the pesky weight of the world on its shoulders, Romans began to recognize their city's beauty. The Renaissance saw the creation of Bernini's fountains, **Saint Peter's Basilica,** and Michelangelo's spectacular paintings on the ceiling of the **Sistine Chapel.** Culture, it seemed, was coming homa to Roma.

Yeah, we know, Florence was the major city for all things Renaissance, but where did you think all those gaudy buildings came from? Popes took some time out of their busy patron-saint-naming schedules to become patrons of the arts. The whole nepotism, simony, and architecture trifecta would ultimately lead to Reformation. Lucky for you, traveler, the buildings got to stay.

During the heyday of Roman Renaissance—May 6, 1527 to be specific—Holy Roman Emperor **Charles V** led a sack on Rome after the Church tried to balance European power by shifting its alliance to France. Charles also imprisoned the man responsible for the switch, **Pope Clement VII** (a different Clement than the one from the Schism fiasco). Lucky for Charles, thousands of loyal soldiers took matters into their own hands, claiming the city and capturing the Pope. Clem graciously gave away the Eternal City and brought the Roman Renaissance to a screeching halt.

let's stay together (1527-1871)

The following centuries gave Rome a little bit of an identity crisis. No worries; much like Madonna, Rome continued to reinvent itself even after thousands of years of love-hate relationships with its fellow countries. Rome spent most of this period under the control of the **Papal States,** an area ruled by the Holy See that was considerably less miniscule than today's Vatican City. The locals sought to throw off the Pope's rule a couple of times and formed reborn Roman Republics in 1789 and 1849. The tenacity of the Popes and the military "might" of the French crushed both of them, though.

In the 1860s, poor Rome was left out of the Italian Unification that brought the boot-shaped country together as one. The Kingdom of Italy was Rome-less; its capital was Florence, for Zeus's sake! But the Franco-Prussian war forced the French to finally give up their stronghold on the Papal States. In 1871, Rome took its rightful place as the capital of Italy.

il duce to today (1900-present)

Fascism rolled into Rome in 1922 when Benito Mussolini, known today as *Il Duce*, marched on the city and declared yet another Empire. Rome reached the enormous one million inhabitants mark in the pre-WWII period. Partially to house them but mainly to celebrate himself (modesty wasn't one of his strengths), Mussolini destroyed many old sections of the city and replaced them with grandiose structures, often made of white marble. Il Duce allied himself with his ideological buddy, Adolf Hitler, forcing Italy into WWII. Though Rome was briefly occupied by the Germans after Mussolini's fall from power in 1943, it was mostly spared from bombings and did not suffer as much as others from the horror of the war.

Post-war, Rome quickly became a major driving force behind the Italian economy. *La Dolce Vita* was the phrase of the day, and even modern day Romans know how to live a sweet life. Today, Rome is a flourishing city known partially for its speeding cars and romantic movies, but above all for the ancient culture that still permeates every corner of the city. On the upside, modern Rome no longer worries about living up to its former Empire status, and can instead focus more on the present while still preserving the past.

CUSTOMS AND ETIQUETTE

If you come across many hospitable Romans (and trust us, you will), they're sure to be warm, loud, opinionated, and ready to feed you. Families are traditionally the center of Italian culture, and their systems and superstitions are very important to them. So here are a few quick dos and don'ts.

italian introductions

Don't be alarmed if Italian introductions aren't as hearty and welcoming as you expect. Make direct eye contact when meeting someone new and don't be surprised if a smile isn't accompanied by a hearty handshake. Once you move past the initial awkward meeting, they'll eventually invite you to use their first name, and now the hearty and welcoming side comes out. Get ready for air-kisses galore (always left cheek first). *Seinfeld* be damned.

roman rules for dining

When it comes to wining and dining with Rome's high class (or any class really), fashionably late is on time. You can show up 15min. late to a dinner and 30min. late to a party and still be good to go. Be sure that when you do arrive, though, you aren't empty-handed. Wait for the hostess before eating or sitting down (or, you know, sneezing or taking a breath). Italians love a good toast as much as a fine wine, so if you have the gift of gab, say a nice *grazie* to your hosts. Finally, follow basic rules for polite eating. Heed the age-old wisdom: "*Let's Go* Reader, strong and able, get those elbows off the table."

FOOD AND DRINK

Along with enriching your mind with art and beauty, you're probably looking to satisfy your body with a few delicious pounds of pizza, pasta, and all things carbohydrate. However, while Italy is rightly known for its carbs, gelato, and wine, food in Rome can be a lot healthier than the Italian ideal. For a truly Roman meal, fresh ingredients are a must. Peas and artichokes, lamb and goat meat, and Italian cheeses are the most common foods, and all staples (and most delicious non-staples) change with the season.

SPORTS AND RECREATION

One might argue that the Italian language sometimes sounds like a lot of shouting, regardless of whether or not you're being yelled at. But, if you mess with Italians and their soccer, you'd better be prepared for a mouthful—and maybe even a fist-full.

Modern soccer, or **futbol** as you should get used to calling it, is just as intense off the field as it is on. There are two major teams in Rome that are forced to share a stadium, and, as one could guess, they and their fans loathe one another. Feel free to cheer for the same team as those around you—lest you get pulled into a heated riot between impassioned fans. The first team, **A.S. Roma** (simply known as Roma to fans), sport maroon and gold uniforms with a picture of the founding brothers being fed by their mother wolf. If you get tongue-tied talking about specifics, just mention **Francesco Totti,** one of Roma's greats, and hope they're too distracted by excitement and adoration to notice you know nothing about him. Fans of the second team, **S.S. Lazio,** will probably be wearing the team's sky-blue uniforms and cheering on one of their more prominent players, **Alessandro Nesta.**

If you find yourself backed into a corner with nothing to say and no way of telling a goal from a touchdown, just say you support team Italia. The national team is the one thing that these mob-like fans can agree on.

FASHION

Italians praise *la bella figura*, good image. Having fashion sense can stand for a lot more than simple good taste. The difference between an an Armani suit and an Ed Hardy trucker hat is the difference between a good first impression and a permanent status on the bad side of an Italian hot-or-not list. Even today you can't walk through the streets of Rome without feeling shamed at the number of model-like Italians strutting leather-clad around monuments. *La bella figura* is about more than fancy clothes—it's the art of style, an aura of confidence. No wonder Italians are so sexy.

HOLIDAYS AND FESTIVALS

HOLIDAY OR FESTIVAL	DESCRIPTION	DATE
Feast of Saint Joseph	Endless array of traditional donuts in Trionfale Quarter. Need we say more?	mid-March
Maratona della Città di Roma	Sign up so all of Rome can watch you run 26 miles through the ancient ruins.	late March
Festa della Primavera	Welcome spring on the azalea-covered Spanish steps, then go see a concert in Trinità dei Monti.	early April
Pesaro Film Festival	Showcases both new directors and classic films.	late June
Spoleto Festival	Top-quality concerts, opera, dance, theater, and film. Spoleto is a couple of hours north of Rome by train.	mid-July
Noianti Festival	Folk music, dancing, parades, and fireworks in Trastevere to honor the Virgin Carmine.	late July

CENTRO STORICO, JEWISH GHETTO, AND TRASTEVERE

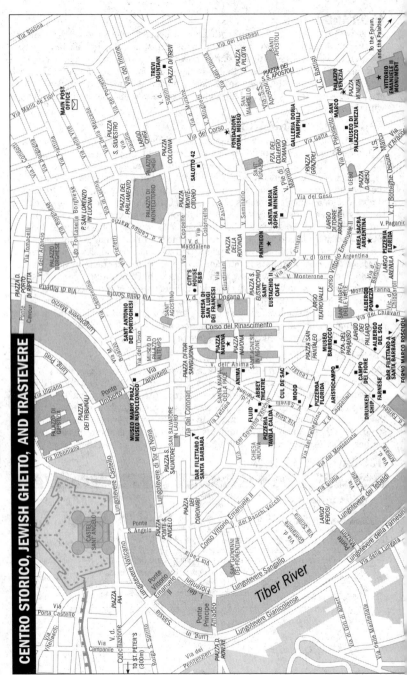

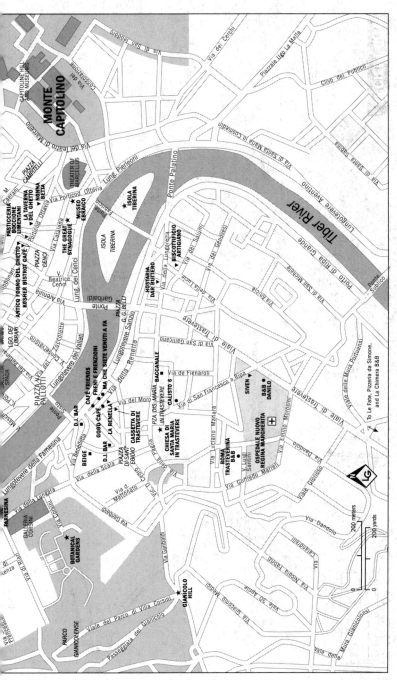

centro storico, jewish ghetto, and trastevere map

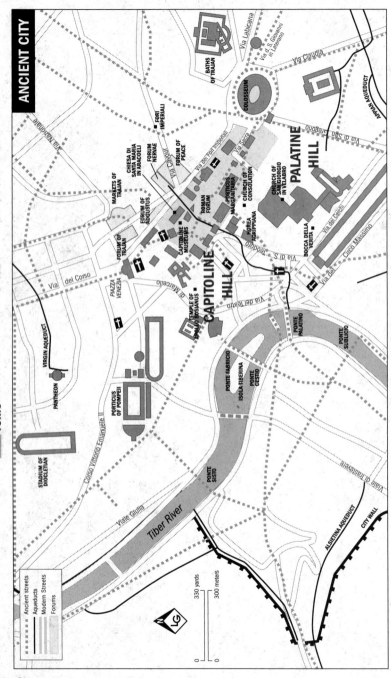

ANCIENT CITY

rome

- Via Labicana
- Via d. S. Giovanni in Laterano
- BATHS OF TRAJAN
- Via Claudia
- APPIAN AQUEDUCT
- COLOSSEUM
- Via di San Gregorio
- FORI IMPERIALI
- FORUM NERVAE
- FORUM OF PEACE
- CHIESA DI SANTA MARIA IN ARACOELI
- MARKETS OF TRAJAN
- FORUM OF AUGUSTUS
- Via dei Fori Imperiali
- Via Sacra
- ROMAN FORUM
- PORTICUS MARGARITARIA
- CHURCH OF CONSOLATION
- CHURCH OF SAN GIORGIO IN VELABRO
- PALATINE HILL
- CAPITOLINE MUSEUMS
- HOREA AGRIPPIANA
- FORUM OF TRAJAN
- Via del Corso
- Via di S. Teodoro
- PIAZZA VENEZIA
- CAPITOLINE HILL
- BOCCA DELLA VERITÀ
- Via dei Cerchi
- Circo Massimo
- Via del Teatro
- Via del Teatro di Marcello
- TEMPLE OF APOLLO SOSIANUS
- PONTE PALATINO
- VIRGIN AQUEDUCT
- PANTHEON
- PORTICUS OF POMPEII
- PONTE FABRICIO
- ISOLA TIBERINA
- PONTE CESTIO
- PONTE SUBLICIO
- STADIUM OF DIOCLETIAN
- Corso Vittorio Emanuele II
- PONTE SISTO
- Viale di Trastevere
- Viale Giulia
- Tiber River
- ALSIETINA AQUEDUCT
- CITY WALL

Ancient streets
Aqueducts
Modern Streets
Forums

330 yards
300 meters

N

826 www.letsgo.com

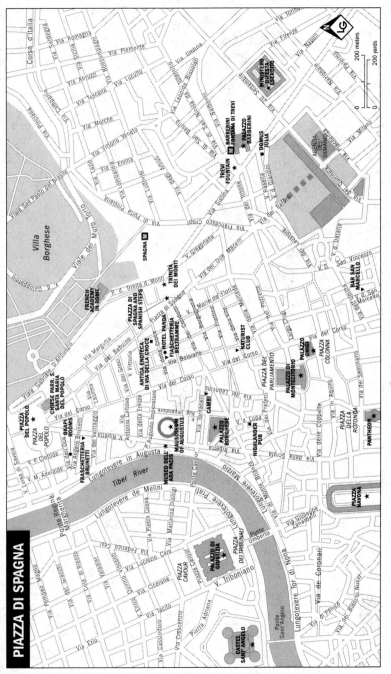

Villa
Borghese

Tiber River

PIAZZA
DEL POPOLO ★

PIAZZA DEL
POPOLO

CHIESE PARR. S.
SANTA MARIA
DEL POPOLO

OKAPI
ROOMS

FRENCH
ACADEMY
IN ROME

SPAGNA M

PIAZZA DI
SPAGNA AND
SPANISH STEPS

TRINITÀ
DEI MONTI

BARBERINI M
★ FONTANA DI TREVI

PALAZZO
BARBERINI

DOMUS
JULIA

TREVI
FOUNTAIN ★

MINISTERO
DELL'
ESERCITO

AGENZIA
DEL DEMANIO

FRASCHETTERIA
BRUNETTI ▼

MUSEO DELL'
ARA PACIS ★

MAUSOLEUM
OF AUGUSTUS ★

ANTICA ENOTECA
DI VIA DELLA CROCE ★

▼ HOTEL PANDA

FIASCHETTERIA
BELTRAMME ▼

NATURIST
CLUB

PALAZZO
GHIGI ★

PIAZZA
COLONNA

CAMBI ★

PALAZZO
BORGHESE ★

PALAZZO DEL
PARLIAMENTO

PALAZZO DI
MONTECITORIO ★

HIGHLANDER
PUB ▼

BAR SAN
MARCELLO

PIAZZA
DELLA
ROTONDA

PANTHEON ★

PALAZZO DI
GIUSTIZIA ★

PIAZZA
DEI TRIBUNALI

PIAZZA
CAVOUR

PIAZZA
NAVONA ★

CASTEL
SANT'ANGELO ★

Ponte
Sant'Angelo

0   200 meters
0   200 yards

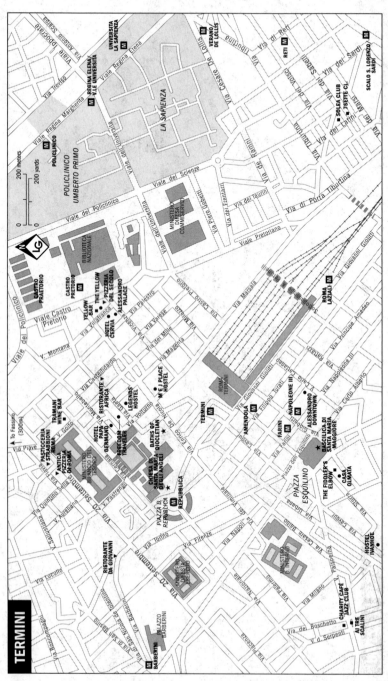

rome

TERMINI

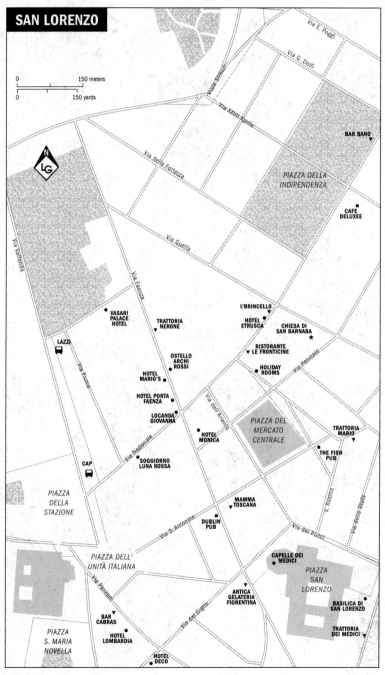

SAN LORENZO

0 — 150 meters
0 — 150 yards

Via E. Poggi

Via G. Dolfi

Prato Strozzi

Via XXVII Aprile

BAR BANO

Via della Fortezza

PIAZZA DELLA INDIPENDENZA

CAFE DELUXEE

Via Guelfa

Via Faenza

VASARI PALACE HOTEL

TRATTORIA NERONE

L'BRINCELLO

HOTEL ETRUSCA

CHIESA DI SAN BARNABA

RISTORANTE LE FRONTICINE

LAZZI

Via Fiume

Via Valfonda

OSTELLO ARCHI ROSSI

HOTEL MARIO'S

HOTEL PORTA FAENZA

LOCANDA GIOVANNA

Via dell'Ariento

HOLIDAY ROOMS

Via Panicale

PIAZZA DEL MERCATO CENTRALE

TRATTORIA MARIO

HOTEL MONICA

THE FISH PUB

Via Nazionale

SOGGIORNO LUNA ROSSA

CAP

PIAZZA DELLA STAZIONE

V. Rosina

Via della Ruta

MAMMA TOSCANA

Via S. Antonino

DUBLIN PUB

Via dei Pucci

PIAZZA DELL' UNITÀ ITALIANA

Via Panzani

CAPELLE DEI MEDICI

PIAZZA SAN LORENZO

ANTICA GELATERIA FIORENTINA

Via del Giglio

BASILICA DI SAN LORENZO

BAR CABRAS

HOTEL LOMBARDIA

PIAZZA S. MARIA NOVELLA

HOTEL DECO

TRATTORIA DEI MEDICI

san lorenzo map

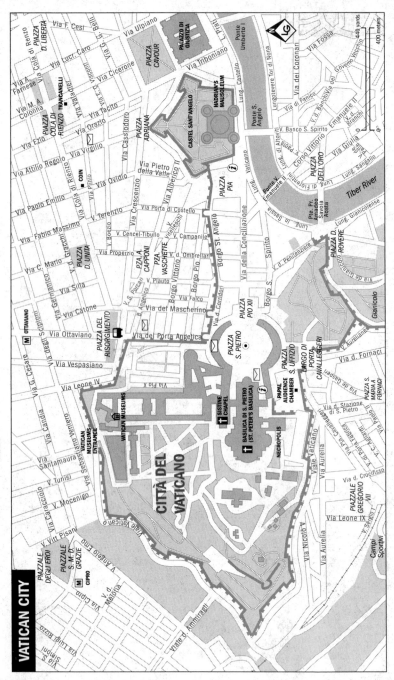

VATICAN CITY

rome

ESSENTIALS

You don't have to be a rocket scientist to plan a good trip. (It might help, but it's not required.) You do, however, need to be well prepared, and that's what we can do for you. Essentials is the chapter that gives you all the nitty-gritty you need to know for your trip: the hard information gleaned from 50 years of collective wisdom and several months of furious fact-checking. Planning your trip? Check. Where to find Wi-Fi? Check. The dirt on public transportation? Check. We've also thrown in communications info, safety tips, and a phrasebook, just for good measure. Plus, for overall trip-planning advice from what to pack (money and as little underwear as possible) to how to take a good passport photo (it's physically impossible; consider airbrushing), you can also check out the Essentials section of www.letsgo.com.

So, flick through this chapter before you leave so you know what documents to bring, while you're on the plane so you know how you can call your parents once you land, and when you're on the ground so you can figure out how to withdraw extra beer money from an ATM. This chapter may not always be the most scintillating read, but it just might save your life.

greatest hits

- **WE ARE ONE.** Poli Sci majors may think of the EU as a bureaucratic nightmare, but it's awesome for you—the **Schengen Agreement** allows you to move between most European countries without going through customs (p. 833).

- **WE ARE ONE, PART TWO.** We have mixed feelings about the **euro.** On one hand, it's awfully convenient to have one currency for most of Europe. On the other hand, the exchange rate is awful (p. 834).

- **ONE-EURO FLIGHTS.** Yes, it's true—**budget airlines** are a wonderful thing. We've compiled the continent's cheapest and most convenient (p. 836).

- **WE AREN'T REALLY ONE.** As integrated as Europe becomes, they'll always speak some wildly different languages. Enter our handy dandy **phrasebook** (p. 841). Can you say "Traveling is awesome"? Can you say it in Czech?

planning your trip

DOCUMENTS AND FORMALITIES

We're going to fill you in on visas and work permits, but don't forget the most important one of all: your passport. **Don't forget your passport!**

visas

Those lucky enough to be EU citizens do not need a visa to globetrot through... the EU. You citizens of Australia, Canada, New Zealand, the US, and most other non-EU countries do not need a visa for stays of up to 90 days, but this three-month period begins upon entry into any of the countries that belong to the EU's **freedom of movement** zone. For more information, see **One Europe** (below). Those staying longer than 90 days may apply for a longer-term visa; consult an embassy or consulate for more information. Note that Turkey is not a member of the EU; for information on visas for the Istanbul leg of your trip, check the **Essentials** section of that chapter.

Double-check entrance requirements at the nearest embassy or consulate for up-to-date information. US citizens can also consult http://travel.state.gov.

Entering many countries to study requires a special visa. Admittance to a country as a traveler does not include the right to work, which is authorized only by a **work permit.** For more information, see the **Beyond Tourism** chapter.

one europe

The EU's policy of freedom of movement means that most border controls have been abolished and visa policies harmonized. Under this treaty, formally known as the Schengen Agreement, you're still required to carry a passport (or government-issued ID card for EU citizens) when crossing an internal border, but, once you've been admitted into one country, you're free to travel to other participating states. Most EU states (the UK is a notable exception) are already members of Schengen, as are Iceland and Norway. In recent times, fears over immigration have led to calls for suspension of this freedom of movement. Border controls are being strengthened, but the policy isn't really targeted against casual travelers, so unless you've been traveling so long that you look like an illegal immigrant, you should still be fine to travel with ease throughout Europe.

TIME DIFFERENCES

Most of the cities in this book are on Central European Time, which is 1hr. ahead of Greenwich Mean Time (GMT) and observes Daylight Saving Time during the summer. This means that they are 6hr. ahead of New York City, 9hr. ahead of Los Angeles, 1hr. ahead of the British Isles, 8hr. behind Sydney, and 10hr. behind New Zealand. However, London is on Western European Time (subtract 1hr. from Central European Time)—a.k.a. Greenwich Mean Time. In addition, Istanbul is on Eastern European Time (add 1hr. to Central European Time).

money

GETTING MONEY FROM HOME

Stuff happens. When stuff happens, you might need some money. When you need some money, the easiest and cheapest solution is to have someone back home make a deposit to your bank account. Otherwise, consider one of the following options.

wiring money

Arranging a **bank money transfer** means asking a bank back home to wire money to a bank wherever you are. This is the cheapest way to transfer cash, but it's also the slowest and most agonizing, usually taking several days or more. Note that some banks may only release your funds in local currency, potentially sticking you with a poor exchange rate; inquire about this in advance.

Money transfer services like **Western Union** are faster and more convenient than bank transfers—but also much pricier. Western Union has many locations worldwide. To find one, visit www.westernunion.com or call the appropriate number: in Australia ☎1800 173 833, in Canada 800-235-0000, in the UK 0808 234 9168, in the US 800-325-6000, or in France 08 00 90 04 07. Money transfer services are also available to **American Express** cardholders and at selected **Thomas Cook** offices.

us state department (us citizens only)

In serious emergencies only, the US State Department will help your family or friends forward money within hours to the nearest consular office, which will then disburse it according to instructions for a US$30 fee. If you wish to use this service, you must contact the Overseas Citizens Services division of the US State Department. (☎+1-202-501-4444, from US 888-407-4747.)

the euro

Despite what many dollar-possessing Americans might want to hear, the official currency of 16 members of the European Union—Austria, Belgium, Cyprus, Finland, France, Germany, Greece, Ireland, Italy, Luxembourg, Malta, the Netherlands, Portugal, Slovakia, Slovenia, and Spain—is the euro.

Still, the currency has some important—and positive—consequences for travelers hitting more than one eurozone country. For one thing, money-changers across the eurozone are obliged to exchange money at the official, fixed rate and at no commission (though they may still charge a small service fee). Second, euro-denominated traveler's checks allow you to pay for goods and services across the eurozone, again at the official rate and commission-free. For more info, check a currency converter (such as www.xe.com) or www.europa.eu.int.

WITHDRAWING MONEY

ATMs are readily available in most major European destinations. To use a debit or credit card to withdraw money from a cash machine (ATM) in Europe, you must have a four-digit Personal Identification Number (PIN). If your PIN is longer than four digits, ask your bank whether you can just use the first four or whether you'll need a new one. Credit cards don't usually come with PINs, so if you intend to hit up ATMs in Europe with a credit card to get cash advances, call your credit card company before leaving to request one.

pins and atms

Travelers with alphabetic rather than numeric PINs may be thrown off by the absence of letters on European cash machines. Here are the corresponding numbers to use: 1 = QZ; 2 = ABC; 3 = DEF; 4 = GHI; 5 = JKL; 6 = MNO; 7 = PRS; 8 = TUV; 9 = WXY. Note that if you mistakenly punch the wrong code into the machine multiple (often three) times, it can swallow (gulp!) your card for good.

TIPPING

Europe is nowhere near homogenous when it comes to common tipping practices, but suffice it to say that no one tips quite as much as Americans. We sometimes include tipping customs in the **Essentials** section of each chapter. When in doubt, check the bill to make sure tip isn't included, and then see what those around you do. Then hope that those around you aren't overly generous or horribly stingy.

TAXES

Members of the EU have value added tax (VAT) of varying percentages. Non-EU citizens who are taking goods home may be refunded this tax for certain purchases. To claim a refund, fill out the form you are given at the shop and present it with the goods and receipts at customs upon departure.

getting around

If you've spent the last month trying to plot out the perfect combination of bus and train routes around Europe, *Let's Go* commends your organizational skills, but you wasted your time (also, you may want to get a life). In the current age of cheap flights, you can take any route you want between Europe's top 10 cities and still do the whole thing on the cheap. Feel like starting in Berlin, then going to Madrid, London, Rome, Prague, and finishing in Barcelona? You can, and it won't cost much. See the **Budget Airlines** box below for some of the companies that offer flights for the same price as the cover charge in Parisian clubs. If you prefer to stay on the land, or want to cut down on your carbon footprint, read on for information on ways to save on bus and train transportation.

BY TRAIN

Trains in Europe are generally comfortable, convenient, and reasonably swift. Second-class compartments are great places to meet fellow travelers. Make sure you are on the correct car, as trains sometimes split at crossroads. Towns listed in parentheses on European train schedules require a train switch at the town listed immediately before the parentheses. If you can, try to buy tickets online in advance of traveling, as prices for long-distance trips can rise close to the day of travel.

   If you plan to take a lot of trains, consider buying a **railpass,** which allows you unlimited travel within a particular region for a given period of time. Almost all countries give students or youths (under 26, usually) direct discounts on regular domestic rail tickets, and many also sell a student or youth card that provides 20-50% off all fares for up to a year.

rail resources

- **WWW.RAILEUROPE.COM:** Info on rail travel and railpasses.
- **POINT-TO-POINT FARES AND SCHEDULES:** www.raileurope.com/us/rail/fares_schedules/index.htm allows you to calculate whether buying a railpass would save you money.
- **WWW.RAILSAVER.COM:** Uses your itinerary to calculate the best railpass for your trip.
- **WWW.RAILFANEUROPE.NET:** Links to rail servers throughout Europe.

BY BUS

Though European trains and railpasses are extremely popular, in some cases buses prove a better option. Often cheaper than railpasses, **international bus passes** allow unlimited travel on a hop-on, hop-off basis between major European cities. **Busabout,** for instance, offers three interconnecting bus circuits covering 29 of Europe's best bus hubs, including all of this book's cities except London and Istanbul. (☎+44 845 026 7514; www.busabout.com $ 1 circuit in high season starts at US$559, students US$539.) **Eurolines,** meanwhile, is the largest operator of Europe-wide coach services. We get misty-eyed just thinking about their unlimited 15- and 30-day passes to 41 major European cities, which include all of our cities except Istanbul. (www.eurolines.com $ High season 15-day pass €345, 30-day pass €455; under 26 €290/375. Mid-season €240/330; under 26 €205/270. Low season €205/310; under 26 €175/240.)

budget airlines

The recent emergence of no-frills airlines has made hopscotching around Europe by air increasingly affordable. Flights (including taxes) can often be bought for as little as €30. The following resources are probably the best way to connect the dots of Europe's best cities.

- **BMIBABY:** To and from most major European cities, and a few less major ones. (www.bmibaby.com.)
- **EASYJET:** Who knew London had so many airports? EasyJet did. (www.easyjet.com.)
- **RYANAIR:** A budget traveler's dream, Ryanair goes most everywhere, with hubs in London, Rome, Paris, and Pisa. (www.ryanair.com.)
- **PEGASUS:** If you think getting to Istanbul is hard, you clearly haven't discovered Pegasus. (www.flypgs.com.)
- **TRANSAVIA:** If Amsterdam's weather gets you down, Transavia will take you to sunnier cities like Barcelona and Istanbul. (www.transavia.com.)
- **WIZZ AIR:** Short hops from Prague to wherever you want. (www.wizzair.com.)

safety and health

In any type of crisis, the most important thing to do is **stay calm.** Your country's embassy abroad is usually your best resource in an emergency; registering with that embassy upon arrival in the country is a good idea. The government offices listed in the **Travel Advisories** feature at the end of this section can provide information on the services they offer their citizens in case of emergencies abroad.

Whenever necessary, *Let's Go* lists specific concerns and local laws in the **Essentials** section of the relevant chapter. Basically, if you want to read about prostitution in Amsterdam, just flip back.

travel advisories

The following government offices provide travel information and advisories:

- **AUSTRALIA: Department of Foreign Affairs and Trade.** (☎+61 2 6261 1111; www.smartraveller.gov.au.)

- **CANADA: Department of Foreign Affairs and International Trade.** Call or visit the website for the free booklet *Bon Voyage, But...* (☎+1-800-267-6788; www.international.gc.ca.)

- **NEW ZEALAND: Ministry of Foreign Affairs and Trade.** (☎+64 4 439 8000; www.safetravel.govt.nz.)

- **UK: Foreign and Commonwealth Office.** (☎+44 845 850 2829; www.fco.gov.uk.)

- **US: Department of State.** (☎888-407-4747 from the US, +1-202-501-4444 elsewhere; http://travel.state.gov.)

PRE-DEPARTURE HEALTH

Matching a prescription to a foreign equivalent is not always easy, safe, or possible, so if you take **prescription drugs,** carry up-to-date prescriptions or a statement from your doctor stating the medications' trade names, manufacturers, chemical names, and dosages. Be sure to keep all medication with you in your carry-on luggage.

immunizations and precautions

Travelers over two years old should make sure that the following vaccines are up to date: MMR (for measles, mumps, and rubella); DTaP or Td (for diphtheria, tetanus, and pertussis); IPV (for polio); Hib (for *Haemophilus influenzae* B); and HepB (for Hepatitis B). For recommendations on immunizations and prophylaxis, check with a doctor and consult the **Centers for Disease Control and Prevention (CDC)** in the US (☎+1-800-232-4636; www.cdc.gov/travel) or the equivalent in your home country.

keeping in touch

BY EMAIL AND INTERNET

Hello and welcome to the 21st century, where you're rarely more than a 5min. walk from the nearest Wi-Fi hot spot, even if sometimes you'll have to pay a few bucks or buy a drink for the privilege of using it. **Internet cafes** and the occasional free internet terminal at a public library or university are listed in the **Practicalities** section of each city.

Wireless hot spots make internet access possible in public and remote places. Unfortunately, they also pose security risks. Hot spots are public, open networks that use unencrypted, unsecured connections. They are susceptible to hacks and "packet sniffing"—the theft of passwords and other private information. To prevent problems, disable "ad hoc" mode, turn off file sharing and network discovery, encrypt your email, turn on your firewall, beware of phony networks, and watch for over-the-shoulder creeps.

BY TELEPHONE

If you have internet access, your best—i.e., cheapest, most convenient, and most tech-savvy—means of calling home is probably our good friend ⌨**Skype** (www.skype. com). You can even videochat if you have one of those new-fangled webcams. Calls to other Skype users are free; calls to landlines and mobiles worldwide start at US$0.023 per minute, depending on where you're calling.

For those still stuck in the 20th century, **prepaid phone cards** are a common and relatively inexpensive means of calling abroad. Each one comes with a Personal Identification Number (PIN) and a toll-free access number. You call the access number and then follow the directions for dialing your PIN. To purchase prepaid phone cards, check online for the best rates; www.callingcards.com is a good place to start. Online providers generally send your access number and PIN via email, with no actual "card" involved. You can also call home with prepaid phone cards purchased abroad.

Another option is a **calling card,** linked to a major national telecommunications service in your home country. Calls are billed collect or to your account. Cards generally come with instructions for dialing both domestically and internationally.

Placing a collect call through an international operator can be expensive but may be necessary in case of an emergency. You can frequently call collect without even possessing a company's calling card just by calling its access number and following the instructions.

international calls

To call Europe from home or to call home from Europe, dial:

- **1. THE INTERNATIONAL DIALING PREFIX.** To call from Australia, dial ☎0011; Canada or the US, ☎011; Ireland, New Zealand, the UK, and most of Europe, ☎00.

- **2. THE COUNTRY CODE OF THE COUNTRY YOU WANT TO CALL.** To call Australia, dial ☎61; Canada, ☎1; Czech Republic, ☎420; France, ☎33; Germany, ☎49; Italy, ☎39; the Netherlands, ☎31; New Zealand, ☎64; Spain, ☎34; Turkey, ☎90; the UK, ☎44; the US, ☎1.

- **3. THE LOCAL NUMBER.** If the area code begins with a zero, you can omit that number when dialing from abroad.

cellular phones

The international standard for cell phones is **Global System for Mobile Communication (GSM).** To make and receive calls in Europe, you will need a GSM-compatible phone and a **SIM (Subscriber Identity Module) card,** a country-specific, thumbnail-size chip that gives you a local phone number and plugs you into the local network. Many SIM cards are prepaid, and incoming calls are frequently free. You can buy additional cards or vouchers (usually available at convenience stores) to "top up" your phone. For more information on GSM phones, check out www.telestial.com. Companies like **Cellular Abroad** (www.cellularabroad.com) and **OneSimCard** (www.onesimcard.com) rent cell phones and SIM cards that work in a variety of destinations around the world.

BY SNAIL MAIL

sending mail home from europe

Airmail is the best way to send mail home from Europe. Write "airmail," *"par avion,"* or the equivalent in the local language on the front. For simple letters or postcards, airmail tends to be surprisingly cheap, but the price will go up sharply for weighty packages. **Surface mail** is by far the cheapest, slowest, and most antiquated way to send mail. It takes one to two months to cross the Atlantic and one to three to cross the Pacific—good for heavy items you won't need for a while, like souvenirs that you've acquired along the way.

receiving mail in europe

There are several ways to arrange pickup of letters sent to you while you are abroad, even if you do not have an address of your own. Mail can be sent via **Poste Restante** (General Delivery). Address Poste Restante letters like so:

> Napoleon BONAPARTE
> Poste Restante
> City, Country

The mail will go to a special desk in the city's central post office, unless you specify a local post office by street address or postal code. It's best to use the largest post office, since mail may be sent there regardless. Bring your passport (or other photo ID) for pickup; there may be a small fee. If the clerks insist that there is nothing for you, ask them to check under your first name as well. *Let's Go* lists post offices in the **Practicalities** section for each city. It is usually safer and quicker, though more expensive, to send mail express or registered. If you don't want to deal with Poste Restante, consider asking your hostel or accommodation if you can have things mailed to you there. Of course, if you have your own mailing address or a reliable friend to receive mail for you, that will be the easiest solution.

climate

Europe is for lovers, historians, architects, beach bums, and... weather nerds? In fact, the smallest continent has quite the diverse climate. Northern European cities like London, Amsterdam, Paris, Berlin, and Prague are often overcast, with cold winters and the chance of rain throughout the year. Summers can be warm but might well not be, while snow is possible but unusual in the winter. Southern European cities close to the Mediterranean are much warmer. Inland cities like Madrid, Rome, and Florence get particularly scorching and dry in the summer, but are still strongly seasonal. Barcelona is more pleasant thanks to being situated on the coast. Istanbul's climate is mostly Mediterranean, but with higher rainfall.

AVG. TEMP. (LOW/ HIGH), PRECIP.	JANUARY			APRIL			JULY			OCTOBER		
	°C	°F	mm	°C	°F	mm	°C	°F	mm	°C	°F	mm
Amsterdam	-1/4	30/39	68	4/13	39/55	49	13/22	55/72	77	7/14	45/57	72
Barcelona	6/13	43/55	31	11/18	52/64	43	21/28	70/82	27	15/21	59/70	86
Berlin	-3/2	27/36	46	4/13	39/55	42	14/24	57/75	73	6/13	43/55	49
Istanbul	3/8	37/46	109	7/16	45/61	46	18/28	64/82	34	13/20	55/68	81
Florence	1/10	34/50	74	7/18	45/65	79	17/31	63/88	41	10/21	50/70	89
London	2/6	36/43	54	6/13	43/55	37	14/22	57/72	57	8/14	46/57	57
Madrid	2/9	36/48	39	7/18	45/64	48	17/31	63/88	11	10/19	50/66	53
Paris	1/6	34/43	56	6/16	43/61	42	15/25	59/77	59	8/16	46/61	50
Prague	-5/0	23/32	18	3/12	37/54	27	13/23	55/73	68	5/12	41/54	33
Rome	5/11	41/52	71	10/19	50/66	51	20/30	68/86	15	13/22	55/72	99

climate

To convert from degrees Fahrenheit to degrees Celsius, subtract 32 and multiply by 5/9. To convert from Celsius to Fahrenheit, multiply by 9/5 and add 32. The mathematically challenged may use this handy chart:

°CELSIUS	-5	0	5	10	15	20	25	30	35	40
°FAHRENHEIT	23	32	41	50	59	68	77	86	95	104

measurements

Like the rest of the rational world, Europe uses the metric system. The basic unit of length is the meter (m), which is divided into 100 centimeters (cm) or 1000 millimeters (mm). One thousand meters make up one kilometer (km). Fluids are measured in liters (L), each divided into 1000 milliliters (mL). A liter of pure water weighs one kilogram (kg), the unit of mass that is divided into 1000 grams (g). One metric ton is 1000kg. Gallons in the US and those in Britain are not identical: one US gallon equals 0.83 Imperial gallons. Pub aficionados will note that an Imperial pint (20 oz.) is larger than its US counterpart (16 oz.).

MEASUREMENT CONVERSIONS	
1 inch (in.) = 25.4mm	1 millimeter (mm) = 0.039 in.
1 foot (ft.) = 0.305m	1 meter (m) = 3.28 ft.
1 yard (yd.) = 0.914m	1 meter (m) = 1.094 yd.
1 mile (mi.) = 1.609km	1 kilometer (km) = 0.621 mi.
1 ounce (oz.) = 28.35g	1 gram (g) = 0.035 oz.
1 pound (lb.) = 0.454kg	1 kilogram (kg) = 2.205 lb.
1 fluid ounce (fl. oz.) = 29.57mL	1 milliliter (mL) = 0.034 fl. oz.
1 gallon (gal.) = 3.785L	1 liter (L) = 0.264 gal.

essentials

phrasebook

ENGLISH	CZECH	DUTCH	FRENCH	GERMAN	ITALIAN	SPANISH	TURKISH
Hello	Dobrý den	Dag/Hallo	Bonjour	Hallo/Tag	Buongiorno	Hola	Merhaba
Goodbye	Nashle-danou	Tot ziens	Au revoir	Auf Wie-dersehen/Tschüss	Arrivederci	Adiós	İyi günler/İyi akşamlar
Yes	Ano	Ja	Oui	Ja	Sì	Si	Evet
No	Ne	Nee	Non	Nein	No	No	Hayır
Please	Prosím	Alstublieft	S'il vous plaît	Bitte	Per favore	Por favor	Lütfen
Thank you	Děkuji	Dank u wel	Merci	Danke	Grazie	Gracias	Teşekkur ederim
You're welcome	Prosím	Alstublieft	De rien	Bitte	Prego	De nada	Bir şey değil
Sorry!	Promiňte!	Sorry!	Désolé!	Es tut mir leid!	Mi scusi!	¡Perdón!	Pardon!
My name is...	Mé jméno je...	Mijn naam is...	Je m'appelle...	Ich bin...	Mi chiamo...	Me llamo...	Ismim...
How are you?	Jak se máš?	Hoe gaat het?	Comment êtes-vous?	Wie geht's (geht es Ihnen)?	Come sta?	¿Cómo estás?	Sen nasılsın?
I don't know.	Nevím.	Ik weet het niet/Geen idee.	Je ne sais pas.	Ich weisse nicht/Keine Ahnung.	Non lo so.	No sé.	Bilmiyorum.
I don't understand.	Nerozumím.	Ik begrijp het niet.	Je ne comprends pas.	Ich verstehe nicht.	Non capisco.	No entiendo.	Anlamadım.
Could you repeat that?	Můžete opakovat, že?	Kunt u dat herhalen?	Répétez, s'il vous plaît?	Können Sie wiederholen?	Potrebbe ripetere?	¿Puede repetirlo?	Lütfen o tekrarla?
Do you speak English?	Mluví anglicky?	Spreekt u Engels?	Parlez-vous anglais?	Sprechen Sie Englisch?	Parla inglese?	¿Hablas español?	İngilizce biliyor musun?
I don't speak ___.	Nemluvím Česky.	Ik spreek geen Nederlands.	Je ne parle pas français.	Ich kann kein Deutsch.	Non parlo italiano.	No hablo español.	Turkçe okuyorum.
Why?	Proč?	Waarom?	Pourquoi?	Warum?	Perché?	¿Por qué?	Neden?
Where is...?	Kde je...?	Waar is...?	Où est...?	Wo ist...?	Dov'è...?	¿Dónde esta...?	...nerede?
What time is it?	Kolik je hodin?	Hoe laat is het?	Quelle heure est-il?	Wie spät ist es?	Che ore sono?	Qué hora es?	Saat kaç?
How much does this cost?	Kolik to stojí?	Wat kost het?	Combien ça coûte?	Wie viel (kostet das)?	Quanto costa?	¿Cuánto cuesta esto?	Ne kadar bu bedeli do?
I am from the US.	Já jsem ze Spojených států.	Ik ben uit de VS.	Je suis des Etats-Unis.	Ich bin von Amerika.	Sono degli Stati Uniti.	Soy de los Estados Unidos.	Ben ABD geliyorum.
I have a visa/ID.	Mám víza/ID.	Ik heb een visum/ID.	J'ai un visa/carte d'identi-fication	Ich habe ein Visum/eine ID.	Ho un visto/carta d'identità.	Tengo una visa/identi-ficación.	Benim bir vizem/ID var.
I have nothing to declare.	Nemám nic k proclení.	Ik heb niets aan te geven.	Je n'ai rien à déclarer.	Ich habe nichts zu verzollen.	Non ho nulla da dichiarare.	No tengo nada para declarar.	Duyurmak için benim hiçbirşeyim yok.
I will be here for less than three months.	I tady bude za méně než tři měsíce.	Ik blijf hier minder dan drie maanden.	Je serai ici pour moins de trois mois.	Ich reste hier für weniger als drei Monate.	Sarò qui per meno di tré mesi.	Estaré aquí por menos de tres meses.	Ben üçten az ay için burada olacagım.

phrasebook

ENGLISH	CZECH	DUTCH	FRENCH	GERMAN	ITALIAN	SPANISH	TURKISH
One-way	Jedním směrem	Enkele reis	Aller simple	Einfache	Solo andata	Ida	Tek yön
Round-trip	Zpáteční	Rondreis	Aller-retour	Hin und zurück	Andata e ritorno	Ida y vuelta	Gidiş dönüş
Hotel/ hostel	Hotel/ubytovna	Hotel/hostel	Hôtel/auberge	Hotel/Herberge	Albergo/ ostello	Hotel/hostal	Otel/pansiyon
I have a reservation.	Mám rezervaci.	Ik heb een reservering.	J'ai une réservation.	Ich habe eine Reservierung.	Ho una prenotazione.	Tengo una reservación.	Benim bir koşulum var.
Single/ double room	Jedno-lůžkový/ dvoulůžkový pokoj	Eenpersoonskamer / Tweepersoonskamer	Chambre pour un/ deux	Einzelzimmer/ Doppelzimmer	Camera singola/ doppia	Habitación simple/ doble	Tek/çift kişilik
I'd like...	Prosím...	Ik wil graag...	Je voudrais...	Ich möchte...	Vorrei...	Me gustaría...	Ben bir... sevecegim.
Check, please!	Paragon, prosím!	Mag ik de rekening!	L'addition, s'il vous plaît!	Die Rechnung, bitte!	Il conto, per favore!	¡La cuenta, por favor!	Hesap, lütfen!
I feel sick.	Je mi špatně.	Ik ben ziek.	Je me sens malade.	Ich bin krank.	Mi sento male.	Me siento mal.	Ben hastayım.
Get a doctor!	Najít lékaře!	Haal een dokter!	Va chercher un médecin!	Hol einen Arzt!	Telefoni un dottore!	¡Llama el médico!	Doktor ihtiyacim!
Hospital	Nemocnice	Ziekenhuis	Hôpital	Krankenhaus	Ospedale	Hospital	Hastane
I lost my passport/ luggage.	Ztratil jsem pas/ zavazadla.	Ik heb mijn paspoort/ bagage verloren.	J'ai perdu mon passeport/ baggage.	Ich habe mein Reisepass/ Gepäck verloren.	Ho perso il mio passaportol/miei bagagli.	Se perdió mi pasaporte/ equipaje.	Ben benim pasaportumu/ bagajımı kaybettim.
Help!	Pomoc!	Help!	Au secours!	Hilfe!	Aiuto!	¡Socorro!	Imdat!
Leave me alone!	Nech mě být!	Laat me met rust!	Laissez-moi tranquille!	Verloren gehen!	Lasciami stare!/Mollami!	¡Déjame!	Beni yalnız bırak!
Go away!	Prosím odejděte!	Ga weg!	Allez-vous en!	Geh weg!	Vattene!	¡Vete!	Git başımdan!
Call the police!	Zavolejte policii!	Bel de politie!	Appelez les flics!	Ruf die Polizei!	Telefoni alla polizia!	¡Llama la policia!	Polis çağırın!

let's go online

Plan your next trip on our spiffy website, **www.letsgo.com.** It features full book content, the latest travel info on your favorite destinations, and tons of interactive features: make your own itinerary, read blogs from our trusty Researcher-Writers, browse our photo library, watch exclusive videos, check out our newsletter, find travel deals, follow us on Facebook, and buy new guides. Plus, if this Essentials wasn't enough for you, we've got even more online. We're always updating and adding new features, so check back often!

essentials

BEYOND TOURISM

If you are reading this, then you are a member of an elite group—and we don't mean "the literate." You're a student preparing for a semester abroad. You're taking a gap year to save the trees, the whales, or the dates. You're an 80-year-old woman who has devoted her life to egg-laying platypuses and figuring out what the hell is up with that. In short, you're a traveler, not a tourist; like any good spy, you don't observe your surroundings—you become an active part of them.

Your mission, should you choose to accept it, is to study, volunteer, or work in Europe as laid out in the dossier—er, chapter—below. More general wisdom, including international organizations with a presence in many destinations and tips on how to pick the right program, is also accessible by logging onto the Beyond Tourism section of www.letsgo.com. We leave the rest (when to go, whom to bring, and how many changes of underwear to pack) in your hands. This message will **self-destruct** in five seconds. Good luck.

greatest hits

- **LET'S STUDY.** We're the student travel guide, so of course we're going to love **study abroad.** This chapter lists organizations that will help you pick a study-abroad program as well as Europe's best universities (p. 844).

- **LET'S STUDY, OUTSIDE THE BOX.** If you want to be the next Antonio Gaudí, you can enroll in **architecture classes** in Barcelona (p. 848). If you want to be the next winner of *Top Chef,* you can sharpen your skills at the **Cordon Bleu** in Paris (p. 847).

- **LET'S VOLUNTEER. Help** clean up London's environment or do some good for the community in Prague (p. 848).

- **LET'S WORK.** If you're going to pad your resume, why not do it in Paris? The **jobs** we list can also help you defray the cost of your travels (p. 850).

studying

As you've doubtlessly already discovered from Googling "study abroad," becoming overwhelmed, questioning whether you want to go in the first place, and then calling your mom (yeah, we've been there), there are a ton of different study-abroad options out there. Don't worry! We're here to help.

First, ask yourself what you want to get out of a study-abroad program. Are you looking for a basic language and culture course that will let you spend as much time as possible engaging with local, um, language and culture? Or are you seeking university-level classes to count for college credit? Second, search study-abroad-specific websites like **www.studyabroad.com, www.goabroad.com,** and **www.westudyabroad.com** for programs that meet your criteria. You can usually search by type of program, desired location, and focus of study. Once you've settled on a few favorites, research them as much as you can before making your decision—determine things like cost, duration, kinds of students in the program, and accommodations provided.

visa information

If you're lucky enough to have an EU passport, stop reading and count your blessings. Non-EU citizens hoping to study abroad in the EU, on the other hand, must obtain a special student visa. The acquisition process can be complicated and requires more pieces of identification than you knew existed, but often if you study abroad with a program rather than enrolling directly, the program will help you with this process. For every country, the best and most up-to-date information can be obtained from your local consulate. Visa applications often have fees attached to them that can range from $30 to $300.

UNIVERSITIES

Say you're a college student who wants to spend a semester abroad in the Netherlands at Heerhugowaard State. In addition to researching on your own as described above, your friendly neighborhood study-abroad office is an excellent place to get your bearings. Make sure that you're proficient in Dutch first, though: most university-level study-abroad programs are conducted in the local language (although many programs offer classes in English and lower-level language courses, too). Especially skilled speakers of Dutch (or whatever; you get the point) may find it cheaper to enroll directly in a university abroad, although getting college credit may be harder.

international programs

AHA INTERNATIONAL

70 NW Couch St., Ste. 242, Portland, OR 97209, USA ☎+1-800-654-2051; www.ahastudyabroad.org

An affiliate of the University of Oregon, the ironically named American Heritage Foundation will set you up to study abroad in major study-abroad destinations like London and Berlin.

$ *Tuition $3730-14,300, depending on the destination and which term you take abroad.*

AMERICAN FIELD SERVICE

71 W. 23rd St., 6th fl., New York City, NY 10010, USA ☎+1-212-807-8686; www.afs.org

Overseeing a network of volunteer organizations in over 50 countries, AFS runs high school exchange programs that send students all over Europe to live with host families and attend local schools full-time. Contact the office in your home country for more details.

i Prices and availability vary over time; consult the website for up-to-date information. Scholarships available. 🕮 *"School Programs" last for a trimester, semester, or year. Intensive and summer programs last 1-3 months.*

AMERICAN INSTITUTE FOR FOREIGN STUDY (AIFS)

River Plaza, 9 W. Broad St., Stamford, CT 06902, USA   ☎+1-866-906-2437; www.aifs.com

With programs in 17 different countries and over 50,000 participants each year, AIFS is one of the oldest and largest cultural exchange organizations out there. Better yet, it's open to both high school and college students. Destinations in Europe cover almost anywhere you'd possibly want to go: London, Berlin, Florence, Rome, Prague, and Paris, to name a few.

i Scholarships available. 💲 *Semester $13,495-16,495; summer $4995-10,995. Prices depend on location and length.*

COUNCIL ON INTERNATIONAL EDUCATIONAL EXCHANGE (CIEE)

300 Fore St., Portland, ME 04101, USA   ☎+1-800-407-8839; www.ciee.org

CIEE not only organizes study-abroad programs for US high school and college students, but they also offer internships and teaching opportunities. They can whisk you away to places like Amsterdam, London, Paris, and Prague.

i Junior status recommended. Scholarships available. 💲 *Academic year $30,400; semester $16,000; summer $3150.*

CULTURAL EXPERIENCES ABROAD (CEA)

2005 W. 14th St., Ste. 113, Tempe, AZ 85281, USA   ☎+1-800-266-4441; www.gowithcea.com

CEA offers summer, semester, or full-year programs in several major European cities. Learn the native language (who knows, Czech could prove to be quite useful) or intern in London while gaining cultural knowledge through planned excursions and guest lectures.

💲 *Semester $10,995-16,595; 3-week summer program $4295.*

EXPERIMENTAL LEARNING INTERNATIONAL (ELI)

1557 Ogden St., Denver, CO 80218, USA   ☎+1-303-321-8278; www.eliabroad.org

A smaller study-abroad organization, ELI combines study programs with internships and other international goodies at campuses in Paris, Florence, and elsewhere.

💲 *Semester $12,595-13,595; summer $1265-5335.*

INSTITUTE FOR THE INTERNATIONAL EDUCATION OF STUDENTS (IES)

33 N. LaSalle St., 15th fl., Chicago, IL 60602, USA   ☎+1-800-995-2300; www.iesabroad.org

A semester in London? A summer in Barcelona? IES has opportunities for enrollment in courses at local universities, language schools, "field study activities" (read: field trips), and term-time and summer internships. They can also help arrange homestays or apartment housing so you won't be homeless while experiencing all of these things.

💲 *Semester $13,885-21,320; summer $6500-7340.*

local programs

The following are just a few of literally thousands of local institutions of higher learning in Europe—culled from some of the continent's hottest study-abroad destinations. For more detail, check out *Let's Go* guides to specific countries.

CEA GLOBAL EDUCATION

2005 W. 14th St., Ste. 113, Tempe, AZ 85281, USA   ☎+1-800-266-4441; www.gowithcea.com

CEA offers small, interactive classes in a wide range of subjects, from the liberal arts and social sciences to international and cultural studies. Students have the option to study at the global campus in Madrid for a summer, semester, or year.

studying

EUROPEAN UNIVERSITY

Ganduxer 70, Barcelona, Spain ☎+34 93 201 81 7; www.euruni.edu

One of the world's top business schools has locations in various European cities, including Barcelona and London The European University offers Bachelors, Masters, and Doctoral of Business Administration degrees. The information for the Barcelona location is listed here.

$ Semester around $7000.

UNIVERSITY OF AMSTERDAM (UVA)

Binnengasthuisstraat 9, Amsterdam, the Netherlands ☎20-525-3333; www.english.uva.nl

Founded in 1632, UvA is the largest university in the Netherlands. Exchange students get a dedicated program with English courses in economics, business, science, law, and everything in between. Don't expect an authentic local academic experience: your classmate might be a clueless foreigner just like you. However, if you are already fluent in Dutch, you may enroll directly in regular courses. If your university lacks an exchange program, you can still pick up a Dutch education through UvA's certificate programs.

i Off-campus housing, varies by faculty. Shorter summer and winter programs are also offered.

$ Exchange students pay tuition to their home university. Certificate programs €2000-4000.

UNIVERSITY COLLEGE LONDON (UCL)

32 Russell Sq., London, UK ☎+44 20 7679 2000; www.ucl.ac.uk

One of the world's top universities, UCL is located in the heart of Central London, adjacent to the British Museum. Students choose four courses per semester out of a pool of tutorials, lectures, and even one-on-one classes. The university helps students find housing in either intercollegiate halls or private apartments.

BOĞAZIÇI UNIVERSITY

OFB Building, Bebek, Istanbul, Turkey ☎+90 212 359 7421; www.intl.boun.edu.tr

Founded in 1863 by two American educators, Boğaziçi is the oldest American university to open outside of the United States. The university is regarded as the best and most popular in Turkey, and has expanded to six campuses across the country. Boğaziçi is famous for its social science, engineering, and applied science programs. Depending on how much studying you actually plan on doing, you might also visit the Van Milligen Library, the first "modern" library in Turkey.

i Contact the Office of International Relations for tuition costs.

JOHN CABOT UNIVERSITY IN ROME

V. della Lungara 233, Rome, Italy ☎+39 6 68 19 121; www.johncabot.edu

According to John Cabot University, whether you're visiting Etruscan ruins, the Colosseum, the Catacombs, or the Vatican, Rome is your "living laboratory." Of course you're more likely to spend your time learning about classics, art, and modern languages than becoming the next Dr. Frankenstein.

i Students live in off-campus residential housing. $ Full year $39,500; includes room, board, books, supplies, personal expenses, and travel.

LANGUAGE SCHOOLS

As renowned novelist Gustave Flaubert once said, "Language is a cracked kettle on which we beat out tunes for bears to dance to." While we at Let's Go have absolutely no clue what he is talking about, we do know that the following are good resources for learning any European language.

A2Z LANGUAGES

3219 E. Camelback Rd #806, Phoenix, AZ 85018 USA ☎+1-888-417-1533; www.a2zlanguages.com

French, German, Italian, Spanish, or German, could all be your newest language acquisition with A2Z's numerous programs, which vary from one location to the

other. All sites service everyone from the complete beginner to the near-master.
$ *$890-5930, depending on program length, number of classes per week, choice of accommodations, and time of year.*

AMERISPAN STUDY ABROAD

1334 Walnut St., 6th fl., Philadelphia, PA 19107 USA ☎+1-800-879-6640; www.amerispan.com

Amerispan started out as Spanish specialists, before they realized they enjoyed offering advice on finding language schools so much that they expanded to many other languages. They now provide helpful information on finding schools in France, Germany, Italy, and Spain.

$ *$320-10,000, depending on program location, length, and choice of accommodations.*

EUROCENTRES

Seestr. 247, Zürich, Switzerland ☎+41 44 485 50 40; www.eurocentres.com

No matter how advanced a speaker you are, Eurocentres has classes in the native language in France, Spain, Germany, and Italy. The schools all provide recreation rooms and free internet access and organize a variety of outings and social activities.

i *16+.*

TOMER TURKISH AND FOREIGN LANGUAGE RESEARCH/APPLICATION CENTRE

Katip Çelebi Mah. Tel Sok. No: 47, Istanbul, Turkey ☎0212 249 1648; www.tomer.ankara.edu.tr

Begun at Ankara University, Tomer has now expanded to nine locations throughout Turkey, including a school in the Taksim neighborhood of Istanbul. Tomer offers instruction in 20 languages, as well as several specialized courses in Turkish for students looking to improve their public speaking, pronunciation, speed reading, and body language.

$ *Prices vary by program.*

SPECIAL-INTEREST SCHOOLS

"But, wait!" we hear you cry, "What if I don't want to study the history and culture of Lisbon? What if I couldn't care less about fulfilling my home school's requirements?" If your tastes are more specific than what a typical university can offer, here's some information on just a handful of alternative schools in Europe.

APICIUS INTERNATIONAL SCHOOL OF HOSPITALITY

Corso Tintori 21, Florence, Italy ☎+39 055 265 81 35; www.apicius.it

At Apicius's campus in Florence, aspiring chefs, sommeliers, bakers, or extreme foodies can study their hearts out, with one-, two-, and four-year professional programs. Amateurs can also indulge in less intense instruction that may include gastronomic walking tours or visits to local farms and markets.

CORDON BLEU PARIS CULINARY ARTS INSTITUTE

8 rue Léon Delhomme, Paris, France ☎+33 1 53 68 22 50; www.cordonbleu.edu

There's no more prestigious training academy for the serious aspiring chef than the original Paris branch of the Cordon Bleu. More tourist-friendly options include two- to four-hour workshops and week-long courses. One-day taste of Provence workshop: €175. Bragging rights: priceless.

$ *1-day cooking class €175.* **i** *Certificate and degree programs available.*

COURTAULD INSTITUTE OF ART

Somerset House, Strand, London, UK ☎+44 20 7872 0220; www.courtald.ac.uk

Based out of central London's Somerset House, the Courtauld Institute of Art is known for both its remarkable painting collection and its challenging art history courses. The Institute is affiliated with the University of London, so some students take classes there as well.

i *Min. 3.5 GPA.*

INSTITUTE FOR ADVANCED ARCHITECTURE OF CATALONIA (IAAC)

Pujades 102 baixos, Barcelona, Spain ☎+93 320 95 20; www.iaac.net

The IAAC combines cutting-edge science with style. Case in point: the "Fab Lab Solar House" (www.fablabhouse.com), a quirky and completely solar-powered home. Look for another creation in the 2012 Solar Decathalon. While the IAAC only admits top-notch architects for Masters degrees, it's worth *echando un vistazo* at their website for current project exhibitions.

$ Annual tuition €14,250; Masters in Advanced Architecture program €28,500.

L'ÉCOLE DU LOUVRE

pl. du Carrousel, Porte Jaujard, Paris, France ☎+33 1 55 35 18 35; www.ecoledulouvre.fr

Installed in the Louvre in 1882, the École du Louvre, dedicated to "making the Louvre into a living center of study," teaches undergraduate, graduate, and post-graduate classes in art history and museum studies as well as an art auctioneer training program. Looking for less of a time commitment? Every Monday, Tuesday, and Thursday evenings, the École organizes free lectures by academics, curators, and other museum professionals.

$ Undergraduate tuition €350. ⏰ Academic year Sept-April. Year 1 candidates must take an entrance exam held in Mar-Apr. Year 2 and 3 candidates must apply before April 15.

ROME UNIVERSITY OF FINE ARTS

V. Benaco 2, Rome, Italy ☎+39 6 85 86 59 17; www.unirufa.it

Are you the next Leonardo? If you answered yes, you should come to RU to refine those skills, big shot. If you sense the potential within you, let RU pump it out of you with its myriad courses on engraving, painting, graphic design, sculpture, and artistic anatomy. The shy beware—"anatomy" art classes in Rome means naked dudes. IES Abroad (☎+1-800-995-2300; www.iesabroad.com) offers semester and full-year programs here.

ℹ Apartment or homestay housing available. $ Full year $34,780; semester $18,670.

volunteering

Got an itch to save the world? We at Let's Go get all types of itches, so we can commiserate. Most people who volunteer abroad do so on a short-term basis at organizations that make use of drop-in or once-a-week volunteers. Local or national volunteer centers are where you want to go for this: they'll marry your ideal interests to your ideal schedule to send you on a honeymoon to your ideal destination. Websites like **www.volunteerabroad.com, www.servenet.org, www.worldvolunteerweb.org,** and **www.idealist.org** also allow you to search for volunteer openings abroad. Just make sure you do your own research, too—a six-week trip to the Galapagos to spot wild boobies may not be what you think it is.

Those looking for longer, more intensive volunteer opportunities usually choose to go through a parent organization that takes care of logistical details and often provides a group environment and support system—for a fee. There are two main types of organizations—religious and secular—although heathens are usually allowed to work for the former, and vice versa. Pay-to-volunteer programs might be a good idea for young travelers who are looking for more support and structure (such as pre-arranged transportation and housing) or anyone who would rather not deal with the uncertainty of creating a volunteer experience from scratch.

AMICS DE LA UNESCO DE BARCELONA

C. Mallorca, 207 Pral, Barcelona, Spain ☎93 452 05 52; www.caub.org

UNESCO is designed to advance the goals of the UN. You're sure to fit in with a motley crew of internationals. A previous project invited *fútbol* fans to write

messages against racism at FC Barcelona's home Camp Nou Stadium.
🕐 *Open M-Th 5-8:30pm.*

AMNESTY INTERNATIONAL
1 Easton St., London, UK   ☎+44 20 7413 5500; www.amnesty.org

Amnesty International is one of the world's most renowned human rights organizations. Contact the office in the country you want to volunteer in for info about paid positions and volunteer work. Internships are available, too.

CARITAS
Ambassadors, 162, Madrid, Spain   ☎91 444 10 00; www.caritas.org

Volunteer with this nonprofit organization whose mission is to eradicate poverty through rehabilitation, advocacy, and social support.

FONDAZIONE FLAMINIA DA FILICAJA
V. Poggio all'Aglione 23, Montaione, Italy   ☎328 62 29 264; www.horseprotection.it

Located 1hr. outside Florence, the Italian Horse Protection Association works to rehabilitate horses that have been abused by their owners. Short- and long-term volunteers help run the daily care of these recovering animals. Sixty horses with adorable names like "Rocket" and "Letizia" need your help!

🍴 *Located in Montaione, 1hr. by car southwest of Florence; accessible by train to Siena and bus to Montaione.*

GEOVISIONS
63 Whitfield St., Guilford, CT 06437, USA   ☎+1-877-949-9998; www.geovisions.org

The fine folks at Geovisions let you volunteer in France, Germany, Italy, and Spain. An example of one program is a homestay in Munich with a German family to whom you teach English for 15hr. per week.

HABITAT FOR HUMANITY
121 Habitat St., Americus, GA 31209, USA   ☎+1-800-422-4828; www.habitat.org

The grandaddy of all volunteer programs, Habitat for Humanity keeps its international acclaim and name-brand appeal with destinations around the world. Volunteers build houses in over 83 countries, including Britain, the Netherlands, Germany, and France.

🕐 *Periods of involvement range from 2 weeks to 3 years.*

INEX
Varšavská 30, 120 00 Prague, Czech Republic   ☎222 362 715; www.inexsda.cz

At these workcamps (somewhere between summer camp and an actual job), volunteers clean up national forests, help out in local community centers, and document Czech historical sights. After-hours activities like campfires and group sing-alongs will fulfill all of your sleepaway camp fantasies.

i *Sessions last 2-3 weeks depending on project. Accommodations provided and include cabins with kitchen access to cook meals. Friendship bracelets optional.*

İNSAN HAK VE HÜRRIYETLERI İNSANI YARDIM VAKFI
Büyük Karaman Cad. Taylasan Sok. No: 3 Pk., Istanbul, Turkey   ☎0212 631 2121; www.ihh.org

The IHH Humanitarian Relief Foundation is an international organization that aims to preserve the natural human rights of all people. Areas of volunteer work include medicine, social services, public relations, and education. Volunteers may choose to participate in one or more fields during their time in Istanbul.

i *Fill out an application form on the IHH website for program description, cost, and duration.*

GO LONDON
237 Pentonville Rd., London, UK   ☎020 7643 1373; www.csv.org.uk

GO London is an environmental volunteer organization that requires little commitment for those just looking to volunteer for a couple of days while staying in the city. Typical volunteers work on city farms, clean up rubbish, and plant

volunteering

gardens. If you're looking for more of a long-term commitment, you can become a GO event leader. The organization will train and then assign you a volunteer group and a project to work on.

i No experience required. Ages 16+.

OXFAM INTERNATIONAL

226 Causeway St., 5th fl., Boston, MA 02114, USA ☎+1-800-77-OXFAM; www.oxfam.org

Oxfam is dedicated to reducing poverty and injustice around the world, focusing in particular on basic human rights, income inequality, and arms reduction. Oxfam has offices in Britain, France, Germany, the Netherlands, and Spain.

PINK POINT

Corner of Raadhuistraat and Keizersgracht, Amsterdam, NL ☎020 428 10 70; www.pinkpoint.org

Pink Point began as an ice-cream cart converted to serve as an informational kiosk at the 1998 Gay Games. Now it welcomes tourists from its central location by the Anne Frank House, next to the busy Rosengracht, and provides information to help gay travelers get the most out of Amsterdam.

SERVICE CIVIL INTERNATIONAL

5474 Walnut Level Rd., Crozet, VA 22932, USA ☎+1-434-336-3545; www.sci-ivs.org

Legal residents of Canada and the US are assigned to workcamps in countries like Germany and Spain with tasks ranging from teaching English to farming.

i 18+. ⏰ Programs last from 2 weeks to 1 year.

UNITED PLANET

11 Arlington St., Boston, MA 02116, USA ☎+1-800-292-2316; www.unitedplanet.org

This international non-profit organizes "volunteer quests" in partnership with local programs in need of volunteers. Several such projects in Italy, Germany, and other European nations offer the opportunity to experience a high level of cultural immersion while doing community service.

working

Nowhere does money grow on trees (though our Researcher-Writers aren't done looking), but there are still some pretty good opportunities to earn a living and travel at the same time. As with volunteering, work opportunities tend to fall into two categories. Some travelers want long-term jobs that allow them to integrate into a community, while others want short-term jobs to finance the next leg of their travels. (Really ambitious people want both.) **Transitions Abroad** (www.transitionsabroad.com) helps potential worker-travelers of all persuasions with its up-to-date online listings for work over any time period. Those who might be skeptical about using this new-fangled "World Wide Web" can also seek out classified ads in local newspapers (no joke), federally run employment offices, and American Chambers of Commerce.

LONG-TERM WORK

If you're planning on spending a substantial amount of time (more than three months) working abroad, search for a job well in advance—they go like pancakes at a dangerously understocked IHOP.

teaching english

In almost all cases, you must have at least a bachelor's degree to be a full-fledged teacher, although college undergrads can often get summer positions teaching or tutoring. Many schools require teachers to have a **Teaching English as a Foreign Language (TEFL)** certificate, or the regional equivalent. You may still be able to find a teaching job without one, but certified teachers often rake in more dough. However, the foreign-language-challenged don't have to give up their dream of teaching. Private

beyond tourism

schools usually hire native English speakers for English-immersion classrooms where the native language is not spoken. (Teachers in public schools will more likely work in both English and the local language.) Placement agencies or university fellowship programs are the best resources for finding teaching jobs. The alternatives are to contact schools directly or try your luck once you arrive at your destination. In the latter case, the best time to look is several weeks before the start of the school year (when no one else can stomach the thought of going back yet).

more visa information

To work legally in any country as a non-citizen, more often than not you need a work permit or a work visa. Citizens of the EU may live and work in any EU country. For everyone else, a visit to your local consulate, a passport, and an official transcript of a job offer is a good start. Again, fees may apply, and they may be anywhere from $30 to $300. Make sure to start your visa application the moment you know you are working in Europe, as the process is long and arduous. First check with your employer or any contacts abroad about permits—usually they are easier to obtain from government organizations within the country in which you plan to work.

DAVE'S ESL CAFE
9018 Balboa Blvd. #512, Northridge, CA 91325, USA   www.eslcafe.com
A two-sided marketplace for ESL teachers and employers, Dave's ESL Cafe has listings around the globe. It's free for teachers, but there are fees for schools and recruiters. The "Job Links" link will lead you to help-wanted ads all over Europe. Plus, Dave is a good-looking guy.

EFINST
Bağdat Cad. Kazım Özalp Sok. 15/4, Istanbul, Turkey   ☎0216 302 7250; www.efdilokulu.com
In just 15 years, EFINST has grown from a small Istanbul office to a national organization with six branches and 2000 students. EFINST offers a variety of contract options, all of which require TESOL or CELTA certification and a university degree. Perfect for the newly graduated who want to do something good while making a little extra cash.
i Provides health insurance and accommodation assistance and Turkish courses if time permits.

INTERNATIONAL SCHOOLS SERVICES
P.O. Box 5910, 15 Roszel Rd., Princeton, NJ 08543, USA   ☎+1-609-452-0990; www.iss.edu
ISS hires teachers and administrators for more than 200 overseas schools. Candidates should have teaching experience and have at least a bachelor's degree. Its American-school job openings are great if you don't speak the local language.

I-TO-I TEACH ENGLISH ABROAD
8 Essex Center Dr., Peabody, MA 01960, USA   ☎+1-877-526-3959; www.onlinetefl.com
I-to-I sets you up with the proper TEFL courses for certification and has job and paid internship listings, including programs for academic purposes and business English.

OXFORD SEMINARS
244 5th Ave., Ste. J262, New York City, NY USA   ☎+1-800-779-1779; www.oxfordseminars.com
If you want to teach English abroad but don't know "their" from "there" from "they're," Oxford might be the place to start. (Or middle school—zing.) Oxford offers TESOL/TESL/TEFL certification courses in the US and Canada and then helps place its graduates at ESL teaching jobs around the world—as long as you've got a

working

bachelor's degree to go along with your Oxford certification. The helpful website provides a ton of helpful information, including detailed explanations of how to obtain work visas for citizens of all different countries hoping to teach abroad.

Ⓢ *TESOL/TESL/TEFL Teacher Training Certification Course $1195.* 🕑 *Courses generally take up 6 days over the course of 3 weeks with a 40hr. online component. Check the website for course locations and dates.*

US DEPARTMENT OF STATE

2201 C St. NW, Washington, DC 20520, USA   ☎+1-202-261-8200; www.state.gov/m/a/os
The US Department of State's Office of Overseas Schools maintains a directory of international schools abroad and can help qualified teachers in the recruitment process. The Department of Defense also operates and directly recruits teachers for its own separate school system for military families.

au pair work

Au pairs are typically women (although sometimes men) aged 18-26 who work as live-in nannies, caring for children and doing light housework in exchange for room, board, and a meager spending allowance or stipend. (Well, "meager" isn't completely fair—sometimes it's just small.) One perk of the job is that it allows you to get to know a new country without large travel expenses. Drawbacks, however, can include long hours and, well, a meager spending allowance. Be warned: much of the au pair experience depends on the family with which you are placed.

AU PAIR CONNECT

www.aupairconnect.com

Your basic pairing service. Au pairs can search for families by nationality as well as by country, so if you want to au pair in Prague but only get along with Londoners, you're in luck.

Ⓢ *Free to register and search. 3 months for access to contact info $45.*

CHILDCARE INTERNATIONAL

Trafalgar House, Grenville Place, London, UK   ☎+44 20 89 06 31 16; www.childint.co.uk

Essentially an au pair and family dating service. France and England are two big destinations. Childcare International also links families with housekeepers and live-in couples for the elderly.

GREAT AU PAIR

1329 Hwy. 395, Ste. 10-33, Gardnerville, NV 89410, USA   ☎+1-800-935-6303; www.greataupair.com

An easy-to-use, US-based organization that matches au pairs with families across the world. Make a profile and search for jobs. Also offers information on visas and immigration and does background checks to all U.S. national caregivers.

i *You can search for jobs without a membership, but must register to access contact info.* Ⓢ *Free registration offers functional access to site. For full access, 1-month membership $60, 3-month membership $120.*

SUNNY AU PAIRS

☎503-616-3026; www.sunnyaupairs.com

Here's another free-to-register au pair database looking for you to punch in your information and connect with a family. Families go through a verification process, so you know you won't be scammed. The website also has in-depth explanations and advice for au pairs.

Ⓢ *Free to register; 6-month membership for host families £70.*

internships and other long-term work

The following list is just a sampling of where you can look to to connect with companies that offer both unpaid and paid internships. Do note that many of these organizations have program or membership fees, and that many of the placements are in semester increments as they mainly work with students.

ASSOCIATION OF INTERNATIONAL DEVELOPMENT AND EXCHANGE (AIDE)

☎+1-866-6-ABROAD, ext. 137; www.aideabroad.org

With an alphabet soup of internships to choose from (Agriculture to Gastronomy), you might end up as an assistant to the events director of a high-quality lifestyle magazine, or in fashion financing. Choose wisely, young grasshopper.

Ⓢ *2- to 6-month placement $1895, plus $230 per week for a shared apartment.*

CA EDUCATION PROGRAMS

112 E. Lincoln Ave., Fergus Falls, MN 56537, USA   ☎+1-218 739 3241; www.caep.org/

Communicating for America coordinates paid internships and other educational experiences with agricultural organizations. Jobs range from farming to wine-making and span the continent from France to the UK to Germany. College credit is also available. Please note that most of these programs require previous experience in the agricultural program or with CA Education Programs in the US.

CDS INTERNATIONAL

440 Park Av., 2nd fl., New York, NY 10016, USA ☎+1-212-497-3500; www.cdsintl.org

Customized internships cater to your previous experience, strengths, and interests. These are unpaid internships, but funding is available through the CDS International Scholarship Fund.

EUROINTERNS

C. Solano 11, Madrid, Spain ☎34 63 754 39 00; www.eurointerns.com

Get real-time experience interning with big-name companies and NGOs like American Express, Amnesty International, Ikea, and INECO, the company that manages public transportation in Spain. A likely gold star on any resume.
Ⓢ *3- to 6-month internship placement €1100.*

GLOBAL EXPERIENCES

209 West St. Annapolis, MD 21401, USA ☎+1-877-432-27623; www.globalexperiences.com

Global Experiences arranges internships with companies in major cities like London. Programs include intensive language training, accommodation, emergency medical travel insurance, and full-time on-site support.
Ⓢ *Semester $5990-9990, depending on location and length of internship.*

INTERNATIONAL ASSOCIATION FOR THE EXCHANGE OF STUDENTS FOR TECHNICAL EXPERIENCE (IAESTE)

10400 Little Patuxent Parkway, Ste. 250, Columbia, MD 21044, USA
☎+1-410-997-3069; www.iaeste.org

IAESTE provides paid overseas internships to university students pursuing technical degrees. Most placements for 8-12 weeks during the summer, but some longer-term placements are also available. Apply through your home country's IAESTE branch.

INTERNATIONAL COOPERATIVE EDUCATION

15 Spiros Way, Menlo Park, CA 94025, USA ☎+1-650-323-4944; www.icemenlo.com

International Cooperative Education provides full-time paid internships (summer and semester) to American college and university students in a number of countries. Type-A workers rejoice: in addition to studying job-related vocabulary and current events, accepted students must write a five-page "paper of intent," a letter of introduction, a 10-page pre-departure paper, and a 15-page final report.
i *Ages 18-30 may apply.* Ⓢ *Application fee $250. Placement fee $1250; includes some housing, work authorization, and visa application fees. Salaries $300-2300 per month.* ☒ *IInternships run for 1-2 academic semesters or 2-3 months in the summer.*

WORKAWAY

www.workaway.info

Workaway connects travelers with host families and organizations who offer room and board in exchange for a few hours of work per day (generally 5hr. per day, 5 days per week). Lots of options to turn your man- or woman-power into a "vacation" of sorts at bed and breakfasts and farms in Europe.
Ⓢ *2-year membership €22, for 2 people €29.*

SHORT-TERM WORK

Different countries have different kinds of odd jobs that can last a week, a month, or anything in between. One popular option is to work several hours a day at a hostel in exchange for free or discounted room and/or board. In some countries, though, this is illegal ("My bad, officer"), so double-check first. Most often, these short-term jobs are found by word of mouth or by expressing interest to the owner of a hostel or restaurant. Due to high turnover in the tourism industry, many places are eager for help, even if it is only temporary. *Let's Go* lists temporary jobs of this nature whenever possible as listings in our coverage of individual cities. In the meantime, some websites to try include **www.easyexpat.com, www.backdoorjobs.com, www.resortjobs. com,** and/or **www.seasonworkers.com.**

tell the world

If your friends are tired of hearing about that time you saved a baby orangutan in Indonesia, there's clearly only one thing to do: get new friends. Find them at our website, www.letsgo.com, where you can post your study-, volunteer-, or work-abroad stories for other, more appreciative community members to read. There's also a Beyond Tourism section that elaborates on non-destination-specific volunteering, studying, and working opportunities. If you liked this chapter, you'll love it; if you didn't like this chapter, maybe you'll find the website's more general Beyond Tourism tips more likeable, you non-likey person.

working

INDEX

index

Index

index

index

index

index

Index

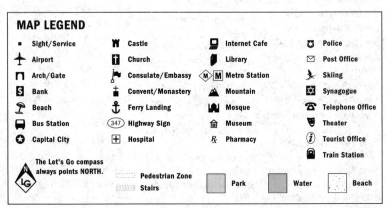

MAP LEGEND

- Sight/Service
- Airport
- Arch/Gate
- Bank
- Beach
- Bus Station
- Capital City

- Castle
- Church
- Consulate/Embassy
- Convent/Monastery
- Ferry Landing
- (347) Highway Sign
- Hospital

- Internet Cafe
- Library
- Metro Station
- Mountain
- Mosque
- Museum
- Pharmacy

- Police
- Post Office
- Skiing
- Synagogue
- Telephone Office
- Theater
- Tourist Office
- Train Station

The Let's Go compass always points NORTH.

- Pedestrian Zone
- Stairs
- Park
- Water
- Beach

index

MAP INDEX

map index

THE STUDENT TRAVEL GUID

Let's Go guidebooks are available at bookstores and through online retailers:

EUROPE

Let's Go Amsterdam & Brussels, 1st ed.
Let's Go Berlin, Prague & Budapest, 2nd ed.
Let's Go France, 32nd ed.
Let's Go Europe 2012, 52nd ed.
Let's Go Europe Top 10 Cities, 1st ed.
Let's Go European Riviera, 1st ed.
Let's Go Germany, 16th ed.
Let's Go Great Britain with Belfast and Dublin, 33rd ed.
Let's Go Greece, 10th ed.
Let's Go Istanbul, Athens & the Greek Islands, 1st ed.
Let's Go Italy, 31st ed.
Let's Go London, Oxford, Cambridge & Edinburgh, 2nd
Let's Go Madrid & Barcelona, 1st ed.
Let's Go Paris, 17th ed.
Let's Go Rome, Venice & Florence, 1st ed.
Let's Go Spain, Portugal & Morocco, 26th ed.
Let's Go Western Europe, 10th ed.

UNITED STATES

Let's Go Boston, 6th ed.
Let's Go New York City, 19th ed.
Let's Go Roadtripping USA, 4th ed.

MEXICO, CENTRAL & SOUTH AMERICA

Let's Go Buenos Aires, 2nd ed.
Let's Go Central America, 10th ed.
Let's Go Costa Rica, 5th ed.
Let's Go Costa Rica, Nicaragua & Panama, 1st ed.
Let's Go Guatemala & Belize, 1st ed.
Let's Go Yucatán Peninsula, 1st ed.

ASIA & THE MIDDLE EAST

Let's Go Israel, 6th ed.
Let's Go Thailand, 5th ed.

Exam and desk copies are available for study-abroad programs and resource centers.
Let's Go guidebooks are distributed to bookstores in the U.S. through Publishers Group Wes and in Canada through Publishers Group Canada.
For more information, email letsgo.info@perseusbooks.com.

ACKNOWLEDGMENTS

BILLY THANKS: My RWs for their endurance and their hilarious stories. Michael for his sass and his sassy editing. Chris for keeping to his schedules and for the Tanjore train. The Soviet/Snuggle Pod for its love, laughs, and coffee (JTR). Google Maps for all its enlightening wisdom. The Format Manual for its insistence on the Oxford comma. NPR for my walks to work. The RLL department for their tutelage. InDesign for always shuttin' down on me. MK for her magical prod abilities. Iya for her humor and noms. Amy and Israel for keeping me sane. Joe for being a #bestie. The residents of 300 Western for laughs, Vinho Verde, and the EBW. Rachel for her coffee breaks. Brandi for being a bee charmer. John for being a beeb. The fam for good ol' support. And Cambridge for a great four years.

DOROTHY THANKS: MPMP for being my favorite and doing more than her share of work. All of the RWs for surviving, and being undaunted by the seemingly endless things asked of them. Pod Sinai for being the best "do your f-ing work-themed" pod of all time. All of Masthead for being sweethearts, especially Sarah. Marykate for being calm and wise. Iya for guerrilla compliments. Grooveshark for being free. Tanjore Tuesdays and Bagel Fridays for providing me with essential nutrients. Finally, the best for last: thanks to the Oxford Commas, for being the harvestest; to Maine, for quickly becoming my favorite state; and to my family, for everything.

LINDA THANKS: The cause for meaning. The Frevolution and those classy Tuesday nights. Israel, for being Israel. Amy for sanity. Michael for winks, tension, and adorableness. Mp styles for sweet jamz and leading the charge. Billy for conducting the chorus of wahh. Spencer for the glory and the primates and the cuddles. Researchers for all their hard work. **Wiz Khalifa** because he deserves a thumbpick somewhere. That man at Dunks for not making me explain myself. All Comrades, all around the world, we salute you. JTR.

MICHAEL THANKS: Billy, for being a phenomenal RM and spotting all the French mistakes I would have surely missed (and for his sass). Linda, because you and The Cause made every day an adventure—спасибо большой, товарищ. Leah, for being my Editor and Quad buddy, and for being one with the earth. Amy, for bringing the word "y'all" into my vocabulary and being an awesome hostess (TT shall continue). Chris, for fielding thousands of nitpicky questions, and for settling Catan with me. Everyone in LGHQ, for always bringing laughs and lots of food. My RWs, for being utterly hilarious and doing a killer job. Al's, for feeding me. My awesome parents, who drove back and forth to bring me home for the weekend. Miranda and Kristin, for being the best friends in the world. And Bryan, for absolutely everything.

SPENCER THANKS: To Linda for fomenting revolution. To Kat, Nicole, Beebs, and RoRo for risking life and limb to bring us intrepid reporting, sterling research, and rib-cracking marginalia. To the legendary sass of Billy and Michael. To Chris for keeping us on shedule. To Iya for being the second most famous Georgian I know. To trivia for simultaneously improving and decimating my self-esteem. To the Red-Headed League. To Proletariat Coffee (and capitalist coffee too). To Electric Ladyland. To Kentucky's finest bourbon, to Cambridge summers and porch-sitting, to Jack Spicer. To CuddlePod, Animal Farm, Whitney's tattoo artistry, Joe's futon, venn diagrams, the office snuggie, headgear of oracular origins, and sleep. To my parents. And most of all to Tanjore Tuesdays for fueling LGHQ through a long, hot summer.

MARY THANKS: Thank you Dorothy, Graham, Mark, Michal, Patrick, Sarah, and everyone at HQ for all of your hard work.

ABOUT LET'S GO

THE STUDENT TRAVEL GUIDE

Let's Go publishes the world's favorite student travel guides, written entirely by Harvard students. Armed with pens, notebooks, and a few changes of clothes stuffed into their backpacks, our student researchers go across continents, through time zones, and above expectations to seek out invaluable travel experiences for our readers. Because we are a completely student-run company, we have a unique perspective on how students travel, where they want to go, and what they're looking to do when they get there. If your dream is to grab a machete and forge through the jungles of Costa Rica, we can take you there. If you'd rather bask in the Riviera sun at a beachside cafe, we'll set you a table. In short, we write for readers who know that there's more to travel than tour buses. To keep up, visit our website, www.letsgo. com, where you can sign up to blog, post photos from your trips, and connect with the Let's Go community.

TRAVELING BEYOND TOURISM

We're on a mission to provide our readers with sharp, fresh coverage packed with socially responsible opportunities to go beyond tourism. Each guide's Beyond Tourism chapter shares ideas about responsible travel, study abroad, and how to give back to the places you visit while on the road. To help you gain a deeper connection with the places you travel, our fearless researchers scour the globe to give you the heads-up on both world-renowned and off-the-beaten-track opportunities. We've also opened our pages to respected writers and scholars to hear their takes on the countries and regions we cover, and asked travelers who have worked, studied, or volunteered abroad to contribute first-person accounts of their experiences.

FIFTY-TWO YEARS OF WISDOM

Let's Go has been on the road for 52 years and counting. We've grown a lot since publishing our first 20-page pamphlet to Europe in 1960, but five decades and 60 titles later, our witty, candid guides are still researched and written entirely by students on shoestring budgets who know that train strikes, stolen luggage, food poisoning, and marriage proposals are all part of a day's work. Meanwhile, we're still bringing readers fresh new features, such as a student-life section with advice on how and where to meet students from around the world; a revamped, user-friendly layout for our listings; and greater emphasis on the experiences that make travel abroad a rite of passage for readers of all ages. And, of course, this year's 16 titles—including five brand-new guides—are still brimming with editorial honesty, a commitment to students, and our irreverent style.

THE LET'S GO COMMUNITY

More than just a travel guide company, Let's Go is a community that reaches from our headquarters in Cambridge, MA, all across the globe. Our small staff of dedicated student editors, writers, and tech nerds comes together because of our shared passion for travel and our desire to help other travelers get the most out of their experience. We love it when our readers become part of the Let's Go community as well—when you travel, drop us a postcard (67 Mt. Auburn St., Cambridge, MA 02138, USA), send us an email (feedback@letsgo.com), or sign up on our website (www. letsgo.com) to tell us about your adventures and discoveries.

For more information, updated travel coverage, and news from our researcher team, visit us online at www.letsgo.com.

THANKS TO OUR SPONSORS

- **ALESSANDRO DOWNTOWN.** Via Carlo Cattaneo 23, Rome, Italy; ☎06-4461950; www.HostelsAlessandro.com
- **ALESSANDRO PALACE & BAR.** Via Vicenza 42, Rome, Italy; ☎06-4461958; www. HostelsAlessandro.com
- **CZECHINN.** Francouzska 76, Prague 101 00, Czech Republic; ☎+420 267 267 600; www.czech-inn.com
- **CITYSTAY HOSTEL.** Rosenstrasse 16, 10178 Berlin-Mitte, Germany; ☎+49 30-23 62 40 31; www.citystay.de
- **GENERATOR HOSTELS.** Storkower Strasse 160, 10407 Berlin, Germany; ☎+49 (0)30 417 2400. 7 Tavistock Place, Russell Square, WC1H 9SE London, United Kingdom; ☎+44 (0)20 7388 7666. Other locations in Copenhagen, Dublin, and Hamburg; www.generatorhostels.com
- **HEART OF GOLD HOSTEL.** Johannistr. 11, 110117 Berlin, Germany; ☎030-29003300; www.heartofgold-hostel.de
- **HELTER SKELTER HOSTEL.** Kalkscheunen Str. 4-5, Berlin, Germany; ☎030-28044997; www.helterskelterhostel.com
- **MARTA GUESTHOUSE.** Via Tacito 41, Rome, Italy; ☎39 06 6889 2992; marta. hotelinroma.com; www.martaguesthouse.com
- **MISS SOPHIE'S.** Melounova 3, 120 00 Prague, Czech Republic; ☎+420 296 303 530; www.miss-sophies.com
- **MOSAIC HOUSE.** Odboru 4, Prague 2, Czech Republic; ☎+420 246 008 324; www.mosaichouse.com
- **OLD PRAGUE HOSTEL.** Benediktská 2, Prague 1, Czech Republic; ☎+420 224 829 058; www.oldpraguehostel.com
- **ODYSSEE HOSTEL.** Grünberger Str. 23, Berlin, Germany; ☎030-29000081; www. globetrotterhostel.de
- **SIR TOBY'S.** Dělnická 24, Prague 7, Czech Republic; ☎+420 246 032 610; www. sirtobys.com
- **SMARTBACKPACKERS.** 48-50 Inverness Terrace, Bayswater, London, United Kingdom; 55-57 Bayham Street, Camden Town, London, United Kingdom; 16 Leinster Terrace, Paddington, London, United Kingdom; and many other locations; www. smartbackpackers.com
- **SUNFLOWER HOSTEL.** Helsingforser Str. 17, Berlin, Germany; ☎030-44044250; www.sunflower-hostel.de

HELPING LET'S GO. If you want to share your discoveries, suggestions, or corrections, please drop us a line. We appreciate every piece of correspondence, whether a postcard, a 10-page email, or a coconut. Visit Let's Go at **www.letsgo.com** or send an email to:

feedback@letsgo.com, subject: "Let's Go Europe Top 10 Cities"

Address mail to:

Let's Go Europe Top 10 Cities, 67 Mount Auburn St., Cambridge, MA 02138, USA

In addition to the invaluable travel advice our readers share with us, many are kind enough to offer their services as researchers or editors. Unfortunately, our charter enables us to employ only currently enrolled Harvard students.

Maps © Let's Go and Avalon Travel
Design Support by Jane Musser, Sarah Juckniess, Tim McGrath

Distributed by Publishers Group West.
Printed in Canada by Friesens Corp.

ISBN-13: 978-1-61237-002-6
ISBN-10: 1-61237-002-0
First edition

SEP 0 6 2012

10 9 8 7 6 5 4 3 2 1

Let's Go Europe Top 10 Cities is written by Let's Go Publications, 67 Mt. Auburn St., Cambridge, MA 02138, USA.

Let's Go® and the LG logo are trademarks of Let's Go, Inc.

QUICK REFERENCE

YOUR GUIDE TO LET'S GO ICONS

📶	Let's Go recommends	☎	Phone numbers	‡	Directions
i	Other hard info	Ⓢ	Prices	🕐	Hours

IMPORTANT PHONE NUMBERS

EMERGENCY: ☎112			
Amsterdam	☎911	London	☎999
Barcelona	☎092	Madrid	☎092
Berlin	☎110	Paris	☎17
Florence	☎113	Prague	☎158
Istanbul	☎155	Rome	☎113

USEFUL PHRASES

ENGLISH	FRENCH	GERMAN	ITALIAN	SPANISH
Hello/Hi	Bonjour/Salut	Hallo/Tag	Ciao	Hola
Goodbye/Bye	Au revoir	Auf Wiedersehen/ Tschüss	Arrivederci/Ciao	Adios/Chao
Yes	Oui	Ja	Sì	Sí
No	Non	Nein	No	No
Excuse me!	Pardon!	Entschuldigen Sie!	Scusa!	Perdón!
Thank you	Merci	Danke	Grazie	Gracias
Go away!	Va t'en!	Geh weg!	Vattene via!	Vete!
Help!	Au secours!	Hilfe!	Aiuto!	Ayuda!
Call the police!	Appelez la police!	Ruf die Polizei!	Chiamare la polizia!	Llame a la policía!
Get a doctor!	Cherchez un médecin!	Hol einen Arzt!	Avere un medico!	Llame a un médico!
I don't understand	Je ne comprends pas	Ich verstehe nicht	Non capisco	No comprendo
Do you speak English?	Parlez-vous anglais?	Sprechen Sie Englisch?	Parli inglese?	¿Habla inglés?
Where is...?	Où est...?	Wo ist...?	Dove...?	¿Dónde está...?

TEMPERATURE CONVERSIONS

°CELSIUS	-5	0	5	10	15	20	25	30	35	40
°FAHRENHEIT	23	32	41	50	59	68	77	86	95	104

MEASUREMENT CONVERSIONS

1 inch (in.) = 25.4mm	1 millimeter (mm) = 0.039 in.
1 foot (ft.) = 0.305m	1 meter (m) = 3.28 ft.
1 mile (mi.) = 1.609km	1 kilometer (km) = 0.621 mi.
1 pound (lb.) = 0.454kg	1 kilogram (kg) = 2.205 lb.
1 gallon (gal.) = 3.785L	1 liter (L) = 0.264 gal.